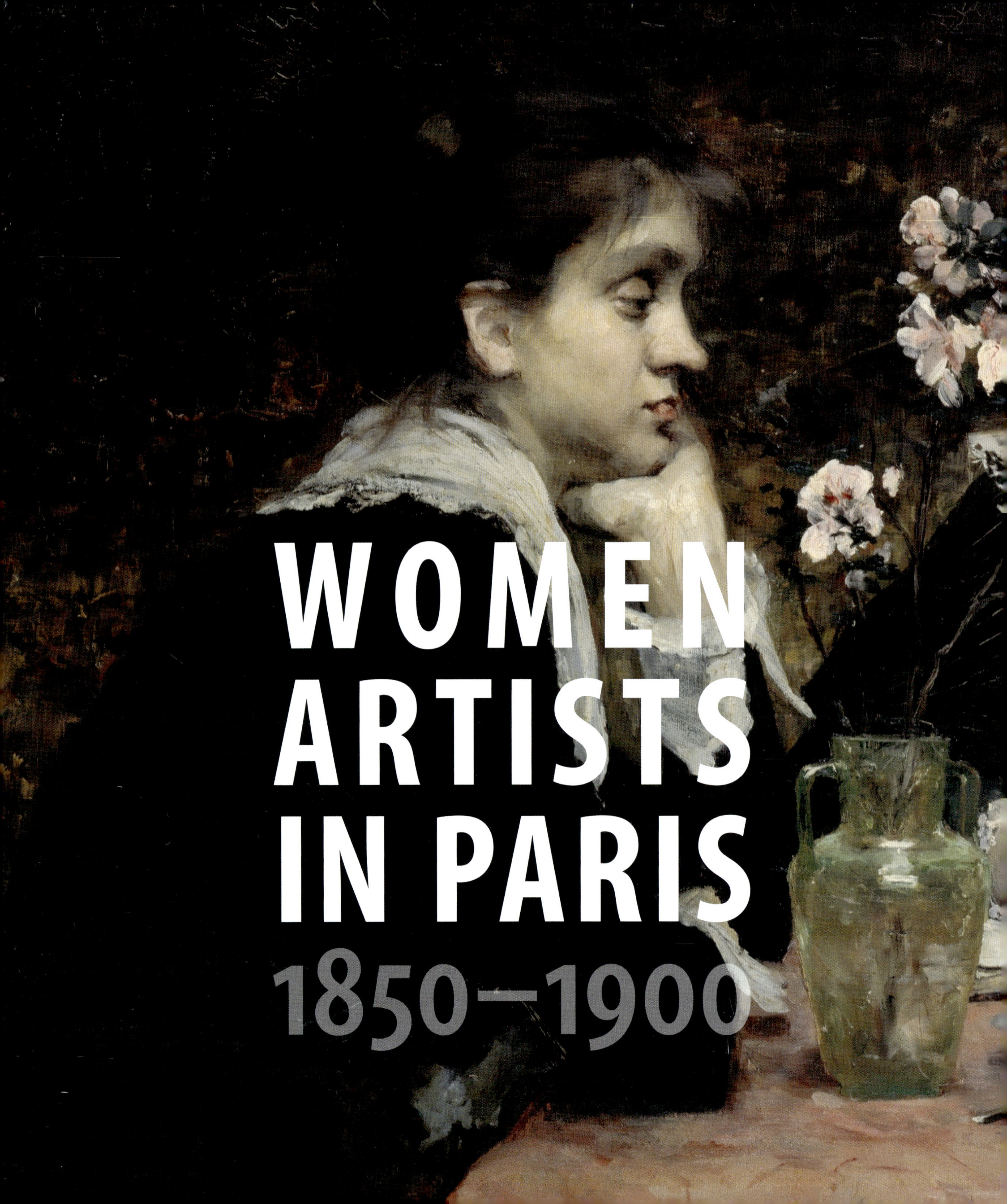
WOMEN
ARTISTS
IN PARIS
1850–1900

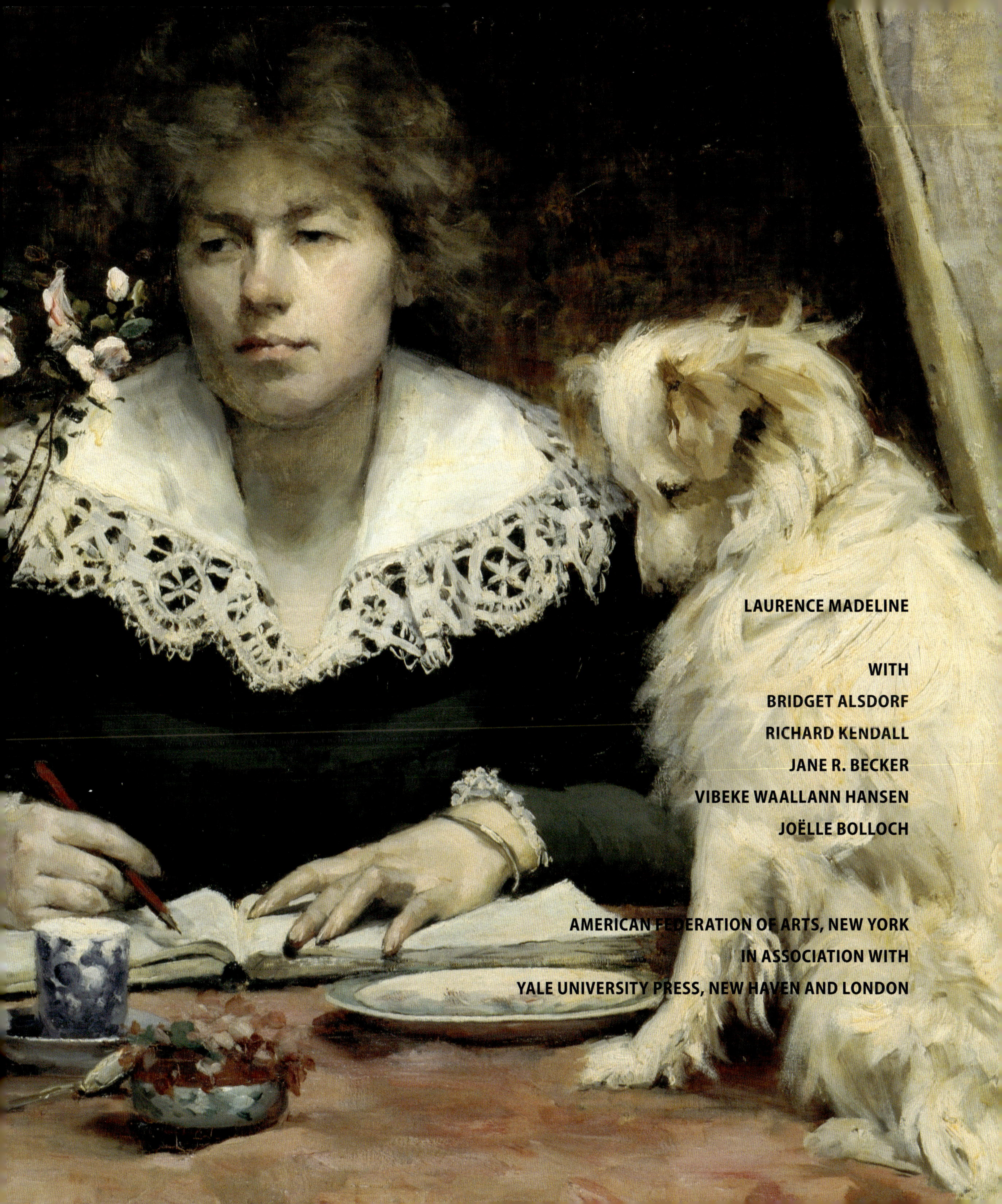

LAURENCE MADELINE

WITH

BRIDGET ALSDORF

RICHARD KENDALL

JANE R. BECKER

VIBEKE WAALLANN HANSEN

JOËLLE BOLLOCH

AMERICAN FEDERATION OF ARTS, NEW YORK

IN ASSOCIATION WITH

YALE UNIVERSITY PRESS, NEW HAVEN AND LONDON

This catalogue is published on the occasion of the traveling exhibition *Women Artists in Paris, 1850–1900*, organized by the American Federation of Arts.

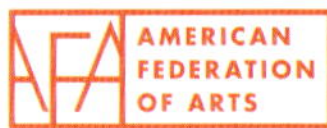

First published in the United States of America in 2017 by

Yale University Press
302 Temple Street
P.O. Box 209040
New Haven, CT 06520-9040
www.yalebooks.com/art

and

American Federation of Arts
305 East 47th Street, 10th Floor
New York, NY 10017
www.amfedarts.org

The American Federation of Arts is the leader in traveling exhibitions internationally. A nonprofit organization founded in 1909, the AFA is dedicated to enriching the public's experience and understanding of the visual arts through organizing and touring art exhibitions for presentation in museums around the world, publishing exhibition catalogues featuring important scholarly research, and developing educational programs.

Women Artists in Paris, 1850–1900 is generously supported by the National Endowment for the Arts. Additional funding is provided by the JFM Foundation, Elizabeth K. Belfer, the Florence Gould Foundation, Monique Schoen Warshaw, the Barbro Osher Pro Suecia Foundation, the Swiss Arts Council Pro Helvetia, Clare McKeon, Steph and Jody La Nasa, Victoria Ershova Triplett, the American-Scandinavian Foundation, and the Finlandia Foundation.

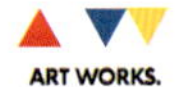

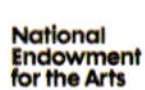

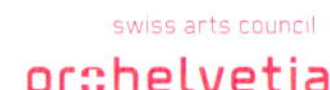

Support for this publication provided by Furthermore: a program of the J.M. Kaplan Fund.

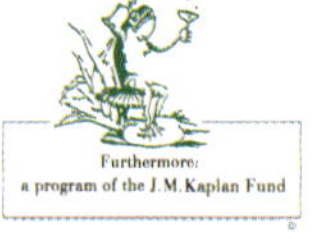

Guest Curator: Laurence Madeline

For the American Federation of Arts:
Managing Curator: Suzanne Ramljak
Associate Curator: Jeremiah William McCarthy
Manager of Publications: Audrey Walen

Women Artists in Paris, 1850–1900 will travel to:
Denver Art Museum, Denver, CO: October 22, 2017–January 14, 2018
Speed Art Museum, Louisville, KY: February 17–May 13, 2018
Clark Art Institute, Williamstown, MA: June 9–September 3, 2018

Designed by Eileen Boxer, boxerdesign.com
Set in Myriad Pro Semicondensed and Kepler Standard Semicondensed
Printed in China through Oceanic Graphic International, Inc.

Library of Congress Control Number: 2016955169
ISBN 978-0-300-22393-4 (hardcover)
ISBN 978-1-885444-45-5 (paperback)

A catalogue record for this book is available from the British Library.

The paper in this book meets the requirements of ANSI/NISO Z39.48-1992 (Permanence of Paper).

10 9 8 7 6 5 4 3 2

Cover illustrations: (front) detail of plate 89; (back) detail of plate 57
Pages ii–iii: detail of plate 11; page v: detail of plate 10; pages 82–83: detail of plate 6; pages 102–3: detail of plate 22; pages 126–27: detail of plate 28; pages 144–45: detail of plate 44; pages 168–69: detail of plate 50; pages 190–91: detail of plate 74; pages 220–21: detail of plate 82

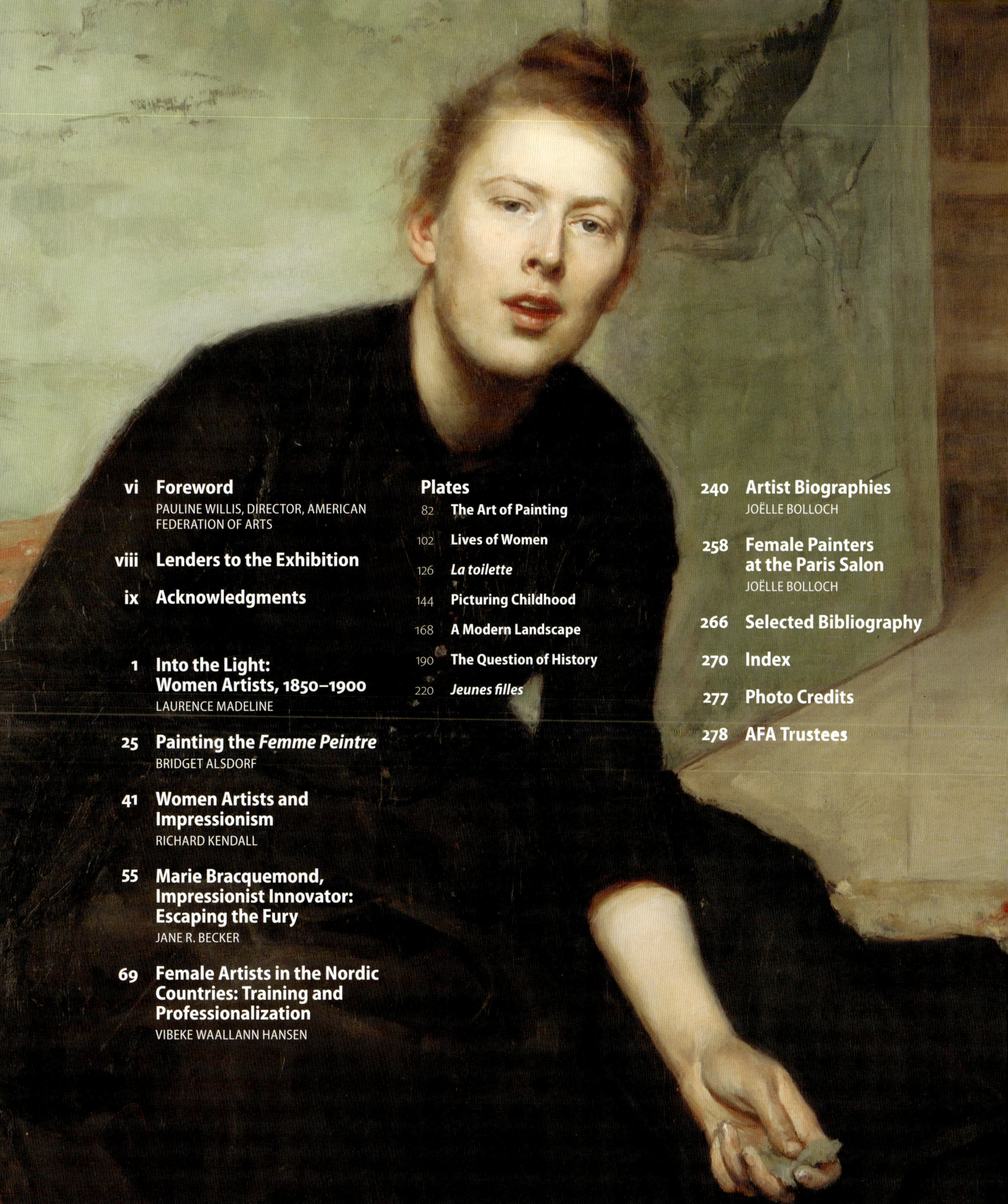

Foreword

It is with great pleasure and pride that the American Federation of Arts presents the groundbreaking exhibition *Women Artists in Paris, 1850–1900*, the first exhibition to broadly survey the art of women painters who worked in France amidst great social and artistic change. As the cultural mecca of the late nineteenth century, Paris lured artists with its wealth of museums, academies, salons, and dynamic urban life. Among these artists were pioneering women who overcame immense obstacles to hone their art and develop their careers, staging what we now recognize as a quiet revolution.

Featuring nearly ninety paintings by thirty-seven women artists, this publication and the traveling exhibition it accompanies move beyond familiar artist names associated with this chapter of art history to bring the creative contributions of lesser-known women to the fore. In addition to their artistic achievements in Paris, these artists often returned to their home countries to work, teach, and establish schools, which empowered future generations of women in the arts. This legacy was not lost on former Vice President of the American Federation of Arts, Cecilia Beaux, when in 1915 she impressed upon our organization the importance of education for artists, without which they would be "a leaf upon the wind, rather than a leaf upon a tree." Today, it gives us great joy to present some of Beaux's most iconic works in this catalogue.

When guest curator Laurence Madeline originally presented this project to us, we recognized that it provided a rare opportunity to offer a new lens onto a widely studied art historical period. This exhibition is a testament to her keen eye, and she has amassed an astounding selection of paintings from private and public collections on both sides of the Atlantic. She brought an originality of thought and a passionate enthusiasm to this project. We also thank the impressive roster of scholars she selected to contribute to this catalogue.

With loans from sixty-eight different lenders in ten different countries, *Women Artists in Paris, 1850–1900* is unquestionably one of the most ambitious exhibitions in the AFA's recent history, and it could not have been realized without the efforts of our committed staff. Suzanne Ramljak, Curator for the AFA, brought her sharp intellect, tenacity, and good humor to this project over the course of several years, expertly guiding the development of this exhibition tour. Associate Curator Jeremiah William McCarthy fully devoted himself to all aspects of the realization of this benchmark exhibition and publication. Shira Backer, former Assistant Curator, provided important assistance for this project in its earlier stages. Our immensely able Head Registrar Elizabeth Abbarno accomplished the intricate and challenging task of organizing loans and tour logistics. Manager of Publications Audrey Walen deftly managed the production of this publication with grace. Rights specialist Gina Broze conscientiously tracked down images for this richly illustrated book, and intern Firozah Najmi far exceeded our expectations. Associate Director for Development Brian Keliher ensured that this project had the support of strong partners, and Manager of Communications and Marketing Natalie Espinosa brought creativity to its presentation.

We also want to acknowledge our colleagues at the participating venues on this national tour. It has been our pleasure to collaborate with the staff of three stellar museums. At the Denver Art Museum, we wish to thank Christoph

Heinrich, Lori Iliff, and Angelica Daneo; at the Speed Art Museum, Louisville, Kentucky, thanks are due to Stephen Reily and Erika Holmquist-Wall as well as former Director Ghislain d'Humières; and at the Sterling and Francine Clark Art Institute, Williamstown, Massachusetts, we express our appreciation to Oliver Meslay and Kathleen Morris.

Women Artists in Paris, 1850–1900 continues the AFA's commitment to exhibitions that share significant scholarly research with the broadest audiences possible. Our partnership with Yale University Press ensures the reach of this important publication, and we are grateful to have collaborated with them. In particular, we appreciate the care and attention given to the project by Kate Zanzucchi, Mary Mayer, and Amy Canonico. Designer Eileen Boxer created a book that conveys the bold yet nuanced nature of this work.

This exhibition's scale required substantial financial support, and we are truly thankful to the distinguished group of patrons who believed in the value of this project and provided critical funding. We would particularly like to thank AFA Chairman Emerita Jan Mayer and the JFM Foundation for their early enthusiasm and support of this project, which helped us secure later gifts and grants from the National Endowment for the Arts, Elizabeth K. Belfer, the Florence Gould Foundation, Monique Schoen Warshaw, the Barbro Osher Pro Suecia Foundation, the Swiss Arts Council Pro Helvetia, Clare McKeon, Steph and Jody La Nasa, Victoria Ershova Triplett, the American-Scandinavian Foundation, and the Finlandia Foundation. The AFA is also deeply grateful to Furthermore: a program of the J.M. Kaplan Fund whose support made this publication possible. Indemnity provided by Federal Council on the Arts and Humanities assisted substantially with insurance costs, and Huntington T. Block Insurance Agency, Inc. graciously provided in-kind support for this exhibition.

Finally, no matter how strong this exhibition's concept, its success would not have been possible without the generosity of lenders from around the world, and to them we would like to extend our deepest gratitude.

PAULINE WILLIS, DIRECTOR, AMERICAN FEDERATION OF ARTS

LENDERS TO THE EXHIBITION

Amon Carter Museum of American Art, Fort Worth, TX

Anders Wiklöf Collection, Andersudde, Åland Islands

ARoS Aarhus Kunstmuseum, Denmark

Art Institute of Chicago

Art Museums of Skagen, Denmark

Birmingham Museum of Art

Brooklyn Museum

Bury Art Museum, United Kingdom

Château-Musée de Dieppe, France

Chrysler Museum of Art, Norfolk, VA

Cincinnati Art Museum

Crystal Bridges Museum of American Art, Bentonville, AR

Denver Art Museum

Dnipropetrovsk State Art Museum, Ukraine

Dorsia Hotel, Gothenburg, Sweden

Finnish National Gallery, Ateneum Art Museum, Helsinki

Galerie St. Etienne, New York

Georgia Museum of Art, University of Georgia, Athens

Gothenburg Museum of Art, Sweden

HAM Helsinki Art Museum

Harvard Art Museums/Fogg Museum, Cambridge, MA

The Hirschsprung Collection, Copenhagen

The John and Mable Ringling Museum of Art, the State Art Museum of Florida, Florida State University, Sarasota

Kunstmuseum Bern, Switzerland

Manchester Art Gallery

Metropolitan Museum of Art, New York

Minneapolis Institute of Art

Drs. Tobia and Morton Mower, Denver, CO

Musée Anne-de-Beaujeu, Moulins, France

Musée d'Art et d'Histoire, Geneva

Musée d'Orsay, Paris

Musée de Gajac, Villeneuve-sur-Lot, France

Musée de Peinture Petiet, Limoux, France

Musée des Augustins, Toulouse, France

Musée des Beaux-Arts, Brest, France

Musée des Beaux-Arts, Pau, France

Musée du Petit Palais, Geneva

Musée intercommunal, Étampes, France

Musée Marmottan Monet, Paris

Museum of Fine Arts, Boston

National Gallery of Art, Washington, DC

The National Museum, Warsaw

National Museum of Art, Architecture and Design, Oslo

National Museum of Women in the Arts, Washington, DC

Palais des Beaux-Arts, Lille, France

Pennsylvania Academy of the Fine Arts, Philadelphia

Petit Palais, Musée des Beaux-Arts de la Ville de Paris

Mr. and Mrs. R. Stephens Phillips, Piedmont, CA

Prins Eugens Waldemarsudde, Stockholm

Private collection, courtesy of Galerie Hopkins, Paris

Private collections

The Royal Collection, Oslo

Smithsonian American Art Museum, Washington, DC

Speed Art Museum, Louisville, KY

Sterling and Francine Clark Art Institute, Williamstown, MA

Tate Britain, London

Bruce and Robbi Toll

UPM-Kymmene Cultural Foundation, Helsinki

Virginia Museum of Fine Arts

ACKNOWLEDGMENTS

I thank here my friends Josseline Erner, who supported the blossoming and fruition of this project, as well as Joëlle Bolloch, who has inspired and encouraged me. Thank you also to Maura Reilly, who proposed this exhibition to the American Federation of Arts, and to Suzanne Ramljak and Jeremiah McCarthy, as well as Shira Backer, with whom I have shared the joys of this long adventure.

I also thank Claude Ghez for his generosity, Jim H. Rubin and Lilly Rubin for their help, warm welcome, and friendship, and my daughters, Raphaëlle and Hortense Madeline-Richet, who always motivate and enlighten me.

I am thinking of all those who have helped and trusted me: Leena Ahtola-Moorhouse; Cédric Angoujard at the Musée des Beaux-Arts, Brest; Hildegard Bachert and Jane Kallir at Galerie St. Etienne, New York; Dr. Maria Balshaw; Céline Barbin; Jean-Christophe Baudequin; Véronique Beauregard, Claire Bernardi, Isabelle Gaëtan, Thomas Galifot, Geneviève Lacambre, Françoise Le Coz, Helena Patsiamanis, and Bruno Roman at the Musée d'Orsay; Jane Becker; Tina Biskop; Mette Bøgh Jensen and Tine S. Haislund at Skagens Museum; Dr. Anna-Maria von Bonsdorff and Timo Huusko at the Finnish National Gallery; Jean-Paul Bouillon; Krista Brugnara; Regina Bühlmann at the Kunstmuseum Bern; Céline Eidenbenz at the Musée d'Art, Valais; Kjell Ekström; Magdalen Evans; Stephanie Herdrich; Marie-Caroline van Herpen at the Galerie Hopkins, Paris; Christian Hoffmann at the Turku Art Museum; Catrin Lundeberg and Anna Meister at Prins Eugens Waldemarsudde; Jean-Yves Marin at the Musées d'Art et d'Histoire, Geneva; Marianne Matthieu at the Musée Marmottan Monet; Katherine McClung-Oakes; Anna Miller at the National Museum in Warsaw; Mary Morton at the National Gallery of Art, Washington, DC; Stéphane Paccoud at the Musée des Beaux-Arts, Lyon; Sylvie Patry at the Barnes Foundation; Ingrid Pfeiffer at the Schirn Kunsthalle; Vibeke Röstorp; Yves Rouart; Alison Smith; Dominique Vazquez at the Musée des Beaux-Arts, Pau; Florence Viguier at the Musée Ingres, Montauban; Anne Wichstrom; and Anna-Maria Wiljanen.

And, finally, thank you to all those who will bring the presentations at Denver, Louisville, and Williamstown to life.

LAURENCE MADELINE, GUEST CURATOR

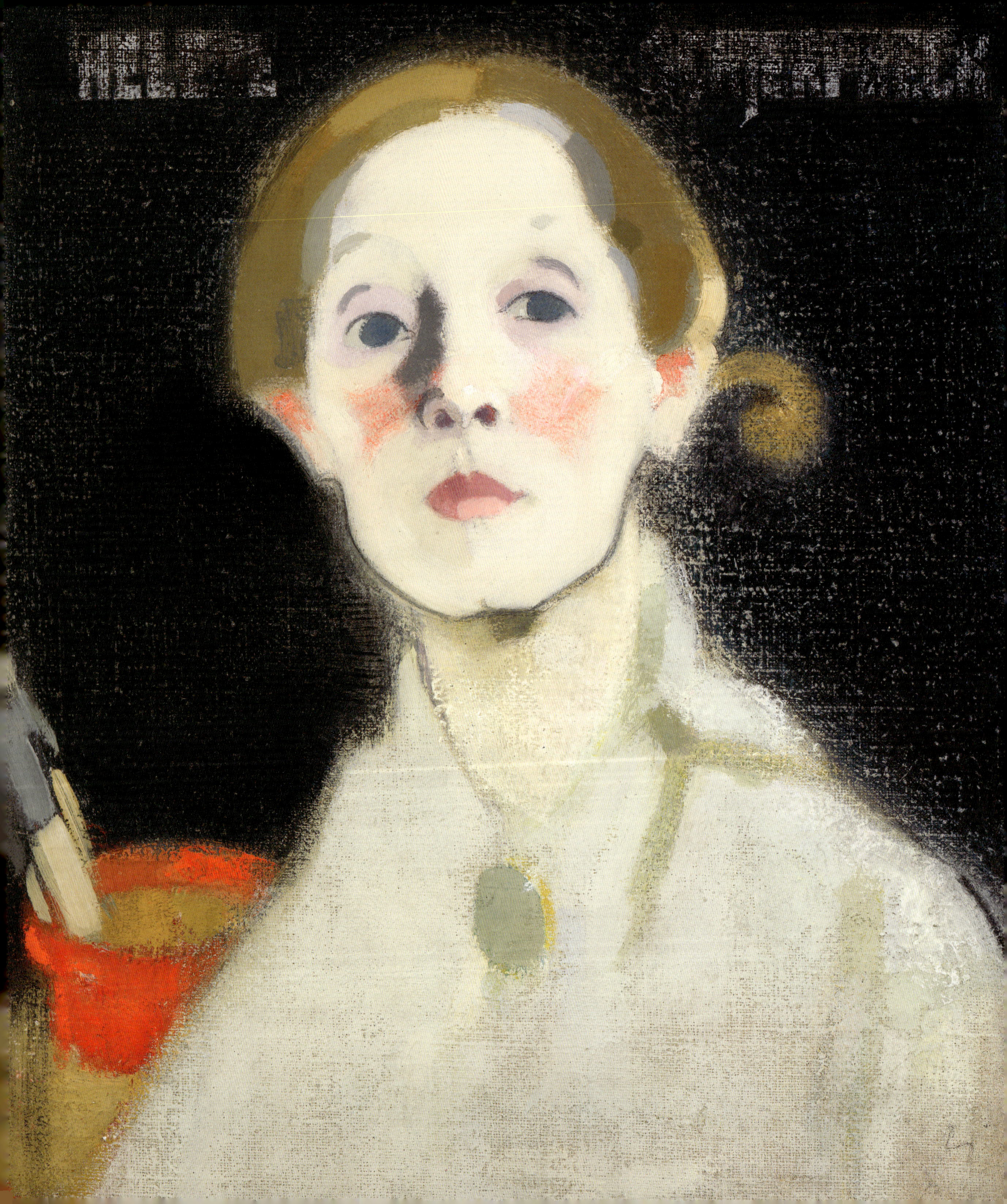

LAURENCE MADELINE

Into the Light: Women Artists, 1850–1900

Nearly a half-century has passed since Linda Nochlin archly posed the question: "Why have there been no great women artists?"[1] In a revolutionary article bearing this title, Nochlin was the first to publicly confront an assumption that had been latent for decades and demonstrate the enormous contributions of women to art history and art education. Nochlin's words uncannily echo the painter Marie Bashkirtseff who, writing under the pseudonym of Pauline Orell in 1881, demanded access for women to the state-sanctioned École des Beaux-Arts (School of Fine Arts): "We are asked with indulgent irony just how many great women artists there have been."[2] In the time between these provocative comments, great strides have been made in expanding the canon, and women artists have come to be viewed in a radically different light. Institutional prejudices and limitations on women's achievements continue to be increasingly challenged, and we have seen female artists conquer, one after another, formerly male-dominated bastions: they are now routinely represented in international contemporary art exhibitions and biennials, and are the beneficiaries of major commissions and sales.

Yet we must remain vigilant. Even in the twenty-first century we find art historians who, though they may acknowledge the growing recognition of contemporary women artists, continue to underestimate the importance of women artists during the second half of the nineteenth century, and ignore the ideological conditioning that holds women as secondary to men. Recent gains in women's participation in the arts now demands an assessment of those who have paved the way—both the women artists who struggled to establish careers in art and the art historians who reinvented the critical language to accommodate them.

It is rather ironic that a retrogressive school of art historical strain, one without any real feminist leanings, would resist the narrative of the heroic revolutionary artist, to rescue from obscurity Salon artists and academicians like William-Adolphe Bouguereau,

Helene Schjerfbeck, *Self-Portrait on a Black Background*, 1915 [detail of fig. 4]

Charles Joshua Chaplin, and partisans of naturalism like Jules Bastien-Lepage.[3] In the process, as art historians have revealed, it was often the conservative critics of the nineteenth century, not the avant-garde, who supported the training of young women artists and guided them through their first steps of public life as they strived for recognition. This exhibition is less concerned with providing a broad historiography of female painters and their critics than with offering a detailed account of a crucial historical episode when women painters from around the world came together in one specific location, during one specific time, to pursue their artistic ambitions.[4]

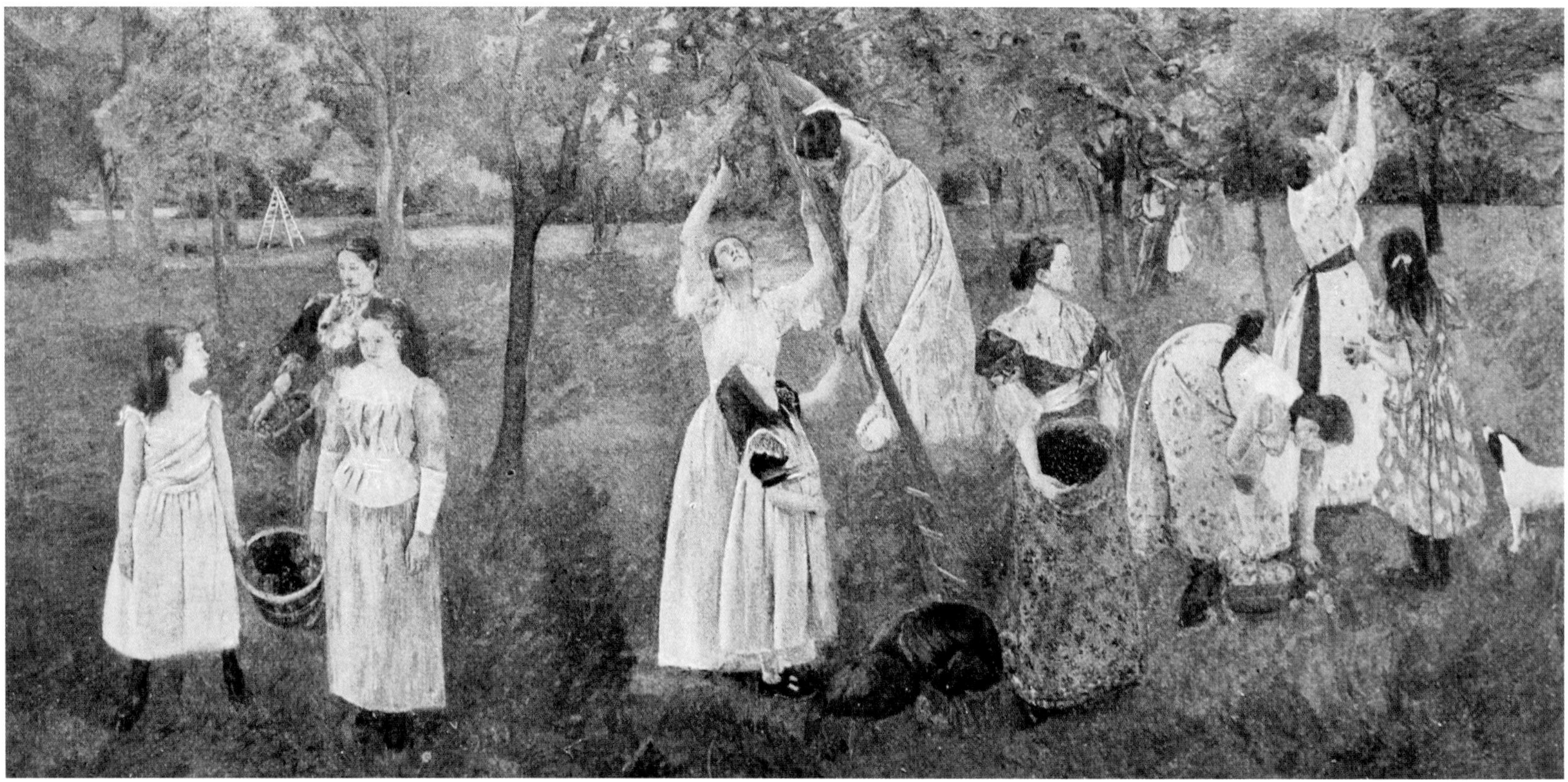

Fig. 1. Mary Cassatt (American, 1844–1926), *Young Women Plucking the Fruits of Knowledge or Science*, central panel from the fresco *Modern Woman*. Three panels, 12 × 64 ft. (3.7 x 19.5 m). Commissioned for the Woman's Building, World's Columbian Exposition, Chicago, 1893 (missing). Published in *Harper's New Monthly Magazine* 86 (May 1893): 837

The female artists who worked in Paris between 1850 and 1900—when the city was unanimously recognized as the world's art capital—witnessed dramatic changes. They saw the emergence of the first avant-garde movements (Realism, Impressionism, Symbolism), the rise of charismatic leaders (Gustave Courbet, Paul Gauguin, Édouard Manet, Claude Monet, Vincent van Gogh), the collapse of the omnipotence of the academies (training, exhibition, and purchases had all been overseen by the Institut de France), and the staggering increase in the number of artists.[5] The latter half of the nineteenth century also saw the determined and methodical advance of women in the art world: in 1865, Rosa Bonheur was awarded the Chevalier of the Légion d'Honneur; in 1881, the Union des Femmes Peintres et Sculpteurs (Union of Female Painters and Sculptors) was created; 1893 witnessed the creation of the Woman's Building at the World's Columbian Exposition in Chicago [fig. 1]; and in 1897, women were finally granted acceptance to the École des Beaux-Arts. "The woman artist is an ignored, little-understood force, delayed in its rise! A social prejudice of sorts weighs upon her; and yet, every year, the number of women who dedicate themselves to art is swelling with fearsome speed," exclaimed Hélène Bertaux, creator of the Union des Femmes Peintres et Sculpteurs, in her inaugural address.[6]

Writing Art History: Myth and Style If art history has not completely achieved the desired revolution, it is clear that certain traditions in discussing art and its history denounced by Linda Nochlin, Rozsika Parker, and their colleagues Whitney Chadwick, Griselda Pollock, and others[7] —the mythification of the artist, for example—do not hinder the study of women artists. Indeed some of these theoretical means, although first defined by men for men (despite Vasari's account of the lives of some women artists), can be equally applied to the study of female artists.[8] Such

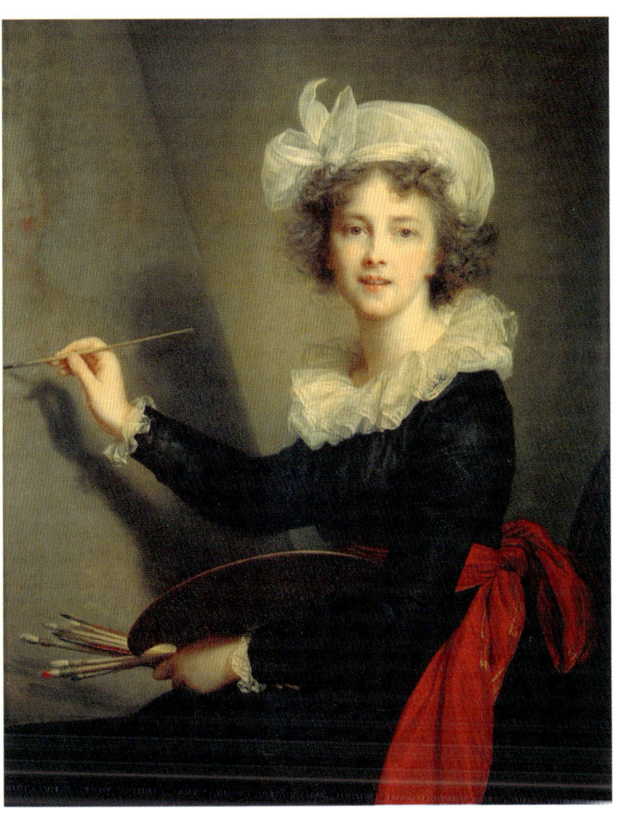

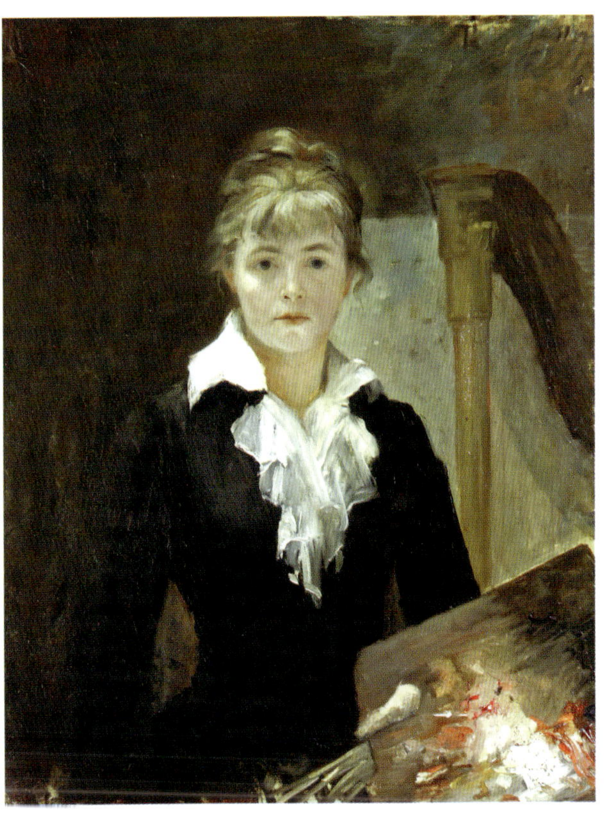

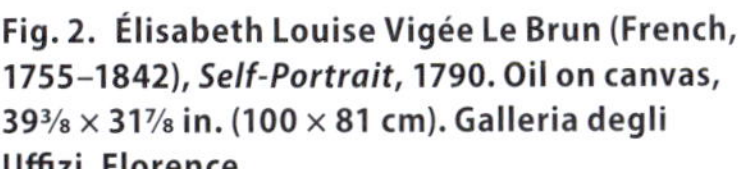

Fig. 2. Élisabeth Louise Vigée Le Brun (French, 1755–1842), *Self-Portrait*, 1790. Oil on canvas, 39⅜ × 31⅞ in. (100 × 81 cm). Galleria degli Uffizi, Florence

Fig. 3. Marie Bashkirtseff (Ukrainian, 1858–1884), *Self-Portrait with Palette*, ca. 1883. Oil on canvas, 36¼ × 28¾ in. (92 × 73 cm). Musée des Beaux-Arts Jules Chéret, Nice

is the case with Élisabeth Louise Vigée Le Brun [fig. 2], the subject of a recent traveling retrospective, which shows how the tropes of the history of art first developed for male artists adapt easily to women.[9] The story recounting how Emperor Charles V served the artist Titian frames our understanding of the anecdote reported by Vigée Le Brun of brushes that Queen Marie Antoinette allegedly picked up for her: "I grabbed my box of colors with such vivacity that it spilled; my paint brushes fell on the floor; I leaned down to correct my blunder. Leave it, leave it, said the queen, you are too far along in your pregnancy to bend down; and, despite complaints, she picked everything up herself."[10] This story, duly reported in the exhibition catalogue,[11] follows another *topos* of painters' lives: precocious talent, the propensity to draw everywhere and at all times. The anecdote of the brushes attests to the glory that the artist readily, and without false modesty, attributed to herself, but the circumstances surrounding the event are so indisputably linked to her own femininity—she was very advanced in her pregnancy—and also to that of the queen, whose grace and kindness Vigée Le Brun seeks to highlight (thereby pointing up the savagery of the revolutionaries who conducted her to the guillotine), that they challenge the essential myth of the powerful bowing before genius. We are witness to the drama of two women (and mothers) meeting, which the painter may have depicted with a gesture of self-effacement or self-censorship, imposed by her female condition.

Marie Bashkirtseff—whose dazzling life is known through her feverish writing in a journal published three years after her death, and her extensive correspondence, published in 1891[12] —continuously highlighted the urgency of her vocation and the obstacles she encountered and sometimes overcame before tuberculosis took her life in 1884 [fig. 3]. These challenges were for the most part tied to the artist's gender. "Now I have no freedom, without which one cannot seriously manage to be something," she proclaimed.[13] She also openly deplored the "terrible prejudices" that young women faced during their artistic training and careers.[14] The public's emotional response to Bashkirtseff's illness and premature death gave rise to a sentimentalism that quickly conferred a desperate grandeur on her oeuvre. In the preface to her published letters, the French Parnassian poet and novelist François Coppée speaks of "a pale and ardent girl . . . an extraordinary hothouse flower, almost miraculously beautiful and fragrant," and nudges her toward the pantheon of heroic artists whose lives were too suddenly cut short while practicing their art: "Mlle Bashkirtseff was no more. She was dead at twenty-six, from a chill she had taken while doing an outdoor study."[15] Coppée intentionally avoided any reference to tuberculosis and created instead a more romantic story of a steadfast artist who died because, disregarding the chill, she could not stop painting.

Although historians and critics may have had an abundance of tools and theories at their disposal, it must be noted that the valorization of certain women painters was accompanied by an emphasis on either their femininity, or the masculine character of their art, or their attitude. In both cases, the very terms that commentators used generated a "gendered" judgment that reined in the study of women's art. Coppée contrasted the delicacy of the "hothouse flower" to Bashkirtseff's virile manner—"Beneath that feminine charm, you sensed the power of iron, truly potent"—obliterating, with his choice of words, any objective view of the artist's painting.[16]

An analysis of *Women Painters of the World, from the Time of Caterina Vigri, 1413–1463, to Rosa Bonheur and the Present Day* (1905), edited by the British art critic Walter Shaw Sparrow, suggests how heavily the gendered gaze has weighed on women's painting.[17] In a groundbreaking tome of eight chapters and over three hundred photographs, Sparrow covered four centuries of female painters working in twelve countries (Italy, Great Britain, the United States, France, Belgium, Netherlands, Germany, Austria, Russia, Switzerland, Spain, and Finland). "What is genius?" he writes in his introduction. "Is it not both masculine and feminine? Are not some of its qualities instinct with manhood, while others delight us with the most winning graces of a perfect womanhood?"[18] This string of questions seems to open a healthy and egalitarian debate, yet the end result is the usual depreciation of women's creativity, on the basis of the claim that there are exclusively feminine qualities that cannot compare to those of men. The few exceptions, such as Rosa Bonheur, only prove the rule. Bonheur was mythologized during her lifetime based on her sexual ambiguity: for male critics of the day, only by assuming all the privileges and

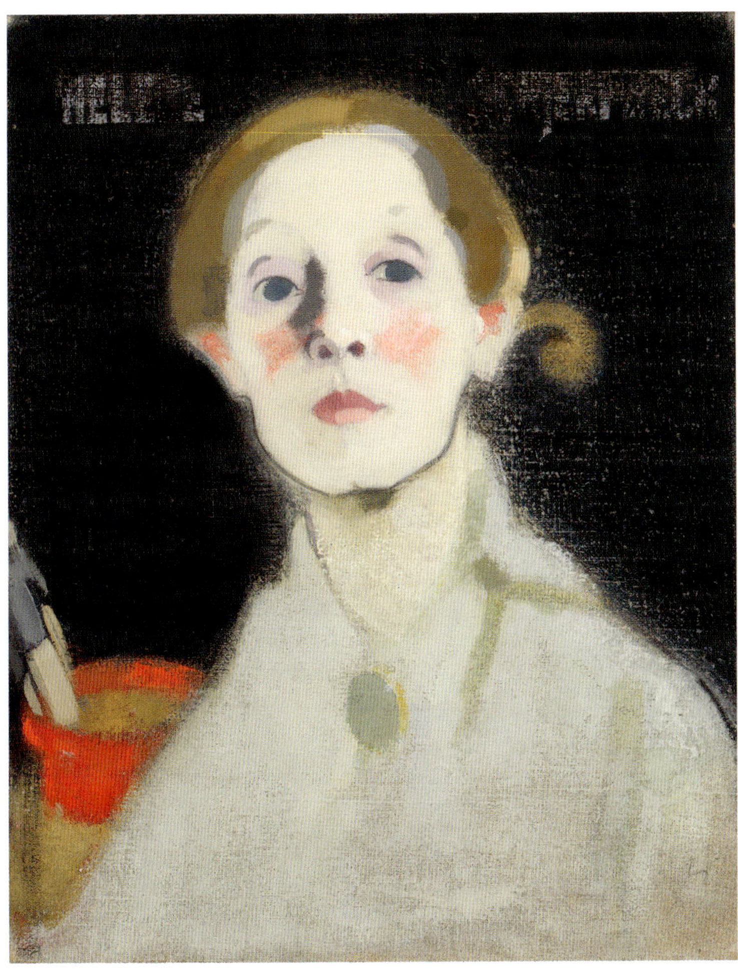

Fig. 4. Helene Schjerfbeck (Finnish, 1862–1946), *Self-Portrait on a Black Background*, 1915. Oil on canvas, 17⅞ × 14⅛ in. (45.5 × 36 cm). Herman and Elisabeth Hallonbladin Collection, Finnish National Gallery, Ateneum Art Museum

attributes traditionally accorded to men could Bonheur be awarded the mantle of a good painter. Critics' differentiation between so-called masculine and so-called feminine qualities set in motion machinery that whittled away at the woman painter's talent. Léonce Bénédite, director of the Musée du Luxembourg, whose portrait was painted by Amélie Beaury-Saurel, wrote the section on French women painters in *Women Painters of the World*.[19] In calling them "specially gifted by their delicate sensitivities," Bénédite is less condescending than Sparrow, who writes of women artists as well tempered in the face of the "emotional life to which women are subject." Sparrow goes on to depict women artists burdened with the "prescient tenderness and grace of [their] nursery nature," and describes the "differing genius of women and men," saying "there is room in the garden of art for flowers of every kind"—an extremely conservative vision of women's art.[20]

These choice terms stand in contrast to the direct and unpretentious words used by Helena Westermarck in her essay "Some Finnish Women Painters."[21] In contrast to Sparrow, Westermarck invented a way of approaching art criticism similar to that in which her compatriots were approaching painting. The parallel is not insignificant. Westermarck, a painter who spent a large part of her time defending the cause of women, abandoned the prejudices that obstructed her male colleagues' gaze and hindered their writing, thus paving the way for a new art and a new discourse. Sensing the importance of Helene Schjerfbeck's works, for example, she wrote, soberly and conclusively: "Her many pictures have been among the best that our women artists have produced."[22] Westermarck mounts one of the first challenges to the assertion, which she vigorously denounced, that there are no great women artists. And indeed Schjerfbeck's 2007 retrospective at the Musée d'Art Moderne de la Ville de Paris offered visitors a rare moment of intellectual and aesthetic discovery of this female genius [fig. 4].[23] The new attention given to many formerly obscure female painters, lifting them to summits previously reserved for their male counterparts, may come as a surprise to some, but it is an outcome brought about by decades of research on and analysis of women's art.

Gender and Dismissal The characterization of feminine and masculine aptitudes appears less defining than the outright rejection of women's artistic aspirations, a denial that cannot be easily attributed to political, social, or aesthetic positions. The Symbolist painter Gustave Moreau, a confirmed bachelor and reactionary, declared in 1891, upon the publication of Marie Bashkirtseff's letters: "The large-scale intrusion of women in the realm of art would be a disaster beyond remedy. What will become of us, when creatures whose minds are as practical and down-to-earth as women's minds are, when creatures so lacking in the true gifts of the imagination, proffer their horrible artistic common sense, supported by claims? This Marie B . . . gives one goose pimples. . . . The poor impassioned idiot, the poor fanatical busybody. And yet she's molding public opinion, she's in charge of an entire high-society coterie. It's enough to make you flee from art and everything related to it, never to return again."[24] At the other end of the political spectrum, even Thadée Natanson, the typically progressive editor of the journal *La revue blanche*, did not hesitate to use the expression "women's inferiority" in a review of the Exposition des

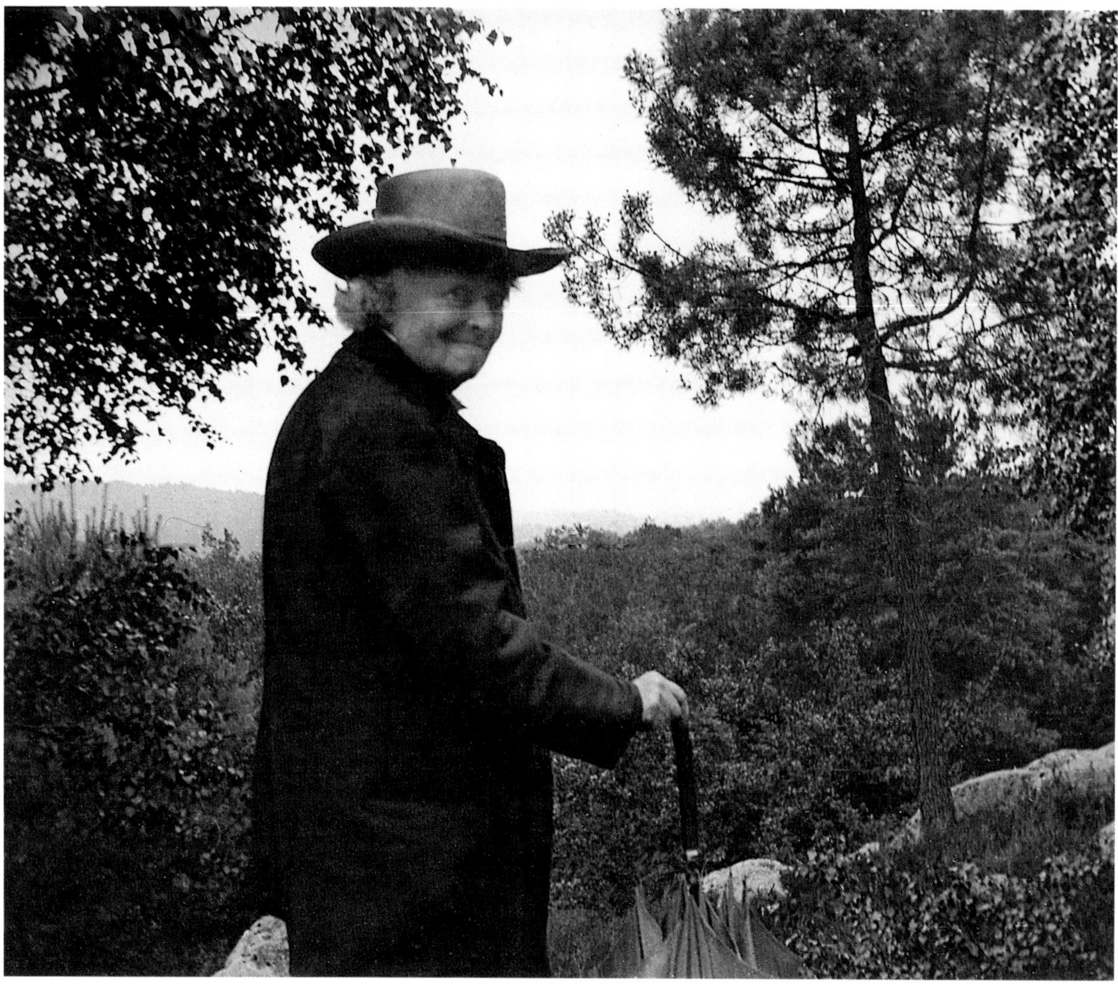

Fig. 5. Portrait of Rosa Bonheur. Photographer unknown

Femmes (Women's Exposition) in 1896: "Between sewing a bodice and composing a painting, from *la toilette* and a work of art, there is a distance that the brains of these ladies—an inferiority of essence or lack of education—cannot span."[25]

Indeed, the intellectual abilities of women were the object of serious scientific debate at the time.[26] That same *Revue blanche*—the journalistic vanguard, if not the avant-garde—also published a tirade by the Swedish writer and painter August Strindberg that left no hope for women: "It is the fate of our age to discover, among other things, that a woman is a scaled-down man, a form whose development was arrested between adolescence and full manhood. This discovery, already anticipated by philosophers from Aristotle to Jean-Jacques Rousseau and Schopenhauer, has been confirmed by scientists such as Darwin, Herbert Spencer, Mill, Haeckel, Virchow, Eduard von Hartmann, Friedrich Nietzsche, the craniologist Welcker, the biologist Letourneau, the physiologist Robin, and the anthropologist Topinard. Woman is inferior to man."[27] Even Rosa Bonheur [fig. 5], mentioned whenever one wants to claim that some women are recognized as having a value equal to men, is summoned forth by Strindberg only to point out that the exception proves the rule, to allude to all the other intellectual shortcomings of women: "The most common flaws to be condemned in women's logic are: . . . that they conclude on the basis of a special case the invalidation of a rule; that is, of what is usually the case. For example, Rosa Bonheur painted good animal paintings, so clearly, woman is not inferior to man (but how about in philosophy, in science, in business, in industry, in engineering?)."[28] As for the other women, those rare other women referenced in public discourse, they are important only when men deem them so: "A few, by way of exception, rise above the common lot, they do so almost always on the condition that we judge them great 'qua women,' and they are always found in fields of secondary value, in art or in literature, never in science! Further, in such cases the constant role of paternal inheritance or some other strong male influence is to be noted."[29]

Certain authors, such as Jacques Lourbet, responded ironically to such radically misogynistic interpretations of science, and denounced Strindberg's allegations: "Mr. Strindberg is a remarkable artist, but in the article titled 'On the Inferiority of Women' he reveals a total lack of critical acumen and shows how ill prepared he is for philosophical speculation. His talent, a product of violence, overheated passion, is able to construct wonderful plays and to elevate him to artistic superiority, but it makes him unsuited for impartial judgments and rigorous deductions that demand a clear and lofty mental serenity. Mr. Strindberg is a significant example of the current tendency to draw from science or pseudo-science what it does not contain."[30] Lourbet goes on to analyze the formidable sexist arsenal at work in his era—"Contemporary science cannot assert, in the name of any established principle, women's 'incurable mental infirmity.' To want to construct permanently the world by examining a few isolated, insufficient, and contradictory facts is mental myopia, the deplorable tendency of simple minds; also and *above all* it is because their arguments are impaired by selfish and, in fact, infantile feelings, that writers have propagated and still profess the contrary opinion: most of men's judgments about women are derived more from buried, inflexible instincts than from enlightened and impersonal reason."[31] And he concluded his book with the encouraging and thunderous call: "COMPLETE FREEDOM FOR WOMEN!"[32]

Even so, belief in woman's inferiority dragged on through the rest of the century. The critic Henry Havard constantly repeated the same litany: "Women have produced no masterpieces in any genre. They did not create St. Peter's Basilica or the *Venus de' Medici* or the *Apollo Belvedere*. They did not invent the fire pump or the hand loom."[33] That refrain profoundly marked the minds of art critics, especially since it came from the philosopher Arthur Schopenhauer. His influence, already strong among French writers in the second half of the nineteenth century, was further advanced by the 1880 publication of a French translation of his aphorisms and miscellaneous writings, in which he wrote, "If we think about it, what more can we expect from women if throughout the world this sex has not produced one single great mind, nor one complete and original work of art, nor, in anything, one work of lasting value."[34] The book, reissued sixteen times by 1900, also made other proclamations that were widely circulated: "Women have neither the emotion, nor the intelligence of music, no more than they have it in poetry or in the fine arts." And, predictably, Schopenhauer dismissed any claims about exceptional women: "Isolated or partial exceptions do not alter the case but, generally speaking, women are and remain the most downright incurable Philistines."[35] In view of the fact that Schopenhauer was a follower of Rousseau, and quoted his statement that "women in general love no art, know nothing about any form of art, and have no genius,"[36] one can easily conceive the abyss of negativity in which women struggled during the nineteenth century.

Alongside these outright proclamations of inferiority, other forces, more insidious but just as damaging, undermined women with their artistic pretensions, and their ambitions tended to weaken as a result. Manet, for example, could imagine no other destiny for Berthe Morisot and her sister Edma than a marriage befitting his own interests. As he wrote to Henri Fantin-Latour, "I am of the same opinion as you, the two Morisot sisters are charming. It's unfortunate that they are not men. As women, however, they could serve the cause of painting, if each were to marry an *académicien*, and sow discord in the camp of these senile old men."[37] Camille Pissarro, also evoking Morisot, reduced her art to her femininity: "You cannot imagine our surprise and emotion upon learning of the death of that distinguished woman, who had such a superb feminine talent."[38] Although Pissarro's respect and affection for Morisot are clear, a nagging doubt remained even among the most open-minded men regarding the essential nature of painting in the feminine. As the painter Virginie Demont-Breton observed, "When someone says of a work of art, 'It's a woman's painting or sculpture,' what he means is, 'it's a weak painting or a mawkish sculpture.'"[39]

Professionalization The world of women invoked by most critics in the second half of the nineteenth century was divided into two realms to which women artists were supposed to adhere: firstly, the decorative arts (enamel, china, tapestry, fans) and minor genres such as the small portrait or still life; secondly, subjects deemed "feminine." For example, Eugène Müntz, perpetuating the view that women were less capable, wrote: "True to their instincts, women embrace by preference the easy genres, those that require elegance rather than energy and invention: watercolor, the miniature, painting on china, and so forth."[40]

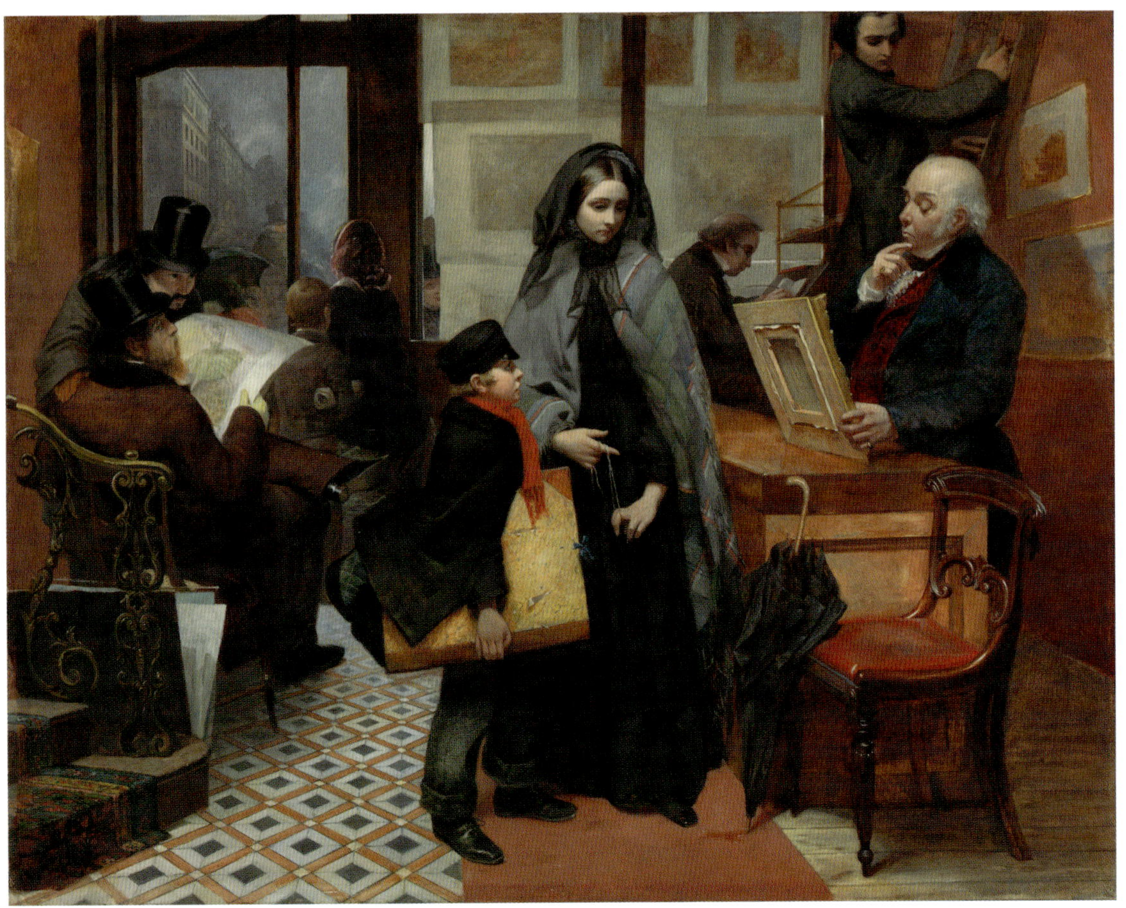

Fig. 6. Emily Osborn (English, 1834–ca. 1913), *Nameless and Friendless (The rich man's wealth is his strong city, etc. Proverbs, x, 15. An impoverished young female artist, accompanied by her younger brother, attempting to sell one of her pictures to a dealer)*, 1857. Oil on canvas, 32½ × 41 in. (82.5 × 103.8 cm). Tate. Purchased with assistance from Tate Members, the Millwood Legacy and a private donor 2009

Yet this belief was already outdated and irrelevant, because male artists too had begun to take an interest in these "easy genres." Manet, Edgar Degas, Pissarro, and Gauguin painted fans; Auguste Renoir, china. And in the 1890s the decorative arts would completely blur the distinction between feminine and masculine art. The question of medium or genre was fundamental during this period and involved glaring incongruities. On one hand, women were expected to limit their ambitions and practice art as an innocuous leisure activity with no consequence for their social situation. Joseph Guichard, the tutor of the Morisot sisters, told their mother: "With natures like those of your daughters, my lessons will not provide them with pleasing little talents; your daughters will become painters." And he warned: "Do you realize what this means? In your upper bourgeois milieu, that will be a revolution, almost, I should say, a catastrophe. Are you really sure that you will not someday curse that art, which, once it has entered this respectfully peaceful home, will become the sole master of your two children's fate?"[41] Strindberg said that a woman "was never forbidden to train her eye, as she busied herself embroidering her woolens, or when she took palette in hand!"[42] He thereby sent women back to their unending, quasi-domestic chores and condemned their incurable lack of taste. On the other hand, however, it was expected that the minor works women produced would allow them to earn an honest living. The professionalization of women's art, which presupposed access to education and exhibition opportunities, was a key issue in the second half of the nineteenth century. Once again, the century was rife with contradictions.

In the first place, it was acknowledged that women needed honorable professions. Emily Osborn's painting *Nameless and Friendless* [fig. 6] has become an icon in the history of women painters. It depicts the vulnerability of a young woman artist in the London of her time. She epitomizes the situation of her sister artists, condemned to earn their living and left to their own devices in an exclusively male and inevitably lecherous environment.[43] Bashkirtseff wrote about such a precarious existence: "the legend of the woman artist, . . . a vagrant and perverted creature, [her nature] incompatible with work or talent, ugly, starving to death, beauty turning bad."[44]

Jeanne Chauvin, in her *Étude historique sur les professions accessibles aux femmes* (*Historical Study of the Professions Accessible to Women*), noted: "Often as well, for various reasons, it is the woman who bears the financial burden of the family; she must therefore practice a profession to support her household." She added that "the principle of freedom of the professions and the idea of equity require that the progressive response prevail: all the professions must be accessible to women."[45]

But whereas Chauvin envisioned true artistic careers for women, facilitated by equal access to education, men generally imagined more modest careers for the fairer sex, far removed from the glory of the Salons. Thirty years earlier, the art historian Léon Lagrange had proposed that women be saved from poverty and perdition by means of art: not dancing, singing, or acting, which are so close to prostitution, but painting, sculpting, and engraving. "The woman painter or engraver will be able to lead a forgotten life in the shadows, never naming herself in public, never appearing before the world's eyes, and yet will find in the exercise of the fine arts sufficient resources for an honorable life."[46] He adds: "The woman painter, though she will not produce great canvasses, will be able to practice painting. What more delicate hand will better know how to decorate the fragile china with which we like to surround ourselves? Who will reproduce on ivory, with a more exquisite sentiment of maternal tenderness, the features of a beloved child? . . . It is from feminine hands, incapable of constructing our great monuments of stone, that industry demands the flimsy edifices that are the first joys of childhood."[47] Lagrange's concern was as much to preserve for men the exclusive domain of great art as it was to direct women toward the minor arts and crafts, in order to assure them a livelihood. He articulated his position clearly: "We are not asking the government to make the École des Beaux-Arts or the École Française de Rome [French Academy in Rome] accessible to women; we are asking that girls, like boys, be allowed to participate in the benefits of drawing lessons, which the primary schools dispense free of charge."[48] Lagrange's argument reveals a crucial paradox: women are supposedly inferior to men; they understand nothing or very little about matters of art, yet they represent a threat, certainly in terms of their numbers.

The ranks of women were in fact increasing in the Salons from one year to the next; meanwhile, men already faced frenzied competition from their male colleagues, whose numbers were also growing. At the Salon, the anguish of having a submission rejected was often followed (after one was finally accepted) by that of a disadvantageous placement, then of negative criticism or indifference, and then of the meager price paid for the work. In addition to these pressures, the possible inclusion of women presented another challenge to male artists, and this was one of the arguments put forth to deny women admission to the École des Beaux-Arts prior to 1897: "As it is, the proletarian masses of male artists are already fairly large; there is no need to add a female contingent. . . . Even if it were possible to determine that there is a certain average level of ability among women, the privilege of pursuing one's talent as a creator falls to men."[49] The task at hand, therefore, was to push aside women to leave room for the men, to send women back home to color. "Male genius has nothing to fear from feminine taste," claimed Lagrange.[50] Meanwhile, at the Académie Julian, one of the foremost private art schools, the lessons provided to both men and women relied a great deal on competition between the sexes, as Bashkirtseff noted: "[Julian] says his women students are sometimes as strong as the men."[51]

With women's first successes at the Salons (those of Louise Breslau and Marie Bashkirtseff especially), the perceived threat became real. In 1889 Pierre Borel, having chivalrously warned women about their male colleagues ("There is no means, however brutal, before which [men] will recoil, in order to thrust aside women once they enter into competition in the closed field of the male professions"), proceeded, once again, to belittle women's talent by circumscribing their field of activity: "To the true and sincere artists, you [women artists] will do no harm; they will hold onto the monopoly on powerful works and the gift of creative force; to you, the light infantry, will fall the realm in which men will always remain inferior, that of the delicate arts, the more intimate and gentler notes; to you, the watercolor and the pastel, the landscape, the flower, the child."[52] Male critics expected women to do paintings of private life, motherhood, childhood, and domesticity—in short, to reveal the secrets of femininity. The exhibitions at the Union des Femmes Peintres et Sculpteurs were supposed to provide "an entryway into feminine genius, to disclose something of the secret feelings of the daughters of Eve."[53] Women artists, as recommended by a critic at *Le temps*, should treat the elegant aspects of life and familiar settings; they should document how women made use of their time.[54]

Impressionism and Femininity The nineteenth-century critics who commented on the works of women artists were intent on defining two distinct principles or geniuses, the masculine and the feminine. Moreover, they were obsessed with demonstrating the existence of a deft and feminine hand and of a sure and masculine eye.[55] They apparently did not realize that the feminine painting they were calling for already existed and this essentially modernist mode of painting was being practiced indiscriminately by both men and women. In condemning the practice by women painters of the full-length portrait and history painting—genres considered too ambitious for feminine abilities—these critics did not see that male painters had begun to turn away from the *grand genre* and were depicting modern life with a fresh eye. The cross-section of paintings presented in this exhibition reveals an artistic comedy of errors in which almost every character masquerades as a member of the opposite sex.

The first plot twist in this comedy emerges with the word *impression*, which gave rise to the term *Impressionism*. The famous critic Louis Leroy, reacting to the title of Monet's *Impression, soleil levant* (*Impression, Sunrise*) at the 1874 exhibition, exclaimed: "Impression indeed, I was sure of it. And I said to myself, since I am impressed, there must be some impression in there."[56] The word *impression* recurred regularly whenever women's attributes were under discussion. August Strindberg, in his supposedly scientific account of woman's nature, emphasized that impressionability. "If we now proceed to a brief consideration of the soul's higher faculties and list them in no particular order (since the information in that area is still very incomplete), we see that the old legend of woman's extreme sensitivity, which is considered a virtue, arises in our minds. If, by that, we understand *impressionability*, that is, a propensity to experience rapid sensations, which a woman is incapable of governing, she will in fact appear superior; but that superiority is itself an imperfection."[57] This claim, widely circulated, can also be found in critiques of the art at the Union des Femmes exhibitions.

Hugues Le Roux, for one, concurred: "Women, who know only themselves, who, in their adorable, childish way, find it impossible to ever see beyond themselves, their own prejudices, impressions, hatreds, loves . . . have no concept of the logical order, the sequence, the absolute value of ideas; in place of all that, they substitute the order and sequence that most pleases them, they recognize the value of events and ideas only insofar as these affect them; they are impressionists in history, in ethics, in literature, in grammar, in logic, in mathematics, in chemistry and, as a result, in painting."[58] The writer S. C. de Soissons penned, more conclusively, "Properly speaking, only a woman has the right to practice the system of the Impressionists; she alone can restrict her efforts, translate her impressions, and mitigate superficiality by means of her incomparable charm, her sweetness and grace."[59]

Leroy's vehement rejection of Monet's painting can accordingly be explained by the following schema: Impressionism = femininity = fear of the loss of virility in art—of the artist's virility, and also that of the unwitting critic. Tamar Garb has brilliantly shown how, beginning in the 1890s especially, critics feminized Impressionism, dismissing it as carefree, frivolous, inconsequential, and superficial, the better to minimize its impact (which, however, they were obliged to acknowledge), and to award the victory to Symbolism, which championed a return to the idea, the concept, and to drawing—all masculine virtues.[60] To further complicate matters, some female painters rejected the Impressionists and other avant-garde movements, believing they represented a threat to the arts, which could be saved only by women. As one female artist urged: "My friends, let us fight that mania for modern singularities. May Art, through us, through women and the character of our works, once more become a civilizing force."[61]

The essence of Impressionism, as Camille Mauclair defined it, lay in the "attempt to limit art to the shock of sensation itself. In pursuit of this aim, it used the most subtle resources of eye and hand; it believed it had found, in the notation of the age, a mental pretext adequate to its whims, and it rejected every general truth in favor of the momentary aspect."[62] With this account, he unconsciously but revealingly cued the end of the Impressionist movement to Berthe Morisot's death: "It was done for, that shimmering Impressionism, an art so feminine that an admirable women, Mme Berthe Morisot, could by her works alone encapsulate all its efforts."[63] It was as if Morisot, a woman and Impressionist, personified the style of painting. When Sparrow wrote, "To Mary Cassatt, Impressionism is a chosen dialect . . . to Berthe Morisot, on the other hand, it was in itself the final word in painting," he was motivated by the same concern to minimize the influence of Impressionism on Cassatt, in order to make her more independent and consequential than Morisot.[64]

Fig. 7. Berthe Morisot (French, 1841–1895), *The Cradle*, 1872. Oil on canvas, 22 × 18⅛ in. (56 × 46 cm). Musée d'Orsay, Paris, RF2849

Fig. 8. Claude Monet (French, 1840–1926), *The Cradle—Camille with the Artist's Son Jean*, 1867. Oil on canvas, 45¾ × 34⅞ in. (116.2 × 88.8 cm). National Gallery of Art, Washington, DC, Collection of Mr. and Mrs. Paul Mellon, 1983.1.25

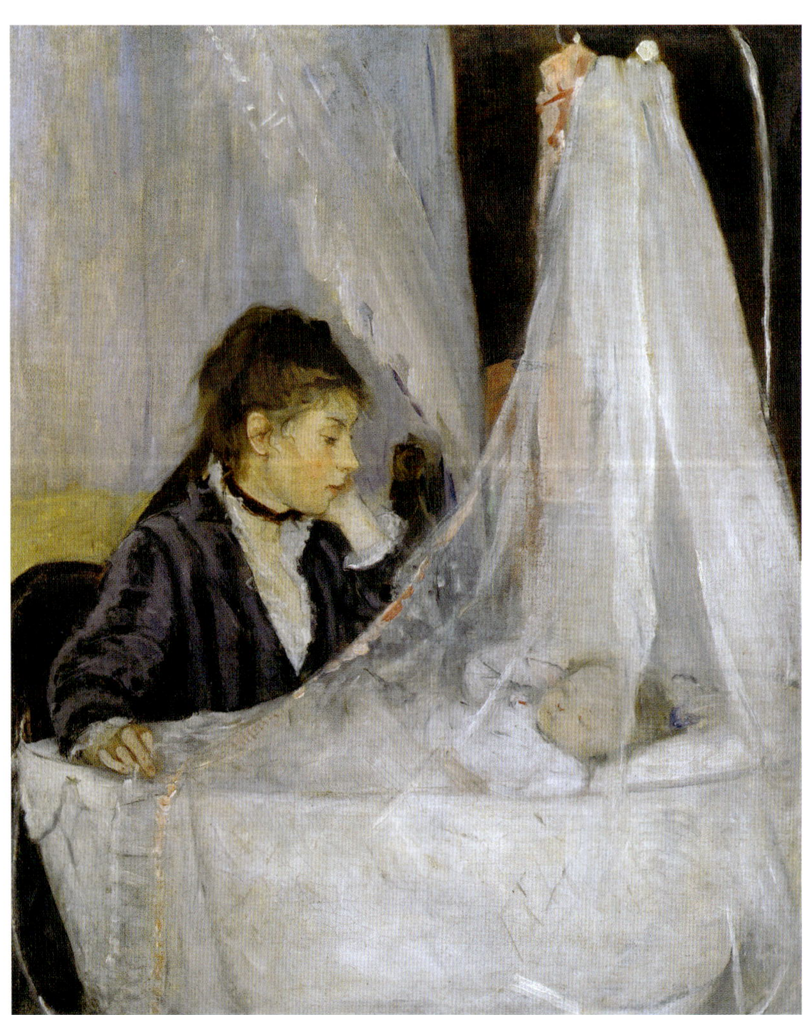

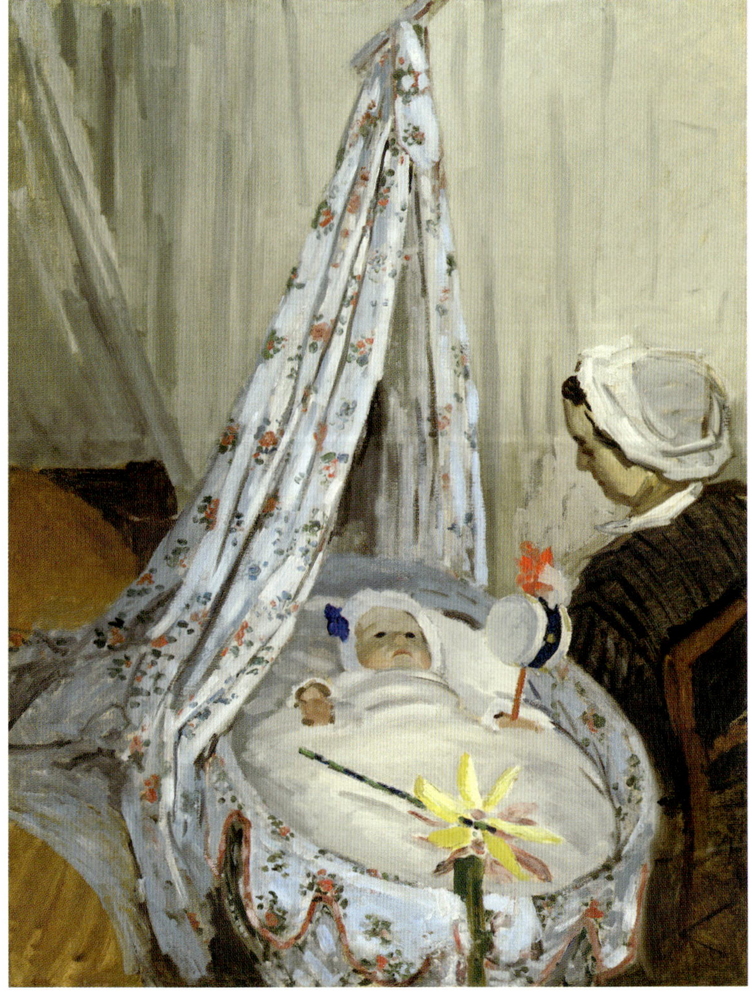

The blurring of women's painting with Impressionism—and this is the second plot twist in our comedy—can also be attributed to the chosen themes: gardens, bouquets, familiar landscapes, intimate scenes, women engaged in their private occupations, mothers, children. This territory was occupied by Manet, Monet, Renoir, Degas, and Pissarro, as well as their female colleagues, Morisot, Cassatt, Marie Bracquemond, and Eva Gonzalès [figs. 7 and 8]. Interestingly, however, many of the women painters who exhibited at the Salon or, like Virginie Demont-Breton, at the Union des Femmes Peintres et Sculpteurs, rejected these minor genres—"a few genre scenes, a large number of portraits, flowers, fruit, a few landscapes, a single full-length portrait"—which were too readily left to them.[65] Instead, they undertook figure and history paintings. And, in a further narrative twist that revealed the critics' blindness and inability to define a feminine art, male painters such as Bouguereau abundantly produced works that provide "an entryway into feminine genius," disclosing "something of the secret feelings of the daughters of Eve," as Le Roux's fantasy would have it [fig. 9]. Meanwhile, Mary Cassatt, whose independence and feminism were beyond dispute, built her entire oeuvre around the feminine and intimate subjects expected from a woman painter.

Fig. 9. William-Adolphe Bouguereau (French, 1825–1905), *Le travail interrompu*, 1891. Oil on canvas, 63 × 39¼ in. (160 × 99.7 cm). Mead Art Museum at Amherst College, 1971.54

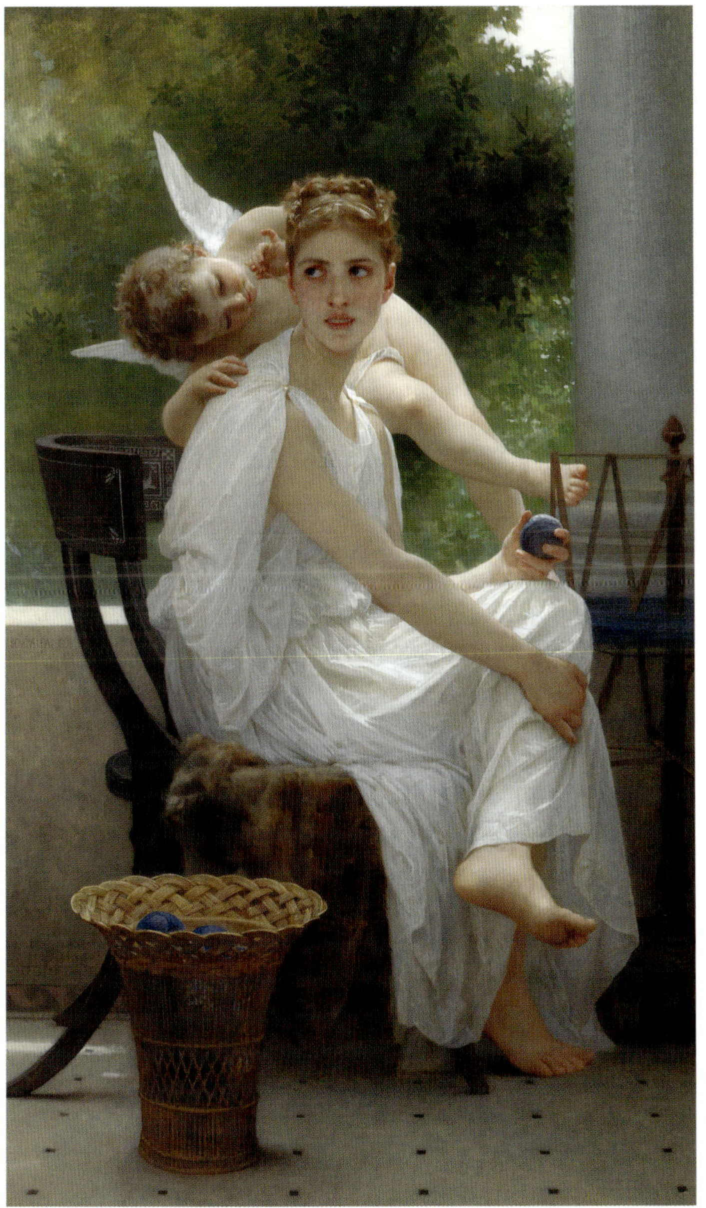

We are thus witness to a curious reversal of roles. In the early 1860s, even as the question of women's artistic training began to be discussed publicly,[66] a whole band of artists (Manet, Degas, Bazille, Monet, Renoir) deserted the lecture halls of the École des Beaux-Arts. Women thronged to the workshops of the Académie Julian, where academic training was gasping its last breath. Bashkirtseff, for example, returned to classical literature, pencil in hand, searching for the edifying, moral, noble, and grand subject from which to make a painting: "Will I really become a painter? The truth is, I leave the atelier only to read Roman histories accompanied by engravings, notes, maps, texts, and translation."[67] Meanwhile, a few men delightedly confined themselves within women's domestic spaces and found their inspiration there. Léon Lagrange wrote, "Man is not made for the wholly sedentary life; woman, by contrast, bears it without ill effect; she also tolerates better the constant vigilance, the active immobility characteristic of the engraver. . . . In some sense, it is only by feminizing himself that a man manages to develop these faculties, which are contrary to his physical constitution, and he always does so at the cost of his strength."[68] Lagrange did not realize that he was anticipating a formidable and salutary scrambling of masculine and feminine positions. Even among the ranks of the Impressionist (and therefore "feminine") painters, it was believed that one woman artist, Mary Cassatt, was more masculine than another, namely, Morisot.[69] Cassatt was masculine because she was unmarried, because she was a better draftsperson, and because she was an American and therefore embodied the sturdy and independent nature of her people.

An Outmoded Plaything, or The Wrong Path It is therefore possible, as Rozsika Parker and Griselda Pollock suggest, that when women were finally admitted to the École des Beaux-Arts in 1897 what they got was a long-coveted toy, but one that, ultimately, was worn out, broken, and no longer appealing.[70] Their relentlessness in demanding absolute and legitimate equality with their male colleagues masked the silent revolution that was demolishing the entire Beaux-Arts system. Because of the frustration women had felt for decades at being denied nude models and anatomy classes and at being barred from competition for the Prix de Rome, the system still retained a certain luster for them.[71] Should this relentless struggle to enter a fortress in ruins be seen as evidence of women's conservatism, their atavistic tendency to imitate? This quality—"mimicry, lack of initiative, fear of being forsaken"[72]—was commonly attributed to women to explain their perceived obstinacy.

The need for an official institution and a master teacher, which accounts for the success of the Académie Julian, has been pointed out several times. Julie-Victoire Daubié, who believed in state action only because the inequalities were such that they could solely find resolution through a strong interventionism, itemized all the privileges refused women—not only the

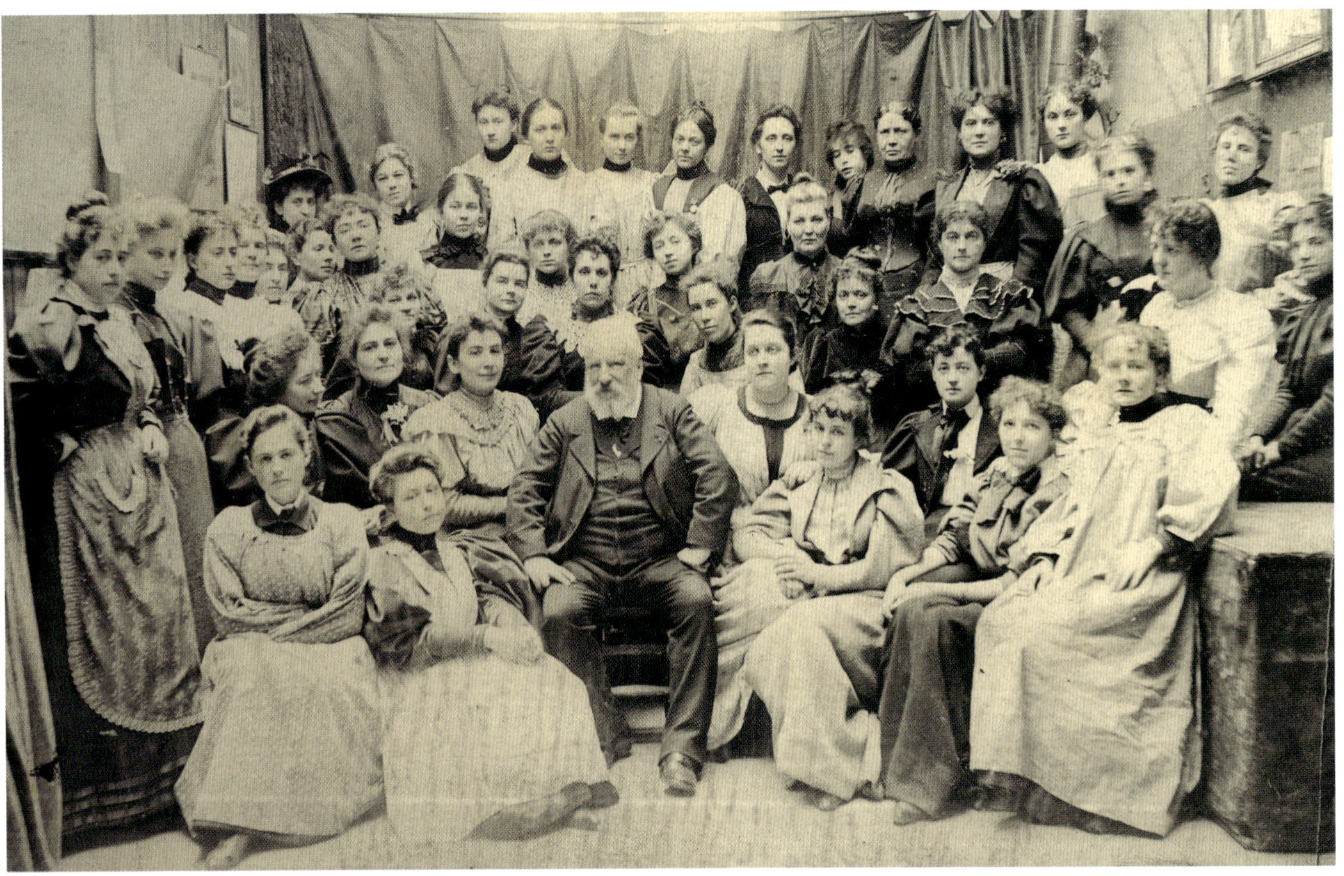

Fig. 10. Atelier Bouguereau, Académie Julian, rue de Berri, Paris, 1896. Photographer unknown. Collection Del Debbio

École des Beaux-Arts and the Prix de Rome but also medals, official commissions, the Légion d'Honneur, the Institut de France. This list indicates the need among women artists for norms and for membership in a social body.[73] Bashkirtseff, who attended a few of Hubertine Auclert's feminist protests, wrote in *La citoyenne* (under the pseudonym Pauline Orell) to lament the conservatism of the other women in the workshop: "Just imagine, of the fifteen women at the Académie Julian, there is not one who would not laugh or cross herself at the idea of women's emancipation, some out of ignorance, others because it is not *comme il faut*."[74]

Raoul Sertat, in reaction to Hélène Bertaux's demand on behalf of the Union des Femmes Peintres et Sculpteurs that women be admitted to the École des Beaux-Arts in the period 1889 to 1890, made reference to that conformism: "The woman artist seems to doubt herself; she is deferential in the extreme toward her masters, and they influence her to such a degree that they pose a danger to her independence."[75] G. Dargenty went even further: "[Women artists display] a blind obedience . . . a slavishness that kills ideas, a religious and therefore irrational admiration of [their] master, the desire to be like him, the conviction that, the closer one gets to him, the better one imitates him, the stronger one becomes!"[76]

Stories about the Académie Julian, which undoubtedly circulated outside its walls, may justify such declarations [fig. 10]. Amélie Beaury-Saurel was in love with Rodolphe Julian, whom she married in 1895. Elizabeth Gardner was also in love with her teacher William Bouguereau, becoming his wife in 1896 and espousing as well his painterly manner. She said: "I know I am criticized for not expressing my individuality with more audacity . . . but I prefer to be known as the best imitator of Bouguereau than to be no one."[77] The American artist Ellen Day Hale warned her friends "to pursue 'friendship' with professors carefully 'against a fault very common among artists of our sex, that of imitating a master and doing nothing original.'"[78] Bashkirtseff explained such attachment to a professor in very rational terms: "Tony is a strong man, a serious artist, an *académicien*, a classicist, and lessons from such people are always excellent. In painting and literature, learn the grammar first; then your nature will tell you whether you should compose plays or little songs." At the same time, she maintained an ambivalent relationship with Jules Bastien-Lepage, whose works she admired enormously and whose style she adopted [fig. 11]: "I love his painting, and it is impossible to view him as a teacher. One wants to treat him as a friend, and his paintings exist to fill us with admiration, awe, and envy. . . . [He] is a lucky man!—I'm a little flustered in his presence. Although he has the physique of a twenty-five-year-old, he has the kindly and unassuming serenity that one sees in great men. . . . I will ultimately come to see him as handsome; in any case, he possesses the infinite charm of people who have merit and forcefulness and who know it, without conceit or foolishness."[79]

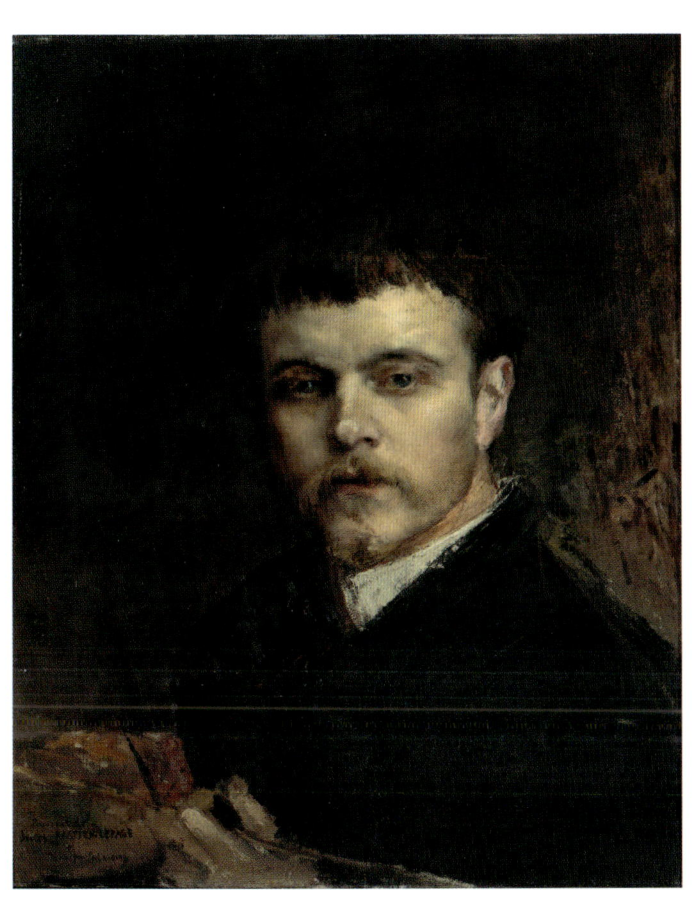

Fig. 11. Jules Bastien-Lepage (French, 1848–1884), *Portrait of the Artist*, ca. 1880. Oil on canvas, 22 × 18⅛ in. (55.5 × 46 cm). Musée d'Orsay, Paris, Gift of Emile Bastien-Lepage and his wife Lucie-Rose Moncuit, 1926, 20040

In the second half of the nineteenth century, women painters, though tethered to a system that had excluded them for decades, undertook initiatives that, given the supposed nature of femininity, ought to have been impossible. In particular, they played a role in the destruction of the Salon's importance and of everything that accompanied it: jury, selection method, medals, mentions in the press. In 1874, disregarding the alarmed advice of Manet and Guichard, Berthe Morisot decided to join the group to which Monet, Cézanne, and Renoir belonged, to secede from the official organization, and exhibit as an independent. Marie Bracquemond followed her, then Cassatt. Eventually, in 1881, dozens of other women artists assembled under the banner of the Union des Femmes Peintres et Sculpteurs. They exhibited together every year, rejecting the Salon's organizational rigidity. It was a lifeline more than an act of sedition, because the other statement by the union was the acceptance of the protégés of sculptor Mme Bertaux to the very official École des Beaux-Arts. Mme Bertaux and her friends, colleagues, and sisters did not understand that the only way to save women and art itself was to turn their backs on the Beaux-Arts system and the academies, which had rejected them for so long.

Yet the Salon and artistic training were still regarded with the greatest seriousness; because it was through these two institutions that women sought to escape another looming threat: amateurism. In literature and painting dating back to ancient times, there are powerful images of elegant women who devoted themselves to the pleasures of painting. Denise Noël rightly cites a precept set down in Baldassare Castiglione's *Il cortegiano* (*Book of the Courtier*), which stipulates that the noblewoman must have "knowledge of what these lords wanted the Courtier to know ... letters, music, painting." She also quotes Mme Roland's memoirs: "I will not make my daughter a *virtuosa*; I will remember that my mother feared I would become a great musician and would devote myself exclusively to painting, because she wanted above all else for me to love the duties of my sex and be a housewife and mother."[80] In the mid-nineteenth century, John Ruskin also wrote on the education of young women. He advised: "Then, in art, keep the finest models before her, and let her practice in all accomplishments be accurate and thorough, so as to enable her to understand more than she accomplishes."[81] Ruskin approved of giving women access to art, but only to make them more submissive to their husbands. The views of the English writer, who exerted a considerable influence, were shared by Marius Vachon, who wrote, more prosaically, "Since 1850, artistic tastes have progressed considerably among women; painting in oil and watercolor is part of the program in all higher education for the upper bourgeoisie and the aristocracy."[82] What was simply part of a good education for girls in the very bourgeois Morisot family became a consuming pastime and then, in Berthe's case, a dangerous career. One might also mention in this context Marie Bashkirtseff, who dreaded being reduced by family members to the despised rank of dilettante: "I'm going downstairs to Mother's salon to receive congratulations from all the imbeciles who believe that the painting I do is that of a woman of high society, and who give the same compliments to Alice and the other little fools."[83] In an effort to combat precisely that relative lack of commitment, the director of the Malerinnenschule Karlsruhe (Painter's School in Karlsruhe) sought to open the doors of his establishment to women: "The prevailing dilettantism, which declares itself openly and pretentiously, is the evil gnawing away at women's artistic practice. The Karlsruhe school must consider its most noble aims the struggle against dilettantism and the strongest encouragement possible of serious and professional work."[84] This peril, however, was considered real and grave. In 1905 Léonce Bénédite, in his introduction to the works of contemporary Frenchwomen, wrote of "the many youthful *amateurs* who constitute the bulk of feminine artists" [fig. 12].[85]

Fig. 12. John Singer Sargent (American, 1856–1925), *The Fountain, Villa Torlonia, Frascati, Italy*, 1907. Oil on canvas, 28⅛ × 22¼ in. (71.4 × 56.5 cm). The Art Institute of Chicago, Friends of American Art Collection, 1914.57

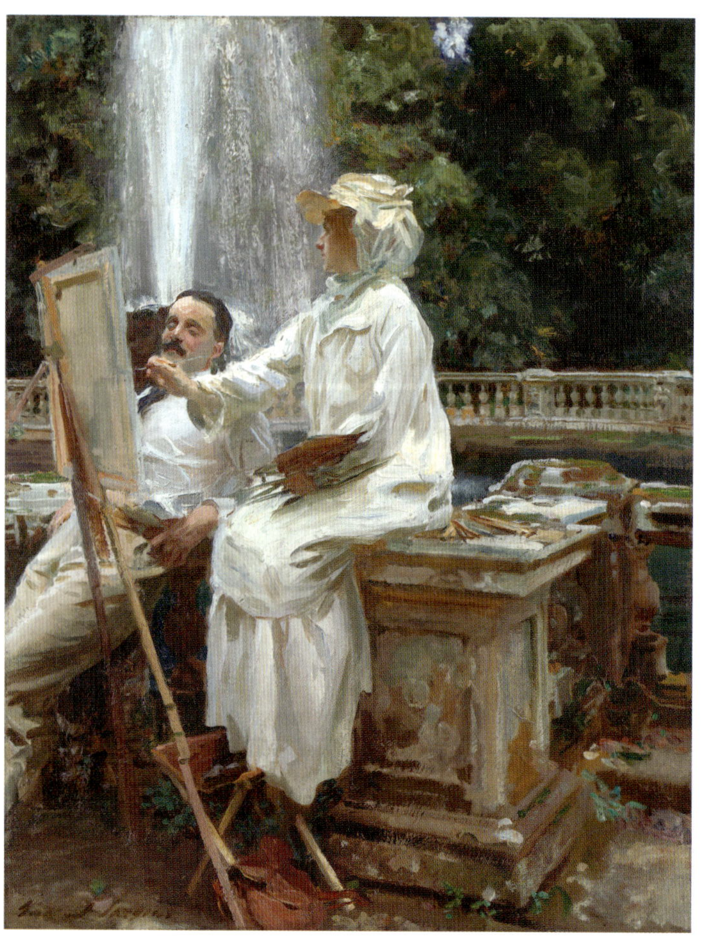

Paris, the Art Capital "Lucky Frenchwomen, you don't know what other countries are like for [young artists], especially the country I came from. You will never understand what France is for us.... A country capable of such delicacy, such pure enthusiasm—one has to love this country! It has proven that the woman artist has a motherland on this earth." So declared the German Swiss Louise Breslau.[86] Breslau's feeling of bliss is not surprising. She had a brilliant career in Paris, obtained commissions and honors (she was the first foreign woman to receive the Légion d'Honneur, in 1901), and moved through various artistic and literary circles, including Degas's. And though it is difficult to reconcile Breslau's statement with what

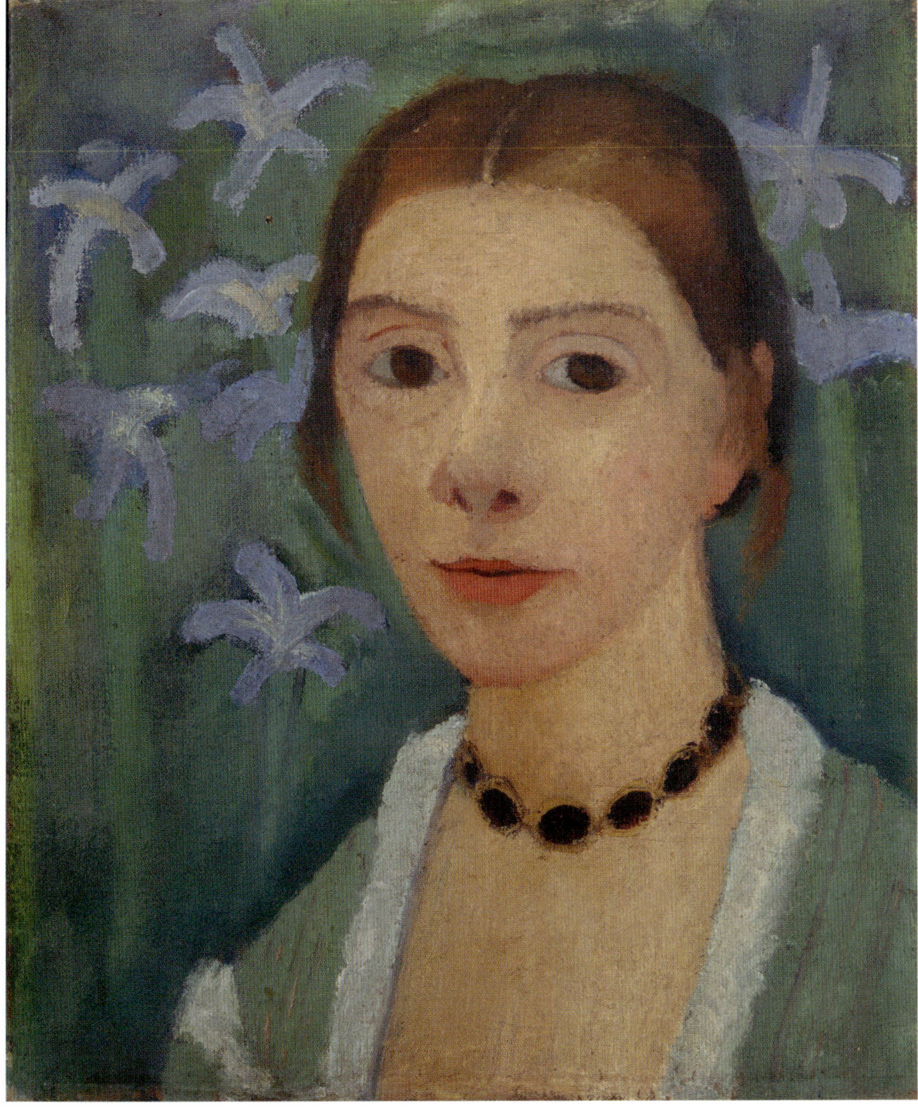

Fig. 13. Paula Modersohn-Becker (German, 1876–1907), *Self-Portrait on a Green Background with Irises*, 1900–1907. Oil on canvas, 16 × 13½ in. (40.7 × 34.5 cm). Kunsthalle Bremen, Acquired in 1967, 972-1967/20

we know about the conditions imposed on women artists, she was not the only one to pay tribute to the French capital. Paula Modersohn-Becker, a German painter, was able to receive training in various schools in her home country that were accessible to women—such as in Berlin, Karlsruhe, and Munich (the academy in that city was considered second only to the Paris school).[87] She traveled constantly between the artist's colony of Worpswede—where she lived among peers and with her painter husband—and Paris. There she discovered the stimulation of museums, exhibitions, artists, and life itself, along with the possibility of completing her training. "I hope to learn many things, particularly because there is a wonderful anatomy class dispensed free of charge at the school of fine arts, which will make up for my inadequate knowledge of anatomy. Yesterday, by means of homework and drawing boards, the knee was brilliantly explained to us. Nowhere else are girls offered such a thing [fig. 13]."[88]

Paris therefore attracted many artists-in-training, some of whom also took courses in Germany from time to time. It was almost a requirement that this training end with a trip to Italy.[89] American women too made Paris their motherland, despite the warm welcome extended to women in several art schools in the United States, such as the Pennsylvania Academy of the Fine Arts in Philadelphia, the School of the Museum of Fine Arts in Boston, and the Art Students League of New York. The Beaux-Arts system in Paris was reputed to be well organized and fiercely devoted to the human figure, and that system would play a role in the professionalism of American schools.[90] In addition, there were museums, Salons (official or independent), and exchanges with male artists who, despite common misogynist beliefs, were often friendly and helpful.[91] All of these visiting students—Americans, Swiss, Finns, Scandinavians, Poles, and French—contributed to Paris's reputation as the capital of the arts.

Ongoing Questions This exhibition attempts to explore the relationships that women artists, temporary and voluntary expatriates, unfailingly established with one another. Yet according to Kirsten Swinth, in the year 1888 alone, there were a thousand American students in Paris.[92] That number suggests the difficulties entailed in connecting the threads. It is well known that Bashkirtseff and Breslau were engaged in a fierce competition at the Académie Julian, as Sophie Schaeppi, Madeleine Zillhardt, and Beaury-Saurel attested.[93] Berthe Morisot is known to have found reading Marie Bashkirtseff's journal an emotional experience. Furthermore, we know that she and Mary Cassatt first met during the Impressionist exhibitions and went together to visit the exhibition of Japanese prints at the École des Beaux-Arts in 1890.[94] It is conceivable that Cassatt ran into Breslau at the home of their mutual friend, Degas. Cassatt, Gonzalès, Marie Petiet,

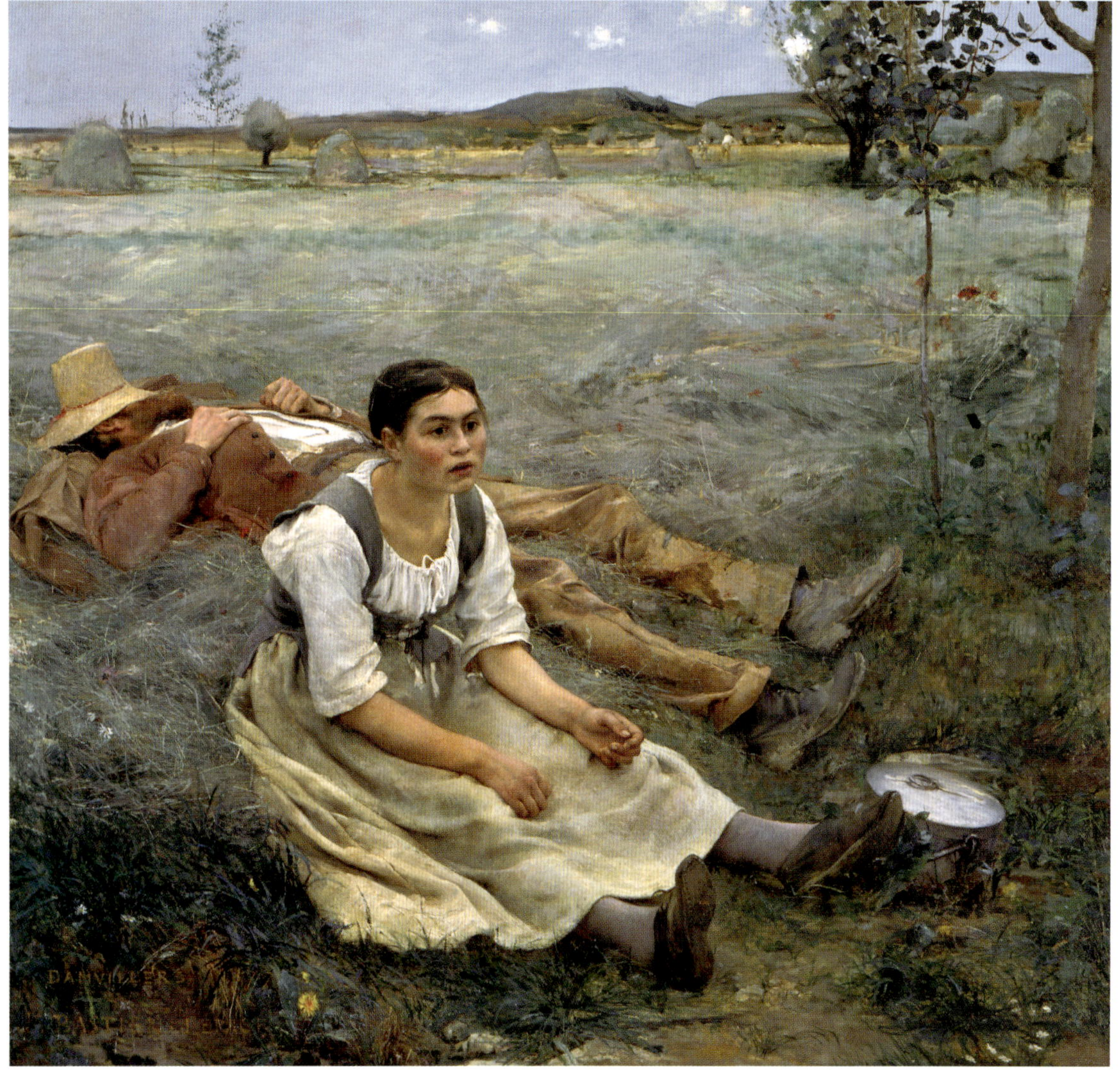

Fig. 14. Jules Bastien-Lepage (French, 1848–1884), *Hay Harvest*, 1877. Oil on canvas, 63 × 76¾ in. (160 × 195 cm). Musée d'Orsay, Paris, RF2748

and Louise Abbéma passed through the "women's studio" run by Jean-Jacques Henner, Chaplin, and Carolus-Duran. Did they meet? We know almost everything about Rosa Bonheur and Anna Klumpke's mutual passion from the moment they met on October 15, 1889,[95] but dates are missing for other friendships and enmities. It is likely that compatriots got together in the area surrounding the capital and at the artists' colonies of Pont-Aven or Concarneau, in Brittany. The Norwegians Harriet Backer and Kitty Kielland may have spent time together in Paris and strengthened their bond of friendship. Artists of different nationalities also kept company with one another. The Finn Helene Schjerfbeck met the Austrian Marianne Stokes at Pont-Aven, where they formed a deep friendship.[96] The Swedish painter Hanna Pauli painted an extraordinary portrait of her Finnish friend Venny Soldan-Brofeldt [plate 10].

These women enlisted a wide range of styles and represented different tastes. The academicism of the Académie Julian predominated, but it was revitalized by Bastien-Lepage's plein-air naturalism, which appealed to many young women artists [fig. 14]. Cassatt, however, remained unconvinced, as her friend Emily Sartain reported: "I do not by any means agree with all the judgments of Miss Cassatt. She is too extreme, she snubs all modern art, has contempt for the Salon paintings of Cabanel and Bonnat, and for all the names that are usually venerated."[97] Likewise, Morisot rejected the ersatz naturalism practiced by Bashkirtseff, which she judged mediocre [fig. 15].

How, then, does one evaluate this rising tide of new work, often chaotic and impetuous? It must be said that art history has not yet completed the inquiries begun in the early 1970s, and the various schools are not treated equally in research on women painters. Scandinavian and Finnish painters have been granted full recognition in the last several decades, so much so that—to the curator's joy and dismay—their paintings have become icons in permanent collections and are not often allowed out on loan. The same cannot be said for French women painters. Although the self-portrait of Bashkirtseff, a Russian who lived mostly in France, is protected almost like a holy relic at the Musée des Beaux-Arts Jules Chéret in Nice, many of her works are unknown or lost [plates 3 and 68]. The works of Virginie Demont-Breton, president of the Union des Femmes

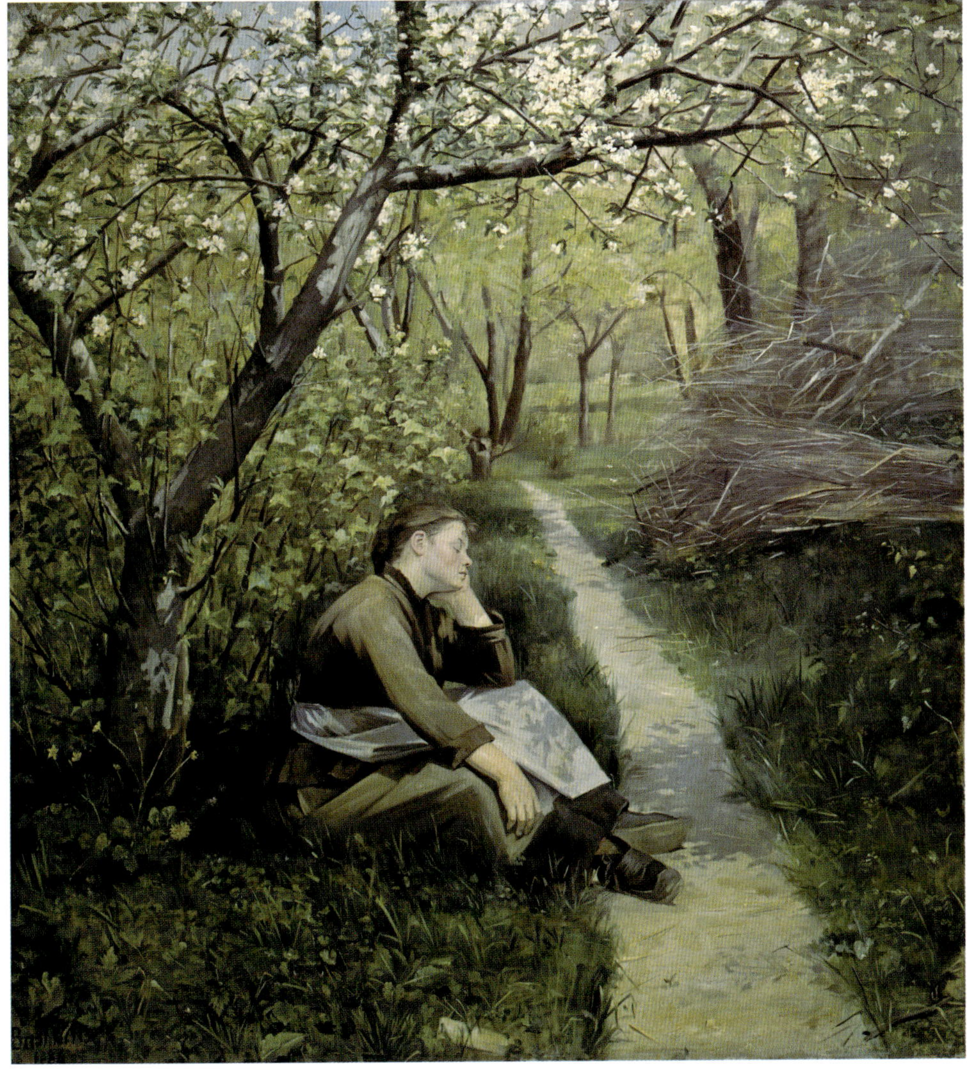

Fig. 15. Marie Bashkirtseff (Ukrainian, 1858–1884), *Spring*, 1884. Oil on canvas, 84⅞ × 78½ in. (215.5 × 199.5 cm). State Russian Museum, St. Petersburg

Peintres et Sculpteurs, though they were honored in her time, are usually misidentified or their locations are unknown. Most of the artists and paintings mentioned by Tamar Garb and Denise Noël in their remarkable and detailed studies have faded into oblivion and are known only through poor-quality reproductions. Of the painters Bénédite chose for the book edited by Sparrow, all or almost all have vanished completely. Excellent surprises can sometimes be had, such as the museum exhibition devoted to Marie Petiet in Limoux, her native town,[98] which resuscitated the works of that interesting artist discussed by Bénédite. But how many entire careers are still lost to us? Of the sixty-four paintings that the state purchased from women painters at the Salon between 1869 and 1900, there are identifiable photographs of only six.[99] In all the other cases, the location of the painting is unknown, or the work is in poor condition, or the work has not been photographed since it was exhibited in one of the various Salons of the late nineteenth century.

A true assessment is difficult, not least because the images we do still have provoke a certain discomfort. Many are mediocre, mawkish, or trivial works. Of all the women painters introduced by the Sparrow book, only a few—Marie Cazin, for example, whose work has largely disappeared—make us regret that we could not really know them [plate 59]. The same discouragement, even exasperation, afflicts anyone curious enough to leaf through the Salon catalogues, where male painters always predominate. One witnesses the almost complete shipwreck of the entire Beaux-Arts system, not merely of the work of women. The proportion of interesting works is the same for the women and the men. Near equality seems to have reigned among those who followed the official avenues. Usually, therefore, the mistake that women artists made was to believe that what had been a male preserve was the most desirable thing. Independent, free, emancipated women such as Morisot, Cassatt, and Schjerfbeck were able to create increasingly original, even brilliant works. The inequality lay rather in the realm of the exceptional, the genius. It was there that the weight of prohibitions, prejudices, and subjugation came to bear. A few years later, however, the example of the geniuses Gauguin and Cézanne would produce the genius of Paula Modersohn-Becker.

Here, the case study of Berthe Morisot is telling. When the artist embarked with Monet, Cézanne, and Degas on the adventure of the first Impressionist exhibition, she turned, instinctively or consciously, in the direction of history. The École des Beaux-Arts denied admission to women; Morisot therefore cobbled together her artistic training far from the official paths. Her paintings were prevented from crossing the threshold of the Salon; so, with her friends, she organized the first secessionist exhibition, in 1874. To counteract decades of scorn and the rejection of women painters by the academic establishment, she deliberately joined the ranks of the renegades, liberating herself from official diktats. She even went so far as to place, on the jacket worn in her self-portrait—at the very spot where Rosa Bonheur sported her Légion d'Honneur medal—a flower, which expressed her rejection of the official systems, as well as her freedom, her passion for nature, liberty, and frivolity [plate 5].

And though Morisot's friendships with other women painters were rooted in strict obedience to bourgeois proprieties, she joined with them to wage a battle for liberation. She went further than they, not only liberating artists from the conditions imposed on their careers but also liberating women from the restrictions placed on the fulfillment of their creative aspirations. The strength of her approach was to accept the constraints imposed by society (small formats, intimate subjects), then to transcend them continually by excavating the same motif, to confer, paradoxically, a greater and greater evanescence on it. Morisot reinvented the codes rather than conforming to them. With Bonheur, who donned men's clothing to paint as she liked, and Schjerfbeck and Modersohn-Becker, who drew the inspiration for their new painting from modern society's alienation, Morisot paved the way for twentieth-century women artists, who would build on their predecessors' inheritance.

The questions raised by women's training and careers governed the selection of works for this exhibition, as well as its organization. Paintings were chosen on the basis of several criteria: their ability to transcend both genre and gender; the artist's desire to introduce something new into the art of the time, something that surpassed the pleasure, charm, and sentimentalism usually expected of a woman painter; and the artist's ability to sustain the long, arduous quest for a women's art. As a result, there are no portraits (other than of artists), nor are there still lifes. That is not because women did not distinguish themselves in those genres: Victoria Dubourg, the wife of Henri Fantin-Latour, produced highly prized paintings of bouquets, so prized, in fact, that they were sometimes attributed to her husband. Madeleine Lemaire, who refused to join the Union des Femmes Peintres et Sculpteurs, was an extraordinarily famous painter of flowers, whose brilliant salon was one of the inspirations for that of Mme Verdurin in Marcel Proust's *À la recherche du temps perdu* (*In Search of Lost Time*). (It is worth noting that Proust, who translated Ruskin's *Sesame and Lilies*, conformed to a great extent to the "Ruskinian" idea that women should practice art to better nurture their sociability, their circle of friendships.)[100] It is also the case that women painters, like their male colleagues, solicited portraits as a means to earn a living, but these fields are too compromised by financial need and convention to reflect the autonomy of the artists who produced them. The nude, though it does entail emancipation from convention, exists in very few examples [fig. 16].

Between the widely depicted flowers and portraits on one hand and the rare nude on the other there is a vast sea of genre scenes: women reading letters, women preparing to go out, women awaiting a visit, women in regional costume, women gathering or selling flowers, children playing, children sleeping. From these we have drawn only sparingly, either because the paintings, though known through different publications,[101] have vanished, or because they did not seem to advance the cause of women. For example, Madeleine Carpentier's *La marchande de fleurs au faubourg* (*Flower Seller in the Suburbs*), like hundreds of works by male painters, demonstrates nothing more than a taste for the anecdotal, for prettiness, an inclination that had been rampant in the Salon since the eighteenth century. There is also that ocean of landscapes, as deep as it is unfathomable, from which we chose a few innovative examples.

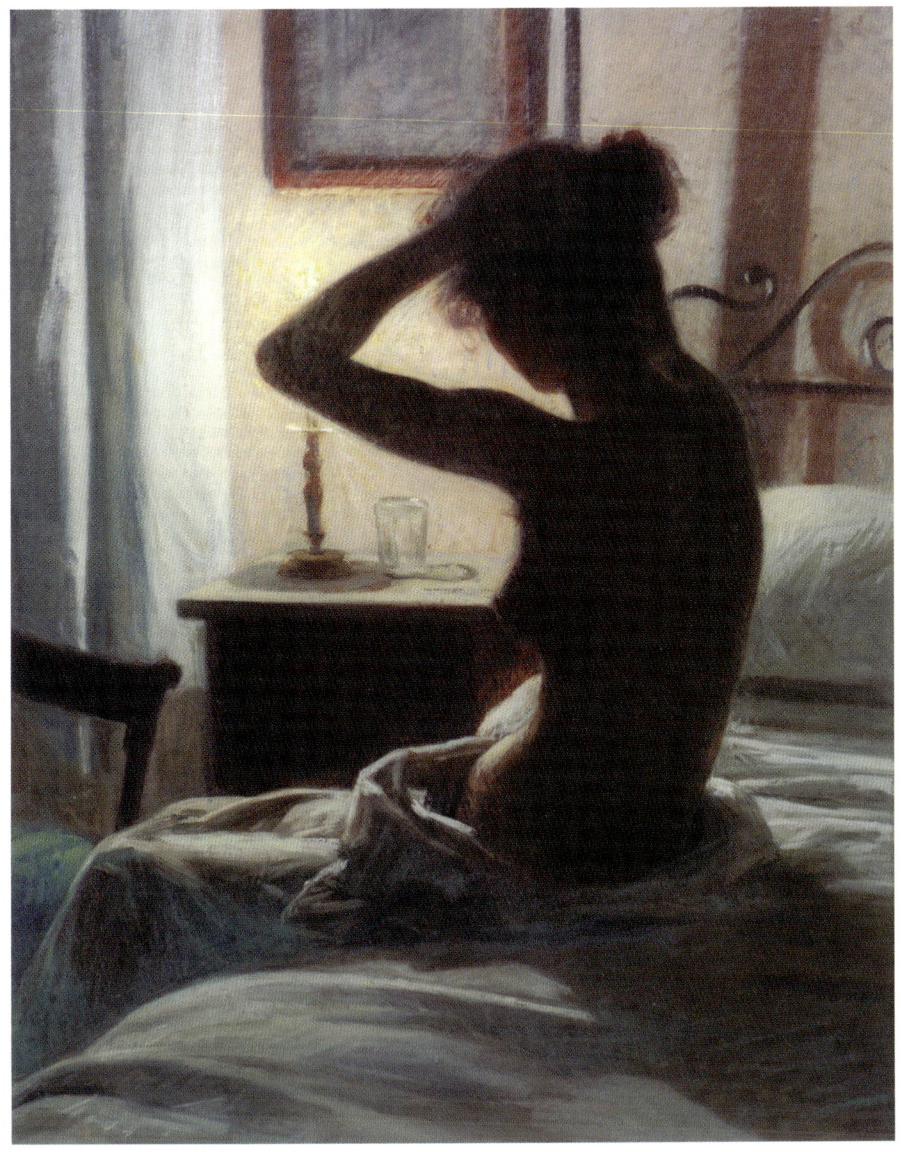

Fig. 16. Elin Danielson-Gambogi (Finnish, 1861–1919), *To Bed*, 1897. Oil on canvas, 27¼ × 19¼ in. (69 × 49 cm). Private collection

Another selection criterion was the wish to illustrate the lives of women who came to Paris from various places, all seeking the same thing: the possibility of acquiring a deeper understanding of their craft (for the most part, they arrived with a strong artistic background) and afterward to make a name for themselves, thanks to the Salon and the entire network of critics, dealers, and art lovers associated with it. German painters, who were able to receive training in their country's art academies, were accordingly less present in Paris. The same can be said of many British artists who, aside from a few exceptions like Lady Butler, Isabelle Dacre, and Annie Swynnerton, largely ignored the French capital.

Though not all countries and not all women painters are included in this exhibition, the international display of paintings offers a stunning vision of a feminist surge in the arts. It shows the extent to which these women artists—viewed with skepticism and confronting so many obstacles—belonged fully to their age. Like their male colleagues, they grappled with the issues of the time: they took on modern subjects, whether rendering life in the country or in the city; they were fascinated with private life, intimate feelings and experiences; they explored the depiction of light and of the ephemeral, impressions. In the late 1890s they moved in the direction of Symbolism and primitive art. And perhaps most tellingly, from their brushes arose the recurring image of the young girl—caught in the liminal stage between adolescence and adulthood—who seems to embody, in her strength, ambitions, dreams, and evanescence, the art itself of these women who, in struggle and in grace, created the future of painting.

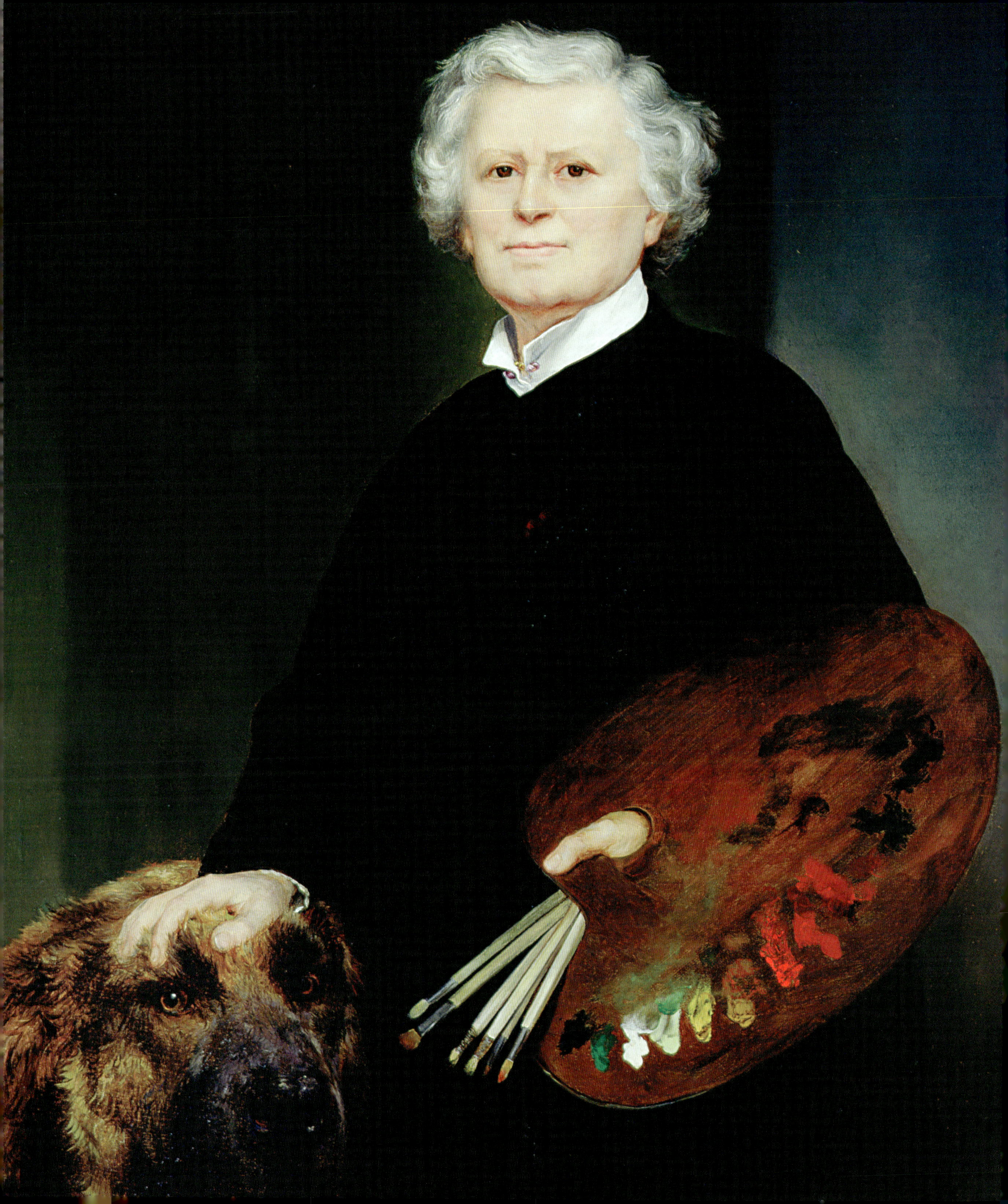

Painting the *Femme Peintre*

"Genius is male," wrote the Goncourt brothers in 1857. The splenetic pair, whose chronicle of the literary and artistic social life of Paris launched the modern genre of malicious celebrity gossip, go on to imagine the autopsies of writers Madame de Staël and George Sand. Suspecting a "hermaphrodite" biology, they assume a physiological foundation for the masculine traits exhibited in these women's life and work.[1] The Goncourts were similarly fascinated by the animal painter Rosa Bonheur, both for her fame and for her rejection of feminine conventions. (Bonheur lived with a woman and had an official permit from the Paris police to dress like a man, allowing her to sketch at the city's slaughterhouses and horse markets without attracting attention.) Desperate to meet her, they finagled an introduction through a mutual friend in 1859. Bonheur dreaded the meeting but felt obliged to do it as a favor. Expressing her dislike for the brothers, she knew "the ways of the world" well enough to be wary and fully on her guard.[2] As expected, they studied her as if she were a circus curiosity, mercilessly dissecting her manners and appearance. They then described her in their *Journal* as a woman with "the head of a little humpbacked Polish Jew," and proceeded to mock her "eternal friend" Nathalie Micas for looking like an old, exhausted mime.[3] The Goncourts reserved their greatest bile for the artists they envied, those whose talent and fame exceeded their own. They were all the more vicious if the artist seemed to them "effeminate" or, even worse, a woman.

The Goncourts' reaction to Bonheur is not exactly typical, but it is certainly telling. It is only a slightly more extreme and rhetorically colorful version of an attitude to women artists than was common among their male peers in nineteenth-century France: a mix of fascination and ridicule, dismissal and disdain. Respect and admiration were rare, and typically expressed in sexist, backhanded terms, lauding women for "painting like a man."[4]

Despite significant progress throughout the nineteenth century in women's access to artistic training and exhibition opportunities, the image of the artist remained

Consuélo Fould, ***Portrait of Rosa Bonheur*****, 1892–94 [detail of fig. 11]**

predominantly male. Creative genius, inspiration, and intellectual interpretation were seen as masculine domains, and bohemian rebellion against bourgeois society was far more risky for women artists than for their male peers. There is excellent scholarship on the various associations, schools, and teaching studios that allowed women artists to advance their careers in mid- to late nineteenth-century France, and this research is frank about the social and institutional barriers that remained, well into the twentieth century and beyond.[5] This essay, while drawing upon that scholarship, will focus on how these artists were perceived and positioned by their colleagues *in paint* and, occasionally, how they responded in representations of their own. Shifting between views of women artists (or the notable lack thereof) in works by male painters of the period and representations by women artists themselves, I aim to illuminate an area of women's artistic culture that has received relatively little attention: the ways their identities as artists were contested on canvas, often in relation to the artistic identities of men.

Competition structured virtually every aspect of the art world in late nineteenth-century Paris—the École des Beaux-Arts, the Salon, the press, and the market. The city was flooded with artists, native and foreign, vying for success, a situation that made it especially difficult for women to find support among their male peers. In fact, artists were even less progressive in recognizing

Fig. 1. Henri Fantin-Latour (French, 1836–1904), *Homage to Delacroix: Cordier, Duranty, Legros, Fantin-Latour, Whistler, Champfleury, Manet, Bracquemond, Baudelaire, A. de Balleroy*, 1864. Oil on canvas, 63 × 98½ in. (160 × 250 cm). Musée d'Orsay, Paris, RF1664

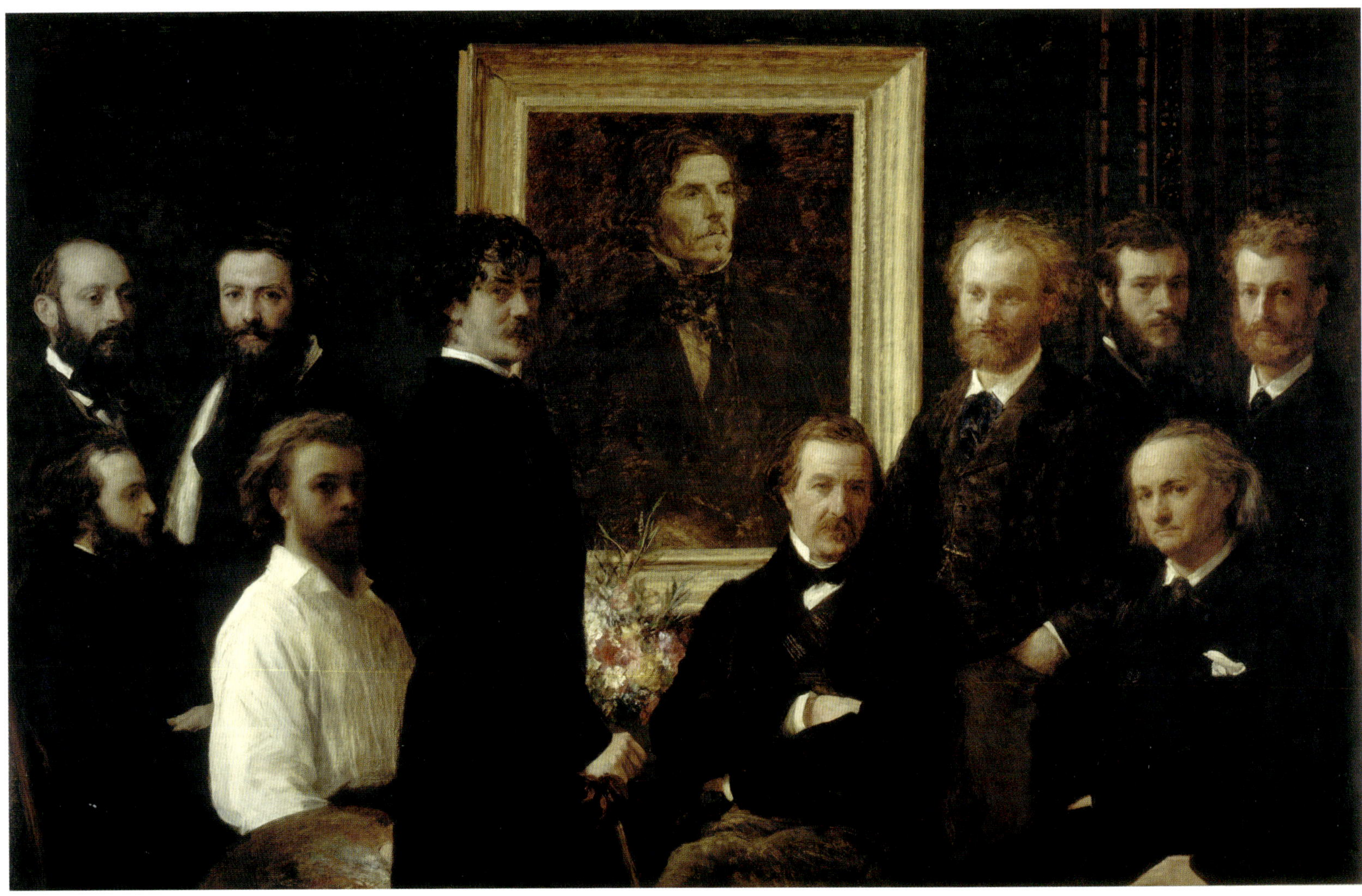

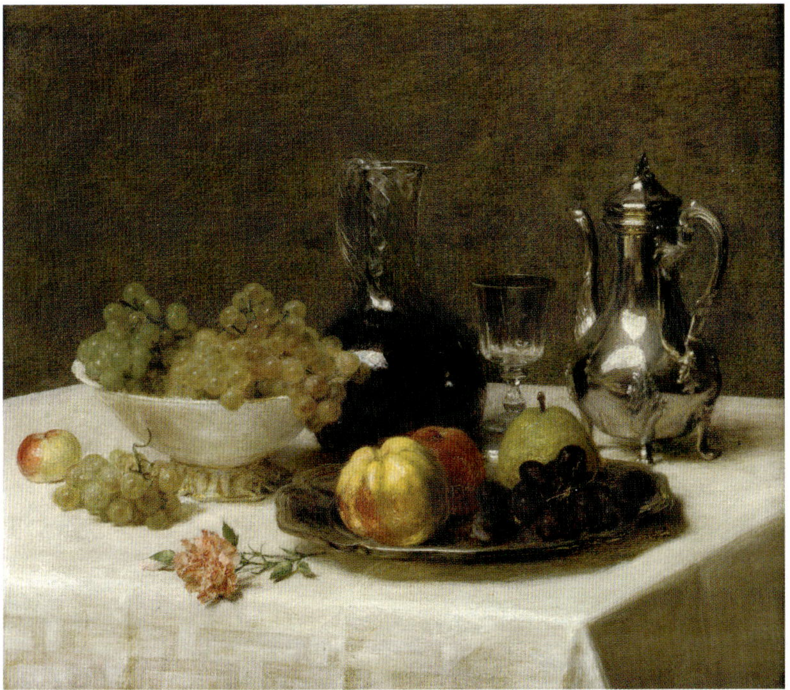

Fig. 2. Victoria Dubourg Fantin-Latour (French, 1840–1926), *Still Life*, 1884. Oil on canvas, 20⅞ × 24¾ in. (53 × 63 cm). Musée de Grenoble, RF3766

the work of women artists than the French state. When the state transferred control of the Salon to artists in 1881, women artists had even greater difficulty gaining admission to the exhibition. The first Salon organized by artists admitted half as many works by women artists as the state-run jury had the previous year.[6] This led to the formation of the Union des Femmes Peintres et Sculpteurs in December 1881, with the aim of forming a separate Salon specifically for the work of women artists. An editorial in the *Gazette des femmes* put it plainly: "Rightly or wrongly, they have judged that at the Salon the male artists falsely claim for themselves the lion's share and treat women's work with excessive disdain."[7] The union gave women artists a regular exhibition venue and a new sense of autonomy over their careers. But although its founders emphasized inclusiveness and mutual support, this association was defined by the same thorny mix of solidarity and rivalry, collectivism and individualism, that defined male artist groups. These tensions were compounded by the added pressure of legitimation: as the main organization representing women artists in France, the union needed to prove that its standards of quality were high.[8] In their struggle to manage their individual and collective reputations as *femmes artistes*, the women of the union disagreed about how to chip away at the pervasive idea of the artist, and of genius, as male.

This idea of the artist was bolstered by painting of the period. Between 1864 and 1885, Henri Fantin-Latour painted five large-scale group portraits of artists, writers, and musicians that forged a new yet still overwhelmingly masculine image of collective artistic identity [fig. 1]. Although their hermetic interior settings suggest a withdrawal from public life, they functioned as painted manifestos at the Salon, announcing a shared aesthetic philosophy as well as a commitment to locating inspiration in mutual admiration and homage. As group portraits, these pictures insisted on the fundamentally collective, reciprocal nature of artistic progress, despite the strain of rivalry and individualism fracturing their forms. But that ideal of collectivity and solidarity hinged in no small part on the exclusion of women, who threatened to disrupt the egalitarian ideal of the homosocial structure.

This exclusion is particularly notable in Fantin's case, since his wife, Victoria Dubourg, was a talented and accomplished artist, known in artistic circles for her intelligence as well as her technical skill.[9] A prolific still-life painter [fig. 2], she regularly exhibited at the Paris Salon and the Royal Academy in London. She shared her husband's devotion to the Old Masters—they were both excellent copyists, and met while painting the same Correggio in the Louvre—as well as his aesthetic commitment to Realism and resistance to Impressionist techniques. She also devoted much of her life to promoting his career and preserving his legacy. And yet there is no indication that Fantin ever considered including her—or any of the other women artists he knew well, such as Berthe Morisot and Marie Bracquemond—in his group portraits. These group portraits track a period of tremendous change in women artists' opportunities in Paris, including the proliferation of private studio schools open to women, their active participation in the Impressionist exhibitions, and the founding of the union. And yet Fantin's image of the artist, and of artistic association, remained adamantly male.

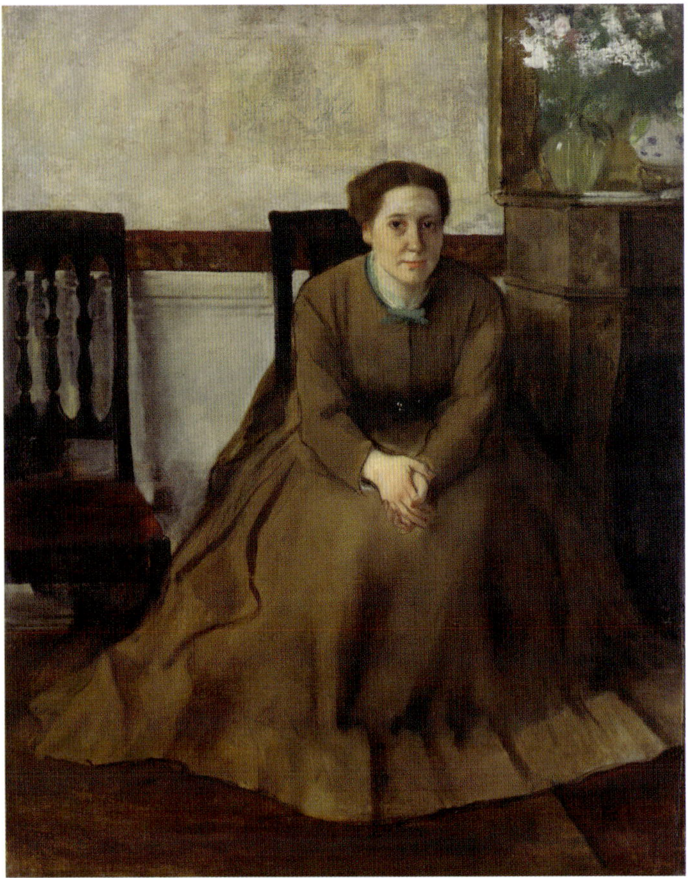

Fig. 3. Edgar Degas (French, 1834–1917), *Victoria Dubourg*, ca. 1868–69. Oil on canvas, 32 × 25½ in. (81.3 × 64.8 cm). Toledo Museum of Art, Gift of Mr. and Mrs. William E. Levis, 1963.45

It is not that Fantin had no interest in painting Dubourg, or that she was unwilling to pose. Fantin painted her reading or simply sitting (never painting) on several occasions, and again in *The Dubourg Family* (1878), where she is defined in relation to her family as a daughter and sister and in relation to Fantin as a wife.[10] Edgar Degas painted her in 1868 or 1869, right around the time of her engagement to Fantin, and his portrait vaguely alludes to Dubourg's vocation in its emphasis on her reddened hands, intelligent eyes, and the bouquet of flowers near her head [fig. 3]. But however arresting this portrait is as an image of unvarnished femininity, engaging candor, and confidence, it is not—at least not explicitly—the portrait of an artist. Degas originally planned to include two paintings on the wall behind Dubourg, more overtly referencing her trade and aesthetic allegiances, but these details were ultimately removed.[11] Dubourg was never painted as a painter, despite her constant presence at the easel both at home and in the Louvre, not to mention the notable success of her work in Paris and London.[12] This fact is all the more remarkable in that Fantin painted two pictures of women artists at work.[13] *The Drawing Lesson* (1879) depicts one of his few students, Louise Riesener, and her friend drawing in his studio, and a study of 1883 depicts another student, the English woman Sarah Budgett, contemplating a blank canvas and a vase of flowers with palette in hand [fig. 4]. Both paintings were highly successful, exhibited internationally to critical acclaim.[14] One can only speculate as to why these women captured Fantin's artistic imagination when Dubourg—at least in her role as a painter—did not. Perhaps he was more comfortable depicting women artists as students. Dubourg was his partner and peer, with a style dangerously close to his own.

Fantin's group portraits never included a female writer or musician, either. *The Toast! Homage to Truth* (1865) featured a nude female model as an allegory of Truth, but the artist destroyed this picture after a disastrous reception at the Salon, due in no small part to the awkward presence of a woman in a room full of men.[15] Victoria Dubourg's absence from *Around the Piano* (1885) is particularly notable, given that she introduced Fantin to the German music—Wagner, Schumann, Brahms—to which this work and so many of his lithographs pay tribute [fig. 5].[16] (She was also an excellent musician. The piano featured in the painting was played primarily by her.) In fact, Fantin initially envisioned a group of women singing around the piano, but abandoned the idea when he could not find enough women to pose.[17] (He did not like to work with professional models, preferring to paint family and friends.) When he sent a sketch of the composition to Ruth Edwards, a close friend and the wife of his dealer in England, he included an explanation as to why there were no women, as originally planned: "I'm not putting in any women. I always paint gatherings of artists, not gatherings of society, which I don't know and which terrify me: you can't do anything with those people these days. They are more and more stupid."[18] A withering and repugnant remark, to be sure, but one whose defensiveness reveals a rare flash of awareness of his group portraits' exclusions. He could not have intended it in reference to his wife or Ruth Edwards, for whom he seems to have had the utmost respect. His association of

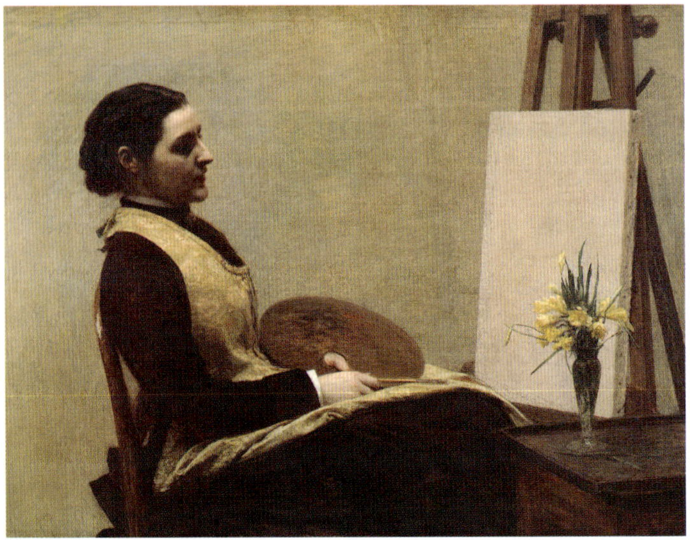

Fig. 4. Henri Fantin-Latour (French, 1836–1904), *Study (Portrait of Sarah Elizabeth Budgett)*, 1883. Oil on canvas, 39⅜ × 52⅜ in. (100 × 133 cm). Musée des Beaux-Arts, Tournai, Belgium

women with the insipid noise of "society," and his rhetorical separation of this society from the gatherings of "artists" he preferred, make clear that he never had women artists in mind.

Including Dubourg in his group portraits, or even depicting her singly as a painter, would have required Fantin to negotiate her status as an artist in relation to his own. What's more, it would have required him to publicly recognize her significance to his work. Dubourg was the more educated and intellectual of the two, with particularly deep knowledge of German literature, philosophy, and music. The painter Jacques-Émile Blanche recounts how she regularly shared literary reviews with her husband, entertained visitors at teatime by translating Hegel, Schopenhauer, and the Ring legend, and translated English criticism of her husband's and other artists' work.[19] Her knowledge and her generosity in sharing it did much to define Fantin's aesthetic interests, shape his social life, and advance his career. In particular, she must have been involved in many aspects of the group portraits, hosting the Monday evening salons that brought their artistic and literary milieu into their home, helping to schedule and coordinate sittings, listening and offering counsel when tensions within the group threatened to boil over, and guiding sitters to the subterranean studio beneath their residence on the rue des Beaux-Arts. Dubourg

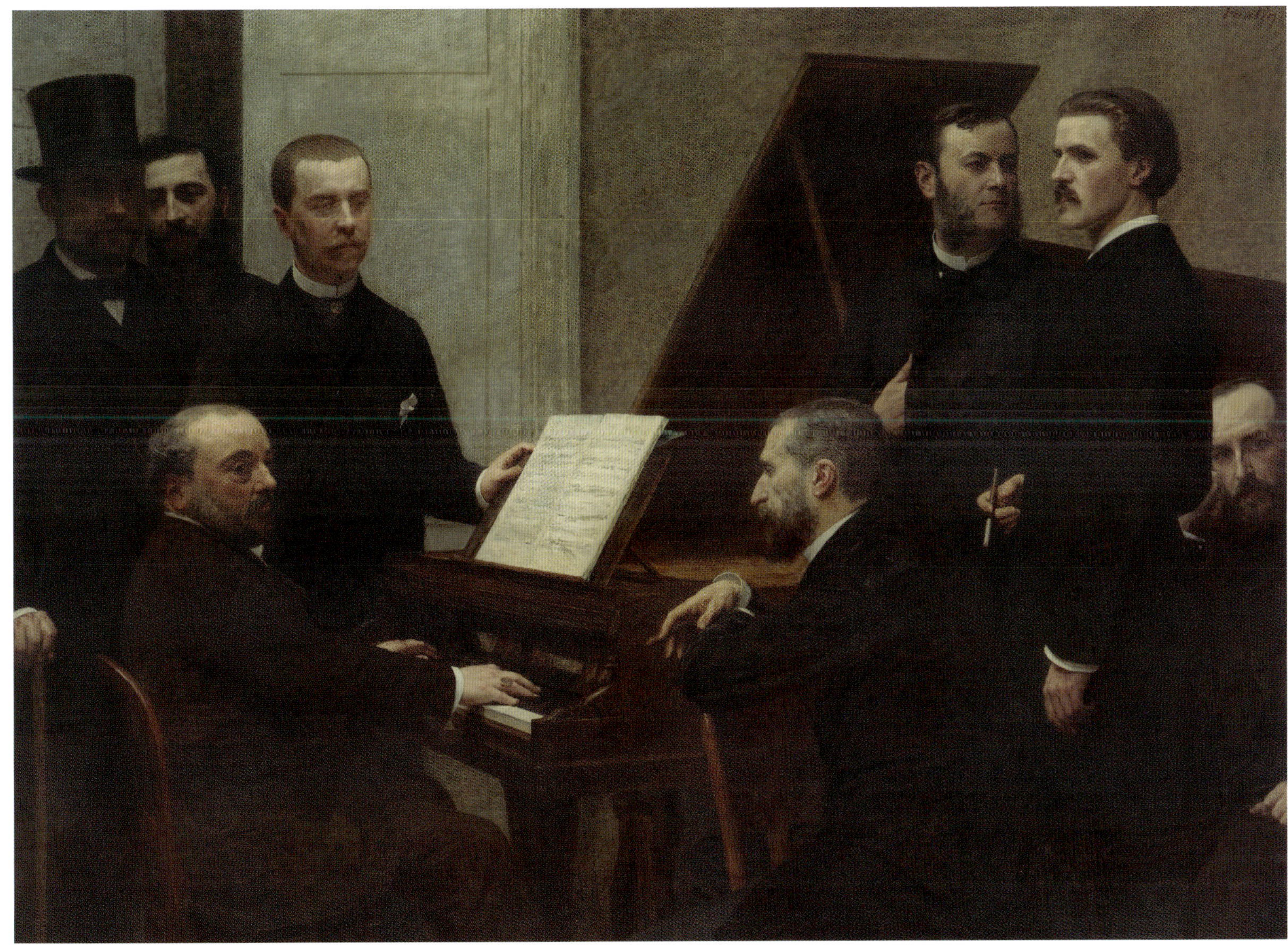

Fig. 5. Henri Fantin-Latour (French, 1836–1904), *Around the Piano: Adolphe Julien, Arthur Boisseau, Emmanuel Chabrier, Camille Benoit, Edmond Maître, Antoine Lascoux, Vincent d'Indy, Amédée Pigeon*, 1885. Oil on canvas, 63 × 87⅜ in. (160 × 222 cm). Musée d'Orsay, Paris, RF2173

had a studio adjacent to Fantin's but also shared his ample, sky-lit space.[20] Photographs of the studio show Fantin's portraits of Dubourg decorating the walls; Dubourg's own portrait of her sister is also prominently displayed.[21] As artists, they worked side-by-side as colleagues, just as they had in the Louvre. They even collaborated on a few canvases, and their work is so close in style and technique that the attribution of several still lifes remains in question. (At least four Dubourg paintings have been sold as Fantins with false signatures. Dubourg was incensed to see this happening even in her lifetime.)[22] No wonder she was "exasperated" by the "unbearable tone" of condescension in Blanche's account of her domestic role.[23] Much more than a great hostess and accommodating translator, Dubourg was a serious artist with a remarkable range of mind.

Fantin was far from alone in relegating women artists to a supporting role outside his paintings. Women rarely appear in nineteenth-century French representations of artistic communities in any medium, visual or literary.[24] It is only slightly more common to find women artists painted singly by male colleagues, and when they are, they are almost always unidentifiable as artists. Degas depicted Dubourg once and Mary Cassatt on several occasions, but never in the act of drawing or painting, although he does depict Cassatt in the Louvre.[25] As far as we know, Dubourg never painted a self-portrait. Cassatt painted two, both on paper in gouache, but only one of them (1878) is finished [fig. 6]. It shows the artist leaning casually on a sofa, capturing her fashionable femininity and determined intensity, but does not show her painting. The other self-portrait (ca. 1880) does depict her in the process of painting, but dissolves into spare, illegible lines around her hands, brush, and paper [see Kendall, fig. 3]. Whether Cassatt abandoned the portrait or chose to leave this area unfinished (more likely the latter, since the work bears her initials), the result is that it comes just shy of making her identity as an artist explicit.

Fig. 6. Mary Cassatt (American, 1844–1926), *Self-Portrait*, 1878. Watercolor, gouache on wove paper laid down to buff-colored wood-pulp paper, 23⅝ × 16⅛ in. (60 × 41.1 cm). The Metropolitan Museum of Art, New York, Bequest of Edith H. Proskauer, 1975, 1975.319.1

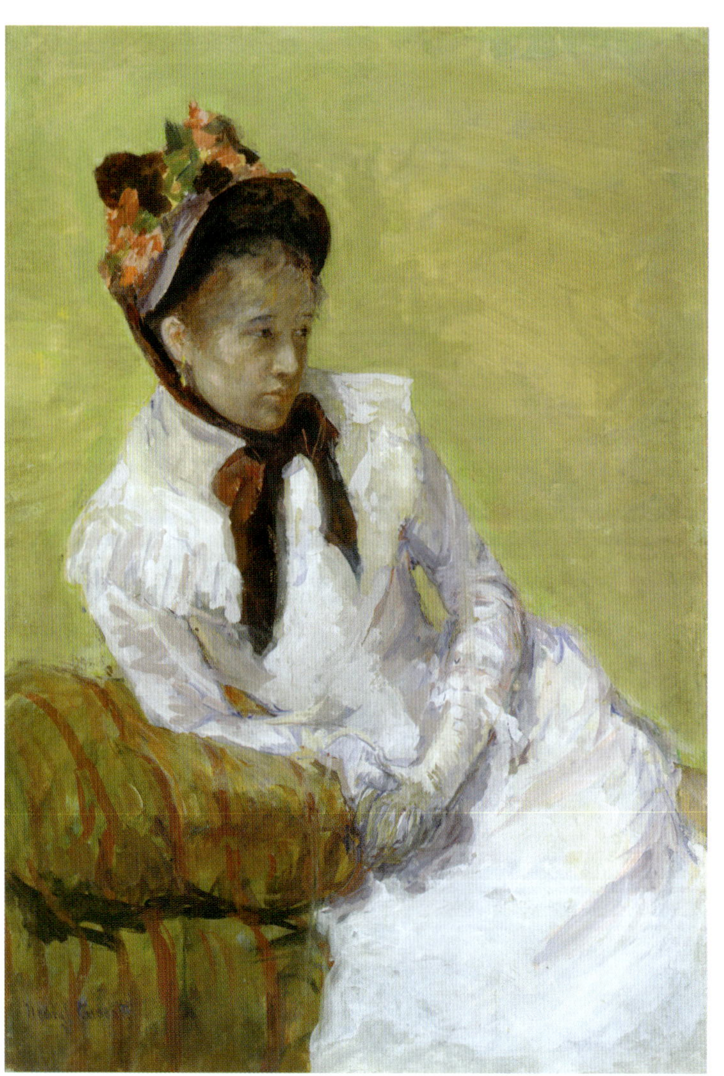

Likewise, Édouard Manet's many paintings of Berthe Morisot show no sign of her vocation. The only woman he—like Fantin—depicted in the role of artist was a student, Eva Gonzalès. His *Portrait of Mlle E.G.* shows her painting a floral still life in Manet's studio, but critics and viewers at the Salon of 1870 judged it awkward and ridiculous [fig. 7]. As Tamar Garb has argued, Gonzalès's "stupefied" expression, wholly impractical white gown, deep décolleté, and unworkmanlike arms made it difficult for the Salon audience to see her as a serious artist. The portrait's harsh reception signaled the difficulty of depicting a woman artist while also satisfying public expectations of feminine refinement, propriety, and charm. Furthermore, Manet's dramatic tonal contrasts and lush, loosely brushed facture insist that Gonzalès's painting is not just indebted to him but is in fact his own.[26] The picture's reappearance in William Orpen's *Homage to Manet*, shown at the New English Art Club in 1909, is perfectly ironic, a further travesty of Gonzalès's already awkward image as a *femme peintre* [fig. 8]. Here that image stands in for Manet's legacy in a room full of men, serving as the backdrop to a group portrait meant to announce the leading artists and critics of British Impressionism.[27]

As these paintings make clear, the status of women artists was contested not only in the realm of social life and institutional politics but also in works of art. When women artists were depicted at work by their male peers, they were usually shown as students following the instruction of a male teacher, or as copyists reproducing an Old Master. An example of the latter, Norbert Goeneutte's *Marcellin Desboutin and His Friends at the Louvre, before a Fresco by Botticelli* (1892) is a playful meditation on the role of women in art, as sources of divine inspiration and diligent reproduction [plate 2]. The painting captures the surge of interest in Botticelli in France during the mid-1880s, following the acquisition of two frescoes by the artist for the Louvre in 1882. Transferred from the Villa Lemmi in Florence, the frescoes were installed at the top of the Daru staircase flanking the entrance to the gallery of large-format French paintings. They quickly became a favorite subject for copyists, especially British and American visitors and women.[28] Goeneutte's scene depicts one of these frescoes, *Venus and the Graces Present Gifts to a Young Girl* (ca. 1483), surrounded by a group of men and a lone female painter, who is working at her easel on what appears to be a full-scale copy. Identified as an English woman,[29] she echoes the slim silhouette of Botticelli's young girl, and the space between her and the group of men—a division made emphatic by her massive canvas—repeats the compositional gap that separates the divine and earthly figures in the fresco.

Fig. 7. **Édouard Manet (French, 1832–1883), *Portrait of Mlle E.G.*, 1870. Oil on canvas, 75¼ × 52½ in. (191.1 × 133.4 cm). The National Gallery, London, Sir Hugh Lane Bequest, 1917, NG3259**

Fig. 8. **William Orpen (Irish, 1878–1931), *Homage to Manet*, 1909. Oil on canvas, 64 × 51 in. (162.9 × 130 cm). Manchester Art Gallery, Purchased from the artist, 1910, 1910.9**

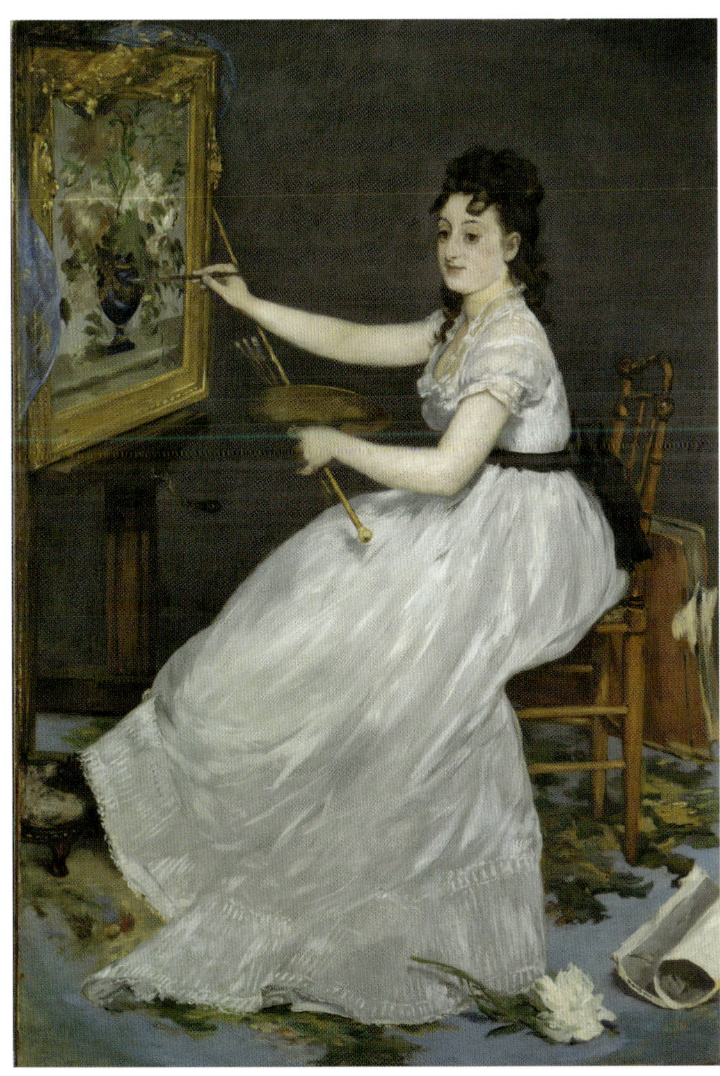

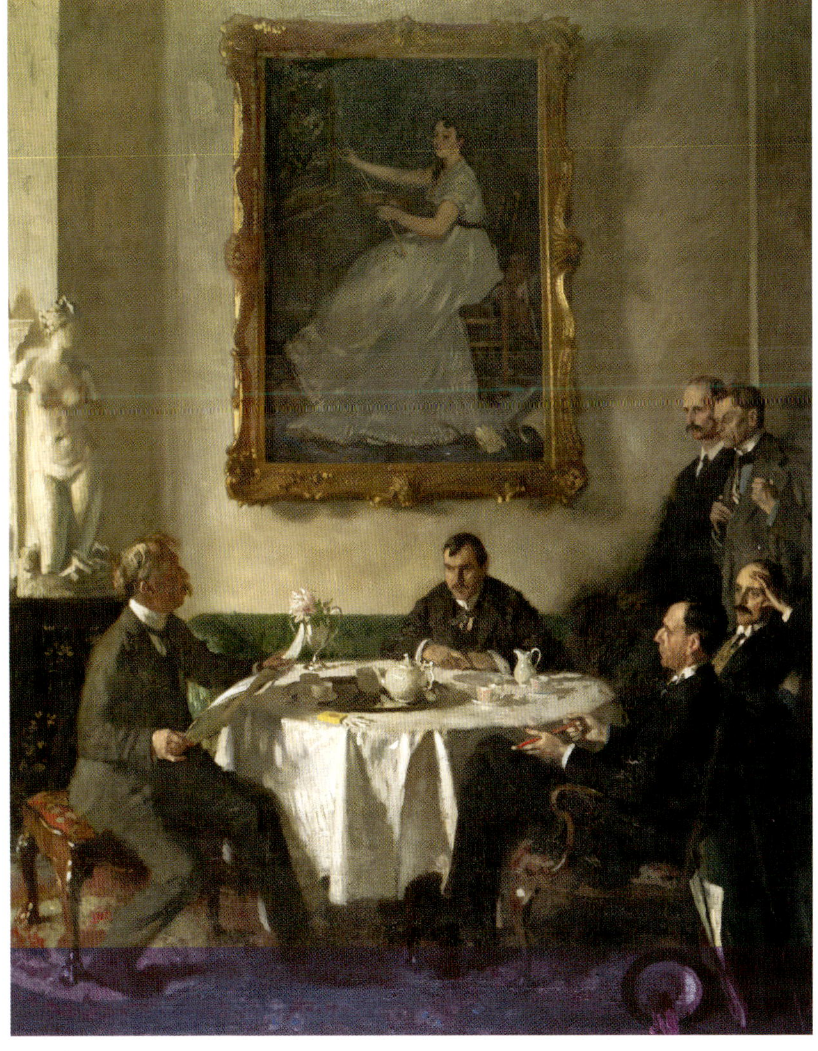

The painting was exhibited in the Salon of 1892, with the group of men identified as the painter and engraver Marcellin Desboutin; the engraver Henri Guérard (who was married to Eva Gonzalès); the critics Roger Marx and Arsène Alexandre; another painter, Victor Vignon; and Goeneutte himself.[30] The central figure in the group, wearing a red cap and scarf, is Desboutin, now better known for his appearance as an archetypal bohemian in pictures by Manet and Degas than for his own work.[31] But in the 1890s he was a widely respected painter and engraver, and he trained Goeneutte in both media. This painting is an homage to him as much as to Botticelli, layering its allegiances in a way likely inspired by Fantin's groups. The difference is that Goeneutte positions his group in relation to women. Like Fantin, he represents his artistic community as exclusively male, but this exclusivity is called into question by the female figures in their midst. Appearing in ideal, mythological form—distanced by layers of time and the picture-within-a-picture motif—or separated by an enormous canvas wall, Goeneutte's female figures are peripheral to the group. Nonetheless, they are a vivid reminder of the shift from model and muse to student and peer that defined women's progress in the art world of nineteenth-century Paris.

Goeneutte delights in the ironic interplay between Botticelli's lithe mythological figures and his modern Parisians, using richly colored scarves of blue and red to link the two most central men to a corresponding feminine divinity in the fresco. The painting's wit hinges on the shift from divine to earthly, Renaissance to modern, feminine to masculine, in its two representational registers. Goeneutte juxtaposes the ideal beauty, creativity, and love that Venus and her retinue represent to the modern "reality" of the art world in fin-de-siècle Paris, where the iconography of gender is removed from the realm of mythological allegory but appears no less absolute. The segregation of male and female artists is unequivocal—virtually architectural—but this segregation is complicated by Goeneutte's dual relationship to the picture as a presence within it and the artist behind the scenes. Although the woman behind the easel occupies the role of copyist within the narrative space of the painting, and Goeneutte is part of the group of male artists and critics representing a more intellectual engagement with art, it is, in fact, Goeneutte who is the copyist of Botticelli's fresco, subsuming the depicted woman's task into his own original composition. The woman's painting remains invisible to anyone but her; we cannot know whether she is copying the fresco faithfully, translating it loosely, or incorporating it into an original composition à la Goeneutte. Whether or not the artist intended it, the painting plays with our stereotypical assumptions about women as copyists and men as creators by blurring the seemingly impassable boundaries between the two.

The strange orientation of the group—all but one of them are posed in profile, rather than facing the fresco—can be explained by Goeneutte's wish to echo Botticelli's composition with his own. But it also suggests that the men may be looking at the fresco's pendant—*A Young Man Being Introduced to the Seven Liberal Arts*—outside the frame [fig. 9]. Goeneutte's arrangement of artists is a mirror image of this fresco's composition, inverting its depiction of a male figure at left encountering seven female figures at right. By incorporating a copy of Botticelli's *Venus and the Graces* into his composition and flipping the figural arrangement and the gender imbalance of the unseen fresco, Goeneutte makes his painting their modern companion piece, an addendum to Botticelli's pair. In order to align himself with the Old Master, he must take on the subservient (feminine) role of copyist. The painting articulates this age-old conundrum of emulation in knowingly gendered terms.

When women artists of this period included themselves in pictures of artistic community, the result tended to revolve less around the hierarchy of homage than around the bonds of friendship essential to their careers. But like Fantin and his colleagues, they used such paintings as an opportunity to define themselves as artists via bonds of association. Although they tended to paint less formalized genre scenes (more like Goeneutte than Fantin) that do not announce themselves as portraits of artist groups, this relative modesty can be deceptive. Louise Abbéma's monumental *Lunch in the Greenhouse* depicts a scene of refined yet relaxed sociability in the winter garden of Sarah Bernhardt's elegant home on the rue Fortuny [plate 24]. Abbéma and Bernhardt were lifelong friends, so close that they were rumored to be lovers, and shared a passion for painting. Abbéma positions her self-portrait behind the fashionable actress, lounging on fur-draped cushions like the mistress of the house. The famous librettist Émile de Najac is seated at left, and Abbéma's parents, along with an unidentified little girl, occupy the center of the painting, further evidence of the intimacy between the artist and her host.[32] Although Abbéma's likeness recedes behind the luminous portrait of Bernhardt in white, and is easy to overlook amid the general profusion of plants, food, and exotic décor, she nonetheless exploits the opportunity to promote her talent by association with Bernhardt, not only Bernhardt's fame, wealth, and cultural sophistication but also the unprecedented respect she had earned as an actress. The painting was not as advantageous for Bernhardt, however, who was skewered in the

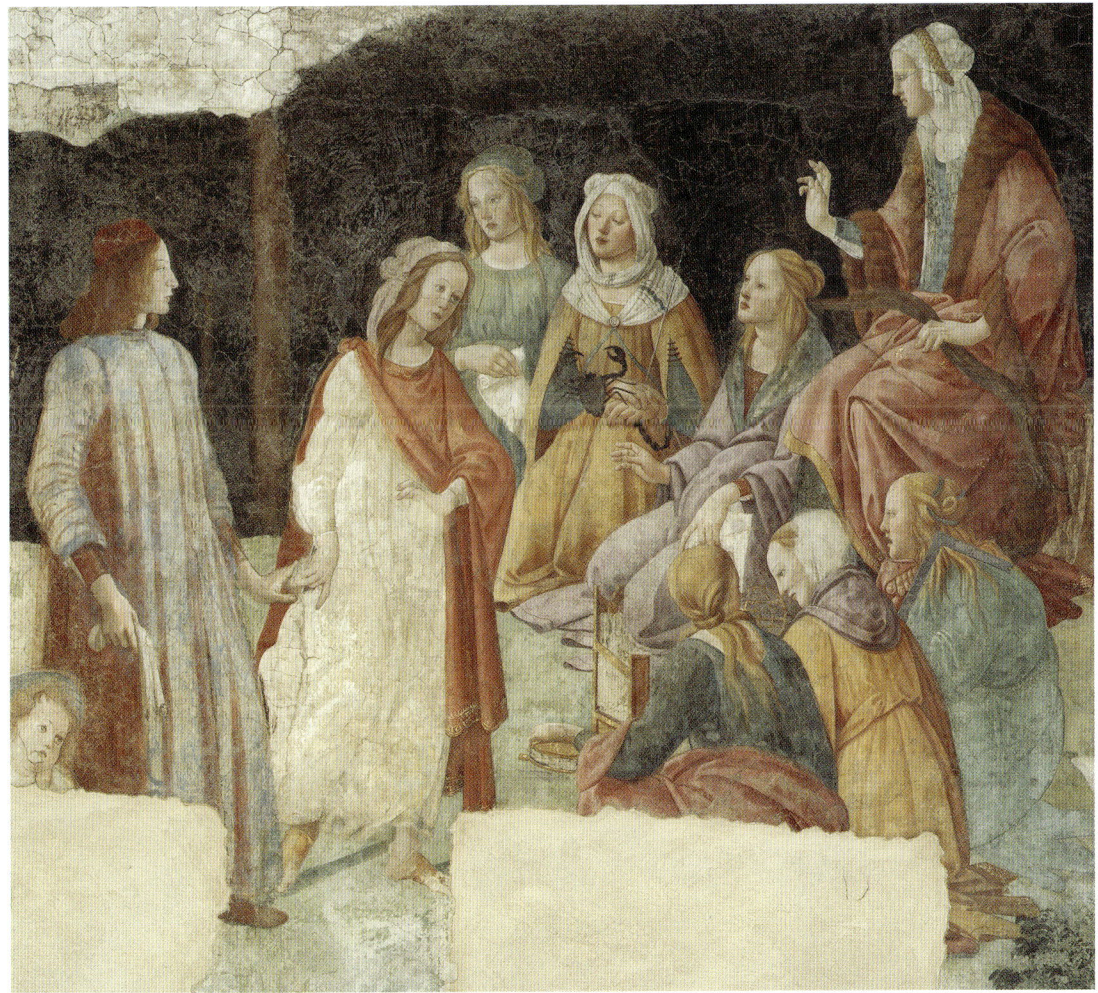

Fig. 9. Sandro Botticelli (Italian, 1445–1510), *A Young Man Being Introduced to the Seven Liberal Arts*, 1483–86. Fresco detached and mounted on canvas, 93¼ × 106 in. (237 × 269 cm). Musée du Louvre, Paris

press in 1878–79 for the "dispersion" of her talent in painting and sculpture. As a public figure engaged in multiple art forms, she was criticized as an amateur dabbler rather than praised as a Renaissance woman.[33]

Louise Catherine Breslau painted several portraits of artist friends, both male and female, throughout her career. But it is her early work *The Friends*, the only one that shows her painting, that proved to be the most important picture of her career [plate 11]. This intimate group portrait of the twenty-four-year-old artist at her easel alongside her roommates, the painter Sophie Schaeppi and the singer Maria Feller, was Breslau's first big success at the Salon, earning her an honorable mention—quite a coup for a young, unknown artist of any gender. By placing herself modestly off to the side, cropped by the picture's right edge, Breslau emphasizes the intensely thoughtful features of her friends—Feller in profile and Schaeppi in the center *en face*. A virtuosically painted white dog joins them at the table, its muzzle demurely tucked into its fluffy chest, in an equally affecting expression of introversion that echoes Breslau's profile, making the two of them a pair.[34] Breslau's self-portrait, a view from behind, is resolutely drab and withdrawn, as if she were reserving her most vivid brushwork, color, and psychological expression for the dog and the portraits of her friends. Despite this act of modesty, the painting made the artist's reputation practically overnight. But it was also caricatured in the satirical press as a family portrait of female dogs,[35] illustrating a preferred means of ridiculing women artists: domesticating them and comparing them to beasts.

Fig. 10. Édouard Louis Dubufe (French, 1819–1883), *Portrait of Rosa Bonheur*, 1857. Oil on canvas, 51⅝ × 38⅝ in. (131 × 98 cm). Chateaux de Versailles et de Trianon, Versailles, France, MV5799; RF1478

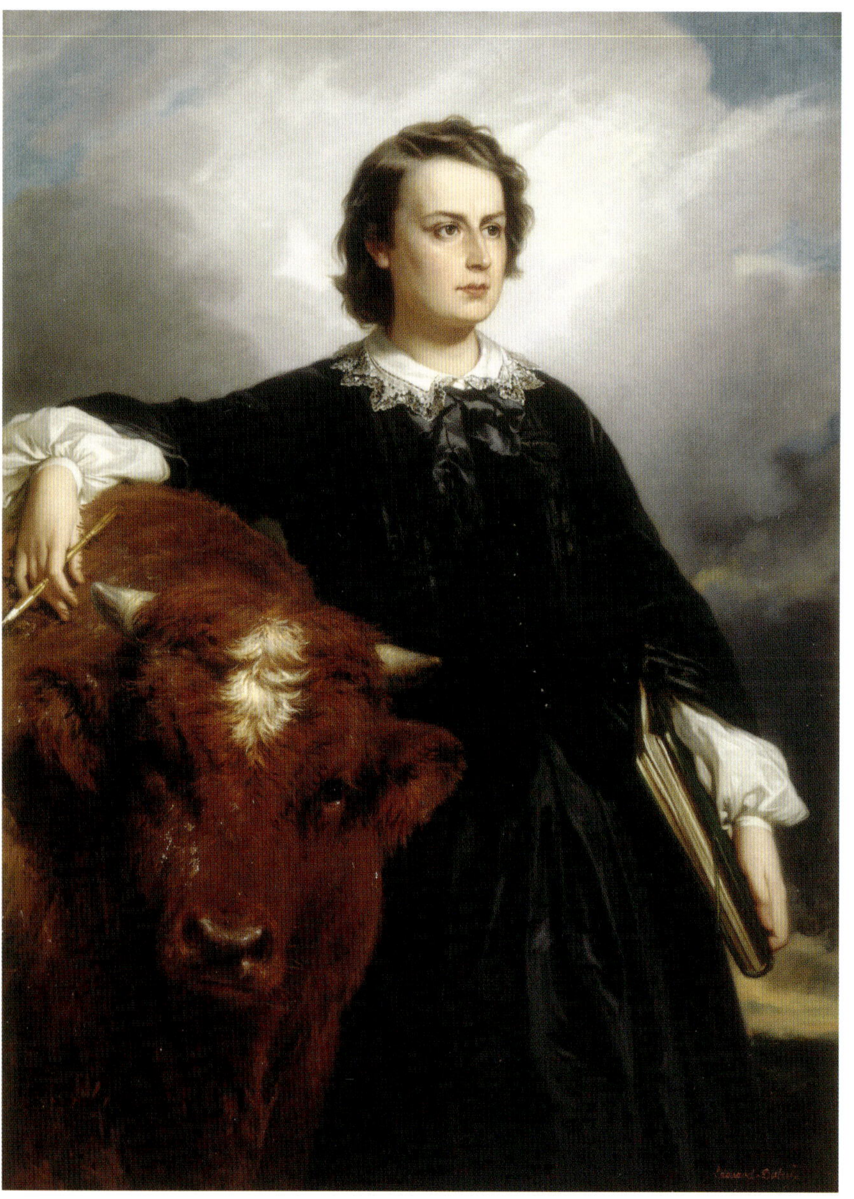

The same year Breslau painted *The Friends*, her rival at the Académie Julian, Marie Bashkirtseff, painted *In the Studio*, a lively and crowded scene of women in Julian's studio school working from a live model [plate 3]. Bashkirtseff makes the competitive yet collaborative atmosphere of the studio apparent and places herself in the center foreground, tipping her palette toward the viewer. The painting is a rare view of the internal dynamics of this crucial training ground for women artists. Although the picture was not Bashkirtseff's idea—Julian ordered her to do it as an advertisement for the studio[36]—it is an important complement to her *Self-Portrait* (ca. 1883), suggesting the close yet fraught web of relationships with both colleagues and teachers that defined her artistic formation [see Madeline, fig. 3]. But by far Bashkirtseff's most vivid picture of the community of women artists in and around the Académie Julian appears in her journal, portions of which were first published in 1887, recounting the rivalry and jealousy, kinship and solidarity, and continual frustration and disappointment that pervaded women's artistic culture in late nineteenth-century Paris. More than her paintings, it is this massive diary full of thwarted ambition, scandalous humor, and feminist rage that made Bashkirtseff a notable figure in the history of nineteenth-century art.[37]

Bashkirtseff's forthright brand of feminism owed a tremendous debt to Rosa Bonheur, the matriarch and role model for all women artists from the mid-nineteenth century forward. Bonheur was an unprecedented and unrepeatable example of critical and financial success, international fame, and freedom from the restrictions of femininity. No woman artist in the nineteenth century or since has managed to do what she did. But as the Goncourts' journal attests, Bonheur too suffered from viciously sexist criticism (especially in France), and she struggled to negotiate her position as an artist and as a woman throughout her career, nowhere more evidently than in her efforts to shape her image as an artist in print and in paint. She collaborated with several of her portraitists, including one who also became her biographer, the American Anna Klumpke, in an effort to take control of her own legacy and mold the public image of the *femme artiste*.[38]

By the mid-1850s, Bonheur was internationally known for monumental works like *Plowing in Nivernais* [plate 72] and *The Horse Fair* (1852–55), both huge successes at the Salon and beyond. She showed the latter painting to Queen Victoria in a private viewing at Buckingham Palace in 1856, and a biography and a monograph were published the same year, when she was only thirty-three.[39] This was also the year that her portrait was painted by Édouard Louis Dubufe, a leading portraitist of high society known especially for his flattering, sentimental depictions of women and children. His *Portrait of Rosa Bonheur*, exhibited at the Salon of 1857, is a striking departure from his usual fare [fig. 10]. Bonheur's stern expression, uncoiffed hair, and funereal black dress already set her apart from the aristocratic women Dubufe typically painted, suggesting that Dubufe had little control over the artist's appearance. But it is the presence of a massive bull next to her that makes her difference wildly clear. As Bonheur recounts in her memoirs, "He started off with me leaning on a table. I began grumbling the second time I posed. That's when he got the idea of having me paint a real live bull's head over the spot where that boring table had been."[40] Bristling at her confinement within stiff portraiture conventions and tired of the monotony of posing, Bonheur leaped at the chance to collaborate with Dubufe and turn her portrait into an animal painting. Taking her image into her own hands, she aligned herself with an animal that epitomized masculine strength and determination. (The artist reportedly said, "In the way of males, I like only the bulls that I paint."[41]) In this way Bonheur became the alpha artist in the portrait transaction, and her bull steals the show. Staring directly out of the picture with the piercing gaze and tilted head of a concerned companion, the animal is a literal bull's-eye that pulls the viewer's attention from Bonheur. Serving as a kind of protector, it seems poised to buffer the artist from public scrutiny, while exemplifying her talents as an *animalier*. Bonheur later reported that Ernest Gambart, her British dealer who commissioned the portrait, was "delighted by the change," especially since it allowed him to sell engravings of it with her signature, increasing their market value (Bonheur's fame far exceeded Dubufe's). This is just one of many instances revealing Bonheur's savvy as a businesswoman, someone who knew how to work with others to manage her image and career.

Decades later, in 1892, when her age made her all the more self-conscious of her image for posterity, Bonheur welcomed the sisters Georges Achille-Fould and Consuélo Fould to her country retreat at By so they could each paint her portrait. Once again, Bonheur collaborated in the construction of her image, painting the dog that her portrait caresses in the bottom left corner of the painting by Consuélo Fould [fig. 11].[42] This time Bonheur cosigned the painting itself:

Fould's signature appears in the lower right-hand corner, while Bonheur's name appears at lower left over the dog's fur, making the collaboration plain. As in Dubufe's portrait, Bonheur places her addition under the protective gesture of her painting arm, claiming the creature as hers, as belonging to her art, while also signaling to the viewer that this part of the painting is *in her hand*.

In these collaborations Bonheur upstages her image-makers with her sensitive, spectacularly realist animals, whose penetrating, empathic gazes make her image look staid in comparison. In doing so, she promotes her talents as an *animalier*, but at the same time necessarily sacrifices her image as a woman. Her public image, her appearance, is juxtaposed to a bull and a dog, with all their connotations of masculinity, incivility, and homeliness. Bonheur jokes about this juxtaposition in a letter to Fould, writing of her effort to make the dog's head "match the calf's head," a self-deprecating allusion to her own image in the painting.[43] By aligning her portrait with an animal, she not only identifies her artistic niche but also plays defiantly with the cruel stereotype of intelligent and talented women as ugly and unfeminine, and makes the most affecting and soulful presence in the picture the animal, rather than herself. In this sense, these pictures are an allegory of the double bind Bonheur had to navigate as a woman artist. Both portrait and self-portrait in one, they indicate how other artists and society at large perceived her—as a woman who, however tremendous her success, still awkwardly occupied the role of artist—while also insisting on how she would like to be perceived, not for her gender or for her appearance but for her *work*.

Fig. 11. Consuélo Fould (French, 1862–1927), *Portrait of Rosa Bonheur*, 1892–94. Oil on canvas, 51½ × 37⅜ in. (131 × 95 cm). Leeds Art Gallery, UK

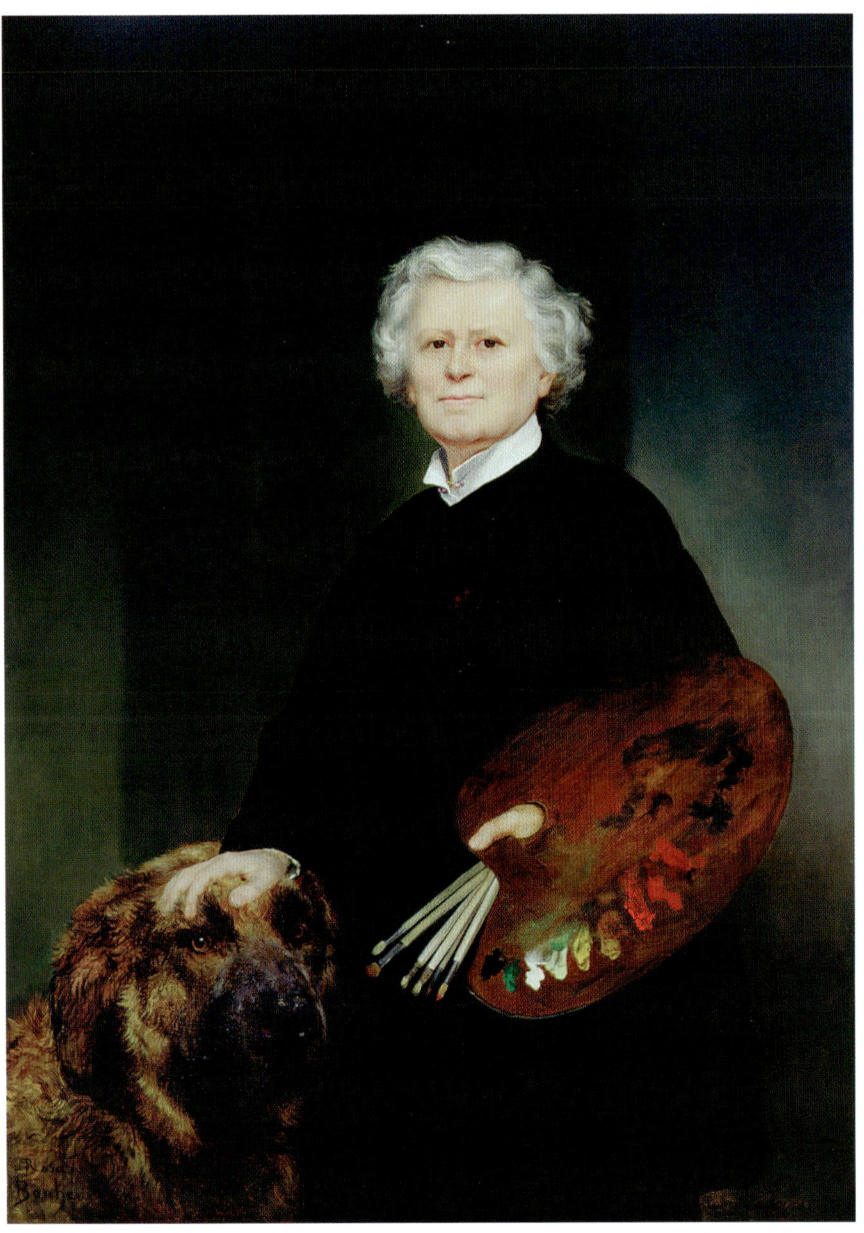

Anna Klumpke recounts in detail her experience painting Bonheur's portrait in 1898 [plate 9], revealing to what extent Bonheur cared about her portrayal and directed the process from beginning to end. Bonheur was concerned about her appearance, particularly as far as it represented her femininity. Her stated desire to be represented in women's clothes was complicated by her repeated resistance to putting them on, and she complained about the fact that "the great portrait painters never asked [her] to pose for them" even while declaring that she would not have liked "sitting for a man."[44] This conflicted attitude toward her womanhood and the restrictions it placed on her status as an artist shows that Bonheur's fame and success did not alleviate her insecurity about the relationship between her feminine and artistic identities.

Her complaint also shows that she had forgotten or wished to disavow Dubufe's portrait, not to mention Nicaise de Keyser's *Great Artists of the Nineteenth-Century French School* (1878), which features Bonheur in the front row.[45] Otherwise, she only entrusted her painted image to women, and largely dictated the pictures herself. Likewise, she asked Klumpke to write her definitive life story in

1898, making clear that she would have editorial control. According to Klumpke, this biography was "one of [Bonheur's] main preoccupations." Her previous biographers had failed to capture her main sources of inspiration, she felt, and it was because Klumpke was a woman that she could trust her "to interpret [her] life for posterity."[46] Bonheur died less than a year later, in 1899.

In 1900 Maurice Denis painted a Fantin-inspired group portrait titled *Homage to Cézanne*, featuring a gathering of nine artists and writers in the shop of art dealer Ambroise Vollard [fig. 12]. Remarkably, the artist's wife, Marthe, appears on the outer margin of the group, ostensibly assembled to admire a still life by Paul Cézanne. Her head tucked behind a frame and her face looking out through a sheer lace veil, Marthe Denis addresses the viewer as if colluding in some kind of secret, with a white-gloved hand holding a lorgnette peeking out behind Bonnard. Marthe was not an artist, but her presence here at least qualifies her as a viewer and a participating

Fig. 12. Maurice Denis (French, 1870–1943), *Homage to Cézanne*, 1900. Oil on canvas, 42½ × 80¼ in. (108 × 204 cm). Musée d'Orsay, Paris, RF1977-137

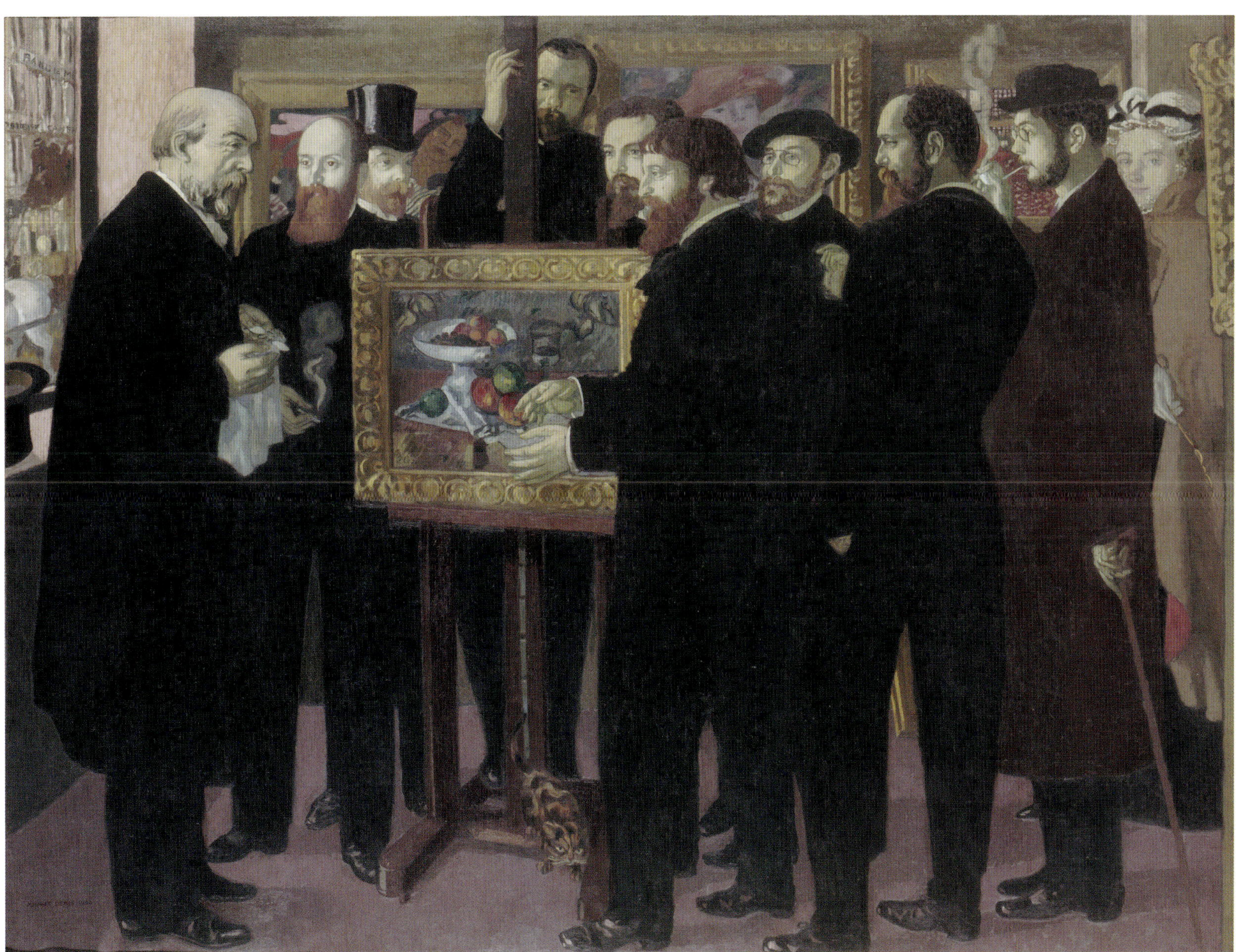

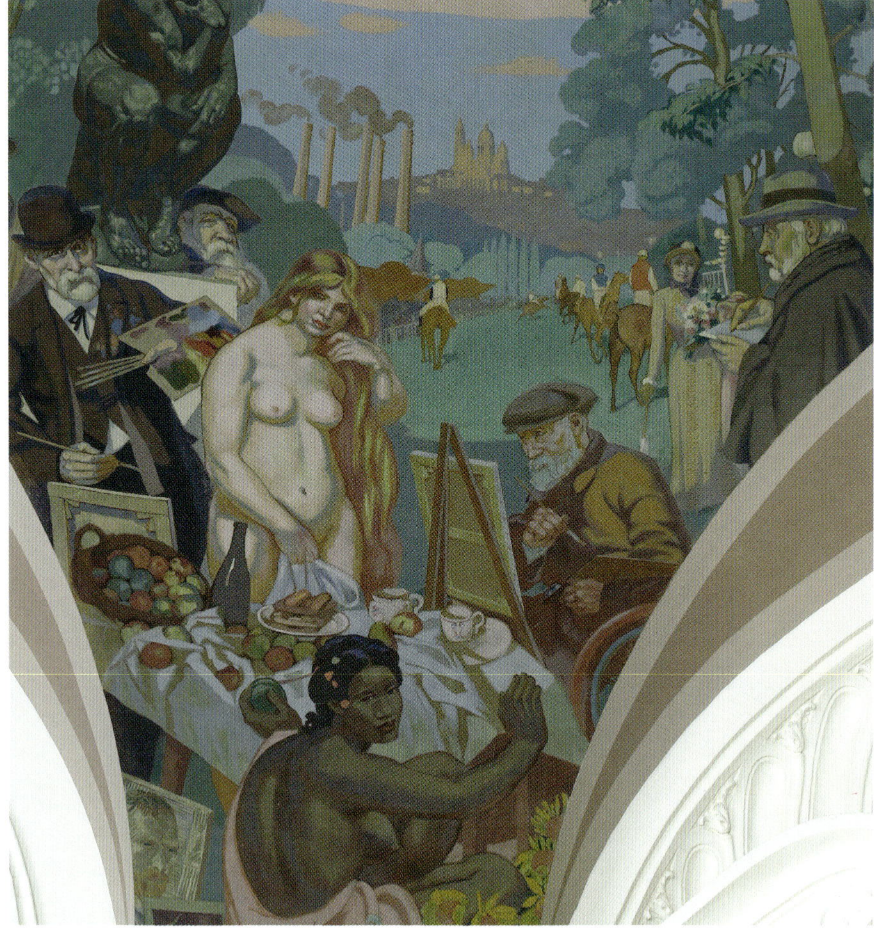

Fig. 13. Maurice Denis (French, 1870–1943), "Histoire de l'art français," detail of the Dutuit Cupola: F section, XIX–XXth centuries, from Monet to Moreau, 1925. Oil on canvas, mounted, diameter: 39 ft. 4 in. (12 m). Musée des Beaux-Arts de la Ville de Paris, Petit Palais, DECOP00G01 (F)

(if marginal) member of the artistic community, unlike the women painted by Gauguin and Renoir who appear as framed objects on the wall behind. By featuring his wife, Denis's *Homage to Cézanne* can be read as a gentle riposte to Fantin's masculine image of the modern group. By 1900 women in Paris were studying at the École des Beaux-Arts and had earned the right to practice law. But as far as their broad cultural status as artists, progress was painfully slow.

Twenty-five years later, Denis would complete a more ambitious and much more public group portrait in the Dutuit Cupola of the Petit Palais, representing the history of French art from the Middle Ages to Monet. His composition features thirty-seven of the nation's most illustrious artists alongside figures plucked from celebrated works of art. Although women are amply represented among the latter—the bare-breasted Marianne from Eugène Delacroix's *Liberty Leading the People*, Jean-Auguste-Dominique Ingres's portrait of his wife, a buxom Rodin nude—only one female artist, Berthe Morisot, is pictured [fig. 13]. Denis admired Morisot's use of color, and positions her between Renoir and Degas, an indication—however subtle—of the crucial role women played in the Impressionist exhibitions. Still, it is hard to celebrate such a minuscule form of recognition. Barely visible in the distance, Morisot holds a bouquet of flowers and a parasol, smiling at the viewer. Unlike her male colleagues in the foreground, she bears no palette or sketchpad to identify her as an artist.[47] Indeed, without an identifying label, few would ever notice that she is there.

For art criticism, the evidence is similarly grim. In 1932 critics were still praising women artists like Breslau for their "male intelligence."[48] On the bright side, this critic was positively reviewing a pioneering exhibition of art by women who had studied at the Académie Julian, an exhibition that brought these women's collective work to public attention for the first time.[49] Women continued to fight for the education, institutional support, and broad social freedoms necessary to develop their talent as artists, without which it was impossible to overturn the pervasive notion of artistic genius as male.[50] Representations of the *femme peintre*—and their marked absence—in later nineteenth-century French painting show how women's status as artists was contested in the pictorial realm. As Rosa Bonheur and her followers came to learn, if they wanted to appear as equals alongside their male peers, they would have to paint those pictures themselves.

1. "Le génie est male," August 20–26, 1857, in Edmond and Jules de Goncourt, *Journal: Mémoires de la vie littéraire*, vol. 1, *1851–1865* (Paris: Laffont, 1989), 295.

2. Rosa Bonheur to Louis Passy, Paris, June 1859, quoted in Theodore Stanton, ed., *Reminiscences of Rosa Bonheur* (New York: Appleton, 1910), 393.

3. Goncourt, *Journal*, entry for March 16, 1857, 241.

4. This recurring theme in the reception of women artists is discussed in Gabriel P. Weisberg, "La reception de Louise Breslau, Rosa Bonheur et Amélie Beaury-Saurel à Paris: La différence sexuelle au coeur du discours," in *Louise Breslau: De l'impressionisme aux années folles*, ed. Catherine Lepdor, Anne-Catherine Kruger, and Gabriel P. Weisberg (Lausanne, Switzerland: Musée Cantonale des Beaux-Arts, 2001), 99–115. For a classic sociological study of artists in nineteenth-century France that includes discussion of how "women were not accepted as professional painters," see Harrison C. White and Cynthia A. White, *Canvases and Careers: Institutional Change in the French Painting World* (Chicago: University of Chicago Press, 1993), 51.

5. A foundational study is Tamar Garb, *Sisters of the Brush: Women's Artistic Culture in Late Nineteenth-Century Paris* (New Haven: Yale University Press, 1994). See also Gabriel P. Weisberg and Jane Becker, eds., *Overcoming All Obstacles: The Women of the Académie Julian* (New York: Dahesh Museum; New Brunswick, NJ: Rutgers University Press, 1999); and Charlotte Foucher Zarmanian, *Créatrices en 1900: Femmes artistes en France dans le milieux symbolistes* (Paris: Mare and Martin, 2015). For a broader historical overview, see Whitney Chadwick, *Women, Art, and Society*, 5th ed. (London: Thames and Hudson, 2012). Séverine Sofio's important study of women artists in Paris from 1750 to 1850, *Artistes femmes: La parenthèse enchantée, XIIIe–XIXe siècles* (Paris: CNRS éditions, 2016), appeared after this essay was in press.

6. Tamar Garb, "Revising the Revisionists: The Formation of the Union des Femmes Peintres et Sculpteurs," *Art Journal* 48, no. 1 (Spring 1989): 64. See also the text by Joëlle Bolloch in this volume.

7. "Union des Femmes Peintres et Sculpteurs," *La gazette des femmes* 2 (January 25, 1882): 1, quoted in Garb, "Revising the Revisionists," 65.

8. Garb, *Sisters of the Brush*, 3–18. On rivalry among women artists, see also Jane Becker, "Nothing Like a Rival to Spur One On: Marie Bashkirtseff and Louise Breslau at the Académie Julian," in Weisberg and Becker, *Overcoming All Obstacles*, 69–113.

9. Georges Rivière, *M. Degas, bourgeois de Paris* (Paris: Floury, 1935), 116, 121.

10. Fantin's paintings of his wife, as confirmed by her annotated catalogue raisonné completed in 1911, include *Reading* (1870; Calouste Gulbenkian Foundation, Lisbon), where she appears with her sister, Charlotte Dubourg; *Mlle Victoria Dubourg* (1873; Musée d'Orsay, Paris); *Mme Fantin-Latour* (1877; Musée de Grenoble); and *Mme Fantin-Latour* (1883; Staatliche Museen zu Berlin). Victoria Dubourg Fantin-Latour, *Catalogue de l'oeuvre complet de Fantin-Latour* (1911; New York: Da Capo Press, 1969). There is at least one other portrait by Fantin, dated 1873, that scholars believe to be of Victoria Dubourg, now in the Museum of Fine Arts, Ghent. She also appears in *The Dubourg Family* (1878; Musée d'Orsay, Paris).

11. A small, framed picture appears on the wall right behind Dubourg's head in a sketch for the painting, in a composition very similar to Degas's 1867–68 portrait of the artist James Tissot. Degas initially included this detail in the oil painting, but then decided to erase it (a ghost of its presence remains). See Henri Loyrette's entry on the painting in Jean Sutherland Boggs et al., *Degas* (New York: Metropolitan Museum of Art, 1988), 142–43.

12. In addition to showing her work regularly at the Paris Salon and the Royal Academy, Dubourg sold many paintings to private collectors. During her lifetime, museums in Paris, Tokyo, and Grenoble acquired her work, and she was awarded the Légion d'Honneur in 1920. Elizabeth Kane, "Victoria Dubourg: The Other Fantin-Latour," *Women's Art Journal* 9, no. 2 (Fall 1998–Winter 1999): 17–18.

13. This point is made by Sylvie Patry in "Victoria Dubourg, 'Femme supérieure et peintre de mérite,'" in *Fantin-Latour: De la réalité au rêve* (Lausanne, Switzerland: Fondation de l'Hermitage, 2007), 169.

14. On these pictures, see Douglas Druick and Michel Hoog, *Fantin-Latour* (Ottawa: National Gallery of Canada, 1983), 252–55, 330–33.

15. For more on this painting and its reception, see my *Fellow Men: Fantin-Latour and the Problem of the Group in Nineteenth-Century French Painting* (Princeton, NJ: Princeton University Press, 2013), 68–104.

16. For a discussion of this painting as a "pictorial document of French Wagnerism" and its relationship to Fantin's Wagner-inspired lithographs, see Anne Leonard, "Picturing Listening in Nineteenth-Century French Painting," *Art Bulletin* 89, no. 2 (June 2007): 267–72.

17. Fantin-Latour to Edwin Edwards, October 3, 1872, in "Copies de lettres de Fantin à ses parents et amis, par Victoria Fantin-Latour," fasc. 2, Bibliothèque Municipale de Grenoble, 184.

18. Fantin-Latour to Mrs. Edwin Edwards, February 25, 1885, in ibid., 207.

19. Jacques-Émile Blanche, *Portraits of a Lifetime*, ed. and trans. Walter Clement (London: Dent, 1937), 41–44, cited in Kane, "Victoria Dubourg," 17.

20. Kane, "Victoria Dubourg," 17.

21. These photographs are reproduced in *Fantin-Latour: De la réalité au rêve*, 178–81. They were taken circa 1901–2, so are not necessarily representative of the studio's decor over time, but the presence of Dubourg's image and work is significant, since the couple knew that these photographs would document the space for posterity.

22. Kane, "Victoria Dubourg," 15, 19n2.

23. Victoria Fantin-Latour to Léonce Bénédite, Buré, May 23 [1919], Fondation Custodia, Frits Lugt collection, inv. 997-A-947, cited in Patry, "Victoria Dubourg," 170. Blanche's anecdotal accounts of his artistic circle were published in 1919 as *Propos de peintre: Première série, de David à Degas* (Paris: Émile-Paul, 1919). His account of Fantin-Latour's home and studio first appeared in an obituary article: "Fantin-Latour," *Revue de Paris*, May 15, 1906, 289–313. Dubourg's "exasperated" reaction was upon her rereading the text when it reappeared in 1919.

24. On the artist as a heroic (and always male) figure in nineteenth-century French literature, see Joy Newton, "The Atelier Novel: Painters as Fictions," in *Impressions of French Modernity*, ed. Richard Hobbs (Manchester, England: Manchester University Press, 1998), 173–89; and, more recently, Eleonora Vratskidou, "L'artiste, héros romanesque de la presse littéraire," in *L'artiste en représentation: Images des artistes dans l'art du XIXe siècle*, ed. Alain Bonnet (Lyon, France: Fage, 2012), 225–35.

25. See Kimberly A. Jones, "'A Much Finer Curve': Identity and Representation in Degas's Depictions of Cassatt," in *Degas / Cassatt* (Washington, DC: National Gallery of Art, 2014), 86–97. Cassatt also posed for Degas as a model.

26. Tamar Garb, "Framing Femininity in Manet's *Portrait of Mlle E. G.*," in *The Painted Face: Portraits of Women in France, 1814–1914* (New Haven: Yale University Press, 2007), 59–99. Victor Fournel mentions Gonzalès's "stupefied eyes" in "Le Salon de 1870," *La gazette de France*, June 8, 1870, cited in Garb, *Painted Face*, 73.

27. On this painting, see Kenneth McConkey, *Impressionism in Britain* (New Haven: Yale University Press, 1995), 11–13.

28. Gabriel Montua, "Botticelli's Path to Modernity: Continental Reception, 1850–1930," in *Botticelli Reimagined*, ed. Mark Evans and Stefan Weppelman (London: V&A, 2016), 87.

29. A series of verses reproduced with an engraving of the painting identifies the copyist as "une blonde anglaise / Mabel ou Nelly." Fichier Moreau-Nélaton, Musée d'Orsay, Paris.

30. These identifications appear in the *Revue encyclopédique* 42 (1892): 1256. They leave one man unaccounted for, and it is not clear who is who, although Desboutin is definitely the figure in red. My thanks to Maud Leyoudec at the Musée Anne-de-Beaujeu for her generosity in sharing documentation on this painting.

31. Manet referred to Desboutin as "le prince des Bohèmes." Maud Leyoudec, "Desboutin à la pointe du portrait," in Bonnet, *L'artiste en représentation*, 71–72.

32. These portrait identifications are drawn from Musée des Beaux-Arts, Pau, *Peintures du XIXème siècle* (Bordeaux, France: Le Festin, 2007), 20.

33. On Bernhardt's "pluridisciplinary" artistic career as an actor, painter, and sculptor, and the sexist criticism she received for this "dispersion" of her talent, see Zarmanian, *Créatrices en 1900*, 158–91.

34. Breslau and the dog are paired looking at the republican newspaper *Le Voltaire* in a preliminary sketch. This sketch also shows an unidentified fourth figure—a man smoking a pipe—seated at the table, but Breslau removed him in the painting to make an all-female group. The sketch, in a private collection, is reproduced in Lepdor, Kruger, and Weisberg, *Louise Breslau*, 42.

35. Stop, "La famille Zoé Chien-Chien," *Le journal amusant*, June 1881.

36. See Becker, "Nothing Like a Rival," 103–5.

37. The full, uncensored text of the journal, covering the years 1860–84, has been available since 2005. Marie Bashkirtseff (transcribed by Ginette Apostolescu), *Mon journal: Texte intégral*, 16 vols. (Paris: Montesson, 2005). During her lifetime, Bashkirtseff published several articles in the feminist journal *La Citoyenne* under the pseudonym Pauline Orell, including "Les Femmes Artistes," March 6, 1881.

38. On Bonheur's self-conscious attention to her artistic legacy, see Francis Ribemont, "Rosa Bonheur, ou les difficiles chemins de la postérité," in *Rosa Bonheur, 1822–1899* (Bordeaux, France: Musée des Beaux-Arts de Bordeaux, 1997), 127–35.

39. Frédéric Lepelle de Bois-Gallais, *Biographie de Madamoiselle Rosa Bonheur* (Paris: E. Gambart, 1856); Eugène de Mirecourt, *Les contemporains: Rosa Bonheur* (Paris: G. Havard, 1856).

40. Bonheur, quoted in Anna Klumpke, *Rosa Bonheur: The Artist's (Auto)biography*, trans. Gretchen van Slyke (Ann Arbor: University of Michigan Press, 1997), 77.

41. Quoted in Stanton, *Reminiscences of Rosa Bonheur*, 366.

42. For correspondence between Bonheur and Consuélo Fould detailing the genesis of this portrait and Bonheur's contribution, see ibid., 258–64.

43. Quoted in Stanton, *Reminiscences of Rosa Bonheur*, 261.

44. Klumpke, *Rosa Bonheur*, 31–62 (quotes on 36–37).

45. This painting was commissioned by Ernest Gambart, so Keyser had no choice but to include Bonheur.

46. Klumpke, *Rosa Bonheur*, 63–75 (quotes on 67, 79).

47. Alain Bonnet, *Artistes en groupe: La représentation de la communauté des artistes dans la peinture du XIXe siècle* (Rennes, France: Presses Universitaires de Rennes, 2007), 52–53. Reproductions of the six sections of Denis's designs for the cupola, including captions naming the figures, were reproduced in "La décoration d'une coupole du Petit Palais par Maurice Denis," *La Renaissance de l'art français et des industries de luxe*, September 1925, 408–13. Morisot's name is misspelled as "Morizot," 413.

48. Anonymous, "De Marie Bashkirtseff à Louise Abbéma," *La revue de Paris* 1, no. 39 (1932): 712.

49. "Une manifestation de l'art chez la femme: L'Académie Julian en 1880 et aujourd'hui," Galerie Charpentier, Paris, January 7–21, 1932.

50. This is Linda Nochlin's seminal argument in "Why Have There Been No Great Women Artists?" *ARTnews* 69, no. 9 (January 1971): 22–39, 67–71.

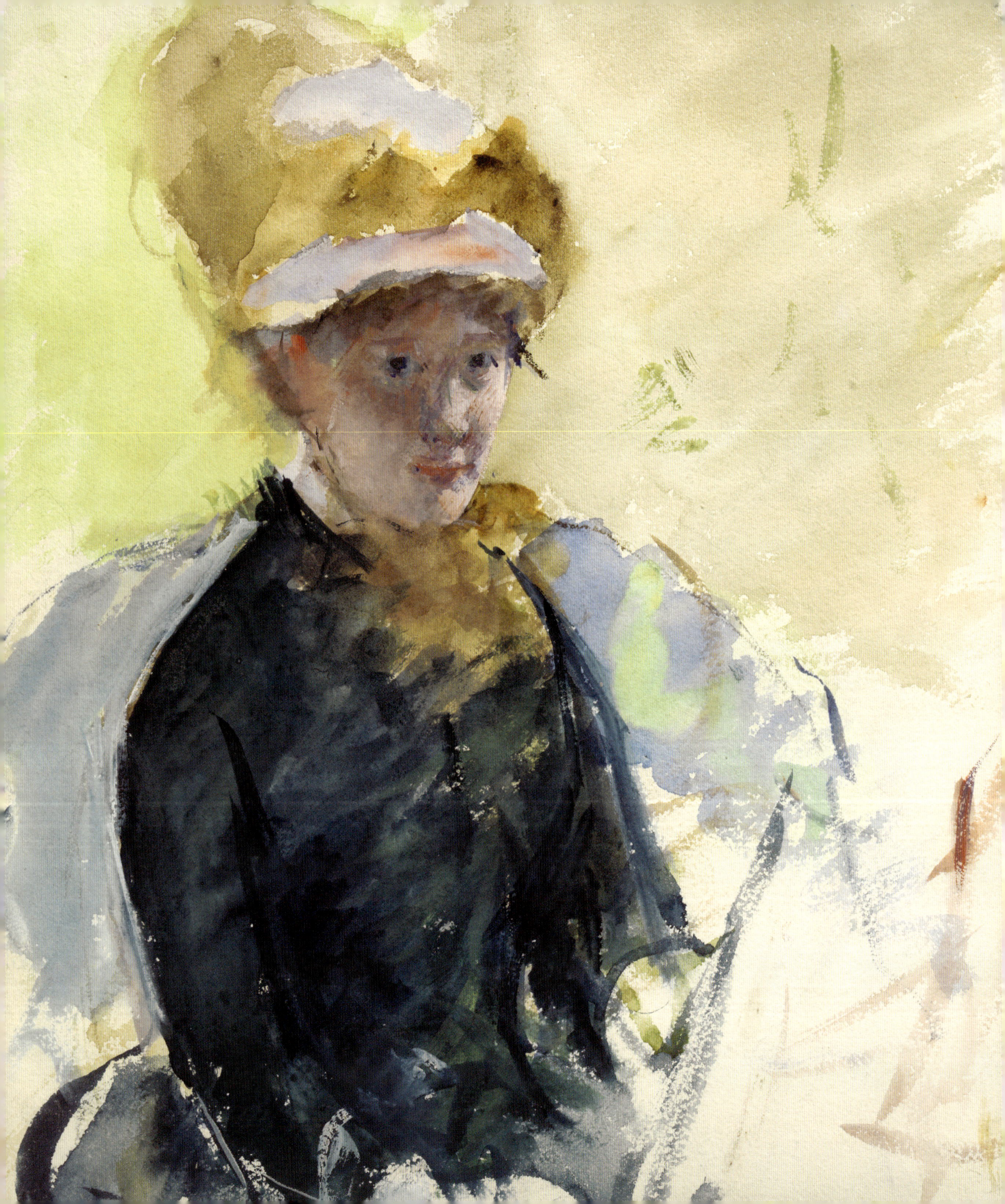

RICHARD KENDALL

Women Artists and Impressionism

The women artists who contributed to Impressionism were a very small minority of the group involved, but disproportionately significant in their collective achievement. Marie Bracquemond, Mary Cassatt, and Berthe Morisot, the three principal figures in question, were all experienced painters who featured in the series of eight Impressionist exhibitions that took place in Paris between 1874 and 1886. Diligent research has identified the majority of pictures that were shown over these years and also brought together much of the art criticism related to them from contemporary newspapers and periodicals.[1] Such sources offer a vivid sense of the upheaval in the visual arts represented by these works and the shifting cast of characters—from the obscure to the now internationally famous—who participated. They reveal, for example, that Bracquemond exhibited just three times and displayed an unusual variety of works in several media, prompting a range of positive and negative responses. Cassatt and Morisot were considerably more prominent; both of them participated in at least half the group's exhibitions, where substantial numbers of their canvases, pastels, and prints were often admired and sometimes sold. The controversy stirred up by the initial displays of pictures by both men and women gradually faded, and doubters were eventually overtaken by sympathizers. While Bracquemond, Cassatt, and Morisot had their share of harsh criticism or found themselves ignored, they were generally treated more politely and sometimes singled out for high praise. At the third group show in 1877, when Morisot presented *La Psyché* (*Mirror*) [fig. 1], the critic Émile Bergerat called her "the most natural painter" on view, and in 1879 another commentator observed of Cassatt that "every one of her portraits" was "a symphony of color."[2]

Before looking more closely at this story, it is important to stress the highly unusual character of the Impressionist exhibitions themselves, which effectively defined the movement in its formative phase. From our vantage point in the twenty-first century,

Mary Cassatt, *Self-Portrait*, ca. 1880 [detail of fig. 3]

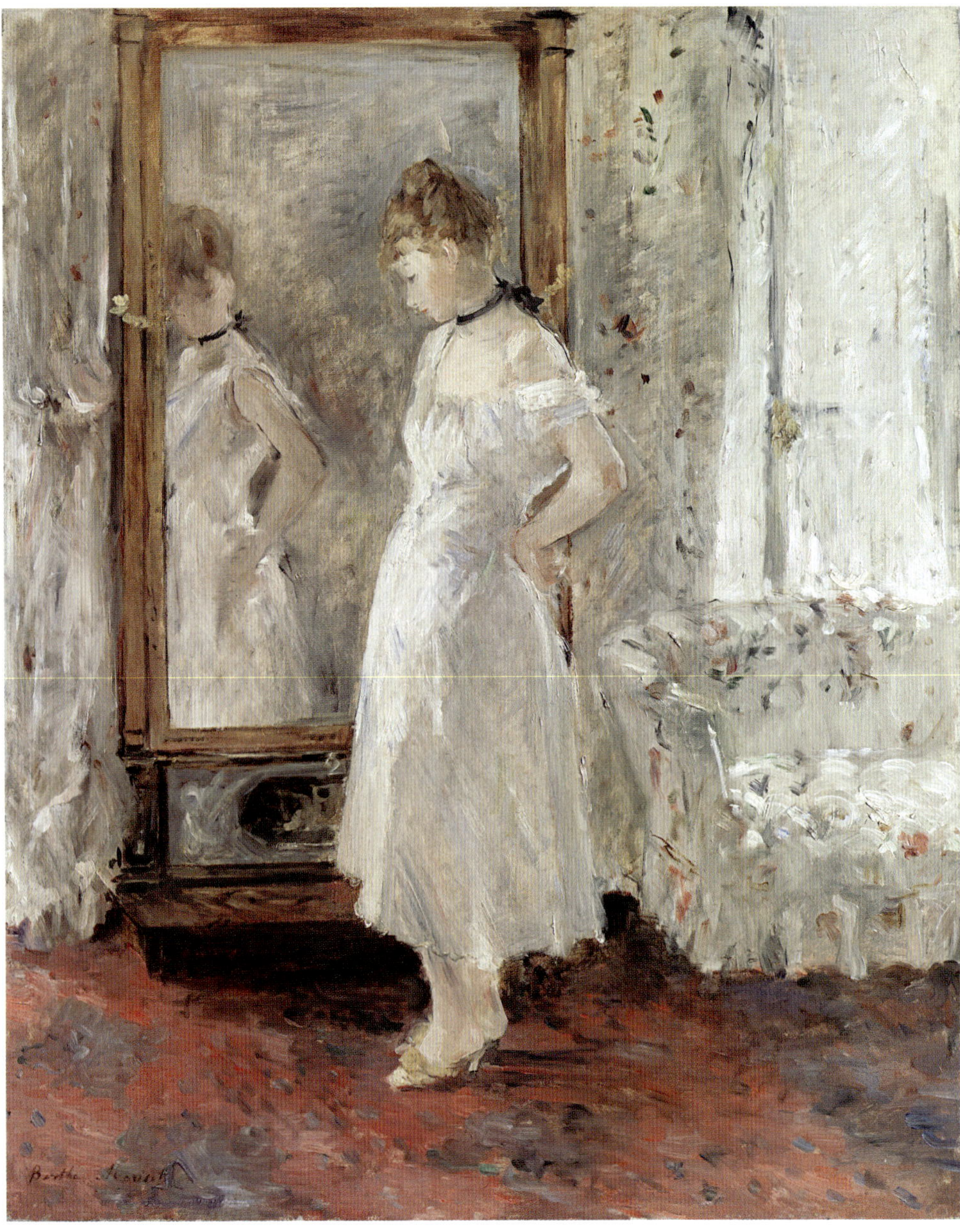

Fig. 1. Berthe Morisot (French, 1841–1895), *La Psyché* (*Mirror*), ca. 1876. Oil on canvas, 25⅝ × 21 in. (65 × 54 cm). Thyssen-Bornemisza Collection, Lugano, Switzerland

these events are often perceived as historic, even heroic occasions. Many hundreds—perhaps thousands—of books, catalogues, and articles have addressed them and the works presented, while claims for their role in the evolution of modernism have reached almost hyperbolic proportions. In reality the original exhibitions were marginal by Parisian standards, irregularly scheduled and haphazardly organized, sometimes at very short notice. There was no formal application or selection process, and each was preceded by a search for appropriate and affordable rooms, which over time included a photographer's premises, dealers' galleries, and an empty apartment. These improvised displays were in sharp contrast to the official Salons that took place in the city each year, when several thousand works of art were selected by a jury and then hung in grand surroundings where they were seen by vast crowds. By comparison the Impressionist shows were small and amateurishly staged, and sometimes lacked focus due to the inclusion of pictures by artists who were marginal to the group enterprise. The shadowy black-and-white etchings of religious and other somber subjects by Alphonse Legros that appeared in quantity in the 1876 show, for example, are impossible to reconcile with the colorful, light-filled scenes of modern life that dominated this same exhibition.[3] Such anachronisms inevitably blurred the impact of the group's presentations and challenged those intrepid Parisians who attended, at first cautiously and over time in large numbers. Some representatives of the press persisted in mocking the works on display and warned of their threat to tradition and even to morality. Responding more lightheartedly to the 1877 exhibition, the caricaturist Cham published a satirical drawing of a pregnant woman being discouraged from entering the third Impressionist exhibition because her condition might be compromised [fig. 2].[4] The critic Philippe Burty was more welcoming and argued that the new group would "have a significant influence over the contemporary French school, with its black, bituminous, or grey coloring."[5] His tone was echoed by several astute and courageous writers, such as Jules Castagnary and Edmond Duranty, who strove to articulate the new phenomenon for the French public.

Equally distorting in our own times has been an obsessive focus on a small minority of exhibitors at these events, while the majority have been allowed to fade into obscurity. Today it is figures such as Claude Monet—whose *Impression, Sunrise* (1872) gave the group its name—along with

Paul Cézanne, Edgar Degas, Camille Pissarro, and Pierre-Auguste Renoir—who typically dominate the popular and even the specialist literature, at the expense of most of their colleagues. Yet historically, almost fifty other male artists showed their work in this context over the years, some appearing only once while a dozen loyal individuals participated in at least half the series of exhibitions. These simple statistics contrast dramatically with the small female contingent who took part: a total of just five women are listed as exhibitors in the entire sequence of eight Impressionist shows over the decade and a half in question, two of whom used pseudonyms and exhibited once but never again.[6] Bracquemond, Cassatt, and Morisot contributed sporadically throughout the cycle, but only once together, in 1880. Morisot was the most persistent of the three, featuring in seven of the eight shows and—like Cassatt—seeming at times to amplify her presence on the gallery walls by presenting a generous number of works. Around sixteen of Morisot's oils and watercolors were included in 1880, for instance, while Cassatt showed some twenty pictures in a variety of media that same year.[7]

Even allowing for these exceptions, however, the issue of women in the Impressionist movement might be considered of little significance to its achievement in numerical terms, other than providing further evidence of male dominance in European public life at this time. Yet the crucial fact is that these women were highly talented and original artists, who richly deserved the praise that was often directed at their exhibited pictures and merited the respect from colleagues and the public that increased over the years. In his typically paradoxical way, Degas acknowledged this situation when he is said to have exclaimed in front of a work by his much-admired friend Cassatt: "No woman has the right to draw like that."[8] Degas, a leading figure in all but one of the

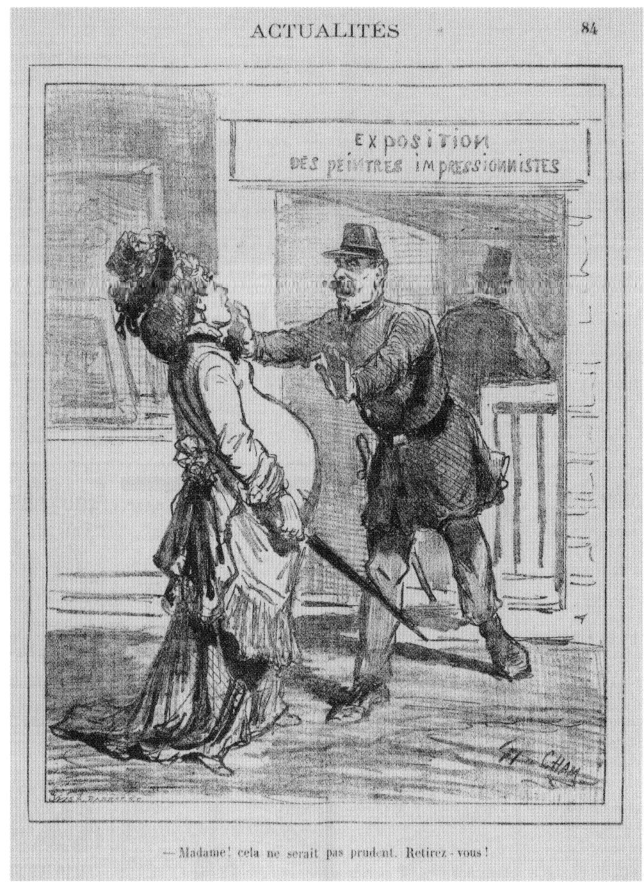

Fig. 2. Cham (Amédée Charles Henri de Noé; French, 1819–1879), "Madame! It is not advisable to enter." ("Madame! Cela ne serait pas prudent. Retirez-vous!"), published in *Le Charivari*, April 16, 1877. Städel Museum, Frankfurt am Main

Impressionist shows, was also among several male colleagues who energetically supported the involvement of Cassatt, Morisot, and Bracquemond in the joint enterprise. Surviving letters and other documents show that he variously urged them to participate,[9] assisted with their installations, and acquired numerous examples of their work for his private collection, sometimes by exchange with pictures of his own.[10] Similarly, Pissarro developed a close, long-lasting, and mutually respectful friendship with Cassatt that is partly recorded in their correspondence, and worked alongside her as they both experimented with new kinds of printmaking.[11] Especially significant here is evidence that Cassatt, a well-financed woman artist, helped to support the less fortunate man through purchases of his paintings when Pissarro and his large family were struggling.

The Artists In approaching the careers of these individuals in more detail, it becomes clear that their early training as painters offers a range of insights into their varied relationships with the late nineteenth-century art world, both as women and as artists. Perhaps surprisingly, it was the American Cassatt who most fully experienced the rigor of a traditional art education that is more usually associated with Europe [fig. 3]. Born in 1844 to a prosperous family of enthusiastic travelers, she first visited Paris as a child and would acquire a fluency in French that served her well. From 1860 onward she studied art in Philadelphia alongside male and female colleagues, learning to draw from the human figure in the classic manner at the celebrated Pennsylvania Academy of the Fine Arts. As in many such institutions at this time, the academy denied young women the opportunity to draw from nude models, which was considered by many to be a prerequisite for a serious artist. Despite this factor, Cassatt worked assiduously and was clearly able to build a solid foundation for the superb draftsmanship of her maturity. Precise copying from approved historic oil paintings followed, now in mixed company. By late 1865 she had returned to Paris and to further traditional instruction from such prominent artists and popular stars of the Salon as Jean-Léon Gérôme and Charles Chaplin. Three years later one of Cassatt's canvases was accepted for the Salon, a crucial step for the young foreigner and one that she would repeat several times. In effect, her persistent labor, refined technique, and respect for the previous generation had been recognized in the city that then dominated European art. Meanwhile, she chose to deepen her understanding of painting by making copies of works in the Louvre and continued to experiment by tackling rural scenes in the Barbizon region. Despite her privileged background, Cassatt was determined to be self-sufficient financially and the equal of her peers, some of whom were increasingly engaged with bold, modern life subjects. There was more travel to Italy and Spain, much of it art-focused, before she decided to make her home in France in 1874. Coincidentally this was the year of the first Impressionist exhibition, but Cassatt arrived in Paris too late to see it and was not to join the group until five years later, when her accomplishments and self-confidence had advanced.

Berthe Morisot's beginnings as an artist were both less dramatic and more focused on Paris itself, where she lived throughout her life. Born three years earlier than Cassatt, she too came from a supportive family of "la grande bourgeoisie" that was sympathetic to the arts, and never needed "to earn a living."[12] Unlike Cassatt, however, Morisot grew up in a capital city where the

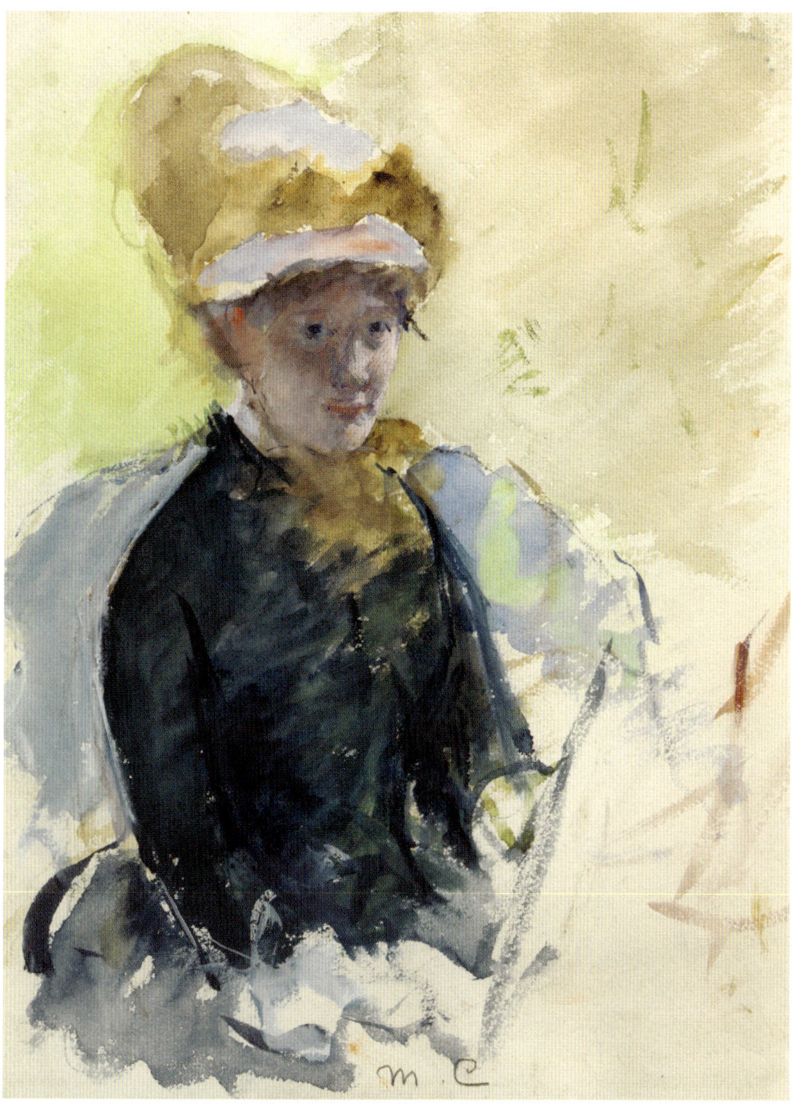

Fig. 3. Mary Cassatt (American, 1844–1926), *Self-Portrait*, ca. 1880. Gouache and watercolor over graphite on paper, 13 × 9⅝ in. (33.1 × 24.6 cm). National Portrait Gallery, Smithsonian Institution, Washington, DC, NPG.76.33

fine arts were in turmoil, as rivalry between the historically based classicists and the more radical romantics still flourished, a tension that was echoed in the training she received. Directly reflecting the Morisot family's status and widespread cultural contacts, Camille Corot—by now a senior painter of timeless landscapes—was chosen "to supervise the artistic development of the young Berthe and her sister Edma."[13] In addition, a pupil of Jean-Auguste-Dominique Ingres—who had led the more severe classicist faction—taught them drawing, and another instructor reported that their startling progress suggested a "revolutionary future."[14] Highly significant for the sisters was the inaccessibility of the state-supported art school in Paris—the École des Beaux-Arts—to all female students, a restriction that lasted until almost the end of the century. This left the Morisots no option other than learning from private teachers and patiently copying pictures from the national collection in the Louvre, a practice that had been followed for centuries. Such copy-making still represented a rite of passage for many aspiring artists, both male and female, while implicitly discouraging original creativity. In their early years, Édouard Manet, Degas, Renoir, and others had also learned from this discipline, but gradually put it behind them as their commitment to topical themes deepened. By 1864 both Berthe's and Edma's Corot-like paintings had been accepted at the Salon and their achievement was briefly noted in the press, attention perhaps encouraged by the presence of Corot himself on that year's jury. Their parents were sufficiently impressed and liberal-minded to commission a purpose-built studio for the aspiring young artists in the family garden, and continued to applaud their efforts and successes as the years passed.

When the inaugural Impressionist exhibition opened in spring 1874, Morisot was the only woman artist who participated, except for one mysterious individual using the pseudonym "Comtesse du Luchaire," who failed to appear in subsequent years.[15] Morisot's own presence was in itself a mark of her open-mindedness and pronounced self-confidence at an otherwise male-dominated occasion, especially given the novelty and implicit challenge of the improvised display. Her characteristic aplomb in such situations had been evolving over several years in the company of established male painters and writers who frankly recognized her intelligence and talent. In the mid-1860s, Morisot already knew Degas, Pissarro, and Félix Bracquemond, while Manet had become a close friend and adviser who also made at least ten memorable and clearly admiring portraits of her [fig. 4]. While Morisot gained privileged insights into the working practices of this controversial figure, she also experienced the indignity of seeing one of her own pictures "improved"—in fact, changed beyond recognition—by her instructor.[16] Morisot's family encouraged such mingling with avant-garde practitioners and thinkers of both sexes, and presumably approved of and supported the sisters' painting expeditions to the Normandy coast, to the south of France, and to Madrid to study the work of Francisco Goya and Diego Velázquez. By the early 1870s, the prominent art dealer Paul Durand-Ruel was already handling some of Berthe's pictures, including oil paintings and pastels, an auspicious development for such a young artist. In 1874 Berthe married Eugène Manet, Édouard's brother, changing her way of life but also formalizing her position in a society that still attached importance to such proprieties. Edma had married earlier and soon provided Berthe with endless artistic opportunities in the form of a pretty young niece, Jeanne. Light-filled watercolors and oil paintings based on mother and child soon preoccupied Berthe, who typically combined the fresh qualities of a rapid sketch with a strongly constructed composition, as in the now celebrated *The Cradle* of 1872, which shows Edma and her baby Blanche [see Madeline, fig. 7]. When this work was included in the pioneering 1874 Impressionist exhibition, the press was almost euphoric, variously describing it as "a little marvel of sentiment, suppleness and lightness"[17] and noting that its delicate execution was "in perfect rapport with the idea to be expressed."[18]

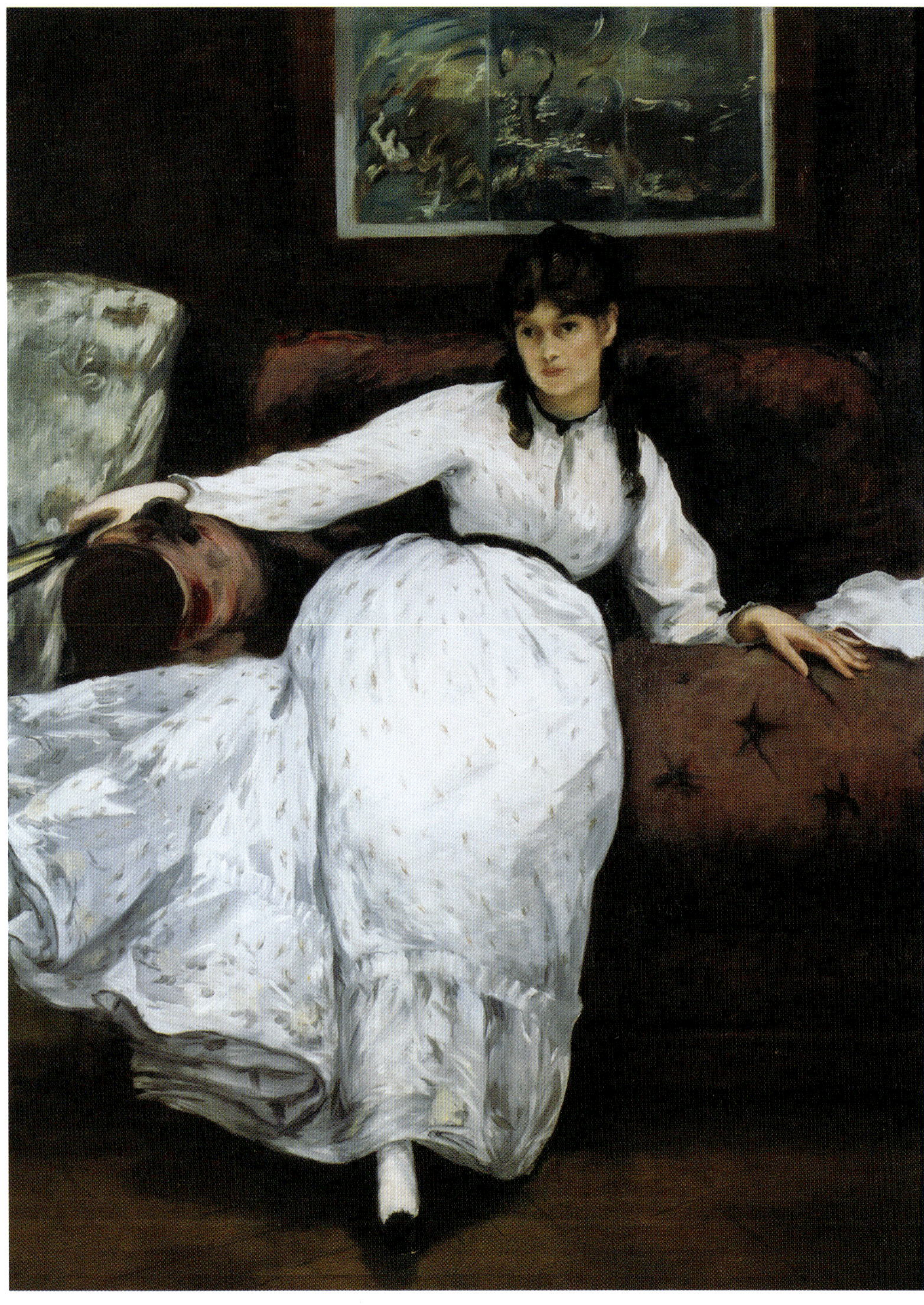

Fig. 4. Édouard Manet (French, 1832–1883), *"Le Repos" (Portrait of Berthe Morisot)*, 1869. Oil on canvas, 141 × 111 in. (358.1 × 282 cm). Rhode Island School of Design

Cassatt was the last of the trio to embrace Impressionism, accepting Degas's invitation to show with the group in 1879. Already experienced and successful elsewhere, Cassatt boldly presented eleven portraits in oil or pastel, the majority depicting women or girls occupied with informal activities. Unusually, her work was hung in a separate space within the exhibition, emphasizing Cassatt's maturity as an artist and her distinctive focus on figures in Parisian interiors that ranged from apartments to theaters. By this date, these collective shows were more widely appreciated and more likely to result in sales. One of Cassatt's canvases was reproduced in the fashionable journal *La vie moderne*, while her new preoccupation with printmaking would further advance and extend her reputation.[19] Again instrumental was Degas, now a close friend and collaborator who literally worked alongside Cassatt as they pushed the boundaries of etching, aquatint, and associated media. In this same year Degas invited Cassatt, Pissarro, and others to join him in producing a journal devoted to their prints, entitled *Le jour et la nuit*. After much effort the journal failed to appear, prompting Cassatt's mother to write, "Degas never is ready for anything."[20] Despite this setback, Cassatt became enthused by printmaking and made her own original advances in the use of color in conjunction with etching, which further boosted her acclaim.[21]

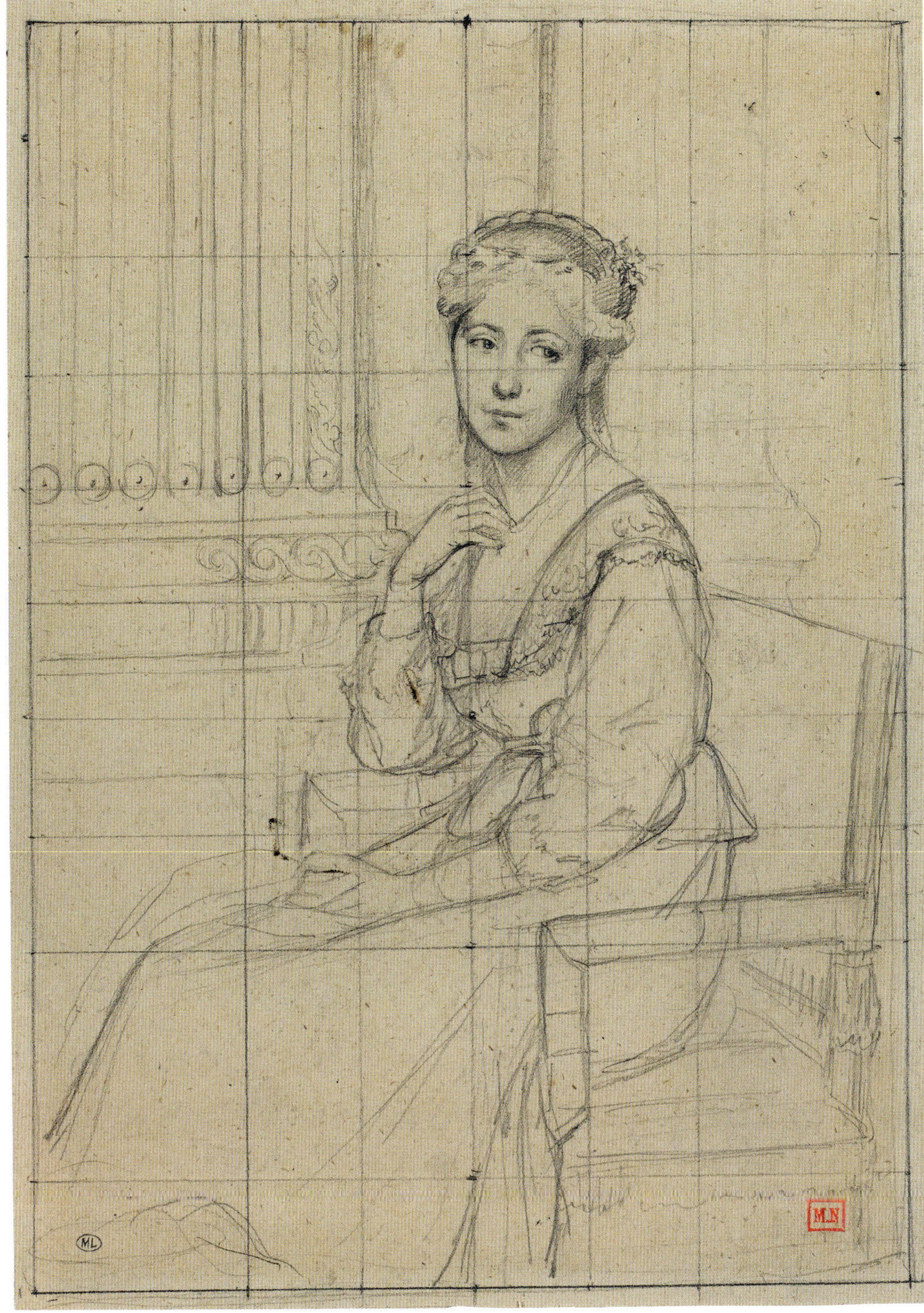

Fig. 5. Marie Bracquemond (French, 1840–1916), *Portrait of the Artist's Sister* (*Portrait de la soeur de l'artiste*), ca. 1860. Drawing (pencil on paper?), 11⅜ × 8¼ in. (28.9 × 20.8 cm). Musée du Louvre, Paris, Département des Arts Graphiques, NR. RF15285, recto

Marie Bracquemond's attachment to Impressionism was briefer and less substantial than that of her female colleagues, but similarly inflected by personal circumstances. Details of her early life are much sparser than those of Cassatt and Morisot, though she is known to have been born in 1840 and learned in her youth to draw in the precise, formal manner of Ingres, whom she briefly met.[22] A surviving pencil study of a seated woman from this period [fig. 5] is highly disciplined in the Ingresque manner, but more lyrical and even sensuous, setting the tone for numerous subsequent pictures of friends and family in interiors and garden settings. In time Marie's art changed again under contrary influences and as a consequence of her marriage to the virtuoso printmaker Félix Bracquemond, who also encouraged his wife toward making decorative designs for china.[23] Félix himself worked for the Haviland ceramic company, becoming director of its design studio and simultaneously advancing as an etcher, engraver, painter, and early proponent of Japanese art. At the inaugural Impressionist exhibition in 1874 he had shown an extraordinary suite of more than thirty finely drawn prints, but it was not until the fourth show in 1879 that Marie joined the group. Here she displayed a trio of cartoons representing the arts that were conceived as decorations for plates.[24] Disregarded by the press, these works were followed at the 1880 group event by Marie's life-size oil portrait of an elegantly clad lady in a garden setting, now known as *The Woman in White* [plate 32], and a smaller study of a modern young couple against a Parisian background.[25] Some critics were won over, referring to the "delicious harmony" of one work, though others were less convinced.[26] In a largely dismissive review in the publication *Le siècle*, Henry Havard damned her with faint praise, noting a "poetic talent" but also referring to "vaporous studies with indecisive tones" that were part of her presentation.[27] In *The Woman in White*, Marie echoed the highly finished manner associated with the Salon, while painting more broadly and presenting her model frontally and frankly in an elaborate dress that seems—deliberately or otherwise—to be incongruous in this garden context. For unknown reasons she did not participate in the next two exhibitions, perhaps due to tensions in her marriage that may be reflected in a severe, almost colorless portrait of Félix that was shown at the final Impressionist exhibition in 1886. Considered to be "extremely assertive," the husband had evidently clashed with his wife artistically and gradually worn her down as Marie pursued various experimental avenues before she "gave up" after 1886.[28]

Women Artists in a Man's World As this brief survey of the careers of Morisot, Cassatt, and Bracquemond demonstrates, the dominance of men in nineteenth-century French art institutions could present practical obstacles to women artists that included limits on their study of the human body and condescending assumptions about their preferred pictorial themes. Serious art was still widely understood to be "man's work," demanding hard physical labor on large canvases or monumental sculptures, vigorous rural expeditions to paint landscapes, and a life undistracted by mundane domestic concerns. More insidiously, perhaps, girls and women were encouraged to use watercolors and pastels as a recreation, addressing modest subjects such as flowers and still lifes while leaving the serious challenges to the many thousands of male artists throughout the country. If the renowned eighteenth-century portraitist Élisabeth Louise Vigée Le Brun and the mid-nineteenth-century animal painter Rosa Bonheur had both overcome such prejudices, they were unquestionably exceptions to a long-standing general rule. The case of Berthe Morisot is of special interest in this context, not least because it was atypical in several ways. With a supportive and liberal family who actively helped to advance her career, she was also spared from financial worry and the possibility of social isolation. Despite these advantages, decorum still decreed that she—like other respectable young women—should not be seen in the city without a parent or companion, while her gender also prevented access to the cafés and bars that Impressionist men frequented and chose for some of their formative meetings. These restrictions inevitably narrowed the available subjects for Morisot's art by comparison with her male colleagues, leading instead to her sustained visual account of family and close friends at home and in the garden and vacation landscapes that she encountered. What might have been monotonous in other hands, however, evolved in her work into an increasingly intense engagement with the act of looking and with the physical practice of painting, as one human being confronted others, using vibrant lines, colors, and marks to respond to their presences. Even a small, broadly brushed watercolor of light falling on a child sitting near a window [fig. 6] could achieve a resonant life under her brush, while arguably echoing a sense of confinement that sometimes haunts Morisot's urban oeuvre. When compared with the output of Monet, Pissarro, Cézanne, and their male colleagues, who were free to roam across the urban and rural landscape to paint what they wished, Morisot's persistent attention to her immediate surroundings can seem claustrophobic.

A sense of the shared achievement of these three women artists as well as their individuality can be found in a comparison of works on similar themes that they created around the 1870s. By the end of this decade, all three had emerged as distinctive contributors to the Impressionist project, earning the respect of male colleagues and of many critics who attended the group exhibitions. Their apprenticeships now in the distant past, Bracquemond, Cassatt, and Morisot—like the men who exhibited beside them in those years—were each increasingly associated with specific types of subject matter and with personal preferences in such aspects of their craft as composition, color, and brushwork. The more astute commentators also reflected on developments within the evolving oeuvres of the contributors, as established themes were revisited and new ones introduced. For the women, as we have seen, their familial circumstances often meant that domestic and personal subjects were prominent in their output, sometimes at the expense of urban themes. But they were on much more even ground when it came to portraiture, a challenge

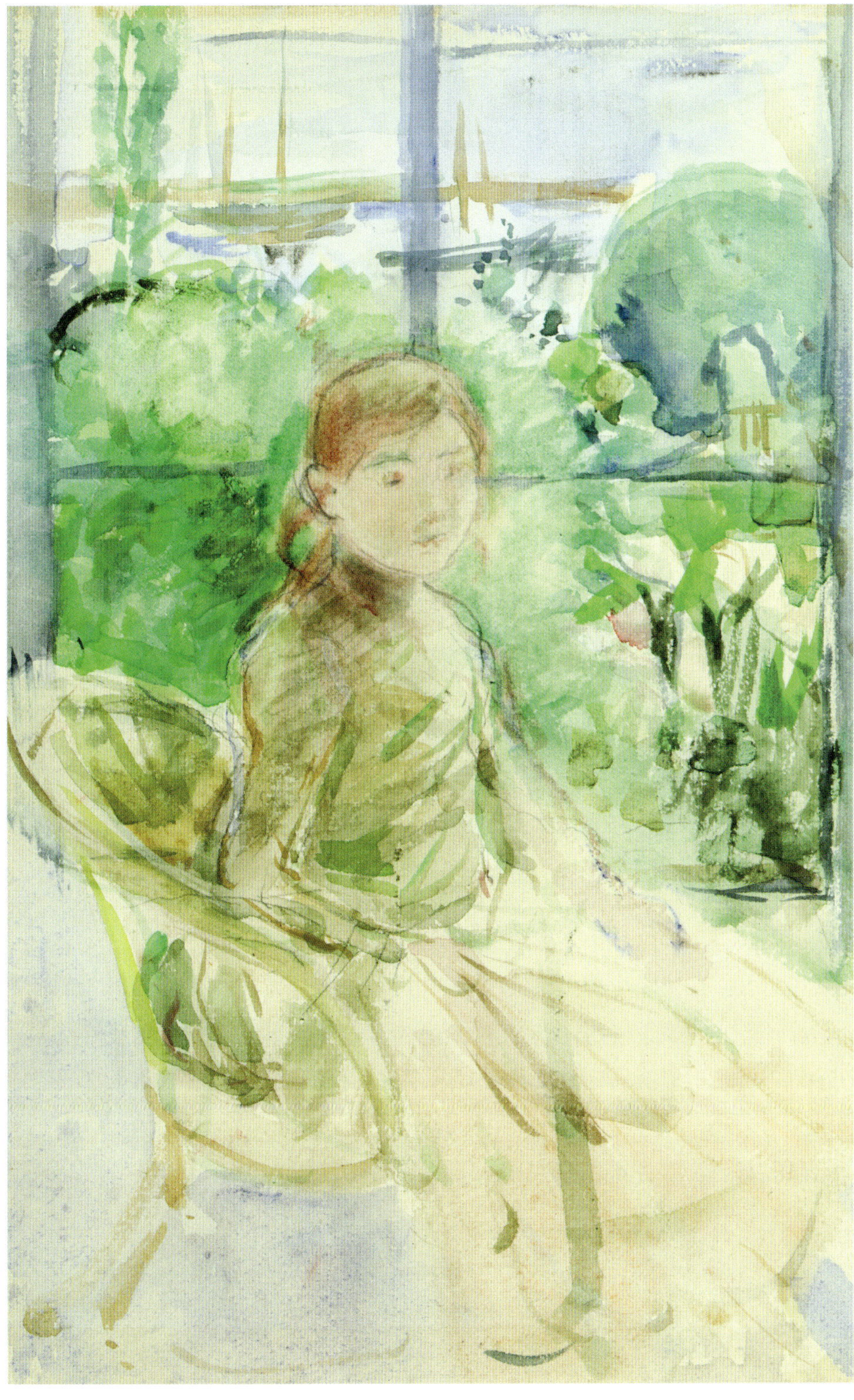

Fig. 6. Berthe Morisot (French, 1841–1895), *Cottage Interior*, 1886. Watercolor, 9⅞ × 6¾ in. (25 × 17 cm). Musée Marmottan Monet, Paris, 6046

that was universally understood and one that invoked comparison with the greatest male and female artists of both past and present. Also attractive to the three women—at least in principle—was the possibility of commissions for portraits, which as well as making money might gratify relatives and friends, and spread word of their skills in society at large. The specific motivation for the portraits has often been lost, but it is clear that Bracquemond, Cassatt, and Morisot all took this challenge very seriously. Portraits dominated the substantial paintings on canvas of all three artists throughout their careers and accounted for the majority of their submissions to the Impressionist shows. By contrast, landscape—especially on a grand scale—was more widely associated with the contributions of Cézanne, Gauguin, Monet, Pissarro, Sisley, and such later adherents as Armand Guillaumin, Paul Signac, and Georges Seurat. Portraiture, it would seem, was a woman's territory.

Berthe Morisot was in many respects the quintessential Impressionist artist, showing her work regularly at the group's exhibitions and remaining loyal to the broad tenets of their early years. The hundreds of pictures in many media that she produced were conceived imaginatively and painted vigorously, while their mainly home-based subjects were familiar to millions of her bourgeois compatriots. A very high percentage of these works were dedicated to the female sex, ranging from members of her extended family to children and friends, some of whom remain unidentified. A case in point is *The Sisters* [plate 30], a small, highly finished canvas that belongs with the artist's more formal early oeuvre. In other circumstances it might be taken for a commissioned picture, of the kind that many French artists still depended on to provide their income. Yet it seems that Morisot rarely chose to follow this professional path, preferring to depict individuals whose appearance was already familiar or those whose demeanor attracted her. Here it was surely the charming sight of two young women who seem to be twins, with identical hairstyles and outfits, who have been persuaded to pose symmetrically on a pale patterned sofa of the kind that features frequently in Morisot's interiors. This is a bold and unusual composition of a type she soon left behind, but one that focuses on the social decorum that presumably surrounded the painted pair and occasionally the artist herself. Yet closer scrutiny reveals a number of subtle deviations from strict symmetry, such as the leaves of a potted plant at upper left and the positioning of the framed fan on the wall, slightly off-center on the canvas. Morisot would revisit this formula with modifications in later works that she showed in public, a reminder of the limited options open to a married woman artist at this time and the formality that dictated life in polite Parisian society. Undated but judged to be from 1869, *The Sisters* was followed over the years by numerous variations on similar motifs that became progressively broader in handling. By the late 1870s, she was using larger brushes and denser applications of paint that resulted in more animated—even agitated—scenes of daily life. Writing of the 1877 exhibition in *La république française*, Philippe Burty devoted a thoughtful and admiring paragraph to Morisot's submissions, noting that she had a "double privilege as a woman and a gifted artist" and comparing her as "a delicate colorist" with the celebrated eighteenth-century pastelist Rosalba Carriera.[29]

Fig. 7. Mary Cassatt (American, 1844–1926), *In the Loge*, 1879. Oil on canvas, 32 × 26 in. (81.3 × 66 cm). Museum of Fine Arts, Boston, The Hayden Collection, Charles Henry Hayden Fund, 10.35

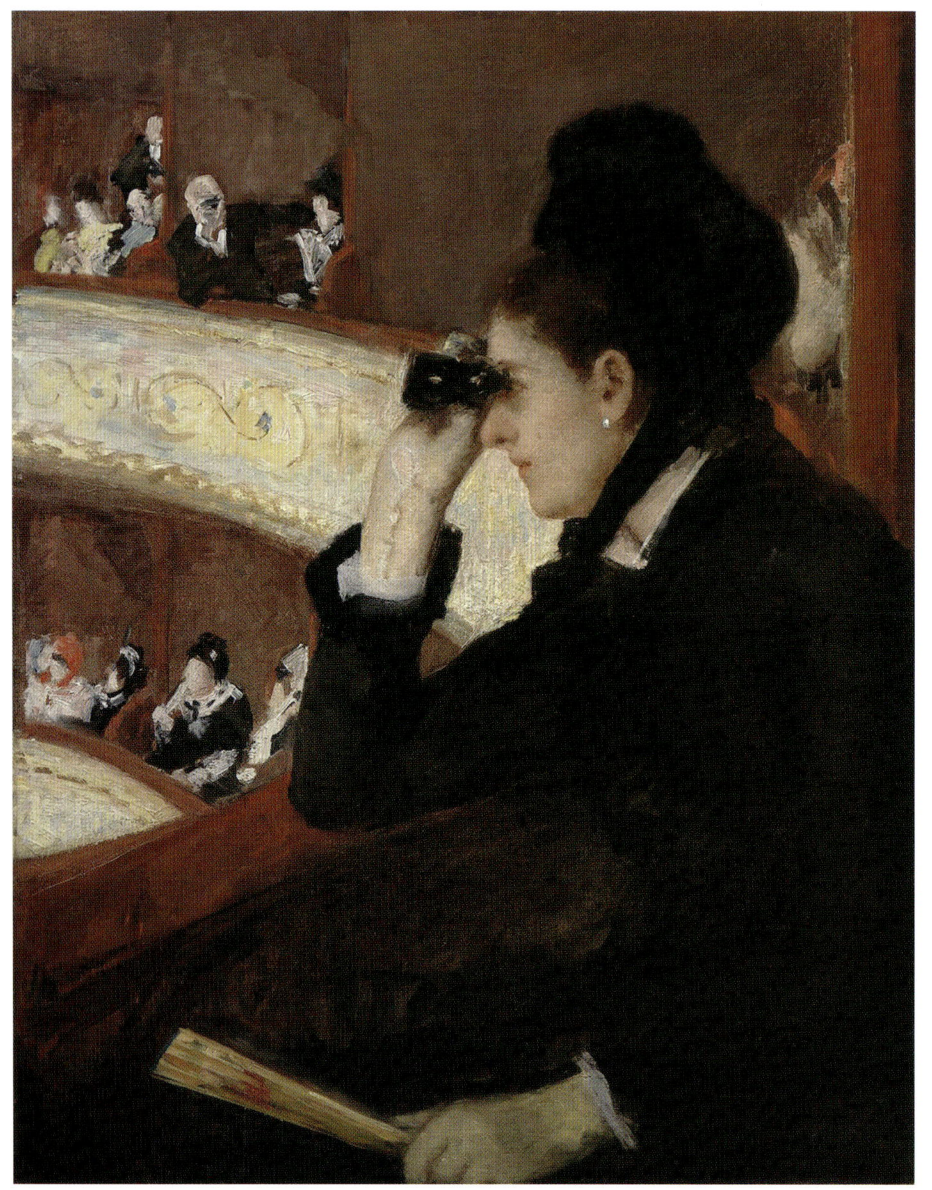

While affected by some of the same constraints, the American Mary Cassatt came from a background that encouraged her to test social boundaries as she and her sister traveled across Europe unaccompanied and—on the evidence of her pictures—visited Paris theaters and museums without male escorts. Her 1879 oil on canvas *In the Loge* [fig. 7] clearly represents a formal public occasion at which two women—the subject and the artist—are sitting close together, though not engaging with each other. There is no evidence of a male companion or chaperone, and the dominant figure is hardly demure; staring brazenly through her opera glasses, she looks not at the stage but instead at other patrons in the theater, perhaps during an intermission. It has often been noted that a blurred male spectator at upper left also seems to be looking in her direction, yet a broad assertion in the context of such works that such a Paris theater was necessarily a "site of sexual commerce" is clearly exaggerated.[30] This anonymous bourgeois woman's body language is confident and assertive, especially given the mixed audience and the public nature of the event, all features that contrast markedly with Morisot's demure subjects in *The Sisters*. While Morisot herself had presumably attended such performances, she never seems to have taken the audacious and imaginative step of reconstructing a comparable occasion from memory.

Cassatt clearly delighted in many aspects of her new world in Paris, exhibiting enthusiastically with the Impressionists and becoming a close friend of Degas, who encouraged her to tackle several kinds of experimental printmaking. So productive was their collaboration that an entire exhibition was devoted to this theme at the National Gallery of Art in 2014, where a number of theater-based prints by both Degas and Cassatt were included to illustrate this unusual rapport.[31] After an often cautious but occasionally scathing reception in the late 1870s, she was treated increasingly well by critics

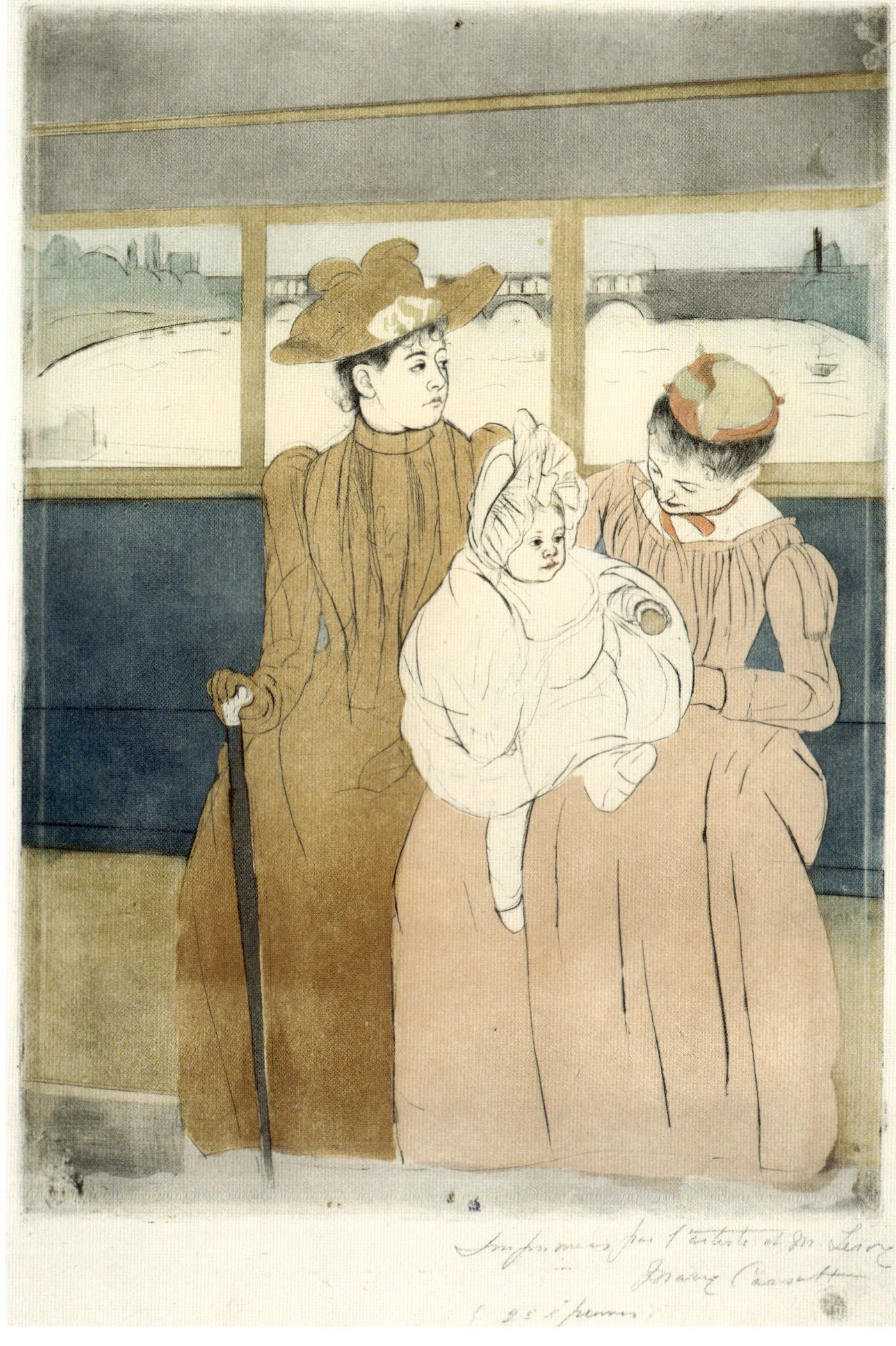

Fig. 8. Mary Cassatt (American, 1844–1926), *In the Omnibus*, 1890–91. Printed with Leroy (French, active 1876–1900), color aquatint with drypoint from three plates, partially printed *à la poupée*, on ivory laid paper, 15¼ × 10½ in. (38.7 × 26.7 cm). The Art Institute of Chicago, Mr. and Mrs. Martin A. Ryerson Collection, 1932.1289

at the four Impressionist shows in which she participated. In a lively 1879 review by Louis Besson, a group of Cassatt's theater portraits was said to have "provoked laughter" among visitors,[32] while another writer acknowledged that she had "taken the bull by the horns" and successfully engaged with "the most difficult subject in art, the portrait."[33] Cassatt went on to make an entirely distinct series of colored etchings in the early 1890s, characteristically devoting many of them to women's and girl's private involvement with bathing and with dressing themselves. Many other paintings, pastels, and prints addressed daily life, where her subjects are seen with their babies and children, playing music, and trying on clothes. One remarkable color print with an almost manifesto-like composition shows two women traveling alone on a tram in central Paris [fig. 8], presumably echoing Cassatt's own independent life in the capital and beyond. Throughout this time she maintained a country property outside the city and lived there alone for extended periods. In 1891 her first one-person exhibition opened in Paris at the Durand-Ruel gallery, and she continued to show and sell her works in France and England, projecting an unashamed independence as an artist and as a woman.

Marie Bracquemond, by contrast with Morisot and Cassatt, combined the roles of mother, as she cared single-handedly for her only son, as well as artist and wife to a self-absorbed and domineering husband. Much of her work presented the domestic landscape as she studied ordinary and sometimes fanciful household scenes and garden views, while her inventiveness found an outlet in exotically colored and intricately drawn designs on porcelain. She nevertheless completed a number of substantial canvases that revealed a sensibility quite distinct from those of Morisot and Cassatt. *Three Women with Parasols* [plate 34] was painted around 1880 and represents a recurrent theme in her work; elegant women in elaborate costumes yet in mundane surroundings. The canvas itself seems flooded with sunlight, which unusually illuminates the three figures from behind and casts them into ominous half-shadow. Dressed in their summer outfits in various shades of pink and peach, they pose self-consciously as if for one of the social photographers who were now invading middle-class life. On closer inspection, all three of Bracquemond's models have somber expressions and thus join the distinctive cast of melancholy women who populate many of her pictures. Carefully prepared in a series of detailed and refined works on paper and canvas, *Three Women with Parasols* was a highly deliberated statement rather than a spontaneous creation, which seems to reflect something of Bracquemond's problematic existence. When a comparable work was presented at the fifth Impressionist exhibition, one critic called it "elegantly drawn"[34] while others protested that Bracquemond's draftsmanship had a precision and a solemnity that was un-Impressionist. Where Morisot celebrated the pleasures of home life and Cassatt's metropolitan imagery expressed her spirited independence, some of Bracquemond's paintings seem like cries for help.

With Bracquemond's sad retreat from painting after the final group show in 1886, an event that all three women again supported, Cassatt and Morisot were left to embody the cause. Morisot persisted with her work as her health gradually faded, still depicting those around her and exploring new themes and formats before her premature death in 1895. Cassatt, the outsider, was now seen to carry the feminist flag and continued to thrive as a daring printmaker and innovative portraitist, refusing as ever to flatter her subjects. In 1892 she was commissioned to make a large mural on the theme of "modern woman" for the 1893 World's Columbian Exposition in Chicago, a considerable honor for an artist whose career had been spent in Europe [see Madeline, fig. 1]. With characteristic panache, Cassatt devised a strong, spare design that showed airy rural spaces where girls and young women played, made music, and picked fruit together in an orchard with not a solitary man in sight. Still determinedly single-minded, she continued to work and travel widely in Europe with family and friends until cataracts limited her sight and her ability to make art. She died in France in 1926.

1. Ruth Berson, *The New Painting: Impressionism, 1874–1886*, 2 vols. (San Francisco: Fine Arts Museums of San Francisco, 1996).

2. Émile Bergerat, "Revue artistique: Les Impressionistes et leur exposition," *Journal officiel de la république française* (April 17, 1877), cited in Berson, *New Painting*, 1:129; F. C. de Syène, "Salon de 1879," *L'Artiste*, May 1, 1879, cited in Berson, *New Painting*, 1:243.

3. Berson, *New Painting*, 2:37–39.

4. Ibid., 1:196.

5. Philippe Burty, "The Paris Exhibitions: Les Impressionistes," *Academy*, May 30, 1874, 616, cited in Berson, *New Painting*, 1:10.

6. Berson, *New Painting*, 2:281.

7. Ibid., 2:151–52, 146–47.

8. Nancy Mowll Mathews, *Mary Cassatt: A Life* (New Haven: Yale University Press, 1994), 303.

9. Edgar Degas, *Letters*, ed. Marcel Guèrin (Oxford: Bruno Cassirer, 1947), 47–55.

10. Colta Ives, Susan Alyson Stein, and Julie Stein, *The Private Collection of Edgar Degas: A Summary Catalogue* (New York: Metropolitan Museum of Art, 1997), 6–104, 897–906.

11. Nancy Mowll Mathews, *Cassatt and Her Circle: Selected Letters* (New York: Abbeville Press, 1984); Janine Bailly-Herzberg, *Correspondance de Camille Pissarro*, 5 vols. (Paris: Presses Universitaires de France, 1980; Paris: Editions du Valhermeil, 1986–91).

12. Anne Higonnet, *Berthe Morisot* (Berkeley: University of California Press, 1990), 8.

13. Charles F. Stuckey, William P. Scott, and Suzanne G. Lindsay, *Berthe Morisot: Impressionist* (New York: Hudson Hills Press, 1987), 17.

14. Ibid., 18.

15. Berson, *New Painting*, 1:9.

16. Stuckey, Scott, and Lindsay, *Berthe Morisot*, 34–36.

17. Etienne Carjat, "L'exposition du boulevard des Capucines," *Le patriote français*, April 27, 1874, 3, quoted in Berson, *New Painting*, 1:14.

18. Jules Castagnary, "Exposition du boulevard des Capucines: Les Impressionistes," *Le siècle*, April 29, 1874, 3, quoted in Berson, *New Painting*, 1:17.

19. Mathews, *Cassatt and Her Circle*, 140.

20. Mathews, *Mary Cassatt*, 146.

21. Nancy Mowll Mathews and Barbara Stern Shapiro, *Mary Cassatt: The Color Prints* (New York: Harry N. Abrams, 1989).

22. Jean-Paul Bouillon, "Marie Bracquemond: The Lady with the Parasol," in *Women Impressionists*, ed. Ingrid Pfeiffer and Max Hollein (Ostfildern, Germany: Hatje Cantz, 2008), 232–33. See also the essay by Jane R. Becker in this volume, especially note 4.

23. Ibid., 234–41.

24. Berson, *New Painting*, 2:105.

25. Ibid., 145, 159.

26. "Un Passant," "Les on-dit," *Le rappel*, April 3, 1880, 2, quoted in Berson, *New Painting*, 1:304.

27. Henry Havard, "L'exposition des artistes indépendants," *Le siècle*, April 2, 1880, 2, quoted in Berson, *New Painting*, 1:284.

28. Bouillon, "Marie Bracquemond," 242.

29. Philippe Burty, "L'exposition des impressionists," *La république française*, April 25, 1877, 3, quoted in Berson, *New Painting*, 1:124.

30. Griselda Pollock, *Mary Cassatt, Painter of Modern Women* (New York: Thames and Hudson, 1998), 144.

31. See Kimberly Jones, *Degas / Cassatt* (Washington, DC: National Gallery of Art, 2014).

32. Louis Besson, "MM. les impressionists," *L'evénement*, April 11, 1879, 2, cited in Berson, *New Painting*, 1:213.

33. Alfred de Lostalot, "Exposition des artistes indépendants," *Les beaux-arts illustrés*, 1879, 82–83, cited in Berson, *New Painting*, 1:229.

34. "L'exposition des indépendants," *Moniteur des arts*, May 21, 1886, 174, cited in Berson, *New Painting*, 1:467.

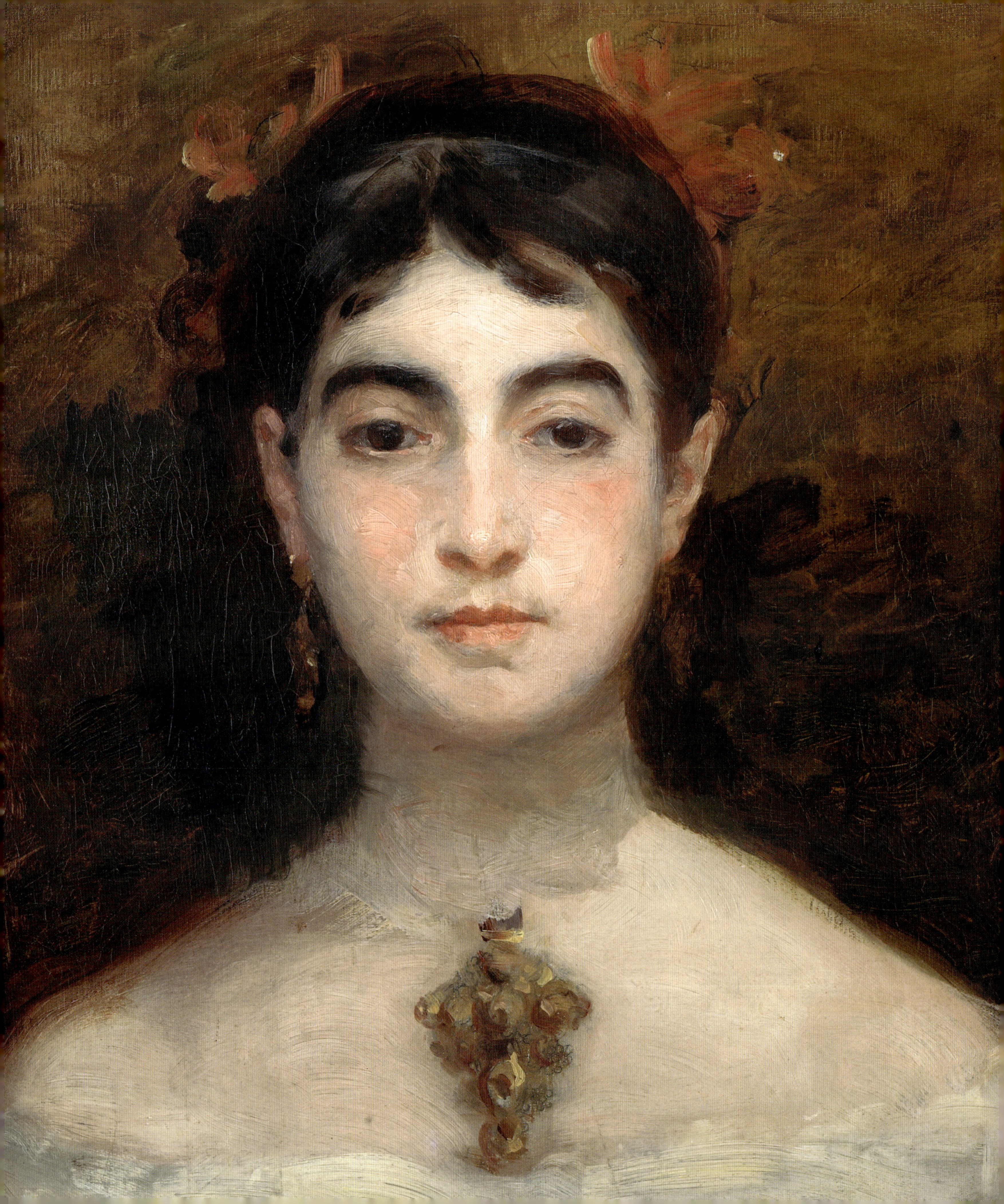

JANE R. BECKER

Marie Bracquemond, Impressionist Innovator: Escaping the Fury

The story of Marie Bracquemond [fig. 1], who pursued first academic art and then Impressionism, only to renounce art-making almost completely in her later years, provides a case study of the trials and triumphs of a woman artist working in Paris in the second half of the nineteenth century. In Bracquemond's case, the obstacles to success included both her social sphere and a lack of access to proper artistic training. As a young suburban mother married to Félix Bracquemond, a well-respected leader in the fields of printmaking and the decorative arts, her particular social sphere was largely specific to her home life. While there has been much discussion of the social difficulties that faced women attempting to become artists in this period in France (as well as in much of the world),[1] few have explored the role of the family in bolstering or discouraging the efforts of young women to participate as fully fledged artists, whether in the Salon or in avant-garde exhibitions. Bracquemond was verbally pummeled day after day, leaving her weary and with little impetus to continue her artistic production. Her main obstacle, her husband, lived under her very own roof. She found escape in often choosing to depict places where women felt most free—the park, the terrace, and gardens—natural liminal spaces, where both she and her subjects were not quite roaming free in the countryside but also not completely shut indoors.

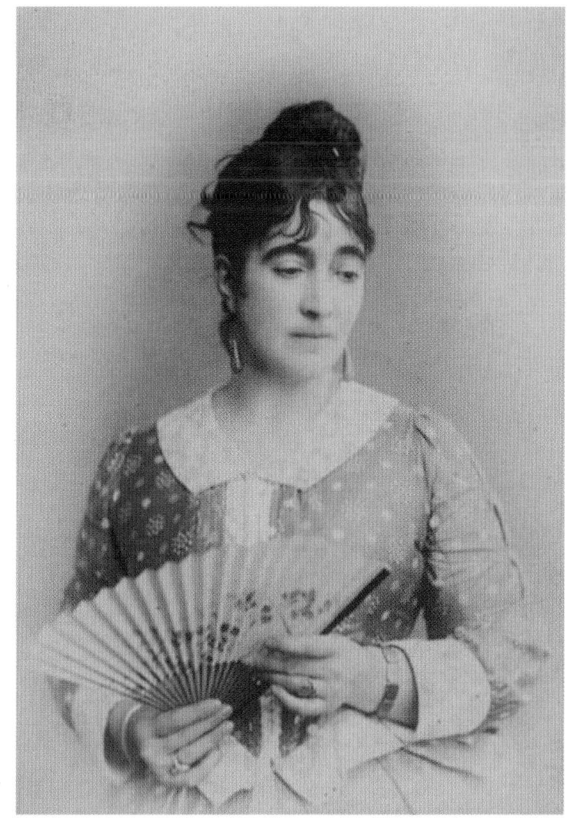

Fig. 1. Marie Bracquemond with a fan, ca. 1886. Photographer unknown

Marie Bracquemond, *Self-Portrait*, ca. 1870 [detail of fig. 5]

Marie Quivoron-Pasquiou Bracquemond was born in Argenton, near Quimper, in Brittany in 1840 to a sea captain father who joined an expedition to the Marquesas Islands shortly after her birth,[2] leaving her mother to raise Marie and her older brother on her own. Her mother soon remarried, deposited her son with an aunt, and led Marie Bracquemond on a nomadic existence, producing another daughter, Louise, along the way. Bracquemond's early years were spent in the Jura Mountains in Switzerland, in Auvergne in the Massif Central, and finally in Étampes, south of Paris, where she began to draw. Her first painting, a birthday present for her mother, was made with pigments she had crushed herself from field flowers; a family friend, noting this ingenuity and drive, presented her with a box of watercolors.[3] While Bracquemond was largely self-taught and never attended an art class or art school, she did take painting lessons with an art restorer in Étampes and was lucky enough to have been introduced to the great Neoclassical master Jean-Auguste-Dominique Ingres through an old family friend and neighbor.[4] Ingres took a liking to Bracquemond's work, gave her advice, and invited her, at only sixteen, to enter two drawings at the Salon of 1857 as a "student of Ingres." The teachers with whom artists associated themselves in the Salon catalogue were of paramount importance in determining the jury's reception of artists' entries; Ingres's great name could open many doors. Despite her age, Bracquemond's drawings were noticed at the Salon,[5] and at the same time Émilien Nieuwerkerke, the director general of French museums, commissioned her to copy important pictures in the Louvre.

Fig. 2. Jean-Auguste-Dominique Ingres (French, 1780–1867), *Venus at Paphos*, ca. 1852. Oil on canvas, 36 × 27¾ in. (91.5 × 70.5 cm). Musée d'Orsay, Paris, Acquired with the help of the Société des Amis du Musée d'Orsay, RF1981 39

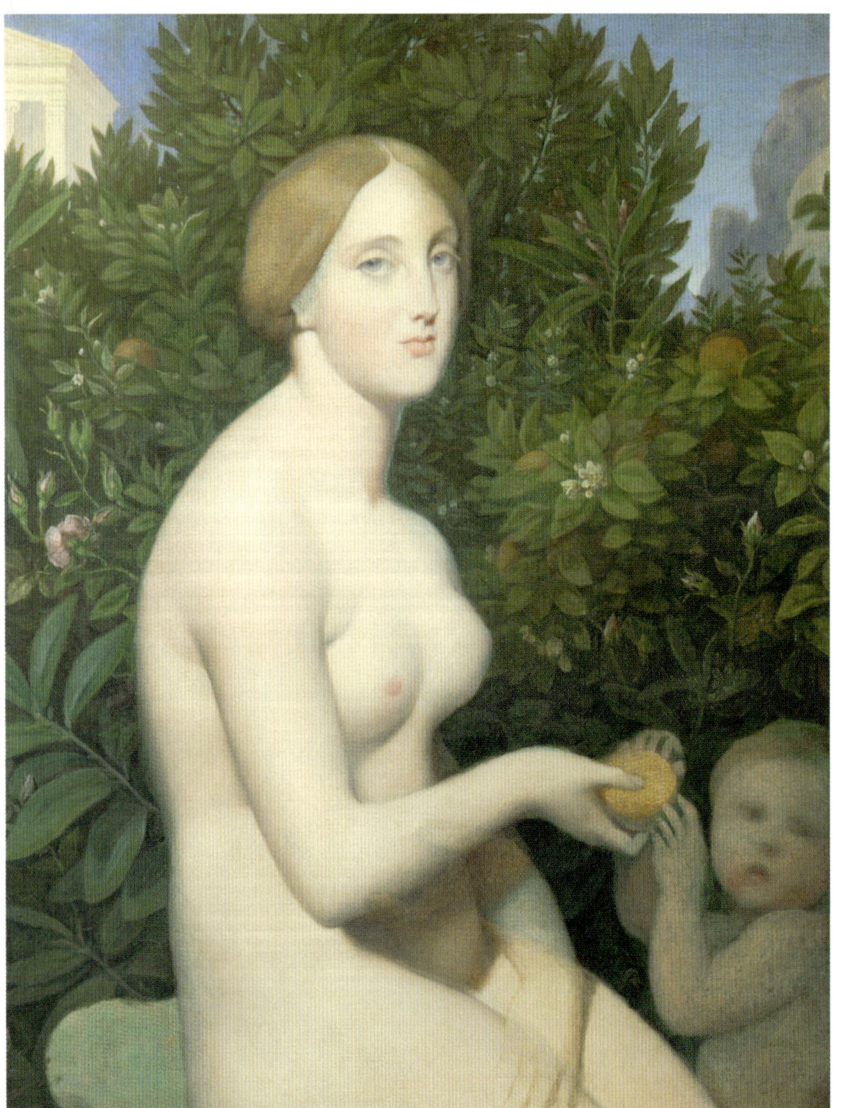

Ingres's influence on Marie Bracquemond was profound, but in the end she chose to leave his studio and to find her own voice. In a letter, she wrote of the limitations Ingres imposed on female painters: "The severity of Monsieur Ingres frightened me, I tell you, because he doubted the courage and perseverance of a woman in the field of painting. He wished to impose limits. He would assign to them only the painting of flowers, of fruits, of still lifes, portraits and genre scenes." At first, he advised her to study with the wife of his student Hippolyte Flandrin, who ran a school where "some rich young ladies try their hand at painting some flowers. But I quickly understood that I could take no part in that school except to waste my time." When, upon seeing Bracquemond's sketches and a portrait of her sister Louise, Ingres admitted she was too advanced for Flandrin, Bracquemond wrote, "There is in me a strong determination to overcome all obstacles. I wish to work at painting, not to paint some flowers, but to express those feelings that art inspires in me. . . . All this will not come to pass in a year, but in any event, I do not wish to return to Monsieur Ingres."[6]

Unlike the other women Impressionists, Marie Bracquemond came from the working class and lacked the access to art training taken for granted by young girls and women from the upper bourgeoisie. There were no drawing and painting lessons at home for Bracquemond, as Berthe Morisot and Mary Cassatt had, and no time spent in a drawing, painting, or printmaking class in an art school or private art teacher's class, as Eva Gonzalès, Cassatt, and many young women who came to Paris from countries near and far had experienced.[7] In these respects, Bracquemond's trajectory—her very entrance into the Salon—was remarkable, her obstacles greater than those of her contemporaries.

In other ways, however, Bracquemond had greater access to the leading artistic minds of her day than many of her female (and male) contemporaries. First, she worked in Ingres's studio, soaking up lessons on the use of line that led to early drawings in an academic mode, such as her *Portrait of the Artist's Sister* [see Kendall, fig. 5], a drawing squared for transfer to canvas with another drawing on the sheet's reverse, *Head of a Muse* [fig. 3]. These drawings owe their rounded faces with heavily shaded chins to Ingres's *Venus at Paphos* [fig. 2], which Bracquemond might have seen in Ingres's studio, as it stayed there until his death; possibly, to his *Madame Duvaucey* (1807; Musée Condé, Chantilly); and, for the muse's head, to *Cherubini and the Muse of Lyric Poetry* (1842; Musée du Louvre, Paris), which she could have seen at the Exposition Universelle of 1855. The lithe fingers of her sister's right hand in the portrait rest weightlessly at her chest, much like the gracefully floating right hand of Ingres's 1823 *Madame Jacques-Louis Leblanc (Françoise Poncelle, 1788–1839)* (Metropolitan Museum of Art, New York), which she also would have seen in the 1855 exhibition. A portrait of her mother, Aline Pasquiou-Quivoron (ca. 1860; Private collection), painted at the same time, reveals the lessons she had absorbed from Ingres on modeling and the importance of line.[8]

Fig. 3. Marie Bracquemond (French, 1840–1916), *Head of a Muse* (*Tête de muse*), ca. 1860. Drawing, 11⅜ × 8¼ in. (28.9 × 20.8 cm). Musée du Louvre, Paris, Département des Arts Graphiques, RF15285-verso

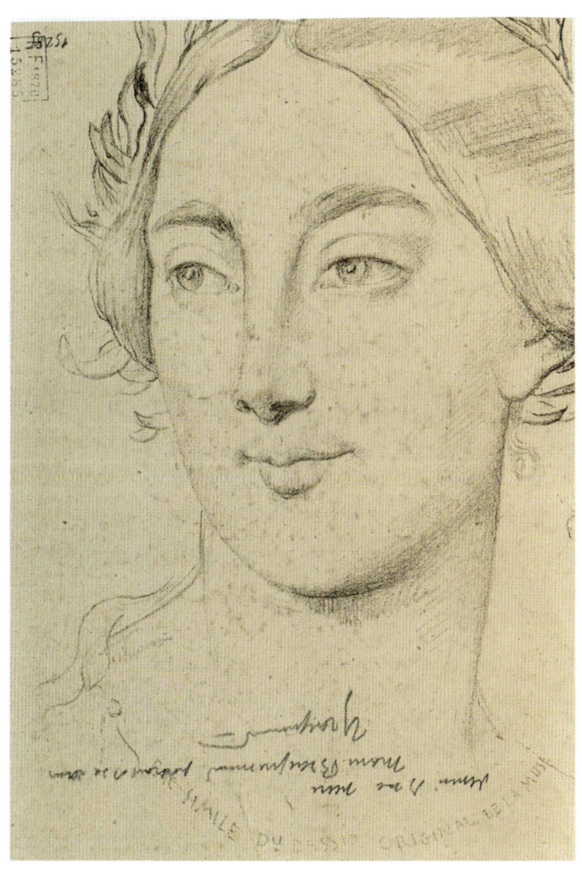

Marie met Félix Bracquemond while copying at the Louvre around 1866 (chaperoned by her mother and sister), and married him soon thereafter, in 1869. As a result she met many of his artist friends, and developed cordial relations with Camille Corot, Édouard Manet, Edgar Degas, Henri Fantin-Latour, Claude Monet, Alfred Sisley, Paul Gauguin, Auguste Rodin, Eugène Carrière, and the art critic and great collector of Japanese prints Philippe Burty. Her time spent discussing and looking at art with Monet, in particular, encouraged her to renounce her Ingresque style of painting, with its dark tones and smooth licked surfaces, in favor of Impressionism's lighter tones and freer brushwork.

Marie's choice to embrace an Impressionist painting style was a thorn in the relationship of the Bracquemonds. This division may seem surprising, given that Félix showed a drawing and etchings with the Impressionists in their first exhibition of 1874, as well as in the same exhibition where Marie first showed, the fourth Impressionist exhibition of 1879. Félix Bracquemond's strongly held beliefs about how best to make art were a force with which to be reckoned. It was, perhaps, this quality that first attracted Marie to the extremely knowledgeable printmaker, with his doggedly held ideas about the nature of successful art-making, in their early days copying together at the Louvre.

Seven years older than Marie, the printmaker, designer, painter, and writer Félix also came from humble origins and also had connections to Ingres: his own teacher, the painter Joseph Guichard, had been a student of Ingres. Félix exhibited drawn and painted portraits in the manner of Ingres at the Salon from 1852 until he gave up painting after 1869. It is for his etchings, however, that he is better known. Showing similar mettle to his self-taught wife, he taught himself the art of etching at age sixteen and led the etching revival in France. In 1862 he founded

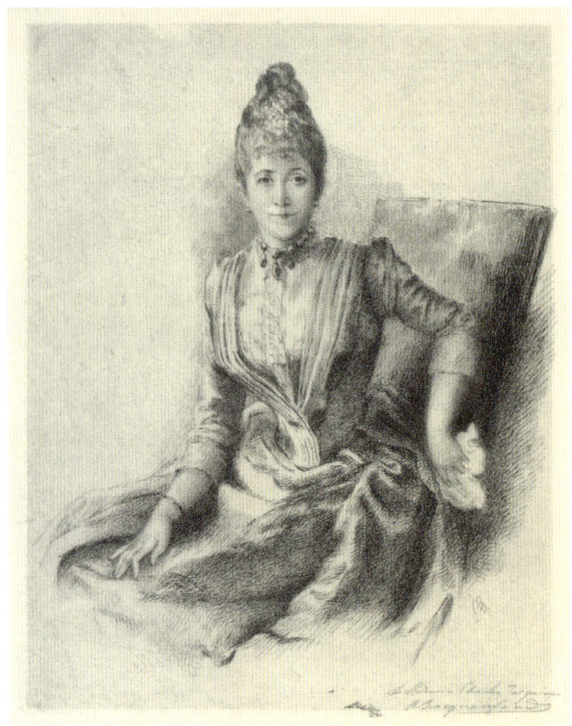

Fig. 4. Marie Bracquemond (French, 1840–1916), *Portrait of Mlle Quivoron*, 1870–90. Etching, 15⅜ × 10⅜ in. (39 × 26.5 cm). The Metropolitan Museum of Art, New York, The Elisha Whittelsey Collection, The Elisha Whittelsey Fund, 1963, 63.625.204

the Société des Aquafortistes, and his etchings won first prize at the Exposition Universelle of 1900 in Paris. He designed furniture, jewelry, tableware, bookbindings, and tapestry, too. A founding member of the Société des Artistes Français in 1881, he also founded the Société des Peintres-Graveurs Français in 1890. One of the circle of artistic and literary avant-garde figures who gathered regularly with Manet at the Café Guerbois, Félix encouraged Manet to take up etching and exhibited with him at the Salon des Refusés in 1863. His friends included the writers Théodore de Banville, Charles Baudelaire, Jules Champfleury, Paul Gavarni, the Goncourt brothers, and Gustave Geffroy as well. Moving quickly from a year spent as the director of the painting studio at the Manufacture de Sèvres to become the head of the Auteuil studio of the Haviland Limoges porcelain factory (located outside Paris) from 1873 to 1880, he designed and oversaw the production of influential new *japoniste* porcelain.[9] From 1878 on, he began to publish art theoretical treatises, most notably his *On Drawing and Color* (*Du dessin et de la couleur*; 1885) on the art of relief and the role of color in design. In short, Félix was a successful artist with many important literary and artistic friends whose appeal for a young woman of lower-class origins with artistic leanings could have rested on these facts alone.

The Bracquemonds' son, Pierre, born in 1870, and the writer Gustave Geffroy, who was close to both Marie and Félix, though, both describe Félix as prone to bouts of fury, particularly about the "right" way to think about and create art. Marie Bracquemond often found herself either caught in the crossfire of his heated arguments with Sunday-luncheon visitors or herself the butt of his anger. Their life together was marked by this fraught dynamic.

Geffroy captured Félix's dogmatic style: "Félix Bracquemond, whom I knew well, for whom I had admiration and felt friendship, was a terrible teacher, at once argumentative and authoritarian. He adored discussion, and always began well, with smiles and clever remarks, but he had the weakness of always wanting too badly to be right, and when anyone stood up to him, he ended up issuing dreadful decrees, made with increasing fury. With how many of his friends did he not fall out, swearing them off for life, only to forget all about it when the friend returned, the following Sunday, at a lunch that went charmingly until the quarrels resumed over dessert! These lunches and these quarrels, these were the Sundays at Sèvres [where the Bracquemonds had settled in 1871], for years. . . . There was in him the obstinacy and the violence of the apostolate."[10] To have lived on a day-to-day basis with such an "art hurricane" cannot have been easy.[11]

Geffroy seems to have sensed that Marie trod on eggshells around her husband. He noted, too, that with a simple charming phrase, she could calm the seethings of her husband, "ready to ignite for art."[12] Yet according to Pierre, Félix often responded, "Your sweetness crucifies me."[13] Pierre's account, in a manuscript entitled "Les idées de Bracquemond," of a rare family outing to visit Félix's student Gaston La Touche in nearby Saint-Cloud gives us a window on Félix's controlling behavior toward his wife, and on her isolation and frustration. Shut away in their home in the still countrified Sèvres, Marie yearned for more interaction with other artists than her husband would allow, and she was "enchanted" at the chance to view another painter's canvases: "This is a joy more vivid for her than for the others. To see new paintings, she who never leaves Sèvres, no longer visits any exhibitions, lives closed up in her house, confined to her solitary thoughts, tormented by her regrets. She would have so much wished to produce with this

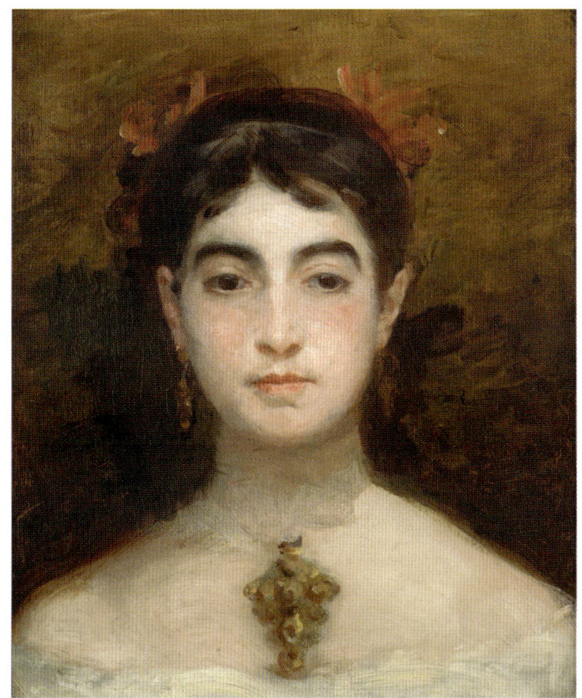

Fig. 5. Marie Bracquemond (French, 1840–1916), *Self-Portrait*, ca. 1870. Oil on canvas, 17¾ × 15⅛ in. (45 × 38.5 cm). Private collection

abundance."[14] Pierre's description of his mother's quashed goals is poignant: "Satisfied with some of her pictures, she wanted to exhibit them, desiring contact with other artists, dreaming of success, wanting to extend her ambition toward a life of struggle and greater production. But her husband was of a very different opinion on the subject"; in fact, he called her ambition "incurable vanity."[15]

The fact that Félix was Marie's teacher as well as her husband only made the power dynamics of their relationship that much more imbalanced. Marie learned both etching technique and ceramic painting from Félix, and her knowledge of Japanese *ukiyo-e* color woodblock prints and their lessons for ceramic design was also indebted to him. He was among the first to discover Japanese prints supposedly when coming upon a copy of Hokusai's *Manga* in Auguste Delâtre's print shop,[16] leading to the craze for Japanese art that became known as *japonisme*. As Félix's student, Marie accepted the discipline Félix imposed as the road to artistic virtue, valuing modeling above all as the goal in art, according to Geffroy.[17] Nine etchings she made under Félix's tutelage demonstrate this approach, among them *Portrait of Mlle Quivoron* [fig. 4], an image of her sister, Louise, who lived with the Bracquemonds at Sèvres. In this etching, Marie's vigorous use of hatched lines emphasizes Louise's strong chin and conveys areas of shadow against the reflective highlights of her satiny dress, displaying a line-based modeling very much in keeping with her husband's teachings. Louise's upright pose, her pursed lips, her intense gaze out to the viewer, and the awkward angle of her left arm back toward the chair, as she holds a handkerchief, all convey an alertness and effort to engage the viewer head-on that is indebted to such predecessors as *Portrait of Madame Regnaud de Saint-Jean-d'Angély* (1799; Musée du Louvre, Paris) by Ingres's contemporary François Gérard, a fellow student of Jacques-Louis David. Louise's relaxed right hand and the highlights on her puff-sleeved dress, meanwhile, recall the Bracquemonds' shared idol Ingres's *Portrait of Madame de Senonnes* (1814; Musée des Beaux-Arts, Nantes), which she probably saw on view in his exhibition in Paris in 1867, if not before. In her paintings, Bracquemond turned away from her aspirations, seen in her contemplative *Self-Portrait* [fig. 5], to less ambitious small canvases of flower portraits and landscapes, more "appropriate" to her gender.[18] A flower painting, *Marguerites*, appeared at the Salon of 1874. It was within her marriage, then, that she experienced both social (familial) and artistic limitations to becoming the artist she might have wished to be.

Still, it has been argued that Marie Bracquemond's physical frailty and inability to complete her own work, rather than her husband's interference, may have been responsible for her limited success. Neil Philip notes that Félix himself participated in the first Impressionist exhibition of 1874, while Marie did not exhibit with them until 1879 (also with him), and that Félix introduced his wife to several of the Impressionists and the critics who championed them.[19] Philip bolsters his argument with Félix's own words, in his account of the visit to La Touche, blaming the artist herself rather than her husband for her limited output: "'She has never turned out masses of work, preferring complete, properly finished pictures. And because she's sick and disheartened, her oeuvre is small. As a result, she's pushed aside as being useless. It's stupid and cruel.'"[20]

It is true that Marie seems to have had some medical difficulties after the birth of her son in 1870, during the Paris Commune, when proper medical care was scarce.[21] Yet Félix's remarks are revisionist at best; at the same time that Félix discounts the judgment of critics who push Marie aside as "stupid and cruel," he cannot help making arguments about his wife's taking on an Impressionist style that show the source of her difficulties to be exogenous to her own health or artistic outlook. When, on the visit to La Touche, she spoke of the new vision Impressionism had brought to her—"all of a sudden, a window opened where the sun and air enter one's home in waves, nature appears to you clearly, enchanted, interesting, [and] one escapes from the stifling atmosphere of the studio"[22]—Félix retorted that this was a "discussion," or rather, an argument, that they had had a thousand times. In front of his student, he then proceeded to criticize what he saw as his wife's artistic lapses, arguing that despite her charming sketches and her ambition to create imaginative scenes, she was limited because she had never dared to truly make the leap to free herself by making painting into a "work of will," not the servile copying of objects. He went on to state that the Impressionism so dear to her had never produced a composed painting, only slices of life.[23]

The Impressionists Marie Bracquemond held in highest esteem were Monet and Pierre-Auguste Renoir. While Félix held his tongue with regard to Renoir, praising, for example, his *Madame Georges Charpentier (Marguérite-Louise Lemonnier, 1848–1904) and Her Children, Georgette-Berthe (1872–1945) and Paul-Émile-Charles (1875–1895)* (1878; Metropolitan Museum of Art, New York)—a painting carefully designed for Salon acceptance—he could not abide the very mention of Monet. Marie protested that Félix shouldn't "rave" against Monet. Never before had anyone arrived at a power of tonal analysis as intense and sweet as in Monet's work, she said, praising the vigor with which he felt his art, the weaving of tones in his shadows, his rich exploration of light, and the sensations he brought forth in her: "He opens my eyes and makes me see better."[24] Félix did finally concede Monet's value as a colorist but noted that those skills rested on a foundation of classical training that his followers lacked and would therefore be unable to equal. Ironically, though, these Monet followers lacking a classical training included Félix's own wife; and in fact Monet's own training was far from a traditional academic one.

Marie exhibited with the Impressionists with Félix in 1879 and 1880, and without him in the eighth and final Impressionist exhibition in 1886. It was Degas who first cajoled Marie into exhibiting with the Impressionists in 1879, alongside her husband. Neither Mary Cassatt nor Marie or Félix Bracquemond deserted the group—as others, like Renoir, did—when news came that those who participated would no longer be allowed to exhibit at the Salon. When in 1880 the posters advertising the Impressionist exhibition left off the names of all three women artists exhibiting—Mary Cassatt, Berthe Morisot, and Marie Bracquemond—one has to wonder why. Degas reported in a letter to Félix shortly before the opening, "Mlle Cassatt and Mme Morisot did not insist on being on the posters. It was done the same way as last year and Mme Bracquemond's name will not appear—it is idiotic. . . . If you insist and Mme Bracquemond insists too, her name can be put on the second thousand posters during the exhibition."[25] While there is no record of Félix's response, artists on the posters were identified by last name only. Félix's role is interesting here, in that he was given the option to replace Marie's name on the poster, but seems to have opted out. While he produced an adoring print of Marie painting her sister outdoors on the terrace of their villa at Sèvres, *The Terrace at the Villa Brancas* [fig. 6], which was published in *L'art* in 1878 and exhibited at the fourth Impressionist exhibition in 1879, he may well have

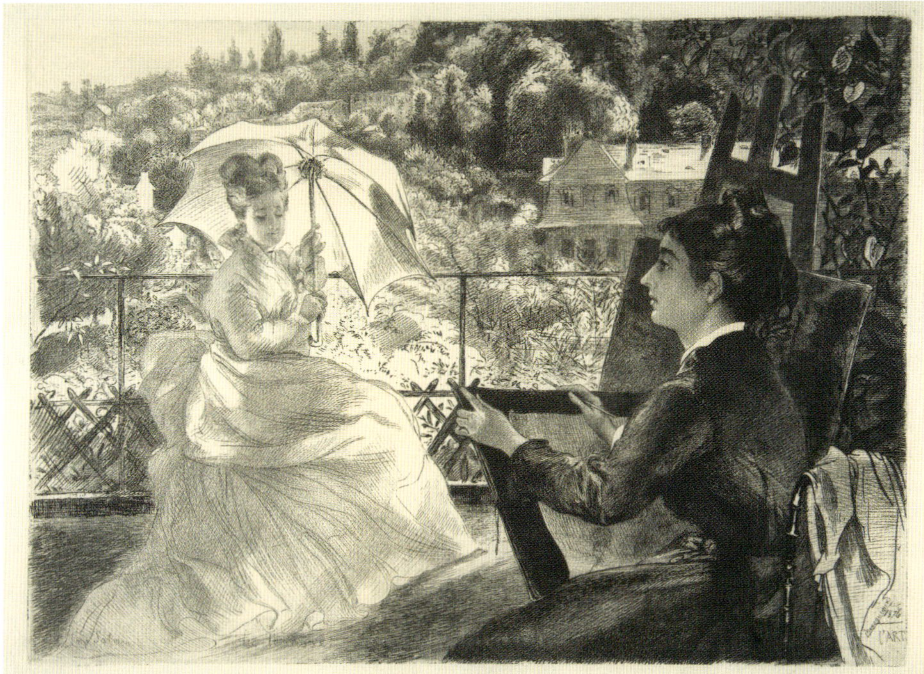

Fig. 6. Félix Bracquemond (French, 1833–1914), *The Terrace at the Villa Brancas*, 1876. Etching, eighth and final state, sheet: 12¾ × 17⅝ in. (32.3 × 44.8 cm); plate: 10¼ × 14⅛ in. (26 × 36 cm). The Metropolitan Museum of Art, New York, The Elisha Whittelsey Collection, The Elisha Whittelsey Fund, 1963, 63.625.13

not been prepared to embrace equal public recognition of his wife alongside himself. Of course, Marie herself may have objected to such public advertisement of her work, but given all that we know of her desire to be treated as a professional artist, that seems unlikely. (Degas's letter also intimated that the painter Gustave Caillebotte may have been behind the decision. Among the possible reasons, surely, was the standard view of the inappropriateness of women appearing publicly as professional artists, not just dilettante painters.) Once included in the Impressionist exhibitions, Marie Bracquemond received overwhelmingly positive comments from the critics, which must have boosted her psychologically.[26]

Even before her appearance at the Impressionist exhibitions, Bracquemond showed a great interest in contemporary fashions in her paintings. Her *Portrait of Madame Théodore Haviland* (ca. 1877; Private collection), created in the period when Félix directed Haviland Limoges's china production at Auteuil, is more a depiction of a highly fashionable dress than of the woman who wears it.[27] The same year, she produced *Woman in the Garden* (Private collection), a full-length portrait of her sister Louise that is decidedly more focused on the subject's fashionable, diaphanous white gown with lace, ruffles, and a black belt than on her relatively small face and features; the bust-length *Portrait of Louise* (also 1877; Private collection), in which her sister is dressed in the same white gown, concentrates more on Louise's facial features, expression, and hands.

The interesting placement of hands seems to have been a lesson that Bracquemond absorbed from Ingres. Her sources for the hands in *Woman in the Garden* may include Ingres's *Madame Moitessier Seated* (1856; National Gallery, London), which she could have seen in Ingres's studio in 1857 or at his exhibition in Paris in 1867; his *Comtesse d'Haussonville* (1845; Frick Collection, New York), on view in Paris in 1855 and 1867; or, again, his *Madame Leblanc*; or even from Ingres's other genres, the hands of Angelica in *Roger Freeing Angelica* (1819; Musée du Louvre, Paris), which was widely reproduced in the nineteenth century. For the pose of the hands in *Portrait of Louise*, a more likely source is Ingres's *Madame Henri Gonse, née Joséphine-Caroline Maille* (1845–52; Musée Ingres, Montauban).

It may well be that *Portrait of Louise* is actually a study for the full-length portrait, which was retitled with the more generic "Woman" to present it as more of a plein-air genre painting. At the fifth Impressionist exhibition of 1880, Bracquemond showed a "Portrait" that has been identified as *The Woman in White* [plate 32], another picture for which her sister modeled wearing the same white gown.[28] White held sway as particularly fashionable in the late 1860s and 1870s, demonstrating that its wearer lived "a leisurely, refined existence," far from physical work and dirt.[29] Pierre Bracquemond called the picture her last painting in a classical technique, and the year 1880 does seem to mark a period of rapid stylistic change in her oeuvre.[30]

In *On the Terrace at Sèvres* [plate 33], believed to have been shown *hors catalogue* in the Impressionist exhibition of 1880 and to be the final study for a painting of the same year in the Diane B. Wilsey Collection, the figure on the right wears a similarly pale, translucent outfit, this time with a cropped overjacket with a rosette at the breast and a fanciful matching hat that was the height of fashion for strolling apparel in 1880. According to Pierre Bracquemond, his aunt modeled for both female figures.[31] This color-dominated retort to Félix's 1876 etching of the artist at work on the same terrace, *The Terrace at the Villa Brancas*, shows the sun kissing the outlines of the contemplative figure at right in particular, giving her a pink halo that her male and female companions lack.

The same year, the fanciful hat reappears in *The Afternoon Tea* [plate 21], a picture of Marie Bracquemond's sister reading at teatime with a snack of grapes in a shaded part of the garden at Sèvres. The focus is fully on Impressionist light and color here, with dappled sunlight coming through the trees to hit the subject's diaphanous, lacy white gown so that it appears blue in parts. The long shadow of her hat gives the upper part of her face a greenish cast, picked up from the dark green trees behind her, while her cheeks, chin, nose, and lips have a roseate glow.

White dresses flank a deep pink one with another rosette pinned at the breast in Bracquemond's over-life-size canvas of women walking in a sunny park, *Three Women with Parasols* [plate 34], formerly in the collection of Gustave Geffroy. Marie worked on the lively poses and contrasting colors in several known extant studies. The final result shows the left figure leaning solicitously toward the central female figure even while her pink parasol angles away from her; the right figure leans slightly away from center, with her left arm raised and white parasol cocked to her left. The model for the two figures flanking the central one appears to have been her sister, Louise, while the model for the central figure is Marie herself. All three figures are in dresses that were the height of fashion around 1880, with the central figure bedecked with a floral corsage and *japoniste* fan. The picture's sense of contemporaneity rests in its fashions and its informal posing. A charcoal study for *Three Women with Parasols* may be the same as "Jeunes filles (carton fusain)," exhibited at the eighth Impressionist exhibition in 1886.[32]

Later in 1886, Gauguin came to stay with the Bracquemonds at Sèvres and taught Marie, contrary to Félix's principles, to use more absorbent, coarsely woven canvases and to integrate the resultant rough surfaces into her work to enhance the modeling of forms. Instead of layering the paint, she was to use the minimally prepared support as her only medium. The fall of the pigments onto these rougher supports left a chalkier-looking surface, as in *Pierre Painting a Bouquet* (1887; Musée Fabre, Montpellier), a portrait of her son earnestly copying from a floral still life; *Winter Landscape* (n.d.; Private collection); *Small Landscape with House* (n.d.; Private collection); and *Under the Lamp* [plate 17]. The last is a portrait of the Sisleys at the Bracquemonds' dinner table in summer twilight under the light of a single gas lamp that makes the outlines of Mme Sisley's figure glow. The light, the steam from the bowl, and Alfred Sisley's face hovering over a barely delineated body create a highly atmospheric effect. The coarse weave of the canvas shows through in the thinly painted area below Sisley's head. Félix cannot have been pleased [fig. 7].

In her time at Auteuil, Bracquemond had mastered the art of colorful ceramic painting to the point that by 1904 Clara Erskine Clement could state, "The progress made in the Haviland faience

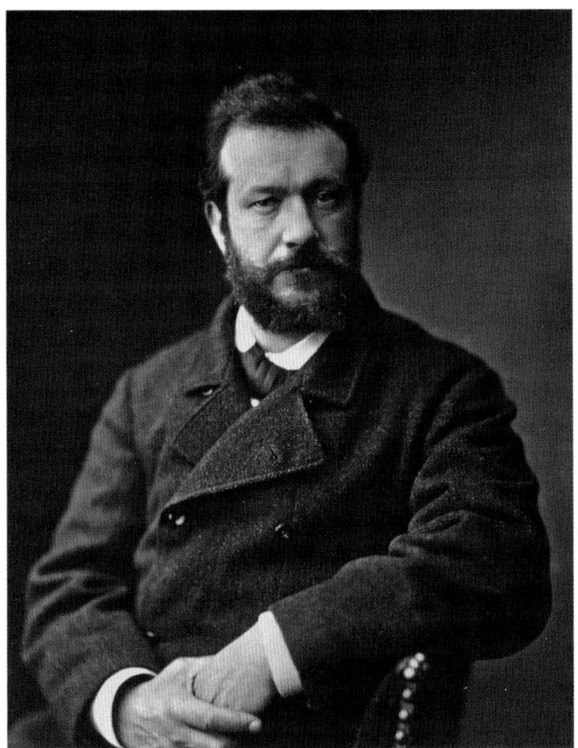

Fig. 7. **Emile Courtin (French, 19th century), portrait of Félix Bracquemond, ca. 1874–78. Published in *Galerie Contemporaine, Littéraire, Artistique* (1878): 5. Private collection**

in the seventies was very largely due to Mme. Bracquemond, whose pieces were almost always sold from the atelier before being fired, so great was her success."[33] Clement noted that Félix was considered the best ceramic artist in France in 1872, and Marie's facility with faience colors was above other artists. In 1879, in the Auteuil period, when she exhibited with her husband at the fourth Impressionist exhibition, Bracquemond displayed an enormous set of three colorful cartoons (location unknown)[34] for the faience tile panels *The Muses* (*Les muses des arts*; location unknown) from the Haviland family's collection, as well as the only faience plate on view in the exhibition. According to Geffroy, the three cartoons together reproduced the size of the actual tiles, seven meters long and three meters high, large enough to take up an entire wall in the second room of the exhibition.[35] She had already shown the actual tile panels at an exhibition of the Union Centrale des Arts Appliqués à l'Industrie with porcelain vessels and plaques in 1876, and Haviland proudly placed the panels on view as an example of the new heights being attained in the decorative arts under his aegis at the Exposition Universelle of 1878. In the panels, each of the traditional seven muses of the arts—Dance, Poetry, Music, Comedy, Sculpture, Architecture, and Painting—was personified by a beautiful woman in flowing robes with the accoutrements of her art. From an old photograph of the actual tile panels, one can see that the plan was for Painting, Sculpture, and Architecture to appear as a tight triumvirate, with Poetry and Music together opposite them.[36] An early design for the panels (private collection) in crayon, watercolor, and gouache attributed to both Bracquemonds (and thereby demonstrating how closely they worked on faience projects) shows the intended outer placement of Dance and Comedy.[37] The final panels, though, were Marie's alone.

Such a subject would have been considered appropriate for women artists at the time, removed enough from the late nineteenth-century painter's bread-and-butter portrait, genre, and landscape subjects (not to mention the more prestigious history painting), especially as it was to be achieved in the lower art form of ceramic painting.[38] *The Muses* have a distinctly eighteenth-century feeling about them that critics noticed. Degas remarked upon the success of this project in a letter to Félix, stating that he was completely "seduced" by it.[39] It is interesting to consider that Marie chose to exhibit a plate and sketches for faience tiles in her first appearance at the Impressionist exhibition; like her husband in this period,[40] she may well have been attempting to promote the idea of the synthesis of the arts (here, decorative arts and painting, rather than the traditional visual arts, music, and literature), particularly given the appropriateness of her theme of the harmony of the seven artistic muses to this endeavor.

Bracquemond's paintings on faience plates hold much interest for those studying *japonisme* in ceramics in late nineteenth-century French decorative arts, a topic that has been explored specifically in relation to Marie Bracquemond in a recent dissertation by Jennifer Criss.[41] Criss states that Bracquemond, along with Cassatt and Morisot, learned of Japan just as female non-artists did, from periodicals addressed to bourgeois women and from the new department stores, where one encountered many Japan-related objects for sale.[42] But Marie's relation to *japonisme* was actually much closer than the other two painters', given her husband's early exposure to and publicity for all things Japanese. Still, Criss makes the intriguing point that it was through associating with an "avant-garde—japonist and Japanese—Other" that Cassatt, Morisot, and Bracquemond (and, presumably, other female artists working in a *japoniste* vein in Paris, such as Anna Bilińska-Bohdanowicz) could break from the restrictive confines of their society, using *japoniste* imagery "as a stepping stone from which they could each explore issues of public and private identity, self, and Other."[43] In other words, *japonisme* provided a form of escape for them greater than the sheer exoticism it provided for their male counterparts. On the one hand, Criss presents *japonisme* as offering Bracquemond the opportunity to present herself artistically as a modern woman and to give herself a voice that was being silenced elsewhere (in the home); on the other hand, Criss notes that while her husband was at Auteuil from 1873 to 1880, she painted ceramics and designed transfer sheets for printing on porcelain and faience for Haviland and Company without ever receiving any compensation for her efforts.[44] Whatever sense of empowerment her *japoniste* work may have given her, Bracquemond's lack of compensation kept her from achieving true parity with her husband in that work, even if hers became the more sought-after pieces.

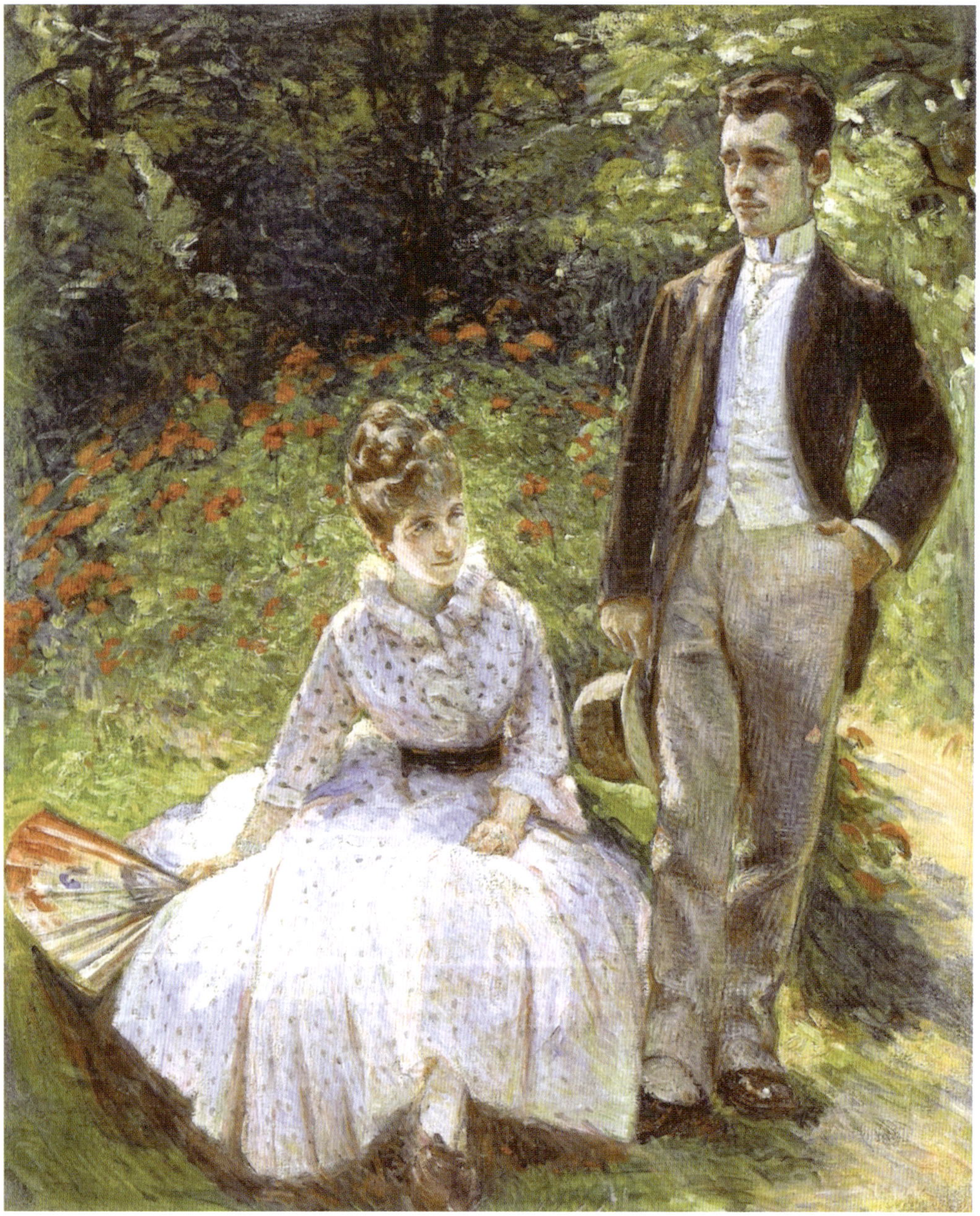

Fig. 8. **Marie Bracquemond (French, 1840–1916), *Pierre and His Aunt Louise in the Garden*, 1886. Oil on canvas, 21⅝ × 18⅛ in. (55 × 46 cm). Private collection**

Morisot, Cassatt, and Bracquemond all abandoned the Salon for Impressionism, and they all refused to participate in group shows specific to women artists or be active in associations of women artists. Once married, Morisot and Bracquemond were drawn to suburbia, the former to Passy, the latter to Sèvres, two of Paris's outlying bedroom communities at the time.[45] While Morisot and Cassatt became friends, Bracquemond kept more to herself, but she did have strong exposure to their work in the Impressionist exhibitions. The three women shared subjects in their art, most strikingly the use of their sisters as models. In fact, were it not for Edma Morisot, Lydia Cassatt, and Louise Quivoron, we would not have the depth of production from any of these three artists available today.

The subject of the separateness of the female sphere has been discussed extensively in relation to Morisot's and Cassatt's art, less so in relation to Bracquemond's. But all that Griselda Pollock has had to say on the subject with regard to the work of the two better-known female Impressionists applies to Bracquemond's imagery of her sister in the garden at Sèvres (*Afternoon Tea*) or on the terrace of their villa there (*On the Terrace at Sèvres*), which in this context may usefully be compared to Morisot's *On the Terrace* (1874; Private collection, Paris), *On the Balcony* (1872; Art Institute of Chicago), *Little Girl Reading* (1888; Museum of Fine Arts, St. Petersburg, FL), and *Interior* (ca. 1871; Private collection, Paris) and Cassatt's

Young Girl at a Window (ca. 1883–84; National Gallery of Art, Washington, DC).[46] Balconies and windows are liminal spaces. For women in the bedroom communities of Paris, they marked the threshold between private domestic lives and a vast public morass to which they had only limited access. The representation of these spaces embodied the artists' shared yearning to move beyond the prescribed domain of their home life. Still others, such as Louise Breslau, depicted that yearning as a true ache to go outside in, for example, *Contre-jour* (1888; Kunstmuseum Bern).

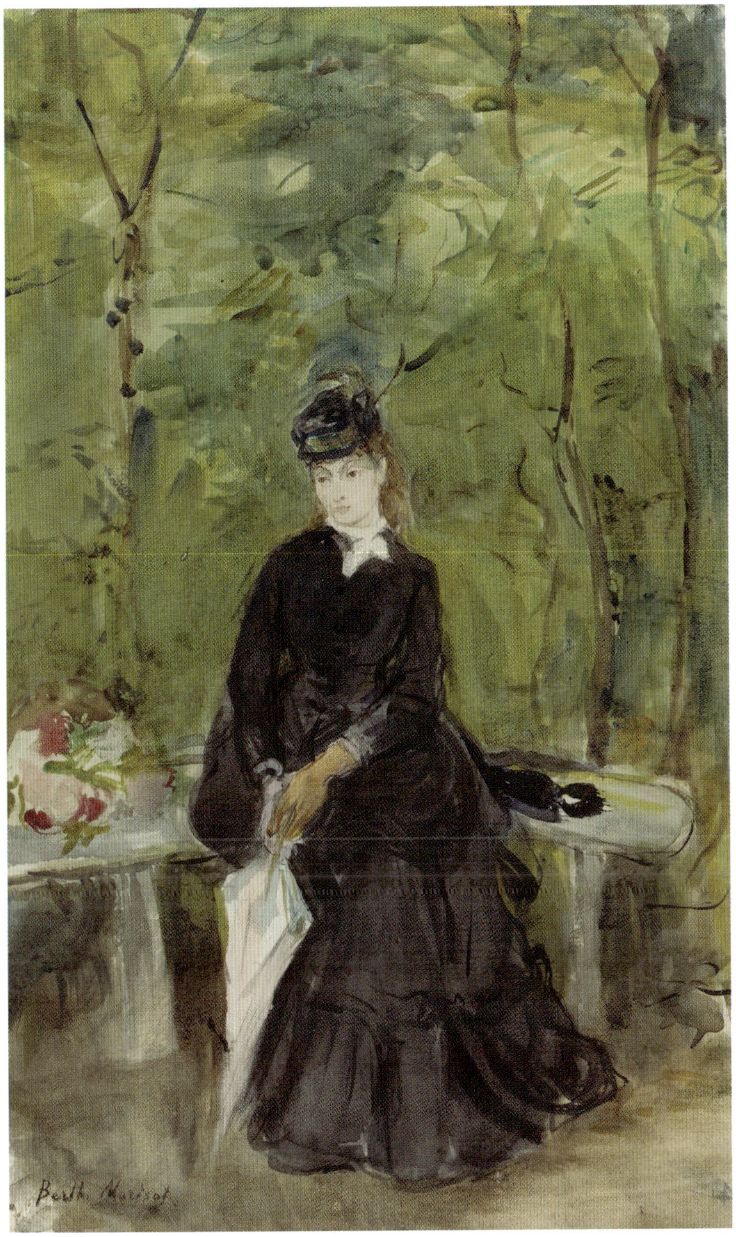

Private gardens could provide a small extension of their private space outdoors. Cassatt, Morisot, and Bracquemond all explored these spaces. From Bracquemond's *The Woman in White* and *Afternoon Tea*, her Monet-inspired *Landscape, Garden Path* (n.d.; Private collection), and one of her last pictures, *Pierre and His Aunt Louise in the Garden* [fig. 8], to Cassatt's *Lydia Crocheting in the Garden at Marly* (1880; Metropolitan Museum of Art, New York) and Morisot's *Eugène Manet and His Daughter in the Garden* (1883; Private collection) and *Butterfly Hunt* (1874; Musée d'Orsay, Paris), the private garden was a small escape to nature.

The large new parks of later nineteenth-century Paris offered a new kind of liberty, a place where women of the bourgeois or higher classes could roam freely in small groups. The newfound freedom women artists felt in public parks was expressed in paintings by a number of women artists, including Morisot's *Girl in a Park* [plate 79]; *Summer's Day* (1879; National Gallery, London), which was identified as *The Lake in the Bois de Boulogne* when it was exhibited in the Impressionist exhibition in 1880; and *The Artist's Sister Edma Seated in a Park* [fig. 9]; as well as more daring images like Cassatt's *Woman and Child Driving* (1881; Philadelphia Museum of Art), where an older woman takes the reigns of a carriage; or Bracquemond's *The Woman in White* and *Three Women with Parasols*, where the women seem to have stopped briefly on a harmonious stroll through the park. Greg M. Thomas explored these images in the context of a broader search for the "invisible *flaneuse*." *Flaneuses* they are not quite, but, as Thomas noted, "they do represent women as competing equally with men for domination and definition of public space. Haussmann's parks were essential to this kind of social imagination; as zones of interchange between the private and public spheres, they opened a hybrid social space in which women could imagine participating on equal terms in public culture."[47] For Bracquemond, such spaces as public and, to a lesser degree, private parks had just this effect. She could imagine a life beyond her everyday existence at home with Félix and Pierre in Sèvres.

Fig. 9. Berthe Morisot (French, 1841–1895), *The Artist's Sister Edma Seated in a Park*, 1864. Watercolor, 9¾ x 6 in. (24.9 × 15.1 cm). National Gallery of Art, Washington, DC, Ailsa Mellon Bruce Collection, 1970.17.159

After 1890 Bracquemond produced barely any art, and none at all for public consumption, until she died a recluse in 1916. For those twenty-six years, she has been said to have "given up," leaving unfinished paintings to lie fallow and giving in to Félix's artistic fury for the good of the harmony of her home. Where Marie might have fared better was in the example of Morisot, who married the enlightened brother of Édouard Manet and continued to exhibit throughout her marriage.

Morisot's sister Edma fared worse than Bracquemond, having trained as a painter alongside her sister but giving up painting upon her marriage out of a sense of duty; this loss was felt by both sisters. For Edma Morisot, her joy in painting lived on, if vicariously, in her sister's exploits. For Berthe Morisot, by contrast, having the outlet of a close relationship with a fellow painter who was at first her "working companion" and later was willing to model for her again and again and who happened to be her sister bolstered her in her ambitions, as Jane Mayo Roos has shown.[48]

Bracquemond's family members continued to support her, too. Her sister was often critical of or defiant about Félix. (Marie's etched portrait of Louise at the Metropolitan Museum of Art conveys something of this defiance.) But while Louise was a companion and confidante, she was not, unfortunately, an artist like Edma Morisot, nor, it seems, was any other woman around Bracquemond. Her son wrote two manuscripts after her death that recorded much of his parents' interactions for posterity, both promoting his mother's work and serving as a cultural memory. Some, like Neil Philip, have called Pierre's attempts bitter, but for us today, they are a window onto the Bracquemonds' world. Even if not verbatim transcriptions, they must convey something of the nature of his parents' interactions as experienced by the person who knew them both most intimately. When we consider the particular roles of each member of Marie Bracquemond's family, then, from Louise to Pierre and Félix, it becomes clear that her family served as both bolster and inhibitor.

Before her final decision to stop painting—however that came about—Bracquemond's escape had been into her work. The stories of late nineteenth-century female artists like Bracquemond and Morisot, working in suburbs outside Paris, have relevance even today for women living in the suburbs and struggling, often after child-rearing, to find a space of their own to work, be productive, and have a sense of belonging. It remains an uphill climb. Marie's search for the liminal spaces of nature gave her hope for a world beyond, a "some day." Today, she would be pleased to see the plethora of contemporary women artists who, together, constitute that new day.

1. See, for example, Linda Nochlin, "Why Have There Been No Great Women Artists?" *ARTnews* 69 (January 1971), reprinted in Thomas B. Hess and Elizabeth C. Baker, eds., *Art and Sexual Politics* (New York: Macmillan, 1973); Ann Sutherland Harris and Linda Nochlin, *Women Artists, 1550–1950* (Los Angeles: Los Angeles County Museum of Art, 1976), 56–57; Tamar Garb, *Women Impressionists* (Oxford: Phaidon, 1986); Tamar Garb, *Sisters of the Brush: Women's Artistic Culture in Late Nineteenth-Century Paris* (New Haven: Yale University Press, 1994); Gabriel P. Weisberg and Jane R. Becker, eds., *Overcoming All Obstacles: The Women of the Académie Julian* (New York: Dahesh Museum; New Brunswick, NJ: Rutgers University Press, 1999); Jane Mayo Roos, "Girls 'n' the 'Hood: Female Artists in Nineteenth-Century France," in *Artistic Brotherhoods in the Nineteenth Century*, ed. Laura Morowitz and William Vaughan (Aldershot, England: Ashgate, 2000), 154–61; and Frances Borzello, *A World of Our Own: Women as Artists since the Renaissance* (New York: Watson-Guptill, 2000).

2. The information about her father, who was previously thought to have died when Bracquemond was very young, is from Ingrid Pfeiffer and Max Hollein, eds., *Women Impressionists* (Ostfildern, Germany: Hatje Cantz, 2008), 302.

3. Jean-Paul Bouillon and Elizabeth Kane, "Marie Bracquemond," *Woman's Art Journal* 5, no. 2 (1984): 21. Bouillon and Kane drew much of their information on the artist and her family from an unpublished manuscript left by Marie's son, Pierre Bracquemond, "La vie de Félix et Marie Bracquemond" (1925), private collection, Paris, to which I have not had access. Bouillon states that the most relevant sections, though, have been published either in their article or in his own contributions to Joel Isaacson, *The Crisis of Impressionism, 1878–1882* (Ann Arbor: University of Michigan Museum of Art, 1980).

4. Gustave Geffroy, "Marie Bracquemond, 1841–1916," preface to *Catalogue des peintures: Aquarelles, dessins et eaux-fortes de Marie Bracquemond* (Paris: Bernheim-Jeune, 1919), 6. See also Bouillon and Kane, "Marie Bracquemond," 22; and Isaacson, *Crisis of Impressionism*, 58. It is possible that there has been some confusion about the nature of the relationship of Marie Bracquemond and Ingres among some scholars because Bouillon has translated these letters into English in multiple, seemingly contradictory ways. Further confounding the issue is the fact that Bouillon is the only scholar who has had access to these letters. Bracquemond more than briefly met Ingres. Her discussions of their encounters in her letters are extensive enough to show the meetings to be influential to her trajectory. She also exhibited under her maiden name in the Salon of 1859 as a "student of Ingres" and is said to have exhibited two drawings, possibly *hors catalogue*, in the Salon of 1857 as his student.

5. Geffroy, "Marie Bracquemond," 6. These drawings may have appeared *hors catalogue*. I have not found a reference to them in the Salon catalogues, but, in the Salon of 1859, she showed a portrait of her family and cited both Ingres and a M. Vassort as her teachers. Bracquemond showed at the Salon under her maiden name (variously identified in the Salon catalogues as Pasquiou-Quivoron, Pasquiou, and Pasquioux) in the 1850s and 1860s and under her married name in 1874 and 1875. This practice diverged from that of Berthe Morisot, who always used her maiden name, whether at the Salon or in the Impressionist exhibitions after her 1874 marriage to Eugène Manet.

6. All quotes in this paragraph from Marie Bracquemond, letter to an unknown addressee, private collection, Paris, quoted in translation in Bouillon and Kane, "Marie Bracquemond," 22.

7. Gonzalès and Cassatt studied in the studio of Charles Chaplin, who specialized in training young women artists. Cassatt had already had the opportunity to study at the Pennsylvania Academy of the Fine Arts and, once in Paris, at the studio of Jean-Léon Gérôme. Others flocked to the Académie Julian and, later, the Académie Colarossi. See Weisberg and Becker, *Overcoming All Obstacles*. Also on the "piecemeal affair" that was women artists' training for centuries, the key missing link of the opportunity to draw the male nude, and the "committed upper-class amateur['s] . . . culture of accomplishment," see Frances Borzello, "Behind the Image," in *Mirror, Mirror: Self-Portraits by Women Artists*, ed. Liz Rideal (London: National Portrait Gallery, 2001), 23–24.

8. Reproduced in Pfeiffer and Hollein, *Women Impressionists*, 233.

9. Félix was among the first to recognize the artistry of Hokusai's woodblock prints, some of which had served as packing around a shipment of Japanese china he received. See Jean-Paul Bouillon, "Remarques sur la Japonisme de Bracquemond," in *Japonisme in Art: An International Symposium* (Tokyo: Kodansha International, 1980), 83–108; and Bouillon and Kane, "Marie Bracquemond," 21.

10. "Félix Bracquemond, que j'ai beaucoup connu, pour lequel j'ai eu et j'ai gardé admiration et amitié, était un terrible maître, à la fois discuteur et autoritaire. Il adorait la discussion, et cela commençait toujours bien avec lui, par des sourires et des malices, mais il avait cette faiblesse de vouloir avoir toujours trop raison, et pour peu qu'on lui tînt tête, cela finissait par des arrêts terribles, rendus avec une fureur croissante. Avec combien de ses amis ne s'est-il pas brouillé à mort, quitte à n'y plus penser quand l'ami revenait, le dimanche suivant, à l'heure du déjeuner, qui se passait d'une façon charmante en attendant le recommencement des querelles au dessert. Ces déjeuners et ces querelles, ce furent les dimanches de Sèvres, pendant des années. . . . Il y avait en lui l'obstination et la violence de l'apostolat." Geffroy, "Marie Bracquemond," 6. All translations are my own unless otherwise noted.

11. "Cet ouragan d'art." Ibid., 7.

12. "Avec quel charme une simple phrase d'elle calmait les bouillonnements passionnés de son mari toujours prêt à s'enflammer pour l'art." Ibid., 8.

13. Bouillon and Kane, "Marie Bracquemond," 22.

14. Jean-Paul Bouillon, "Une visite de Félix Bracquemond à Gaston La Touche," *Gazette des Beaux-Arts* 112 (March 1970): 168, quoted in translation in Elizabeth Kane, "Marie Bracquemond: The Artist Time Forgot," *Apollo* 117 (February 1983): 121. Pierre's manuscript recounting the visit to La Touche is undated; however, based on paintings by Monet referred to in the manuscript, it is possible to give an earliest possible date for the visit as in the late 1890s and a *terminus ante quem* of 1914, the year of Félix's death.

15. Pierre Bracquemond, unpublished manuscript, quoted in translation in Isaacson, *Crisis of Impressionism*, 59; Félix quoted in Bouillon and Kane, "Marie Bracquemond," 25.

16. Jean-Paul Bouillon, "Félix(-Auguste-Joseph) Bracquemond," in *From Monet to Cézanne: Late 19th-Century French Artists*, ed. Jane Turner (New York: St. Martin's Press, 2000), 42.

17. Geffroy, "Marie Bracquemond," 7.

18. See Bouillon and Kane, "Marie Bracquemond," 23, which does not provide examples of these canvases. On the gendering of the painting genres, see many of the sources in note 1.

19. Neil Philip, "Felix Bracquemond and Impressionism," *Adventures in the Print Trade* (blog), June 20, 2012, http://adventuresintheprinttrade.blogspot.com/2012/06/felix-bracquemond-and-impressionism.html.

20. Bouillon in Pfeiffer and Hollein, *Women Impressionists*, 240. The original French quotation is in Bouillon, "Une visite," 172.

21. Bouillon and Kane, "Marie Bracquemond," 22; Geffroy, "Marie Bracquemond," 7.

22. "C'est tout d'un coup une fenêtre ouverte par où le soleil et l'air entrent à flots chez vous, la nature vous apparaît claire, enchantée, aintéressante [*sic*], on échappe à l'atmosphère étouffante de l'atelier." Bouillon, "Une visite," 169.

23. "Une oeuvre de volonté." Ibid.

24. "Il m'ouvre les yeux et me fait voir mieux." Ibid.

25. Degas to Bracquemond, n.d., in Edgar-Germain-Hilaire Degas, *Letters*, ed. Marcel Guérin (Oxford: Bruno Cassirer, 1947), letter 33, 55–56, cited in Charles S. Moffett, "Disarray and Disappointment," in *The New Painting: Impressionism, 1874–1886* (San Francisco: Fine Arts Museums of San Francisco, 1986), 294.

26. For Marie Bracquemond's critical reception at the Impressionist exhibitions, see Ruth Berson, *The New Painting: Impressionism, 1874–1886*, 2 vols. (San Francisco: Fine Arts Museums of San Francisco, 1996), 1:210, 219, 226, 228, 233, 235–36, 241, 243–44, 252, 266–67, 269, 273–74, 276, 284, 290, 294, 296, 299–300, 302, 304, 306, 312, 315, 320, 427, 433–34, 437, 442, 447–48, 450, 452, 459, 464, 467, 471, 473, 474. While any in-depth discussion of her critical reception at the Impressionist exhibitions is beyond the scope of this essay, it remains a fertile area for future exploration.

27. The painting is reproduced (reversed and cropped, according to Bouillon in Isaacson, *Crisis of Impressionism*, 62) in J. and L. d'Albis, "La céramique impressionniste: L'atelier Haviland d'Auteuil et son influence," *L'oeil* 223 (February 1974): 47. It is dated to 1877 by Bouillon in Pfeiffer and Hollein, *Women Impressionists*, 236–37.

28. *The Woman in White* also appears in the background of a later watercolor-and-black-ink painting of Bracquemond's known as *Interior of a Salon* (after 1880; Musée d'Orsay, Paris), which brings an Impressionist plein-air light study into a light-filled salon with its cropped, sunny window, shadow-stained rug, and cheery flowering plant.

29. Birgit Haase, "Fashion en Plein Air," in *Impressionism, Fashion, and Modernity* (Chicago: Art Institute of Chicago; New York: Metropolitan Museum of Art, 2012), 104.

30. Isaacson, *Crisis of Impressionism*, 58.

31. Pierre Bracquemond, unpublished manuscript, quoted by Bouillon in ibid., 65.

32. Isaacson, *Crisis of Impressionism*, 66.

33. Clara Erskine Clement, *Women in the Fine Arts from the Seventh Century B.C. to the Twentieth Century A.D.* (Boston: Houghton, Mifflin, 1904), 60. Gustave Geffroy also noted that her earthenware pieces were very much in demand for their strong use of arabesque lines and their beautiful colors. "Histoire de l'impressionnisme: Marie Bracquemond," *La Vie artistique* 3 (1894): 272.

34. Reproduced from an old photograph in a private collection, Paris, in Isaacson, *Crisis of Impressionism*, 60–61, figs. 15–17.

35. On the size of the overall cartoon for the project, see Geffroy, "Histoire," 271; on its appearance in the second room, see Ronald Pickvance, "Contemporary Popularity and Posthumous Neglect," in Moffett, *New Painting*, 252.

36. Reproduced in Pfeiffer and Hollein, *Women Impressionists*, 235, fig. 5.

37. Ibid., fig. 8.

38. On the understanding of the decorative arts, especially porcelain and fans, as feminine, and the ability to trace the history of that idea to the eighteenth century, see the excellent essay by Sonia Coman, "The Bracquemond-Rousseau Table Service of 1866," *Journal of Japonisme* 1 (2016): 24.

39. It is not clear if Degas was referring to the tiles at the Exposition Universelle or the cartoons at the Impressionist exhibition; the letter is undated. But in another letter to Bracquemond of May 13, 1879, he sent compliments to Marie for her cartoons in the Impressionist exhibition. See Marcel Guérin, ed., *Lettres de Degas* (Paris: Grasset, 1945), 4:43, 45, cited by Bouillon in Isaacson, *Crisis of Impressionism*, 61n5.

40. See Coman, "Bracquemond-Rousseau Table Service," 34–35.

41. Jennifer T. Criss, "*Japonisme* and Beyond in the Art of Marie Bracquemond, Mary Cassatt, and Berthe Morisot, 1867–1895" (PhD diss., University of Pennsylvania, 2007). An in-depth study of both Bracquemonds' ceramic production is beyond the scope of this essay.

42. Ibid., 5.

43. Ibid., 7–8. On Bilińska-Bohdanowicz, see, for example, her *Woman with a Japanese Parasol* (1885), reproduced in Weisberg and Becker, *Overcoming All Obstacles*, fig. 40.

44. This last is according to extant records. Criss, "*Japonisme* and Beyond," 21, 20n29, respectively.

45. On the role of Passy, in particular, in Morisot's art, see Kathleen Adler, "The Spaces of Everyday Life: Berthe Morisot and Passy," in *Perspectives on Morisot*, ed. T. J. Edelstein (New York: Hudson Hills Press, 1990), 35–44; and Kathleen Adler, "The Suburban, the Modern and 'Une Dame De Passy,'" *Oxford Art Journal* 12 (1989): 3–13.

46. See Griselda Pollock, "Modernity and the Spaces of Femininity," in *Vision and Difference: Femininity, Feminism and Histories of Art* (London: Routledge, 1988), 50–90.

47. Greg M. Thomas, "Women in Public: The Display of Femininity in the Parks of Paris," in *The Invisible Flaneuse?: Gender, Public Space, and Visual Culture in Nineteenth-Century Paris*, ed. Aruna d'Souza and Tom McDonough (Manchester, England: Manchester University Press, 2006), 46.

48. Roos, "Girls 'n' the 'Hood," 168–73.

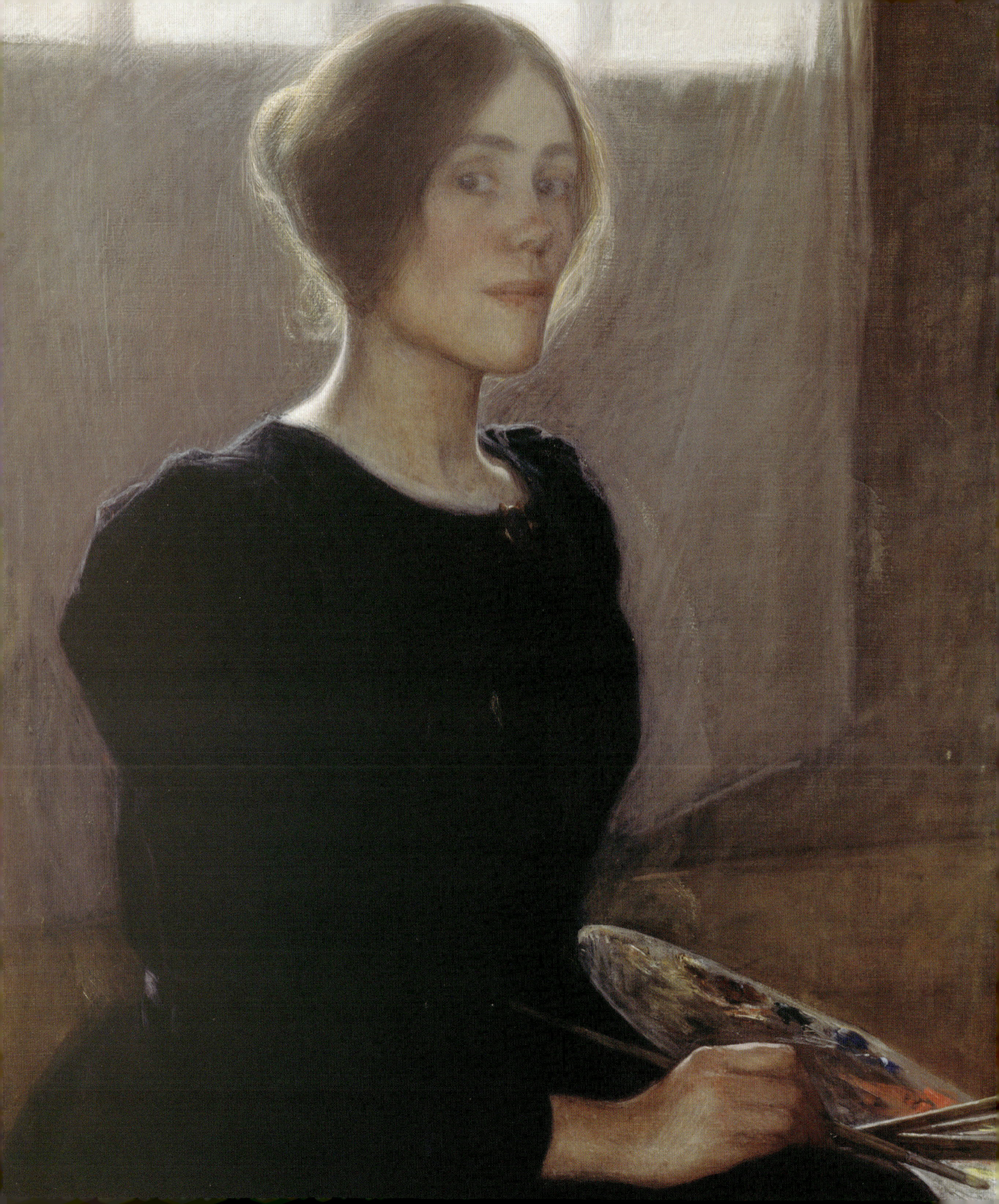

VIBEKE WAALLANN HANSEN

Female Artists in the Nordic Countries: Training and Professionalization

Women in the Nordic countries were among the very first to win the right to vote,[1] and from the initial women's rights movements of the nineteenth century and up till the present day, gender equality has gained ever stronger ground as a social and political ideal in these countries. The participation of Nordic women in the workforce ranks among the highest in Europe,[2] and the Nordic countries are widely regarded as an ideal in gender equality. Given the current situation, one might easily believe that Nordic female painters of the late nineteenth century were more privileged than their sister painters on the Continent in their acceptance, opportunities, and rights. But what were conditions actually like for Nordic women of the era who wished to establish a professional career and, more specifically, a professional career as an artist?

In regard to culture, ideas, and mentalities, the Nordic countries—Denmark, Norway, Sweden, Finland, and Iceland—are often treated as a single entity, given their linguistic similarities and a shared history that has spanned well over a thousand years. I shall begin this essay by presenting a few common traits that typified the nineteenth-century debate on gender relations in the Nordic countries. When it came to specific training opportunities, exhibition venues, and markets for female artists, differences did exist within the Nordic countries. Still, throughout the entire nineteenth century, there were close bonds between artists from the various Nordic countries, not least because they all met one another in foreign art metropoles such as Munich, Berlin, and Paris. This applied just as much to women as to men, and in the final part of the essay we shall take a closer look at the women's attachment to Paris and their exploits and triumphs in the Parisian art scene.

Elin Danielson-Gambogi, *Self-Portrait*, 1900 [detail of fig. 5]

The Debate on Gender Relations in the Nordic Countries In 1795, some eighty or so years before Nordic women began in earnest to move to Paris to pursue their art, the Enlightenment philosopher Mary Wollstonecraft made a journey of her own to Scandinavia, and the following year she published the travel account *Letters Written during a Short Residence in Sweden, Norway, and Denmark*. At the time, Wollstonecraft was known for her groundbreaking and controversial treatise *A Vindication of the Rights of Woman* (1792), which was translated soon after into French and German and a decade later also into Danish. In *Letters*, one of the topics she addresses is the concept of liberty: "The Norwegians appear to me to be the most free community I have ever observed. . . . From all I can gather, the inhabitants of Denmark and Norway are the least oppressed people of Europe. The press is free. They translate any of the French publications of the day, deliver their opinion on the subject, and discuss those it leads to with great freedom, and without fearing to displease the government."[3]

From her British homeland, Wollstonecraft was well accustomed to class divisions and rigid hierarchical structures, so that to her the Nordic countries likely seemed particularly egalitarian. The fact that Wollstonecraft, as an experienced traveler influenced by Enlightenment ideals, perceived Scandinavia as an uncommonly free region suggests a social structure in those countries that would provide fertile grounds for the idea of women's liberation.[4]

For female artists of the late nineteenth century, however, a more immediately impactful text was John Stuart Mill's essay *The Subjection of Women* from 1869.[5] The essay was translated that same year into Danish by the noted critic Georg Brandes, who also wrote an impassioned foreword. At the time, Brandes was the Nordic standard-bearer for cultural radicalism and wielded a tremendous amount of influence over the artists, writers, and art critics of the age. In the ongoing Nordic debate on gender and artistic professions, Brandes argued that women and men were endowed with the same artistic potential and that it was only historical and social contingencies that had led to male dominance in the field. Brandes therefore welcomed women into the world of art with open arms. He knew many of the era's artists and authors personally, enjoying for example a close friendship with the Danish painter Marie Krøyer and frequenting the famous artists' colony in Skagen along the northern Danish coast, where he had many adherents [fig. 1].

In the foreword to his translation of Mill, Brandes notes that he himself had long wanted to write a defense of women's rights, but that *The Subjection of Women* had rendered this moot, because it "has reinforced my confidence in the validity of my ideas, even as it has articulated them in an infinitely more ample and robust manner than I myself would ever have been able to achieve."[6] Brandes also used the foreword to attack a key argument that had been proposed against women's participation in the workforce, namely, the "aesthetic argument": "This insipid aestheticizing of a single femininity, one that must be cultivated through ignorance and subjugation in order to truly blossom, merits no reply. For nothing is beautiful save that which unfolds without duress. . . . The intimidated, the crippled, the artificially stunted, is always ugly, and just as ugly is that which suffocates, which stunts, which intimidates. We treat our women's spirits as the Chinese treat their women's feet, and like the Chinese we carry out this operation in the name of beauty and femininity."[7]

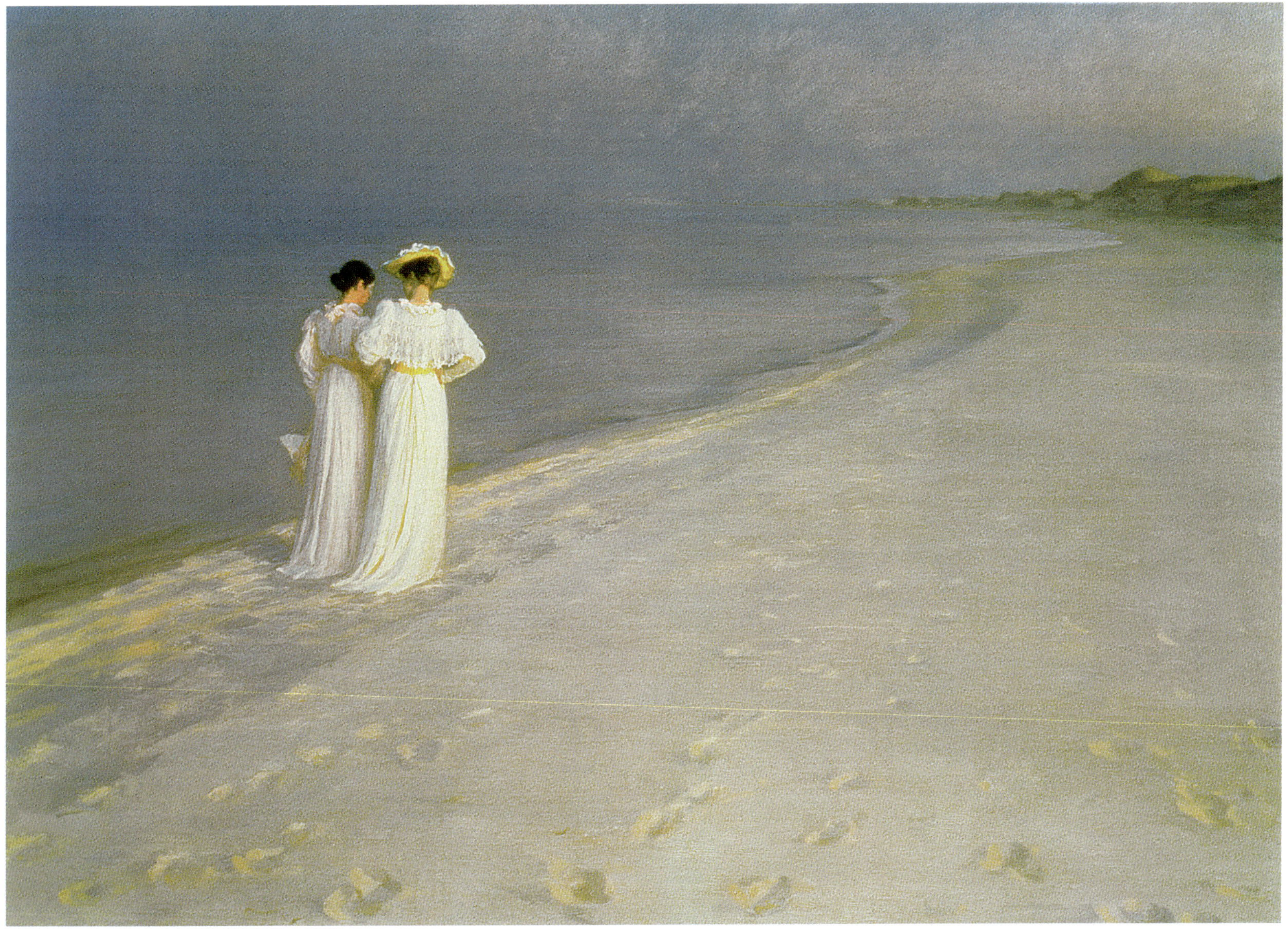

Fig. 1. P. S. Krøyer (Danish, 1851–1909), *Summer Evening on Skagen's Southern Beach with Anna Ancher and Marie Krøyer (Sommeraften på Skagen Sønderstrand med Anna Ancher og Marie Krøyer)*, 1893. Oil on canvas, 39⅜ × 59 in. (100 × 150 cm). Art Museums of Skagen, Denmark, SKM 1288

Brandes persuaded Nordic authors and artists to look at themselves as essential participants in the public debate, emboldening them to believe in art's potential to help bring about a better, more egalitarian society. In Norway, for example, the community of artists and authors known as the Christiania Bohemians began to champion the cause of free and equal love between men and women. A young Edvard Munch frequented this coterie, and his later depictions of women as a mature artist are but one example of how the Nordic art and literature of the time addressed and added nuance to representations of women [fig. 2]. Munch's women are rarely occupied with embroidery, child-rearing, or other domestic chores that in many ways were the only acceptable activities for middle-class women. In general, women's rights issues were taken up by leading artists and authors of both genders in the Nordic countries, and through their advocacy such issues made their mark on the Nordic identity.[8]

Throughout the entire nineteenth century, a striking number of Nordic women with artistic ambitions took part in the struggle for gender equality. As early as 1854, the Norwegian author

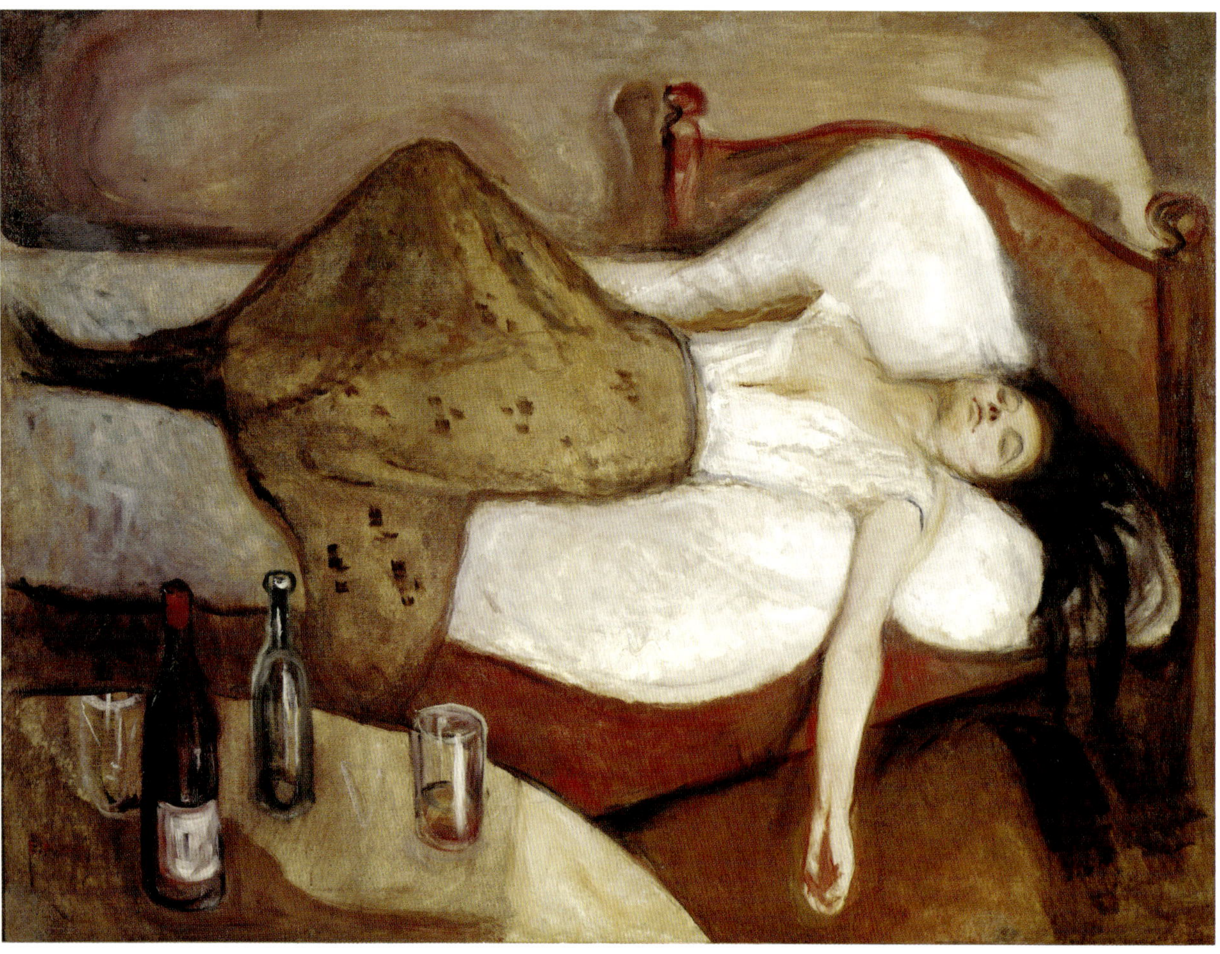

Fig. 2. Edvard Munch (Norwegian, 1863–1944), *The Day After*, ca. 1894. Oil on canvas, 45¼ × 59⅞ in. (115 × 152 cm). National Gallery, Oslo

Camilla Collett tackled the issue in her celebrated novel *Amtmannens døtre* (The governor's daughters), and in 1872 she supported Mill's ideas in her essay "Om Kvinden og hennes Stilling" (On woman and her position). Also in the 1870s, the Norwegian painter and women's rights activist Aasta Hansteen wrote an encomium on Mill entitled "Befrieren" (The liberator), hailing him as a savior in a world where women, in Hansteen's view, were as fettered as Russian serfs or the slaves of past societies.[9] In Sweden, author Fredrika Bremer played a similar trailblazing role as a women's rights activist. During a lengthy sojourn in the United States from 1849 to 1851, Bremer came into contact with the nascent women's rights movement and became inspired by their strategies. During the nineteenth century, art had the power to act like a powder keg, and Bremer's novel *Hertha* (1856) proved highly explosive indeed. The novel swayed public opinion and expanded the national conversation on gender issues, ultimately leading the Swedish parliament, the Riksdag, to pass a resolution whereby unmarried women could apply to receive full legal rights as an adult at the age of twenty-five. Bremer was internationally renowned, and her books were sold all over Europe. She has later been venerated as a feminist pioneer in Sweden, and one of the country's oldest women's rights organizations, the Fredrika Bremer Association (founded in 1884), is named in her honor.[10]

Female Artists' Training Opportunities in the North As elsewhere in Europe before 1850, few women in the Nordic countries worked professionally as visual artists. Only with the emergence of the middle-class women's rights movement did their numbers increase markedly.[11] The struggle of nineteenth-century women to earn the right to an education, a professional career, and legal autonomy coincided with the growth of a modern art market, and such an open market for buying and selling art allowed significantly more artists, both men and women, to work professionally. The number of artists in Europe rose significantly in the latter half of the nineteenth century. It is known that registered female artists in the United Kingdom soared from 278 in 1841 to around 1,000 in 1871. In Denmark at least 200 female artists were active during the nineteenth century.[12] From the 1870s on, the number of female artists in Norway, Finland, and Sweden also rose markedly.

Why exactly was the artist's vocation such an alluring one for middle-class women? Part of the explanation lies in a changed outlook on art. As the art market expanded, modern art came to be seen as a commodity and a decorative object, no longer only something wealthy patrons commissioned to portray themselves or represent their values. With this development, painting in some ways fell into the province of middle-class women throughout the nineteenth century, namely, that of creating decorative objects for the home. The creative pursuits of women, formerly regarded as the work of amateurs, were increasingly professionalized over the course of the century. In the debate on women's participation in the workforce, the conventional view at the time was that if a women was to have an occupation, then artist was one of the more decorous and suitable choices.[13] But even though artistic activity was accepted, there was a long way to go before women's creative endeavors were deemed on a par in ambition and scope with those of men. The "perfect" female artist engaged in the lesser genres—miniature painting, ivory carving, printmaking, embroidery, porcelain decoration, weaving, or jewelry design.[14] As the Victorian art critic John Ruskin phrased it, "The woman's intellect is not for invention or creation but sweet ordering, arrangement."[15]

Women in the Nordic countries also encountered such opinions, though female artists in Sweden were somewhat better off than their Nordic sisters: a class for women—or "womenfolk" (*Fruntimmer*), to use the terminology of the day—was offered at the Royal Academy of Fine Arts in Stockholm from as early as 1864.[16] As in most other areas of society, there was initially a relatively sharp gender divide at the academy, but this would change during the 1870s, with student cohorts that included Julia Beck, Caroline Benedicks-Bruce, Karin Larsson (née Bergöö), Mina Carlson-Bredberg, Emma Löwstädt-Chadwick, and Hanna Pauli (née Hirsch), all of whom traveled to Paris during the 1870s and 1880s. Naturally enough, the dedicated class for women enticed an increasing number of female artists to enroll at the academy in Stockholm. By the end of the 1870s there were so many female artists in Sweden—the year 1880 saw the hundredth female student enroll at the academy—that the profession was regarded as proper and respectable for women.[17] But despite the academy's woman-friendly admittance policy and the great increase in the number of female artists, the battle was far from won. Paris, at the time the epicenter of European art, meant greater freedom and greater opportunity and therefore attracted many of the Swedish women who yearned to become artists.

In contrast to the academy in Stockholm, the Royal Danish Academy of Fine Arts in Copenhagen was a relative latecomer in admitting women, accepting its first female students in 1888. Indeed,

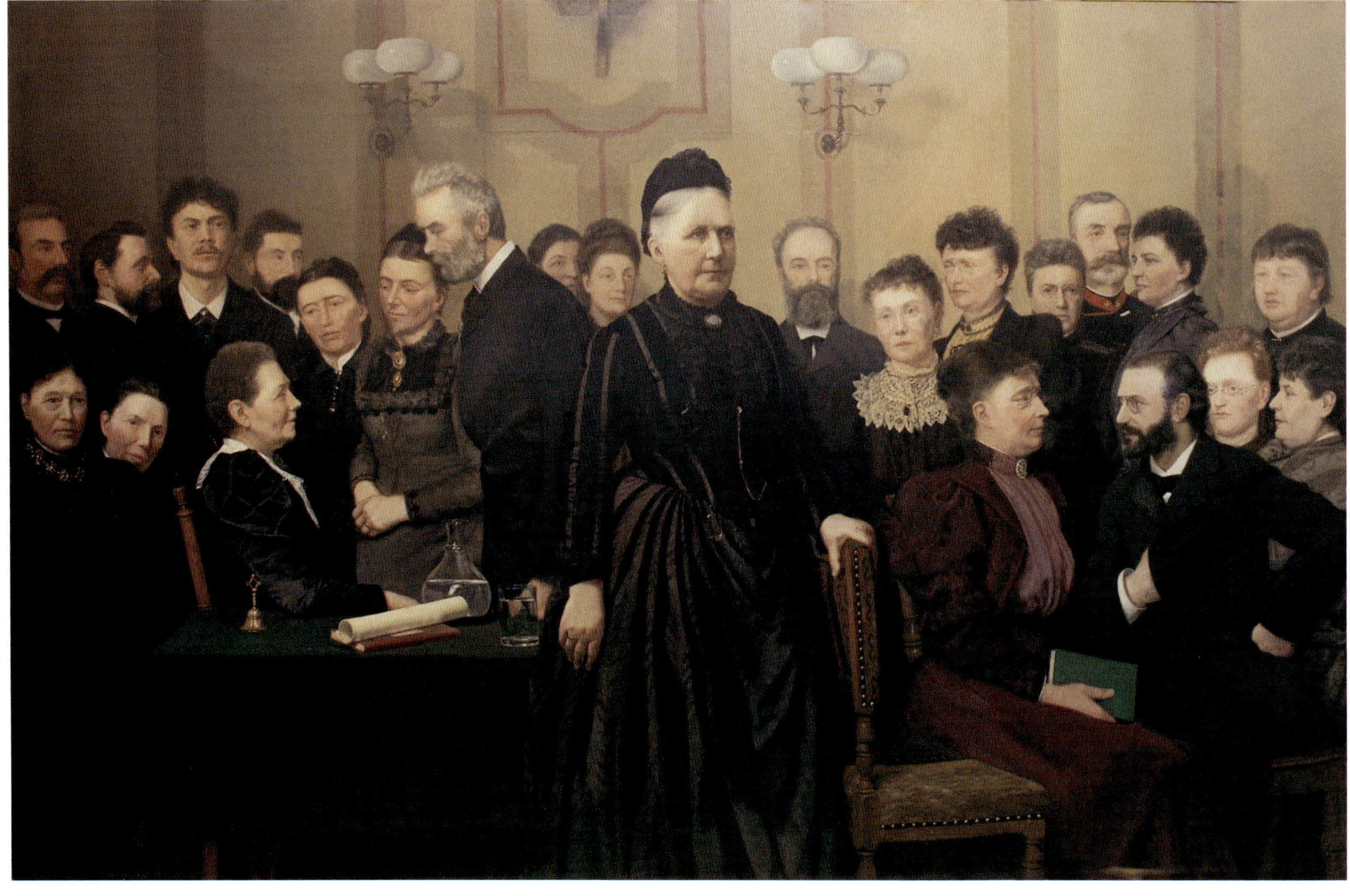

Fig. 3. Marie Luplau (Danish, 1848–1925), *From the Early Days of the Women's Suffrage Movement*, 1891–97. Oil on canvas, 58⅝ × 92½ in. (149 × 235 cm). Folketinget, Copenhagen

not until the 1870s had the debate on whether women should be allowed into the academy even become a major issue in the Danish cultural debate. But as women became more active in public life, industrialization increased the need for them in the workforce, and recognition also grew that they needed to be educated. Vilhelm Kyhn's private school of drawing and decorative arts for women, founded in 1876 by the Danish Women's Society, which sought to boost the opportunities for women to be gainfully employed in the decorative arts sector, served as an alternative to the academy in Copenhagen. Kyhn's school was not an unqualified blessing, however; its existence—as the painter Johanne Krebs argued in a series of articles in the *Politiken* newspaper in 1888—served as a "cushion," allowing the authorities to delay opening up the Royal Danish Academy to women. That same year, several women petitioned the Danish government to admit women to the academy, complaining that Kyhn's school was insufficient artistically, and that it was both expensive and difficult to study abroad.[18] Finally, in fall 1888, a women's department was established at the academy, with Johanne Krebs as its leader.[19] The painter Marie Luplau, one of those who had signed the petition earlier that year, was also active both in the fight for universal suffrage and in the women's rights movement in general. A few years later, she depicted her sisters in the struggle for the right to vote in the painting *From the Early Days of the Women's Suffrage Movement* [fig. 3].

In Norway, the women's rights movement coincided with the founding of a national community of artists and what we may call the breakthrough of Norwegian painting.[20] Norway, which was under Swedish rule at the time, did not have its own academy of the arts, and there were few venues for exhibiting and selling works of art. An urban, middle-class culture had yet to fully develop, and few people had purchasing power, so there was little demand for art. All this changed from the 1870s on. The artists of the new generation, including the aforementioned Christiania Bohemians, strove to create a domestic environment for art in the Norwegian capital of Christiania (modern-day Oslo). During the 1880s efforts were made to make artists' organizations more democratic, with an important outcome being the founding of an artist-run exhibition in 1882 in which female painters were included from the very first showing. The Norwegian women often began their training as artists in Christiania at Knud Bergslien's private school, before continuing their studies abroad in the great artistic centers of Munich, Berlin, or Paris; only a handful availed themselves of the opportunity to attend the Royal Academy of Fine Arts in Stockholm. The female artists who enjoyed the greatest success at home in Norway in the 1880s and 1890s were Harriet Backer, Kitty Kielland, Asta Nørregaard, and Oda Krohg, representatives of a golden age of Norwegian painting. But at the same time Norwegian women like the sculptor Ambrosia Tønnesen and the painters Sigrid Bølling, Leis Schjelderup, and Valborg Olsen-Dubois were also enjoying artistic careers in Paris.[21]

Finland's artistic heritage, like Norway's, is also of relatively recent vintage; not until the mid-nineteenth century did the Finns establish their own art society and academy of art. As in Norway, too, the Finnish artistic community was small, there were few exhibition venues, and the market was limited. The fact that few men sought admittance to the private art schools, however, gave women easier access, and many female students attended the Finnish Art Society's courses. Although women were not particularly encouraged, the number of female artists continued to grow.[22] The letters, diaries, and notebooks of these women provide insight into how it felt to be an ambitious woman during the nineteenth century. In her memoirs, the painter, writer, and women's rights activist Helena Westermarck recalls how "a young girl's hard work could often be met with distrust or antipathy, since, at the time, it was still not a matter of course that she could tread her own path outside the confines of the house."[23] In one of her letters from 1882, the painter Elin Danielson-Gambogi complained that her neighbors viewed her artistic endeavors as nothing more than an aimless diversion, and that they probably believed that embroidery was more fitting for a woman. "How much happier are men in this regard," she lamented, "as they are allowed to dedicate their time to whatever pursuit they have chosen as their calling in life."[24]

Paris: The Mecca of Art for Nordic Women Throughout the nineteenth century, the most important venues of learning for artistically ambitious women were private studios. There were many such studios in Paris, and as we have seen, there were also private art schools in the various Nordic capitals. The number of such institutions grew during the 1880s, with a few Nordic women establishing their own schools of drawing and painting. Marie Luplau and Emilie Mundt founded a school of drawing for women in Copenhagen in 1878 and ran it for no less than thirty-five years. In 1885 Marie Krøyer and Agnes Slott-Møller founded the Lille Malerskole

(Little School of Painting) in Copenhagen, where the women shared the expenses for models and localities.[25] In Christiania, the leading male artists Christian Krohg and Erik Werenskiold offered lessons to female painters in the early 1880s. After returning from Paris, Harriet Backer opened her own school of painting in Christiania in 1892, running it herself for twenty years. There were also private alternatives to the Royal Academy of Fine Arts in Stockholm, such as Kerstin Cardon's school of painting, which she founded after returning home from Paris in 1875 and ran until 1911.

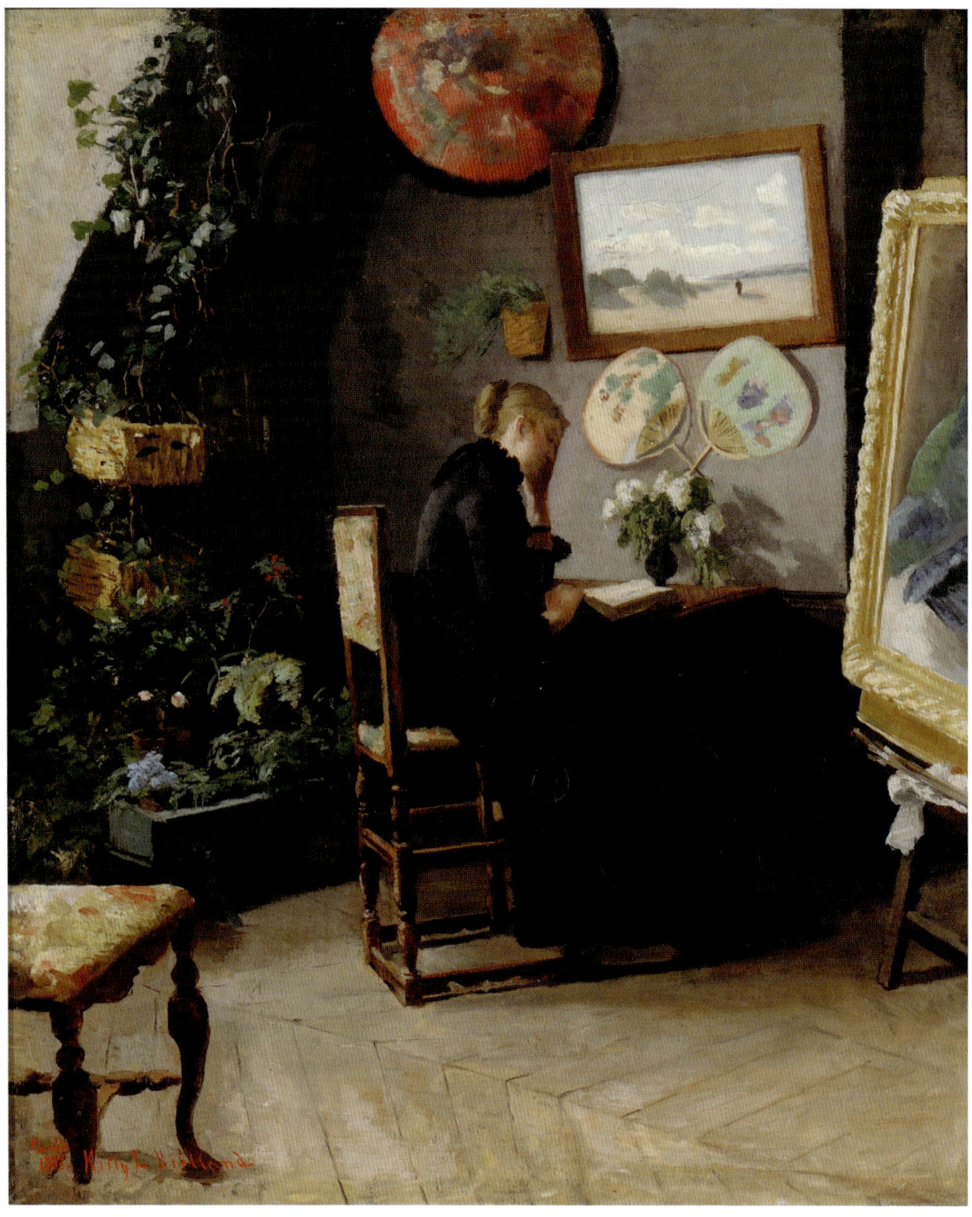

Fig. 4. Kitty Kielland (Norwegian, 1843–1914), *Ateliérinteriør (or Portrait of Harriet Backer)*, 1883. Oil on canvas, 16⅞ × 14⅝ in. (43 × 37 cm). Lillehammer Kunstmuseum, Norway

Nordic female artists, among them the Swedish painter Sophie Adlersparre, had found their way to the French capital earlier in the nineteenth century, but it was during the 1870s that their number rose sharply, and during the following decade a great many female artists from the Nordic countries were working and training there. Compared with Paris, the northern capitals were like small towns, not least in regard to the art market and exhibition opportunities. It was in Paris that Nordic artists such as Anna Ancher, Backer, Eva Bonnier, Kielland, Hanna Pauli, and Helene Schjerfbeck acquired a new modern style of art. Even though there were training opportunities for women in their home countries and the struggle for women's liberation was in full swing, they found a greater degree of freedom in Paris. Moreover, Paris was at the time the city of choice for the ambitious artist. Above all, in Paris the women could dedicate themselves to their artistic pursuits without feeling that they had neglected the "womanly" duties they were expected to perform as members of a household. Hanna Pauli's *The Artist Venny Soldan-Brofeldt* [plate 10] has often been interpreted as reflecting the liberated lifestyle of Nordic women in Paris at the time.

For these women, the premier schools of art in Paris were the Académie Julian, the Académie Colarossi, and the Académie Trélat. Not until 1896 did the École des Beaux-Arts open its doors to women, but this drawback was alleviated by the fact that many of the artists who taught at Trélat, Julian, and Colarossi were the same as those who taught at the École. Other private academies stressed the importance of upholding the propriety of middle-class women with strict rules, but these do not seem to have appealed much to the Nordic women, who were primarily interested in the most professional instruction.[26] Their letters and diaries testify that they often worked from morning to evening, and then used their spare time to visit the Louvre or other venues of art.

Of the many private schools that offered lessons in drawing and painting, the most important was the Académie Julian, where women also had the opportunity to draw from a live nude model.[27] Many of the Nordic women attended short-term classes there, though a few also studied there over a longer period.[28] Of the school's teachers, Léon Bonnat, Jean-Léon Gérôme, and Alfred Stevens were most important to the Nordic painters. Bonnat, who had the greatest number of Nordic students, both women and men, told the Swedish artist Gustaf Cederström that he was especially impressed by the skills and output of the Swedish women.[29]

Elin Danielson-Gambogi, Hanna Pauli, and Venny Soldan studied at the Académie Colarossi in the 1880s, with Danielson-Gambogi also participating in one of the classes for men. Students at Mme Trélat de Vigny's Académie Trélat included Backer, Asta Nørregaard, Schjerfbeck, Ada Thilén, Hildegard Thorell, Bertha Wegmann, and Westermarck. The Nordic women formed a close network, forging many bonds of friendship during their years in Paris. Some of them lived together, while others shared studios. Though some stayed in Paris for a brief period, others, such as Backer and Kielland, lived there for more than a decade [fig. 4].

Achievements The Nordic women in Paris largely adhered to the rather conventional *juste milieu* (middle way), a conciliatory style that upheld the rules of academism while appropriating many of the avant-garde traits of Realism and Impressionism. As did their male colleagues, they admired Édouard Manet, Claude Monet, and other Impressionists, though few took the plunge to become full-fledged Impressionists themselves (the same can be said of the male Nordic artists). However, some women did advance beyond the *juste milieu*, and a few were even regarded as provocative at home in the Nordic countries. Both the Danish and Finnish press accused the Finnish painter Helena Westermarck's *An Important Question, or The Ironers* [fig. 6], for example, of being nihilistic and overly direct, with one critic dismissing it as "repulsive" and contending that it evinced far-left political sympathies.[30] Hanna Pauli's portrait of her friend Venny Soldan was also denounced as indecent, proof of the debauched, bohemian lifestyle that this generation of female artists enjoyed, at least as imagined by certain contemporaries.[31] In reality, however, only a small number of these women lived bohemian or otherwise controversial lives. Indeed, the vast majority tried to adapt to the norms of the day. Elin Danielson-Gambogi was an artist who questioned the conventional roles allotted to women, stating that she wanted to live and create art like a man, and she was likely one of the examples people had in mind when they claimed to detect moral turpitude in the lifestyles of the female artists. According to the mores of the time, Danielson-Gambogi did indeed live a bohemian life: she had many affairs, publicly enjoyed tobacco, wine, and parties, lived alone, and supported herself until she married as a thirty-seven-year-old. Her self-portraits radiate a supreme sense of self-confidence, and the confrontational gaze we encounter in several of these works can perhaps be interpreted as a sign of opposition and steely resolve [fig. 5].

It has often been noted that female painters of the nineteenth century opted for conventional motifs such as portraits, genre scenes, pictures of children, or still lifes. This is true to a certain extent, but many Nordic women dedicated themselves either in part or exclusively to modern plein-air painting: the Swede Julia Beck, the Finn Fanny Churberg [plate 53], and the Norwegian

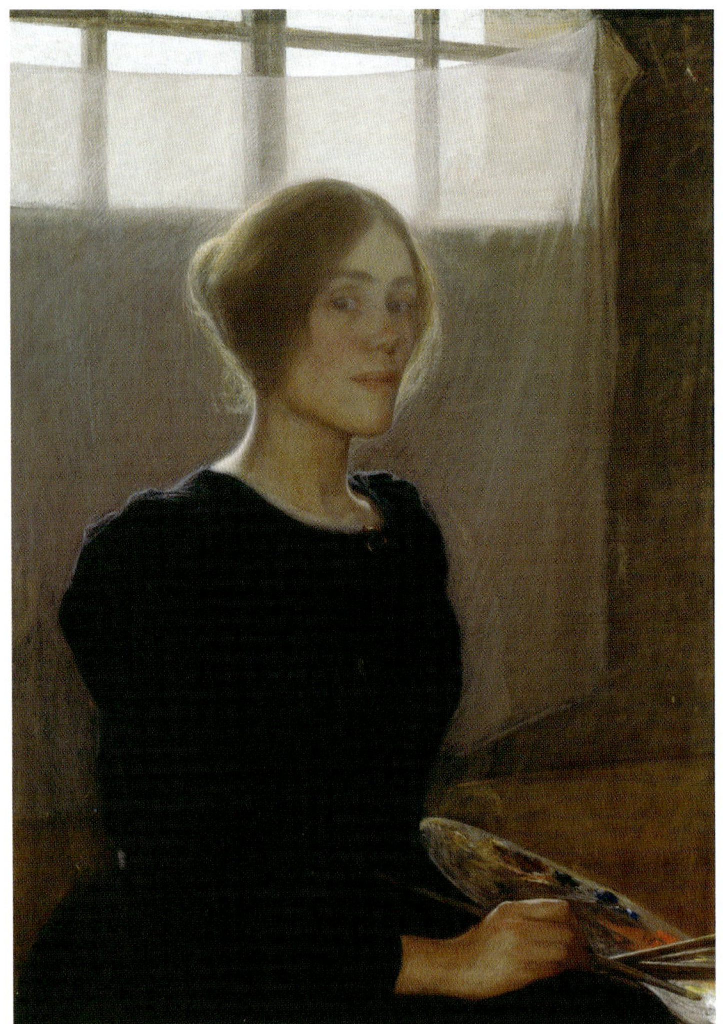

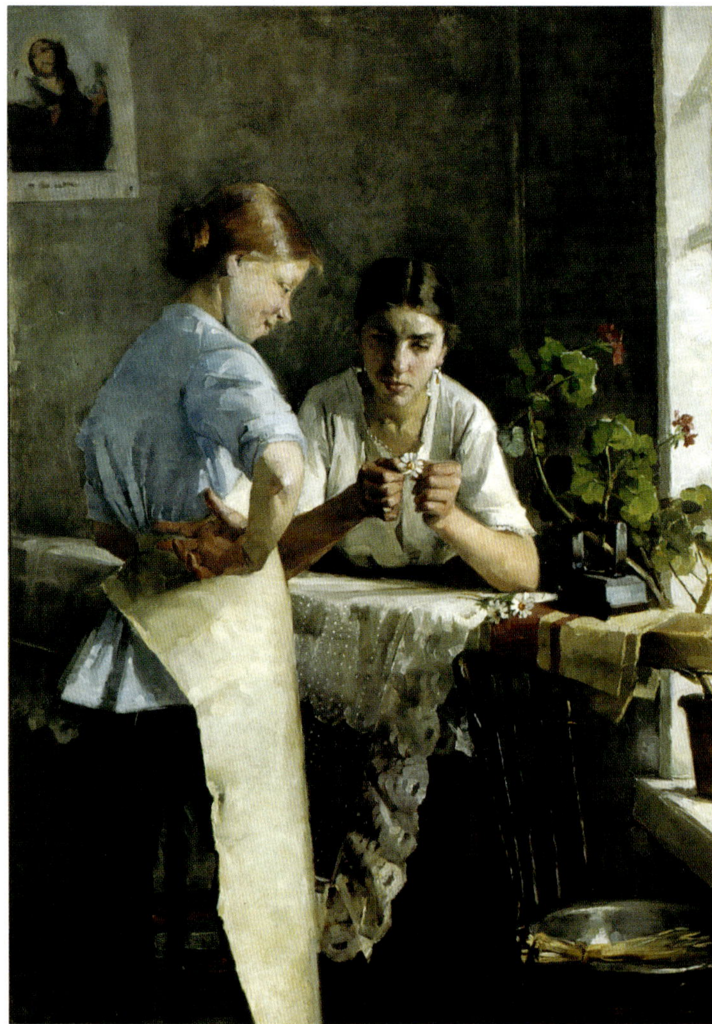

Fig. 5. Elin Danielson-Gambogi (Finnish, 1861–1919), *Self-Portrait*, 1900. Oil on canvas, 37¾ × 25¾ in. (96 × 65.5 cm). Antell Collections, Finnish National Gallery, Ateneum Art Museum, Helsinki, A I 760

Fig. 6. Helena Westermarck (Finnish, 1857–1938), *An Important Question, or The Ironers (Strykerskor)*, 1883. Oil on canvas, 49¼ × 35 in. (125 × 89 cm). Private collection

Kitty Kielland [plates 50 and 51] were all particularly innovative and consistent practitioners of this genre. Beck was active in Paris for a number of years; she displayed her work there annually, and was also among the Nordic artists whose works were acquired by the French state. Other Nordic women with a similar level of success in Paris included Caroline Benedicks-Bruce, Sigrid Bølling, Agnes de Fummier, and Ambrosia Tønnesen. Despite such impressive artistic achievements, Beck and several of her female colleagues were written out of art history, and it was first during the 1980s that they were rediscovered by scholars who applied a women's studies perspective to Nordic art history.[32]

Kielland became one of the most consistent plein-air painters in the Norwegian Realist generation and was represented at the Expositions Universelles in Paris in 1889 and 1900 with four and three paintings, respectively. Kielland also showed her works at the salons of the Société des Artistes Français and the Union des Femmes Peintres et Sculpteurs. Her close colleague Harriet Backer made her debut at the Salon in 1880 with the painting *Solitude*. Backer's later work *Interior from Rochefort-en-Terre, Bretagne* [fig. 7] shows that her years in Paris and her studies of French art had induced her to change her style. Backer also participated at the Expositions Universelles in 1889 and 1900, with two and three paintings, respectively, while Hanna Pauli participated with three paintings in both 1889 and 1900. Many of the Nordic women were thus

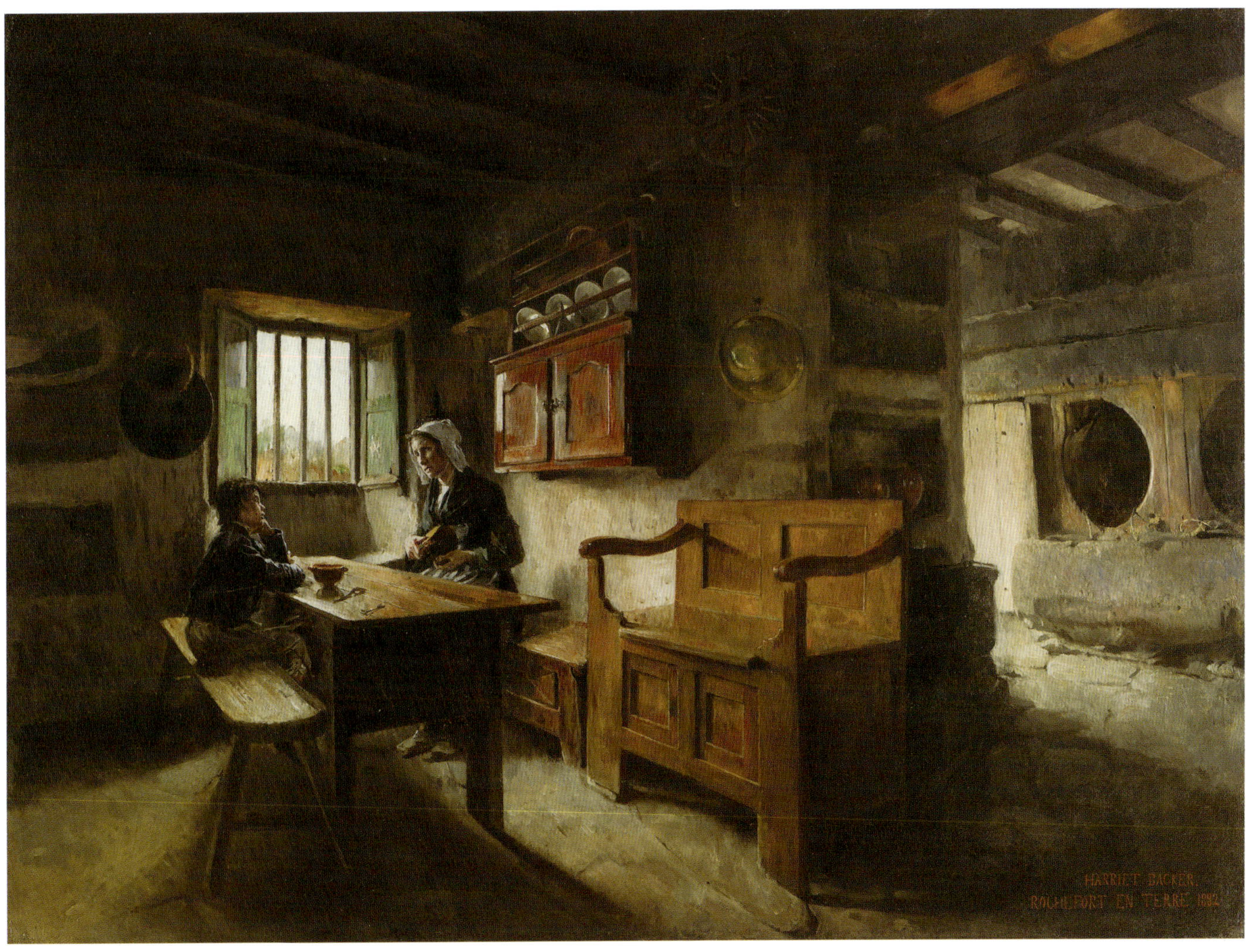

Fig. 7. Harriet Backer (Norwegian, 1845–1932), *Interior from Rochefort-en-Terre, Bretagne (or Interior with Figures, Bretagne)*, 1882. Oil on canvas, 12¼ × 16⅛ in. (31 × 41 cm). The Royal Collections, Norway, NG.M.03328

allowed to represent their home countries at the Expositions Universelles, and they were also honored with medals. The Finnish artist Maria Wiik, for instance, won several medals, including a bronze medal in 1900, a medal Danielson-Gambogi also achieved for her painting *Mother* (1893).

Even though they received artist's grants, were taught in Paris, and enjoyed a certain amount of success at exhibitions, the vast majority of these women ended their careers upon marrying and having children. One of the exceptions is the Danish artist Anna Ancher (née Brøndum). Ancher studied in Copenhagen from 1875 to 1878, and in 1889 she studied briefly in Paris in the studio of Pierre Puvis de Chavannes along with Marie Krøyer. At the age of twenty-one, in 1880, she married Michael Ancher, a painter who was ten years older than she, but despite her early marriage, she continued to work as an artist. She and her husband seem to have enjoyed a coequal and stimulating bond as artists, as testified to by the painting *Judgement of a Day's Work* [plate 12].

The Long Journey from Amateur to Professional The obstacles to Nordic women receiving instruction as artists had been abolished by the 1880s and 1890s, but their struggle was far from over. Women might return from Paris to find new and more modern attitudes to being a woman and an artist, but in actual practice the artist community in the north, as elsewhere in Europe, was dominated by men until well into the twentieth century. Indeed, many women artists felt more or less ostracized upon their return. In Stockholm, for example, women were barred from the prominent artist's club Konstnärsklubben, and as late as 1907, the bylaws of the newly founded artist's collective De Unge (The Young) explicitly excluded women. In reaction, an association of Swedish female artists, Föreningen Svenska Konstnärinnor, was founded in 1910. Upon its founding, the members stressed that the association had not been established because it was desirable to keep women apart from men, but that it was a necessary evil because men organized exhibitions without inviting women.[33]

Although many Nordic women were allowed to represent their countries at prestigious foreign expositions, other benchmarks of inclusion paint a different picture. They rarely received public commissions in their home countries; they were hardly ever invited to serve as jury members; and they were largely ignored by their national galleries of art. Moreover, they stood outside of the artistic community in the sense that they did not assume positions of power. In Norway, Backer served as a member of the annual Autumn Exhibition's jury in 1890 and of the National Gallery's board and acquisition committee from 1898 on, but she was very much an exception.[34]

That so many women from the north in particular set out to be artists in the latter half of the nineteenth century is in itself telling, suggesting a social openness to women participating in the workforce and entering the public arena. Many prominent Nordic men stood up to defend the "new woman" and "female emancipation." But the flip side of this development—that so many of these female artists abandoned their careers upon marrying—is also indicative of a social structure that made it difficult to combine family life and a career. Even women who married fellow artists set their careers to one side or lowered their ambitions. A lack of continuity and a dearth of spare time seem to be among the main reasons why these women were surpassed by their husbands and gradually let go of their artistic ambitions. The late nineteenth-century women who fought for equal conditions within the field of art took a giant leap forward from the amateurism that prevailed earlier in the century, but being a woman and an artist in this pioneering era demanded an exceptional stamina and strength of will. There were obstacles aplenty, and many sacrifices had to be made. Many of the women who so optimistically made their way to Paris in the 1870s and 1880s soon discovered that talent and ability were only part of the game of art.

1. In 1906 Finland, at the time an autonomous grand duchy in the Russian Empire, became the first nation in Europe to give women the vote. Norway and Denmark (which included faraway Iceland) followed in 1913 and 1915, respectively, while Sweden did not introduce universal suffrage until 1921.

2. Tor Petter Bø, "Høy yrkesdeltakelse blant kvinner i Norden," *Samfunnsspeilet*, no. 1 (2004), https://www.ssb.no/arbeid-og-lonn/artikler-og-publikasjoner/hoy-yrkesdeltakelse-blant-kvinner-i-norden.

3. Mary Wollstonecraft, *Letters Written during a Short Residence in Sweden, Norway, and Denmark* (1796; repr., New York: Oxford University Press, 2009), 41, 45. At the time when Wollstonecraft was journeying around Scandinavia, Norway was under Danish rule, which is why she refers to the two countries as one when speaking of freedom of the press. Norway's union with Denmark, with Danish as the official language, lasted from 1380 to 1814, when Norway instead entered into a union with Sweden, only in 1905 declaring independence. Finland, for its part, was under Swedish rule from 1155 to 1809 and under Russian rule from 1809 until 1917.

4. Hilde Danielsen, Eirinn Larsen, and Ingeborg W. Owesen, *Norsk likestillingshistorie, 1814–2013* (Oslo: Fagbokforlaget, 2013), 34.

5. Mill's wife Harriet Taylor Mill was also an important figure and participated in most of his endeavors, though the extent and nature of their collaboration is still being debated. See Dale E. Miller, "Harriet Taylor Mill," *The Stanford Encyclopedia of Philosophy*, ed. Edward N. Zalta, winter 2015, http://plato.stanford.edu/archives/win2015/entries/harriet-mill/.

6. Georg Brandes, foreword to John Stuart Mill, *Kvindernes underkuelse*, 2nd ed., trans. into Danish by Georg Brandes (Copenhagen: Gyldendalske Boghandels Forlag, 1885), 6. All translations from the Scandinavian languages are my own.

7. Brandes, foreword, 7.

8. Danielsen, Larsen, and Owesen, *Norsk likestillingshistorie*, 149.

9. In 1870 four major articles by Aasta Hansteen were published in the Norwegian newspaper *Dagbladet* in support of Mill. *Store norske leksikon*, s.v. "Aasta Hansteen," https://nbl.snl.no/Aasta_Hansteen.

10. Linda L. Clark, *Women and Achievement in Nineteenth-Century Europe* (New York: Cambridge University Press, 2008), 60–61.

11. As with gender studies in general, research on Nordic female artists of the nineteenth century has grown as a field since the 1980s. Prior to this interest, many of these women were more or less omitted from art history. Recent studies have repeatedly shown that many women from the Nordic countries set off to strike "artistic gold" in Paris toward the end of the nineteenth century. For a recent major work in this field, see Vibeke Röstorp, *Le mythe du retour: Les artistes scandinaves en France de 1889 à 1908* (Stockholm: Stockholm University Press, 2013).

12. Clark, *Women and Achievement*, 83.

13. Tamar Garb, "Men of Genius, Women of Taste: The Gendering of Art Education in Late Nineteenth-Century Paris," in *Overcoming All Obstacles: The Women of the Académie Julian*, ed. Gabriel P. Weisberg and Jane R. Becker (New York: Dahesh Museum; New Brunswick, NJ: Rutgers University Press, 1999), 115.

14. Garb, "Men of Genius, Women of Taste," 119.

15. Ruskin, quoted in Clark, *Women and Achievement*, 93.

16. Elsewhere, the Royal Academy of Arts in the United Kingdom had already created classes for women in 1837, before allowing women general admittance in 1861. In the Netherlands, women were admitted from 1863 at the Royal Academy of Art in Amsterdam.

17. Barbro Werkmäster, "Frigjord eller bunden?," in *De drogo till Paris: Nordiska konstnärinnor på 1880-talet*, ed. Lollo Fogelström and Louise Robbert (Stockholm: Liljevalchs Konsthall, 1988), 15.

18. Birthe Møller Nielsen, "Två systrar i Paris: Emma och Ludovica Thornam," in Fogelström and Robbert, *De drogo till Paris*, 211.

19. Royal Danish Academy of Fine Arts, "Undervisning for kvinder: 1870'erne–1920'erne," http://www.kunstakademiet.dk/da/billedkunstskolerne/billedkunstskolernes-historie/undervisning-kvinder-1870erne-1920erne.

20. Anne Wichstrøm, *Kvinneliv, kunstnerliv: Kvinnelige malere i Norge før 1900* (Oslo: Gyldendal, 1997), 8.

21. Vibeke Röstorp has documented that more Nordic artists, both women and men, have enjoyed active careers in Paris than previously thought; see Röstorp, *Mythe du retour*, 128, 232, and the appendix, which contains an overview of Norwegian and Swedish artists who participated in French salons from 1889 to 1908. For more on the three Norwegian women, see also Line Ruud, "Académie Julian: En studie av tre norske kvinners opphold på 1880-tallet—Leis Schjelderup, Sigrid Bølling og Valborg Olsen-Dubois" (master's thesis, University of Oslo, 2003).

22. Riitta Konttinen, "Kvinnor berättar om kvinnor: Bilder av kvinnliga finska konstnärers genombrott," in *Når kvinder fortæller: Kvindelige malere i Norden 1880–1900*, ed. Jorunn Veiteberg (Copenhagen: Kunstforeningen, 2002), 86.

23. Riitta Konttinen, "Finska konstnärinnors 1880-tal: Ljus, luft och färg," in Fogelström and Robbert, *De drogo till Paris*, 222.

24. Ibid.

25. "Marie Krøyers skjebne," NRK, http://www.nrk.no/kultur/marie-kroyers-skjebne-1.11088552.

26. Riita Konttinen, "Nordic Women Artists in Paris," in *Á Paris! Nordic Artists in Paris in the Late 19th Century*, ed. Kati Kivimäki (Helsinki: Gallen-Kallela Museum, 1996), 34.

27. Garb, "Men of Genius, Women of Taste," 127.

28. Female students included Mina Carlson-Bredberg, Emma Löwstädt-Chadwick, Sigrid Bølling, Jenny Nyström, Hanna Rönneberg, Valborg Olsen-Dubois, Amanda Sidwall, and Leis Schjelderup.

29. Inga Zachau, "Julia Beck," in Fogelström and Robbert, *De drogo till Paris*, 39.

30. Konttinen, "Kvinnor berättar om kvinnor," 90.

31. Konttinen, "Nordic Women Artists," 33.

32. Vibeke Röstorp, "Svenska friluftsmålare i Frankrike," in *Ljusets magi: Friluftsmåleri från sent 1800-tal*, ed. Anna Meister and Karin Sirén (Stockholm: Prins Eugens Waldemarsudde, 2016), 210. There has recently been further documentation that Beck was a highly productive artist who participated at various French salons every year, sometimes with more than one painting. Röstorp, *Mythe du retour*, 277 and 315–406.

33. Görel Cavalli-Björkman, "Svenska konstnärinnors förening," in *Kvinnor som målat* (Stockholm: Nationalmuseum, 1975).

34. Wichstrøm, *Kvinneliv, kunstnerliv*, 58.

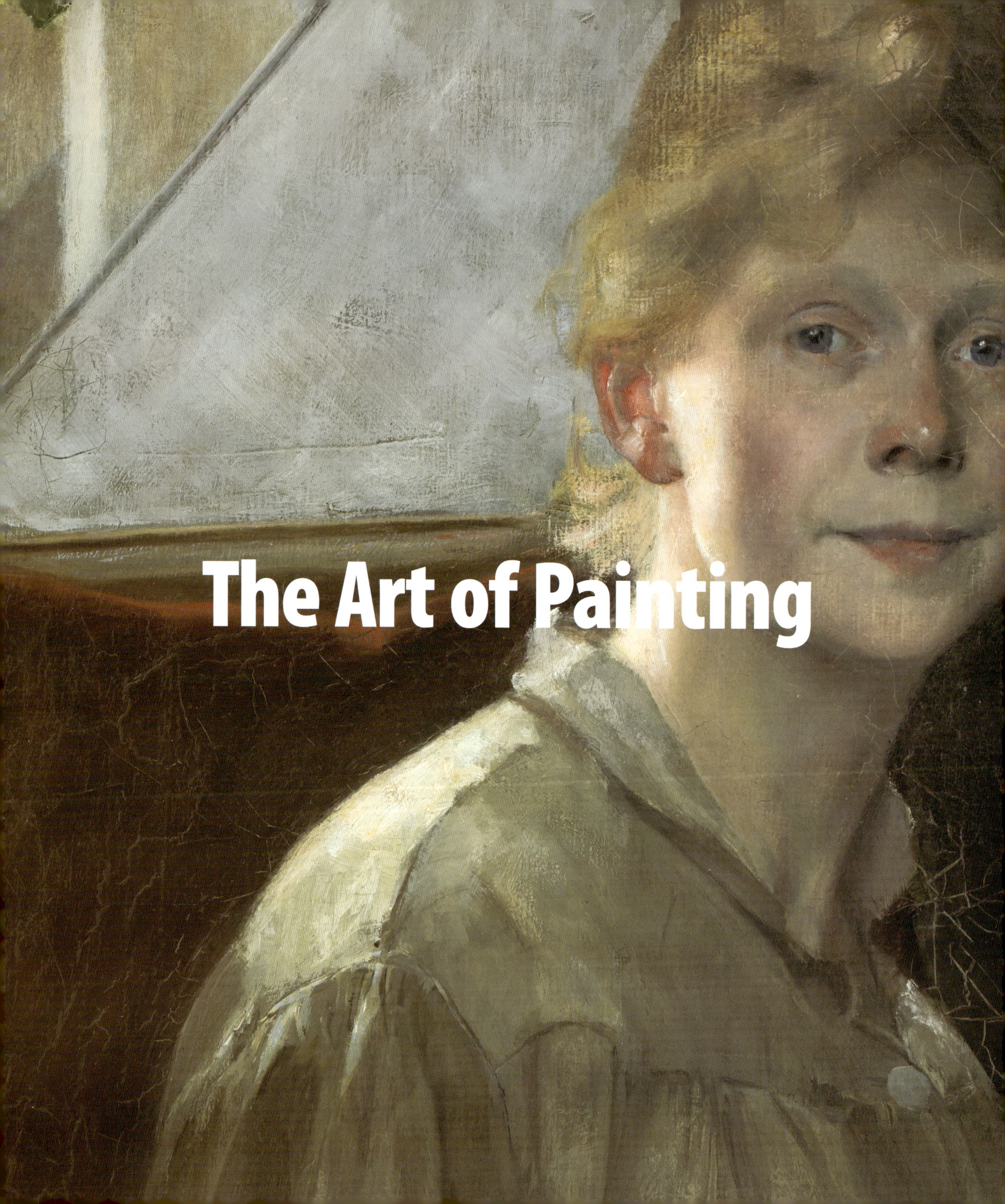
The Art of Painting

Self-portraits, and representations of one artist by another, are familiar topoi throughout the history of painting. In the nineteenth century, women painters readily engaged in such portraiture and, like their male counterparts, sought to create an image of themselves and their contemporaries and, moreover, a claim for their art. However, this practice takes on a distinct quality when women serve as both painter and model. The legitimization of painters—through the act of holding a brush and standing by an easel—comes as a result of a series of struggles and acts of renunciation, to which these paintings bear witness.

When women painters are represented in the second half of the nineteenth century, they rarely display the self-assurance and panache that the French royal court allowed Élisabeth Vigée Le Brun and Adélaïde Labille-Guiard in their self-portraits a century earlier, and that Édouard Manet conjures in his portrait of Eva Gonzalès [see Alsdorf, fig. 7]. Instead, they reveal a self-imposed restraint required by their social condition as women, as the question of appropriateness in women's public presentation was still a matter of debate. From the sixteenth century forward—codified in the writings of Giorgio Vasari—the archetype of the woman artist who finds acceptance, because she is either noble by birth or considered so through her virtue and behavior, dominates. Surely male artists respected Berthe Morisot for her dignified attitude and reserved manner, which conformed to their expectations of feminine behavior, as much as for her talent.

Edma Pontillon's portrayal of her older sister, *Portrait of Berthe Morisot* [plate 4], illustrates one young woman artist bridling another's spirit with a dark dress and concentrated visage. The same can be said of the self-portraits of Elizabeth Nourse and Mina Carlson-Bredberg [plates 8 and 6], which illustrate the determination of women painters and, at the same time, their conflicting desire to avoid the eccentricities allowed—indeed encouraged—in work of their male counterparts. Marie Bashkirtseff's lively *In the Studio* [plate 3] depicts the artist at the Académie Julian working alongside her peers, each outfitted in the latest fashions of the day, but the artist portrays herself more discreetly in *Self-Portrait with Palette* [see Madeline, fig. 3], choosing instead to highlight the intensity and determination of her gaze.

Given that women did not have access to the education offered by the École des Beaux-Arts until 1897, and the bulk of their training occurred in special courses or workshops reserved exclusively for their sex, their encounters with male artists were often limited to the public space of the museum. Although a certain degree of freedom could be found at the Louvre—here, the Morisot sisters met Henri Fantin-Latour, then Édouard Manet and Edgar Degas, and Victoria Dubourg and Marie Quivoron-Pasquiou met their future husbands, Fantin-Latour and Félix Bracquemond, respectively—social proprieties still required modesty in conduct and dress. Accordingly, the female copyist in Norbert Goeneutte's *Marcellin Desboutin and His Friends at the Louvre, before a Fresco by Botticelli* [plate 2] wears somber velvet while contemplating her canvas. A strident voice in this debate is that of the art critic and co-founder of *La revue blanche*, Thadée Natanson, who used his pen to publicly denounce the men's clothing that Rosa Bonheur adopted, with special permission from the police, in order to detract attention from herself while working unaccompanied outdoors. In Anna Klumpke's *Rosa Bonheur* [plate 9], the sitter exhibits an entirely masculine rigor, proudly displaying on her jacket the first Légion d'Honneur rosette awarded to a woman painter. In contrast, Berthe Morisot, in an act of defiance somewhat tempered by her epoch, paints in her *Self-Portrait* [plate 5] an embroidered floral pattern on her chest—an unofficial and free emblem.

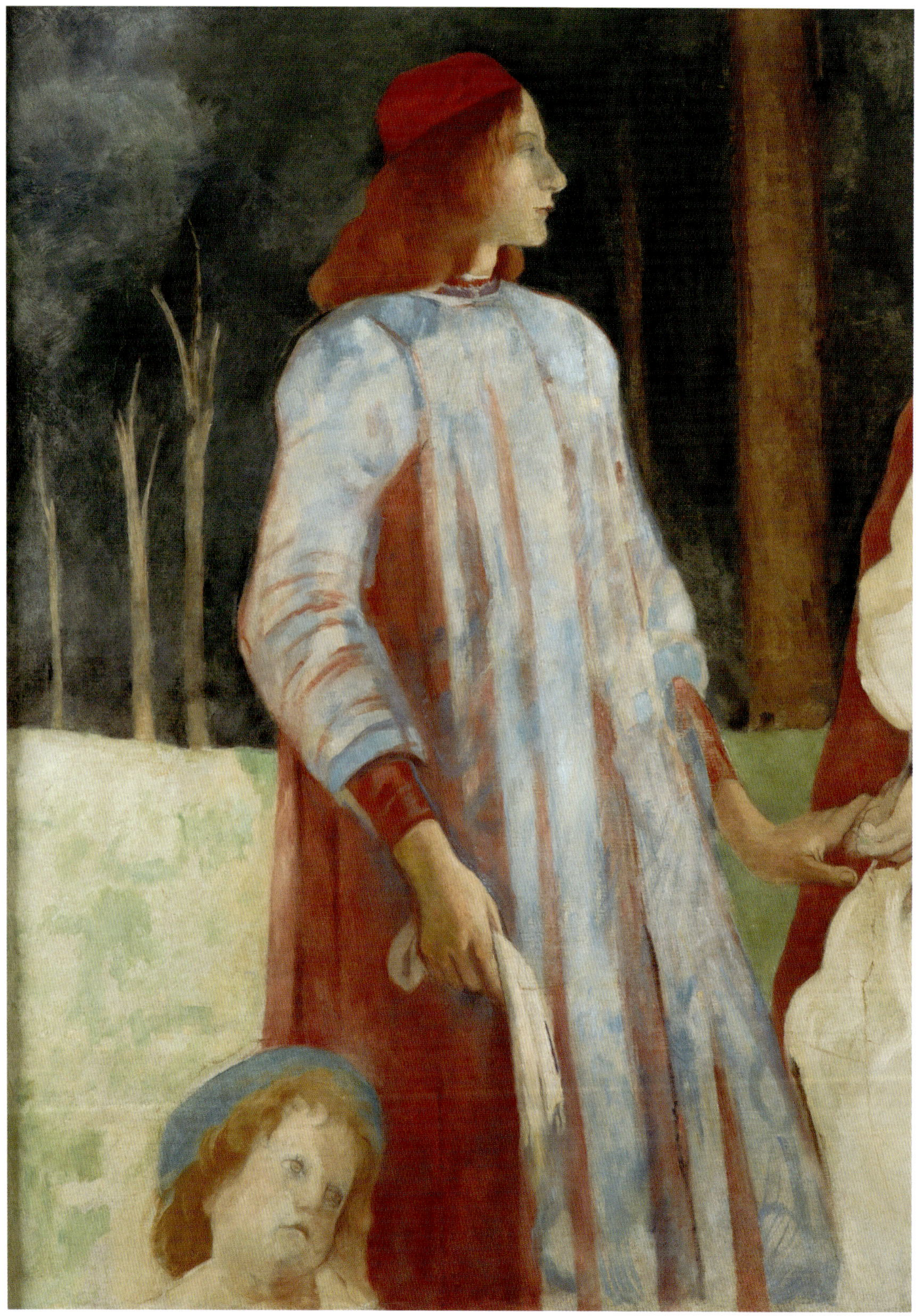

PLATE 1 HELENE SCHJERFBECK, *FIGURE STUDY (COPY AFTER "YOUTH PRESENTED TO THE SEVEN LIBERAL ARTS" BY SANDRO BOTTICELLI IN MUSÉE DU LOUVRE) (COPY D'APRÈS UNE FRESQUE DE SANDRO BOTTICELLI AU MUSÉE DU LOUVRE)*, 1884
Oil on canvas, 47⅞ × 37⅝ in. (121.5 × 95.5 cm). UPM-Kymmene Cultural Foundation, Helsinki, UKKS429

PLATE 2 NORBERT GOENEUTTE, *MARCELLIN DESBOUTIN AND HIS FRIENDS AT THE LOUVRE, BEFORE A FRESCO BY BOTTICELLI*, 1892
Oil on canvas, 27¼ × 35 in. (69.3 × 89 cm). Musée Anne-de-Beaujeu, Moulins, France

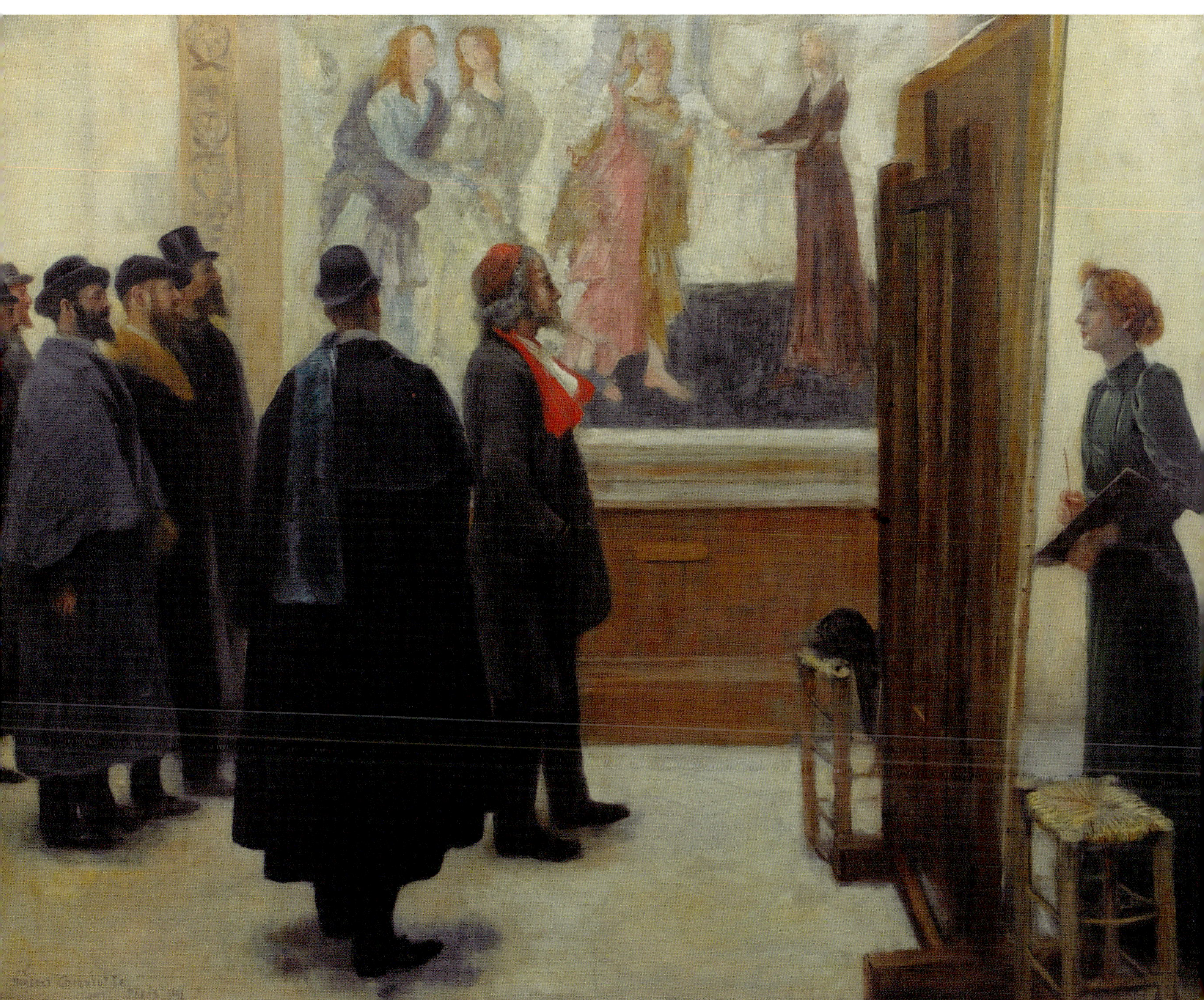

PLATE 3 MARIE BASHKIRTSEFF, *IN THE STUDIO*, 1881

Oil on canvas, 60⅝ × 73¼ in. (154 × 186 cm). Dnipropetrovsk State Art Museum, Ukraine, KH-4234

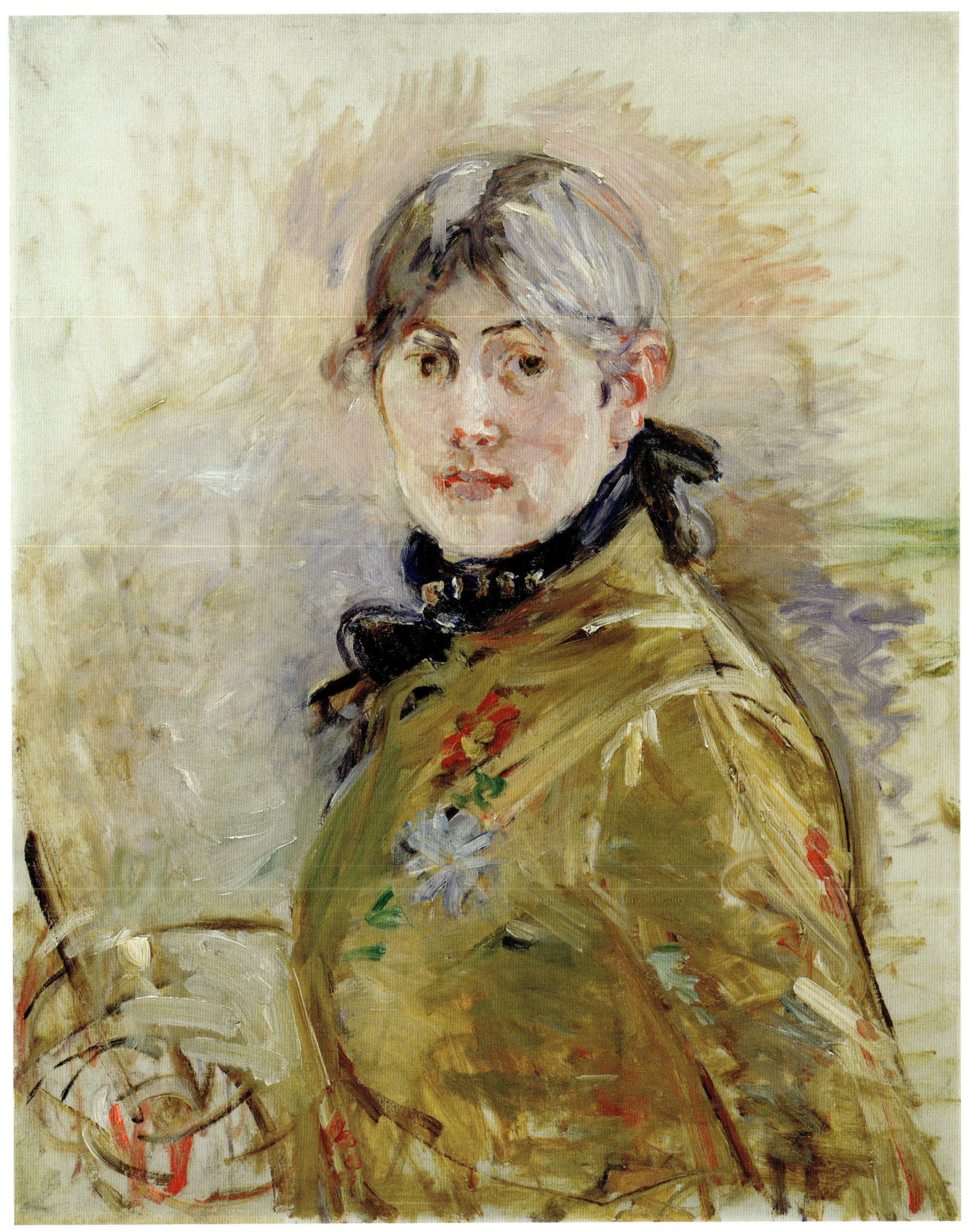

PLATE 4 EDMA PONTILLON, *PORTRAIT OF BERTHE MORISOT*, CA. 1865

Oil on canvas, 39 × 28 in. (100 × 71 cm). Private collection, Paris

PLATE 5 BERTHE MORISOT, *SELF-PORTRAIT*, 1885

Oil on canvas, 24 × 19¾ in. (61 × 50 cm). Musée Marmottan Monet, Paris, 6022

PLATE 6 MINA CARLSON-BREDBERG, *SELF-PORTRAIT* (*SJÄLVPORTRÄTT*), 1889

Oil on canvas, 36 × 29¾ in. (91.5 × 75.5 cm). Prins Eugens Waldemarsudde, Stockholm, W1488

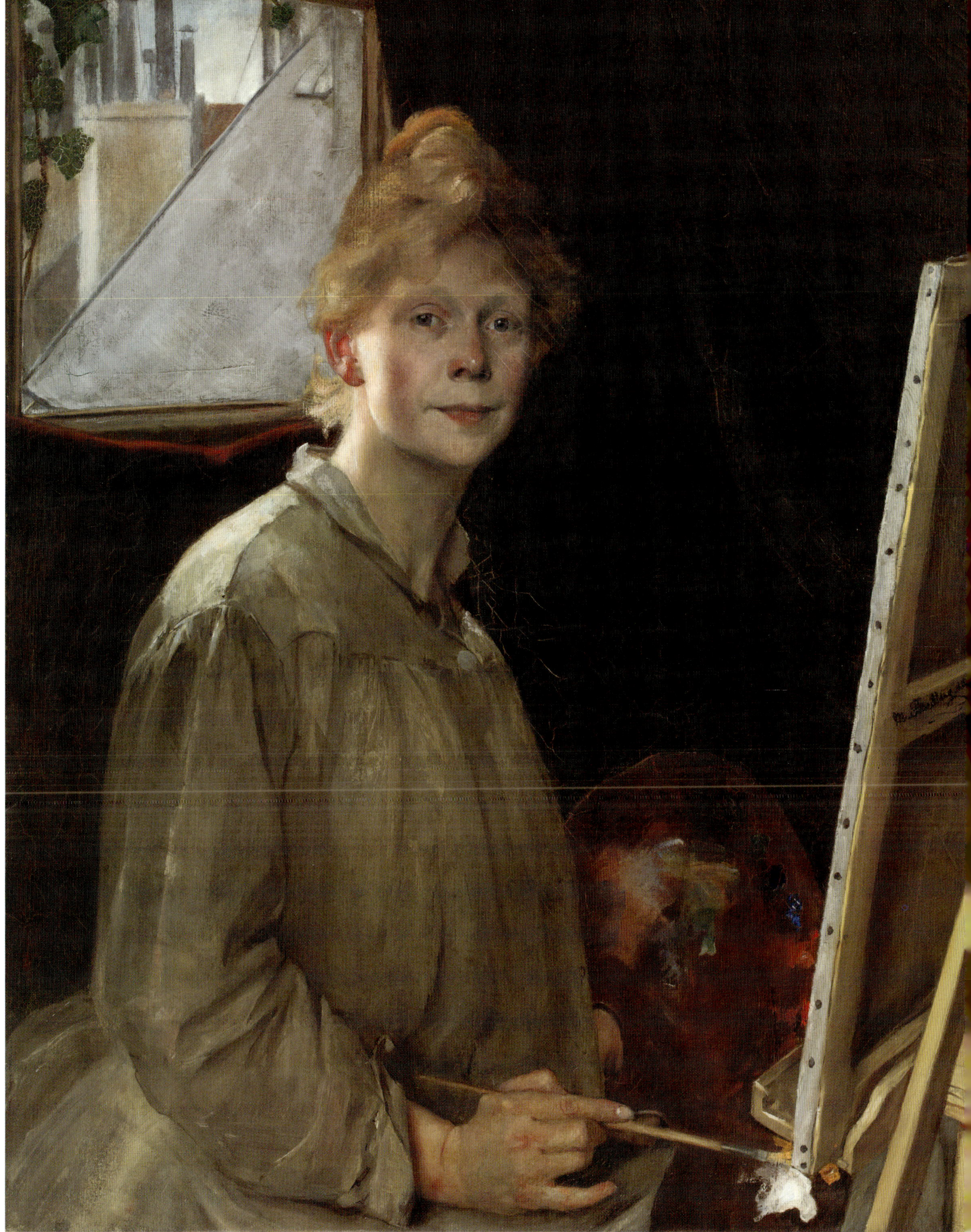

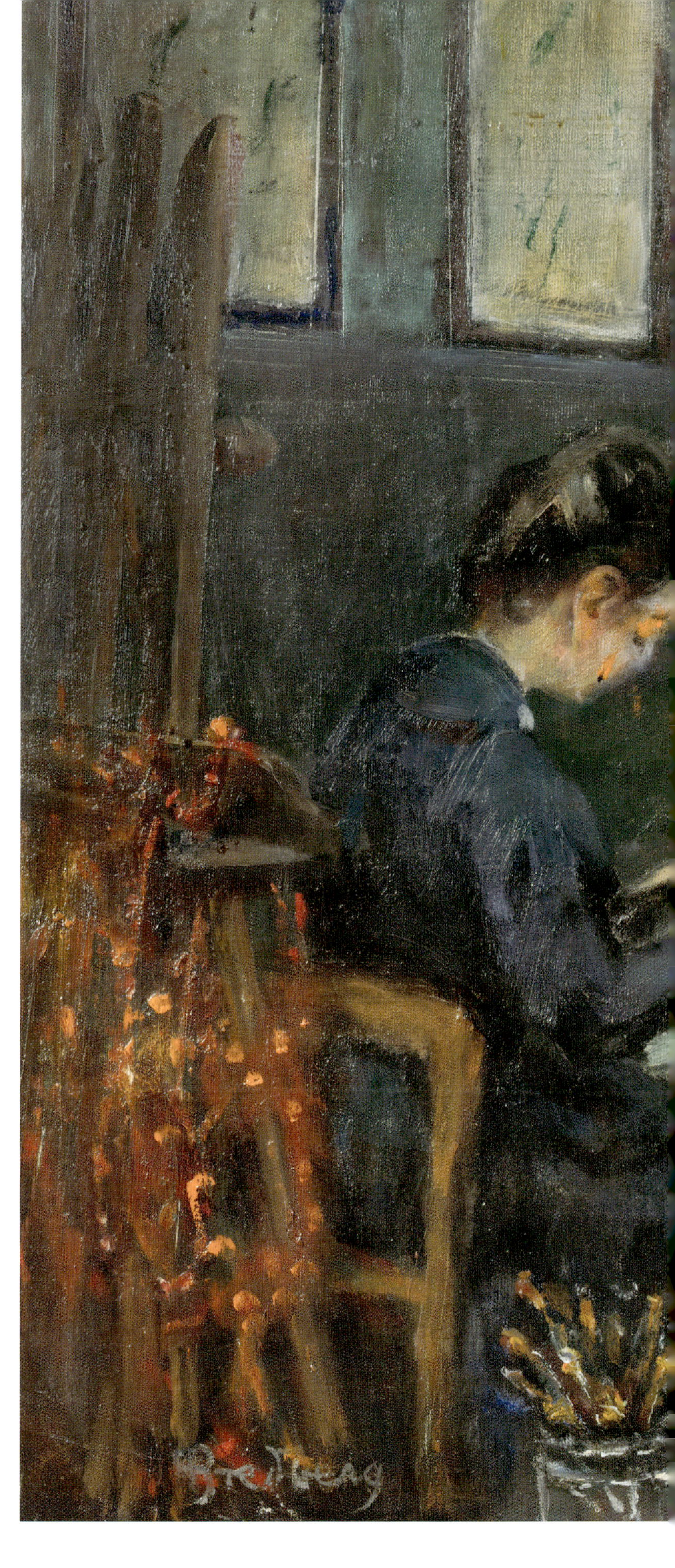

PLATE 7 MINA CARLSON-BREDBERG, *ACADÉMIE JULIAN, MADEMOISELLE BESON DRINKING FROM A GLASS* (*ACADEMIE JULIAN. MADEMOISELLE BESON DRICKER UR ETT GLAS*), N.D.

Oil on canvas, 20⅞ × 29⅛ in. (53 × 74 cm). Dorsia Hotel, Gothenburg, Sweden

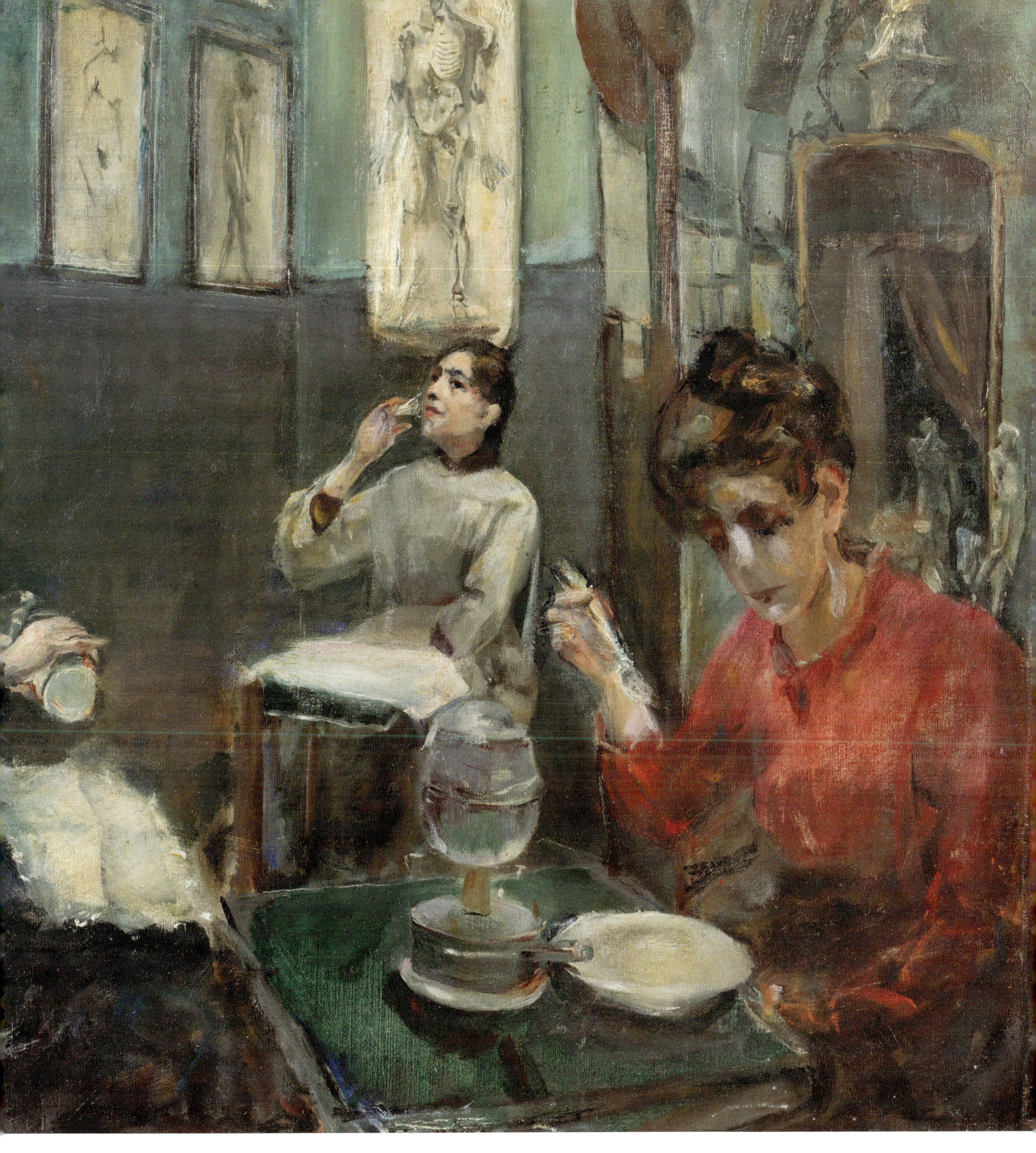

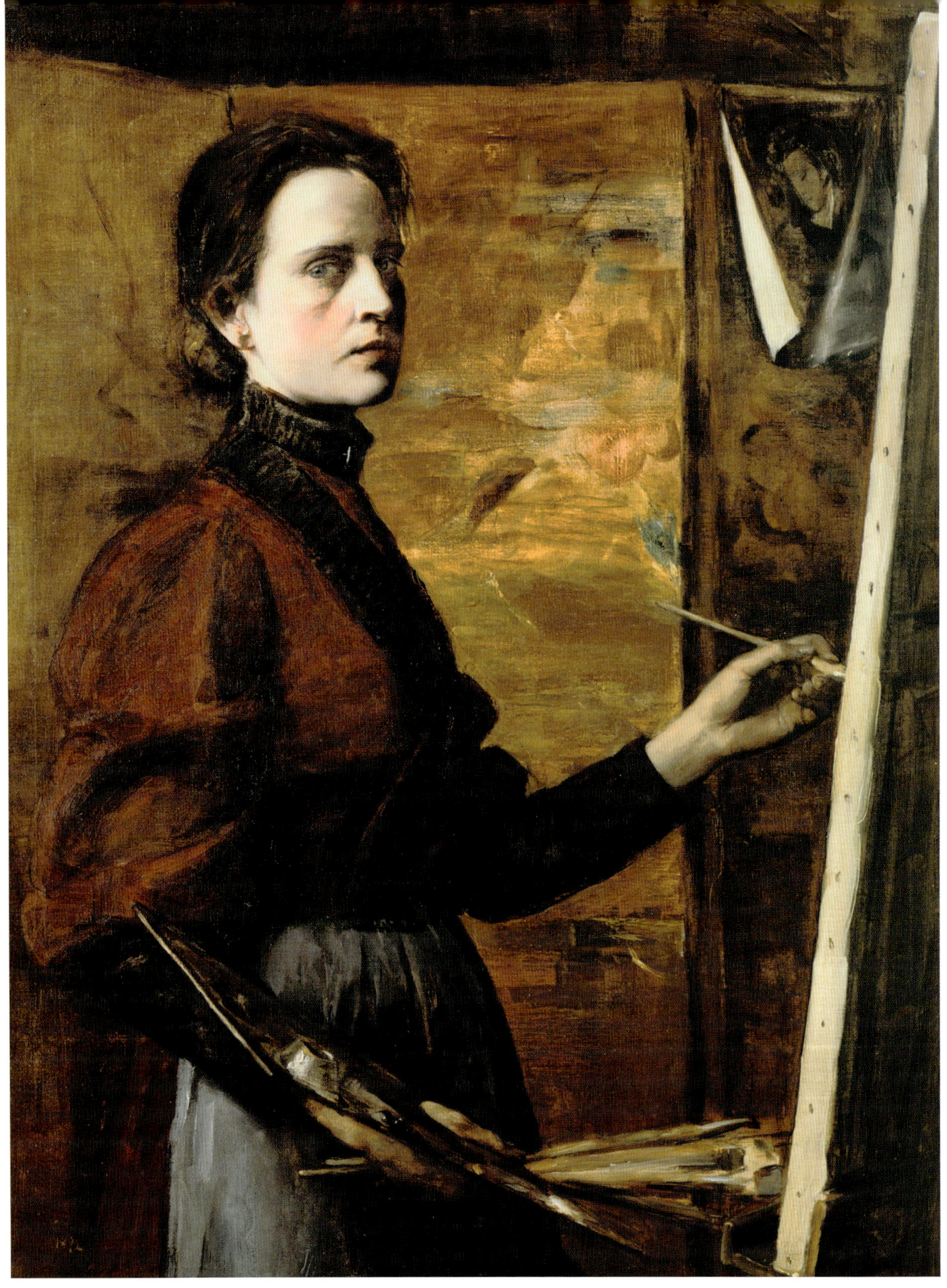

PLATE 8 ELIZABETH NOURSE, *SELF-PORTRAIT*, 1892
Oil on canvas, 39 × 29½ in. (99 × 75 cm). Private collection

PLATE 9 ANNA ELIZABETH KLUMPKE, *ROSA BONHEUR*, 1898
Oil on canvas, 46⅛ × 38⅝ in. (117.2 × 98.1 cm). Metropolitan Museum of Art, New York, Gift of the artist, in memory of Rosa Bonheur, 1922, 22.222

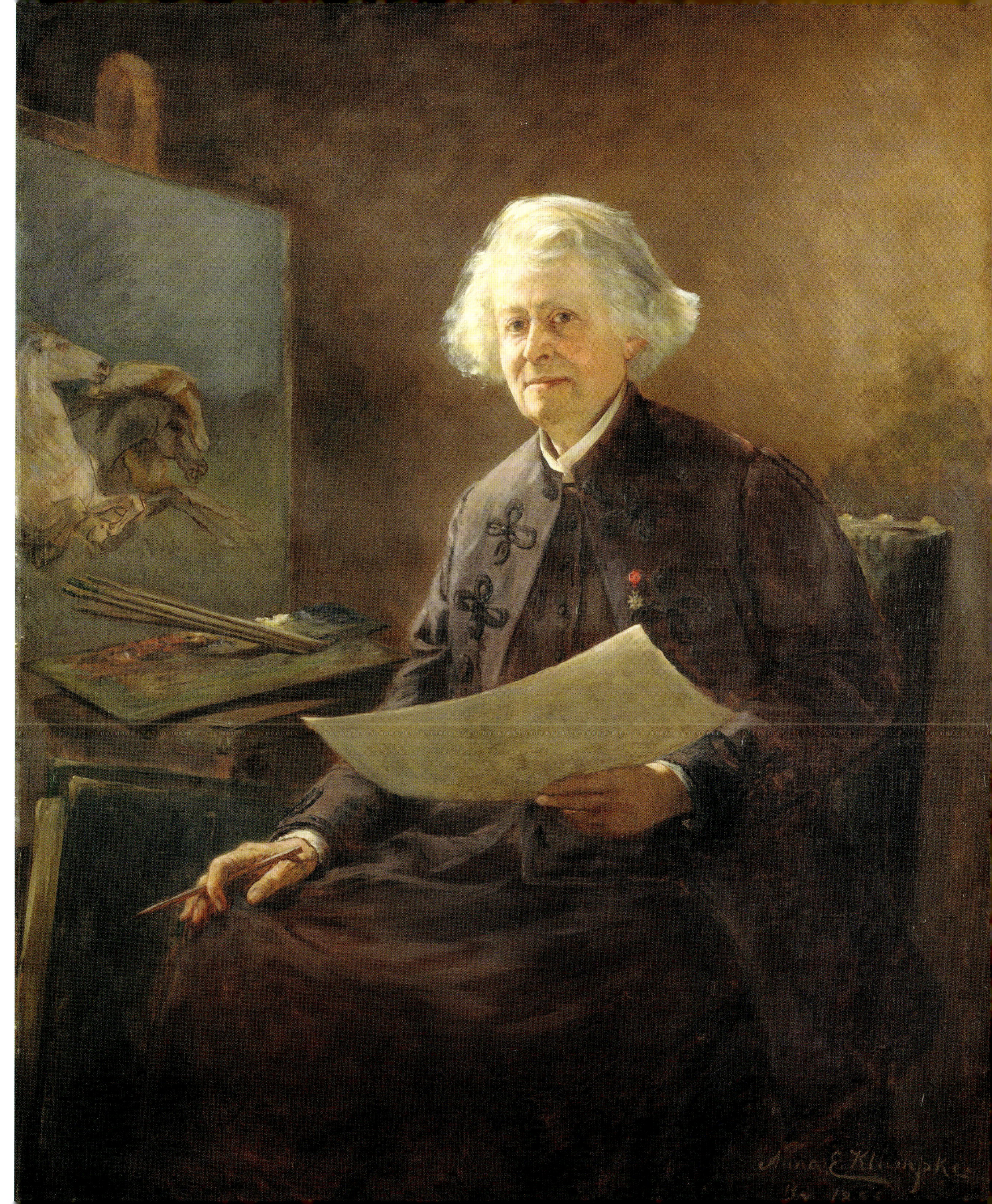
Anna E Klumpke

PLATE 10 HANNA PAULI, *THE ARTIST VENNY SOLDAN-BROFELDT*, 1886–87

Oil on canvas, 49⅜ × 52¾ in. (125.5 × 134 cm). Gothenburg Museum of Art, Sweden, GKM 444

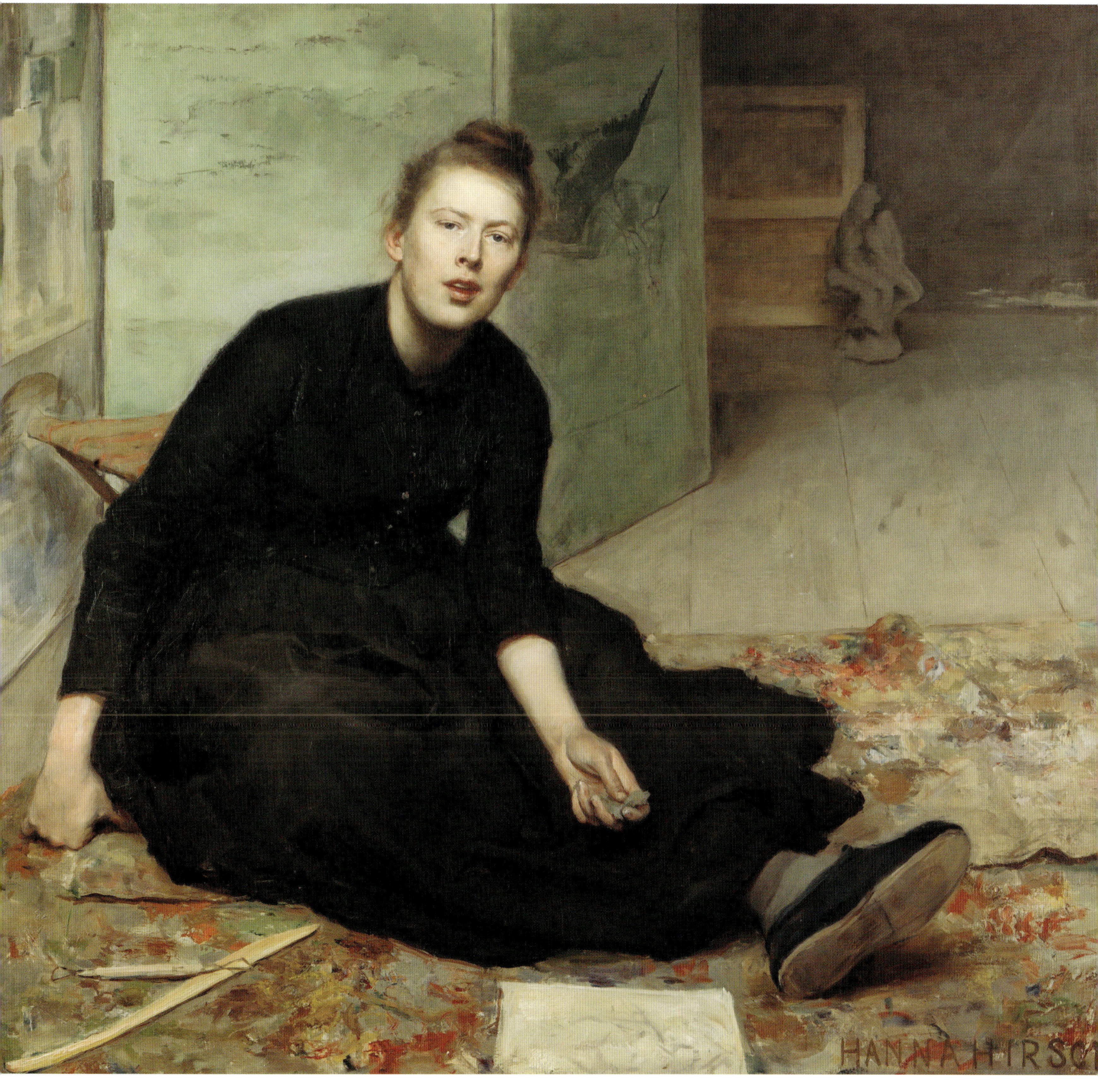
HANNA HIRSC

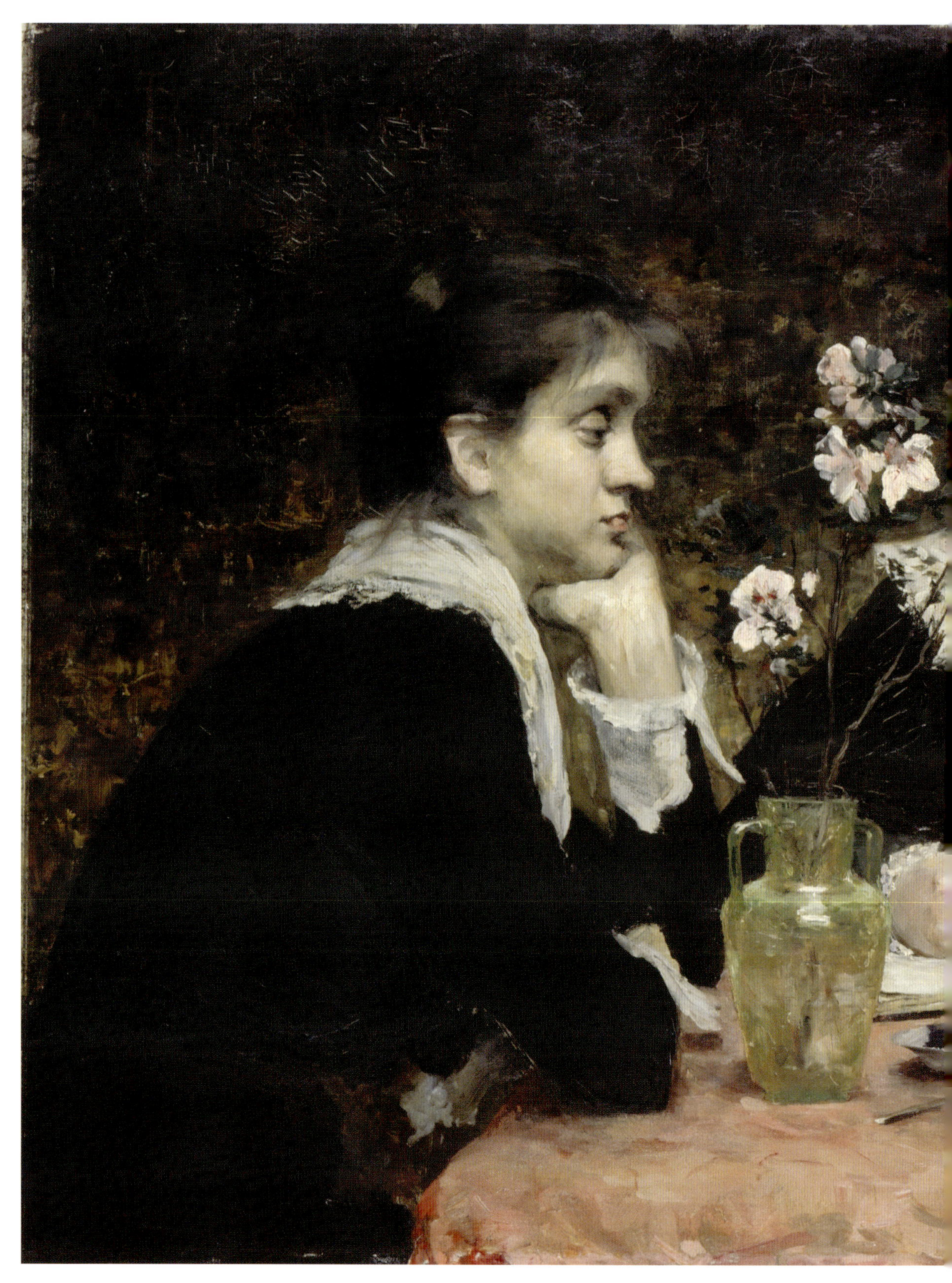

PLATE 11 LOUISE CATHERINE BRESLAU, *THE FRIENDS* (*LES AMIES*), 1881

Oil on canvas, 33½ × 63 in. (85 × 160 cm). Musée d'Art et d'Histoire, Geneva, 1883–0002

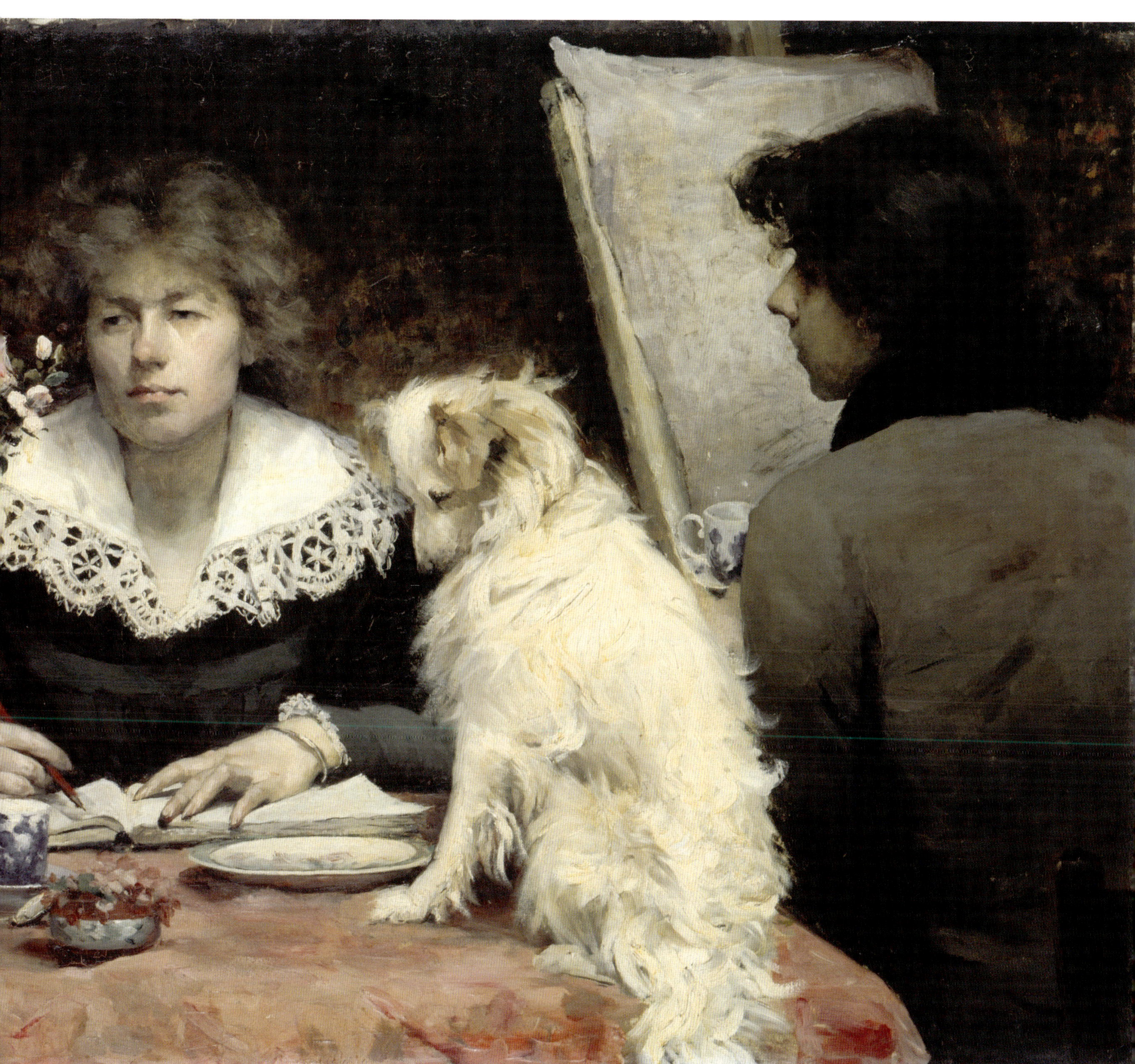

PLATE 12 ANNA AND MICHAEL ANCHER, *JUDGEMENT OF A DAY'S WORK* (*DAGENS ARBEJDE BEDØMMES*), 1883

Oil on canvas, 32⅞ × 40½ in. (83.5 × 103 cm). Art Museums of Skagen, on deposit 1991 from the National Gallery of Denmark, DEP9

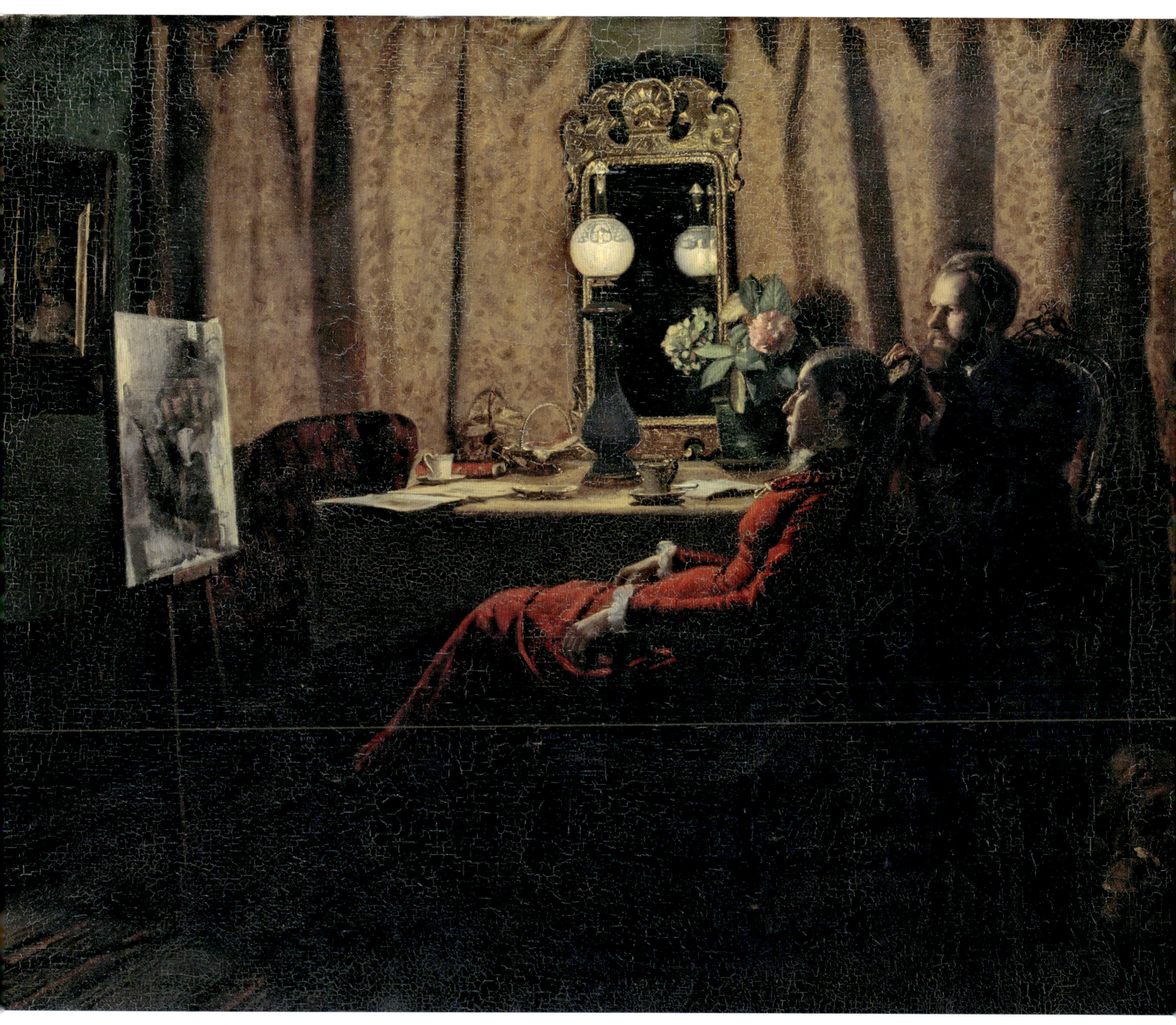

Paintings depicting women absorbed in manual or intellectual activity within a domestic setting are not the invention of women painters. Jean-Siméon Chardin, Vilhelm Hammershøi, Édouard Manet, Jean-François Millet, Claude Monet, and Johannes Vermeer, as well as other male artists, frequently painted women focused on their reading or handiwork. Their interpretations of this theme, however, do not share the same characteristics as those of similar works produced by women. Few male figures can be found in such paintings by women, and those who are depicted are often seen from the back or along the margins of the composition. It is as if women artists took more pleasure in a private world, seemingly unwilling or unable to enter the domain of men, even as male artists increasingly found a source of inspiration in the feminine sphere.

Perhaps this is a response by women artists to the admonitions of critics, largely male, who expected them to open windows onto their daily lives and who, above all, resisted their ability to exceed the boundaries of a closed world. This is readily apparent in Anna Ancher's *Young Woman Arranging Flowers* [plate 13], where the artist simultaneously elevates and makes secret the simplest and most delicate of household tasks. It must be acknowledged, though, that women painters were afforded little freedom of unaccompanied social movement. Consequently, they often painted domestic life, tending to confer grandeur and importance on what, by overwhelming consensus, had long been deemed secondary or negligible. Concomitant developments, such as the collapse of history painting, with its battles and sagas, and the evolution of public sensibility, made these everyday scenes, which the Impressionists and their followers also captured, much more desirable.

These slices of life present a calm yet unyielding curiosity about modernity, which, with the democratization of certain social rituals—illustrated in Louise Catherine Breslau's gathering for *Tea at Five O'Clock* [plate 15] and Louise Abbéma's vast canvas, *Lunch in the Greenhouse* [plate 24]—and burgeoning tastes for the exotic, such as *japonisme*, transformed the domestic space. At the same time, a rejection of certain unsettling aspects of modern life elevated the home to the status of refuge in works such as Harriet Backer's *Evening, Interior* [plate 22].

In these quiet scenes where story or anecdote is suspended, such as Mary Cassatt's *Portrait of an Elderly Lady in a Bonnet: Red Background* [plate 23] and the artist's *Woman Standing, Holding a Fan* [plate 19], the rendering of atmosphere and light effects, as well as the formal qualities of brushstroke, spatial composition, and color palette, is now essential to representations of the lives of women. A sitter's gaze—an element of fascination for Cassatt in *The Reader* [plate 20]—becomes, in Amélie Beaury-Saurel's *Dans le bleu* [plate 16], a metaphor for the creativity and introspection of women who were moving from a hidden life devoted to the private practices of reading or writing to a truly artistic and public role.

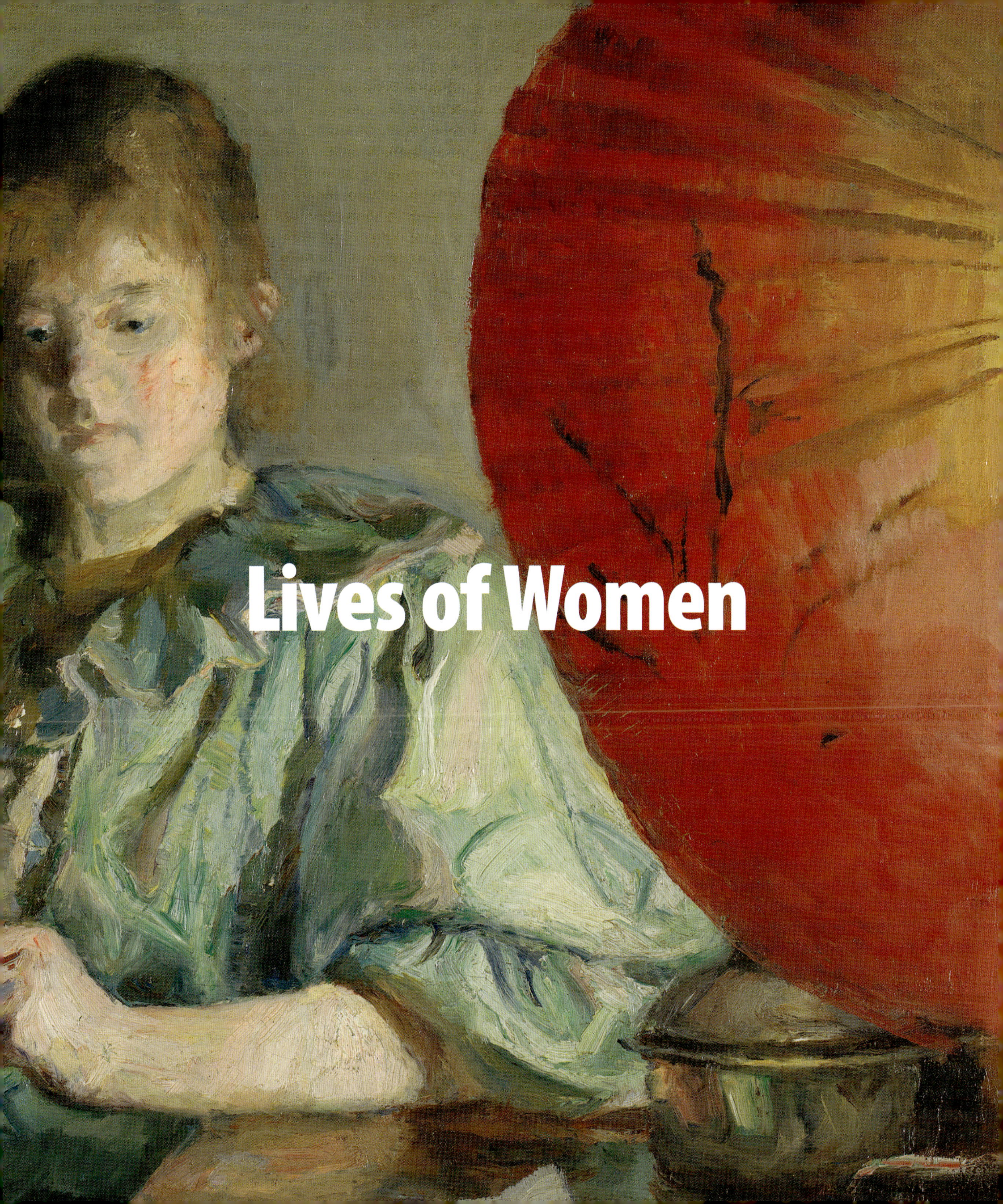

Lives of Women

PLATE 13 ANNA ANCHER, *YOUNG WOMAN ARRANGING FLOWERS*, CA. 1885

Oil on canvas, 22½ × 19½ in. (54.5 × 40.5 cm). ARoS Aarhus Kunstmuseum, Denmark, AAK-M 113

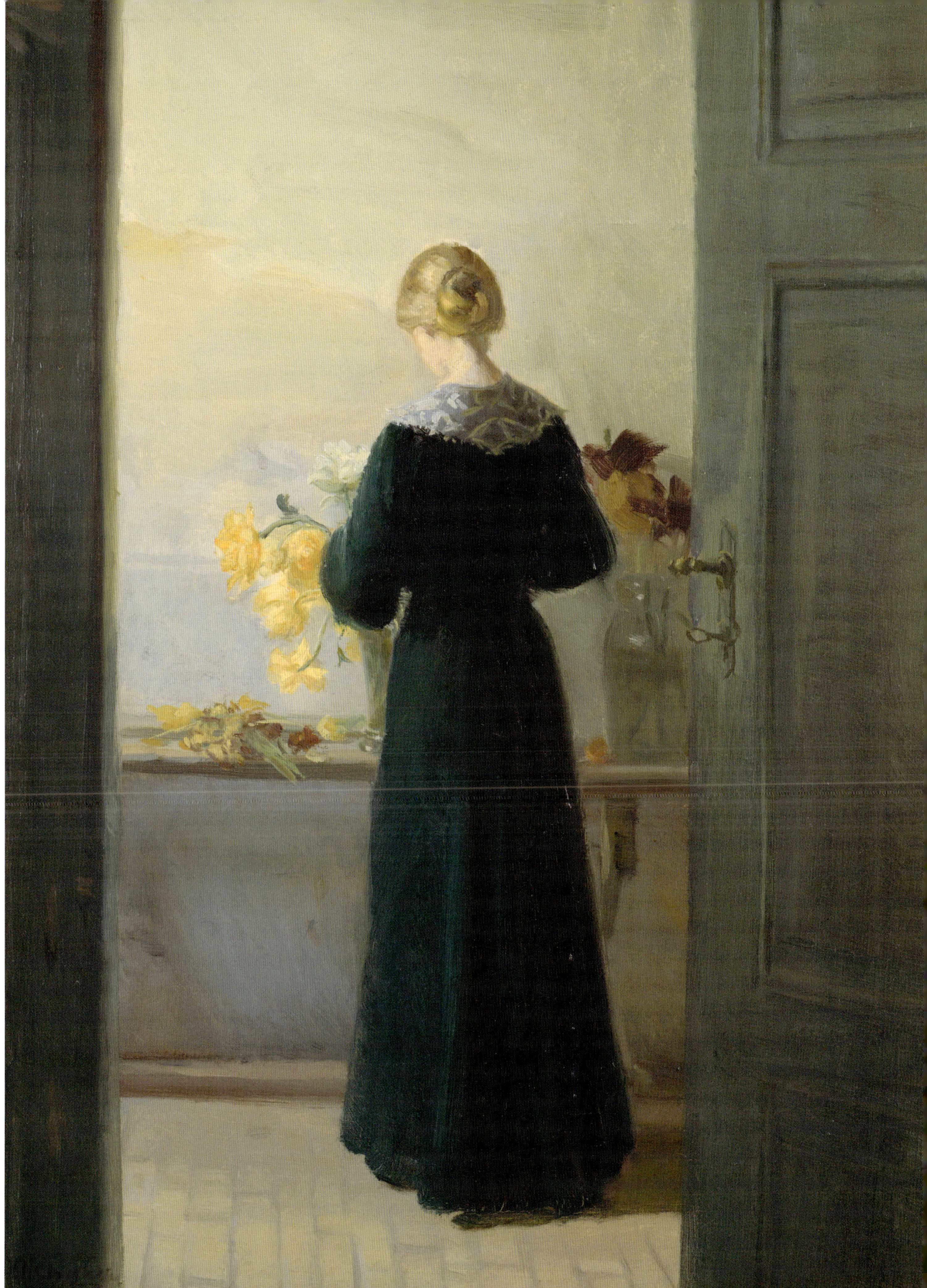

PLATE 14 **ANNA ANCHER,** ***AN OLD WOMAN IN HER ROOM, MRS. BRAT*** **(*EN GAMMEL KONES I SIN STUE. MADAM BRAT*), 1888**
Oil on canvas, 11¾ × 9⅞ in. (30 × 25.2 cm). The Hirschsprung Collection, Copenhagen

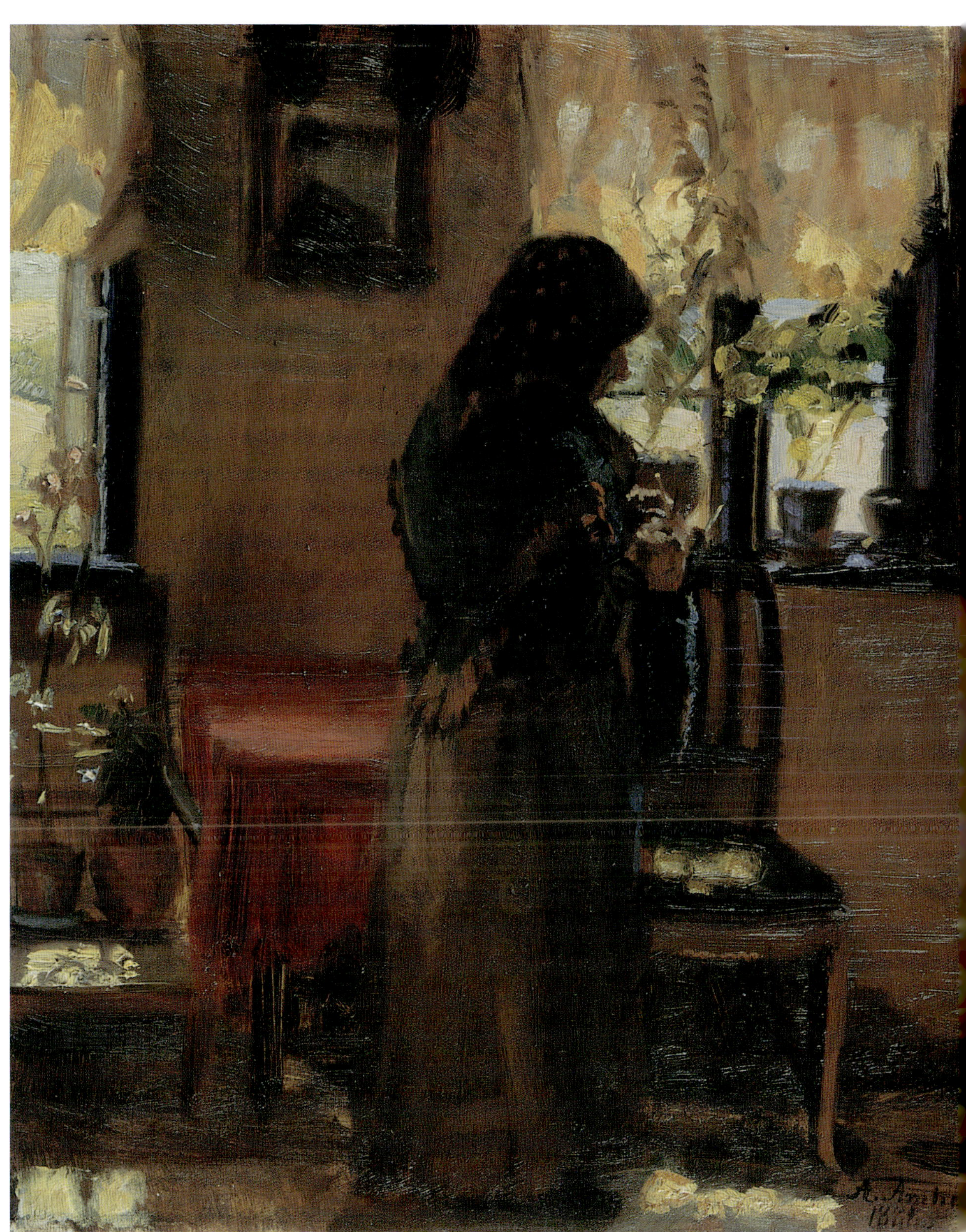

PLATE 15 LOUISE CATHERINE BRESLAU, *TEA AT FIVE O'CLOCK*, 1883

Oil on canvas, 59¼ × 59⅝ in. (150.5 × 151.4 cm). Gottfried Keller Foundation, Federal Office of Culture, Bern, deposited at the Kunstmuseum Bern, Switzerland, G1032

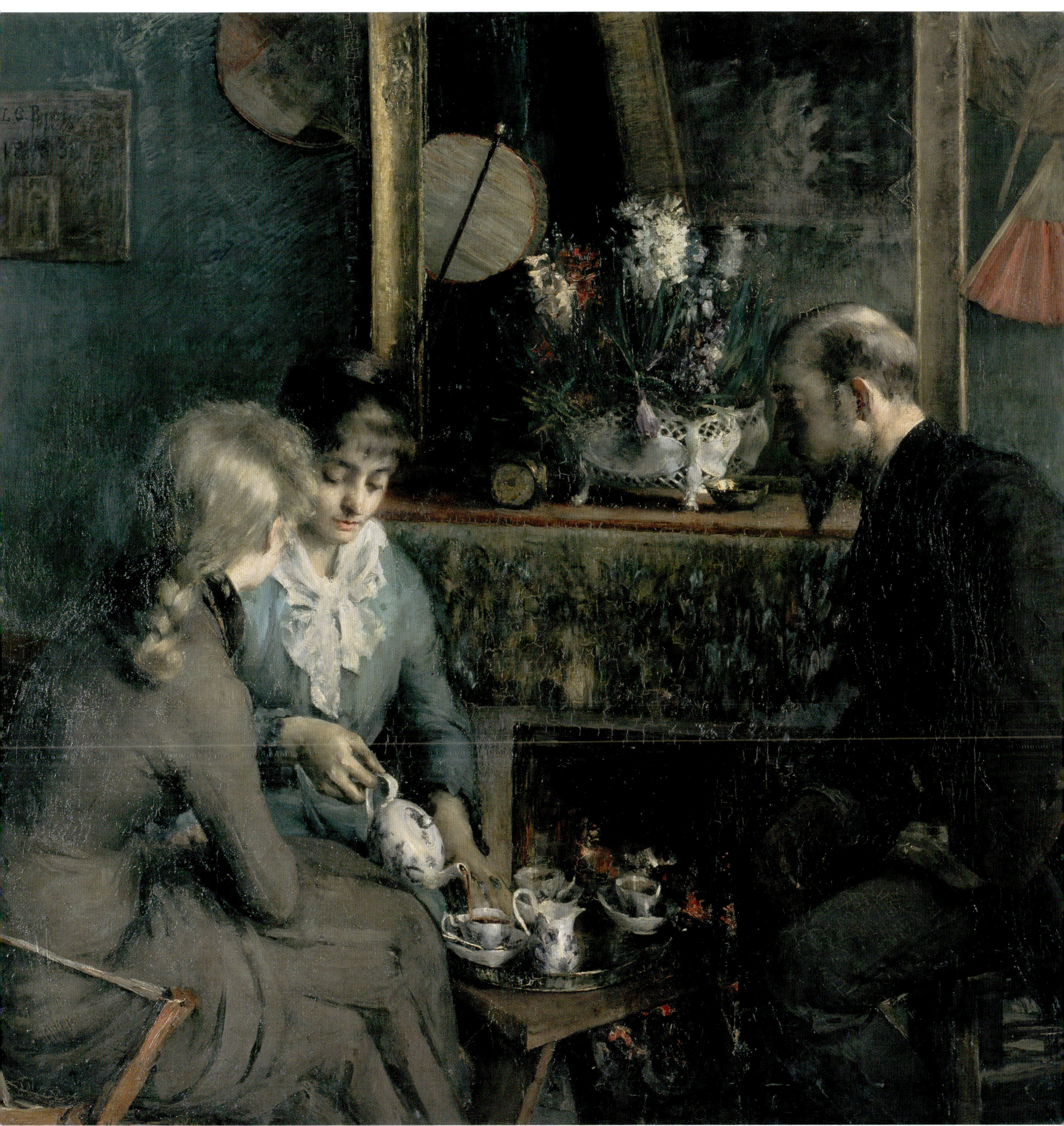

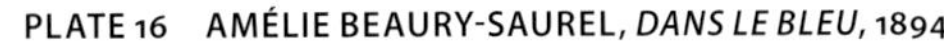

PLATE 16 AMÉLIE BEAURY-SAUREL, *DANS LE BLEU*, 1894

Pastel on canvas, 29½ × 32¼ in. (75 × 82 cm). Musée des Augustins, Toulouse, RO494

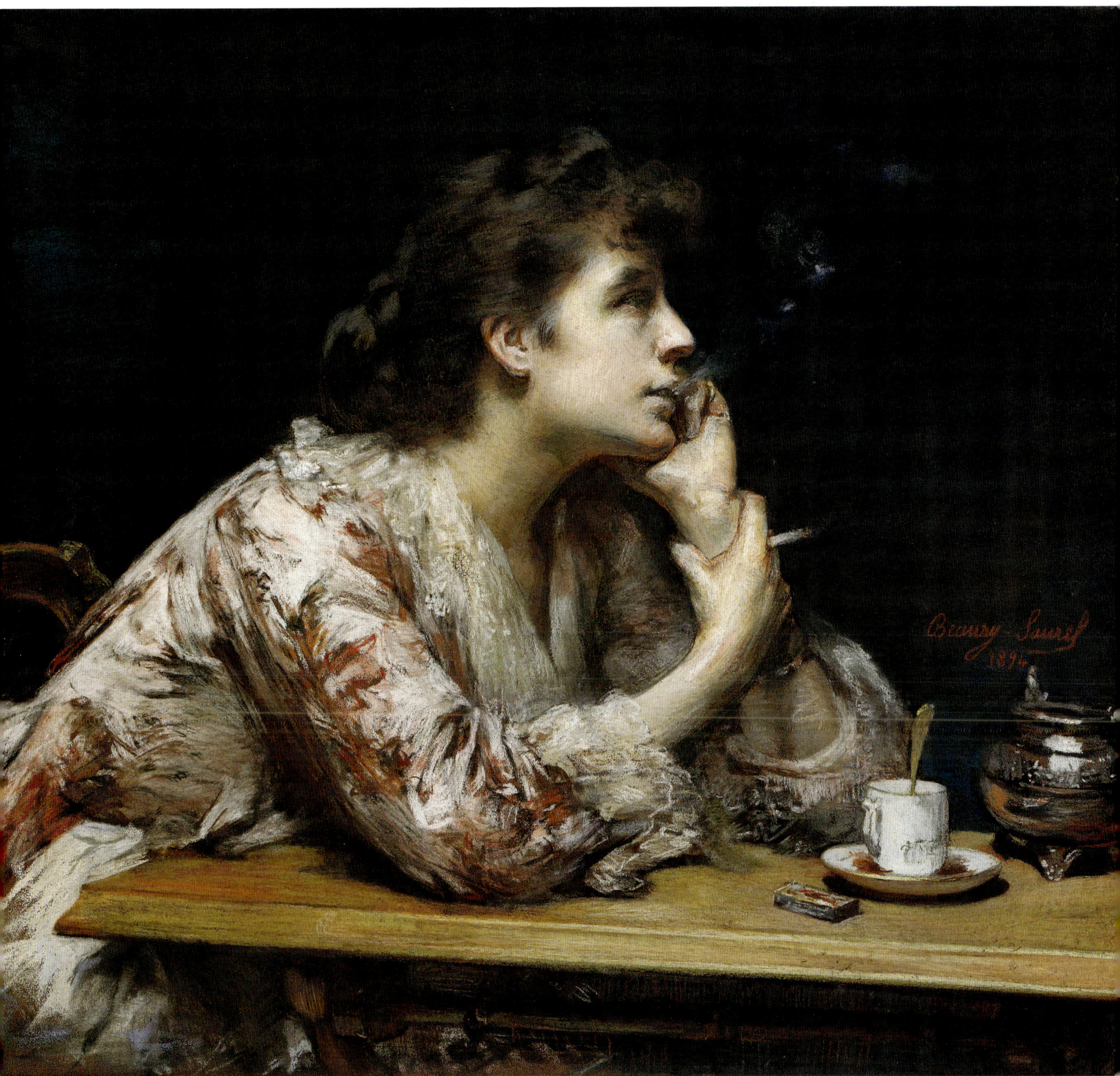
Beaury-Saurel
1894

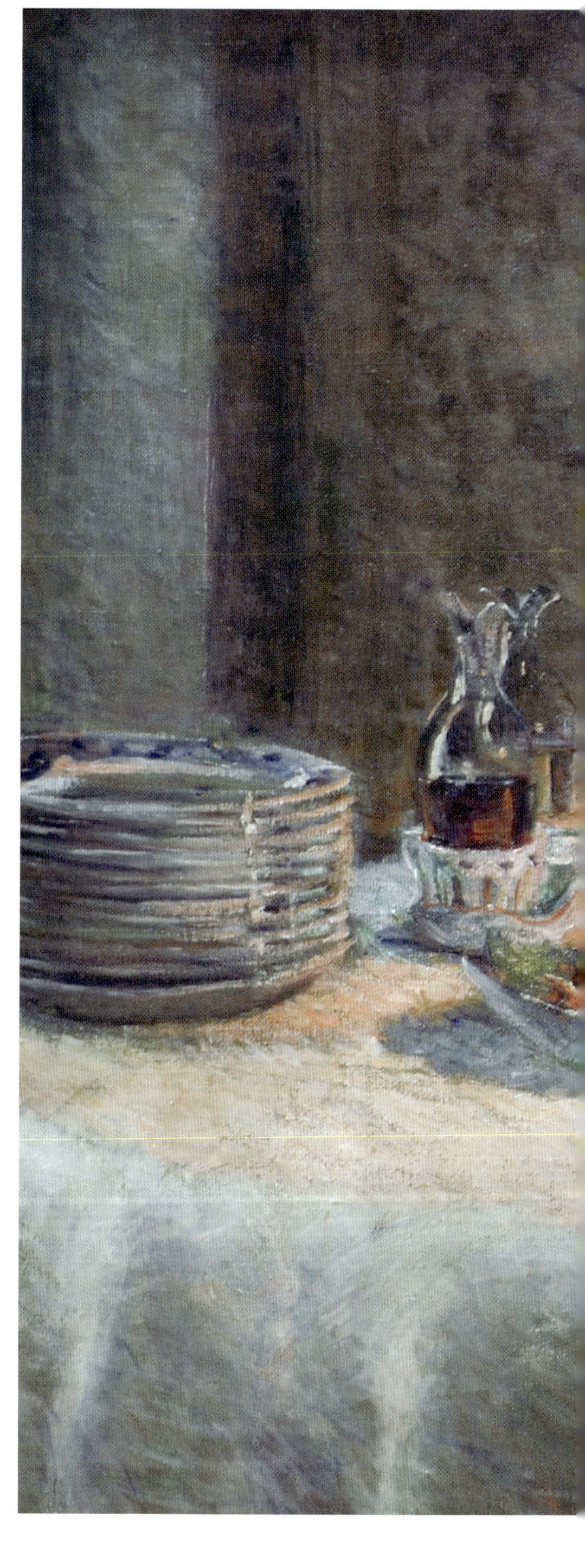

PLATE 17 MARIE BRACQUEMOND, *UNDER THE LAMP*, 1887

Oil on canvas, 27 × 44½ in. (68.6 × 113 cm). Collection of Mr. and Mrs. R. Stephens Phillips, Piedmont, CA

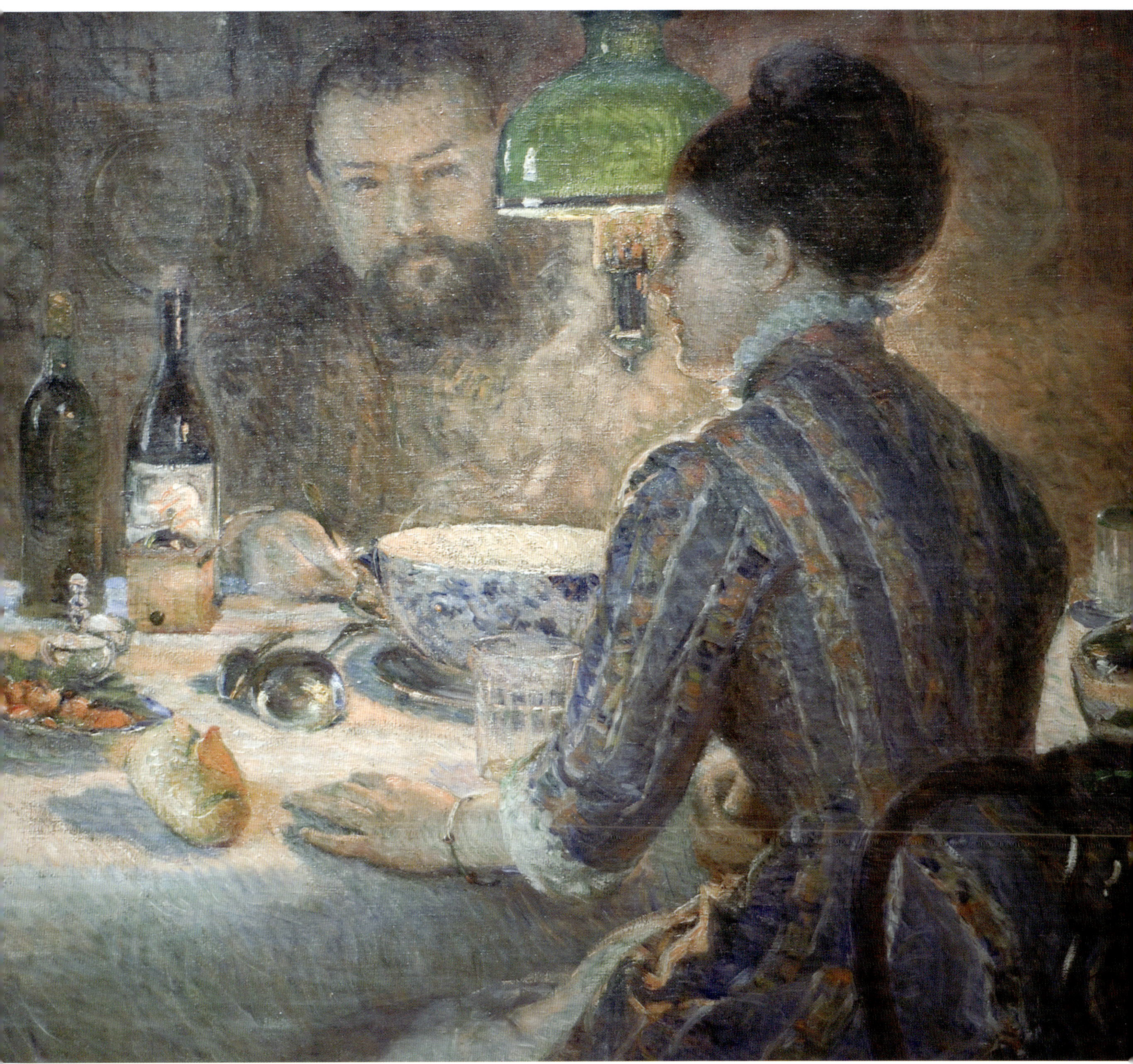

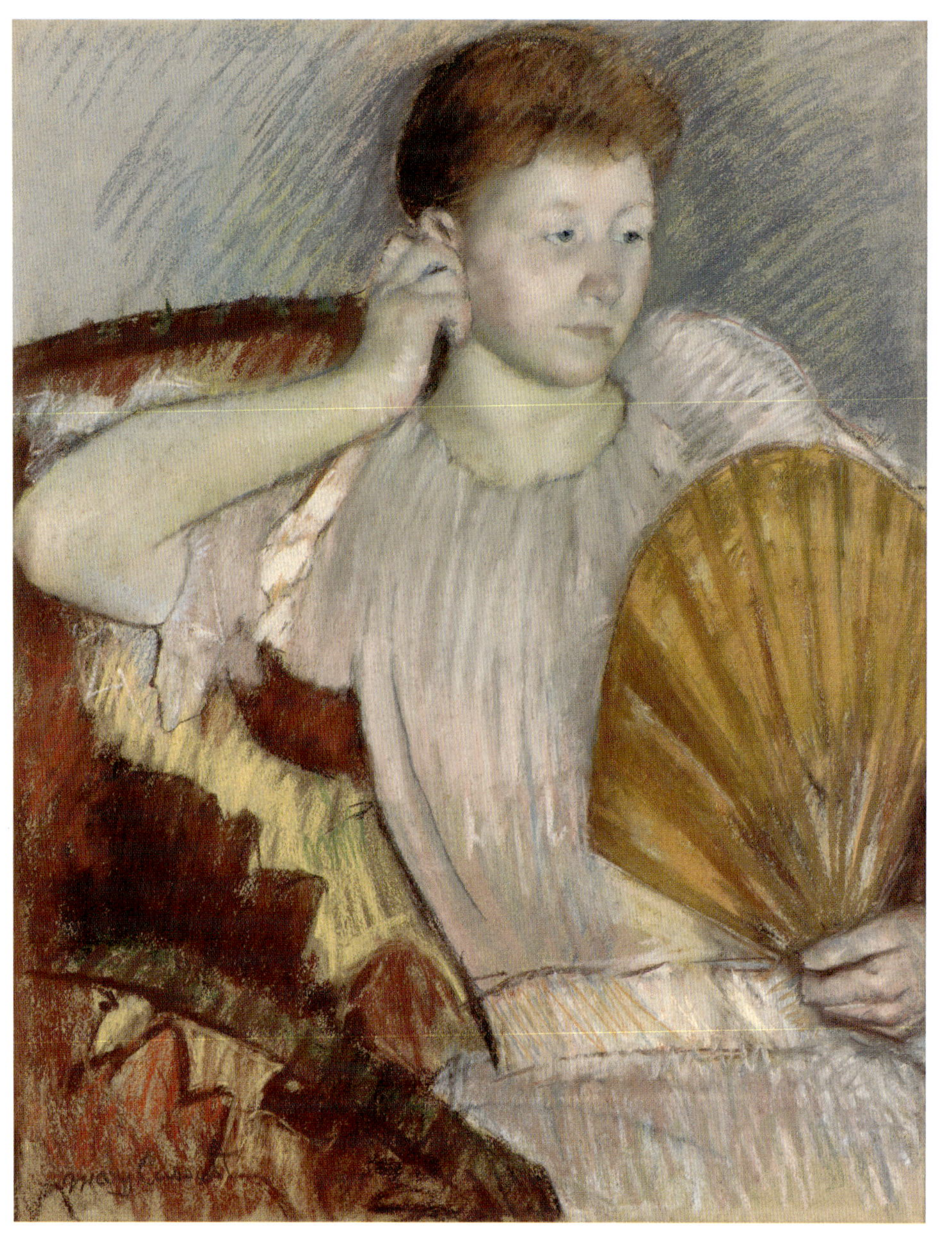

PLATE 18 MARY CASSATT, *WOMAN WITH FAN* (*FEMME Á L'ÉVENTAIL*), 1891–92

Pastel on tan wove paper, 26 × 20 in. (66 × 50.8 cm). Collection of Drs. Tobia and Morton Mower, Denver, CO

PLATE 19 MARY CASSATT, *WOMAN STANDING, HOLDING A FAN*, 1878–79

Distemper with metallic paint on canvas, 50⅝ × 27¾ in. (128.6 × 70.5 cm). Amon Carter Museum of American Art, Fort Worth, TX, 2011.20

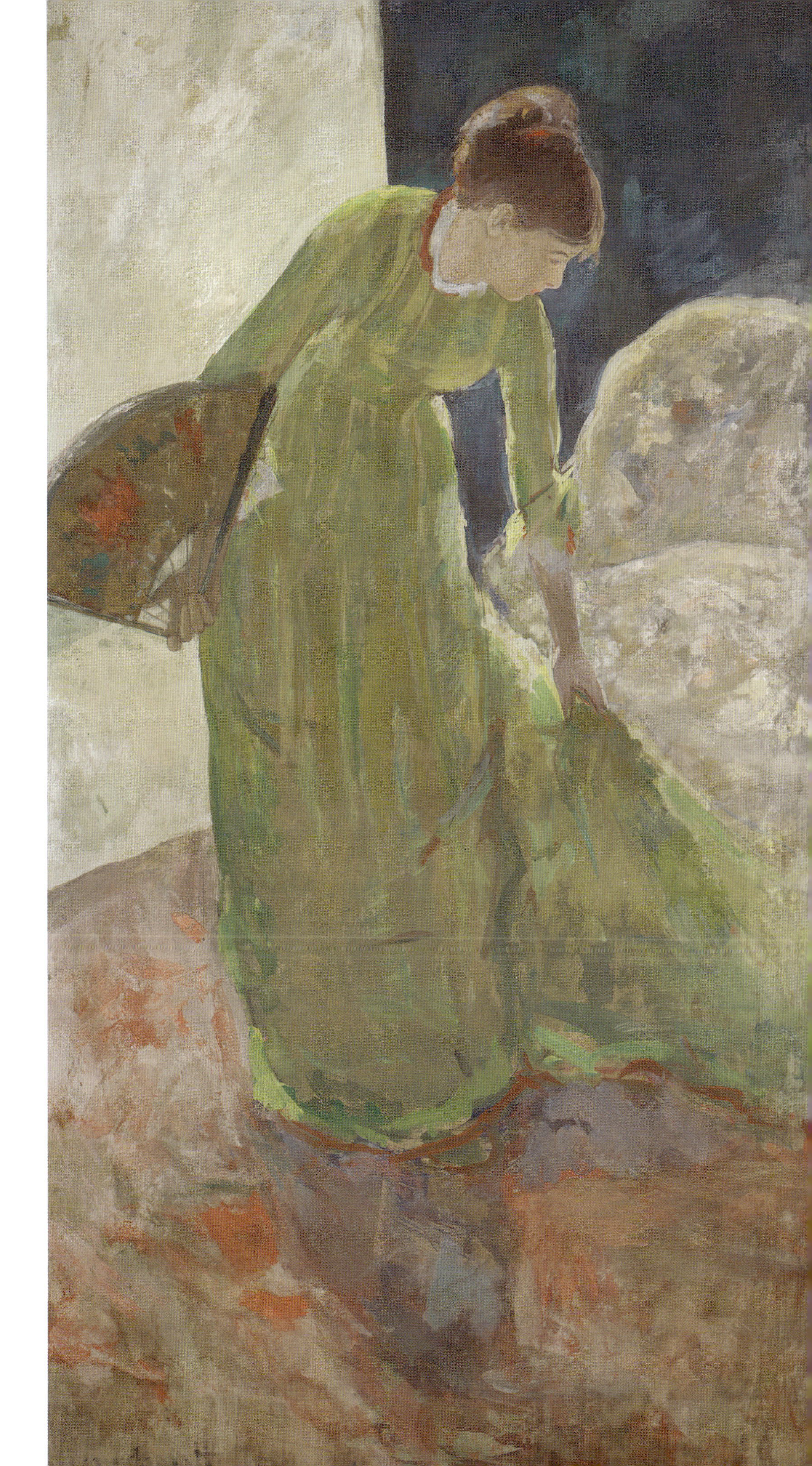

PLATE 20 MARY CASSATT, *THE READER*, 1877

Oil on canvas, 32 × 25½ in. (81.3 × 64.8 cm). Promised Gift to Crystal Bridges Museum of American Art, Bentonville, AR

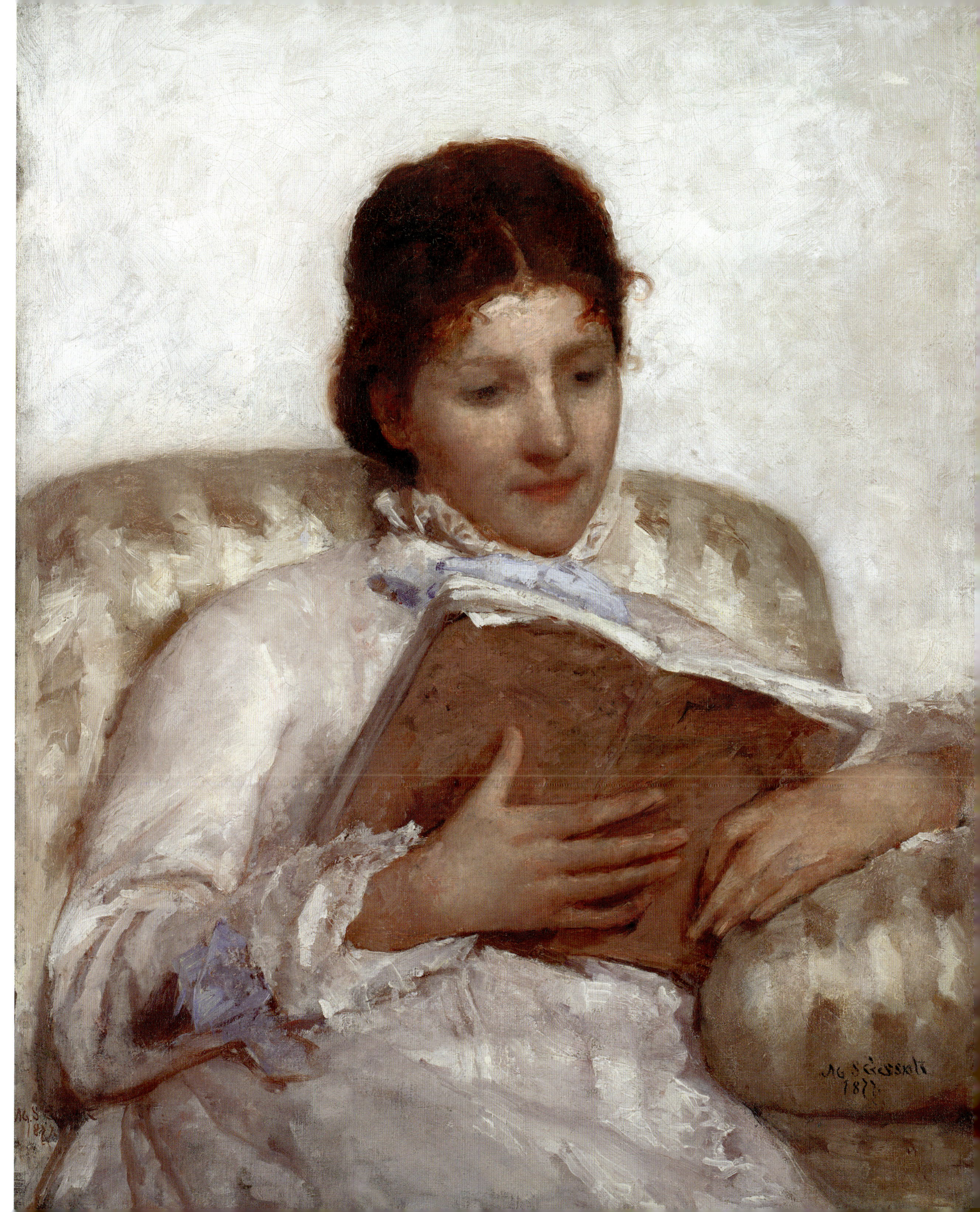

PLATE 21 **MARIE BRACQUEMOND, *THE AFTERNOON TEA* (*LE GOÛTER*), 1880**

Oil on canvas, 32⅛ × 24¼ in. (81.5 × 61.5 cm). Petit Palais, Musée des Beaux-Arts de la Ville de Paris

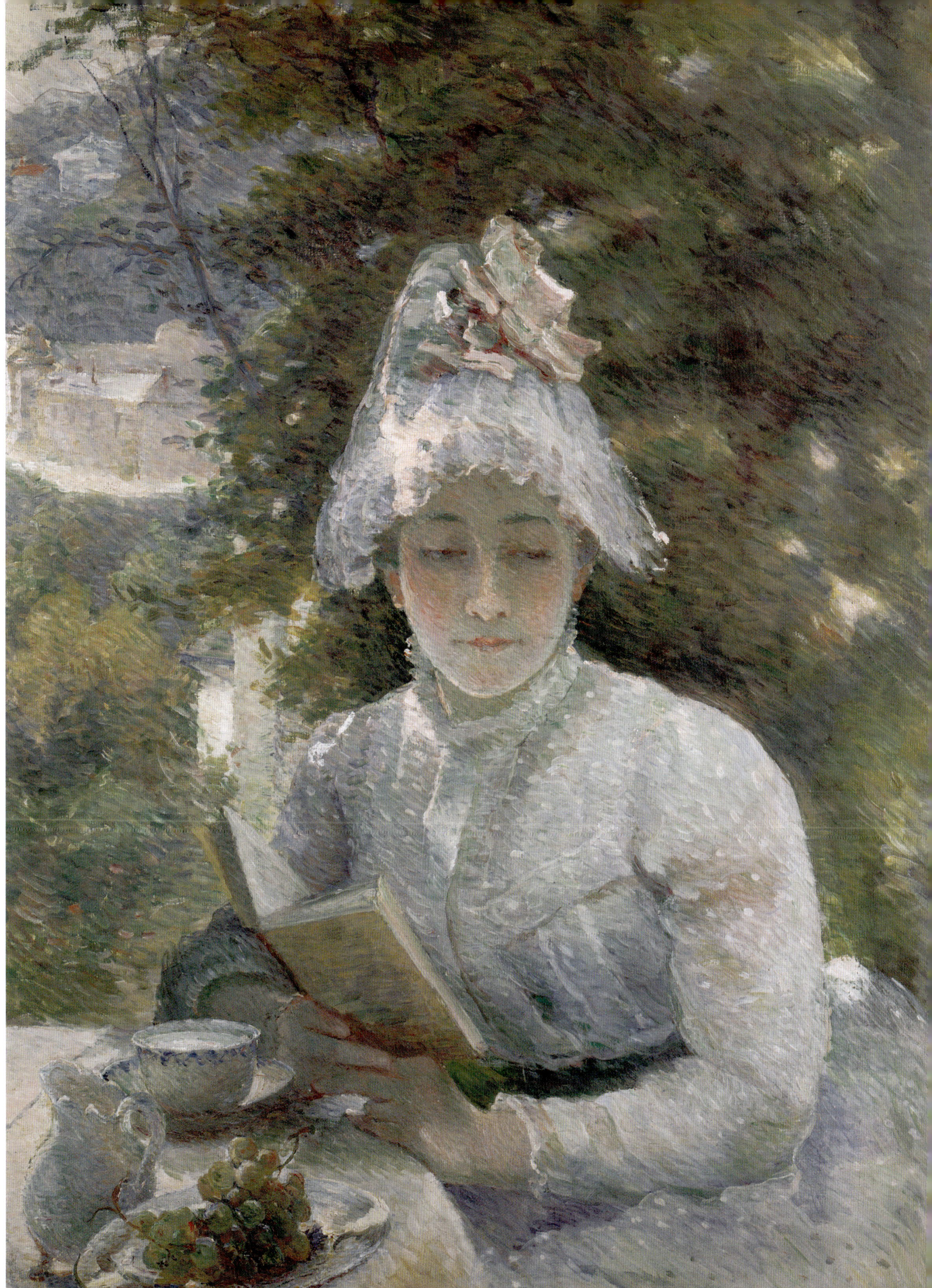

PLATE 22 HARRIET BACKER, *EVENING, INTERIOR* (*AFTEN, INTERIOR*), 1890

Oil on canvas, 32 × 34 in. (81.3 × 167.6 cm). National Museum of Art, Architecture and Design, Oslo, NG.M.02216

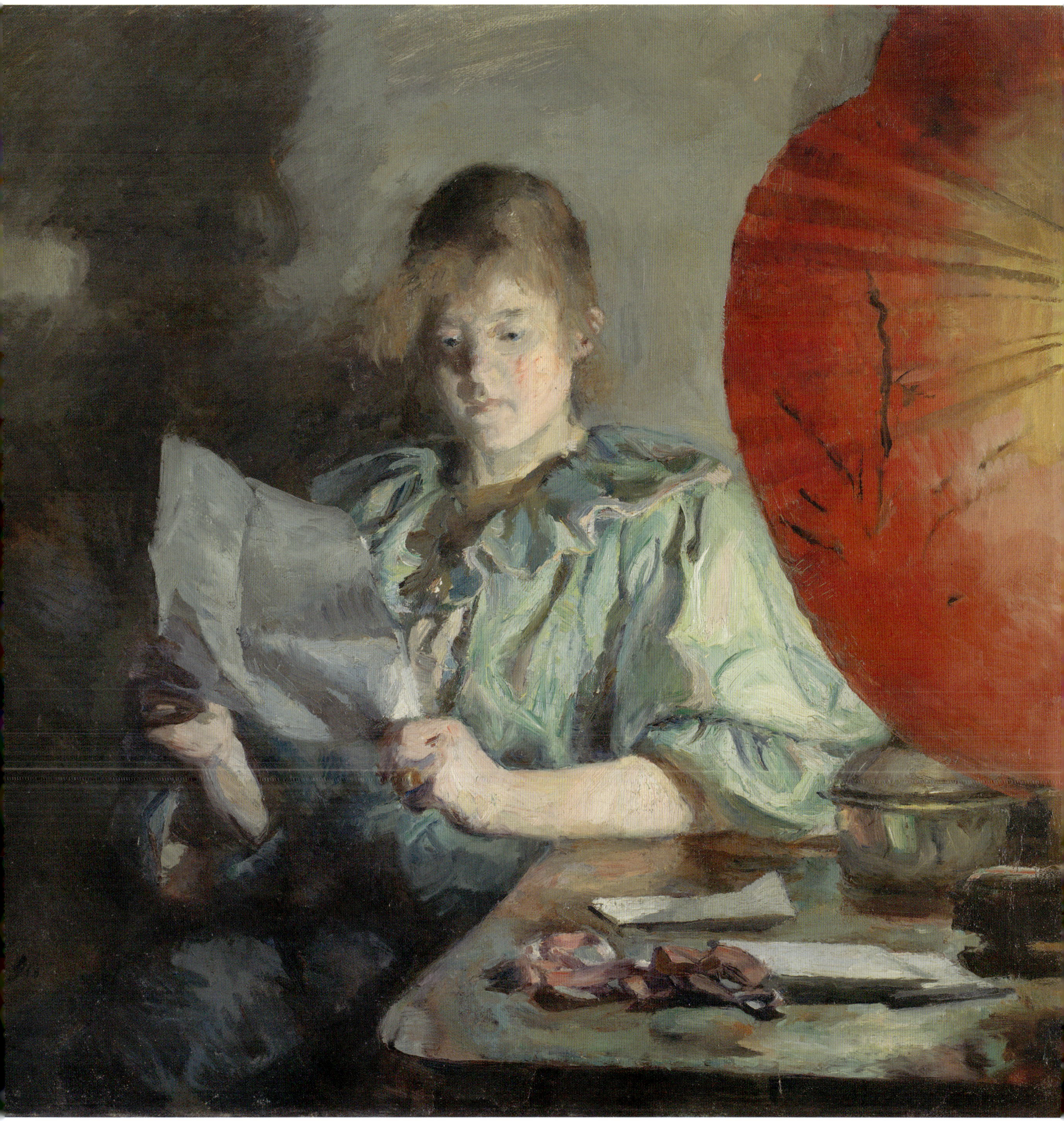

PLATE 23 MARY CASSATT, *PORTRAIT OF AN ELDERLY LADY IN A BONNET: RED BACKGROUND* (*ÉTUDE DE FEMME ÂGÉE EN CHAPEAU: FOND ROUGE*), CA. 1887

Oil on canvas, 32 × 25½ in. (81.3 × 64.8 cm). Birmingham Museum of Art, Gift of Mahdah R. Kniffin Estate

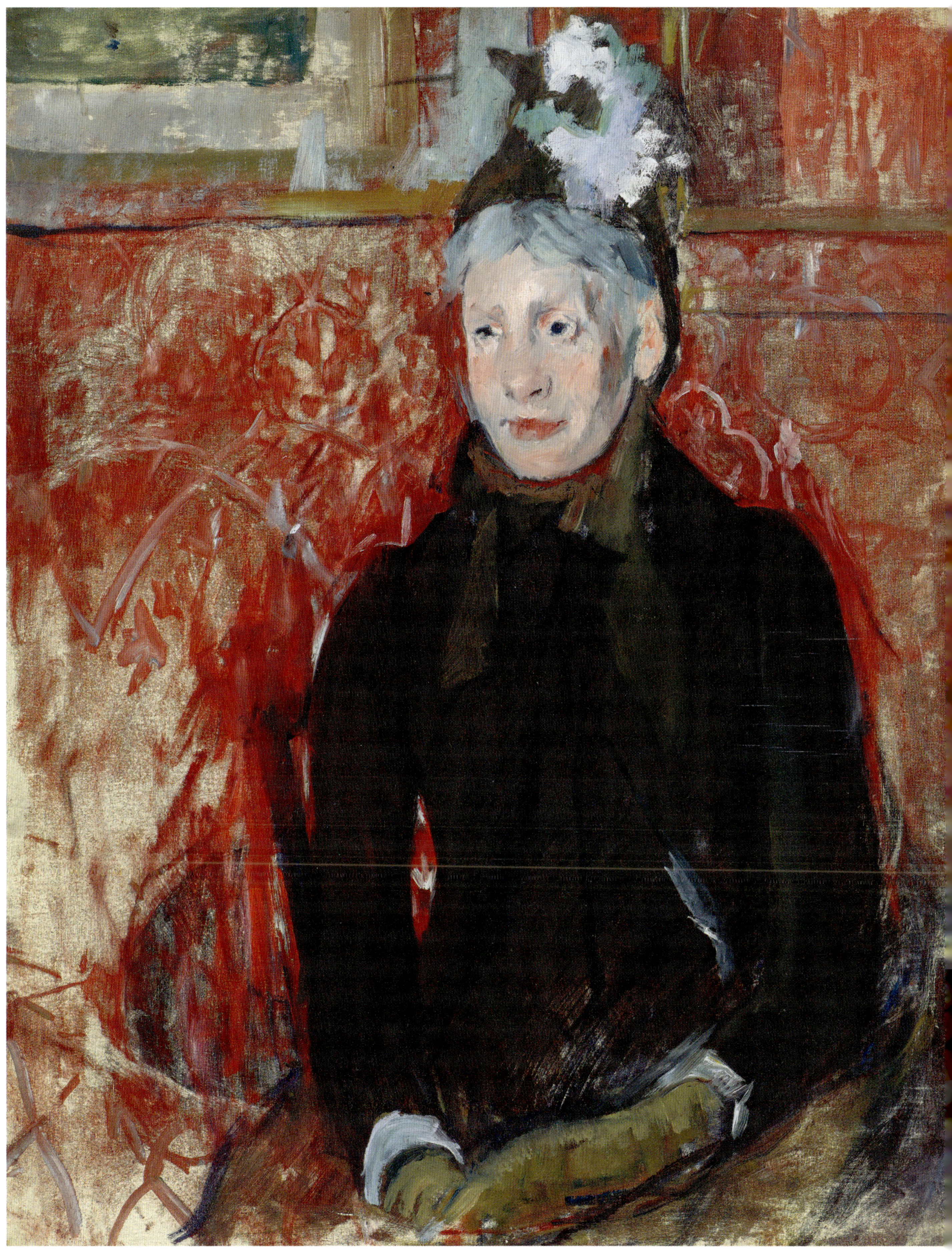

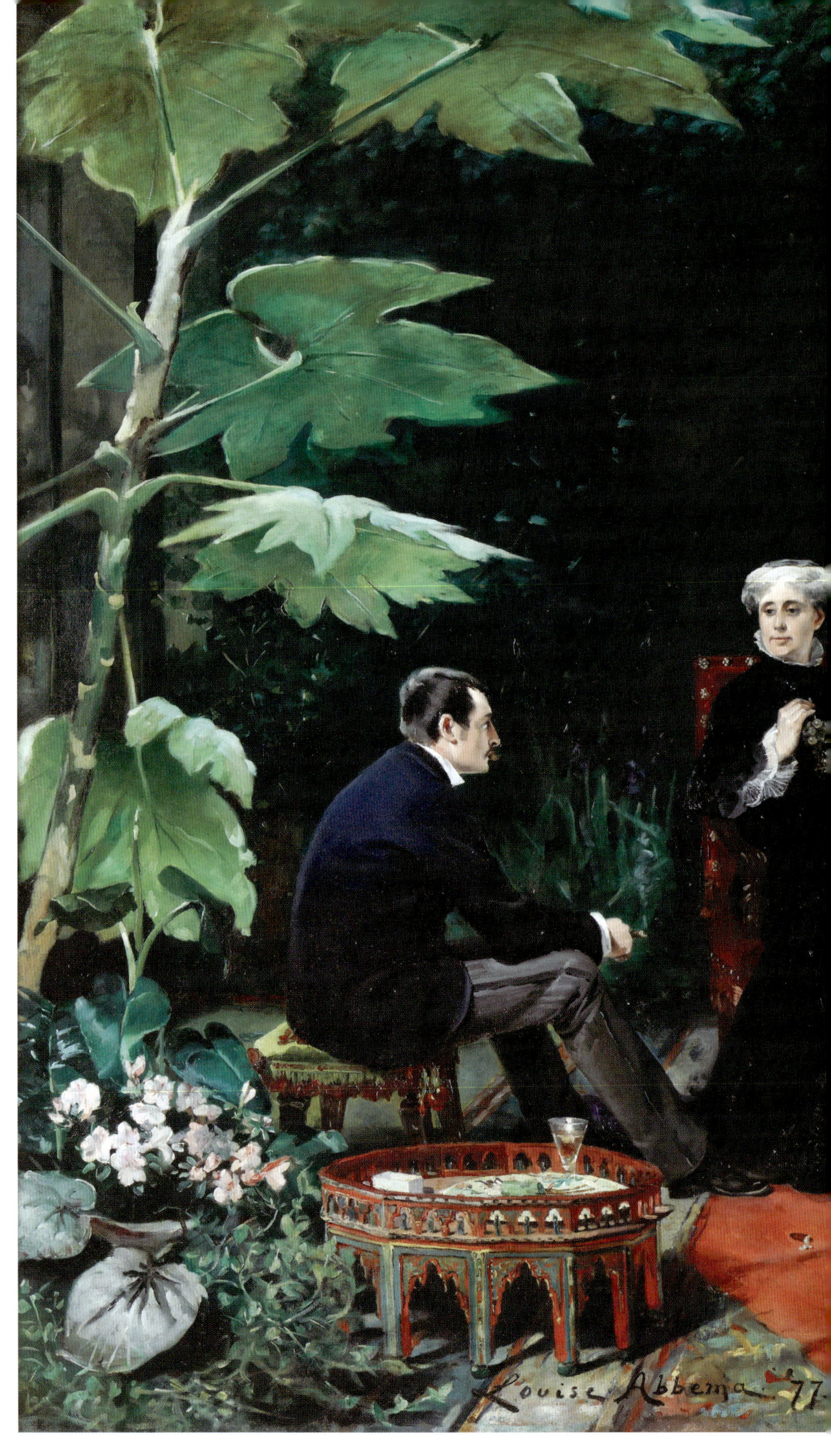

PLATE 24 LOUISE ABBÉMA, *LUNCH IN THE GREENHOUSE* (*LE DÉJEUNER DANS LA SERRE*), 1877

Oil on canvas, 76⅜ × 121¼ in. (194 × 308 cm). Musée des Beaux-Arts, Pau, France, 878.1.1

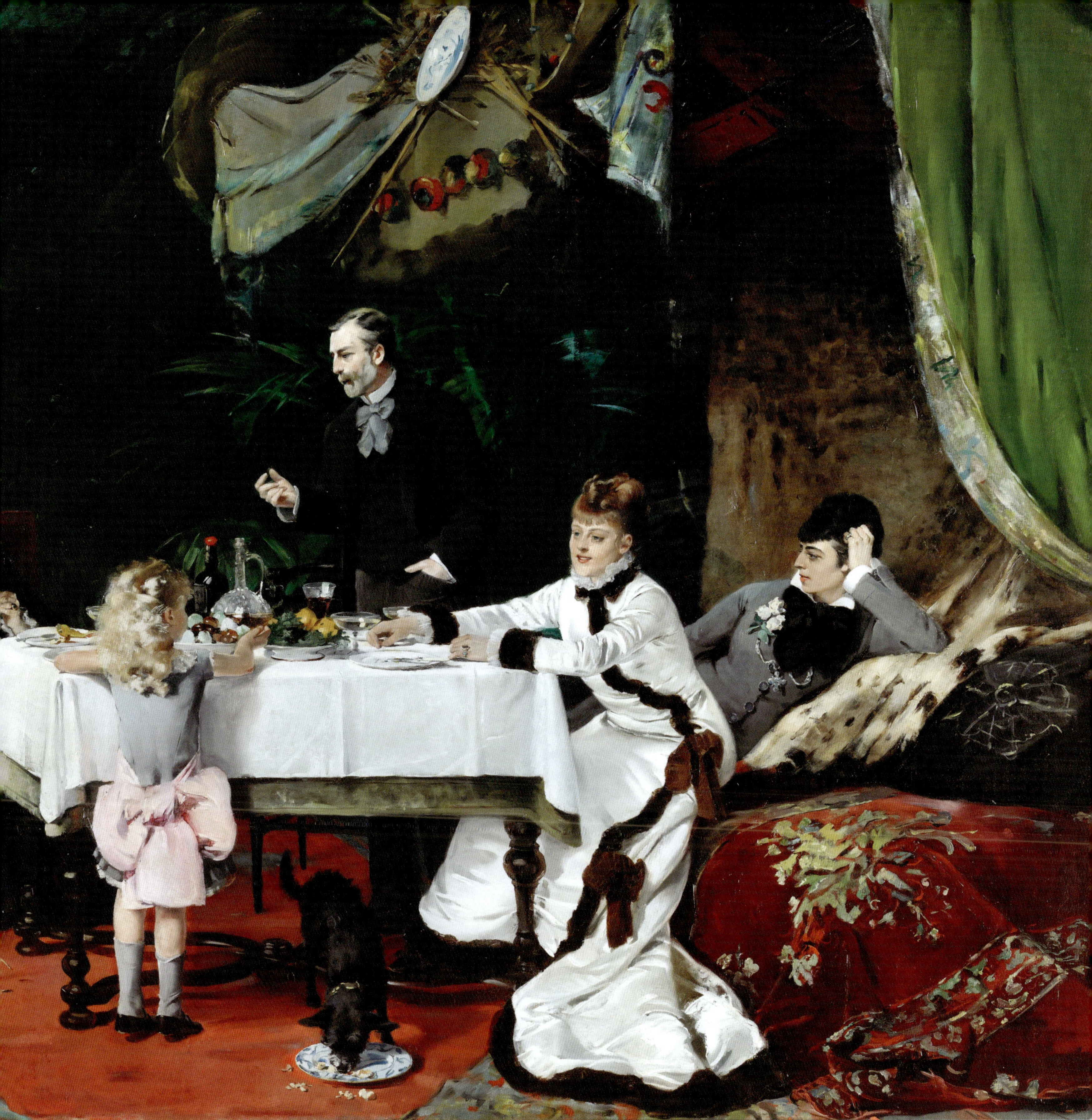

The staunchly conservative critic Hugues Le Roux declared: "Frenchwomen, and Parisian women in particular, are so tasteful in their alterations, are such good colorists in combining the pieces of an ensemble, are so truly artistic in their ability to furnish their homes, that one would expect to find more creativity, charm, and verve in their works of art."[1] This statement no doubt affirms the pointlessness of women's painterly pursuits: women presumably should have a large enough arena to express their originality through the composition of their clothing and the design of their interiors. Indeed, in the face of such cruel criticism, what uselessness for women to desire to leave the private space of their boudoirs.

The same declaration might also be viewed as an invitation to consider the brilliant representations of the social ritual of *la toilette* by Louise Abbéma, Cecilia Beaux, Marie Bracquemond, and Berthe Morisot as merely an extension of feminine talent—in effect, a transposition of a woman's capacity to dress herself into an ability to paint. Extending the critic's view even further, one might ultimately conclude that clothing, even more than painting, is the business of women, and that a woman painting a gown would therefore be a pleonasm, or an artistic tautology.

And yet the art of dressing—clothing and fashion—is, more broadly, fundamental to the social life of the nineteenth century. The novelist Honoré de Balzac wrote, "Clothing is the expression of society. . . . It is at once science, art, habit, and feeling."[2] The representation of costumes, then, is a subject matter that painters seize upon. Firstly, clothing is seen as the embodiment of modernity, as Edmond Duranty observed: "What we need is the special note of the modern individual, in his clothing, his social habits, at home or in the street."[3] The desire of women artists to imbue the secular objects of *la toilette* with symbolic—almost sacred—potential is evident in Eva Gonzalès's *The Pink Slippers* [plate 26], where the artist turns an elegant pair of evening shoes into a mysterious, seductive, and enigmatic portrait of modern life.

Secondly, both formally and aesthetically, clothing allowed an artist to demonstrate her mastery in rendering fabric—for example, its transparency or sheen. In so much of this work—Marie Bracquemond's *The Woman in White* [plate 32], Mary Shepard Greene Blumenschein's *Un Regard Fugitif* [plate 28], Louise Abbéma's *Among the Flowers* [plate 31], and Cecilia Beaux's *Sita and Sarita (Woman with a Cat)* [plate 29]—white dominates. Each artist illustrates how the act of adorning oneself, of making oneself more beautiful with fabrics and makeup, could be viewed as a metaphor for painting, which was supposed to "correct" or "idealize" nature. Furthermore, images of women in front of a mirror, with skillfully made-up faces and deftly coiffed hair—foregrounded in Morisot's *Woman at Her Toilette* [plate 27]—posit an equivalence between painting and dressing.

Male painters, such as Édouard Manet [see Kendall, fig. 4], James McNeill Whistler, Claude Monet, Alfred Stevens, and James Tissot—perhaps most emblematically in *The Most Beautiful Woman in Paris (The Fashionable Beauty)*—were just as apt to take interest in women's attire, which was vastly more colorful than their own overwhelmingly black costumes. Their attention to fashion illustrates a growing concern, exactly the same for men and for women, to render the spectacle, customs, and sartorial splendor of modern life. Above all, there was a desire to decipher, like the poet Stéphane Mallarmé (a columnist for the fashion review *La dernière mode*) and the novelist Marcel Proust—through his detailed accounts of Odette Swann's outfits—what fashion, through its complex visual codes, has to say about the world.

1. Hugues Le Roux, "La vie à Paris," *Le temps*, March 5, 1882.
2. Honoré de Balzac, "Traité de la vie élégante," *La mode*, October 6–November 6, 1830.
3. E. L. Duranty, *La nouvelle peinture, à propos du groupe d'artistes qui expose dans les galleries Durand-Ruel* (Darius: E. Dentu, 1876), 24.

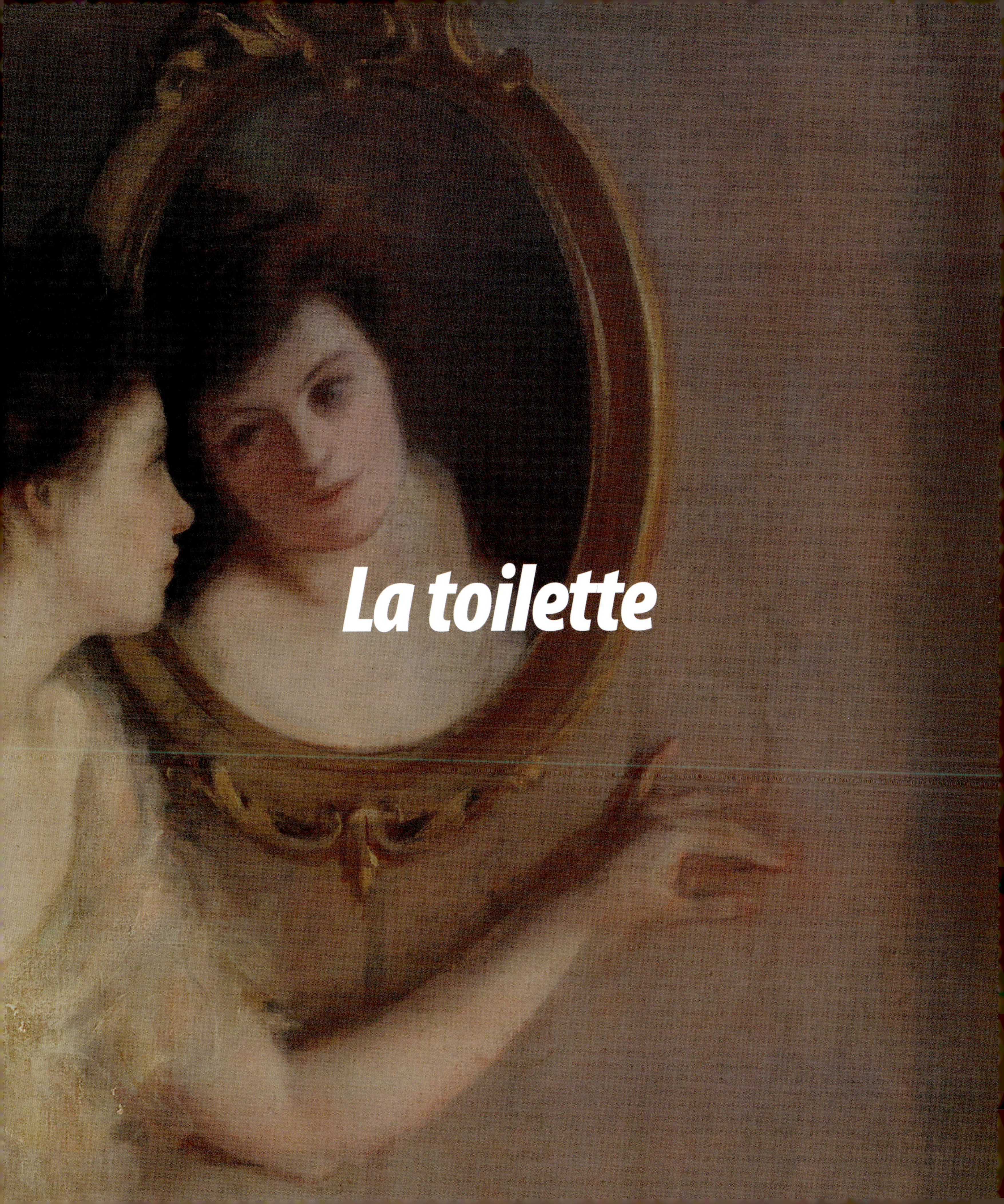

La toilette

PLATE 25 BERTHE MORISOT, *THE BATH*, 1885–86

Oil on canvas, 36¼ × 28⅞ in. (92.1 × 73.3 cm). Sterling and Francine Clark Art Institute, Williamstown, MA, 1955.926

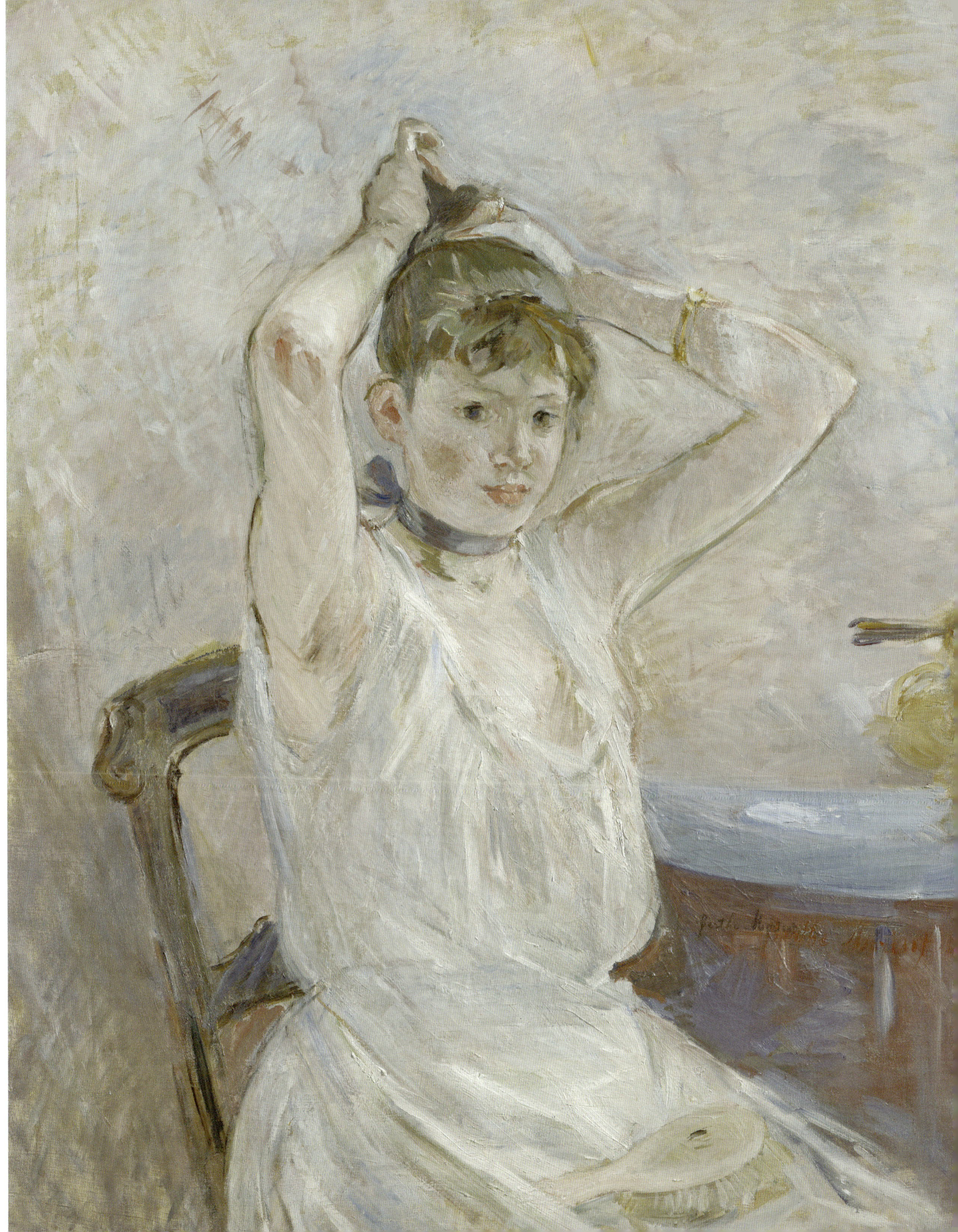

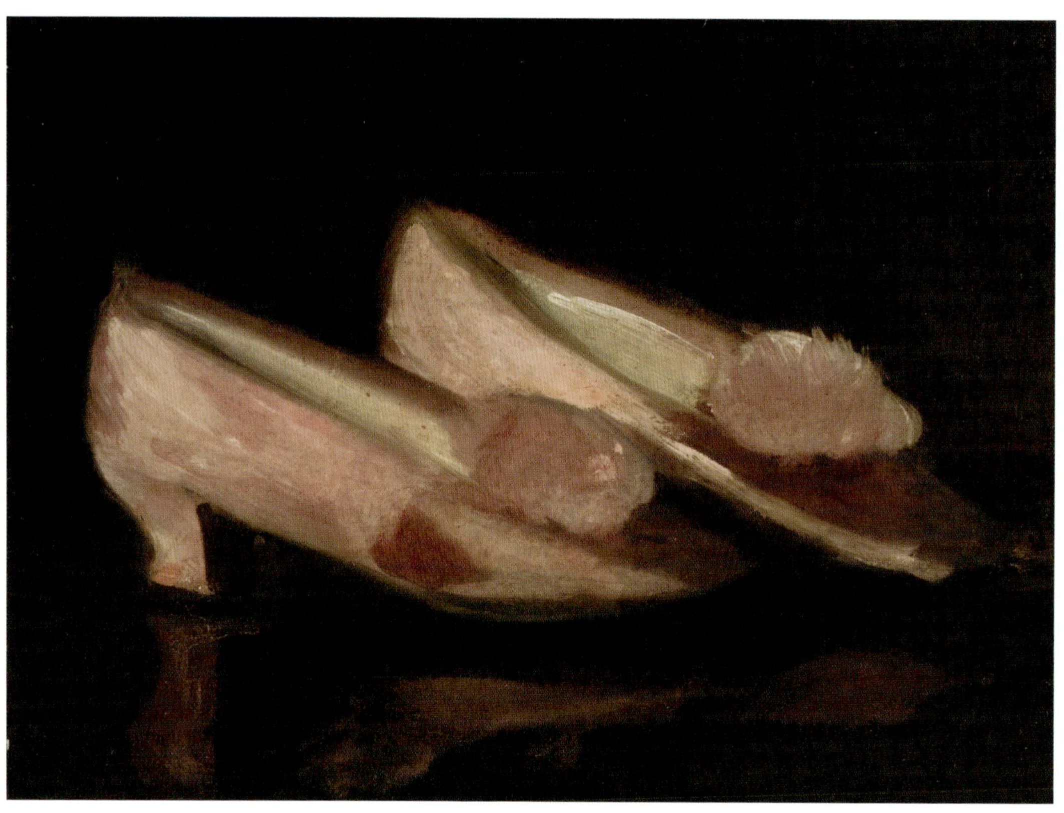

PLATE 26 EVA GONZALÈS, *THE PINK SLIPPERS*, 1879–80

Oil on canvas, laid down on panel, 10¼ × 13¾ in. (26 × 35 cm). Private collection, courtesy of Galerie Hopkins, Paris

PLATE 27 BERTHE MORISOT, *WOMAN AT HER TOILETTE*, 1875–80

Oil on canvas, 23¾ × 31⅝ in. (60.3 × 80.4 cm). Art Institute of Chicago, Stickney Fund, 1924.127

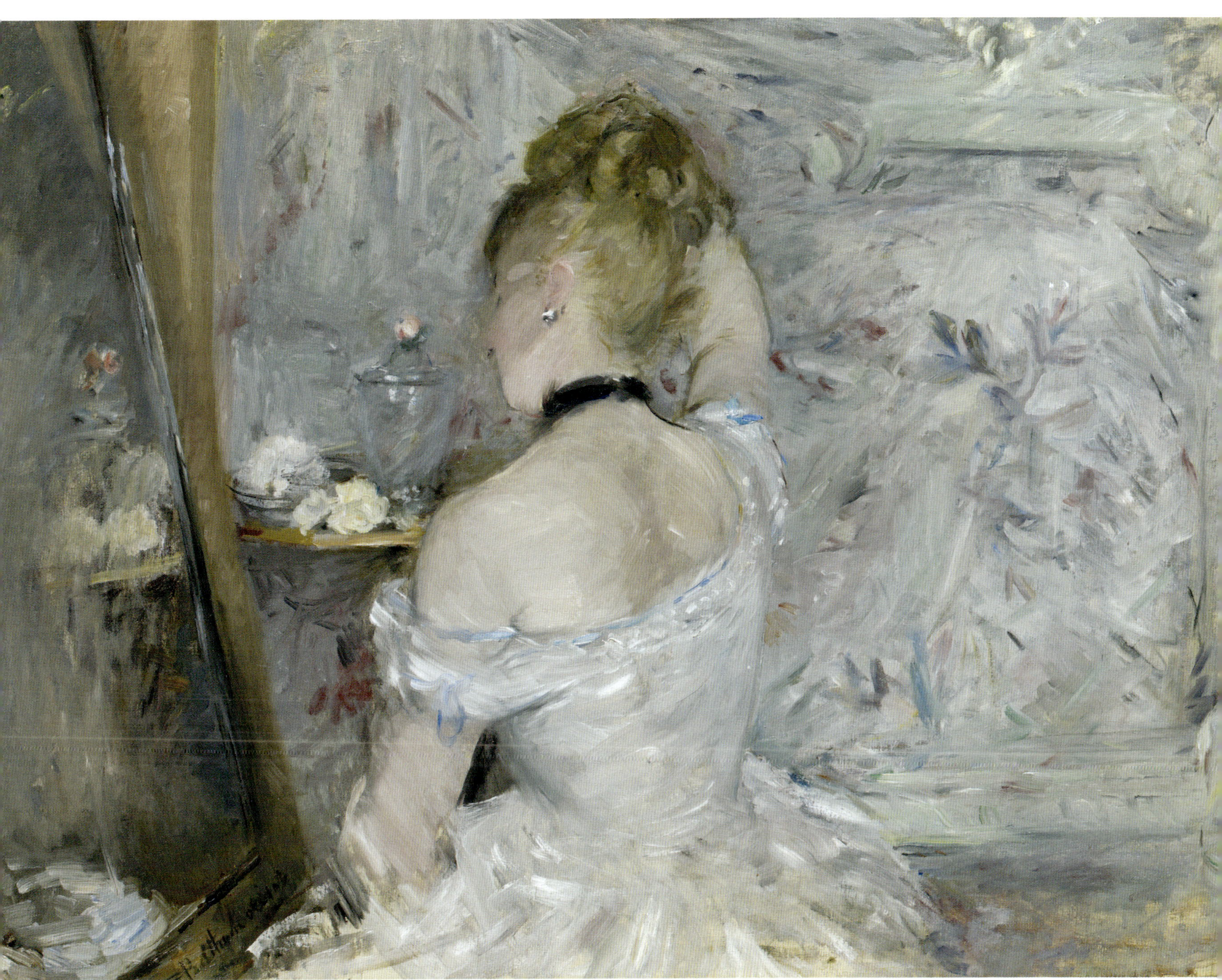

PLATE 28 MARY SHEPARD GREENE BLUMENSCHEIN, *UN REGARD FUGITIF*, 1900

Oil on canvas, 51¾ × 36¼ in. (131.4 × 92.1 cm). Brooklyn Museum, Gift of Mr. and Mrs. Sidney W. Davidson, 57.95

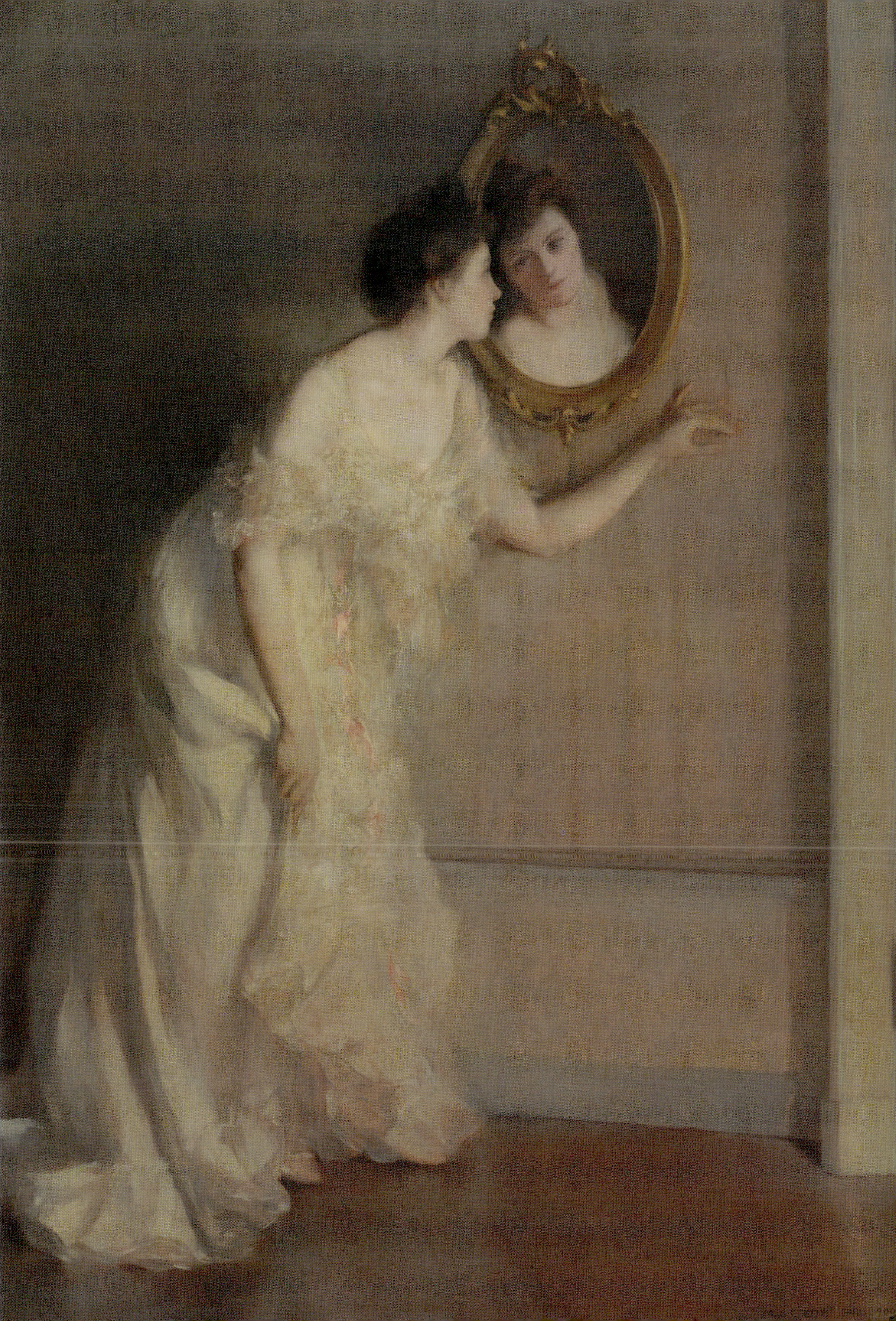

PLATE 29 CECILIA BEAUX, *SITA AND SARITA (WOMAN WITH A CAT)* (*SITA ET SARITA [FEMME AU CHAT]*), 1893–94

Oil on canvas, 44⅝ × 33 in. (94.5 × 63.5 cm). Musée d'Orsay, Paris, gift of the artist, 1921, RF1980-60

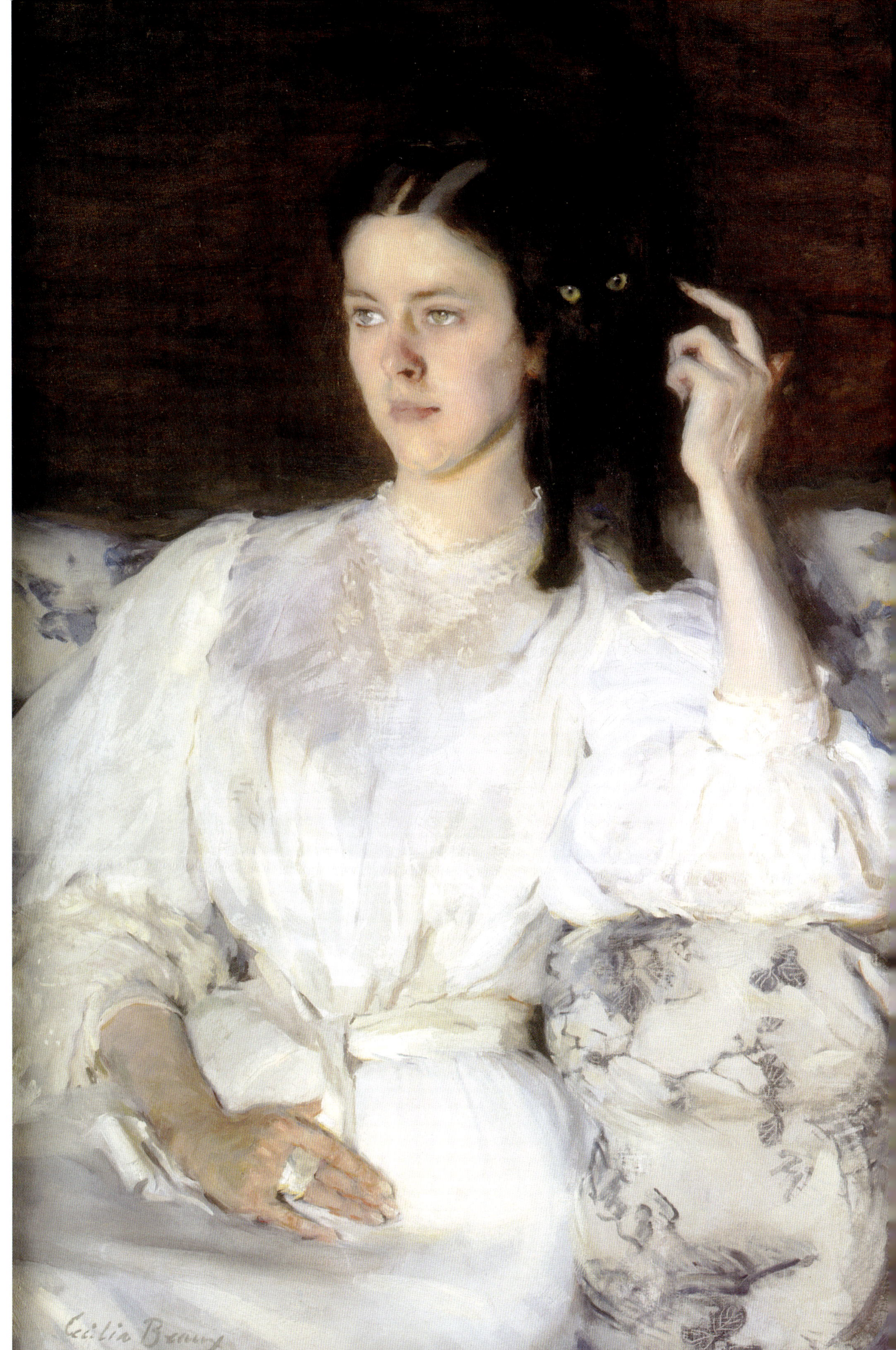

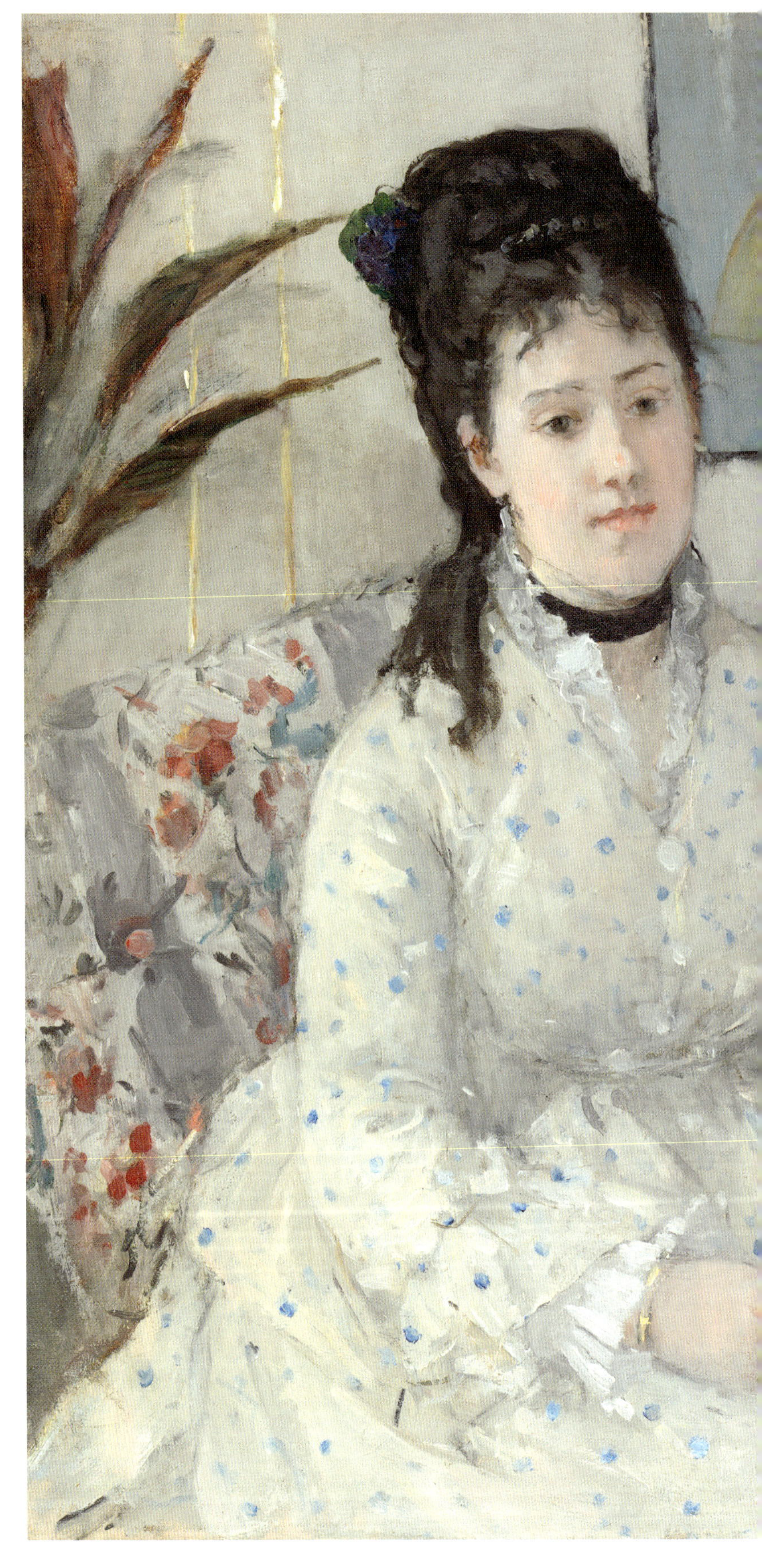

PLATE 30 BERTHE MORISOT, *THE SISTERS*, 1869

Oil on canvas, 20½ × 32 in. (52.1 × 81.3 cm). National Gallery of Art, Washington, DC, Gift of Mrs. Charles S. Carstairs, 1952.9.2

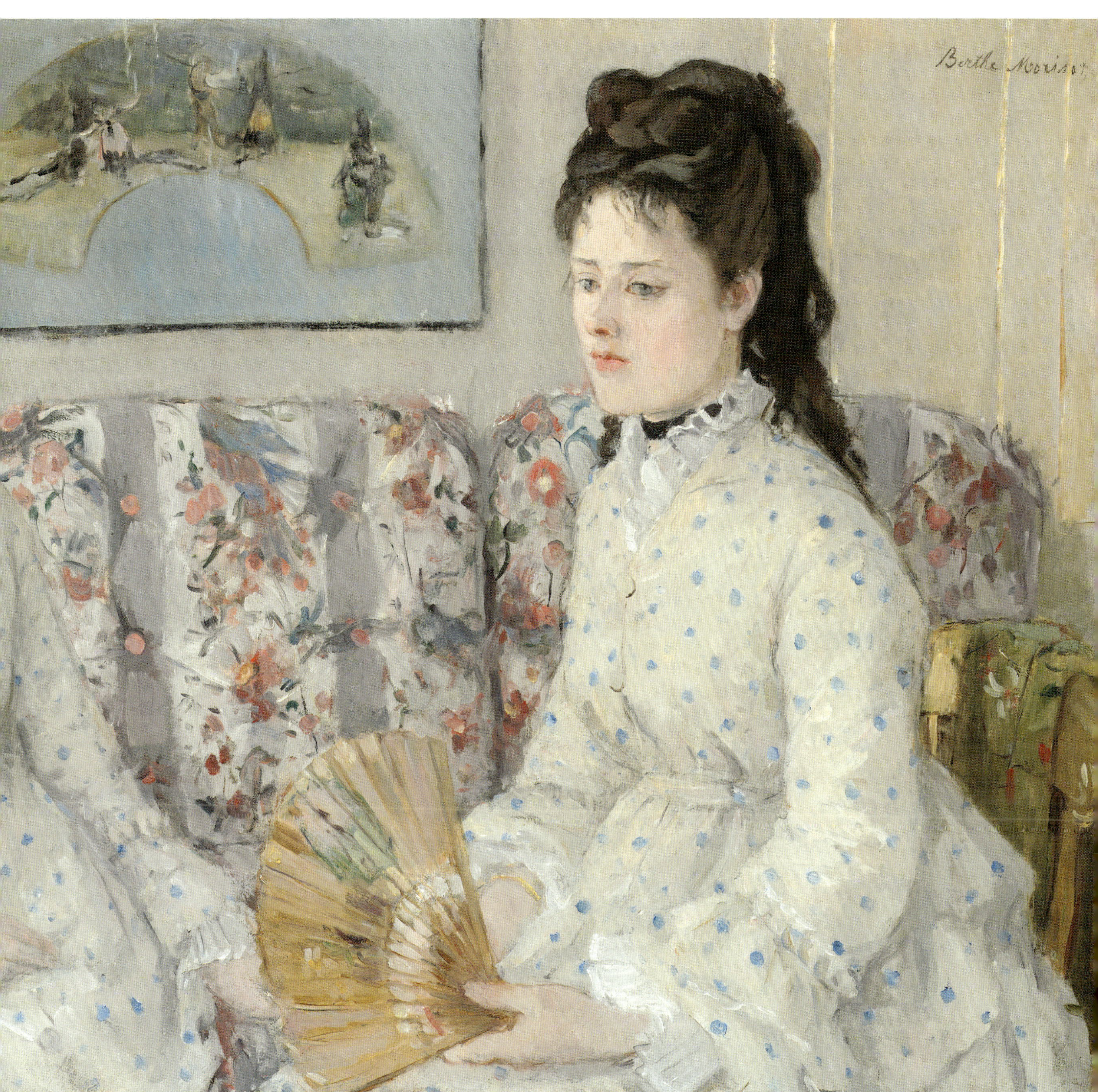
Berthe Morisot

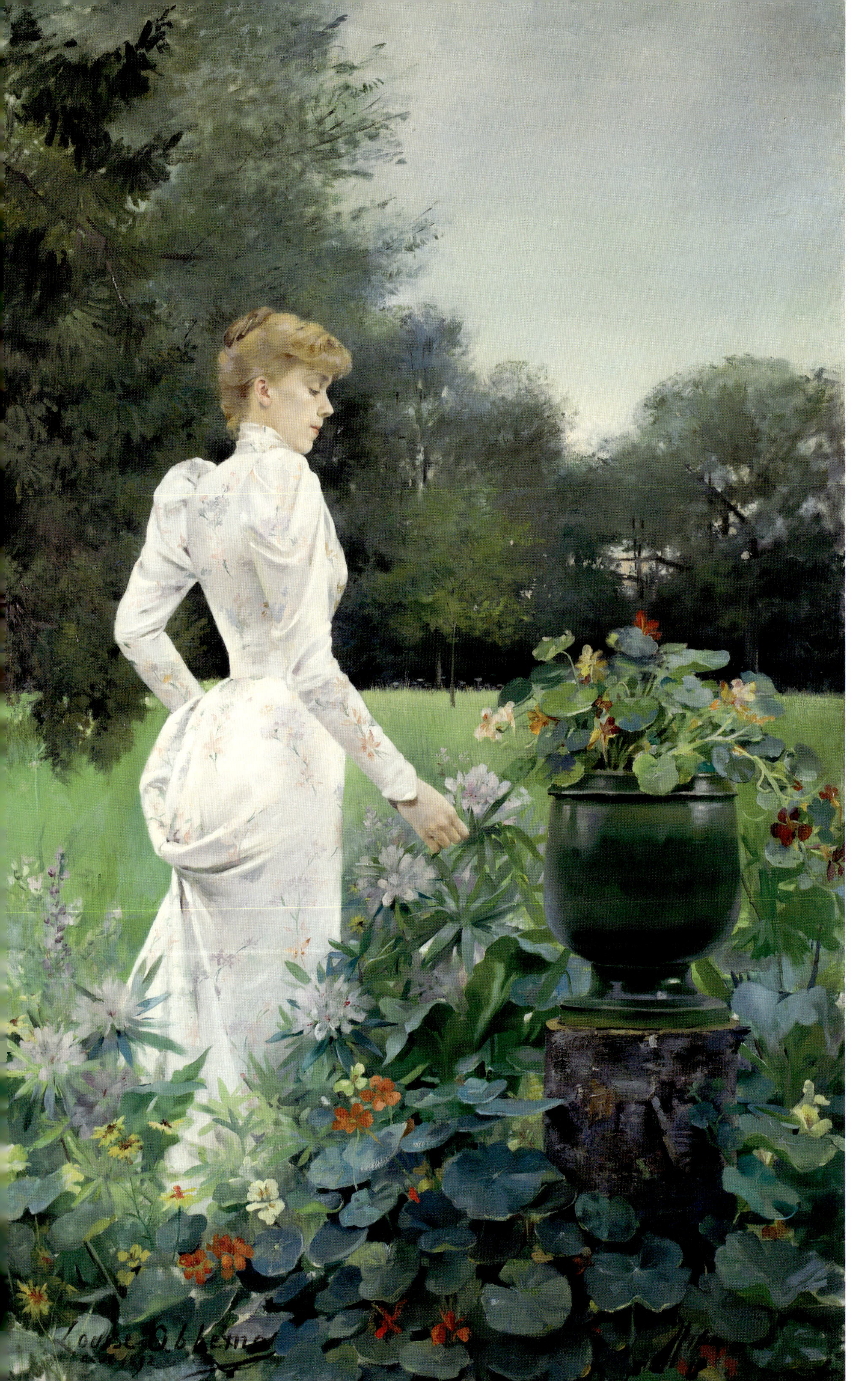

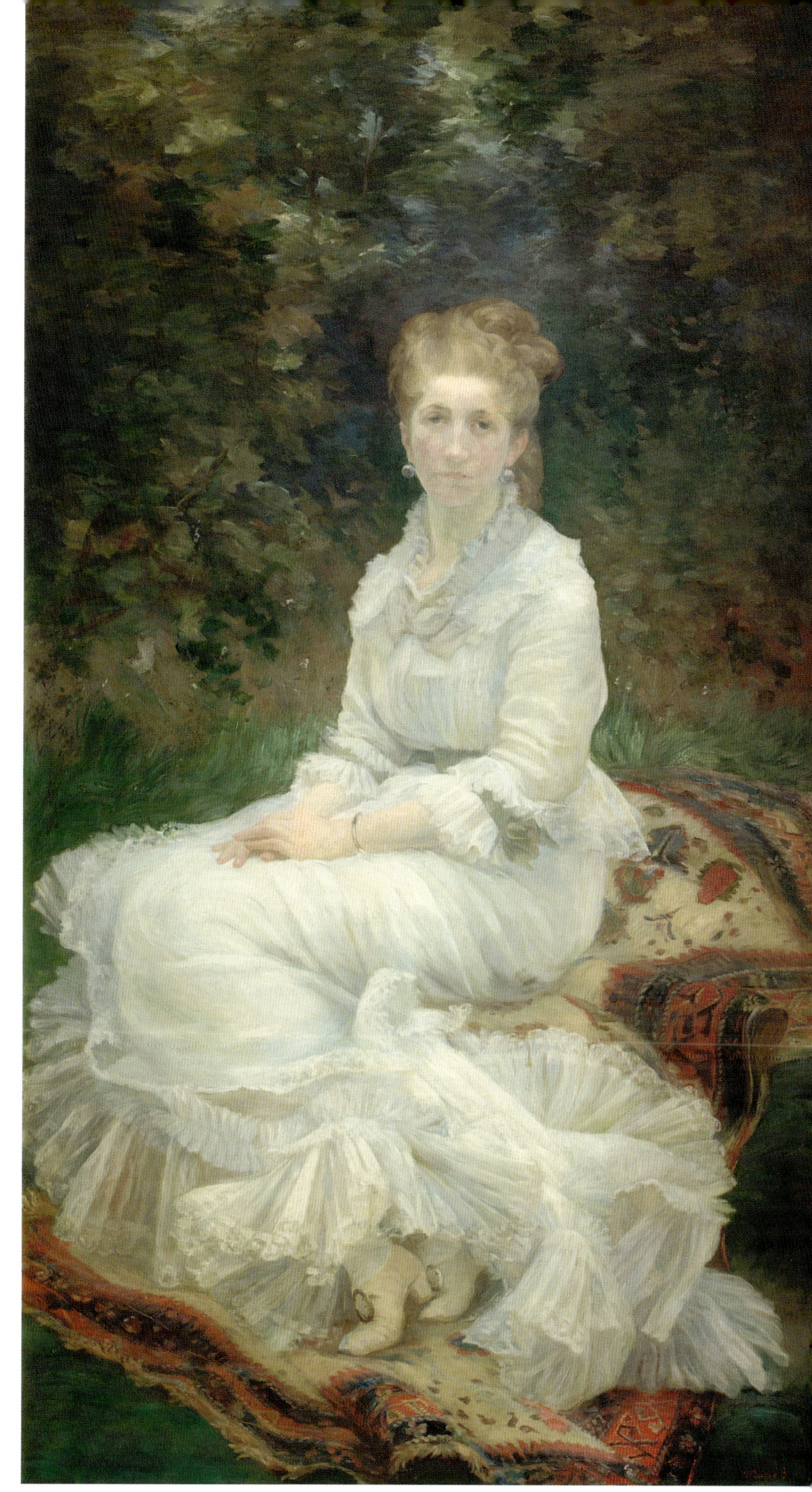

PLATE 31 LOUISE ABBÉMA, *AMONG THE FLOWERS* (*DANS LES FLEURS*), 1892
Oil on canvas, 78 × 48⅜ in. (198 × 123 cm). Musée intercommunal, Étampes, France

PLATE 32 MARIE BRACQUEMOND, *THE WOMAN IN WHITE* (*LA DAME EN BLANC*), 1880
Oil on canvas, 71 × 41⅜ in. (180.5 × 105 cm). Musée d'Orsay, Paris, on deposit at Musée de Cambrai, RF2751

PLATE 33 MARIE BRACQUEMOND, *ON THE TERRACE AT SÈVRES* (*SUR LA TERRASSE À SÈVRES*), 1880

Oil on canvas, 34⅝ × 45¼ in. (88 × 115 cm). Musée du Petit Palais, Geneva

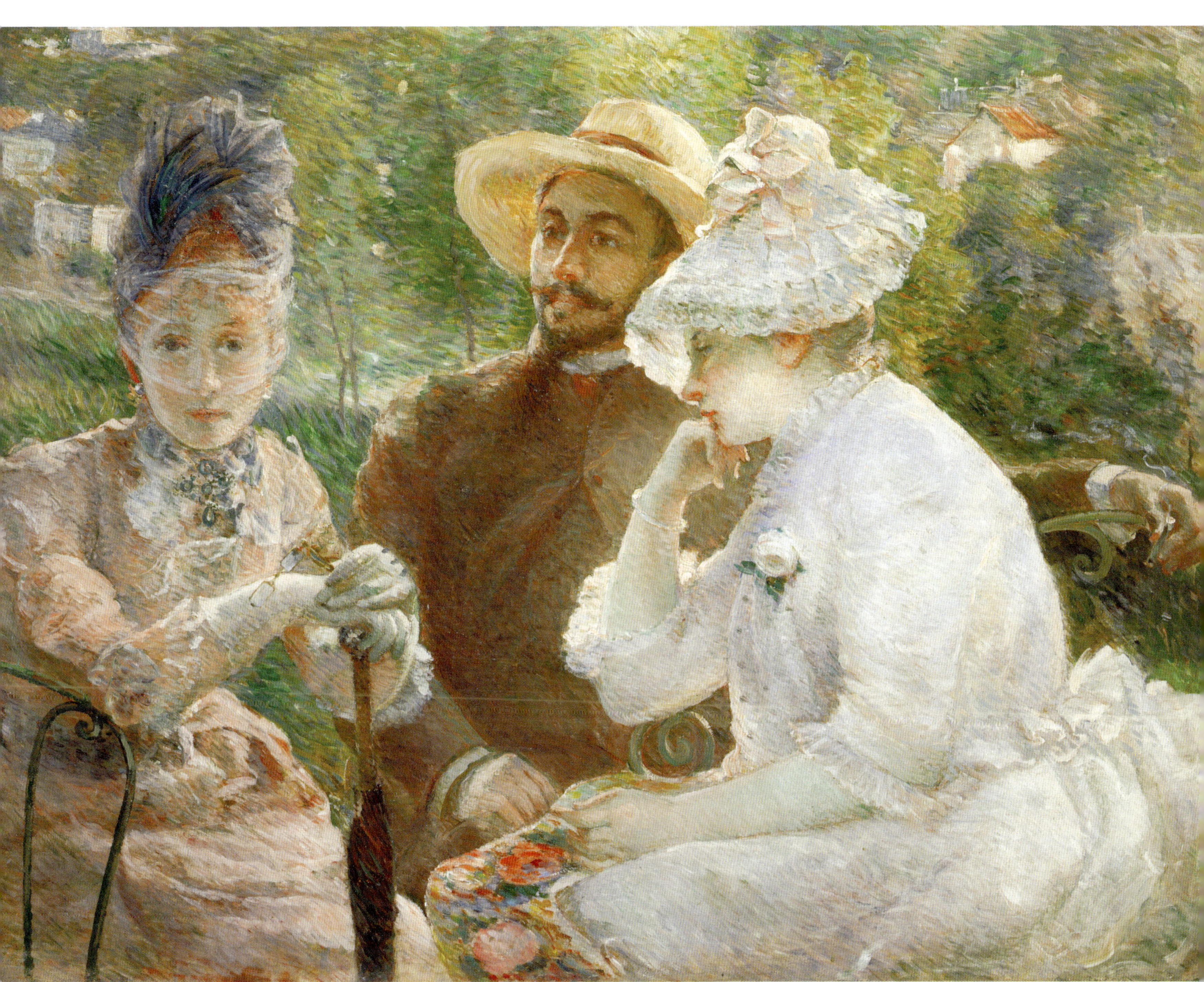

PLATE 34 MARIE BRACQUEMOND, *THREE WOMEN WITH PARASOLS* (*TROIS FEMMES AUX OMBRELLES [LES TROIS GRACES]*), CA. 1880

Oil on canvas, 54¾ × 35 in. (139 × 89 cm). Musée d'Orsay, Paris, Bequest of Gustave Geffroy, 1926

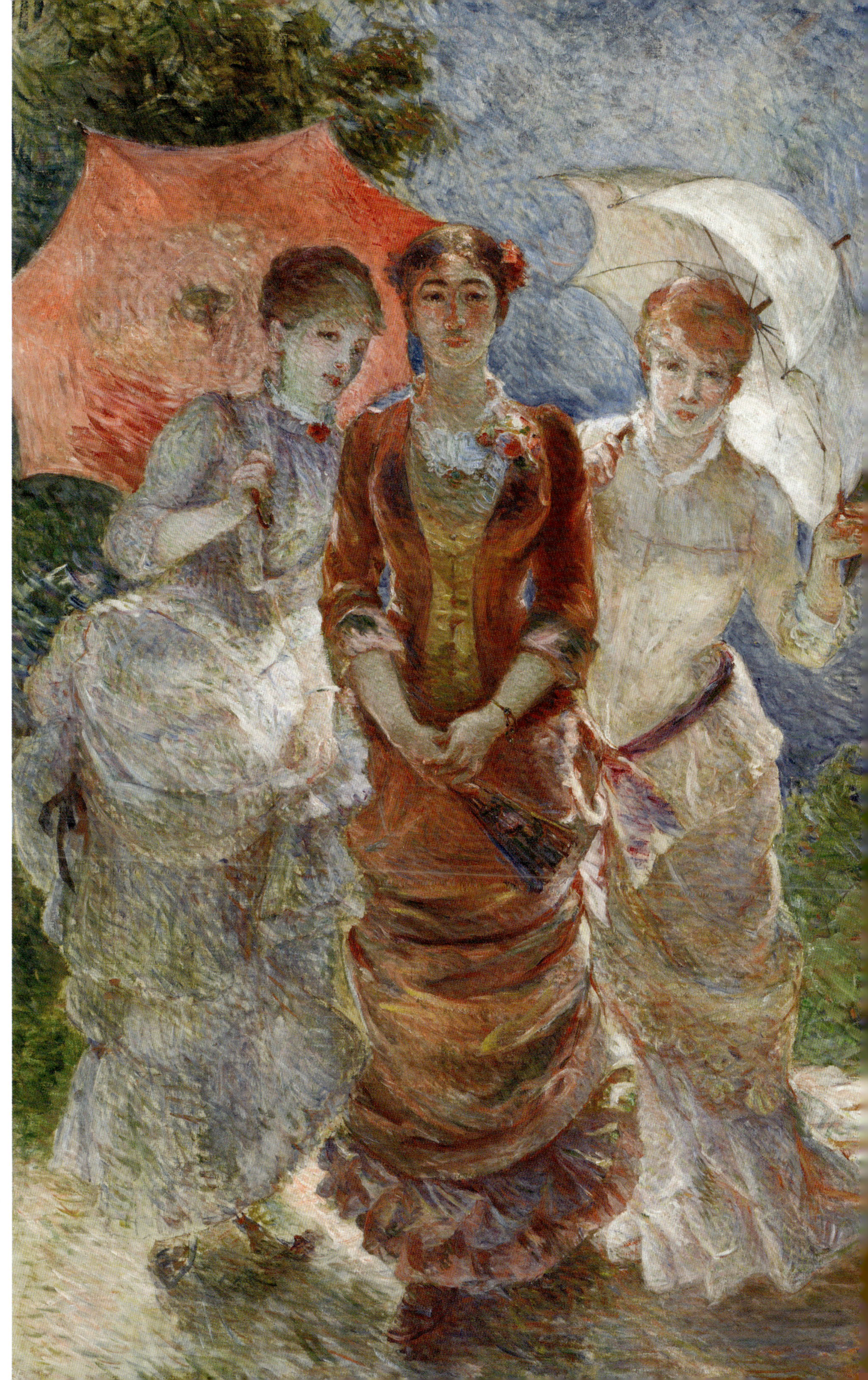

The cultural status of children, heretofore virtually ignored, changed in the late eighteenth century, just as women were attempting to find their place in the art world. Childhood came to be viewed as an important stage in the formation of subjectivity, as well as symbolizing the perpetuation of a lineage. New attention was lavished upon children, and their portrayal elicited strong emotional responses. Élisabeth Vigée Le Brun's *Self-Portrait with Her Daughter*, a great success at the Salon of 1787, thrust the artist into the public eye and become the iconic image for maternal tenderness.

This child-centric phenomenon became more pronounced in the nineteenth century, as revealed in the period's paintings: portraits of children or of parents with their children, and scenes depicting children at play. It so happened that these two developments—women's growing artistic aspirations and the new cult of childhood and motherhood—coincided, and it seemed naturally to fall on women painters to represent this burgeoning subject. From this point on, the relationship between feminine creativity and motherhood would become highly ambivalent. Popular opinion held that motherhood was a woman's sole destiny. As Arthur Schopenhauer proclaimed, "Women in truth exist entirely for the propagation of the race, and their destiny ends here."[1] Accordingly, women's involvement in the practice of art quickly came to be perceived as a danger to the family. Rosa Bonheur abandoned the idea of having a family, dedicating herself completely to her art. Meanwhile, her sister Juliette Peyrol Bonheur was praised in the *Journal des femmes artistes* for her ability to reconcile the then-opposing concepts of "great art" and "family duties."[2]

This ambivalence extended to the choice of subject matter. As both an artist and a woman, the female painter was encouraged to devote herself to themes that men seemed less capable of handling, especially childhood, and to place her sensibility in the service of a "maternalistic" message. More categorically, Joris-Karl Huysmans wrote that "only a woman can paint childhood. There is a particular feeling there that a man cannot render."[3] However restrictive and inaccurate these proclamations may have been (Edgar Degas, Claude Monet, and Pierre-Auguste Renoir also painted children), mothers, children, and families were subjects commonly chosen by women painters, who repeatedly engaged the religious prototype of the Madonna and Child, evoking the sacredness of procreation and the profound quality of motherhood. In both Cecilia Beaux's *The Last Days of Childhood* [plate 40] and Elizabeth Nourse's *A Mother* [plate 39], parent and child are depicted with an unparalleled level of intimacy that excludes any other presence—even that of the father—in a masterfully captured state of fusion.

Mary Cassatt—Huysmans's heroine—specialized in maternal scenes and portraits of children, instilling in them a practical realism that averts any temptation to sentimentality. With *Children Playing on the Beach* [plate 35], two toddlers appear isolated from the world and absorbed in their play, embodying in a nearly universal way the enchanted first years of life. Berthe Morisot made her daughter the center and driving force of her painterly practice through works such as *The Artist's Daughter, Julie, with her Nanny* [plate 36], while her delicate and allusive technique followed the girl's slow metamorphoses. At the other end of the spectrum, an unsettling mix of innocence and savagery characterizes Paula Modersohn-Becker's *Three Bathing Boys by the Canal* [plate 48]. Children, sometimes far from the protective cocoon of the family and a prime target of the modern world's violence and injustices, also represented a desire to revitalize painting through a return to primitivism, instinct, and archaism, which had been attributed to the child since Jean-Jacques Rousseau in the late eighteenth century.

1. Arthur Schopenhauer, *Parerga and Paralipomena: Short Philosophical Essays*, trans. E. F. J. Payne (Oxford: Oxford University Press, 1974).
2. *Journal des femmes artistes*, May 15, 1891, 4.
3. Joris-Karl Huysmans, "L'Exposition des Indépendents en 1881," in *L'art moderne* (1883; repr., Paris: Stock, 1902), 256.

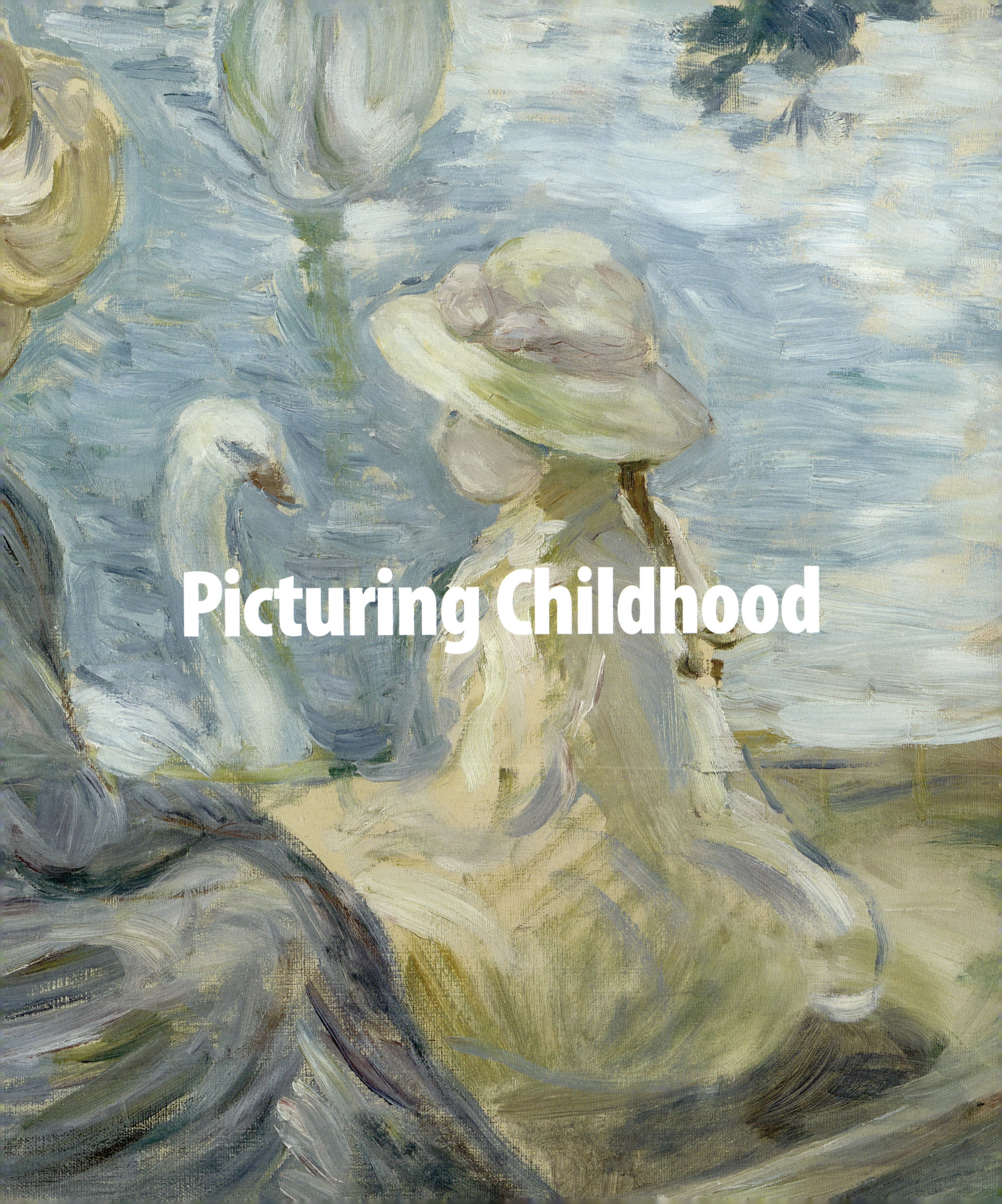
Picturing Childhood

PLATE 35 MARY CASSATT, *CHILDREN PLAYING ON THE BEACH*, 1884

Oil on canvas, 38⅜ × 29¼ in. (97.4 × 74.2 cm). National Gallery of Art, Washington, DC, Ailsa Mellon Bruce Collection, 1970.17.19

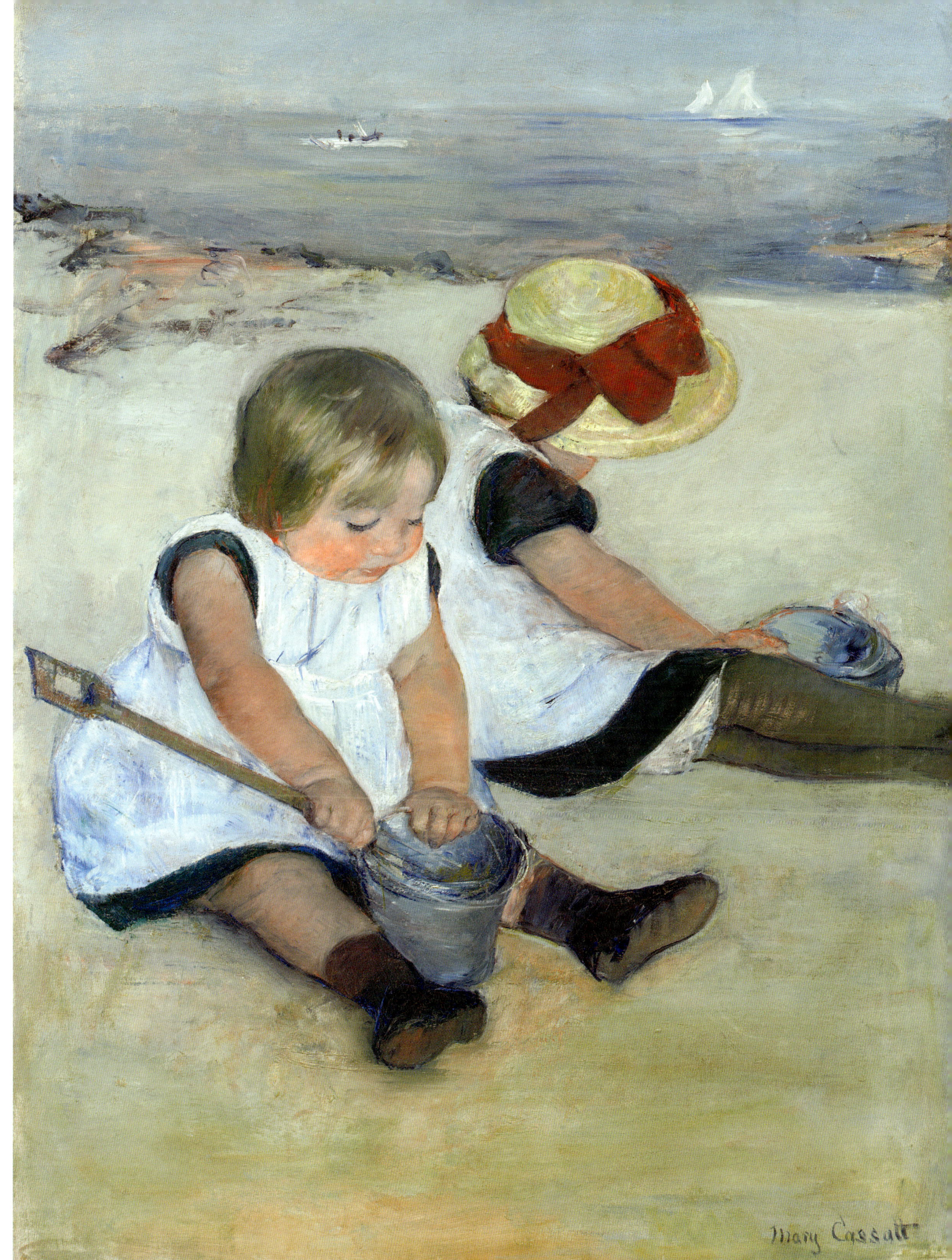
Mary Cassatt

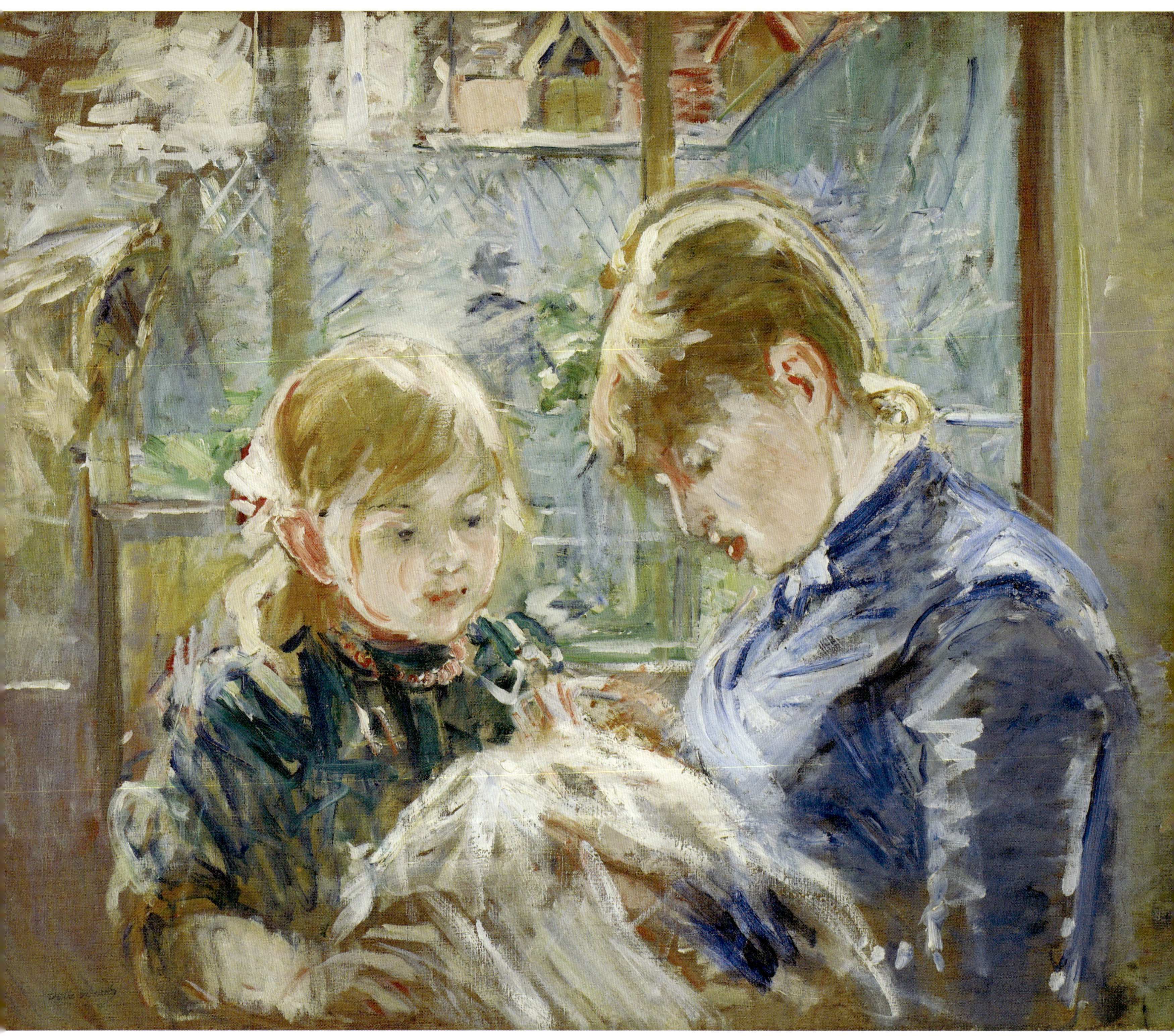

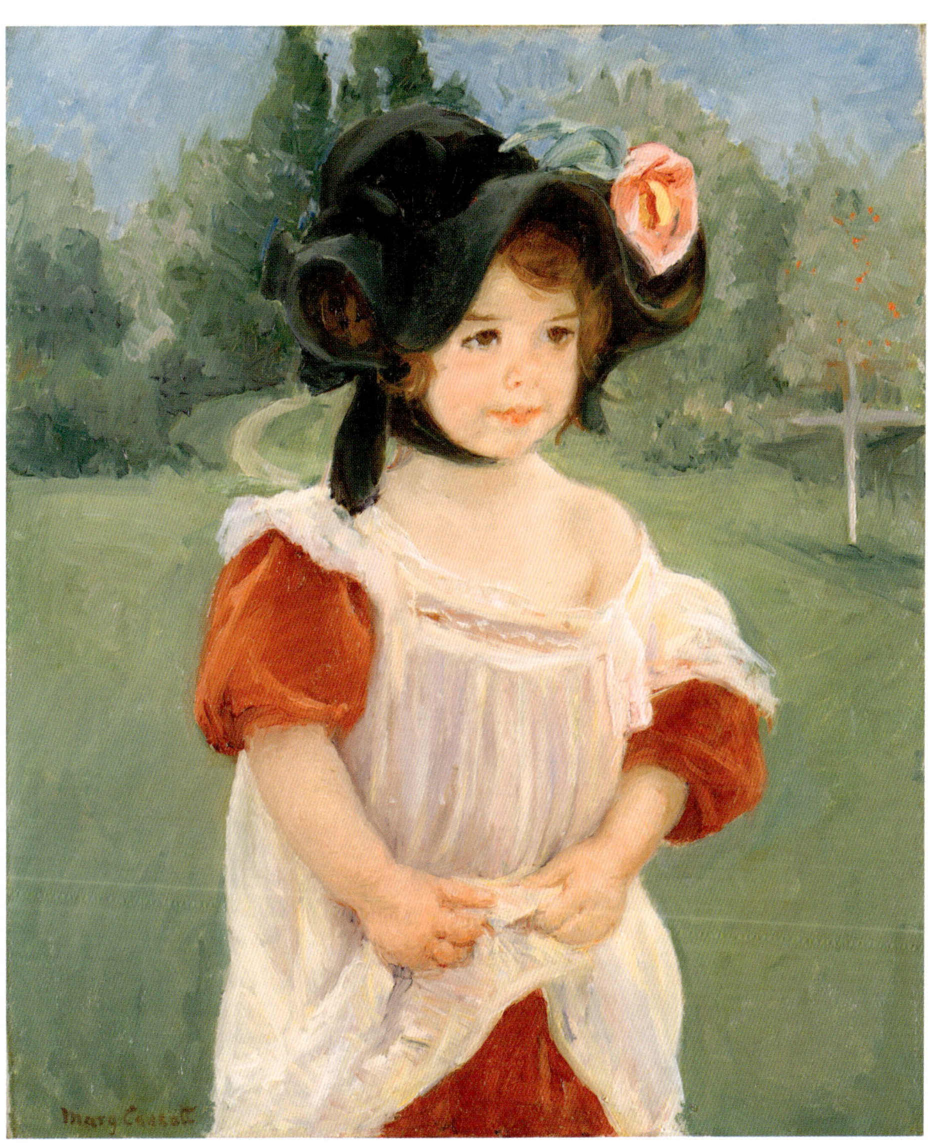

PLATE 36 BERTHE MORISOT, *THE ARTIST'S DAUGHTER, JULIE, WITH HER NANNY*, CA. 1884

Oil on canvas, 22½ × 28 in. (57.2 × 71.1 cm). Minneapolis Institute of Art, The John R. Van Derlip Fund, 96.40

PLATE 37 MARY CASSATT, *SPRING: MARGOT STANDING IN A GARDEN* (*FILLETTE DANS UN JARDIN*), 1900

Oil on canvas , 26¾ × 22¾ in. (67.9 × 57.8 cm). Metropolitan Museum of Art, New York, Bequest of Ruth Alms Barnard, 1981, 1982.119.2

PLATE 38 CECILIA BEAUX, *ERNESTA (CHILD WITH NURSE)*, 1894

Oil on canvas, 50½ × 38⅛ in. (128.3 × 96.8 cm). Metropolitan Museum of Art, New York, Maria DeWitt Jesup Fund, 1965, 65.49

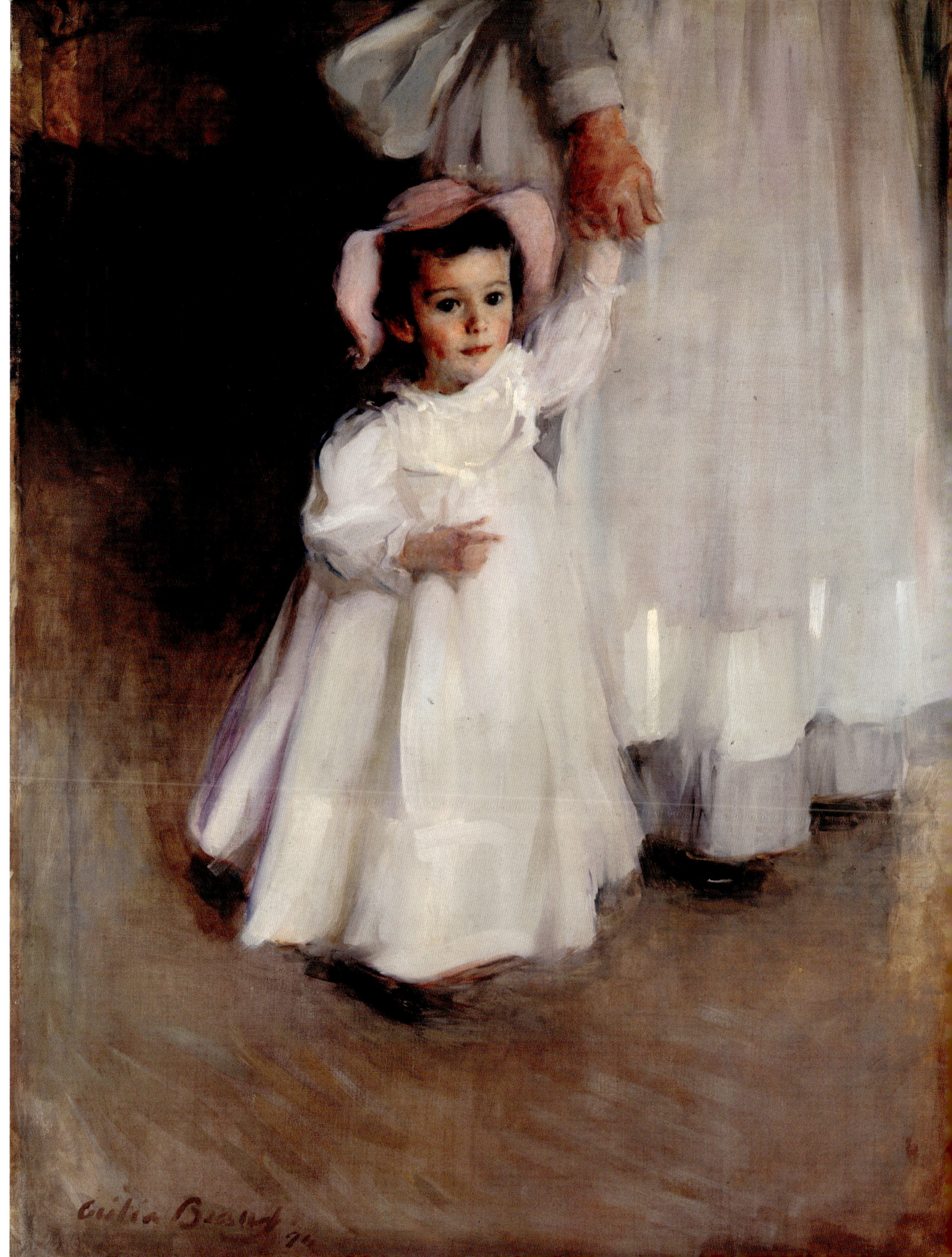
Cecilia Beaux
'94

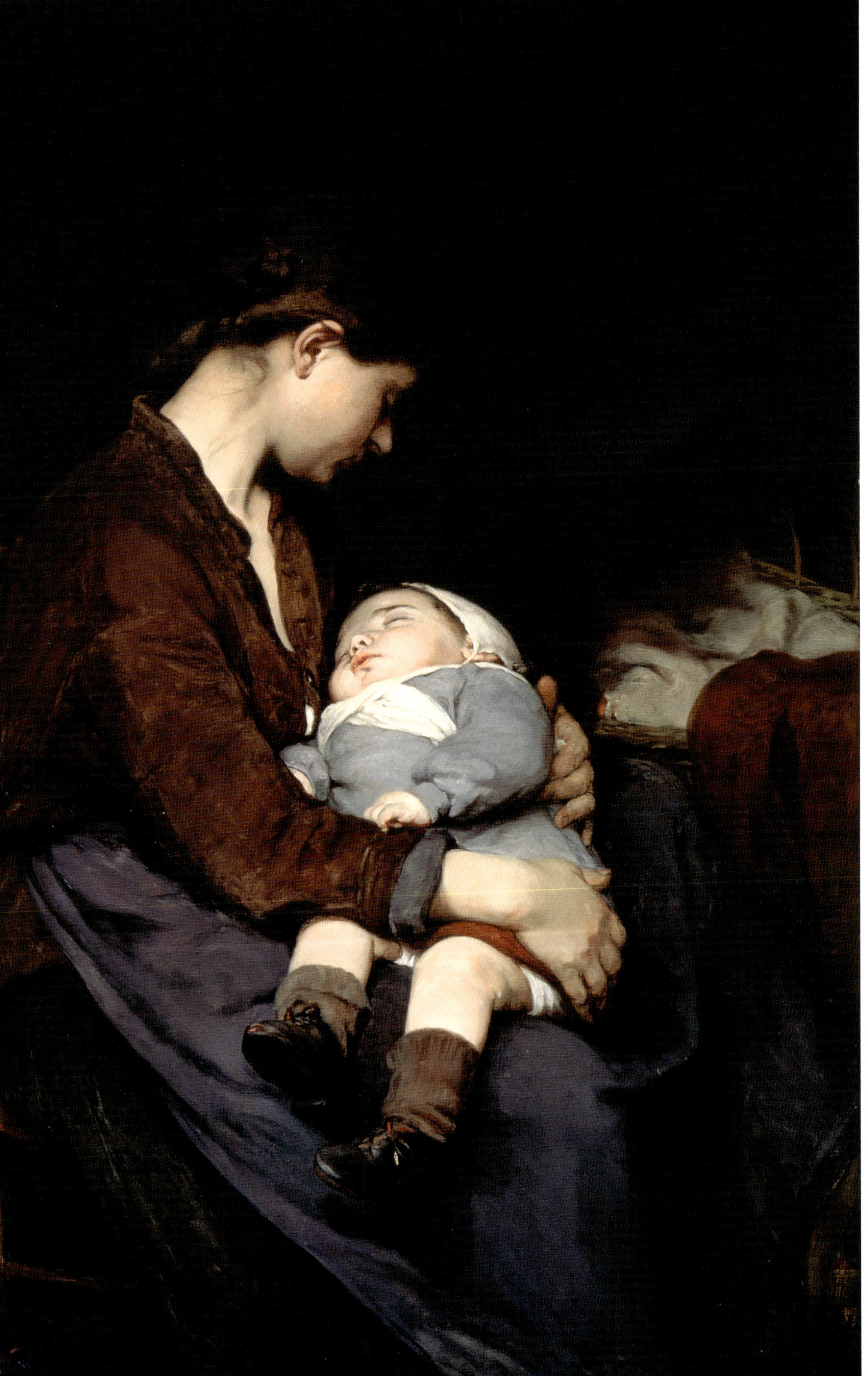

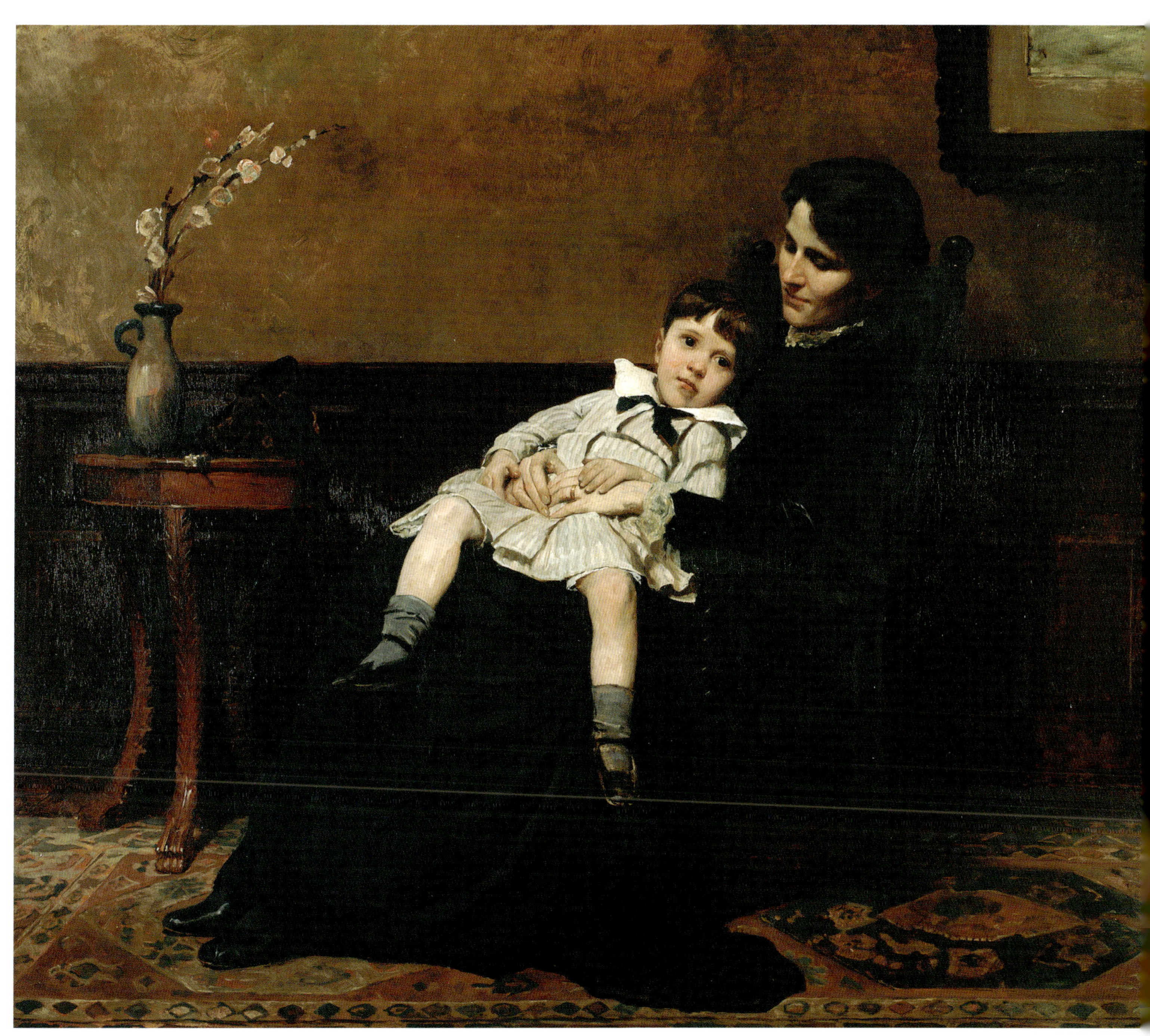

PLATE 39 ELIZABETH NOURSE, *A MOTHER* (*UNE MÈRE*), 1888

Oil on canvas, 45½ × 32 in. (115.6 × 81.3 cm). Cincinnati Art Museum, Gift of The Procter & Gamble Company, 2003.93

PLATE 40 CECILIA BEAUX, *THE LAST DAYS OF CHILDHOOD* (*LES DERNIERS JOURS D'ENFANCE*), 1883–85

Oil on canvas, 45¾ × 54 in. (116.2 × 137.2 cm). Pennsylvania Academy of the Fine Arts, Philadelphia, Gift of Cecilia Drinker Saltonstall, 1989.21

PLATE 41 PAULA MODERSOHN-BECKER, *NURSING MOTHER IN FRONT OF BIRCH FOREST*, 1905

Oil on cardboard, cradled, 28¼ × 20 in. (71.8 × 50.8 cm). Private collection, Bedford, NY

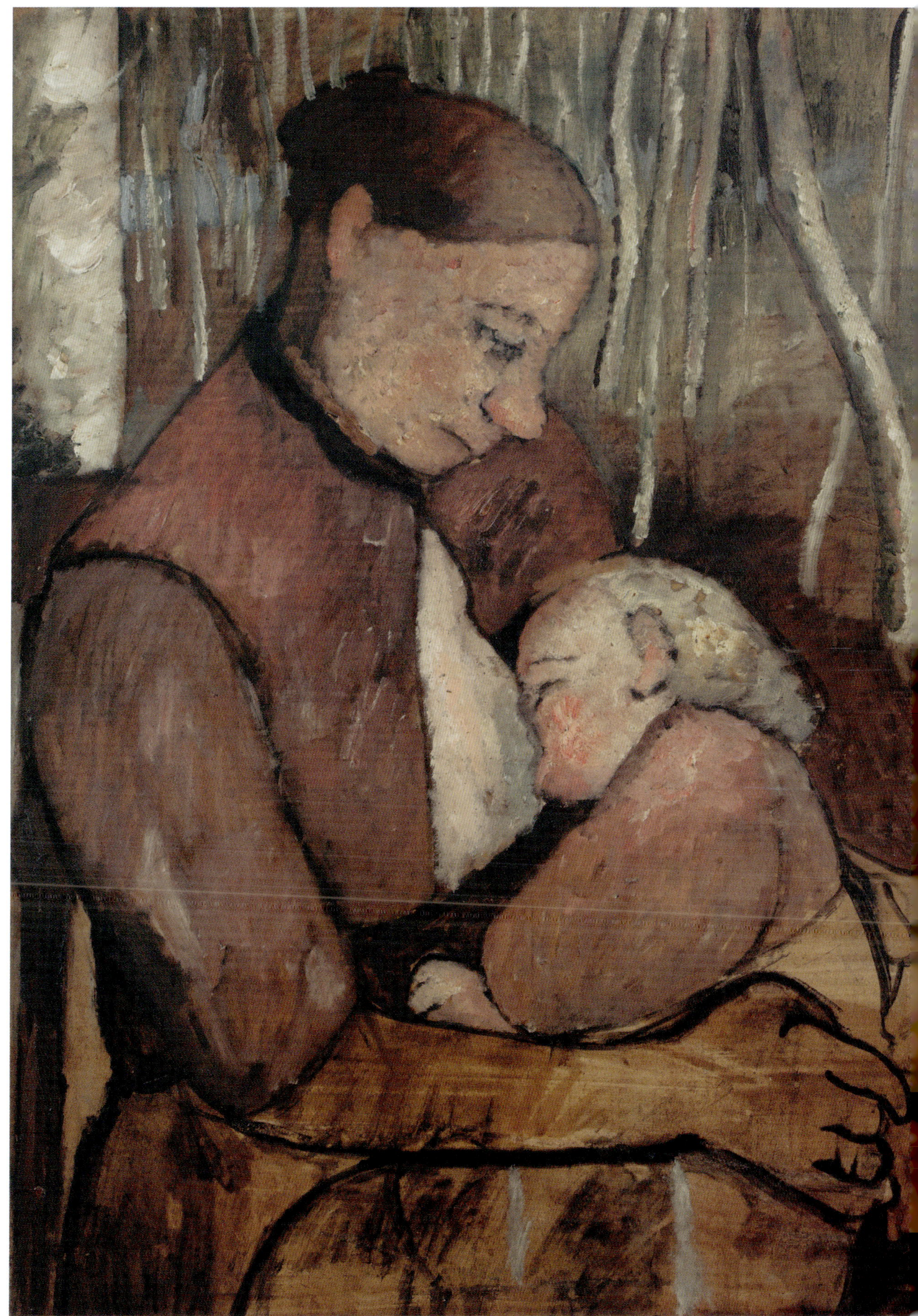

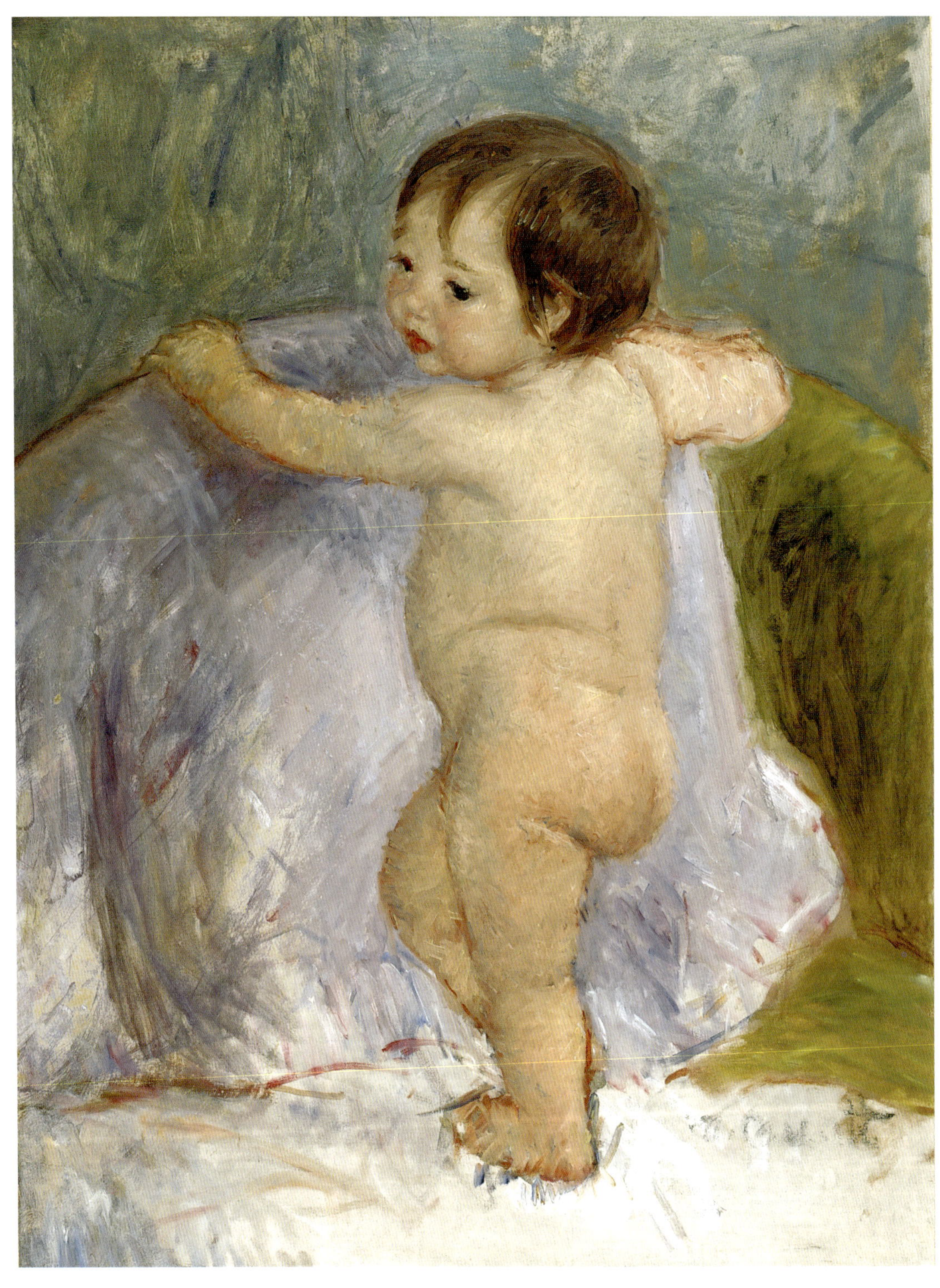

PLATE 42 MARY CASSATT, *THE CHILD*, CA. 1905

Oil on canvas, 29⅞ × 21⅝ in. (75.9 × 54.9 cm). Speed Art Museum, Gift of Mrs. Blakemore Wheeler, 1964.22

PLATE 43 MARY CASSATT, *CHILD PICKING A FRUIT* (*ENFANT CUEILLANT UN FRUIT*), 1893

Oil on canvas, 39½ × 25¾ in. (100.3 × 65.4 cm). Virginia Museum of Fine Arts, Richmond, Gift of Ivor and Anne Massey, 75.18

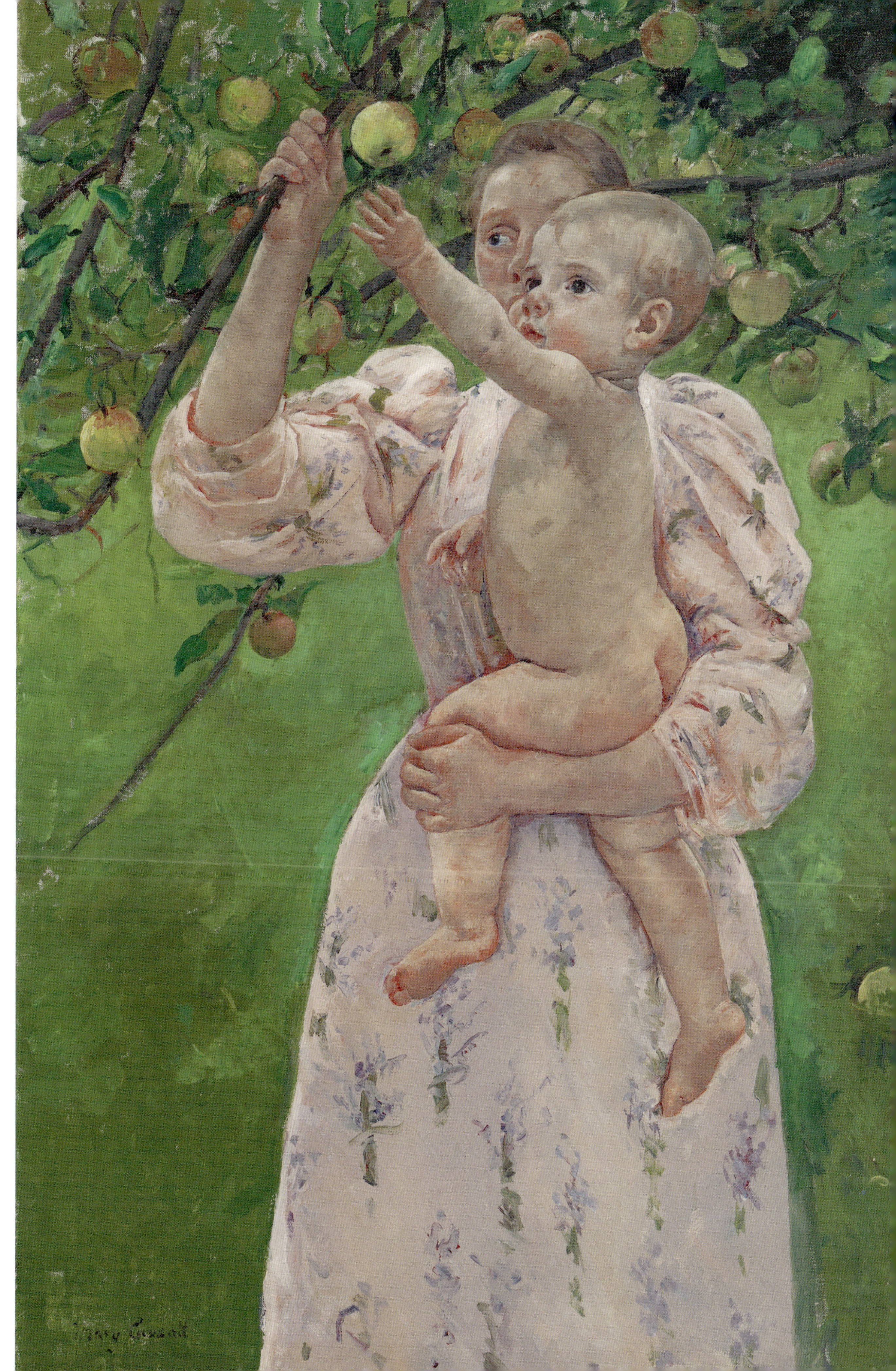

PLATE 44 BERTHE MORISOT, *ON THE LAKE* (*SUR LE LAC*), CA. 1884

Oil on canvas, 25½ × 30½ in. (64.8 × 77.5 cm). Private collection, Denver, CO

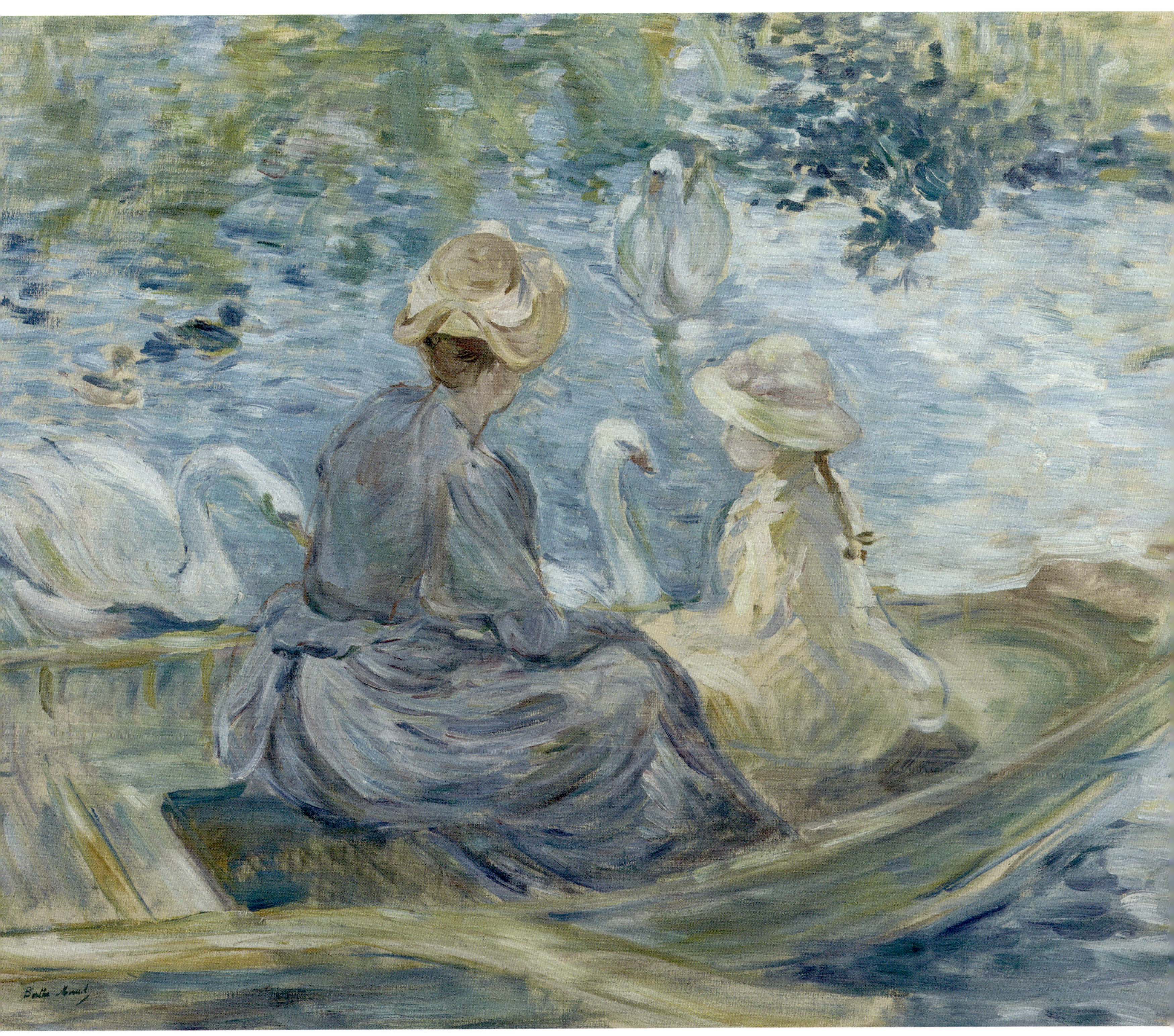

PLATE 45 BERTHE MORISOT, *GIRLS AT THE WINDOW (JEANNE AND EDMA BODEAU)* (*FILLETES À LA FENÊTRE*), 1892

Oil on canvas, 57⅝ × 35 in. (146.5 × 89 cm). Collection of Bruce and Robbi Toll

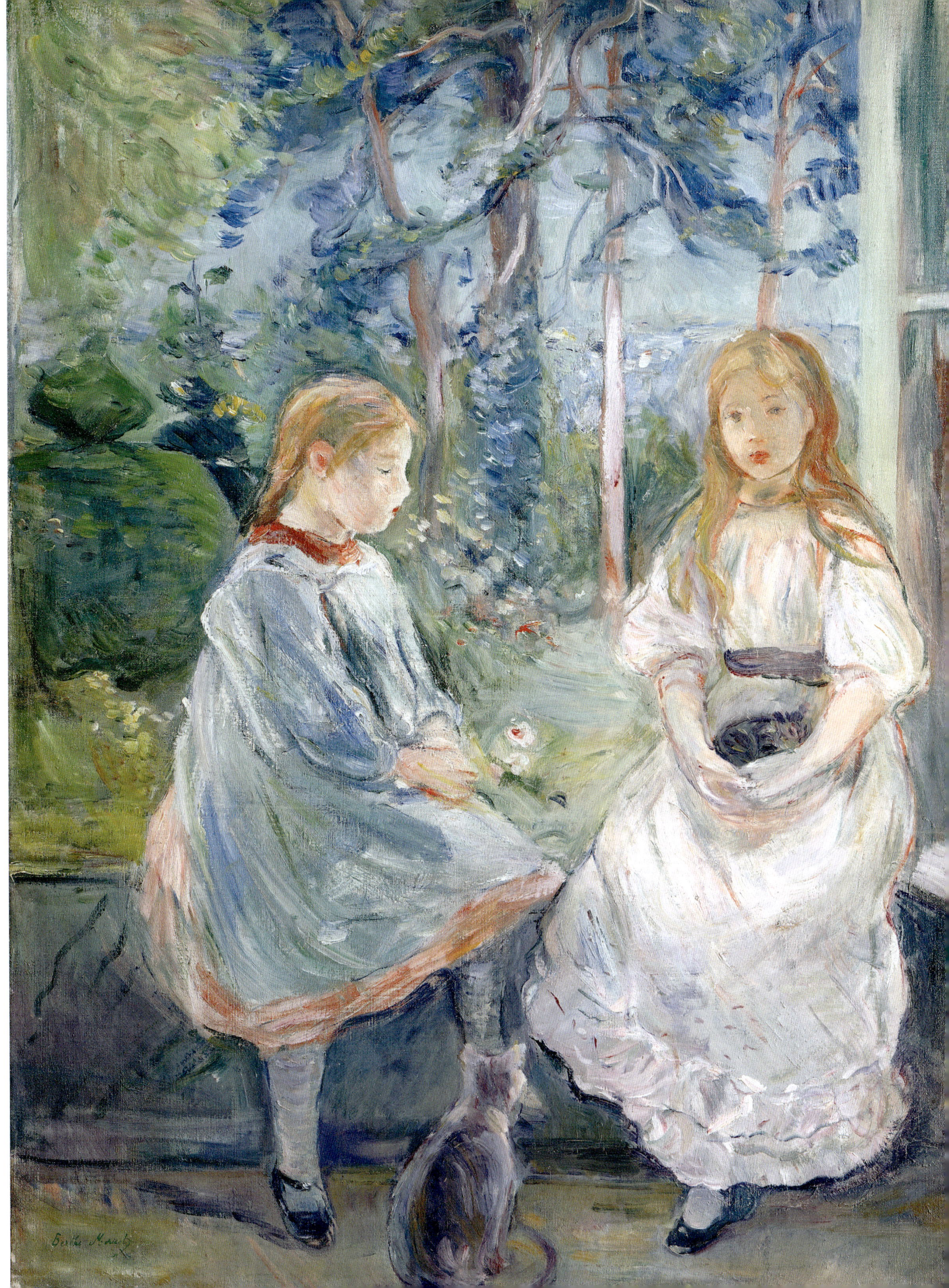

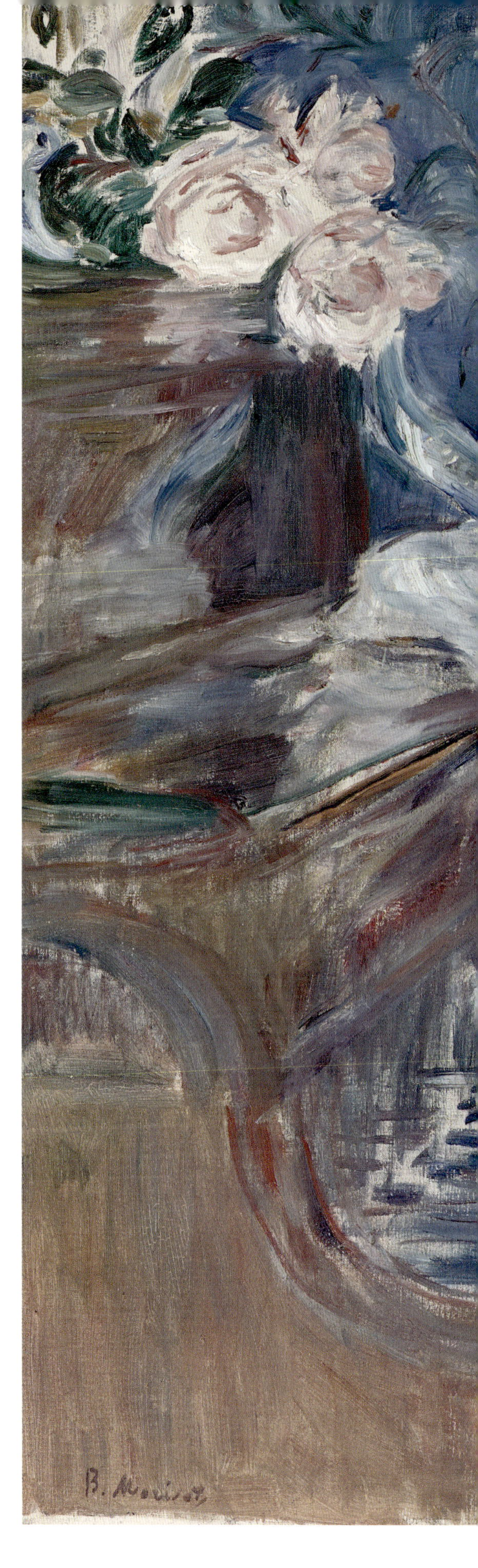

PLATE 46 BERTHE MORISOT, *LUCIE LEON AT THE PIANO*, 1892

Oil on canvas, 25⅝ × 31½ in. (65 × 80 cm). Collection of Drs. Tobia and Morton Mower, Denver, CO

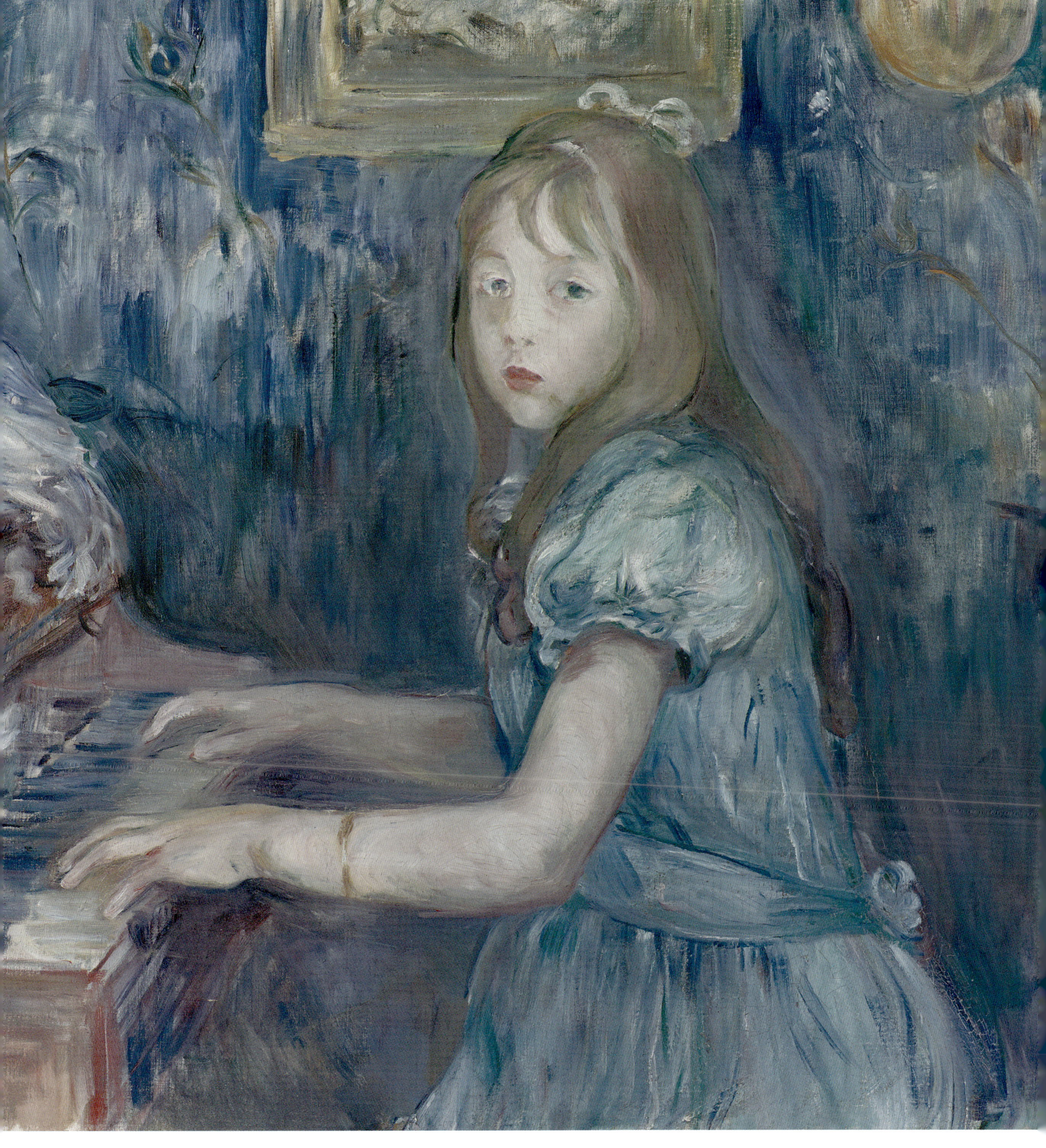

PLATE 47 HARRIET BACKER, *BIG BROTHER PLAYING*, 1890

Oil on canvas, 19⅞ × 24¼ in. (50.5 × 61.5 cm). Gothenburg Museum of Art, Sweden, GKM 0798

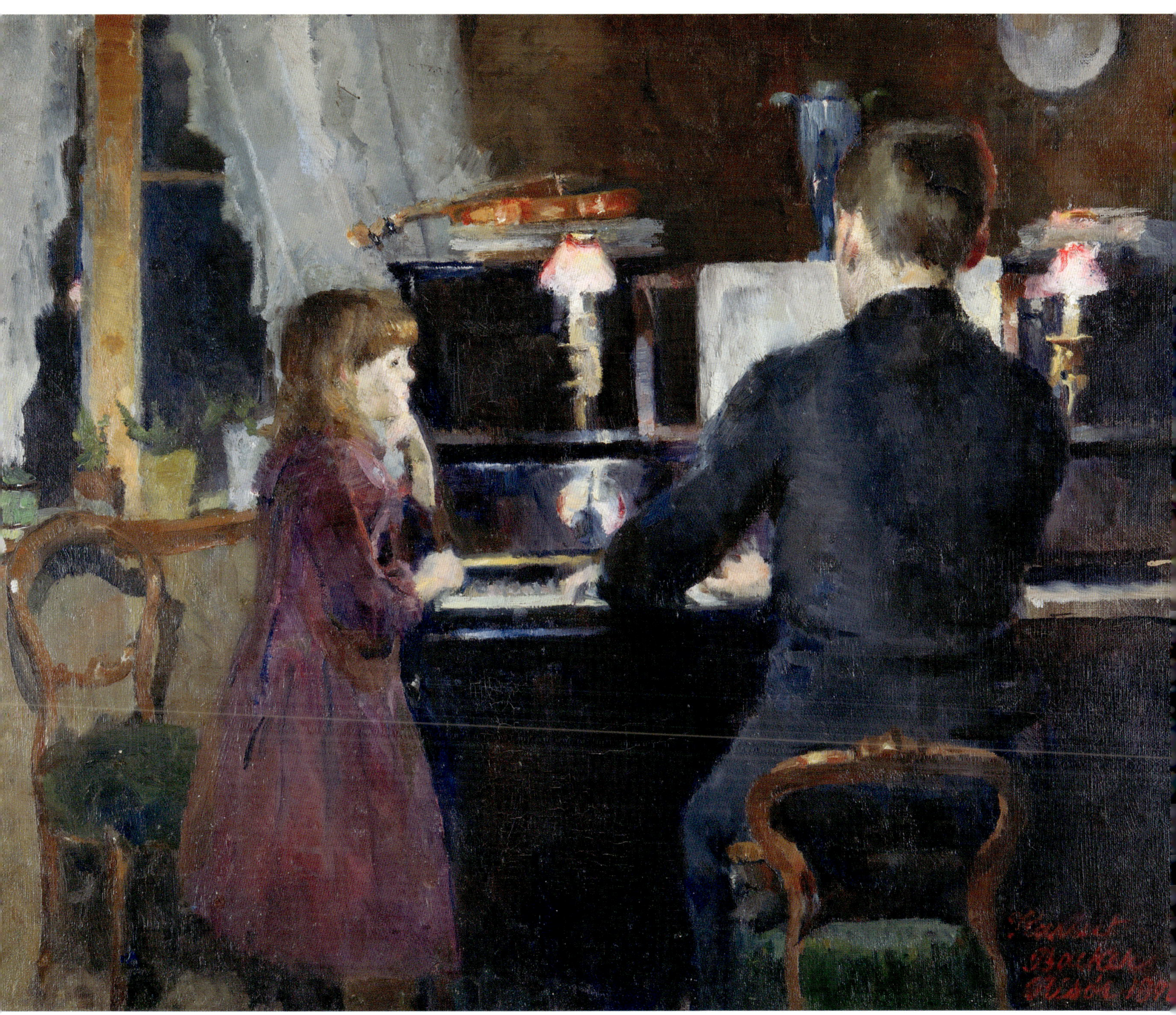

PLATE 48 PAULA MODERSOHN-BECKER, *THREE BATHING BOYS BY THE CANAL*, 1901

Oil on cardboard, mounted on wood, 21⅜ × 15½ in. (54.3 × 39.4 cm). Courtesy Galerie St. Etienne, New York

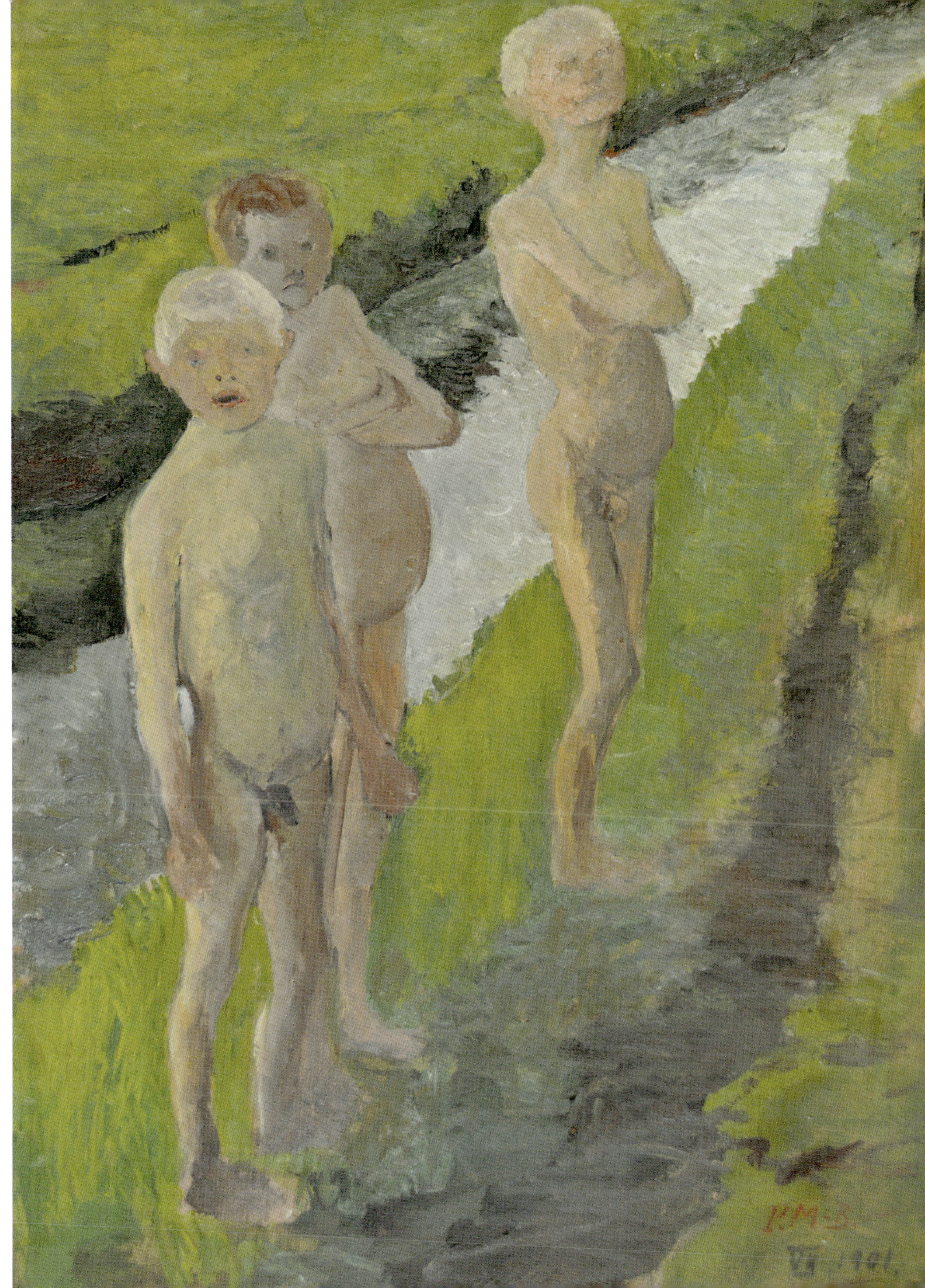
P.M-B.
VII. 1901.

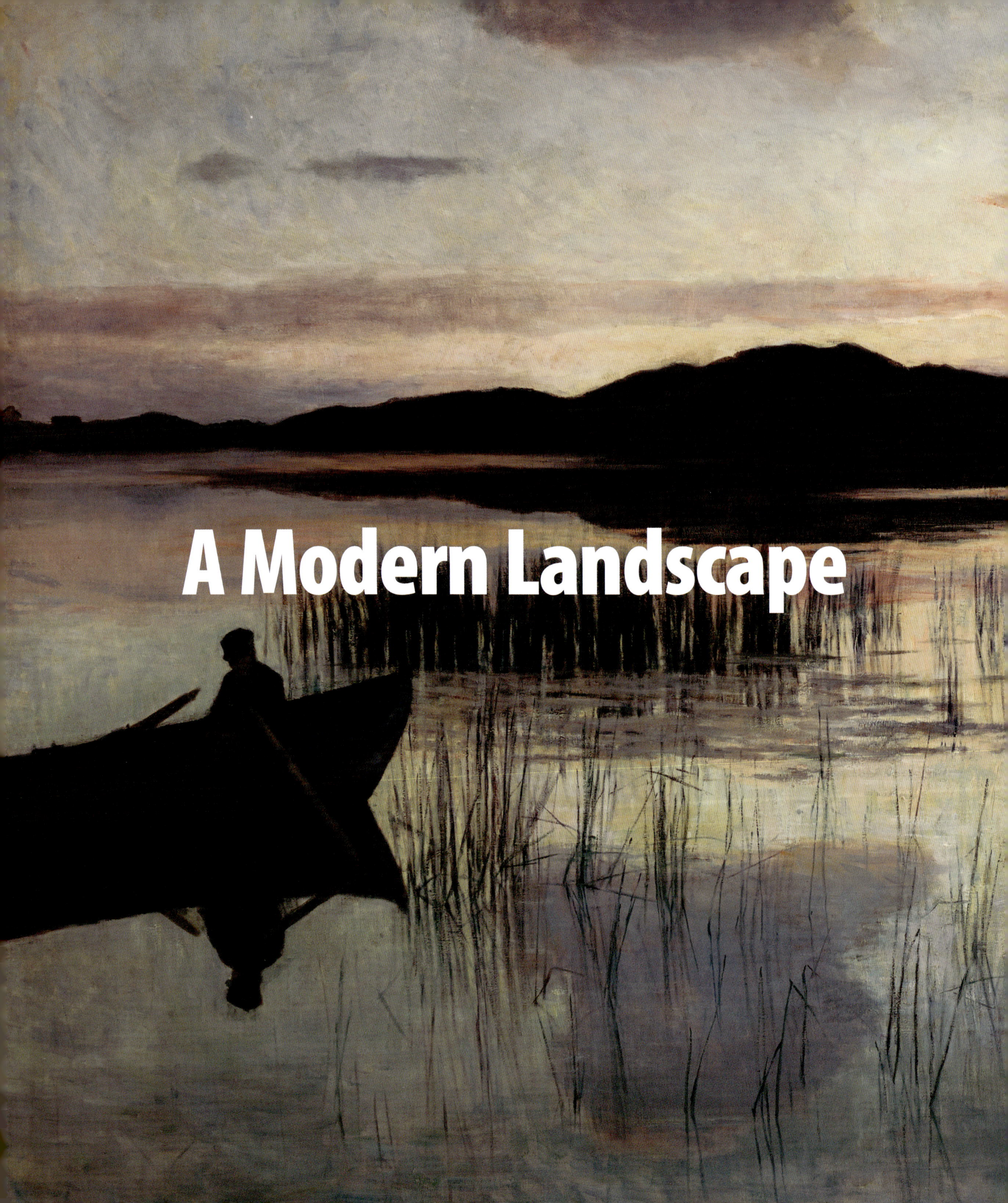

A Modern Landscape

A vast distance separates the elegant and refined landscape paintings expected of well-brought-up women artists and the varied and robust works they ultimately produced, thereby contributing to the renewal of a genre that had been codified since the founding of the Académie Royale de Peinture et de Sculpture two centuries before. Women artists were active participants in the shift from Realism to Impressionism and Symbolism during the late nineteenth century.

Berthe Morisot visited Camille Corot at his country house in Ville d'Avray and learned from him how to paint outdoors. Eventually, she would exhibit alongside Claude Monet, Camille Pissarro, and Pierre-Auguste Renoir, and show Édouard Manet how to paint the brightness of daylight. Morisot was captivated by gardens—nature writ small—which competed in her art with human figures: children, young women, mothers, nannies, and fathers—even her own daughter and husband in *A Lesson in the Garden* [plate 56]. Morisot's landscapes are those of a city dweller in love with flowers, trees, lakes, and rowboats. Through landscape painting, women artists often demonstrated their broader engagement with the modern world: the banks of the Seine, the dynamism of the city, which charmed Anna Bilińska in *Unter den Linden in Berlin* [plate 58], and the beaches of Normandy, depicted by Eva Gonzalès, and of Brittany, by the Swedish artist Mina Carlson-Bredberg.

Interest in local scenery, which caught the eye of painters who had returned to their native region or country after time in Paris, served to revitalize landscape painting and renew women's relationship to nature. Harriet Backer, Fanny Churberg, and Hanna Pauli found grandeur and mystery in the landscapes of Scandinavia or Finland. Kitty Kielland's *Stokkavannet* [plate 50] balances an evocation of the atmospheric light effects on placid water with a precise attention to Stokkavannet lake, an area of Norway relatively unspoiled by human activities.

The melancholic realism of Marie Cazin's *Evening* [plate 59] and Fanny Churberg's *Waterfall* [plate 53] revealed that Impressionism was not the only mode of approach to landscape. Although most of the artists who trained in Paris then went on to plant their easels around the villages of Île de France, Brittany, or Normandy, others' concerns extended beyond the strict observation of light. They became part of the major current of European Symbolism; Helene Schjerfbeck's *The Door* [plate 60] attests to the potent role played by women in this movement. This painting, which educes feelings of closure or withdrawal from the interior landscape of the Chapelle de Trémalo in Pont-Aven, counters the quest that impelled Schjerfbeck and her female contemporaries to cross the physical and symbolic borders of the garden and enter the wilds. The impulse to fulfill the dual role assigned them was summed up by John Ruskin in his famous 1864 lecture, "Lilies: Of Queens' Gardens," when he posited that women should not only maintain the home and its surroundings but also understand and preserve the larger forces and secrets of nature.

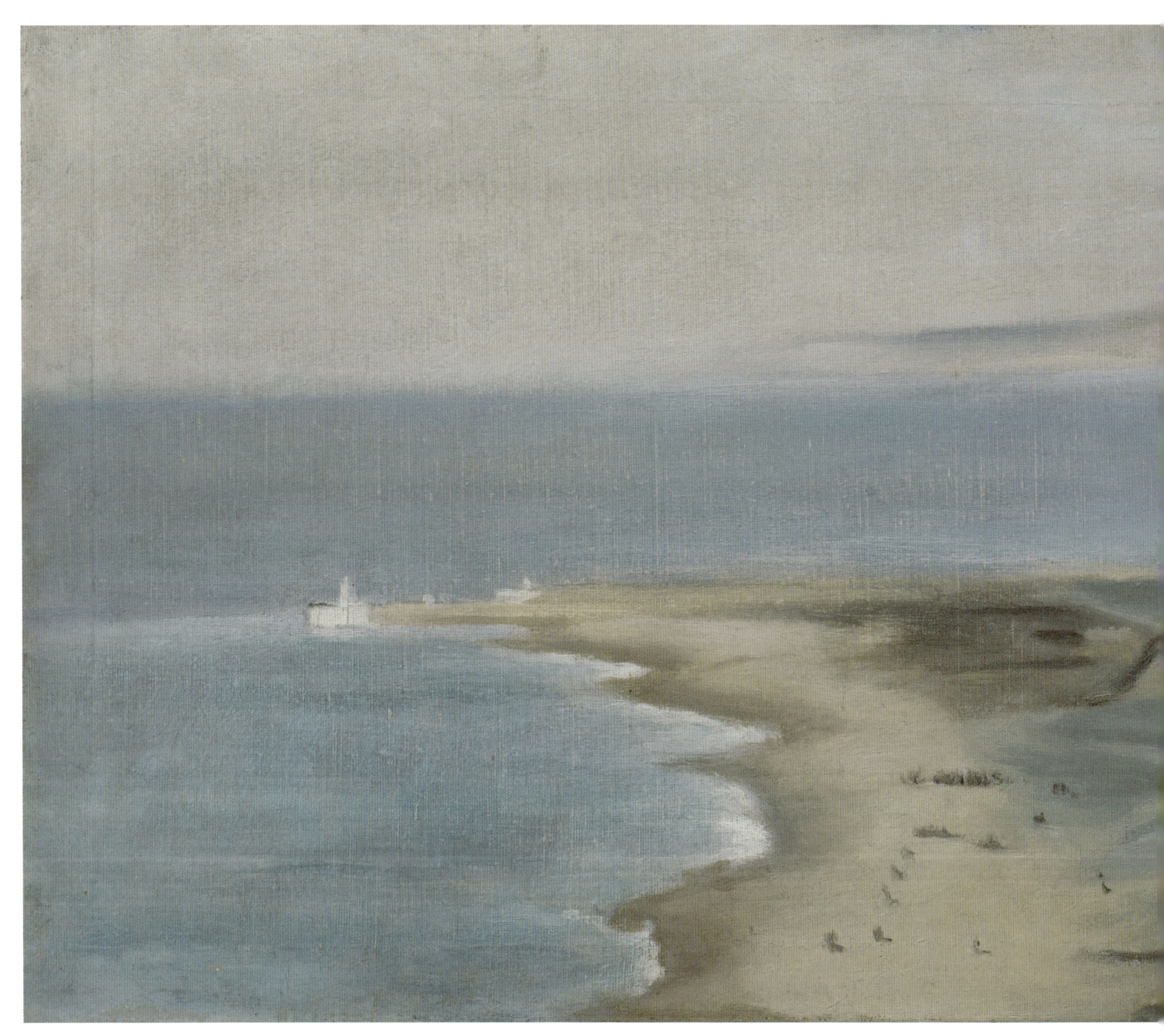

PLATE 49 EVA GONZALÈS, *THE BEACH OF DIEPPE (VIEW FROM THE CHÂTEAU)* (*LA PLAGE DE DIEPPE, VUE DEPUIS LA FALAISE OUEST*), 1871–72
Oil on canvas, 11¼ × 27½ in. (28.5 × 70 cm). Château-Musée de Dieppe, France, 973.15.1

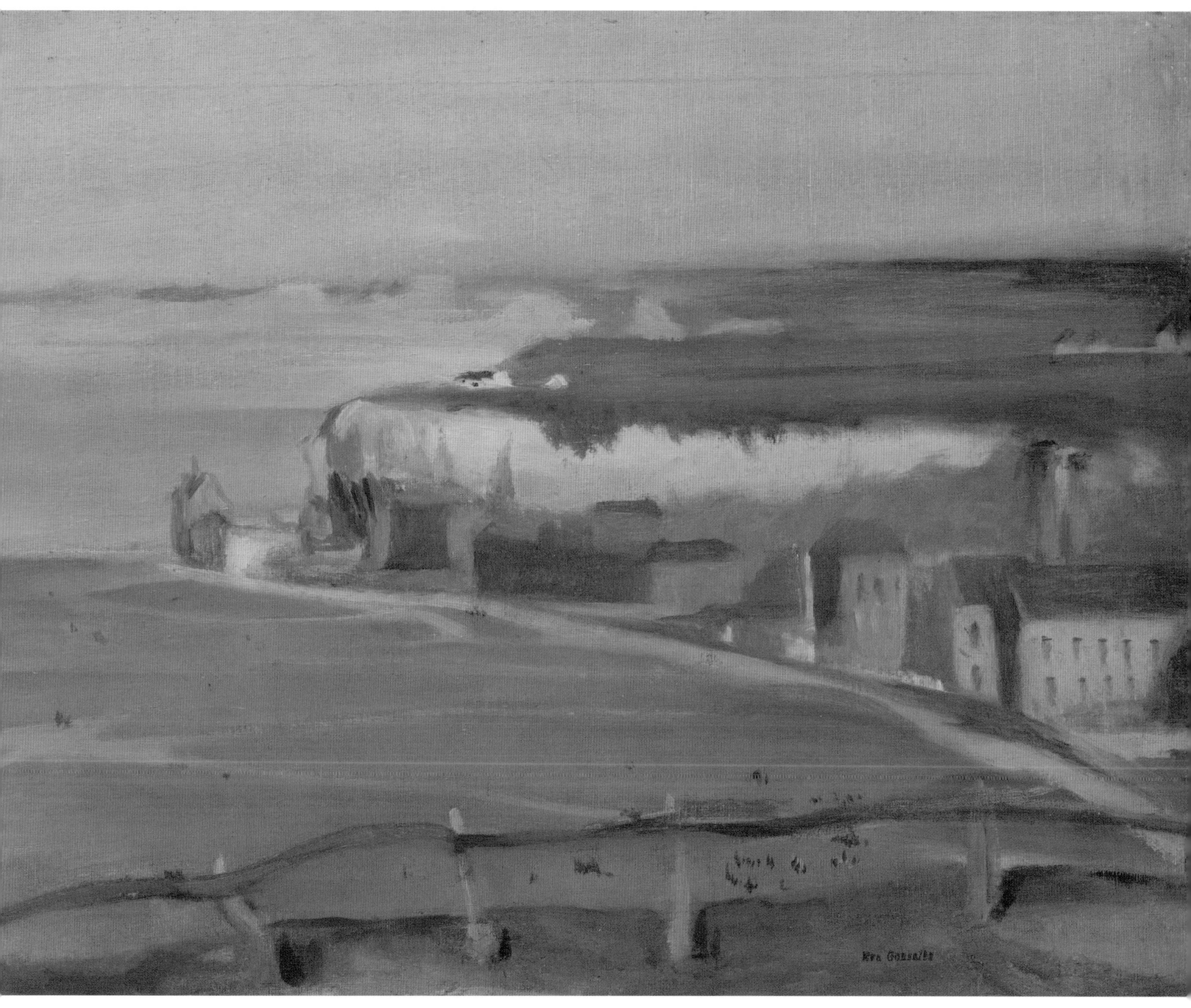

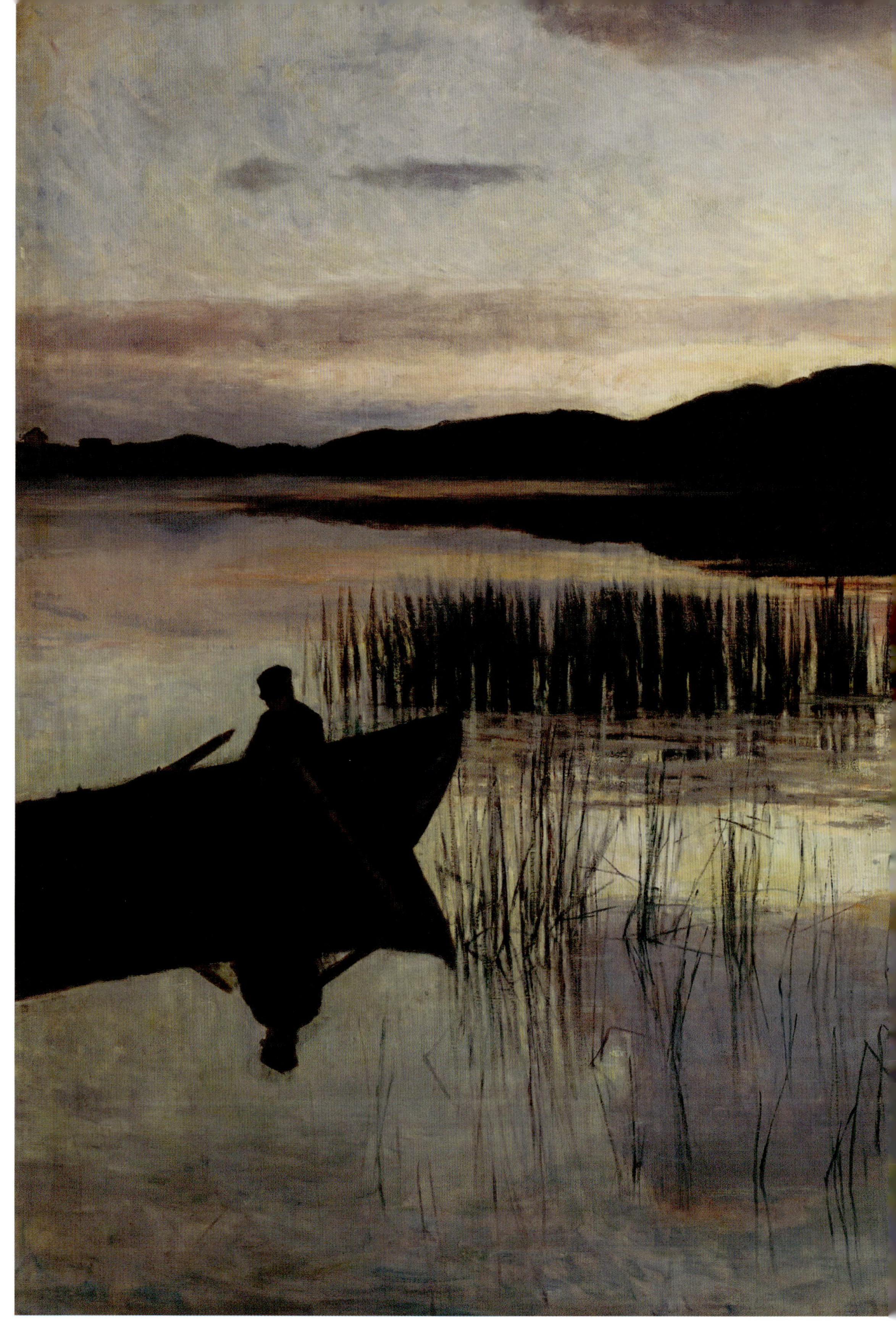

PLATE 50 KITTY KIELLAND, *STOKKAVANNET*, 1890

Oil on canvas, 45¼ × 78¾ in. (115 × 200 cm). The Royal Collection, Oslo, DKS.001128

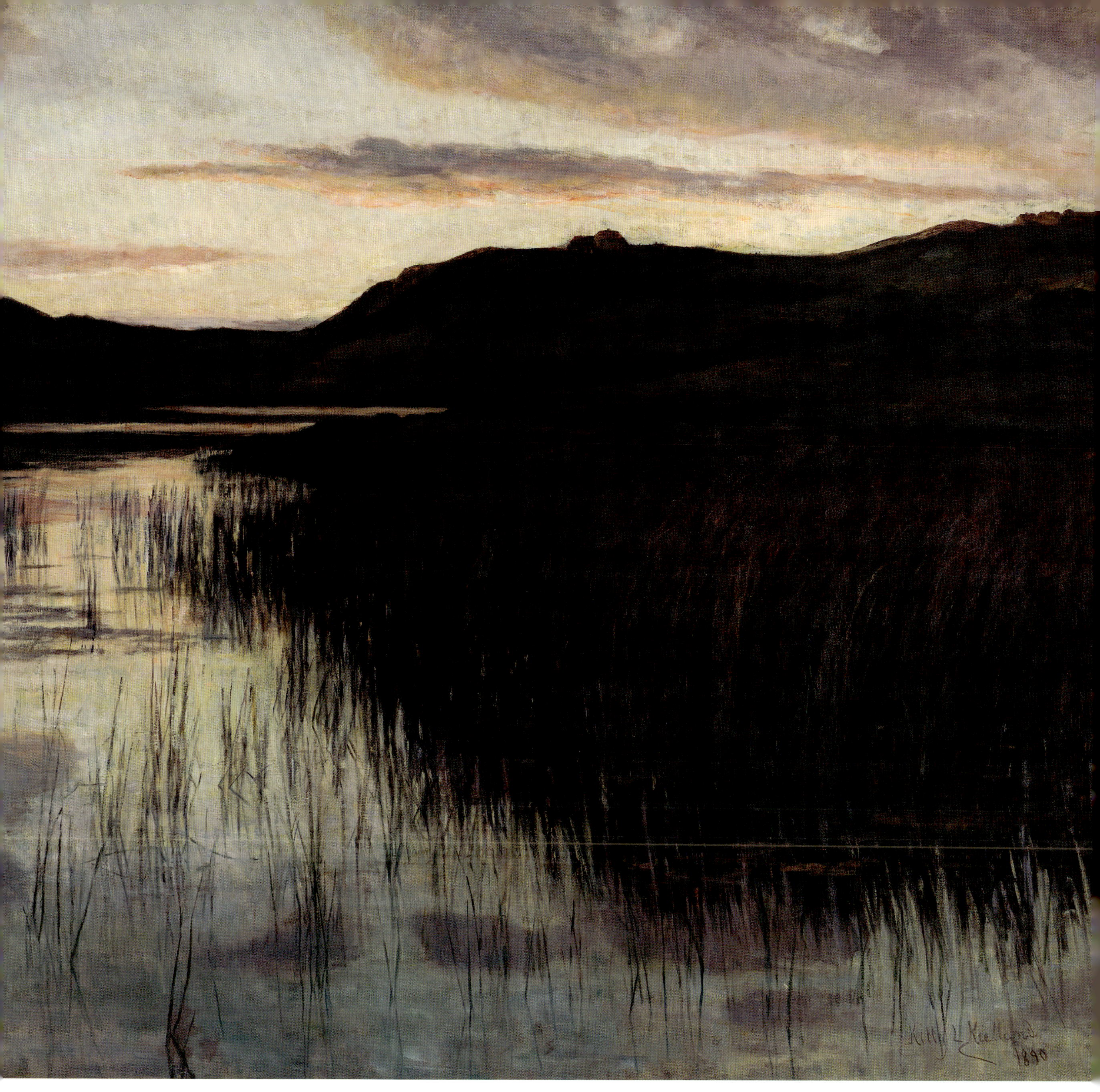
Kitty L. Kielland
1890

PLATE 51 **KITTY KIELLAND, *VIEW OF JOTUNHEIMEN*, 1896**

Oil on canvas, 20 × 37¾ in. (50.8 × 94.6 cm). Private collection, Maryland

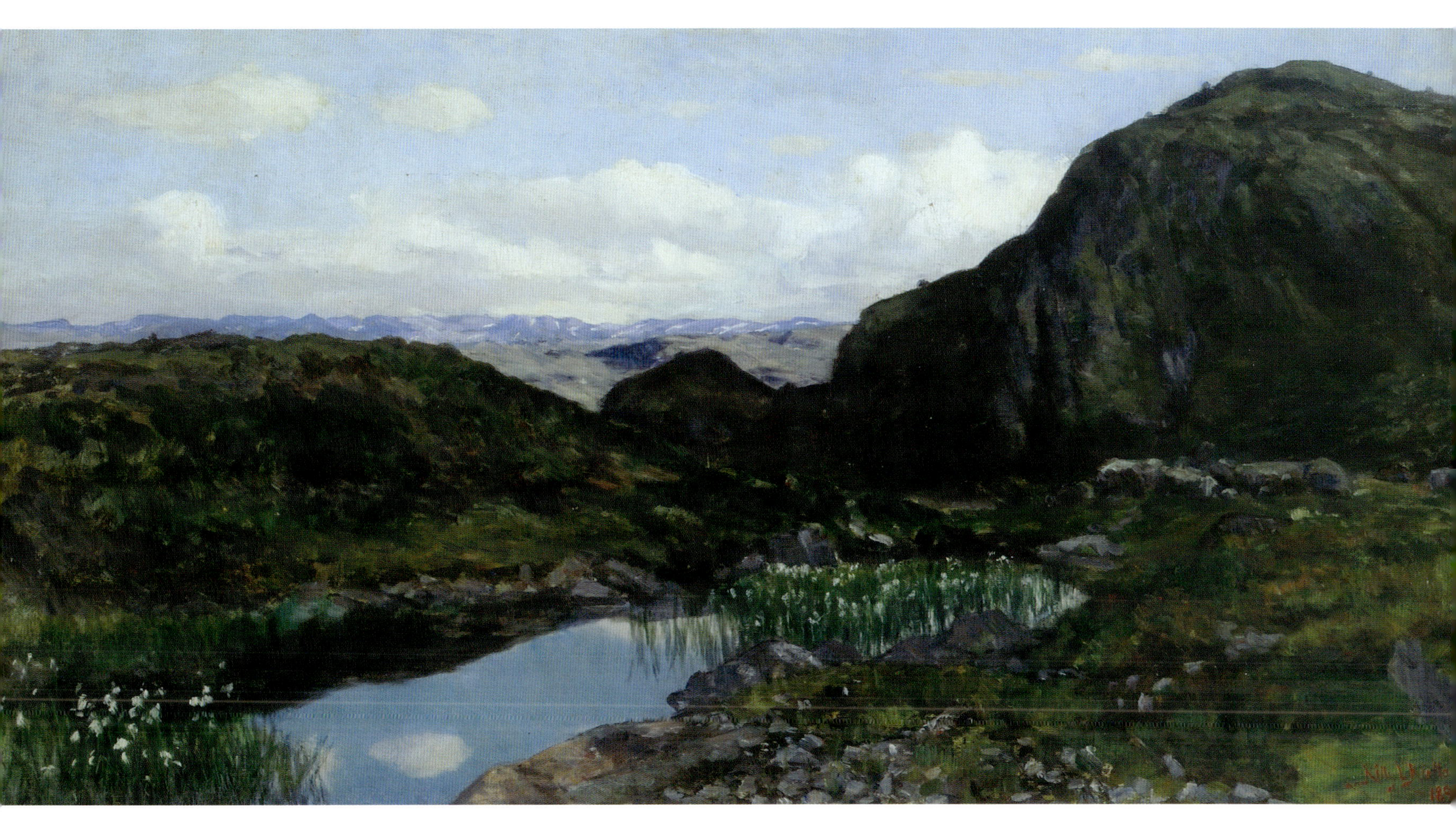

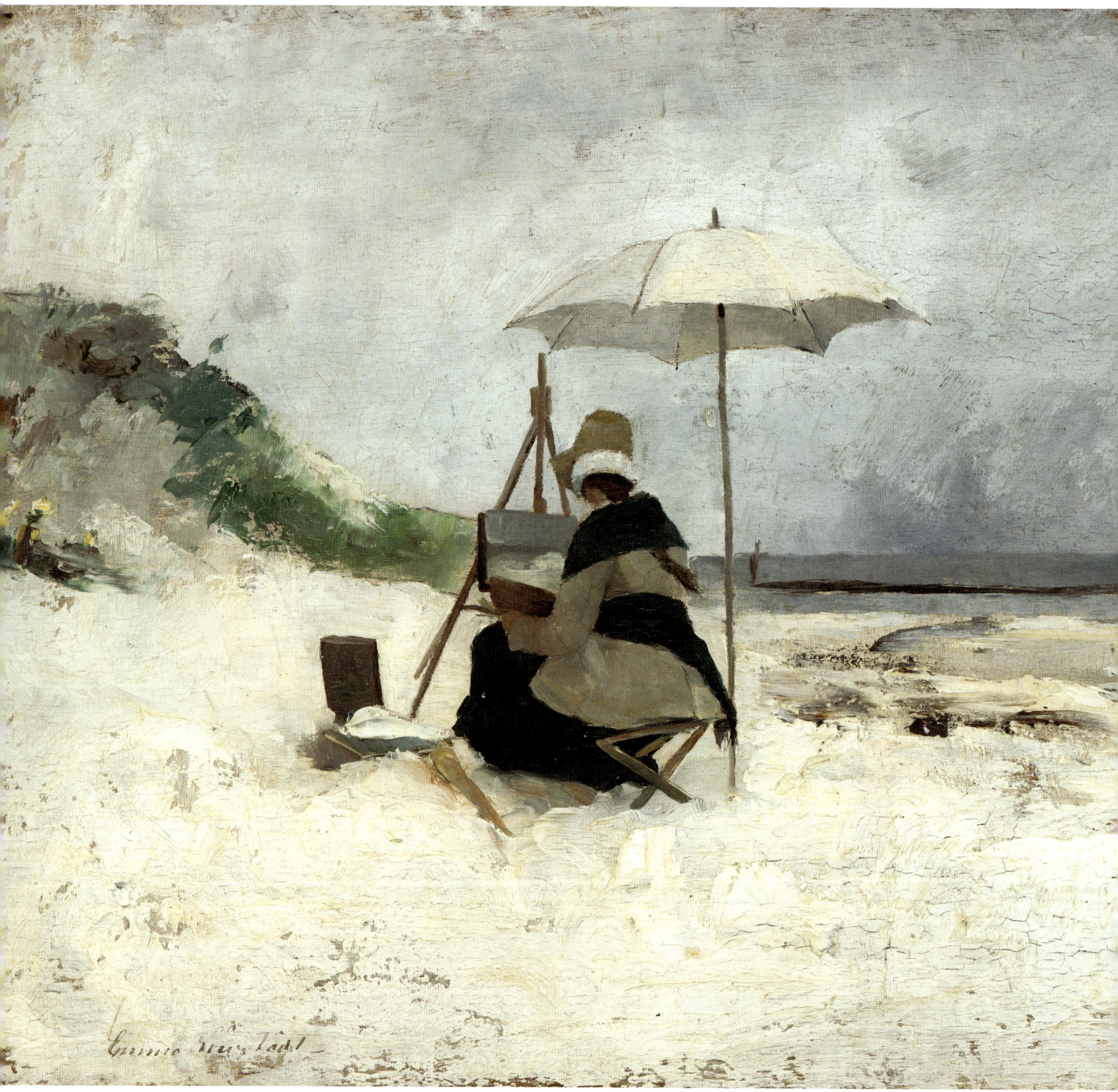

PLATE 52 EMMA LÖWSTÄDT-CHADWICK, *BEACH PARASOL, BRITTANY (PORTRAIT OF AMANDA SIDWALL)*, 1880
Oil on panel, 11⅜ × 19¾ in. (29 × 50 cm). Private collection, Stockholm

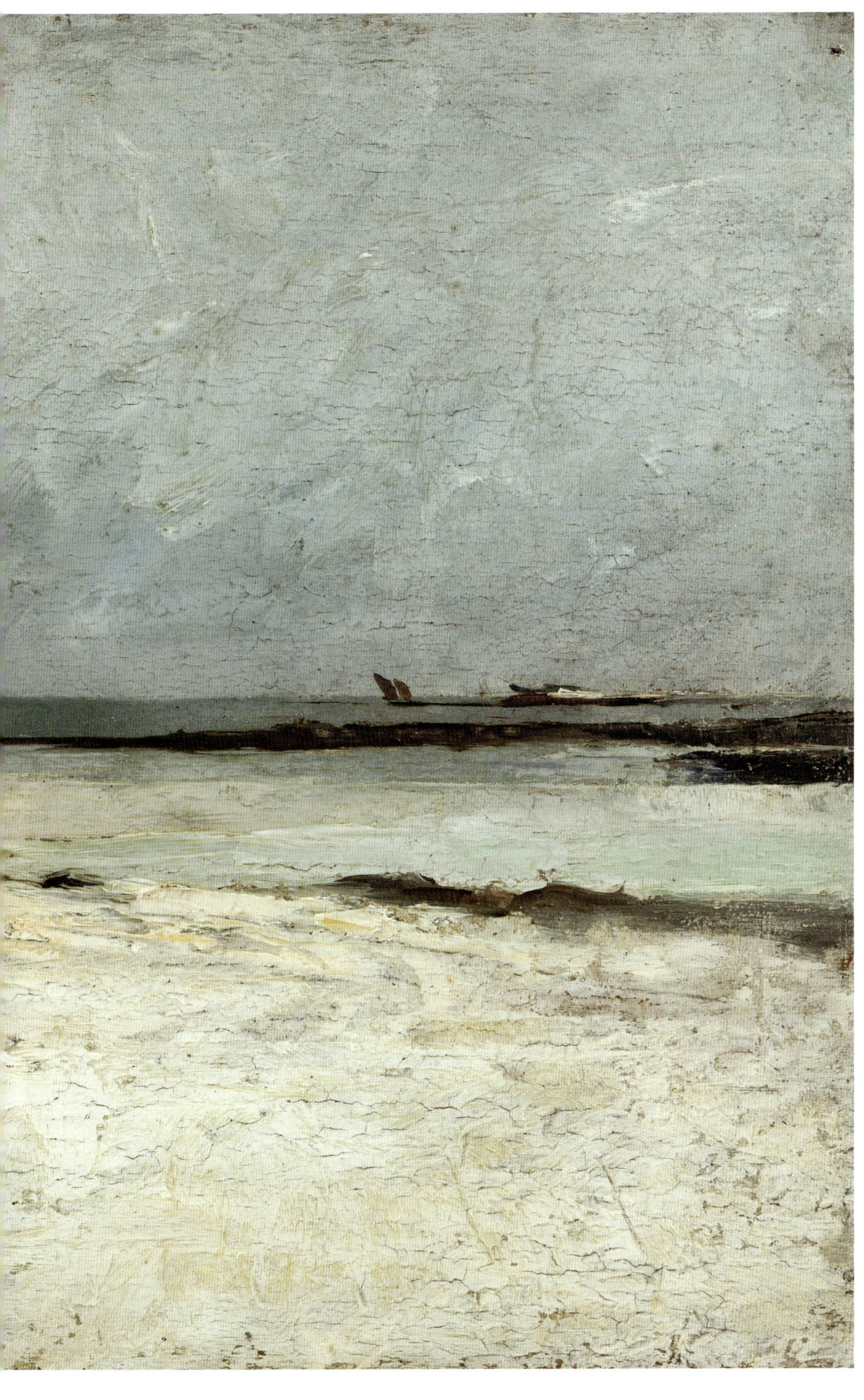

PLATE 53 FANNY CHURBERG, ***WATERFALL***, 1877

Oil on canvas on plywood, 11¾ × 18⅞ in. (30 × 48 cm). Gift from Arvid Sourander, Finnish National Gallery, Ateneum Art Museum, Helsinki, A III 2350

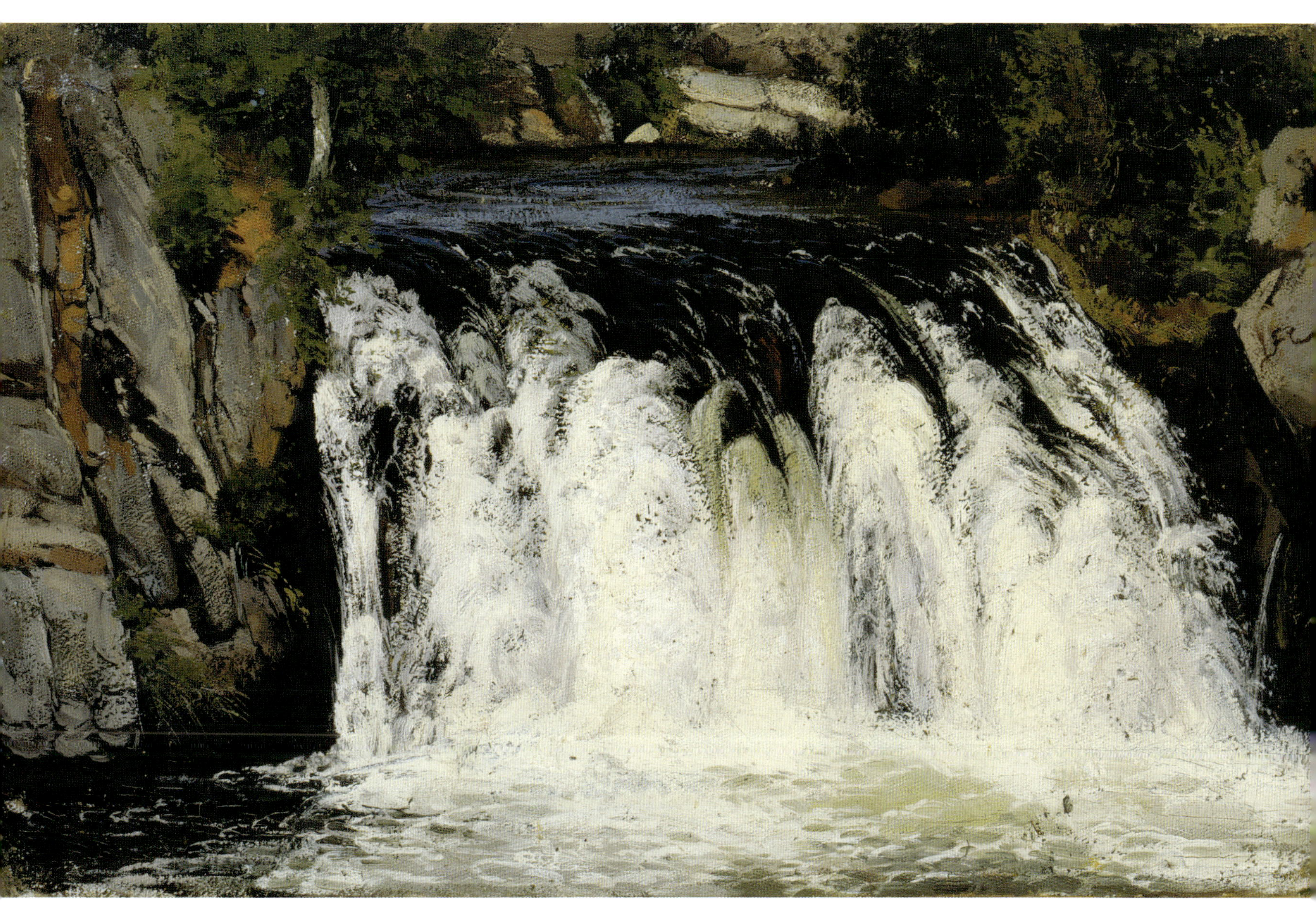

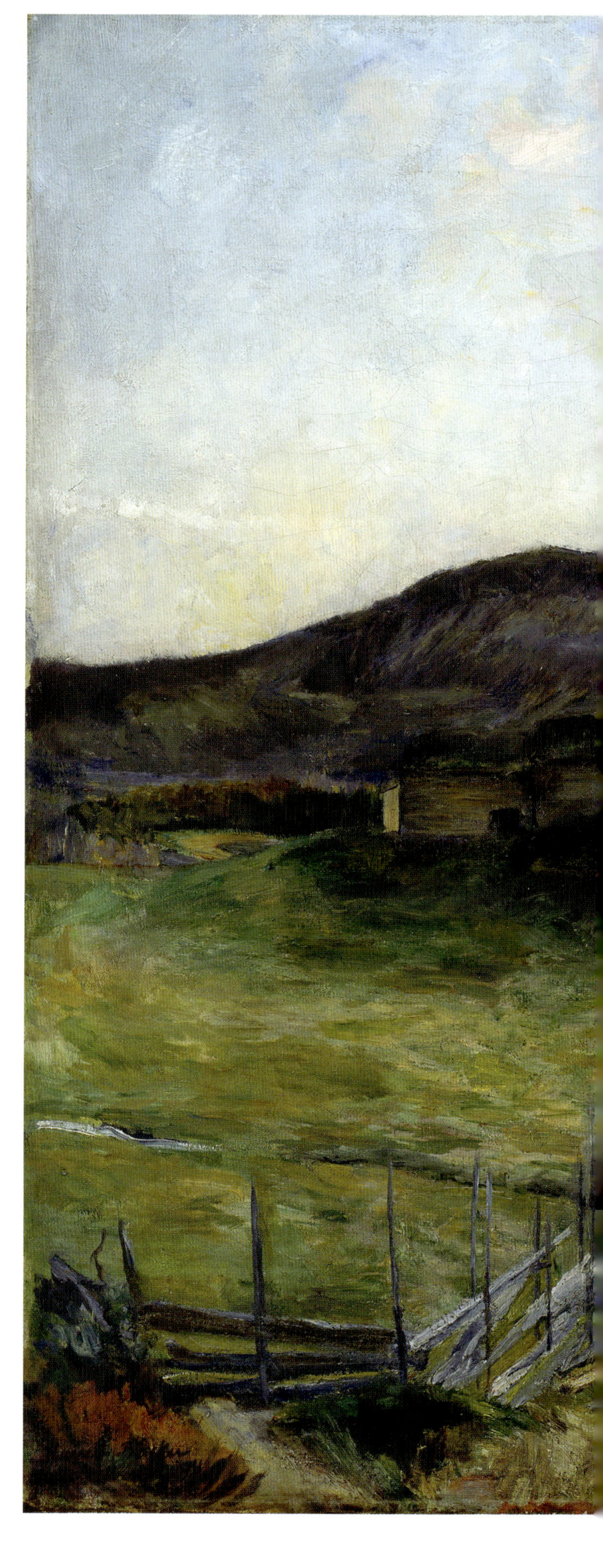

PLATE 54 HARRIET BACKER, ***AUTUMN AT STRÅLSJØEN*** **(*FRA STRÅLSJOEN, HØST*), 1894**

Oil on canvas, 30⅛ × 44⅛ in. (76.5 × 112 cm). National Museum of Art, Architecture and Design, Oslo, NG.M.01035

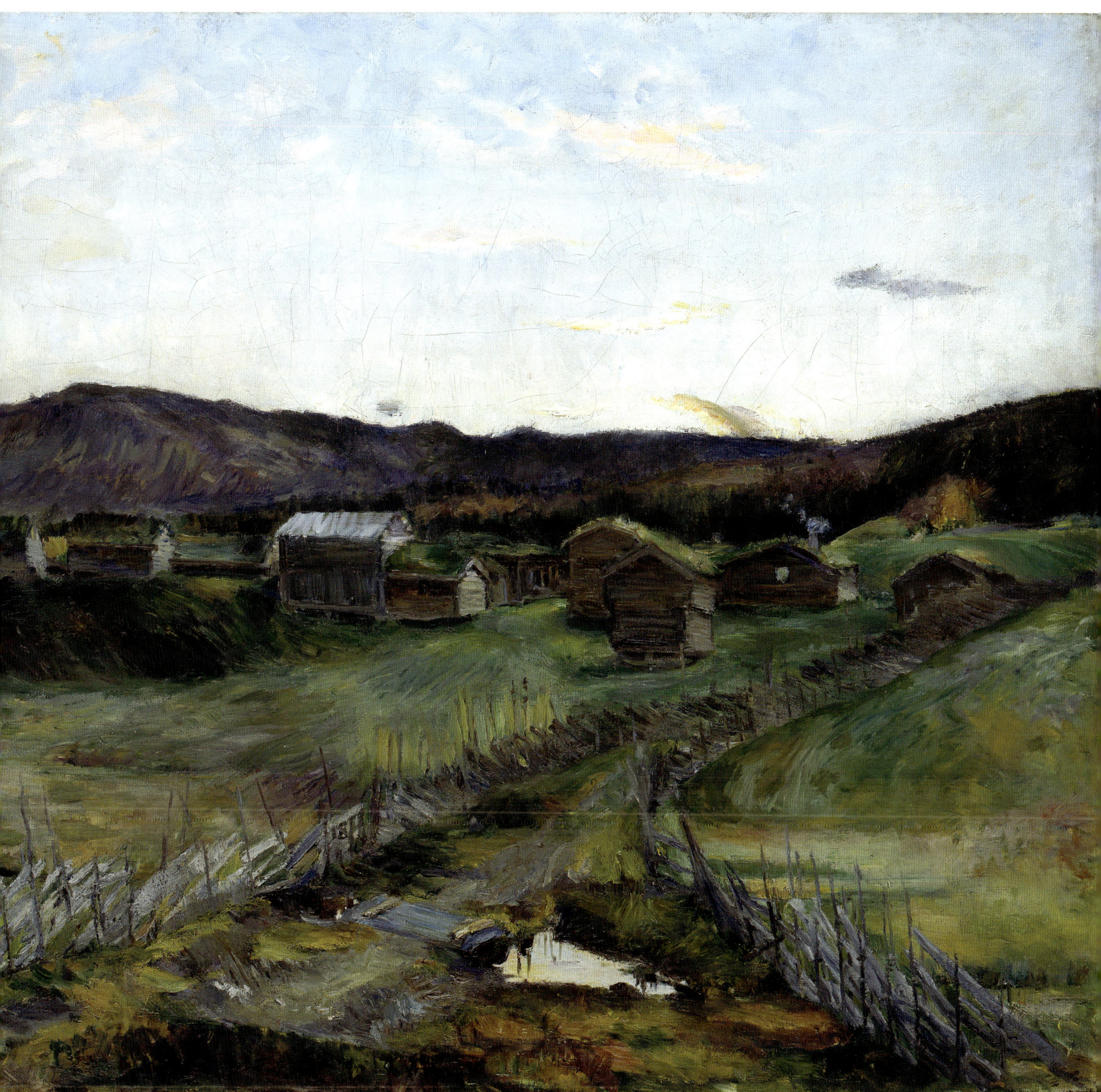

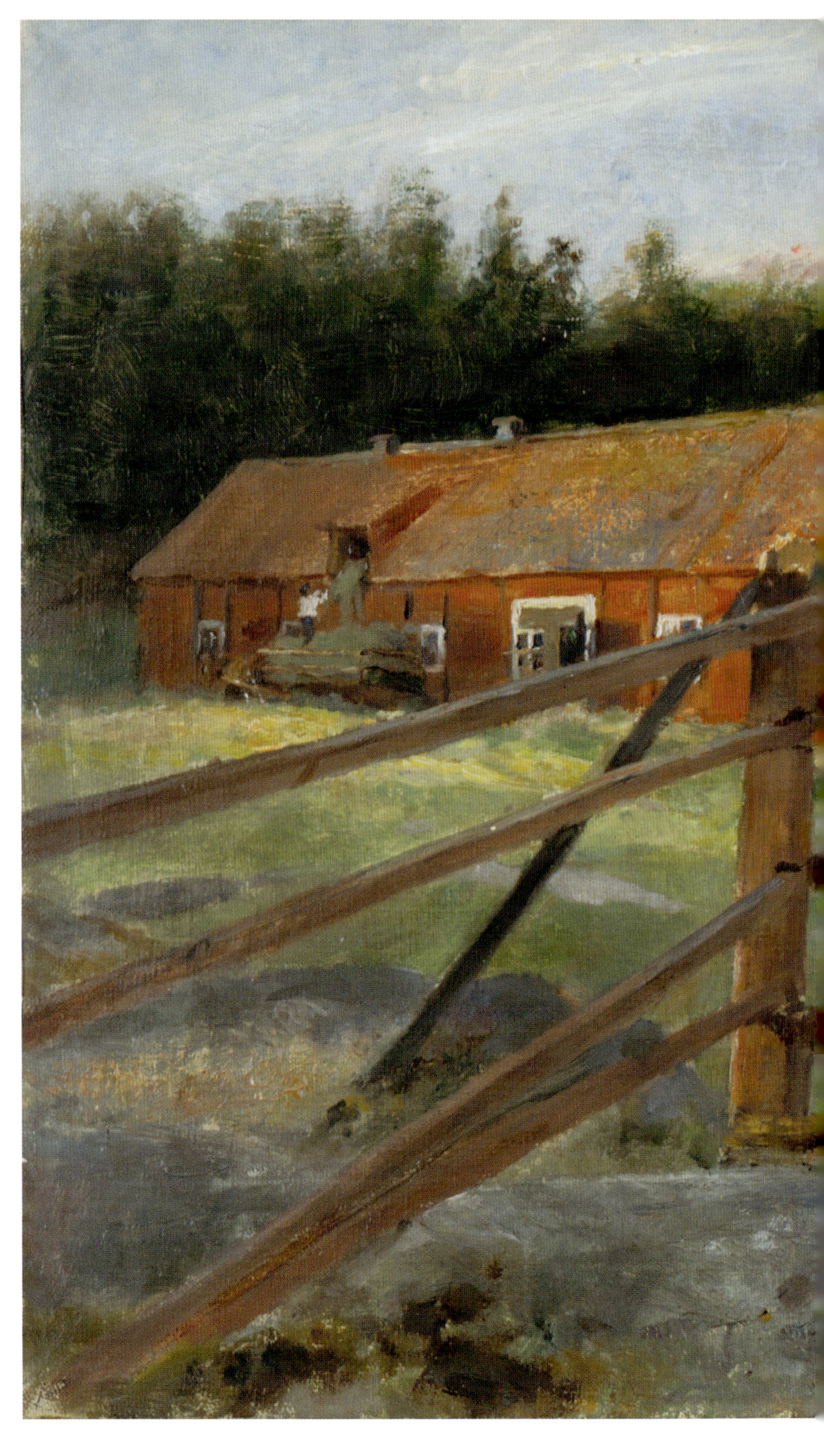

PLATE 55 HANNA PAULI, *THE FARM*, 1887

Oil on canvas, 13 × 21⅝ in. (32.5 × 55 cm). Gothenburg Museum of Art, Sweden, F 120

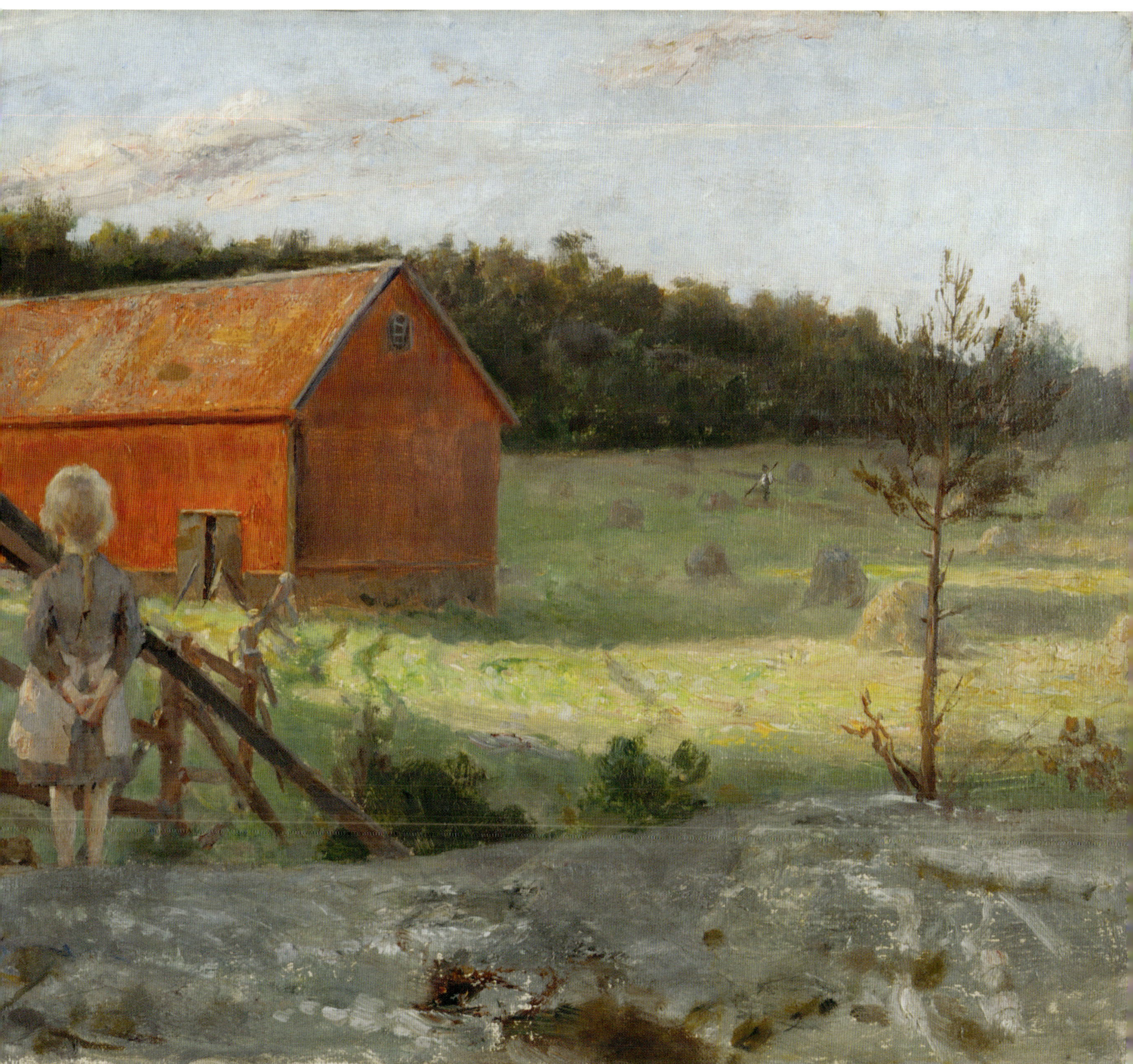

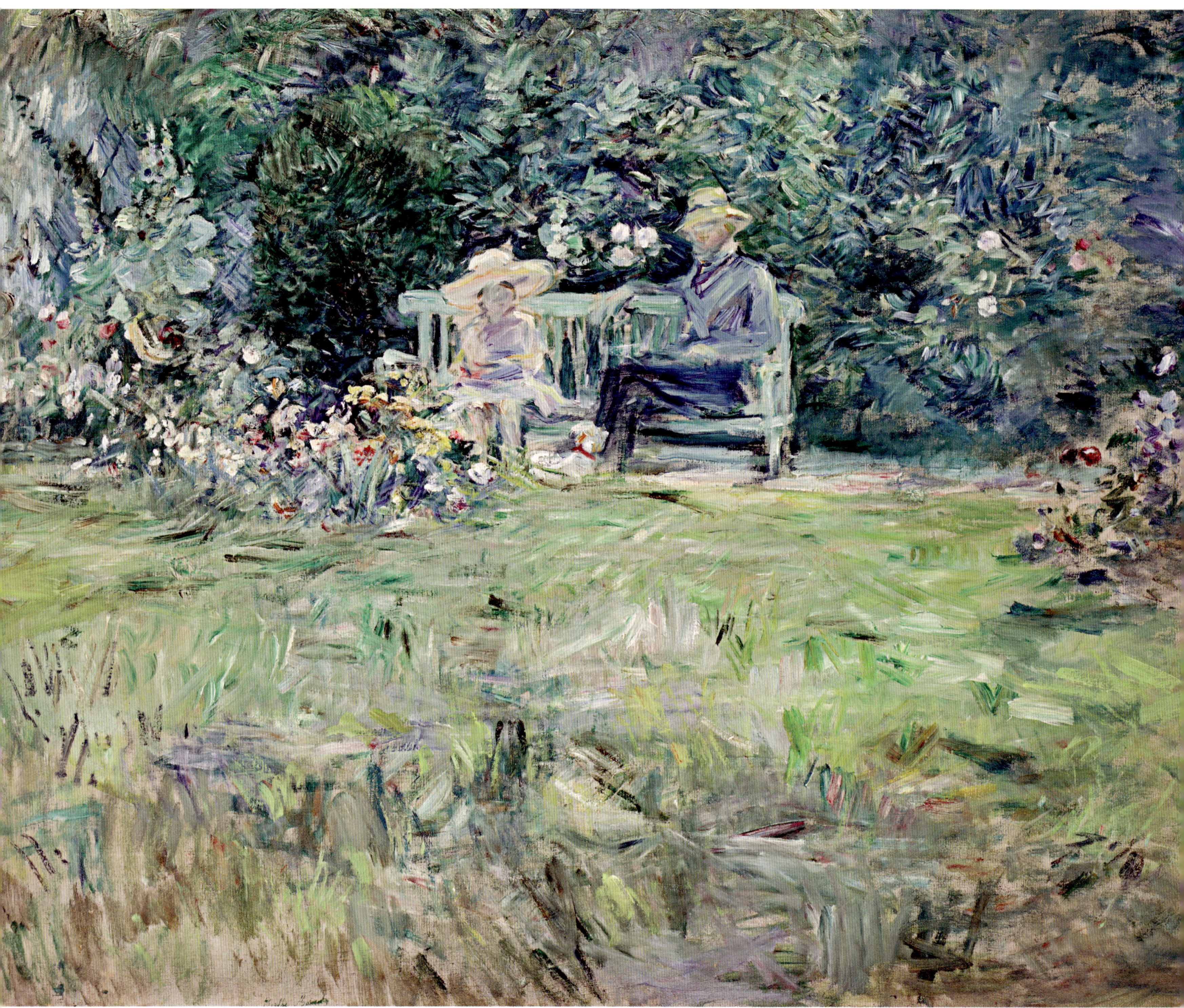

PLATE 56 BERTHE MORISOT, *A LESSON IN THE GARDEN*, 1886

Oil on canvas, 23⅝ × 28¾ in. (60 × 73 cm). Collection of Frederic C. Hamilton, bequeathed to the Denver Art Museum, TL-32569

PLATE 57 MARY CASSATT, *AUTUMN, PORTRAIT OF LYDIA CASSATT*, 1880

Oil on canvas, 36⅜ × 25¾ in. (92.5 × 65.5 cm). Petit Palais, Musée des Beaux-Arts de la Ville de Paris

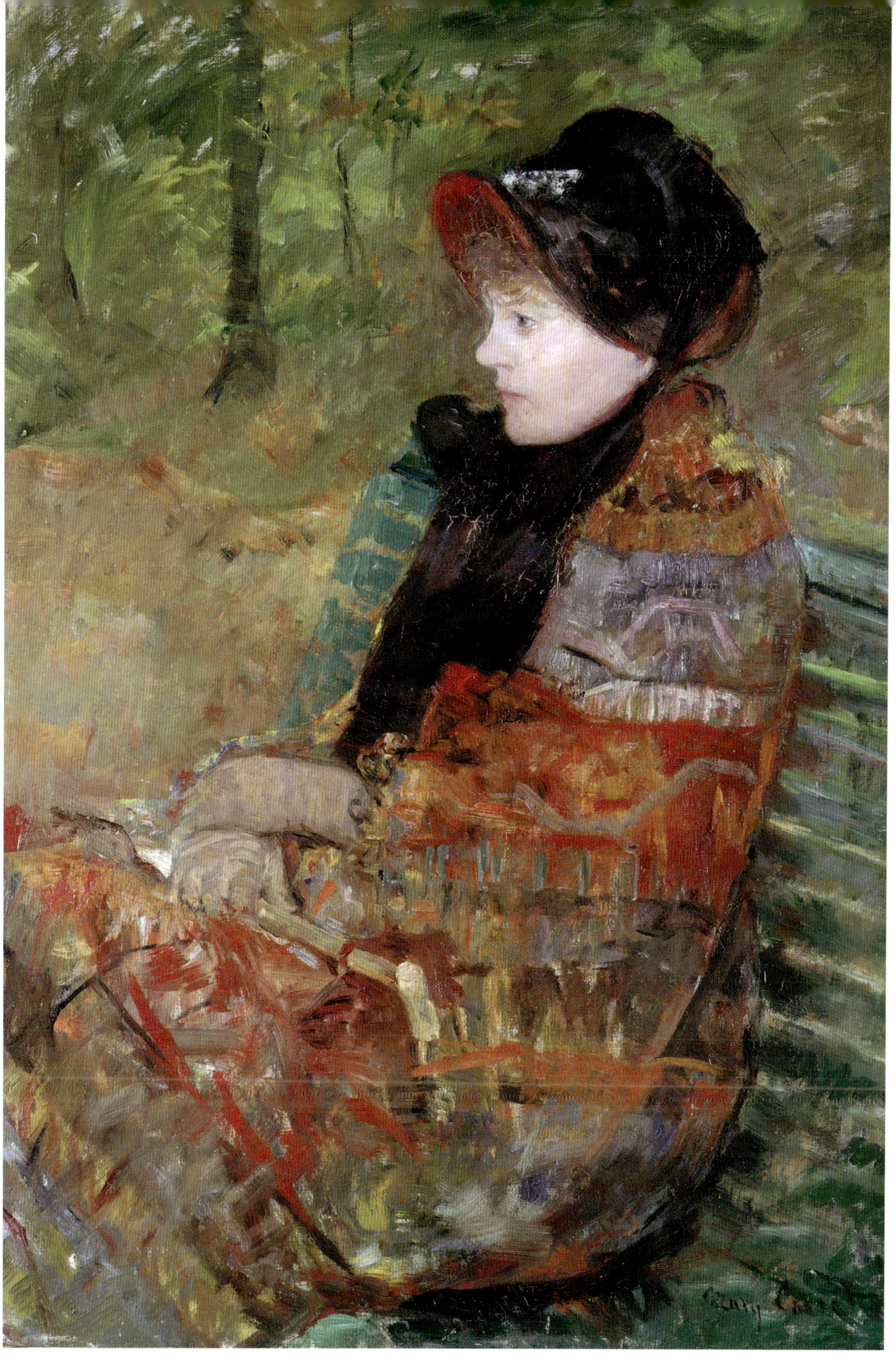

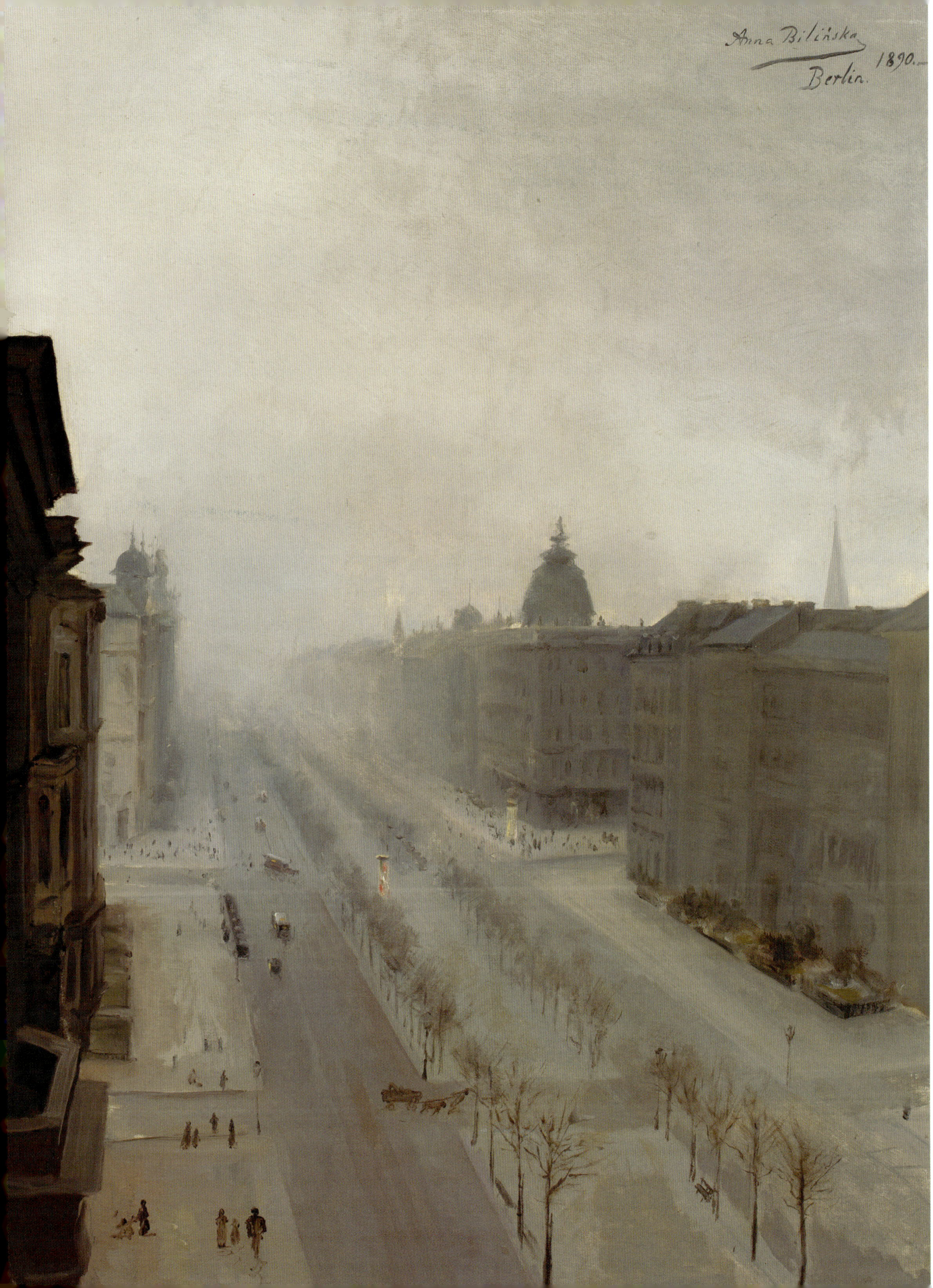

Anna Bilińska 1890
Berlin

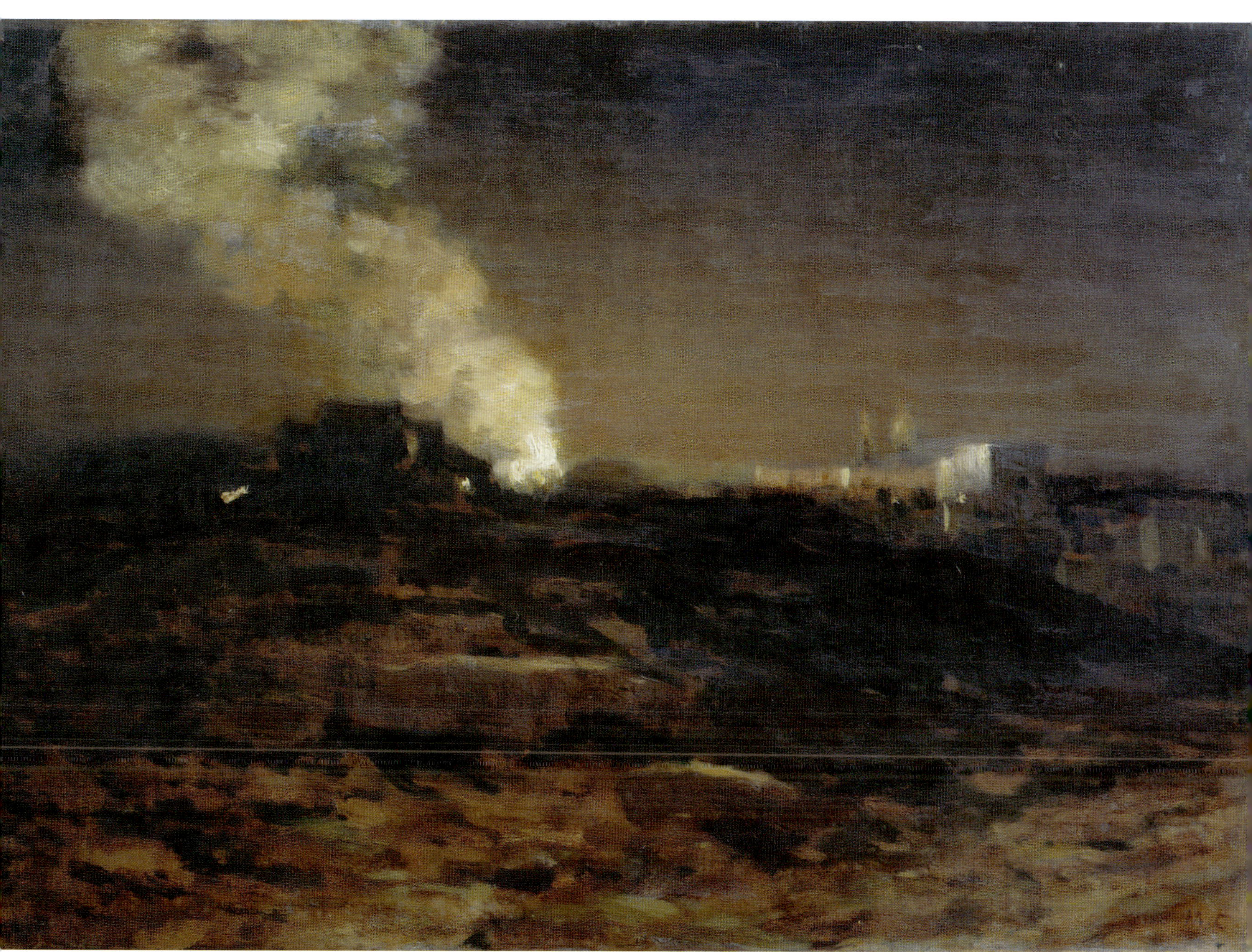

PLATE 58 ANNA BILIŃSKA, *UNTER DEN LINDEN IN BERLIN*, 1890

Oil on canvas, 32¼ × 23⅝ in. (82 × 60 cm). The National Museum, Warsaw

PLATE 59 MARIE CAZIN, *EVENING*, CA. 1884–88

Oil on canvas, 12⅞ × 18⅛ in. (32.7 × 46 cm). Tate: Bequeathed by Mrs. Mary James Mathews in memory of her husband Frank Claughton Mathews, 1944, N05571

PLATE 60 HELENE SCHJERFBECK, *THE DOOR*, 1884

Oil on canvas, 16 × 13 in. (40.5 × 32.5 cm). Finnish National Gallery, Ateneum Art Museum, Helsinki, A IV 3680

To judge by critics at the time, history painting was not meant for women, who lacked the necessary training provided by the École des Beaux-Arts and did not "possess the energy of inventiveness," rendering them unfit to convey the noble feelings of heroic subjects.[1] Nor would this be the arena in which women enjoyed success. "Very few large works, no history paintings," concluded the critic from *Le siècle* upon visiting the first exhibition of the Union des Femmes Peintres et Sculpteurs.[2] Nonetheless, Virginie Demont-Breton attempted to open new avenues for women painters that would lead to the *grand genre*. She proposed that women should place in its service their capacity to probe "the tenderness, but also the anxieties, the harrowing sorrows of life," and to ultimately represent women as heroines.[3]

Such encouragement from the president of the Union des Femmes Peintres et Sculpteurs, along with reflections on the subject compiled by artist Marie Bashkirtseff in her journal, gives an inkling of the uncertainty among women painters regarding their potential subject matter. While Bashkirtseff made artistic forays based on Roman history, she also felt compelled to paint a contemporary subject such as *Young Woman Reading "The Question of Divorce" by Alexandre Dumas*.[4] She imagined a painting of "Ophelia" or a "Carnival Scene," and then proceeded to paint *The Meeting* [plate 68]—possibly the "urchins around a carriage entrance" referenced in her diary—and wax enthusiastic about urban life as a series of "admirable pictures."[5]

Should a painter continue the strict adherence to history paintings' source material: the Bible, mythology, allegory, and great literature? This was the view espoused by Elizabeth Jane Gardner Bouguereau and Annie Louisa Swynnerton with *Mater Triumphalis* [plate 62], her rare symbolic personification of the glory of motherhood. Maybe one should chart a middle course, seeking out men and women in daily life who possess the inestimable qualities of classical heroes. Asta Nørregaard's *Peasant Woman from Normandie* [plate 73], Virginie Demont-Breton's epic *The Tormented* [plate 76], and Elizabeth Nourse's *Fisher Girl of Picardy* [plate 77] all cast their female subjects as everyday heroines while avoiding sentimentality or melodrama. Each of these artists turned to the fields and sea to find ways of illustrating enduring virtues such as bravery and piety.

Or should an artist take an interest in the modern world and its new customs? Anna Klumpke, Mary Cassatt, Marie Bashkirtseff, and Annie Hopf set out on that path, opened by the advent of Realism in the late 1840s, and fueled by their readings of Émile Zola. This direction, however, was often refused by other women, who denounced "that shameful, so-called *naturalist* literature."[6] The unresolved questions of subject matter raised by Bashkirtseff and seen in paintings such as Helene Schjerfbeck's noble *Churchgoers (Easter Morning)* [plate 75] demonstrate that the woman painter, even more than her male counterparts—who dictated the rules or had rejected them several decades earlier—had to choose, above all else, autonomy and fidelity to her own perception.

1. Eugène Müntz, "Le Salon: Essai de statistique," *La chronique des arts et de la curiosité*, May 31, 1873, 215.
2. Henry Havard, "Exposition de l'Union des Femmes Peintres et Sculpteurs," *Le siècle*, January 25, 1882.
3. Virginie Demont-Breton, *Journal des femmes artistes*, May 17, 1897.
4. *Journal de Marie Bashkirtseff*, vol. 2 (Paris: Charpentier, 1890), 86–87, 168. This work, originally titled *Jeune femme lisant la Question du Divorce d'Alexandre Dumas* when it was exhibited at the Salon of 1880, was sold as *Portrait of a Young Woman Reading* at Sotheby's day sale in London on November 27, 2012.
5. Ibid., 346, 376.
6. *La femme*, August 1, 1890.

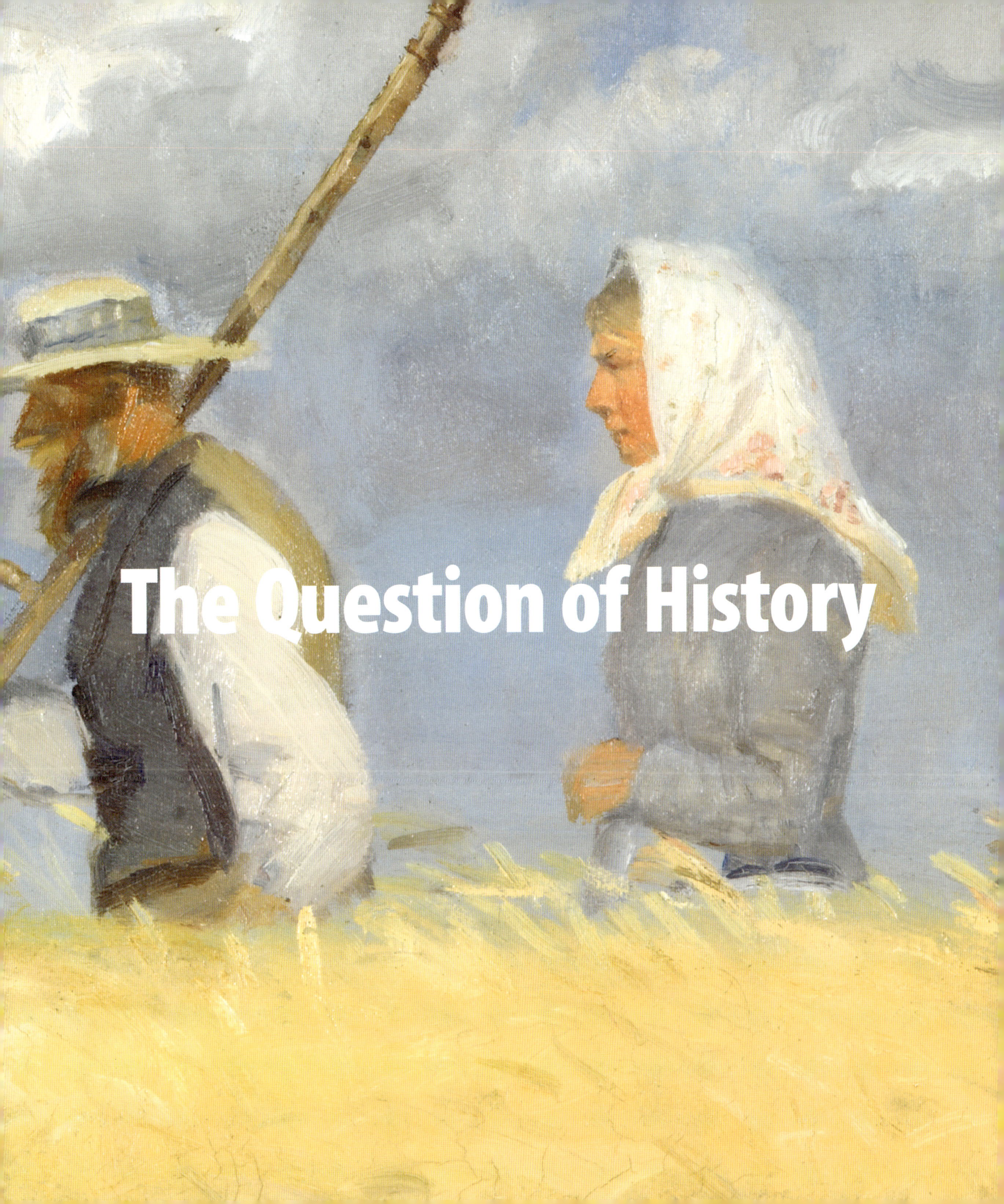
The Question of History

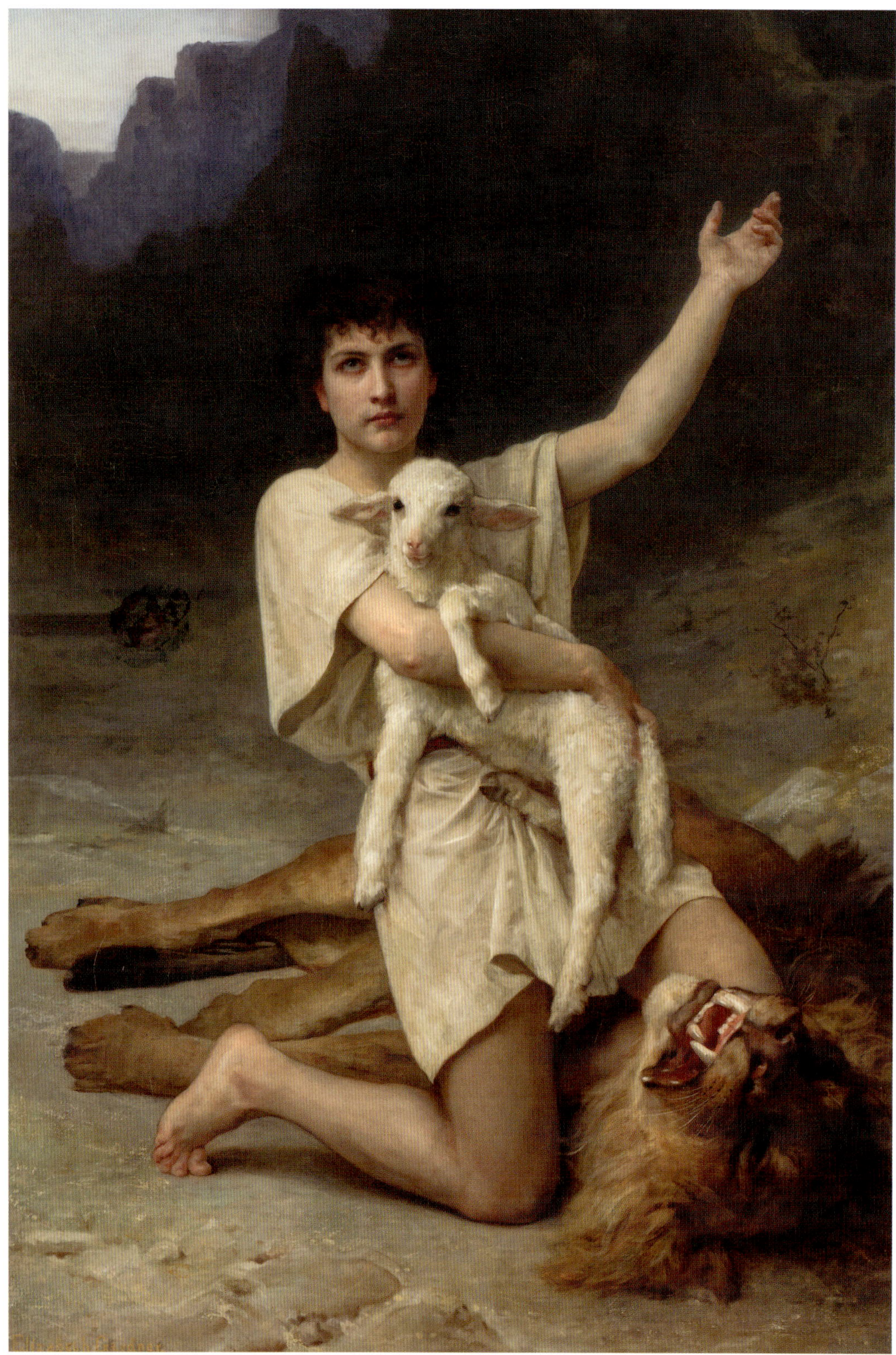

PLATE 61 ELIZABETH JANE GARDNER BOUGUEREAU, *THE SHEPHERD DAVID*, CA. 1895

Oil on canvas, 60½ × 41⅜ in. (153.7 × 105.1 cm). National Museum of Women in the Arts, Washington, DC, Gift of Wallace and Wilhelmina Holladay, 1986.24

PLATE 62 ANNIE LOUISA SWYNNERTON, *MATER TRIUMPHALIS*, 1892

Oil on canvas, 65¾ × 26¾ in. (167 × 68 cm). Musée d'Orsay, Paris, Gift of Edmund Davis, 1915, RF1977-432

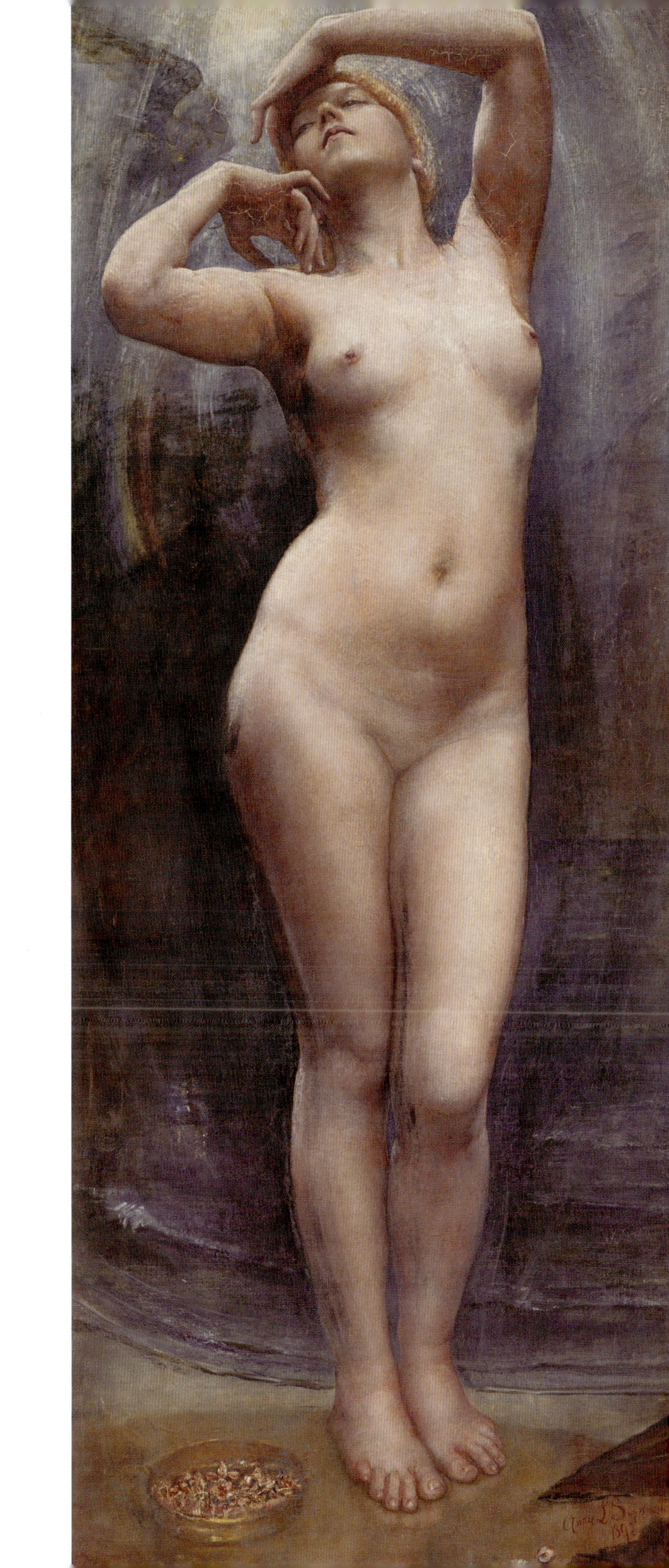

PLATE 63 MARY CASSATT, *OFFERING THE PANAL TO THE BULLFIGHTER*, 1873

Oil on canvas, 39⅝ × 33½ in. (100.6 × 85.1 cm). Sterling and Francine Clark Art Institute, Williamstown, MA, 1955.1

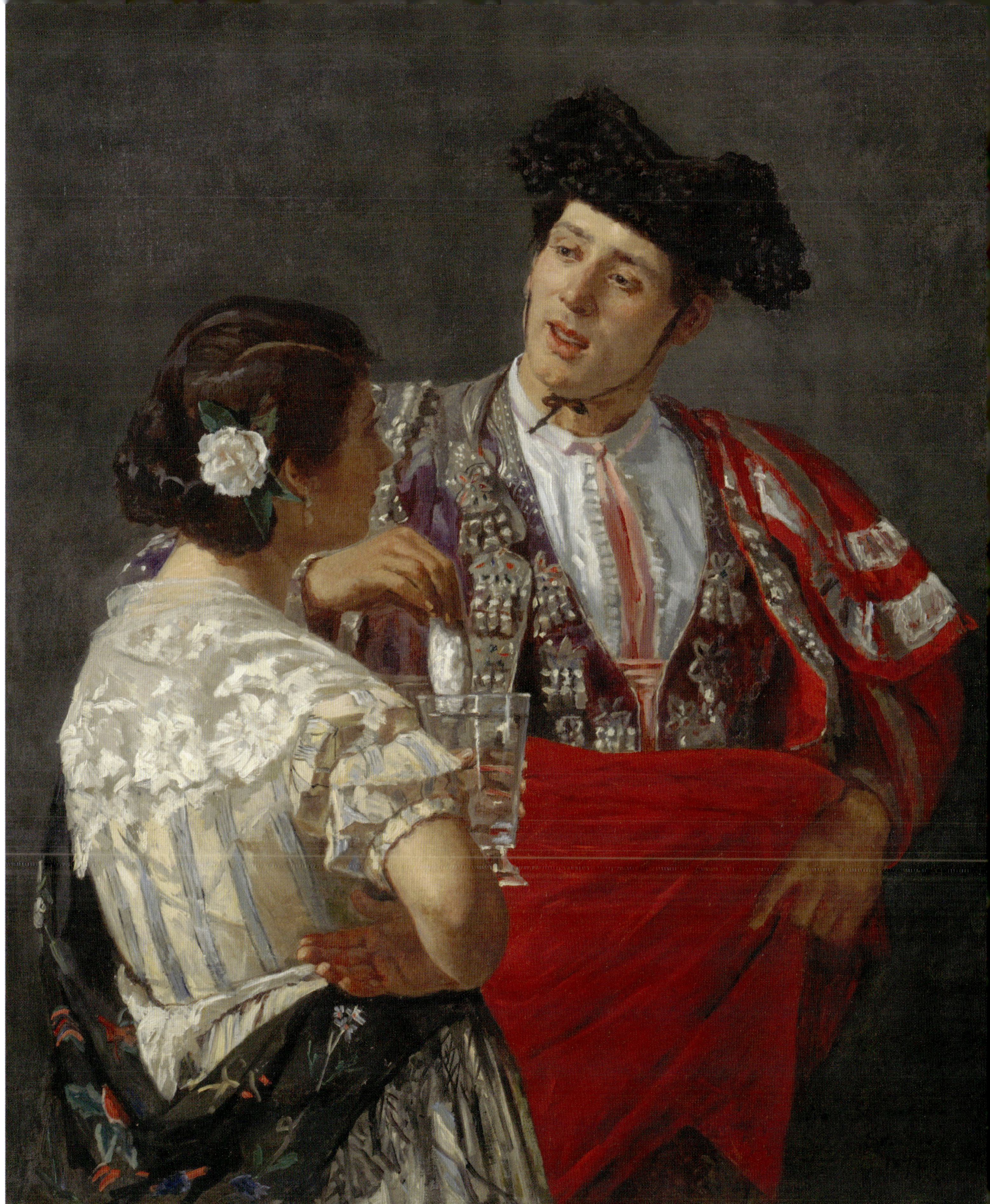

PLATE 64 ANNIE HOPF, *AUTOPSY (PROFESSOR POIRIER, PARIS)*, 1889

Oil on canvas, 44⅞ × 57⅞ in. (134 × 142 cm). Kunstmuseum Bern, Switzerland

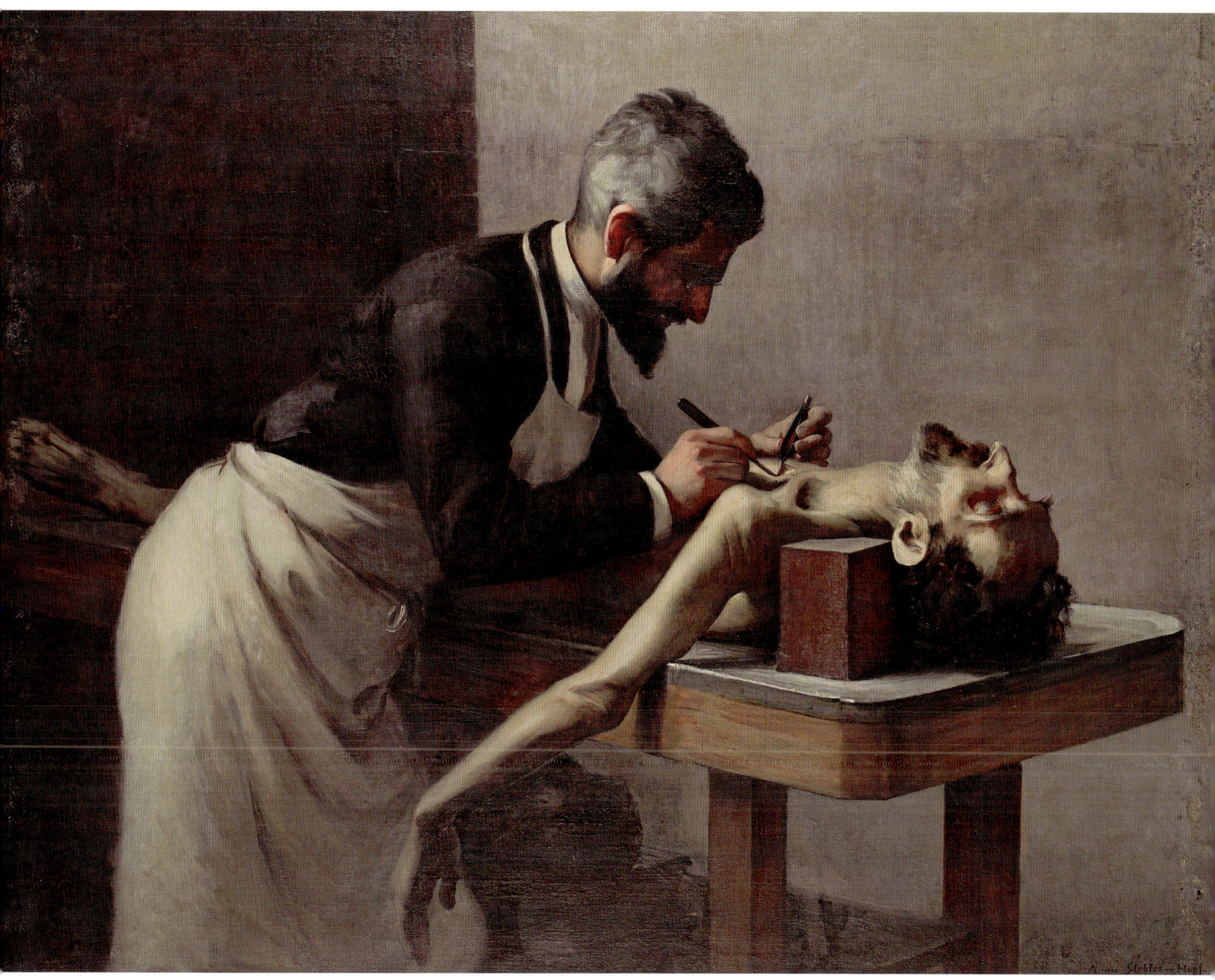
Annie Stebler-Hopf

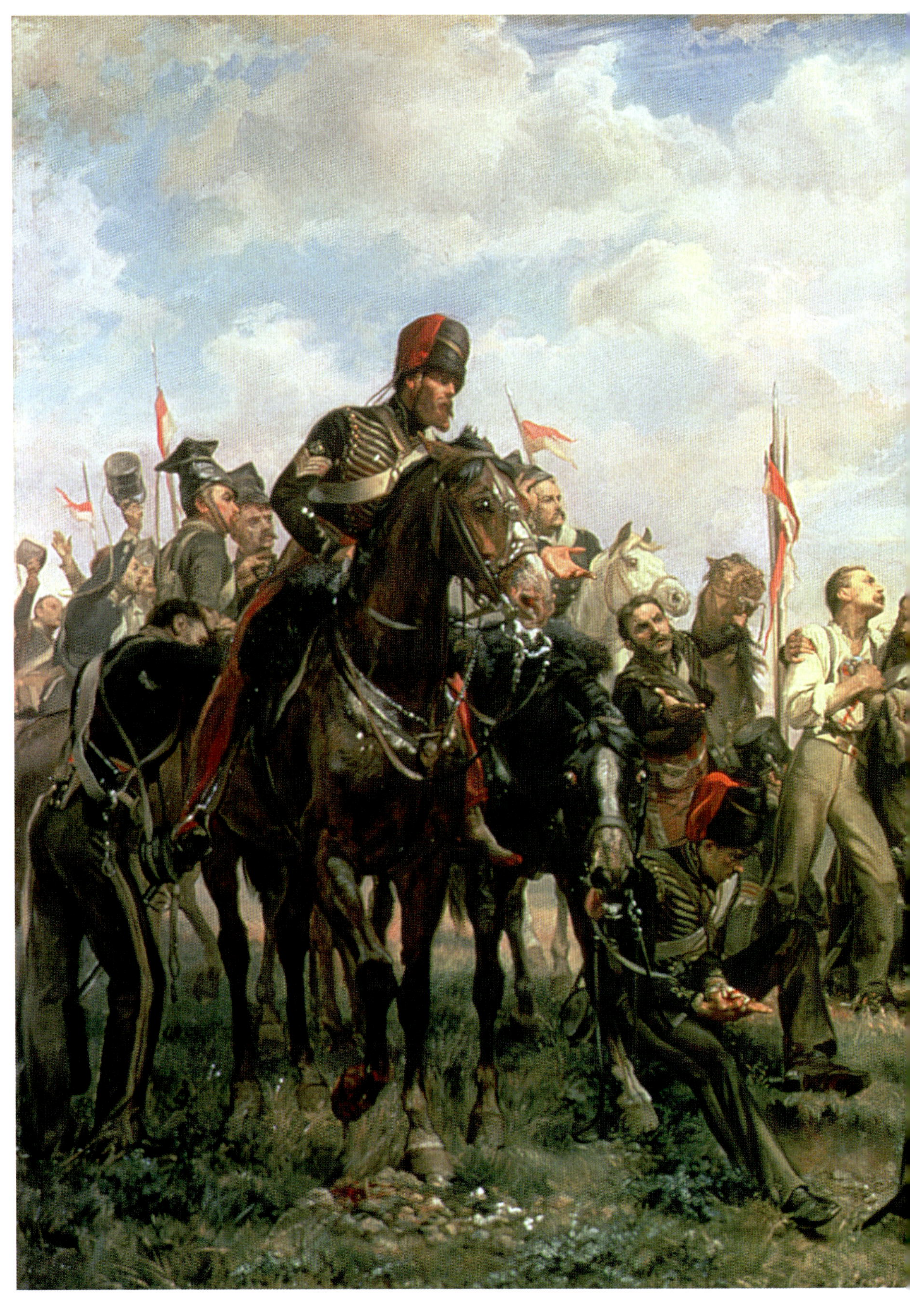

PLATE 65 **LADY ELIZABETH BUTLER, *BALACLAVA*, 1876**

Oil on canvas, 40⅝ × 73⅝ in. (103.4 × 187.5 cm). Manchester Art Gallery, Gift from Robert Whitehead, 1989, 1898.13

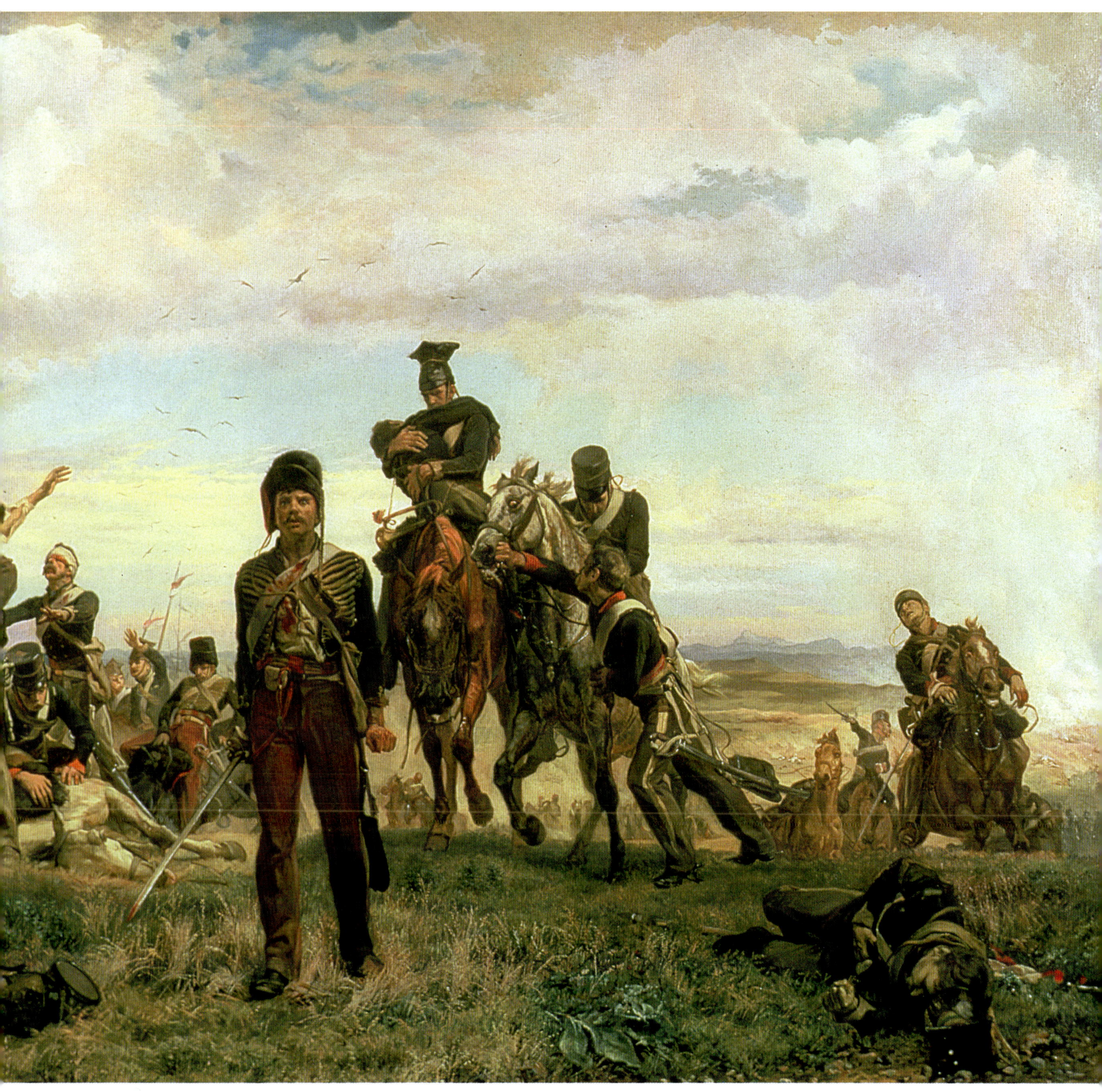

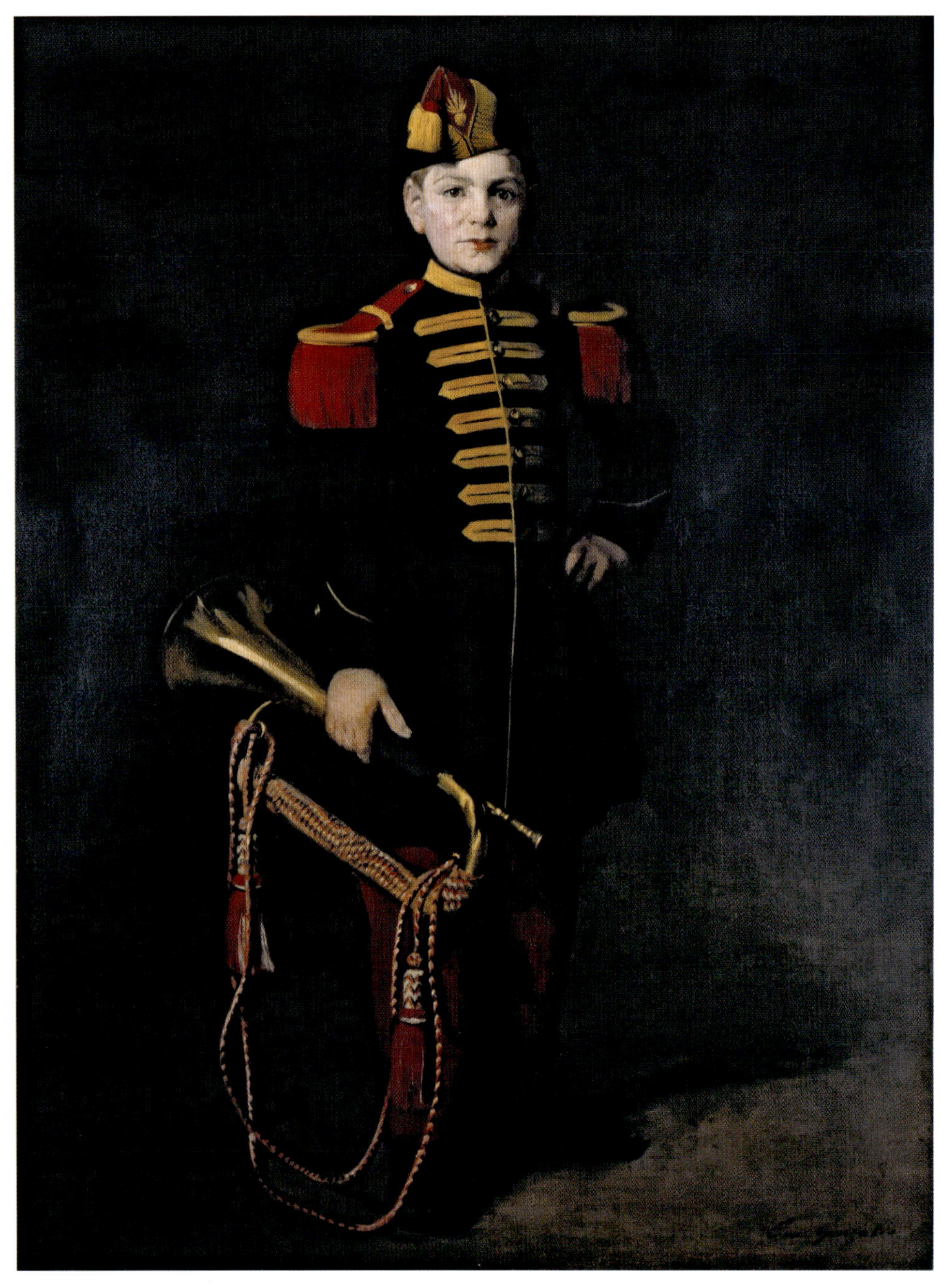

PLATE 66 **EVA GONZALÈS, *SOLDIER BOY* (*L'ENFANT DE TROUPE*), 1870**

Oil on canvas, 52⅜ × 42⅞ in. (133 × 109 cm). Musée de Gajac, Villeneuve-sur-Lot, France

PLATE 67 **LADY ELIZABETH BUTLER, *LISTED FOR THE CONNAUGHT RANGERS: RECRUITING IN IRELAND*, 1878**

Oil on canvas, 41⅞ × 66⅝ in. (106.4 × 169.3 cm). Bury Art Museum, Gift from Robert Whitehead, United Kingdom, BUYGM:0434:1937

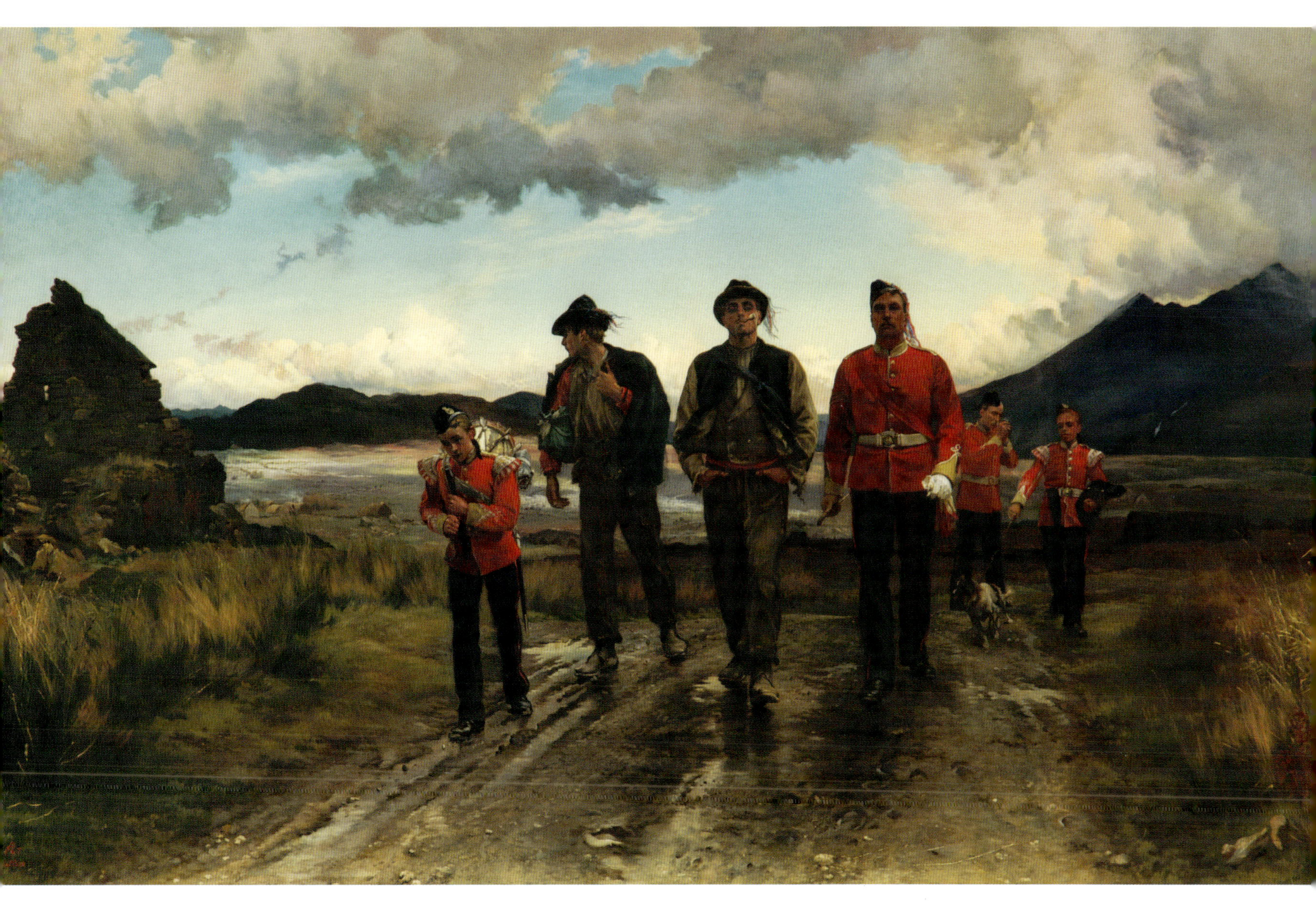

PLATE 68 **MARIE BASHKIRTSEFF, *THE MEETING* (*UN MEETING*), 1884**

Oil on canvas, 76 × 69⅝ in. (193 × 177 cm). Musée d'Orsay, Paris, RF442

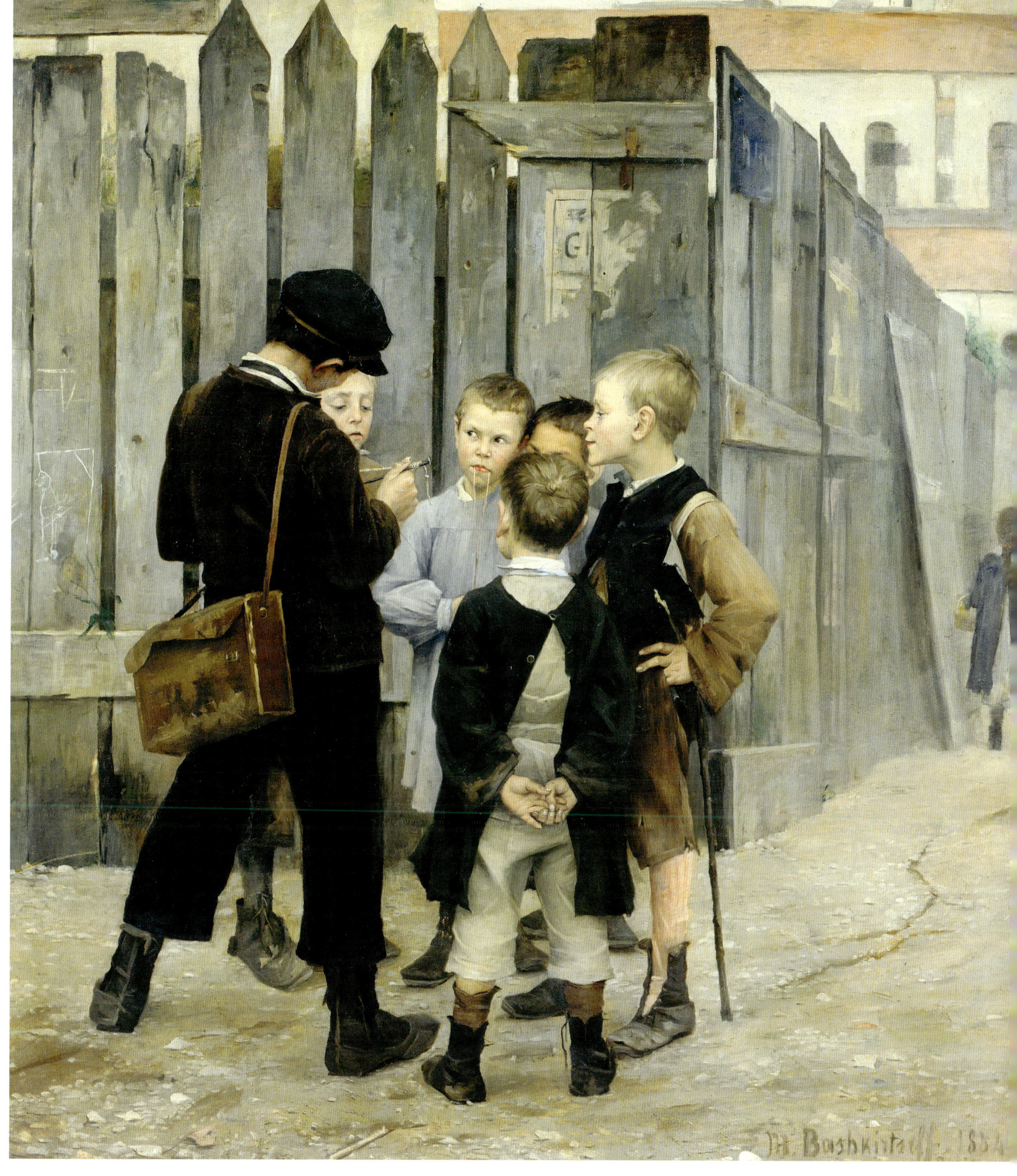

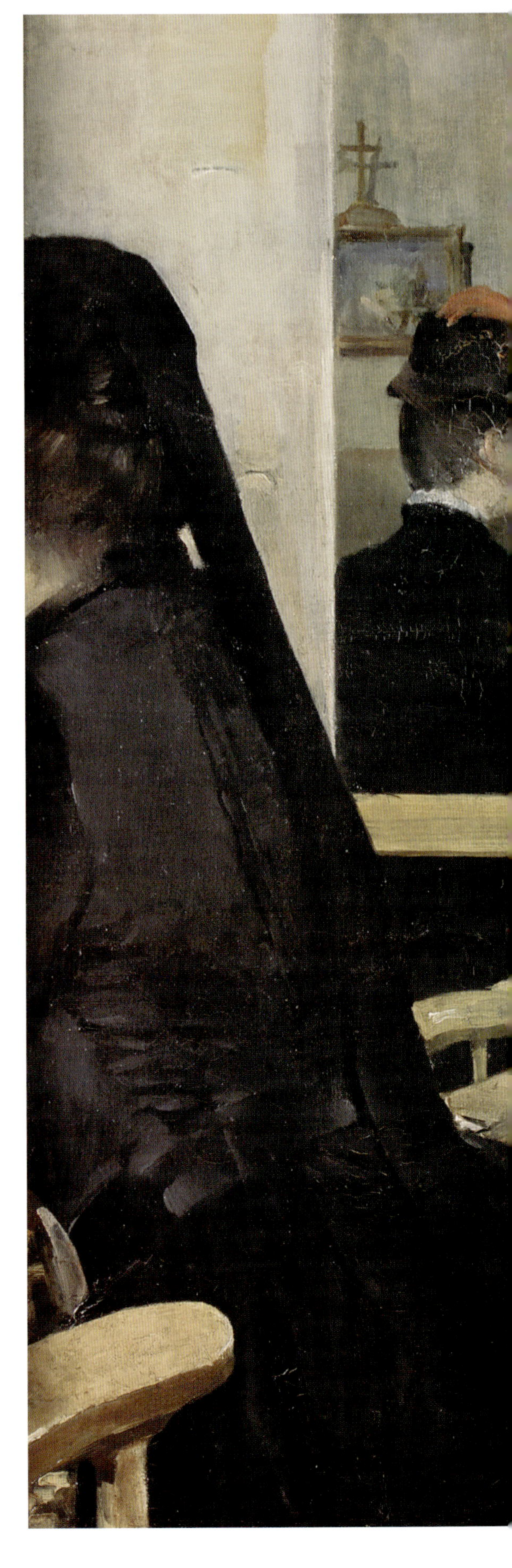

PLATE 69 JULIE DELANCE-FEURGARD, *THE MARRIAGE* (*LE MARIAGE*), 1884

Oil on canvas, 38⅜ × 51⅜ in. (97.5 × 130.5 cm). Musée des Beaux-Arts, Brest, France, 974.39.2

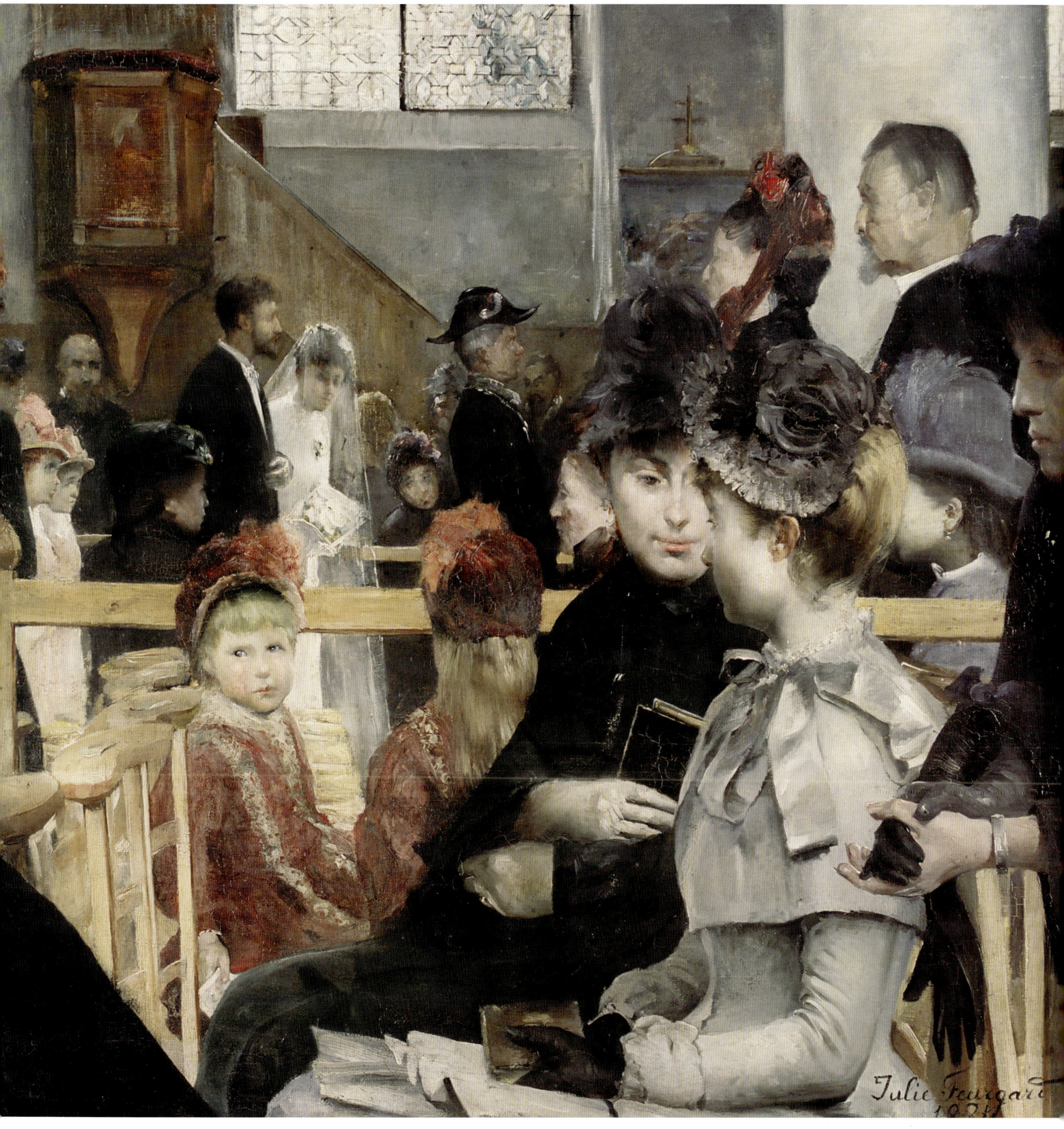
Julie Feurgard

PLATE 70 MARIE PETIET, *YOUNG WOMEN IN CHURCH* (*LES JEUNES FEMMES À L'ÉGLISE*), N.D.

Oil on canvas, 50 × 37⅜ in. (127 × 95 cm). Musée de Peinture Petiet, Limoux, France, 881-030

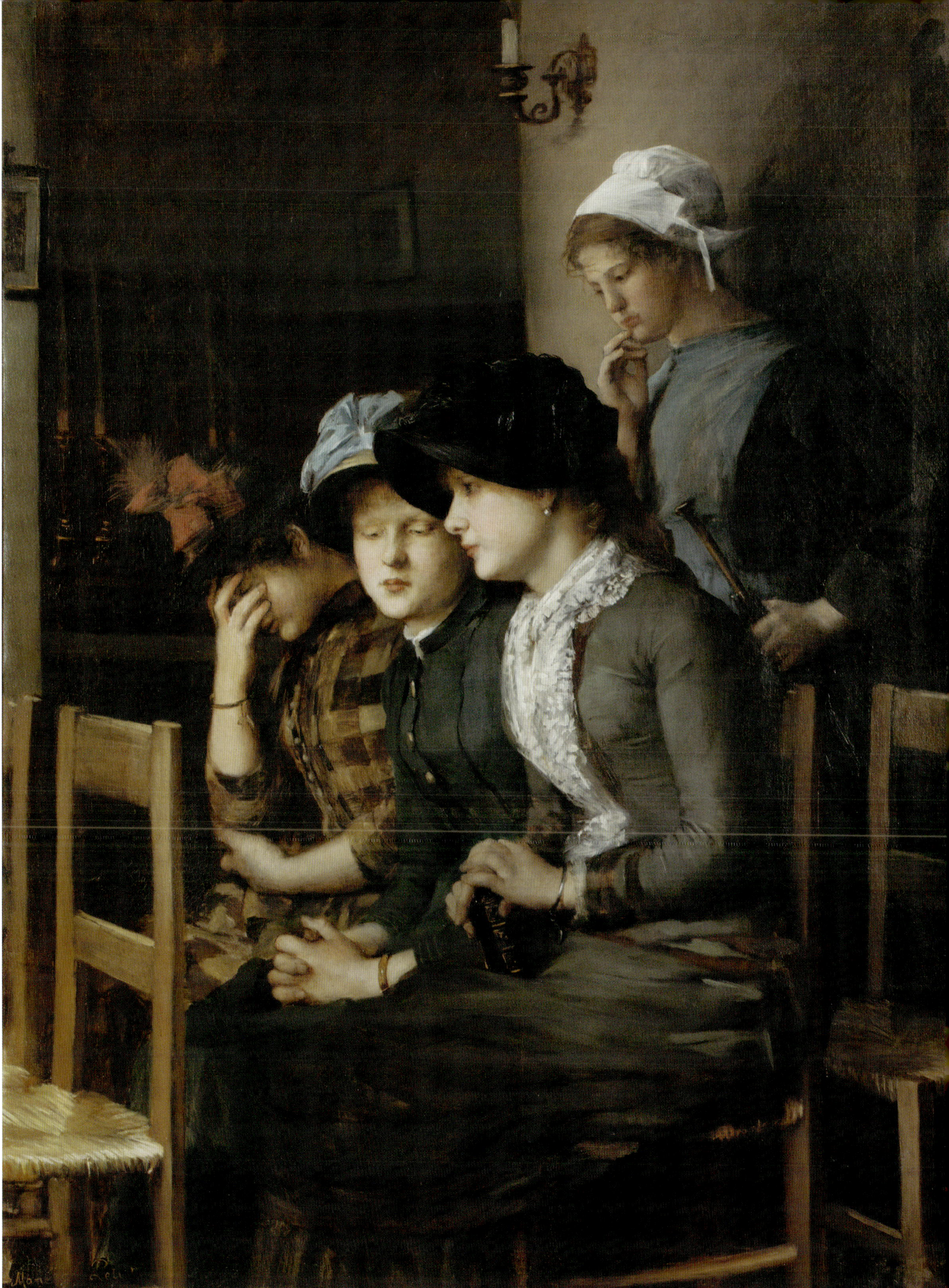

PLATE 71 **ANNA ELIZABETH KLUMPKE, *IN THE WASH-HOUSE*, 1888**

Oil on canvas, mounted on wood, 79 × 67 in. (200.7 × 170.2 cm). Pennsylvania Academy of the Fine Arts, Philadelphia, Gift of the artist, 1890.1

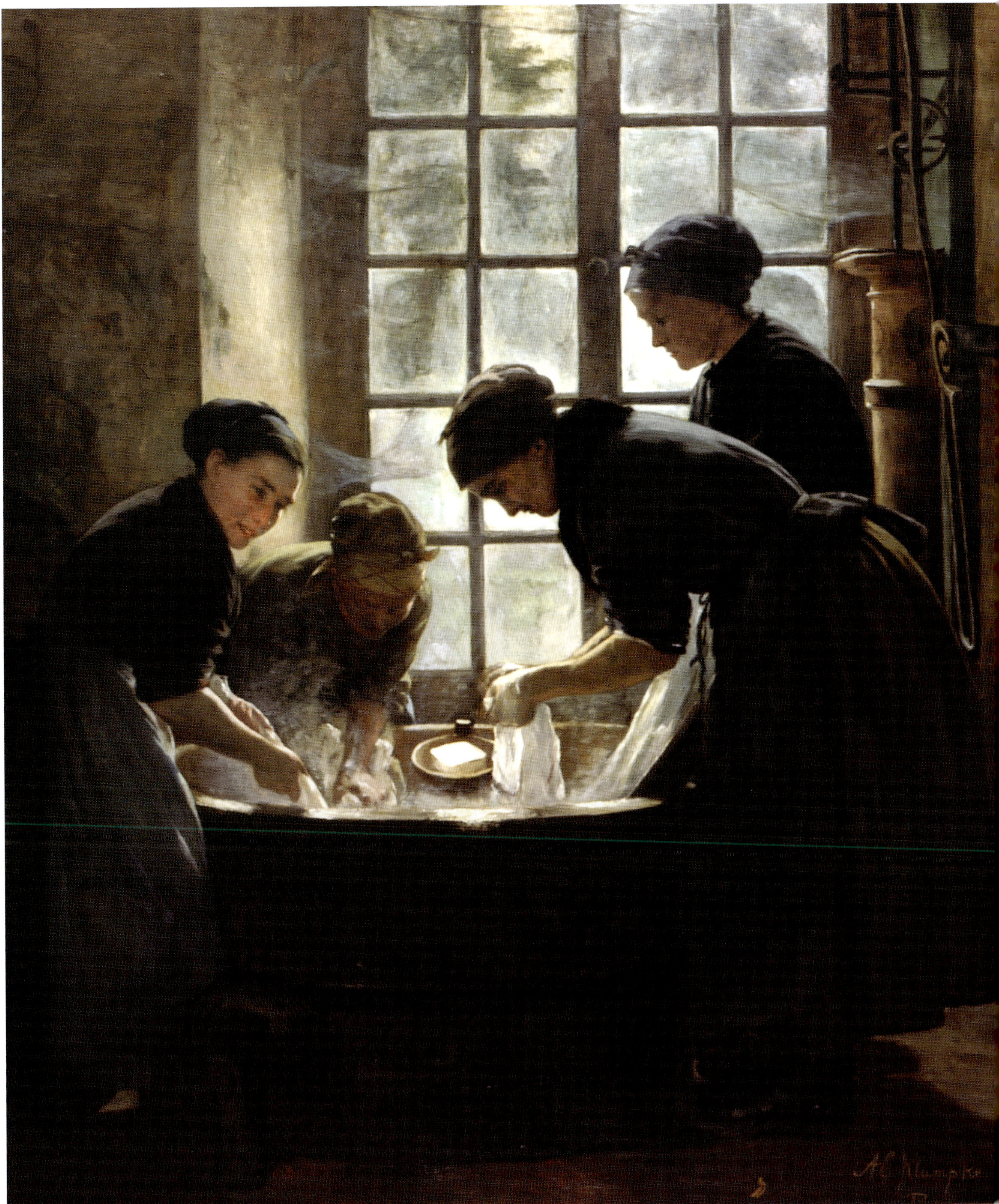

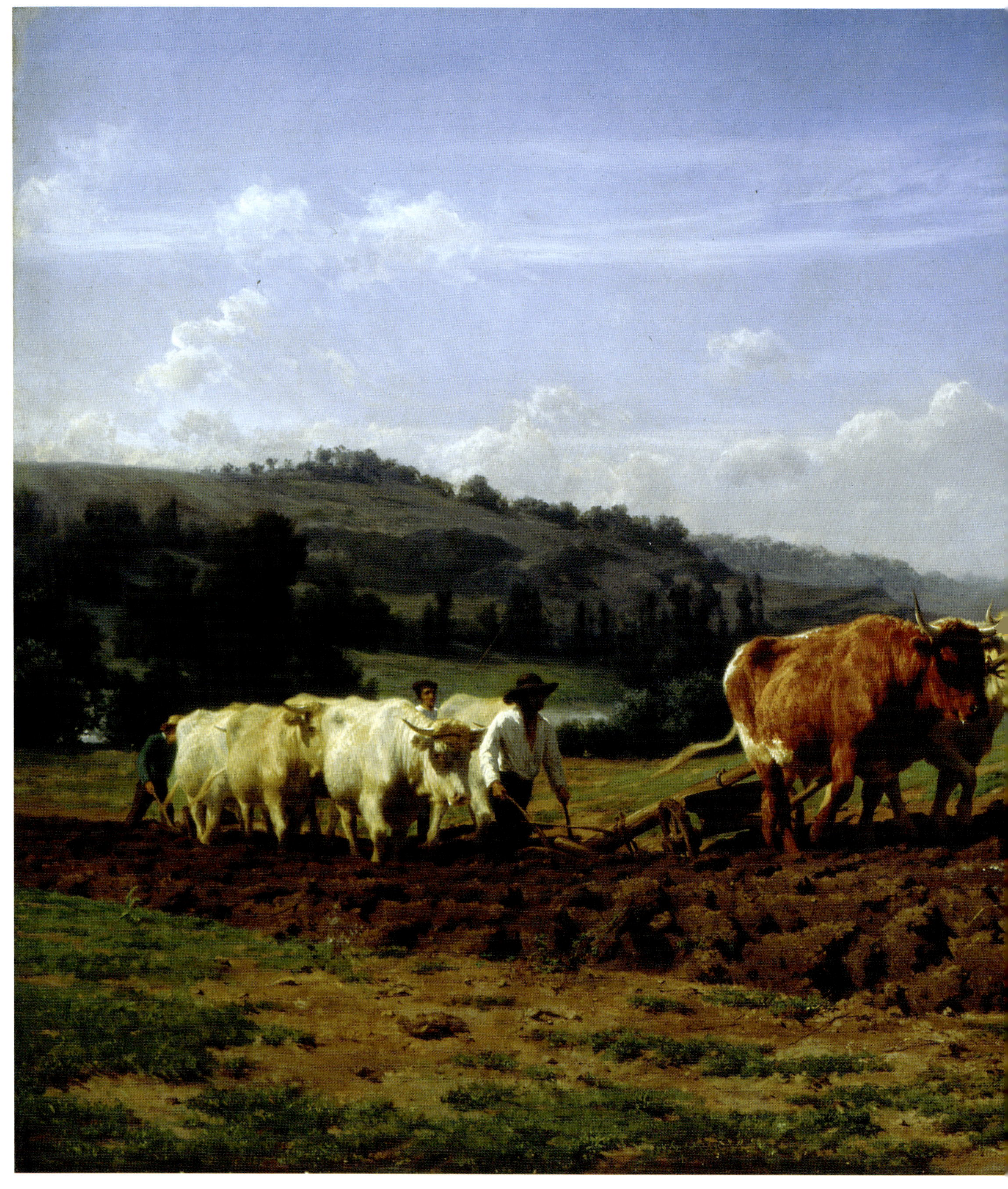

PLATE 72 ROSA BONHEUR, *PLOWING IN NIVERNAIS* (*LABOURAGES NIVERNAIS*), 1850

Oil on canvas, 52½ × 102 in. (133.4 × 259.1 cm). Bequest of John Ringling, 1936, SN433. Collection of The John and Mable Ringling Museum of Art, the State Art Museum of Florida, Florida State University, Sarasota, FL

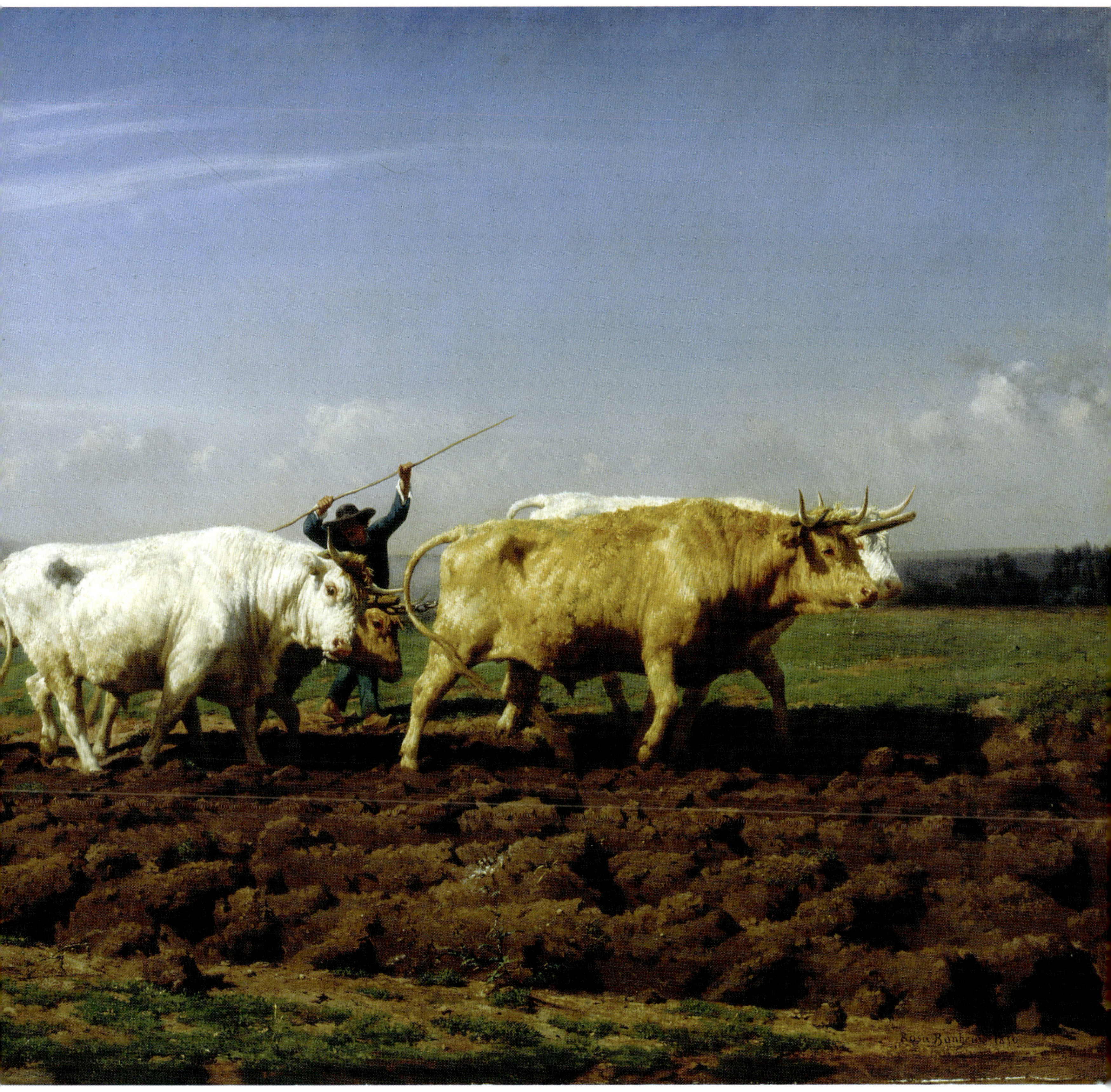
Rosa Bonheur

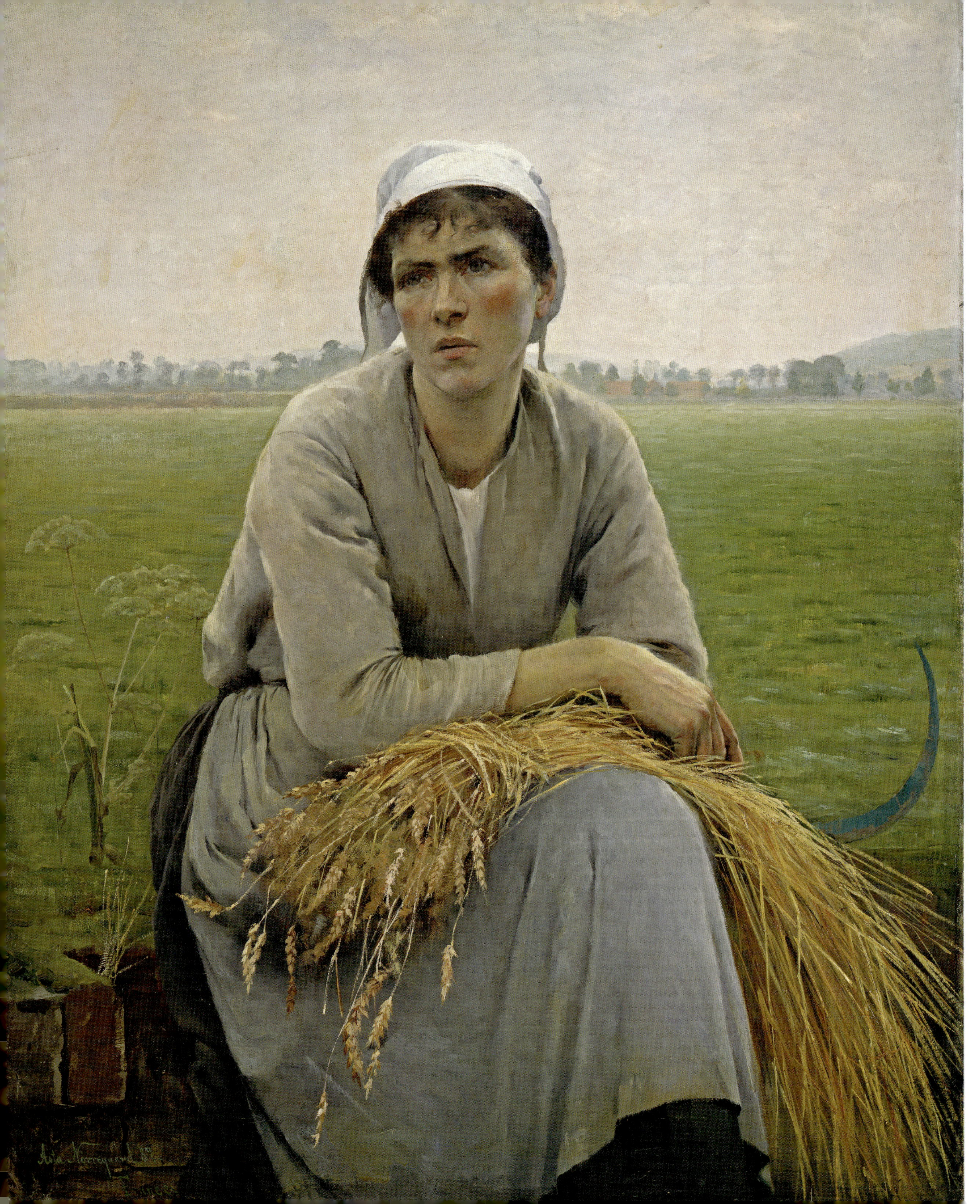

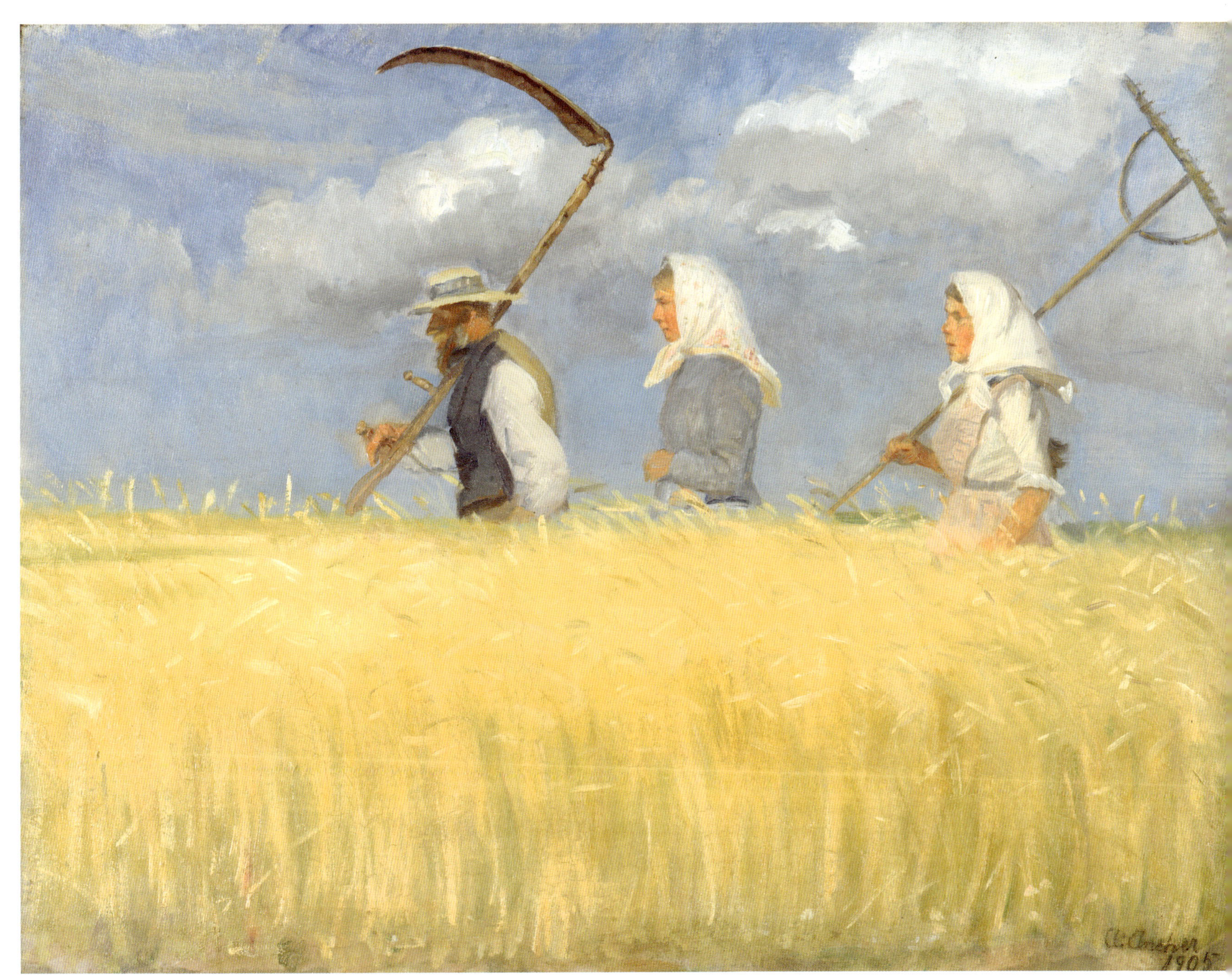

PLATE 73 ASTA NØRREGAARD, *PEASANT WOMAN FROM NORMANDIE*, 1889

Oil on canvas, 41 × 33½ in. (104 × 85 cm). National Museum of Art, Architecture and Design, Oslo, NG.M.03608

PLATE 74 ANNA ANCHER, *THE HARVESTERS* (*HØSTARBEJDERE*), 1905

Oil on canvas, 17⅛ × 22⅛ in. (43.4 × 56.2 cm). Art Museums of Skagen, Denmark, SKM1465

PLATE 75 HELENE SCHJERFBECK, *CHURCHGOERS (EASTER MORNING)* (*KIRKKOVÄKEÄ*), 1895–1900

Oil on canvas, 27½ × 37⅜ in. (70 × 95 cm). Finnish National Gallery, Ateneum Art Museum, Helsinki, A 1991 71

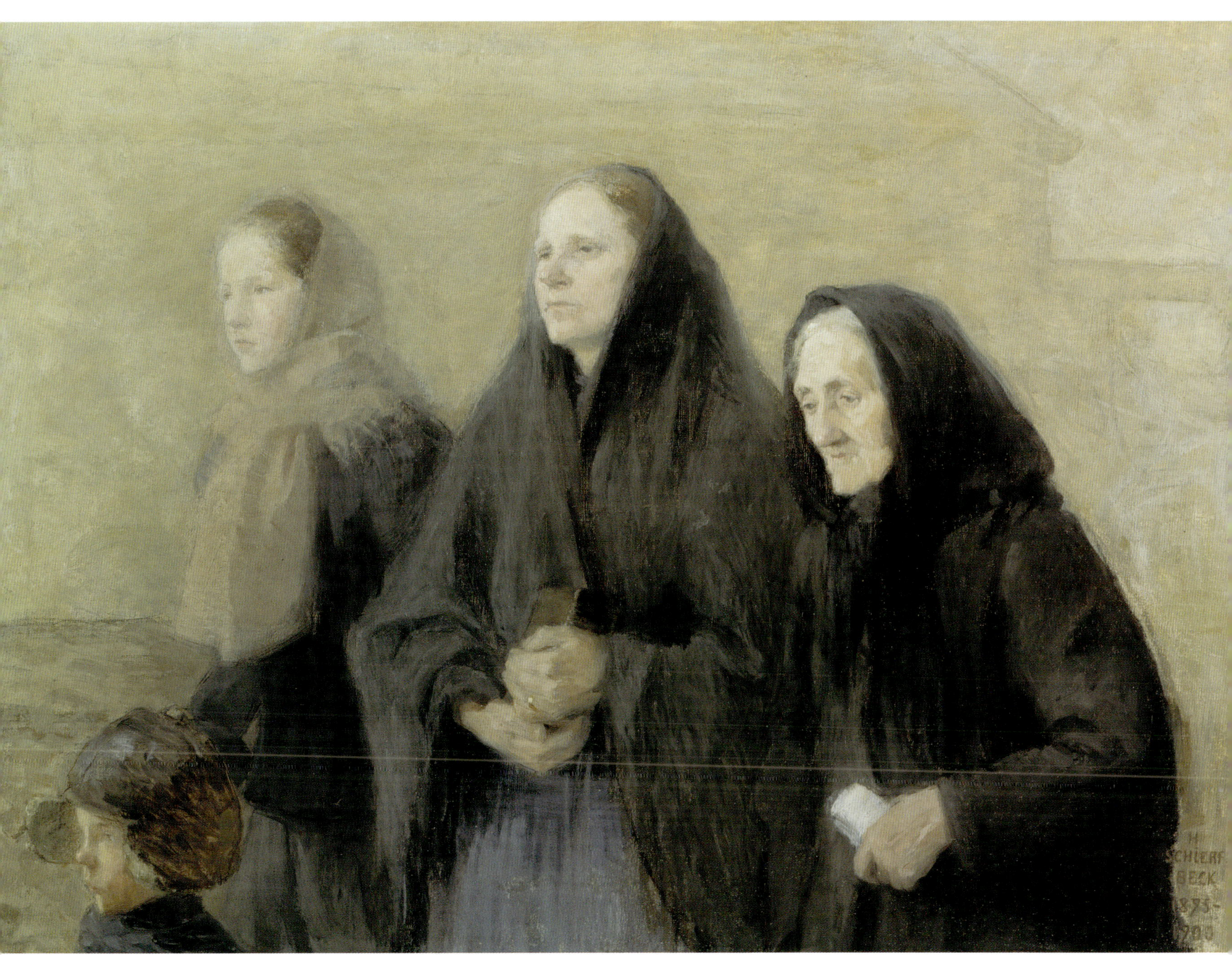

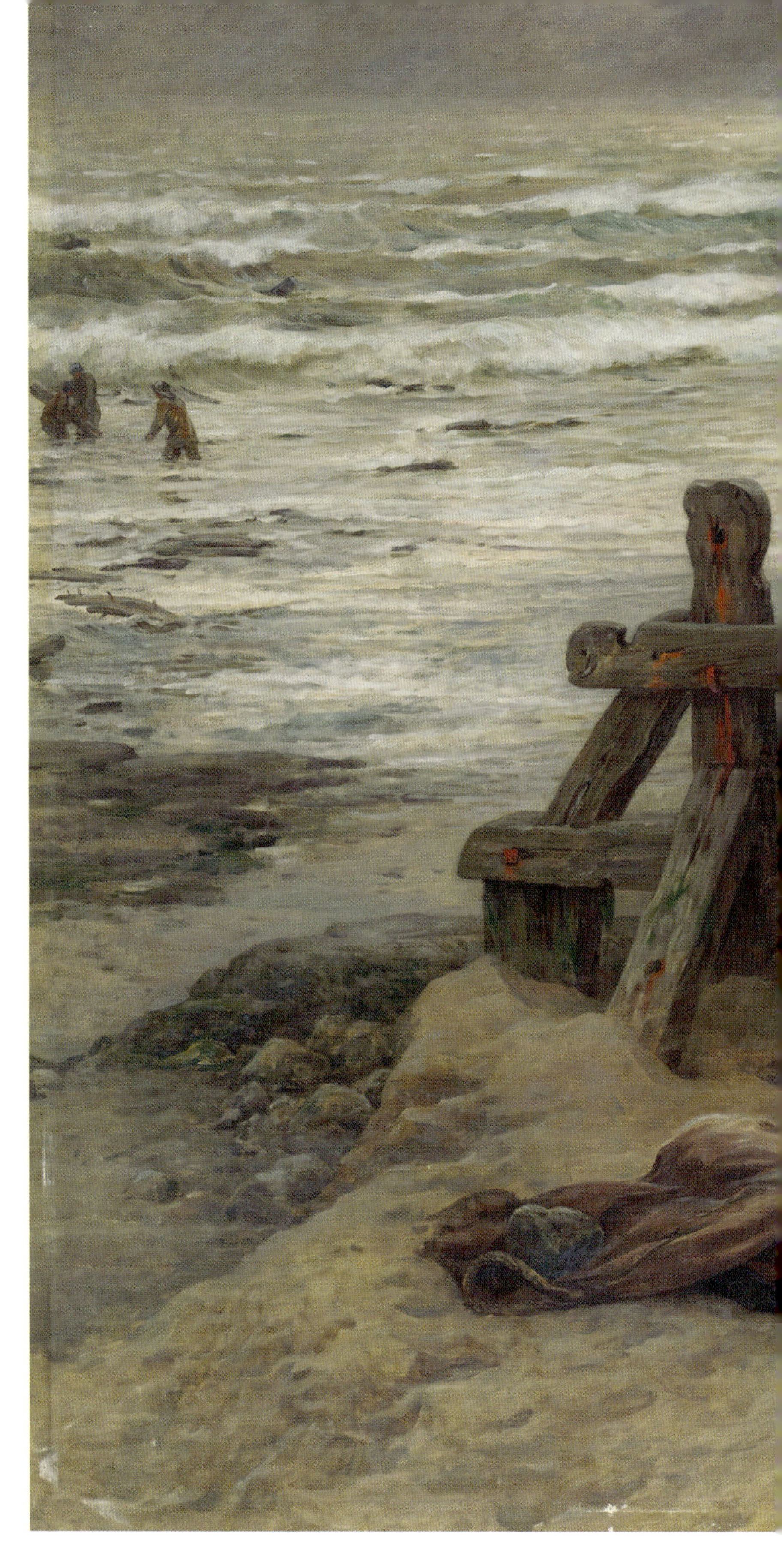

PLATE 76 VIRGINIE DEMONT-BRETON, *THE TORMENTED* (*LES TOURMENTÉS*), 1905
Oil on canvas, 60⅝ × 80¾ in. (154 × 205 cm). Palais des Beaux-Arts, Lille, France, P 1664

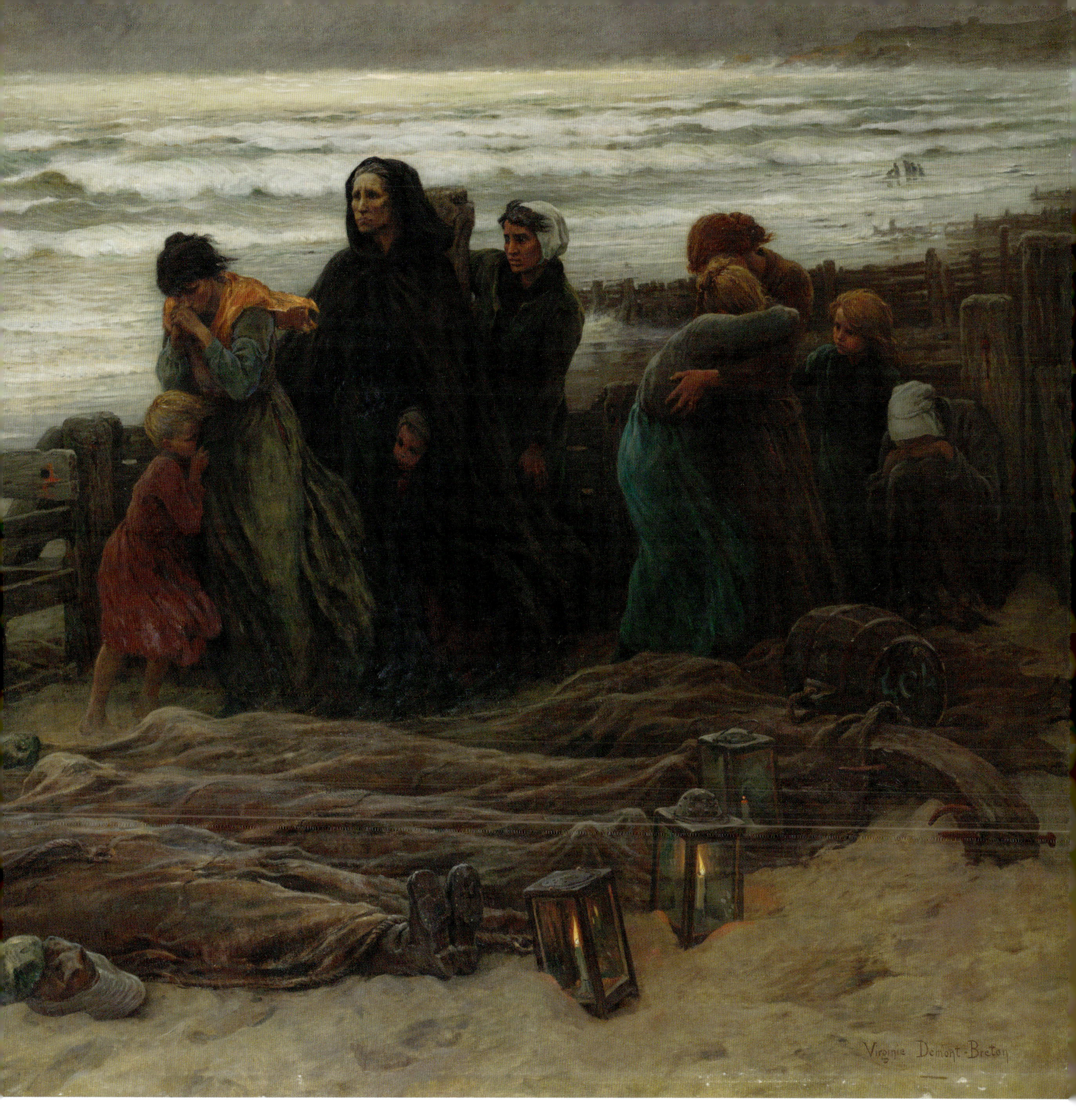
Virginie Demont-Breton

PLATE 77 ELIZABETH NOURSE, *FISHER GIRL OF PICARDY*, 1889

Oil on canvas, 46¾ × 32¼ in. (118.7 × 82 cm). Smithsonian American Art Museum, Washington, DC, Gift of Elizabeth Pilling, 1915.3.1

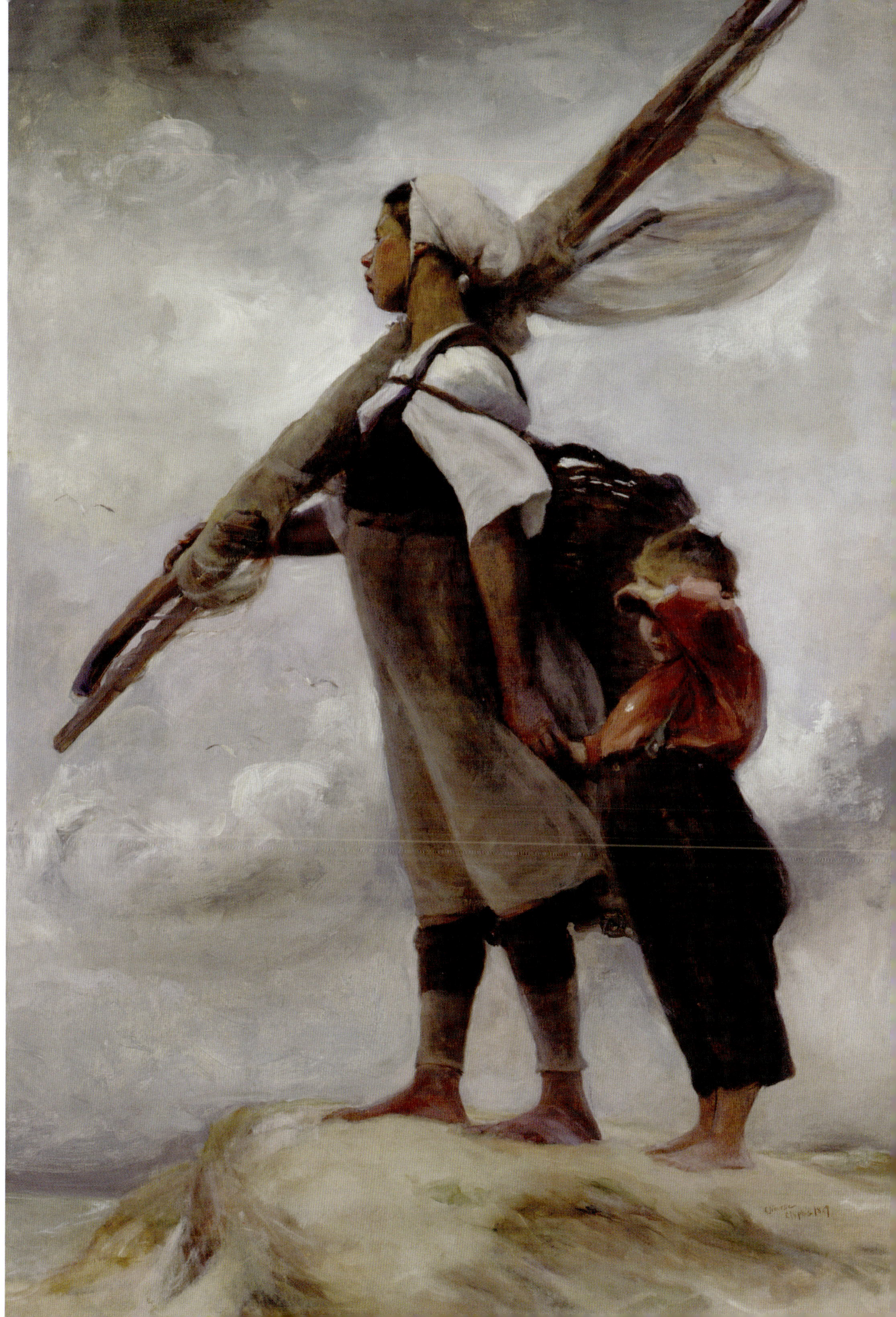

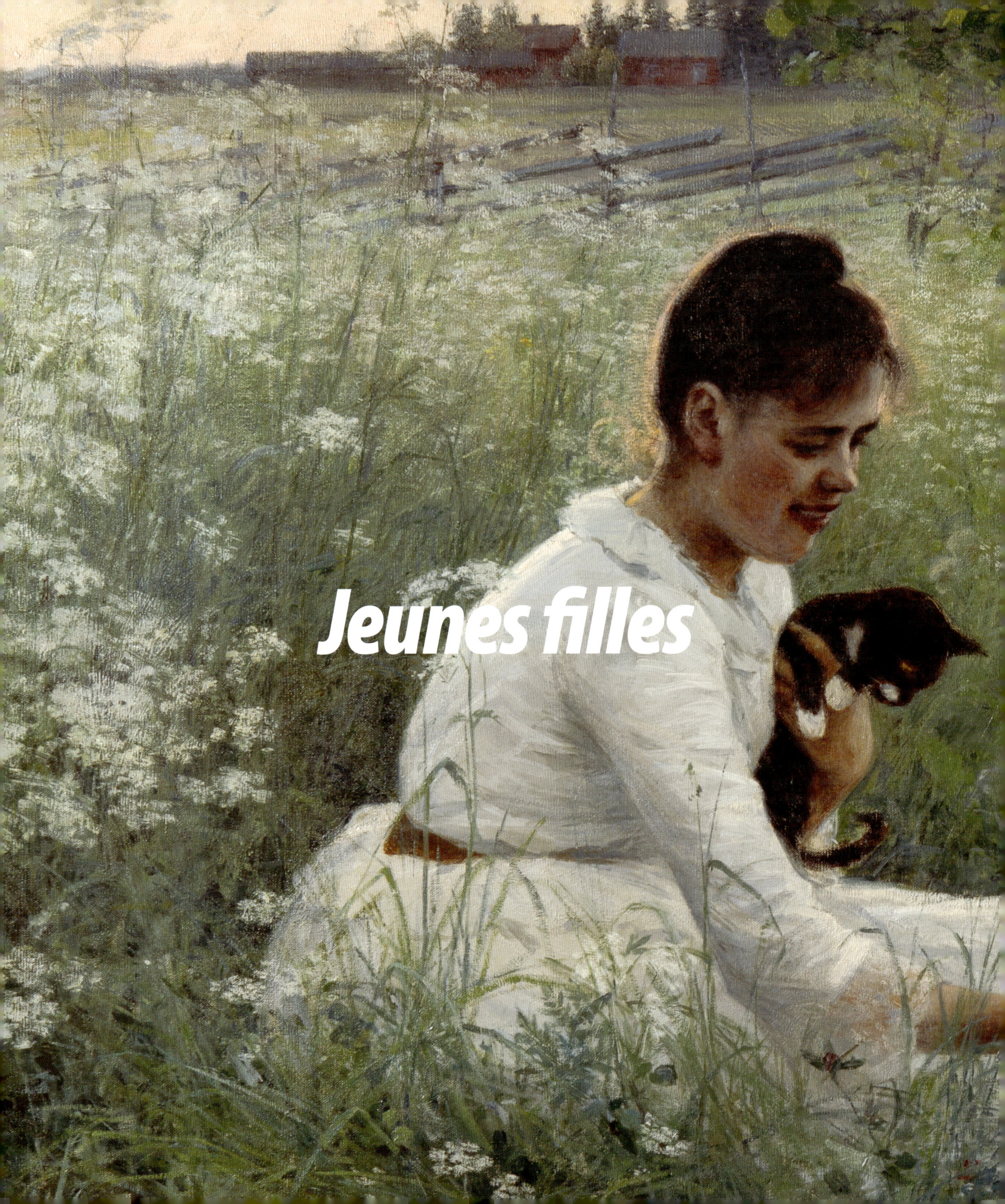

Jeunes filles

Although representations of *jeunes filles*—girls navigating the liminal stage between adolescence and adulthood—may relate to the same concerns raised by the depiction of children, it nonetheless remains a distinct theme. Just as childhood was a creation of the late eighteenth century, young ladies became increasing visible in the nineteenth century, when the average marrying age for girls rose, and with it the urgent need to prepare them to fulfill their expected duties. Lost in thought as she glimpses a passing locomotive, the protagonist of Marianne Preindlsberger-Stokes's *The Passing Train* [plate 81] is located somewhere on the border of the "provincial" and the modern, and caught between the promise and uncertainty of adolescence. Lilla Cabot Perry's dual portraits of her three daughters, *Open Air Concert* [plate 83] and *The Trio, Tokyo, Japan* [plate 84], document their maturation over the course of almost a decade.

It would seem natural for women painters to portray this transitional identity with which they are intimately acquainted, having passed through this stage themselves: "Woman is essentially idealistic, romantic, from the first springtime of her adolescence and before beginning her own love story."[1] Such romantic ideals readily come to the fore in these depictions, where the constraints of good breeding and the shackles of morality can also be discerned. In *La Confidence* [plate 78], Elizabeth Jane Gardner Bouguereau represents two girls sharing a secret, succinctly presenting the key themes tied to nineteenth-century notions of budding womanhood: first, the need for proper guidance, good advice, and others in whom to confide; second, the birth of love, which will lead to marriage, itself the condition for woman's true blossoming and fulfillment; and third, the preservation of purity and virginity, as symbolized by the unbroken jug.

Stokes's *Death and the Maiden* [plate 87] references a score by Schubert to allude to the ancient iconography of a young lady intimately coupled with death, the specter of the threats looming over adolescent girls (tuberculosis and other diseases, prostitution, unhappy marriage). This theme was prevalent in Symbolist painting, and Helene Schjerfbeck treated it with a certain remove in her *The Schoolgirl II (Girl in Black)* [plate 86]—the gaze of the Finnish pupil solemnly suggests an off-canvas presence.

Alongside these somber images, in Berthe Morisot's *Girl in a Park* [plate 79] and Elin Danielson-Gambogi's *Girl and Kittens in a Summer Landscape* [plate 82], the young subjects also embody curiosity, the pleasure of discovery, hope, and grace. In Ellen Thesleff's portrait of her sister, *Thyra Elisabeth* [plate 88], the artist adumbrates a halo to suggest a wakening power. And then there is Thesleff's *Echo* [plate 89], which presents a girl discovering, in a sudden cry, the power of her own voice as it resounds against the landscape. This release suggests a vital communicative energy that perhaps anticipates the future autonomy of young and grown women alike.

1. Virginie Demont-Breton, "La femme dans l'art," *Journal des artistes*, July 12, 1896.

PLATE 78 ELIZABETH JANE GARDNER BOUGUEREAU, *LA CONFIDENCE*, CA. 1880

Oil on canvas mounted on aluminum, 68 × 47⅛ in. (172.7 × 119.7 cm). Georgia Museum of Art, University of Georgia; Original gift of Mr. George Seney to the Lucy Cobb Institute, Athens, GA. GMOA 00.67

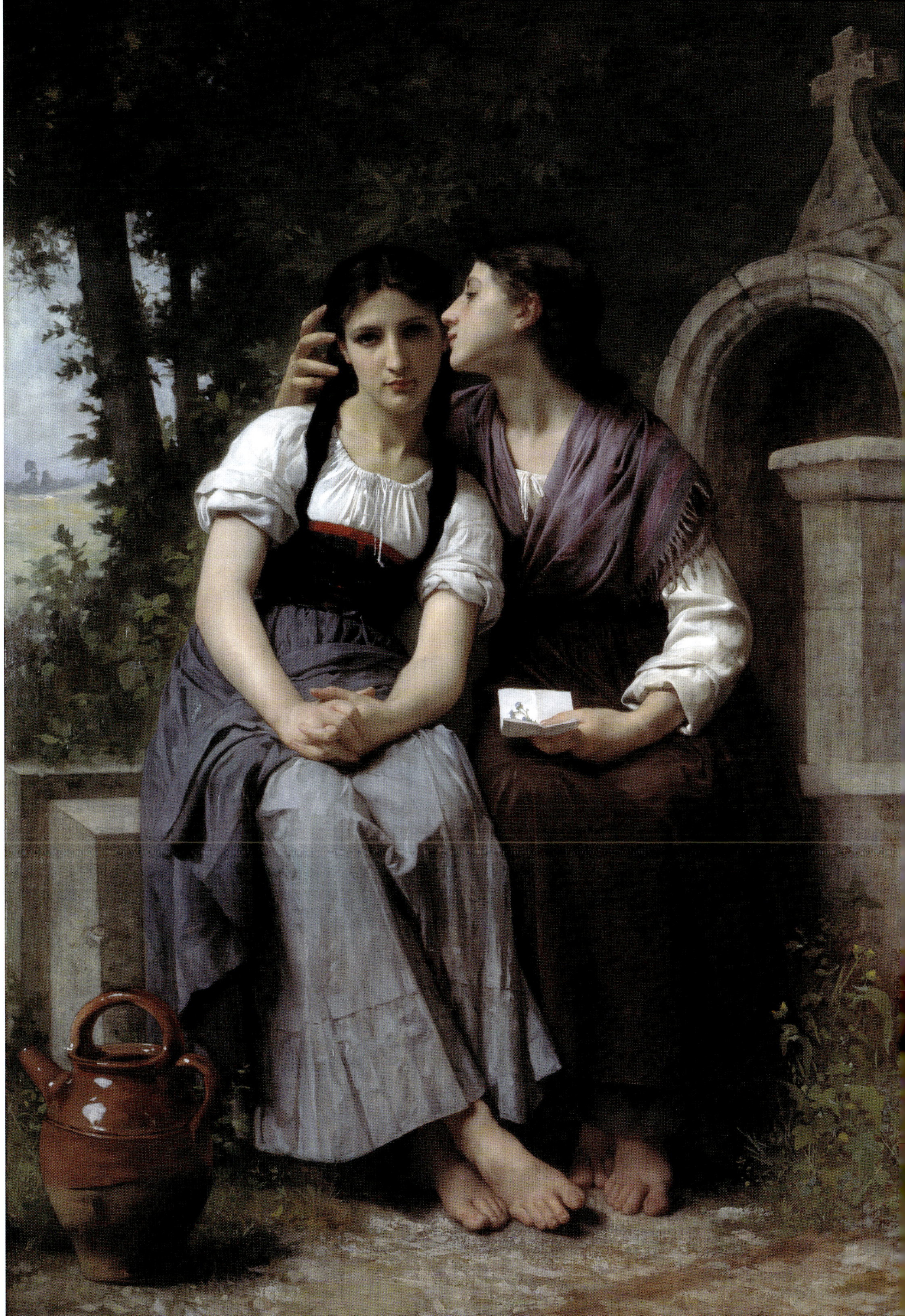

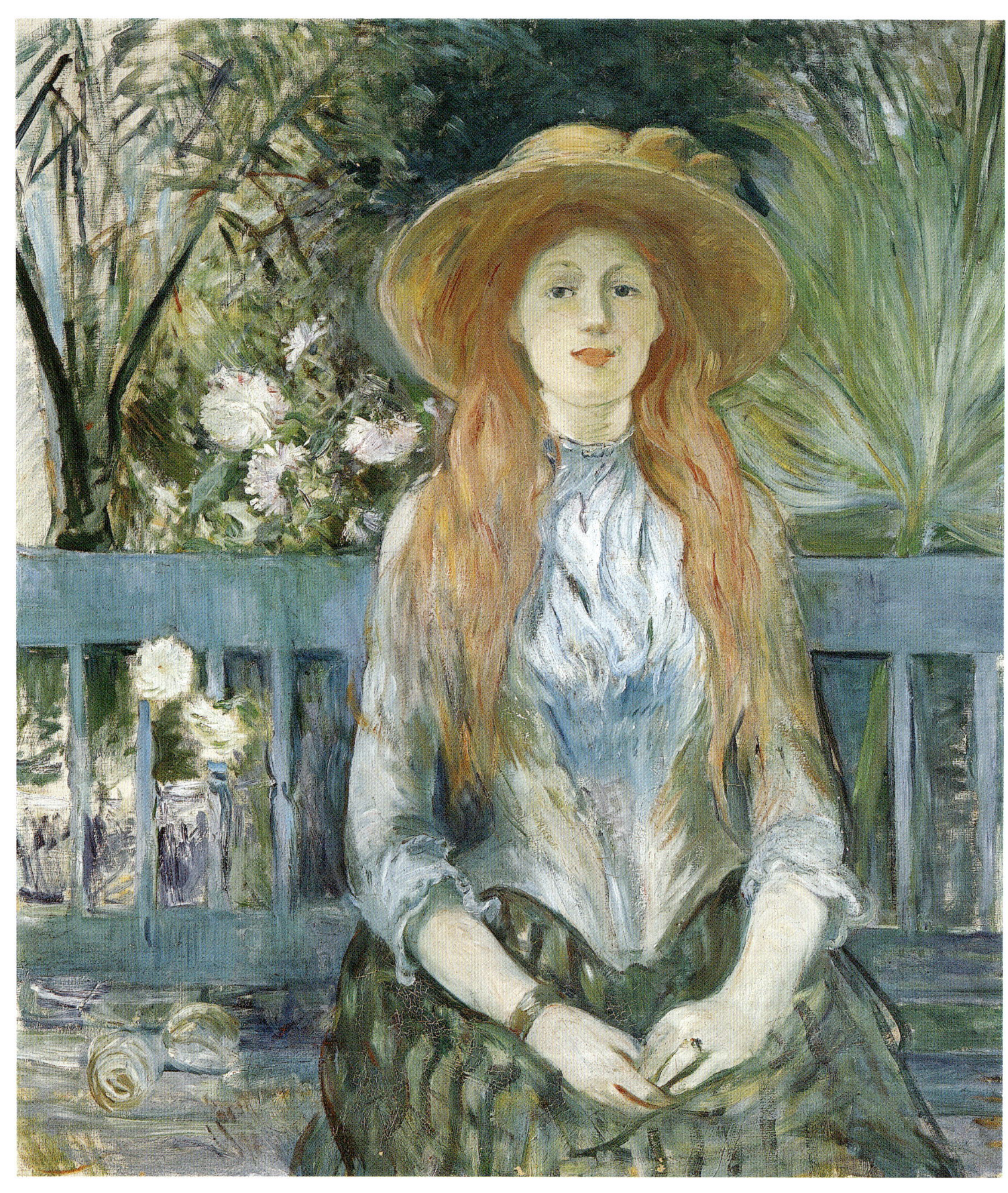

PLATE 79 BERTHE MORISOT, *GIRL IN A PARK* (*JEUNE FILLE DANS UN PARC*), 1888–93

Oil on canvas, 35⅜ × 31⅞ in. (90 × 81 cm). Musée des Augustins, Toulouse, RO708

PLATE 80 BERTHE MORISOT, *THE CHERRY TREE*, 1891

Oil on canvas, 57⅝ × 35 in. (146.5 × 89 cm). Collection of Bruce and Robbi Toll

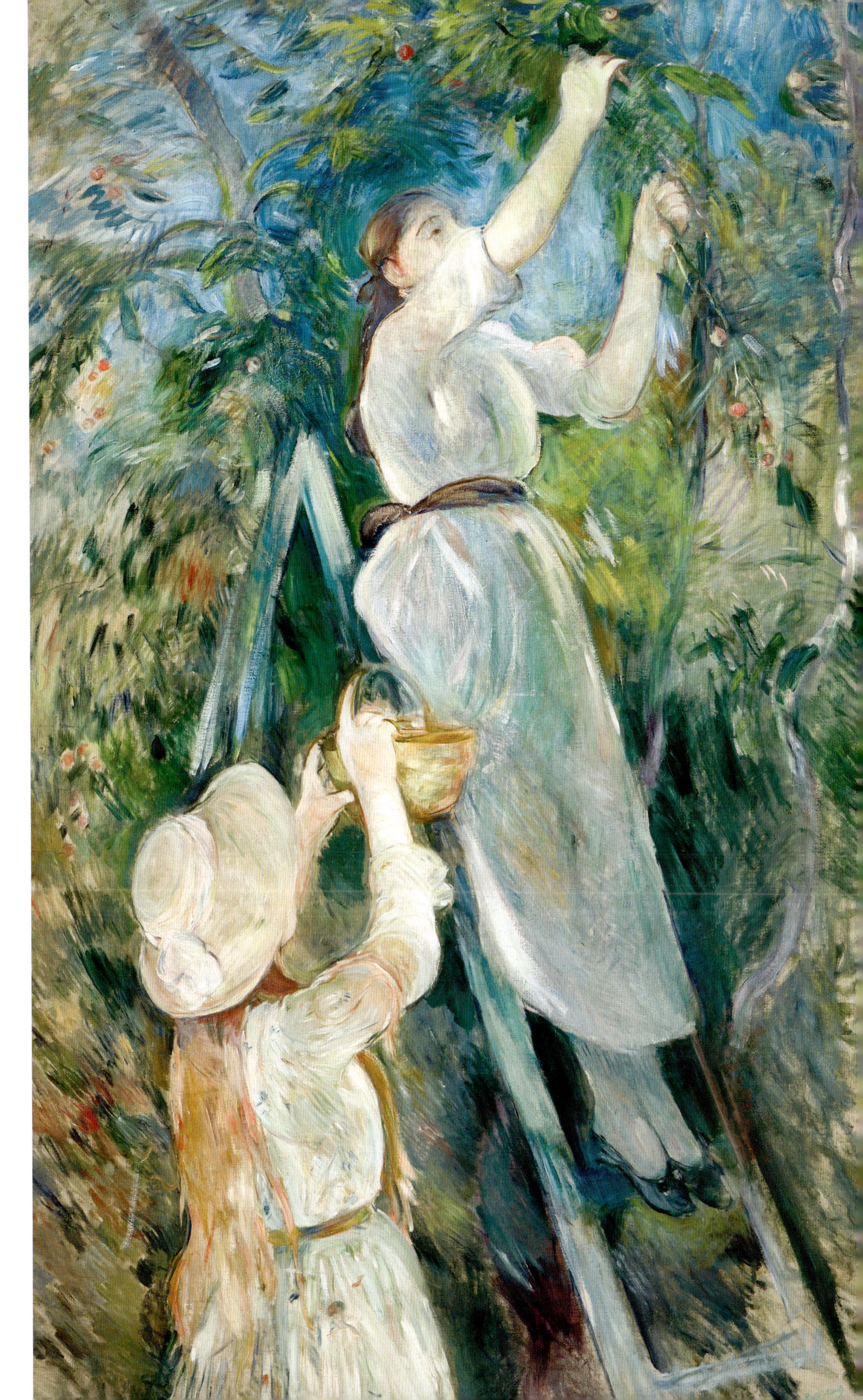

PLATE 81 **MARIANNE PREINDLSBERGER-STOKES, *THE PASSING TRAIN*, 1890**

Oil on canvas, 24 × 30 in. (61 × 76.2 cm). Private collection

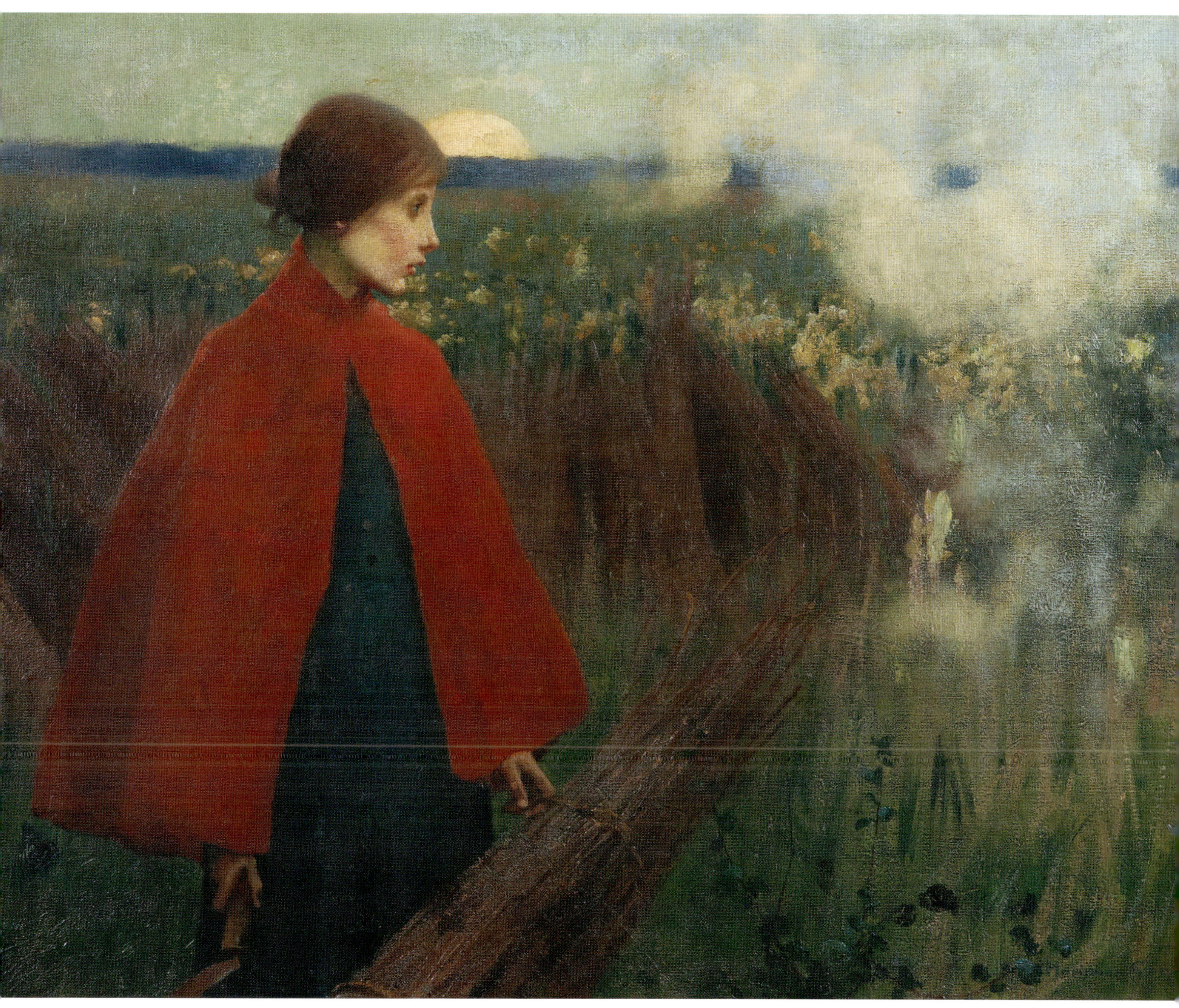

PLATE 82 ELIN DANIELSON-GAMBOGI, *GIRL AND KITTENS IN A SUMMER LANDSCAPE*, 1892

Oil on canvas, 43¼ × 54 in. (110 × 137 cm). UPM-Kymmene Cultural Foundation, Helsinki, UKK S56

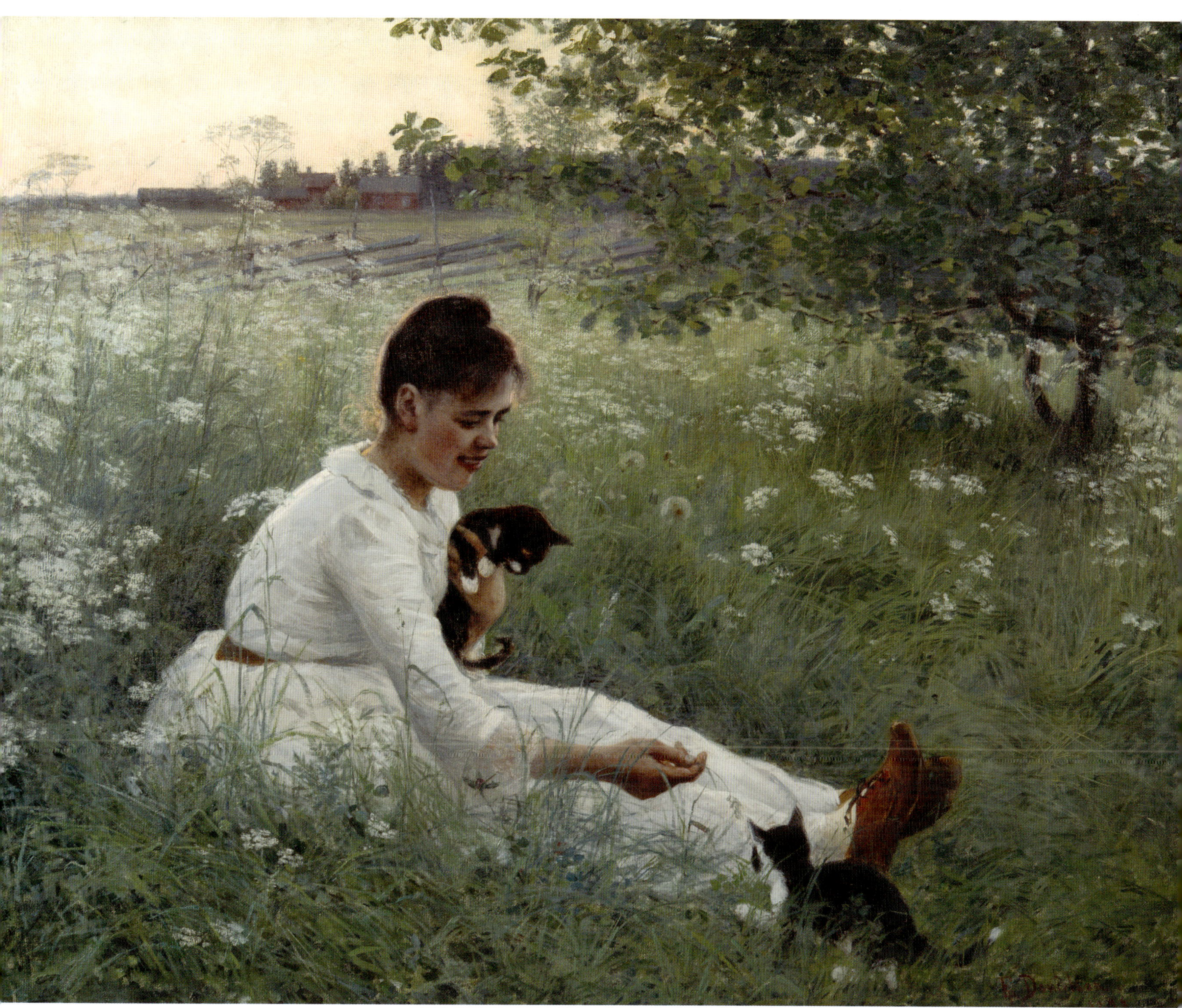

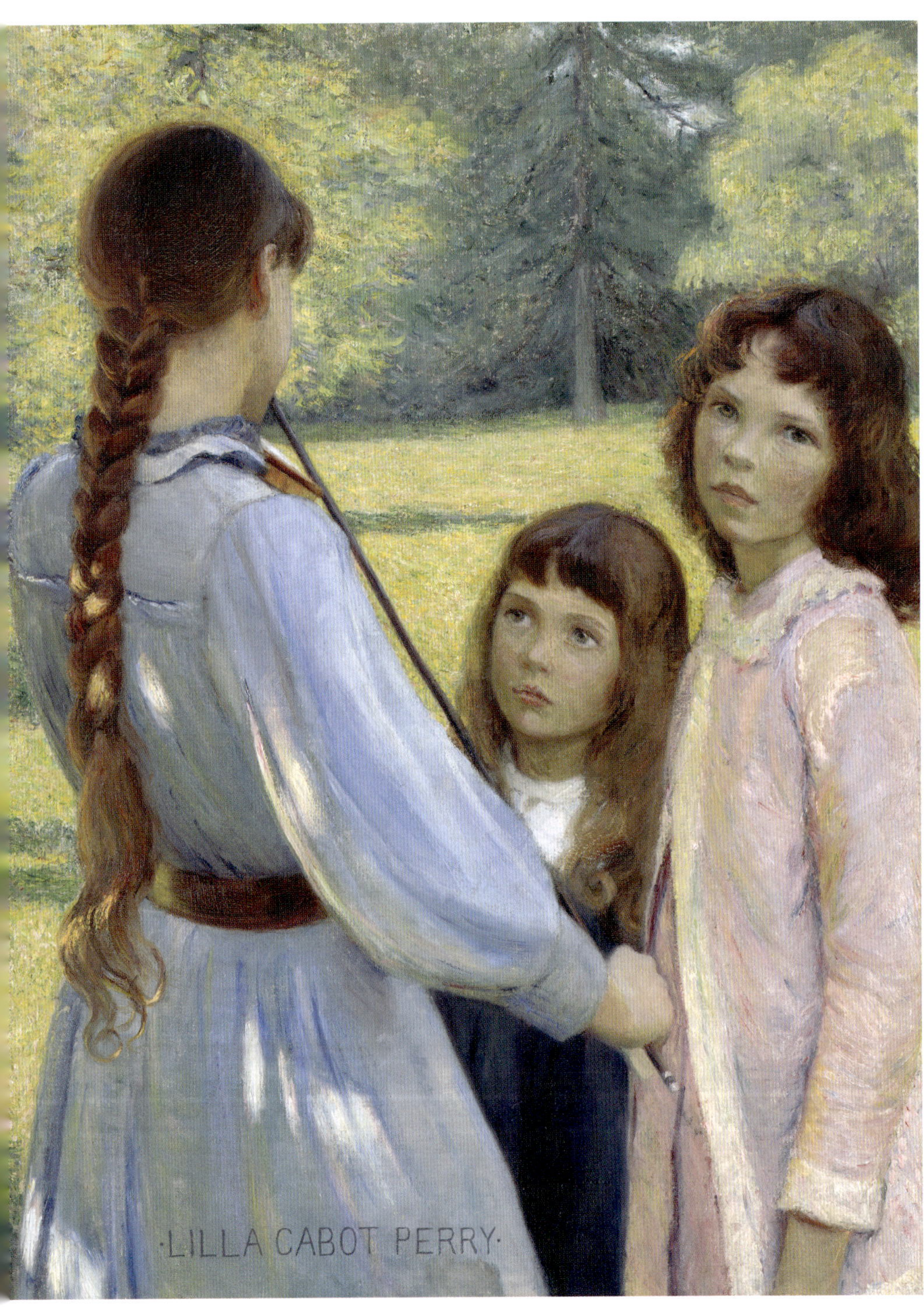

PLATE 83 **LILLA CABOT PERRY, *OPEN AIR CONCERT*, 1890**

Oil on canvas, 39¾ × 30⅛ in. (101 × 76.5 cm). Museum of Fine Arts, Boston, Gift of Miss Margaret Perry, 64.2055

PLATE 84 **LILLA CABOT PERRY, *THE TRIO, TOKYO, JAPAN*, 1898–1901**

Oil on canvas, 29¾ × 39⅜ in. (75.6 × 100 cm). Harvard Art Museums/Fogg Museum, Cambridge, MA, Friends of the Fogg Art Museum Fund, 1952.117

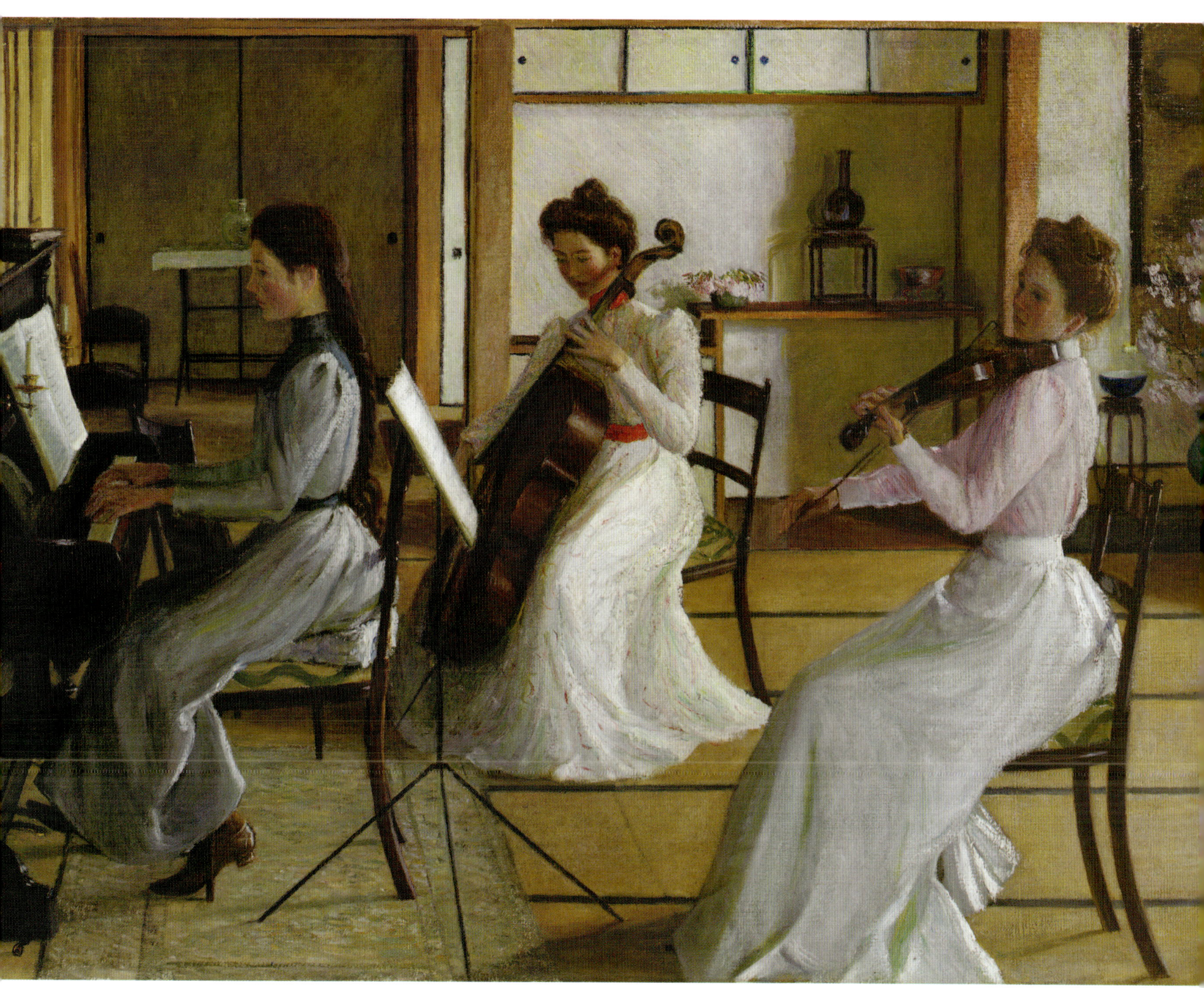

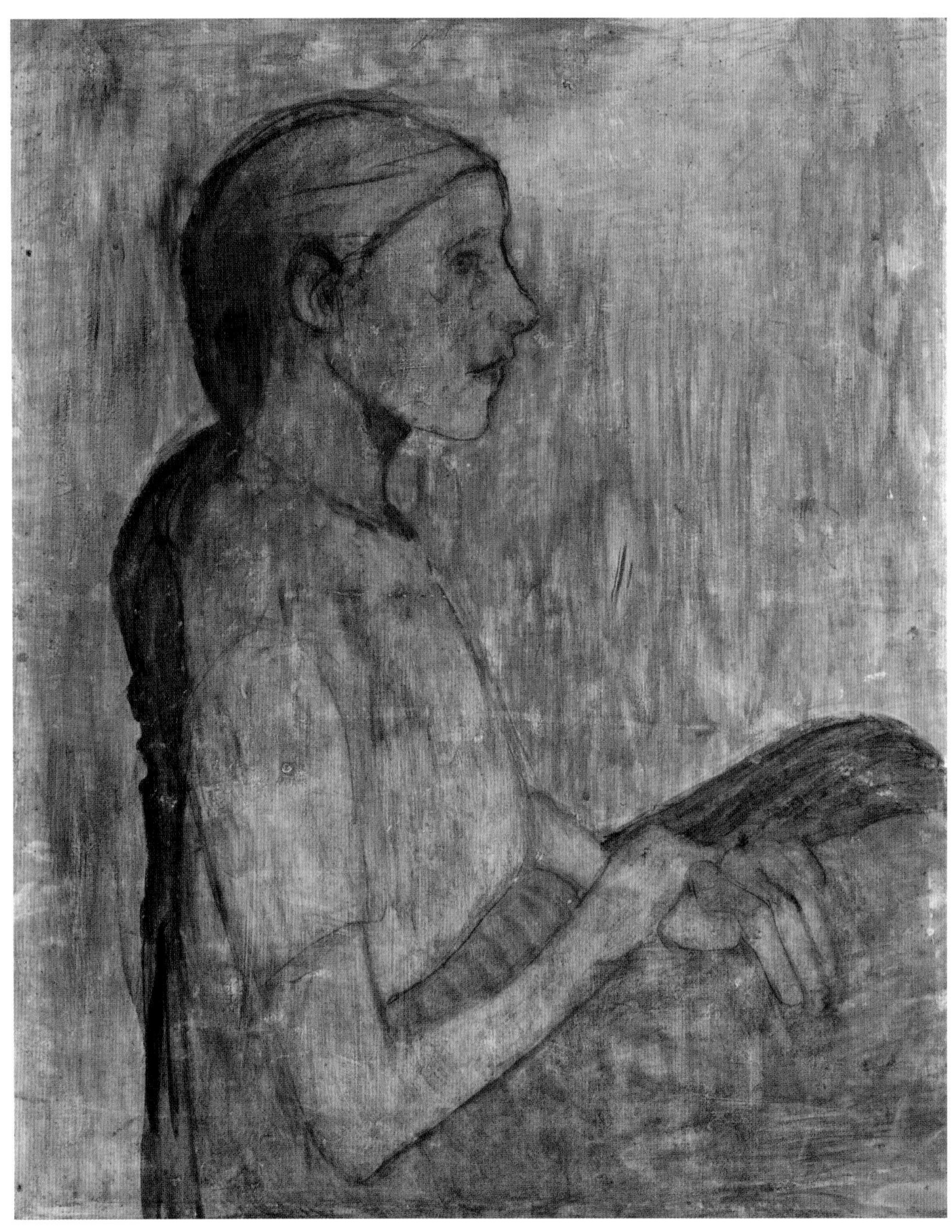

PLATE 85a and b PAULA MODERSOHN-BECKER
Verso: ***SELF-PORTRAIT: A STUDY IN BLACK, GRAY, AND WHITE*, CA. 1898–1900**
Mixed media on cardboard, 27½ × 22 in. (69.9 × 55.9 cm)
Recto: ***GIRL WITH A BABY AMONG BIRCH TREES*, 1905**
Oil on cardboard, 27½ × 22 in. (69.9 × 55.9 cm)
Chrysler Museum of Art, Norfolk, VA, Gift of Margaret S. Travers in memory of Arnold F. Strauss, M.D., and Marjory Spindle Strauss, 94.21

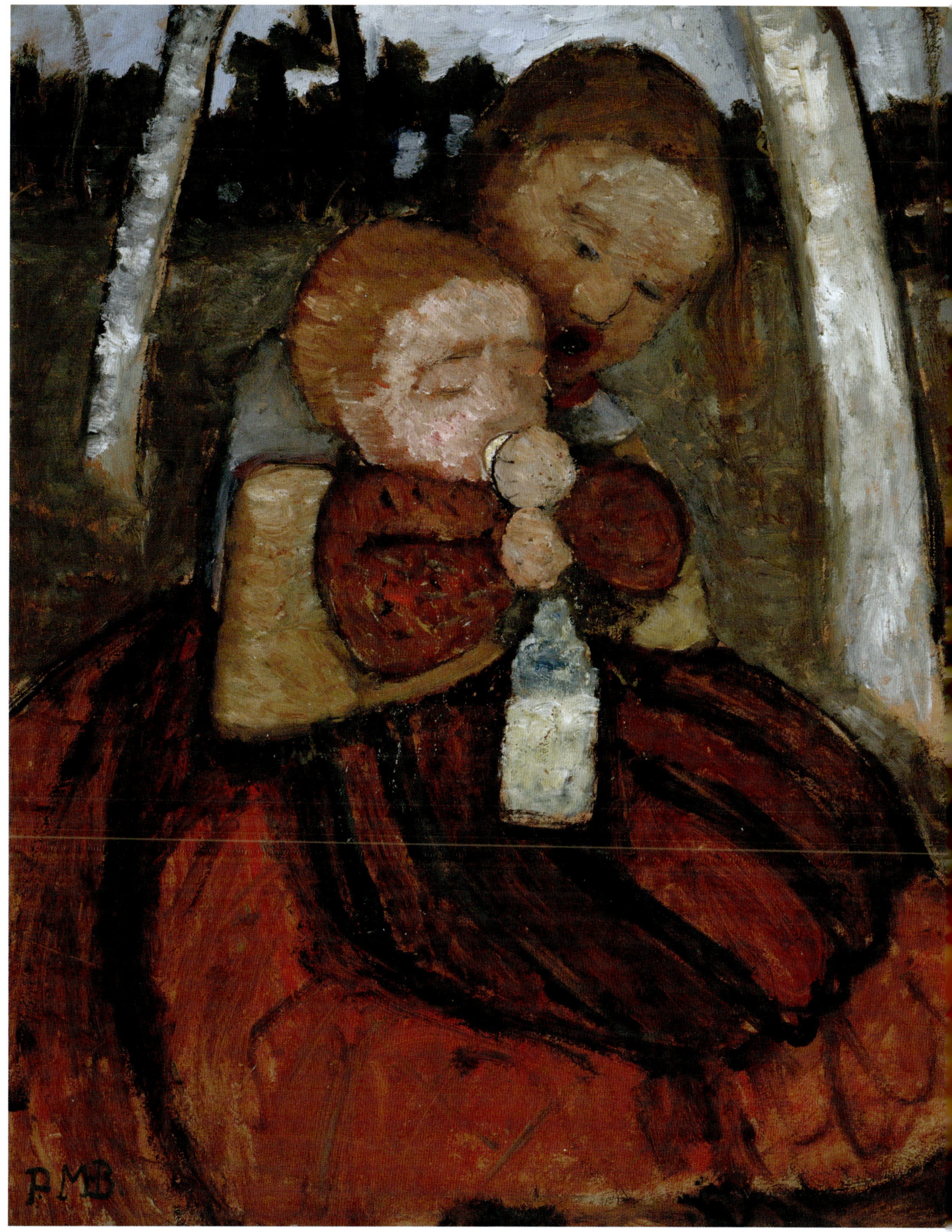

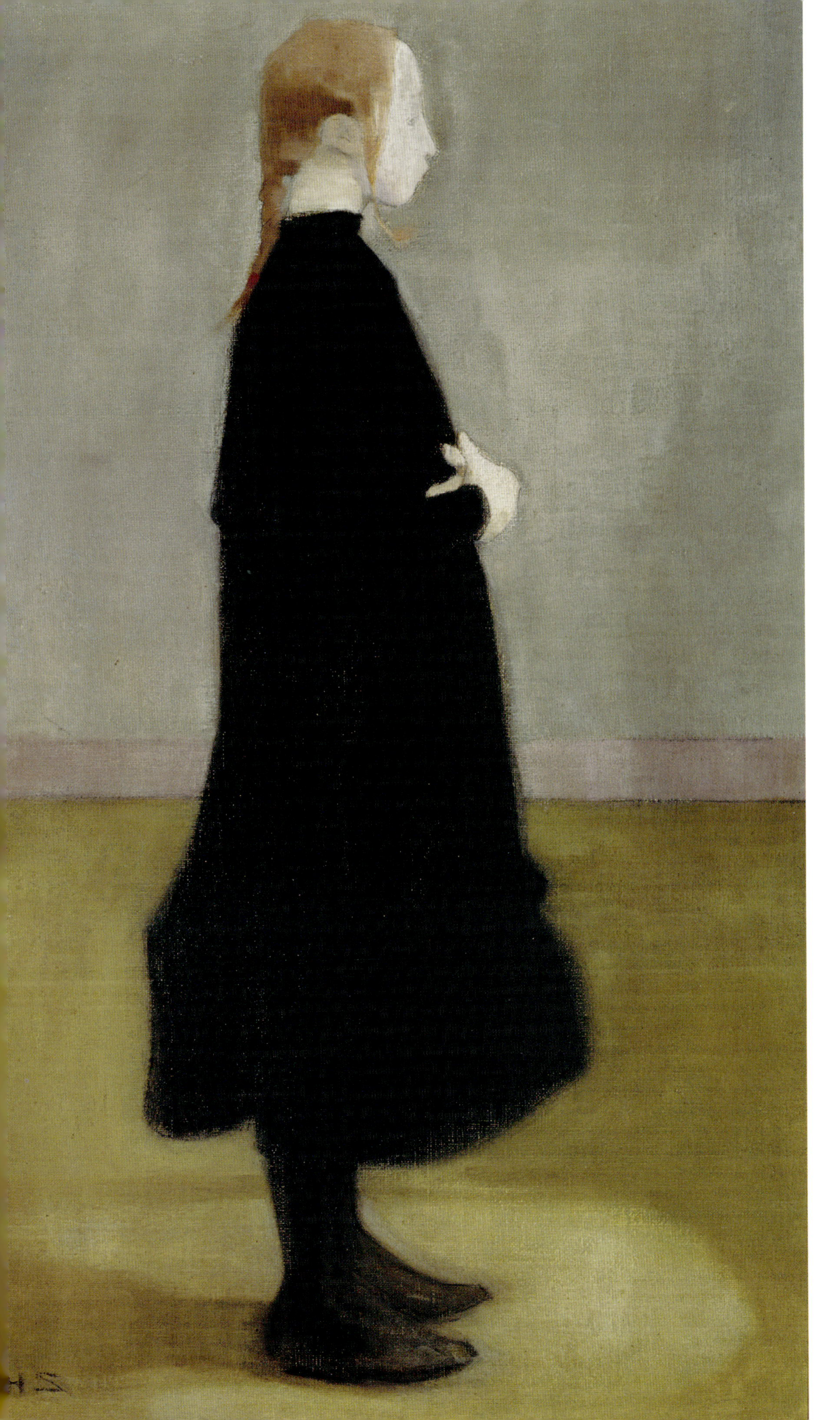

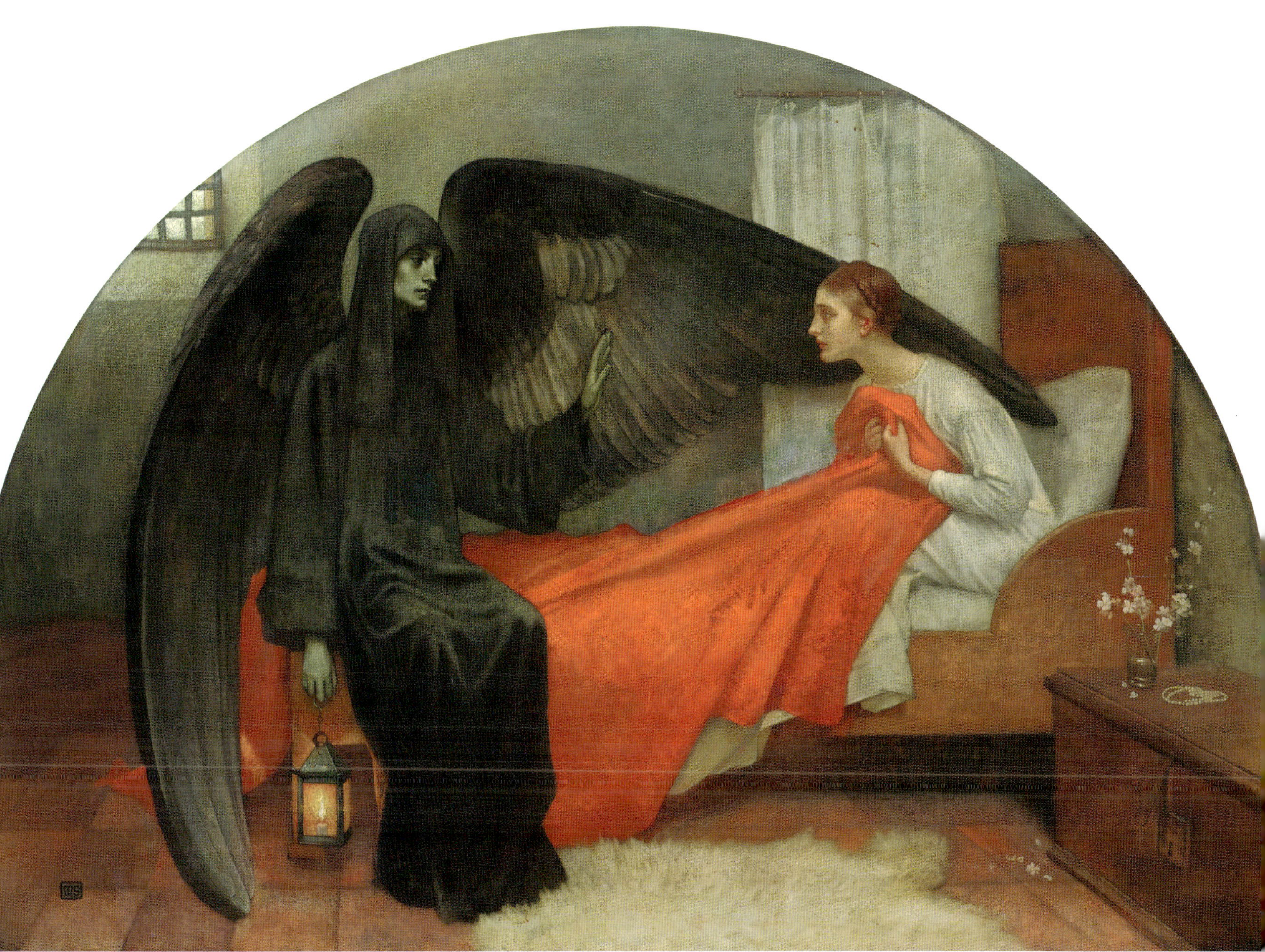

PLATE 86 HELENE SCHJERFBECK, *THE SCHOOLGIRL II (GIRL IN BLACK)*, 1908

Oil on canvas, 28 × 16 in. (71 × 40.5 cm). Herman and Elisabeth Hallonblad Collection, Finnish National Gallery, Ateneum Art Museum, Helsinki, A II 1062

PLATE 87 MARIANNE PREINDLSBERGER-STOKES, *DEATH AND THE MAIDEN* (*LA JEUNE FILLE ET LA MORT*), 1908

Oil on canvas, 37⅜ × 53⅛ in. (95 × 135 cm). Musée d'Orsay, Paris, RF1978-36

PLATE 88 ELLEN THESLEFF, *THYRA ELISABETH*, 1892

Oil on canvas, 16 × 13½ in. (41.5 × 34.5 cm). HAM Helsinki Art Museum, The Katarina and Leonard Bäcksbacka Collection

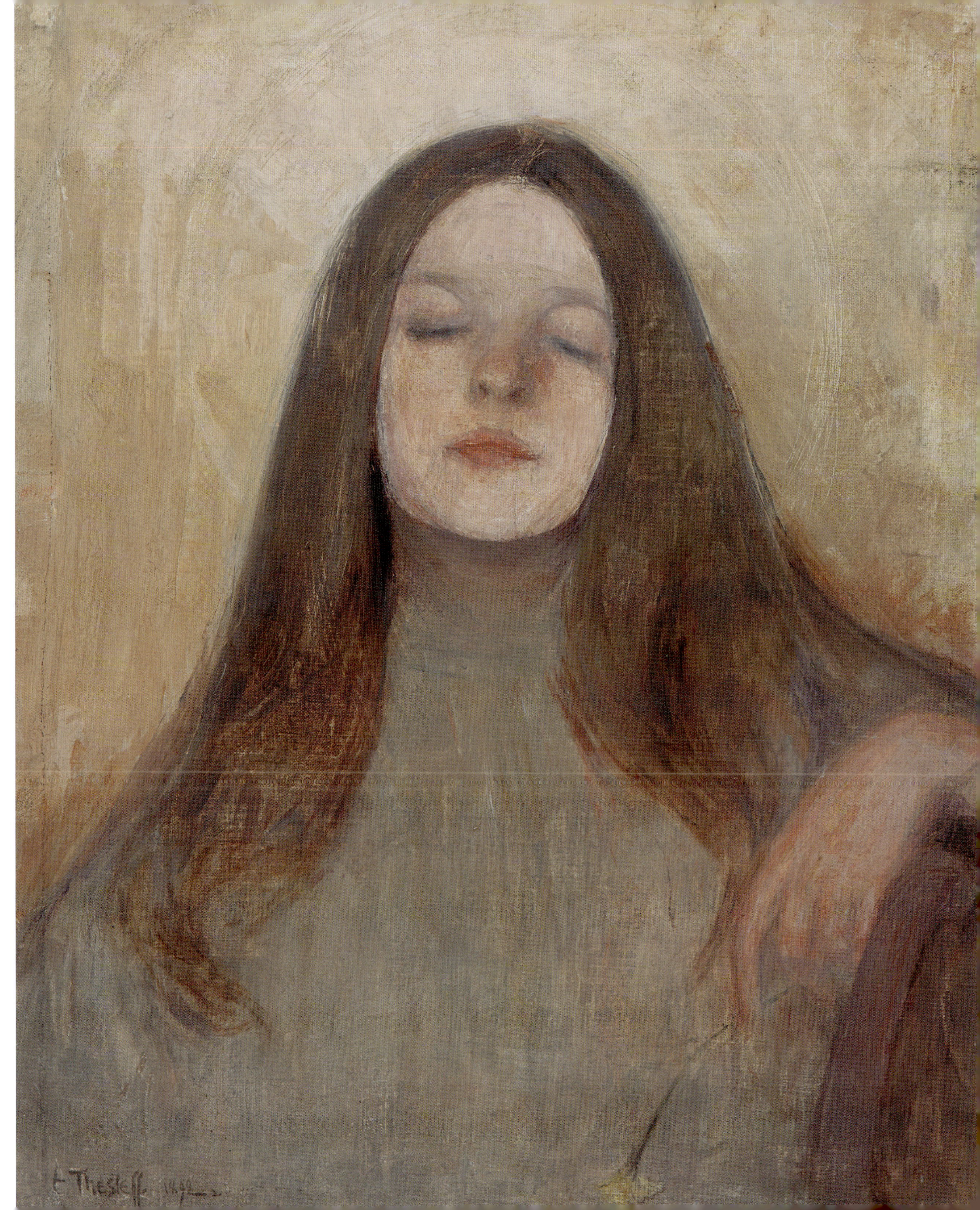
E. Thesleff.

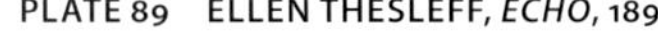

PLATE 89 ELLEN THESLEFF, *ECHO*, 1891

Oil on canvas, 24 × 17⅛ in. (61 × 43.5 cm). Anders Wiklöf Collection, Andersudde, Åland Islands

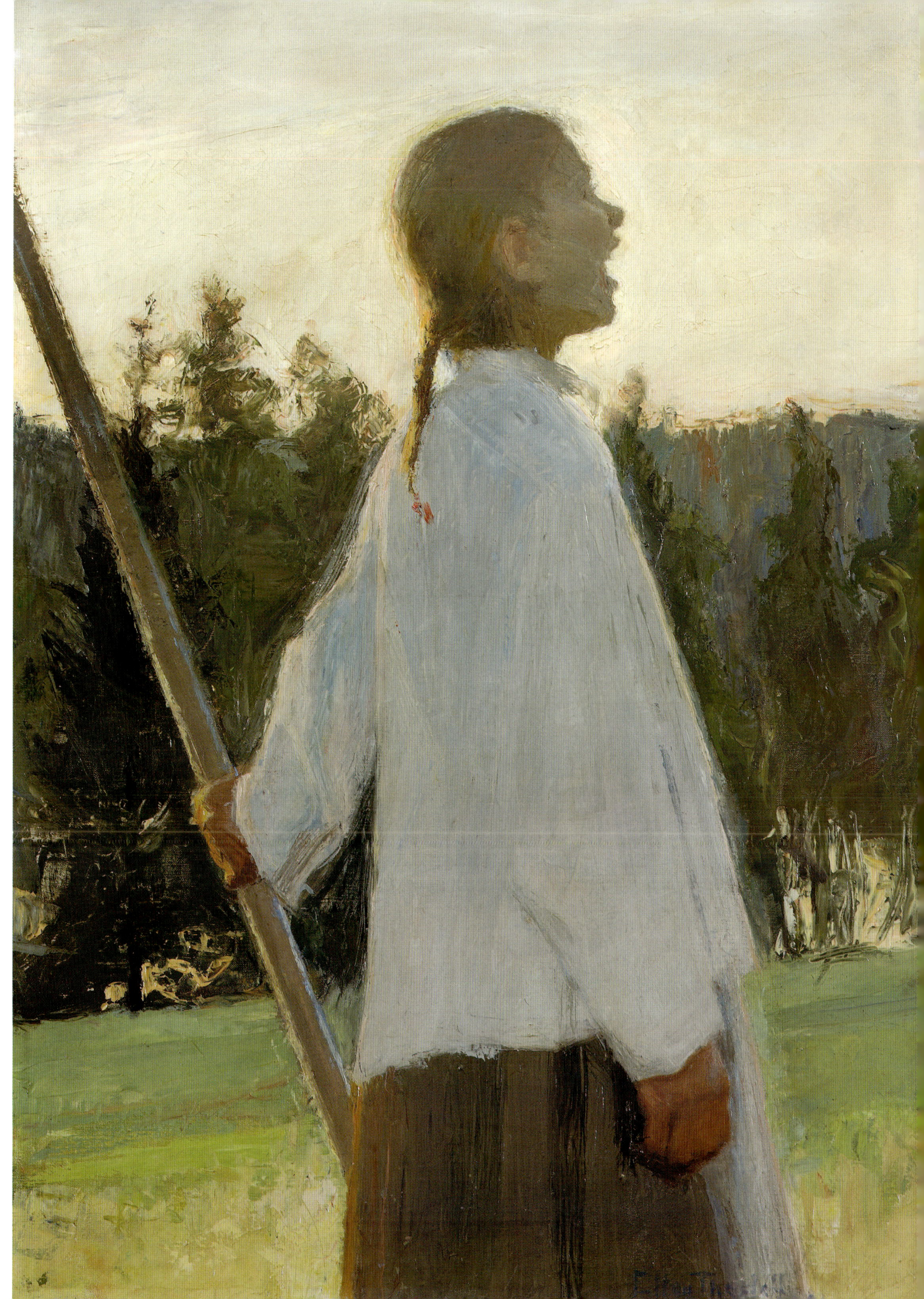

JOËLLE BOLLOCH

WITH CONTRIBUTIONS BY
MAGDALEN EVANS, JEREMIAH WILLIAM MCCARTHY, AND ANNA MEISTER

Artist Biographies

Louise Abbéma

ÉTAMPES, FRANCE, 1853–PARIS, 1927

The sole daughter of viscount Emile-Léon Abbéma and Henriette-Anne-Sophie d'Astoin, Louise Abbéma was born in the little village of Étampes. Her interest in drawing was encouraged by her father, in particular during the family's stay in Italy between 1859 and 1867, where they made visits to museums. Upon her return to Paris, Abbéma began copying works at the Louvre and then briefly studied in the studio of painter Charles Chaplin. She quickly moved on to the "women's studio" opened in 1874 by Carolus-Duran and Jean-Jacques Henner. At the 1876 Salon she presented *Portrait of Sarah Bernhardt*, which she had painted the preceding year. Abbéma and Bernhardt first met in 1871. The artist wanted to depict the actress, and first made many sketches before asking the actress to pose for a painting. A great friendship soon developed between the two, which some interpreted as a love affair. Bernhardt, who was also a sculptor and had a studio in her mansion on rue Fortuny, carved a marble bust of Abbéma, currently housed at the Musée d'Orsay. Abbéma, in turn, designed the interiors for one of the salons in Bernhardt's mansion.

Abbéma exhibited at the Salon on forty-five occasions. Her first participation dates to 1874, when she presented *Portrait de Mme ****, allegedly a portrait of her mother, which has disappeared; her last was in 1926. The artist was acknowledged several times during her career, including receiving an honorable mention in 1881, a bronze medal at the 1900 Exposition Universelle, and the medal of honor in 1906—making her only the fourth woman to receive that distinction, after Rosa Bonheur, Virginie Demont-Breton, and Louise Breslau.

She was well connected in artistic circles in Paris, as well as with politicians and the press, and was awarded numerous commissions. The work Abbéma produced is eclectic: floral subjects, etchings, watercolors, and pastels as well as portraits, decorative panels, illustrations for art reviews, fans, and advertising designs. She was one of the few artists of the time to be the subject of annual solo exhibitions at the important Galerie Georges Petit, located on rue Godot-de-Mauroy in Paris.

Abbéma's status as a successful, unmarried artist, as well as her sober style of dress and presumed relationship with Bernhardt, led to an undeserved reputation as a feminist. However, some of her remarks and actions contradict that: she refused to participate in Union des Femmes Peintres et Sculpteurs exhibitions, but in 1893 agreed to show at the Chicago World's Columbian Exposition, in the Woman's Building where women artists' works were gathered.

Louise Abbéma died four years after Sarah Bernhardt, and was buried in the Montparnasse Cemetery in Paris. —JB

Anna Ancher, née Brøndum

SKAGEN, DENMARK, 1859–1935

Anna Kirstine Brøndum was born on August 18, 1859, in Skagen, the northernmost town in Denmark. Located on the east side of the Skagen Odde peninsula, Skagen originally developed as a fishing village and summer destination, and Brøndum's family capitalized on early tourism to the area by opening an inn. Artists were drawn to Skagen, particularly during the summer, for its picturesque landscape and the intensity of its sunlight, which is unparalleled throughout Denmark. From the 1880s to the end of the century, the artists' colony at Skagen flourished, with artists frequently housed at the Brøndum family hotel. Internationally famous artist Peder Severin Krøyer's arrival in 1882 cemented Skagen's place as a premier artists' destination.

At the age of sixteen, Brøndum became engaged to the artist Michael Ancher. She spent the next three winters studying in Copenhagen with the painter Vilhelm Kyhn. After Kyhn suggested that Brøndum give up making art and prepare to be a wife and mother, she ended her studies with him and returned home to Skagen, where she found reassurance within the town's burgeoning artistic community. She and Michael married in 1880, and the couple welcomed their daughter Helga three years later.

As Danish women were occluded from study at the Royal Danish Academy of Fine Arts, Ancher frequently traveled abroad to find inspiration and seek artistic training: in 1881 she visited Gothenburg, Sweden, and in 1882 she traveled to Germany and Vienna. Scholars frequently cite the influence of Dutch Golden Age painters on Ancher's development, and it is likely that she saw their paintings during this Vienna trip. In 1883 she and her husband jointly painted *Judgement of a Day's Work*, a visual document of both their romantic and artistic relationships. Two years later, Ancher spent time in Amsterdam, Belgium, and Paris, during which time she painted *Young Woman Arranging Flowers*. This now-iconic work demonstrates many of the painterly concerns that would occupy the artist for the rest of her career: the elevation of an everyday task, the effect of light on varied surfaces, and the solitary female figure caught in a moment of mental absorption.

At the end of 1888, Ancher made a second trip with Michael to Paris, where she studied under Pierre Puvis de Chavannes. During this period, she painted *An Old Woman in Her Room, Mrs. Brat*, and the remarkable portrait of her peer, the Norwegian painter Kitty Kielland (1889).

Upon their return home, the Anchers created a world unto themselves at Skagen, along with Krøyer and his wife, artist Marie Krøyer; in his magisterial *Summer Evening on Skagen's South Beach* (1893), Krøyer pictures Anna and Marie walking arm-in-arm along the edge of the sea. While the work of both P. S. Krøyer and Michael Ancher tended to be larger in scale and often devoted to heroic depictions of Skagen's fishermen and social rituals, Anna Ancher's work was much more intimate, combining a fidelity to nature with an expressive use of color. In this regard, her unique interpretation of Danish modernity surpassed that of all other painters of her generation.

Ancher was awarded medals for her submissions to the Paris Expositions Universelles of 1889 and 1900. Throughout her life, she regularly submitted work to the annual Charlottenborg salons in Copenhagen—nearly two hundred works from 1880 to 1935, culminating in a memorial retrospective of the artist's work in 1935. The Royal Danish Academy of Fine Arts awarded her medals in 1903 and 1904, and King Christian X of Denmark honored her with the prestigious Ingenio et Arti medal in Copenhagen in 1913. In 1916 Ancher participated in the founding of the Association for Women Artists, which sought to increase educational and exhibition opportunities for women artists in Denmark, and in 1924 the artist received the first Tagea Brandt Travel Scholarship—awarded to Danish women who have advanced science or the arts—which allowed her to study in Italy.

Ancher died in Skagen on April 15, 1935, and in 1984 a selection of her letters was published by Herluf Stokholm. Major exhibitions devoted to her work include *Women Artists in Skagen* (1987; Skagens Museum), *Anna Ancher: 1859–1935* (1994; Niedersächsisches Landesmuseum, Hannover), *I Am Anna* (2009; Skagens Museum), and *A World Apart: Anna Ancher and the Skagen Art Colony* (2013; National Museum of Women in the Arts, Washington, DC). The majority of Ancher's work is held at the Skagens Museum and at Michael and Anna Ancher's home, which was turned into the Anchers Hus Museum in 1967. —JWM

Harriet Backer

HOLMESTRAND, NORWAY, 1845–OSLO, 1932

Born into a wealthy family in Holmestrand, Norway, Harriet Backer was encouraged by her parents to study drawing, an art form in which she had displayed talent since infancy. When she was twelve, the family moved to the Norwegian capital, Oslo—at the time called Christiania, a name it maintained until 1924—about forty-five miles from Holmestrand.

Backer frequented the city's many art schools until 1874, before embarking, along with her sister—who would become the celebrated pianist/composer Agathe Backer-Grondahl—on voyages to Germany and Italy. She made copies of artworks by the Old Masters in museums and continued her training, studying in Munich at Eilif Peterssen's workshop from 1874 to 1878. That year she left for Paris, where she remained for about ten years. She studied first alongside Léon Bonnat and Jean-Léon Gérôme and then with Jules Bastien-Lepage, who taught at Mme Trélat de Vigny's workshop, one of the rare spaces open to women. Here she rubbed shoulders with young foreign artists, including the Finn Helene Schjerfbeck and Marianne Stokes, of Austrian origin. She also met her compatriot Kitty Kielland, with whom she shared housing.

In 1880 Backer received an honorable mention for her painting *Solitude*, which had been admitted to the Salon. The following year she left with Kielland for Concarneau, a small port frequented at the time by many artists. The two friends then traveled through Norway, reaching Jaeren, in 1884, then Risor and Fleskum, where the painter Christian Skredsvig settled after having traveled to Paris and exhibited at the 1881 Salon. During this journey, accompanied by Erik Werenskiold, another Norwegian artist trained in Paris, Backer painted the interiors of farms and medieval churches.

Backer returned for a few more years to Paris before definitively resettling in her native country. She received a silver medal for *Chez moi* (*My House*), a painting that she exhibited at the 1889 Exposition Universelle, the fourth held in Paris during the centenary celebration of the French Revolution. She then established a school for painters in the Norwegian capital, where her notable students included Halfdan Johnsen Egedius and Harald Oskar Sohlberg.

Harriet Backer died in Oslo on March 25, 1932, at age eighty-seven. She left behind about two hundred canvases, a good number of which may be found in museums in Norway—in Oslo and at the Stavanger Art Museum, which maintains in its collection more than two thousand works of Norwegian and international art—and in the United States, notably at the St. Louis Art Museum. In 1983 the Stiftelsen Modum Blaafarvevaerket in Modum, Norway, presented the exhibition *Harriet Backer, 1845–1932, Kitty L. Kielland, 1843–1914*. In 2012 the same foundation again presented the work of Backer and Kielland, this time along with that of other women artists, including Asta Nørregaard, in an exhibition titled *Women in Art*. —JB

Marie Bashkirtseff, née Maria Konstantinovna Bashkirtseva

GAVRONTSIY, UKRAINE, 1858–PARIS, 1884

Marie Bashkirtseff came from a noble and wealthy family. After her parents separated, she lived with her mother in the Kharkiv region of Russia and received a French education. Before age twelve she had already traveled through Europe and lived in Vienna, Baden, and Geneva. Gifted with languages, she spoke Russian, French, English, and Italian.

In 1870 the family settled in Nice. Bashkirtseff was surrounded by her mother, her grandfather, her aunt, her uncle, her young brother Paul, her cousin Dina, and a friend of the family, a physician who accompanied them. She read extensively, the classics as well as contemporary authors, and took up writing; her *Journal*, which was later published, was written in French. Early on, she dedicated herself to singing, but had to give up this pursuit when she contracted tuberculosis. Turning to painting, she convinced her mother to sell the Nice property and move to Paris. Upon their arrival, she signed up for the Académie Julian, where she studied from 1877 to 1884. Her canvas *In the Studio* (also known as *L'atelier Julian*) represents the most well-known image of this institution. Bashkirtseff's *Journal*—full of anecdotes about her life at the studio, its professors, other students, her friends and enemies, and her successes and failures—presents a picture of an ambitious painter who considered Louise Breslau to be her principal rival.

Bashkirtseff exhibited her work at the Salon from the beginning of the 1880s, won an honorable mention in 1883, and the following year was represented in the painting section with *The Meeting*, one of her most celebrated paintings today. She was linked to several lovers, but never married. She took up positions in favor of women's emancipation, notably regretting that they were not admitted to the École des Beaux-Arts, as evidenced by articles published under the pseudonym Pauline Orell in *La citoyenne*, a magazine created in 1881 by Hubertine Auclert.

Bashkirtseff forged a great friendship with Jules Bastien-Lepage, with whom she shared aesthetic choices. But if Bastien-Lepage was interested in rural life, Bashkirtseff was more attracted by urban life, whose misery she depicts in a naturalist style. She produced an important body of work in her brief life, leaving behind portraits and street scenes as well as some sculptures, but many of her works were destroyed during World War II.

Marie Bashkirtseff died at age twenty-five, on October 31, 1884, due to complications from tuberculosis, a few days before the death of her friend Jules Bastien-Lepage, stricken by cancer. They saw each other until the end, assisted by Bashkirtseff's cousin Dina and Bastien-Lepage's brother.

In 1885 the Union des Femmes Peintres et Sculpteurs organized a posthumous exhibition in Bashkirtseff's honor. The state acquired *The Meeting*, today held at the Musée d'Orsay in Paris. A few years later her *Journal* was published. Early versions were largely sugar-coated by her family; in 1995 the Cercle des Amis de Marie Bashkirtseff published an edition that is loyal to her manuscript. —JB

Amélie Beaury-Saurel

BARCELONA, 1848–PARIS, 1924

Partly raised in Spain, where she was born, Amélie Beaury chose to add Saurel to her surname to honor her mother's family, which dated back to the Komnenos dynasty, Byzantine emperors of the eleventh century.

After a stay in Corsica, the family settled in France. Beaury-Saurel enrolled in the Académie Julian, where she managed expenses for the women's studio, serving as an intermediary between instructors and students and representing the students' interests. In her *Journal*, Marie Bashkirtseff, also a student at the studio, speaks with a certain annoyance of the woman she calls "the Spaniard."

During the 1873 Salon, Beaury-Saurel presented her first work of art, a portrait, and declared herself a student of a certain M. Coeffier. She returned to the Salon in 1879 with two works, this time identifying herself as a student of Tony Robert-Fleury, the main instructor of the women's studio at the Académie Julian. Through the years she added William-Adolphe Bouguereau, Gustave Boulanger, Jean-Paul Laurens, Jules Lefebvre, and Jean-Joseph Benjamin-Constant to the list of her instructors.

In 1883 Beaury-Saurel obtained a third-class medal for *Portrait de Mlle S.*, and she was rewarded in the Expositions Universelles in both 1889 and 1900. She also participated in the 1891 Black and White Salon in Paris, where her canvas *Le travail de M. Frey, maître d'armes* (*The Work of M. Frey, Master of Arms*) received the honorary award. In 1895 she married Rodolphe Julian and began teaching at the women's studio, but she did not neglect her professional career, only strengthening her reputation as a portraitist. Her portrait of journalist and militant feminist Séverine (Caroline Rémy de Guebhard) appeared at the 1893 Salon, along with likenesses of the painter Jean-Paul Laurens and Léonce Bénédite, curator of the Musée du Luxembourg in Paris, among others.

Upon Rodolphe Julian's death in 1907, Beaury-Saurel regained control of the academy's management with the help of her nephews, Jacques and Gilbert Dupuis. She repurchased the house that Julian had acquired in Provence and renovated it in her husband's memory as a home for his family, especially his sister and niece, Andrée Magdeleine Husson, who wrote novels under the name André Corthis.

Amélie Beaury-Saurel died in Paris on May 30, 1924, at the age of seventy-five. —JB

Cecilia Beaux

PHILADELPHIA, 1855–GLOUCESTER, MASSACHUSETTS, 1942

Cecilia Beaux was born in Philadelphia to a French father and an American mother, who died twelve days later. Their distraught father returned to France after his wife's death, and Cecilia and her sister Aimée were raised by their maternal grandparents in a cultural environment that encouraged the development of their artistic talents. Cecilia received instruction from Catherine Ann Drinker, a painter and family friend, and then from the German artist Francis Adolf Van der Wielen. She made a living as a drawing teacher before gaining admission to the Pennsylvania Academy of the Fine Arts, where she studied with American landscape painter William Sartain. She also crossed paths with Thomas Eakins, who influenced her, although he was never her instructor.

Beaux refused several marriage proposals, preferring to dedicate herself to her career. Moving to Paris, she frequented the Académie Colarossi and the Académie Julian, where she was registered in 1889 as a student of William-Adolphe Bouguereau, Tony Robert-Fleury, and Jean-Joseph Benjamin-Constant. At the 1887 Salon she showed *The Last Days of Childhood*, a double portrait of her sister and nephew, for which she had already received the Mary Smith Prize in Pennsylvania. After participating in the 1889 Salon, she left France, first spending time with other artists at Concarneau, a port on the Brittany coast.

In 1895 Beaux became the first female professor at the Pennsylvania Academy, where she taught portraiture—the genre she is best known for—and drawing for twenty years. She painted both commissioned portraits and, above all, portraits of family members and friends. She was influenced by Japanese art and its way of illustrating motifs, and several of her works evoke those of the English painter James McNeill Whistler.

At the end of the 1890s, while continuing to teach in Philadelphia and spending her summers in a house she built in Gloucester, she settled in New York. There she moved in elite social circles, and her elevated social life was reflected in her portraits; in 1903 she painted Eleanor Roosevelt and her daughter Ethel at the White House. She exhibited her work in the United States and in France, where she maintained contacts, having become a member of the Société Nationale des Beaux-Arts, and participated and received awards in several Salons. In 1919, commissioned by the US War Portraits Commission, she traveled to Europe to paint portraits of war heroes such as the Frenchman Georges Clemenceau.

In 1924 Beaux broke her hip in a bad fall. Although she continued to paint, her production rate diminished. Her autobiography, *Background with Figures*, was published in 1930, and in 1935 the American Academy of Arts and Letters held a major retrospective of her work. She died at age eighty-seven on September 7, 1942. Her archives are found at the Smithsonian Institution's Archives of American Art and at the Pennsylvania Academy of the Fine Arts. —JB

Anna Bilińska-Bohdanowicz

ZLATOPIL, UKRAINE, 1857–WARSAW, 1893

Anna Bilińska was born in Kiev, Ukraine, where her father practiced medicine. The family settled in Viatka, currently Kirov, in Russia, and she began to study drawing with Michal Elwiro Andriolli, a painter and architect famous for his illustrations of Adam Mickiewicz's poem *Pan Thadeus*. She then trained under Wojciech Gerson, one of the most representative painters of the Polish realist movement, who taught at the School of Fine Arts in Warsaw, which Bilińska started attending in 1877.

Bilińska embarked on a voyage through Europe in the early 1880s, visiting Munich, Salzburg, Vienna, and Italy before settling in Paris, where she enrolled in courses at the Académie Julian. She is listed in the archives as a "naturalized Polish painter from Ukraine," and a student of Tony Robert-Fleury and William-Adolphe Bouguereau between 1882 and 1889. Starting in 1885, she presented works at the Salon, obtaining a third-class medal in 1887 for a self-portrait (now in the National Museum, Krakow), and a silver medal at the 1889 Exposition Universelle.

In 1892 Bilińska married Antoni Bohdanowicz, a doctor, with whom she returned to Warsaw with the intention of opening an art school. On May 1, 1893, when the Paris Salon opened its doors, *Portrait de Mlle R.*, presented by Anna Bilińska-Bohdanowicz, still residing on rue de Fleurus in Paris, was listed as number 190 in the Salon's catalogue. The artist never saw her work in the Salon, however; she had died the previous month, in Warsaw, following cardiac complications.

The bulk of Anna Bilińska-Bohdanowicz's work, composed mostly of portraits, is now held in museums in Warsaw and Krakow. A number of her canvases that were stolen from the National Museum in Warsaw during World War II have recently reappeared on the market. One of them, *Négresse* (*A Negress*; 1884), went on sale at Grisebach, in Berlin, in 2011. The following year, it was returned to the National Museum. —JB

Rosa Bonheur

BORDEAUX, 1822–THOMERY, FRANCE, 1899

Marie-Rosalie Bonheur was born on rue Saint-Jean-Securin in Bordeaux. Her mother, Sophie Marquis, born to unknown parents, was adopted by a rich businessman who, on his deathbed, revealed that he was her real father. Marquis married her drawing instructor, the painter Raymond Bonheur, with whom she had four children. Three became painters: Rosa, Auguste, and Juliette. The youngest, Isidore, became a sculptor. The family settled in Paris in 1929, and four years later Sophie died, exhausted by maternity and work. Raymond remarried a few years later and had one more child, Germain.

At the age of thirteen, Rosa Bonheur left school. She spent her time drawing at her father's workshop before beginning to visit the Louvre regularly to make copy sketches, which she sold and which became her first source of income. At age nineteen she exhibited for the first time at the 1841 Salon, with *Goats and Sheep* and *Two Rabbits*. The interest in painting animals shown in these works would be enduring. In 1845 she received a third-class medal, her first, and in 1848 she won a first-class medal with *Oxen and Bulls of Cantal*. After this, she quickly gained a name for herself, and soon received her first commission from the French state. Her painting *Plowing in Nivernais* achieved great success at the following Salon.

In 1849, after her father passed, Bonheur became director of the École Gratuite de Dessin pour les Jeunes Filles, a position she held until 1860. She continued to exhibit at the Salon and, after 1853 when her painting *The Horse Fair* confirmed her fame, she was exempted from submitting her works for jury selection to future Salons.

Bonheur shared her life with Nathalie Micas, whom she had known since they were seventeen and twelve years old, respectively; they would remain companions, traveling and working together until death separated them in 1889. Bonheur attained international success with *The Horse Fair*, which she and Micas took to London to present to Queen Victoria, then later to the United States, where it was purchased by an American who donated it to the Metropolitan Museum of Art.

After 1855 virtually all of Bonheur's paintings were sold in advance, and she no longer exhibited at the Salon. In 1860 she and Micas moved to By, where Bonheur restored a château and built a large workshop. Empress Eugénie visited her for the first time in 1864, returning the following year to give Bonheur the Grand Cross of the Légion d'Honneur, making her the first female artist to receive this distinction. In 1894 she was promoted to "officer" rank.

Shortly after the death of Nathalie Micas, Rosa Bonheur met the American artist Anna Klumpke, who wished to paint her portrait. Klumpke became Bonheur's companion and moved to By, where she wrote her friend's biography. In 1893 Bonheur traveled to Chicago to present works at the Woman's Building at the World's Columbian Exposition.

The 1899 Salon reunited Anna Klumpke's *Portrait of Rosa Bonheur* and *Cows and Bulls of Auvergne*, Bonheur's first submission in over forty years. On May 25 of the same year, she died of pneumonia, leaving Klumpke as her heir. In 1908, having created the Rosa Bonheur Prize at the Society of French Artists, Klumpke published a biography of Rosa Bonheur. —JB

Marie Bracquemond

ARGENTON-EN-LANDUNVEZ, FINISTÈRE, FRANCE, 1840–SÈVRES, HAUTS-DE-SEINE, FRANCE, 1916

Marie Quivoron-Pasquiou was born on December 1, 1840, in a rather unhappy home, her parents having made an "arranged" marriage. Her father, a marine captain, died shortly after her birth, and her mother remarried quickly. The couple left Brittany for Jura, then Switzerland, and finally Limousin, where Marie's half sister,

Louise, who often served as Marie's model, was born in 1849. The family finally settled in Étampes, near Paris, and the young girl began an apprenticeship with the painter Auguste Vassort, who provided lessons to a few of the town's female students. She later met and studied with Jean-Auguste-Dominique Ingres, but found his attitudes toward female painters intimidating and frustrating. Bracquemond left his studio and began receiving commissions; notably, the court of Empress Eugénie asked her to paint an image of Cervantes in prison. She then became a copyist at the Louvre, authorized by the Count of Nieuwerkerke, general director of museums.

Around 1866 she met Félix Bracquemond, also a painter and engraver, at the Louvre. She married him two years later, and they had a son, Pierre—who would also become a painter—the following year. The two began to collaborate on the manufacturing of porcelain for Haviland, where Félix was artistic director between 1872 and 1881. Marie designed several models for Haviland, notably a ceramic panel on the theme of art's muses that she showed at the 1878 Exposition Universelle, winning admiration from Edgar Degas.

In her plein-air portraits, landscapes, and still lifes, Bracquemond progressively adopted the style of the Impressionists, one of four women who exhibited with this group. She showed with the Impressionists in 1879, 1880, and in the last Impressionist exhibition in 1886.

The couple socialized with several artists, including Degas, Henri Fantin-Latour, Paul Gauguin, Auguste Rodin, and Alfred Sisley. Gauguin had a particularly strong influence on Marie's technique. Félix did not appreciate her shift away from the style of Ingres, and in the face of his opposition, Marie gradually abandoned painting. Her work, nevertheless, drew the interest of several critics, including Philippe Burty and Gustave Geffroy, who in 1919 wrote the preface to the catalogue of a solo exhibition at the Galerie Bernheim-Jeune in Paris, where close to one hundred Bracquemond canvases were shown.

Long relegated to her husband's shadow, Marie Bracquemond today receives deserved recognition, in part thanks to numerous exhibits that help to rediscover female painters long neglected by art historians. The couple's only son, Pierre, left a testimony dedicated to his parents, *La vie de Félix et Marie Bracquemond*. —JB

Louise Catherine Breslau

MUNICH, 1856–NEUILLY-SUR-SEINE, FRANCE, 1927

Marie Louise Catherine Breslau was the eldest of four daughters. Born in Germany, she spent her infancy in Zurich, Switzerland, where her father worked as an obstetrician and gynecologist. Her father died when she was ten years old. In fragile health and suffering from asthma, she was sent to a convent near Lake Constance, where she fought off boredom by drawing. For a while she took courses with local artist Eduard Pfyffer, but soon decided to go to Paris, attracted by the Académie Julian's reputation. She studied there under the direction of Tony Robert-Fleury. In 1879 she was admitted to the Salon for the first time, exhibiting *Tout passe!* (*Everything Passes!*), a self-portrait with two friends. Shortly afterward, she left the Académie Julian and opened her own studio, where she made a living from commissions, thanks to her prestige as a portraitist.

Breslau principally painted portraits and interior scenes, although she ventured into plein-air painting during trips to Brittany, a region that had attracted numerous artists since the 1860s, where exchanges between artists, male and female, were easier than in Paris. She exhibited regularly at the Salon until about 1890, receiving an honorable mention in 1881 and a gold medal at the 1889 Exposition Universelle, where she represented Switzerland (she gained Swiss nationality in 1892). She joined the Société Nationale des Beaux-Arts in 1890, not only exhibiting in its salons—where three of her works were purchased by the state, in 1891, 1893, and 1897—but serving on the jury, along with another woman, Madeleine Lemaire. In 1901 she became the third woman, and first foreign woman, to receive the Légion d'Honneur.

Breslau often worked in pastel for her commissions, while favoring oils for her personal creations. During World War I she painted numerous paintings of soldiers and infirmaries. Afterward, commissions became rare, and she progressively retired from public life, dedicating herself to flower paintings.

Louise Breslau died in 1927. Madeleine Zillhardt, her muse, model, and companion for close to four decades, inherited her estate, and a few years later donated about sixty of Breslau's works, mostly pastels and drawings, to the Musée des Beaux-Arts in Dijon. In 1932 Zillhardt published *Louise Catherine Breslau et ses amis* (*Louise Catherine Breslau and her Friends*).

Several exhibitions have been dedicated to Louise Breslau. The École des Beaux-Arts organized a commemorative exhibition shortly after her death, and in 1932 she figured in a retrospective at the Galerie Charpentier in Paris, dedicated to women trained at the Académie Julian. —JB

Lady Elizabeth Butler, née Elizabeth Southerden Thompson

LAUSANNE, SWITZERLAND, 1846–GORMANSTON, IRELAND, 1933

During her lifetime, Lady Elizabeth Butler became one of the most celebrated artists in Great Britain.

Born to wealthy British parents in Switzerland, Thompson was a precocious talent. At the age of sixteen, she enrolled in classes at South Kensington Art School, but quickly became frustrated that female students were denied access to living models. In 1869 Thompson and her sister Alice—who, writing under the pen name Alice Meynell, would become one of the era's most visible female art critics—traveled to Florence, where Elizabeth became a student of Giuseppe Bellucci at the Accademia di Belle Arti and copied the frescos of Andrea del Sarto, Pontormo, and Franciabigio at the Basilica della Santissima Annunziata. The following year she went to Rome and produced *The Magnificat*, a depiction of the Visitation that was exhibited for the Pope in 1870.

Thompson frequently visited Paris and became familiar with the work of Rosa Bonheur, as well as the military painters Édouard Detaille and Alphonse de Neuville. Although she submitted numerous religious paintings to the Royal Academy, the artist was rejected by the institution until 1873, when she put forward an imagined scene from the Franco-Prussian War entitled *Missing*. Beginning with this work, Thompson would almost exclusively focus on military scenes, and that winter she started the painting that catapulted her to fame, *Call the Roll after an Engagement, Crimea*, more popularly known as *The Roll Call*. Depicting a row of beleaguered yet stoic troops during the Crimean War, this work was based on Thompson's extensive research: she purchased soldier's equipment and uniforms, read firsthand accounts from the war, and interviewed veterans. Displayed at the Royal Academy in 1874, the work caused an immediate sensation; prints of the work and photographs of the artist were widely circulated, and eventually Queen Victoria acquired the painting.

The following year Thompson began work on *The 28th Regiment at Quatre Bras*, which she based on Captain William Siborne's account of the Battle of Waterloo. Her exhaustive preparation included studying the anatomy of horses at the circus, purchasing a field to serve as the setting, requesting the British army to organize military exercises so she could observe smoke patterns, and even going so far as to ask specific troops to charge her on horseback. When the work was exhibited at the Royal Academy, John Ruskin praised its refinement, but—with a chauvinism characteristic of the era—he noted that he never expected such quality from a woman painter. Later that year, Thompson returned to Paris and visited Detaille's studio. She also illustrated her sister's collection of poems, *Preludes*, in 1895; although Meynell's poetry attracted little attention upon its release, she eventually became a noted author, suffragette, editor, and art critic.

In 1876 Thompson displayed *Balaclava* at the Fine Arts Society. This second Crimean subject depicts an event during the Battle of Balaclava, which resulted in substantial British causalities. *The Return from Inkerman*, the artist's third portrayal of the Crimean War, was exhibited in 1877 along with two other works at a solo exhibition at the Fine Arts Society and the following year at the Exposition Universelle in Paris. In 1877 Thompson married William Francis Butler, a major in the British Army, and the two moved to Ireland, where Butler began to work on *Listed for the Connaught Rangers*. Exhibited at the Royal Academy in 1879, this work is notable for its poignant depiction of child soldiers. This same year Butler narrowly missed election to the Royal Academy; no female had been elected to the position of royal academician (RA) since the organization's inception.

From 1880 onward, Butler continued to depict military themes, influenced by travels with her husband on his expeditions, especially their time in Egypt. In 1885 her sister passionately argued against barring women artists from life drawing classes in public schools, and in 1886 Butler's husband was knighted. After 1905 then-General Butler retired and the couple moved to Bansha, Tipperary, but continued to travel extensively. Butler had five solo exhibitions from 1900 to 1920, but never again reached the level of critical success she achieved in the final decades of the 1800s. She died in Ireland on October 2, 1933, a month before her eighty-seventh birthday, survived by five children.

In her autobiography, published in 1922, Butler wrote, "I never painted for the glory of war, but to portray its pathos and heroism."—JWM

Mina Carlson-Bredberg

STOCKHOLM, 1857–1943

Wilhelmina Bredberg, the daughter of a Swedish government official, was born into an upper-class family, which had both literary and artistic interests: her great uncle was the famous newspaper publisher and critic Lars Johan Hierta, and her parents frequently entertained noted architects, playwrights, and politicians of the day. At the advice of a family friend, Bredberg—then in her late teens—began to take painting lessons in Stockholm, first at Kerstin Cardon's private school, and then alongside Amanda Sidwall, who had returned to Stockholm after her study at the Académie Julian. When Bredberg was twenty, she and a family friend, Vilhelm Swalin, were seen kissing; as the convention of the day demanded, the couple then had to marry. During this time, Bredberg turned away from painting.

The marriage dissolved seven years later, but shortly before, Bredberg traveled to Paris, where she attended the Académie Julian from 1883 to 1887, studying under Jules Lefebvre and Gustave Boulanger. There, she occasionally acted as *massière* (assistant to the teaching artist) and made a number of friends, among them the Swiss-German painter Louise Catherine Breslau, one of her generation's more successful female painters; their friendship lasted many years. Compared to life in Sweden, social norms were a bit looser in Paris, but, nevertheless, women were not able to appear publicly on their own and could only visit restaurants in a group or escorted by a man. As a result, Bredberg and her female artist-friends often met at each other's studios and commonly ate their meals at home. *Académie Julian, Mademoiselle Beson Drinking from a Glass* evokes the artist's milieu during this period. From 1888 to 1890, Bredberg then studied under Carolus-Duran. In 1889 Bredberg received an honorable mention at the Exposition Universelle for her submission, *Self-Portrait*, which depicts the artist in her combined home/studio with a confident smile playing on her lips.

After her return to Stockholm in 1890, she taught at the art school established by the artist Elisabeth Keyser, a friend and fellow Académie Julian student. In this period, it was quite common for female artists to teach painting in order to supplement their incomes. During the first half of the 1890s, Bredberg traveled abroad almost yearly and visited countries including England, Germany, and Italy. In France, she made friends with Lewis Foreman Day, a key figure in the Arts and Crafts movement, and she stayed repeatedly with Day and his wife in London. Through them she met the movement's leading figures William Morris and Walter Crane.

In 1895 Mina Bredberg married Georg Carlson, who was head of a Swedish government office. Her husband does not seem to have been very sympathetic to her art. According to a relative, sculptor Anita Brusewitz Hansson, Carlson thought that his wife spent too much time painting, thereby neglecting their home, and the artist frequently said to her nieces: "Girls, remember to think about how lucky you are not to be married!" With her husband's death in 1920, Carlson-Bredberg's artistic production again increased.

Mina Carlson-Bredberg was a versatile artist who painted landscapes, city views, interiors, religious and genre motifs, as well as floral still lifes, and also worked in the graphic arts. Like many women artists, as time went on, she painted a number of excellent portraits, especially of children and women, as such commissions were easy to secure. Since the market for female artists was much more limited than that for males, Swedish institutions and museums hardly ever bought works by female artists; as a consequence, many of the best works by Swedish women artists from this period are in private ownership in Sweden and abroad. Paintings by the artist can be found in the permanent collections of the following Swedish institutions: the Nationalmuseum, Prins Eugens Waldemarsudde, and the Gothenburg Museum of Art. —AM

Mary Cassatt

ALLEGHENY, PENNSYLVANIA, 1844–MESNIL-THÉRIBUS, OISE, FRANCE, 1926

Mary Stevenson Cassatt was the fourth child of a wealthy family—her father was a banker—whose French ancestors had moved to the United States in 1662. After her brother was diagnosed with bone cancer, the family traveled to Europe, first to France and then to Germany, in search of treatment. During these travels, Cassatt learned French and German, and visited museums. After the boy's death in 1855, the family returned to Pennsylvania, and Cassatt began her initiation in drawing, in 1860 enrolling in the Pennsylvania Academy of the Fine Arts in Philadelphia. Disappointed by the curriculum, she decided to return to Paris in 1865. In 1866 she studied, accompanied by friend and compatriot Eliza Haldeman, with Paul-Constant Soyer. Cassatt and Haldeman also enrolled in classes with Charles Chaplin, studying portraiture, and obtained their certificates as copyists at the Louvre.

Cassatt presented her first work at the Salon, *La mandoline* (*The Mandolin Player*), in 1868, under the name Mary Stevenson, listing herself as a student of Chaplin and Soyer; in the 1870 Salon, she registered as a student of Soyer and Charles Bellay. In 1870, with the outbreak of the Franco-Prussian War, she returned to Pennsylvania, but came back to Europe in the fall of 1871, visiting England, Italy, Spain, and Belgium, and again settling in Paris. In the Salons of 1872, 1874, and 1875, she appears under the name Cassatt.

Edgar Degas showed interest in Cassatt's work and, following the rejection of her work by the 1877 Salon, encouraged her to exhibit with the Impressionists, which she agreed to during the group's four last exhibitions, between 1879 and 1886.

In 1886 the art dealer and amateur painter Paul Durand-Ruel traveled to the United States with some three hundred Impressionist canvases, which he wanted to make known on the other side of the Atlantic. As the former classmate of Louisine Elder, the wife of the great collector Henry Osborne Havemeyer, Cassatt advised the couple on their purchases, thus contributing greatly to the diffusion of these Impressionist works in America.

Cassatt's later work was greatly influenced by Japanese art, which she discovered in 1890 during an exhibition of prints. She presented numerous etchings in exhibits dedicated to her by Paul Durand-Ruel and then Ambroise Vollard.

In the mid-1890s Cassatt bought the Château de Beaufresne in Mesnil-Théribus, Oise, where she would spend her summers while continuing to work and travel. Increasingly hampered by blindness, she stopped painting around 1914. She died in Mesnil-Théribus in 1926, at the age of eighty-two.

Although she spent most of her life in France, the majority of Mary Cassatt's canvases are held in American museums. She is a member of the National Women's Hall of Fame in Seneca Falls, New York, which preserves the memory of female American citizens particularly illustrious in their domains, including art. —JB

Marie Cazin

PAIMBEUF, FRANCE, 1844–EQUIHEN, FRANCE, 1924

Born Marie Guillet, Cazin was the daughter of an engraver who encouraged her to practice drawing during her apprenticeships. She attended the École Gratuite de Dessin pour les Jeunes Filles in Paris, studying under Juliette Peyrol, Rosa Bonheur's sister. She met fellow painter Jean-Charles Cazin at the Musée du Luxembourg, and they married in 1867. After her marriage, Marie Cazin collaborated with her husband, a painter, sculptor, and primarily ceramist, while also pursuing her solo career. The couple visited Touraine, and then London; in the catalogue for the 1876 Salon, where they both exhibited—Marie presenting *Un étang en Picardie* (*A Pond in Picardie*)—they are listed with a London address.

Cazin exhibited in the Painting and Drawing section of the Salon until 1882, when she shifted to sculpture, submitting a bronze mask, *Tristesse* (*Sadness*), in 1882. A bust of David was accepted the following year. Her most famous work, *Les jeunes filles* (*The Young Girls*), was accepted in 1886 and purchased by the state in 1899.

In 1891 Marie and Jean-Charles become members of the Société Nationale des Beaux-Arts, which placed more importance on the decorative arts than did the Société des Artistes Français. Marie exhibited until 1914. She created several monumental sculptures, often linked to her family life, dedicating a group of them to her brother-in-law, the doctor Henri Cazin, and to Dr. Perrochaud, Henri's father-in-law and founder of the hospital in Berck, where the sculpture resides. Her monument to the memory of her husband, who died in 1901, is today visible in the public garden in Samer, in Pas-de-Calais; she also made a funerary monument for his tomb in Borme-les-Mimosas.

During World War I, Cazin retired to Equihen, in Pas-de-Calais, where the family had acquired a vast coastal estate. The couple's only son, Jean-Michel, born in 1869, followed in his parents' footsteps, practicing sculpture and ceramics. In 1917, while he was visiting the destroyer *La Rafale* with his wife in the port of Dunkerque, a torpedo exploded, killing him and leaving his wife nearly blind.

From that point, Cazin dedicated herself to perpetuating the memory of her husband and son, notably hoping to transform the Equihen estate into a museum. At her death, in 1924, her sister, Célie Heseltine, donated numerous of the couple's works of art, and their son's, to the Musée des Beaux-Arts de Tours. Several decades later, a museum opened in Jean-Charles Cazin's native town of Samer, named after him, where some of Marie's art is conserved. —JB

Fanny Churberg

VAASA, FINLAND, 1845–HELSINKI, 1892

Fanny Churberg's physician father died when she was twenty, leaving her a comfortable inheritance that granted her rare financial independence. After attending girls' schools in Porvoo and Vyborg, she settled in Helsinki, where she took her first drawing classes, between 1865 and 1867, from Alexandra Frosterus, Emma Gyldén, and Berndt Lindholm. Subsequently she traveled to Dusseldorf to study under the guidance of Carl Ludwig, and then to Paris, where she chose as professor Swedish landscape artist

Wilhelm von Gegerfelt, who had also been in Dusseldorf and was well acquainted with the modern art market thanks to the dealer Goupil.

In the spring of 1873, Churberg participated in a Finnish Art Society exhibition, presenting two large-scale landscapes. Critics dubbed her work "promising [but] strange," a label that stuck to the artist's work throughout her brief career. After an initial period dedicated chiefly to landscapes, she turned to still lifes. Unlike other female Finnish artists who studied in Paris, Churberg never exhibited outside of her country. In 1879 she was awarded the Premier Prix Dukaat by the Finnish Art Society. Despite this recognition, she never gained popularity among critics and the public, who judged her painting too violent. She abandoned painting around 1880.

In June 1878 Churberg made a final trip to Paris to visit the Exposition Universelle, where she became interested in the traditional work of female artisans. She soon became interested in the cause of women who work in the manual trades and began to write art criticism, publishing numerous articles on feminism and Finnish art. She participated in the Society of Friends of Finnish Handicraft, where she played a crucial role.

Churberg died in 1892, not yet fifty. Her recognition arrived posthumously, when in 1919 gallery owner Gösta Stenman dedicated a retrospective to her in Helsinki. Attitudes have evolved, and the freedom in her paintings is no longer met with shock. —JB

Elin Danielson-Gambogi

NOORMARKKU, FINLAND, 1861–ANTIGNANO, ITALY, 1919

Elin Danielson was ten years old when her father, Karl Emil Danielson, committed suicide, despondent at the failure of the family farm. Her mother, Rosa Amalia Gestrin, encouraged Elin to continue her studies, with the financial help of her brother, who would be a longtime supporter of the young girl. At fifteen, Danielson entered Helsinki's Finnish Art Society Drawing School, where, in addition to drawing technique and painting, she studied painting on porcelain, training that proved invaluable in enabling her to support herself. In 1880 she obtained a teaching diploma, having taken classes with the painter Adolf von Becker, whose private school was attended by several young Finns, including Helene Schjerfbeck and Ellen Thesleff.

In 1883 Danielson received a grant to travel to Paris. There she enrolled at the Académie Colarossi, received training from the painters Gustave Courtois and Raphaël Collin, and began to study sculpture under Auguste Rodin. In the summertime she left the capital for the artists' communities in Brittany, where the landscapes were a perpetual source of inspiration. It was here that she met the naturalist painter Jules Bastien-Lepage, who inspired her to lighten her palette. Danielson divided her time between France and Finland, where she worked outdoors under the leadership of Victor Westerholm in a group known as the Önningeby colony, similar to the Danish group Skagen, led by the couple Michael and Anna Ancher, or the Worpswede group in Germany made famous by Paula Modersohn-Becker.

Danielson participated in several exhibits in Finland. Her favorite subjects tended to be portraits of women engaged in ordinary daily work. The artist was critical of conditions for women, and demonstrated an indifference to prevailing social mores, entertaining relationships with several artists, among them the Norwegian sculptor Gustav Vigeland.

A new grant allowed Danielson to travel to Florence in 1895. She returned the following year and soon afterward settled permanently in Italy, near Livorno. In 1898 she married the Italian painter Raffaello Gambogi, thirteen years her junior. The couple influenced each other mutually, for years participating together in exhibitions in France and Italy. Danielson-Gambogi achieved a certain success in Italy, taking home a prize given by Florence, and one of her paintings was bought by King Umberto I. But the situation quickly deteriorated. Gambogi, who suffered from mental problems, abandoned his wife, leaving her financially insecure. The outbreak of World War I made it difficult for her to sell her work and impossible for her to see her native country before her death, in 1919, following a bout of pneumonia. —JB

Julie Delance-Feurgard

PARIS, 1859–1892

Little is known of the life of Julie Delance-Feurgard. Catalogues for the Salon, where she exhibited at least between 1880 and 1888, establish that she was born in Paris and lived at Sannois, a little town northwest of Paris. This information is backed by the testimony of her friend Louise Breslau, who, questioning the value of her training at the Académie Julian, found refuge for a few weeks in the spring of 1886 at Feurgard's house at Sannois, where Breslau painted a portrait of her friend at her easel under a flowering apple tree. In her letters, Breslau describes the creation of this painting, today in the Musée Cantonal des Beaux-Arts de Lausanne in Switzerland.

Feurgard studied at the Académie Julian, alongside Breslau and the Swiss artist Sophie Schaeppi. She also studied with Paul-Louis Delance, whom she married in 1886; the following year, her painting *Un coin d'omnibus* (*A Corner of the Train*) is listed in the Salon catalogue, with the number 707, under the name Delance-Feurgard residing at rue Saint Ferdinand in Paris; Delance, whose painting is listed under the number 706, gave the same address. For submissions to the Salon, starting in 1884, she declared herself a student of Jean-Léon Gérôme and Léon Bonnat.

During her short career, Delance-Feurgard exhibited at the Paris Salon until 1888, then at the salons of the Société Nationale des Beaux-Arts, where she was a member, and at those of the Union des Femmes Peintres et Sculpteurs, created in 1881 by Hélène Bertaux. In 1886 she received an honorable mention at the Salon; in 1889 she garnered the same award at the Exposition Universelle. She also exhibited in numerous provincial exhibits, notably in Bordeaux and Toulouse.

On several occasions, Delance-Feurgard attracted the attention of critics. In the report on the 1888 Salon in *L'art français*, the critic Firmin Javel dwells at length on *La Crèche* (*The Nativity Scene*), emphasizing the touching side of these "children who ignore the kisses of their mothers," a painting that is "blackened by ideas" but "full of light and clarity," in which a "great sense of modern art" is unleashed.

In his 1907 memorial to his secretary and companion Gabriel de Yturri, *Le chancelier des fleurs*, Robert de Montesquiou honors Julie Feurgard in a passage about Louise Breslau's portrait of Yturri: "In passing, a detail; in his untiring kindness to me, Mademoiselle Breslau's model was infinitely delighted with the revelation that was made to him, by this painter, of the talent of Mademoiselle Feurgard, an admirable and illuminated artist, whom he made carry out a series titled 'Prières.' These are masterpieces." This work, *Prières de tous: Douze poésies enluminées par Mademoiselle Feurgard* (*Everyone's Prayers: Twelve Poems Illuminated by Mademoiselle Feurgard*), was finally published in Paris in 1924 by the Société d'Editions d'Art et d'Histoire, more than thirty years after the artist's death in 1892, following the birth of her daughter, Alice. Delance-Feurgard was thirty-three years old. —JB

Virginie Demont-Breton

COURRIÈRES, PAS-DE-CALAIS, FRANCE, 1859–PARIS, 1935

Virginie Élodie Marie Thérèse Breton grew up surrounded by painting. Her father, Jules Breton, and uncle, Émile Breton, were both recognized artists. Encouraged by her father to pursue the study of nature, she quickly learned to use a brush. In 1880 she married the landscape artist Adrien Demont, a native, like her, of northern France. The following year, at just twenty years of age, she had her first submission to the Paris Salon accepted.

The couple settled in the Parisian region of Montgeron but soon discovered Wissant, a little village on the Opale coast, between Blanc-Nez and Gris-Nez, where they oversaw construction of the Typhonium, a neo-Egyptian villa by the Belgian architect Edmond De Vigne. Virginie Demont-Breton experienced a string of successes, winning a gold medal in 1883 at the International Colonial Exposition in Amsterdam and, the same year, gaining exemption at the Paris Salon from jury selection for future salons. The state purchased her painting *La plage* (*The Beach*) for the Musée du Luxembourg in Paris before it was shipped to the Musée des Beaux-Arts, Arras, where it remains today. A second purchase by the state followed in 1898. Her painting *Les hommes de la mer* (*Men of the Sea*) currently resides in the Musée de Picardie, Amiens.

Very sensitive to the treatment of men and women in the artistic scene in particular, in 1883 Demont-Breton joined the Union des Femmes Peintres et Sculpteurs, founded two years earlier by Hèléne Bertaux, and she served as the group's president from 1895 to 1901. Thanks to the union, the École des Beaux-Arts opened its doors to women, and they were allowed to compete for the Prix de Rome.

After their arrival in Wissant, the couple was joined by young painters equally seduced by the site and its residents. The group, which was active between 1890 and World War I, would become known as the Wissant school, counting among its members Félix Planquette, Georges Maroniez, and Henri and Marie-Geneviève Duhem.

At the beginning of her career, Demont-Breton chiefly painted portraits, children and families, or historic scenes. At Wissant she discovered landscapes, but the local residents and their difficult lives became the chief focus of her work—notably fishermen engaged with the rough sea, and the anguish of their families following accidents at sea.

In 1893 Demont-Breton formed part of a delegation of French artists at the Woman's Building, a pavilion reserved for women at the World's Columbian Exposition in Chicago. The following year she was decorated by the Légion d'Honneur, making her the second woman to receive the distinction; Rosa Bonheur had accepted the honor close to thirty years earlier, in 1865.

Virginie Demont-Breton died in Paris in 1935, seven years after her husband. Besides her painted work, she left behind poems, reassembled under the title *Tenderness in the Harrow* (*Tendresses dans la tourmente*). Several of her paintings are in the collections of French museums, in Paris and in the north, as well as in Belgium and Holland. —JB

Elizabeth Jane Gardner Bouguereau

EXETER, NEW HAMPSHIRE, 1837–SAINT-CLOUD, FRANCE, 1922

We know little about the infancy of Elizabeth Jane Gardner, though we can surmise she came from a wealthy family that supported her studies at Lasell College in Newton, Massachusetts, founded in 1851 as a place for young girls to receive training in, among other subjects, drawing and watercolor. At Lasell she formed a friendship with one of her professors, Imogene Robinson, who she joined in Paris in 1864 after a stay in Boston, where she had gone to continue her training.

As the École des Beaux-Arts did not allow women to enroll until 1891, Gardner trained in private studios, including those of Ange Tissier and Hugues Merle. In 1868 Gardner, Eliza Haldeman, and Mary Cassatt were the first female artists born in the United States to have works accepted in the Paris Salon. Gardner exhibited *Les trois amis* (*The Three Friends*) and *Nature morte: Raisins, etc.* (*Still Life: Grapes, etc.*); Haldeman, a student of Paul-Constant Soyer, presented *Une paysanne* (*A Peasant Woman*); while Cassatt, then identifying herself as Mary Stevenson, a student of Soyer and Charles Chaplin, presented *La mandoline* (*The Mandolin Player*).

Gardner then enrolled at the Académie Julian, where she studied with Jules Lefebvre and William-Adolphe Bouguereau. She was very influenced by Bouguereau's painting style and his choice of subjects, in particular his focus on historical, religious, or mythological scenes. She exhibited at the Salon twenty-five times, between 1868 and 1896, when she married Bouguereau, her fiancé since 1879. She often said she preferred "to be known as the best imitator of Bouguereau than . . . a nobody." She obtained an honorable mention in the Salon of 1879 and a third-class medal in 1887, which exempted her from submitting to the jury for future Salons. During the Exposition Universelle of 1889 she received a bronze medal, and she also participated in the Chicago World's Columbian Exposition in 1893, exhibiting in the Woman's Building.

In 1896 more than two hundred canvases painted by and belonging to her former professor, Imogene Robinson, were destroyed in a fire. Gardner came to the aid financially of Robinson, with whom she had remained close. In 1905 Bouguereau died at age seventy-nine. Gardner, suffering from rheumatism, soon ceased painting.

In the 1980s the artist's great-niece, Miriam Gardner Dunnan, donated archival documents, correspondence, and photographs from the archives of Gardner and Bouguereau to the Smithsonian's Archives of American Art. Several of Gardner's works are in the collection of the National Museum of Women in the Arts in Washington, DC. —JB

Eva Gonzalès

PARIS, 1849–1883

Born in Paris in an intellectual and bourgeois environment—her father was a novelist and wrote for newspapers like *Le siècle*, and her mother was a musician—Eva Gonzalès and her younger sister Jeanne were encouraged by their parents to study painting. From age sixteen, Eva trained with Charles Chaplin, before studying alongside Édouard Manet, to whom she was introduced by Alfred Stevens. In Manet's studio she crossed paths with Berthe Morisot, who, like Eva, became the instructor's model as well as a student. Although she named Chaplin as her instructor at her first Salon, in 1870, the painting that she presented, *The Child of the Troupe*, clearly evokes Manet's *The Fife*, which had been refused by the Salon jury four years earlier. At the same 1870 Salon, Manet presented *Portrait of Mlle E.G.*, which depicts the model painting a still life.

Gonzalès participated in the Salon des Refusés in 1873 as well as in 1875, when she exhibited *A Box at the Theatre des Italiens*, rejected by the official Salon jury for its masculine vigor. Her sister, Jeanne, and Henri Guérard served as models for the painting. She married Guérard a few years later, in 1879. Like Manet, Gonzalès refused to participate in Impressionist exhibitions, although her name remains linked to the group nonetheless. She persisted in her desire to be admitted to the official Salon, and in 1879 she succeeded: a second version of *A Box at the Theatre des Italiens* was accepted.

Gonzalès progressively distanced herself from Manet's influence, lightening her palette little by little. She and Guérard often visited the Saint-Siméon farm on the Normandy coast, a locale discovered by the painter Eugène Boudin, which attracted numerous artists, including Claude Monet. Gonzalès and her husband met, among others, the painters Norbert Goeneutte, Paul Cézanne, and Félix Bracquemond.

Gonzalès died from an embolism on May 6, 1883, shortly after the birth of her son, Jean-Raymond, and one week after the death of Manet. She was only thirty-four years old. Henri Guérard later married her sister, Jeanne.

Eva Gonzalès left behind a body of work composed chiefly of portraits and interior scenes. During the last years of her life, she exhibited at the Galerie Georges Petit in Paris, and one of her canvases was chosen for the centenary exhibition of French art during the 1900 Exposition Universelle. Today she is regularly exhibited as the artist most associated with the other great women painters of Impressionism, including Mary Cassatt, Berthe Morisot, and Marie Bracquemond. —JB

Annie Hopf

THUN, SWITZERLAND, 1861–ZURICH, 1918

Very little is known about the early life of Annie (or Anny, or Anna) Hopf, or Stebler-Hopf. Born in Thun, in the district of Bern, Switzerland, she trained in Berlin with the painter Karl Gussow, a German artist who taught at the Staatliche Akademie der Bildenden Künste in Karlsruhe before becoming a professor at the Berlin Arts Academy between 1876 and 1881.

In 1882 Hopf moved to Paris, soon followed by Ottilie Roederstein, another Swiss student of Gussow. Both artists shared the same address in Paris, living at 77 rue Notre-Dame de Champs. It is speculated that they were a couple; Roederstein later was the romantic partner of Elisabeth Winterhalter, the first female German surgeon, with whom she lived until her death.

During her years in Paris, Hopf took courses at the Académie Julian under the name Stebler-Hopf, though the dates of her enrollment are not specified. In Salon catalogues between 1884 and 1890, she identified herself as a student of Luc-Olivier Merson and of Tony Robert-Fleury, one of the more celebrated instructors at the Académie Julian, and gave her name as Anna Hopf. Roederstein also presented work at the 1885 Salon.

Subsequently, Hopf moved to Zurich, likely in 1890. A catalogue from the Swiss Society of Fine Arts mentions two works by an Annie Hopf, a portrait and landscape, at an exposition in Lucerne in August and September 1894.

Letters from Hopf to the Swiss writer Maria Waser are today gathered in the archives of the Swiss national library. In 2008 the exhibition *Lost Paradise, der blick des engels* at the Paul Klee Center in Bern included work by Annie Stebler-Hopf. At the Kunstmuseum Bern, which houses *Autopsy (Professor Poirier, Paris)*, this work is presented as having been painted by "the unknown Bern artist Annie Stebler-Hopf." Unlike numerous women artists from the same era, Annie Stebler-Hopf does not seem to be the subject of recent research. She remains to be discovered. —JB

Kitty Kielland

STAVANGER, NORWAY, 1843–CHRISTIANA [OSLO], NORWAY, 1914

Kitty Kielland was born to a wealthy family in Stavanger, a town in southwestern Norway. Her brother, Alexander Kielland, became a celebrated writer. At an early age, Kielland had ambitions for an artistic career, but although she was allowed to take painting and drawing courses, she was not encouraged to follow this route for long. Not until she was thirty years old, when an inheritance gave her independence, did she leave for Germany and begin formal training with Hans Gude, a Norwegian painter who then worked in Karlsruhe, after having earlier taught in Dusseldorf.

Many Norwegian artists were in Germany at the time, and Kielland found a number of them in Munich, where she lived between 1875 and 1878, training with Eilif Peterssen. She arrived in Jaeren, in the south of Norway, following the advice of Gude, who had been impressed by the region's landscapes. Kielland completed numerous sketches there, before her return to Munich. The Jaeren region and its peat bogs were a recurrent theme in her work: she returned to the region often, notably with her friend Harriet Backer, whom she met in Paris and who was similarly trained.

After arriving in Paris in 1879, Kielland fell under the influence of the landscape artist Léon Pelouse, who worked in Brittany—in the Concarneau region, where Kielland would spend the summer of 1881 with Backer—before becoming the director of the painting school in Cerney, near Paris. Kielland exhibited regularly at the Salon between 1879 and 1889, alternating between landscapes of Norway and of Brittany. Between 1881 and 1889 she lived on the rue de l'Université with Backer. Four of her paintings figured in the Norwegian section at the 1889 Exposition Universelle, among them *After the Rain*, which earned her a silver medal.

Upon returning to Norway in 1889, Kielland continued to paint and, like many of her colleagues, became engaged in the fight for women's emancipation. Ravaged by senility, she died in 1914 in Christiania, which become Oslo ten years later. The Stavanger Kunstmuseum, in her hometown, holds several of her paintings, alongside those of other notable Norwegian painters: Knut Baade, Harriet Backer, Lars Hertervig, Christian Krohg, Olaf Lange, Edvard Munch, Eilif Peterssen, and Carl Sundt-Hansen. A street in the Baerum neighborhood of Oslo bears Kielland's name.

In 1983 an exhibition at the Modums Foundation reunited Kitty Kielland with her friend Harriet Backer. More recently, in 2012, the same foundation's exhibition *Women in Art* presented the two artists again, alongside other women, including Asta Nørregaard. —JB

Anna Elizabeth Klumpke

SAN FRANCISCO, 1856–1942

The eldest of eight children, three of whom died at a young age, Anna Klumpke suffered health problems during her infancy. At age three she suffered a bad fall and broke her femur. Two years later, she fell again. Her mother took her to Berlin to undergo a treatment that lasted over a year. It was not a great success: Klumpke would limp all her life. Her parents divorced when she was fifteen, and Mme Klumpke took her five children to Göttingen, Germany, where her sister lived. Two years later the family moved to Switzerland, near Lake Geneva. After two years in a boarding school, Klumpke studied at home before departing again, this time for Paris, in October 1877.

She began training with Pierre Auguste Cot, a popular painter at the time and member of the Salon jury, at a studio where she found a friend, Ellen Day Hale. Klumpke spent a lot of time in museums, notably at the Musée du Luxembourg, where contemporary works purchased by the state were exhibited. There she made numerous copies, including one of Rosa Bonheur's *Plowing in Nivernais*. She also trained under the painter Félix de Vuillefroy-Cassini before joining the Académie Julian, like many foreign artists residing in Paris.

Klumpke made her first submission to the Salon, *Une excentrique* (*An Eccentric*), in 1882. She exhibited regularly for several years, winning an honorable mention in 1885 for her *Portrait de Mlle A. K.* She took a trip to Boston, where she completed her training while teaching classes, returning to Paris in time to participate in the Exposition Universelle of 1889, where she obtained a bronze medal.

Under the pretext of serving as a translator for a horse dealer, Klumpke approached Rosa Bonheur, someone she admired greatly. The two women got along and saw each other regularly. Klumpke's portrait of Rosa would be showcased at the 1899 Salon, later to be installed in Bonheur's property in By, where the two women lived as a couple after the death of Bonheur's first companion, Nathalie Micas. Klumpke continued her career as a portraitist, and a number of her works now reside in American museums.

Bonheur made Klumpke her sole heir, and Klumpke began writing her friend's biography, which appeared in 1908. After Bonheur's death, Klumpke divided her time between France and San Francisco. She created the Prix Rosa Bonheur at the Société des Artistes Français, which led to her being named a Chevalier of the Légion d'Honneur in 1924.

Anna Klumpke died in San Francisco in 1942. Her ashes were sent to France and deposited at the Micas family tomb, close to Nathalie and Rosa, at the Père Lachaise Cemetery in Paris. —JB

Emma Löwstädt-Chadwick

STOCKHOLM, 1855–VILLENEUVE-LÈS-AVIGNON, FRANCE, 1932

Emma Löwstädt came from a rather well-to-do family, and at the age of nineteen, she began her artistic training at the Swedish Royal Academy of Fine Arts. In 1879 she was given a monetary prize, which enabled her to travel through France for the summer, visiting Paris, Brittany, and the village of Villerville. Upon graduation the following year, Löwstädt's father funded her second trip to Paris. In the French capital, Löwstädt studied under Tony Robert-Fleury at the Académie Julian, and it was there that she became friends with Marie Bashkirtseff. The two shared a studio for some time. Later, she also studied under landscapist Jean-Charles Cazin.

In the summer of 1880, Löwstädt, accompanied by her peer Amanda Sidwall, traveled to Concarneau on the Brittany coast. Sidwall was mainly a genre painter, and had her biggest success at the Salon two years later with *La première leçon*, which was most advantageously placed and received high praise. In *Beach Parasol, Brittany (Portrait of Amanda Sidwall)*, Löwstädt depicted her friend and fellow artist painting on the beach in the stunning light of the west coast of France. Like most Swedish artists in France during this time, Löwstädt painted *en plein air*, but, often, such landscapes are not ends in themselves, but backdrops for figures and genre scenes. The artist's early works included many Breton motifs: fishermen and their families, and shepherdesses with herds of sheep or goats.

In 1881 Löwstädt debuted at the Paris Salon with *Portrait of Mlle C*, and from then on, she exhibited regularly. In 1882 her work *Départ pour la mer* (*Departure for the Sea*) was reviewed in a French newspaper with backhanded praise—typical of the time—for having "no show of hesitation or female fragility." Löwstädt received honorable mentions at the Salon of 1887 and the 1889 Exposition Universelle. In general, Swedish female artists were successful on the Parisian scene because of their training at the Swedish Royal Academy, which opened its doors to female students in 1865, over three decades before the École des Beaux-Arts.

While in France, Löwstädt became acquainted with the village of Grez-sur-Loing—an artists' colony located a short train ride from Paris primarily populated by Scandinavian and English-speaking artists. This picturesque town on the river Loing offered many motifs. Perhaps it was in Grez that she first met her husband-to-be, the wealthy American painter Francis (Frank) Chadwick. The two were married in 1882, and Löwstädt-Chadwick, who previously had to rely on her father's financial support, had no further economic worries. The two had several homes—including an apartment in Paris as well as the Pension Laurent at Grez, which they purchased in 1891 and offered as a guest house for fellow artists—and took painting trips to England, Italy, North Africa, Spain, Sweden, and the United States. Unlike many of her peers, Löwstädt had no plans to quit painting once she married.

In 1885 Löwstädt-Chadwick was one of only a handful of women artists who signed a proclamation that demanded the Swedish Royal Academy reform and modernize. This protest led to the formation of Konstnärsförbundet (The Artists' Union), which later became enormously influential on the Swedish art scene. Only nine female artists, Löwstädt-Chadwick among them, were included among the sixty-eight artists in the group's first exhibition.

Later in life, Emma Löwstädt-Chadwick painted less and took up etching, at which she also excelled. In his influential chronicle about the Artists' Union, *History of the Artists' Union I* and *II* (*Konstnärsförbundets historia I* and *II*)—which covered a substantial part of Swedish art history between the 1870s and 1920—Swedish art historian Sixten Strömbom wrote, in 1945: "Emma Löwstädt was probably the one amongst all the *målarflickor* [girl painters] of the 1880s who was in possession of the most robust and consistent talent."—AM

Paula Modersohn-Becker

DRESDEN, GERMANY, 1876–WORPSWEDE, GERMANY, 1907

The third of seven children, Paula Becker was born in February 1876 to a cultivated, wealthy family, where the children received an education that included music, drawing, and literature. Becker spent the first twelve years of her life in Dresden, until the family left in 1888 for Bremen, where the father, Carl Woldemar Becker, had been hired as a building engineer.

During a sojourn in London, where her parents sent her to perfect her English, Becker began drawing. Upon her return to Bremen, she entered a school for teachers at her father's desire, but, unenthusiastic about that career, secured permission to attend courses with the painter Bernhard Wiegandt. She would study with Wiegandt from 1893 to 1895, working from live models. The first portraits she painted of her family, as well as her first self-portrait, date to this period. In September 1895 she also obtained her diploma as an instructor.

The following year, Becker traveled to Berlin, where she took courses at the Berlin Artist Association, a painting school reserved for women who did not have access to the Fine Arts School. Here, she painted her first nudes. In 1897 she was accepted to study with Jeanna Bauck, a Swedish painter who encouraged Becker to continue her training in Paris.

Becker's family spent the summer of 1897 in Worpswede, Germany, home to an artist community that Becker had already admired thanks to works of art exhibited at the Kunsthalle in Bremen in 1893. Provided with a small stipend, she decided to return to Worpswede in September 1898, a stay that was originally meant to be a quick visit, but was prolonged. She studied with Fritz Mackensen and met several people who would be important during the course of her life: Clara Westhoff, a sculptor who became a dear friend; Otto Modersohn, her future husband; and Heinrich Vogeler. Becker's style inclined to simplifying forms and colors, which did not match the aesthetic celebrated by critics, so she decided to leave for Paris on December 31, 1899. There she again met Westhoff, who wanted to become a student of Rodin, and enrolled in the Académie Colarossi, which accepted women. Discovering the work of the Nabis, she succeeded in convincing Modersohn and Fritz Overbeck to travel to Paris to visit the Exposition Universelle. Modersohn's wife stayed behind in Worpswede, where she died, leaving him widowed and in charge of their little girl, Elsbeth. Paula and Otto returned together to Worpswede, where they wasted little time in announcing their engagement; they married in May 1901. When the poet Rainer Maria Rilke visited Worpswede in 1900, he became friends with Modersohn-Becker. He later married Clara Westhoff in 1901.

From this time on, Modersohn-Becker attempted to reconcile her family life with her work as an artist. Liberated by marriage from the need to make a living, she painted a great deal. In 1903 and 1905 she made two more trips to Paris. Otto did not approve of his wife's stylistic evolution and her desire for independence, and the couple separated in 1906. Modersohn-Becker returned to Paris, but then the couple reconciled and returned to Worpswede later that year. On November 2, 1907, she gave birth to a girl, Mathilde. It was a difficult birth, and Modersohn-Becker was on enforced bedrest for a lengthy period. She died of a pulmonary embolism on November 20, 1907.

Although Paula Modersohn-Becker's career lasted a mere fourteen years, she left behind 750 paintings, 13 etchings, and roughly 1,000 drawings. During her life, she only sold two paintings, to her friends Rilke and Vogeler. —JB

Berthe Morisot

BOURGES, FRANCE, 1841–PARIS, 1895

Berthe Morisot was born in Bourges, at a time when her father was prefect of the department of Cher. Two sisters—Yves, born in 1838, and Edma, in 1839—preceded her, and a brother, Tiburce, would be born in 1848. In 1852 the family moved to Paris. Berthe's mother, the great-great-niece of the painter Jean-Honoré Fragonard, offered her daughters painting lessons at a very young age, choosing Joseph Guichard as their professor. His training suited the girls very well, and he declared himself impressed by their talent. Sensing that they could become great painters, he warned: "In your upper bourgeoisie milieu, that will be a revolution, almost, I should say, a catastrophe!" Edma and Berthe persisted, wishing to experiment with painting outdoors. Guichard entrusted them to the landscape painter Achille Oudinot, who put them in contact with Camille Corot. The Morisot family, far from discouraging the girls, rented a summer house in Ville d'Avray so that they might be closer to Corot.

In 1864 the Salon jury accepted two landscapes from each of the sisters, who cited the training of Guichard and Oudinot, but did not mention the influence of Corot, who was not officially their instructor.

The sisters frequented the Louvre and were familiar with the realm of copyists. They met, among others, Édouard Manet, who would play a great role in their lives. The Manet and Morisot families met at parties frequented by painters, musicians, and writers, organized by a bourgeoisie class that was both social and avant-garde. The eldest Morisot girl, Yves, married Théodore Gobillard in 1866, and Edma married Adolphe Pontillon about two years later, quickly thereafter abandoning her career as a painter. Berthe Morisot, on the contrary, pursued hers. She was very close to Édouard Manet, and he often used her as a model, and sought to influence her painting, though she did not always appreciate his intervention to "correct" her canvases. In 1874 she married Eugène Manet, Édouard's brother, and their daughter, Julie, was born in 1878.

Little by little Berthe's painting began to distance itself from Manet's, as she adopted a lighter palette more in line with that of Corot, a shift appreciated by Edgar Degas. With Claude Monet, Camille Pissarro, Alfred Sisley, and some others, Degas created the Société Anonyme des Peintres, Sculpteurs et Graveurs, which organized a salon of its own, independent of the official Salon. Despite the opposition of Manet, who never joined, Morisot decided to exhibit with this group, which would become the Impressionists. At their first salon, in 1874, she presented *The Cradle* (1872), a depiction of her sister Edma watching her daughter Blanche as she slept. She exhibited in every Impressionist salon except the fourth, in 1879, which followed the birth of her daughter. Morisot was the only women to appear at the first salon, but was later joined by Marie Bracquemond and Mary Cassatt. In February 1887 she was invited to exhibit in Brussels with a group of avant-garde artists, Les XX, including Georges Seurat and Pissarro.

The health of Eugène Manet, then fifty-nine, began to deteriorate; he died on April 13, 1892. That same year, Morisot refused Les XX's invitation to the group's Brussels exhibition, but her husband encouraged her to organize an individual exhibition at the Parisian gallery Boussod et Valadon, founded by Adolphe Goupil. The exhibition received wide acclaim.

Having contracted pulmonary congestion while caring for her daughter, Berthe Morisot died on March 2, 1895. Julie received the support of the Impressionist group and of Stéphane Mallarmé, her tutor. The year following Morisot's death, in March 1896, Durand-Ruel, with the help of Degas, Henri Rouart, and Julie Manet, presented a retrospective that gathered four hundred of the artist's canvases. Today, the Musée Marmottan Monet in Paris conserves the biggest collection of works by Berthe Morisot, whose remains rest at the Passy Cemetery. —JB

Asta Nørregaard

CHRISTIANIA [OSLO], NORWAY, 1853–OSLO, 1933

Asta Elise Jakobine Nørregaard and her elder sister lost their parents, Hans Peter Nørregaard and Elise Jacobine Hesselberg, at an early age. In 1874–75 Nørregaard began to study at Knud Bergslien's school for women in Christiania, where Harriet Backer was a classmate. Then she left Norway for Germany, enrolling in courses in Munich taught by the Norwegian painter Eilif Peterssen.

Having obtained a grant from the Schaffer endowment, Nørregaard traveled to Paris, where she would remain from 1879 to 1884. There she discovered painting outdoors, which was in vogue at the time. She became better known, however, for her portraits, which show the influence of Léon Bonnat, her instructor. Nørregaard exhibited at the Salon on two occasions. In 1881 the jury accepted her painting *L'attente du Christ* (*The Expectation of Christ*). In the Salon catalogue she declared herself a student of Peterssen and provided an address on rue Carnot in Paris. In 1882 she presented two portraits; the address she gave, that of Peterssen's house on avenue de l'Opéra, demonstrated her bond with the instructor.

Upon returning to Norway in 1885, the year in which she participated at the Exposition Internationale in Anvers, Nørregaard made Christiania her base while she traveled around Europe, particularly France and Italy. She produced more than three hundred portraits of men and women from the upper middle class and high society. Among her models was Edvard Munch, who posed for her starting in 1885, when he was just twenty-two years old. She also painted the portrait of King Haakon VII, the son of the king of Denmark Frederic VIII, who was named king of Norway in 1905.

The gallery founded in 1870 in Christiania by the merchant Christian Walfrid Blomqvist dedicated several solo exhibits to Nørregaard between 1893 and 1925. She participated in the 1889 Exposition Universelle in Paris, and in various group exhibitions in several Nordic countries between 1880 and 1890.

In 1905 the National Academy of the Arts in Christiania opened its doors after efforts led by Harriet Backer, Kitty Kielland, and Nørregaard, among others. In 1920 she received the Gold Medal from the king, a distinction created in 1908 by Haakon VII to reward achievements in the arts, sciences, and industries.

Nørregaard died in 1933 in Oslo. Most of her work is held in museums in Oslo, including an ensemble of sixty-six paintings and drawings at the National Museum. In 2012 an exhibition at Blaafarveværket, a museum built at a former mining site about one hour from Oslo, highlighted the work of eight women artists: Backer, Marie Hauge, Kielland, Nørregaard, Signe Scheel, Elisabeth Sinding, Nina Sundbye, and Marie Tannæs. —JB

Elizabeth Nourse

CINCINNATI, 1859–PARIS, 1938

Elizabeth Nourse was born to a Catholic family in Ohio. She and her twin sister, Adelaide, were the youngest of ten children. At age fifteen, Nourse entered the McMicken School of Design in Cincinnati, one of very few women to be admitted, where she was taught by the painter Thomas Satterwhite Noble, the school's director. There she studied watercolor. After seven years at the school she was offered a teaching post, but chose instead to dedicate herself to her own art.

Following the death of her parents, in 1882, and Adelaide's marriage to the engraver Benn Pitman, Nourse moved to New York to continue her training. On her return to Cincinnati, she began to paint portraits, and worked on landscapes and watercolors during summers in the country.

In 1887 Nourse settled in Paris with her sister Louise, where she enrolled briefly at the Académie Julian, studying with Gustave Boulanger and Jules Lefebvre. In 1888 she presented *A Mother* at the Salon; the painting is today held at the Cincinnati Art Museum.

Throughout her career Nourse painted landscapes, scenes of motherhood, and portraits, taking as her subjects rural life, women at work, and peasants and black women and girls. Her work shows her interest in the culture and inhabitants of the various countries she visited, notably in Europe and northern Africa.

In 1895 Nourse was the first woman elected to the Société Nationale des Beaux-Arts, a group that five years previously had broken off from the Société des Artistes Français to organize its own salon. It was at the Société Nationale salon that the French state acquired, in 1910, Nourse's painting *Les volets clos* (*Closed Shutters*) for the Musée du Luxembourg; the painting is now held at the Musée d'Orsay in Paris. In 1899 Nourse became president of the American Women's Art Association in Paris.

Nourse was honored both in France and the United States, earning medals at exhibitions in Chicago, Nashville, St. Louis, and San Francisco. Supporting herself and her sister Louise with her artwork throughout her career, without a personal fortune, a teaching post, or a husband, she was a perfect example of the "New Woman" described by American journalist Sarah Grand in 1894 and popularized by the writer Henry James—a woman who chose her own career, claimed the right to travel, and rejected the role of housewife and mother.

Nourse remained in France during World War I, aiding refugees and the wounded and organizing the raising of funds from her American and Canadian friends to help. After the death of her sister in 1927, she fell prey to depression. She died in 1938.

In 1983, a retrospective exhibition, *Elizabeth Nourse, 1859–1938: A Salon Career,* was held in Washington, DC, and Cincinnati. —JB

Hanna Pauli

STOCKHOLM, 1864–SOLNA, SWEDEN, 1940

Hanna Pauli was born Hanna Hirsch, one of eight children of Pauline Meyerson and the music editor Abraham Hirsch, whose paternal grandfather, David Hirsch, immigrated to Sweden from Germany and obtained Swedish nationality in 1821.

Hirsch trained at the Royal Academy of Fine Arts under August Malmström—a professor there from 1867 to 1894 and director from 1887 to 1893. At the academy she met future portrait painter Eva Bonnier, seven years her elder. The two met again in Paris, in the Académie Colarossi, and became housemates. Hirsch stayed in the French capital from 1885 to 1887; her portrait of her Finnish friend and fellow student Wendla Irene Soldan Brofeldt, more commonly known as Venny Soldan, was accepted at the 1887 Salon.

Most of the young artists enrolled at the Académie Colarossi or the Académie Julian at this time, when the avant-garde was breaking away from academic painting, steered a middle path between the two, though a few, such as Lilla Cabot Perry, took up Impressionism enthusiastically. The majority, like Hirsch, were more inclined toward naturalism, admiring painters such as Jules Bastien-Lepage or Jules Breton.

In 1887 Hirsch married Georg Pauli, who had been similarly trained. Along with other Swedish painters and sculptors, Georg Pauli formed part of the group Opponenterna (the Opponents), created in 1885 and inspired by the art they encountered in Paris. The couple spent one year in Italy. A few years later, upon returning to Sweden, Georg Pauli was named director of the school of painting and drawing affiliated with the Gothenburg Museum.

Hanna Pauli concentrated on portraits, often depicting writers from the couple's entourage—Verner von Heidenstam; Selma Lagerlöf, whose works Georg Pauli illustrated; and the Swedish feminist writer Ellen Key, with whom Hanna shared ideas, and whom she depicted lecturing to a group of friends at the Pauli household.

She received a third-class medal at the 1889 Exposition Universelle in Paris, and the art historian Léonce Bénédite cited her among Swedish artists in his account of the 1900 fair: "Leading a series of talented portraitists is M. Bjôrk, author of *Portrait of Prince Eugène*... followed by MM. Bergh and Thegerstrôm, Mrs. Hanna Pauli, M. Georg Pauli, M. Aron Gerle, etc."

Hanna Pauli died in 1940, having established a reputation as both a significant artist and a modern thinker. —JB

Lilla Cabot Perry

BOSTON, 1848–HANCOCK, NEW HAMPSHIRE, 1933

Raised in a rich Boston family (her father was a surgeon), Lilla Cabot was introduced to literature and music at a very early age. Although she worked on some sketches in childhood, she only undertook serious training at age thirty-six, after her marriage to the English literature professor Thomas Sergeant Perry, under the guidance of an old Académie Julian student, the portraitist Alfred Quinton Collins.

With their three girls, born respectively in 1876, 1880, and 1884, the couple traveled extensively before spending two years in Paris from 1887 to 1889. Perry enrolled in the Académie Colarossi, spending a lot of time studying the Old Masters at the Louvre. During visits to Spain, Italy, and England, she copied paintings found in the great museums. After spending some months in Munich, where she worked alongside Fritz von Uhde, who had opened a private school, she returned to Paris and enrolled in the Académie Julian. In 1889 two of her canvases, both portraits, were accepted by the Salon des Indépendants. That same year she saw an exhibition of Claude Monet's work at the Galerie Georges Petit, which she admired greatly. Between 1889 and 1909 the Perrys spent most summers in a rented house in Giverny, very close to Monet, and the two artists met. This meeting proved to be a decisive encounter in her life and career. Although he did not accept students, Monet advised Perry, who adopted plein-air painting techniques and the Impressionists' use of light.

After a journey to Belgium and the Netherlands, Perry returned to Boston, where she promoted Impressionism through conferences and exhibits. Pursuing her own work, she represented Massachusetts at the 1893 World's Columbian Exposition in Chicago with seven paintings. Her work received recognition in the 1890s, an acknowledgment that represented the beginning of the acceptance of Impressionist painting on the North American continent. Additionally, Perry exhibited at the salon of the Société Nationale des Beaux-Arts in Paris between 1894 and 1897 before following her husband to Japan, where he taught at Tokyo's Keiogijiku University. Japan was a new source of inspiration for the artist, who produced more than eighty paintings during her three years in Tokyo.

Returning to Boston in 1901, the artist received a bronze medal at the 1904 Louisiana Purchase Exposition in St. Louis with a portrait of Alice, the youngest of her three daughters. In the following years, she faced problems with her health and began to accept commissions for portraits to alleviate some financial burdens. She again traveled to Paris, where her paintings were well received at the Salon des Indépendants. Returning to Boston she exhibited in various galleries and became involved with the Guild of Boston Artists, a very conservative foundation.

Personal woes plagued Perry's successes in later years. Her second daughter, Edith, was institutionalized in a sanitarium; Perry herself suffered from diphtheria, and spent two years convalescing in South Carolina; her husband died in 1928, following a bout with pneumonia. Yet even in this difficult period, Perry found occasions to renew her inspiration, notably through the discovery of new landscapes, her favorite subject.

Lilla Cabot Perry died at age eighty-five, leaving behind an abundant body of artwork and several volumes of poetry. —JB

Marie Petiet, later Marie Dujardin-Beaumetz

LIMOUX, AUDE, FRANCE, 1854–LA BEZOLE, AUDE, FRANCE, 1893

Marie Petiet's mother died a few days after her birth, on July 21, 1854, and she was raised by her father, Léopold Petiet, and her uncle Auguste, wealthy landowners. Both men were amateur painters; they maintained a studio in La Bezole castle, their residence near Limoux, and another studio in Limoux itself, where they chiefly copied works of the Old Masters. Petiet at first copied alongside them, but at eighteen she painted her first original work, *Autoportrait au chevalet* (*Self-Portrait with Easel*).

The Petiets also owned property in Paris, on rue de la Pompe. An examination of Salon catalogues—Petiet exhibited regularly at the Salon from 1877 until 1885—shows different studio addresses, sometimes Limoux and sometimes Paris. Petiet studied in Paris between 1877 and 1883 with the painter Jean-Jacques Henner, who not only encouraged her to concentrate on representing the human figure but also helped her win acceptance from the Salon jury.

Around 1882 Léopold Petiet asked military painter Étienne Dujardin-Beaumetz to immortalize on canvas one of the heroes of the 1870 Franco-Prussian War, General Lapasset, who came from a family native to Limoux. Marie and Étienne met during this commission and married in 1886, a year after the death of Léopold, who had opposed their union, disapproving of the progressive politics of his future son-in-law.

Petiet often used as models subjects from her own circle in Limoux, usually women, placed in settings meant to evoke working-class professions. The young women represented in *Les blanchisseuses* (*The Laundrywomen*), for example, have been identified, and none were in fact laundrywomen. Aside from some still lifes and rare landscapes, portraits represent more than half of the work left behind by the artist.

After marrying, the couple settled in La Bezole, and Marie continued to paint and exhibit. Interestingly, until 1885 she relied solely on her father's training; starting in 1887 she listed Henner as one of her instructors. From this point on, she exhibited her art under the name Beaumetz-Petiet.

Marie Petiet died in 1893, before she turned forty. Most of her work is in the collections of the Musée de Peinture Petiet in Limoux, in a building originally granted to the municipality in 1880 by her father, and which previously held a drawing school. —JB

Edma Pontillon, née Marie Edma Caroline Morisot

VALENCIENNES, FRANCE, 1839–PARIS, 1921

Edma Morisot was born in 1839, the second of four children. Her elder sister, Yves, was born in 1838; Berthe, another girl, followed in 1841; and a boy, Tiburce, in 1848. Until 1852 the family lived in Bourges, where the father was a prefect, before settling in Paris.

As was typical in bourgeois families, the children received an artistic education, drawing, painting, and music being considered necessary to the cultural education of young girls, preparing them for their future lives as wives who could hold their own in society. But for Edma and her younger sister Berthe, there was more involved. Recognizing their early ambition and talent for painting, their mother—a descendant of the painter Jean-Honoré Fragonard—encouraged them to begin serious instruction. After early training with the classical painter Geoffroy-Alphonse Chocarne, they were entrusted to a student of Jean-Auguste-Dominique Ingres, Joseph Guichard. Their talent impressed him so much that he warned the family of the risks facing bourgeois women who embark on careers in painting. Nevertheless, Edma and Berthe, not content as copyists at the Louvre or workshop students, wished to paint plein-air landscapes, and were supported by their family. They continued their training under the guidance of the landscape painter Achille Oudinot. The Morisot family rented a house in Ville d'Avray, close to where Camille Corot lived and worked. Corot played an advisory role to the two sisters.

During sessions as copyists at the Louvre, Edma and Berthe crossed paths with Henri Fantin-Latour, who presented them to Édouard Manet. The two sisters were very close, with no tendency toward rivalry. Both were admitted to the 1864 Salon, with each sister submitting two landscapes. The preceding year Edma had started to work successfully in portraiture, depicting her sister Berthe in front of her easel. Edma exhibited at the Salon each year until 1868.

In 1869 Edma married a marine officer, Adolphe Pontillon. Among the witnesses was Adolphe Thiers. Following her husband to Lorient, she abandoned all artistic activity. Edma continued to maintain an abundant correspondence with Berthe, in which she often expressed nostalgia for the time when they worked together, and made pastel copies of some of her sister's canvases, among them fragments of *Vénus allant demander les armes à Vulcain*, *La natte*, *Jeunes femmes à leur toilette*, and *Devant la psyché*.

For her part, Berthe often visited her sister; in 1869 she painted her sister in *The Harbor at Lorient*, which she later offered to Manet. Edma served as a model for two of Berthe's most celebrated canvases, today in the collections of the Musée d'Orsay in Paris: *The Cradle*, in which Edma watches over her daughter Blanche, born in 1871, and *Chasing Butterflies*, in which she appears with her two daughters, Blanche and the elder Jeanne, born in 1870.

Edma Pontillon died in Paris in 1921. —JB

Helene Schjerfbeck

HELSINKI, 1862–SALTSJÖBADEN, SWEDEN, 1946

Helene Schjerfbeck began drawing at a very early age. She enrolled at the Finnish Art Society Drawing School, Helsinki, at age eleven, where she first met Helena Westermarck. The painter Adolf von Becker, impressed by the young girl's talent, taught her oil painting techniques he had learned during his stay in Paris. In 1879, at the age of seventeen, Schjerfbeck received a prize from the Finnish Art Society.

In 1880 Schjerfbeck was awarded a grant to study in Paris, where she enrolled in Mme Trélat de Vigny's workshop. Together with Marianne Preindlsberger, a young woman painter of Austrian origin later known as Marianne Stokes, she traveled around France. In Pont-Aven, in Brittany, Schjerfbeck met and became engaged to a painter. However, the engagement was called off when her handicap, from an earlier hip fracture, caused his parents to object to the marriage. After a brief return to Finland, in 1884 Schjerfbeck enrolled at the Académie

Colarossi in Paris. Three years later, she traveled to St. Ives, in Cornwall, where she again met Marianne Stokes and her husband, Adrian.

After this period, Schjerfbeck returned to Finland and began to teach at the Drawing School. Health problems forced her to resign her teaching post, and she relocated to Hyvinkää in 1902, an isolated village thirty miles north of Helsinki, where she cared for her ailing mother. Schjerfbeck remained there for ten years. This was a period of artistic and social isolation, during which she was removed from the fight for Finnish independence as well as Akseli Gallen-Kallela's national romantic movement, contributing to her marginalization.

After Hyvinkää, Schjerfbeck moved to Tammisaari where she lived until 1940, creating landscapes, still lifes, and portraits. Starting in 1913, she began to return to the artistic scene; in 1914 she was the only Finnish woman artist invited to participate in the Baltic Exhibition in Malmö, Sweden, and that year the Finnish Art Society also exhibited a number of her works. Her self-portraits represent the most remarkable work of this period. She continued to exhibit until her death in 1946 at a sanatorium in Saltsjöbaden, Sweden, where she found refuge after the Soviet Union's invasion of Finland in 1939.

In 2007 the Musée d'Art Moderne de la Ville de Paris held a retrospective of Schjerfbeck's work. The 150th anniversary of her birth was commemorated with exhibitions at several Finnish museums, most notably the Ateneum Museum in Helsinki; Tammisaari on the south coast and Vaasa on the west coast also presented festivities in her honor. —JB

Mary Shepard Greene Blumenschein

NEW YORK, 1869–TAOS, NEW MEXICO, 1958

Mary Shepard Greene Blumenschein is relatively unknown today, but during her lifetime she attained an exceptional level of institutional success for a woman artist.

Shepard Greene's father died when she was fifteen, and she and her mother and brother were left with a sizeable fortune. Her mother encouraged her interest in art, sending her to Pratt Institute in Brooklyn, where she studied under John Barnard Whittaker. In 1889 after completing her studies, Shepard Greene and her mother—her brother was enrolled in medical school—moved to Paris; what was intended as a brief sojourn quickly became a new life.

Shepard Greene's artistic training in the capital city was formative: she attended classes at the Académie Julian, and then spent nearly fifteen years as a pupil of the Salon painter Raphaël Collin, whose academicism left an indelible impression. After her Salon debut in 1896, Shepard Greene frequently exhibited in Paris and the United States, and major successes quickly followed. In 1900 she garnered a third-class medal for her Salon submission, *Un Regard Fugitif*, and the following year this painting was exhibited in the Seventieth Annual Exhibition of the Pennsylvania Academy of the Fine Arts. In 1902 she became the second American woman (the first was Mary Cassatt) to earn a second-class medal at the Salon, with *Une petite histoire* (*A Little Story*), and this work was chosen to be exhibited the following summer at the Worcester Art Museum, where Cecilia Beaux served on the jury. She referred to this work as her chef d'oeuvre. She also received a silver medal at the 1904 Louisiana Purchase Exhibition, held in conjunction with the St. Louis World's Fair—Lilla Cabot Perry took bronze.

On June 29, 1905, Shepard Greene married artist Ernest L. Blumenschein. At the time of their marriage, and unlike most artist couples of the age, she was the more famous painter, as he had only found success with commercial illustration, and he strove to equal her in reputation. The couple moved into a large artist studio in the fashionable Latin Quarter, and they spent days visiting the Louvre and painting side-by-side in their apartment. During this time, she also began to work as an illustrator.

In 1909 she became pregnant with a girl (she lost her first child, a son, two days after his birth), and on May 29 the expectant couple and the artist's mother sailed back to New York City. After the birth of her daughter, Helen, Mary continued to illustrate novels—most notably Marjorie Benton Cooke's popular 1914 romance *Bambi*—and paint. She regularly exhibited with the National Association of Women Artists and at the Art Institute of Chicago and the National Academy of Design, which awarded her the 1915 Julia A. Shaw Memorial Prize for *The Princess and the Frog* (1909), which illustrates a Grimm fairy tale. In 1917 her mother died, and in 1919 she reluctantly moved full-time to Taos, New Mexico, where Ernest had been seeking artistic inspiration each summer since 1910. In 1928, just as her mother had done for her at the age of nineteen, Blumenschein took her daughter to Paris to study art, where they remained for two years. Upon returning to Taos, she continued to paint, and her works from this period manifest her interest in the regional style of the Southwest. Eventually she turned her attention to jewelry making, with exhibitions at the Museum of International Folk Art and the Museum of Fine Arts, both in Santa Fe. Blumenschein died in 1958, after a lengthy battle with heart disease. The following year, Helen Blumenschein donated *Husking Corn* (1939) to the Harwood Museum of Art in Taos in her mother's memory.

Sketches from her time in Paris, including a self-portrait, can be found in the Blumenschein Home and Museum in Taos, New Mexico. Her correspondence is divided between the Fray Angélico Chávez History Library, in the New Mexico History Museum, Santa Fe, and the Archives of American Art at the Smithsonian Institution, Washington, DC. Although a surfeit of biographical information is available on the artist, including Helen Blumenschein's *Recuerdos: Early Days of the Blumenschein Family* (1979), no monographic study of Mary Shepard Greene Blumenschein's artistic contributions exists. —JWM

Marianne Stokes, née Preindlsberger

GRAZ, AUSTRIA, 1855–LONDON, 1927

Marianne Preindlsberger was born into a merchant-class family in Graz, Austria's second-largest city, where her mother, Agnes, ran a dress shop while her father, Franz, a businessman, also encouraged his children's artistic talents. Having studied at the city's drawing academy, Preindlsberger won a prize in her youth that enabled her to study for five years in Munich, where she lived with an aunt. She visited Vienna, where in 1875 Johann

Strauss the Younger, then at the height of his fame, dedicated to her a lively polka-mazurka, although the circumstances behind this story are unknown. Records show that she fulfilled her ambition to reach Paris by 1880, when she was listed as a student under Léon Bonnat and Jean-Léon Gérôme at the Académie Trélat. She also studied with Pascal Dagnan-Bouveret, and then in 1882 enrolled at the Académie Colarossi. There, she met two Finnish artists, Helene Schjerfbeck and Maria Wiik, with whom she had more in common than being young women studying fine art in a foreign city. The women shared a similar approach to technique and subject matter, and Preindlsberger later encouraged both to come paint in Cornwall.

Gustave Courtois came every week to look at their studies and several other French artists, such as Raphaël Collin, also made occasional visits. Work hours were strictly regimented, beginning at eight o'clock, with different models provided for morning and afternoon sessions. On Saturday afternoons the students visited galleries and museums in the city. In 1882 Preindlsberger won Colarossi's silver medal in the expressive head competition. In 1883 her first chance to exhibit in public was provided by the Société des Amis des Arts de Seine et Oise in Versailles, and, later that year, she and Schjerfbeck shared lodgings at the Hotel Mont-Blanc at 14 rue de la Seine. Soon after, the two, along with Wiik, set out for western France, cementing a friendship with Schjerfbeck that would last for the rest of Preindlsberger's life.

The strong influence of Dagnan-Bouveret's and Bastien-Lepage's "square brush" technique was evident in the oil paintings of most of the artists who congregated annually in the western French colonies. Preindlsberger was no exception, and after three years of study she submitted a painting, *Reflection*, to the 1883 Salon. Her charming account of waiting anxiously for two weeks for news brings to life the anxiety of this first important marker in her career. This debut was swiftly followed by more plein-air studies in Brittany, and it was there that she met the British painter Adrian Stokes, whom she married in Graz in 1884. Beginning in 1885, Marianne Stokes had an international audience, and eventually displayed her work at the 1893 World's Columbian Exposition in Chicago. That year she completed *The Passing Train*; in this painting the model wears the same cape, although in bright red rather than brown, as the young Madonna in *Hail Mary*, a medal winner at the World's Fair of two years earlier. *Passing Train* was shown at the Carnegie Institute and later purchased by the Cleveland Museum of Art; it was deaccessioned after World War II and entered a private collection in England. The serious face in sharp profile of a young girl collecting kindling echoes the artist's *Polishing Pans* of 1887.

A devout Catholic, Stokes then turned to religious themes, having found inspiration on a visit to Italy in 1887, with paintings such as *Angels Entertaining the Holy Child* and *St. Elizabeth of Hungary Spinning Wool for the Poor*. From the late 1890s, Stokes favored romantic medieval themes such as *The Page*, based on a poem by Heinrich Heine, and *Aucassin and Nicolette*. Executed in a tempera technique that achieved Pre-Raphaelite brilliance of color and with minute attention to detail, her subject matter and naive style led the art critic Alice Meynell to describe her as "a Primitive in art and heart."

The Stokeses searched for new inspiration in the Netherlands in 1899, and in 1905 made the first of five visits to what was then Hungary, which resulted in 1909 in a jointly illustrated book and an exhibition in Budapest in 1910. Marianne's delicate tempera portraits of the folk costumes of what is now Slovakia and Romania remain among her most highly coveted works. *Death and the Maiden* of 1908 is unusual for this period in that it is painted in oil. Elected an associate of the Royal Watercolor Society in 1923, Marianne Stokes died in London in 1927.

In 2009 Wolverhampton Art Gallery organized a touring exhibition of Stokes's work, accompanied by the publication of the first monograph on the artist by a great-great niece of Adrian Stokes, Magdalen Evans. —ME

Annie Louisa Swynnerton, née Robinson

MANCHESTER, ENGLAND, 1844–HAYLING ISLAND, ENGLAND, 1933

Annie Louisa Robinson was born on February 26, 1844, in Hulme, an area of Manchester just south of the city center. One of six daughters, Robinson began her institutional artistic training rather late, enrolling at the Manchester School of Art in 1869 at age twenty-five. In 1871 a scholarship allowed her to travel to Rome, where she shared a studio with fellow Manchester artist Susan Isabel Dacre. The two traveled to Florence to study sculpture, and after 1876 the pair went to Paris, where they studied at the Académie Julian from 1877 to 1879. Upon returning home in 1879, Robinson—along with two of her sisters and Dacre—founded the Manchester Society of Women Painters. The society offered life drawing classes to women and held annual group exhibitions of members' work. Robinson served as founding secretary, and Dacre as founding president. The broader art historical importance of this network of female artists—one of the few to flourish outside of central London—remains to be studied.

Throughout her life, Robinson frequently traveled to Rome, where in 1883 she married the sculptor Joseph Swynnerton, and the couple remained in Rome until his death. Several of her works from this period are inspired by Italian locales or religious motifs: *The Olive Gatherers* presents a panoramic landscape of Lombardy's mist-covered fields, *Assisi* depicts the hill town's characteristic architecture, and *An Italian Mother and Child* casts a peasant and her toddler as a Renaissance Madonna and Child. Toward the end of the 1880s, Swynnerton became an active suffragette, and as her public profile and popularity increased, she exhibited widely throughout the 1890s at the Royal Academy, London; the Royal Scottish Academy; and the Royal Glasgow Institute; as well as with the Society of Women Artists, the Royal Society of Portrait Painters, and the New English Art Club.

In 1890 and 1892 Swynnerton painted *Cupid and Psyche* and *Mater Triumphalis*, respectively. Each vertically oriented composition features a heavily modeled figure set against a flat background, a stylistic idiom she developed from her study of sculpture. Alongside such allegorical and symbolic paintings, Swynnerton produced numerous portraits, landscapes, and genre scenes, and in 1895 she became the second woman to be asked to serve on the selection jury for the Liverpool Autumn Exhibition. Swynnerton was included in

Walter Shaw Sparrow's 1905 compendium *Women Painters of the World*, in the section devoted to "Modern British Women Painters." Sparrow reproduced her immensely popular *The Sense of Sight*, and the painter Ralph Peacock singled out a distinctive feature of Swynnerton's painterly imagination: her remarkable ability to reproduce eyes, or in his words, "blue eyes . . . so blue."

Joseph Swynnerton died in 1910, and although Annie continued to travel, she eventually settled at Hayling Island, off England's south coast. In 1922 Swynnerton was elected associate member (ARA) of the Royal Academy, London. Although two women artists, Mary Moser and Angelica Kauffman, were founding members of the institution, rules formally excluded women from election as members, and only in 1936 did Dame Laura Knight become the first woman royal academician (RA) with full rights. Toward the end of her life, Swynnerton's eyesight began to suffer, and although she still exhibited, she frequently submitted works painted at an earlier date. On October 24, 1933, the artist died on Hayling Island. Her gravestone at St. Mary's Church in South Hayling reads "I have known love and the light of the sun."

Swynnerton left behind more than two hundred paintings that cannot easily be categorized, as they traverse European Symbolism, Pre-Raphaelitism, and British Impressionism, yet no monographic study of her work exists. Manchester Art Gallery has the largest public collection of paintings by the artist; additional major works can be found in the Glasgow Museums; the Musée d'Orsay, Paris; the Royal Academy of Arts, London; the Tate, London; and the Walker Art Gallery, Liverpool. —JWM

Ellen Thesleff

HELSINKI, 1869–1954

Ellen Thesleff came from a musical family—she herself sang and played piano—and her father was an amateur painter. When she was sixteen the family moved to Kuopio, a university town about 250 miles north of Helsinki, where she enrolled in Adolf von Becker's private painting academy, studying alongside Helene Schjerfbeck and Akseli Gallen-Kallela. In 1888 Thesleff continued her training at the Finnish Art Society Drawing School in Helsinki, where her teacher was Gunnar Berndtson.

Like many of her compatriots, Thesleff went to Paris to continue her training. In 1891 she enrolled at the Académie Colarossi, where she studied under Gustave Courtois and Pascal Dagnan-Bouveret. Subsequently she traveled to Italy, spending time in Florence, where she focused on the art of the Renaissance. In Italy Thesleff met Gordon Craig, who introduced her to the technique of wood engraving. She was also influenced by Symbolism, and admired the French painter Pierre Puvis de Chavannes as well as the Impressionists. Along with Willy Finch and Magnus Enckell, Thesleff participated in the creation of the group Septem, which introduced Impressionism to Finland. Her own work focused on portraits—an image of her sister, *Thyra Elisabeth*, evokes the French painter Eugène Carrière—and landscapes.

She traveled often, and exhibited in Florence, Moscow, Paris, Stockholm, and St. Petersburg. Thesleff received a bronze medal at the 1900 Exposition Universelle in Paris. In Finland she spent most of her time at her family's home in Murole, near Ruovesi.

Thesleff never married, and continued painting until the end of her life. In 1944 she participated in the exhibition *Finsk Nutidskonst, 1914–1944*, organized by the Finnish Association of Contemporary Art, and was selected as an honorary member of the Artists Society of Finland. In 1951 she received the Pro Finlandia medal, given by the nation's president since 1945 to Finnish artists.

Today Ellen Thesleff's works are held mainly in Helsinki, at the Kuopio Museum and the Ateneum Musem, which dedicated an exhibition to the artist in 1998. —JB

Female Painters at the Paris Salon

This study is focused on women's increasing presence on the artistic stage during the latter half of the nineteenth century, as indicated by their presence at the Salon. It is partly the result of research conducted by Denise Noël, who, in her thesis "Female Painters at the Salon, 1863–1889" investigated the professionalization of that group of female painters who participated in the official art market.[1] In using the participation of female artists in the Paris Salon as a criterion, Noël joins Harrison and Cynthia White, who studied the careers of nineteenth-century painters through a "cross section of all the artists considered professionals on the national stage."[2] To support their work, the authors relied on a list of artists whose works were accepted many times by Salon juries that was compiled in the nineteenth century by Emile Bellier and Louis Auvray.[3] The information gathered and presented here is the result of systematic analysis of each of the Salon catalogues from the second half of the nineteenth century, which allow a thorough review of the presence and evolution of women on the art scene.

The Salon was born with the establishment of the Académie Royale de Peinture et de Sculpture (Royal Academy of Painting and Sculpture) on January 20, 1648, by Jean-Baptiste Colbert, who hoped to eliminate the guild system inherited from the Middle Ages. Guilds governed all aspects of the professional careers of painters and sculptors, from their training to authorizing the sale of their work, limiting access to professional careers to members only. The advent of the Académie Royale put an end to these prerogatives and promoted a new image of artists, one that no longer considered them as artisans and merchants.

The Académie Royale's first exhibition took place in 1667. Little information exists regarding the exhibition's content, and little more regarding the exhibitions that followed it, in 1669 and 1671. Starting in 1673, the exhibitions are better documented. Their organization fluctuated during the different political regimes in France, with modifications in registration, jury selection, the number of submissions allowed, and compensation. Despite political instability, the exhibition, after undergoing a period of irregularity, stabilized in 1831 and became an annual event. It was initially held in the galleries of the Palais-Royal and the courtyard of the Hôtel Richelieu. Starting in 1699, it began taking place at the Louvre's Grande Galerie, then later moved to the Salon Carré at the Louvre. This last site eventually gave the exhibition its name; it became known as the Paris Salon, even after it moved to the Palais de Tuileries in 1849.

Between 1848 and 1900, the Beaux-Arts ministry assumed responsibility for organizing the Salon, under the guidance of several successive ministers (interior and education).[4] By 1881 the Société des Artistes Français (Society of French Artists) was created with the encouragement of Edmond Turquet, undersecretary of state at the Beaux-Arts ministry, who asked artists who had already exhibited at the Salon to become incorporated.

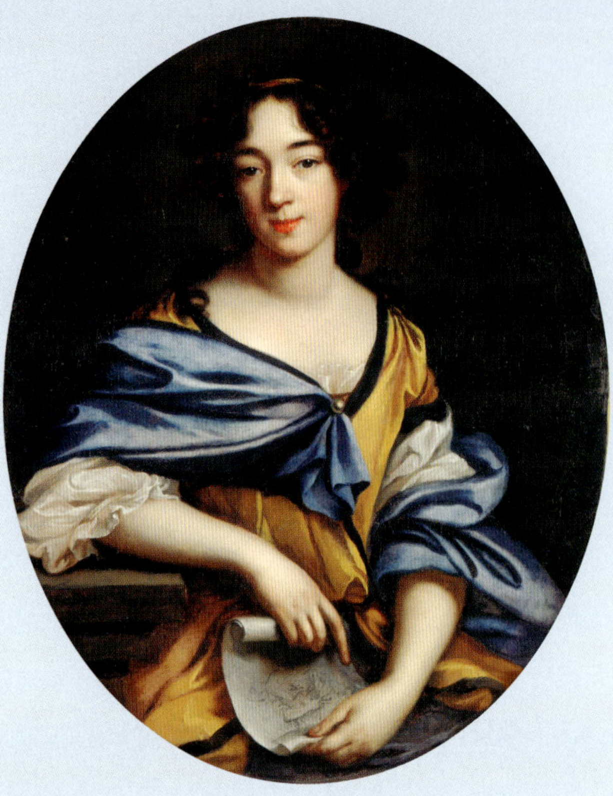

Fig. 1. Elisabeth Sophie Chéron (French, 1648–1711), *Self-Portrait*, 1672. Oil on canvas, 34⅝ × 28¾ in. (88 × 73 cm). Musée du Louvre, Paris, 3239
Sophie Chéron was the fourth woman painter admitted to the Académie Royale, after Catherine Duchemin (in 1663) and Madeleine and Genevieve Boullogne (in 1669). This was her reception piece in 1672.

The 1848 exhibition, which opened its doors on March 15, was atypical, coming shortly after the February Revolution, in which several artists took part. In response to the enthusiasm for the newly created Second Republic, the Salon was declared "free"—that is, without jury. In 1900 the Salon was eclipsed by the fifth Exposition Universelle, a world's fair that included decennial and centennial exhibits. In the years between these two events, the evolution of French artistic life accelerated: independent and competing Salons multiplied; the professions of art merchant and art critic evolved; and an increasing number of independent studios challenged the monopoly that the École des Beaux-Arts had over the training of artists. The official Salon began to lose its prestige, and artists built their careers beyond its walls. The Salon, however, continued its essential missions: provide a gathering space for artists and an exhibition space for the public, and sell the works of the exhibiting artists. Much like their male colleagues, female artists wished to see their work shown in these exhibitions and to profit from the subsequent advantages.

Quantitative Evolution of the Presence of Women Artists at the Salon Until the end of the eighteenth century, women did not have any significant presence at the Salon; only members of the Académie Royale were allowed to show their work. For nearly a century and a half—between 1663, when the first woman was admitted, until the eve of the Revolution—only fifteen women (thirteen painters and two sculptors) exhibited at the Salon [fig. 1]. An additional restriction was imposed in 1783, when the number of women accepted to the Salon was limited to four [fig. 2], "a sufficient number to honor talent," claimed the Earl of Angiviller, the director general of the king's buildings; "Women will never be useful for the progress of the arts. The decency of their gender keeps them from working on art painted from life and in public schools established and founded by Your Majesty."[5] Among the forty-five painters who showcased their work in 1767, two were women; four were included in the forty-six artists in 1787, and three were among the forty-eight artists exhibiting in the last show organized by the Académie Royale, in 1789. The following Salon, in 1791, was dedicated to "freedom": participants were no longer required to be members of the Académie, and women represented nearly 12 percent of the artists, compared to a little less than 6 percent in 1789. This was their only gain following the Revolution: the Institut de France, which replaced the Académie Royale, closed its doors to them, as did the Académie des Beaux-Arts, created in 1816. Not only were women barred from the title of academician, but after the abolition of the Académie Royale, those women who had previously received the title lost it. As a result, for almost two centuries no female was admitted into the Académie des Beaux-Arts.[6]

Paris hosted forty-six Salons between 1848 and 1900.[7] With 729 participants, the 1853 Salon hosted the smallest number of artists. The number of participating artists in painting and drawing sections failed to reach 1,000 on only two occasions; nineteen Salons featured between 1,000 and 2,000 artists; twenty, between 2,000 and 3,000; three, between 3,000 and 4,000; and the 1880 Salon assembled the largest number of exhibitors, with 4,261 in the painting and drawing sections.[8] The varying numbers result from changes in the Salon's regulations that altered the makeup of the jury and its selection process, the process of exemption for previous Salon prize recipients, the existence, or lack thereof, of quotas for works of art allowed per artist and per section, and limits on the total number of works received. These factors influenced not only the number of exhibitors and works of art accepted but also, in varying degrees of significance, the proportion of women artists represented.

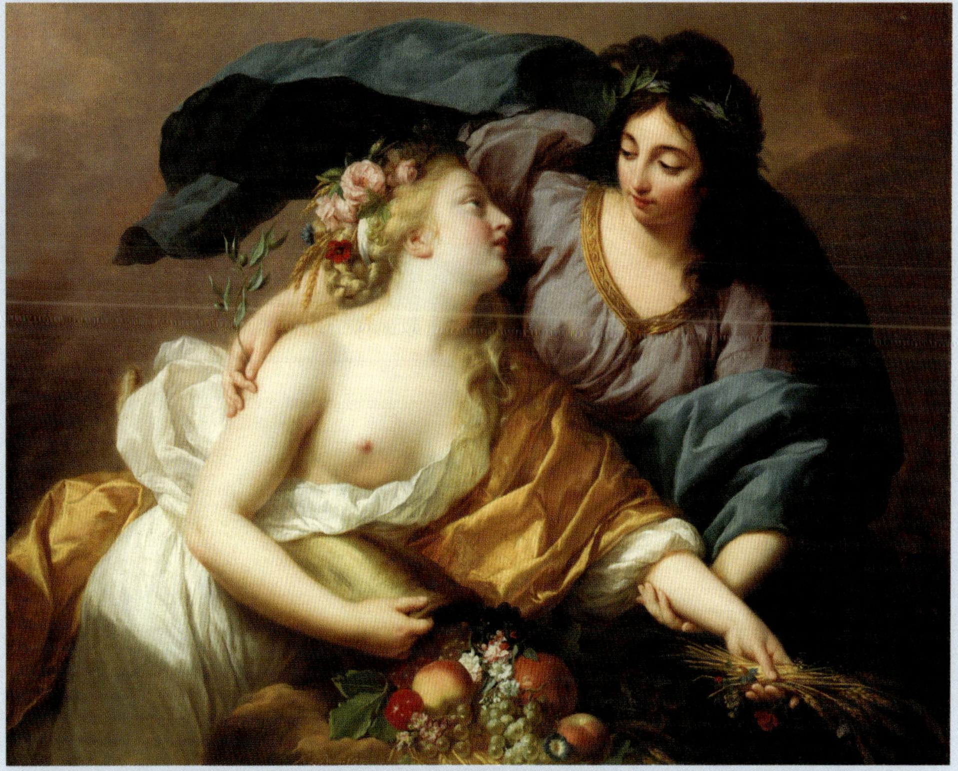

Fig. 2. Élisabeth Louise Vigée Le Brun (French, 1755–1842), *Peace Bringing Abundance* (*La Paix ramenant l'Abondance*), 1780. Oil on canvas, 40⅜ × 52⅛ in. (102.5 × 132.5 cm). Musée du Louvre, Paris, 3052
This picture, presented by Vigée Le Brun for her reception to the Académie Royale in 1783, was also exhibited at the Paris Salon in the same year.

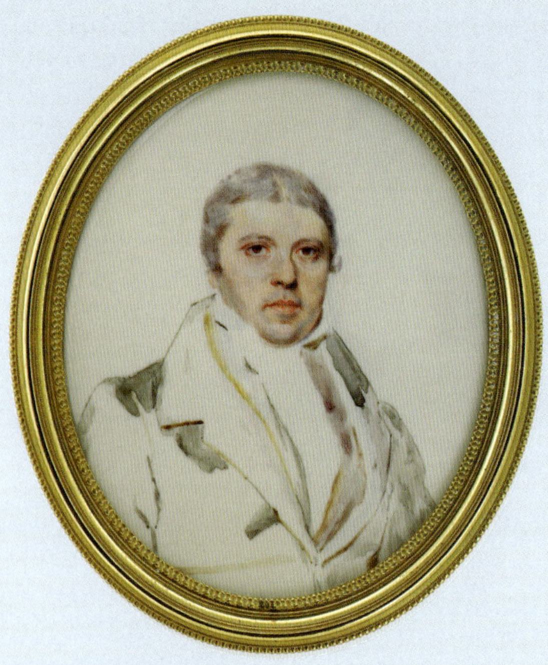

Fig. 3. Lizinka Aimée Zoé de Mirbel (French, 1796–1849), *Portrait of Ingres*, 1834. Ivory miniature, 4⅛ × 3⅜ in. (10.4 × 8.5 cm). Musée du Louvre, Paris, 31339 recto
Mme de Mirbel was cited as a teacher by many women into the 1870s, more than twenty years after her death.

The jury selection process and its resulting composition affected the number of works of art admitted each year. The 1848 Salon assembled a large number of participants: close to 2,000 exhibitors and more than 4,500 paintings and sketches. This abundance is likely linked to the fact that submissions that year were not subjected to jury approval. The percentage of women (15.8 percent of exhibitors and 13.2 percent of works of art) was relatively high. Women were particularly well represented outside the realm of painting, forming over one-third of exhibitors showcasing work that fell generally under the banner of graphic arts, such as pastels, watercolors, porcelains, enamels, miniatures, and illustrations. Can it be considered a coincidence that the number of women admitted diminished sharply between 1852 and 1863, a decade during which initially half the juries were represented by elected artists and half by appointed male academics, and in subsequent years, when juries were entirely made up of appointed academicians? The number of works of art presented by women rested below 10 percent.

In 1863, the jury rejected close to 3,000 artworks. This severity unleashed a strong reaction from the artists, who obtained from the emperor permission to present a temporary exhibition, the Salon des Refusés.[9] Women were proportionally better represented here than at the official Salon, making up 12.6 percent of exhibitors and 13.3 percent of total artworks, compared to 11.2 percent and 9.1 percent, respectively, in the official Salon. In this period it's worth noting that despite ever-changing methods of selection, varying number of members elected or appointed by the academy or administration, and varying degrees of acceptance of artists or members of the Institut de France and those with awards or medals, no woman ever formed part of a jury.

In another regulation that militated against the presence of women, nearly every year members of the institute and decorated artists were automatically exempted from submitting for jury selection. Since women were not admitted to the institute, and not until 1865 was the Légion d'Honneur granted to a woman,[10] in 1853 none of the 74 exempted artists were women. In 1864 those awarded medals in previous Salons were also automatically exempted, and only 7 of the 269 exempted artists were women. In 1884, when those exempted included standouts and medal winners, again women represented 7 of the 348 artists not required to submit to the jury; thus, of 2,016 male artists, 341—close to 17 percent—were exempted, while only 1.5 percent of the 452 female artists were exempted.

The number of works permitted by artists in each section was another decisive factor. Even in years when there was no quota on the number of works presented, women showed only one or two works, while individual male artists tended to present more works. The 1855 Salon, with its section dedicated to the fine arts at the Exposition Universelle, provides the most significant example. Twenty-eight countries, in addition to France, participated, and artists were permitted to present as many works for the fair as they wished. Alexandre Decamps presented the most works: 46. Jean-Auguste-Dominique Ingres presented 39 works, while Eugène Delacroix submitted 35, and Gustave Courbet contributed 11.[11] The average number of works presented by male artists was 2.7, while women submitted 1.6 on average. Most women exhibited one work; ten exhibited three works, one presented four works, and only two, Henriette Browne and Elise Wagner, submitted five works. Rules also authorized the exhibition of works of art already showcased in previous Salons. Male artists took advantage of this, Abel de Pujol presenting two works he had already shown in 1817 and 1819. Many works exhibited by men in the years 1820 to 1830, when women were not strongly represented, were shown in multiple Salons. Finally, works admitted to the Exposition Universelle included art lent by private and public owners, such as ministries, museums, and churches. Since publicly owned artworks were overwhelmingly by male artists, and every work mentioned in the Salon catalogue as being acquired by the emperor or the state—roughly fifty works of art—was signed by a man, 1855 was the worst year for women at the Salon: they represented less than 7 percent of artists, and less than 5 percent of total works of art (3.4 percent among paintings, and 10.9 percent among drawings).

Progressively, female participation grew to over 20 percent midway after 1877. After a slight dip between 1884 and 1886, it continued to climb, breaking the 30 percent barrier in 1899. If we separate those women who presented paintings from those who submitted graphic works, we notice immediately that representation among the second group is much higher, never falling below 20 percent, and reaching up to 60 percent during certain years, compared to the proportion of female painters, long hovering near 10 percent and never passing 16 percent. The percentage of women painters tended to decrease over the years, while the percentage focused on the graphic arts climbed. A comparison with male artists proves illuminating. In the 1877 Salon, 27 percent of women fell into the painting category, 73 percent into the drawing category. For men, the percentages are reversed: 72 percent were painters and 28 percent were draftsmen.

These developments came amid a substantial change in the number of exhibitors overall, which increased until 1880, and then declined. The increase was not linear: the numbers dropped starting in 1872, and increased progressively in the following years. The reasons are tied to political events within Paris. The 1871 Salon was canceled and the following year's exhibition opened in the Élysée Palace, part of which was occupied by the Ministry of Finance after the ministry's headquarters were destroyed during the period of the Paris Commune known as *la semaine sanglante* (the bloody week), in which 20,000 revolutionaries were killed. The space dedicated to the exhibition decreased by nearly half, with close to a 50 percent decrease in the number of works displayed, a reduction that did not significantly change the percentage of female exhibitors. The 1880 Salon reached a milestone: more than 4,200 exhibitors presented over 6,000 works, an exorbitant number that triggered scathing criticism. The French state decided to withdraw from the organization of future Salons, entrusting that endeavor to the Société des Artistes Français. Society members elected a ninety-member collective—with fifty representing painting and the rest drawing and the graphic arts—to organize the 1881 Salon. No women were among them. The board of directors and the jury was composed of 40 men. Starting the following year, the number of works admitted would be fixed: initially, a maximum of 2,500 paintings and 800 drawings, then 1,800 and 600, descending to 1,200 and 300, respectively, in 1900. These limits, even if not scrupulously respected, nonetheless avoided an excess of works. Starting in 1863, regulations stipulated how many artists' works would be allowed in each category. Exhibitors could present a maximum of two works for each category, which was lowered to a single work per category in 1900. We can see that this rule favored women's representation.

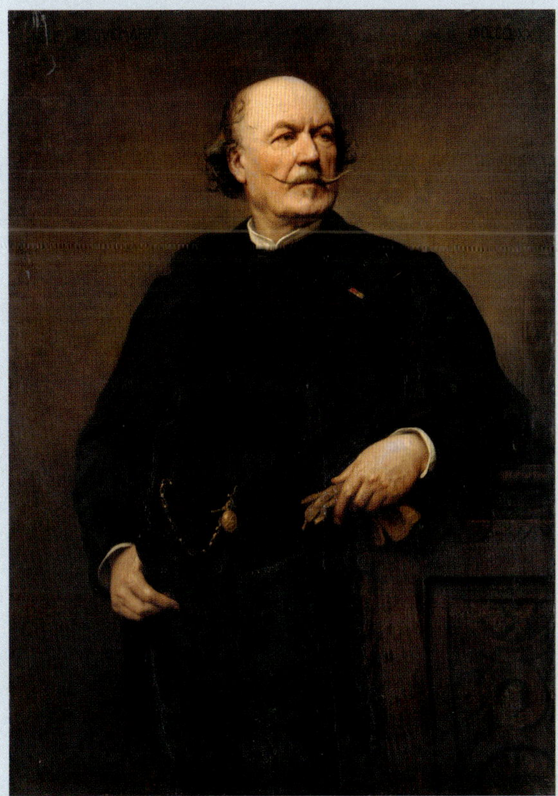

Fig. 4. Nélie Jacquemart (French, 1841–1912), *Portrait of Maréchal Canrobert*, 1870. Oil on canvas, 49¼ × 23¼ in. (125 × 59 cm). Musée National du Château de Compiègne, C.46.007
Nélie Jacquemart is one of many female students who attended the studio of Léon Cogniet; more than forty exhibitors claimed him as teacher at the Salon of 1870, when this painting appeared.

Training Methods and Types of Works Produced by Women Marie Bashkirtseff, writing under a pseudonym in 1881, analyzed the problems women faced when seeking artistic training: "I won't surprise anyone by saying that women are excluded from the École des Beaux-Arts like they are virtually everywhere. We accept them, however, at the School of Medicine, so why not at the École des Beaux-Arts? Mystery. . . . Thus, those of you who loudly proclaim to be stronger, more intelligent, better endowed than us, you monopolize for yourselves one of the most beautiful schools in the world, where you are lavished with every compliment. As for the women you call frail, weak, bounded, many of which are denied the same ordinary freedom to come and go by the word *convenience*, you do not grant them the same encouragement or protection, on the contrary."[12]

The unequal training methods Bashkirtseff denounced lasted until the end of the century. Not until 1897 did a decree end the ban on women's admission to the École des Beaux-Arts, and it was three more years before painting studios were effectively opened to female students. Female artists continued their struggle—under the notable impetus of Hélène Bertaux, who in 1881 created the Union des Femmes Peintres et Sculpteurs (Union of Female Painters and Sculptors), and Virginie Demont-Breton, who led the union between 1895 and 1901—before obtaining the right to attend the Prix de Rome in 1903.[13]

What, then, were the strategies available to women before the turn of the century? Following a well-established tradition, some women studied under a father, brother, or husband. During this time, among women who declared that they had at least one teacher, rarely do over 10 percent cite a man in the family as that teacher: the percentage rests between 7 and 13 percent until the end of the 1870s, then falls to less than 4 percent by the end of the 1890s. With only occasional exceptions, the percentage of women who declared a father, brother, or husband as a teacher is greater in the painting section than in the graphic arts section. Virginie Demont-Breton, who studied painting under her father, Jules Breton, and Juliette Peyrol, who learned to paint under the guidance of her father, Raymond Bonheur, showed paintings in the Salons; while Delphine de Cool, who was trained by her father, Paul Marie Fortin, a porcelain painter in Limoges, made a name for herself as a miniaturist and porcelain painter.

Several Parisian public schools that focused on the graphic arts welcomed students free of charge. In 1863, fourteen such schools existed, seven of them dedicated to women. For the most part they were directed by women, a number of whom exhibited at the Salon. Delphine de Cool headed a school on rue de l'Arbre-Sec in the first arrondissement, Mme Mac Nab led a school in the ninth arrondissement, and Léonide Poisson ran a school in the nineteenth arrondissement. Starting in 1803, another alternative was offered by the École Gratuite de Dessin pour Jeunes Personnes (Free School of Drawing for Young People), created by Mme Frère de Montizon. Renamed the

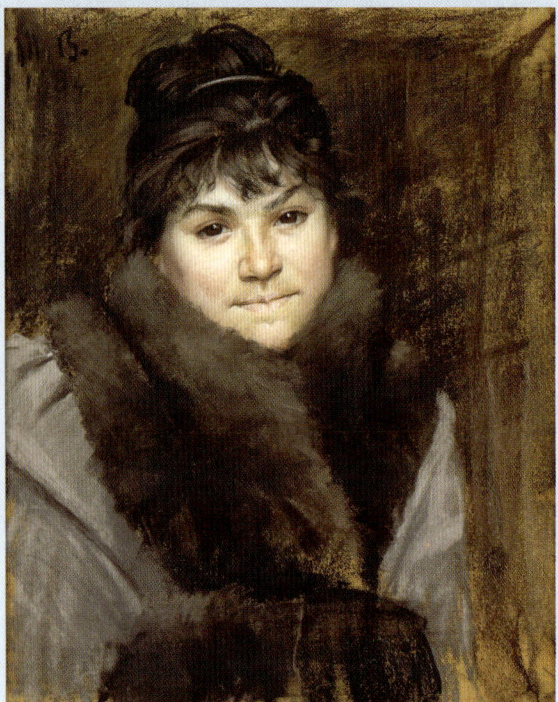

Fig. 5. Marie Bashkirtseff (Ukrainian, 1858–1884), *Portrait of a Young Woman* (*Portrait d'une jeune femme*), 1884. Pastel, 22 × 18¼ in. (56 × 46.5 cm). Musée d'Orsay, Paris, RF1565-recto
Marie Bashkirtseff was one of most famous young women who attended the Académie Julian. She left testimonials, both in her diary and in her paintings, of the atmosphere there.

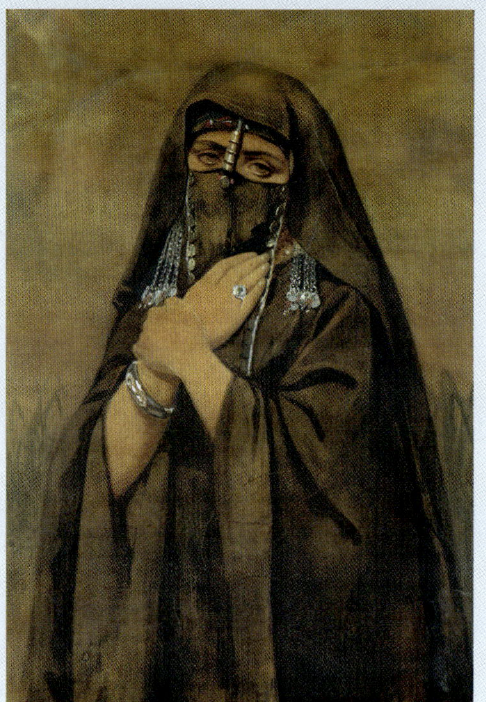

Fig. 6. Mathilde-Létizia Wilhelmine Bonaparte, called Princess Mathilde (French, 1820–1904), *A Fellah* (*Une fellah*), 1861. Tempera and oil on paper, 36¼ × 24½ in. (92 × 62.2 cm). Musée des Beaux-Arts, Nantes, 1588
Princess Mathilde was awarded an honorable mention at the Salon of 1861. Her entry consisted of four watercolors, including this one.

École Gratuite de Dessin pour les Jeunes Filles (Free School of Drawing for Young Girls) and then the École Gratuite de Dessin pour les Demoiselles (Free School of Design for Ladies), its direction passed from its founder to Raymond Bonheur and then to Rosa Bonheur, who served as both director and the school's only teacher between 1849 and 1860, and, finally to Nelly Marandon de Montyel. The young women who attended often came from modest families and hoped to find prospects for employment, as Léopold Bellan argued in his report on the distribution of subsidies to public design schools in 1896.[14] Bellan analyzed fifteen schools, which received subsidies according to the number of their students and the "usefulness" of their training. Mme Latruffe-Colomb's school in the seventeenth arrondissement, for example, received increased grants because "students obtain important results during general studies, and above all find the means to use the knowledge acquired in class in the industry." Other schools named as standouts were those directed by Mme Thoret, Mme Keller, Mme de Chatillon, and Mme Mac Nab, located in the sixth, seventh, eighth, and ninth arrondissements, respectively. These women were often claimed as teachers by women showing works at the Salons, essentially in the drawing section.

Among the women who exhibited at the Salon between 1852 and 1900,[15] many more—rarely fewer than 20 percent, and in some years up to 45 percent—named at least one woman among their teachers, compared to the low percentage of those who claimed training by a male family member. Generally speaking, the percentage of women who had women teachers is much higher for exhibitors in the graphic arts than for painters. Female teachers comprised between one-third and one-half of the instructors declared by female students in the years when porcelains and miniature paintings were most numerous at Salons: between 1875 and 1880, porcelains represented more than half of the works exhibited by women in the graphic arts category, and again between 1893 and 1900, when between 40 and 60 percent of works exhibited by women were miniatures. Mme de Mirbel, a renowned miniature painter [fig. 3] who died of cholera in 1849, must be added to the list of oft-cited teachers: she was named frequently as a teacher, even into the 1870s.[16] Delphine de Cool, who collaborated with the Manufacture de Sèvres, was named by thirty-five students in 1875, forty-four in 1876, sixty-eight in 1877, eighty-one in 1878, and sixty-eight in 1879—all years when between 50 and 65 percent of works exhibited by women artists in the graphic arts were porcelains; in 1885, when the percentage of porcelains fell to 21 percent, only nineteen students named her. Mme Latruffe-Colomb was declared as a teacher for forty-seven miniaturists in the Salon catalogue of 1897, a number that seems high, given that the previous year, Léopold Bellan had mentioned that only seventy-three students were enrolled in her school in the seventeenth arrondissement, and between fifty-five and sixty were regulars in her course.

For their part, men rarely selected a female teacher. In the 1877 Salon, only two men, exhibitors in the drawing section, claimed female instructors, though close to 800 works were presented—80 percent of them designs, pastels, or watercolors, with porcelains and enamels representing 16 percent, and miniatures less than 2 percent. In the same category, women exhibited 550 works: 21 percent were designs, 11.4 percent, miniatures, and 67 percent, porcelains.

Finally, a great number of Salon artists studied alongside recognized artists who opened private studios while continuing to serve in official roles. Some of these workshops accepted a growing number of women, who viewed them as a good introduction to the Salon. Before 1880, prominent studios were directed by Léon Cogniet, Charles Chaplin, Ange Tissier, Thomas Couture, and, between 1874 and 1889, the "women's studio" opened by Carolus-Duran and Jean-Jacques Henner. The number of students claiming Cogniet [fig. 4] as instructor increased between 1863 (27 women and 117 men) and 1870 (45 women and 178 men). The numbers then decreased among women, who turned instead to the "women's studio" (28 in 1880, 31 in 1884,

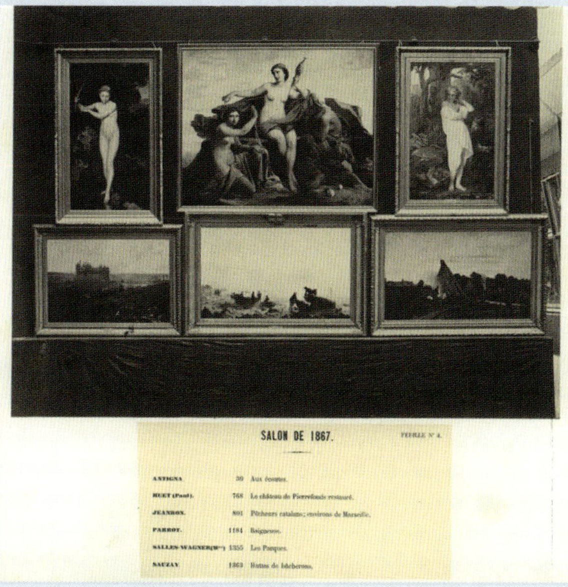

Fig. 7. Photo album of works purchased by the state from the Salon of 1867, plate 4, showing *The Fates* by Mme Adelaide Salles-Wagner, 1867, at top center. Photographic print on albumen paper, 24 3/8 × 18 1/8 in. (62 × 46 cm). National Archives, France, ARCG0105

36 in 1888), while the rate of men remained stable.

During the last quarter-century numerous women benefited from the creation of free, privately run, open-access studios that admitted both genders, principally the Académie Colarossi and the Académie Julian, which allowed them access to nude models. Given that the archives of the Colarossi have disappeared, we focus principally on the second academy, opened in 1868 in the passage des Panoramas by Rodolphe Julian, who began accepting women in 1873 [fig. 5]. Mixed studios attracted young foreigners, notably English and Americans but also many Scandinavians. To further attract French students, Julian soon replaced the mixed studio with a woman-only one, as mixed studios with live nude models remained taboo in certain families.

Segregation by gender, however, did not disappear completely. It manifested itself notably through money; fees were twice as high for women as they were for men, a measure seen as weeding out amateurs, who were supposedly more numerous among women than men. But the fame of the Académie Julian loomed large, sustained by its teachers: first, professor Tony Robert-Fleury, who was soon followed in mixed studios by Gustave Boulanger, Jules Lefebvre, and William-Adolphe Bouguereau, all decorated graduates of the École des Beaux-Arts and, importantly, members of the Salon jury. In similar fashion, Robert-Fleury was cited as teacher by 23 women and 22 men in 1880, numbers that increased to 43 women and 39 men in 1884, then 69 women and 64 men in 1888. It is difficult to know whether his prestige came from his popularity as an instructor or his title as professor at the Académie Julian. Gradually, some former female students were given the responsibility of directing studios, among them Amélie Beaury-Saurel, a regular exhibitor at the Salon starting in 1874, who married Rodolphe Julian in 1895. Studio instructors were often behind artists' first appearances at the Salon. Moreover, if they were also jury members, their students' chances of success increased. Many foreign artists arrived in Paris to study, exhibiting their art with varying frequency, and some of them built careers in art. Among the 1,076 female foreigners admitted to the Salon between 1873 and 1900, 110, or roughly 10 percent, frequented the Académie Julian.[17] The exhibitors to emerge from these studios were represented primarily in the Salon's painting category; when they were recognized in the graphic arts category, it was mainly via pastels or watercolors.

Recognition, Rewards Distribution, Public Procurement Despite losing its status as a virtual monopoly, the Salon remained crucial to artistic life, giving artists the opportunity to present their work for critique by the public and experts as well as to gain recognition. It was through the Salon that awards and medals were distributed and the French government made its acquisitions. We can trace the recognition of female artists in three ways: through the granting of medals or awards; by tracing the number of works by women included in celebrated publications, notably in the *Catalogue illustré du Salon*; and finally through the number of works purchased at Salons by the French government and religious or public authorities.

In the second half of the nineteenth century, the distribution of awards is notable. While 201 men were honored by the Légion d'Honneur with various types of awards between 1848 and 1880, after which these awards were no longer distributed during Salons, no women received an award. Before 1900, only two female painters were honored by the Légion d'Honneur outside the Salon: Rosa Bonheur in 1865 and Virginie Demont-Breton in 1894.[18] There are similarly telling figures regarding the awarding of medals: no woman won a medal of honor or Salon prize among the 38 awarded; 4 won first-class medals out of 125 granted; 10 won second-class medals, out of 537; 46 won third-class medals among 829; 189 women won honorable mentions out of 1,467 awarded [fig. 6]; and 8 women received "unique" medals out of the 273 granted (this distinction existed only between 1864 and 1870). If among the forty-six Salons examined here, women made up 19 percent of exhibitors, they represented only 11.4 percent of those awarded medals in the least prestigious category, honorable mentions, and between 0 and 5.6 percent in other categories.

The *Catalogue illustré du Salon*, published by François Guillaume Dumas, appeared annually starting in 1879. The publication was initially billed as "authorized" by the minister of arts and public education. Subsequently it was "approved" by the same ministry, which cut ties with the publication when the Salon's organization transferred to the Société des Artistes Français. The number of works by women included in the catalogue was far less than the actual number of works by women shown at the Salons: while paintings by women represent between 10 and 14 percent of all works shown between 1879 and 1886, the percentage of works by women reproduced in the catalogue varied between 1.2 and 4.5 percent. This percentage rose gradually to around 8 percent between 1887 and 1893, while the percentage of women who presented works remained substantially within the same range, 10 to 12 percent. In the end of the period between 1894 and 1900, a balance was established between the percentage of works by women presented and that of works reproduced.

Purchase of an artist's work at the Salon by the French government was viewed as an accolade, guaranteeing exposure in public collections such as at the Musée du Luxembourg or on

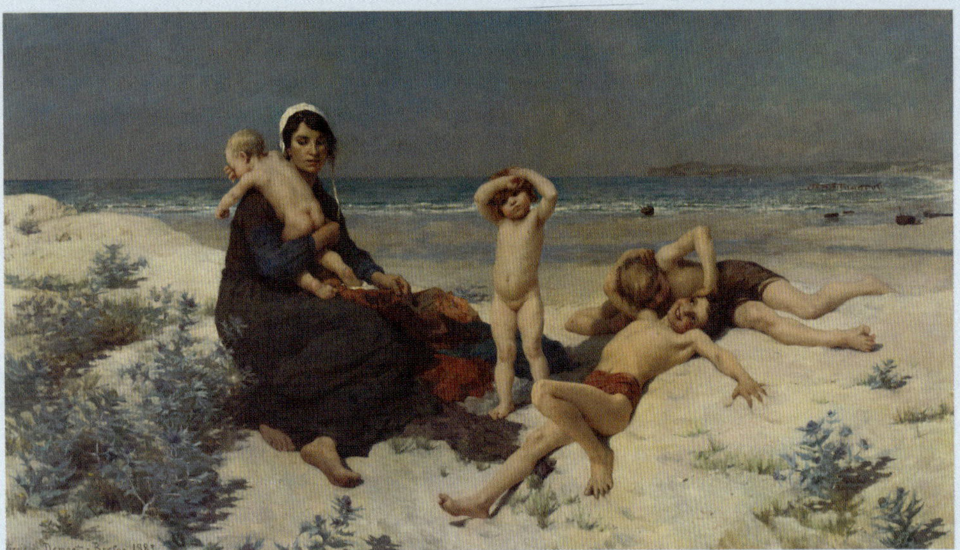

Fig. 8. Virginie Demont-Breton (French, 1859–1935), *The Beach* (*La plage*), 1883. Oil on canvas, 74¾ × 137 in. (190 × 348 cm). Musée des Beaux-Arts, Arras, RF376
This painting was acquired by the state at the 1883 Salon. Another painting from the same artist was purchased from the Salon of 1898.

the walls of a provincial museum. If other public authorities purchased the work, it would be seen at a corresponding location, like a city hall or church. Between 1864 and 1900, 2,732 works of art shown during Salons were purchased, with 84 of them, or 3 percent, signed by women. Starting in 1864, illustrated albums were published annually containing the works purchased at every Salon. These albums, dubbed Albums Michelez, taken from the name of the photographer, have served as a source for these calculations [fig. 7].[19] Some artists saw their works purchased on several occasions: the miniaturist Delphine de Cool had works purchased in 1864, 1866, 1870, and 1872; the marine life painter Élodie La Villette sold works from Salons in 1876 and 1878; the government acquired two paintings by Laure de Chatillon in 1866 and 1869, two works by Virginie Demont-Breton [fig. 8] in 1883 and 1898, two canvases by Angèle Delasalle in 1898 and 1900, and four paintings and a tapestry cartoon by Eléonore Escallier [fig. 9] between 1865 and 1880. For her part, Rosa Bonheur benefited in 1849 from a government purchase of her great painting *Plowing in Nivernais*, today in the Musée d'Orsay's collection in Paris.

An examination of Salon reviews sheds light on the way their contemporaries viewed women's works. We will focus on the year 1878 through the lens of two publications of that year: the annual *L'année artistique*, and the June 17 issue of the *Gazette des femmes* devoted to the review of the Salon. In the first, Victor Champier highlights the works that garnered critics' attention: among some 140 works cited, only 4 belong to women—two portraits, one ceiling decoration, and one landscape.[20] In the second, Jean Alesson focuses on no less than seventy-eight works by women in the painting category, including biblical and historical scenes, genre scenes, seascapes and landscapes, paintings of animals, flowers, and fruits, portraits and torsos, and still lifes.[21] He also cites one hundred or so works from the graphic arts category. We can assume that some of these works from women could have attracted widespread critical attention had their signatures not discredited them in advance.

With supporting data, it is possible to confirm that, contrary to popular belief, women were able to develop strategies that assured their presence on the artistic stage, most notably at the Salon, in significant numbers. On average, they represented 19 percent of exhibitors in the painting and graphic arts categories between 1848 and 1900, and the number increased to close to 30 percent toward the end of this period. Has the inclusion of women in the arts actually improved today? A study of artists represented at the 2015 Foire Internationale d'Art Contemporain (International Contemporary Art Fair, or FIAC) in Paris shows that among the 1,732 artists, 412, or 23.7 percent, were women.

Why, then, is the presence of women on the French artistic stage in the second half of the nineteenth century so little known? It may primarily be the result of prejudice concerning a woman's role in society, a prejudice evoked in 1896 by Virginie Demont-Breton in her essay "La femme dans l'art": "When we say of a work of art, 'It's a woman's painting or sculpture,' by this we understand, 'It's a weak painting or a pretty sculpture.' And when we judge a serious work that emanates from a woman's brain and hands, we say, 'It's painted or sculpted like it came from a man.' This look at two expressions is sufficient to prove, without need for further comment, that there is an initial bias against women's art."[22]

How many women are entitled to a spot in history? Certain names emerge, like those of Rosa Bonheur, Virginie Demont-Breton, Louise Breslau, Marie Bashkirtseff, and Victoria Dubourg, for example, as well as certain women associated with the Impressionist movement—all of whom participated in Salons during the 1860s and 1870s—like Berthe Morisot, Mary Cassatt, Eva Gonzalès, and Marie Bracquemond. Perhaps it is best to quote Marie Bashkirtseff, writing under the pseudonym of Pauline Orell: "With indulgent irony, we are asked how many great female artists there have been. There have been many, gentlemen! And it's surprising given the enormous difficulties that they have encountered."[23]

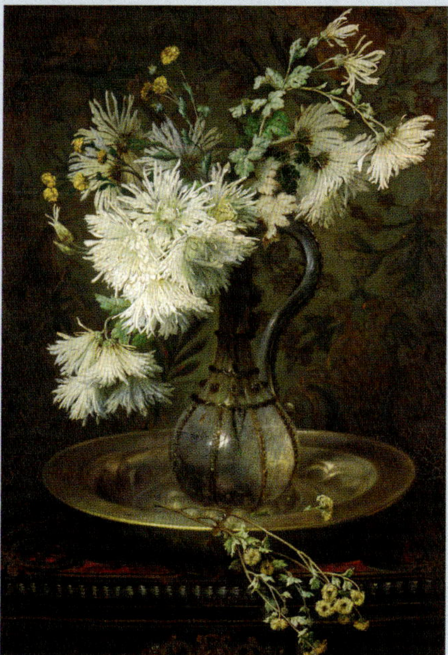

Fig. 9. Marie Caroline Eléonore Escallier (French, 1827–1888), *Chrysanthemums* (*Les Chrysanthèmes*), ca. 1869. Oil on canvas, 27½ × 21⅝ in. (70 × 55 cm). Musée d'Orsay, Paris, RF 602
Eléonore Escallier experienced some fame in her lifetime but has since fallen into obscurity: the state bought five of her works, including *Chrysanthemums,* through the Paris Salons, and she won a medal in 1868.

Sources

For Salon catalogues, see:

Pierre Sanchez and Xavier Seydoux, *Les catalogues des Salons*, with an introduction by Dominique Lobstein, volumes V–XIX published by Echelle de Jacob, Paris, 2001–10.

The numbered catalogues accessible on Gallica, http://gallica.bnf.fr, the digital library of the Bibliothèque Nationale de France, and on https://archive.org, digitized by the University of Illinois at Urbana-Champaign.

The database "Salons et expositions de groupes 1673–1914," accessible at http://salons.musee-orsay.fr, which is a joint project of the Musée d'Orsay and the Institut National d'Histoire de l'Art (INHA), supported by the Ministère de la Culture et de la Communication. I thank Axelle Huet and Ophélie Ferlier, who allowed me to consult the database prior to its public release in June 2016.

For Salon acquisitions, see:

The photo albums of works of art purchased by the French state, principally at the Paris salons, available in the Archim database, Archives Nationales, http://www.culture.gouv.fr/documentation/archim/dossiers.htm.

The "Base Michelez" database by the Musée d'Orsay, only available in person. In addition to information available on the Archim database, the current locations of works of art are listed, thanks to Jacqueline Henry.

For the Académie Julian:

L'Académie Julian website, which gathers academy students and professors (a list compiled from documents submitted to the Archives Nationales and referenced 63 AS, Fonds de l'Académie Julian).

Acknowledgments: Thank you to the teams at the Musée d'Orsay's documents center and library for their always warm welcome and their precise help, to Dominique Lobstein for her proofreading and kind attention, and to Serge Bolloch for his patience and keen skill with the calculator.

1. Denise Noël, "Les femmes peintres au Salon, 1863–1889" (PhD diss., Université Paris VII–Denis Diderot, 1997).

2. Harrison and Cynthia White, *La carrière des peintres au XIXème siècle* (Paris: Flammarion, 2009), 110.

3. Emile Bellier de la Chavignerie and Louis Auvray, *Dictionnaire général des artistes de l'École Française depuis l'origine des arts du dessin jusqu'à nos jours*, 2 vols. (Paris: Librairie Renouard, 1882).

4. In establishing the figures and statistics for the "official" Salons, I do not include the so-called Impressionist salon exhibitions organized by independent artist societies starting in 1874, nor those organized by the Société Nationale des Beaux-Arts starting in 1890, nor those other exhibitions that adopted the name Salon, but were not official Salon exhibitions.

5. Anatole de Montaiglon, *Procès-verbaux de l'Académie Royale de Peinture et de Sculpture, 1648–1793*, vol. 8, *1769–1779* (Paris: J. Baur, 1888), 152–54.

6. No female painters were accepted; only one female sculptor, Brigitte Terziev, was accepted in 2007.

7. The Salon that opened on December 30, 1850, was extended until March 6, 1851. Salons became biannual events between 1853 and 1863. The 1871 Salon was canceled following the Paris Commune uprisings.

8. Certain Salons gathered paintings and drawings in one section, while others divided works into two sections. The calculations presented here were made based on indications provided by the Salon catalogues. A small margin of error exists because the catalogues do not always present information in the same fashion. Given that men and women are in the same situation, that margin of error may affect absolute values, but not the calculation of percentages.

9. The list of works presented in the Salon des Refusés was printed in the publication produced in the official addendum to the Salon catalogue.

10. Rosa Bonheur was the first woman to be granted the Grand Cross of the Légion d'Honneur, which was done by special decree. Two women artists, Rosa Bonheur and Jeanne Herbelin, gained exemption from jury selection by winning sufficient recognition to join the ranks of their male counterparts. As is written in the 1855 Salon catalogue, "Having obtained all the medals that artists can receive, enjoying in the future prerogatives that their eminent talents merit, their works of art will be exhibited without subject to review by the jury." Between 1848 and 1880, the Salon catalogue included the list of artists decorated with the Légion d'Honneur. Later this distinction was not presented at the Salon.

11. In 1855 Gustave Courbet organized his own exhibition at the Pavillon du Réalisme, located on the margins of the Exposition Universelle. Here he showed about forty works, among them *L'atelier du peintre*, which was rejected by the official Salon.

12. Pauline Orell [Marie Bashkirtseff], "Les femmes artistes," *La citoyenne*, no. 4 (March 6, 1881).

13. Lucienne Heuvelmans was the first recipient, in 1911, in the sculpture category. Women obtained the right to compete for the Prix de Rome in 1903, and it took eight years for one of them to win the prize.

14. Account presented by Léopold Bellan, Paris municipal council record no. 66, 1896, Bibliothèque Nationale de France, Paris.

15. The names of instructors do not appear in the Salon catalogues during 1848, 1849, and 1850/51.

16. For deceased artists to later be claimed as instructors was not uncommon. Is that proof of fidelity from former students, or the desire to continue to benefit from an artist's prestige? In any case, we still find students of Delacroix, Ingres, or Courbet in the 1880s, although these artists died in 1863, 1867, and 1877 respectively.

17. Women born overseas were recorded as foreigners. Notes in the Salon catalogue still do not make it known which artists were naturalized French citizens. This choice may impact the total numbers, but less so the percentages and developments during the period under review. Birth place was not indicated in the Salon catalogues before 1852. Seventy-one or so foreigners who exhibited works between 1852 and 1872, before the Académie Julian was opened to women, have not been included in the calculation.

18. They were followed by Louise Breslau in 1901, Louise Abbéma and Madeleine Lemaire in 1906, Amélie Beaury-Saurel in 1923, and Anna Klumpke in 1924.

19. The album from 1889 was not located during research for this essay.

20. Victor Champier, *L'année artistique, 1878* (Paris: A. Quantin, 1879).

21. Jean Alesson, "Les femmes artistes au Salon de 1878 et à l'Exposition Universelle," *Gazette des femmes*, June 17, 1878. Jean Alesson is the pseudonym used by Anatole Alès, writer and bibliographer. He founded *Le bas bleu*, dedicated to women, in 1873. The name changed to *Les gauloises* the following year.

22. Virginie Demont-Breton, "La femme dans l'art," *Revue des revues*, March 1, 1896, 451.

23. Orell, "Les femmes artistes."

Selected Bibliography

Adler, Kathleen. "The Suburban, the Modern and 'Une Dame de Passy.'" *Oxford Art Journal* 12, no. 1 (1989): 3–13.

Alesson, Jean. "Les femmes artistes au Salon de 1878 et à l'Exposition Universelle." *Gazette des femmes*, June 17, 1878.

Alexandre, Arsène. *Louise C. Breslau*. Paris: Les Editions Rieder, 1928.

Baillio, Joseph, and Xavier Salmon. *Élisabeth Louise Vigée Le Brun*. Paris: Réunion des Musées Nationaux, 2015.

Bailly-Herzberg, Janine. *Correspondance de Camille Pissarro*. 5 vols. Paris: Presses Universitaires de France, 1980; Paris: Editions du Valhermeil, 1986–91.

Bashkirtseff, Marie. *Journal de Marie Bashkirtseff*. 2 vols. Paris: Charpentier, 1887–90.

———. *The Journal of a Young Artist, 1860–1884*. Translated by Katherine Kernberger. New York: Cassel, 1889.

———. *Lettres de Marie Bashkirtseff*. Paris: Charpentier, 1891.

Bastien-Lepage, Jules, and Serge Lemoine. *Jules Bastien-Lepage, 1848–1884*. Paris: Nicolas Chaudun, 2007.

Beaux, Cecilia. *Background with Figures: Autobiography of Cecilia Beaux*. Boston: Houghton Mifflin, 1930.

Bellier de la Chavignerie, Emile, and Louis Auvray. *Dictionnaire général des artistes de l'École Française depuis l'origine des arts du dessin jusqu'à nos jours*. 2 vols. Paris: Librairie Renouard, 1882.

Bengtsson, Eva-Lena, and Barbro Werkmäster. *Kvinna och konstnär i 1800-talets Sverige*. Lund, Sweden: Signum, 2004.

Berson, Ruth. *The New Painting: Impressionism, 1874–1886*. 2 vols. San Francisco: Fine Arts Museums of San Francisco, 1996.

Bø, Tor Petter. "Høy yrkesdeltakelse blant kvinner i Norden." *Samfunnsspeilet*, no. 1 (2004). https://www.ssb.no/arbeid-og-lonn/artikler-og-publikasjoner/hoy-yrkesdeltakelse-blant-kvinner-i-norden.

Boime, Albert. "The Case of Rosa Bonheur: Why Should a Woman Want to Be More Like a Man?" *Art History* 4, no. 4 (December 1981).

Bona, Dominique. *Berthe Morisot: Le secret de la femme en noir*. Paris: Livre de Poche, 2002.

Bonheur, Rosa. *Reminiscences of Rosa Bonheur*. Edited by Theodore Stanton. New York: Appleton, 1910.

Bonnet, Alain. *Artistes en groupe: La représentation de la communauté des artistes dans la peinture du XIXe siècle*. Rennes: Presses Universitaires de Rennes, 2007.

———, ed. *L'artiste en représentation: Images des artistes dans l'art du XIXe siècle*. Lyon, France: Fage, 2012.

Bonnet, Marie-Jo. "Femmes peintres à leur travail: De l'autoportrait comme manifeste politique." *Revue d'histoire moderne et contemporaine* 49, no. 3 (2002–3): 140–67.

Borel, Pierre. "L'exposition des femmes peintres." *La nouvelle revue*, March–April 1889.

Borzello, Frances. *A World of Our Own: Women as Artists since the Renaissance*. New York: Watson-Guptill, 2000.

Bouillon, Jean-Paul. "Remarques sur la Japonisme de Bracquemond." In *Japonisme in Art: An International Symposium*. Tokyo: Kodansha International, 1980.

———. "Une visite de Félix Bracquemond à Gaston La Touche." *Gazette des beaux-arts* 112 (March 1970): 161–77.

Bouillon, Jean-Paul, and Elizabeth Kane. "Marie Bracquemond." *Woman's Art Journal* 5, no. 2 (1984): 21–27.

Bracquemond, Marie. *Catalogue des peintures, aquarelles, dessins et eaux-fortes de Marie Bracquemond*. Paris: Bernheim-Jeune, 1919.

Breakell, Mary. "Marie Bashkirtseff: The Reminiscence of a Fellow-Student." *The Nineteenth Century and After* 62 (July 1907): 110–25.

Brummer, Hans Henrik, ed. *Konstnärsparet Hanna och Georg Pauli*. Stockholm: Carlssons, 1997.

Brusewitz-Hansson, Anita. *Mina Carlson-Bredberg: Från Lidingö till Björnholmen*. Stockholm: Stockholms Stadsmuseum, 1971.

Busch, Gunter, and Liselotte von Reinken, eds. *Paula Modersohn Becker in Briefen und Tagebüchen*. Frankfurt: S. Fischer Verlag, 1979. Translated by Arthur S. Wensinger and Carole Clew as *Paula Modersohn Becker: The Letters and Journals*. New York: Taplinger, 1983.

Carter, Alice. *Cecilia Beaux: A Modern Painter in the Gilded Age*. New York: Rizzoli, 2005.

Cavalli-Björkman, Görel. "Svenska konstnärinnors förening." In *Kvinnor som målat*. Stockholm: Nationalmuseum, 1975.

Chadwick, Whitney. *Women, Art, and Society*. 5th ed. London: Thames and Hudson, 2012.

Champier, Victor. *L'année artistique, 1878*. Paris: A. Quantin, 1879.

Cheney, Liana. *Essays on Women Artists: "The Most Excellent."* New York: Edwin Mellen Press, 2003.

Clark, Linda L. *Women and Achievement in Nineteenth-Century Europe*. New York: Cambridge University Press, 2008.

Claude, Roger-Marx. *Les Impressionnistes*. Paris: Hachette, 1956.

Clement, Clara Erskine. *Women in the Fine Arts from the Seventh Century B.C. to the Twentieth Century A.D.* Boston: Houghton, Mifflin, 1904.

Clement, Russell T., Annick Houzé, and Christiane Erbolato-Ramsey. *Women Impressionists: A Sourcebook*. Westport, CT: Greenwood Press, 2000.

Coman, Sonia. "The Bracquemond-Rousseau Table Service of 1866." *Journal of Japonisme* 1, no. 1 (2016): 17–40.

Cosnier, Colette. *Marie Bashkirtseff: Un portrait sans retouches*. Paris: Pierre Horay, 1985.

Criss, Jennifer T. "*Japonisme* and Beyond in the Art of Marie Bracquemond, Mary Cassatt, and Berthe Morisot, 1867–1895." PhD diss., University of Pennsylvania, 2007.

D'Albis, J. and L. "La céramique impressionniste: L'Atelier Haviland d'Auteuil et son influence." *L'oeil* 223 (February 1974): 47 ff.

Danielsen, Hilde, Eirinn Larsen, and Ingeborg Winderen Owesen. *Norsk likestillingshistorie 1814–2013*. Bergen, Norway: Fagbokforlaget, 2013.

Dargenty [Arthur d'Echerac]. "Union des femmes peintres et sculpteurs." *Courrier de l'art* 10 (March 7, 1890).

Darrieussecq, Marie. *Être ici est une splendeur: Vie de Paula M. Becker*. Paris: P.O.L., 2016.

———. *Paula Modersohn-Becker*. Paris: Musée d'Art Moderne de la Ville de Paris, 2016.

Daubié, Julie-Victoire. *La femme pauvre au dix-neuvième siècle, III: Condition professionnelle*. 2nd ed. Paris: Ernest Thaurin, 1870.

Degas, Edgar-Germain-Hilaire. *Letters*. Edited by Marcel Guèrin. Oxford: Bruno Cassirer, 1947.

Demont-Breton, Virginie. "La femme dans l'art." *Journal des artistes*, July 12, 1896.

———. "La femme dans l'art." *Revue des revues*, March 1, 1896.

———. *Journal des femmes artistes*, May 17, 1897.

D'Souza, Aruna, and Tom McDonough, eds. *The Invisible Flaneuse?: Gender, Public Space, and Visual Culture in Nineteenth-Century Paris*. Manchester, England: Manchester University Press, 2006.

Dunford, Penny. *A Biographical Dictionary of Women Artists in Europe and America since 1850*. Philadelphia: University of Pennsylvania Press, 1989.

Duranty, E. L. *La nouvelle peinture, à propos du groupe d'artistes qui expose dans les galleries Durand-Ruel* (Darius: E. Dentu, 1876).

Edelstein, T. J., ed. *Perspectives on Morisot*. New York: Hudson Hills Press, 1990.

Evans, Magdalen. *Utmost Fidelity: The Painting Lives of Marianne and Adrian Stokes*. Bristol: Sansom, 2009.

Fidell-Beaufort, Madeleine. "Elizabeth Jane Gardner Bouguereau: A Parisian Artist from New Hampshire." *Archives of American Art Journal* 24, no. 2 (1984): 2–9.

Fogelström, Lollo, and Louise Robbert, eds. *De drogo till Paris: Nordiska konstnärinnor på 1880-talet*. Stockholm: Liljevalchs Konsthall, 1888.

Foucher, Charlotte. "Madame Pygmalion: Le rire transgressif de la femme artiste au passage du siècle, XIX–XX." In *Rire et émancipation feminine*. Paris: L'Harmattan, 2013.

Foucher-Zarmanian, Charlotte. *Créatrices en 1900: Femmes artistes en France*. Paris: Mare and Martin, 2016.

Frontisi-Ducroux, Françoise. "'La fille de Dibutade,' ou l'inventrice inventée." In *Cahiers du genre* 2, no. 43 (2007): 133–51.

Garb, Tamar. "Berthe Morisot and the Feminizing of Impressionism." In *Perspectives on Morisot*, edited by T. J. Edelstein, 57–66. New York: Hudson Hills Press, 1990.

———. *The Body in Time: Figures of Femininity in Late Nineteenth-Century France*. Seattle: University of Washington Press, 2008.

———. *The Painted Face: Portraits of Women in France, 1814–1914*. New Haven: Yale University Press, 2007.

———. "Revising the Revisionists: The Formation of the Union des Femmes Peintres et Sculpteurs." *Art Journal* 48, no. 1 (Spring 1989): 63–70.

———. *Sisters of the Brush: Women's Artistic Culture in Late Nineteenth-Century Paris*. New Haven: Yale University Press, 1994.

———. *Women Impressionists*. Oxford: Phaidon, 1986.

Geffroy, Gustave. "Histoire de l'Impressionnisme: Marie Bracquemond." *La vie artistique* 3 (1894): 68–74.

Genêt-Delacroix, Marie-Claude. *Art et état sous la IIIème République: Le système des Beaux-Arts*. Paris: Sorbonne, 1992.

Goetz, Adrien, Michaël Vottero, Louis-Antoine Prat, Bernard Grassin Champernaud, and Jérôme Merceron. *Femmes peintres et salons au temps de Proust de Madeleine Lemaire à Berthe Morisot*. Paris: Hazan, 2010.

Goncourt, Edmond and Jules de. *Journal: Mémoires de la vie littéraire*. Vol. 1, *1851–1865*. Paris: Laffont, 1989.

Gonnard, Catherine, and Élisabeth Lebovici. *Femmes artistes/artistes femmes: Paris, de 1880 à nos jours*. Paris: Hazan, 2007.

Goodyear, Frank, and Elizabeth Bailey. *Cecilia Beaux: Portrait of an Artist*. Philadelphia: Pennsylvania Academy of the Fine Arts, 1974.

Groom, Gloria, ed. *Impressionism, Fashion, and Modernity*. Chicago: Art Institute of Chicago; New Haven: Yale University Press, 2012.

Gynning, Margareta. "Det ambivalenta perspektivet: Eva Bonnier och Hanna Hirsch-Pauli i 1880-talets konstliv." PhD diss., Uppsala University, Sweden, 1999.

———, ed. *Pariserbref: Konstnären Eva Bonniers brev 1883–1889*. Stockholm: Klara, 1999.

Harris, Ann Sutherland, and Linda Nochlin. *Women Artists, 1550–1950*. Los Angeles: Los Angeles County Museum of Art, 1976.

Havard, Henry. "Exposition de l'Union des Femmes Peintres et Sculpteurs." *Le siècle*, January 25, 1882.

Hedges, Elaine, and Ingrid Wendt, eds. *In Her Own Image: Women Working in the Arts*. New York: Feminist Press, 1980.

Heller, Nancy G. *Women Artists: An Illustrated History*. New York: Abbeville Press, 1987.

Hess, Thomas B., and Elizabeth C. Baker, eds. *Art and Sexual Politics*. New York: Macmillan, 1973.

Higonnet, Anne. *Berthe Morisot*. Berkeley: University of California Press, 1990.

———. "Situation critique de la féminité." In *La Critique d'art en France, 1850–1900, actes de colloque (1987)*, 121–33. Saint-Etienne: Université de Saint-Étienne, Centre interdisciplinaire d'études et de recherches sur l'expression contemporaine, 1989.

Hirshler, Erica E. *A Studio of Her Own: Women Artists in Boston, 1870–1940*. Boston: MFA Publications, 2001.

Hobbs, Richard, ed. *Impressions of French Modernity*. Manchester, England: Manchester University Press, 1998.

Holland, Clive. "Lady Art Students' Life in Paris," *International Studio* 21 (1904): 230.

Hovelaque, Emile. "Artistes contemporains: Mlle Louise Breslau," *Gazette des beaux-arts*, 3rd ser., 34 (September 1, 1905): 195–206.

Isaacson, Joel. *The Crisis of Impressionism, 1878–1882*. Ann Arbor: University of Michigan Museum of Art, 1980.

Ives, Colta, Susan Alyson Stein, and Julie A. Steiner. *The Private Collection of Edgar Degas: A Summary Catalogue*. New York: Metropolitan Museum of Art, 1997.

Jones, Kimberly A. *Degas / Cassatt*. Washington, DC: National Gallery of Art, 2014.

Kane, Elizabeth. "Marie Bracquemond: The Artist Time Forgot." *Apollo* 117 (February 1983): 118–21.

———. "Victoria Dubourg: The Other Fantin-Latour." *Women's Art Journal* 9, no. 2 (Fall 1998–Winter 1999): 15–21.

Kivimäki, Kati, ed. *Á Paris! Nordic Artists in Paris in the Late 19th Century*. Helsinki: Gallen-Kallela Museum, 1996.

Klumpke, Anna. *Rosa Bonheur: The Artist's (Auto)biography*. Translated by Gretchen van Slyke. Ann Arbor: University of Michigan Press, 1997.

Lacambre, Geneviève. *Le Musée du Luxembourg en 1874*. Paris: Réunion des Musées Nationaux, 1974.

Lagrange, Léon. "Du rang des femmes dans les arts." *Gazette des beaux-arts* 8, no. 1 (1860): 30–43.

Larsson, Karin. *Emma Löwstädt-Chadwick: Une artiste-peintre suédoise en France*. Paris, 2010.

Lepdor, Catherine, Anne-Catherine Kruger, and Gabriel P. Weisberg. *Louise Breslau: De l'impressionnisme aux années folles*. Lausanne, Switzerland: Musée Cantonale des Beaux-Arts, 2001.

Lepelle de Bois-Gallais, Frédéric. *Biographie de Mademoiselle Rosa Bonheur*. Paris: E. Gambart, 1856.

Leroy, Louis. "L'exposition des impressionnistes." *Le Charivari*, April 25, 1874.

Lewis, Mary Tompkins, ed. *Critical Readings in Impressionism and Post-Impressionism: An Anthology*. Berkeley: University of California Press, 2007.

Lourbet, Jacques. *La femme devant la science contemporaine*. Paris: Félix Alcan, 1896.

Lübbren, Nina. *Rural Artists' Colonies in Europe, 1870–1910*. Manchester, England: Manchester University Press, 2001.

Manoeuvre, Laurent. *Les pionnières: Femmes et impressionnistes*. Rouen: Editions des Falaises, 2016.

Mathews, Nancy Mowll. *Cassatt and Her Circle: Selected Letters*. New York: Abbeville Press, 1984.

———. *Mary Cassatt: A Life*. New Haven: Yale University Press, 1994.

Mathews, Nancy Mowll, and Barbara Stern Shapiro. *Mary Cassatt: The Color Prints*. New York: H. N. Abrams, 1989.

Mauclair, Camille. "Les Salons de 1896." *La nouvelle revue*, May–June 1896.

Meister, Anna, and Karin Sirén, eds. *Ljusets magi: Friluftsmåleri från sent 1800-tal*. Stockholm: Prins Eugens Waldemarsudde, 2016.

Mirecourt, Eugène de. *Les contemporains: Rosa Bonheur*. Paris: G. Havard, 1856.

Moffett, Charles S. *The New Painting: Impressionism, 1874–1886*. San Francisco: Fine Arts Museums of San Francisco, 1986.

Montesquiou-Fezensac, Count Robert de. "Une Maître-Femme: Mademoiselle Breslau." *Art et decoration* 15 (April 15, 1904): 134–42.

Moreau, Gustave. *Écrits sur l'art*. Vol. 2, *Théorie et critique d'art*. Edited by Peter Cooke. Preface by Geneviève Lacambre. Fontfroide, France: Bibliothèque Artistique et Littéraire, 2002.

Morineau, Camille. *Elles @centrepompidou: Artistes-femmes dans la collection du Musée National d'Art Moderne–Centre de Création Industrielle*. Paris: Centre Pompidou, 2010.

Morisot, Berthe, and Denis Rouart. *Correspondance de Berthe Morisot avec sa famille et ses amis: Manet, Puvis de Chavannes, Degas, Monet, Renoir et Mallarme: Documents réunis et présentés*. Paris: Quatre Chemins–Éditart, 1950.

Müntz, Eugène. "Le Salon: Essai de statistique." *Chronique des arts et de la curiosité*, May 31, 1873.

Musée d'Art Moderne de la Ville de Paris. *Helene Schjerfbeck, 1862–1946*. Paris: Paris Musées, 2007.

Musée d'Orsay and Musée National de l'Orangerie. *Qui a peur des femmes photographes?: 1839–1945*. Vanves, France: Hazan, 2015.

Musée Marmottan Monet. *Berthe Morisot 1841–1895*. Paris: Editions Hazan, 2012.

Natanson, Thadée. "XV Salon des Femmes Peintres et Sculpteurs." *La revue blanche* 10 (1896): 187.

National Museum of Women in the Arts. *Voices of Freedom: Polish Women Artists and the Avant-Garde, 1880–1910*. Washington, DC: National Museum of Women in the Arts, 1991.

Neue Gesellschaft fur bildende Kunst, Berlin. *Das Verborgene Museum I: Dokumentation der Kunst von Frauen in Berliner öffentlichen Sammlungen*. Berlin: Hentrich, 1987.

Nieriker, May Alcott. *Studying Art Abroad and How to Do It Cheaply*. Boston, 1879.

Nochlin, Linda. *Femmes: Art et pouvoir*. Paris: Jacqueline Chambon, 1993. Originally published as *Women, Art and Power: And Other Essays*. New York: Harper and Row, 1988.

———. "Why Have There Been No Great Women Artists?" *ARTnews* 69, no. 9 (January 1971): 22–39, 67–71. Reprinted in *Art and Sexual Politics: Why Have There Been No Great Women Artists?*, edited by Thomas B. Hess and Elizabeth C. Baker, 1–43. New York: Macmillan, 1973.

Noël, Denise. "Les femmes peintres au Salon, 1863–1889." PhD diss., Université Paris VII–Denis Diderot, 1997.

———. "Les femmes peintres dans la seconde moitié du XIXe siècle." *Clio: Femmes, genre, histoire* 19 (2004). doi: 10.4000/clio.646.

Orell, Pauline [Marie Bashkirtseff]. "Les femmes artistes." *La citoyenne*, no. 4 (March 6, 1881).

Parker, Rozsika, and Griselda Pollock. *Old Mistresses: Women, Art and Ideology*. London: Routledge, 1981. Reprint, London: L. B. Tauris, 2013.

Patry, Sylvie. "Victoria Dubourg, 'Femme supérieure et peintre de mérite.'" In *Fantin-Latour: De la réalité au rêve*. Lausanne: Fondation de l'Hermitage, 2007.

Patry, Sylvie, Hughes Wilhelm, and Sylvie Patin. *Berthe Morisot, 1841–1895*. Paris: Réunion des Musées Nationaux–Grand Palais, 2002.

Petiet, Marie. *Marie Petiet: Être femme au 19e siècle*. Cinisello Balsamo, Milan: Silvana, 2014.

Pfeiffer, Ingrid, and Max Hollein, eds. *Women Impressionists*. Ostfildern, Germany: Hatje Cantz, 2008.

Philip, Neil. "Felix Bracquemond and Impressionism." *Adventures in the Print Trade* (blog), June 20, 2012. http://adventuresintheprinttrade.blogspot.com/2012/06/felix-bracquemond-and-impressionism.html.

Pollock, Griselda. *Mary Cassatt, Painter of Modern Women*. New York: Thames and Hudson, 1998.

———. *Vision and Difference: Femininity, Feminism and Histories of Art*. London: Routledge, 1988.

Ribemont, Francis. *Rosa Bonheur, 1822–1899*. Bordeaux, France: Musée des Beaux-Arts de Bordeaux, 1997.

Rideal, Liz, ed. *Mirror, Mirror: Self-Portraits by Women Artists*. London: National Portrait Gallery, 2001.

Rivière, Georges. *M. Degas, bourgeois de Paris*. Paris: Floury, 1935.

Roos, Jane Mayo. "Girls 'n' the 'Hood: Female Artists in Nineteenth-Century France." In *Artistic Brotherhoods in the Nineteenth Century*, edited by Laura Morowitz and William Vaughan, 154–61. Aldershot, England: Ashgate, 2000.

Röstorp, Vibeke. *Le mythe du retour: Les artistes scandinaves en France de 1889 à 1908*. Stockholm: Stockholm University Press, 2013.

Rouland, Norbert. *À la découverte des femmes artistes: Une histoire de genre*. Aix-en-Provence, France: Presses Universitaires d'Aix-Marseille, 2016.

Rubin, James. *Impressionism*. London: Phaidon, 1999.

Ruskin, John. *Sesame and Lilies*. London, 1865.

Ruud, Line. "Académie Julian: En studie av tre norske kvinners opphold på 1880-tallet—Leis Schjeldrup, Sigrid Bølling og Valborg Dubois-Olsen." Master's thesis, University of Oslo, 2003.

Sanchez, Pierre. *Dictionnaire de l'Union des Femmes Peintres et Sculpteurs: Répertoire des artistes et liste de leurs œuvres, 1882–1965*. Dijon, France: Échelle de Jacob, 2010.

Sauer, Marina. *L'entrée des femmes à l'École des Beaux-Arts, 1880–1923*. Paris: École Nationale Supérieure des Beaux-Arts, 1990.

Schopenhauer, Arthur. *Pensées, maximes et fragments*. Translated by Jean Bourdeau. Paris: G. Baillière, 1880. Reprint, Paris: Alcan, 1900. Page references are to the Alcan edition.

Sertat, Raoul. "Les femmes artistes." *Le public*, February 24, 1890.

Sofio, Séverine. *Artistes femmes: La parenthèse enchantée, XVIIIe–XIXe siècles*. Paris: CNRS, 2016.

Soissons, S. C. de. *Boston Artists: A Parisian Critic's Notes*. Boston, 1894.

Sparrow, Walter Shaw, ed. *Women Painters of the World, from the Time of Caterina Vigri, 1413–1463, to Rosa Bonheur and the Present Day*. London: Hodder and Stoughton, 1905.

Stebler-Hopf, Annie, to Waser, Maria. Correspondence, 1911–14. Swiss Literary Archives SLA, Swiss National Library, Bern.

Strindberg, August. "De l'infériorité de la femme et comme corollaire de la justification de la situation subordonnée selon les données dernières de la science." *La revue blanche* 8 (1895).

Strömbom, Sixten. *Konstnärsförbundets historia I: Till och med 1890*. Stockholm: Bonnier, 1945.

———. *Konstnärsförbundets historia II: Nationalromantik och radicalism, 1891–1920*. Stockholm: Bonnier, 1965.

Stuckey, Charles F., William P. Scott, and Suzanne G. Lindsay. *Berthe Morisot: Impressionist*. New York: Hudson Hills Press, 1987.

Swinth, Kirsten. *Painting Professionals: Women Artists and the Development of Modern American Art, 1870–1930*. Chapel Hill: University of North Carolina Press, 2001.

Tappert, Tara Leigh. *Cecilia Beaux and the Art of Portraiture*. Washington, DC: Smithsonian Institution Press / National Portrait Gallery, 1995.

Turner, Jane, ed. *From Monet to Cézanne: Late 19th-Century French Artists.* New York: St. Martin's Press, 2000.

Union des Femmes Peintres et Sculpteurs. *Catalogue des oeuvres de Mlle Bashkirtseff.* Paris: Ludovic Baschet, ed., 1885.

Vachon, Marius. *La femme dans l'art, les protectrices des arts, les femmes artistes.* Paris: J. Rouam, 1893.

Vaisse, Pierre. *La Troisième République et les peintres.* Paris: Flammarion, 1995.

Veiteberg, Jorunn, ed. *Når kvinder fortæller: Kvindelige malere i Norden, 1880–1900.* Copenhagen: Kunstforeningen, 2002.

Vigée-Lebrun, Louise. *Souvenirs de Madame Louise-Elisabeth Vigée-Lebrun.* 3 vols. Paris: H. Fournier, 1835.

Weeks, Charlotte. "Lady Art Students in Munich." *Magazine of Art,* 1881, 343–47.

Weinberg, H. Barbara. *The Lure of Paris: Nineteenth-Century American Painters and Their French Teachers.* New York: Abbeville Press, 1991.

Weisberg, Gabriel P. *The Realist Tradition: French Painting and Drawing, 1830–1900.* Cleveland: Cleveland Museum of Art / Bloomington: Indiana University Press, 1980.

———. *Redefining Genre: French and American Painting, 1850–1900.* Washington, DC: Trust for Museum Exhibitions, 1995.

Weisberg, Gabriel P., and Jane R. Becker, eds. *Overcoming All Obstacles: The Women of the Académie Julian.* New Brunswick, NJ: Rutgers University Press, 1999.

Wichstrøm, Anne. *Kvinneliv, kunstnerliv: Kvinnelige malere i Norge før 1900.* Oslo: Gyldendal, 1997.

Wollstonecraft, Mary. *Letters Written during a Short Residence in Sweden, Norway, and Denmark.* 1796. Reprint, New York: Oxford University Press, 2009.

Yeldham, Charlotte. *Women Artists in Nineteenth-Century France and England: Their Art Education, Exhibition Opportunities, and Membership of Exhibiting Societies and Academies, with an Assessment of the Subject Matter of Their Work and Summary Biographies.* Vol. 1. New York: Garland, 1984.

Zalta, Edward N., ed. *The Stanford Encyclopedia of Philosophy,* winter 2015 ed., http://plato.stanford.edu.

Zillhardt, Madeleine. *Louise-Catherine Breslau et ses amis.* Paris: Portiques, 1932.

Index

Page references in *italics* refer to illustrations.

C

M

N

Photo Credits

All images of works are collection and courtesy the lenders unless indicated below. Numerals refer to page numbers, with "a" corresponding to left or top and "b" to right or bottom.

© Muriel ANSSENS, Musée des Beaux-Arts Jules Chéret: 3b

Photo © The Art Institute of Chicago: 16, 51, 131

© Art Museums of Skagen: 190–91, 213

ArtDigitalStudio, Paris: 88

Philippe Benoist IMAGES BLEU SUD: 207

Bridgeman-Giraudon / Art Resource, NY: 46

Photo: Dominic Brown, DGA Brown Photography: 227

© Bury Art Museum, Greater Manchester, UK: 201

CAPEHART: 225

© Christie's Images / Bridgeman Images: 161

Cincinnati Art Museum, Ohio, USA / Bridgeman Images: 152

Courtesy Crystal Bridges Museum of American Art, Bentonville, Arkansas. Photography by Robert LaPrelle: 117

Collection André Del Debbio: 14

© Den Hirschsprungske Samling: 107

Courtesy Denver Art Museum / Photo: Jeff Wells: 114, 144–45, 159, 162–63

Dnipropetrovsk State Art Museum, Dnipropetrovsk / Bridgeman Images: 87

Photo: Jonathan Dorado, Brooklyn Museum: 126–27, 133

Photo: Lars Engelhardt: 82–83, 91, 92–93, 176–77

Finnish National Gallery / Hannu Aaltonen: 189, 215, 234

Finnish National Gallery / Yehia Eweis: x, 5

Finnish National Gallery / Pirje Mykkänen: 78b

Finnish National Gallery / Jukka Romu: 179

Finnish National Gallery / Kari Soinio: 68, 78a

Gothenburg Museum of Art, Sweden: 165, 182–83

© Gothenburg Museum of Art 2015 / Hossein Sehatlou: v, 97

© HAM / Hanna Kukorelli: 237

Photo: Jan Haug, Royal Collection, Oslo: 168–69, 172–73

© Kunsthalle Bremen, Der Kunstverein in Bremen; Photo: Lars Lohrisch: 17

© C. Lancien, C. Loisel / Réunion des Musées Métropolitains Rouen Normandie: 54, 59

Leeds Museums and Galleries (Leeds Art Gallery), UK / Bridgeman Images: 24, 36

Photo: Erich Lessing / Art Resource, NY: 12a, 56, 141

© Lillehammer Art Museum / Photo: Thomas Widerberg: 76

Manchester Art Gallery, UK / Bridgeman Images: 31b, 198–99

Photo: Daniel Martin: 224

Mead Art Museum, Amherst College, MA, USA / Bridgeman Images: 13

www.metmuseum.org: 95, 149, 151

Minneapolis Institute of Art: 148

© Musée Anne-de-Beaujeu & Maison Mantin (Moulins): 85

© Musée d'art et d'histoire, Ville de Genève / Bettina Jacot-Descombes: ii–iii, 98–99

Musée des Beaux-Arts, Bordeaux: 6

© Musée des Beaux-Arts de Brest Métropole: 204–5

Musée des Beaux-Arts, Tournai, Belgium / Bridgeman Images: 28b

Musée du Louvre, Dist. RMN-Grand Palais / Art Resource, NY: 260

Musée Marmottan Monet, Paris, France / Bridgeman Images: 49, 89

Museo Thyssen-Bornemisza / Scala / Art Resource, NY: 42

© National Gallery, London / Art Resource, NY: 31a

© The National Museum of Art, Architecture and Design, Oslo; Photo: Børre Høstland: 102–3, 120–21

© National Museum of Art, Architecture and Design, Oslo; Photo: Jacques Lathion: 180–81, 212

Photo: Ole Hein Pedersen: 105

© Petit Palais / Roger-Viollet: 38

Photography Incorporated: 28a

© President and Fellows of Harvard College; Photo: Imaging Department: 231

Private Collection / The Stapleton Collection / Bridgeman Images: 63

© RMN-Grand Palais / Art Resource, NY / Photo: Daniel Arnaudet: 33

© RMN-Grand Palais / Art Resource, NY / Photo: Gérard Blot: 27, 34, 261, 262b

© RMN-Grand Palais / Art Resource, NY / Photo: Bulloz: back cover, 119, 185

© RMN-Grand Palais / Art Resource, NY / Photo: Adrien Didierjean: 47, 57

© RMN-Grand Palais / Art Resource, NY / Photo: Philippe Fuzeau: 259

© RMN-Grand Palais / Art Resource, NY / Photo: Lagiewski: 258

© RMN-Grand Palais / Art Resource, NY / Photo: Hervé Lewandowski: 15, 18, 26, 29, 37, 139, 193, 235, 262a, 264

© RMN-Grand Palais / Art Resource, NY / Photo: Stephane Marechalle: 216–17

© RMN-Grand Palais / Art Resource, NY / Photo: René-Gabriel Ojéda: 135

© RMN-Grand Palais / Art Resource, NY / Photo: Thierry Ollivier: 124–25

© RMN-Grand Palais / Art Resource, NY / Photo: Patrice Schmidt: 143

© RMN-Grand Palais / Art Resource, NY / Photo: Jan Schormans: 203

© RMN-Grand Palais / Art Resource, NY / Photo: Michel Urtado: 265

Scala / Art Resource, NY: 3a, 72

Skagens Museum, Denmark / Bridgeman Images: 71

© SMK Photo: 101

Photo: Kjell Söderlund: front cover, 239

Courtesy, Special Collections & Archives, David O. McKay Library, Brigham Young University, Rexburg, ID: 2

Städel Museum/ARTOTHEK: 43

Photo: Gregory Staley: 175

Photo: Lee Stalsworth: 192

© State Russian Museum, St. Petersburg: 19

Sterling and Francine Clark Art Institute, Williamstown, MA / Bridgeman Images: 129

© Sterling and Francine Clark Art Institute, Williamstown, MA / Photo: Michael Agee: 195

© Tate, London 2016: 8, 187

Photo: Matias Uusikylä: 84, 220–21, 229

© Ville de Dieppe: 170–71

© Virginia Museum of Fine Arts / Photo: Travis Fullerton: 157

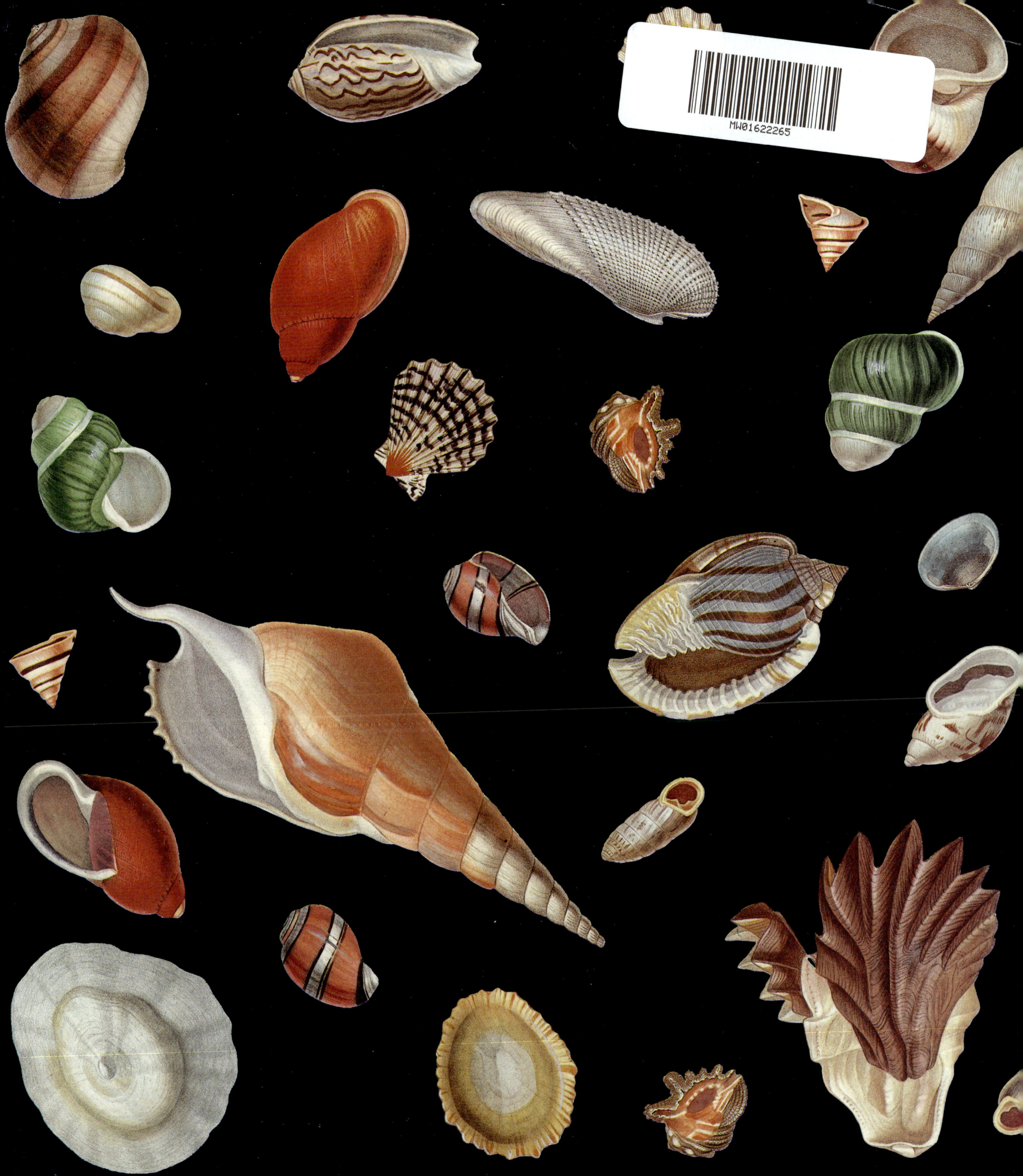
MW01622265

Janet Ryan-Finlayson
11338 So. 2700 West
So. Jordan, Utah 84065
801-254-0967

SOWERBY'S BOOK OF SHELLS

Janet,
I hope you treasure this volume as much as I treasure your friendships. Each year that passes is like another whorl on a shell – watching our families change and grow.
Enjoy both the book and the days that pass.
Sandi '92

SOWERBY'S
BOOK OF
SHELLS

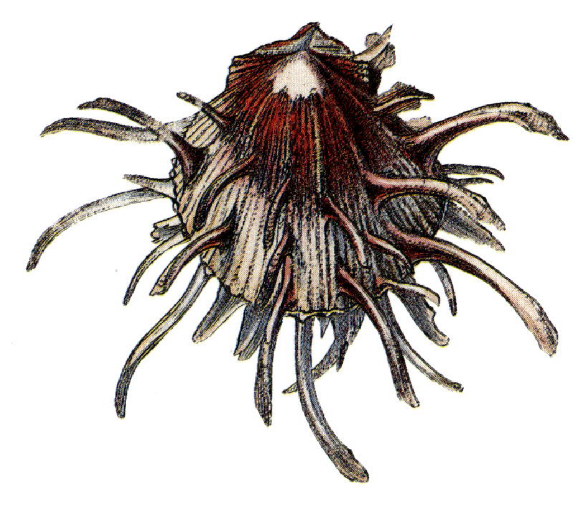

STUDIO EDITIONS
LONDON

Originally published 1852 by
Henry G Bohn, York Street, Covent Garden
as A Conchological Manual.
This edition includes additional
prints taken from
Dictionnaire Universel d'Histoire Naturelle
by Charles d'Orbigny

This edition published 1990 by Studio Editions Ltd.
Princes House, 50 Eastcastle Street,
London W1N 7AP, England

ISBN 1 85170 440 X

Printed and bound in Czechoslovakia

FOREWORD

The Sowerby family was distinguished during the eighteenth and nineteenth centuries for its contributions to the literature of natural history. The Sowerbys are remembered now chiefly for the several thousand hand coloured plates they produced, many of them being the corporate efforts of the family working as a team. The author of *A Conchological Manual* was the second and the most prolific of three members of the family who successively bore the name George Brettingham and added significantly to the literature of natural history. He was very knowledgeable about conchology, wrote extensively about the subject and illustrated his writings with accurate engravings.

The first edition of his *Conchological Manual*, to which his father made important contributions, was first published in 1839. The fourth and last edition, extensively revised and illustrated with extra plates, appeared in 1852. Sowerby's book was intended for the shell collector rather than the serious scientific student and as such had popular appeal. The illustrations show typical examples of the various genera and are, as they always were, the book's principal attractions. He would have been the first to admit that his knowledge of conchology was more wide ranging than profound.

This re-issue of the fourth edition differs in several respects from the 1852 issue. In the original there were two folding tables comparing the conchological systems of De Blainville and Lamarck. These tables have been omitted as irrelevant and of little interest to the modern student. The woodcut vignettes, illustrating shell features, were originally presented in groups of two, three, four or more. Here they have been placed adjacent to the relevant portions of the text. Except for the frontispiece the 29 hand coloured plates were originally grouped together, but in this edition they have been distributed evenly through the text. The most substantial innovation, however, is the addition of a dozen hand coloured plates of shells culled from the multi-volume *Dictionnaire Universel d'Histoire Naturelle*, edited by Alcide Charles Victor Dessalines d'Orbigny and published at Paris between 1839 and 1849.

Each volume of this work is comparable in format to *A Conchological Manual*, the illustrative plates being hand coloured etchings. The exquisite illustrations of shells are based on original drawings by Jean Gabriel Prêtre, a highly talented artist who specialized in the very difficult art of shell portraiture. They make an attractive supplement to the hand coloured lithographs of G.B. Sowerby Junior and allow us to compare French and English styles of conchological illustration. Clearly the French favoured a more delicate and more highly coloured style. Also they seem to have preferred their gastropod (or univalve) shells to be shown upside-down. The orientation of these shells as shown by Sowerby is the one now adopted almost universally, although even today some French conchologists adopt the 'upside-down' style in their publications.

No useful purpose would be served by trying to make Sowerby's original text conform with modern linguistic and scientific requirements. It is now appreciated as a period piece and would gain nothing from drastic revision. In its original published form *A Conchological Manual* is now a costly item obtainable only from the antiquarian book trade. This attractively designed and augmented re-issue of its 1852 edition is a handsome substitute.

S. PETER DANCE
January 1990

NAMES OF AUTHORS ABBREVIATED

Adans. Adanson. Author of "Voyages du Senegal".
Bl. Blainville. Author of "Manuel de Malacologie et de Conchyliologie", &c.
Brod. W.J. Broderip, Esq. Author of various descriptions of shells in the Zoological Journal, &c.
Brongn. Brongiart. Author of "Memoire sur les terrains du Vicentin, d'Italie, de France, et d'Allemagne," &c.
Brug. Bruguière. Author of "Dictionaire des Vers testacés, dans l'Encyclopédie," &c.
Cuv. Baron Cuvier. Author of "Regne Animal," &c.
Defr. Defrance. Contributor to the "Annales des Sciences Naturelles," &c.
Desh. Deshayes. Author of "Coquilles fossiles des environs de Paris," &c.
D'Orb. D'Alcide d'Orbigny.
Drap. Draparnaud. Author of "Histoire Naturelle des Mollusques terrestres et fluviatiles de la France," &c.
Fer. De Ferussac. Author of "Histoire Naturelle des Mollusques terrestres et fluviatiles," &c.
Flem. Fleming.
Gmel. Gmelin. Author of an edition of Linnæus's "Systema Naturæ," &c.
Guild. Rev. Lansdowne Guilding.
Hübn. Hübner.
Humph. The late George Humphrey.
Lam. Lamarck. Author of "Animaux sans Vertebres," &c.
Lin. Linnæus. Author of "Systema Naturæ," &c.
Mont. Montague. Author of "Testacea Britannica," &c.
Montf. Montfort. Author of "Histoire Naturelle des Mollusques," &c.
Müll. Müller. Author of "Vermium terrestrium et fluviatilium Historia," "Zoologia Danica," &c.
Ranz. Ranzani. Author of "Considerations sur les Balanes," &c.
Schum. Schumacher.
Sow. Sowerby. The late and present James. Authors of "Mineral Conchology," &c. George Brettingham, Senr., "Genera of Shells," "Species Conchyliorum," &c. G. B. Jun. "Conchological Manual," "Conchological Illustrations," "Thesaurus Conchyliorum," Description of New Shells in the Zoological Proceedings, &c.
Sw. Swainson. Author of "Zoological Illustrations," "Exotic Conchology," and Treatises in "Lardner's Cabinet Cyclopedia," &c.
Turt. Turton. Author of "British Shells."

INTRODUCTION

The Science of Conchology affords a very delightful and instructive amusement for the leisure hours of those who, retiring occasionally from the more active pursuits of life, seek pleasure in the quiet contemplation of some of the smaller, but not less wonderful operations of creative wisdom. And, although the study of shells would be more complete, and rank higher in the scale of philosophical pursuits, were it always accompanied by that of the animal inhabiting them, it nevertheless presents means of intellectual gratification, to many who cannot follow it beyond the cabinet and the boudoir. These may examine with admiration and mental improvement, the beautiful colouring and architecture of these wonders of the deep, they may exercise their taste and judgment in the selection and arrangement of specimens, and their discrimination in detecting and appreciating the distinctions upon which the arrangement is founded.

It is but little that can be known of the subject without forming a collection of greater or less extent; for, as it would be uninstructive merely to delight the eye with the bright colours and elegant form of shells, without possessing correct information respecting them, so it would be insipid and useless to learn technicalities without being acquainted, by personal observation, with the subjects to which they are applied. The first endeavour should, therefore, be to obtain a few shells as examples of the larger divisions, and, when these are understood, to proceed with the smaller groups, until a collection be formed to represent as many generic forms as possible. It may be as well here to advise those who are forming a collection to be very particular, in every practicable instance, to have the shells properly named at the time of purchasing; as it will save much trouble, and materially assist in the attainment of the desired object. To this end, recourse should be had to those naturalist tradesmen, who unite the attainment and diffusion of real scientific knowledge with their commercial pursuits.

Supposing, however, that the person who desires to learn the science, possesses a small parcel of unarranged and unnamed shells, without any previous acquaintance with the subject, the following introductory explanations, are drawn up with the view of enabling him, without further assistance, to obtain a general insight into its principles, equal to that of those who have studied it long and laboriously. To effect this, he must read them, carefully comparing the descriptions with the figures referred to, and with the specimens which he may have at command.

After describing the nature of the science and defining its objects, we shall proceed to explain the structure of those objects, and the manner of their growth. We shall then enter somewhat minutely into the principles of classification, the distinctions upon which they are founded, and some of the technical terms used to express them. After which we shall pass through the arrangement of Lamarck, defining the general divisions adopted under the terms of "*Classes, Orders,* and *Families,*" as far as they are capable of definition. The subdivisions of the latter into *genera* will only be entered into so far as to enumerate the principal of them, the more minute descriptions being reserved for the alphabetical part of the work.

Let none be discouraged by the number of generic distinctions proposed and adopted in modern times; for *if well defined*, they will be found to facilitate rather than encumber the science. The knowledge of species must be the foundation of every system, and the greater their number, the more necessary it becomes to subdivide them; if, for instance, all the species now known were to have been included in the 50 genera of Linnæus, a single genus would have contained many hundreds of incongruous species, in which case it would be much more difficult to remember them, than if they were to be divided into a far greater number of genera. Every well marked division, tends to simplify the subject, and to facilitate the researches of the student.

NATURE OF THE SCIENCE

Conchology is the study of shells, viewed and described as to what they are either in themselves, or in relation to the soft, inarticulate animals which produce them, and of which they form a part. These animals are called Mollusca, and perhaps the best general description of them will be found in De Blainville's "Manuel de Malacologie et de Conchyliologie." The following is a translation, "Animal in pairs, the body and its appendages soft, inarticulate (not jointed), enveloped in a muscular skin, commonly called the mantle, which is extremely variable in form, and has developed either within or upon it a calcareous portion, consisting of one or several pieces, commonly called a shell."

The term Mollusca was formerly restricted to those soft animals which were destitute of shells, although possessing in other particulars, the characters described above, and it was used in order to distinguish them from the TESTACEA, which were covered or internally supported by calcareous parts. In the system of Linnæus, the soft portions are first arranged under the general designation of "Vermes Mollusca," and described without regard to the presence, absence, or character of the shells; and then the shells are separately characterized under the appellation of "Vermes Testacea," without any further notice of the animal, than an indication of the genus to which it belongs; thus the animal of Cypræa is said to be a Limax, and that of Tellina a Tethys.

The nearest approach to correctness, and the most philosophical method of study will be found in the modern system, adopted by Lamarck and his followers, of observing these animals as a whole, and arranging them according to the assemblage of characters which they present; of course taking into consideration the existence or non-existence, the form and structure of the shell, on the same principle, which, in arranging the vertebrated animals would lead us to study the hair, hoof, nails, claws, &c. as well as the other parts.

At the same time, it must be admitted that there are many private collectors of Shells who would find it a difficult, if not impossible task to study minutely and successfully the soft parts of the Mollusca. Ladies, for instance, could not be expected to handle with pleasure and perseverance, these bodies, which in order to be preserved from putrefaction, must be kept in spirits; and yet such persons may, with improvement and advantage to their own minds, enjoy the interesting and scientific amusement of studying and arranging the clean and beautiful shells which are so easily preserved, and so exquisitely beautiful in their structure. Let it also be remembered, that if shells had not been rendered commercially valuable, by the zeal and emulation manifested by *mere* Conchologists for the possession of rare specimens, few travelling merchants and sea captains would have thought them worthy of a corner in their cabins. In this case, few specimens being brought to the country, the more Philosophical Naturalist would have been left without the means of obtaining materials to work upon, or of attracting public attention to his favourite pursuit.

On account of these and other considerations, it has been thought advisable that the present work should bear a purely conchological character. The peculiarities of the shells alone being detailed for the assistance of those who collect and study them, while at the same time, in deciding upon their affinities and places, in the arrangement, it will be necessary sometimes to adopt conclusions arrived at by those who have studied the animal in all its parts. And the conviction must be expressed, that if ever a complete Natural System shall be formed it will result from the labours of the last mentioned class of naturalists.

DEFINITION OF A SHELL

Before entering minutely into the description of shells, it will be necessary to distinguish from the true testaceous Mollusca two kinds of animals, which have formerly been associated with them. Of these, the first is the class of CRUSTACEA, consisting of crabs, crayfish, &c. These differ from shell-fish, not only in structure and chemical composition, but also in the fact that the animal has jointed limbs, and that the substance of the flesh is inseparable from the hard external covering, which invests each particular joint as with a sheath; whereas the Molluscous animal is but partially attached to its shell, from which it possesses the power of partly withdrawing and returning. The second class is that to which the sea-urchin, or Echinus, belongs, of which there are many genera and species. The testaceous covering of Echini is composed of a number of small pieces, placed edge to edge, forming a more or less globular external covering to the flesh, which is supported in the centre by a number of bones leaning upon each other in a pyramidal form. The *test* is of a fibrous texture, guarded on the outside with moveable spines, which turn on ball and socket joints.

A true shell is composed of one or more calcareous pieces, commonly called valves, each piece formed by a series of layers, applied obliquely upon each other, in such a manner that each new layer begins within, and terminates a little in advance of the one before it.

The Cirripedes, however, although their testaceous pieces will correspond with this definition, are otherwise so connected with the crustacea, that they do not enter into the study of Conchology.

STRUCTURE AND GROWTH

We shall now endeavour to describe the manner in which the growth of each separate valve, or each regularly formed shell, proceeds from the nucleus.

Before the young animal has left the egg, if it be an *oviparous* species, or the body of the parent if *viviparous*, the nucleus of the shell is generally formed, and specimens are sometimes preserved in which the young shell is seen within the egg, as in the cut, fig. 1, 2; or adhering to the inner surface of the full-grown shell by the dried mucus of the animal, as seen in fig. 3.

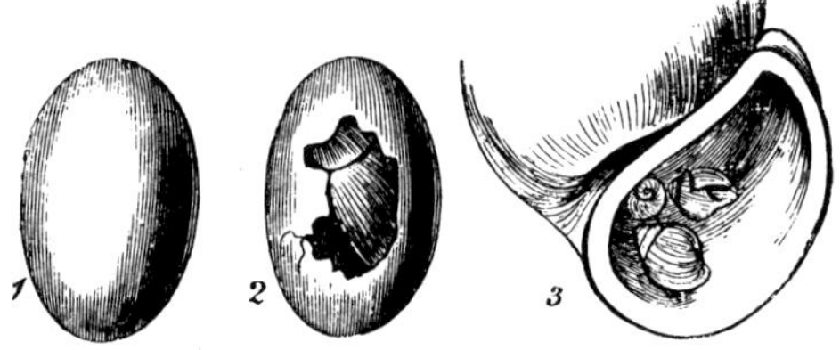

1. Egg of a Bulinus. 2. The same broken, shewing the young shell. 3. The young of a Paludina, as seen in the aperture of the shell.

In both cases, the nucleus is generally of a more horny and transparent composition than the parts subsequently produced. As soon as the animal is hatched, or, in other words, leaves the egg or body of the parent, of course it begins to increase in size, and to require a corresponding enlargement in the shell. To effect this, a small quantity of mucous substance, secreted by the mantle of the animal, is deposited on the edge of the aperture. When this is dry and become sufficiently hard, it is lined by a more calcareous secretion; and these together form a new layer, which is followed by others in succession; each new layer being larger than the one that preceded it until the whole being complete, the full-grown animal is invested with a shell commensurate with its own proportions. Thus from the apex or nucleus the formation proceeds, as it were, downwards, taking the shape of the part which secretes it, on which it is in a manner moulded.

The nucleus, or first formed portion, may for technical purposes be considered, mathematically, as the apex of a spiral cone. And here it must be observed, that whether the shell consists of one or several pieces, each piece has a distinct nucleus, and the process of formation is separately repeated with each. The word *cone* is used for convenience, and its meaning extended so as to include all those structures which commencing at a point enlarge downwards.

From the apex, the next layer is deposited on its edge, and advancing beyond it necessarily adds to its extent. Thus, suppose for the sake of illustration, the part marked *a* in the diagram, fig. 4, to represent a nucleus, the cross lines (*l*) will shew the consecutive layers which enlarge their circle as they add to their numbers. This disposal of shelly matter into layers is marked externally by concentric striæ, or *lines of growth*, while on the inside, the edges of the laminæ are consolidated into a kind of enamel. If a perpendicular section of a solid portion of a shell were magnified, it would present, in many instances, an appearance resembling the diagram, fig. 5; *a* may be taken to represent the horny part of the layers which form the outer coating, named "*Periostaca*," or "*Epidermis*;" the undulating line *b*, is formed by the edges of the calcareous layers, and causes the striæ, or lines of growth, which are often distinguishable on the surface of the shell; the space *c* is the middle part of those layers, and at *d* they are consolidated into the enamel which lines the interior.

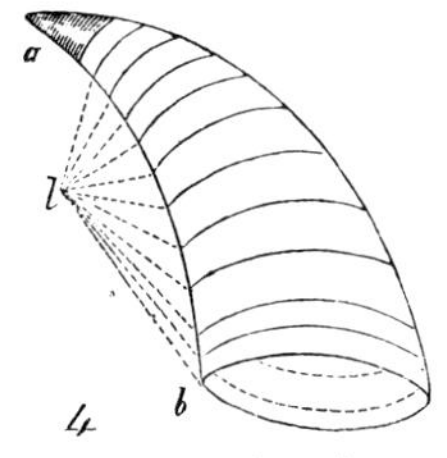

4. *Imaginary cone. a. Apex. b. Base. l. Lines of growth.*

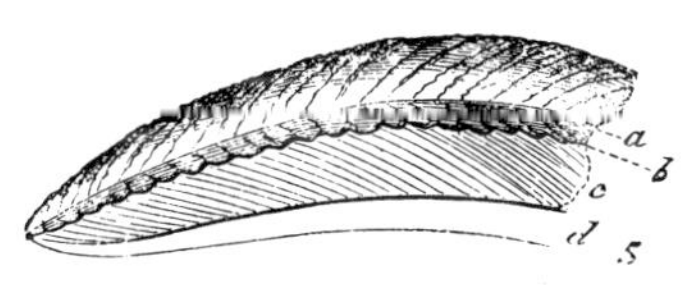

5. *Supposed section of a part of a solid shell.*

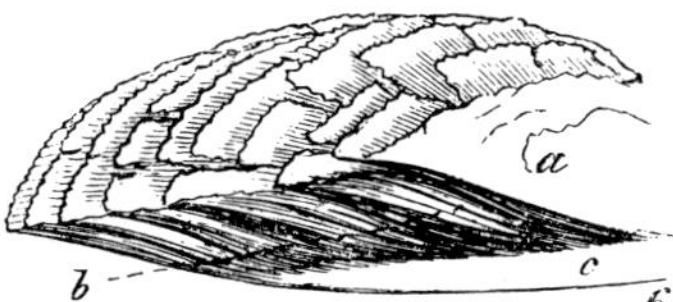

6. *Section of an oyster shell enlarged.*

In some species the layers are irregularly grouped together, and their edges overlap each other, so that they are easily separable, and advancing beyond each other, give a leafy appearance to the external surface. This structure is termed *foliaceous*. A very familiar instance of this may be observed in the common oyster. If a specimen of this shell be broken, the substance will be seen to exhibit a degree of looseness, and a magnifying glass will enable the student to trace distinctly the laminæ of which it is composed. The accompanying representation of a magnified section (fig. 6) will shew at *a*, the external surface, with the foliations or leaves; at *b*, the parcels of layers which form them; and at *c*, the pearly structure produced by their consolidation, and by the subsequently deposited enamel which covers their external surface.

CLASSIFICATION

The classification of shells, that is, their systematic arrangement into *classes*, *orders*, *families*, *genera* and *species*, cannot be made to depend entirely upon the characters observable in them, viewed by themselves; for this reason, that many similarly formed shells belong to animals perfectly distinct, and that many molluscous animals are found to agree with each other in every respect but in the form of their testaceous support. There are, however, many important distinctions to be observed in the shells themselves, leading to the establishment of many of those very divisions, which would afterwards be confirmed by an examination of the soft parts. It is desirable to attend, as far as means and opportunity will allow, to *all* the points of difference, in order to form, or even to appreciate, a generic or wider distinction. It will therefore be our endeavour to explain the general principles upon which those distinctions are formed, and the manner in which they are applied and expressed in detail by scientific writers.

NUMBER OF PIECES, OR INDEPENDENTLY FORMED PARTS

The first, most simple and obvious division of shells, is that which results from the number of separate pieces composing them. Hence the distinction implied by the terms UNIVALVE, or consisting of a single piece; BIVALVE, or composed of two pieces; and MULTIVALVE, or composed of more than two. For an example of *univalve*, take a common whelk; for a *bivalve*, take a muscle or scallop; and for a *multivalve*, the *chiton*.

But although this arrangement may appear at first sight perfectly easy and plain, some explanation will be necessary in order to guard the student against understanding the above expressions in their strictest sense, without qualification. Thus the univalves are said to consist of a single piece, or spiral cone; but it would be more correct to speak of this piece as forming either the whole or principal part of the shell: for there is in many instances, a much smaller flattened piece attached to the foot of the animal, which being drawn in when it retires, closes the aperture as with a kind of door, to which in fact the word valve might be very properly applied; it is called, however, the *operculum*, of which the little horny plate, frequently drawn out by means of a pin from the aperture of a periwinkle, will present a familiar example.

The same may be said respecting the bivalves; for besides the principal portions or valves of which the shell is composed, there are in many species, one or two smaller separate portions, named "*accessary plates*" by some authors. They are fixed by means of cartilages, on the back of the hinge.—The engraving, fig. 7,

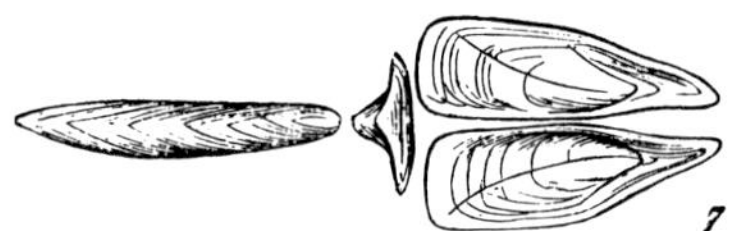

7. *Accessary valves of a Pholas.*

represents the accessary valves of a species of Pholas, which was on this account arranged by Linnæus with the Multivalves. Nearly allied to the Pholades is a set of shells to which De Blainville has given the name "*Tubicolæ*," or inhabitants of tubes. In this case, the bivalve shell is connected with a testaceous tube or pipe, to which it is attached either by one or by both valves, or in which it lies attached only by the cartilages of the animal. In the genus Aspergillum, the two small valves are soldered into the sides of the tube in such a manner as to constitute a part of it. One of these shells, called the Water-spout, might be taken up by a person not aware of its real nature, and regarded as a pipe or tube prettily fringed, and nothing more; but upon a closer examination, he would find the two valves, the points of which are visible from the outside of the tube.

HABITS – *Land, Fresh-water, or Marine Shells*

Another distinction, leading to important results in classification, is that which is derived from the nature of the element breathed by the Mollusc. And although this consideration belongs more especially to the study of the animal itself, yet the habits of the animal materially influence the structure of the shell.

The Terrestrial or Land Molluscs live on land, breathe air, and feed on plants and trees.—Those who find pleasure in horticultural pursuits will at once call to mind a too familiar example of these Molluscs in the common garden snail. The Land-shells are all univalves, and constitute a family in the Lamarckian system under the name "*Colimacea*" or snails, corresponding with the Linnean genus Helix.—They are generally light in structure and simple in form.

The Aquatic, or Fresh-water Molluscs, such as the Planorbis, commonly called the Fresh-water Snail; the Unio—known by the name of Fresh-water Muscle, is found in ponds, ditches and rivers. The *epidermis* of these is generally of a thick, close-grained character, and they are subject to corrosion near the umbones.

The Marine, or *sea-shells*, belong to all the classes and orders, and include by far the greater number of species. They vary in the habits of the animal, and consequently in the situations in which they are found. Some are found buried in sand and marine mud, and are named "*Arenicolæ*" or inhabitants of sand; others in holes of rocks and other hard substances, then they are named "*Petricolæ*,"—some of these latter form the holes in which they live by corroding or eating away the stone. A section of these form the family of "*Lithophagidæ*," or stone-eaters, of Lamarck. Others, again, take up their parasitical abode in the bodies of animals, and feed upon their substance; as for instance, the Stylifer, which is found in the vital part of star-fish, and Coronula, and Tubicinella, found buried in the skin of the whale.

LOCOMOTION – *Attached, Unattached*

A much more subordinate source of distinction arises from the freedom or attachment of the shells. Some of them float or walk freely in their natural element; others are fixed or attached to foreign bodies. Among those which are attached, there is again a difference as to the *mode* of attachment. Some are united to foreign bodies by means of a glutinating substance, secreted by the animal, and joining part of the surface of the shell to that of the stone, coral or other substance. In this way shells are fixed to each other in groups; this is the case with the Spondyli among bivalves, and the Serpulæ among univalves. M. de Blainville applies the term "*Fixæ*" to these shells. Others are kept in a particular place by means of a *Byssus* or Tendinous fibrous line or bunch of silky hairs, acting as a cable, and allowing the Mollusc to ride as it were at anchor. This Tendon is connected with some part of the animal from which it passes through an opening or hiatus in the shell, as in the Terebratula and the Mytilus.

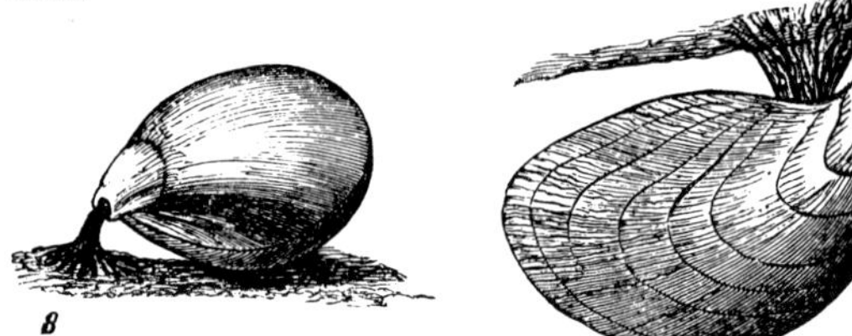

In the former, represented by the cut, fig. 8, the tendon passes through a perforation in the upper valve; and in the latter, Mytilus, fig. 9, the byssus passes out between the valves.

Before proceeding to explain the characters of the different groups, according to the modern system of classification, it may be desirable to explain the terms by which the different parts and characters are described, and to shew the manner in which the shells are measured. For this purpose we shall treat of the general divisions separately. We begin with

UNIVALVE SHELLS

In considering Univalves merely with reference to their mathematical construction, the first point demanding our attention is, whether they are symmetrical or non-symmetrical, or, in other words, whether a straight line drawn through the shell would divide it into two equal parts. The greater part of univalves are non-symmetrical, being rolled obliquely on the axis; but many are symmetrical, being rolled horizontally on the axis. The Nautilus presents an illustration of the latter; the Snail is a familiar example of the former.

Symmetrical Univalves

In describing these it will be well to commence with the most simple form, such as the Patella,—taking a conical species as an example. In this it will be observed that there is no winding or curvature, but a simple depressed cone, and that the line *a*, *p*, divides it into two equal parts.

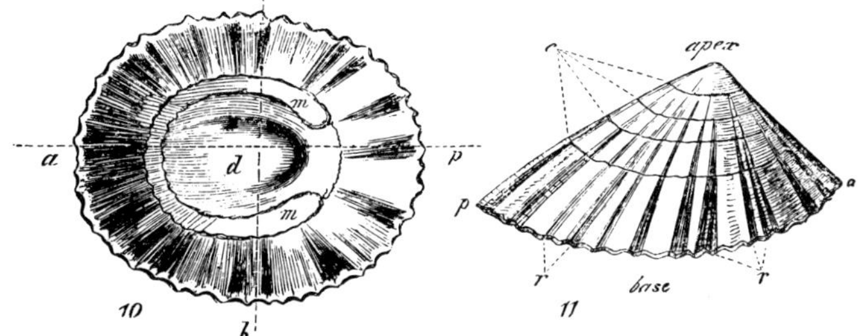

The *anterior*, *a*, (*cut*, fig. 10) is known by the interruption of the muscular impression which surrounds the central disc (*d*). This interruption of the muscular impression is in the place where the head of the animal lies in the shell. The impression itself is caused by the fibrous muscle which attaches the animal to the shell. The apex (*a*) in Patella, generally leans towards the anterior (*a*) part of the shell, and away from the posterior (*p*); and this circumstance has caused some mistakes, because in Emarginula the apex leans towards the posterior; and students, instead of examining the muscular impression, which is the only criterion, have only noticed the direction in which the apex turned, and concluded that to be the anterior, towards which it inclined. The lines or ribs running from the base to the apex of the shell, in the direction *r*, are called *radiating* lines; and those which encircle the cone in the direction *c c*, from front to back, are very properly described as *concentric*. The *length* is measured from front to back in the line *e*; the breadth, from side to side, in the line *b*; and the depth from the apex to the base.

Let it be observed that patelliform, or limpet shaped shells are not all symmetrical; Umbrella, Siphonaria, Ancylus, &c. will form exceptions, of which we have yet to speak. And the learner may also be reminded that the Limpets themselves are not *all* regular in their form: for as they adhere to rocks and other rough surfaces, and are so little locomotive, in many instances they partake of the inequalities of the surface, and conform to its irregularities. This adherence is not affected by any agglutinating power in the animal, nor by any tendinous process like that described above; but simply by means of the foot of the animal acting as a sucker.

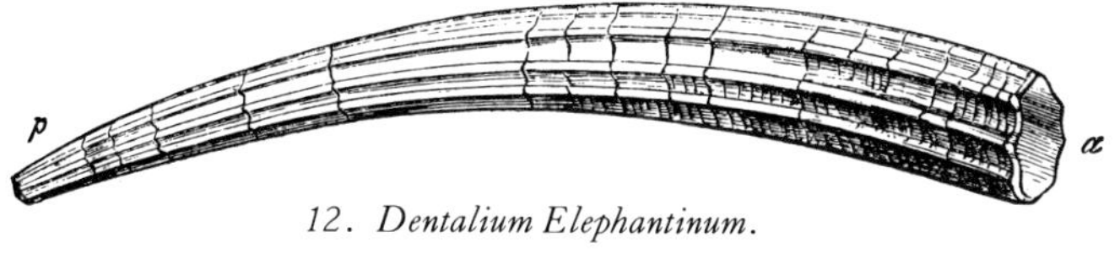

12. *Dentalium Elephantinum.*

The next variation in symmetrical univalves is to be observed in the tubular, curved form, the example of which will be the Dentalium, fig. 12.

This has an opening at the anterior termination *a*, called the aperture. The opening at the posterior end (*p*) is named a fissure, or perforation. The ribs running along the sides of the shell are *longitudinal*, or radiating. And the lines round the circumference are *lines of growth*, or *concentric*—each one having in succession, at earlier stages of growth, formed the aperture. They are described as concentric or transverse.

Symmetrical Convolute Univalves

The Nautilus, the Spirula, the Scaphite, and the Ammonite are the leading types of this form; but when we use the term symmetrical, in reference to these, the word must not be understood in its strictest sense, for no shell is *perfectly* symmetrical: but it means that there is no perceptible difference in the proportion of the two sides; as in the human body, the right side is larger and more powerful than the left, yet to a degree so small that it gives no apparent bias to the figure.

CHAMBERED SHELLS

Many of the shells now under consideration are chambered, that is, the internal cavity is divided into separate compartments by plates reaching across it, named *Septa*; and the only connection between the chambers is formed by the small pipes passing through them, to which the name of Siphon is attached.

Septa

The septa are *simple* in some species, as in the Nautilus, fig. 13. In others they are undulated, having waved edges, as in some species of Ammonites; in others they are *angulated*, as in Goniatites, fig. 480 in the plates; and in the greater number of instances, among the Ammonites, they are *arborescent*, or branched.

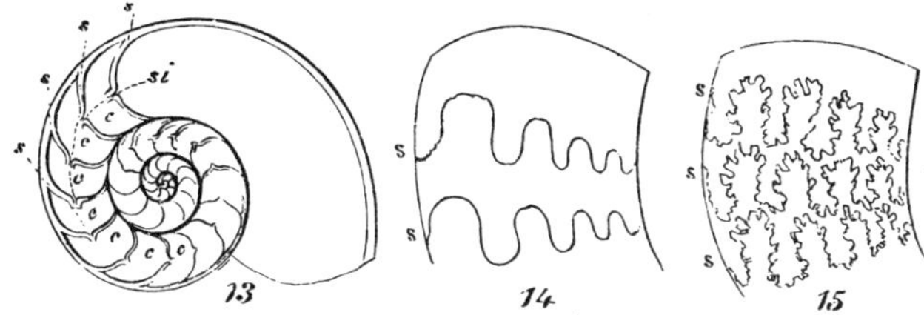

13. *Section of Nautilus.*—14. *Undulating Septa.*—
15. *Arborescent Septa.*

In the above section of a Nautilus, fig. 13, diminished in size, shewing the whorls and chambers (*c*), it will be seen that the edges of the septa (*s*) are formed in one simple curve. In fig. 14, the upper part of an Ammonite, the undulating line will be seen; and in fig. 15 a specimen is given of the arborescent septa.

Siphon

The Siphon is *dorsal* when placed near the outside of the whorls; *central* when near the middle; and *ventral* when near the inside of the whorl, or that part which leans against the last volution. When it passes uninterruptedly from one chamber to another, it is described as *continuous*, as in the case of Spirula; when, on the other hand, it only passes through the septum a little distance, and opens into the chamber, as in Nautilus, it is *discontinuous*.

Whorls of Symmetrical Univalves

They are *disunited* when they do not touch each other, as in the case of Spirula (fig. 471 in the plates); but in the contrary case they are said to be *contiguous*. In some species of Nautilus the whorls overwrap each other in such a manner that the early whorls are entirely covered by the last, the edges of which reach to the centre of the disk; the spire is then said to be *hidden*; as in the Nautilus Pompilius. In Nautilus umbilicatus the spire is nearly hidden, the whorls not quite covering each other; but in the greater number of the Ammonites, the largest part of the preceding whorl is seen. To express the degree in which the whorls overwrap each other, has caused much difficulty in concise descriptions. Perhaps it would be well to apply the term *spiral disc* to so much of the shell as is seen besides the last whorl, and to describe it as large or small in diameter, compared with the whole: or to say that the whorls of the spire are half, or one-third, or one-fourth covered, as the case may be.

Aperture of Symmetrical Univalves

In Ammonites Blagdeni and some others the aperture is of an oblong square; it is then said to be *sub-quadrated*; in Nautilus triangularis it is *angulated*; in Ammonites Greenoughi it is of an interruped oval shape, described as *elliptical*. In the greater number of Orthocerata, it is rounded or *circular*. The entrance of the last whorl into the aperture of some rounded species of Nautilus causes it to take a *semi-lunar* form; if rounded at the sides it is said to be *reniform* or kidney-shaped: if pointed at the sides it is *semi-lunar*; and in some species of Ammonites, it is five-sided or *quinquelateral*.

Measurement of Symmetrical Conical Univalves

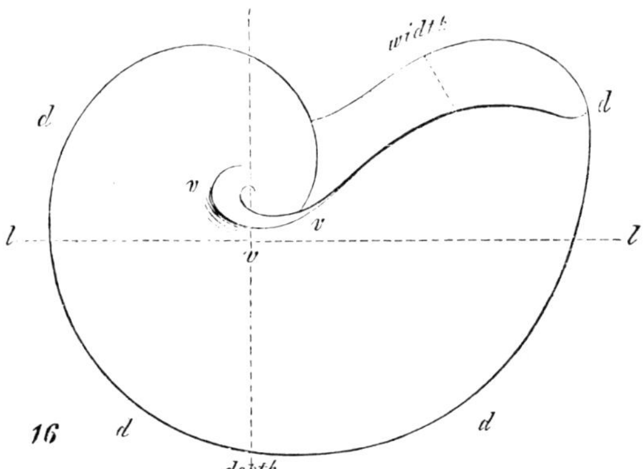

The *width* is measured across the aperture, which is the widest part of the shell. The *length* (*l*) from the dorsal part (*d*) of the aperture to the dorsal part of the *whorl* (*d*) on the opposite part of the shell. The *ventral* part of the whorls is that nearest to the axis, and the *dorsal* that which forms the outline of the figure.

NON-SYMMETRICAL UNIVALVES

These are *conical, irregular, spiral,* or *convolute*. The *conical* form is when there is no enrolment of the apex. Although the Patellæ were described as symmetrical, there are several species of Patelliform shells which are not symmetrical. In Umbrella, for instance, the apex is oblique, the shells being placed obliquely on the animal. In the genus *Siphonaria*, there is a grove on one side, where the brachia or gills of the animal rest. In the genus Ancylus, it will be observed that the apex bends on one side, and the animal is like the Limnæa, which has a spiral shell. The cup and saucer Limpets, or Calyptrædæ, present a group which requires to be described differently from the symmetrical or true Limpets. Their structure is very curious, and they vary considerably among themselves, some of them being simply conical, others nearly flat, or discoidal, and others more or less spiral. But their principal peculiarity consists in their having a small internal process or plate, commonly named their *septum*, variously shaped.

Septa of Limpets

The septa of Limpets assume a variety of forms, the principal of which will be seen in the accompanying engravings.

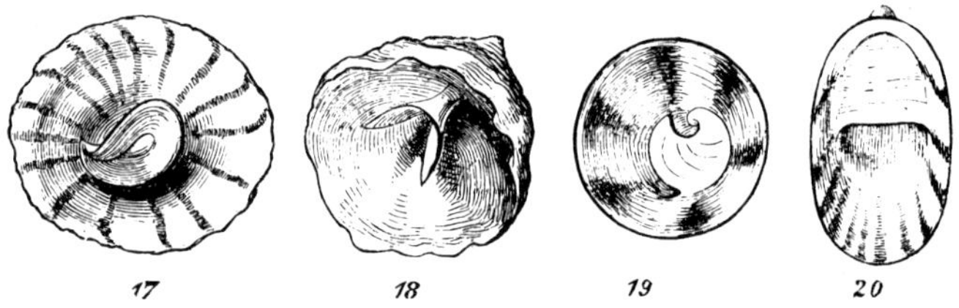

The form from which the group derives its generic appellation is that of the cup-shaped or *Cyathiform* species (fig. 17). In the Crepidulæ, or Slipper-Limpets, the septum is flat, reaching across the opening, like the deck of a vessel; it is then described as *transverse* (fig. 20). In Calyptræa Equestris, it has two prominent points, and is described as *bi-furcated* (fig. 18). In another species, it is a three-sided plate rather spiral at the apex (fig. 19).

Measurement of Cup and Saucer Limpets

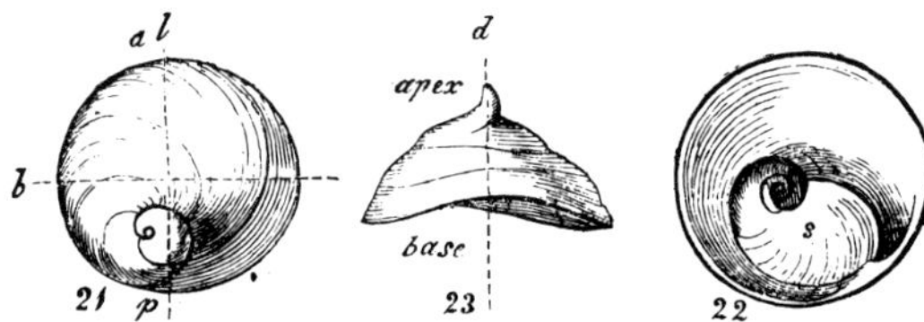

The line marked *a, p, l l,* indicates the direction in which the shell is to be measured for *length*. *a* indicates the *anterior*, *p* the *posterior*. The line *d* (fig. 23), from the apex to the base, is the *depth*. The line *b* (fig. 21), is in the direction of the breadth.

Irregular non-symmetrical Univalves

Serpuliform shells are irregularly twisted hollow tubes, which were formerly considered to have been secreted by a kind of worm, but now known to be the shells of true Molluscs, of a kind not very widely differing from those which have regularly spiral shells. The greater part of these are attached to foreign bodies, or to each other in groups. Some are attached by the whole length of the shell, they are then said to be *decumbent*. Some of these are coiled round like the Spirorbis, the little white shell seen on the carapace of the Lobster or on leaves of sea-weeds; they are then said to be discoidal; others again, such as the *Vermetus*, approach more nearly to the spiral form. The deviation from the regular spire only taking place after the first few first volutions.

SPIRAL NON-SYMMETRICAL UNIVALVE

As these constitute the largest class, it will be necessary to dwell upon them in detail. First as to *measurement*.

The length is measured from the apex, to that part of the aperture *a* (fig. 24), at the greatest distance from it. The *breadth* is in the opposite direction. The *anterior*, or front part of the aperture, is marked *a*, where the head of the animal protrudes.

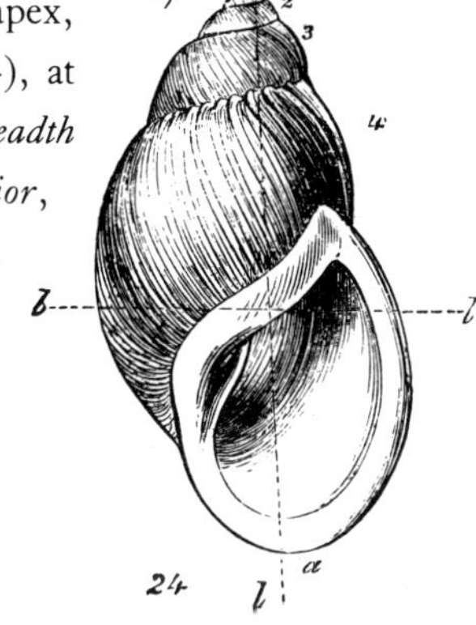

Spire of non-symmetrical Univalves

In counting the whorls of which the spire consists, we commence at the apex, and reckon downwards to the last, or body whorl. The spire is described as being long or short in relation to the aperture: in which case, all that is above the aperture is measured with the spire. Its apex requires particular notice, as the character of the whole shell frequently depends upon the particulars observable in this part. It is sometimes *obtuse*, or blunt; sometimes *acute*, or sharp. In the Cones it is frequently flat, and in Planorbis it is concave. It is sometimes of a different structure from the rest of the shell, retaining the horny and transparent appearance which characterized it when the animal was first produced. The Tritons present an instance of this, although it is not always observable, owing to the tenderness of the substances which causes it to break or fall away in many specimens. A very remarkable instance also occurs in Bulinus decollatus (cut, fig. 27, 28), so named, because the apex, to the depth of several whorls, falls off, and the shell is *decollated*. In this, and many more instances, among Pupæform land shells, the occurrence of this circumstance seems to be by no means rare or accidental, a provision having been made for filling up the opening by a septum. A *papillary apex* is one

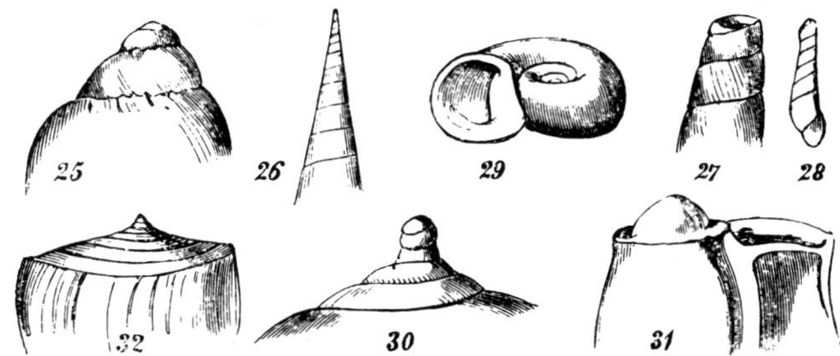

Fig. 25, obtuse; 26, acute; 27, 28, decollated; 29, concave; 30, papillary; 31, mammellated; 32, discoidal.

which is swelled at the extremity into a little rounded knob, or nipple; and a *mammellated* apex is one which is rounded out more fully.

Whorls

The spire is described as consisting of *numerous* or *few* whorls, and sometimes the number of them is particularly stated. A whorl consists of one turn of the spiral cone. The whorls are described as *flattened*, when their sides are not much bulged out: when the contrary is the case, the whorls are said to be *ventricose*, and either *rounded* or *angulated*. The degree of rapidity with which the whorls become enlarged presents an important source of distinction. The *suture*, or seam, which separates one whorl from another is also noticed as being *distinct* or otherwise; *canaliculated*, or grooved; or covered by an enamel, which in some instances is even *tumid* or swelled into a ridge.

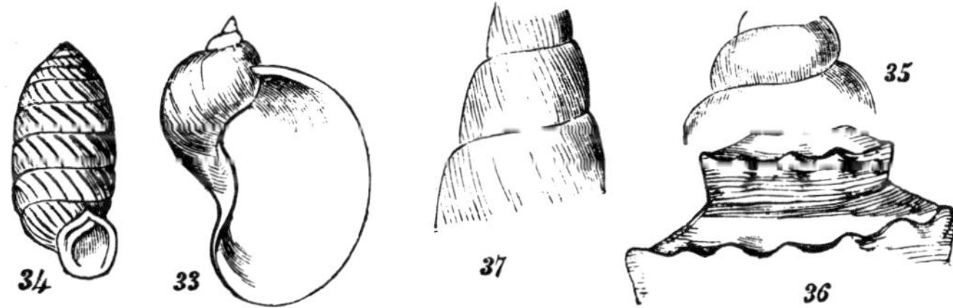

Fig. 33, few; 34, numerous; 35, rounded, ventricose; 36, angular, ventricose; 37, flattened.

Suture.

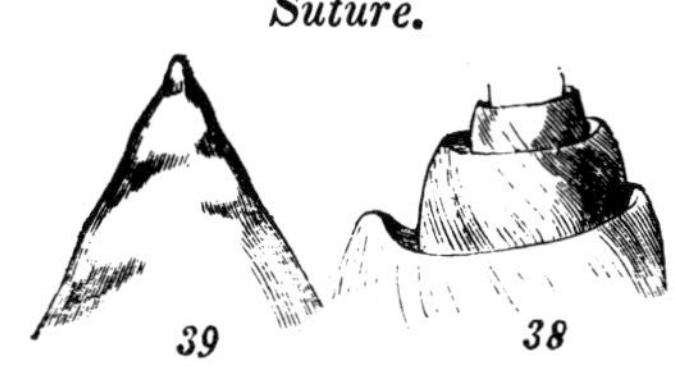

Fig. 38, canaliculated; 39, enamelled.

Varices

Varices are caused by periodical rests or stoppages in the growth of the shell, when the edge of the aperture thickens, and renders the shell as complete as when full grown. Again, after an interval, another check takes place, and another thickened edge is formed, and so on in succession, until the animal arrives at maturity, and the shell is full-grown. The thickened edges successively forming the aperture, remain visible on the outside, through all the subsequent stages. When these rests take place at frequent periods, the varices will of course be numerous, as in Harpa and Scalaria. They occur at regular or irregular distances, varying in shape and other characters. When the varices occur at regular intervals, and form a connected ridge from whorl to whorl up the spire, they are said to be *continuous*, as in Ranella; when on the contrary, the varix on one whorl does not come in contact with that on the other, they are described as *discontinuous*. In order to distinguish a regular varix from a mere external ridge, it will be sufficient to notice whether its edge overlaps the external surface, and whether it resembles the open edge of the aperture, which true varices do.

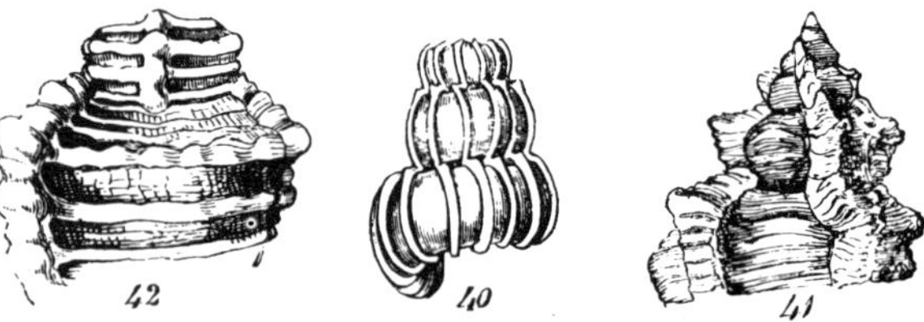

Fig. 40, numerous; 41, few, continuous; 42, few, discontinuous.

Aperture

The aperture or opening of the spiral tube, was formerly called the "mouth;" a term calculated to convey an erroneous impression, when applied to a part of the shell which has no correspondence with the mouth of the animal. The word *aperture* is used by modern writers in a general sense, including the cavity, its edges, and the canals. The cavity itself is distinguished in various shells as to its shape, which depends much upon the degree of modification produced by the last whorl. In some cases, as in Cyclostoma, where the aperture stands apart from the last whorl, the shape is round, or nearly so. The Scalaria presents a good example of this. In others, where the inner edge or lip, wrapping over the body whorl is nearly straight, the aperture is *semi-lunar*, or half-moon shaped: this is remarkable in the "*Neritacea*" of Lamarck, named, on that account, "*hemi-cyclostomata*" by De Blainville. In a great number of instances, the lower part of the body whorl enters obliquely into the upper part of the aperture, the result being a *pyriform*, or pear-shaped opening. The aperture is described as *long* when it is largest in the direction of the axis, and *wide*, in the contrary case. The *anterior* is the part at the greatest distance from the apex, and the body whorl; the *posterior*, the part nearest to the apex. Thus some apertures are described as *posteriorly contracted* and *anteriorly widened*, or the reverse. A *linear* aperture is one contracted in its whole length, as in Cypræa. When the whorls are angulated, a *trigonal* aperture is the result, as in many species of Trochus. Some are *transversely oval*, that is in an opposite direction to the axis, and others *longitudinally oval*. When the whorls are formed with two outer angles, a somewhat quadrated aperture is formed. There are other variations too numerous to mention.

Apertures

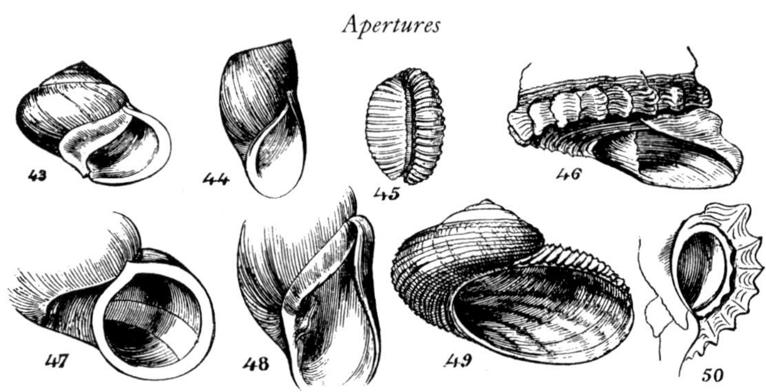

Fig. 43, Helicina, semilunar; 44, Pirena, pyriform; 45, Cypræa, linear; 46, Trochus, trigonal; 47, cyclostoma, rounded; 48, Chilina, posteriorly contracted; 49, Stomatia, transversely oval; 50, Murex, longitudinally oval.

The entire edge of the aperture described generally, is named the *Peritreme*, but this term can only be conveniently applied in cases where, in some at least of its characters, it is the same all round, so that one descriptive term is applicable to the whole. As, however, this is of rare occurrence, it is found convenient in descriptions to separate the inner from the outer lip. In a great number of instances, this is done naturally, by a canal, or notch at the anterior or lower extremity, and by the posterior union of that part which overlays the body whorl with the other portion. At these two points the outer and inner lips separate from each other: we therefore describe the

Canals of the Aperture

When there is neither notch nor canal, anteriorly or posteriorly, interrupting the edge of the aperture, it is described as *entire*. When there is a notch or sinus at the anterior extremity, it is said to be *emarginated*. When the edge of this notch is expanded, and drawn out in the form of a beak, it is said to be *canaliferous*, or to have a *canal*. When, in addition to this, the lips are thickened and contracted posteriorly near their junction, and drawn out so as to form a groove, it is said to be *bi-canaliculated*, or to have two canals. The *anterior canal* is said to be long or short, according to the proportion which it may bear to the rest of the shell. Thus the canal of Ranella ranina (fig. 393 in the plates), may be described as *short*; while that of Murex haustellum, (fig. 396, pl.) is *long*. When it is wide near the aperture, and becomes gradually contracted towards its termination, it is said to be *tapering*, as in Pyrula (fig. 388, pl.); when the termination is sudden, it is described as *truncated*. If, on placing the shell upon a plane, with the aperture downwards, the canal is seen to rise upwards, it is *recurved*. In Buccinum and Nassa it is turned suddenly over the back, and forms a short, curved elevation; it is then described as *recurved* and *varicose*. If the edges meet, so as to form a tube, it is said to be closed, as in some species of Murex and Typhis. The posterior canal is, in some cases, *free*, or standing out from the spire, as in some species of Ranellæ; while in others it is *decumbent*, running up the sides of the spire, as in Rostellaria (fig. 402, pl.).

Canals

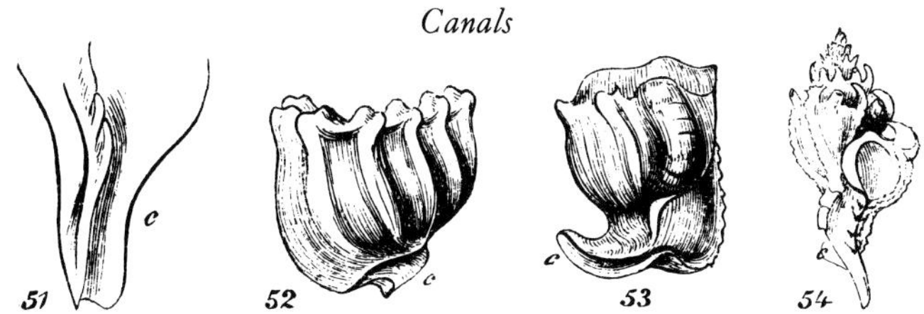

Fig. 51, Fasciolaria, truncated; 52, Nassa, recurved, varicose; 53, Cerithium, recurved; 54, Typhis, closed.

Lips, or edges of the Aperture

The part of the edge of the aperture next to the body whorl is named the *inner*, or *columellar* lip. Posteriorly it commences at the point of union with the outer lip, where that touches the body whorl, the junction being generally marked by an angle, and sometimes by a canal. Anteriorly it terminates where there is generally seen a notch or canal, or sudden angle from which the outer lip proceeds. The part which setting out from the body whorl, and proceeds outwards at a distance from the axis, till it reaches the anterior canal or notch (or its place in case of absence) is named the *outer lip*. In many cases the edges are united in such a manner, that it is difficult to distinguish where the inner lip terminates, and the outer lip commences: when this is the case, it is usual to describe the margin or peritreme, as a whole, without distinguishing the parts. The *outer* lip, sometimes called the *right* lip, or *labrum* of continental writers, is sometimes *acute*, not being of thicker substance than the remainder of the shell. In other cases it is *obtuse*, or thickened and rounded at the edge. When thickened and turned backwards it is described as *reflected*; when, on the other hand, it is turned inwards towards the axis, as in the Cyprædæ, it is *inflected*, or involute. When it is *toothed*, a distinction must be observed as to whether the dentations are external or internal. If the teeth are small and numerous, it is *denticulated*; if larger, it is *dentated*; when expanded into a kind of wing, as in some species of Strombus and Rostellaria, it is described as *alated*; and a family in Lamarck's system is named "Alatæ," from this very circumstance. In some of those which are expanded, the expansion is divided into separate, attenuated portions, they are then said to be digitated.

Outer Lips

The *inner* lip, sometimes named the *columellar* lip, or "*labium*," is subject to similar variations as to thickness, dentition, &c. That portion of it which lies upon the body whorl is frequently distinguished from that which intervenes between it and the notch or canal. De Blainville, restricting the term *lip* "bord gauche" to the former portion, applies the term "columella" to the latter; and in some instances this may be the more convenient method of describing the part in question. The columellar lip is sometimes *detached* entirely from the body of the shell, as in Murex haustellum; in others it is *decumbent*, or lying over the last whorl, although quite distinct, and in some cases, *thickened*, *callous*, or *tumid*.

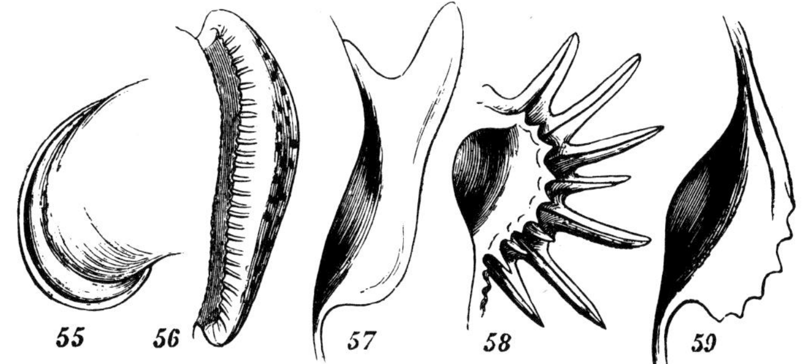

Fig. 55, Helix, reflected; 56, Cypræa, involute, denticulated; 57, Seraphs, alated; 58, Murex, digitated; 59, Rostellaria, dentated.

At the lower or anterior part, sometimes called the *columella*, there are in many instances flattened, laminated folds; these are particularly conspicuous in the genera Cymba and Melo, where, being obliquely spiral and laminar, they are extremely elegant, presenting to the eye graduated repetitions of the line of beauty. In other cases, as in the Turbinellæ, they are more horizontal and thickened.

In some cases the columella is swelled into a varicose mass; as in Oliva, Ancillaria, &c.; it is then described as *tumid* or *varicose*. It is sometimes *tortuous*, and sometimes straight, and is susceptible of many variations, too minute and particular to be described in this part of the work.

Columellar Lips

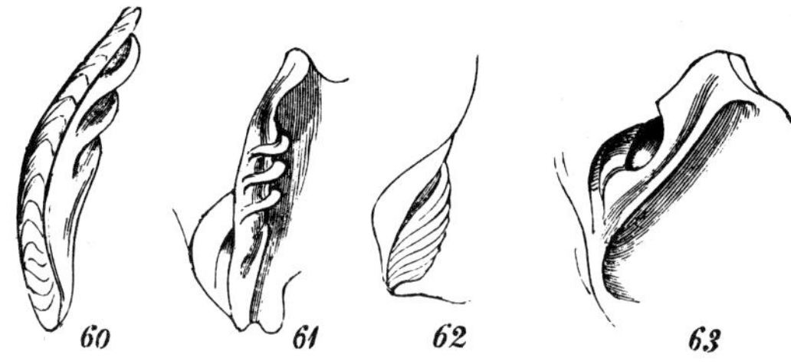

Fig. 60, Melo, obliquely plaited; 61, Turbinellus, horizontally plaited; 62, Ancillaria, varicose, tortuous; 63, Natica, straight.

OPERCULUM

The aperture of many species of shells remains constantly open; but in a great number of species it is occasionally closed, whenever the animal is retracted within the shell, by a calcareous or horny piece called the operculum. This must be distinguished in the first instance from another kind of calcareous covering, which in some univalve shells serves to close the aperture during a certain portion of the year. This piece, named the *epiphragm*, although hardened and shelly in appearance, is no real part of the animal or of the shell; being only a secretion temporarily hardened, for the purpose of defending the animal from external influences during the *hibernating or torpid* season, to be dissolved when the season is at an end. On examining this piece, it will be observed that it is not formed in regular layers like the rest of the shell; while the true operculum is of a regularly laminated structure, having a nucleus and receiving obliquely deposited additions, either in a lateral, spiral or concentric direction. It is attached to the posterior part of the foot on the upper surface; and when the animal retires within its shell, that part of the foot enters last, drawing the operculum after it, and thus closing the aperture.

Opercula of Spiral Univalves

The opercula of various shells differ in the first place as to their chemical composition. They are sometimes formed principally of calcareous matter, like the rest of the shell, as in Neritina, Nerita, and some others. They are *corneo-calcareous*, when upon an internal lamina of horn there is a thickened layer of shelly matter. This is the case with shells of the genus Turbo and Phasianella, which are on this account distinguished from those of the genus Trochus; the opercula of the latter being horny or *corneus*.

The size of the operculum is distinguished by comparison with the rest of the shell; thus, those of Strombus, Cassis, &c. are small; while those of Cyclostoma and others are large, filling up the cavity at its outer edge.

The direction in which the successive layers are deposited, forms another ground of distinction. The disc is formed in some instances of a series of whorls, the apex or nucleus being more or less central; if these whorls are numerous, the operculum is described as *multispiral*, as in shells of the genus Trochus; if few, as in Cyclostoma, it is *paucispiral*. In some instances the flattened spire consists of but one whorl, it is then *unispiral*; and when scarcely one turn is completed, it is described as *subspiral*. When the layers are applied upon each other in such a manner that the nucleus is central, and the edges of the subsequent layers are extended beyond each

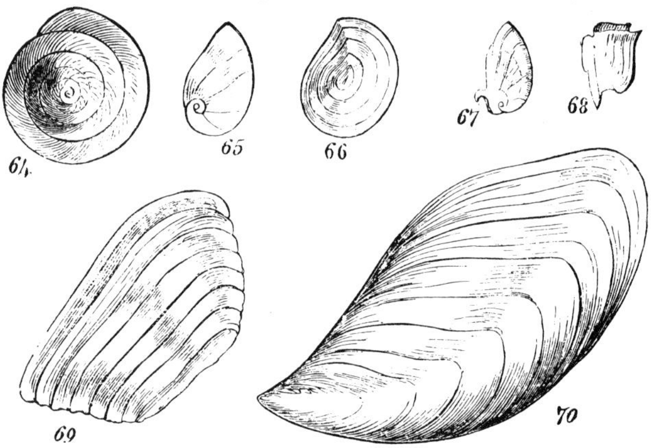

Fig. 64, multispiral; 65, paucispiral; 66, concentric; 67, articulated; 68, radiated; 69, lammellated; 70, unguiculated.

other all around, so as to form rims, the operculum is described as *concentric*; if the nucleus is lateral, or at one side without being spiral it is *lammellated*; and when it forms a terminal point, enlarging in the form of a finger-nail or claw, it is *unguiculated*. In the operculum of a Neritina, there is a lateral process, by means of which it is locked into the columella, the term *articulated* is then applied. In that of Navicella, there is also a process which appears to radiate from the nucleus, it has therefore been described as a *radiated* operculum.

BIVALVE SHELLS

Bivalve shells, named Conchacea by Lamarck, are those which consist of two principal portions united to and folded upon each other by means of a hinge. The pieces united compose the shell, while each piece separately is called a valve. Considering the bivalve shell as a whole, it will be necessary, in the first instance, to describe the position in which it is to be observed, in order to give the student a clearly defined notion of what is intended, when terms expressive of height, depth, length, breadth, &c. are used, as well as when the anterior and posterior extremities are spoken. For this purpose, we must suppose the animal to be living and creeping along the bed of the sea by means of its foot; where this foot protrudes, will be the *ventral margin*, and the opposite part the *dorsal margin* of the shell. There will then be a valve on each side; and if we further suppose the animal to be walking forward with its back to the observer, the *right* and *left* valves will correspond with his right and left sides.

Measurements

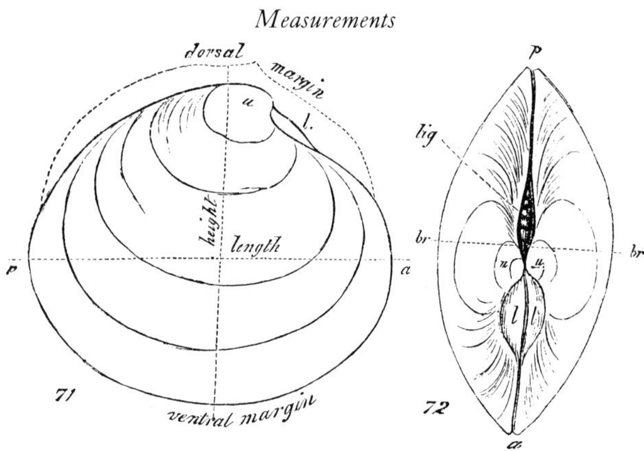

The *length* will be measured from *anterior* (*a*) to *posterior* (*p*), and the lines of growth running in the same direction will consequently be *longitudinal* or *concentric*; *transverse* of some authors. The height will be from the umbones (*u*), to the *ventral margin*, and lines or bands in that direction are termed *radiating*; longitudinal, according to some authors.

The points from which the growth of the shell commences, are called the *umbones*; these usually turn towards the anterior part of the shell: if this circumstance fails to point out the *anterior*, the opposite may in many cases be distinguished by the muscular impressions of the mantle, the sinus or winding of which, if any, is always near the *posterior* muscular impression; and in all cases where there is an external ligament, it is on the posterior side.

There is sometimes an external impression near the front of the umbones, which forms a semicircle on each valve; the space within this semicircle is called the *lunule* (wood-cut, fig. 71); a corresponding depression, when it exists on the posterior margin near the umbones, is named the *escutcheon* or *posterior area*.

Hinge

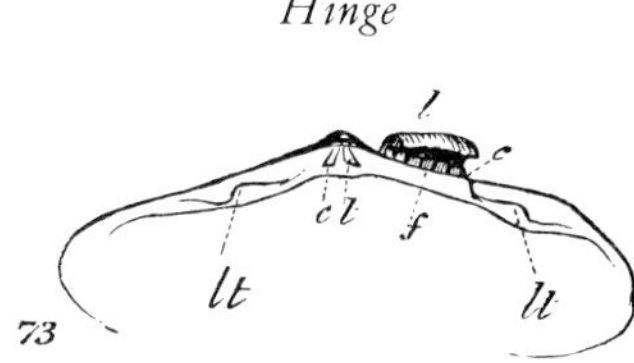

Fig. 73, l t, lateral teeth; c t, cardinal teeth; c, cartilage under the ligament; l, ligament; f, fulcrum of the ligament.

The *hinge* of the shell is on the *dorsal* margin, and is composed of the various apparatus by which the two valves act upon each other in opening and shutting. It consists of a *ligament*, which is placed on the dorsal margin, just at the back of the umbones, and unites the two valves together; and the *cartilage* or thick gristly elastic substance, sometimes found close to the *ligament*, to which it then forms an inner coating, and sometimes received into a pit within the shell. It serves the purpose of keeping the shell open when not forcibly closed by the adductor muscles. An inner layer of shelly matter upon which are placed teeth, and pits to receive them on the two valves reciprocally. Each of these it will be necessary to explain more fully; observing, at the same time, that in some species of Bivalves these parts may be wholly or partially wanting. Thus we meet with some shells, such as the Muscle, without teeth; and in the group containing Pholas, &c. the hinge is destitute of teeth and ligament, the two valves being kept together by loose cartilages, and by the stone in the hollow of which they are confined.

Ligament and Ligamentary Cartilage of the Hinge

These two distinct substances have been described by many writers, as though, composing the same mass, they were of one substance; but the difference may very easily be explained. The *true ligament* is external, being fixed on the edge of one valve behind the umbones, and passing over in an arch to the corresponding edge of the other, very correctly retaining the name of *ligament*, because it serves the purpose of binding the two together. The thick, elastic substance, which Mr. Gray names the *cartilage*, is sometimes found in connexion with the ligament, so as to form one mass with it, although it is always separable and placed within it: it is sometimes placed quite within the shell, and separated from the ligament, in a pit or hollow formed for its reception in the hinge lamina, near the centre. It is found in both valves, and being elastic, the portion in one valve presses against that in the other, so as to keep the valves apart, unless voluntarily closed by the adductor muscles of the animal. The ligament is sometimes spread over an external area, as in Arca, while the cartilage is placed in several grooves of the same area, beneath the outer covering.

Hinge lamina, Teeth and Fulcrum of the Ligament

In a great variety of cases, there is a thickening of the substance of the shell within, under the dorsal margin; this is named the hinge lamina. It is sometimes merely callous; but in many cases it has raised *teeth* in both valves, those in one valve entering into corresponding cavities in the other. Those which are placed immediately below the umbones, and seem to take their rise from beneath them, are called *cardinal teeth*; those at a distance from the umbones, which are seen to lie along the upper margin of the shell are named *lateral teeth*.

When the cardinal teeth terminate in a double point, which is not unfrequently the case, they are said to be *bifid*. The lateral teeth, in various species, are distinguished as terminating *near* to, or at a *distance* from the umbones. In the Nuculæ and Arcæ there is a row of teeth placed across the hinge lamina. In which case, the lateral cannot be distinguished from the cardinal teeth.

Muscular Impression

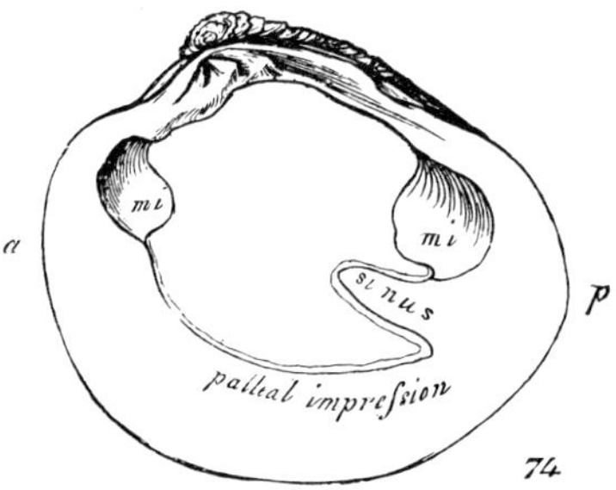

Fig. 74. a, anterior; p, posterior; m i, muscular impressions.

Lamarck divides the Bivalve shells into two general orders; the first is named "Dimyaria," having two adductor muscles; and the second, "Monomyaria," having but one. These adductor muscles are used for the purpose of drawing the valves together, being composed of contractile fibrous gristle, fastened firmly to the inner surface of each valve. The place where they are thus fixed may be seen when the animal is removed by depressed areas, which are generally pretty well defined and are named *muscular impressions*. Where there is but one adductor muscle, there will be but one of these impressions near the centre of each valve, but in the Dimyaria, where there are two, the impressions are seen, one on the anterior, and one on the posterior of each valve, just below the *hinge* lamina. They are sometimes *complex*, that is, composed of several portions in a group; but in general, they are simple and well defined.

They are also described as large or small, in proportion to the size of the shell; regular or irregular in form. The animal is attached to the inner surface by the fibrous portions of the mantle, which creates a linear impression or *cicatrix*, commonly described as the *palleal impression*, or muscular impression of the mantle. It runs near the ventral margin from one muscular impression to the other, sometimes in a smooth *continuous* line or band, and sometimes in an interrupted series of small impressions. Near the point of union with the posterior muscular impression, there is sometimes a more or less considerable winding inwards towards the centre of the shell, and back again towards the point of union. This is named the *sinus*, and is distinguished as being *angular* or *rounded*, large or small, according to the species. When it enters towards the centre of the shell in a tongue-shaped outline it is said to be *ligulate*. Where it exists it affords a certain index to the posterior side of the shell; as it is the region through which the excretory tubes pass.

Umbones

These are the prominent points of the dorsal edge, where the growth of the shell commenced, and are called beaks, by some English writers. In some instances they are close to each other; in others they are rendered distant from each other by the intervention of areas in the hinge, as in Spondyli, &c. In Pectunculus they are *straight*; in Venus *curved* towards the anterior margin; in Isocardia, *spiral*; in Chama, spirally *decumbent*; in Diceras, *free*. In shells subject to external corrosion, the process commences at the umbones.

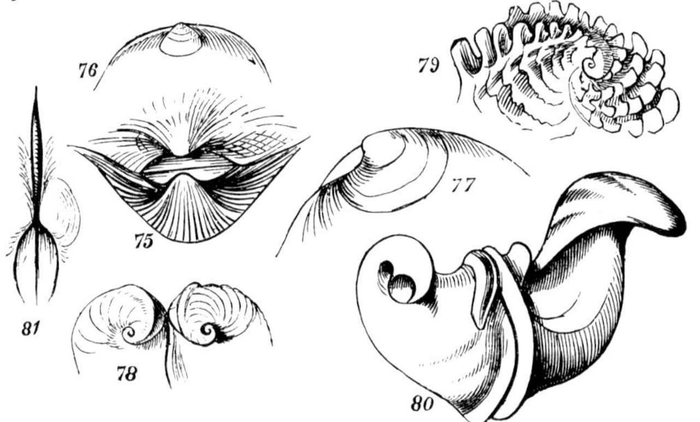

Fig. 75, distant; 76, straight; 77, curved; 78, spiral; 79, decumbent; 80, free; 81, close.

GENERAL CHARACTER OF BIVALVES

When the *breadth* is spoken of, the distance between the most convex parts of both valves, when closed, is intended; but when an expression implying *thickness* is used, it refers to the substance of each valve: it is important to bear this in mind, as many persons have been misled by descriptions in which the distinction has not been attended to. Glycimeris (fig. 67 in the plates) is a *thick* shell, but Anatina (fig. 69 in the plates) is a *broad* one.

Regularity

A great number of Bivalves are extremely regular in their form. Their animals are generally locomotive, and the shells consequently free from those obstructions in growth which occur to stationary shells. The latter, being confined to a particular position, or particular spot, modify their shape according to the substance with which they come in contact, and thus become irregular. This is generally the case with shells which are attached to submarine substances, such as Spondyli, Oysters, &c.; and the degree of irregularity will depend upon the extent of surface involved in the attachment. In the case of fixed shells, the attached valve is usually termed the under valve, and the other which moves freely upon the hinge, is termed the upper valve.

Form and Proportions

Bivalves are said to be *equivalve* when the two valves correspond in extent, breadth, and thickness; and of course *inequivalve* in the contrary case. They are *equilateral* when a line drawn from the umbones to the ventral margin would divide the shell into two nearly equal parts; and of course *inequilateral* in the opposite case, which occurs in the great majority of instances.

A Bivalve is said to be *compressed*, when the distance is small from the most prominent part of one valve to that of the other. It is *cylindrical* when lengthened, and more or less rounded in its breadth, as in Lithodomus (fig. 161 in the plates.) It is *cordiform* when the shape presents a resemblance to an imaginary heart, as in Cardium cardissa (fig. 122 in the plates), and in the Isocardia (fig. 126 in the plates). It is *linguiform* when it resembles a tongue in shape, as in Vulsella (fig. 185 in the plates); *rostrated* when it protrudes at either extremity, and terminates in a kind of point, as in Sanguinolaria Diphos (fig. 99 in the plates); *truncated* when it ends in a square or angle, as if cut off; an example of which may be seen in Solen (fig. 60 in the plates).

Other Bivalves are distinguished as being *auriculated*, or having processes flattened and expanded on either side of the umbones, as in Pecten (cut, fig. 82). When there is one of these on each side of the umbones, it is *bi-auriculated*; when only on one side, it is *uni-auriculated*. When the expansion is very broad, as in Unio alatus (fig. 142 in the plates), and in the Hammer Oyster (cut, fig. 83), the term *alated* is used.

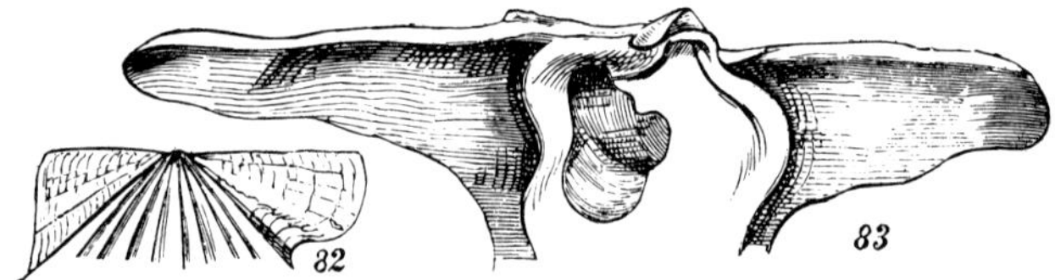

Fig. 82, auriculated; 83, auriculated, alated.

With regard to these alated species of *Uniones*, it is necessary to observe that they are also "*adnate*," as it is termed; the two valves being joined to each other by the dorsal edge of the expanded parts, and united so completely in substance with each other, that they cannot be separated without being broken. Many other terms are used to express differences in Bivalves, but being equally applicable to Univalves and Multivalves, as well as to them, they will be explained at large in the alphabetical part of the work.

MULTIVALVE SHELLS

These are of three different kinds; the first, the "*dorsal*" as they are termed by Linnæus, because they form a ridge in the back of the animal. They are composed of eight pieces, or separate valves, placed in a longitudinal series, being joined to each other by inserted lamina, and named *Articulata* by De Blainville, on that account. The genus Chiton is the only example of this kind of Multivalve.

The second kind, not shells of true Mollusca, M. De Blainville terms the *lateral* bivalves, the pieces being placed in pairs on each side of the animal; these compose the "Pedunculated Cirripedes," or Lepadæ.

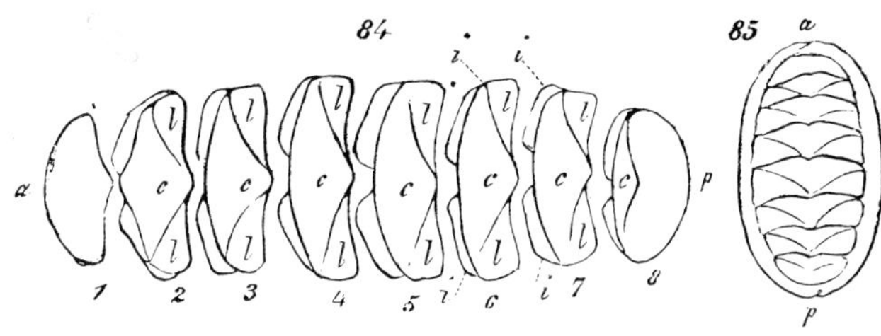

Fig. 84, 85, Chiton. a, anterior; p, posterior; d, dorsal ridge; l l, lateral areas of the valves; c c, central areas; i i, inserted lamina; m, margin.

They differ considerably in the number and arrangement of the valves; the small ones, which are found near the peduncle in some species, are sometimes termed accessary valves; those which form the edge through which the bunch of Cilia protrude, are termed *ventral*, and those on the opposite side *dorsal*. The extremity joining the peduncle is the basal, or anterior; and the upper extremity is the apicial, or posterior.

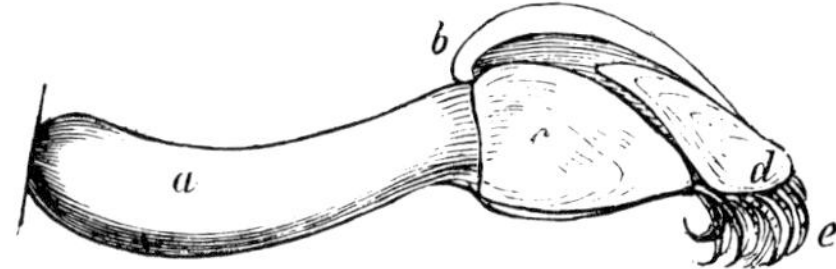

Fig. 86, Lepas. a, peduncle; b, cavina; c, scutum; d, tergam; e, cirri.

The third kind are termed *coronular* by De Blainville, and compose the order Sessile Cirripedes of Lamarck; they consist of a number of valves placed against each other side by side in a circle, supported on a plate, or tube, or cup, and closed by an operculum composed of two or more valves.

The *basal support* is sometimes thick and flat, sometimes forming an elongated tube, and sometimes hollowed out into a cup. In other species it is altogether wanting. The operculum always consists of more than one piece, generally of two pairs: they are either articulated to each other by serrated edges, and placed against each other conically, as in Balanus, or they lie flat in two pairs against each other. Through the ventral pair the *cirri* protrude.

The *parietal* valves, composing the principal part of the shell, vary in number, form and position. The *anterior* valves are placed on the same side with the cirri; the *posterior*, those on the opposite side; and those which remain between on each side are the lateral valves. In many cases, particularly in Balanus, each valve is separated into the *prominent* and *depressed* areas, and the inserted

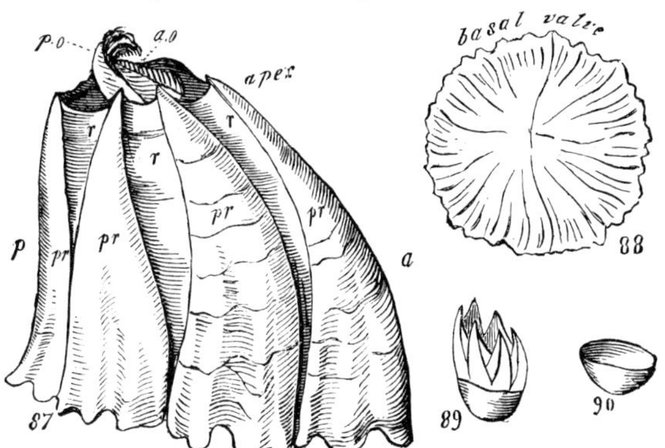

lamina. In some instances, the parietal portion is formed by a single rounded piece.

In the accompanying cut (87), the prominent areas are distinguished by the letters *pr*, and the depressed areas by *r*; the posterior valves of the operculum are marked *p. o.*, and the anterior *a. o.* The basal valve (fig. 88) belongs to a Balanus. Fig. 89 is an Acasta, the cup-shaped base of which is represented at fig. 90.

In the foregoing explanations we have omitted many of those general terms which, relating to external characters, are applicable to shells in almost every division of the system. It may be as well, however, to enumerate a few of them in this place, although they are explained under their respective letters in the alphabetical part of the work.

When bars or ribs, or large striæ are crossed by others radiating from the umbones, shells are said to be *cancellated*, as represented in cut, fig. 91. When there is a series of nodules or spines on the upper part of the whorls, they are *coronated*, as shewn in cut, fig. 92. When a series of projecting parts overlay each other, in the manner of tiles, as in the cut, fig. 93, the word *imbricated* is applied. When characterized by a regular series of ridges, radiating from the apex, they are *pectinated*; the species of Chiton, a single valve of which is represented in cut, fig. 94, has received the specific name of *pectinatus*, in consequence of this character. Shells are said to be *plicated* when characterized by angular bendings or foldings in their surface, as shewn in cut, fig. 95. A remarkable instance of this is seen in the Ostræa Crista-Galli. When the margin of any shell has a series of minute notches, resembling the teeth of a saw, it is said to be *serrated*; when covered with raised points or spines it is *aculeated*; and when striated in both directions, it is *decussated*; when covered with a number of raised rounded points, it is *granulated*; and having a series of these points placed in a row, near or upon the edge, it is *denticulated*, as already explained in reference to the outer lips of

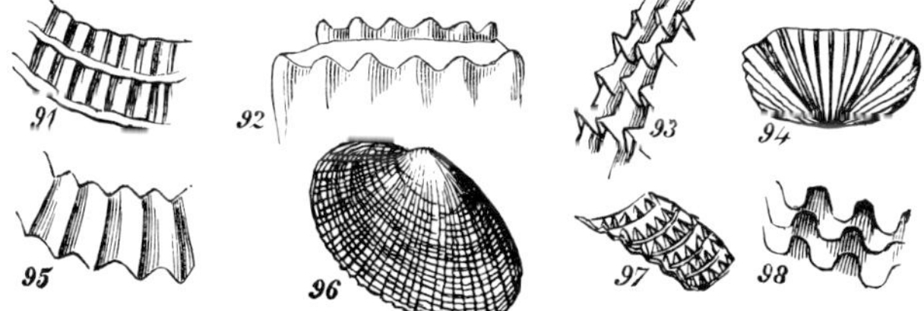

External surface. Fig. 91, cancellated; 92, coronated; 93, imbricated; 94, pectinated; 95, plicated; 96, decussated; 97, muricated; 98, foliated.

Spiral Univalves. When the external surface is rendered uneven by raised knobs, it is said to be *tuberculated*; and if rendered rough and prickly by sharp points it is *muricated*, as in the cut, fig. 97. The term *reticulated* is applied to fine raised lines, crossing each other, and resembling fine net work.

By the foregoing general observations and explanations, it is trusted that the reader will be prepared for the following exposition of the general arrangement of Lamarck, and the principles upon which it is founded.

GENERAL ARRANGEMENT ACCORDING TO LAMARCK

In Lamarck's "Histoire Naturelle des Animaux sans Vertebres," he divides the invertebrata into classes, the 9th, 10th and 11th of which include animals possessed of shells properly so called. These are the Annelides, the Cirripedes, the Conchifera, and the Mollusca.

The class Annelides constitutes the 9th, and is divided into three orders, namely, the "Apodes," "Antennees," and "Sedentaires;" the last of which, the *Sedentaria*, alone contains testaceous animals. This order includes tubular shells, which with the exception of Dentalium, are irregularly twisted, and attached to each other, or to extraneous substances. The first family, *Dorsalia*, contains the genus Siliquaria (plates, fig. 1), known from the Serpulæ, by the slit which passes through the whole length of the shell on the upper surface of the tube. The second family, *Maldania*, has the genus Dentalium (plates, fig. 2), a species of which are commonly known by the name of "tooth shells;" these are regularly formed, curved, conical tubes, open at both extremities. The third family, *Serpulacea*, includes the genera Serpula, Spirorbis, Galeolaria, Vermilia, Spiroglyphus, and Magilus. The only shell that a learner would be likely to place among these incorrectly, according to the system, is the Vermetus (plates, fig. 345), which being regularly spiral at the apicial extremity, has been placed among the Mollusca; to which situation the whole of the shells under consideration have a better title than is generally supposed. It may here be mentioned that the Serpulacea are provided with opercula.

Class Cirripedes

This class constitutes the tenth of invertebrated animals and receives its name from the jointed and ciliated branchia which protrude between the opercular valves. They are Multivalve shells, and were all included in the single genus Lepas in the system of Linnæus, and are commonly known by the name "Barnacles." Lamarck has, however, divided them into two distinct orders. First, the *Sessile* Cirripedes, or those which being composed of several valves, joined to each other, side by side in a circle, are attached to each other, or to submarine bodies by the basal portion of their own substance, and form a hollow, irregular cone, with the aperture above closed by an operculum consisting of two or more valves. Secondly, the *Pedunculated Cirripedes*, which are composed of valves placed in pairs against each other, so as to form a flattened disc attached by means of a tendinous tube called a peduncle. The first of these orders includes the genera Tubicinella, Coronula, Platylepas, Clitia, Conia, Elmineus, Catophragmus, Octomeris, Balanus, Creusia, Nobia, Savignium, Pyrgoma, Adna, Megatréma. The second contains the genera Sepas, Scalpellum, Alepas, Pollicipes, Anelepas, Lithotrya, Ibla, Conchoderma, Dichelaspis.

The study of this class is not properly connected with Conchology. It is now regarded as a sub-class of Crustacea.

Class Conchifera

The shell of a conchiferous animal is always bivalve, composed of two pieces placed opposite to each other, joined at the dorsal margins by an elastic hinge. All true bivalve shells belong to animals of this class; and the correspondence between the shell and the animal is so true that on examining an empty bivalve shell we can not only determine that its inhabitant belonged to this class, but also decide on the particular order and family in which it should be placed, without seeing the soft parts.

The first general division of Conchifera is that which results from observing the muscular impressions, or marks made on the inner surface of the valve by the insertion of the adductor muscles. All Conchifera are divided into two orders, as follows:

First Order, *Conchifera Dimyaria*

Having two adductor muscles, and consequently two impressions in each valve. They are separated into the following families:

1. *Tubicolæ* (plates, fig. 44 to 54), having shelly tubes besides the valves. This family contains the genera Aspergillum, Clavagella, Teredina, Teredo, Xylophaga, Fistulana, and Gastrochæna.
2. *Pholadaria* (plates, fig. 55 to 59), cylindrical, living in holes in rocks pierced by animals. Lamarck places in this family the genera Pholas and Gastrochæna, the last of which belongs more properly to the family Tubicolæ, as placed above.
3. *Solenaceæ* (plates, fig. 60 to 68), longitudinally (transversely, Lam.) elongated, open at the anterior and posterior extremities. This family contains the genera Solen, Pholadomya, Panopæa, Glycimeris, (Solecurtus) and Solenimya.
4. *Myaria* (plates, fig. 69 to 76), ligament internal. A spoon-shaped ligamentary pit in one or both valves. Shell generally gaping at one or both extremities. This family includes the genera Anatina, Mya, Anatinella, Kelladiæ, Lyonsia, Myochama, Cleidotherus.
5. *Matracea* (plates, fig. 77 to 88), the cartilage placed in a trigonal pit, with a small external ligament. The genera Lutraria, Mactra, Crassatella, Erycina, Ungulina, Amphidesma, and Solenimya belong to this family, the last of which ought to have been placed among the Solenacea, as above.
6. *Corbulacea* (plates, fig. 89, 90), inequivalve, with an internal ligament resembling the Mactracea, but differing in having one valve deeper than the other, although regular shells. This small family contains only the genera Corbula and Pandora.
7. *Lithophagidæ* (plates, fig. 91 to 97), irregular, terebrating, living in holes of rocks. The genera are Saxicava, Petricola, and Venerirupis.

8. *Nymphacea* (plates, fig. 98 to 110), ligament external, generally placed upon a prominent fulcrum, which passes from the inside to the outside of the hinge; valves generally gaping at the extremities. This family contains the genera Sanguinolaria, Psammobia, Psammotæa, Tellinides, Corbis, Lucina, Donax, Capsa, and Crassina.
9. *Conchacea* (plates, fig. 111 to 121), regular, having several cardinal teeth and sometimes lateral teeth. The Conchacea constitute one of the most beautiful and numerous families of the class; they present equivalve shells, which are always regular, unattached, and in general closed, especially at the sides; they are always more or less inequilateral. They are divided into the *fluviatile* and *marine Conchacea*, the first containing the genera Cyclas, Cyrena, and Galathæa, found in rivers; and the second, Cyprina, Cytherea, Venus, and Venericardia.
10. *Cardiacea* (plates, fig. 122 to 130). This family, which resembles the last in some general characters, are also regular and equivalve, and are generally provided with radiating ribs, which are seldom seen in the Conchacea. The genera enumerated in this family are Cardium, Cardita, Cypricardia, Hiatella, and Isocardia.
11. *Arcacea* (plates, fig. 131 to 138). These are known by having a row of numerous small teeth on the cardinal hinge in each valve. The genera included are, Cucullæa, Arca, Pectunculus, Nucula.
12. *Trigonacea* (plates, fig. 139 and 140). It is doubtful whether this family should remain distinct. As of the two genera placed in it, the first Trigonia, is thought by some naturalists to have strong affinities with Nucula, in the family of Arcacea; and the latter, Castalia, certainly belongs to the Nayades.
13. *Nayades* (plates, fig. 141 to 152). These are fresh water shells, covered on the outside by a thick horny epidermis, and pearly within. They include the genera Unio, Hyria, Anodon, Iridina.
14. *Chamacea* (plates, fig. 153 to 155), inequivalve, irregular, foliaceous, attached; containing the genera Diceras, Chama and Etheria.

Second Order, *Conchiferra Monomyaria*

Having one adductor muscle, and therefore only one impression in each valve. They are separated into the following families:

1. *Tridacnacea* (plates, fig. 156 & 157), transverse, equivalve, with an elongated muscular impression, near the centre of the ventral margin; margin undulated at the termination of the radiated large ribs. The genera Tridacna and Hippopus are included.
2. *Mytilacea* (plates, fig. 158 to 162), generally regular, with the hinge linear, without teeth, occupying the greater part of the dorsal margin. This family includes the genera Modiola, Mytilus, Pinna.
3. *Malleacea* (plates, fig. 163 to 170), shell generally thin, inequivalve, irregular, foliaceous, with the hinge linear. This family contains the genera Crenatula, Perna, Malleus, Avicula, Meleagrina.
4. *Pectinides* (plates, fig. 171 to 178). The pectinides are generally regular or nearly so, with the shell solid; the greater part of them are auriculated at the dorsal margin, and generally characterized by ribs radiating from the umbones. The genera are Pedum, Lima, Plagiostoma, Pecten, Plicatula, Spondylus, Podopsis.
5. *Ostracea* (plates, fig. 180 to 192). The shells of this family are irregular, generally attached and foliaceous. They compose the genera Gryphæa, Ostræa, Vulsella, Placuna, Anomia.
6. *Rudistes* (plates 193 to 200). This family is composed of a particular association of shells, which appear on one side to be connected with the Ostracea; and on the other to approach the Brachiopoda. They differ from Ostracea in having no hinge or ligament, and only resemble them in their irregularity and foliaceous structure. The following six genera are placed by Lamarck in this family:—Sphærulites, Radiolites, Calceola, Birostrites, Discina, Crania. Of these, Calceola, Discina, and Crania are shewn to belong to the Brachiopoda.
7. *Brachiopoda* (plates, fig. 201 to 219). The shells of this family are inequivalve, equilateral, and attached to marine bodies by a tendon passing through one of the valves. The animals have, near their mouth, two elongated, ciliated arms, which are spirally rolled when at rest. The following genera are enumerated by Lamarck, Orbicula, Terebratula, Lingula.

MOLLUSCA

Lamarck applies, or rather restricts, this name to those invertebrated animals, which while they are inarticulate in all their parts, have the head sufficiently advanced at the anterior part of the body to be distinguished; which is not the case with the Conchifera. All the shells are univalve, and are divided into six orders, namely, the Pteropoda, which have wing-shaped natatory organs or fins, and have *light, thin transparent, nearly symmetrical* shells; the Gasteropoda, with the foot not distinguishable from the rest of the body, have *patelliform, open* and *scarcely spiral* shells; the Trachelipoda with the foot distinct and attached to the neck of the animal, have *spiral, non-symmetrical* shells. The Cephalopoda, with arms covered by suckers, surrounding the head of the animal, have generally *symmetrical convolute* shells. The Cephalopoda are divided into C. *polythalamia*, which have the internal cavity divided into chambers by septa, as in the Nautilus; and the C. *Monothalamia*, which are not so divided, as the Argonauta. The order *Heteropoda* contains the genus Carinaria alone.

Order *Pteropoda*

This order, containing hyaline, symmetrical, non-spiral shells, as above described, is not divided into families, but contains the following genera, Hyalæa, Cleodora, Limacina, Cymbulia; the first of which, although composed of a single piece, resembles a bivalve so nearly, that Linnæus actually placed it in his genus Anomia.

Order *Gasteropoda*

With the exception of the genus Bulla and Vitrina, the last of which forms a passage into the next order, the shells contained in this order are *patelliform, open, and scarcely spiral*. They are divided into the following families:

1. *Phyllidiana* (plates, fig. 227 to 231), containing the genera Chiton, Chitonellus, and Patella, the two former of which present the only exception to the statement above made, that all the shells of Mollusca were univalve.
2. *Semiphyllidiana* (plates, fig. 232 and 233). Of the two genera contained in this family, Pleurobranchus is broad, thin, and slightly spiral at the apex, and Umbrella is flat, circular, with a central apex.
3. *Calyptracea* (plates, fig. 234 to 246). The patelliform shells of this family, although united by no other general characters, are brought together by the characters of the animals which produce them. The genera are Parmophorus, Emarginula, Siphonaria, Fissurella, Pileopsis, Calyptræa, Crepidula, Ancylus.
4. *Bulleana* (plates, fig. 247 to 258), contains the genera Bulla and Bullæa.
5. *Aplysiacea* (plates, fig. 254 and 255). The genera Aplysia and Dolabella are both expanded, somewhat flattened shells, with the apex placed at one extremity, and slightly spiral.
6. *Limacinea* (fig. 256 to 263). Many of the animals (slugs) are without shells; some, as the Limax, or common garden slug, have a slightly developed calcareous piece, hidden beneath the mantle, and of others the shells are scarcely spiral. The genera included in this family are, Parmacella, Limax, Testacella, Vitrina.

Order *Trachelipoda*

All the remaining spiral non-symmetrical shells are arranged in this order, which is divided into the following families:

1. *Colimacea* (plates, fig. 264 to 307). With the exception of the few contained in the family of Limacina, which ought not to be separated from this order, the whole of the land-shells are contained in this family, and although it is difficult to notice any one character by which terrestrial shells may be distinguished from others, few at all conversant with the subject are liable to mistake them. There is a general lightness and simplicity of form, which, though not clearly definable, is generally understood. The following distribution of genera by Lamarck, is generally acknowledged to require numerous modifications; the genera are Helix, Carocolla, Anostoma, Helicina, Pupa, Clausilia, Bulinus, Achatina, Succinea, Auricula, Cyclostoma.
2. *Lymneana* (plates, fig. 308 to 312). The shells of this family are found in fresh water, wells, ditches, and ponds. They are of a light horny structure, and simple form. The genera Planorbis, Physa, and Lymnea are placed in this family by Lamarck.
3. *Melaniana* (plates, fig. 313 to 317). These are also found in fresh water, principally in rivers; they are thicker than those of the last family; and the greater part of them have elevated spires composed of numerous whorls. This family contains the genera Melania, Melanopsis, Pirena.
4. *Peristomata* (plates, fig. 318 to 322). These are also fresh-water shells, having opercula, and covered by a smooth green, or greenish-brown epidermis. They differ from the last family in having the peritreme entire. The genera are Valvata, Paludina, and Ampullaria.
5. *Neritacea* (plates, fig. 323 to 333). The peculiarity of the shells of this family consist in the inner lip being flattened and rather straight at the inner edge. The genera are Navicella, Neritina, Nerita, Natica, and Janthina, the last of which forms an exception to the general character, and is placed by De Blainville in a family by itself.
6. *Macrostomata* (plates, fig. 334 to 341), so named, on account of the large open aperture which they present in comparison to the spire. The shells of this family, which contains the genera Stomatia, Stomatella, and Haliotis, are pearly within.
7. *Plicacea* (plates, fig. 342 to 344), contains the genera Tornatella and Pyramidella.
8. *Scalariana* (plates, fig. 345 to 352). The genera Vermetus, Scalaria and Delphinula, seem to have been placed in this family, by Lamarck, on account of the whorls being distinct from each other.
9. *Turbinacea* (plates, 353 to 371). The shells contained in this family are all more or less globose, or angular, thickened and pearly within. The following genera are included in this division by Lamarck, Solarium, Rotella, Trochus, Monodonta, Turbo, Planaxis, Phasianella, and Turritella.
10. *Canalifera* (plates, fig. 372 to 401). The numerous genera of which this family is formed, namely, Cerithium, Pleurotoma, Turbinella, Cancellaria, Fasciolaria, Fusus, Pyrula, Ranella, Murex, Triton, are distinguished by having at the anterior termination of the aperture, a more or less elongated canal.
11. *Alatæ* (plates, fig. 402 to 406). These are known by having the outer lip more or less expanded and generally a posterior canal leaning towards the spire. The genera are Rostellaria, Strombus, and Pteroceras.
12. *Purpurifera* (plates, fig. 407 to 429). In these, the canal, if such it may be called, is extremely short, and turning abruptly backwards, produces a kind of varix at the lower part of the whorl. The genera enumerated in this family are Cassidaria,

Cassis, Ricinula, Purpura, Monoceras, Concholepas, Harpa, Dolium, Buccinum, Eburna, Terebra.

13. *Columellata* (plates, fig. 430 to 433). The shells of this family are emarginated at the anterior extremity of the aperture, and the inner lip is characterized by plates or folds, which with the exception of those on Columbella are distinct. The genera are Mitra, Voluta, Marginella, Volvaria, Columbella, the latter of which would be better placed among the Purpurifera.
14. *Convolutæ* (plates, fig. 444 to 462). The well-known shells contained in this family are distinguished for the small proportion of the spire, if any, which remains uncovered by the last whorl. They might be well divided into two groups, the first containing the genera Ovulum and Cypræa, under the name of Cypræadæ, which are truly convolute, having the spire entirely hidden; and the second containing the genera Oliva, Ancillaria, and Conus.

Order *Polythalamous, or Chambered Cephalopoda*

The greater part of the shells belonging to this order are symmetrical, and the internal cavity is divided into separate compartments, by plates called *Septa*. It is divided into the following families:

1. *Orthocerata* (plates, fig. 463 to 470), containing the genera Belemnites, Orthoceras, Nodosaria, Hippurites, And Conilites. Hippurites certainly has no affinity with the Cephalopoda, but is ascertained to be a bivalve shell, properly belonging to the family Rudistes; the other genera are straight, elongated, and conical.
2. *Lituacea* (plates, fig. 471), containing the genera Spirula, Spirulina, and Lituola, the two latter of which are microscopic.
3. *Cristacea, containing the microscopic genera Renulina, Orbiculina, and Cristellaria.*
4. *Spherulacea*, containing the microscopic genera Miliola, Gyrogona, and Melonia.
5. *Radiolacea*, containing the microscopic genera Rotalites, Lenticulina, Placentula.
6. *Nautilacea* (plates, fig. 472 to 476). This family contains the following genera—Discorbites, Siderolites, Polystomella, Vorticialis, Nummulites, and Nautilus; the two latter of which alone are now received in cabinets of shells, the four former belonging to that class of microscopic fossils, now termed Foraminifera; the genus Nummulites, although large, may probably belong to the same class, and perhaps it would have been better to have included the remaining genus, Nautilus, in the next family, from which it differs in having the septa which divided the chambers simple at their edges.
7. *Ammonacea* (plates, fig. 477 to 484). The edges of the septa of these are all more or less sinuous and complicated. This family contains the following genera, Ammonites, Ammonoceras, Baculites, and Turrilites, the latter of which presents a singular anomaly in having an oblique spire, like that of the order Trachelipoda, while it is divided into chambers by sinuous septa.

Order *Monothalamous Cephalopoda*

The only shells included in this order belong to the genera Argonauta (plates, fig. 485), placed here by Lamarck, and Bellerophon (plates, fig. 486 and 487), a fossil genus subsequently added.

Order *Heteropoda*

The singular and beautiful transparent shell contained in this order, under the generic name Carinaria, forms a covering to a small portion of an animal, equally remarkable and equally distinct from those of all other orders.

The above arrangement, although far from perfect and requiring numerous modifications, is perhaps liable to as few objections as any other yet proposed, and will certainly be more easily understood by those who have not the opportunity of studying the soft parts of the animal.

Class, ANNELIDES

Order, Sedentaria

Fam. Dorsalia

FIG.

1. Siliquaria anguina. Agathirses, Montf.

Fam. Maldania

2. Dentalium octogonum.
3. Pharetrium fragile, with the outer tube broken. Cæcum, fig. 565. To be added to this family.

Fam. Serpulacea

4. Serpula bicarinata.
5. Spirobis Nautiloides, on sea-weed.
6. Galeolaria decumbens, on a Conia.
7. Vermilia triquetra.
8. Spiroglyphus, on a portion of Patella.
9. Magilus antiquus, old shell. Campulotus, Guild. (from Guerin.)
10. The same, in a young state.
11. Leptoconchus striatus.
12. Stylifer astericola.
13. The same, in a portion of Star-fish.

Class, CIRRIPEDES

Order, Sessile Cirripedes

14. Tubicinella Balænarum.
15. Coronula Testudinaria. Chelonobia, Leach, Astrolepas, Kelin.
16. ——Balænaris. Cetopirus, Ranz.
17. ——diadema. Diadema, Ranz.
18. Chthalamus, Ranz. (from Blainville.)
19. Platylepas pulchra, Leach. One valve separate, showing the inside.
20. Clitia Verruca, Leach. Octhosia, Ranz. Verruca, Schum.
21. Conia porosa. Teraclita, Schum.
22. Elminius Leachii.
23. Catophragmus imbricatus, (from Sowerby's Genera.)
24. Octomeris angulosus, (from Sow. Gen.)
25. Balanus tintinnabulum.
26. ——Montagui. Acasta, Leach.
27. ——galeatus, Conoplæa, Say.
28. Creusia gregaria. *b*. showing the internal structure.
29. Nobia grandis.
30. Savignium crenatum.
31. Pyrgoma cancellata
32. Adna Anglicum.
33. Megatrema semicostata.

(30–33: Pyrgoma, Auct.)

Daracia, fig. 489, 490. To be added to this family.

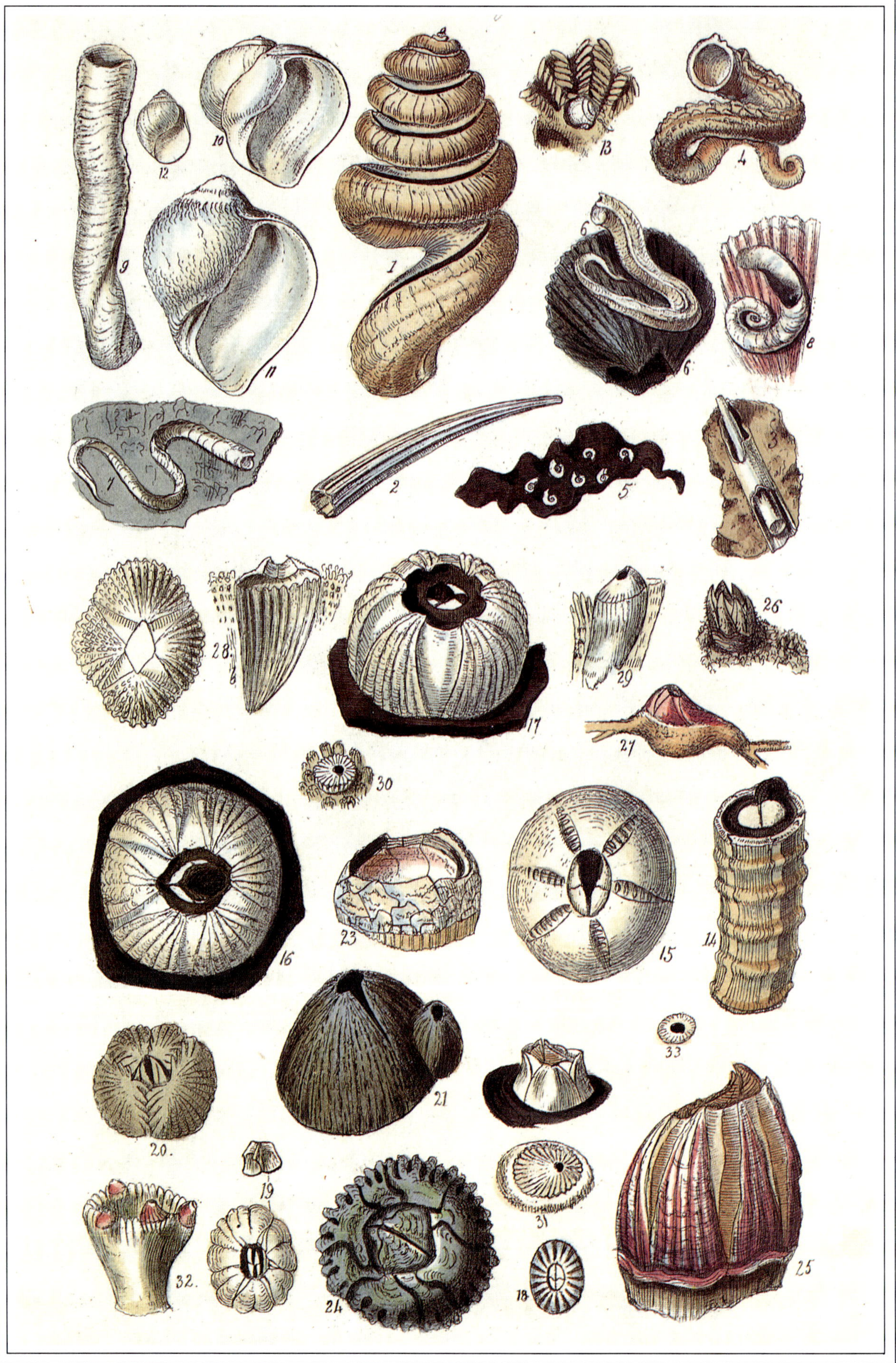

CONCHOLOGICAL MANUAL

ABIDA. Leach, 1819. A genus founded on a species of Pupa, which has the peristome slightly reflected, and numerous plaits in the aperture. Pupa Juniperi, Pupa secale, *Draparnaud*. Great Britain; also Central and Southern Europe.

ABRA. Leach, 1817. *Fam*. Mactracea. A genus composed of Amphidesma tenue, *Lamarck*, prismaticum, and other small thin species. British Channel and Mediterranean. Pl. xxiv. f. 496.

ABSIA. Leach. Lithotrya, Sowerby. *Fam*. Pedunculated Cirripedes.

ACAMAS. Montfort. Belemnites multiforatus, Blainville. A species described as being perforated at the apex, by a stellated perforation. No species of Belemnite at present known agreeing with the description; it is supposed to have been taken from a broken specimen.

ACANTHIZA. Fischer. Monoceras, *Lamarck*.

ACANTHOCHETES. Leach, 1819. A name given to Chitones, having bunches of bristles at the sides of the valves. Ex. Ch. fascicularis, Pl. xxiv. fig. 506.

ACANTHOPLEURA. Guilding, 1835. A generic name given to species of Chiton having bristles on the margin. Ex. Ch. spinosus, f. 227.

ACARDO. Lam. 1801. Umbrella. Lam. 1812.

ACARDO. Commerçon. Described from a pair of bony plates, taken from the vertebræ of the Whale, and mistaken for a bivalve shell, destitute of a hinge.

ACARDO. Swainson. See Aphrodite, Lea. C. Greenlandicum, Pl. vi, fig. 123*.

ACASTA. Leach. *Order*, Sessile Cirripedes, *Lamarck*. Balanus *Montagui*, Sowerby. A small genus separated from Balanus, on account of the cup-shaped base, but re-united by Sowerby, who shews, in his Genera of Shells, that this is a merely accidental circumstance, resulting from the situations in which the shells acquire their growth. If, for instance, the Balanus be attached to a flat surface, in an open situation, the base will be short and flat; if it be placed in a hollow among other growing substances, it will be lengthened out in order that the aperture of the shell may be even with the outer surface of the surrounding mass; and if, as in the Acastæ, it be imbedded in a soft and loose substance, the base, being left to itself, will take a regular form. The Acastæ are found imbedded in sponges. Also found in the Pacific ocean and Philippines. *Ex*. Balanus Montagui, of Great Britain, Pl. i. fig. 26.

ACAVUS. Montfort, 1810. *Fam*. Limacinea, Blainville; Colimacea, Lamarck. A division of the genus Helix, which may be considered synonymous with De Ferrusac's sub-genus Helicogena. De Montfort has given H. Hæmastoma, as an example. Plate xiii. fig. 267.

ACCESSARY VALVES, are the smaller or less important testaceous plates, found on the hinge or dorsal margins of the true valves of some shells. Example, the small plates on the hinge of Pholas, fig. 55, *a*. The Pholades were placed by Linnæus and Bruguière among multivalve shells.

ACEPHALOPHORA. Blainville (*a*, without; κεφαλε, head.) The third class of the type Malacozoaria, Bl. including all bivalve shells, the animals of which have no distinct head. This class corresponds with the Conchifera of Lamarck, and is divided into the orders Palliobranchiata, Rudistes, Lamellibranchiata, and Heterobranchiata, the last of which contains no genera of testaceous Mollusca.

ACHATINA. Auctorum. *Fam*. Colimacea, Lam. (from Achates, an agate.) *Fam*. Limacineæ, Bl. *Gen*. Polyphemus, Montf.—*Descr*. Shell oval or oblong, sub-turrited, light, thin; aperture oval, or pyriform; outer lip sharp; columella smooth, tortuous, truncated, so as to form a notch at its union with the outer lip.—*Obs*. It is from this notch that we are enabled to distinguish Achatinæ from Bulini, which, moreover, generally have a reflected outer lip. The Polyphemi of Montfort have an undulation in the centre of the outer lip. Achatina Virginea, fig. 286. Polyphemus Glans, fig. 288. These land shells are found in various parts of the globe, but attain the greatest size and richness of colouring in tropical climates; particularly in the West India Islands. Mr. Reeve's monograph contains 129 species. Subulina, f. 514, has an elongated spire, it is otherwise an Achatina. Pl.

ACHATINELLA. Swainson, 1828. A genus of shells, differing from Achatina in having the inner edge of the outer lip thickened, and a slight groove near the suture of the spire. Reeve's monograph contains 45 species. Fig. 287.

ACHELOIS. Montf. Conilites Achelois. Knorr. Supp. T.4. fig. 1.

ACICULA. Risso, 1826. Achatina Acicula, Auct. Cionella, Jeffreys.

ACIONA. Leach, 1815. Scalaria, Lamarck, 1801.

ACMÆA. Pattelloidea, Gray. Lottia, Gray.

ACME. Hartmann. A genus formed of Turbo fuscus, Walker. Auricula lineata, Drap. thus described—"Shell sub-cylindrical, with a blunt tip; mouth ovate, simple, thin, slightly reflected over the pillar, forming a slight perforation." The animal is said to resemble a Cyclostoma, but has no operculum. Auricula lineata, Drap. Hist. 57, t.3, fig. 20, 21. Southern Europe.

ACTEON. Montf. Tornatella, Lam.

ACTINOCAMAX. Stokes. A genus of Belemnitiform Fossils.

ACULEATED. Beset with sharp spines, as the margin of Chiton aculeatus, fig. 227.

ACUMINATED. Terminating in a point, as the apex of Melania subulata, fig. 313.

ACUS. Humphrey. Terebra of Lamarck.

ACUTE. Sharp, pointed, or sharp-edged.

ADDUCTOR MUSCLE. That which draws the two valves of a shell together, and leaves a mark on the inner surface of each, called the MUSCULAR IMPRESSION.

ADELOSINA. D'Orb. A genus of microscopic Foraminifera.

ADEORBIS. Wood. A genus of Trochæform shells, approaching Delphinula, and represented by Ad. subcarinata. Pl. xxviii. f. 588.

ADESMACEA. Bl. (*a*, without; Δεσμα, *desma*, ligament.) The 10th family of the order *Lamellibranchiata*, Bl. composed of Mollusca which either bore tubular dwellings in rocks, wood, &c. or live in testaceous tubes, their shells being consequently destitute of the hinge ligament. The action of opening and shutting the valves being limited to the narrow space to which they are confined, or else the valves themselves being soldered into the tube, renders it unnecessary for them to have a ligament to keep them in their places. The genera Pholas, Teredina, Fistulana, and Septaria, belong to this family, which corresponds in part with the families Tubicolaria and Pholadaria, of Lamarck.

ADNA. Leach. One of the genera separated by Leach from *Pyrgoma*, and characterized as consisting of an upper valve, supported on a funnel-shaped base, which is not buried in the coral to which it is attached, Like Pyrgoma, but is seen externally. The operculum consists of four valves. British Channel and Mediterranean. Adna Anglicum, Pl. i. fig. 2.

ADNATE. A term applied by some authors to those shells belonging to the family of Unionidæ, which have the valves joined together at the dorsal margin, not like other bivalves, by a distinct ligament, but by the substance of the shell itself, the valves appearing to grow together in such a manner that they cannot be separated without one of them being broken, as will be seen in our figure of Dipsas plicatus, fig. 142. This circumstance has been made the foundation of specific and even generic distinctions, for which however it is insufficient, because many species which when young are "adnate," when fully grown have their valves joined together only by a ligament.

ÆGLIA. Say. A division of "Unionidæ," described as having the "shell cuneate; bosses prominent; cardinal teeth much compressed, placed on one side of the bosses. Æglia ovata, *Say*. Occidens *Lea*. Am. Tr. iii. pl. 10." Lardner's Encyclopedia of Malacology.

AGANIDES. Montf. ORBULITES. Lam. Pl. xxiii. f. 479*.

AGAROMA. Gray, 1839. A genus of shells, of which Voluta hiatula is the type.

AGATHIRSES. Montf. SILIQUARIA, Auct.

AGINA. Turton, 1822. Corbula, Brug. 1792.

AKERA. Bl. The fourth family of the order Monopleurobranchiata, Bl. containing the genera Bulla, Bullæa and Bellerophon, which, excepting the last, constitutes the family Bullæana, Lam.

AKERA. Müller. A genus of extremely light horny shells, belonging to the family of Bullidæ. Six species are described in Mr. Adams' Monongraph, No. 11. Sowerby's Thesaurus. *Ex*. Bulla Hanleyi, f. 247.

ALÆA. Jeffreys. A genus of minute land shells, resembling *Vertigo*, but separated because they are dextral, while Vertigo is sinistral. A. marginata, Pupa marginata, Drap. found in marshy ground, roots of trees, moss &c. Britain and Southern and Central Europe. Pl. xiv. f. 292.

ALASMODON. Say. MARGARITUM. *Ex*. A. complanatus, pl. vii. fig. 141. Schum.

ALATÆ. Lam. A family of the order Trachelipoda, Lam. containing the following genera, which may be thus distinguished:

1. ROSTELLARIA. Sinus close to the canal; including *Hippochrenes, and Aporrhais*. Fig. 402 to 404.
2. STROMBUS. Sinus not close to the canal. Fig. 406.
3. PTEROCERAS. Same, digitated. Fig. 405.

ALATED. (From Ala, a wing.) Winged, a term applied to shells when any portion of them is spread out in any direction, as in fig. 403. Hippochrenes, Montf. and fig. 147, Unio Alatus.

ALATUS. Humphrey. STROMBUS, Auct.

ALCADIA. Gray? (B. M. Syn. p. 134.) Helicinæ which have a notch in the aperture. A distinction which it is impossible to maintain. See HELICINA.

ALCADIA. Gray. Helicina major, &c. Species with a notch, Pl. xiv. fig. 306, 307.

ALECTRION. Montf. BUCCINUM Papillosum, Auct. fig. 422.

ALEPAS. Rang. A genus of Pedunculated Cirripedes, either without any shell, or with a scarcely visible valve on each side near the orifice.

ALVANIA. Leach, M.S. Risso, 1818. A very imperfectly described genus, founded on a single species in the British Museum collection, labelled by Leach, A. globella. We figure the Cray fossil, A. ascaris. Pl. xxviii. fig. 586.

ALVEOLINA. D'Orbigny. A genus of microscopic Foraminifera.

AMALTHŒA. Schumacher, 1817. A generic name given to the small flattish species of Capulus.

AMALTHUS. Montf. A. margaritaceus, Montf. is a species of AMMONITES, described as a very flat, keeled, with an angular aperture. It belongs to the family Ammonacea, Lam.

AMATHINA. Gray, Syn. 1840. Pileopsis, or Capulus tricarinatus.

AMARULA———? A genus composed of MELANIA Amarula, Auct. and similar species.

AMBIGUÆ. Lam. The fourth section of the order Conchifera Dimyaria, containing the family Chamacea, fig. 153 to 155.

AMICULA. Gray, 1842. A genus formed for the reception of CHITON vestitus, the valves of which are covered by an integument; so as to be almost hidden externally. Pl. xxiv. fig. 507.

AMIMONUS. Montf. CONILITES ungulatus, Knorr. A species distinguished only by being slightly curved; *Fam*. Orthocerata, Lam.

AMMONACEA. Bl. The fourth family of the order Polythalamia, Bl. or chambered shells, described as thin, chambered, discoidal, convolute, symmetrical, generally compressed, with visible whorls. This last character is used in De Blainville' System to distinguish the Ammonacea from the Nautilacea. This family contains the genera Discorbites, Scaphites, Ammonites, and Simplegas.

AMMONACEA. Lam. The seventh family of Polythalamous Cephalopoda. Lam. containing the genera Ammonites, Orbulites, Ammonoceras, Turrilites, and Baculites, to which may be added Amalthus, Simplegas, Ellipsolites, Nautellipsites, Hamites, Icthyosarcolites, and other genera mentioned in the list of figures 477 to 484.

AMMONITES. Auct. (from Jupiter Ammon.) *Fam*. Ammonacea, Lam. and Bl.—*Descr*. Symmetrical, convolute, discoidal, orbicular; chambers numerous, divided by lobated, branched, or sinuous septa, perforated by a siphon; aperture generally more or less modified by the last whorl. The fossils of the secondary strata which compose this genus are numerous and well known: they are vulgarly termed "snake-stones", and some of them are extremely beautiful, particularly when the external structure is exhibited by a section. There is some difficulty in distinguishing them from the Fossil Nautili, for although the whorls, being visible, and the septa *sinuous*, may be taken as the characteristics of the Ammonites, yet there are several species which partake the characters of both. The Orbulites of Lamarck (fig. 479) for instance, have sinuous septa like Ammonites, but the last whorl covers those which precede it as in Nautilus. Simplegas Montf. and Bl. (fig. 475) has the whorls visible externally, and the septa simple. Ammonites is figured in the plates—Pl. xxii. fig. 478.

AMMONOCERAS, or AMMONOCERATITES. } Lam. (from *Ammon* & Κερας, ceras, horn.) The shells described under this Lamarckian genus present an anomaly which is considered by Mr. G. B. Sowerby, sen., as merely accidental. They resemble the Ammonites in internal structure, but instead of being spirally convolute, they are merely curved like a horn. *Ex.* (copied from De Blainville) Pl. xxii. fig. 477.

AMPHIBOLA. Schum. 1817? A genus formed for the shell usually named Ampullaria avellana, fig. 538.

AMPHIBULIMA. Lam. 1812. SUCCINEA Patula, Auct. (fig. 266) was first published in the Ann. du Mus. D'Hist. Nat. under the name Amphibulima cucullata. The generic name was afterwards abandoned by its author, and the species stands in his system as Succinea cucullata. West Indies. Pl. xiii. fig. 266.

AMPHICERAS. Gronovius, 1781. OVULA, Bruguière; OVULUM, Sowerby.

AMPHIDESMA. Lam. (from Αμφω, *ampho, ambo,* Δεσμος, *desmos, ligamentum*). *Fam* Mactracea, Lam.—*Descr.* Equivalve, oval or rounded, sub-equilateral, sometimes rather gaping at the sides, with slight posterior fold; hinge with one or two cardinal teeth in each valve, and two elongated lateral teeth, distinct in one valve, nearly obsolete in the other; ligament short, separated from the cartilage, which is elongated and couched obliquely in an excavation of the hinge.—*Obs.* In most bivalve shells, the cartilage and ligament are united in one mass, or placed close to each other; the contrary in this case gives rise to the name, which signifies *double ligament.* This circumstance distinguishes the genus Amphidesma from Tellina, which in other respects it greatly resembles. From Lutraria it may be known by its distinct lateral teeth, and also by its valves being nearly close all round, while the Lutrariæ gape anteriorly. The species do not appear to be numerous; no fossil species are known. A. *Reticulatum*, fig. 85. West India Islands, Brazil, Coast of the Pacific, &c. Pl. iv. fig. 85; Pl. xxiv. fig. 495.

AMPHIPEPLEA. Nilson, 1822. The type of this proposed genus is LIMNEA glutinosa, Auct. Gray's edition of Turton, page 243, Pl. ix. fig. 103. The shell is polished, and the inner lip expanded.

AMPHISTEGINA. D'Orb. A genus of microscopic Foraminifera.

AMPLEXUS. J. Sowerby. A. *Corralloides*, fig. 463. A singularly formed fossil, described as nearly cylindrical, divided into chambers by numerous transverse septa, which embrace each other with reflected margins. It occurs in the Dublin limestone, and resembles a coral or madrepore. Pl. xxi. fig. 463.

AMPLEXUS. A generic name proposed by Captain Brown for HELIX pulchella. Drap. 112, tab. 107–134; and other similar species. Zurama, Leach.

AMPULLARIA. Lamarck, 1801. (*Ampulla*, a rounded vessel.) *Fam.* "Peristomiens," Lam. Ellipsostomata, Bl.—*Descr.* Spiral, globular, sometimes discoidal, frequently umbilicated, covered with a rounded, horny epidermis; spire short; whorls rapidly enlarging; aperture elliptical, rounded anteriorly; peristome nearly or quite entire, thickened, and slightly reflected; operculum, testaceous, annular, with a sub-central nucleus.—*Obs.* This genus of fresh-water shells of which a few fossil species occur, is easily distinguished from other genera by obvious characters, particularly by a thick, horny, greenish-brown epidermis, and the rotundity in form. One species (fig. 320) the A. Cornu-arietis, (*Genus*, MARISA, Gray), which forms the type of Lamarck's genus Planorbis, requires notice on account of its flatness, but may be known by the aperture which in the Ampullaria is longer than wide, and in Planorbis the contrary. Lanistes, Montf. is described from a *reversed* species of Ampullaria, fig. 319. The Ampullaria is vulgarly called the Idol Shell, and is said to be held in high veneration by the South American savages. The animal has a large bag, opening beneath, placed on the side of the respiratory cavity. It is supposed that the animal has the power of filling this bag with water, and that it is thus enabled to live a long time out of water. Ampullariæ have been brought as far as from Egypt to Paris *alive*, packed in sawdust. East and West Indies, North Africa, South America, &c. Pl. xiv. fig. 318.

AMPULLINA. Blainville, 1825. Part of the genus HELICINA, Auct.

AMUSIUM. Megerle, 1811. A generic name for species of Pecten, which are flat and smooth outside. Pecten Pleuronectes.

ANALOGOUS. A term applied to certain species of fossil shells, which present a certain degree of resemblance to recent species; but which are not sufficiently similar to warrant the use of the term "identical," or any other implying that they are of the same species.

ANASTOMA or ANOSTOMA. Fischer. (from Ανα, *ana*, backwards; Στομα, *stoma*, mouth) *Fam.* Colimacea, Lamarck. A genus of land shells so named from the singular circumstance of the last whorl taking a sudden turn and throwing the mouth upwards; so as to present it on the same plane with the spire; the animal walking with the spire of the shell downwards resting on the foot. In other respects, these shells resemble other Helices; and belong to De Ferrusac's division "Helicodonta." *Tomogerus* is the earlier, and therefore, correct name for this genus. *T. depressum* is represented in figs. 271, 272. The nearest approach to this genus will be found in the fossil shell named Ferrusina by Grateloup, Strophostoma by Deshayes, which however, has no teeth in the aperture and is provided with an operculum like Cyclostoma. South America. Pl. xiii. figs. 271, 272.

ANATIFER. Brug. ANATIFA, Lam. This name, which signifies Duck-bearing, has been given to the shells commonly called Barnacles, on account of an absurd notion entertained among the ancients, that they inclose the young of the Barnacle duck, in an embryo state. The beautiful bunch of jointed arms, the ciliæ of which serve the purpose of agitating the water, so as to draw in food by the current, were supposed to be the feathers of the future bird. For a description of these shells, see PENTELASMIS; and fig. 34.

ANATINA. Lam. (*That which belongs to a duck*) *Fam.* Myaria, Lam. Pyloridea, Bl.—*Descr.* Thin, transparent, generally equivalve, inequilateral, transverse, marine; hinge with a spoon-shaped process in each valve, containing the cartilage.—*Obs.* Some species included in the genus Anatina of authors, A. striata, for instance, have not the spoon-shaped prominence, but in its place a small, testaceous, moving appendage, connected with the interior of the hinge. These are now separated, and form the genus LYONSIA. The genus Næara, Gray, is composed of Anatina longirostrum, and similar species, which have not the bony appendage, while the spoon-shaped prominence is small, and only found in one valve. Mya is distinguished from Anatina, by the thickness of the shell, and also by having the prominence only in the hinge of one valve. Pl. iii. fig. 69.

ANATINELLA. G. B. Sowerby. (1835). (Diminution of *Anatina.*) A genus so named from its resemblance to Anatina, from which it differs in being destitute of the internal appendage, and having no sinus in the palleal impression. *Ex.* Anatinella Sibbaldii, fig. 70.

ANATOMUS. Montf. Tom. 2, plate 279. A microscopic shell, apearing, from the figure, to resemble SCISSURELLA.

ANAULAX. Roissy? ANCILLA, Lamarck.

ANCILLA. Lam. (1801.) ANCILLARIA. Lam (1822.) (*A handmaid.*) *Fam.* convolutæ, Lam. Angyostomata, Bl.—*Descr.* Smooth, oblong, subcylindrical. Spire short, sutures hidden by enamel. Aperture long, anteriorly emarginated and somewhat effuse. Columella tortuous, oblique, tumid, truncated.—*Obs.* The Ancillariæ are pretty shining shells, enveloped almost entirely by the soft parts of the animal..They resemble Oliva, from which they are distinguished by the suture of the spire being filled up with shelly enamel, nearly covering the surface. The whorls in Oliva being separated by a distinct canal. Ancillaria may be known from Terebellum by the tumid varix at the base of the columella. The well known Ivory shell, Eburna glabrata, *Lam.* must retain its name, and be removed, with several congeners from this genus. The recent species are found in the Islands of the Indian Ocean and Australian Seas. Eburna glabrata is represented in the plates fig. 455; Ancillaria cinnamonea, fig. 456.

ANCULOTUS. Say, 1825. *Fam.* Melaniana, Lam. Ellipsostomata, Bl. A genus proposed to include some fresh-water shells resembling those of the genus Melania, the differences between them being that the spire of Anculosa is more depressed, and the anterior of the outer lip more angulated than in Melania. On an examination of the different species, however, it will be found that this is quite unsatisfactory, as a generic distinction; because the same species which have short flattened spires, do not always have angulated apertures. An example of each from N. America is represented, Pl. xiv. fig. 314.

ANCYLUS. Geoffroy, 1767. *Fam.* Calyptracea, Lam. Otides, Bl.—*Descr.* Thin, obliquely conical, patelliform; apex acute, turned sidewise and backwards; aperture oval; margin simple.—*Obs.* Although the little fresh-water shells described under this name, resemble those of the genus Patella, the animals which produce them are nearly allied to Lymnea. And, it may also be observed, that the shells themselves differ from Patella in not being quite symmetrical, having the apex turned on one side. A. fluviatilis, Pl. xiii. fig. 246. Pl. xxiv. figs. 510, 511.

ANDROMEDES. Montf. VORTICIALIS, Dam. *Fam.* Nautilacea, Lam. A genus of microscopic Foraminifera.

ANELASMA. Darwin. Cirrip. P. 169. A genus of pedunculated Cirripedes distinguished from ALEPAS in important respects, but like in having no shell.

ANGULITES. Montf. A genus composed of species of fossil NAUTILI, described by De Blainville as not umbilicated, with a dorsal keel and angular aperture. NAUTILUS triangularis, Buffon.

ANGIOSTOMATA. Bl. The third family of Siphonobranchiata, Bl. described as differing little from the family of Entomostomata, but having long, narrow, straight apertures, and the columellar lips straight or nearly so. Were it not for the admission of the genus Strombus into this family, it would correspond with COLUMELLARIA and CONVOLUTÆ of Lamarck.

ANNELIDES. The ninth class of invertebrated animals, divided into three orders, namely, A. Apodes, A. Antennés, and A. Sedentaires. The last only contains families of testaceous Mollusca. The animals are vermicular, some naked, others inhabiting shelly tubes. See SEDENTARY ANNELIDES.

ANNULAR OPERCULUM is one which has the nucleus central, or nearly so, the other layers surrounding it in flattened rings. The term concentric is also applied. See Introduction.

ANNULATED. (Annus, a ring.) Composed of, or surrounded by rings, as in the case of Tubicinella, fig. 14.

ANODONTA. Cuvier, 1798. *Fam.* Submytilacea, Bl. Nayades, Lam. A genus composed of such species of NAYADES as have no teeth on the hinge. Europe, North America, &c. The example given is A. Cataractus, Pl. viii. fig. 152.

ANOMALINA. D'Orb. A genus of microscopic Foraminifera.

ANOMALOCARDIA. Schum. 1817. Venus flexuosa, and similar species. See THESAURUS Conchyliorum, Pl. xiii.

ANOMIA. *Fam.* Ostracea, Lam. and Bl.—*Descr.* Irregular, inequivalve, sub-equilateral, foliaceous, pearly within; adhering to marine substances by means of a bony appendage, which passes through a large circular opening in the lower valve; muscular impression divided into three irregular portions; hinge destitute of teeth with a short cartilage.—*Obs.* The Linnæan genus included not only the shells to which the description above given would apply, but also many other genera, such as Crania, Orbicula, Terebratula, &c. which belong to the Brachiopoda, and are perfectly distinct. The Anomiæ are found in Europe, N. America, Moluccas, Philippine Islands, &c. Fig. 186, in the plates, is a somewhat reduced representation of a full grown specimen of A. Ephippium. Fig. 187, the hinge of the under valve, with the bony process. Fig. 188, the hinge showing the opening through which it passes, Pl. xi. figs. 186, 187, 188.

ANOSTOMA. See ANASTOMA, and TOMOGERUS.

ANASTES. Klein. A genus formed of those species of Patella which have a produced, recurved beak. Helcion, Montf. *Ex.* Patella pellucida, fig. 230.

ANSULUS or ANSYLUS. See ANCYLUS.

ANTENOR. Montf. A genus of microscopic Foraminifera.

ANTERIOR. In Bivalves is the side on which the head, or part analogous to the head of the animal lies; it is known in the shell by the umbones, which if turned at all, are turned towards that part. If there be a sinus in the impression of the mantle, it is always on the posterior part of the shell. If the ligament be placed only on one side of the umbones, it is only on the posterior side. The anterior of a *spiral univalve* is that part of the outer lip which is at the greatest distance from the apex. Of a *symmetrical conical univalve* such as Patella, it is that part where the head of the animal lies, indicated by the interruption of the muscular impression. Of *Brachiopoda*, that part which is farthest from the umbones and which corresponds with the ventral margin in other Bivalves. The anterior of *symmetrical, convolute univalves*, is the outer or dorsal part of the aperture, or that part which is farthest from the spire. Lamarck and other Conchological writers have occasioned much confusion by their errors on this subject; describing the same part of a shell at one time anterior, at another posterior; but generally the reverse of the above arrangement, which is founded upon the natural position of the animal, and generally adopted. The anterior will be indicated by the letter *a*, in figs. 119, 421, 229, 34, 202.

ANTIGONA. Schum. 1817. A genus composed of VENUS cancellata, Lam. (fig. 119.) and similar species.

ANTIQUATED. This word, signifying *out of date*, is occasionally used to express that species of composition which constantly occurs in shells, by each fresh deposit or layer of calcareous matter, forming a new margin, which being replaced by its successor, is no longer used as the margin, and is consequently said to be out of date.

APEX. This term does not apply to the natural position of a shell, but is used in a mathematical sense, to indicate the nucleus or first formed part; which may be considered as the point of the spiral cone. From this point, the shell enlarging rapidly or slowly as it descends, takes a spiral, arched, straight, oblique, convolute, or irregularly spiral course. The apex is indicated by the letter *a*, in fig. 282 and 466.

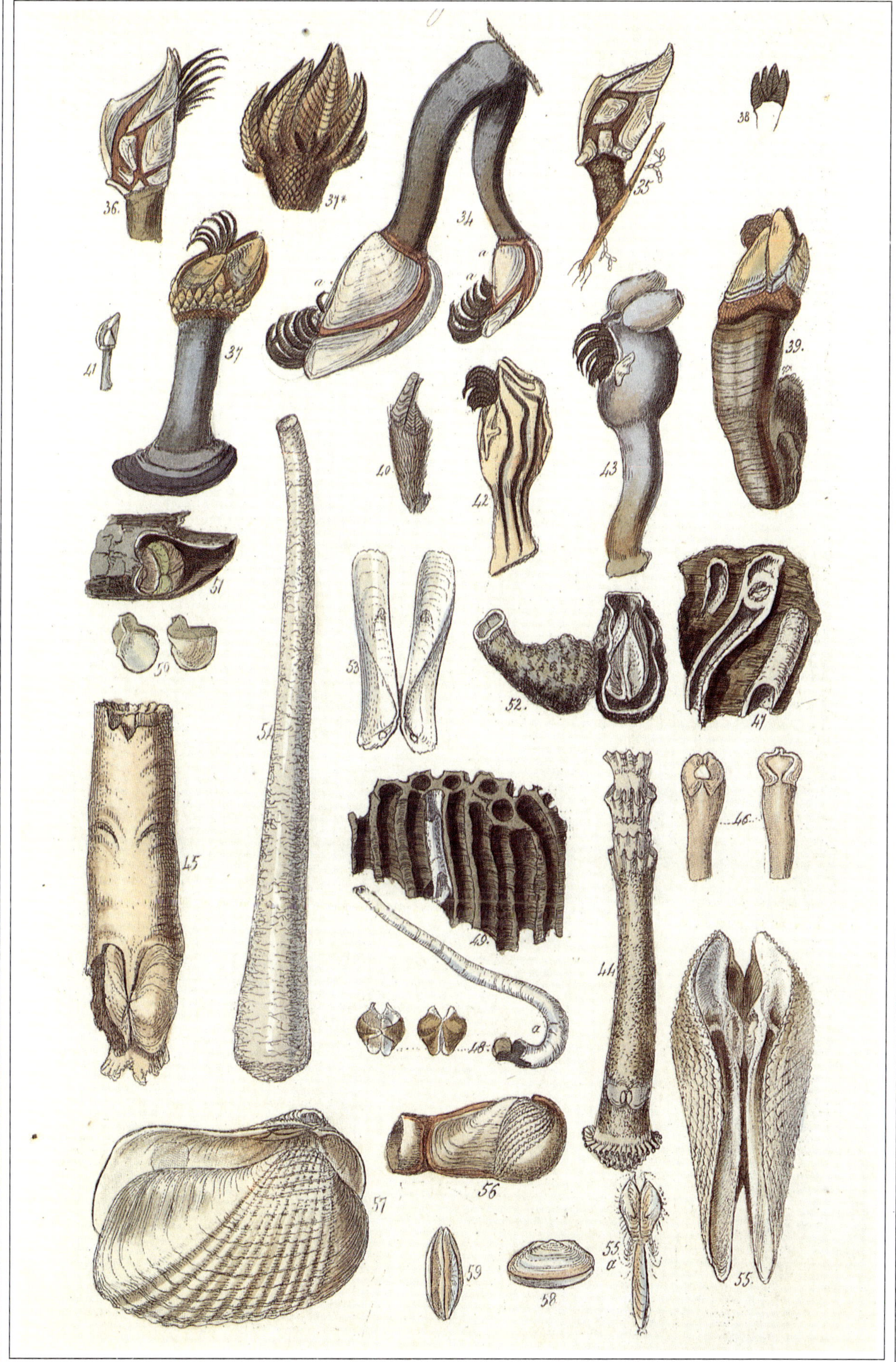

Order, Pedunculated Cirripedes

34. Lepas anatifer. Pentelasmis Anatifera.
35. Scalpellum vulgare.
36. Peronii. (Smilium. Leach.)
37. Pollicipes polymeus. Ramphidoma, Schum.
37*. Pollicipes mitellus. Capitulum, Klein.
38. Lithotrya Rhodiopus. (Brisnæus.)
39. Lithotrya dorsalis. Absia, Leach, Litholepas, Bl.
40. Ibla Cuvieriana.
41. Pæcilasma Warwickii. Octolasmis, Gray.
42. Cineras vittatus. } Conchoderma.
43. Otion Cuveriri } Conchoderma.

Class, CONCHIFERA

Order, C. Dimyaria

Fam. Tubicolaria

44. Aspergillum vaginiferum. Penicullus, Brug.
45. Clavagella, a fossil species.
46. Teredina personata.
47. Lignite, pierced by Teredinæ.
48. Teredo navalis; *a*, tube, (from Sowerby's Genera.)
49 Wood bored by the Teredo.
50. Xylophaga dorsalis. Xylotrya, Leach.
51. The same, in wood. (This would be more properly placed in Pholadaria.)
52. Gastrochaena Modiolina, in the tube (from Sowerby's Genera.)
53. Fistulana Clava } (From Sowerby's Genera.)
54. Tube of the same. } (From Sowerby's Genera.)

Fam. Pholadaria

55. Pholas Dactylus; *a*, plates of the hinge.
56. ——papyracea. Pholadidæa.
57. Pholadomya candida.
58. Galeomma Turtoni.
59. Front view of the same. (Here Xylophaga should be placed, see Tubicolaria.) Triomphalia, fig. 566. To be added to this family.

APERTURE or MOUTH. The entrance to the spiral cavity of univalve shells. The parts of the aperture are separately described, as follows: The *inner lip* or *labium* is that part which lies over the preceding whorl of the shell. It terminates anteriorly, or towards the lower part in what is termed the *columella*, so called because it forms a kind of axis on which the volutions turn. The outer lip, sometimes called the labrum, is on the opposite side, or the farthest from the axis. If the edges of the inner and outer lips unite all round, they are described as composing the *peritreme*. In fig. 318, the aperture is marked by the letter *a*.

APHRODITE. Lea. (from Αφροδιτη, Greek name of Venus.) ACARDO, Swains. A genus composed of CARDIUM Grœnlandicum, Auct. fig. 123,* and other similar species of Cardium, the teeth of which are either wholly wanting, or very indistinct. Northern Ocean. Pl. vi. fig. 123.*

APICIAL. Belonging to the apex. The apicial extremity of the aperture of a univalve shell, is that which is nearest to the apex of the spire.

APLEXA. Fleming. 1824. A genus composed of PHYSA Hypnorum, Drap. &c. and described as having the inner lip simple, and not spread over the body whorl.

APLODON. Rafinesque. A genus proposed to be established at the expense of the genus HELIX, but upon what grounds does not appear from the imperfect description, which is unaccompanied by a figure.

APLUSTRUM. Schum. A genus formed for the reception of some species of BULLA which have the spire uncovered. *Ex.* Bulla Thalassiarchi, fig. 289. Three species are enumerated by Mr. Adams in his Monograph of the Bullidæ in Sowerby's Thesaurus, Pl. xi.

APLYSIA. Gmel. 1790. (*a*, without; Πλυω, to wash.) *Fam.* Laplysiens, Lam. Aplysiana, Bl.—*Descr.* Horny, transparent, clypeiform, or shield-shaped, placed horizontally on the back of the animal, with its convex side uppermost: apex slightly in-curved.—*Obs.* The animal producing this shell has derived its name from the purplish liquor which it exudes, when disturbed. In contour, it has been fancied to present a certain likeness to a hare crouching, and on this account was called *Lepus marinus*, or sea hare, by the ancients. The shell bears a strong resemblance to Dolabella, which, however, is much thicker, and more testaceous. The species are found in the Mediterranean, European, and West Indian Seas. A. Petersoni. Pl. xiii. fig. 254.

APLYSIACEA. Bl. The second family of the order Monopleurobranchiata, Bl. The animals composing this family are either destitute of shells, or are provided with internal ones, which are flat, open, oblique, with the apex or nucleus slightly incurved, not distinctly spiral. This family contains the genera Aplysia and Dolabella. The first sub-spiral, with the apex terminal; shell thin, horny. Fig. 254. The second the same, but thick and shelly. Fig. 255.

APOLLON. Monft. RANELLA. Lamarck.

APOROBRANCHIATA. Bl. The first order of the second section of Paracephalophora Monoica, Bl. The Thecosmata is the only family of this order containing any approach to shells, these are Hyalæa and Cymbulia.

APORRHAIS. Da Costa, 1778. A genus formed of ROSTELLARIA Pespelicani, *Auct.* and similar species. Although the shell presents no characters to distinguish it generically from Rostellaria, those who have examined the soft parts are convinced that it is distinct. Of the three species now known and figures in part I. of Thesaurus Conchyliorum, by the Author, one is common on our own coast, and in the Mediterranean. See ROSTELLARIA; and our plates: Pl. xviii. fig. 404.

AQUATIC. A term applied by some authors to those species of Molluscous animals, which inhabit fresh water, either in rivers or salt water standing pools, as distinguished from the marine or Mollusca. See Fresh-water.

AQUILLUS. Montf. TRITON Lampas, Cutaceus, &c. Auct. Placed by De Blainville in the division of the genus Triton, which is described as having a short spire, being covered with tubercles and umbilicated. Triton Cutaceus. Pl. xviii. fig. 309.

ARCA. Linn. (Anglicè, a boat.) *Fam.* Arcacea, Lam.—*Descr.* Obliquely transverse, subquadrate, equivalve, or nearly so, inequilateral, thick, ventricose, longitudinally ribbed, dentated near the inner margins; hinge rectilinear, forming a flat, external area, upon which the ligament is spread in cross rows, and having a series of small, regular teeth, extending on both sides of the umbones in each valve; muscular impressions distant.—*Obs.* The shells composing this genus are easily distinguished from those of all other bivalve shells, by the straight, linear row of small notched teeth, and by the area between the umbones. The genus *Cucullœa* makes the nearest approach to it in this respect, but it may easily be known from it by the outermost teeth on each side of the row being oblique, and lengthened out; and also by the prominent edge of the muscular impression. These shells are recent, found in various marine localities; fossil, in the tertiary deposits. The Arca Noæ, formerly regarded as the type of this genus, has, with several other species, been separated from it under the name of Bysso-area, by Swainson, on account of an hiatus in the ventral margin, to admit the passage of a byssus; this is not found in the true Arcæ. The true Arcæ are mostly tropical. Mr. Reeve's Monograph contains 122 species. Arca Antiquata, fig. 121. Byssoarca Noæ, 132. Pl. vii.

ARCACEA. Lam. A family of the order Conchifera Dimyaria, characterized by a series of teeth placed on the hinge in a line. The genera may be distinguished as follows,

1. ARCA. Hinge straight; valves close. Fig. 131.
2. BYSSO-ARCA. Valves gaping. Fig. 132.
3. CUCULLÆA. Distant teeth oblique; posterior muscular impression prominent. Fig. 133.
4. PECTUNCULUS. Hinge curved. Fig. 134.
5. NUCULA. The same, with a pit in the centre of the hinge, including Myopara and Crenella. Figs. 135 to 137.
6. SOLENELLA. Fresh water, oval; a series of teeth on one side of the hinge, only two or three on the other. Fig. 138.

ARCHAIAS. Montf. A genus of microscopic Foraminifera.

ARCHONTE. Montf. HYALÆA, Auct.?

ARCINELLA. Schum. 1817. ACANTHIZA, Fischer. 1807. Claimed as a prior name for MONOCEROS, Lamarck. CHAMA Arcinella, Auct.

ARCTICA. Schum. CYPRINA. Lamarck.

AREA. A flat space or disc, on any part of a shell. *Ex.* the triangular space on the hinge of Arca, fig. 132, and Spondylus.

ARENACEOUS. (Arena, sand.) Of a sandy texture, as the sand tubes surrounding the bodies of some of the Annellides, named Arenaria on this account. But the word is more commonly used to intimate the habits of the animal, burrowing with its shell in the sand.

ARETHUSA. Montf. A genus of microscopic Foraminifera.

ARGONAUTA. Lamarck. Commonly called the "Paper Sailor." *Fam.* Pteropoda, Bl. *Order* Cepholopoda Monotholamia, Lam.—*Descr.* Light, thin, transparent, or nearly so, symmetrically convolute, carinated by a double row of tubercles, terminating smooth or tuberculated ribs radiating towards the centre; aperture large, elongated; peritrême acute, interrupted by the body whorl.—*Obs.* The exquisitely beautiful, light and delicate fabrics included under the above name are inhabited by a molluscous animal named the *Ocythöe*,

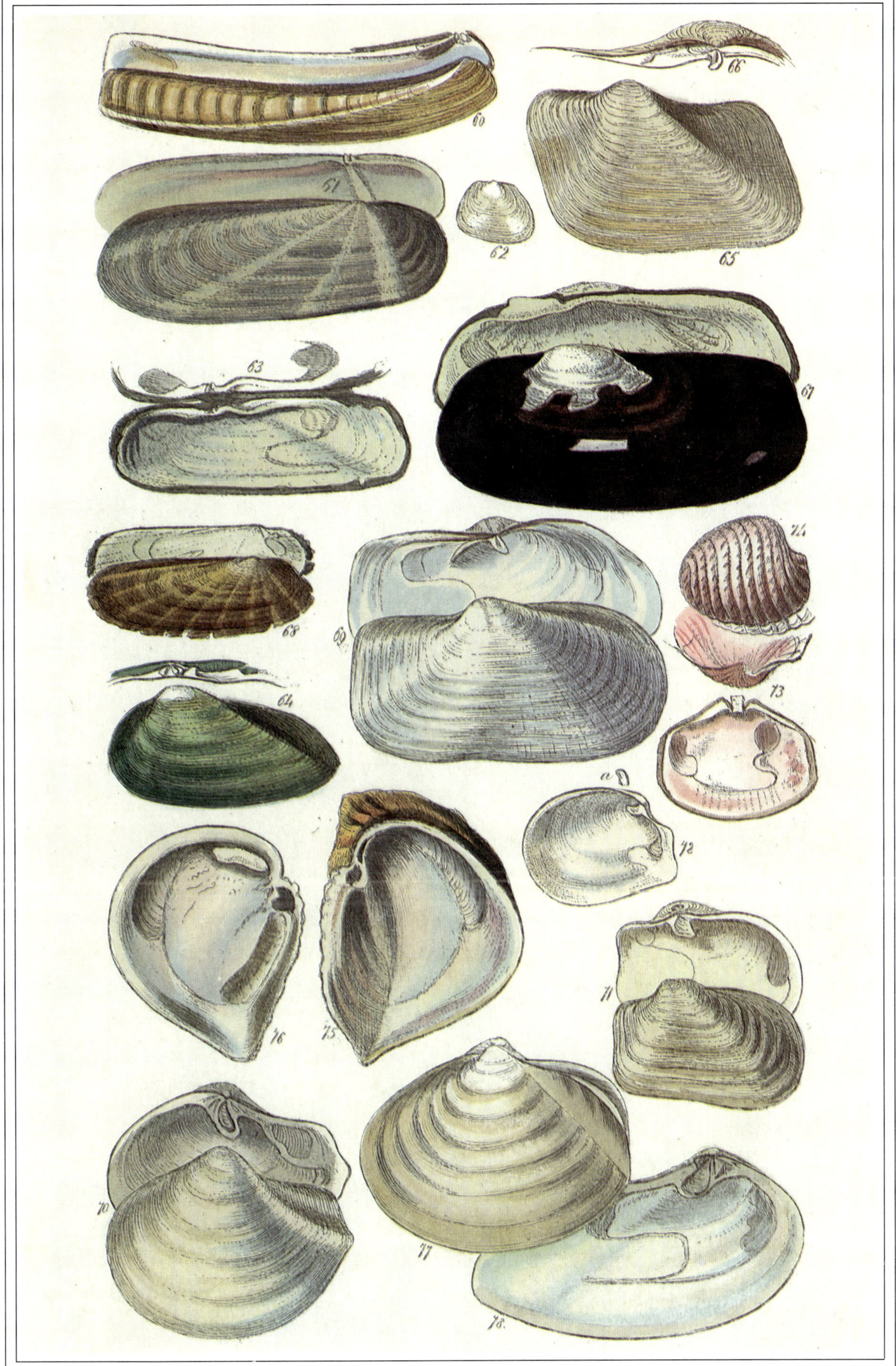

Fam. Solenacea

60. Solen ensis. Ensis, Schum. Ensatella, Sw.
61. Solen radiatus. Solenocurtus, Bl. Leguminaria, Schum. Siliqua, Megerle.
62. Lepton squamosum, (from Turton.)
63. Novaculina gangetica.
64. Glanconome Chinensis.
65. Panopæa Australis. } (From Sowerby's Genera.)
66. Hinge of Panopæa Faujasii. } (From Sowerby's Genera.)
67. Glycimeris Siliqua.
68. Solenimya Mediterranea.

Fam. Myaria

69. Anatina rostrata. Auriscalpium, Megerle.
70. Anatinella Sibbaldii.
71. Mya tuncata.
72. Periploma inæquivalvis. Osteodesma, Desh. *a*, bone of the hinge, (from Blainville.)
73. Myochama anomioides; lower valve with clavicle, and hinge of upper valve.
74. External view of the same, attached to a Trigonia.
75. Cleidothærus Chamoides, attached valve.
76. Upper valve of the same, with the clavicle.

Lyonsia, 491, 492.
Næra, 493–5.
Turtonia, fig. 567.
Poronia, fig. 568.
Kellia, fig. 569.
Montacuta, fig. 570.
Pythina, fig. 571.
Syndosmya, fig. 572.
Cochlodesme, fig. 573.
Myodora, fig. 574.
} To be added to this family

Fam. Mactracea.

77. Lutraria papyracea. Ligula, Leach. Carinella, Adans.
78. ——Solenoides. Cutellus——?

which is provided with tuberculated arms. These, hanging over the sides of the aperture, give to the whole the appearance of a vessel propelled by oars: a poetical illusion further heightened by the broad, flat membranes of the two arms, which, when vertically expanded, present an idea of sails. Pliny has described the Nautilus (the name has been changed by the moderns) as sailing gracefully on the Mediterranean waters; and Pope has versified the idea in the well known lines–

"Learn of the little Nautilus to sail,
Spread the thin oar and catch the driving gale."

Scientific men have long been engaged in the interesting discussion, whether the animal really belongs to the shell in which it is found, or whether, having destroyed the rightful owner, it has possessed itself of the "frail bark." It is now, however, proved beyond the shadow of a doubt that the Argonaut is the testaceous part of the Ocythöe, and that the broad membranes which in some representations have been artificially placed as sails, are naturally bent backwards over the shell like the mantle of some other molluscs. The interesting experiments of Madame Power, in the Mediterranean, have contributed very materially to lead the investigations of naturalists to a satisfactory conclusion. This lady kept a cage under water, in which Argonautæ were bred in great numbers, giving her an opportunity of tracing the gradual development of the shell in all its stages, from the elastic and transparent nucleus to the full grown "Paper Sailor." Pl. xxiii. fig. 485.

ARGUS. Poli, 1795. Equivalve pectens, like P. opercularis.

ARIANTA. Leach, 1819. A sub-genus of land shells, containing Helix arbustorum, Auct. (Gray, Turton, p. 137.)

ARION. Ferrussac, 1817. A genus of slugs, originally described as having no shells, but the shell of which is now ascertained to be a Limarella.

ARROW-HEADS. One of the names by which fossils of the genus Belennites were formerly known.

ARTEMIS, or ARTHEMIS. Poli: Dosinia? Scopoli. A genus of bivalve shells, distinguished from those of the genus Cytheræa by having a rounded, denticular form, and a deep, angular sinus in the palleal impression; although palleal impressions of the Veneres are subject to great variations, this may be considered a pretty well defined genus. The author is preparing a Monograph in the Thesaurus Conchyliorum, containing 60 species. A. lincta, Pl. vi. fig. 118.

ARTICULATED. (Jointed.) Applied to distinct parts of shells, which are fitted or jointed into each other, as the valves of Chitones and those of Balani. The operculum of Nerita is said to be *articulated* to the columella, having a small process by which it is as it were locked under the edge. See *Introduction*. The word is also applied to the Cirri, which protrude from the oral openings of Cirripides.

ARTICULINA. D'Orb. A genus of microscopic Foraminifera.

ASIPHONIBRANCHIATA. Bl. The second order of Paracephalophora Dioica, Bl. Consisting of spiral univalves, which have no notch or canal at the anterior part of the aperture. This order is divided into the families Goniosomata, Cricosomata, Ellipsostomata, Hemicyclostomata, and Oxystomata.

ASPERGILLUM. Lam. (From *Aspergo*, to sprinkle.) *Fam.* Tubicolæ, Lam. Pyloridea, Bl.—*Descr.* The small, equal equilateral valves are cemented into, so as to form part of, a large tube; the umbones are slightly prominent outside. The tube is elongated, rather irregular, granulated with sandy particles, and terminated at the base by a convex disc, which is perforated by small pores, elongated into tubes round the edge, presenting a resemblance to the spout of a watering pot, whence the name is derived. *Loc.* New Holland, Java, New Zealand, Red Sea. Aspergillum Vaginiferum. Pl. ii. fig. 44.

ASSIMINEA. Leach, 1819. *Fam.* Turbinacea, Lam.—*Descr.* Inclining to oval, light, thin, covered with a horny epidermis, spire produced into an acute pyramid; whorls slightly angulated in the centre, rounded beneath; aperture elliptical, slightly modified by the last whorl; inner lip planed; outer lip thin; operculum horny, subspiral. Found in brackish water; one species may be procured abundantly on the muddy shores of the Thames, in Kent. There are also species from Calcutta, China, Tahiti, and Australia. Without comparing the animals, it is difficult to distinguish this genus from some species of Littorina. A. Grayana. Pl. xvi. fig. 363.

ASTACOLUS. Montf. A genus of microscopic Foraminifera. Cristellaria Crepidula, Lam.

ASTARTE. J. Sowerby, 1816. (Name of a Sidonian goddess, *Ashtaroth* in Scripture.) *Fam.* Nymphacea, Lam. Genus Crassina, Lam.—*Descr.* Suborbicular, equivalve, inequilateral, thick, compressed; hinge with two solid diverging teeth in the right valve, one tooth and a slight posterior elevation in the left; muscular impressions, two in each valve, uniform, united by a simple palleal impression; ligament external.—*Obs.* This genus differs from Venus, Cytheræa, &c. in not having a posterior sinus in the impression of the mantle. The hinge also differs in having but two cardinal teeth. Astarte differs from Crassatella in having no internal cartilage in the hinge. Some of the species are British, others are from America, and one from Sicily. The fossils occur in Crag, Lower Oolite, &c. A. Danmoniensis. Pl. v. fig. 110.

ASTROLEPAS. Klein. Coronula Testudinaria, Auct. Chelonobia, Leach. Fig. 15.

ATLANTA. Lesueur. *Fam.* Pteropoda, Lam. and Bl.—*Descr.* Spiral, convolute, transparent, fragile, compressed, with a broad, fimbriated, dorsal keel, and a narrow aperture. This shell, which is called "*corne d'ammon vivant*," is found in the Atlantic. The small Pteropod, figured in Sowerby's Genera as Limacina, belongs to this genus. Atlanta Helicialis, Pl. xii. fig. 220.

ATLAS. Lesueur. A genus of Bullidæ without any shell.

ATRACTODON. Charlesworth. (Mag. Nat. Hist. 2nd series, vol. 8. p. 218.) A genus proposed for the admission of a singular fossil-shell, found on the beach at Felix-stone, of which the following are the characters:—fusiform, aperture equalling the spire in length, terminating anteriorly in a slightly recurved canal; columellar lip smooth, curved, thickened posteriorly into a blunt tooth; spire obtuse.—*Obs.* This shell would be a Fusus were it not for the tooth on the posterior extremity of the columellar lip. The only species known is regularly striated in a spiral direction, and named A. elegans.

ATRYPA. Dalman. A genus of brachipodous bivalves, distinguished by the valves being nearly equal, and the umbones not separated by an intermediate area. A. reticulata, Pl. xi. fig. 302.

ATTACHED. Shells are attached to marine substances by various means; in some cases by a *byssus*, or a bunch of tendinous fibres passing through an opening between the valves, which gape at their margins to admit a free passage, as in the genera Byssoarca and Mytilus. In other cases the byssus is of a more compact substance, and passes through a perforation in the shell itself. This is the case with many of the brachiopodous shells, in some species of which the perforation is in the point of the umbones, a specimen of which is represented in the Introduction. This species of attachment does not keep the animal motionless, although it is confined to a particular spot. Other shells are attached by a portion of their own substance, as in Chama, Spondylus, Serupla, &c. in which instances, the attached valve is motionless, and is termed the under valve. The pedunculated Cirripedes are attached by a tubular tendinous process, called a peduncle.

ATURIA. Bronn. A genus typified by Nautilus zigzag, having an angularly lobed septum. Edwards. Cephalopoda of London clay. P. 54.

ATYS. Montf. 1810. A generic name including those species of BULLA, which are described as "convolute, with the last whorl covering the rest and hiding the spire, the apex rounded at both ends." In Sowerby's Thesaurus Mr. Adams enumerates 22 species. Bulla Naucum, Auct. fig. 250.

AURICLE. (A little ear.) See AURICULATED.

AURICULA. Lam. 1801. (Dim. from *Auris*, an ear.) *Fam.* Auriculacea; Bl. Colimacea, Lam.—*Descr.* Oval or oblong, cylindrical or conical; aperture long, narrow, generally narrowest in the centre; rounded anteriorly, with two or three strong folds on the inner lip, and the outer lip thickened, reflected, or denticulated; spire short, obtuse, epidermis horny, brown.—*Obs.* The above description includes the A. coniformis, f. 298. and several other conical species with narrow apertures, which formed the genus *Melampus*, Montf. and *Conovulus*, Lam. The latter author suppressed his genus on ascertaining the Conovuli to be land shells. We exclude, however, the A. Dombeyana, Lam. f. 300. and several similar species, which being more rounded, having thin outer lips and but one fold on the columella, are described under the generic name *Chilina*, Gray. It appears rather more doubtful whether the Auriculæ are marine or fluviatile, but the animals appear to be amphibious. The Auriculæ are principally found in salt marshes of tropical climates, some small species are found on the southern European coasts, as far north as Britain and south as Tierra del Fuego. The Auriculæ formed a part of the genus Voluta of Linnæus, f. 297. A. Judæ, f. 298. A. Coniformis, Pl. xiv.

AURICULATED. Some bivalve shells, such as *Pecten*, fig. 171, 172, have a flat, broad, somewhat triangular appendage on one or both sides of the umbones, called an *auricle*, or little *ear*. If on one side only, they are said to be *uni-auriculated*; if on both, they are said to be *bi-auriculated*.

AURICULACEA. Bl. The second family of the order Pulmobranchiata, thus described: "shell thick, solid; aperture more or less oval, always large, rounded anteriorly, and contracted by teeth or folds on the columella." This family is included in the genus Voluta of Linnæus, on account of the plaited columellar lip, a character by which that heterogenous assemblage of shells is distinguished. It forms part of the family of *Colimacea*, Lam. from which they differ not only in general form, but also in the fact of the animals being partly amphibious, always living (according to De Blainville) on the sea shore, and being occasionally covered with water for a short time. It contains the general Pedipes, Auricula, Pyramidella.

AURIFERA. Blainville, OTION, Auct.

AURIFORM. (From *Auris*, an ear; *forma*, shape.) Ex. *Haliotis*, fig. 338.

AURISCALPIUM. Megerle, 1811. ANATINA, Lam. 1812. Laternula, Bolton, 1798.

AVICULA. Lam. (From *Avis*, a bird.) *Fam.* Mallacea, Lam. Margaritacea, Bl.—*Descr.* Inequivalve, inequilateral, foliaceous, subquadrate, oblique, pearly; hinge rectilinear, lengthened into auricular appendages, with a small indistinct tooth in each valve, an elongated, marginal, ligamentiferous area, and an hiatus in the left valve, for the passage of a byssus; one circular muscular impression, near the centre of each valve, with a series of smaller ones arranged in a line towards the umbones.—*Obs.* The Meleagrinæ of Lamarck, Margaritiferæ, Schum. included in this description, consist of the more rounded species, and do not present the elegant obliquity of form, nor the wing-like auricles from which the genus Avicula receives its name. The Aviculæ are pearly within. From A. margaritiferæ, a young specimen of which is figured in the plates, fig. 164, is obtained oriental pearls. This is an example of Meleagrina. A. Hirundo, fig. 163, belongs to the genus Avicula of Lamarck. It is, however, needless to continue the separation. Avicula are from E. and W. Indies, Mexico, Coasts of the Pacific, Mediterranean, British Islands, &c. Fossil species occur in the London clay, &c. Pl. ix. fig. 163, 164.

AXINEA. Poli, 1795. A generic name used by some authors in preference to PECTUNCULUS of Lamarck, as claiming the priority.

AXINUS. J. Sowerby.—*Descr.* Equivalve, transverse; posterior side very short, rounded, with a long ligament, placed in a furrow, extending along the whole edge; anterior side produced, angulated, truncated, with a flattish *lunule* near the beaks. The late Mr. James Sowerby, who described this shell in the Mineral Conchology, did not consider his genus as established, not having seen the hinge. It is stated to have been previously named Thyassira; but CRYPTODON, Turton, is the first name accompanied by true character.

AXIS. The imaginary line, round which the whorls of a spiral shell revolve. The extremities of the axis are pointed out in fig. 379, by the letters, a. a. See "Columella."

AZECA. Leach. Gray, 1840. *Fam.* Colinacea, Lam.—*Descr.* "Animal like Bulinus, with subcylindrical, rather obtuse shell, covered with a polished periostraca (epidermis); aperture pear-shaped, curved and pointed at the top; the margin thick, obtuse, united all round and toothed; the axis imperforated." Gray's edition of Turton's British Shells, page 189.—*Obs.* The Turbo Tridens of Montagu, upon which this genus is founded, resembles Bulinus lubricus in general form and character. Both these shells differ from the true Bulini in having the peritreme entire, and in being pellucid and glossy. Azeca differs from Bulinus lubricus in having three teeth in the aperture, two on the inner lip and one on the outer. Not seeing the necessity for creating a genus on grounds so slight, I have simply transcribed the description given above, leaving others to form their own conclusions as to the propriety of separating this shell from the genus Bulinus. Britain, Central and Southern Europe. Azeca Tridens, Pl. xiv. fig. 290.

AZEMUS. Ranzani. CONIA, Leach.

BACULITES. Lam. *Fam.* Orthocerata, Bl. Ammonacea, Lam.—*Descr.* Straight, conical, tubular, laterally compressed; chambers divided by very sinuous lobed septa, the last elongated; aperture elliptical; siphon dorsal.—*Obs.* This genus differs from Orthoceras in the same manner in which Ammonites differs from Nautilus, having its septa sinuated and branched. A Baculite might be described as a straight Ammonite. This genus is known only in a fossil state. It is found in the Cretaceous Limestone of Maëstricht and Valognes. B. Faujasii. Pl. xxiii. fig. 484.

BALANUS Brug. (an Acorn; "gland de mer." Fr.) *Order* Sessile Cirripedes, Lam. *Fam.* Balanidea, Bl.—*Descr.* Shell composed of six valves articulated to each other side by side in a circle, by the insertion of lamina; closed at the base by a flat, cylindrical or cup-shaped valve, by which it is generally attached; and at the apex by a conical operculum, consisting of four valves in anterior and posterior pairs. Each valve of the shell is divided into a rough triangular portion pointed towards the apex, and a flat area on each side.—*Obs.* This description includes the *Acasta* of Leach, which growing in sponges, has the base cup-shaped; *Conoplœa* of Say, which being attached to the stems of Gorgonia and sea-weeds has the base elongated and lanceolate, and *Chirona*, Gray. Balanus is the only genus of Sessile Cirripedes the shells of which consist of six parietal valves, except *coronula*, which has no shelly base, is flatter, and has the valves of the operculum placed horizontally. The Balani are common in all seas, adhering to rocks, corals, floating timber, and to each other. The fossil species are found in the newest strata, at Bordeaux, Paris, &c. Fig. 25. B. Tintinnabulum; 26. *Acasta* Montagui; 27. Balanus galeatus, *Conoplœa*, Say. Pl. i. figs. 25 to 27.

BALANIDEA. Bl. The second family of the class Nematopoda, Bl. corresponding with Sessile Cirripedes, Lam., and consisting of Coronular Multivalves, which are fixed, and in a manner soldered to submarine substances, by the base of the shell; as distinguished from the Lepadicea, Bl., Pedunculated Cirripedes, Lam., which are attached by a fleshy stalk. The Balanidea are composed of two sets of valves, besides the shelly plate or base on which they rest. The first, called the Parietal valves, are arranged so as to surround the body of the animal; the second, called the Opercular valves, are placed horizontally, so as to cover the aperture.

BALEA. Prideaux. Gray. 1824. *Fam.* Colimacea, Lam.—*Descr.* Spiral, turrited, concentrically striated, sinistral, and covered with a thin brown epidermis; spire composed of numerous whorls, gradually increasing in size; aperture small, sub-quadrate; peritreme entire, slightly thickened, with a very slight fold on the columella; axis perforated.—*Obs.* A genus of small land shells, found in moss at the roots of trees in Britain, not very nearly resembling any other land shells, except Clausilia, from which they differ in not having the clausium. They have been placed in Helix by De Ferrusac, and in Pupa by Draparnaud. *Helix perversa*, Fer. *Pupa perversa*, Drap. B. fragilis, Pl. xiv. fig. 296.

BARBATA. Humphrey. 1797. Dipsas. Leach. 1817.

BARNACLES. Pentelasmis, Auct. (fig. 34.) Called Anatifa, by Linnæus and Lamarck, from the ancient notion that they were the eggs or embryo of the Barnacle Duck. See Anatifer.

BASE. In all shells which are attached to sub-marine substances the base is that part of the shell which forms the point of attachment—as for instance, the attached valve of Spondylus, the basal plate of Balanus, the lower part of the peduncle of Pentelasmis: in unattached Bivalves, the margin opposite to the umbones, where the foot of the animal, or the part analogous to it, protrudes; in spinal univalves, the aperture, which rests on the back of the animal when walking. Lamarck and some other authors have used the term *base* as simply opposed to apex, and apply it to the anterior of the aperture.

BATOLITES. Montf. Hippurites, Auct.

BEAK. The Apices, or points of the valves of a bivalve shell, generally termed Umbones, in descriptions. Also any part which is rostrated or drawn out like a beak.

BEAKED. See Beak and Rostrated.

BEAR'S PAW-CLAM. The common name for Hippopus maculatus, a representation of which is given in the plates, fig. 156.

BELEMNITES. Lamarck. 1801. (Βελεμνον, *belemnon*, a dart, or arrow.) *Fam.* Orthocerata, Bl. and Lam.—*Descr.* Straight, conical, consisting of two parts; the *external* portion forming a thick solid sheath, with a cavity at the base to admit the internal portion or nucleus, which is mathematically conical, and is divided into chambers by smooth simple septa perforated by a lateral siphon—*Obs.* These singular fossils, which are found in most secondary beds, have long attracted the attention of philosophers as well as the ignorant, from whom they have received the various appellations of Thunder-Stones, Petrified Arrows, Petrified Fingers, Devil's Fingers, Spectre Candles, &c. The above description is framed to include the genera Hibolithes, Porodragus, Cetocis, Acamas, and Paclites of De Montfort, and Actinocamax, Stokes. Pl. xxii. fig. 466 to 468.

BELLEROPHON. Montf. 1810. (or Bellerophus).—*Descr.* Convolute, symmetrical, umbilicated with a double dorsal ridge; aperture wide, semilunar.—*Obs.* The fossils composing this genus resemble Nautilus in general appearance, but not being chambered shells they approach very near to Argonauta, from which they differ in the thickness of their shell and in roundness of their external form. This genus is erroneously placed by De Montfort among chambered shells, and by De Blainville next to Bulla. It belongs to the Monothalamous Cephalopoda of Lamarck. This fossil is found principally in the Carboniferous Limestone. B. tenuifasciata. Pl. xxiii. fig. 486, 487.

BELOPTERA. The bony support of a species of Cuttlefish, partly resembling Sepia.

BEZOARDICA. Schum. part of the genus Cassidea, Swainson. Cassis glauca, &c.

BIAPHOLIUS. Leach. A genus believed to be identical with Hiatella.

BI-AURICULATED. Having two auricles placed at the sides of the umbones, as in Pecten, fig. 171. See Auriculated.

BIFID. Divided, double.

BIFRONTIA. Deshayes. 1833. Also Omalaxis. Desh. 1830. *Fam.* Turbinacea, Lam.—*Descr.* Discoidal, planorbicular, with whorls sometimes not contiguous; umbilicus deep, keeled at the margin; aperture subtriangular, somewhat dilated; outer lip acute, separated by a deep notch at both extremities.—*Obs.* We do not see any reason for separating this genus from Solarium, except the last mentioned character. The few fossil species which this genus contains (Solarium disjunctum, Bifrons, &c.) are found principally in the Paris basin. Solarium Bifrons. Pl. xvi. fig. 354.

BI-FURCATE. Double pronged, or having two points. *Ex.* the internal appendage of Calyptræa Equestris, fig. 234.

BIGENERINA. D'Orb. A genus of microscopic Foraminifera.

BILABIATED. Having the edge of the outer lip as it were doubled, by one part of the lip being more thickened and reflected than the other, so as to form a ledge, or second lip.

BILOBATE. Having two prominent parts, as the outer lip of Rostellaria Pes-Pelecani, fig. 404.

BIPARTITE. Composed of or divided into two parts; as the valves of Platylepas, fig. 19, each of which has a septiform division in the centre; also the area on the hinge of the Spondylus. See Frontispiece.

BIROSTRA. Sw. A genus composed of species of Ovulum, which have elongated extremities, as for instance, Ovulum Volva, fig. 442.

BIROSTRITES. Lam. (Double Beak.) A fossil formerly considered as a distinct bivalve shell, with conical umbones, and placed in the family of Rudistes by Lamarck, but now known to be an internal cast of Sphærulites. Pl. xi. fig. 196.

BITHINIA. Gray. 1824. A genus described as differing from Paludina, in having the operculum shelly, and the mouth of the shell thickened internally. Paludina impura, Auct. Pl. xxv. fig. 537.

BITOMUS. Montf. A microscopic shell, deriving this general appellation, from the appearance of a double aperture.

BIVALVE. A shell composed of two equal, or nearly equal principal parts, each part having a separate nucleus, turning upon each other by means of a hinge. The class Conchifera of Lamarck, and Acephalophora of De Blainville severally include the whole of the bivalve shells; the latter name being derived from the fact that the animals have not distinct heads, and neither eyes nor tentacula. All bivalve shells are marine or fresh-water. They form the class Dithyra of Aristotle. It may be observed that some of the Acephalophora, the Pholades, for example, have small testaceous pieces fixed on the hinge, which are called accessory valves. These are still fairly bivalve shells, although the genus Pholas has been placed by some writers among the multivalves.

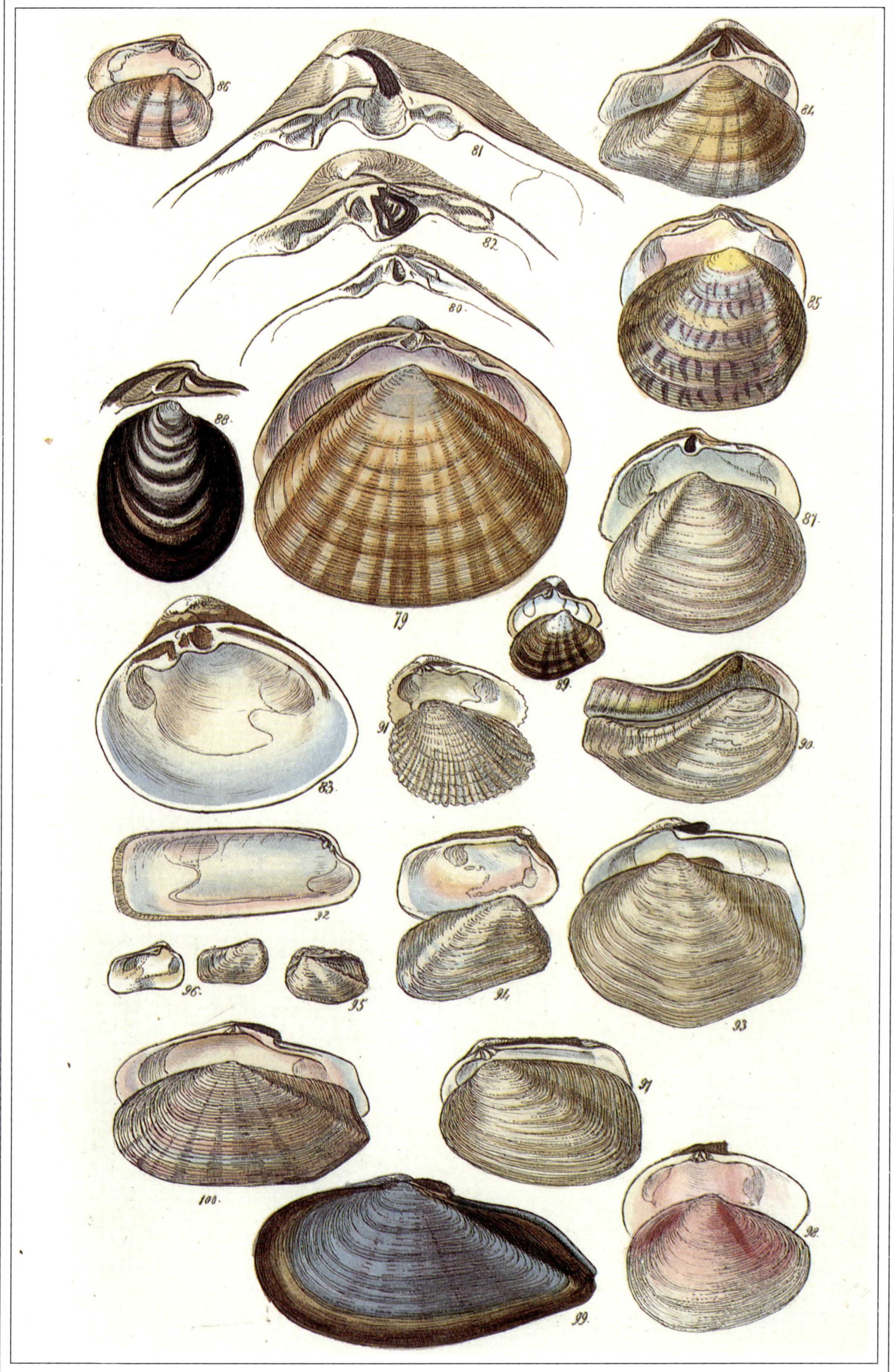

79. Mactra Stultorum.
80. ——plicataria. Spisula? Gray.
81. ——Spengleri. Schizodesma, Gray.
82. ——bicolor. Mulinia, Gray.
83. Gnathodon cuneatus. Clathodon, Conrad.
84. Crassatella rostrata.
85. Amphidesma reticulatum.
86. Erycina plebeja. mesodesma, Desh.
87. Cumingia mutica.
88. Ungulina transversa, (from Sowerby's genera.)
Abra, fig. 495. } To be added
Ervilia, fig. 497. } to this family.

Fam. Corbulacea

89. Corbula nucleus.
90. Pandora rostrata. Potamomya, fig. 498, 499. To be added to this family.

Fam. Lithophagidæ

91. Petricola Roccellaria.
92. ——Carditoidea. Coralliophaga, Bl.
93. Thracia corbuloides.
94. Saxicava rugosa.
95. Hiatella biaperta.
96. Sphænia Binghamii.
97. Venerirupis vulgaris.

Fam. Nymphacea.

98. Sanguinolaria rosea. Lobaria, Schum.
99. ——Diphos. Soletellina, Bl.
100. Psammobia Ferroensis. Gari, Schum.

BIVONIA. Gray. Vermetus glomeratus, Brown.

BOAR'S TUSK. A common name given to shells of the genus Dentalium. One particular species has received a specific name in accordance with a supposed resemblance, namely, Dentalium Aprinum, (of a Boar.)

BONELLIA. Desh. Nisso, Risso, ante. A genus formed, in the first instance, for the reception of Bulinus terebellatus, Lam. which Mr. G.B. Sowerby, in his Genera of Shells, united with the genus Pyramidella. M. Deshayes, however, in his new edition of Lamarck, makes the genus Bonellia include several species which I have arranged in the genus Eulima. From the remarks of M. Deshayes, tom. 8, p. 286, 287, we are led to suppose that the estimated difference between Eulima and Bonellia consists in the latter having the axis perforated; or in other words, umbilicated. After remarking "que Mr. Sowerby, junr. confond deux choses bien distinctes, sous le nomme d'Eulima," M. Deshayes gives the following description of his genus, (translated) "shell turriculated, smooth, polished, with the apex acute and laterally inclined; axis perforated throughout its length; aperture small, entire, angular at the extremities; columella simple and without folds; outer lip thin, simple, nearly parallel with the longitudinal axis." That author further remarks, "Mr. Sowerby, junr. à signalé cinqu espèces vivant, que nous rapportons à notre genre." (Sowerby, junr. Conchological Illustrations, parts 52 and 53; Bohn, York Street, Covent Garden.) The species thus selected are E. splendidula, E. marmorata, E. interrupta, E. imbricata, E. brunnea; the two last of which have the umbilicus so inconsiderable, as to be scarcely distinguishable from other species, which M. Deshayes has left in the genus Eulima, and which have a slight hollow, almost approaching to a perforation, behind the columella. Eulima marmorata, (Bonellia, Desh.) is figured in the plates. Pl. xv. fig. 348.

BODY WHORL. The last whorl, constituting the bulk of the shell.

BORELIS. Montf. Melonia, Bl. A genus of microscopic Foraminifera.

BORER or PIERCER. A term applied to those species of Acephalopodous Mollusca, which bore holes as dwellings in the rocks, as the Pholades, and some others.

BRACHIOPODA. Lam. A family of symmetrical bivalves belonging to the third section of Lamarck's *order* "Conchifera Monomyaria," described as bivalve (generally symmetrical) adhering to marine bodies, by a tendon passing through the shell, having no true ligament. What most distinguishes this family and renders it remarkable is the structure of the animal. It has two elongated, tendril-shaped arms. When the animal is in a state of repose these arms are coiled up spirally and enclosed in the shell, but when required for use, are unfolded and extended. This family contains the genera Orbicula, Terebratula and Lingula, in the system of Lamarck, to which may be added Thecidium, Productus, Spirifer, Magas, Pentamerus, Crania, Strigocephalus, Strophomena, and some others enumerated in the explanation of figures 201 to 219. The above genera may be thus distinguished.

1. Orbicula. Umbones central; byssus passing through a hole in the flat valve. Fig. 201.
2. Atrypa. Without foramen or space between the valves. Fig. 203.
3. Producta. The same, valves produced, overwrapping: including Leptæna. Fig. 206, 206*.
4. Terebratula. Hinge of the upper valve produced beyond that of the other, with a pit or foramen; including *Delthyris, Orthis, Trigonosemus, Magas, Strophomena*. Fig. 202, 205, 207, 208, 209.
5. Spirifer. The same, with deep triangular area; spiral folds in the interior; including *Trigonotreta* and *Cyrtia*. Fig. 204, 214, 215.
6. Thecidium. Large valve attached; curved ridges in the inner surface; two jutting points or teeth on the hinge. Fig. 216.
7. Crania. Attached by the surface of the valve; muscular impressions four, forming a face. Fig. 197, *a, b*.
8. Pycnodonta. Irregular; hinge with raised pointed teeth. Fig. 217, 218.
9. Pentamerus. Valves divided by septa; including *Gypidia*. Fig. 210 to 213.
10. Lingula. Valves equal, gaping, with a peduncle. Fig. 219.

BRACHISTOMA. Swainson. 1840. Clavatula, Lamarck. 1801.

BRANCHIFERA. Bl. The second family of the order Cervicobranchiata, containing the following genera of symmetrical univalves:—Fissurella, Emarginula, and Parmophorous.

BRISNÆUS. Leach. *Order*. Pedunculated Cirripedes. Lam. B. Rhodiopus. Part of the genus Lithotoya. Pl. ii. fig. 37.

BROCCHIA. Brown. Patella sinuata?

BRODERIPIA. Gray, 1847. Part of the genus Scutella, Broderip-type, Scutella rosea. Pl. xxiv. gigs. 508, 509.

BRONTES. Montf. 1810. This generic name is given to such species of Murex as have a very long, closed canal; with a short spire, circular aperture, and are destitute of spires and ramifications. Brontes (Murex) Haustellum, Pl. xvii. fig. 396.

BRYOPA. Gray, 1840. Clavagella aperta, &c.

BUCARDIA. Schum. Isocardia, Auct.

BUCCINUM. Linn. *Fam*. Purpurifera, Lam. Entomostomata, Bl.—*Descr*. Subovate or oblong, covered with an epidermis; spire turrited, consisting of few whorls; aperture wide, subovate, terminating anteriorly in a very short canal, reflected over the back; outer lip simple, slightly reflected; inner lip spread over a portion of the body whorl, terminating in a thick, smooth columella; operculum horny. *Hab*. British Seas, Northern Ocean, and Coast of Africa. Most of the fossil species occur in Crag, some in upper marine formation and London clay.—*Obs*. There are considerable difficulties in keeping this genus distinct from others nearly related to it, into which many of the species run by imperceptible gradations. The genus *Nassa* has been separated on account of the little notch, which terminates the columella. Some species of Terebra so nearly resemble the Buccina, that it is difficult to say where one genus ends and the other begins. Mr. Reeve's Monograph contains 118 species. T. Buccinoides, fig. 427. Buccinum Undatum, the common Whelk, Pl. xix. fig. 421.

BUFO. Montf. A generic division of the species composing Ranella, characterized as having the shell not umbilicated. The above character is scarcely sufficient in some cases, even as a specific distinction. Ranella Ranina, Pl. xvii. fig. 394.

BULBUS. Humph. Rapella, Swainson. A genus formed for the reception of Pyrula papyracea, Auct. (fig. 389), and similar species. Rapanus, Montf.

BULIMIMA. Montf. A genus of microscopic Foraminifera.

BULIMULUS. Leach. 1826. *Fam*. Colimacea, Lam. The author is unacquainted with the characters by which the two or three species included in this genus are to be distinguished from Bulinus. We have represented, (fig. 283), Bulimulus trifasciatus, Leach, (Bulinus Guadaloupensis, Auct.) This occurs in the same limestone which encloses the half fossilized human remains from the Grand Terre of Guadaloup. Several species are described by the Rev. L. Guilding in the Zoological Journal, namely, the B. Undulatus, Antiguensis, and

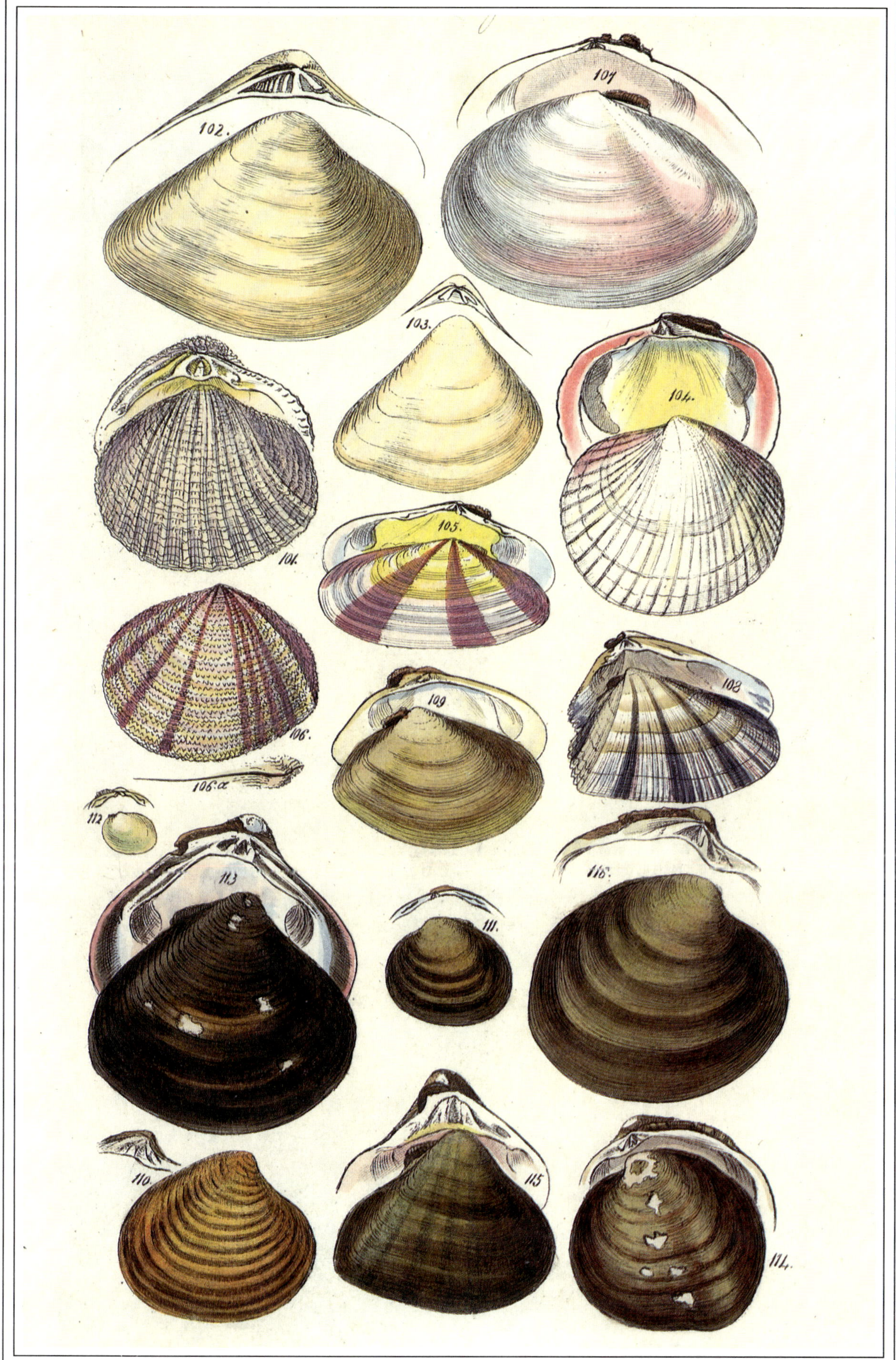

101. Corbis fimbriata. Fimbria, Megerle.
102. Grateloupia Moulinsii, (from Lea.)
103. Egeria triangulata, (from Lea.)
104. Lucina tigerina.
105. Tellina radiata.
106. ——lingua-felis; *a*, showing the fold in the ventral margin.
107. Tellinides rosea.
108. Donax cuneatus.
109. Capsa Braziliensis, young.
110. Astarte Danmoniensis. Crassina, Lam.

Diplodonta, fig. 576. Cryptodon, fig. 575.	To be added to this family.

Fluviatile Conchacea

111. Cyclas rivicola. Cornea, Megerle.
112. Pisidium amnicum. Pisum, Megerle.
113. Cyrena fuscata. Corbicula, Megerle.
114. Cyrenoides Dupontia.
115. Potamophila radiata. Galathæa, Lam. *v.* ventral margin. Pera, fig. 500. To be added to this family.

Marine Conchacea

116. Cyprina vulgaris. Arctica, Schum.

Proteus; but neither from the shells themselves, nor from the figures of the animal, can we draw any information as to the generic character; the difference alleged by Mr. Swainson and Mr. Gray being a comparative thinness in the outer lip. Pl. xiv. fig. 283.

BULINUS. Brug. (Bulinus, Lam.) *Fam.* Colimacea, Lam. Limacinea, Bl.—*Descr.* Oval or oblong, light, covered with a thin epidermis; spire obtuse, variable in length and in the number of whorls, which are generally few; aperture wide, oval, rounded anteriorly; outer lip simple, usually reflected, joining the columella without a sinus; inner lip reflected over part of the body-whorl. The Bulini are land shells, found in many parts of the world.—*Obs.* The genus Bulinus can only be distinguished from Helix by its oval form; it forms part of the genus Helix of De Ferrusac, under the sub-generic designation of Cochlostyla. It is known from Achatina by the absence of the notch at the point of union between the inner and the outer lips. The young are produced from eggs, which are as firm and opaque as those of birds. (See Introduction.) Bulinus rosaceus, fig. 282. B. Guadaloupensis, fig. 283. B. Lionetianus, fig. 284. B. lubricus, fig. 285. Many new species were brought to this country by Mr. Cuming, and are represented in the Conchological Illustrations, published by the Author at 50, Great Russell Street, Bloomsbury, (in parts 21, 22, 23, 26, 27, 30, 31, 34, 35, 137 to 146, 185, 186.) Species occur in Europe, West Indies, Brazil, and South America generally. Reeve's Monograph contains 662 species. Some small species are British. Pl. xiv. fig. 282.

BULLA. Auct. *Fam.* "Bulléens," Lam. Akera, Bl.—*Descr.* Generally thin, smooth, oval, oblong or cylindrical, more or less convolute; spire short, depressed, or hidden by the last whorl; aperture long, wide in front, gradually narrowing towards the spire; outer lip thin; inner lip spread over a part of the last whorl.—*Obs.* The shells composing this genus are very variable in form. The light horny species with an elastic lip is called Akera, fig. 247. The more decidedly convolute species with hidden spires are the Atys, Montf. B. Naueum, fig. 250. B. Lignaria, fig. 251, is Scaphander of Leach. The light, thin species, with extremely wide aperture, fig. 248, is Bullæa aperta, Lam. The genus Bullinula of Dr. Beck, consists of those species which have more produced spines, fig. 253. The Bullæ are marine, and inhabit all climates. The fossil species occur in tertiary beds. Since the first edition of this work was published, a very valuable monograph of the family by Mr. Adams has appeared in Sowerby's Thesaurus, part 11, in which the animals and their shells are arranged in the following genera or subgenera, Bullina, Aplustrum, Hydatina, Cornatina, Utriculus, Akera, Scaphander, Bulla, Haminea, Atys, Cylichna, Volvula, Linteria, Cryptopthalmus, Phaneropthalinus, Sormetus, Philine, Doridium, Chelidonura, Gasteropteron, and Atlas. Fig. 247 to 253.

BULLÆA. Lam. BULLA aperta, Auct. fig. 248.

BULLÆANA. ("Bulléens, Lam.") A family belonging to the first section of Lamarck's order, Gasteropoda, containing the genus Bulla. The genera Bullæa, Akera, Aplustra, Atys, Scaphander, Bullinula, into which it has been divided, may all be fairly included under the name BULLA.

BULLIA. Gray. 1834. A genus of shells partly resembling Buccinum, and Terebra in general form, being more elongated than the former and more ventricose than the latter. Mr. Gray remarks in the Synopsis of the British Museum, page 114, that the Bulliæ resemble the Nassæ in most characters, "but they have a very large, broad foot, and the hinder part of the inner lip of the shell being extended beyond the mouth, forms a raised enamelled band round the suture of the whorls, as is also the case with the Ancillariæ and some Volutes." Bullia vittata, fig. 427, is an example of the genus. The name Subula is given by De Blainville to the other species of Terebra, so that if both these genera were admitted, the old genus Terebra must be expunged. Pl. xx. fig. 427.

BULLIDÆ. See BULLA.

BULLINA, FER. BULLINULA. Beck. Species of BULLA, with produced conical spires, fig. 253. Three species are enumerated by Mr. Adams in his Monograph in Sowerby's Thesaurus Conchyliorum.

BYSSOARCA. Sw. 1835. (*Byssus* and *Arca.*) *Fam.* Aracea. Lam. A genus of bivalve shells, composed of the Arca *Noæ*, and several other species, separated from the genus Arca on account of their shells being attached by means of a byssus passing through an hiatus in the ventral margins. B. *Noæ*, fig. 132. The species occur in Southern Europe, East and West Indies, China; also, on the coasts of Great Britain. Pl. vii. fig. 132.

BYSSOMYA. Payr. 1826. (*Byssus* and *Mya.*) De Blainville states that, although the shell of this proposed genus resembles Saxicava, the animal is sufficiently different to justify the separation.

BYSSUS. (Βυσσος, byssus, ancient name for linen.) The tendinous fibres by which some Bivalves are as it were anchored or moored to submarine substances. A fine example of this is to be seen in the Pinnæ, which bear some resemblance to large Mussel Shells, and have an hiatus in the margin of the valves, through which a bunch of silken fibres passes. In the British Museum there is preserved a pair of gloves, which have been woven of these fibres. The Byssus is peculiar to some bivalve shells, such as Mussels, Hammer Oysters, Arca Noæ, &c.

CÆCUM. Fleming. A genus of minute shells resembling Dentalia, as if truncated, &c. the opening filled by a kind of septum. The position of this genus in the system is not yet accurately ascertained. Cæcum trachea, British Mollusca, Pl. lxix. fig. 4; our figure, Pl. xxvii. fig. 565.

CALCAR. Montf. 1817. (a spur.) A genus composed of TROCHUS STELLARIS, Lam. and other depressed species of Trochus which are characterized by a stellated keel round the angle of the last whorl; but not including T. Imperialis, which is the genus Imperator, Montf. The difference consists in the latter being umbilicated, and the former not. T. stellaris, fig. 358.

CALCAREOUS. (*calx*, lime.) A term applied to a shell, or to its operculum, which is composed principally of lime or shelly matter, as is usually the case, in distinction from one which is of a horny, membranaceous texture. The greater number of shells are calcareous, but it forms an important point of distinction with regard to the operculum. The only difference between the genera Trochus and Turbo, as at present established, depends upon the calcareous or shelly, and the corneous or horny, texture of the operculum.

CALCEOLA. *Fam.* Rudistes, Lam. and Bl.—*Descr.* Equilateral, inequivalve, triangular; umbones separated by a large triangular disc in the lower valve; cardinal margin straight, linear, dentated, lower valve large, deep; upper valve flat, semi-orbicular, forming a kind of operculum to the lower.—*Obs.* This singular shell, known only in a fossil state, in the Palæozöic beds, is placed by Linnæus in the genus Anonia. Lamarck places it among his Rudistes, but Mr. Sowerby, in his genera of shells, states that it should be added to the family of Brachiopoda. C. Sandalina, Pl. xi. fig. 194, 195.

CALANTICA. Gray. Part of Scalpellum.

CALLIA. Gray, 1840? A genus described as having a peculiarly polished shell like Pupina, but wanting the notch, Pl. xxv. fig. 528.

CALLIPARA. Swainson. VOLUTA bullata; Sowerby's Thesaurus Conchy-

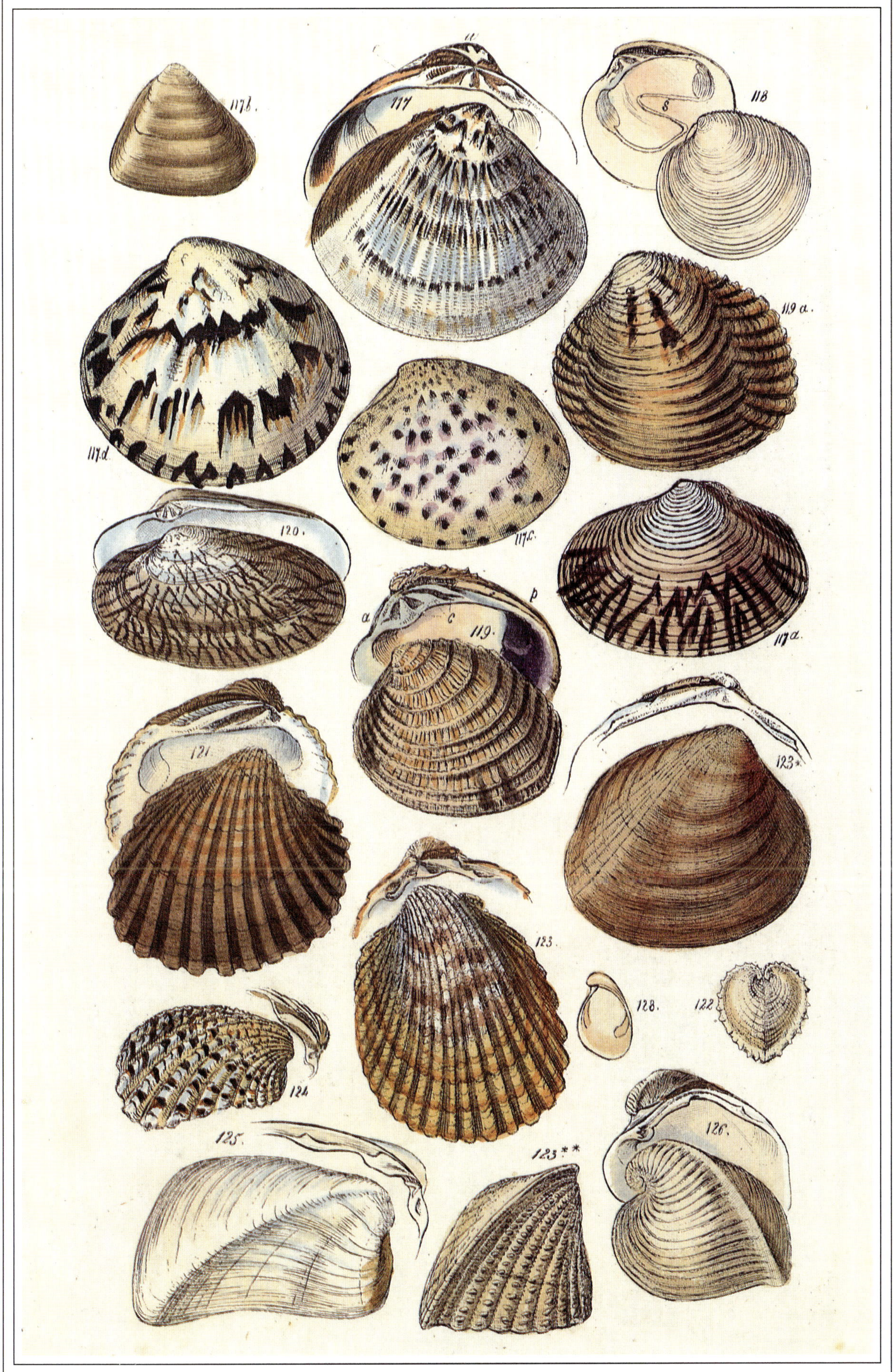

117. Cythera Meretrix; *e*. escutcheon.
117. *a*. C. Meroe; *Gen*. Meroe.
117. *b*. C. Tripla; *Gen*. Trigona.
117. *c*. C. Maculata; *Gen*. Chione.
117. *d*. C. Castrensis.
118. Artemis lincta; *s*, sinus in the palleal impression.
119. Venus cancellata. Antigona, Schum. *a*. anterior; *p*. posterior; *c*. cardinal teeth.
119. *a*. V. Verrucosa. Dosina, Schum.
120. Pullastra Textile.

Fam. Cardiacea

121. Venericardia, recent species, resembling V. planicostata, Lam.
122. Cardium Dionæum. Cardissa, Sw. Hemicardium. Nonnull.
123. ——angulatum.
123*.——Greenlandicum. Aphrodita, Lea, Acardo, Sw.
123**.——hemicardium. *Gen*. Hemicardum.
124. Cardita calyculata.
125. Cypricardia angulata.
126. Isocardia Moltkiana.
128. Hippagus Isocardioides, (from Lea.)

liorum, Pl. liii. fig. 88.

CALLISOSTOMA. Sw. A genus of shells separated from TROCHUS, and thus described: "Imperforate; spire elevated, acute; aperture broader than high, transversely ovate, hardly sinuated at the base, and slightly oblique; shell always smooth, and often polished." C. zixyphina is mentioned as an example.

CALLISCAPHA. Gray? IRIDINA Nilotica, Sow. Zool. Journ. 1. pl. 2. Separated from Iridina on account of the hinge margin being smooth.

CALLITHEA. Sw. A sub-genus of Mitræ, consisting of those species, which like M. sanguisuga, have the "spire and aperture of nearly equal length: internal channel nearly obsolete; shell with longitudinal linear ribs, crossed by transverse striæ and bands; base contracted." Swainson, Mallac. Lard. Cyclop.

CALLOCHITON. Gray, 1847. Chiton lævis, &c.

CALLOSITY. A term used in general zoology to express those hard horny tumidities formed in the skin of some animals (such as the Dromedary, for instance) in those parts which are most frequently used. It is not used in this sense by Conchologists, who apply it to those undefined tumidities or bumps which appear on the inner surface and hinge of some bivalve shells, and to the thickening over the umbilicus of Natidæ. Glycimeris, fig. 97; Natica, fig. 327, 328.

CALPURNUS. Montf. 1810. OVULUM *verrucosum*, Auct. Distinguished by the small circular tubercle at the back of each extremity of the shell. Pl. xx. fig. 441.

CALYPTRACEA. Lam. A family belonging to the first section of the order Gasteropoda, Lam. the shells of which are described as always external, covering the animal, and having no operculum. The genera contained in this family may be thus distinguished:

1. CALYPTRÆA. Conical; apex central, septum spiral, cup-shaped, or forked; including *Infundibulum*, fig. 234 to 238.
2. CREPIDULA. Apex terminal; septum flat, reaching half way across the aperture. Fig. 239.
3. CAPULUS. Conical; apex obliquely curved, no septum. Fig. 240.
4. EMARGINULA. Apex curved backwards; a notch in the anterior margin; including *Parmophorus*. Fig. 241, 242.
5. CEMORIA. A slit *near* the apex. Fig. 244.
6. FISSURELLA. A slit *upon* the apex. Fig. 245.
7. RIMULA. A slit near the margin. Fig. 243.
8. ANCYLUS. Apex curved sidewise. Fig. 246.

CALYPTRACEA. Bl. The second family of the order Scutibranchiata. Bl. thus described: "Shell more or less conical, not spiral, or very slightly so; aperture large and entire." The genera included in this family are Crepidula, Calyptræa, Capulus, Hipponyx, and Notrêma.

CALYPTRÆA. Lamarck. *Fam.* Calyptracea. Lam. and Bl.—*Descr.* Conical, patelliform, irregular, with an internal, lateral, salient plate or septum, varying in form.—*Obs.* The species of this genus or family are divided very properly in the British Museum Synopsis according to the character of the septum, reserving the name (Calyptræa (or Calyptra) for species with a forked septum, C. equestris, fig. 234. The name CRUCIBULUM is applied to the "cup and saucer" division; GALERUS to the species with a half-spiral septum, fig. 236; TROCHITA to the trochæform, spiral species (INFUNDIBUM, Montf.) fig. 237; and Crypta to CREPIDULA, Lamarck, with a septum across the shell, fig. 239, Pl. xii.

CAMERIMA. Brug. NUMMULITES, Auct.

CAMILLUS. Montf. A genus founded upon a minute, spiral, shell, with a triangular aperture, turned over the back of the last whorl. It is figured in Soldani's Testacea Microscopica.

CAMITIA. Gray, described——? (adopted from his Synopsis.) A genus founded on a very interesting shell brought by Mr. Cuming from the Isle of Luzon, Philippines. It is round and flat, and in general appearance like a Rotella; but the Columella presents very singular characters, being quite separated from the body whorl by a spiral slit, and from the outer lip by a deep notch under a strong tooth. Behind the Columella is a spiral canal. Ex. C. pulcherrima, Pl. xxviii. fig. 590.

CAMOSTRÆA. Roissy? CLEIDOTHERUS, Stutchbury.

CAMPULOTUS. Guettard, 1759. MAGILUS, Montfort, 1810. The former is therefore used by some authors on the ground of priority.

CANALICULATED. Applied generally to any distinct groove or canal.

CANAL. A groove which characterizes some spiral univalves, where the inner and outer lips unite at the front part of the aperture. This canal is drawn out in some shells to a considerable length, in others it is turned abruptly over the back. The family Canaliferæ, Lam. (fig. 372 to 401) are all provided with this canal.

CANALIFERA. *Canalifères,* Lam. A family belonging to the order Trachelipoda. Lam. nearly corresponding with the family Entomostrata in De Blainville's system, and described as having a canal of greater or less extent at the anterior part of the aperture. This canal is sometimes straight, sometimes tortuous, and in some genera it is recurved over the back of the shell. All the shells have an operculum, and the thickness of the perfectly formed outer lip does not increase with age. The Canalifera are characterized by having a canal, in distinction from the Purpurifera, which have only a notch. This family contains the following genera:

1. CERITHIUM. Club-shaped. Fig. 372.
2. POTAMIS. The same, fresh water. Fig. 377.
3. NERINEA. The same, with internal folds. Fig. 374.
4. TRIPHORA. Anterior and posterior canals closed, so as to present three openings. Fig. 375, 376.
5. TELESCOPIUM. Pyramidal, trochiform. Fig. 378.
6. PLEUROTOMA. A slit on the outer part of the outer lip; including *Clavatula*. Fig. 379, 381.
7. TURBINELLA. Three horizontal folds on the columella. Fig. 382, 383.
8. SPIRILLUS. Spire papillary; one fold on the columella. Fig. 384.
9. CANCELLARIA. Three folds, and internal costæ. Fig. 385.
10. FASCIOLARIA. Oblique folds, the lowest the largest. Fig. 386
11. FUSUS. Fusiform; no folds on the columella. Fig. 317.
12. PYRULA. Pear-shaped. Fig. 388 to 390.
13. STRUTHIOLARIA. Outer lip thickened; sinuated. Fig. 391.
14. RANELLA. Two rows of varices; a canal at each extremity of the aperture. Fig. 393, 394.
15. MUREX. Three or more rows of varices; only one distinct canal. Fig. 395, 396.
16. TYPHIS. A tubular perforation between each varix. Fig. 307.
17. TRITON. Varices not in rows. Fig. 398 to 401.

CANCELLARIA. Lamarck, 1801. (From *Cancellatus*, cross-barred, like window-frames or net work.) *Fam.* Canalifera, Lam. Entomostomata, Bl.—*Descr.* Oval, thick, cancellated; spire generally short, pointed; aperture sub-ovate, emarginated anteriorly, pointed at the posterior extremity: outer lip marked within by transverse ridges; inner lip spread over part of the body whorl, terminating in a straight, thick obtuse columella, with several strong oblique folds. *Hab.* Indian Ocean, Coast of Africa, America, and West Indies. Fossils found in London Clay and Calc-grossier of Paris. Differing from Turbinellus in

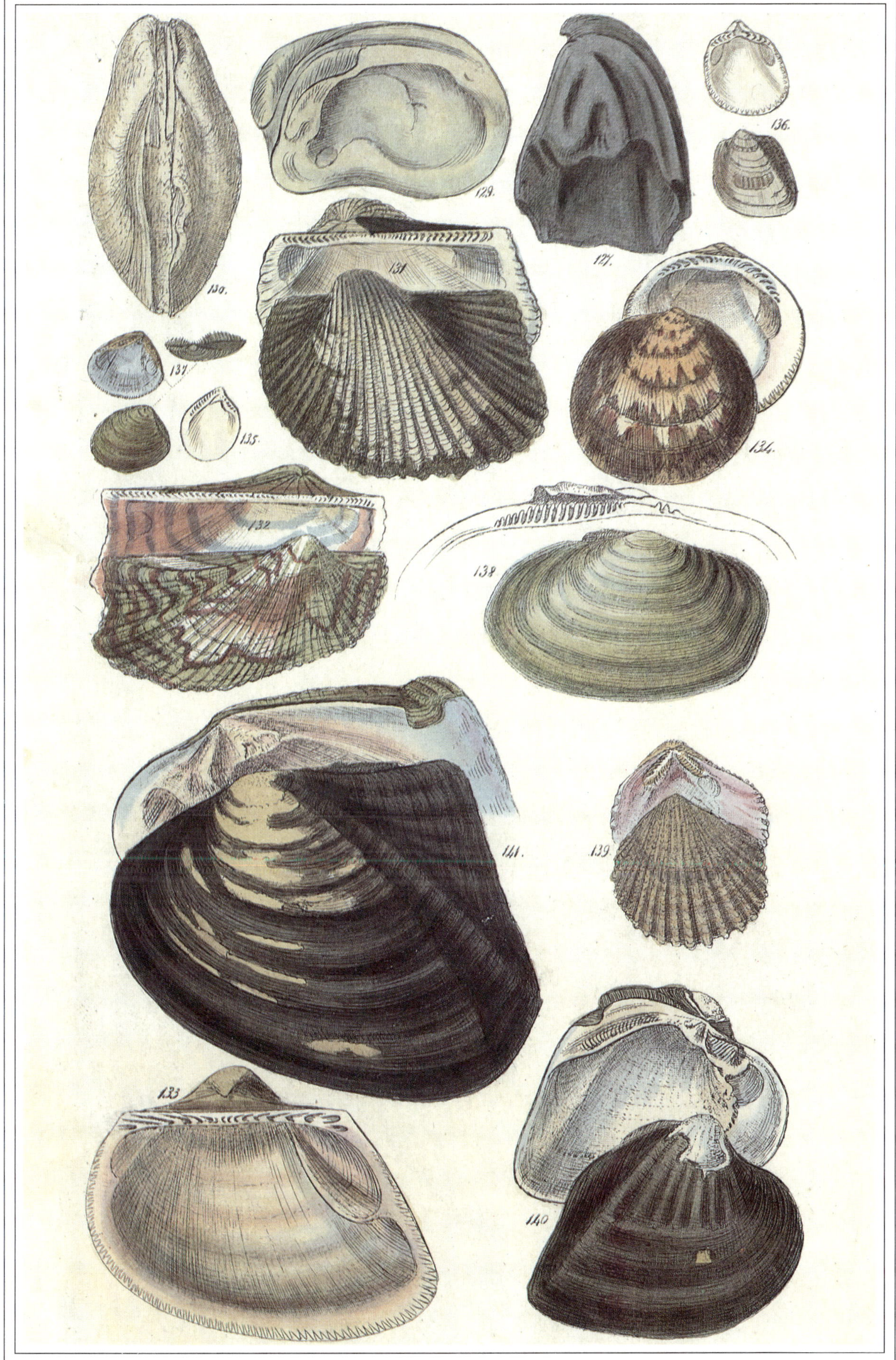

127. Megalodon cucullatus, (from Sow. Min. Con.)

129. Hippopodium ponderosum, (from Sow. Min. Con.)

130. Pachymya gigas, (from Sow. Min. Con.)

Cardilia, fig. 581, 582.
Papyridea, fig. 503, 504.
Pleurorynchius, fig. 505.
} To be added to this family.

Fam. Arcacea

131. Arca antiquata.

132. Bysso-arca Noæ.

133. Cucullæa auriculifera, (from Sowerby's Genera.)

134. Pectunculus pilosus.

135. Myopara costata, (from Lea.)

136. Crenella.

137. Nucula margaritacea, three views.

138. Solenello Norrissii.

Leda, fig. 578.
Nucinella, fig. 579.
} To be added to this family.

Fam. Trigonacea

139. Trigonia pectinata.

140. Castalia ambigua. Tetraplodon pectinatus, Spix.

Fam. Nayades

141. Alasmodon complanatus, Say. Margaritana, Schum.

form and in the transversely ribbed inside of the outer lip. Fig. 315. C. reticulata.—*Obs*. The latest enumeration of the species of this genus is contained in a catalogue published by Mr. G. B. Sowerby, senior, accompanying the author's figures of the new species, amounting to 38 in parts 9 to 13 of the Conchological Illustrations. The greater part of these new species were brought to this country by Mr. Cuming. The monograph subsequently published by the author in pl. ix. of the Thesaurus Conchyliorum, contains 68 species. See our plate xviii. fig. 385.

CANCELLATED. (From *Cancellatus*, cross-barred.) Applied generally to any shells which are marked by ridges crossing each other as Cancellaria, fig. 385.

CANCILLA. Sw. A sub-genus of Mitræa, described as having "the whorls crossed by transverse linear ribs; inner canal wanting, plates very oblique; form slender; outer lip thin." *Ex*. M. Isabella, M. sulcata.

CANCRIS. Montf. CREPIDULINA, Bl. A genus of microscopic Foraminifera.

CANOPUS. Montf. A genus of microscopic Foraminifera.

CANTHAPLEURA. Swainson, 1840. ACANTHOPLEURA, Guilding, 1835. C. spinosus. fig. 227, and similar species of Chiton.

CANTHARIDUS. Montf. 1810. TROCHUS IRIS, Auct. and analogous species. ELENCHUS, Humph. Pl. xxv. fig. 543.

CANTHARUS. Montf. A genus of microscopic Foraminifera.

CANTHIDOMUS. Swainson, 1840. A sub-genus of Melanopsis, thus described: "spire generally short; whorls coronated with spines, or marked with longitudinal ribs; base obtuse. C. costata, Sow. Gen. f. 3." Melanopsis costata. Pl. xiv. fig. 315.

CANTHORBIS. Sw. A sub-genus of the sub-family Trochinæ, Sw. Described as being "nearly disc-shaped: spire but slightly raised; the margin of the body-whorl flattened, and serrated with flat spines; inner lip united to the outer; pillar and aperture as in the last. (Tubicanthus) C. imperialis. Mart. 173. f. 1714," This sub-genus appears to include those species of which De Montfort's genera Imperator and Calcar are formed.

CAPITULUM. Klein. POLLICIPES Mitellus, Lam. Pl. ii. fig. 37*.

CAPRELLA. Guilding, 1825. PLEKOCHEILUS. Also of Guilding, AURICULA Caprella, Lam. Pl. xxv. fig. 522, 523.

CAPRINA. D'Orb. DICERAS. Auct.?

CAPRINUS. Montf. (Conch. Syst. t. 2, p. 143.) The figure appears to be intended to represent Helix Nux-denticulata.

CAPSA. Lamarck. *Fam*. Nymphacea, Lam.—*Descr*. Equivalve, transverse, subequilateral, subtrigonal; cardinal teeth, two in one valve, a notched one in the other; lateral teeth remote, obsolete; an external ligament; two muscular impressions in each valve; a large sinus in the muscular impression of the mantle.—*Obs*. This genus is so nearly related to Donax, that it is difficult to distinguish it at first sight. The Capsæ, however, have not the short, plain, straight, posterior side, the distinct lateral teeth, nor the crenulated margins which characterize nearly all the Donaces. They are found in the British Channel, Brazil and coast of Pacific Ocean. They are known from Eyrcina by not having the pit in the hinge for the ligament. C. Braziliensis. Pl. v. fig. 109.

CAPULUS. Montf. 1810. *Fam*. Calyptracea, Lam.—*Descr*. Obliquely conical, posteriorly recurved; apex pointed, sub-spiral; aperture large, rounded, oval; with two muscular impressions, lateral, meeting behind; epidermis horny, rather velvety. Britain, Mediterranean, West Indies, California, Australia. *Ex*. C. ungaricus. Pl. xii. fig. 240.

CARDIACEA. (Cardiacées, Lam.) A family of the order Conchifera Dimyaria, Lam. Most of the genera of shells contained in this family are included in the very extensive family of Conchacea, in the system of De Blainville. They are described as having irregularly formed cardinal teeth. Most of the species are ventricose, and have regular radiating ribs. The family contains the genera Cardium, Cardita, Cypricardia, Hiatella, Isocardia, and others enumerated in the explanation of figures 122 to 130. Their characters may be thus explained.

1. CARDIUM. Two cardinal and two lateral teeth in each valve, including *Hemicardium, Papyridea* and *Aphrodita*, in the last of which the teeth are nearly obsolete. Fig. 122, 123, 123*, 123**.
2. VENERICARDIA. Two oblique cardinal teeth, one elongated; including *Cardita*, which has the umbones nearly terminal. *Pachymya* may probably be included, but the hinge is not known. Fig. 121, 124, and 130.
3. HIPPOPODIUM. One elongated cardinal tooth. Fig. 129.
4. MEGALODON. Hinge broad, septiform, with a large tooth in the centre of one valve. Fig. 127.
5. ISOCARDIA. Teeth laminar; umbones spiral. Fig. 126.
6. CARDILIA. The same with a septiform posterior laminar tooth.
7. HIPPAGUS. Shaped like Isocardia, without teeth. Fig. 128.

CARDILIA. Desh. 1837. HEMICYCLONOSTA. *Fam*. Cardiacea, Lam. A genus formed for the reception of Isocardia semi-sulcata, Lam. and a small fossil shell, which Deshayes had formerly named Hemicyclonosta Michelini; thus described, (translation) "shell oval, oblong, longitudinal, white, heart-shaped, ventricose, with large prominent umbones; hinge with a small cardinal tooth and a pit at the side; a spoon-shaped projection for the reception of the internal ligament; anterior muscular impression rounded, not deep; the posterior being upon a thin, horizontal lamina, projecting in the anterior." Deshayes further remarks that although the animal is unknown, the relations of the genus may be established by means of the shell alone. Two families contain all the shells which have the internal ligament inserted in a spoon-shaded projection; in the one, that of the Anatinæ, the ligament is supported upon a little bone, which is not soldered to the hinge; in the other, that of the Mactraceæ, this little bone has no existence. In the former, all the shells are inequivalve; in the latter equivalve. And M. Deshayes, considering that the valves are equal, and that there is no separate bone to the hinge, is of opinion that the genus ought to be placed near the Lutrariæ, and not far from the Anatinæ. C. semisulcata, pl. xxiv. fig. 501, 2.

CARDINAL MARGIN. The edge of a bivalve shell on which the teeth is placed.

CARDINAL TEETH. The teeth upon the hinge directly beneath the umbones of a bivalve shell, as distinguished from the lateral teeth, which are placed at a distance on each side. In Venus, fig. 119, the cardinal teeth are marked by the letter *c*.

CARDIOCARDITES. Bl. A genus separated from CARDITA, Auct. Thus described, (translation) "oval species, with the inferior margin nearly straight, or a very little inflated, crenulated and completely closed. *Ex*. La C. Ajar, Adans. Seneg. pl. xvi. fig. 2."

CARDISSA. Megerle, 1811. A genus composed of those species of CARDIUM *Auct*. which are heart-shaped. *Ex*. C. dionæum, fig. 122. and C. Cardissa.

CARDITA. Brug. 1789. *Fam*. Cardiacea, Lam. Submytilacea, Bl.—*Descr*. Equivalve, inequilateral, ovate, subquadrate or oblong, marked externally by ribs radiating from the umbones and terminating in a

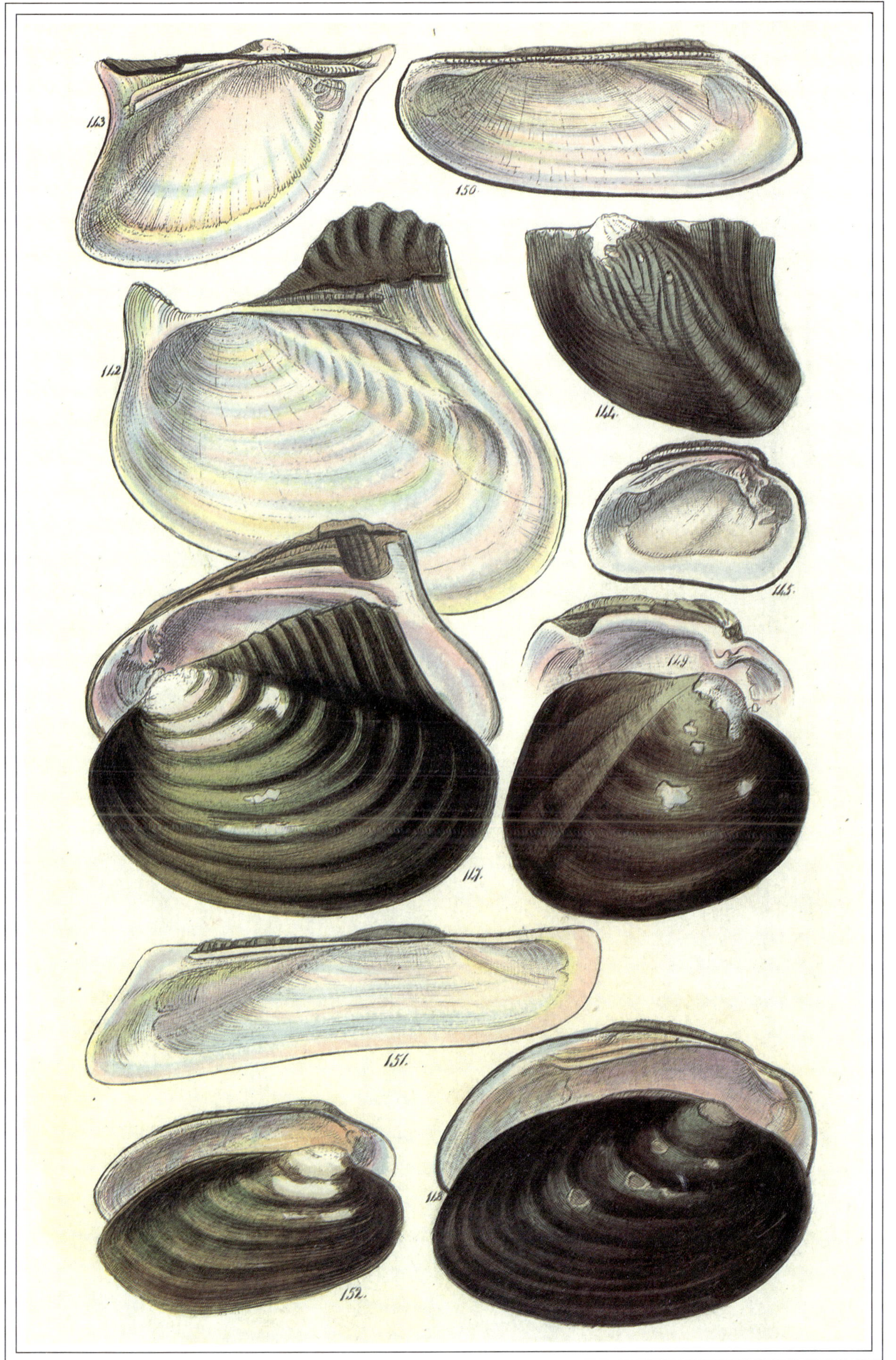

142. Dipsas plicatus, Leach.
Cristaria, Schum.
143. Hyria corrugata, Lam.
Paxyodon, Schum. Triplodon.
144. Syrmatophora, Sow. Prisodon,
Schum. Diplodon, Spix.
145. Unio littoralis, Lam. Mysca.
ovata, Turton.
147. ——Alatus. Symphynota, Lea.
148. ——Atratus, Lam. Naia, Sw.
149. Monocondylæa Paraguayana.
150. Iridina elongata.
Pleiodon, Conrad.
151. Mycetopus
solenoides, D'Orb.
Spatha, Lea.
} Platiris Lea.
152. Anodon Cataractus.

crenulated margin on the inner surface; cardinal teeth in one valve, one long, thick, oblique; another short, more straight; in the other valve one long, oblique, thick. Muscular impressions two in each valve, rather oval; palleal impression not sinuated.—*Obs.* This description includes Lamarck's genus Venericardia, which, although consisting of the more oblong species, is not considered sufficiently distinct to justify the separation. Cypricardia is distinguished from this genus by a remote lateral tooth. Mediterranean, Africa, East Indies, &c. Cardita calyculata, fig. 124.

CARDIUM. Linn. *Fam.* Cardiacea, Lam. Conchacea. Bl.—*Descr.* Equivalve, sub-equilateral, sometimes gaping posteriorly, ornamented on the outside by ribs radiating from the umbones; cardinal teeth, two in each valve, locked into each other cross-wise, lateral teeth, two in each valve, remote; muscular impressions, two in each valve; palleal impression entire. Ligament external, inflated.—*Obs.* Although this genus includes many remarkable forms, the characters are so easily defined that there is no difficulty in distinguishing it from any other genus. The principal forms are Cardium Angulatum, fig. 123, and C. Hemicardium, fig. 123**; Cardium Grœnlandicum, fig. 123*. (Aphrodite) Cardium Dionæum, fig. 122, (Cardissa) and Apertum, fig. 503, 4. (Papyridea.) Pl. vi. It is somewhat surprising that this genus, which contains some of the most beautiful forms of bivalve Testacea, should have been left till quite lately without any attempt to revise the species and settle the synonyms. The monograph in the Author's Conchological Illustrations contains sixty species from all climates. Pl. vi. fig. 122, 123, 123*, 123**. Pl. xxiv. fig. 503, 504.

CARINARIA. Lamarck, 1801, *Class*, Cephalopoda. *Division*, Monothalamia, Lam. *Fam.* Nectopoda, B.—*Descr.* Symmetrical or nearly so, conical, thin, glassy, fragile, patelliform; with a fimbriated dorsal keel; apex convolute, bent forwards; aperture oval, pointed at the dorsal extremity. *Hab.* Amboyna, Indian Ocean, and Mediterranean Sea.—*Obs.* A most singular and beautiful shell, remarkable for its transparency, its fragile structure, and the dorsal keel, whence it derives its name. It was once so rare that a single specimen of the large species realized a hundred guineas. C. Mediterranea. Pl. xxiii. fig. 488.

CARINATED. (From *Carina*, a keel.) Applied to any shell having a raised, thin ledge, passing round a whorl or any other part of a shell, as in Carinaria, fig. 488.

CARINEA. Swainson, 1840. Ultimus, Montf. 1810. Ovulum gibbosum, Auct. fig. 343, and similar species.

CARINELLA. Adanson. Lutraria papyracea, Lam. *Fam.* Mactracea, Lam. Fig. 77.

CARINIDEA. Swainson, 1840. Infundibulum. Montf. 1810.

CAROCOLLUS. Montf. *Fam.* Colimacea, Lam.—*Descr.* Orbicular, depressed, with the outer side of the whorls angulated or keeled, whorls few; peritreme reflected; columella contiguous to the axis; epidermis thin.—*Obs.* This genus differing from Helix only in the whorls being angulated, is hardly distinct enough from the latter to justify the separation. In De Ferrusac's system these species constitute the division Helicigona, of the genus Helix. C. Lamarckii, fig. 277. East and West Indies, Philippines, South America and Europe. Pl. xiii. fig. 277.

CARTILAGE. See Ligament.

CARYCHIUM. Müller, 1774. *Fam.* Auriculacea, Bl. Colimacea, Lam.—*Descr.* Oblong or cylindrical, with gradually increasing whorls, few in number; aperture straight, short, with a fold on the columella.—*Obs.* This genus of minute land shells differs from Auricula chiefly in the soft parts. De Ferrusac enumerates three species, C. Lineatum, C. Corticaria, (*Odostomia*, Flem.) and C. Minimum, fig. 301. De Blainville places it in his genus Auricula, as "species with two folds and a posterior tooth on the columella," giving a figure of A. Mysotis as his example, and quoting the name Phitia, Gray. Europe. Pl. xiv. fig. 301.

CASSIDARIA. Lam. 1812. Should be Morio. Montf. 1810, on the ground of priority. (From Cassis.) *Fam.* Purpurifera, Lam. Entomostomata, Bl.—*Descr.* Oval, ventricose, spirally grooved and tuberculated, with a short turrited spire and a large aperture, terminating anteriorly in a recurved canal; outer lip thickened, reflected, undulated or denticulated; inner lip expanded over a part of the body whorl and the columella, with part of its lower edge free.—*Obs.* The recent species of this genus are not numerous; the few fossil species occur in the tertiary strata. C. carinata is found in "Calc-grossier" and London Clay. In general form this resembles Cassis, but is at once distinguished by the canal, which does not turn abruptly back, but is slightly curved upwards. Oniscia (C. Oniscus, &c. Lam.) is distinguished by the shortness of the canal, and the granulated surface of the inner lip. C. Echinophora. Mediterranean. Pl. xix. fig. 407, 408.

CASSIDEA. Sw. (From Cassis.) A genus composed of those species of the genus Cassis, Auct. which have the "aperture wide; outer lip never broad or flattened, but sometimes slightly inflected; inner lip spreading, but never dilated or detached beyond the base into a prominent rim." East Indies. *Ex.* C. Glauca. C. Bezoardica. Schum. 1837. Pl. xix. fig. 411.

CASSIDULUS. Humph. The genus Pyrula being restricted to the fig-shaped species, this name is used for the turrited and turbinated species that remain. C. melongena, &c. but not including P. perversa. Fulgur. Montf.

CASSIDULINA. D'Orbigny. A genus of microscopic Foraminifera.

CASSIS. Browne, 1756. (A helmet.) *Fam.* Purpurifera, Lam. Entomostomata, Bl.—*Descr.* Oval or triangular, ventricose, thick, generally tuberculated, with a short varicose spire; aperture long, sometimes narrow, with the outer lip thickened and reflected, generally denticulated; the inner lip spread over the surface of the body whorl, indented and incrassated at its inner edge; canal turned suddenly over the back of the shell.—*Hab.* Seas of tropical climates. The fossil species are rare, occurring in the tertiary strata.—*Obs.* The large, common species of this well known genus are used for shell cameos and as ornaments on chimney pieces, grottos, &c. and are remarkable for the triangular disc, presented by the inner lip, which, in many species, is thickened and spread over the front of the body whorl and the angulated outer lip. The smaller, more rounded species, which have widened apertures, have been separated by Swainson, under the generic name Cassidea. The C. rufa, coarctata, &c. are formed by Mr. Stutchbury into a new genus under the name Cypræcassis, for reasons which will be stated under the word. Cassidaria is distinguished by the gradual curve of the canal. Mr. Reeve's monograph contains 43 species. C. tuberosa (diminished.) Pl. xix. fig. 410.

CASTALIA. Lamarck, 1819. *Fam.* Trigonées, Lam.—*Descr.* Fluviatile, equivalve, inequilateral, trigonal, with corroded umbones; hinge with two laminar, transversely striated teeth, one of which is posterior, remote from the umbones, short, divided, the other anterior, elongated; epidermis thick; internal surface pearly. Lamarck, in describing this shell, states that he regards it as intermediate between Trigonia and Unio. It should, however, certainly have been placed in the family of "Nayades," and perhaps should form a part of the genus Unio itself. C. ambigua, Lam. Pl. vii. fig. 140.

CATILLUS. Brong. INOCERAMUS, Sowerby. CATILLUS. Humph. 1797. CIMBER. Montf. 1810. NAVICELLA. Lamarck, 1822. Pl. x. fig. 158.

CATOPHRAGMUS. Sow. (From Κατω, *beneath*; φραγμος, *a place paled in.*) *Order*, Sessile Cirripedes, Lam.—*Descr*. Eight principal valves, cemented side by side in a circle; eight small pointed valves beneath, covering the joints of the upper circle, and numerous still smaller valves forming the base of the shell; operculum, four valves.—*Obs*. Catophragmus is the only genus of Sessile Cirripedes, which consists of eight principal valves, excepting Octomeris. The latter genus has not the accessary pieces from which the former derives its name. C. imbricatus. Pl. i. fig. 23.

CAUDAL CANAL. The elongated hollow process which terminates the aperture anteriorly of some univalve shells. For instance, Murex Haustellum, fig. 396, has an elongated caudal canal.

CELLANTHUS. Montf. VORTICIALIS, Bl. A genus of microscopic Foraminifera.

CELLULACEA. Bl. The second order of Cephalophora, Bl. consisting of doubtful microscopic bodies, with a number of variously arranged shells, as distinguished from the true Polythalamia, Bl. or chambered shells. See FORAMINIFERA.

CEMORIA. Leach. 1819. A small patelliform shell, differing from Fissurella, in having the fissure placed behind the apex, which is produced, pointed and incurved. It is the Patella Fissurella, Müll. Patella Noachina, Chemn. F. Noachina, Sow. Puncturella, Lowe. Scotland and Tierra del Fuego. Cemoria Flemingii. Pl. xiii. fig. 244.

CENTRAL. A term used to indicate the position of the muscular impression of a bivalve shell when it is near the centre of the inner surface. It is also applied to the siphon perforating the septum of a chambered shell when it is placed near the centre of the plate. *Sub*-central is also used as a comparative term, to indicate the position of the siphon, or of the muscular impression, is *near* the centre. Thus in Placuna (fig. 184), the muscular impression is central: in Exogyra (fig. 183), it is *sub*-central.

CEPA. Humph. 1797. ANOMIA, Linn. Müller. 1776.

CEPHALOPHORA. Bl. The first class of Malacozoæ, Bl. Divided into: *Order* 1. Cryptodibranchiata; 2. Cellulacea; 3. Polythalamacea. The first consisting of Cuttle-fish, &c. which are destitute of shells; the second composed of those microscopic cellular bodies, which are regarded as shells by some authors; and the third containing the true chambered shells.

CEPHALOPODA. Lam. (Cephalopodes.) (Κεφαλη, *kephale*, head; πους, ποδος, *podos*, foot.) The fourth order of the *class* Mollusca, Lam. containing molluscs, which are characterized by having a series of arms surrounding the head, which is placed above a sack-shaped body. This order is divided into Polythalamia, or many-chambered shells) Monothalamia, or single-chambered Cephalopoda: and Sepiaria, or cuttle-fish. Fig. 463 to 488.

CERATISOLEN. Forbes. PHARUS, Leach. Ms. Gray. Syn. Brit. mus. A genus formed for the reception of Solen legumen, which differs from the true Solens, or razor shells, in having the umbones nearly central, &c.

CERATODES. Guild. 1828. Marisa, Gray. 1824. (Κερατωδης, like a horn.) A genus composed of the flat, orbicular species of AMPULLARIA, Auct. which present so near a resemblance to the Planorbes, as to have been considered as belonging to them. Planorbis has, however, a horny texture, and no operculum, and it is always *reversed*. Pl. xv. fig. 320, represents Ampullaria (Ceratodes) Cornu-arietis.

CERIPHASIA. Swainson, 1840. A sub-genus of Melanianæ, thus described, "Cerithiform; outer lip thin, dilated at the base; aperture small, slightly emarginate, without any internal groove; inner lip thin. C. sulcata, Sw. fig. 38. p. 204." (Sw. Lard. Cyclop. Malac. p. 342.)

CERITHIDEA. Swainson. Part of POTAMIS, sp. decollatus, with rounded whorls, and spread outer lip sinuous at the base.

CERITHIOPSIS. Forbes and Hanley, 1851. A genus of shells distinguished from Cerithium on purely anatomical grounds. Ex. C. tuberculare. British Moll. Pl. xci. figs. 7, 8. p. 365.

CERITHIUM. Adanson, 1757. *Fam*. Canalifera, Lam. Entomostomata, Bl.—*Descr*. Elongated, ribbed, tuberculated, or rarely smooth, with a lengthened, turrited, pointed, pyramidal spire, consisting of numerous whorls; aperture sub-quadrate, terminated anteriorly by a tortuous canal; outer lip thickened, sometimes reflected, expanded; inner lip thickened posteriorly; operculum horny, spiral, with numerous whorls.—*Obs*. The fresh-water shells described as Cerithia by Lamarck, are separated under the name Potamis, and may be known by the thick, horny epidermis. Triphora, Desh. has the canal closed, except at the extremities. Cerithium Telescopium, does not appear to present the same characters as the other Cerithia, and has been separated by some writers under the generic name Telescopium. Cerithium Aluco, fig. 372. Mediterranean, East and West Indies, Coasts of the Pacific, Gallapagos, Australia, &c. Some small species are British. Fossils are numerous in the tertiary beds. Pl. xvii. fig. 372.

CERVICOBRANCHIATA. Bl. The second order of Paracephalophora Hermaphrodita, Bl. containing symmetrical patelliform shells, divided into the families Retifera and Branchifera.

CETOCIS. Montf. *Fam*. Orthocerata, Lam. and Bl. Placed by De Blainville in his section of Belemnites, characterized as having small folds at the apex. *Ex*. B. Penicillatus.

CETOPIRUS. Ranz. CORONULA BALENARIS, Auct. Pl. i. fig. 16.

CHÆNA. Gray. FISTULANA, Lamarck.

CHAMA. Linnæus. *Fam*. Chamacea, Lam. and Bl.—*Descr*. Inequivalve, irregular, thick, foliaceous, attached by the umbone of the lower and larger valve. External ligament placed in a groove, following the curve of the umbones. Umbones spiral, coiled round on the back of the valves; hinge with a thick, crenated, lengthened tooth, in one valve, entering a corresponding cavity in the hinge margin of the other; muscular impressions, two in each valve, distinct, lateral.—*Obs*. The Linnæan genus Chama, included the beautiful shells now called Tridacna. These are exceedingly different from the true Chamæ, being regular and unattached. The Chama (Tridacna) gigas, when at its full age and development, is the largest shell known. Specimens have occurred weighing upwards of 500 lbs., and measuring two feet across. Diceras may be known from Chama by the spiral horns into which the umbones are produced; Isocardia, by the regularity of the shells, and it is hardly necessary to mention Spondylus, which may be known by the triangular disc between the umbones; Cleidothærus, Stutch. which resembles Chama in general form, has a separate bony appendage attached to the hinge, and may, moreover, be distinguished by its elongated muscular impression. 55 species are contained in Mr. Reeve's Monograph. E. and W. Indies. Ch. Lazarus, Pl. ix. fig. 153.

CHAMACEA. Bl. The seventh family of the order Lamellibranchiata, Bl. containing the genera Chama, Diceras, Etheria, Tridacna, Isocardia and Trigonia.

CHAMACEA. Lam. A family belonging to the order Conchifera Dimyaria, Lam. described as inequivalve, attached, irregular; with or without a single rough tooth on the hinge; with two lateral muscular impressions in each valve. This family contains the genera:

1. Chama. Leafy; umbones spiral. Fig. 153.
2. Etheria. Very irregular, pearly, without teeth. Fig. 155.
3. Diceras. Like Chama, but with the umbones free, produced. Fig. 154.

CHAMBERED. When the cavity of a shell is not continuous, but is divided by shelly diaphragms or septa, it is said to be chambered. This is the case with the shells of the Polythalamous Cephalopoda, as in the Nautilus (see Introduction). The character is not confined to these, as it occurs in some species of Spondyli, and in several turrited univalves.

CHAMOSTRÆA. De Roissy. Cleidothærus. Stutch.

CHARYBS. Montf. A genus of microscopic Foraminifera.

CHELIBS. Montf. A genus of microscopic Foraminifera.

CHELIDONURA. Adans. Sowerby's Thesaurus, 1850. A sub-genus of Bullidæ, the shell of which is thus described, "hid in the thickness of the mantle, thin, very open, scarcely spiral, with the right border ending in a point."

CHELINOTUS. Swainson. A genus of "Haliotidæ," Sw. including Velutina, Lam. a species of Sigaretus from Tonga, and Coriocella, Bl. Thus described, "Animal cheloniform, broad; depressed; the mantle larger than the shell, lobed in front; tentacula two, short, obtuse; eyes basal; mouth circular; shell ear-shaped, thin, fragile, imperforate; pillar none."

CHELONOBIA. Leach. Coronula Testudinaria, Auct. Pl. i. fig. 15.

CHEMNITZIA. D'Orbigny. A genus of small transparent shells, resembling Scalariæ in some respects, but without varices. C. varicula. Pl. xxviii. fig. 585.

CHERSINA. Humph. Part of Achatina, Lam.

CHICOREUS. Montf. 1810. A generic division of the genus Murex, consisting of such species as have three ramified varices. *Ex.* M. inflatus, fig. 395.

CHILINA. Gray. *Fam.* Auriculacea, Bl. Colimacea, Lam.—*Descr.* Oval, thin, covered with an olive green epidermis; spire rather short, consisting of few whorls; aperture large, oval, rounded anteriorly; outer lip thin, joining the inner lip without a sinus; inner lip spread over part of the body whorl, terminating in a thick columella with one or two folds.—*Obs.* These shells differ from the true Auriculæ in the thinness of the outer lip. C. Dombeyana (Auricula Dombeyana, Auct.) Fig. 300. The illustrated catalogue published by the author (Sow. Conch. illustr. parts 135, 136) contains 13 species. Rivers of South America. Pl. xiv. fig. 300.

CHILOTREMA. Leach, 1819. A sub-genus of Helix, containing Helix lapicida. Auct. Gray, Turton, p. 440.

CHIMOTREMA.—— ? Belongs to Helix.

CHIONE. Megerle. Cytheræa maculosa, (fig. 117, c.) sulcata, circinata, &c. Auct. and other similar species. See Thesaurus Conchylium, No. 12, and our figure. Pl. vi. fig. 117, c.

CHISMOBRANCHIATA. Bl. The second order of the first section of Paracephalophora Monoica, Bl. Those Mollusca belonging to this order which have shells, have them either internal or external, but always scutiform, with depressed spires and wide, haliotoid, oblique apertures, without a columellar lip properly so called. This order partly answers to the family Macrostomata, in the system of Lamarck. It contains the genera Coriocella, Sigaretus, Cryptostoma, Oxinoe, Stomatella, and Velutina.

CHITON. Lamarck. (χιτον, an integument), *Fam.* Phyllidiana, Lam. *Class*, Polyplaniphora, Bl.—*Descr.* Oval, consisting of eight arched valves arranged in a series across the body of the animal and fixed in the skin which forms a rim around them, sometimes scaly, spinose, or rugose, sometimes smooth.—*Obs.* The genus Chiton, commonly called "Coat of Mail," from its resemblance to jointed armour, remains to the present day in exactly the same state with regard to its boundaries as that in which Linnæus found it, and in which he left it. That illustrious Naturalist placed it among the multivalves in his purely Conchological system, although the animal is totally different from the Cirripedes. The shells are prettily marked, and are found attached to the rocks in all seas of Tropical and Southern climates, but fossil species are almost unknown. Fig. 227, C. Spinosus. The genus is divided in the British Museum Synopsis, according to the character of the marginal integument into the genera Lophiuns, *Ex.* Chiton squamosus; Radsia, *Ex.* Chiton Barnesii; Callochiton, *Ex.* Ch. lævis; Ischnochilon, *Ex.* Ch Textile; Leptochiton, *Ex.* Ch. cinereus; Conicia, *Ex.* Ch. elegans; Acanthapleusa, *Ex.* Ch. spinosa; Chiton, *Ex.* Ch. gigas; Schizochiton, *Ex.* Ch. inscisus; Corepheum, *Ex.* Ch. Echinalus; Planiphora, Ornithochiton, Enoplochiton, Mopalia, Katharina, Cryptochiton, Cryptoconchus, Amicula, Acanthochetes, Chitonellus, Eryphiochiton, Metopoma. Our Plate xii. fig. 227, 228. Pl. xxiv. fig. 506, 507.

CHITONELLUS. Lam. (From *Chiton.*) Separated by Lamarck from Chiton, on account of the valves being placed at a greater distance from each other, the soft integument of the animal intervening. C. striatus. Philippines. Pl. xxii. fig. 228.

CHLOROSTOMA. Swainson. A sub-genus of "Trochinæ." Sw. (Trochus) of which C. argyrostoma is given as an example. Sw. Lard. Cyclop. p. 350.

CHORUS. Gray, 1850. Monocerous Giganteus. Lesson.

CHRYSOAR. Montf. Probably a species of Orthoceras.

CHRYSODOMUS. Swainson, 1840. "Distinguished from Fusus, by the comparative shortness of the basal channel, and the ventricose or enlarged shape of the body whorl. The beautiful orange-mouthed Whelk of England is a typical example; and the few others known are of a very large size, and chiefly found in Northern Seas, where they represent the more elegant Fusi of tropical latitudes; the outer lip is always thin and smooth." Sw. p. 90, paragraph 78, described at page 308.

CHRYSOLUS. Montf. Polystomella, Bl. A genus of microscopic Foraminifera.

CHRYSOSTOMA. Swainson, 1840. A genus of the family "Rotellinæ," Sw. Thus described, "Shell turbinate; the whorls few and convex; aperture effuse, round; inner lip thickened just over, and almost concealing the umbilicus. Nicobaricus, Martini, 182 fig. 1822–5." Sw. Lard. Cyclop. Malac. p. 327. Pl. xxv. fig. 542.

CHTHALAMUS. Ranz. *Fam.* Balanidea, Bl. *Order*, Sessile Cirripedes, Lam.—*Descr.* "Shell much depressed, valves thick, thickened at the base, with prominent areas; operculum nearly horizontal, composed of four valves."—*Obs.* This description would apply generically to the shell called Platylepas in the British Museum, only nothing is said about the prominent plates jutting from the internal surface of the valves. The difference between this genus and Balanus consists principally in the horizontal position of the operculum, and general flatness of the shell. C. stellatus. Pl. i. fig. 18.

CIBICIDES. Montf. A genus of microscopic Foraminifera.

CIDARIS. Swains. 1840. A genus composed of Turbo Smaragdus, petholatus, and other similar species. The word Cidaris is, however, already in use for a genus of Echinæ.

CIDAROLLUS. Montf. A genus of microscopic Foraminifera.

CILIATED. (Ciliæ, hairs.) Having minute hairs as in Orbicula, Lingula, &c. and the jointed feelers of the Cirripedes.

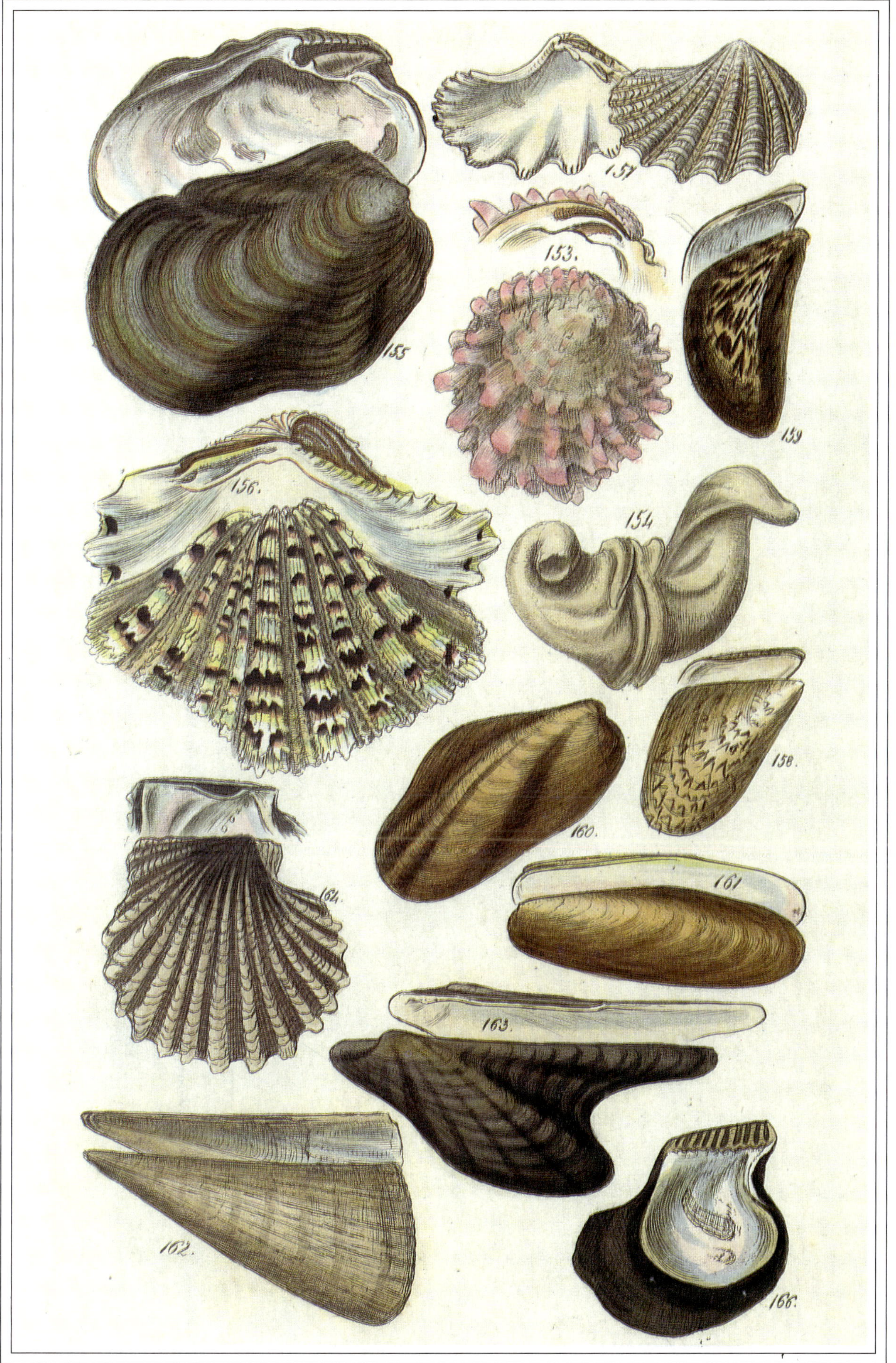

Fam. Chamacea

153. Chama Lazarus. Jataronus, Adanson.
154. Diceras perversum, (from Sowerby's Genera.)
155. Etheria semilunata.

Order, MONOMYARIA

Fam. Tridacnacea

156. Hippopus maculatus.
157. Tridacna elongata.

Fam. Mytilacea

158. Mytilus achatinus.
159. ——polymorphus. Dreissina.
160. Modiola Tulipa.
161. Lithodomus Dactylus.
162. Pinna saccata.

Fam. Malleacea

163. Avicula Hirundo.
164. ——margaritifera. Meleagrina, Lam.
.166. Perna Ephippium.

CIMBER. Montf. 1810. NAVICELLA. Lamarck, 1822. "Cimber" claims priority.

CINERAS. Leach (*Cinereus*, ash-coloured.) Included by Darius with Otion, under the name CONCHODERMA. Olfus, 1814. *Order*, Pedunculated Cirripedes, Lam.—*Descr.* Animal with a quadrilateral body, supported on a fleshy peduncle, with an opening in front of the upper part for the passage of a bunch of ciliated tentacula. Immediately above this aperture is a pair of small elongated valves, placed in a nearly horizontal position; at the lower part is another tripartite pair placed perpendicularly, one on each side, and a narrow, angulated, keel-shaped piece placed at the back.—*Obs.* The nearest approach to this genus is Otion. (C. Vittatus.) Found upon substances floating in the sea. Pl. ii. fig. 42.

CINEREOUS. (*Cinereus.*) Ash-coloured.

CINGULA. Fleming, 1828. RISSOA, Freminville, 1814.

CIONELLA. Jeffreys. ZUA, Leach, MS. Gray, 1840. *Fam.* Colimacea, Lam.—*Descr.* Oblong or elongated; last whorl large; apex rather acute; columella, sub-interrupted; aperture canaliculated, sub-effuse at the base; margins very unequal; no umbilicus. BULINUS octonus, lubricus, acicula, &c. Auct. C. lubrica. Pl. xiv. fig. 285.

CIRCE. Schum. Distinguished from CYTHERÆA by the total want of Pallæal sinus, and by a peculiar flatness near the umbones. The monograph in Thesaurus Conchyliorum, by the Author (No. 12) contains sixteen pieces. Circe pectinata and C. scripta, represent the two groups. Circe scripta, Pl. xxvii. fig. 577.

CIRRIPEDES. Lam. The tenth class of invertebrated animals, so named from the curled and ciliated branchia which protrude from the oval aperture of the shells. The class Cirripedes of Lamarck constitutes the entire genus *Lepas* of Linnæus. They are divided into two sections; first, Sessile Cirr. attached by the basal portion of the shell; second, Pedunculated Cirr. supported upon a peduncle. Figs. 14 to 45.

CIRROBRANCHIATA. Bl. The first order of Paracephalophora Hermaphrodita, Bl. This order has been formed for the purpose of giving a place in the system to the genus Dentalium. The animal of which has lungs, consisting of numerous filaments, having their basal origin in two radical lobes under the dock.

CIRRUS. J. Sowerby (cirrus, a tendril.) *Fam.* Turbinacea, Bl. and Lam.—*Descr.* Spiral, conical, with a hollow axis; whorls contiguous, numerous, rounded, or slightly angulated.—*Obs.* This fossil genus resembles Trochus, from which it is known by the deep funnel-shaped umbilicus. C. nodosus. Pl. xvi. fig. 349.

CISTULA. Humph. Part of CYCLOSTOMA, Lam. C. fimbriata. See Thesaurus Conchyliorum.

CLANCULUS. Montf. 1810. TROCHUS *Pharaonis*, Lam.—*Obs.* This, with several other species, belong more properly to MONODONTA, Lam. ODONTIS, Sow. Pl. xvi. fig. 361.

CLATHODON. Conrad. GNATHODON, Gray.

CLATHRUS. Oken, 1815. The species of Scalaria, which have the whorls contingent. *Ex.* Scalaria Clathrata.

CLAUSILIA. Drap. 1805. (*Clausium*, a valve or folding door.) Colimacea, Lam. Limacinea, Bl.—*Descr.* Spire elongated, consisting of many volutions; aperture small, sub-quadrate, having several tooth-shaped folds in the columella. A small, elastic shelly plate, attached to the columella within, called the Clausium, its office being to enclose the aperture when the animal has retired within the shell.—*Obs.* This last character distinguishes it from the Pupæ, to some of which it bears a very near resemblance.—*Hab.* Land, in the central and southern parts of Europe, several British species. C. Macascarensis. Pl. xiv. fig. 295.

CLAUSIUM. A name applied to the beautiful contrivance whence the genus Clausilia derives its name, consisting of a little bony tortuous plate, placed in a groove in the columella. Here it serves the purpose of a door, which, when not prevented by counteracting pressure, springs forward on its elastic ligament, and encloses the animal in his retirement. The aperture is opened by pushing back the clausium into the groove.

CLAUSULUS. Montf. Conch. Syst. 1, 179. A genus of microscopic Foraminifera.

CLAVA. Humph. CERITHIUM, Lam.

CLAVAGELLA. Lamarck, 1818. (*Clava*, a club.) *Fam.* Tubicolæ, Lam. Pyloridea, Bl.—*Descr.* Two irregular flattish valves, one fixed or soldered, so as to form part of the side of an irregular shelly tube; the other free within the tube near the base.—*Obs.* The shells composing this genus are found in stones, madrepores, &c. and appear to form the connecting link between Aspergillum, which has both valves cemented into the tube; and Fistulana, in which both are free. Found recent on the coast of Malta and New South Wales. A fossil species. Pl. ii. fig. 45.

CLAVALITHES. Swainson, 1840. A genus composed of some fossil shells, separated from the genus Fusus, which, having the general form of Turbinella Rapa, &c. are considered by Swainson, as holding an intermediate station between Fusus and the Turbinellidæ.—*Descr.* "Unequally sub-fusiform; the body whorl, and spire, being conic; and the canal suddenly contracted and attenuated; terminal whorls papillary; inner lip thick; pillar smooth, C. longævus, clavellatus, Noæ, ponderosus, Sw."—*Obs.* The papillary spire may form a sufficient reason for separating this genus from Fusus, while the absence of plates on the columella places them at a still greater distance from Turbinella. Pl. xxvi. fig. 548.

CLAVATE. When one extremity of the shell is attenuated, and the other becomes suddenly ventricose or globular, it is said to be Clavate. *Ex.* Murex Haustellum, fig. 396.

CLAVATULA. Lamarck, 1801. The generic name by which Lamarck originally distinguished those species of Pleurotoma which were remarkable for the shortness of their canals. In his system, however, they are re-united to Pleurotoma. P. Strombiformis. BRACHISTOMA, Swainson. Pl. xvi. fig. 381.

CLAVICANTHA. Swainson, 1840. CLAVATUTA, Lamarck, 1801. A genus separated from Pleurotoma, Lam. consisting of species, which are described as "thick, sub-fusiform; the surface rugose, and the whorls sub-coronated; channel short; slit assuming the form of a short, broad sinus. C. imperialis, E. M. 440, spirata, E. M. 440, fig. 5, conica, E. M. 439, fig. 9, echinata, E. M. 439, fig. 8, Auriculifera, E. M. 439, fig. 10."

CLAVICLE. (*clavis*, a key.) A little key. This term is applied to the bony appendage in the hinge of some species of Anatina, (those included in the generic term Lyonsia) Cleidothærus, Myochama, &c.

CLAVULINA. D'Orb. A genus of microscopic Foraminifera.

CLEIDOTHÆRUS. Stutchbury, 1835. (Θαιρος, hinge, Κλεις, clavicle.) *Fam.* Chamaceæ or Myariæ, Lam.—*Descr.* Inequivalve, irregular, solid, attached; with one cardinal, conical tooth in the free valve, entering a corresponding indenture in the other; and an oblong shelly appendage, fixed by an internal cartilage in a groove under the umbones; muscular impressions, two in each valve, one elongated, the other uniform.—*Obs.* This shell is like Chama in general form, but is distinguished by the clavicle or shelly appendage from which its name is derived. Pl. iii. figs. 75, 76.

CLEMENTIA. Gray, 1840. Venus Papyracea. Wood's Supplement, fig. 8. See Monograph of Veneridæ, forthcoming in Pt. xiii. xiv. Thesaurus Conchyliorum, by the Author.

CLEODORA. *Per. et Les. Fam.* Pteropoda, Lam. Thecosomata, Bl.—*Descr.* Thin, transparent, pyramidal, with flat alate sides, and oval aperture. Pl. xii. fig. 221, C. cuspidata.

CLISIPHONITES. Montf. Microscopic. Lenticulina, Bl.

CLITHON. Montf. 1810. Neritina Corona, spinosa, &c. Auct. fig. 325.

CLITIA. Leach. *Fam.* Balanidea, Bl. *Order*, Sessile Cirripedes, Lam.—*Descr.* Sub-conical, compressed, consisting of four unequal valves, two larger and two smaller, joined together side by side, by the interlocking of their dentated edges, a process somewhat like that which joiners call dove-tailing. Operculum, consisting of two unequal pointed valves.—*Obs.* Clitia is known from Creusia, by the articulations of the valves, and by the operculum, which in Creusia consists of four valves. C. Verruca, (Lepas Verruca, Gmelin.) Britain and Peru. Pl. i. fig. 20.

CLOSE. The margins of a bivalve shell are described as being close, when there is no hiatus between them in any part, otherwise they are described as *gaping*.

CLOTHO. Faujas. *Fam.* Conchacea, Bl. More properly belonging to the Pyloridea, Bl.; and the Lithophagidæ, Lam.—*Descr.* "Oval, nearly regular, longitudinally striated, equivalve, sub-equilateral; hinge consisting of a bifid tooth, curved like a crochet, larger in one valve than in the other." This description is translated from Blainville, who states that he has never seen the shell. Annales du Museum D'Histoire Naturelle, tom. 9, pl. 17, fig. 4–6.

CLYPEIFORM. (*Clypeus*, a shield.) Open, flat, shaped like a shield or buckler, as Umbrella, fig. 233, and Parmaphorus, fig. 242.

CLYPIDELLA. Sw. A sub-genus of Fissurella, described as having one extremity of the shell slightly raised. C. pustula, Sow. Gen. fig. 3.

COAT OF MAIL. A common name given to shells of the genus Chiton, on account of their resemblance to jointed armour.

COBRESIA. Hübner. Vitrina, Draparnaud.

COCHLEATE. (*Cochleare*, a spoon.) Applied to any shell or part which is hollow and oval, as Patellæ, &c. The cavity containing the cartilage in Mya, fig. 71, is Cochleate.

COCHLICELLA. One of the sub-genera into which De Ferrusac has divided the genus Helix, consisting of Bulinus decollatus, fig. 279, and similar species. See Helix.

COCHLICOPA. Fer. A sub-genus of Helix, partly corresponding with Polyphemus of De Montfort, and consisting of species of Achatina, which have the outer lip undulated.

COCHLITOMA. Fer. A sub-genus of Helix, corresponding with the genus Achatina, Auct. not including those with undulated outer lips.

COCHLODESMA. Couthoy. Boston Journal. Forbes and Hanley. British Mollusca. *Fam.* Myaria. Thin, inequivalve; muscular impressions connected by a deeply sinuated palleal impression; hinge with spoon-shaped process in each valve, with a cartilage; external ligament slight; beaks fissured. Distinguished from Thracia by the character of the hinge. *Ex.* C. prætemis. Pl. xxvii. fig. 573.

COCHLODINA. Fer. A sub-genus of Helix, including the genus Clausilia, Auct.

COCHLODONTA. Fer. A sub-genus of Helix, containing Pupa Uva, Auct. &c.

COCHLOGENA. Fer. A sub-genus of Helix, containing pupiform shells, such as Azeca tridens, fig. 290.

COCHLOHYDRA. Fer. A sub-genus of Helix, composed of the genus Succinea, Auct.

COCHLOSTYLA. Fer. A sub-genus of Helix, composed of the genus Bulinus, Auct.

COLIMACEA. Lam. This Family, of the order Trachelipoda, Lam. includes all land shells, which might with propriety be divided into three sections, the first of which contain the following well known genera:–

1. Succinea. Oval, transparent, oblique; animal amphibious. Fig. 265, 266.
2. Helix. The type of which is the common snail shell. The separation of *Carocolla*, on account of the angulated whorls, or that of *Geotrochus*, on account of the turbinated shape, cannot be well maintained. Fig. 264, 267, 268, 273 to 276, 278 to 281, 294.
3. Anostoma. The aperture turned up towards the spire. Fig. 271, 272.
4. Streptaxis. Whorls excentric. Fig. 269, 270.
5. Bulinus. Oval; aperture entire, including *Bulimulus*, *Balea*, *Cionella*, *Azeca*. Fig. 282 to 285, 289, 290, 296.
6. Achatina. A notch terminating the columella. Fig. 286 to 288.
7. Pupa. Cylindrical; including *Vertigo*, *Alœa*, &c. Fig. 291 to 293.
8. Clausilia. Cylindrical, with a clausium. Fig. 295.

Obs. The above are united in the system of De Ferrusac under the generic name Helix, and divided into sub-genera as explained under that word.

The next section, included in the family Auriculacea, Bl., contains the genera Auricula, Chilina, Carychium, Marinula, Scarabæus, and Partula. Fig. 297 to 302.

The third section contains the following genera of land shells with opercula.

1. Cyclostoma. Aperture round; operculum spiral. Fig. 303, 304.
2. Nematura. Last whorl contracted; operculum spiral. Fig. 305.
3. Helicina. Aperture semi-lunar or angulated; operculum concentric. Fig. 306, 307.
4. Pupina. Shell polished; operculum concentric; aperture round. Fig.
5. Strophostoma. Aperture turned up towards the spire, like Anostoma, but said to have an operculum. Only known fossil. Fig. 97.

COLUMBELLA. Lamarck, 1801. (Columba, a dove.) *Fam.* Columellata, Lam.—*Descr.* Thick, oval, or angular; with short spire, and long narrow aperture, contracted in the centre, and terminating in a short canal; outer lip thickened and dentated; inner lip irregularly crenated. Epidermis thin, brown. Operculum very small, horny.—*Obs.* Those species of Mitra, which resemble Columbella in shape, may easily be distinguished by the plaits on the columella. The Columbellæ are marine, and few fossil species are known. Fig. 430, C. Mercatoria. Swainson has divided this genus into the following: *Columbella*, consisting of C. Mercatoria, &c.; *Pusiostoma*, consisting of the Strombiform species; *Crassispira*, which is most probably a Cerithium; *Nitidella*, consisting of the smooth species; *Conidea*, consisting of the more conical species; another set of the more conical species has been removed from this family, and placed in that of the "Coninæ," but as they are separated by no essential character, we suppose this has merely been done for the purpose of completing the "circle" of the last mentioned family, which otherwise would not have reached the required number of five. Mediterranean, East and West Indies, South America, Coast of California, Gallapagos, &c. The Monograph of this genus in the Author's Thesaurus Conchyliorum, contains 102 species. Plates 36 to 40. Our figure, Pl. xx. fig. 430.

COLUMELLA. The column formed by the inner sides of the volutions of a spiral univalve. It is sometimes described as the inner lip of the aperture, of which it forms a part; but the term would be more properly confined to that portion of the inner lip which is seen below the body whorl, over which the remainder of the lip is frequently spread. All the inner edge of the aperture, including that part of it which covers the body whorl, is called the columellar lip. In fig. 431, the anterior termination of the columella is indicated by the letter *c*. The axis, is an imaginary line drawn strictly through the centre of the whorls, whether their inner edges form a solid column or not.

COLUMELLAR LIP. The inner lip. See COLUMELLA.

COLUMELLATA. Lam. A family of the order Trachelipoda, Lam. containing the following genera:–

1. MITRA. Elongated; aperture narrow; strong folds on the columella; including *Mitrella*, *Mitreola*, *Tiara*, and *Conohelix*. Fig. 431, 432.
2. MARGINELLA. Outer lip reflected; including *Volutella*, *Persicula*, *Gibberula*, and *Glabella*. Fig. 437.
3. COLUMBELLA. Outer and inner lips denticulated or granulated. Fig. 430.
4. VOLUTA. Outer lip thickened; folds on the columella; aperture generally wide; apex papillary; including *Scaphella*, *Harpula*, *Volutilithes*, *Cymbiola*. Fig. 433, 436.
5. MELO. Shell comparatively light; spire short, sometimes hidden; apex round, spiral; folds on the columella laminar. Fig. 435.
6. CYMBA. Upper edge of the aperture separated from the body whorl by a flat disc; apex mammillated, irregular; folds on the columella thick. Fig. 434.
7. VOLVARIA. Cylindrical; aperture long, narrow; folds on the columella small; spire hidden. Fig. 439.

COLUS. Humphrey. 1797. FUSUS COLUS, Lamarck, and similar species. Pl. xviii. fig. 387.

COMPLANARIA. Swainson, 1840. A subgenus of ALASMODON, (Unio), thus described, "shell winged; the valves connate; the bosses very small and depressed; cardinal teeth two or three; lateral teeth represented by irregular grooves. C. gigas (Unio), Sow. Man. fig. 141. Alasmodon complanatus, (Say) C. Rugosa, Sw."

COMPRESSED. Pressed together, or flattened. The application is the same as in common use. A Patella may be described as a vertically compressed cone. A Ranella, on account of the two rows of varices skirting the whorls, appears, as it were, laterally compressed. A bivalve shell is said to be compressed when it is flat, that is, when only a small cavity is left in the deepest part when the valves are closed. Perhaps the Placuna placenta, fig. 184, is the most remarkable instance of this character.

CONCAMERATIONS. (*Con*, with, *camera*, a chamber.) A series of Chambers joining each other, as in Nautilus, Spirula, &c.

CONCENTRIC. A term applied to the direction taken by the lines of growth in spiral and other shells, (*longitudinal* of some authors.) Every fresh layer of shelly matter forms a new circle round an imaginary line, drawn through the centre of the spiral cone, down from the nucleus. When the edges of the successive layers are marked by any external characters, the shell is said to be concentrically striated, banded, grooved, costated, &c. A fine illustration of the latter character is to be seen in the Scalaria or Wentletrap, fig. 351. Lines, bands, ribs &c. in the opposite direction, (*transverse* of some authors), are "radiating" in bivalves, as the ribs of Cardium, fig. 123, and "spiral" in univalves, that is, following the direction of the whorls, as the bands of colour in Pyramidella, fig. 342.

CONCHACEA. Bl. The eighth family of the order Lamellibranchiata, Bl. The shells are described as follows: nearly always regular, valves closed all round; apices curved towards the anterior: dorsal hinge complete, with teeth and ligament; the latter external or internal, short and thick; two distinct muscular impressions, united at the lower part by a parallel impression, which is frequently sinuated at the posterior. The genera described in this family are divided into three sections. First, those which are regular, and have distant lateral teeth, Cardium, Donax, Tellina, Lucina, Cyclas, Cyprina, Mactra, and Erycina. Second, those which are regular, and have no distant lateral teeth, Crassatella and Venus. Third, those which are irregular, Venerupis, Coralliophaga, Clotho, Corbula, Sphænia, and Ungulina.

CONCHACEA. Lam. A family of Lamarck's order Conchifera Dimyaria. Regular, unattached in general, closed at the sides. They are always more or less inequilateral. The *Marine* Conchacea are those which inhabit the sea. The fluviatile Conchacea are those which are found in rivers, ponds, &c. Each of these contain various genera, which may be arranged as follows:–

Fluviatile

1. CYRENELLA. Three cardinal teeth; ligament long; shell thin. Fig. 114.
2. CYCLAS. Thin, oval; cardinal and lateral teeth; anterior side shortest, including *Pera*.
3. PISIDIUM. The same, with the posterior side shortest. Fig. 112.
4. CYRENA. Thick; cardinal and lateral teeth. Fig. 113.
5. POTAMOPHILIA. Two thick cardinal teeth. Fig. 115.

Marine

1. CYPRINA. Two cardinal teeth, and one remote lateral tooth. Fig. 116.
2. VENUS. Three cardinal; no lateral teeth. Fig. 118, 119, 119*a*.
3. CIRCE. Short lateral tooth, like Cytherea; no sinus in the palleal impression.
4. CYTHEREA. Several cardinal teeth; one very short lateral tooth. Fig. 117, 117*a*, 117*b*, 117*c*, 117*d*.
5. MEROE. Short lateral tooth, like Cytherea; wedge-shaped, with a deeply hollowed hinge area.
6. PULLASTRA. Cardinal teeth notched, shape long, otherwise like Venus. Fig. 120.
7. ASTARTE. Three cardinal teeth; ligament short. Fig. 110.

CONCHIFERA. Lam. The 11th class of Invertebrata, consisting of all those animals which have bivalve shells. Lamarck divides the class into Dimyaria, which have two adductor muscles; and Mononyaria, which have but one.

CONCHODERMA. Olfers, 1814. A name under which Mr. Darwin, in his recent work on Cirripedes, unites the pedunculated cirripedes commonly known and described in this book as "CINERAS" and "OTION."

CONCHOLEPAS. Lamarck, 1801. (CONCHA, a shell; lepas, a stone or rock.) *Fam.* Pupurifera, Lam. Entomostomata, Bl.—*Descr.* Oval, imbricated, thick; with a very short spire and large oval patelliform aperture, terminating anteriorly in a slight emargination; outer lip crenated, with two produced points or teeth towards the anterior; inner lip smooth, nearly flat, reflected over the last whorl, so as nearly or entirely to cover it; operculum horny. Marine, only one species known, from Peru.—*Obs.* This shell is placed near Patella by Lamarck, on

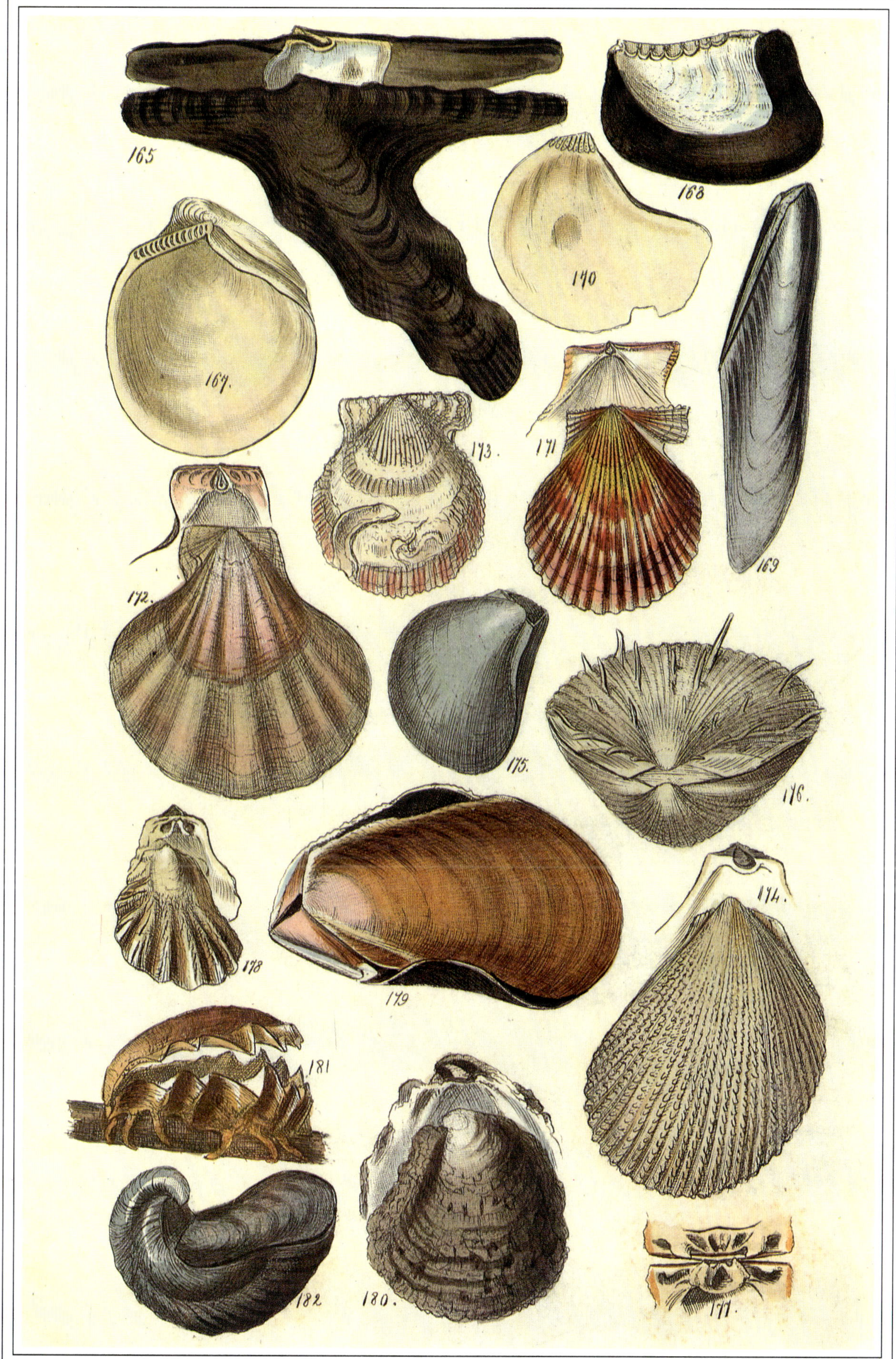

165. Malleus Vulgaris. Himantopoda, chum.

Fam. Brachopoda

167. Catillus Lamarckii. Inoceramus, Sow. (from Blainville.)
168. Crenatula mytoloides.
169. Gervillia aviculoides.
170. Pulvinites Adansonii.

(from Sowerby's Genera.) [applies to 168–170]

Fam. Pectinides

171. Pecten varius. Janera, Schum.
172. ——Plica. Decadopecten, Rüppell.
173. Hinnites Pusio. Pecten Pusio, Lam.
174. Lima squamosa.
175. Dianchora striata, (from Sow. Min. Con.)
176. Plagiostoma spinosum, (from Sow. Min. Con.)
177. Spondylus Americanus, Hinge. (See Frontispiece.)
178. Plicatula gibbosa. Harpax, Parkinson.
179. Pedum Spondyloideum, (from Sow. Gen.) Hemipecten, fig. 580. To be added.

Fam. Ostracea

180. Ostrea edulis.
181. ——Folium. Dendostrea, Sw.
182. Gryphæa incurva.

account of its large open aperture; but having a horny operculum, and resembling Purpurea in other respects. Concholepas Peruviana. Pl. xix. fig. 418.

CONCHOTRYA. Gray. (*Concha*, a shell; Τρυο, (*tryo*) to bore.) *Order*, Pedunculated Cirripedes, Lam.—*Descr*. Five pieces, two pairs ventral, one single; shaped like Pentelasmis. Found in holes.

CONCHYLIOMORPHITE. A term used by De Blainville to designate the cast or model of a fossil shell, formed by a siliceous substance which has entered or surrounded it when in a liquid state, and subsequently become hardened into flint. The shell has afterwards decomposed or fallen off by accident, leaving its external or internal characters to be conjectured from the monumental impressions that remain.

CONE. A common name for shells of the genus Conus.

CONE. This mathematical term is used by conchologists in its utmost latitude of signification to express a body, which in its formation, commences in a small point, called the apex, and increases in width towards the base. It is applied to all shells, whether the increase in width be gradual or sudden; or whether in its growth it takes a straight, oblique, curved, or spirally-twisted course. In this sense, a bivalve would be described as a pair of rapidly enlarging, oblique cones, and the aperture of every spiral shell would be its base. But this phraseology being in disuse, it is only mentioned here that it may be understood when occasionally met with.

CONELLA. Swainson. A genus composed of species of the genus Columbella, Lam. which have a conical form, and which, on that account, are considered by Swainson as belonging to his family of Coninæ. Swains. Lardner, Cyclop. Malac. described at p. 312. C. picata, Sw. fig. 17. a. p. 151.

CONFLUENT. A term applied to two parts of a shell when they gradually flow into each other, as, for instance, the inner and outer lips of Univalves when they pass into each other at the anterior extremity, without the intervention of a notch or angle.

CONIA. Leach. *Fam*. Balanidea. *Order*, Sessile Cirripedes, Lam.—*Descr*. Four rather irregular valves, of porous structure, placed side by side, so as to form a circular cone, supported at the base on a shelly plate, and closed at the aperture by an operculum consisting of four valves in pairs. Distinguished from Creusia by its porous structure and by its flat support; that of Creusia being cup-shaped. Conia porosa. Pl. i. fig. 21.

CONICAL. A term applied in the ordinary sense, and not as explained above, under the word CONE.

CONIDEA. Swainson. A genus separated from Columbella, Lam. thus described, "Mitra shaped, fusiform; spire equal to or longer than the aperture; the whorls tumid; outer lip slightly gibbous above, contracted below; margin not inflected; striated within; inner lip terminating in an elevated ridge, but with the teeth obsolete. C. semipunctata, (*Columbella*, Lam.) Mart. 44. fig. 465, 466." Africa.

CONILITES. *Fam*. Orthocerata, Lam. & Bl.—*Descr*. "Conical, straight or slightly curved; having a thin external covering, independent of the nut or alveole, which it contains. Alveole transversely chambered, sub separable." (Translated from Lam.)—*Obs*. The difference between Belemnites and Conilites is that the external sheath of the latter is thin, and not filled up with solid matter, from the point of the alveole to the apex, as in the former. De Blainville places in this genus the genera Thalamulus, Achelois and Antimomous, Montf. two of which are figured, Knor. Sup. Fab. iv. fig. 1. 1. 8, 9. Conilites Pyramidatus, Pl. xxii. fig. 470.

CONILITHES. Swainson. A sub-genus of Coronaxis, Sw. (Coni, with coronated whorls) thus described, "Conic; spire considerably elevated; the aperture linear, C. antediluvianus, Sow. Gen. fig. 1."

CONOHELIX. Swainson, 1843. IMBRICARIA, Schum. 1817. (*Conus and Helix*.) The generic name given to those species of Mitra which are conical in form. C. marmorata, Pl. xx. fig. 432.

CONOPLÆA. Say. *Order*, Sessile Cirripedes, Lam. A genus composed of Balani, attached to the stems of Gorgonia, having their bases elongated. *Ex*. Balanus Galeatus, Pl. i. fig. 27.

CONOPLEURA. Hinds, Voyage of the Sulphur. P. 24, pl. vii. fig. 223. Described as "coniform, or involute, with the spire conically elevated, with a deep posterior sinus, the edge of which is callous; outer lip smooth, columella rather lengthened; aperture linear; scarcely any canal." (Translated.) Remarkable for the series of fossils formed by the successive elevations of the edge of the sinus at the suture. Only one species is known. *Ex*. C. strians, Pl. xxviii. fig. 596.

CONORBIS. Swainson. A genus composed of species of CONUS, such as C. dormitor, (Sowerby, gen. fig. 8) which have elevated spires and the upper part of the outer lip deeply sinuated. Mr. Swainson considers these fossil species as analogous to the Pleurotomæ. Sw. Lard. Cyclop. Malac. p. 312.

CONOVULUS. Lamarck, 1812. MELAMPUS, Montfort, 1810. Conical species of Auricula, which have the outer lip simple. *Ex*. fig. 298, Auricula coniformis.

CONTIGUOUS. A term applied to the whorls of spiral shells when they rest upon, or touch each other. This is the case in a great majority of instances. When, on the contrary, there is a space between the whorls, they are said to be non-contiguous, detached, or free. Examples of non-contiguous whorls are to be seen in Scalaria, fig. 351 (in this case, the distance between the whorls is small), and in Crioceratites, fig. 482. A "*Columella contiguous to the axis*," is when in the centre of the shell and takes the place of the imaginary line which forms its axis.

CONTINUOUS. Carried on without interruption, as the siphon in Spirula, the varices in Ranella, fig. 394, which, occurring in a corresponding part of each whorl, form a continuous ridge.

CONULARIA. Miller. A genus of Orthocerata, described as conical, straight, or nearly so, divided into chambers by imperforate septa; aperture half closed; apex solid, obtuse; external surface finely striated. Resembling Orthoceras, but wanting the siphon. Pl. xxii. fig. 449.

CONUS. Linnæus. (Κωνος, a cone.) *Fam*. Enroulées, Lam. Angyostomata, Bl.—*Descr*. Conical, convolute, with a short spire, consisting of numerous whorls; and narrow lengthened aperture, terminating in a slight emargination at each extremity; outer lip thin; epidermis thin; operculum small, pointed, horny.—*Obs*. This well-known genus of shells is easily distinguished from any other, by its conical form, its smooth columella, its narrow aperture, and thin outer lip. The form of the spire varies from flat and even partially concave, to a regular pyramidal cone; and the upper edges of the whorls are rounded in some species, angulated in others, and in some are waved or coronated. The variety of marking and the numerous delicate tints of these shells have caused them to be highly appreciated by amateur collectors; and many species, as the C. Ammiralis, or admiral; the C. Gloria Maris, or Glory of the Sea; the C. Cedonulli ("I yield to none"), and others, have always produced good prices in the markets. We give figures of the principal forms, as expressed in the genera proposed by De Montfort, of Rhombus, Hermes, Rollus and Cylinder, in figures 459 to 462. Many new species were brought to this country by Mr. Cuming, and are represented in parts 24, 25, 28, 29; 32, 33, 36, 37; 54, 55, 56, 57; 147, 148; 151 to 158 of the Conchological Illustrations, by G. B. Sowerby, jun. See CORONAXIS, Swainson. The cones are mostly tropical, some are found as far north as the Mediterranean, and south as

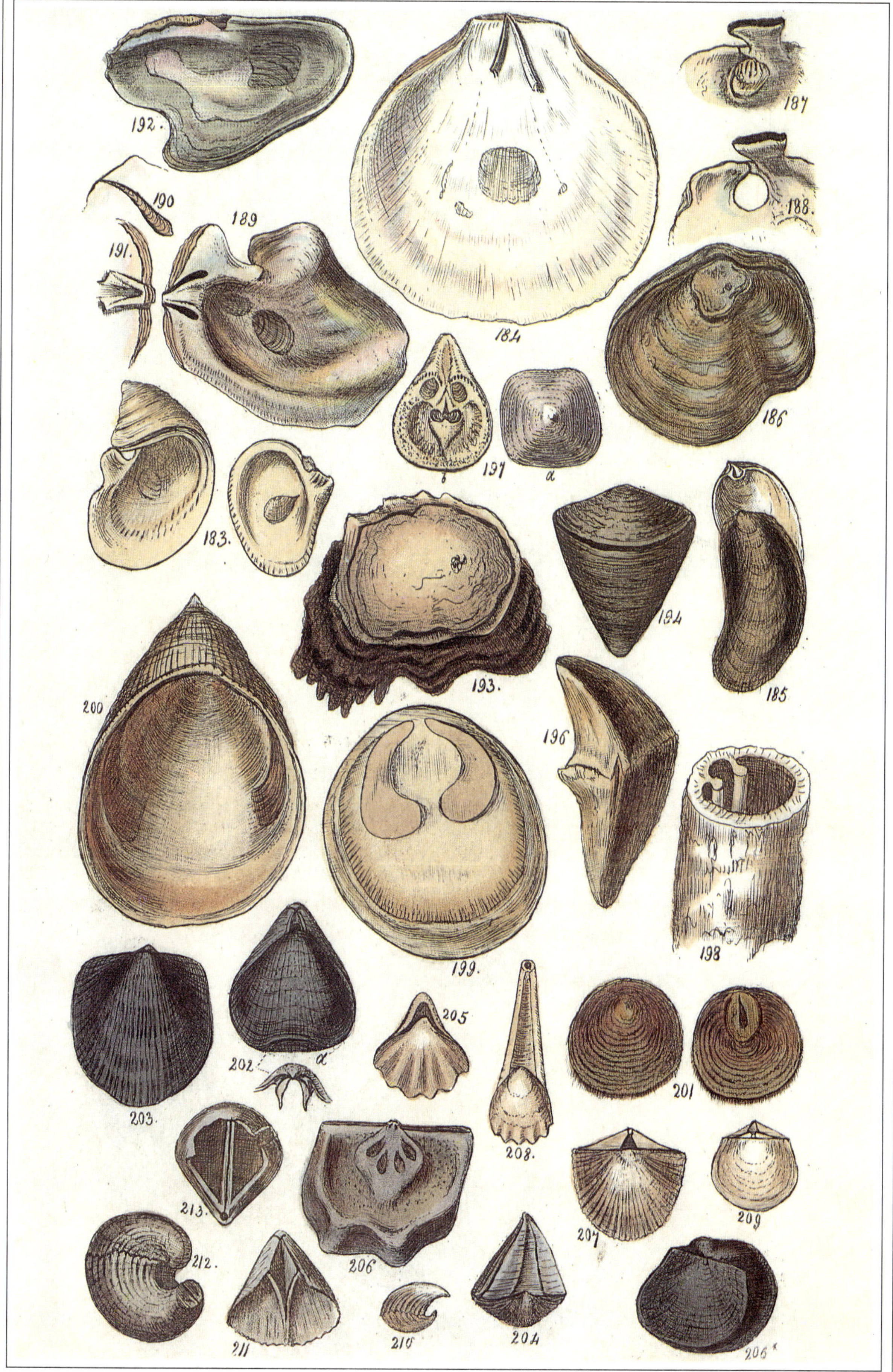

183. Exogyra conica, (from Sow. Min. Con.)
184. Placuna Placenta. *Gen.* Placenta, Schum.
185. Vulsella lingulata.
186. Anomia Ephippium.
187. Hinge of the same, with bony process.
188. Hinge, shewing the fissure.
189. Placunanomia Cumingii.
190. Hinge of the same, shewing the fissure.
191. Hinge of the unattached valve.
192. Mulleria. (from Sow. Gen.)

Fam. Rudistis

193. Sphærulites foliacea. (Radiolites is more conical.)
194. Calceola Sandalina.
196. Birostrites inæquiloba, internal cast of Sphærulites.
197. *a.* Crania personata, dorsal valve; *b.* C. antiquata, interior. (This would be more properly placed in Brachiopoda.)
198. Hippurites Cornucopia, (from Blainville.)
199. Hipponyx Cornucopia, attached valve.
200. Upper valve of the same.
201. Orbicula lævis.
202. Terebratula Psittacea; *a.* anterior margin.
203. Atrypa reticularis. Trigonoteta, König.
204. Cyrtia exporrecta.
205. Delthyris plycotes, (from Dalman.)
206. Leptæna depressa, Dalman. Producta, Sow. (from Sow. Gen.)
206*. Producta antiquata.
207. Orthis basalis, Dalman. Strophomena, Rafinesque.
208. Trigonosemus Lyra, König.
209. Magas pumilus, Sow.
210. Gypidia conchidium, (from Dalman.)
211. Interior of the large valve of the same, (from Dalman.)
212. Pentamerus Aylesfordii, (from Sow. Min. Con.)
213. ——lævis.

the Cape of Good Hope. The most beautiful species are from the East and West Indies. Pl. xxi. fig. 459 to 462.

CONVOLUTÆ. (Enroulées, Lam.) A family of the 2nd section of the order Trachelipoda, Lam. the genera of which may be distinguished as follows:–

1. Cypræa. Lips thickened, inflected, with teeth; spire hidden including *Cypræovulum, Luponia, Trivia*. Fig. 444 to 450, and Cyprædia. Pl. xxvi. fig. 564.
2. Ovulum. Lips thickened, inflected, with slight crenulations; spire hidden. Fig. 440 to 443.
3. Erato. Lips thickened, inflected; spire visible; a groove down the back. Fig. 454.
4. Terebellum. Cylindrical, open at the anterior extremity; columella smooth; suture of the spire canaliculated. Fig. 451, 452.
5. Oliva. Columella plaited, swelled into a varix at the anterior. Fig. 457, 458.
6. Ancillaria. The same, but the suture of the spire covered with enamel. Fig. 455, 456.
7. Conus. Turbinated, numerous whorls; spire flat or short, conical: columella smooth. Fig. 459 to 462.

CONVOLUTE. (*Con*, together; *volvo*, to revolve.) This term can be strictly applied only to symmetrical shells, signifying that the volutions are parallel to each other in a horizontal direction, as in the Ammonites, &c.; but the term is also commonly used in describing such shells as Conus, in which, the direction of the whorls being scarcely oblique, the last whorl almost entirely covers those which precede it. This is the case with Lamarck's family of Enroulées. Fig. 440 to 462.

CORALLIOPHAGA. Blainville, 1825. Cypricardia Coralliophaga, Lam.—*Descr*. Oval, elongated, finely striated from the apex to the base, cylindrical, equivalve, very inequilateral; umbones slightly raised and quite anterior; hinge nearly the same in both valves; two small cardinal teeth, one of which is bifid, placed before a kind of lammellated tooth, beneath a very slender external ligament; two small, distant, muscular impressions, united by a striated palleal impression, which is strongly striated posteriorly.—*obs*. This shell, which is found in the empty holes of dead Lithodomi, in some instances conforming its shape to its situation, differs from Cypricardia of Lamarck, principally in its cylindrical form. C. Carditoidia, Pl. iv. fig. 92.

CORBICULA. Megerle, 1811. Part of Cyrena, Lam.

CORBIS. Cuvier, 1817. (*A basket*.) *Fam*. Nymphacea, Lam.—*Descr*. Transverse, oval, thick, ventricose, equivalve, sub-equilateral, free, cancellated, with denticulated internal margins; hinge with two cardinal and two lateral teeth in each valve; of the latter, one near and one remote from the umbones; muscular impressions lunulate, two in each valve, united by an entire palleal impression, without a sinus.—*Obs*. This genus, of which only two or three recent species are known, resembles many species of Venus and Cytherea in general form; but differs in having lateral teeth, and in the palleal impressions, which in all the Veneres, &c. is sinuated. From Lucina it may be known, not only by its oval form, but also by the muscular impressions, which, in Lucina, are produced into an elongated point; it will also be distinguished from Tellina, by the want of a posterior fold in the valve, for which that genus is remarkable. C. Fimbriata is an inhabitant of the Indian Ocean. Several fossil species are found in the recent formations, above the chalk, at Grignon and Hautville. Pl. v. fig. 101.

CORBULA. Bruguière, 1792. (*A little basket*.) *Fam*. Corbulacea, Lam. Conchacea, Bl.—*Descr*. Inequivalve, sub-equilateral, transverse, gibbose, not gaping; cardinal tooth in each valve, conical, curved, prominent, inserting its extremity into a pit in the opposite hinge; cartilage attached to the tooth of the smaller valve, and the pit in the larger; muscular impressions, two in each valve, distant, rather irregular; palleal impression posteriorly angulated. *Obs*. The shells composing this genus were placed in Mya by Linnæus, but differ from the true Myæ in having a sinus in the palleal impression, and a prominent ligamentiferous tooth in each valve, whereas the Myæ have but one. The Corbulæ are marine, some species inhabiting the British coasts. Fossil species occur abundantly in green sand, London clay, crag, and corresponding formations. C. Nucleus, Pl. iv. fig. 89.

CORBULACEA. (Corbulées, Lam.) A family of the order Conchifera Dimyaria, Lam., containing the genera:–

1. Corbula, with a prominent curved tooth. The Fresh-water species has been separated under the name *Potamomya*. Fig. 89.
2. Pandora. Thin, pearly, no teeth. Fig. 90.

CORDIFORM. (*Cor*, a heart.) Heart-shaped, a term applied generally to any shell which may be fancied to resemble a heart in shape, as Isocardia, fig. 126, and Cardium Dionæum, fig. 122.

CORETUS. Adamson, 1757. Planorbis.

COREPHIUM. Browne. Chiton echinatus, and similar species with spires on the marginal integument.

CORIACEOUS. (*Corium*, leather.) Of the substance of leather. *Ex*. the integument into which the valves of Chitones are inserted.

CORIOCELLA. Bl. The animal designated by this name is described by De Blainville as being without any traces of shell, either internal or external. This must have arisen from the imperfection of the specimen described, probably deprived by accident of its shell. The testaceous appendage of the Coriocella is now well known to naturalists. It is a milky white, transparent shell, shaped like Sigaretus.

CORNEA, and Pisum, Megerle. Cyclas, Lam.

CORNEO-CALCAREOUS. A term used to express the mixture of horny and shelly matter which enters into the composition of some shells, Aplysia, for instance. It is also applied to those Opercula, which are horny on one side, and testaceous on the other, as that of Turbo.

CORNEUS. Horny. A species of Patella has had the specific name corneus given to it, because its texture more nearly resembles that of a horn than that of a shell. The epidermis of fresh-water shells is of a similar composition.

CORNUCOPIA. Humph. Lepas, Linn.

CORONALES. See Coronular Multivalves.

CORONATED. (*Corona*, a crown.) Applied to shells when ornamented with a series of points, tubercles, &c. round the upper edges of the volutions. *Ex*. Conus Nocturnus, fig. 459.

CORONAXIS. One of the two genera into which Swainson divides the genus Conus, consisting of those species which have a row of tubercles on the upper edge of the whorls, an arrangement by which he would in many instances, not only separate between two individuals of the same species, but also between two parts of the same shell; for instances occur in which the earlier whorls are coronated, while the body whorl and the penultimate are perfectly plain.

CORONULA. (*Corona*, a crown, dim.) *Order*, Sessile Cirripedes, Lam. *Fam*. Balanidea, Bl.—*Descr*. Six radiated valves, joined side by side in a circle, forming a depressed cone; internal structure of the valves, porous or chambered; thickened at the base; operculum consisting of four valves in pairs; imbedded horizontally in a cartilaginous substance.—*Obs*. The shells composing this genus are found partly imbedded in the skin of whales, and the shells of tortoises, and are therefore destitute of the shelly foundation on which the Balani and other Coronular Multivalves are supported. C. Testudinaria, (Chelo-

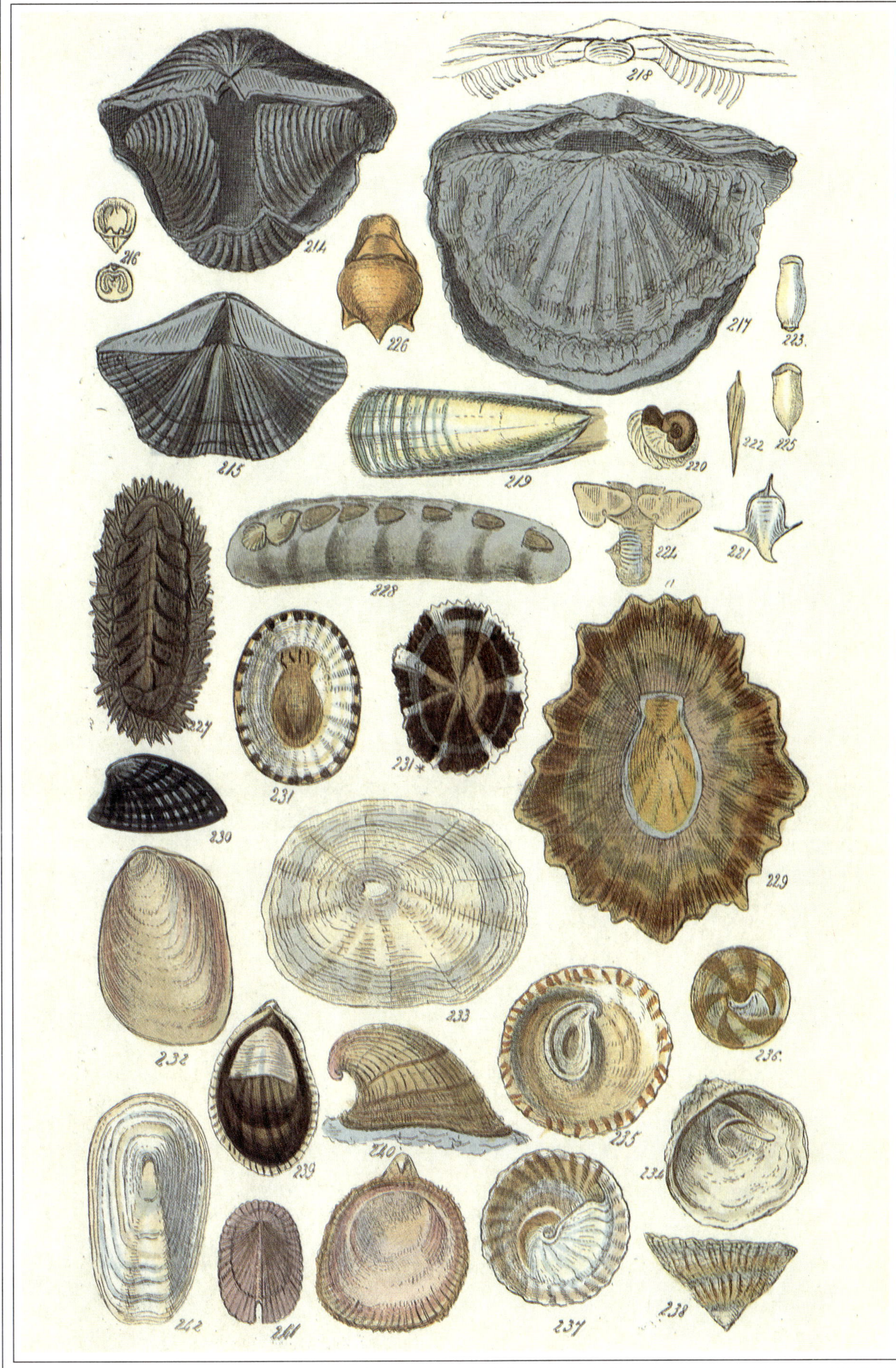

214. Spirifer trigonalis. 215. ——dorsatus. } Trigonotrata, König, (from Sow. Gen.)

216. Thecidium recurvirostrum. (Here should come Crania, see Rudistes.)

217. Pycnodonta radiata, (from Fischer.)

218. Hinge of the same.

219. Lingula Anatina.

Class, MOLLUSCA

Order, Pteropida

220. Atlanta helicialis.

221. Cleodora cuspidata.

222. Creseis spinifera.

223. Cuviera columella.

224. Spiratella limacinea, with animal; Limacella, Lam. Limacina, Cuvier. (from Blainville.)

225. Vaginula Daudinii.

226. Hyalæa tridentata. Archonte, Montf. Spiralis, fig. 581.

Order, Gasteropoda

Fam. Phyllidiana

227. Chiton spinosus.

228. Chitonellus striatus, (from Sow. Gen.)

229. Patella oculus; *a*. anterior.

230. Patella pellucida. Helcion, Montf. Ansates, Klein.

231. Patelloida Antillarum. Lottia, Gray.

231*. Siphonaria Sipho. Phakellopleura, fig. 506. Amicula, fig. 507.

Fam. Semiphyllidiana

232. Pleurobranchus membranaceus.

233. Umbrella indica. Gastroplax, Bl.

Fam. Calyptracea

234. Calyptræa Equestria.

235. ——extinctorium.

236. ——auriculata.

237. ——Pileus. Infundibulum, Montf.

238. Side view of the same.

239. Crepidula Porcellana.

240. Capulus ungaricus, two views. Pileopsis, Lam.

241. Emarginula fissura.

242. Parmophorus elongatus. Scutus, Montf.

NOBIA, Leach), fig. 15. C. Balænarum, (CETOPIRUS, Ranz.) fig. 16. C. Diadema, (DIADEMA, Ranz.) fig. 17. Pl. i. fig. 15, 16, 17.

CORONULAR MULTIVALVES are those which have their parietal valves joined together side by side in a circle, surrounding the body of the animal, so as to form a sort of coronet. This is the characteristic of the Sessile Cirripedes of Lamarck's system, the Balanidea of De Blainville.

CORRODED. (*Corrodo*, eat away, consume.) The umbones, apices, and other thick parts of shells, are frequently worn away or consumed by the action of the element in which they exist. As the thickest parts of some shells are the most subject to this operation; it appears to the author to arise from the outer surface of the shell, being less under the influence of the animal juices than the other parts; and therefore, more exposed to the influence of the surrounding element. This, however, is not the case with respect to the Nayades and other fresh-water shells; with these, corrosion does not take place until after the thick epidermis which covers them, becomes wounded by some means or other, and then the animal thickens its shell within as fast as it is corroded without.

CORTALUS. Montf. (Conch. Syst. 1. 115.) A genus of microscopic Foraminifera, placed by De Blainville in a division of the genus Rotalites.

COSTATED. Ribbed, as Cardium Angulatum, fig. 123.

COSTELLARIA. A sub-genus of the genus Tiara, Sw. (Mitra.) C. rigida. Swainson, Zool. Ill. 1st series, pl. 29.

COWRY. A common name for shells of the genus Cypræa.

CRANIA. Retzius, 1788. (*Cranium*, a skull.) *Fam.* Rudistes, Lam. *Order*, Pallio-branchiata, Bl.—*Descr.* Inequivalve, equilateral, irregular, sub-quadrate; upper valve patelliform, conical, with the umbo near the centre; lower valve attached by its outer surface; muscular impressions, 4 in each valve; two large, posterior, distant; two small, near to each other, central. No hinge teeth; no ligament.—*Obs.* This genus properly belongs to the Brachiopoda, Lam. It differs from Orbicula in the mode of attachment, which in the latter, is by a byssus passing through the lower valve, and not by the valve itself. Hipponyx has only two muscular impressions in each valve. The name of this genus is derived from the inner surface of the attached valve, which presents a remarkable resemblance to the facial portion of a human skull. The appearance is caused by the situation and elevated edges of the muscular impressions. Coasts of Britain and Mediterranean. The monograph in Thesaurus contains four species. Pl. xi. fig. 197.

CRASSATELLA. Lamarck, 1801. (*Crassus*, thick.) *Fam.* Mactracea, Lam. Conchacea, Bl.—*Descr.* Equivalve, inequilateral, close, thick, rounded anteriorly, rostrated posteriorly, with denticulated margins, smooth, or ribbed transversely; hinge with a triangular pit containing the cartilage, two anterior cardinal teeth, and a posterior depression in one valve; one anterior tooth and a slight anterior marginal elevation, and a posterior elevation in the other valve. Muscular impressions distant, strongly marked. Palleal impression not sinuated.—*Obs.* The few recent species known are marine, several being brought from the coasts of New Holland. Fossil species are found in Calcaire-grossier and London clay. The Crassatella are known from the Veneres, &c., by the ligamentary pit in the hinge, and from Lutraria and Mactra by the thickness and closeness of the shell. C. rostrata. Pl. iv. fig. 84.

CRASSINA. Lamarck, 1818. ASTARTE. J. Sowerby, 1816.

CRASSIPEDES. Lam. (*Crassus*, thick; *pes*, foot.) The first section of the order Conchifera Dimyaria, Lam. In this section the foot of the animal is thick, and the shell gapes considerably. It is divided into the families Tubicolæ, Pholadidæ, Solenidæ, and Myaria. Fig. 44 to 76.

CRASSISPIRA. Swainson. A sub-genus of COLUMBELLA, Auct. for which Mr. Swainson quotes "Pleurotoma Bottæ, Auct." Crassispira fasciata, Sw. Lardn. Cyclop. Malac. p. 313.

CRENATED. (*Crena*, a notch.) Applied to small notches, not sufficiently raised or defined, to be compared with teeth. *Ex.* The hinge of Iridina, fig. 150.

CRENATULA. Lamarck, 1819. *Fam.* Malleacea, Lam. Margaritacea, Bl.—*Descr.* Compressed, foliated, irregular, sub-equivalve, inequilateral, oblique; umbones terminal; hinge linear, nearly straight, with a series of excavations, containing the cartilage, while the intervening ridges are covered with the ligament, properly so called. Muscular impression oblong, indistinct.—*Obs.* This genus is known from Perna by the hinge, which in the latter is composed of a series of regular, straight, ligamentary grooves placed across it. In Crenatula also there is no passage for the byssus, as in Perna. C. Mytiloides, pl. x. fig. 168.

CRENELLA. Brown. A genus composed of MODIOLA discors and similar species, having an oblique division between the anterior and posterior portions of the shell, and a crenulated hinge margin.

CRENELLA. ——? See TRIGONOCÆLIUS. Pl. vii. fig. 136.

CRENULATED. Finely crenated or notched.

CREPIDULA. Lamarck, 1801. CRYPTA, Humph. is used in Gray's Synopsis as being the prior name, although it only appeared by name in a catalogue. (*Crepidula*, a little slipper.) *Fam.* Calyptracea, Lam. and Bl.—*Descr.* Oval, irregular, patelliform: apex lateral, incurved, or sub-spiral; external surface convex, smooth, with a flattish septum reaching nearly half across the cavity; epidermis light brown.—*Obs.* The difference between this genus and Calyptræa is that in the latter the septum is more free from the sides of the shell, so that, instead of forming a regular plate, covering half the aperture, it assumes a variety of shapes, and in some is cup-shaped, in others forked, and in some forms a little angular shelf. Indeed, the variations are so numerous that I think it would be better to throw the two genera into one, and then divide them into smaller groups. Some species of Calyptræa are farther removed from each other with respect to the characters of the septum and general form of the shell, than they are from the Crepidulæ. Fig. 239. Mediterranean, North and South America, East and West Indies, New South Wales, &c. Pl. xii. fig. 239.

CREPIDULINA. Bl. CRISTELLARIA, Lam. Microscopic.

CRESEIS. Rang. 1828. *Order*, Pteropoda, Lam.—*Descr.* Thin, fragile, transparent, pyramidal, pointed; with a dorsal ridge produced into a point at the edge of the aperture.—*Obs.* The species found in the Mediterranean is named C. Spinifera, from its resemblance to a thorn. Pl. xii. fig. 222.

CREUSIA. Leach. (*Creux*, se. Fr. a cavity.) *Fam.* Balanidea. Bl. *Order*, Sessile Cirripedes, Lam.—*Descr.* A depressed cone, consisting of four valves, supported upon, and jointed to, a cup-shaped cavity formed in the Madrepores, in which it resides. Aperture quadrilateral, closed by an operculum of four valves.—*Obs.* This genus is distinguished from Pyrgoma, which is supported on the edge of a similar cup-shaped cavity, by the paries being composed of four valves, whereas in Pyrgoma, it consists of a single piece. East Indies. C. Gregaria. Pl. i. fig. 28.

CRICOSTOMATA, Bl. The second family of Asiphonibranchiata, Bl. It is thus described: "shell equally (with the animal) variable in general form, but of which the aperture, always nearly round, is completely closed by the shelly or horny operculum; whorls few, and apex sublateral." This family agrees in some measure with the family Turbinacea of Lamarck, and with the genus Turbo in the system of Linnæus. It contains the genera Pleurotomaria, Delphinula, Turritella,

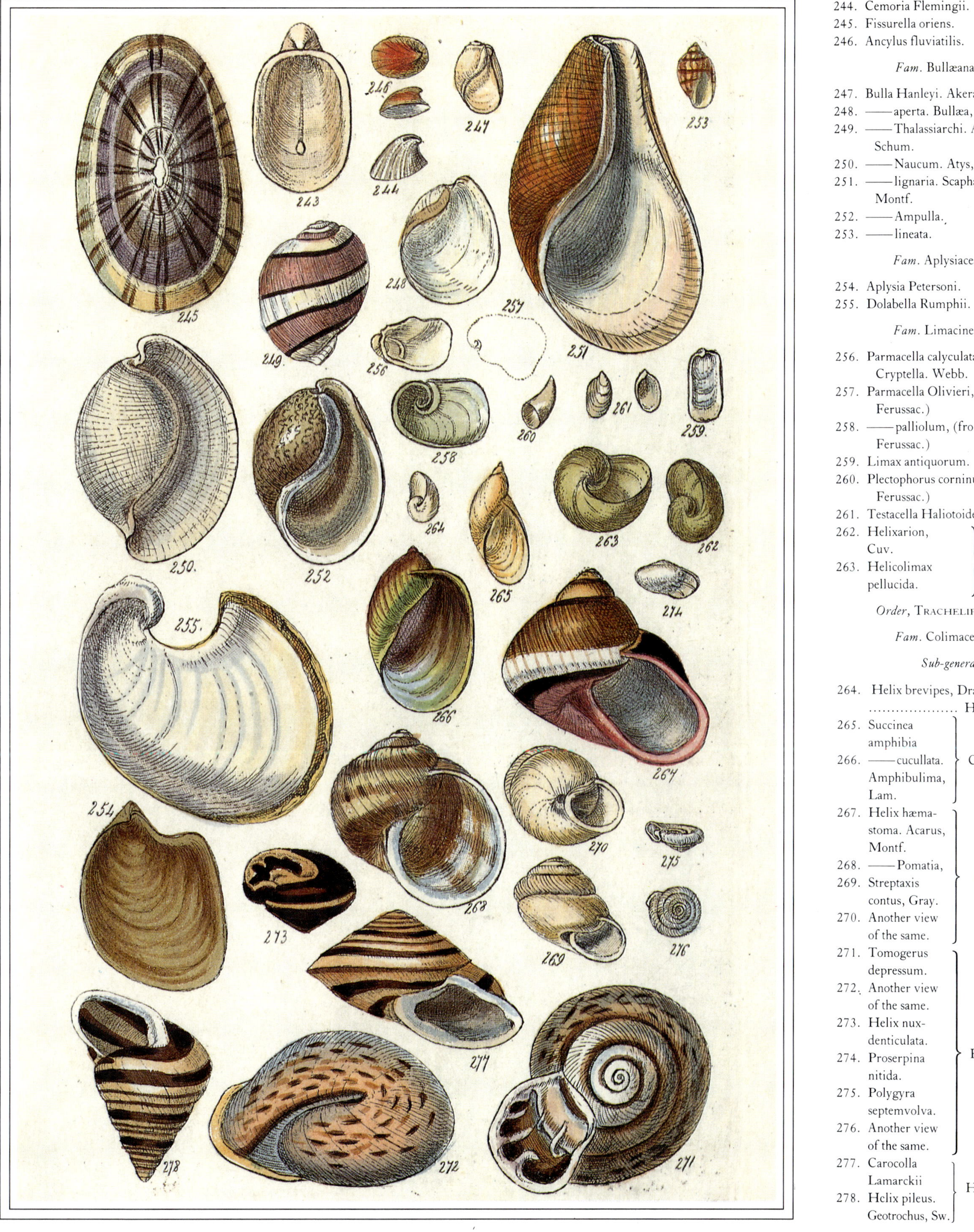

243. Rimularia Blainvillii.
244. Cemoria Flemingii.
245. Fissurella oriens.
246. Ancylus fluviatilis.

Fam. Bullæana

247. Bulla Hanleyi. Akera, Müller.
248. ——aperta. Bullæa, Lam.
249. ——Thalassiarchi. Aplustrum, Schum.
250. ——Naucum. Atys, Montf.
251. ——lignaria. Scaphander, Montf.
252. ——Ampulla.
253. ——lineata.

Fam. Aplysiacea

254. Aplysia Petersoni.
255. Dolabella Rumphii.

Fam. Limacinea

256. Parmacella calyculata, Cryptella. Webb.
257. Parmacella Olivieri, (from de Ferussac.)
258. ——palliolum, (from de Ferussac.)
259. Limax antiquorum.
260. Plectophorus corninus, (from de Ferussac.)
261. Testacella Haliotoidea.
262. Helixarion, Cuv. } Vitrina, Drap.
263. Helicolimax pellucida. } Cobresia, Haubner.

Order, TRACHELIPODA

Fam. Colimacea

Sub-genera of De Fer.

264. Helix brevipes, Drap. .... Helicophanta.

265. Succinea amphibia
266. ——cucullata. Amphibulima, Lam.
} Cochlohydra.

267. Helix hæmastoma. Acarus, Montf.
268. ——Pomatia,
269. Streptaxis contus, Gray.
270. Another view of the same.
} Helicogena.

271. Tomogerus depressum.
272. Another view of the same.
273. Helix nuxdenticulata.
274. Proserpina nitida.
275. Polygyra septemvolva.
276. Another view of the same.
} Helicodonta.

277. Carocolla Lamarckii
278. Helix pileus. Geotrochus, Sw.
} Helicigona.

Proto, Scalaria, Vermetus, Siliquaria, Magilus, Valvata, Cyclostoma, and Paludina.

CRIOCERATITES. A genus composed of species of Ammonites, with disconnected whorls. C. Duvallii. Pl. xxiii. fig. 482.

CRIOPUS. Poli. CRANIA, Auct.

CRISTACEA. Lam. The third family of Polythalamous Cephalopoda, Lam. This family is described as including shells of the following characters: "Multilocular, flattened, nearly reniform; the chambers gradually increasing in length, as they approach the outer arched margin, and appearing to revolve round an eccentric, more or less marginal axis. The Cristacea contain the genera Renulina, Cristellaria, and Orbiculina."

CRISTACEA. Bl. The third family of Polythalamia, Bl. containing the genera Crepidulina, (Cristellaria, Lam.) Oreas and Linthuris.

CRISTARIA. Schum, 1817. DIPSAS Plicatus, Leach. ANODON tuberculatus, Fer.

CRISTELLARIA. Lam. CREPIDULINA, Bl. *Fam.* Cristacea, Lam. and Bl.—*Descr.* Semidiscoidal, chambered; whorls contiguous, enlarging progressively; spire eccentric, sublateral; septa imperforate. Microscopic.

CRUCIBULUM. Schum. 1817. The "cup and saucer" division of Calyptrææ.

CRYPTA. Humph. See CREPIDULA, Lam.

CRYPTELLA. Webb, 1833. (Κρυπτω, to conceal.) TESTACELLUS Ambiguus of Ferrusac. Published in Sowerby's Genera of Shells as PARMACELLA calyculata.—*Descr.* A small patelliform shell, with a very short papillary spire; and the aperture irregularly expanded. Canary Islands. Pl. xiii. fig. 256.

CRYPTOCHITON. Gray, 1847. Chiton Amiculatus. The valves of which are entirely covered.

CRYPTOCONCHUS. Bl. A genus composed of species of Chiton, the valves of which are covered by the integument, as Chiton porosus of Burrows. Ch. amiculatus of Pallas.

CRYPTOCONCTUS. Bl. Chiton porosus, the valves of which are covered, with the exception of a narrow dorsal ridge.

CRYPTODIBRANCHIATA. Bl. The first order of the class Cephalophora, Bl. containing families of molluscous animals destitute of shells.

CRYPTODON. Turton, 1822. A genus of Lucinæform shells, differing from that genus in the character of the hinge and palleal impressions, and having a fold at the posterior side of the shell. Partially described by J. Sowerby, under the name Axinus, and named Thyatira, besides several other names by Leach. C. Sinuosum. Pl. xxvii. fig. 575.

CRYPTOTHALMUS. Ehrenherg. A sub-genus of Bullidæ, the shells of which are thus described in Adams's Monograph, No. 11 Sowerby's Thesaurus: "Shell fragile, horny, scarcely involute, destitute of columella and spire; aperture wide."

CRYPTOSTOMA. Bl. 1825. Differs from SIGARETUS, Lam. principally in the soft parts of the animal. De Blainville remarks that he is acquainted with only two species (from the Indies), which he can with decision refer to the genus, but he thinks that many of the Lamarckian Sigareti may very properly be found to belong to it, as soon as the soft parts shall be known. The species which he figures is Cryptostoma Leachii. (Manuel de Malacologie, pl. xlii. fig. 3.)

CTENOCONCHA. Gray. Described as having many characters common with the Solens, the teeth like Nucula, but the cartilage entirely external. SOLENELLA, Sow.?

CUCULLÆA. Lamarck, 1801. (*Cucullus*, a hood.) *Fam.* Arcacea, Lam.—*Descr.* Sub-quadrate, nearly equivalve, sub-equilateral, deep; hinge rectilinear, with a series of angular teeth, small near the umbones; larger and more oblique towards the extremities; umbones separated by a flat external area, on which the ligament is spread. Anterior muscular impression produced into a sharp-edged plate or ledge, projecting from the side of the shell. Posterior muscular impression flat and indistinct.—*Obs.* This genus very much resembles Arca in general form, but differs in the oblique, lengthened character of the remote teeth, and in the singularly prominent edge of the muscular impression. China. C. Auriculifera. Pl. vii. fig. 133.

CUCUMIS. Klein. MARGINELLA, Auct.

CULTELLUS. Schum. 1817. *Ex.* L. Solenoides. Pl. iii. fig. 78.

CUMA. Humph. Part of FUSUS and FASCIOLARIA, Lam.

CUMINGIA. Sowerby, 1833. *Fam.* Mactracea, Lam.—*Descr.* Equivalve, inequilateral, transverse, rounded anteriorly, subrostrated posteriorly. Hinge with a central spoon-shaped cavity in each valve, containing the cartilage; a very small anterior cardinal tooth in each valve; two lateral teeth in one valve, none in the other: muscular impressions two in each valve, distant; palleal impression with a very large posterior sinus.—*Obs.* The species known at present are found in sand, in the fissures of rocks in Tropical climates. They resemble Erycina in general form and character, but differ in having the internal cartilage placed in a prominent spoon-shaped process, while that of Erycina is contained in a hollow which sinks under the umbones. This genus should be placed near Amphidesma. Cumingia mutica. Pl. iv. fig. 87.

CUNEIFORM. (*Cuneus*, a wedge.) Wedge-shaped, as Donax, fig. 108.

CUNEUS. Megerle, 1811. MEROE, Schumacher, 1817. Pl. vi. fig. 117. *a*.

CURVED. Arched or bent. *Ex.* Dentalium, fig. 2.

CUVIERIA. Rang. 1827. (Baron Cuvier.) *Class*, Pteropoda, Lam.—*Descr.* Thin, transparent, glassy, cylindrical, rounded and inflated at the closed extremity, compressed towards the opening, so as to render it oval. This genus differs from Vaginula in being rounded, instead of pointed, at the lower extremity. Mediterranean. C. Columella. Pl. xii. fig. 223.

CYCLAS. Brug. *Fam.* Conques Fluviatiles, Lam. Conchacea, Bl.—*Descr.* Orbicular, thin, subovate, ventricose, sub-equilateral, equivalve; cardinal teeth minute, one more or less complicated in the left valve, two divering in the right; lateral teeth elongated, compressed, laminar, acute doubled in the left valve; ligament external; epidermis thin, horny.—*Obs.* The Cyclades are viviparous, and abound in ditches, ponds, slow streams, &c. in Europe and North America. The genus Pisidium has been separated on account of a difference in the animal, and may be known from Cyclas by being less equilateral, and the anterior side being the longest. C. Rivicola. Pl. v. fig. 3.

CYCLOBRANCHIATA. Bl. The third order of the second section of Paracephalophora Monoica, Bl. containing no genera of Testaceous Mollusca.

CYCLOCANTHA. Swainson, 1840. A genus of "Trochidæ," consisting of Turbo stellaris and T. Calcar, and corresponding with the genus Calcar, Montf.

CYCLONASSA. Swainson. A genus of "Nassinæ," Sw. consisting of Nassa Neritoidea, and corresponding with the genus Cyclops, Montf.

CYCLOPHORUS. Montf. 1810. A generic name proposed for those species of Cyclostoma, Auct. which have an umbilicus. C. Involvulus would be the type of this genus. Pl. xiv. fig. 304.

CYCLOPS. Montf. Nassa Neritoidea, Auct. Pl. xix. fig. 424.

CYCLOSTOMUS. Montf. 1810. (κυκλος, *cyclos*, round; στομα, *stoma*, mouth.) *Fam.* Colimacea, Lam. Cricostomata, Bl. A genus of land shells varying in shape from that of Pupa to that of a flat orb; the aperture is generally circular and the peritreme uninterrupted, thickened, and sometimes reflected, the operculum is shelly and spiral. Two other genera of land shells are provided with opercula, and consequently might be confounded with this genus. In Helicina, the operculum is concentric and the peritreme is not continuous; while in the small genus hitherto almost unknown of Pupina, the peritreme is not continuous, and there is a glassy enamel over the whole of the external surface. The Monograph in Sowerby's Thesaurus contains 175 species. The generic names Cyclostoma, Licina, Cyclophorus, Cyclotus, Myxostoma, Pterocyclos, Farcinea, Myodoctoma, and Pomatias, represent the principal forms. Pl. xiv. fig. 303, 304. Pl. xxv. fig. 529.

CYCLOTUS. Guild. A sub-genus of Cyclostoma, consisting of those species which are discoidal, as C. Planorbulum. Thesaurus Conchylium. Pl. xxv. fig. 83 to 86; and the species in our plate xxv. fig. 531.

CYLICHNA. Loven. Cylindrella, Swainson. Volvaria. Brown. A sub-genus of Bullidæ, consisting of animals with shells, thus described in Adams's Monograph, No. 11, Sowerby's Thesaurus: "Cylindrical; sphire none; apex umbilicated; columella callous, with a single plait."

CYLINDER. Montf. 1810. Conus textile, Auct. (fig. 461) and other species having a cylindrical form.

CYLINDRA. Schumacher, 1817. Voluta crenulata, Lamarck, and other species like Conohelix, but cancellated.

CYLINDRELLA. Sw. Cylichna.

CYLINDRICAL. (Κυλινδρος, a cylinder.) This like other mathematical terms is used with great latitude by Conchologists, and applied to any shell the sides of which are nearly parallel, with the extremities either rounded, flat, or conical. *Ex.* Oliva, fig. 457.

CYLLENE. Gray, 1839. *Fam.* Purpurifera, Lam.—*Descr.* Oval, thick, with a short acute spire; an oval aperture terminating anteriorly in a slight emargination, posteriorly in a short canal; a fold at the lower end of the body whorl; outer lip thick, striated within; angle of the whorls tuberculated.—*Obs.* This genus of small marine shells resembles Voluta in general character, but differs in having a smooth columella without folds. Recent, Pacific Ocean; Fossil, London clay. Pl. xix. fig. 425.

CYMBA. Broderip. (*Cymba*, a boat or skiff.) *Fam.* Columellaria, Lam.—*Descr.* Smooth, ventricose, with a very short, mammillated, rude spire; and a very large, wide aperture, terminated anteriorly in a deep emargination; posteriorly in a flat ledge, which separates the outer lip from the body whorl; columella with three or four oblique, laminar, projecting folds, terminating in a point; outer lip thin, with its edge sharp; epidermis smooth, brown, covered partly or entirely by the glassy enamel, which, commencing with the outer lip, spreads over the body of the shell.—*Obs.* These very elegant shells, found in Africa, are distinguished from the true Volutes by the shapeless, mammillated apex of the short spire, by the large size of the aperture, and by the horizontal ledge which separates the outer lip from the body whorl. The genus Melo, also separated by Mr. Broderip from the Volutes, agrees with Cymba in some respects, but differs in the regularity of the spire. Pl. xx. fig. 434, C. Porcina. Nine species are enumerated in the Monograph by the Author, pt. 8. Thes. Conchyliorum.

CYMBIOLA. Swainson, 1840. The generic name for a group of Volutes, described as "armed with spinous tubercules, sometimes smooth, but never ribbed; spiral whorls gradually diminishing in size, but not distorted; apex thick and obtuse; pillar with four plaits." Mr Swainson remarks that this genus is chiefly distinguished by the obtuse, but not irregular spire. The typical species are stated to be V. Rutila and V. Vespertilio, fig. 433. Tropical.

CYMBIUM. Adanson, Melo, Broderip.

CYMBULIA. Peron and Leseur, 1810. (Dim. from *Cymba.*) *Fam.* Pteropoda, Lam. An extremely light, cartilaginous covering of a molluscous animal, so named from its similarity in shape to a boat. We mention it here on account of its similarity to the shelly or glassy covering of other Pteropods, to which, although membranaceous, it is evidently analogous. The Cymbuliæ are found in the Mediterranean.

CYNODONTA. Schum. 1817. Scolymus, part. Swainson. Represented by our figure 382.

CYPRÆA. Linnæus. *Fam.* Enroulées, Lam. Angyostomata, Bl.—*Descr.* Oval or oblong, ventricose, convolute, covered by an enamel, generally smooth and shining. Spire short, nearly hid. Aperture long, narrow, terminating in a short canal at both extremities. Outer lip dentated, thickened, inflected. Inner lip dentated, thickened, reflected over part of the body whorl.—*Obs.* These shells are so distinguished by the two rows of teeth arranged on each side of the aperture; the thickened front formed by the inner and outer lips; and the enamel deposited over the back of the shell from the mantle of the animal which envelopes it, that there is no danger of confounding them with any other genus, except in a young state. Before they have arrived at the full growth, the front is not thickened, and the outer lip is thin, not inflected, nor are the teeth formed. In this state the shell resembles, in some degree, an Oliva. Some species are striated, ribbed or tuberculated, but the generality are smooth. Most species belong to tropical climates, only one to Great Britain. The C. Moneta is current as money in some parts of Africa, and many species are worn as ornaments by the South Sea Islanders. The colouring in most species is exceedingly rich, and arranged in every variety of spots, patches, rings, lines, bands and clouds. The species most esteemed by collectors are C. Mappa, C. Testudinaria, C. Pustulata, C. Aurora, C. Princeps, of which only two specimens are known, C. Leucodon, &c. See also Cypræovulum, Trivea and Luponia. The fossil species are principally from the Calc-grossier, the London Clay, Crag, &c. The latest revision of this genus has been effected by Mr. G. B. Sowerby, sen., who has published a complete catalogue in the author's Conchological Illustrations. This catalogue enumerates 130 species, the whole of which are figured in parts 1 to 8, 101 to 131 of the above mentioned work. Pl. xxi. fig. 445 to 450.

CYPRÆCASSIS. Stutch. (Cypræa and Cassis.)—*Descr.* Shell, when young, striated, reticulated, or tuberculated; outer lip simple: when mature, outer lip involute and toothed; columellar lip also toothed; aperture straight, anteriorly terminated by a recurved canal, posteriorly by a shallow channel. Animal with the mantle bilobed; operculum none.—*Obs.* The reasons given for separating this genus from Cassis, are, 1st, That the shells of the latter have an operculum, while those of the proposed genus have none. 2nd, That the Cypræcassides do not form a complete, thickened lip, before the full period of their growth, like the Cassides. 3rd, That the Cypræcassides have no epidermis. The species mentioned as probably belonging to Cypræcassins are C. rufa, the type; C. coarctata, and C. Testiculus, Auct. The establishment of this genus has been opposed on the ground that indications of epidermis are discoverable in some specimens of C. rufa; that some specimens of the same species and Testiculus have been examined, and found to have formed slightly thickened and dentulated outer lips at very early periods of growth, while many of the other Cassides are destitute of varices, and

279. ——algira. Zonites, Montf.
280. ——citrina. Naninia, Gray. } Helicella.
281. ——epistilum .... Helicostyla.
282. Bulinus rosaceus; *a*. apex.
283. ——Guadaloupensis; Bulinulus, Leach.
284. ——Lyonetianus. Gibbus, Montf. } Cochlostyla.
285. ——lubricus. Cionella, Jeffreys.
286. Achatina virginea Liguus, Montf.
287. Achatinella, Sw. } Cochlitoma.
288. Polyphemus Glans, Montf. . . . Cochlicopa.
289. Bulinus decollatus, *a*. in a young state . . . Cochlicella.
290. Azeca tridens, Jeffreys. Turbo tridens, Gmelin. .. Cochlogena.
291. Pupa Uva.
292. Alæa marginata; Jeffreys.
293. Vertigo pusilla.
294. Megaspira Ruschenbergiana } Cochlodonta.
295. Clausilia Macascarensis; *a*. a break, to shew the clausium
296. Balea fragilis, ... } Cochlodina.
297. Auricula Judæ.
298. ——coniformis. Conovulum, Lam. Melampus, Montf.
299. Pedipes Adansonii.
299*. Scarabæus imbrium.
300. Chilina Dombeyana.
301. Carychium minimum.
302. Partula Australis.
303. Cyclostoma ferrugineum.
304. ——Involvulus. Cyclophorus, Montf.
305. Nematura Deltæ.
306. Helicina major.
307. Operculum of the same.

Macrospira, fig. 514.
Stenopus, fig. 516, 516.
Abida, fig. 518.
Gonidomus, fig. 519.
Truncatella, fig. 520, 521.
Caprella, fig. 522, 523.
Pupina, Callia, fig. 524–528.
Megalomastoma, fig. 529.
Cyclotus, fig. 530.
Pterocyclos, fig. 531.
Trochatella, fig. 532.
Strophostoma, fig. 534–536.
Stoastoma, fig. 582. } To be added to this family.

Fam. Lymneana

308. Limnæa stagnalis.
309. ——auricularia. Radix, Montf.
310. ——castanea. Physa, Drap.
311. Planorbis corneus.
312. Planaria nitens, (from Lea.)

Fam. Melaniana.

313. Melania subulata. Melas, Montf.
314. Melania præerosa and monodontoides. Anculosa, Say.
315. Malanopsis costata. Faunus, Montf.
316. Pirena terebralis.
317. Pasithæa striata, (from Lea.)

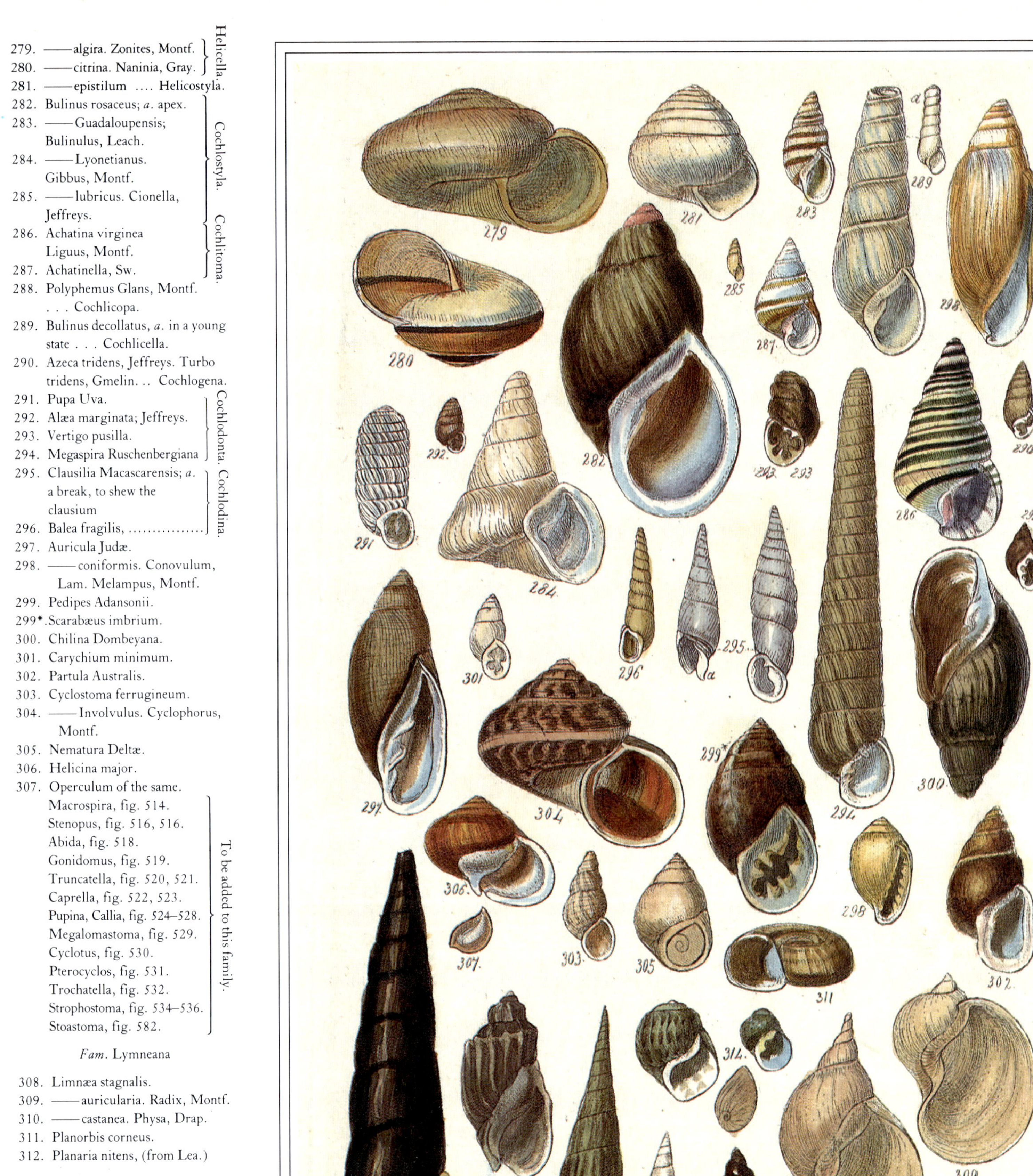

that an operculum of C. coarctata was brought to this country by Mr. Cuming. It is probable, however, that an increased knowledge of facts might go far to establish the separation. C. Testiculus, Pl. xix. fig. 412.

CYPRÆADIA. Swainson, 1840. A genus of the family "Cypræidæ," Sw. thus described:—"Cypræform; the base contracted; the body whorl not flattened beneath; shell cancellated; aperture of equal breadth throughout; a few thickened, short teeth on the pillar; lip at the base, which is not internally concave. C. cancellata, Sw. Fossil only, differing from Trivea in its contracted base, in the inequality of its aperture, and the equal convexity of the inner lip within." (Sw. Lardn. Cyclop. Malac. p. 325.) Cyprædia, Pl. xxvi. fig. 564.

CYPRÆLA. Swainson. Calpurnus, Montf. Ovulum verrucosum, fig. 441.

CYPRÆOVULUA. Gray. 1832. A genus of Cypræidæ thus described, "shell like a cowry, but front end of columella covered with regular cross-ribs, like the rest of the base, internally produced into an acute toothed ridge. Shell pear-shaped, cross-ridged." C. capense. South Africa. Pl. xxi. fig. 444.

CYPRICARDIA. Lam. *Fam.* Cardiacea, Lam.—*Descr.* Equivalve, inequilateral, subquadrate, transversely elongated, with the anterior side very short; hinge with three cardinal teeth and one remote lateral tooth in each valve; ligament external.—*Obs.* This genus is distinguished from Cardita by the three cardinal teeth. The mollusca of this genus are marine. Pacific Ocean. C. angulata, Pl. vi. fig. 125.

CYPRINA. Lamarck, 1818. *Fam.* "Conques Marines," or Marine Conchacea.—*Descr.* Equivalve, inequilateral, sub-orbicular; umbones curved obliquely; hinge with three diverging cardinal and one remote lateral teeth in each valve; ligament external; muscular impressions two in each valve; palleal impression having a slight posterior sinus; epidermis thick, rough brown.—*Obs.* The Cyprinæ belong to the Northern Hemisphere. The recent species are not numerous. Fossil species are found in the tertiary deposits. Cyprina may be known from Venus by the remote lateral tooth and the thick epidermis. C. vulgaris, Pl. v. fig 116.

CYRENA. Lamarck, 1818. *Fam.* Fluviatile Conchaceæ, Lam. Conchacea, Bl.—*Descr.* Suborbicular, equivalve, inequilateral, ventricose, corroded at the umbones, thick, covered with a thick epidermis; hinge with three cardinal and two remote lateral teeth in each valve. Muscular impressions two in each valve; palleal impression not sinuated.—*Obs.* This genus is distinguished from Venus, Cytherea and Cyprina, by having two remote lateral teeth; and from Cyclas by the thickness of the shell. This genus is mostly fluviatile; the recent species are tropical, and the fossil are found in the newest formations. C. fuscata. Pl. v. fig. 113.

CYRENELLA. Desh. See CYRENOIDA.

CYRENOIDA. Joannis, 1835. CYRENELLA, Desh. *Fam.* Conques Fluviatiles, Lam.—*Descr.* Equivalve, subequilateral, ventricose, thin, covered with a reddish brown epidermis, coroded at the umbones, with a slight posterior fold. Hinge thin, with three diverging cardinal teeth in each valve, and a very slight posterior fold in the right valve. Ligament not very tumid.—*Obs.* This fresh-water shell differs from Cyclas and Cyrena in the lateral teeth, and from the later in the thinness of the shell. Pl. v. fig. 114.

CYRTIA. Dalman. (Κυρτος, curtos, gibbose.) *Fam.* Brachiopoda, Lam.—*Descr.* "Hinge rectilinear; with the back elevated into a semicone or half-pyramid, the cardinal side perpendicularly *plane.*"—*Obs.* This genus of fossil Brachiopoda forms part of the genus Spirifer, Sow. C. exporrecta, (Anomites exporrecta, Nonnull.) Pl. xi. fig. 204.

CYTHARA. Schum. 1817. Cancellaria Cytharella. LAMARCK.

CYTHEREA. Lam. *Fam.* "Conques Marines," Lam.—*Descr.* Equivalve, inæquilateral, oval, lenticular, or sub-trigonal; hinge with two or more short, diverging cardinal teeth, and one anterior approximate lateral tooth in each valve.—*Obs.* The Cythereæ are distinguished from the Veneres by the lateral tooth. The Monograph of this genus, in No. 12. Thesaurus Conchyliorum contains, apart from Meroe, Artemis and Circe, 115 species. See MERETRIX. C. MERETRIX. Pl. vi. fig. 117, and 117, *a. b. c. d.*

CYRTULUS. Hinds. 1844. A genus founded on a turbinella-like shell, thus described, (translation) "fusiform; the two last whorls turbinated, the spire suddenly rising; aperture linear, ending in a short effuse canal; columella much arched, callous above; outer lip acute; umbilicus small; epidermis smooth." C. scrotinus. Pl. xxviii. fig. 594.

DACTYLINA. Gray. Syn. B. Mus. Pholas Dactylus, and other species, with several accessory valves. Pl. ii. fig. 55.

DACTYLUS. Schum. 1837. Species of ACTÆON or TORNATELLA, which have a duplicate fold at the lower part of the columella. T. solidula.

DACTYLUS. Humph. MARGINELLA, Auct.

DAPHNELLA. Hinds. Voyage of the Sulphur, p. 25. Pl. vii. fig. 19, 20, 21. "Among the smaller Pleurotomaceæ are a few shells of a thin fragile structure, elongated in form, the outer lip acute and separated from the last whorl so as to leave a sinus, aperture of a lengthened oval, scarcely any canal, and with the surface usually transversely striated. These form a very distinct group, and may be separated with advantage under a proper head; the best known of these is probably Lymnæformis Kiener." *Ex.* D. Marmorata, our Pl. xxviii. fig. 593.

DARACIA. Gray. A subgenus of Pyrgoma, including a species which is remarkable for the irregularity of its form. It grows upon a species of Monticularia, and the margin takes the shape of the lobes by which it is surrounded. The aperture is large, and completely closed by the operculum. Daracia (Pyrgoma) Monticulariæ. Pl. xxiv. fig. 489, 490.

DATE. A common name given to shells of the genus Pholas, on account of their cylindrical form and consequent resemblance to the fruit. For the same reason the name Pholas Dactylus has been given by Naturalists to the species which we represent, fig. 66.

DEAD SHELL. A term used among collectors to signify that the shell has been exposed on the sea-shore after the animal has ceased to live. A shell in this condition is worn down by attrition, and loses its beauty and brilliancy of colouring by being subject to the action of salt water. A dead shell may be known by a certain hoary whiteness spread over its surface.

DECACERA. Bl. The second family of the order Cryptodibranchita, Bl. containing the genera Calmar and Sepia, which have no shells.

DECADOPECTEN. Rüppell. PECTEN *Plica*, Linn. Having a plicated hing. Pl. x. fig. 172.

DECOLLATED. (*Decollari*, to be beheaded.) The apex or nucleus of some shells being composed of a more fragile substance than the rest, has a tendency to fall off. The reason of this probably is that the animal withdrawing from that part, leaves it unprotected. When the part falls off, the hole is stopped up by a septum filling the cavity of the volution, so as to exclude the air: the shell is then said to be decollated. *Ex.* Bulinus decollatus, fig. 289.

DECUSSATED. Intersected by striæ crossing each other. *Ex.* Rissoa, fig. 346.

DELPHINULA. Montf. (*Delphinus*, a dolphin.) *Fam.* Scalariens, Lam. Cricostomata, Bl.—*Descr.* Orbicular, depressed, thick, rugose; whorls few, angulated, branched at the angles; aperture pearly, rounded or

Fam. Peristomata

318. Ampullaria fasciata. Amphibola; *a.* aperture.
319. ——Guinaica. Lanistes, Montf.
320. ——Cornu-arietis. Ceradotes, Guild.
321. Paludina Bengalensis.
322. Valvata piscinalis.

Bithinia, fig. 537.
Amphibola, fig. 538.
Pachylatra, fig. 539.
Paludomus, fig. 583. } To be added to this family.

Fam. Neritacea

323. Navicella elliptica.
324. Neritina virginea. Theodoxus, Montf.
325. ——spinosa. Clithon, Montf.
326. ——perversa. Velates, Montf. (from Sow. Gen.)
327. Natica mamilla. Polinices, Montf.
328. ——lineata.
330. Nerita peloronta. Peloronta, Oken.
331. Neritopsis granosa.
332. Pileolus plicatus.
333. Janthina fragilis.

Fam. Macrostomata

334. Sigaretus concavus.
335. Stomatia Phymotis.
336. Stomatella imbricata.
337. Velutina lævigata. Galericulus, Nonnul.
338. Haliotis rubra, young.
339. ——tricostalis, Lam. Padollus, Montf.
340. Scissurella elatior, magnified. } (from Sow. Gen.)
341. Pleurotomaria reticulata. } (from Sow. Gen.)

Vanicoro, fig. 584. To be added to this family.

Fam. Plicacea

342. Pyramidella terebellum.
343. Tornatella solidula. Acteon, Montf.
344. Monoptygma elegans, (from Lea.) Ringicula, fig. 540, 541. To be added to this family.

Fam. Scalariana

345. Vermetus lumbricalis.
346. Rissoa reticulata.
347. Eulima labiosa.
348. ——marmorata. Bonellia, Desh.

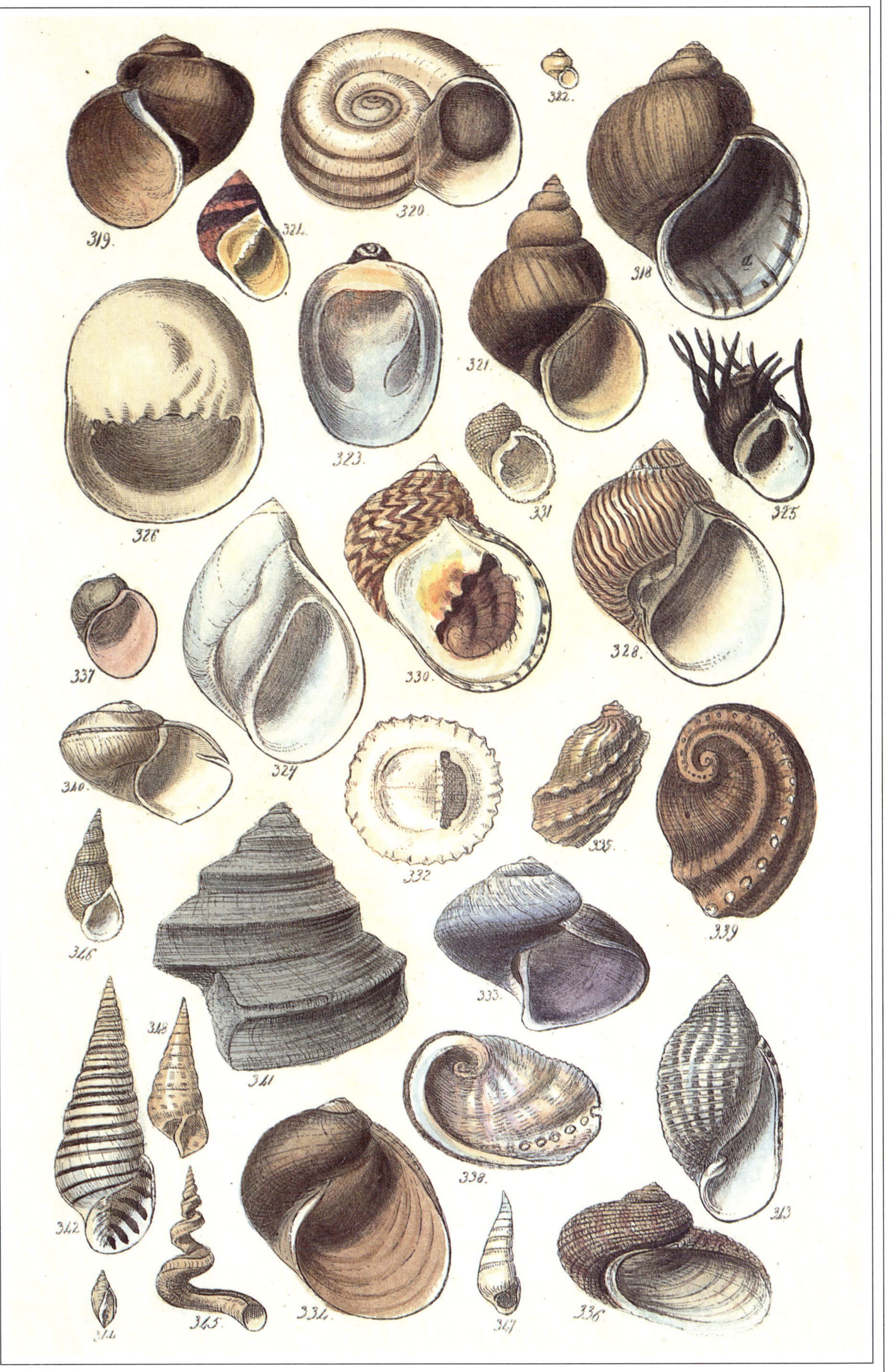

sub-quadrate; peritreme continuous, thickened; operculum horny, composed of numerous whorls.—*Obs.* Several fossil species are found in the tertiary deposits. D. laciniata. Pl. xvi. fig. 352. Recent species belong to tropical climates.

DELTHYRIS. Dalman. *Fam.* Brachioponda, Lam.—*Descr.* Hinge more or less rounded, with distant umbones; both valves convex; with the umbo of the largest rostrated and deltoid, with a hollow. This genus forms part of the genus Spirifer, Sow. D. Plycotes, Dalman. Pl. xi. f. 205.

DELTOID. (Δ, *delta.*) Triangular.

DENDOSTREA. Swainson, (1840). (Δευδρσν, *dendron*, tree; οστρεον, *ostreon*, oyster.) Ostrea *Crista-galli*, and other species which are attached to stems of sea-weed and corallines, by means of arms thrown out from the innter surface of the lower valve. Ostrea Folium. Pl. x. f. 181.

DENTALIUM. Linnæus (*Dens*, a tooth.) *Fam.* Maldania, Lam. *Order*, Cirrobranchiata, Bl.—*Descr.* Tubular, arched, increasing in size towards the anterior extremity, open at both ends; small aperture sometimes having a lateral fissure; large aperture round; external surface ribbed, striated or smooth.—*Obs.* The well known shells composing this genus are shaped very much like an elephant's tusk, and are not liable to be confounded with any other genus. The fossil species are sometimes termed Dentalithes, from *dens*, a tooth, and *lithos*, a stone. The Dentalia, being true molluscs, are not rightly placed among the Annelides. D. octogonum. Found on sandy shores in most climates. Pl. i. f. 2.

DENTATED. Having teeth or raised points.

DENTICULATED. (Denticulatus, Lat.) Having little teeth or raised points.

DEPRESSED. Flattened, pressed down, as the spires of some shells.

DEXTRAL Spiral Shells. Place the point of a spiral shell towards the eye, with its mouth downwards; if, as in most instances, the aperture be on the right side of the axis, it is a *dextral* shell, if otherwise, it is *sinistral* or *reversed*. Balea (fig. 296), and Clausilia (fig. 295), are examples of reversed shells.

DEXTRAL Valve. Take a bivalve shell closed, place it before the eye, with the umbones uppermost, and the posterior side, which may be known by the ligament towards the observer, whose right side will then correspond with the right valve of the shell.

DIADEMA. Ranz. CORONULA Diadema, Auct. Pl. i. fig. 17.

DIADORA. Grey. CEMORIA, Leach.

DIANCHORA. Sowerby. *Fam.* Pectinides, Lam. *Order*, Palliobranchiata, Bl.—*Descr.* Inequivalve, attached, oblique, subtriangular; attached valve, having an opening in the place of the umbo; the other valve auriculated, with an obtuse umbo; hinge without teeth.—*Obs.* The green sand fossils contained in this differ from Plagiostoma in being attached. D. striata. Pl. x. f. 175.

DIAPHANOUS. (Δια, *dia*, through; φαινω, *phaino*, to shine.) Transparent.

DIAPHRAGM. (διαφραγμα, a partition.) This term is applied to the septa, by which the chambers of multilocular and other shells are divied from each other.

DICERAS. Lamarck. (Δυς, *dis*, double; Κερας, *ceras*, horn.) *Fam.* Chamacea, Bl. and Lam.—*Descr.* Inequilateral, inequivalve, attached by the point of the umbo of the larger valve; umbones prominent, spirally twisted and grooved; hinge with one large thick tooth in the larger valve; muscular impressions, two in each valve.—*Obs.* The prominent spiral umbones, which gives to this genus its name, with the circumstance of its being attached by the point of one of them, is sufficient to distinguish it from any other. Although it appears to approach Isocardia in some characters, in others it will be found still more nearly to resemble Chama. In fact, from being attached and irregular, the shells composing this genus have been regarded as Chamæ with produced umbones. The singular fossil shells composing this genus, are found in granular limestone, near Geneva in Normandy. D. perversum. Pl. ix. fig. 154.

DICHÆLASPIS. Darwin. Cirrip, p. 115. OCTOLASMIS, Gray. HEPTALASMIS, Leach. A genus of pedunculated cirripides, the shell of which is thus described: "Valves 5, generally appearing like 7, from each section being divided into two distinct segments, united at the rostral angle; carina generally extending up between the terga, terminating downwards in an imbedded disc, or fork, or cup." Ex. D. Warwickii (imperfect figure.) Pl. 2. f. 41.

DIDONTA. Schum. SAXICAVA. Auct.

DIFFUSE. (*Diffundo*, to spread out, to dilate.) A term applied to the aperture of a univalve shell, when it is spread out or widened into a flat surface, or digitations. *Alated* is another term used to express the same character. Thus the shells belonging to the family of Alatæ, in the system of Lamarck, are *diffuse* in the outer lip. Fig. 402 to 406.

DIGITATED. (*Digitus*, finger.) Branched out in long points, as Ricinula, fig. 413.

DILATED. Expanded, spread. This term has the same application as diffuse and alated, explained above. The outer lip of Rostellaria Columbaria, fig. 403 (Hippochrenes, Montf.), will serve as an example.

DIMORPHINA. D'Orb. A genus of microscopic Foraminifera.

DIMYARIA. (Δις, *dis*, double; μυσν, *myon*, muscle.) The first order of Conchifera, Lam, including those molluscs which have two adductor muscles, and consequently two muscular impressions in each valve. The Conchifera Dimyaria are divided into Crassipedes, Tenuipedes, Lamellipedes, and Ambiguæ, fig. 44 to 155.

DIODONTA. Deshayes. A genus formed for the reception of Tellina fragilis. Hanley, in Sowerby's Thesaurus Conchyliorum. P. 319, pl. lvi. fig. 14, and similar species.

DIOICA. Bl. The first division of the class Paracephalophora, Bl. It is divided into the orders Siphonobranchiata and Asiphonibranchiata, Bl.

DIONE. A generic term used to distinguish the group of Cytheræa represented by C. Dione. See Monograph of Cytheræa, No. 12, pl. cxxxii. fig. 98. Sowerby's Thesaurus Conchyliorum.

DIPLODON. Spix. HYRIA Syrmatophora, Lam. fig. 144, and UNIO multistriatus, Lea, are doubtfully quoted by Lea as belonging to this apparently ill-defined genus of Nayades.

DIPLODONTA. Brown. Resembles LUCINA, but without the ligneate elongation of the muscular impression. D. rotundata. Forbes and Hanley, British Mollusca. Our figure, pl. xxvii. fig. 576.

DIPSAS. Leach, 1817. A genus or sub-genus of Nayades, the distinctive character of which is "having a linear tooth under the dorsal edge." D. plicatus, pl. viii. fig. 142.

DISCINA. Lam. ORBICULA, Auct.

DISCODOMA. Sw. A sub-genus of Lucerninæ, Sw. (Helix), thus described, "teeth none; aperture angulated; the inner lip nearly obsolete; the outer only slightly thickened; margin carinated."

DISCOIDAL. (*Discus*, a circular plane.) A spiral shell is said to be discoidal, when the whorls are so horizontally convolute as to form a flattened spire. *Ex.* Planorbis, fig. 311. Orbulites Discus, fig. 479.

DISCOLITES. Montf. A genus of microscopic Foraminifera.

DISCONTINUOUS. Interrupted. *Ex.* The siphon of Nautilus is discontinuous, i.e. its termination in one chamber does not reach to its

349. Cirrus nodosus, Sow.
350. Euomphalus pentangulus, (from Sow. Min. Con.)
351. Scalaria Pallassii. Aciona, Leach.
352. Delphinula laciniata.
Chemnitzia, 585.
Alvania, 586.
Odostomia, 587.
} To be added to this family.

Fam. Turbinacea

353. Solarium perspectivum.
354. ——Bifrons. Bifrontia and Omalaxis, Desh.
355. Orbis Rotella, (from Lea.)
356. Another view of the same.
357. Rotella vestiaria, Pitonellus, Montf.
358. Trochus stellaris, Lam. Calcar, Montf. Turbo, Sow.
359. ——maculatus. Tectus, Montf.
360. ——agglutinans. Phorus.
361. ——Pharaonis. Clauculus, Montf.
362. Margarita tæniata.
363. Littorina vulgaris.
363*. Assiminea Grayana.
364. Lacuna pallidula.
365. Planaxis sulcata.
366. Monodonta labeo; Odontis, Sow.
367. Phasianella variegata.
368. Turbo setosus. Marmarostoma, Sw.
369. Tuba striata, (from Lea.)
370. Turritella imbricata.
371. Monotygma, Gray.
Chrysostoma, fig. 542.
Elenchus, fig. 543.
Adeorbis, fig. 588.
Teinostoma, fig. 589.
Camitia, fig. 589.
Mesalia, fig. 591.
Eglesia, fig. 592.
} To be added to this family.

Fam. Canalifera

372. Cerithium Aluco, front.
374. Nerinea Goodhallii, (from Geol. Trans.)
375. Triphora plicata, (from Deshayes.)
376. End view of the same.
379. Pleurotoma Babylonia; *a*, *a*, extremities of the anix.
381. ——strombiformis, Clavatula, Lam.

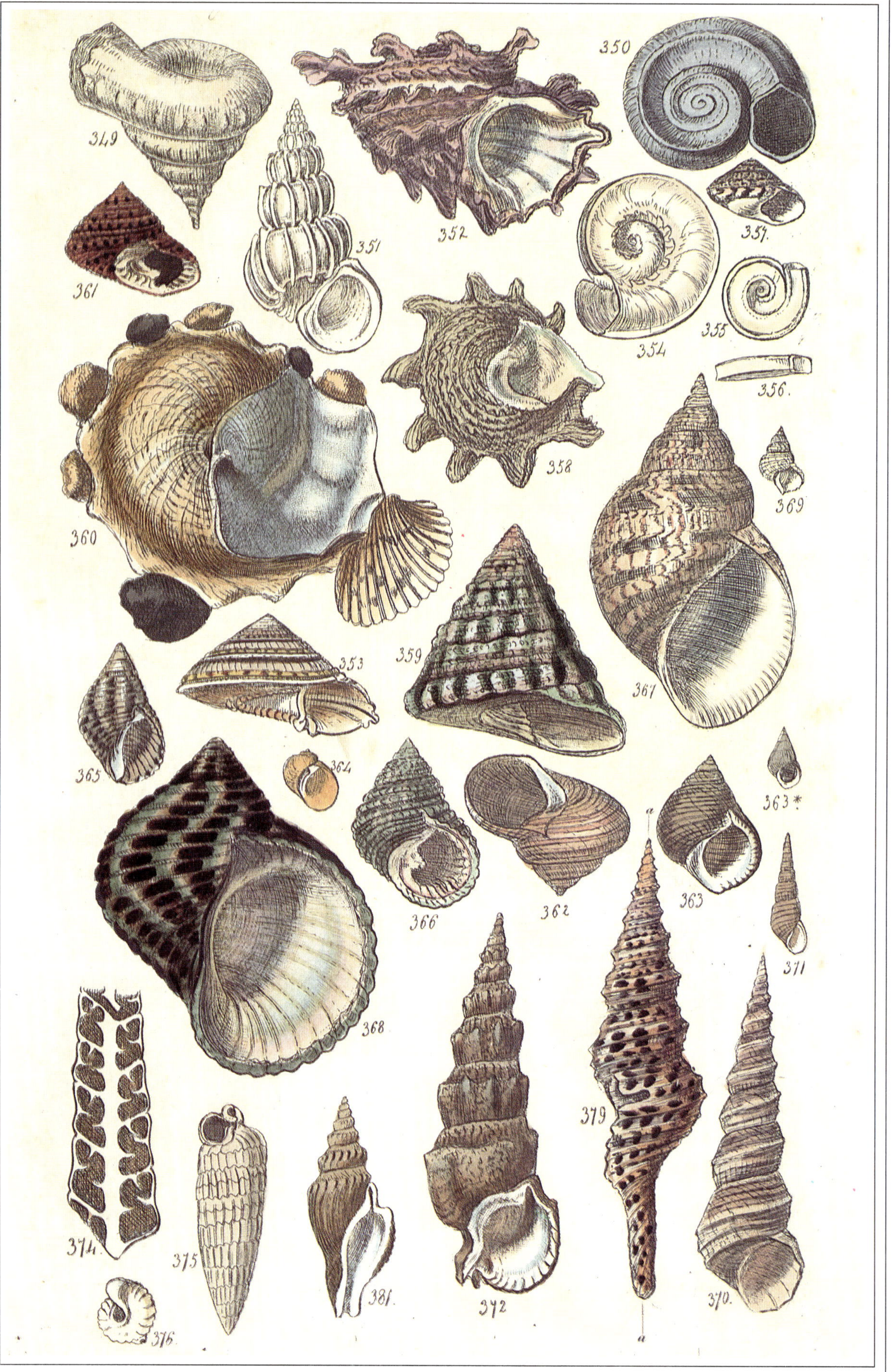

commencement in the next. The varices of Triton, occurring in different parts of the whorls, do not form the continuous ridges which characterize the generality of the Ranellæ.

DISCORBITES. Lam. A genus of microscopic Foraminifera.

DISTANT. The teeth on the hinge of a bivalve shell are said to be distant when they are said to be remote from the umbones.

DIVARICATED. Diverging, meeting in a point, as the teeth on the hinge of Placuna, fig. 184.

DOLABELLA. Lamarck (Dim. from *Dolabra*, a hatchet.) *Fam.* Aplysiacea, Lam. and Bl.—*Descr.* Hatchet-shaped, arched, covered with a horny epidermis; posteriorly attenuated, thickened, sub-spiral, anteriorly plane, broad, thin; posterior margin reflected.—*Obs.* The two or three species of Dolabella known are inhabitants of the Indian Ocean. They were placed by Linnæus in his very convenient genus Bulla, under the name of B. dubia. Pl. xiii. fig. 255, Dolabella Rumphii.

DOLIUM. Brown, (1756.) (*a tun.*) *Fam.* Purpurifera, Lam. Entomostomata, Bl.—*Descr.* Thin, ventricose, oval, or globular, with a short spire; large aperture terminating in a reflected canal, and spirally ribbed or grooved external surface; outer lip crenated; inner lip reflected over part of the body whorl, which terminates in a tumid varix; epidermis light, horny. Mediterranean and East Indian.—*Obs.* This genus is distinguished from Cassis by the outer lip, which is not reflected. The species which are not so round as the others, as D. Perdix, Auct. have been separated under the name Perdix, as if generically distinct. Mr. Reeve's Monograph contains fourteen species. Dolium Maculatum. Pl. xix. fig. 420.

DONAX. Linnæus. *Fam.* Nymphacea, Lam. Conchacea, Bl.—*Descr.* Equivalve, inequilateral, trigonal, with the anterior side short, straight, plane; the posterior side elongated, drawn to a narrow, rounded termination; hinge with two cardinal teeth in one valve, one in the other, and one or two, more or less remote lateral teeth; ligament external; muscular impressions two in each valve; palleal impression sinuated posteriorly.—*Obs.* The Capsæ have not the crenated margins, the short anterior side, and the distinct lateral teeth, which characterise the Donaces. Some species of Erycina resemble Donax in general form, but are at once distinguished by the ligamentary pit in the hinge. The Donaces inhabit sandy shores in all climates. D. cuneatus. Pl. v. fig. 108.

DORSAL. A dorsal shell is one placed upon the back of the animal. The dorsal margin of a bivalve shell is that on which the hinge is placed; the opposite margins are termed ventral. The dorsal surface of a spinal univalve is that which is seen when the aperture is turned from the observer. The dorsal valve is the uppermost in Brachiopodous bivalves. The dorsal part of a symmetrical convolute univalve, such as the Nautilus and Ammonite is that part of the whorls which is at the greatest distance from the spire, that is, the outer part of the whorls. Thus the situation of the siphon is said to be dorsal when it pierces the septum near the outer edge of the whorls. The dorsal part of symmetrical conical univalves, such as Patella, is the upper part, on which the apex is placed.

DORSALLIA. Lam. (*Dorsum*, the back.) The first family of the order Annelides Sedentaria, Lam. containing the genera Arenicola, not a shell, and Siliquaria, fig. 1, which is now considered as a true mollusc, and placed next to Vermetus.

DOSINA. Schum. Venus Verrucosa, Casina, and similar species. Fig. 119, *a*.

DREISSINA. 1835. Mytilus Polymorphus. Auct. fig. 159. This genus differs from Mytilus principally in the characters of the animal. The shell is characterized by a small septiform plate under the hinge within. Fluviatile, Europe and Africa. Pl. ix. fig. 159.

EBURNA. This name belongs to the species "glabrata," described in this book as an Ancillaria. "Latrunculus" is given by Gray for the present genus. Ancillaria glabrata, fig. 455. (*Eburneus*), ivory. *Fam.* Purpurifera, Lam. Entomostomata, Bl.—*Descr.* Oval, thick, smooth, turrited, umbilicated; spire angulated, acute, nearly as long as the aperture; aperture oval, terminating anteriorly in a canal, posteriorly in a groove; outer lip slightly thickened with an anterior notch, which terminates in a spiral fold surrounding the body whorl; umbilicus generally covered by the thickened columellar lip.—*Obs.* (A. glabrata, fig. 455.) The Eburnæ resemble in some respects the genus Buccinum, but a glance at the figure will enable the reader to distinguish a true Eburna from all other shells. Fig. 426 is Eburna Zeylanica. A catalogue of 9 species is given in part 20 of the Conchological Illustrations published by the Author, accompanied by figures of several species.

ECHIDNIS. Montf. Described as a straight, chambered, annulated, fossil shell, computed from the extremely gradual increase in diameter of the fragments to be at least sixteen feet long. Found in marble from the Pyrenees.

ECHINELLA. Swainson. A sub-genus of Monodonta. Sw. Malac. page 352.

EFFUSE. (*effundo*, to pour out.) The aperture of an univalve shell is said to be effuse when there is a notch in the margin which would suffer a liquid to escape, and thus prevent it being filled to the brim.

EGEON. Montf. A genus of microscopic Foraminifera.

EGERIA. Lea. (Contrib. to Geol. p. 49, pl. 1.) A genus of fossil bivalves, described as very variable in form, with or without lateral teeth, sometimes a crenated margin, &c. The only certain characters appear to be that they have two diverging cardinal teeth in each valve, one of which is bifid; and an external ligament. Lea states that the Egeriæ should be placed between the Sanguinolariæ and the Psammobiæ, which two latter genera have been united by Sowerby. E. Triangulata, from the tertiary formation of Alabama. Pl. v. fig. 103.

EGLESIA. Gray. Reeve's Monograph (2 species.) Conch. Iconica. "Shell elongated, turrited; whorls numerous; sutures depressed; columella flatly thickened; squarely angled at the base; aperture small, rounded; margins almost joined, not reflected." Distinguished from Turritella by the angular depression of the upper part of the whorls, and by the consequent straightness of the outer lip.—*Obs.* There are certain species of so-called Scalariæ; such as Sc. Australis, Sc. Diadema, Sc. Crenata, &c. of Sowerby's Thesaurus, which perhaps might be added to this genus with propriety. See our Pl. xxviii. fig. 592.

ELENCHUS. Humph. A genus composed of Trochus Iris, Auct. and other similarly formed species. It is the same as Cantharidus of Montfort. Pl. xxv. fig. 543.

ELEPHANT'S TUSK. The common name given by dealers to shells of the genus Dentalium. *Ex.* D. octogonum, fig. 2.

ELEVATED. A term which is applied by some conchological writers to the spire of an univalve shell when it consists of numerous whorls drawn out into a telescopic form. Other authors use the term *elongated*, or the more simple one '*long*,' to express the degree of elevation.

ELLIPSOLITHES. Montf. (Ελλειψις, *ellipsis*, oval; λιθος, *lithos*, stone.) A genus composed of Ammonites, which instead of being regularly orbicular, take an elliptical or oval form. This character appears to be accidental, as some individuals of the same species, both of Nautilus and Ammonites, are round, while others are compressed into an oval form.

ELLIPSOSTOMATA. Bl. (Ελλειψις, *ellipsis*, oval; στωμα *mouth*.) The third family of the class Asiphonibranchiata, Bl. The shells of this family are described as of various forms, generally smooth; the aperture longitudinally or transversely oval, completely closed by a horny or shelly operculum. This family contains the genera Rissoa, Phasianella, Ampullaria, Helicina, and Pleuroceras.

ELLIPTICAL. (Ελλειψις, *ellipsis*.) Oval. Applied to any shell or part of a shell, having that form.

ELMINEUS. Leach. *Order*, Sessile Cirripedes, Lam.—*Descr.* Four unequal valves, arranged circularly side by side, forming a quadrate cone; aperture large, sub-quadrate, irregular; operculum composed of four valves, in pairs.—*Obs.* This genus differs from Conia in the structure of the shell, the latter being porous. Elmineus Leachii. Pl. i. fig. 22.

ELPHIDIUM. Montf. (Conch. Syst. t. 1. p. 15.) A genus of microscopic Foraminifera.

EMARGINATED. (*e*, out; *margo*, border.) Notched or hollowed out. Applied to the edges or margins of shells, when instead of being level they are hollowed out, as the outer lip of Oliva, fig. 457, at the base, and the ventral margins of some bivalves.

EMARGINULA. Lamarck, 1801. (*e*, out; *margo*, border.) *Fam.* Calyptracea, Lam. Branchifera, Bl.—*Descr.* Patelliform, oblong or oval; anterior margin notched or emarginated; apex posteriorly inclined; muscular impressions wide.—*Obs.* Emarginula elongata, of some Authors, PARMOPHORUS of De Blainville is commonly called the Duck's bill limpet, from its shape. The Emarginulæ may be known from Patellæ and other neighbouring genera, by the notch or slit in the anterior edge. In the genus Rimula, Defr. fig. 243, this slit is near the apex, and does not reach the margin. Recent species occur in all climates, but are not numerous. Fossil species are still more rare, occurring in the Calcairegrossièr, Crag and Oolite. E. fissurata, Pl. xiii. fig. 241.

ENDOSIPHONITES. A genus composed of Ammonites, having the siphon close to the body whorl. Pl. xxii. fig. 476.

ENDOTOMA. Rafinesque. A genus of microscopic Foraminifera.

ENOPLOCHITON. Gray. Chiton niger, &c.

ENROULEES. Lam. See CONVOLUTÆ.

ENSATELLA. Swainson, 1840. Ensis, Schum. 1817.

ENSIS. Schum. 1817. SOLEN ensis. Auct. and similar species, fig. 60.

ENTALIS. Defr. DENTALIUM duplicatum, Bl. PHARETRIUM, König. This genus is described as a small tube, within a larger one, the smaller extremity of the inner tube projecting beyond that of the outer one. Deshayes, who describes this genus, expresses a conviction that the soft parts of the animal must be entirely different from those of the animal of Dentalium. The genus PHARETRIUM, as described by König in his "Icones Fossilium Sectiles," is evidently identical with Entalis. It is placed by him in the family of Pteropoda, but being a fossil shell, there is some difficulty in finding its place in the system. See plates, fig. 3.

ENTELLITES. Fischer. A genus composed of species of TEREBRATULA, SPIRIFER, and PRODUCTUS, Auct. having the hinge large and the umbones short. ORTHIS? Dalman.

ENTIRE. (Integra.) Not interrupted, not emarginated. The peritrême of a univalve shell is said to be entire when not interrupted by canals or by the body whorl. *Ex.* Cyclostoma, fig. 304. The palleal impression is entire, when continued without interruption, or without a sinus.

ENTOMOSTOMATA. Bl. The second family of the order Siphonibranchiata, Bl. The shells of this family are described as differing but little from those contained in the family of Siphonostomata of the same author, both with regard to the soft parts, and their testaceous covering. This family partly answers to the Purpuriferæ in the system of Lamarck, and contains the genera Subula, Cerithium, Melanopsis, Planaxis, Terebra, Eburna, Buccinum, Harpa, Dolium, Cassidaria, Cassis, Ricinula, Cancellaria, Purpura, Concholepas.

EOLIDES. Montf. A genus of microscopic Foraminifera.

EPIDERMIS. (Επι, *epi*, over or upon; δερμα, *derma*, skin.) The fibrous, horny, external coating of shells, called by the French, "*Drap marin*," or marine cloth. Lamarck objects to the name Epidermis, because he does not consider the substance as answering to the cuticle or scarf skin of the human body, but more analogous to the nails and hair. Gray calls it the PERIOSTRACUM, from the membranous skin covering the bones of quadrupeds.

EPIPHRAGM. The membranaceous or calcareous substance by which some species of molluscs close the aperture of the shell, when they retire within it to hibernate. When the animal wishes to come forth from his hiding-place, again to breathe the air, the edges of the Epiphragm are detached by a chemical process, so that it drops off. The name *Hibernaculum* has also been given to this covering. It must not be confounded with the operculum, which is a permanent portion of the shell, and is used as a door, fitted to the foot of the animal and moved at will to pen or close the aperture of the shell, whereas the Epiphragm is produced for the occasion from a mucous secretion of the animal and dissolved at the edges when no longer, wanted, when it drops off.

EPISTYLA. Swainson, 1840. A subgenus of the genus HELIX. E. conical. Sw. Helix Epistylium, fig. 281.

EPONIDES. Montf. A genus of microscopic Foraminifera.

EQUILATERAL. (*Æquus*, equal; *latus*, side.) Equal-sided. A term applied to bivalve shells, when a line drawn down perpendicularly from the apex would divide the shell into two equal parts. *Ex.* Pectunculus pilosus, fig. 134.

EQUIVALVE. (*Æquus*, equal, *valva*, a valve.) A term applied to a bivalve shell when the valves are equal to each other in dimensions.

ERATO. Risso, 1826. *Fam.* Convolute, Lam.—*Descr.* Ovate, more or less angulated, smooth or granulated, with a dorsal scar, spire short, aperture large, angulated, emarginated; columella slightly crenated; outer lip reflected, denticulated on the inner edge. Suture of the whorls covered with enamel.—*Obs.* This genus of shells resembles Marginella in form, but has no folds on the columella. Having a scar or groove down the back it may be considered intermediate between Marginella and Cypræa. In the Author's Conchological Illustrations, seven species are enumerated and figured. E. Maugeriæ. Pl. xxi. fig. 454.

ERUCA. Sw. A subgenus of Clausilia. Sw. Malac. p. 334.

ERVILIA. Turton, 1822. A genus described as "oval, equivalve, equilateral, closed. Hinge with a single erect tooth closing between two small diverging ones in the opposite valve: lateral teeth none. Ligament internal. E. nitens. Turt. Mya. nitens, Auct." Pl. xxiv. fig. 497.

ERYCINA. Lam. *Fam.* Mactracea, Lam. Conchaecea, Bl.—*Descr.* Ovate or triangular, transverse, equivalve, inequilateral, smooth; hinge with a ligamentary pit, two diverging cardinal and two lateral teeth in each valve; muscular impressions two in each valve; palleal impressions sinuated. East and West Indies and Mediterranean.—*Obs.* This genus is distinguished from *Mactra* and *Lutraria* by the cardinal teeth being placed one on each side of the ligamentiferous pit; whereas in the last named genera they are both placed on the anterior side. E. Plebeja. Pl. iv. fig. 86.

ESCUTCHEON. The impression on the posterior dorsal margin of some bivalve shells. That on the anterior margin is named the lunule. The escutcheon is pointed out by the letter *e* in some of the figures of Cythereæ. Fig. 117, *a. b. c.*

ETHERIA. Lam. 1808. *Fam.* Chamacea, Lam. and Bl.—*Descr.* Irregu-

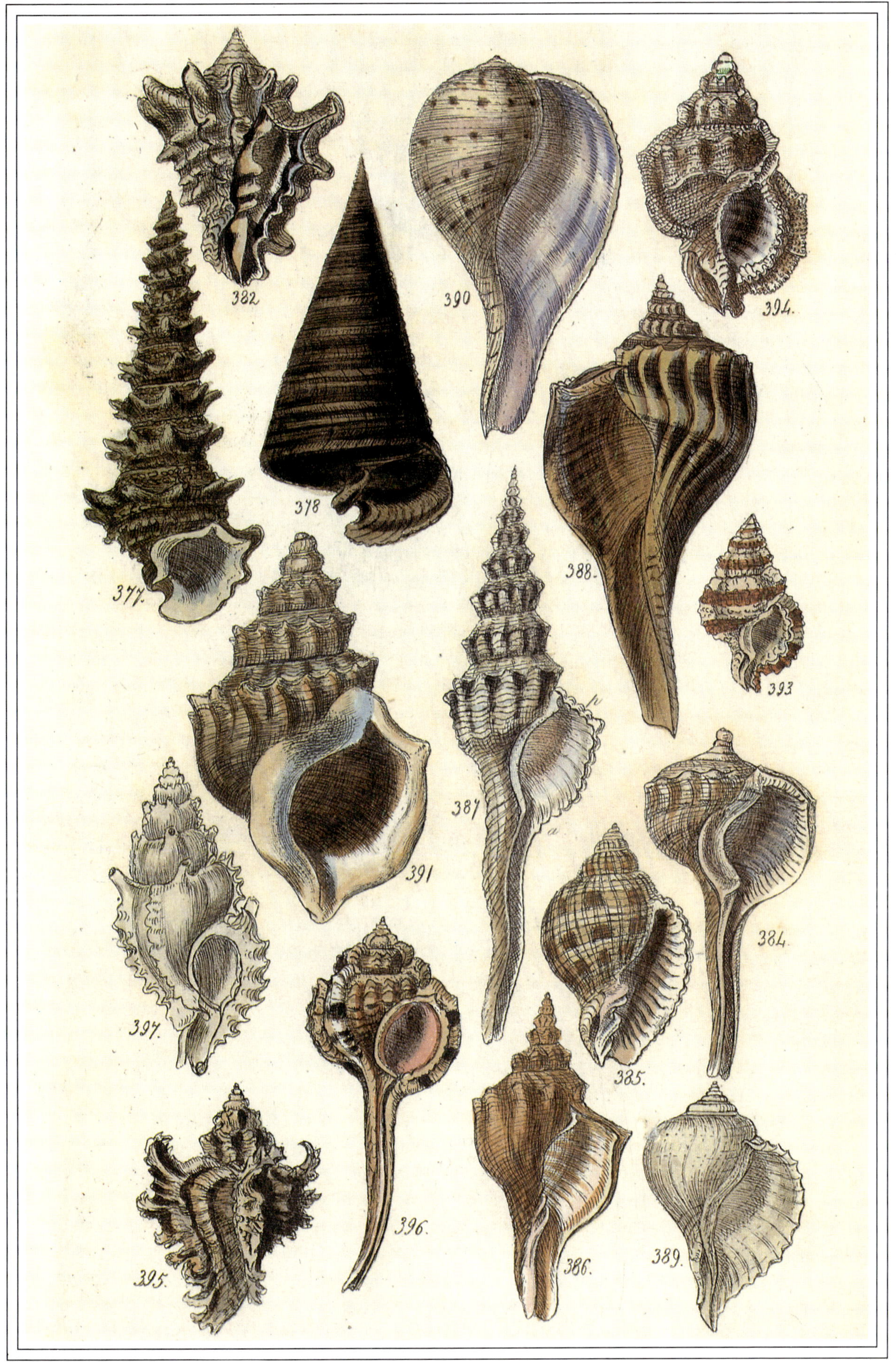

377. Potamis muricata. Pyrazus, Montf. Tympanostomata, Schum.
378. Cerithium Telescopium. *Gen.* Telescopium.
382. Turbinella corniger. Scolymus, Swainson.
384. Spirillus. *Gen.* Pyrella, Sw. Turbinella spirillus, Auct.
385. Cancellaria reticulata.
386. Fasciolaria Trapezium.
387. Fusus Colus; *a*, anterior of the aperture; *p*. posterior.
388. Pyrula perversa. Fulgur, Montf.
389. ——papyracea. Rapanus, Schum. bulbus, Humph. Rapella, Sw.
390. ——Ficus. Ficula, Sw.
391. Struthiolaria straminea.
393. Ranella ranina. Apollon, Montf.
394. ——neglecta. Bufo, Montf.
395. Murex inflatus. Chicoreus, Montf.
396. ——haustellum. Brontes, Montf.
397. Typhis tubifer, (from Deshayes.)

lar, inequivalve, inequilateral, foliaceous, pearly within, covered by an olive green epidermis without; hinge callous, undulated, destitute of teeth; ligament partly external, partly internal, passing through the hinge on a somewhat raised, callous area in the lower valve. Muscular impressions elongated, two in each valve, united by a slender palleal impression. Rivers of Africa.—*Obs.* The irregular, unequal air-bubbles of the inner surface, whence this genus derives it name, are very brilliant in some species, and atone, in some measure, for the rugged ugliness of the exterior. In its irregular form, foliated structure, and toothless hinge, it resembles OSTREA, from which it differs in having two muscular impressions. E. semilunata. Pl. ix. fig. 155.

EULIMA. Risso, 1826. *Fam.* Scalareins, Lam.—*Descr.* Elongated, smooth, pyramidal; spire long, composed of numerous whorls; apex acute, slightly tortuous; aperture oval, rounded anteriorly, acute at the posterior union with the body whorl; outer lip slightly thickened; columella smooth. Fig. 347, E. labiosa, fig. 348, E. splendidula. A complete illustrated Monograph of this genus of pretty shining little shells, consisting of 15 known species, is given in parts 52 and 53 of the Conchological Illustrations by the author. Pl. xv. fig. 347, 348.

EUOMPHALUS. J. Sowerby. *Fam.* Scalariens, Lam.—*Descr.* Orbicular, planorbular spire, with three or four volutions, imbricated above; smooth below; aperture of a round polygonal form; umbilicus large, penetrating to the apex of the shell.—*Obs.* This genus of fossils very nearly resembles Delphinula. The main difference appears to be that the whorls do not increase so rapidly in size in the former as in the latter. Fossil, in the Carboniferous Limestone. Pl. xvi. fig. 350.

EUTROPIA. Humphrey. Gray's Synopsis, Phasianella, Lamarck.

EXOGYRA. Say. A genus of fossil bivalves described as resembling Chama in shape and Ostræa in structure, having but one muscular impression in each valve. Pl. xi. fig. 183.

EXSERTED. Standing out, protruding.

EXTERNAL. An external shell is one which contains the animal and is not covered by the mantle.

FARCIMEN. Troschel, 1847. Pupæform species of CYCLOSTOMA. *Ex.* C. tortum. Thesaurus Conchyliorum, Pl. xxviii. fig. 181, 182: and our figure. Pl. xxv. fig. 529.

FASCIATED. (*fascia*, a band.) Banded or striped. *Ex.* Carocolla marginata, fig. 277.

FASCICULATED. (From fasciculum.) A little bunch of hairs or bristles against each end of each valve, characterizes some species of the genus Chiton, which are termed fasciculated species.

FASCIOLARIA. Lamarck, 1801. *Fam.* Canalifera, Lam. Siphonostomata, Bl.—*Descr.* Elongated, fusiform, ventricose; spire conical, consisting of a few rounded or angulated whorls; aperture wide, terminating in a long straight open canal: columella lip with several oblique folds, the lower of which is larger than the rest; operculum horny, pyriform.—*Obs.* This genus is known from Fusus by the folds on the columella; from Turbinella, by their obliquity and the last being larger than the rest. Mr. Reeve's Monograph contains 16 species. East and West Indies and Australia. F. trapezium. Pl. xvii. fig. 386.

FASTIGIELLA. Reeve. Zool. Proc. 1851. A genus composed of the single species figured, whose characters (as to the shell) place it half way between Turritella and Cerithium. *Ex.* F. carinata, Reeve. Pl. xxviii. fig. 598.

FAUNUS. Montf. Part of MELANOPSIS, Auct.

FERRUGINEOUS. Of an iron rust colour.

FERUSSINA. Grateloup. STROPHOSTOMA, Deshayes. The latter being the Latin name must be dropped. *Ex.* Pl. xxv. fig. 534–5–6.

FIBROUS. A shell is said to be of a fibrous structure when a fracture would present a series of perpendicular fibres, as Pinna.

FICULA. Swainson, 1840. A generic group of shells, consisting of those species of PYRULA. Auct, which have the true pear-shaped character. P. Ficus. Pl. xvii. fig. 300.

FIMBRIA. Megerle. CORBIS, Cuvier.

FIMBRIATED. Fringed; as Murex fimbriatus, a delicate white species, with broad fringed varices.

FISSURE. (*Fissura*, a slit.) A slit or cut, a narrow perforation, as in Emarginula and Fissurella.

FISSURELLA. Lamarck, 1801. (*Fissura*, a fissure.) *Fam.* Calyptracea, Lam. Branchifera, Bl.—*Descr.* Patelliform, oval or oblong, radiated; apex anterior, perforated.—*Obs.* The Fissurellæ are known from Patellæ by the performation in the apex. Fig. 245. The catalogue published by the author in the Conchological Illustrations, enumerates 68 species. Pl. xiii. fig. 245.

FISTULANA. Lam. (*Fistula*, a pipe.) *Fam.* Tubicolæ, Lam. Adesmacea, Bl.—*Descr.* A transversely elongated, equivalve, in equilateral bivalve, enclosed by a septum within the widest, closed extremity of a straight calcareous tube. Fistulana is known from Gastrochæna by the straightness of the tubes, and the oblong state of the valves. Fistulana Clava. Pl. ii. fig. 53, 54.

FLEXUOUS. Having windings or bendings. *Ex.* The Tellinæ are known by the twist or flexuosity in the posterior ventral margin of the shell.

FLORILLUS. Montf. A genus of microscopic Foraminifera.

FLUVIATILE. (Fluviatilis.) Belonging to a river or running stream. *Ex.* Limnæa fluviatilis.

FLUVIATILE CONCHACEA. See CONCHACEA.

FOEGIA. Gray, 1840. ASPERGILLUM. Novæ Zelandiæ.

FOLIATED, or FOLIACEOUS. (From *folium*, a leaf.) When the edges of the successive layers of which a shell is composed are not compacted but placed apart from each other, projecting like tiles, the shell is said to be of a foliated structure. The common Oyster, fig. 180, presents a familiar example.

FORAMINIFERA. D'Orb. (*Foramen*, a hole or pit) An order established for minute many chambered internal shells, which have no open chamber beyond the last partition. Lamarck, D'Orbigny, and other writers have placed them among the Cephalopoda in their systems, but Du Jardin, on comparing the fossils with some recent species of the same class, arrived at the conclusion, now generally adopted, that they constitute a distinct class, much lower in degree of organization than even the Radiata. Not recognizing these microscopic bodies as shells, properly so called, but considering them sufficiently numerous and interesting to form a distinct branch of study, I do not think it desirable to describe the genera, or to present any arrangment of them in this work.

FORNICATED. Arched or vaulted, as the exfoliations on the costæ of Tridacna Elongata, fig. 157.

FORSAR. Gray, 1840. Is it not a Trichotropis?

FOSSIL SHELL. A shell is considered to be in a fossil state when, the soft parts having ceased to exist, it is deprived of all its animal juices, has lost all, or nearly all its natural colour, and its thus changed in its chemical composition, when little or nothing is left but a mere bone, which is embedded in a sedimentary deposit. In this state it is fragile, prehensible to the tongue, and either destitute of colour or tinged with the diluted mineral matters which prevade the stratum in which it lies. In some cases, the mineral composition of the shell is so completely changed as no longer to present its proper structure, consisting of

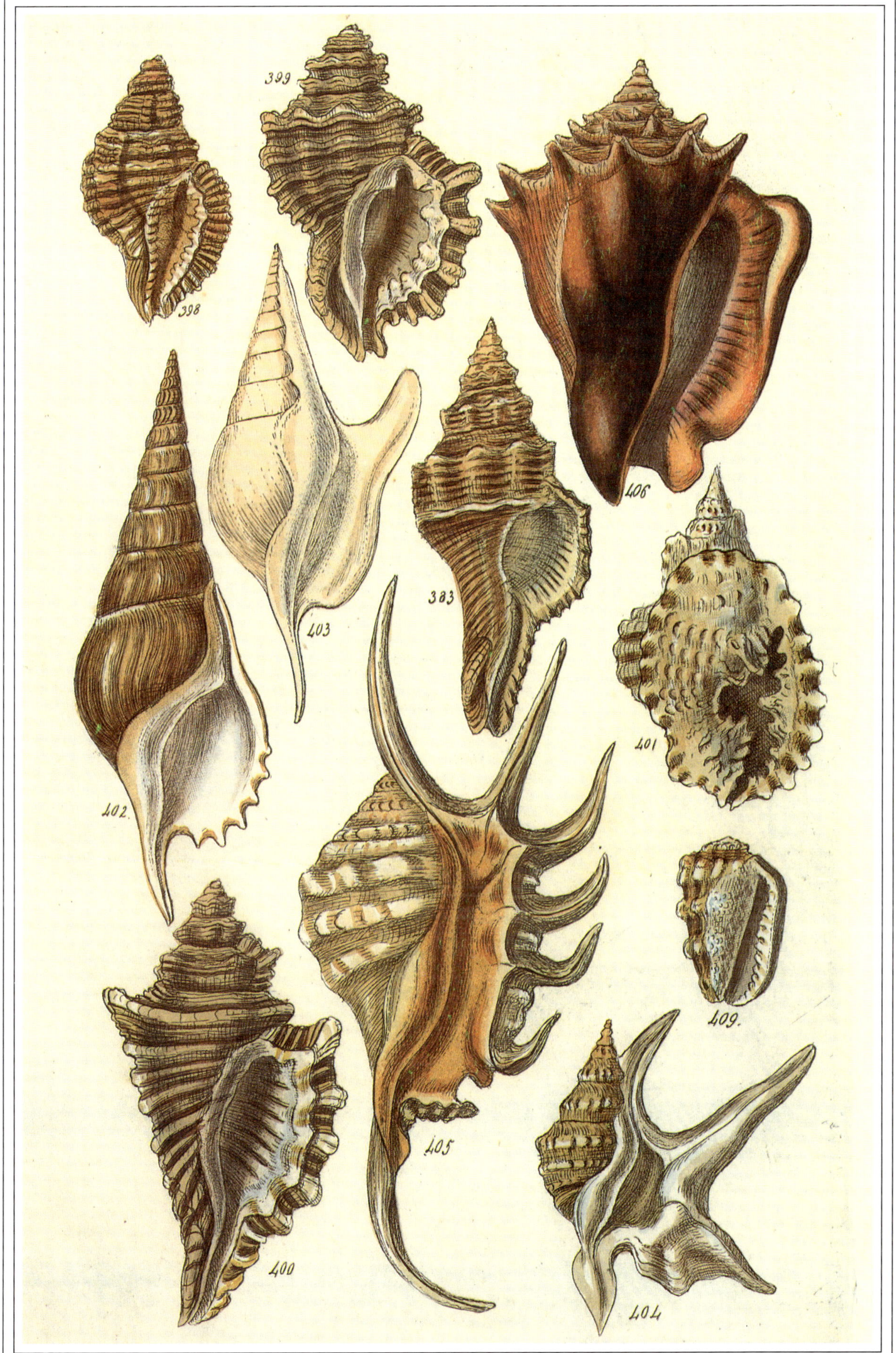

383. ——polygona. Polygonum, Schum.

398. Triton pilearis.

399. ——cutaceus. Aquillus, Montf.

400. ——Lotorium. Lotorium, Montf.

401. ——anus. Persona, Montf.

Fam. Alatæ

402. Rostellaria curvirostrum.

403. ——columbaria. Hippochrenes, Montf. (from Sow. Gen.)

404. ——Pes-pelicani. Aporrhais, Petiver.

405. Pteroceras aurantiacum.

406. Strombus pugilis.

Clavalithus, fig. 548.
Leiostoma, fig. 549.
Pyrella, fig. 550.
Tomella, fig. 551.
Myristica, fig. 552.
Vitulina, fig. 553.
Cyrtulus, fig. 594.
Trophon, fig. 595.
Conopleura, fig. 596.
Mangelia, fig. 597.
Frastigiella, fig. 598.
Hindsia, fig. 599.

} To be added to this family.

Fam. Purpurifera

409. Oniscia Oniscus. Cassidaria.

successive oblique layers of shelly matter; but is altered into a fibrous structure, composed of rhomboidal particles. An example of this will be found in the Belemnites, which if broken, shew the perpendicular fibres. In other cases, the matter which has entered and filled up the cavities of the shell has become silicified, or changed into flint, and the shell itself has been decomposed and fallen off, so as to leave nothing but an external or internal cast of its form, in flint. This is called a Conchyliomorphite by continental writers. Some of the most important of Geological data are obtained by a minute comparison of fossil shells, found in various beds, with recent ones presenting the nearest resemblance to them. Some species of fossil shells are considered as identical with recent species. And many Geologists seek to fix the chronology of the different strata by the number of species which they inclose bearing a resemblance to the recent species. Indeed, all who would study Geology with success, will find it indispensably necessary to obtain a thorough knowledge of Conchology.

FRAGELLA. Swainson, (1840.) CLANCULUS, Montf. 1810. A sub-genus of Monodonta, consisting of M. Pharaonis (fig. 361), and similar species.

FRAGILE. (*Fragilis.*) Tender, easily broken.

FREE SHELL. One that is not attached.

FREE VALVE. In attached bivalve shells, one only is fixed; the other is then *free*, as far as to the action of opening and shutting.

FRESH-WATER SHELLS, (sometimes described as aquatic) are those which inhabit rivers, running pools and ditches, in which case they are *fluviatile*; or wells and ponds of standing water, &c. Fresh-water shells are either thin and horny in their texture, as the Limneana of Lamarck; or are covered with a compact, smooth, horny epidermis. They are generally simple in form, subject to corrosion where the epidermis is wounded or broken, and are circumscribed with regard to the classes and genera to which they belong. The family of Nayades includes nearly all the fresh-water bivalves; and the Melaniana and Limneana are the principal among univalves.

FRONDICULARIA. Defr. A genus of microscopic Foraminifera.

FRONT. The surface of a shell on which the aperture appears.

FULCRUM. That part of a shell on which any other part rests or turns. The term is applied more particularly to the tumid part in the hinge or bivalve shells on which the ligament is fixed.

FULGUR. Montf. 1810. PYRULA perversa, Auct. and such other species as have an angulated spire. Fig. 388.

FUSIFORM. (*Fusus*, a spindle.) Shaped like a spindle, swelling in the centre and tapering at the extremities. *Ex.* Fusus, fig. 387.

FUSUS. Lamarck, (1801.) (A spindle.) *Fam.* Canalifera, Lam. Siphonostomata, Bl.—*Descr.* Fusiform, turrited, with many rounded whorls; aperture generally oval, terminating in a long straight canal; operculum horny, pyriform.—*Obs.* The Fusi are subject to considerable variations in form. The recent species are numerous and do not appear to be confined to any climate. The fossil species are also numerous, chiefly abounding in the tertiary formations. Mr. Reeve's Monograph contains 79 species. The recent species are mostly tropical. Pl. xvii. fig. 387, F. Colus. Priority has been claimed for the generic name "Colus," used by Humphrey in 1797, but without any description.

GADILA. Synopsis of Brit. Mus. Dentalium Gadus. Martyn.

GALATHÆA. Brug. 1798, POTAMOPHILA, Sow. MEGADESMA. Bowd.

GALEA. Klein. PURPURA, Auct.

GALEOLARIA. Lam. (From Galea, a helmet or crest.) A genus composed of species of SERPULA, Auct. Distinguished as being fixed by the side of the shell, and having the anterior extremity erect, the aperture terminating in a tongue-shaped projection.—*Obs.* This genus is said by Lamarck to resemble Vermilia in other respects, but to differ in having the anterior part raised. Africa and Australia. G. decumbens. Pl. i. fig. 6.

GALEOMMA. Turton, 1835. *Fam.* PHOLADARIA, Lam.—*Descr.* Thin, oval, equivalve, equilateral, with the ventral margin gaping; hinge with one cardinal tooth in each vale; muscular impressions two, approximate; palleal impression interrupted, not sinuated; ligament small, partly internal, partly external, fixed on a prominent fulcrum.—*Obs.* The wide hiatus in the ventral margins of this equilateral shell prevents the possibility of confounding it with any other. Four or five recent species are known, one of which is found on the coast of Sicily, and also in the British Channel. *Fam.* "Kelliadæ." G. Turtoni. Pl. ii. fig. 28, 29.

GALERICULUS. (*Galericulum*, a little cap or bonnet.) VELUTINA, Auct. fig. 337.

GALERUS. Humph. Species of CALYPTRÆA, Lam. With an obliquely spiral septum. *Ex.* C. Chinensis.

GAPING. (*Hians.*) Bivalve shells are said to gape when the margins do not meet all round. *Ex.* Gastrochæna, fig. 52.

GASTEROPODA. Lam. (Γαστηρ, *gaster*, belly; πους, ποδος, *pus*, *podos*, a foot.) The second order of the class Mollusca, Lam. containing those molluscous animals whose organs of locomotion are ventral. Most of the shells belonging to this order are patelliform, placed upon the back of the animals, which rest or crawl upon the belly. This order is divided into Pneumonobranchiata, that is, those which breathe air, or land molluscs; and Hydrobranchiata, or those which breathe water, marine or fresh-water molluscs. Fig. 227 to 263.

GASTEROPTERA. Meckel. A genus of Bullidæ without any shell.

GASTRANEA. Schum.? CORBULA, Act.

GASTRIDEA.? Pseudoliva Swainson, 1840. Eburna plumbea. Sowerby. Pl. xxvi. fig. 547.

GASTROCHÆNA. Spengler, 1780. (Γαστηρ, *gaster*, belly; χαινω, *chaino*, gape.) *Fam.* Pholadaria, Lam. Pyloridea, Bl.—*Descr.* Equivalve, regular, inequilateral, with a wide, oblique, ventral hiatus, inclosed in a curved pyriform tube. Differing from Galeomma in being a free, oblique shell; from Fistulana, in the oval shape of the valves, and the curve of the tube; from Aspergillum and Clavagella, in both valves being free.—*Obs.* The Gastrochænæ are found in the hollows of massive shells or other marine substances. G. Modiolina. Pl. ii. fig. 62.

GASTROPLAX. Blainville. UMBRELLA, Lam. De Blainville described this genus from a specimen in which the shell had been, probably by accident, placed upon the under part of the animal, and not discovering his error until afterwards, gave it the above name.

GENA. Gray. Part of Stomatella, Lamarck.

GEOMITRA. Swainson. A sub-genus of Geotrochus, Sw. founded on a trochiform species of Helix, with coronated nodules on the whorls. Helix bicarinata, Sow. Zool. Journ. 1, pl. iii. fig. 7. Sw. page 166 and 332.

GEOPHONUS. Montf. Conch. Syst. t. 1, p. 19. A genus of microscopic Foraminifera.

GEOTROCHUS. Swainson, (1824.) HELIX pileus, Auct. (fig. 278), and other trochiform species. Divided into the sub-genera Pithohelix, Geotrochus, Hemitrochus, Gonidomus, and Geomitra. Sw. p. 165 and 166, described at page 331. Pl. xiii. fig. 278.

GEOVULA. Swainson. A sub-genus of Melampus (Auricula), consisting of oval species, resembling Auricula Midæ, fig. 297.

GERVILLIA. Defr. *Fam.* Margaritacea, Bl. Malleacea, Lam.—*Descr.*

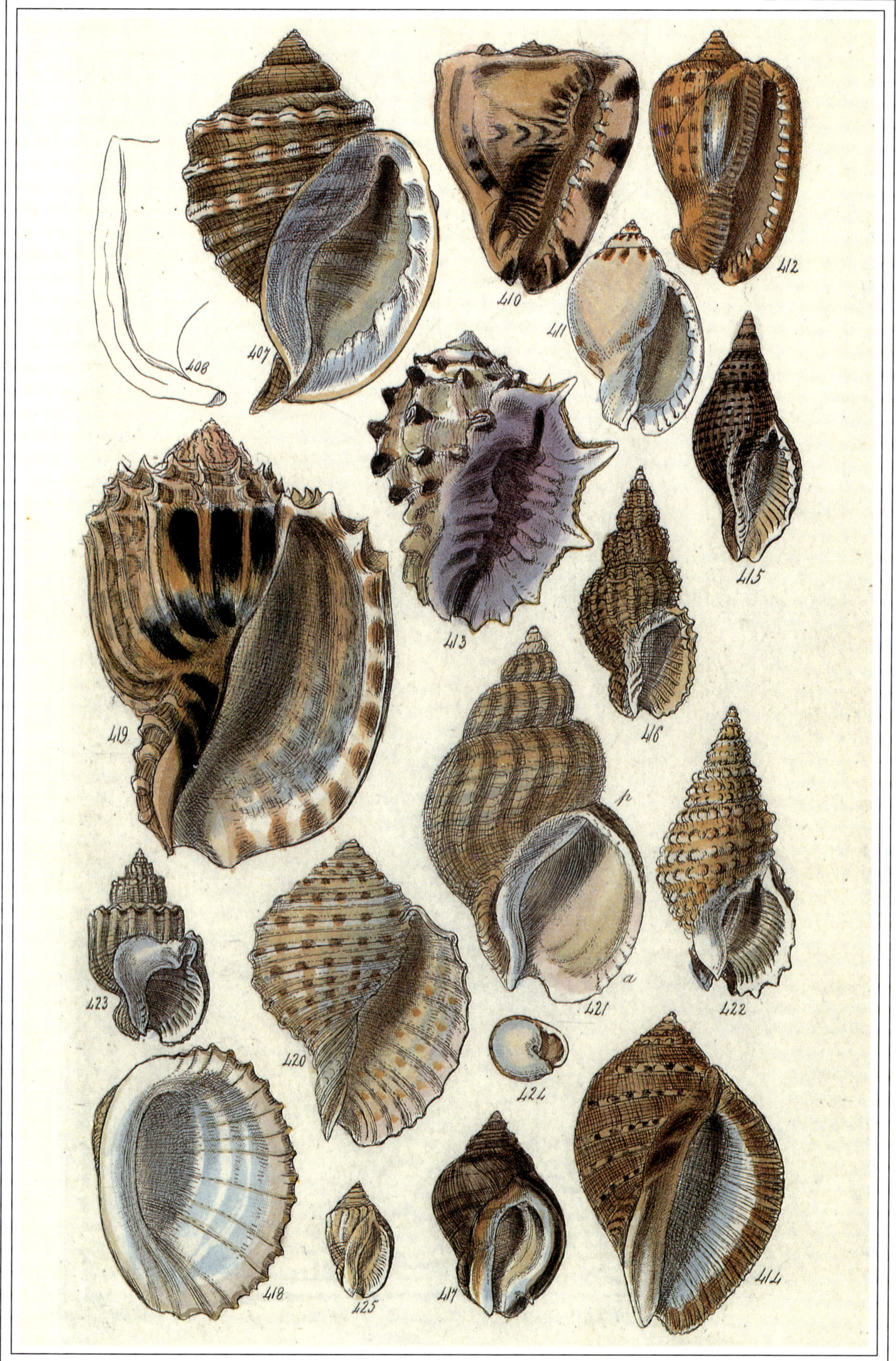

407. Cassidaria echinophora. Morio, Montf.
408. Side view of the outer lip, to shew the canal.
410. Cassis tuberosa, reduced.
411. ——erinaceus. Cassidea, Sw.
412. ——testiculus. Cypræcassis, Stutchbury.
413. Ricinula horrida. Sistrum, Montf.
414. Purpura persica.
415. Tritonidea (*Pollia*, Gray.) articularis.
416. Phos senticosa.
417. Monoceros crassilabrum.
418. Concholepas Peruviana.
419. Harpa ventricosa.
420. Dolium maculatum.
421. Buccinum undatum; *a*, anterior of the aperture; *p*. posterior.
422. ——papillosum. Alectrion, Montf.
423. Nassa arcularia.
424. ——neritoidea. Cyclops, Montf.
425. Cyllene, Gray.

Equivalve, oblong, oblique; hinge long, straight, having small, irregular, transverse ligamentary pits.—*Obs.* This genus of fossil shells, found at various geological periods, from the Lias to the Baculite limestone in Normandy, is now extinct. In general form it resembles Avicula, but in the hinge it approaches Perna. G. Avicularis. Pl. x. fig. 169.

GIBERULA. Sw. A genus separated from MARGINELLA, Auct. and thus described, "sub-oval; spire slightly prominent; top of the outer lip dilated and gibbous; base of the inner lip with plaits; inner lip broad, spreading, G. Zonata. Enc. Méth. 374, f.6."

GIBBOSE or GIBBOUS. (*Gibbosus.*) Bunched out, embossed, having a lump or swelling of any kind. *Ex.* Bulinus Lyonetianus, (fig. 284) named Gibbus by De Montfort. Ovulum gibbosum.

GIBBUS. Montfort, (1810.) BULINUS *Lyonetianus*, Lam. PUPA, Bl. Pl. xiv. fig. 284.

GLABELLA. Swainson, 1840. MARGINELLA Glabella (fig. 437), Goodallii, Auct. and similar species.

GLANDINA. Schum. 1817. POLYPHEMUS, Montf.

GLANDIOLUS. Montf. A genus of microscopic Foraminifera.

GLAUCONOME. Gray, 1829. *Fam.* Solenacea, Lam.—*Descr.* Oblong or oval, transverse, slightly ventricose, equivalve, inequilateral; margins close, rounded anteriorly, somewhat acuminated posteriorly; hinge teeth, three in each valve, of which the central in one, and the posterior in the other, are bifid; muscular impressions anterior, elongated, marginal; posterior sub-quadrate; palleal impression, having a long sinus; ligament oblong, external; epidermis thin, horny, green, folded over the margins.—*Obs.* C. Chinensis was the first species described, since which eight more have been added, in a monograph by Reeve, several of which were brought by Mr. Cuming from the Philippine Islands. Pl. iii. fig. 64.

GLOBIGENERA. D'Orb. A genus of microscopic Foraminifera.

GLOBOSE. (*Globosus.*) Rounded like a globe or ball, as the species of Helix, represented in fig. 268.

GLOBULARIA. Swainson, 1840. A sub-genus of Natica, consisting of globose species. (Sw. p. 345.) *Ex.* N. Lineata, fig. 328.

GLOBULUS. Sow. Min. Con. Part of AMPULLARIA, Auct.

GLOSSUS. Poli, 1795. ISOCARDIA Moltkiana, and similar species. Pl. vi. fig. 126.

GLYCIMERIS. Lamarck, 1799. *Fam.* Solenacea, Lam. Pyloridea, Bl.—*Descr.* Equivalve, transverse, oblong, thick, compressed, gaping at both extremities; hinge callous, without teeth; ligament large, external, prominent; epidermis thick, black, horny, folded over the margins; muscular impressions two, distant, running into the irregular palleal impression which unites them.—*Obs.* But few species of this singular genus are known; Lamarck describes two species from the Northern Seas. Blainville is of opinion that they belong to the family of the Nayades. G. Siliqua. Pl. 3. fig. 67.

GNATHODON. Gray, 1837. (Γναθος, *gnathos*, jaw-bone; οδος, οδοντος, *odontos*, tooth.) *Fam.* Mactracea, Lam.—*Descr.* Ovate, posteriorly angulated, equivalve, thick, ventricose, inequilateral, covered with a greenish brown epidermis; umbo distant, prominent; hinge having in one valve a sharp, angular, notched, cardinal tooth, and two lateral teeth, the posterior of which is elongated, and the anterior angulated, tortuous, shaped like a jaw-bone; in the other valve, two cardinal and two lateral teeth, the anterior of which is wedge-shaped; ligament internal, cuneiform, placed in a deep cardinal pit proceeding from the umbones; muscular impressions two; palleal impression having a slight sinus.—*Obs.* Only one species is known, G. cuneatus, fig. 83, from New Orleans. It is known from all other shells by the character of the hinge. Pl. iv. fig. 83.

GONIATITES. De Haan. A genus composed of species of Ammonites, Auct. in which the last whorl covers the spire and the sinuations of the septa are angulated. Pl. xxiii. fig. 480. G. striatus.

GONIDOMUS. Swainson. A sub-genus of Geotrochus, Sw. PUPA pagodus, Auct. Sw. p. 332. Pl. xxv. fig. 519.

GONIOSTOMA. Swainson, 1840. A sub-genus of Bulimus, thus described, "spire elongated, of few whorls; aperture contracted at each end; lips margined; the pillar curving inwards; the base slightly notched. G. erubescens, *Sw.* Zool. Journ. i. pl. 5, f. 2." Sw. p. 335.

GONIOSTOMATÆ. Bl. A family belonging to the order Asiphonibranchiata, Bl. containing the genera Solarium and Trochus.

GONOSPIRA. Swainson, 1840. A sub-genus of Pupa, thus described, "spire perfectly cylindrical, of equal thickness, the tip obtuse, with the whorls large; aperture oval; lips thickened; pillar with or without a plait. G. polanga, *Desh.* Lesson, Voy. pl. 8, f. 8." Sw. p. 333.

GRANULATED. (*Granum*, a grain.) Covered with minute grains, rough. The granulated lip of Oniscia, (fig. 409) will serve as an example.

GRATELOUPIA. Desmoulins, 1828. *Fam.* Nymphacea, Lam.—*Descr.* Equivalve, inequilateral, sub-cuneiform, rounded anteriorly, sub-rostrated posteriorly; hinge with three cardinal teeth, a series of five or six irregular, small diverging teeth behind the umbones, and one lateral anterior tooth in each valve; ligament external; muscular impressions two; palleal impression sinuated posteriorly.—*Obs.* This genus (Donax irregularis, Bast.) is only known in a fossil state. Pl. v. fig. 102. G. Moulinsii.

GRYPHÆA. Lamarck, 1801. (From Gryps, a griffin.) *Fam.* Ostracea, Lam.—*Descr.* Inequivalve, free; lower valve large, concave; with the umbo prominent, incurved: upper valve small, flat, opercular; hinge toothless, with a curved, depressed area; one muscular impression.—*Obs.* These shells, which approach the Oysters, are of a more regular form, and are remarkable for the curved, produced beak of the lower valve. They are only known in a fossil state, belonging to the more ancient strata. Fig. 182, G. incurva. The recent species mentioned by Lamarck is not a true Gryphæa. Pl. x. fig. 182.

GYMNOLEPAS. A generic name used by De Blainville to include OTION and CINERAS, Leach. See CONCHODERMA.

GYMNOSOMATA. Bl. The second family of the order Aporobranchiata, in the system of De Blainville. The animals belonging to this family are destitute of shells.

GYPIDEA. Dalman. A genus of Brachiopoda, thus described, "Larger valve with the umbo rostrated, remote from the hinge; with the canal large, deltoid; bilocular within." PENTAMERUS, Sow. G. Conchidium, copied from Dalman. Pl. xi. figs. 210, 211.

GYROGONA. Lam. A genus of microscopic Foraminifera.

GYROIDINA. D'Orb. A genus or microscopic Foraminifera.

HALIA. Risso. PRIAMUS, Beck. Fig. 545.

HALIOTIDÆ. Sw. A sub-genus of Calyptræa. CALYPTRÆA dilatata. Sowerby's Genera of Shells, fig. 9.

HALIOTIS. Linneæus. (αλς, *als*, sea; ους, ωτος, *otos*, ear.) *Fam.* Macrostomata, Lam. Otides, Bl.—*Descr.* Auriform, broad, depressed, pearly within, rough, costated, tuberculated without; spire short, flat, consisting of one or two whorls; aperture wide; ovate; columella laminar, flat, oblique; a spiral series of perforations running along the dorsal margin.—*Obs.* The splendid shells belonging to this genus are remarkable for the pearly iridescence of the inner surface, and the row of holes following the course of the spire. The soft parts are eaten in Guernsey and Jersey, and reckoned delicious. They belong to temperate and tropical climates. Fig. 338, H. rubra. 339, Padollus, Montf. Mr. Reeve's monograph contains 73 species.

HALIOTOID. (*Haliotis*, and ειδος, *eidos*, form.) Ear-shaped.

HAMIFORM. (*Hamus*, a hook.) Curved at the extremity.

HAMINEA. Leach. A genus of Bulridæ, the shells of which are thus described by Adams in his Monograph, No. 11, Sowerby's Thesaurus, "shell convolute, horny, thin, transversed, grooved, destitute of columella or spire."

HAMITES. Parkinson. (*Hamus*, a hook.) *Fam.* Ammonacea, Lam.—*Descr.* Elongated, cylindrical, chambered, recurved at the smaller extremity, annulated; septa lobed and sinuated.—*Obs.* This remarkable fossil from the Baculite limestone in Normandy, differs from Baculites in being curved at one extremity, a circumstance from which its name is derived. Some small species are found in chalk-marl, Folkestone. H. cylindricus. Pl. xxiii. fig. 484.*

HARPA. Humphry, 1797. (*Harpa*, a harp.) *Fam.* Purpurifera, Lam. Entomostomata, Bl.—*Descr.* Oval, ventricose, longitudinally and regularly costated; spire short, with rounded, dome-like whorls; aperture wide, emarginated; outer lip thickened, reflected, composing the last costa or rib; inner rib polished, spread over part of the body whorl, terminating in a point.—*Obs.* This beautiful genus of shells is so clearly defined by the regular, longitudinal ribs that adorn the external surface, suggesting the idea of a stringed instrument, that there is no danger of confounding it with any other. H. multicostata; (Buccinum costatum, Linn.) and H. ventricosa, are among the most elegant of the testaceous productions of the sea both in form and colouring; the former is rare. The recent species are not numerous, they inhabit the Indian Ocean. A fossil species occurs at Grignon, near Paris. Mr. Reeve's Monograph contains 9 species. *Ex.* H. ventricosa. Pl. xix. fig. 419.

HARPAX. Parkinson. Part of Plicaula, Auct.

HARPULA. Swainson, 1840. A group of shells separated from Voluta, Auct. thus described, "shell generally tuberculated or longitudinally ribbed; apex of the spire papillary, smooth, and in general distorted; pillar with numerous distinct plaits; the upper, small and slender, the lower, thickest and shortest."—*Type*, H. Vexillum. (Voluta, Auct.) Thesaurus Conchyliorum. Pl. l. fig. 54, 55; Pl. xxvi. fig. 557.

HAUSTATOR. Montf. A genus proposed to include those species of Turritella, Auct. which have angulated whorls.

HAUSTELLARIA. Swainson, 1840. Brontes. Montf. 1810. A sub-genus of Murex, consisting of species with long canal and no spines. Murex haustellum, fig. 396.

HAUSTRUM. Humph. Purpura, Lamarck.

HELCION. Montfort, 1810. A genus composed of species of Patella, which have the apex distinctly and prominently bent forwards. *Ex.* P. pellucida. Pl. xii. fig. 230.

HELENIS. Montf. A genus of microscopic Foraminifera.

HELICELLA. Fer. One of the sub-genera into which De Ferussac has divided the genus Helix, consisting of depressed species with large umbilicus, such as Helix Algira, (Gonites Montf.) fig. 279.

HELICIFORM. Shaped like shells of the genus Helix.

HELICIGONA. One of De Ferussac's sub-genera of the genus Helix, consisting of angulated species, such as Carocolla Lamarckii, fig. 277.

HELICINA. Lamarck, 1801. Rotella, Lamarck, 1822.

HELICINA. Lamarck, 1822. Olygira, Sacy. *Fam.* Colimacea, Lam. Ellipsostomata, Bl.—*Descr.* Globose, compressed, or angulated, generally light and thin; aperture trigonal or semi-lunar; outer lip thickened and generally more or less reflected; inner lip spread over the body whorl, frequently callous near the columella, which is short, and terminates in a notch, angle, or slight callosity.—*Obs.* This genus of land shells, distinguished from the genus Helix, by having an operculum and a thickened columellar lip, differs also from Cyclostoma in having the apterture semicircular or angular, the peritrême discontinuous and the operculum concentric. These shells are generally small in size, and simple in form. Lamarck describes only three or four species. Mr. Gray described some others in the Zoological Journal. 73 species are given in the Monograph, No. 1, Sowerby's Thesaurus. "Oligyra" of Say is given to this genus in Gray's Synopsis, because Lamarck applied "Helicina" first to Rotella. Helicina Major and similar species having a notch in the peritrême, have been separated under the name Alcadia (our figs. 306, 307.) H. Aureola, Thesaurus Conchyliorum, Pl. i. fig. 43, 4, 5, having a peculiar contraction near the outer lip, is named genus "Lucidella," and the sharp-keeled, Carocolla-formed species (our figs. 532, 533), has been named genus "Trochatella." The passage by intermediate species is, however, so gradual, that these generic distinctions can hardly be maintained.

HELICITES. Bl. Part of the genus Nummulites, Lam. Rotalites and Egeon, Montf.

HELICOGENA. Fer. A sub-genus of Helix, consisting of species, which, like the common garden snail, fig. 268, are globose and simple in form.

HELIOCOLIMAX. Fer. Vitrina, Drap. H. Pellucida, Pl. xiii. fig. 263.

HELICOPHANTA. Fer. A sub-genus of Helix, consisting of ear-shaped species with large open apertures.

HELICOSTYLA. Fer. A sub-genus of Helix, consisting of species with numerous whorls, as H. Epistylium, Pl. xiv. fig. 281.

HELISOMA. Sw. A sub-genus of Planorbis. Sw. p. 337.

HELIX. Linnæus. *Fam.* Colimacea, Lam.—*Descr.* Orbicular, light, generally globular; spire short, last whorl ventricose, aperture oblique, peritreme reflected, interrupted by the most prominent part of the body whorl; columella confluent with the outer lip, and contiguous to the axis of the shell. No operculum; a thin epidermis.—*Obs.* The land shells composing this genus are found in all parts of the world; the common snail, H. Aspersa, is well known as a destructive animal in our gardens. The genera Helix, Achatina, Bulinus, Clausilia, Anostoma, &c., have been united under one generic name by De Ferussac, and again divided under the following sub-generic names, each of which we shall illustrate by a figure. Genus Helix: *Sub-genus* 1, *Helicophanta*, consisting of species with large apertures, like Vitrina; Helix brevipes. *S. gen.* 2, *Cochlohydra*, Succinea Amphibia, Drap. *S. gen.* 3, *Helicogena*, consisting of the common species with the last whorl large; Helix Hæmastoma, H. Contusa, (Streptaxis, Gray,) H. Aspersa. *S. gen.* 4, *Helicodonta*, consisting of species with teeth or folds on the columella; Polydonta, Montf. Anostoma, Helix Nux-denticulata. *S. gen.* 5, *Helicigona*, Carocolla, Geotrochus. *S. gen.* 6, *Helicella*, consisting of depressed species with a large umbilicus; H. Citrina (Naninia, Gray.) *S. gen.* 7, *Helicostyla*, consisting of species with a simple aperture, like the Helicogenæ, but with the whorls increasing very gradually; H. epistylium. *S. gen.* 8, *Cochlostyla*, Bulinus. *S. gen.* 9, *Cochlitoma*, Achatina. *S. gen.* 10, *Cochlicopa*, Polyphemus Glans. *S. gen.* 11, *Cochlicella*, Bulinus decollatus. *S. gen.* 12, *Cochlogena*, Azeca tridens. *S. gen.* 13, *Cochlodonta*, Pupa Uva. *S. gen.* 14, *Cochlodina*, Clausilia macascarensis, Balea fragilis. The last three sub-genera are included in the genus Odostomia of Fleming. We give an example of each of these sub-divisions, for the sake of presenting the reader with the principal variations to which the genus is subject. The established genera will be characterized in their places. Pl. xiii. fig. 254 to 281.

HELIXARION. Ferussac, 1819. Vitrina, Drap. Differing from Helicolimax in the structure of the animal. Pl. xiii. fig. 262.

HEMICARDIUM. Swainson, 1840. (ἡμισυς, *hemisus*, half, Καρδια, *cardia*, heart.) CARDIUM Hemicardium, and several similar species. Pl. vi. fig. 123***.

HEMICYCLA. Sw. A sub-genus of Helix.

HEMICYCLONOSTA—see CARDILIA.

HEMICYCLOSTOMATA. Bl. The fourth family of Asiphonibranchiata, Bl. described as "more or less globular, thick, flattened on the under side; spire very short; aperture large, semilunar, entire; its outer edge hollowed; its inner or columellar edge straight, sharp and septiform." This family answers to the genus *Nerita* of Linnæus, and to the family Neritacea of Lamarck. It contains the genera Natica, Nerita, Neritina, and Navicella.

HEMIMACTRA. Swainson, 1840. A sub-genus of Mactra, thus described: "General form of *Mactra*, but the cardinal teeth entirely wanting; cartilage internal, central, in a large triangular cavity; lateral teeth ½, distinct, lateral, striated: connected to the *Glycimeri*. H. gigantea, *Lam.* v. 472. No. 1. grandis, *Sw.* Sp. Nov." Sw. p. 369.

HEMIMITRA. Sw. A sub-genus of Paludomus, Sw. (Melanianæ.)

HEMIODON. Sw. A sub-genus of Anodon, described as having "Tubercles or undulations on the hinge margin. H. undulatus, purpurascens and areolata."

HEMIPECTEN. Adams and Reeve. Mollusca of the Samarang. A genus belonging to the family of Pectinidæ, thus described, "attached, inæquivalve, irregular, hyaline, upper valve simple anteriorly, very slightly auriculated posteriorly; lower valve simple anteriorly, conspicuously auriculated posteriorly, deeply sinuated and denticulated beneath the auricle; hinge edentulate, ligament slightly marginal with a small cartilage in a central cavity. Hemipecten Forbesianis, *Reeve.* Conch. Icon." Our Plate xxvii. fig. 580.

HEMISINUS. Sw. A sub-genus of Melania, thus described: "General shape of *Melania*; but the base of the aperture is contracted and emarginate; outer lip crenated. H. lineolata, Griff. Cuv. xii. pl. 13. fig. 4."

HEMITOMA. Sw. A sub-genus of Emarginula, thus described: "Patelliform; the fissure not cut through the shell, but merely forming an internal groove. H. tricostata, *Sw.* Sow. Gen. fig. 6."

HEMITROCHUS. Sw. A sub-genus of Geotrochus, Sw. H. hæmastroma. Sw. p. 331.

HEPTALASMIS. Leach. (Ἑπτα, *hepta*, seven; ελασμα, *elasma*, plate.) A small shell resembling Pentelasmis, from which it differs in the number of valves, being composed of seven valves according to Leach, and of eight according to Gray, who counts the dorsal valve, which is jointed, as *two*, and names his genus Octolasmis, the appearance of seven valves being caused by the scuta being entirely or partially divided into two segments. M. Darwin has decided not to retain either of the names, implying the apparent number of valves but to name the genus. DICHELASPIS. *Ex.* D. Warwickii. Pl. ii. fig. 41.

HERCOLES. Montf. A microscopic shell, appearing from De Montfort's figure to resemble TROCHUS *Imperialis* in shape.

HERION. Montf. LENTICULINA, Bl. Microscopic.

HERMAPHRODITA. Bl. The third sub-class of Paracephalophora, Bl. divided into, Sect. 1, *symmetrical*, containing the orders Cirrobranchiata and Cervicobranchiata; Sect. 2, *non-symmetrical*, order, Scutibranchiata.

HERMES. Montfort, 1810. A genus composed of CONUS *Nussatella*, Auct. and other elongated, cylindrical, striated species. Pl. xxi. fig. 460.

HETEROBRANCHIATA. Bl. The fourth order of the class Acephalophora, Bl. containing no testaceous mollusca.

HETEROPODA. Lam. The fifth order of the class Mollusca, Lam. This order contains but one genus of shells, viz. Carinaria, fig. 488.

HETEROSTEGINA. D'Orb. A genus of microscopic Foraminifera.

HIATELLA. Daudin. Fam. Lithophagidæ, Lam. A genus composed of species of Saxicava, Auct. which have sharp, angulated, posterior ridges, a circumstance which occurs to many species in a young state, which afterwards become rouonded off. Hiatella biaperta. Pl. iv. fig. 95.

HIATULA. Sw. A genus proposed to include those species of Oliva, Auct. which have widened apertures. *Ex.* O. Subulata. Pl. xxi. fig. 458.

HIBOLITHES. Montf. A genus composed of species of Belemnites, Auct. which are swelled towards the apex, and contracted near the centre. B. Hastatus, Auct. Pl. xxii. fig. 468.

HIMANTOPODA. Schum. MALLEUS, Auct.

HINDSIA. A. Adams, Zool. Prac. 1851. A genus composed of Triton Acuminata, (Reeve's Monograph) and similar species, of which there are about a dozen, agreeing with each other remarkably well in characters, which separate them from other groups. They have no distinct varices, properly so called, such as distinguish the true Tritons, excepting a large one immediately behind the aperture, which is rather small, with the lips produced and detached. The general form over the back, but long and slightly recurved. *Ex.* T. acuminatum. Pl. xxviii. fig. 599.

HINGE. The edge of the bivalve shells near the umbones, including the teeth and ligament.

HINNITES. Defrance, 1831. A generic name proposed for PECTEN PUSIO, Auct. remarkable for the irregularity of the outer surface, which would almost lead to the belief of its being an attached shell. The monograph of this genus in the Author's Thesaurus Conchyliorum contains three species. Pl. xx. fig. 173, H. Pusio.

HIPPAGUS. Lea. (*Horse boat.*) A minute fossil shell, resembling Isocardia in form, but destitute of hinge teeth. H. Isocardioides. Pl. vi. fig.f 128.

HIPPOCHRENES. Montfort, 1810. Species of ROSTELLARIA, Auct. with the outer lip spread. R. Columbaria. Pl. xviii. fig. 403.

HIPPONYX. Defrance, 1819. (Ἱππος, *hippos*, horse; ονυξ, *onyx*, nail or hoof.) *Fam.* Rudistes, Lam.—*Descr.* Inequivalve, sub-equilateral, rather irregular, destitute of ligament and hinge teeth; lower valve attached, flat, sub-orbicular, with a muscular impression, composed of two lunulate portions, meeting at one extremity, and presenting the form of a horse-shoe; upper valve conical; with the apex inclined backwards, and the muscular impression marginal.—*Obs.* The earlier naturalists having only met with the upper valve of these shells, placed them among the patelliform univalves; to some of which, particularly Pileopsis, they bear a very strong resemblance. The species of Hipponyx are numerous, and till lately only known in a fossil state. The recent species belong to tropical climates: the fossil species are found in the tertiary beds. The monograph in the Thesaurus Conchyliorum contains five species. H. cornocopia. Pl. xi. figs. 199, 200.

HIPPOPODIUM. Conybeare. J. Sowerby, 1819. *Fam.* Cardiacea, Lam.—*Descr.* Equivalve, obliquely transverse, heavy, deep, inequilateral, umbones incurved; ventral margin sinuated, so as to give a bilobed appearance to the shell; hinge incrassated, with one rugged oblique tooth.—*Obs.* These fossils are found in the upper beds of Lias. H. Ponderosum. Pl. vii. fig. 129.

HIPPOPUS. Lam. (Ἱππος, *hippos*; πους, *pous*, foot.) *Fam.* Tridacnacea, Lam.—*Descr.* Equivalve, inequilateral, regular, subquadrate;

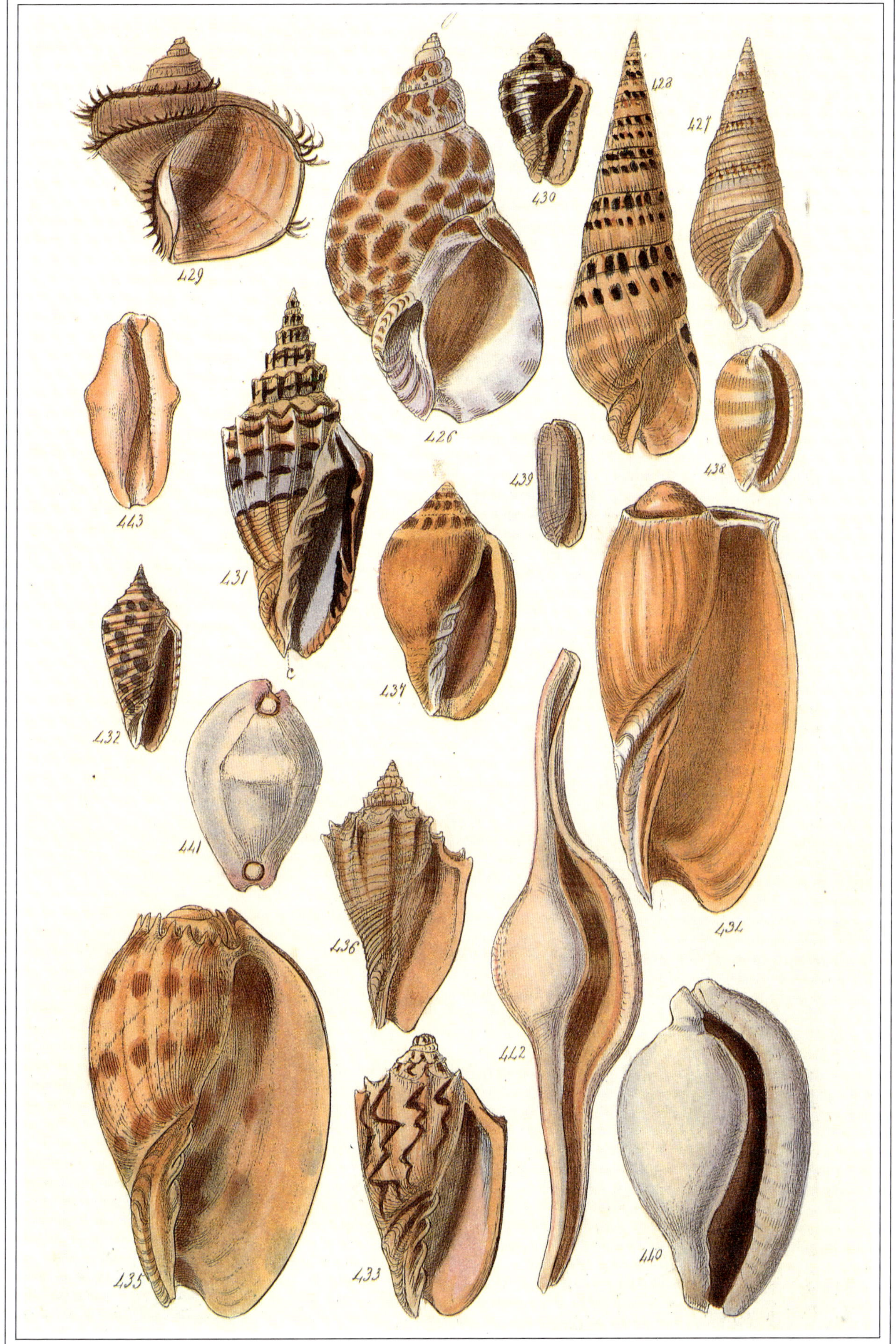

426. Eburna Zeylanica.
427. Bullia vittata.
428. Terebra maculata. Subula, Bl.
429. Trichotropis bicarinata.
Polytropa, fig. 546.
Vexilla, fig. 544.
Gastridium, fig. 545.
Daphnella, fig. 593.
} To be added to this family.

Fam. Columellata

430. Columbella mercatoria.
431. Mitra plicaria; *c.* termination of the columella.
432. Conohelix marmorata.
433. Voluta Vespertilio. Cymbiola, Sw.
434. Cymba porcina.
435. Melo Æthiopicus.
436. Volutilithes spinosus.
437. Marginella Glabella. Glabella, Sw. Cucumis, Klein.
438. ——persicula. Volutella, Sw. Persicula, Schum.
439. Volvaria concinna.
Harpula, fig. 557.
Mitreola, fig. 558.
Mitrella, fig. 559.
Nitidella, fig. 560.
Pachybathron, fig. 600.
} To be added to this family.

Fam. Convolutæ

440. Ovulum Ovum.
441. ——verrucosum. Culpurnus, Montf.
442. ——Volva. Radius, Montf.
443. ——gibbosum. Ultimus, Montf.

lunule closed, flat, with crenulated edges; ventral margin deeply undulated; external surface fluted, with radiating ribs, which are transversely fringed with rows of tubular spines; hinge margin thick, with two long, compressed posterior lateral teeth in one valve, three in the other; ligament marginal, external.—*Obs*. The shell thus described is rightly separated from Tridacna, on account of the anterior dorsal margins being closed; whereas in Tridacna there is a wide hiatus. Only one species of this genus is known, which receives its name from its resemblance in form to a horse's foot, when held with the flat anterior dorsal margin downwards. Few shells are found to concentrate so many beauties as the Hippopus Maculatus, commonly called the Bear's-paw-clam; the delicate whiteness of the interior, the undulating edge, the radiated fluted columns, adorned at intervals by crisped fringes, and the richness of the variegated colouring, are such as to secure the admiration of the most superficial observer. From the Indian Archipelago. H. Maculatus. Pl. ix. fig. 156.

HIPPURITES. Montf. *Fam*. Orthocerata, Lam. Rudistes, Bl.—*Descr*. Tubular, rude, irregular, attached; lower valve cylindrical, more or less lengthened, apparently divided into sections by septa (considered by some authors as merely projecting layers of growth) having one or two lateral tubes within; upper valve round, flat, fixed on the aperture of the tubular valve like an operculum.—*Obs*. This genus is known only in a fossil state, and but very imperfectly. Lamarck places it among his chambered Cephalopoda, &c. De Blainville, considering it a true Bivalve, enumerates it among his Rudistes. Cretaceous group. H. Cornucopia. Pl. xi. fig. 198.

HYALÆA. Lamarck, 1799. (*Hyalus*, glass.) *Fam*. Pteropoda, Lam. Thecosomata, Bl.—*Descr*. Globose, glassy, transparent, with a triangular opening at the upper part where the dorsal portion advances beyond the ventral; ventral portion vaulted; dorsal more flat; lower extremity tridentate.—*Obs*. The singular structures composing this genus were formerly taken for bivalves, and named Anomia Tricuspidata, &c. They are now known to belong to the class of molluscous animals, called Pteropoda, from the wing-shaped organs of locomotion. A species of Hyalæa occurs in Sicily in a fossil state. Recent species are found in the Mediterranean, Atlantic, and Indian Oceans. H. Tridentata. Pl. xii. fig. 226.

HYALINA. Schumacher, 1827. Marginella pallida, Thesaurus Conchyliorum, Pl. viii. Marginella, Pl. lxiv. fig. 108.

HYALINA. Studer. VITRINA, Drap.

HYALINE. (*Hyalus*, glass.) Glassy, thin, transparent.—*Ex*. Carinaria Mediterranea, fig. 488.

HYDATINA. Schumacher. A sub-genus of Bullidæ, the shells of which are thin and inflated, and have flat, visible spires. B. venillum is an example of four species described in M. Adams' Monograph, Part 11, Sowerby's Thesaurus.

HYDROBRANCHIATA. Bl. The first section of the order Gasteropoda, Lam. containing Molluscs which breathe water only; divided into the families Tritoniana, Phyllidiana, Semiphyllidiana, Calyptracea, Bullæana, and Aplysiana.

HYGROMANES. Fer. A sub-division of Helix, containing H. limbata, Auct. &c. Gray's Turton, p. 143.

HYPOTHYRIS. Phillips, King, 1846. A genus represented by Terebatula psittacea. Pl. xi. fig. 202.

HYRIA. Lamarck, 1819. A genus composed of species of Nayades, distinguished by their alated dorsal margins, and lamellated lateral teeth. South America. HYRIA corrugata, fig. 143, Hyria Syrmatophora. Pl. viii. fig. 144.

HYRIDELDA. Swainson, 1840. A genus of "Hyrianæ," Sw. described as differing from HYRIA, Auct. in having a cardinal as well as a lateral tooth in each valve. Sw. p. 380.

HISTRIX. Humphrey, 1797. RICINULA, Auct.

IBDRUS. Montf. CAROCOLLA, Lam.

IBLA. Leach, 1825. *Fam*. Pedunculated Cirripedes, Lam.—*Descr*. Four valves, posterior pair elongated, anterior pair short, triangular; pedicle cylindrical, contracted at the base, hairy.—*Obs*. I. Cuveriana, is brought from Kangaroo Island. Pl. ii. fig. 40.

ICTHYOSARCOLITES. Desmarest. *Fam*. Ammonacea, Lam.—*Descr*. Chambered, slightly arcuate, laterally compressed; septa simple, leaving triangular articulations imbricated like the thick muscles of a fish.

ILOTES. Montf. ORBICULINA, Bl. A genus of microscopic Foraminifera.

IMBRICARIA. Schumacher, 1817. CONOHELIX, Sw. 1833. See MITRA.

IMBRICATED. (*Imbrex*, a tile.) A shell is said to be imbricated when the superficial laminæ are arranged over each other in the manner of tiles.

IMPERATOR. Montfort, 1810. A genus composed of species of the genus TROCHUS, Auct. with whorls angulated and stellated, having an umbilicus. *Ex*. T. Imperialis.

IMPRESSION. See MUSCULAR IMPRESSION.

INCRASSATED. (*Crassus*, thick.) Thickened, as the hinge of Glycimeris, fig. 67.

INCURVED. Turned inwards or bent forwards. Applied to symmetrical shells, when the point of the apex turns towards the anterior extremity, as in Patella. The apex of a shell is said to be curved when it is bent inwards, but not sufficiently so to be described as spiral. *Ex*. Ammonocesas, Lam. fig. 477.

INDENTED. (*In*, in; *dens*, a tooth.) Exactly the reverse of DENTATED; meaning a series of small cavities, such as might be produced by the entrance of teeth. The cast of a dentated surface would be indented.

INEQUILATERAL. (*Æquus*, equal; *latus*, a side.) A term applied to a bivalve shell when its extent on one side of the umbones is greater than that on the other. When the sides are nearly equal, the term *sub-equilateral* is used.

INEQUIVALVE. (*in; æquus*, equal; *valva*, valve.) The two principal valves differing from each other in diameter or convexity.

INFERIOR VALVE is that which is attached to sub-marine bodies. Only applied to attached bivalves.

INFEROBRANCHIATA. Bl. The fourth family of the second section of Paracephalophora Monoica, Bl. containing no testaceous mollusca.

INFLATED. Swelled, as Bulla, fig. 250, 252. This term can only be applied to rotund shells of a light, thin texture.. In other cases we should use the word VENTRICOSE.

INFLECTED. Turned inwards. This term is applied to the outer lip of a spiral shell when it turns towards the body whorl. This is the case in Cypræa, fig. 446. See REFLECTED.

INFUNDIBULUM. Montfort, 1810. (*A funnel*.) A genus formed of those species of CALYPTRÆA, Lam. which, having a spiral septum, so nearly resemble Trochus that some authors have placed them in that genus. One species named Patella Trochiformis. Recent from South America, fossil from the tertiary beds. Calyptræa (Infundibulum) Pileus. Pl. xii. fig. 237, 238.

INNER LIP. That edge of the aperture of a univalve shell which is near to the imaginary axis, as distinguished from the outer lip, or that which is on the opposite side.

INOCERAMUS. Sow. *Fam*. Malleacea, Lam. Margaritacea, Bl.—*Descr*. Thick, inequivalve, sub-equilateral, triangular, deep, with the umbones incurved; hinge formed of a series of transverse grooves.—

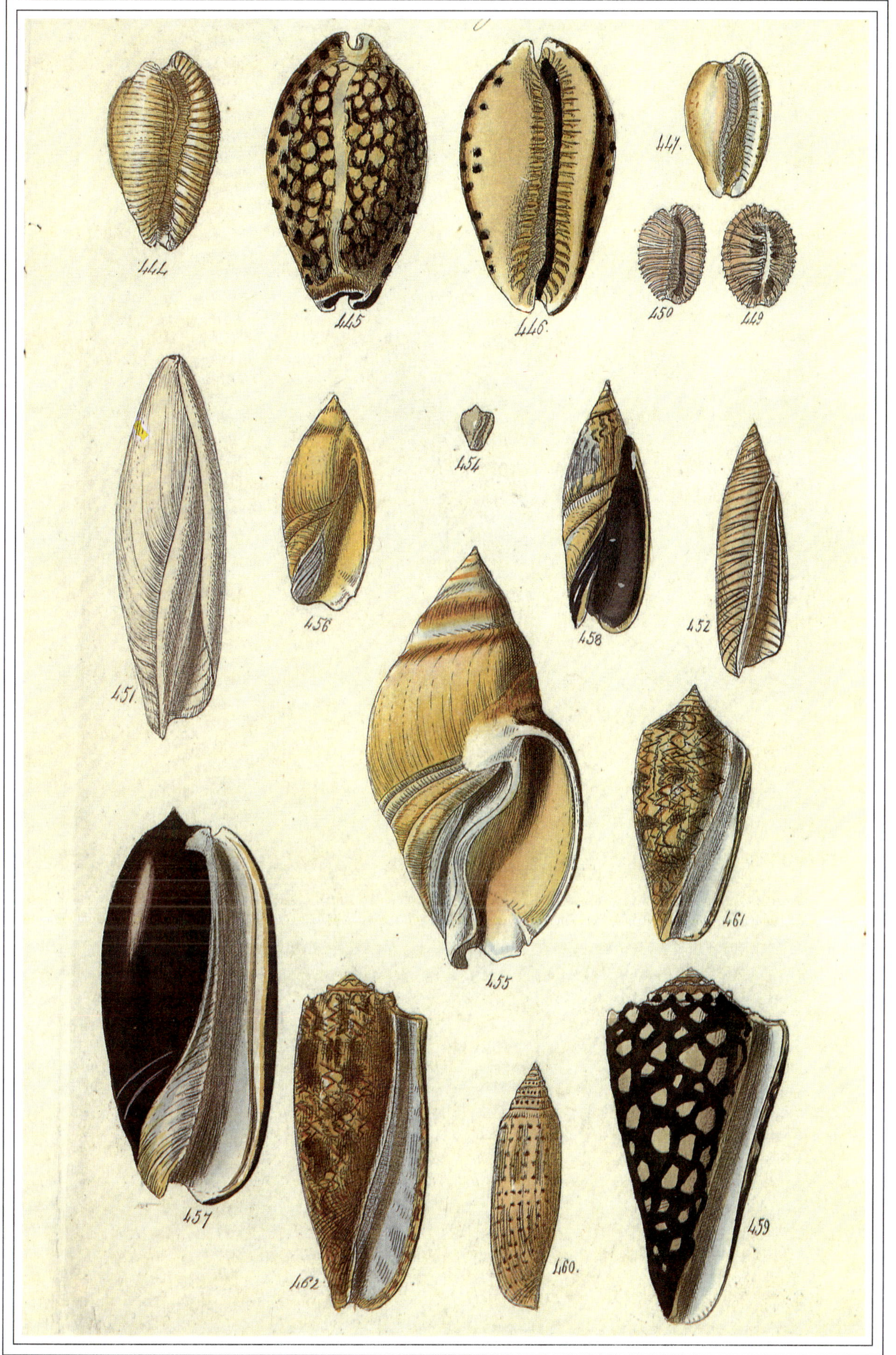

444. Cypræovulum capense.
445. Cypræa arabica, back.
446. The same, front.
447. Cypræa Algoensis. Luponia, Gray, front.
449. ——Pediculus. Trivia, Gray, Back.
450. The same, front.
451. Terebellum convolutum. Seraphs, Montf.
452. ——subulatum, front.
454. Erato Mangeriæ.
455. Ancillaria glabrata. Anolax, Brongn.
456. ——cinnamonea.
457. Oliva Maura.
458. ——subulata. Hiatula, Sw.
459. Conus nocturnus. Rhombus, Montf.
460. ——Nussatella. Hermes, Montf.
461. ——Textile. Cylinder, Montf.
462. ——geographus. Rollus, Montf.

Lamprodoma, fig. 561.
Cyprædia, fig. 564.
} To be added to this family.

Obs. The larger valves of these fossil shells resemble the larger valve of Gryphæa; but the hinge is quite distinct. The species described in Mineral Conchology are found in the blue marl, at Folkestone, and in the chalk. I. Lamarckii, (Catillus, Brong.) Pl. x. fig. 167.

INTERNAL CAST. The mould of a fossil shell, composed of matter which entered the shell in a soft state, and has subsequently hardened, when, the shell dropping off, the hardened substance which filled it is left to represent its internal form.

INTERNAL LIGAMENT. A term used by some conchological writers signifying that the ligament of a bivalve shell is placed within the closed part of the hinge, so as not to be seen when the valves are shut. But the substance, formerly called the internal ligament, is now distinguished from the true ligament both in structure and use; and is now more properly called the cartilage, so that when the ligament is said to be internal, it must be understood that the internal cartilage is unaccompanied by any ligament properly so called, and when a shell is described as having two ligaments, as in the case of Amphidesma, it means that the two substances are so far removed from each other in the hinge that they are no longer confounded together.

INTERNAL SHELL is one which is enclosed in the soft parts of the animal, as a bone is enclosed in the flesh of a human body. The Limax, or common garden slug, which as a testaceous shield beneath its mantle, is an instance of this.

IO. Lea, 1842. A genus composed of several species of fresh-water shells which are considered as differing from Melaniæ in having the anterior termination of the aperture produced into a point in some degree resembling the caudal canals of shells belonging to the family of Canalifera, which are marine. Io fusiformis and spinosus are described and figured in Lea's work.

IPHIGENIA. Schum. 1817. Capsa, Lamarck.

IPHIGENIA. Gray, 1821. A sub-genus of Clausilia, C. biplicata, &c. Auct. Gray's Turton, p. 214.

IRIDEA. Sw. A genus of "Hyrianæ," Sw. thus described:– "Oblong ovate; bosses small, depressed, sulcated; inner cardinal tooth placed between the outer. I. granosa, *Lam*. En. Méth. 248. fig. 9."

IRIDINA. Lamarck, 1818. A genus belonging to the Nayades, and resembling the Anodontæ, Auct. but its peculiar characteristic is that the hinge lamina is tuberculated or crenulated in its whole length. Sowerby unites all the genera of the family into the genus Unio. I. Elongata. Pl. viii. fig. 150.

IRREGULAR SHELLS, are those which, being attached to, or imbedded in other marine bodies, have no constant form, but are modified in shape according to the substances to which they are fixed, as the Chamacea, fig. 153 to 155.

IRUS. Oken. Comprehending Pandora, Petricola, Saxicava, &c.

ISCHNOCHITON. Gray. Chiton vestitus, and similar species.

ISOCARDIA. Lamarck, 1801. (Ισος, *isos*, similar; Καρδια, *cardia*, heart.) *Fam*. Cardiacea, Lam. Chamacea, Bl.—*Descr*. Cordiform, regular, equivalve, ventricose, with distant, diverging, involute, free umbones; hinge with two compressed cardinal teeth in each valve, and one distant compressed lateral tooth; ligament external, bifid, diverging in the direction of the umbones.—*Obs*. The shells composing this genus are remarkable for the beautiful curvature of the diverging umbones. European and Chinese Seas, I. Moltkiana. Pl. vi. fig. 126.

JANIRA. Schum. 1817. A genus composed of species of Pecten, Auct. having oblique plicæ or calli on each side of the ligamentary pit. *Ex*. P. plica, fig. 172. Decadopecten, Rüppell.

JANTHINA. Bolton, 1798. (*Janthum*, a violet.) *Fam*. Neritacea, Lam. Oxystomata, Bl.—*Descr*. Sub-globose, thin, fragile; spire short, consisting of few whorls; aperture angulated, at the anterior junction of the inner and outer lips; columella tortuous, contiguous to the axis; outer lip thin, sinuated in the centre.—*Obs*. The shells composing this genus are celebrated for their beautiful purple colour. The animal possesses a small vesicular process, which keeps it floating on the surface of the water; it exudes a purple secretion when irritated. It is occasionally floated on to the shores of most temperate and tropical countries. J. Fragilis. Pl. xv. fig. 333.

JATARONUS. Adanson. Chama, Auct.

JEFFREYSIA. Alder. A genus of small shells separated from Rissoa on the ground of a peculiarity in the operculum. *Ex*. J. Diaphana, Forbes and Hanley. British Mollusca, No. 30. Pl. cli. fig. 76.

JESITES. Montf. A minute fossil resembling Galeolaria.

JODAMIA. Defr. A genus resembling Birostrites, except that in Jodamia one valve overwraps the other, while in Birostrites the circumference of the valves is equal.

JOUANNITIA. Desmoulins. Pholas semicandata.

KATHARINA. Gray. Chiton lumiatus, &c. The external part of the shell is small.

KEEL. A flattened ridge, resembling the keel of a ship. As that on the back of Carinaria vitrea, fig. 488, and those on the whorls of some spiral shells. A shell characterized by a keel or keels is said to be carinated.

KELLIADÆ. A family of small bivalve shells divided into the following genera, viz.—

Montacuta, Turton. M. bidentata? Pl. xxvii. fig. 570.
Turtonia, Hanley. T. minuta. Pl. xxvii. fig. 567.
Kellia, Montagu. K. orbicularis. Pl. xxvii. fig. 569.
Poronia, Recluz. P. rubra. Pl. xxvii. fig. 568.
Lepton, Turton. L. squamosum. Pl. iii. fig. 62.
Galeomma, Turton. G. Turtoni. Pl. ii. fig. 58, 59.

With the exception of the two latter, the distinctions of the above genera depend so much on anatomical grounds that our readers must be content for the present with a characteristic figure of each.

Pythina, Hinds, may be added to this family. Pl. xxvii. fig. 571.

KELLIA. Turton. See Kelliadæ, K. orbicularis. Pl. xxvii. fig. 569.

LABIS. Oken. Monodonta, Lam.

LABIUM, or inner lip,—is used to express that side of the aperture which is nearest to the axis and generally contiguous to the body whorl. The lower part of this, when sufficiently distinct from that part which overwraps the body whorl, is called the Columella.

LABRUM, or outer lip,—is the edge of the aperture at the greatest distance from the axis.

LACINEA. Humph. Chama, Lam.

LACUNA. Turton, 1828. *Fam*. Turbinacea, Lam.—*Descr*. Globose, thin, covered with a smooth epidermis; spire short, consisting of few rapidly increasing whorls; aperture semilunar, rounded at the extremities; columella oblique, reflected over part of the umbilicus; umbilicus forming a lengthened area behind the columella. Northern shores. L. Pallidula. Pl. xvi. fig. 364.

LAGENULA. Montf. A genus of microscopic Foraminifera.

LAMELLARIA. Montagu. Sigaretus. Auct. (The thin, hyaline species.)

LAMELLATED. (*Lamella*, a thin plate.) When the layers of which a shell is composed, instead of being compacted into a solid mass, are separated, overlaying each other in the manner of tiles, with the edges prominent, the structure is said to be lamellated or foliaceous.

LAMELLIBRANCHIATA. Bl. The third order of the class Acephalophora, Bl. consisting of bivalve shells, divided into the families

Ostracea, Subostracea, Margaritacea, Mytilacea, Polydontes, Sybmytilacea, Chamacea, Conchacea, Pylorides, Adesmacea.

LAMELLIPEDES. Lam. (*Lamella*, a thin plate, *pes*, a foot.) The third section of the order Conchifera Dimyaria, containing bivalves, with the foot of the animal broad and thin; divided into the families Conchacea, Cardiacea, Arcacea, Trigonacea, Nayades. Fig. 111 to 152.

LAMPAS. Montf. LENTICULINA, Bl. A genus of microscopic Foraminifera.

LAMPRODOMA. Swainson. A genus of "Olivinæ," Sw. thus described:– "Mitriform; spire produced, conic; resembling MITRELLA in shape, but the suture is channelled; the aperture effuse at the base, contracted above; lower half of the pillar with 6 to 7 plaits. Volutella, Zool. Ill. ii. series, pl. 40. f. 1. (*fig.* 86.)" Sw. p. 321. Pl. xxvi. fig. 561.

LAMPROSCAPHA. Sw. A sub-genus of "Anodontinæ," Sw. thus described:– "Shell not winged, elongated, pod-shaped; teeth none; bosses near the anterior extremity. Tropical America only? L.? elongata. *Sw.* Zool. Ill. i. 176. ensiforme, *Spix.* Braz. Test. siliquosa. Braz. Test. pygmæa. Ib." Sw. p. 381.

LANCEOLATE. Lengthened like a lance.

LANISTES. Montfort, 1810. Reversed species of AMPULLARIA. Pl. xv. fig. 319.

LAPLYSIA. See APLYSIA.

LAPLYSIACEA. Lam. (properly Aplysiacea.) A family belonging to the first section of the order Gasteropoda, Lam. containing the genera Aplysia and Dolabella. Fig. 254, 255.

LARVA. Humph. Part of FISSURELLA, Lam.

LATERAL. (*Latus*, a side.) The lateral teeth are those which, taking their rise near the umbones, proceed to some distance towards the sides of the shell; as distinguished from the cardinal teeth, which receive their full development close to the umbones. Lateral muscular impressions are those which are placed at a distance from each other, on the opposite sides of the shell.

LATIAXIS. Sw. A genus of "Eburninæ," Sw. corresponding with the genus Trichotropis. Sow. (Sw. Malac. p. 306.)

LATRUNCULUS. Gray. The name "Eburna" being used for Ancillaria Glabrata, this is required for the genus described in this book as "Eburna."

LATIRUS. Montfort, 1810. A genus composed of a species of FUSUS, Auct. which have an umbilicus and are turriculated. L. polygonus.

LAURIA. Gray, 1840. A sub-genus of PUPA, containing P. umbilicata, & c. (Gray's Turton, p. 193.)

LEDA. Schum. 1817. Those species of Nucula, Lamarck, which have a rostrated form. Leda caudata. Pl. xxvii. fig. 578.

LEGUMINARIA. Schum. 1817. SILIQUA, Megerle, 1811. A genus composed of species of SOLEN, Auct. which have an internal longitudinal bar or rib. Fig. 61. S. Radiatus, Lam.

LEILA. Gray, 1840. Described as having the hinge smooth like Iridina, but having a "sharp siphonal inflection." (Syn. B. M. p. 142.) Anodon esula.

LEIODOMUS. Sw. A genus of "Buccininæ," Sw. consisting of Terebra vittata and other similar species. This genus corresponds with Bullia, Gray.

LEIOSTOMA. Swainson. A genus of "Fusinæ," Sw. thus described, "Equally fusiform," (with Fusus) "but ventricose in the middle; shell entirely smooth, almost polished; inner lip thickened, and vitreous; base of the pillar very straight. Fossil only. (*fig.* 75.) L. bulbiformis. En. Méth. 428. f. 1." Pl. xxvi. fig. 549.

LEMBULUS. Leach. A genus composed of oval species of NUCULA, resembling N. margaritacea, fig. 137.

LENDIX. Humph. PUPA, Lam.

LENGTH. See MEASUREMENT.

LENTICULAR. (*Lens.*) Of a circular, convex form, as Pectunculus, fig. 134.

LENTICULINA. Lam. A genus of microscopic Foraminifera.—*Descr.* Lenticular, sub-discoidal, compressed, convolute, symmetrical; aperture notched; chambers few in number; visible on the exterior, radiating from the centre of the disk.

LEPADICEA. Bl. The first family of the class Nemantopoda, Bl. This family consists of the same animals which constitute the Pedunculated Cirripedes of Lamarck, and part of the genus Lepas in the system of Linnæus. It contains the genera Gymnolepas, Pentalepas, Polylepas and Litholepas.

LEPAS. (Δεπας, *lepas*, a rock.) The Linnæan name Lepas contains all the Cirripedes or Multivalves, the different kinds of which are not distinguished in the accounts given by early writers of the habits of the animals. (Fig. 14 to 43.) It was formerly applied to the Limpets or Patella. In fact, the ancient definition was "Concha petræ adhærens," and would apply to any shells attached to rocks. Mr. Darwin, however, in his work on the Lepadæ, has very properly restricted the term "Lepas" to the genus described in this work as Pentelasmis. Pl. ii. fig. 34.

LEPTÆNA. Dalman. A genus belonging to the Brachiopoda; and thus described:– "Hinge compressed, rectilinear, frequently exceeding the width of the shell." It forms part of the genus Producta, Sow. Fig. 206, L. depressa.

LEPTOCHITON. Gray. Chiton Cinereus, Chiton Cajetanus, and similar species.

LEPTOCONCHUS. Rüppell. (Λεπτος, *leptus*, thin; Κογχος, *conchos*, shell.) This shell resembles a young MAGILUS in general appearance, although the animal is said to differ. In the young Magilus also, the inner lip is reflected over the body whorl, which is not the case in Leptoconchus. Red Sea. Pl. i. fig. 11.

LEPTOCONUS. Swainson. A sub-genus of Conus, consisting of Conus grandis, amadis, duplicatus, Australis, &c. Sw. p. 312.

LEPTOLIMNEA. Swainson. A sub-genus of Limnea, described as being nearly cylindrical. Limnea elongata, Sow. Gen. fig. 6.

LEPTON. Turton, 1822. SOLEN Squamosus, Montague, and other species described as "flat, nearly orbicular, equivalve, inequilateral, a little open at the sides. Hinge of one valve with a single tooth, and a transverse linear lateral one on each side; of the other valve, with a cavity in the middle and transverse deeply cloven lateral tooth on each side, the segments of which divaricate from the beak." See KELLADIÆ, L. squamosum. Pl. iii. fig. 62.

LEPTOSPIRA. Swainson. A sub-genus of Bulinus, thus described: "Spire excessively long, sub-cylindrical; body whorl largest; outer lip thickened; aperture oval; no teeth, striata, *Sw.* Chem. 153. f. 1226. signata *Sw.*" Sw. p. 335.

LEUCOSTOMA. Swainson. A genus of "Achatina," Sw. described as resembling Achatinella, but having a "thick pad," at the top of the "upper lip," and another over the base. L. variegata, Sw. Lardn. Cyclop. Malac. fig. 24. 172.

LEVENIA. Gray, 1847. Cassis Coarctatum, &c.

LICINA. Browne, 1756. CISTULA. Humphreys, 1797. CYCLOSTOMA fimbriata, and Thesaurus Conchyliorum. Pl. xxviii. fig. 145, 146, and similar species having a broad fringed margin.

LICIUM. Humph. OVULA, Lam. (Ovulum.)

LIGAMENT. (From *Ligo*, to bind.) The true ligament is always external, and serves the purpose of binding the two valves of a shell together externally by the posterior dorsal margins. There is another substance, called by Gray the *Cartilage*, which is elastic and of a condensed fibrous structure, placed within the ligament, either close to it, or at a more interior part of the shell; it is sometimes contained in a pit, formed for its reception, in the centre of the hinge. The substance, being elastic, keeps the valves open, unless drawn together by the counteracting force of the adductor muscles. When conchologists speak of a shell as having the ligament external, the real meaning is that these two substances are so close together as in appearance to constitute one body placed outside the shell so as to be seen when the valves are closed. When two ligaments are spoken of, as in Amphidesma, the meaning is that the cartilage occupies a separate place on the hinge.

LIGAMENTIFEROUS. (*Ligamentum*, a ligament, *fero*, to bear.) Having or containing the ligament, as the cardinal pit in Mya, fig. 71.

LIGULA. Leach. A genus containing the more rounded and less gaping species of LUTRARIA, Auct. Fig. 77, Lutraria Papyracea.

LIGULATE. (*Ligula*, a slip, a shoe-latchet.) Thin, slender, like a slip, or neck of any thing, as the anterior muscular impression of Lucina, fig. 104.

LIGUMIA. Swainson. A sub-genus of Unio, thus described:– "Very long and pod-shaped; bosses depressed; cardinal teeth moderate. S. recta, Lam. vi. l. p. 74." Sw. p. 378.

LIGUUS. Montf. 1810. A genus containing species of ACHATINA, Auct. which have rounded apertures and lengthened spires, differing from his POLYPHEMI, which have lengthened apertures. A. virginea, Auct. fig. 286, is the type of this genus.

LIMA. Brug. 1797. (Lima, a file.) *Fam.* Pectinides, Lam. Subostracea, Bl.—*Descr.* Equivalve, inequilateral, compressed, oblique, auriculated, oval, radiately ribbed or striated, imbricated, covered with a light brown epidermis; hinge with a triangular disc between the umbones, divided in the centre by a triangular ligamentary pit without teeth; muscular impression one, sub-lateral, sub-orbicular.—*Obs.* The shells thus described are marine, two or three species being found on our coasts, and fossil species occuring in Lias, inferior Oolite, Calcaire-grossiér, &c. They differ from Pecten in having a wide hiatus for the passage of a byssus, by which they are occasionally attached, and also in the triangular disc, which separates the umbones. The animal makes use of the valves of his shell for swimming, working them like fins or paddles, and by this means proceeding at a rapid rate through the waters. The Monograph of this genus in the Author's Thesaurus Conchyliorum contains 13 species. Plates 21, 22. L. Squamosa, Pl. x. fig. 174.

LIMACINA. Cuv. (*Limax*, a snail.) Fam. Pteropoda, Lam.—*Descr.* Papyraceous, fragile, planorbicular, sub-carinated, obliquely convolute; spiral side rather prominent, the other side umbilicated; aperture large, entire, not modified, peristome sharp.—*Obs.* This is SPIRATELLA, Bl. The shell figures as Limacina in Sowerby's Genera, under "pteropoda," is an *Atlanta*. Our representation of Spiratella Limacinea, fig. 224 is copied from Blainville.

LIMACINEA. Lam. A family of the order Gasteropoda, Lam. including the following genera:–

1. CRYPTELLA. Spire mammillated; a septum. Fig. 256.
2. PARMACELLA. Flat, haliotoid, spiral. Fig. 257, 258.
3. TESTACELLUS. Sub-spiral. Fig. 261.
4. LIMAX. Incomplete. Fig. 259.
5. PLECTROPHORUS. Conical. Fig. 260.
6. VITRINA. Heliciform, hyaline. Fig. 262, 263.

LIMACINEA. Bl. The third family of the order Pulmobranchiata, Bl. Described as containing shells very variable in form, most frequently inclining to globular or oval; the apex always obtuse; aperture variable, but never emarginated. All the Limacinea are phytophagous and terrestrial. This family answers to the genus Helix of Linnæus and to the Colimacea of Lamarck, leaving out the Auriculacea. It contains the genera Succinea, Bulinus, Achatina, Clausilia, Pupa, Partula, Helix, Vitrina, Testacella, Limacella, Limax.

LIMAX. Linnæus. Limacinea, Lam. and Bl.—*Descr.* Internal irregular, sub-quadrate, scutiform, crystalline; apex rounded, indistinct; epidermis, light brown, thin, extending beyond the margin.—*Obs.* The shell is placed under the scutellum of the common garden slug. L. Antiquorum. Pl. xiii. fig. 259.

LIMNACEA. Bl. The first family of the order Pulmobranchiata, Bl. The shells of this family are described as thin, with the outer lip always sharp. It contains the genera Limnea, Physa, Planorbis.

LIMNEANA. Lam. A family of the order Trachelipoda, Lam. containing the following genera:–

1. LIMNÆA. Spire produced; including *Physa*. Fig. 308 to 310.
2. PLANORBIS. Spire orbicular; including *Planaria*. Fig. 311, 312.

LIMNEA. Lamarck, 1801. (Λιμνας, *limnas*, lacustrine.) Fam. Limnacea, Lam. and Bl.—*Descr.* Oblong, light, thin; spire variable in length, acute; last whorl large, aperture large, longitudinal, entire; inner lip spread over a portion of the last whorl; columella forming an oblique fold; outer lip rounded at each extremity, thin.—*Obs.* These light horn-coloured shells are common in standing pools, ponds and ditches, in various parts of Europe. They resemble the Amber shell (Succinea) in shape, but the animal of the latter is amphibious, and the shell of a bright amber colour. L. Stagnalis, fig. 308. L. auricularia, fig. 309. (RADIX, Montf.) The reversed species have been separated under the name Physa, fig. 310. Other generic names have been given to other species. Pl. xiv.

LINES OF GROWTH. The concentric striæ or lines formed by the edges of the successive layers of shelly matter deposited by the animal by which it increases the shell. The outer edge of the aperture is always the last line of growth.

LINGUIFORM. (*Lingua*, tongue; *forma*, form.) Tongue-shaped.

LINGULA. Lam. 1801. (Dim. from *lingua*, tongue.) *Fam.* Brachiopoda, Lam. Palliobranchiata, Bl.—*Descr.* Equivalve, oblong, depressed, thin, equilateral, gaping and pointed at the umbones, gaping and truncate or trilobate at the opposite extremities, attached by a fleshy pedicule fixed to the umbones.—*Obs.* This is the only bivalve shell which is pedunculated, in which respect it constitutes a singular anomaly. The ancient writers, seeing the valves separate, placed it in their systems under the name Patella Unguis. There are several recent species found in the Moluccas, and some fossils in sandy indurated marl, and in alluvium of Suffolk. L. Anatina, fig. 219, is so named from its resemblance to a duck's bill. Mr. Sowerby's Monograph of this genus in the Author's Thesaurus Conchyliorum contains 7 species. Plate 67. See our Plate xii. fig. 219.

LINGULINA. D'Orb. A genus of microscopic Foraminifera.

LINTERIA. Adams. Sowerby's Thesaurus, Pl. 11. 1850. A sub-genus of Bullidæ, the shells of which are thus described: "oval, depressed; aperture with a slight canal above; inner lip with a cup-shaped appendage, spiral within."

LINTHURIS. Montf. Conch. Syst. 2. 154. A genus of microscopic Foraminifera.

LIP. See LABIUM and LABRUM.

LIPPISTES. Montf. A genus of microscopic Foraminifera.

LITHODOMUS. Cuv. (Λιθος, *lithos*, stone; Δωμα, *doma* house.)

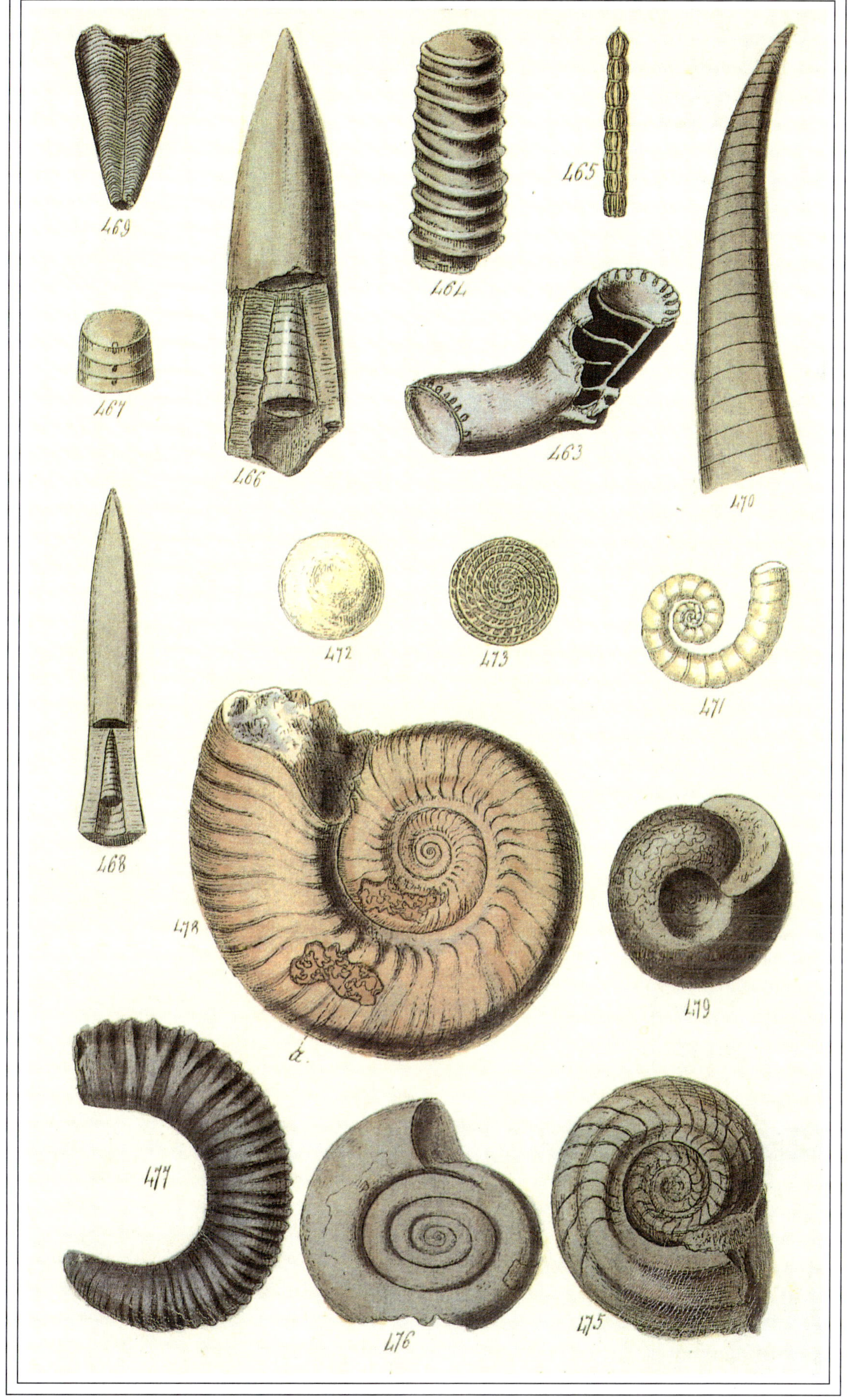

Order. Cephalopoda

First Division. Polythalamous Cephalopoda

Fam. Orthocerata

463. Amplexus coralloides, (from Sow. Min. Con.)
464. Orthoceratites annulatus.
465. Nodosaria æqualis.
466. Belemnites, with the outer coat broken to shew the alveole.
467. ——portion of the alveole separated.
468. ——hastatus. Hibolithes, Montf. (from Blainville.)
469. Conularia quadrisulcata.
470. Conilites pyramidatus, (from Blainville.)

Fam. Lituacea

471. Spirula Peronii.

Fam. Nautilacea

472. Nummulites buticularis, outisde. Helicites, Bl. Camerina. Brookes.
473. The same inside, to shew the chambers.
474. Nautilus pompilius, young. See Frontispiece.
475. Simplegas sulcata.
476. Endosiphonites. (From Camb. Philos. Trans.)

Fam. Ammonacea

477. Ammonoceras, (from Blainville.)
478. Ammonites; *a*, break in the shell, showing the sinuous septa.
479. Orbulites crassus. Globulites, Nonnul. Angulites, Montf. reduced.

Fam. Mytilacea, Lam.—*Descr.* Transverse, elongated, cylindrical, equivalve, with the extremities rounded, and the posterior extremity rostrated; umbones not prominent, terminal; hinge straight, destitute of teeth; ligament linear, most conspicuous within; muscular impressions two.—*Obs.* The shells composing this genus differ from Modiola, not only in the cylindrical form, but also in the circumstance fromwhich the generic name is derived, *i.e.* of their living in stones. Thus, while the form and structure of the shell bring it near the Mytili or Muscle shells, the habits of the animal cause it to approach the Lithophagi, or rock-eating molluscs of Lamarck. L. Dactylus is the Mytilus Lithophagus of ancient authors. Pl. ix. fig. 161.

LITHOLEPAS. Bl. (Λιθος, *lithos*, stone; λεπας, *lepas*, rock.) De Blainville, LITHOTRYA, Sowerby.

LITHOPHAGIDÆ. Lam. (Λιθος, *lithos*, stone; Φαγω, *phaga*, eat or gnaw.) A family of the Conchifera Dimyaria, Lam. consisting of terebrating bivalves, gaping anteriorly, having no accessary valves; and containing the genera Saxicava, Petricola, Venerupis, to which are added other genera enumerated in explanation of figures 91 to 97. Notwithstanding the numerous genera which have been created, I think that the most convenient arrangement will be to reduce them to two, thus–

1. PETRICOLA, with distinct cardinal teeth, including Clotho, Venerirupis and Coralliophaga. Fig. 91, 92, 97.
2. SACICAVA, without teeth, including Biapholius, Hiatella, Sphænia, Byssomya, and Thracia. Fig. 93 to 96.

LITHOPHAGUS. Megerle, 1811. LITHODOMUS. Cuvier, 1817.

LITHOTRYA. G.B. Sowerby. (Λιθος, *lithos*, stone; τρυω, *truo*, to bore through.) *Fam.* Pedunculated Cirripedes, Lam.—*Descr.* Eight unequal valves, forming a laterally compressed cone, the lower central valves being very minute; pedicle fleshy, scaly at the upper extremity; fixed at the base in a patelliform shelly support.—*Obs.* This genus derives its name from the power possessed by the animal of making dwelling holes in stones or pieces of rock. The remarkable shelly cup at the base of the pedicle is regarded as analogous to the shelly base of the Balanus, so that this genus seems to form an intermediate link between the Sessile and Pedunculated Cirripedes of Lamarck. West India Islands. L. dorsalis, Pl. ii. fig. 39.

LITIOPA. Rang. 1829. *Fam.* Turbinacea, Lam.—*Descr.* "Shell not very thick, horny, with a slight epidermis, rather transparent, conical with whorls somewhat rounded; the last being larger than all the rest together; with the apex pointed, longitudinally grooved; aperture oval, larger anteriorly than posteriorly, with the lips disunited, the right lip simple, separated from the left by a rather indistinct notch, or a slight sinus in the contour. The left slightly reflected backwards, so as to form a kind of salient margin with the anterior extremity of the columella, which is united, rounded, arcuated and slightly truncated at the anterior."—*Obs.* The Molluscous animals, whose shells are thus described, are found in the Mediterranean, and are remarkable for the power of suspending themselves from the sea-weed on which they live, by a thread resembling a spider's web. The general appearance of the shell presents a medium between Phasianella and Littorina, but it is apparently destitute of an operculum.

LITTORINA. Ferussac. (*Littus*, the sea-shore.) *Fam.* Turbinacea, Lam.—*Descr.* Turbinated, thick; spire acuminated, consisting of a few whorls, about one-third of the axis in length; aperture entire, large, rounded anteriorly; outer lip thickened within, acute; columella rather flattened; operculum horny, spiral with rapidly increasing volutions.—*Obs.* The shells composing this genus are known from Turbo and Phasianella by the horny operculum; and from Trochus, which has also a horny operculum, by the small number of the whorls. The Littorinæ, among which may be enumerated the common Periwinkle, are, as the name implies, found on sea shores, feeding upon sea-weed, in all parts of the world. L. Vulgaris. Pl. xvi. fig. 363.

LITUACEA. Bl. The second family of Polythalamacea. Bl. The shells are described as chambered, symmetrical, convolute in part of their extent, but constantly straight towards the termination. The genus Spirula, which is admitted into this family, does not properly belong to it, any more than to the Lituolæ of Lamarck, in which it is also placed. It does not agree with the descriptions of either. This family partly corresponds with the "Lituolées," Lam. and contains the genera Lituola, Ichthyo, sarcolites, Spirula, Hamites and Ammonoceras.

LITUACEA. Lam. A family of the order Polythalamous Cephalopoda, Lam. containing the genus Spirula, fig. 471.

LITUITUS. Montf. SPIROLINA, Lam. Microscopic.

LITUOLA. Lam. A genus of microscopic Foraminifera.

LITUOLÆ. Lam. The third family of Polythalamous Cephalopoda, Lam. the shells of which are described as partially spiral, the last whorl continuing in a straight line. The transverse septa which divide the chambers, are in general pierced by a siphon which breaks itself off before it reaches the succeeding septum. This family contains the genera of microscopic Foraminifera Lituola and Spirolina. The genus Spirula, also placed in this family, does not by any means agree with Lamarck's definitions, "the last whorl continuing in a straight line."

LITUUS. Hump. CYCLOSTOMA? Lam.

LIVID. (From *lividus.*) Of a pale, dull, blue colour. The adjective is sometimes used as a specific name. *Ex.* Conus *lividus*, Sanguinolaria *livida*.

LOBARIA. Schum. SANGUINOLARIA rosea, Lam. (fig. 98) and other similar species.

LOBATE or LOBED. Divided into two parts.

LOBATULA. Fleming. A genus composed of two very minute species of chambered shells. Serpula lobata and S. concamerata, Mont. Test. Brit. 515.

LOMASTOMA. Rafinesque. An imperfectly defined genus, probably belonging to the Limnacea.

LONGITUDINAL. Lengthwise. Longitudinal striæ, ribs, &c. are those which radiate from the apex and follow the spiral direction of the whorls, in spiral shells; and from the umbo to the ventral margin in bivalves. The term "decourantes" is employed by French conchologists. The bands in Achatina, fig. 286, are longitudinal or spiral.

LOPHUERUS. Poli. Chiton squamosus, and similar species. The marginal insegment in regular scales.

LORICULA pulchella. G.B. Sowerby, Jun. Ann. Nat. Hist. Vol. XII. 1843, p. 260. Darwin, Fossil lepadæ, p. 84. A very beautifully formed Cirripede, found in the lower chalk, near Rochester, Kent. The specimen is in Mr Wetherell's collection.

LORIPES. Poli. A genus composed of a species of LUCINA. Auct. in which the cartilage is wholly internal. *Ex.* Lucina divaricata.

LOTORIUM. Montf. 1810. A genus composed of species of TRITON, Auct. in which the aperture is effuse. T. Lotorium, Pl. xviii. fig. 400.

LOTTIA. Gray, 1833. PATELLOIDA, Quoy and Gaimard.

LUCERNA. Humph. A generic name applied to some species of HELIX included in De Ferussac's sub-genus Helicogena.

LUCERNELLA. Sw. A genus of "Lucerninæ," Sw. thus described: "Teeth on both sides of the aperture; surface regularly and distinctly striated. Circumference convex."

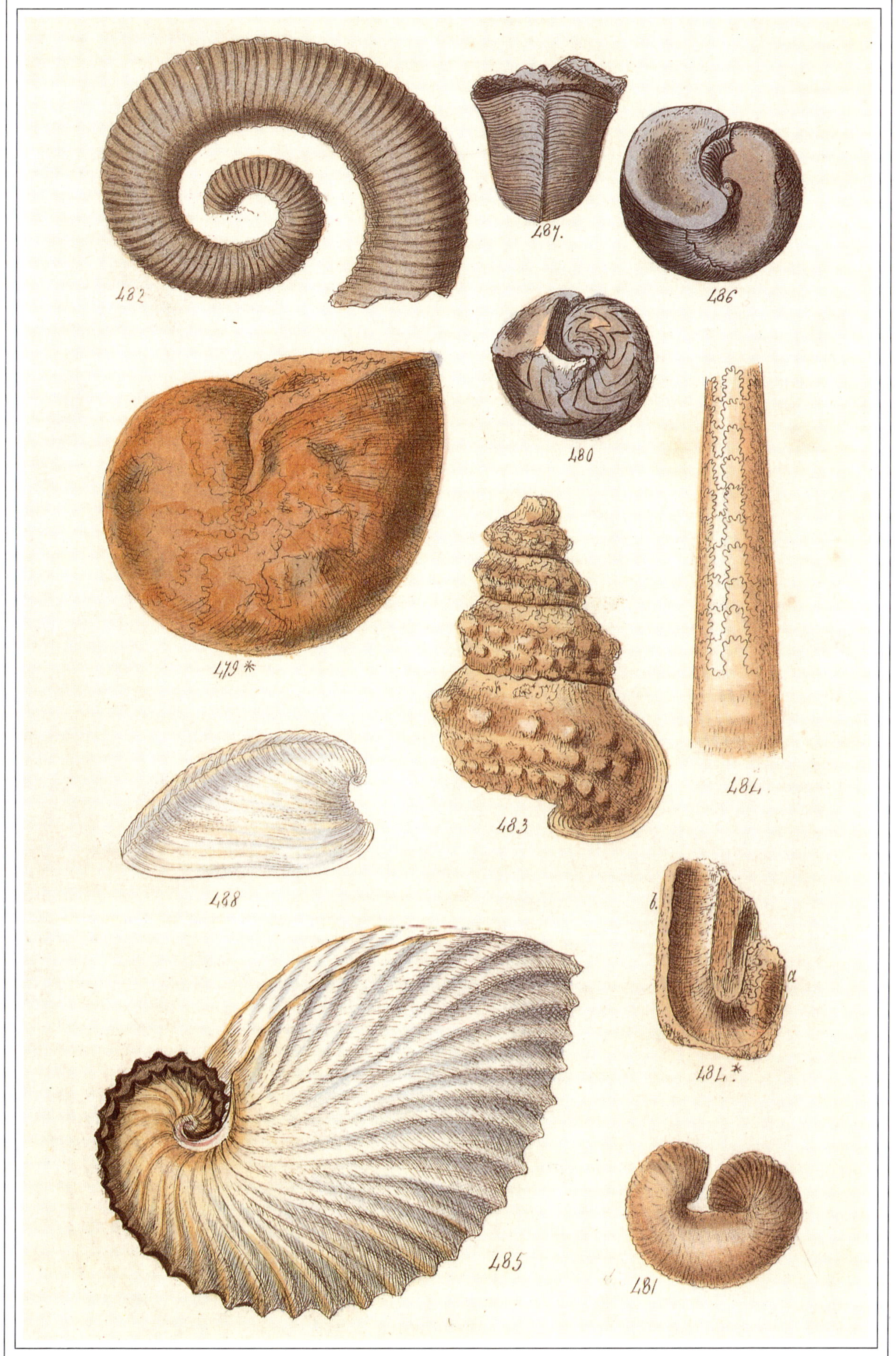

479*.——discus. Aganides, Montf.
480. Goniatites striatus.
481. Scaphites æqualis.
482. Crioceratites Duvallii.
483. Turrilites tuberculatus.
484. Baculites Faujasii. Portion near the centre.
484*. Hamites cylindricus; *a*, internal cast of part of the shell; *b*, hollow external cast of the remainder.

Second Division. Monothalamous Cephalopoda

485. Argonauta Argo.
486. Bellerophon tenuifasciata, (from Sow. Gen.)
487. The same, shewing the dorsal keel.

Order. Heteropoda

488. Carinaria Mediterranea

LUCIDELLA. Swainson, 1840. Helicina or Oligyra, species contracted near the outer lip. H. aureola. Thesaurus Conchyliorum, Pl. i. fig. 43, 4, 5.

LUCIDULA. Sw. A sub-genus of "Lucerna," Humph. thus described: "Aperture transverse, both lips much thickened and united; the outer with marginal obsolete teeth at the base; umbilicus closed. Barbadensis, *Lam.* No. 49. p. 78. Fêr. Moll. pl. 47, 2, 3, 4."

LUCINA. Brug. 1792. *Fam.* Nymphacea, Lam. Conchacea, Bl. *Descr.* Equivalve, inequilateral, orbicular, lenticular, radiately striated; hinge with, generally, two minute cardinal teeth, which are sometimes nearly obsolete, and two lateral teeth, on each side of the umbo in one valve, one in the other; ligament external, partly hidden by the margins of the valves when closed. Muscular impressions two in each valve, the anterior one produced into an elongated, ligulate band, the posterior short and semi-rotund; impression of the mantle not sinuated.—*Obs.* The shells of this genus resemble Amphidesma in general form, but are distinguished by the external ligament, the elongated muscular impression, and the want of a sinus in the palleal impression. East and West Indies, and European shores. L. Tigerina. Pl. v. fig. 104.

LUCINOPSIS. Forbes and Hanley. Nov. 1848. Venus undata pennant. Differing slightly from Artemis in the hinge and palleal sinus. See Sowerby's Thesaurus, Pl. 13.

LUNULATE. (*Luna*, the moon, dim.) Moon-shaped, having the form of a crescent. Applied most frequently to muscular impressions. The word semilunar is sometimes used, perhaps with greater accuracy, to express the same shape.

LUNULE. An impression on the anterior dorsal margin of some bivalve shells. The similar impression on the posterior dorsal margin is called the *escutcheon*.

LUPONIA. Gray, 1832. A genus composed of species of Cypræa, Auct. which are described as having the anterior of the columellar lip crossed by several irregular ridges, without any distinct marginal ones, internally narrow, flat; the shell pear-shaped, smooth, or cross-ribbed. *Ex.* C. Algoensis, Luponia Algoensis, Gray, Pl. xxii. fig. 447.

LUTRARIA. Lamarck. 1799. (*Lutum*? mud.) *Fam.* Mactracea, Lam.—*Descr.* Thin, equivalve, inequilateral, transverse, oblong or ovate, gaping at both extremities; hinge with one double and sometimes one single cardinal tooth in each valve, and a triangular, oblique pit with a prominent margin, containing the ligament; muscular impressions distant; palleal impression having a large sinus.—*Obs.* This genus differs from Mactra in the entire absence or indistinctness of lateral teeth. Fig. 77, L. Papyracea. (Ligula, Leach.) Fig. 78. L. Solenoides. Sandy and muddy shores. Pl. iii. fig. 77, 78.

LUTRICOLA. Blainville, 1825. Lutraria. Lam. 1799. Fig. 77, 78.

LYCOPHRIS. Montf. A microscopic fossil described as resembling Nummulites, but having a granulated surface.

LYMNADEA. Sw. A sub-genus of "Mysca," Turton, in the family of Nayades, Lam. thus described: "Posterior hinge margin elevated and winged; the valves connate; the surface smooth. L. alata *Sw. Ex.* Conch. (fig. 48.) fragilis. *Sw.* Zool. Ill. compressa, *Lea.* Am. Tr. iii. pl. 12. f. 22." Sw. p. 379.

LYMNEA. See Limnea.

LYMNEUS. Lam. See Limneana.

LYONSIA. Turt. Inequivalve, species of Anatina, Auct. which have no spoon-shaped cavity in the hinge, but an accessary piece. L. striata, Pl. xxiv. fig. 491, 492.

LYRIA. Swainson. Voluta Nucleus, Thesaurus Conchyliorum, Pl. v. fig. 108.

LYRODON. Goldf. Trigonia?

MACLURITES. Lesœur. Journ. des Scienc. Nat. Philad. t. 1. p. 312. pl. 13. fig. 2, 3.

MACOMA. Leach. Venus tenuis, Bl. and similar species, described as "Clothed with an epidermis; striated, compressed, oval; the summits not very prominent; two bifid teeth upon the right valve and a single undivided one upon the left."

MACRODITUS. Montf. Lenticulina, Bl. A genus of microscopic Foraminifera.

MACROSPIRA. Guild. 1840. Subulina, Beck, 1837. A genus composed of Helix Octona, Auct. *Ex.* Subulina octona, Pl. xxv. fig. 514.

MACROSTOMATA. Lam. (Μακρος, *macros*, long; στομα, *stoma*, mouth.) A family belonging to the first section of the order Trachelipoda, the shells belonging to which are described as haliotoid or ear-shaped, with a very large aperture, destitute of an operculum. This family contains the following genera, which may be thus distinguished.

1. Velutina. Globose, with velvety epidermis. Fig. 337.
2. Stomatia. Ear-shaped; pearly within; including Stomatella. Fig. 335, 336.
3. Sigaretus. The same, not pearly; including *Cryptostoma*, Fig. 334.
4. Coriocella. The same, thin, transparent.
5. Haliotis. The same, not thin, nor transparent; with holes; including *Padollus*. Fig. 338, 339.
6. Scissurella. Heliciform, with a slit near the aperture. Fig. 340.
7. Pleurotomaria. Trochiform, with a slit at the edge of the aperture. Fig. 341.

MACTRA. Linn. (*Mactra*, a kneading trough.) *Fam.* Mactracea, Lam. Conchacea, Bl.—*Descr.* Usually thin, equivalve, sub-equilateral, subtrigonal, slightly gaping at the extremities; hinge with one cardinal tooth, divided into two parts, diverging from the umbo, with sometimes a very small laminar tooth close to its side; a deep triangular pit near the centre, containing the cartilage; one long, lateral tooth on each side of the umbo in one valve, received between two in the other; muscular impressions two, lateral; palleal impression with a small sinus.—*Obs.* This genus contains many species of beautiful shells found in various parts of the world, some of which are common in Britain. Fossil species are not numerous, they occur in the tertiary strata. The principal forms are represented by M. Splengleri, fig. 81. (Schizodesma) M. gragilis, fig. 80, (Spisula) M. bicolor, fig. 82, (Mulinea) and M. Stultorum, fig. 79. Pl. iv. fig. 79 to 82.

MACTRACEA. Lam. A family of the order Conchifera Dimyaria, Lam. Sect. Tenuipes. The cartilage placed in a trigonal pit with a small external ligament. The genera may be thus distinguished.

1. Lutraria. No lateral teeth, shell gaping. The short species constitute the genus *Ligula*. Fig. 77, 78.
2. Mactra. Lateral teeth, shell closed. This genus has been divided into mactra, Mulinia, Schizodesma and Spisula, by Mr. Gray. Fig. 79 to 82.
3. Gnathodon. Teeth serrated, thick, one angular. Fig. 83.
4. Crassatella.Shell thick, lateral teeth. Fig. 84.
5. Amphidesma. A distinct external ligament, internal ligament oblique. Fig. 85.
6. Erycina. A short tooth on each side of the cartilaginous pit in each valve. Including Mesodesma. Fig. 86.
7. Ungulina. Ligament flat, divided. Fig. 88.

MACULATED. (From *Macula*, a spot.) Spotted or patched. This term is applied by conchological writers, to those shells which are coloured in spots or small patches. In the same sense it is also used as a specific

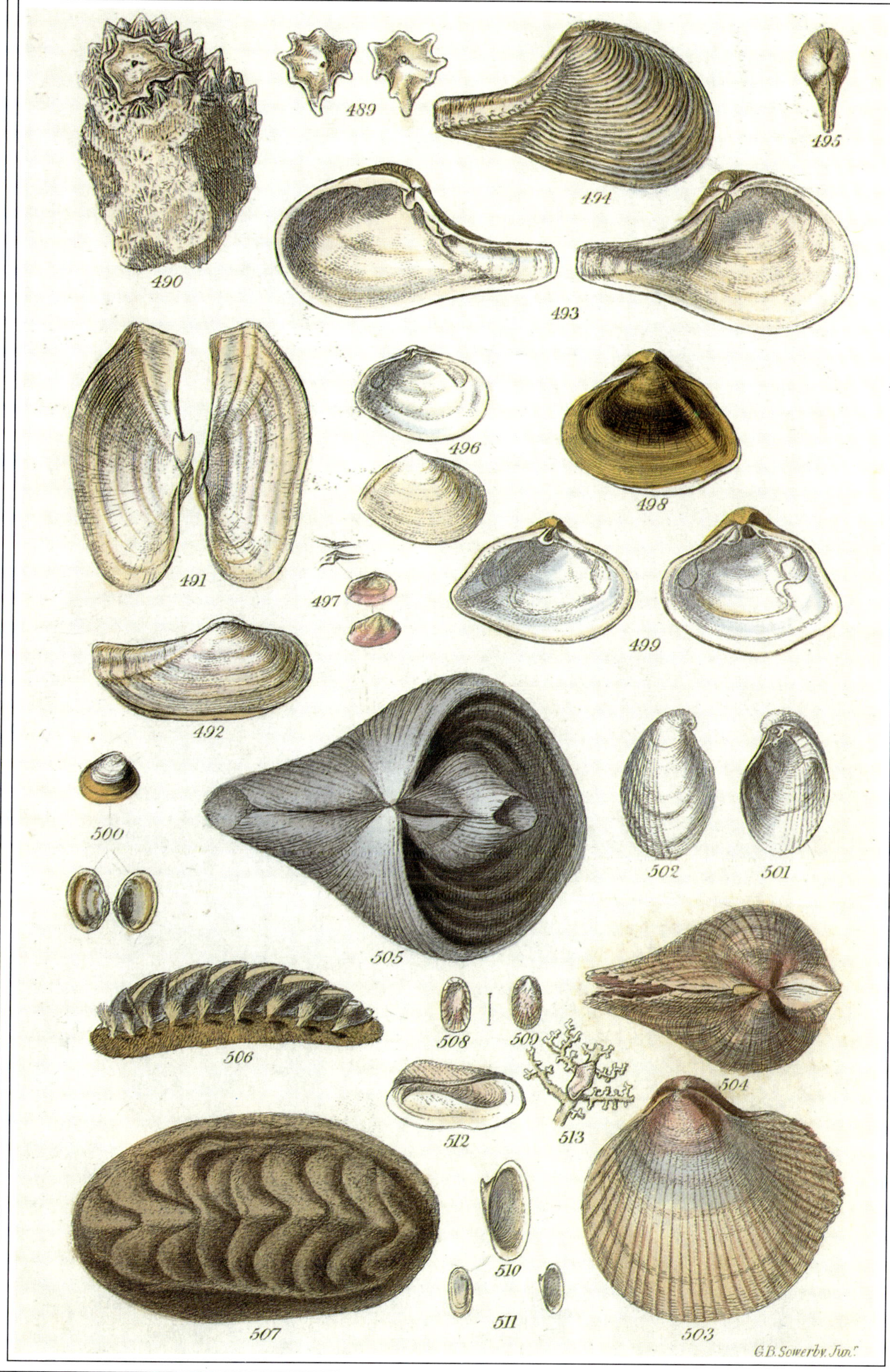

489. Pyrgoma monticularia. *Sub-genus*, Daracia, Gray, back and front.

490. The same, in situ.

491. Lyonsia Norvegica. Anatina, Nonnul. Inside view of both valves.

492. Outside, with the valves closed.

493. Næara longirostrum, Anatina longirostris, Lam. Inside of both valves.

494. Outside, with both valves closed.

495. A smaller species of Næara, shewing the inequality of the valves.

496. Amphidesma tennis. Abra. Leach.

497. Ervillia nitens.

498. Potamomya, of some authors. A fresh-water shell, resembling Corbula. Outside, valves closed.

499. Inside of both valves.

500. Cyclas amnica. Pera, Leach.

501. Cardilia semisulcata. Isocardia semisulcata. Lam. Internal view.

502. External view of the same valve.

503. Cardium apertum. Papyridea, Sw.

504. The same, shewing the umbones.

505. Pleurorynchus, fossil, (from Mineral Conchology.)

506. Chiton fascicularis. Phakellopleura, Guild.

507. ——amiculatus. Amicula Gray.

508. Scutella, Brod. Internal view.

509. External view of the same.

510. Ancylus, a reversed species, illustrating the genus Velletia, Gray, enlarged view.

511. The same, natural size.

512. Pedicularia. Enlarged figure, (copied from Swainson.)

513. The same, natural size, growing on coral.

name. As for instance, Cytherea maculata, fig. 167, c. and Hippopus maculatus, fig. 156.

MAGAS. Sow. (Μαγας, *magas*, a board, a deck.) *Fam.* Brachiopoda, Lam.—*Descr.* Equilateral, inequivalve; one valve convex, with a triangular area, divided by an angular sinus in the centre; the other valve flat, with a straight hinge line and two small projections; a partial longitudinal septum, with appendages attached to the hinge within. Differing from Terebratula in having a triangular disc, and not a circular perforation. Magas pumilus. Fossil in chalk. Pl. xi. fig. 209.

MAGILUS. Montf. *Fam.* Cricostomata, Bl. Serpulacea, Lam.—*Descr.* Thick, tubular, irregular, contorted; rounded above, keeled beneath, free; apicial extremity convolute, heliciform, ovate or sub-globose; aperture elliptical.—*Obs.* This shell when in a young state presents the characteristics of a regularly formed spiral univalve, living in holes in madrepores. As the madrepore increases in bulk, the animal gives an eccentric course to the shell, in order to have its aperture even with the surface, and leaving the nucleus or young shell behind, fills it up with calcareous matter to reside in the open extremity of the tube. Red Sea and Mauritius. Campulotus is the original name for this genus. Pl. i. fig. 9, 10.

MALACOTA. Schum. Otion. Leach. Conchoderma.

MALACOZOA. Bl. (Μαλακος, *malacos*, soft; εν, *in*, τεμνω, *temno*, cut; Ζωον, *zoon*, animal.) Or articulated mollusca. The sub-type in De Blainville's system, comprehending those with multivalve shells.

MALDANIA. Lam. The second family of the order Annelides Sedentaria. The only genus of shells described in this family is Dentalium, fig. 2, to which may be added Pharetrium, König, fig. 3. It is doubtful however whether the latter do not belong to an unknown genus of Pteropodous Mollusca.

MALEA. Valenciennes. A genus composed of Dolium latilabrum, Kiener, and other similar species. D. ringens, &c.

MALENTOZOA. Bl. (Μαλακος, *malacos*, soft; εν, *in*, τεμνω, *temno*, cut; Ζωον, *zoon*, animal.) Or articulated mollusca. The sub-type in De Blainville's system, comprehending those with multivalve shells.

MALLEACEA. Lam. A family belonging to the order of Conchifera Monomyaria. Containing the following genera of irregular pearly bivalves.

1. Avicula. Hinge linear, simple, including *Meleagrina*. Fig. 163, 164.
2. Perna. Hinge with linear grooves, including *Pulvinites*. Fig. 166, 170.
3. Gervillia. Shaped like Modiola, with irregular grooves. Fig. 162.
4. Crenatula. Hinge with a series of pits. Fig. 168.
5. Catillus. Like Perna, but more regular and convex. Fig. 167.
6. Malleus. A triangular disc on the hinge, and two auricles. Fig. 165.

MALLEUS. Auct. (*Malleus*, a hammer.) *Fam.* Malleacea, Lam. Margaritacea, Bl.—*Descr.* Equivalve, inequilateral, foliaceous, trilobate, undulated, irregular, attached by a byssus passing through a sinus in one valve; hinge rectilinear, lengthened by two auricles; with a small disc under the umbones, containing the ligament, and a groove containing the cartilage; muscular impressions one in each valve, large, uniform, and one or two others extremely minute.—*Obs.* Malleus Vulgaris, the type of this genus, is a most singular shell, commonly called the "Hammer Oyster," from the peculiarity of its shape. It belongs to the Linnean genus Ostrea, from which it differs in being attached by a byssus. M. Vulgaris, Pl. x. fig. 165.

MAMILLARIA. Sw. A sub-genus of Natica, corresponding with Polinices of Montfort, having the spire small and the umbilicus filled. *Ex.* Natica Mamilla, Auct. fig. 327.

MAMMILLA. Schum. 1817. Natica melanostoma.

MAMMILLATED. (*Mammula*, a little teat.) A term applied to the apex of a shell when it is rounded like a teat. *Ex.* Voluta Vespertilio, fig. 433.

MANGELIA. Leach. A genus consisting of small shells which approach the clavate form of the Pleurotomæ. They are angularly fusiform, ribbed, and turrited; the aperture is long and narrow, the outer lip thickened, turned inwards and denticulated, with an angle and slight sinuosity above; the inner lip is more or less granulated or denticulated. *Ex.* M. Citharella, Leach. This was the first species known, and it was placed by Lamarck among the Cancellariæ, to which it has little affinity. M. Reeve's Monograph contains about 70 species, the great majority of which were brought new from the Philippines by Mr. Cuming. Mangelia Coronata, Hinds. Pl. xxviii. fig. 597.

MARGARITA. Leach. (*Margarita*, a pearl.) A genus of small shells resembling the genus Trochus, from which it differs in having an operculum consisting of few whorls. M. tæniata, fig. 362. Mr. G. B. Sowerby, sen. has enumerated 15 species in a list accompanying the figures published by the author of this manual in Nos. 132 to 134 of his Conchological Illustrations.

MARGARITACEA. Bl. The third family of Lamellibranchiata, Bl. The shells belonging to it are described as irregular, inequivalve, inequilateral, black or horny without, pearly within; hinge auriculated, scarcely developed, and without teeth. The ligament is variable and there is a large sub-central muscular impression. This family contains the genera Vulsella, Malleus, Pinna, Crenatula, Inoceramus, Catillus, Pulvinites, Gervillia and Avicula.

MARGARITACEOUS. (*Margarita*, a pearl.) Pearly.

MARGARITANA. Schum. 1817. Alasmodonta. Say, 1840. A sub-genus of Uniones, composed of species having "one cardinal tooth," and no lateral teeth. *Ex.* M. Complananta, fig. 141.

MARGARITIFEROUS. (*Margarita*, pearl; *fero*, to bear.) Pearl-bearing. Applied to shells which form pearls; as Meleagrina Margaritifera, or Pearl-bearing Oyster.

MARGINAL. Near the margin or edge.

MARGINATED. (*Margo*, edge.) Having an edge or border thicker than the rest of the shell, from which circumstance the little genus Marginella derives its name.

MARGINELLA. Lamarck, 1801. Porcellana. Adanson, 1757. (A little rim or border.) *Fam.* Columellaria, Lam. Angyostomata, Bl.—*Descr.* Ovate, smooth, shining, with a short, sometimes hidden spire; aperture narrow, emarginated; columella with several oblique folds; outer lip neatly reflected.—*Obs.* This genus of pretty little shells differs from Voluta, in the reflection of the outer lip. The animal covers the greater part of the shell with the mantle, and by continually depositing vitreous matter gives it a bright polish, which, together with the delicately neat arrangement of colours in most species, renders them exceedingly beautiful. The Marginellæ are marine and tropical. A few fossil species are found in the Calc-grossier. Fig. 437. M. Glabella, genus Glabella, Sw. Sowerby's Monograph in Thesaurus Conchyliorum enumerates 108 species. It will be seen that priority may be claimed for the name "Porcellana" for this genus. Pl. xx. fig. 437.

MARGINULINA. D'Orb. A genus of microscopic Foraminifera.

MARINE CONCHACEA. See Conchacea.

MARINE TESTACEA. Those shell-fish which inhabit seas, lakes, &c.

of salt water, in distinction from the *Aquatic* Testacea, or those which are found in rivers, ponds or stagnant pools of fresh water: and also from the *Land* Testacea, which live on land and breathe air. The great proportion of shells belong to the former class, those of the latter two classes being limited in their nubmer, and in the genera to which they belong.

MARINULA. King. A genus of small shells resembling Auricula and Pedipes, described as "Ovate, sub-solid, with aperture ovate entire; columella bidentate, uniplicated towards the base, with large sub-remote teeth; the largest uppermost; no operculum."

MARISA. Gray, 1824. CERATODES, Guilding. AMPULLARIA Cornu-arietis, Lamarck. See our fig. 323.

MARMAROSTOMA. Sw. A genus of "Trochidæ," Sw. thus described: "Umbilicus deep; spire of few whorls, much depressed, and obtuse; inner lip obsolete; base even more produced than in *Senectus*, but never distinctly channeled. M. versicolor. Mont. 176. f. 1740, 1741, undulata. Chem. 169. f. 1640, 1641." Sw. p. 348. The operculum is thick, rounded, and with a canal near the outer edge.

MARPESSA. Gray. A sub-genus of Clausilia, C. bidens, &c. Auct. Gray's Turton, p. 212.

MARTESIA. Leach. A genus composed of those species of PHOLAS, Auct. which are described as short, cuneiform, nearly closed at both extremities, having several accessary pieces on the middle of the back, and two marginal, lower down. The Monograph of the genus PHOLAS, in Sowerby's Thesaurus Conchyliorum, No. 10. Ph. striata, sp. 29, fig. 40 to 44, and other similar species.

MEASUREMENT. The most usual method of stating the measurements of various kinds of shells is as follows: *symmetrical convolute univalves*, the length is from anterior to posterior; the depth from ventral to dorsal; the breadth, from side to side of the aperture, as marked on the diagram, page 18. Of *symmetrical conical univalves*, length, from front to back; breadth from side to side; depth from apex to base. Of *spiral univalves*, length, from apex to anterior of the columella or axis of the shell; breadth, across from the outer lip to the opposite side. Of *non-symmetrical bivalves*, the length is from the anterior to the posterior margin; breadth, from the greatest convexity of one valve to the corresponding part of the other; depth, from the ventral to the dorsal margin. See Introduction.

MEGADESMA. Bowd. (Μεγας, *megas*, great; δεσμα, *desma*, ligament.) POTAMOPHILA, Sow. GALATHÆA, Lam.

MEGADOMUS. Sw. A sub-genus of Unio, thus described: "Only one lateral tooth in each valve; cardinal teeth two; posterior hinge margin winged. M. gigas, *Sw.*." Sw. p. 378.

MEGALODON. Sow. (Μεγας, *megas*, great; οδος, *odos*, tooth.) *Fam.* Cardiacea, Lam.—*Descr.* Equivalve, longitudinal, acuminated at the umbones, thick; hinge forming an incrassated septum across the cavity of the shell, with a large bifid tooth in the right valve, and one irregular and one pointed in the left; ligament long, external.—*Obs.* The general form, the thickened hinge reaching across the cavity of the valve and the terminal umbones serve to distinguish this genus from Cardita, to which, however, it is nearly allied. M. cucullatus, Pl. vii. fig. 127.

MEGALOMASTOMA. Guild. A sub-genus of Cyclostoma, thus described: "Cylindrical, resembling *Pupa*, but has a horny operculum; spire not thickened; teeth or fold on the pillar none, flavula *Sw.* En. Méth. 461. f. 6. brunnea *Guild.* (*fig.* 97. *g. h.* 1.) Sw. p. 336." Mr. Gray applies the name to those species which have "a groove or ridge in front of the mouth near the pillar." *Ex.* Cyclostoma Flavulum, Sowerby's Thesaurus Conchyliorum, Pl. xxiv. fig. 66, 67; and our fig. (same species?) Pl. xxv. fig. 529.

MEGARIMA. Rafinesque. A genus proposed to include species of TEREBRATULA, Auct. which are smooth and nearly equivalve. T. lævis, T. crassa, T. truncula.

MEGASPIRA. Lea. (Μεγας, *megas*, great, and spire.) M. Ruschenbergiana, (fig. 294) is a pupiform land shell, remarkable for the length of its spire, which consists of no less than twenty-five close set, narrow, gradually increasing whorls. The outer lip is simple, slightly thickened; the inner lip has a tooth on the body-whorl, and two folds on the columella. Only one species of this singular shell is known. Pl. xiv. fig. 294.

MEGATHYRUS. D'Orbigny. A genus of Brachiopoda represented by M. cistellula. Forbes and Hanley, British Mollusca, and Teretrabula decollata, Sowerby's Thesaurus Conchyliorum. Pl. lxxi. fig. 68 to 70.

MEGATREMA. Leach. M. S.? A genus composed of those species of PYROGOMA, Auct. which have a large aperture. Pl. i. fig. 33.

MELACANTHA. Sw. A sub-genus of Melania. Sw. p. 341.

MELAFUSUS. Sw. A sub-genus of Melanopsis. Sw. p. 341.

MELAMPUS. Montf. CONOVULUM, Lam. A genus composed of species of AURICULA, Auct. of a conical form. A. conoidalis, fig. 298.

MELANIA. Auct. (Μελας, *melas*, black.) *Fam.* Melaniens, Lam. Ellipsostomata, Bl.—*Descr.* Turrited; spire generally elongated, acute; aperture entire, oval or oblong, pointed at the posterior extremity, rounded anteriorly, with a kind of indistinct canal or sinuosity; epidermis thick, generally black.—*Obs.* In common with other fresh-water shells, the Melaniæ are frequently found with corroded apices. This genus is known from Melanopsis by the absence of the notch at the anterior part of the aperture. The Melaniæ occur in rivers of warm climates. The fossil species are frequent in upper marine formations. Pl. xiv. fig. 313.

MELANIANA. Lam. (Melaniens.) A family belonging to the first section of the order Trachelipoda. The genera contained in it may be distinguished as follows.

1. MELANOPSIS. Aperture notched; columellar lip thickened above; including *Pirena*. Fig. 315, 316.
2. MELANIA. Aperture not notched; columellar lip not thickened; including *Auculosa*, *Pasithœa*, *Io*. Fig. 313, 314, 317.

MELANITHES. Sw. A sub-genus of Melanopsis. Sw. p. 341.

MELANOIDES. Olivier. MELANOPSIS. Fer.

MELANOPSIS. Fer. *Fam.* Melaniana, Lam. Entomostomata, Bl.—*Descr.* Oval or oblong, fusiform; spire acute, sometimes elongated; aperture oblong or oval, pyriform, with a distinct notch at the anterior extremity; columella tortuous, callous, thickened at the extremity near the spire; epidermis thick, horny, generally black. Subtropical.—*Obs.* This description includes the two first species of the genus Pirena, Lam. The Melanopsides are known from the Melaniæ by the notch in the aperture. M. costata. Pl. xiv. fig. 315.

MELAS. Montf. MELANIA, Auct.

MELATOMA. Sw. A sub-genus of Melanopsis. Sw. p. 341.

MELEAGRINA. Lam. MARGARITA. A genus composed of the Pearl Oyster and similar species, separated from Avicula on account of the roundness of their general form, but re-united by Sowerby. For generic characters, see Avicula. M. margaritifera. Pl. ix. fig. 164.

MELEAGRIS. Montf. TURBO Pica, Auct. and similar species, having the aperture oblique, the columella gliding imperceptibly into the outer lip, and having an umbilicus.

MELINA. Schum. BERNA, Auct.

MELO. Brod. (*Melo*, a melon.) *Fam.* Columellaria, Lam.—*Descr.* Light, ventricose, oval, with a light greenish brown epidermis, spire short, papillary, regular, sometimes hidden by the last whorl; aperture

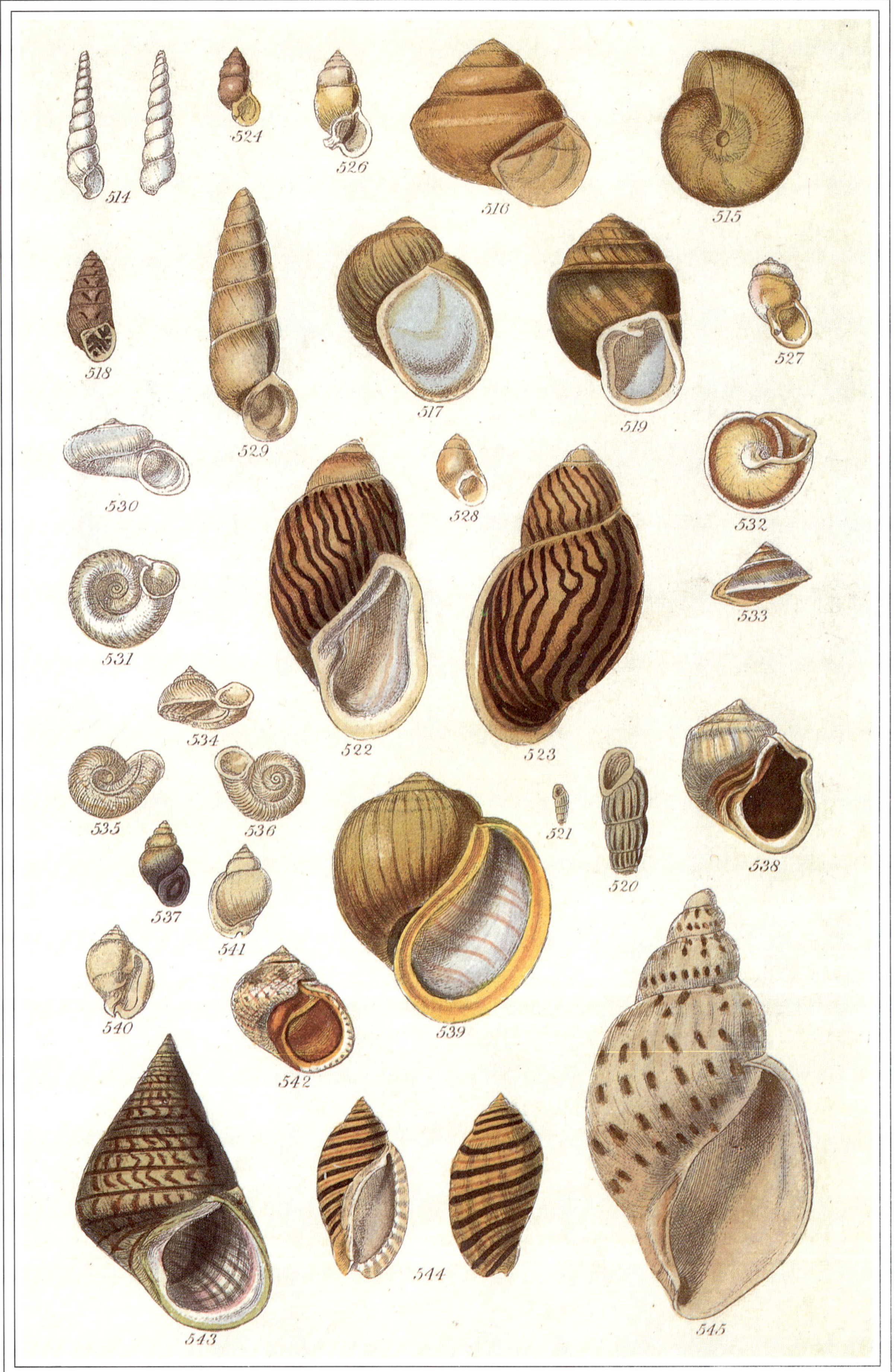

514. Achatina? octona. Macrospira, Guild.
515. Stenopus cruentatus, Guild. Under side.
516. ——lividus.
517. Helix, the aperture covered by the epiphragm.
518. Pupa secale, Drap. Abida, Leach.
519. ——pagoda. Gonidomus, Sw.
520. Truncatella, enlarged figure.
521. The same, natural size.
522. Auricula caprella. *Gen.* Caprella, Nonnul. Front view.
523. The same, dorsal view.
524. Pupina vitrea.
526. ——antiquata.
527. ——Namezii.
528. ——lubrica. Callia? Gray.
529. Cyclostoma, flavulum. Megalomastoma, Guild.
530. ——Planorbulum. Cyclotus, Guild.
531. ——a smaller species, with the complicated notch at the posterior part of the aperture. Pterocyclos, Benson.
532. Helicina acutissima, nobis. View of the under side. Trochatella, Sw.
533. The same in profile.
534. } Strophostoma, Desh. Three views.
535. }
536. }
537. Paludina impura. Bithinia, Gray?
538. Ampullaria avellana. *Amphibola Schum.*
539. A species of Ampullaria, having a thickened ledge on which the shelly operculum rests. Pachystoma, Guild. changed to Pachylabra, Sw.
540. Ringicula, Desh. A fossil species, front view.
541. Back view of the same.
542. Turbo nicobaricus. Chrysostoma, Sw.
543. Trochus Iris. Elenchus, Humph.
544. Purpura vexilla. *Gen.* Vexilla, Sw.
545. Halia. Achatina priamus, Auct.

large, nearly as long as the whole shell, emarginate anteriorly; outer lip thin; columella slightly curved, with four or five laminar, oblique, prominent plaits.—*Obs*. The genus Melo has been separated from *Voluta* principally on account of the largeness of the aperture, the lightness of the shell and the thinness of the outer lip. Melo differs from Cymba in the regularity of the spiral apex, and in the greater rotundity of the shell. The Melons are beautifully coloured large shells, found in the seas of the old world. The Melo Indicus has a certain resemblance to a Melon. Ten species are enumerated in the Monograph, Pt. viii. Thesaurus Conchyliorum, by the author. M. Æthiopicus. Pl. xx. Fig. 435.

MELONIA or MELONITES. A genus of microscopic Foraminifera.

MERCENARIA. Schum. VENUS Mercenaria, Auct. The Money shell which passes current for cash, under the name "Wampum," among the North American Indians.

MERETRIX. Lam. 1801. Original name for Cytherea, Lam. 1818. In the British Museum Synopsis it is proposed to confine this genus to the species resembling Cyth.' meretrix, &c. After, however, removing Meroe, Circe, and Arthemis, from Lamarck's Cytheræa, it appears difficult to make any further divisions. In preparing the Monograph for No. 12 of the Thesaurus Conchyliorum, the author found the succession of forms so gradual, that it was impossible to make a rest at any given point. Pl. vi. fig. 117, *a. b. c. d.* d.

MEROE. Schum. CUNEUS, Mergerle, (prior.) CYTHEREA Meroe, sulcata, scripta, hians, Auct. and similar species. The Monograph, Thesaurus Conchyliorum, No. 12, contains seven species. Pl. vi. fig. 117, *a*.

MESALIA. Gray. Reeve Conch. Icon. "Shell acuminately turrited, rounded at the base, columella flatly twisted, receding; margin of the aperture below the columella sinuated and reflected;" distinguished from TURRITELLA by the character of the columella, which is receding and flattened. Reeve's Monograph contains three species. *Ex*. M. brevialis. Pl. xxviii. fig. 591.

MESODESMA. Desh. ERYCINA, Lam. according to G. B. Sowerby.

MESOMPHYX. Rafinesque. A genus proposed to be separated from HELIX, Auct.

MICROTOMA. Sw. A genus of "Purpurinæ," Sw. thus described, "Pillar very broad and curving inwards; aperture effuse; the notch at the base small and nearly obsolete; spire very short, patula Mart. 69. f. 758, 759. Persica. En. Méth. 397. f. 1. unicolor. *Sw*. Chem. f. 1449. Sw. p. 301." Purpura Persica. Fig. 414.

MILIOLA. Lam. A genus of microscopic Foraminifera.

MISILUS. Montf. A genus of microscopic Foraminifera.

MITRA. Lam. (*Mitre*.) *Fam*. Columellaria, Lam. Angyostomata; Bl.—*Descr*. Oblong, thick, covered with a light brown epidermis; spire long, turrited, acute; aperture emarginated anteriorly; outer lip thickened; columella with several oblique, thick plaits.—*Obs*. The pretty shells composing this genus differ from Marginella, not only in general form, but in the outer lip not being reflected. Some species of Voluta, of a more elongated shape than the rest, present a near approach to the most ventricose of the Mitræ. The apex of Mitra, however, is always acute, while that of Voluta is generally papillary. The aperture of the former is narrow and the inner lip thickened, the contrary being the case with the latter. The shells of this genus are varied in colouring, which is generally rich; and also in form, some being angulated, some plicated, some coronated and others smooth. The species are mostly tropical; very few occur so far north as the Mediterranean. Fossil species are numerous in the Eocene beds. Fig. 431. M. Plicaria. Fig. 432. Conohelix marmorata, Sw. Pl. xx.—The Mitræ are thus divided in Gray's British Museum arrangement: *Mitra*, typified by the common M. episcopalis; *Zierliana*, Gray, certain short, thick-lipped strombiform species, M. Ziervoglii; *Turris*, Montf. of which our figure is an example; *Cylindra*, like Conohelix, but cancellated, M. Dactylus; and Conohelix (our fig. 432), to which is given the prior name, Imbricaria, Schum.

MAITRELLA. Sw. A genus consisting of MITRA Fissurella, casta, Olivæformis, and similar species, described as "Rather small; olive-shaped; unequally fusiform; always smooth and polished, and sometimes covered with an epidermis; base obtuse and effuse; spire nearly or quite equal to the aperture; plaits of the pillar few, oblique, and extending beyond the aperture, which is smooth internally." Sw. p. 321. M. Fissurata, E.M. 371. f. 1. Olivarii, f. 2. Dactylus, 372. f. 5. *Ex*. Mitra bicolor. Pl. xxvi. fig. 559.

MITREOLA. Sw. A genus of "Mitranæ," Sw. thus described: "Small; unequally fusiform; the base obtuse; inner lip, typically thickened, inflected, and either toothed or tuberculated; plaits on the pillar distinct, the inferior largest; tip of the spire sometimes papillary; aperture without either striæ or groove." Sw. p. 320, M. Monodonta, M. Trebellum. Zool. Illustr. II. 128. f. 1. f. 2. dPl. xxvi. fig. 558.

MODIOLA. Lam. (*Modiola*, a little measure.) *Fam*. Mytilacea, Lam.—*Descr*. Equivalve oblique, cuneiform, inequilateral, thin, with the anterior side short and narrow, slightly gaping to admit the passage of a byssus, and the posterior side elongated, broad, sub-quadrate; hinge thin, toothless, rectilinear, with a long, partly external ligament; muscular impressions two in each valve; palleal impression irregular, not sinuated.—*Obs*. This genus differs from Mytilus, to which the common muscle belongs, in the anterior margin being rounded out beyond the umbo, which in Mytilus is terminal. The Lithodomi may be known from this genus by their cylindrical form. M. Tulipa. Pl. ix. fig. 160.

MODULUS. Gray, 1840. Species of Monodonta. Lamarck, typified by Trochus modulus.

MOLLUSCA. (From *Mollis*, soft.) The twelfth class of invertebrated animals with univalve shells or none; divided into the following orders: Pteropoda, Gasteropoda, Trachelipoda, Cephalopoda, Heteropoda, fig. 220 to 488. The term mollusca is also used in a general sense to include the classes Conchifera and Molusca of Lamarck, corresponding with the type Malacozoa of De Blainville.

MONEY COWRY. Cypræa Moneta, which passes current in some parts of Africa and the East Indies.

MONILEA. Sw. A sub-genus of Monodonta. Sw. p. 352.

MONOCEROS. Lamarck. ACANTHIZA, Fischer. (Μονος, *monos*, single; Κερας, *ceras*, horn.) *Fam*. Purpurifera, Lam.—*Descr*. Ovate, thick, covered with a brown epidermis; spire short, consisting of few whorls; aperture emarginated anteriorly; columella rather flat; outer lip thick, with a prominent tooth near the extremity.—*Obs*. This genus resembles Purpura, in every respect, except in having the tooth from which the name is derived. A catalogue of 16 species by Mr. Sowerby, sen. is published with figures of 14, in parts 48 to 67 of the Conchological Illustrations by the author. The species belong to the South American coasts of the Pacific Ocean. Priority is claimed for the name ACANTHIZA (Fischer, 1807) for this genus. Pl. xix. fig. 417.

MONOCONDYLÆA. D'Orb. A sub-genus of Uniones, described as equivalve, inequilateral, sub-rotund or angulated; hinge consisting of a large, obtuse, round cardinal tooth in each valve, with no lateral teeth. Monocondylæ (Unio) Paraguayana. Pl. viii. fig. 149.

546. Purpura crispata. Polytropa, Sw.
547. Pseudoliva plumbea. Gastridium, Sow.
548. Fusus longevus. Clavalithes, Sw.
549. ——bulbiformis. Leiostoma, Sw.
550. Pyrella, Sw. Turbinella Spirillus, Auct.
551. Pleurotoma lineata. Tomella, Sw.
552. Pyrula melongena. *Gen.* Myristica, Sw.
553. Murex vitulinus, *Gen.* Vitulina, Sw.
554. Typhis Sowerbii.
555. A brown variety of the same.
556. Typhis Cumingii.
557. Voluta Vexilum. Harpula, Sw.
558. Mitra monodonta. Mitreola, Sw.
559. ——bicolor. Mitrella, Sw.
560. Columbella nitidella. *Gen.* Nitidella, Sw.
561. Oliva volutella. *Gen.* Lamprodoma, Sw.
562. ——marua.
563. Cypræa Globulus.
564. ——pulchella, fossil. *Gen.* Cyprædia, Sw.

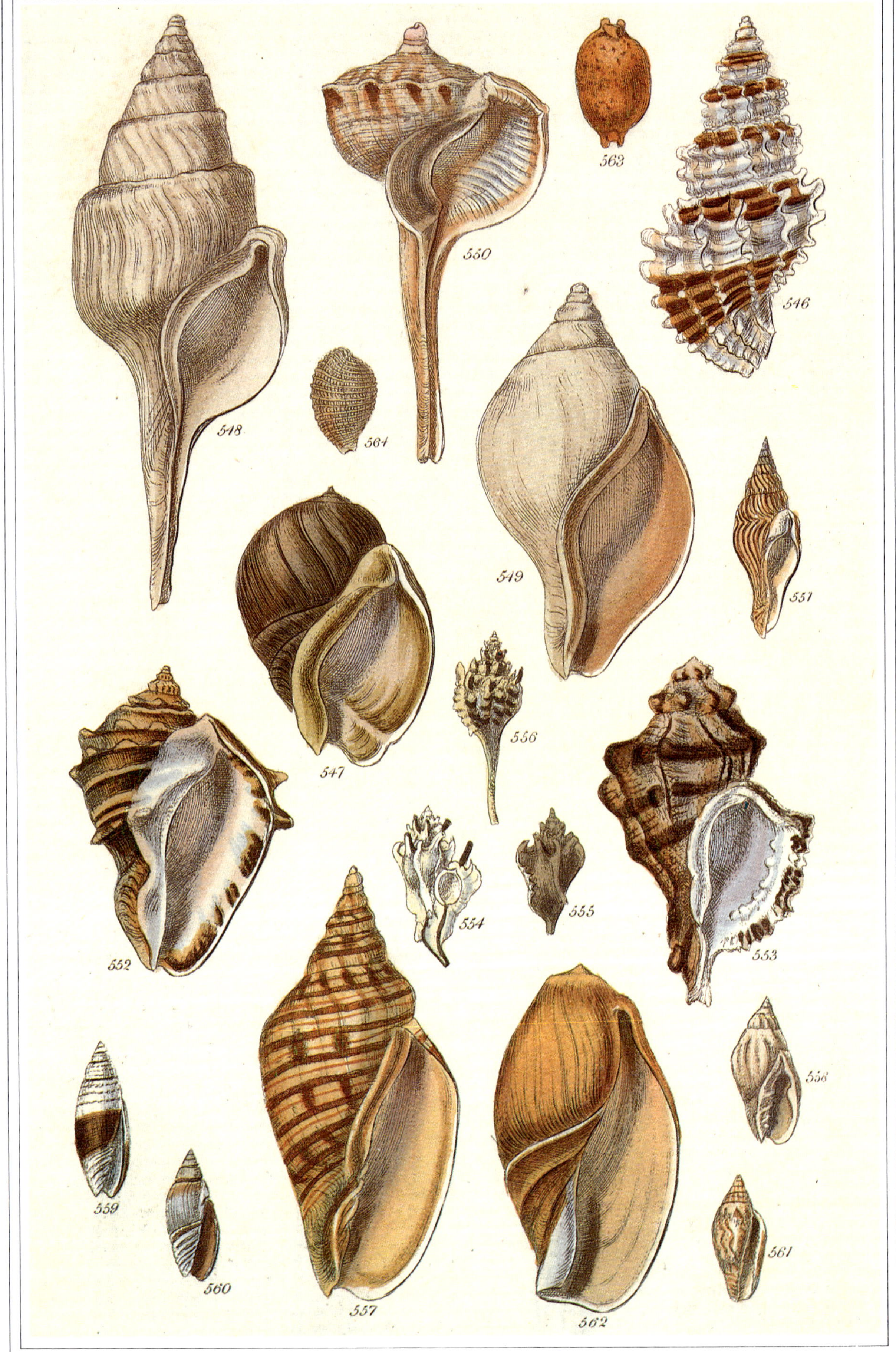

MONODONTA. Lam. ODONTIS, Sow. A genus separated from Trochus, Auct. on account of the tooth or notch with which the columella abruptly terminates. M. labeo. Pl. xvi. fig. 366.

MONOICA. Bl. The second sub-class of the class Paracephalophora, Bl. divided into the orders Pulmobranchiata, Chismobranchiata, Monopleurobranchiata, in the first section; and Aporobranchiata, Polybranchiata, Cyclobranchiata, Inferobranchiata, and Nucleobranchiata, in the second.

MONOMYARIA. Lam. (Μονος, *monos*, single; μυον, *myon*, muscle.) The second order of Conchifera, consisting of those bivalve shells which have but *one* principal muscular impression in each valve. The Monomyaria are thus divided: First section, containing the families Tridacnacea, Mytilacea, Malleacea; second section, containing the families Pectinides, Ostracea; third section, containing the families Rudistes, Brachiopoda.

MONOPLEUROBRANCHIATA. Bl. The second order of the first section of Paracephalophora Monoica, Bl. The animals are described as having the lungs branched, situated at the right side of the body and covered more or less completely by the operculiform mantle, in which there is sometimes enveloped either a flat or a more or less involute shell, with a large entire aperture. They have either rudimentary or auricular tentacula, or none. This order, which includes mollusca with haliotoid or patelliform shells, is divided into the following families: *Fam.* 1. Subaplysiacea; 2. Aplysiacea; 3. Patelloidea; 4. Acera.

MONOPTYGMA. Lea. A genus of small shells resembling Tornatella, but having a strong, oblique fold in the centre of the columellar lip. M. elegans. Pl. xv. fig. 344.

MONOTHALAMIA. (Μονος, *monos*, single; Θαλαμος, *thalamos*, chamber.) The second division of Cephalopoda, Lam. containing only one genus, namely Argonauta.

MONOTHYRA. A term used by Aristotle to designate spiral univalves.

MONOTIGMA. Gray. A genus founded on the species represented. It is a turrited shell, but we are unacquainted with the characters of the genus. Pl. xvi. fig. 371.

MONTACUTA. Turton, 1822. (See KELLIADÆ.) M. bidentata. Pl. xxvii. fig. 570.

MOPALIA. Gray. CHITON, Hindsii, &c.

MORIO. Montf. 1810. CASSIDARIA, Lamarck, 1812. (The former should be used.) C. Echinophora, fig. 407.

MOTHER OF PEARL. This beautiful substance, which is so much resorted to for ornamental purposes, constitutes the thickened coating of the internal surface of the shell named by scientific collectors, Meleagrina Margaritifera, commonly called the Pearl Oyster, a young specimen of which is figured (164) in our plates. The reason why this substance is called mother-of-pearl is that the true pearls are produced from its surface. They arise principally from accident or disease, and are sometimes artificially produced by pricking the outside of the shell while the animal is living. The animal is allowed to live until it has formed a pearl over the wounded part.

MOULINSIA. Grateloup. PUPINA, Vignard. A genus of small land shells with enamelled surface and spiral operculum. See PUPINA.

MOURETIA. Gray. "*Gadin*," Adanson. A genus of patelliform shells, described as differing from SIPHONARIA (the original Mouretia of Adanson) in the situation of the siphon, which in Mouretia is close to the place where the muscular impression is interrupted to leave a space for the head; while in Siphonaria it is nearly half way between the anterior and posterior ends of the shell.

MOUTH. The aperture or opening of univalve shells.

MULINIA. Gray. A genus composed of species of MACTRA, Auct. described as having the ligament (properly so called) internal, and lateral teeth simple. M. bicolor; Mactra, Auct. Pl. iv. fig. 82.

MULLERIA. Fer. *Fam.* Ostracea. Lam.—*Descr.* Irregular, subquadrate, inequivalve, inequilateral, foliaceous, attached, pearly within, green, horny without; hinge irregular, with a partly external ligament, passing to the interior, through a sort of sinus.—*Obs.* This remarkable shell resembles Etheria in general form and appearance, but is distinguished by having only one muscular impression. It is so rare that, although not very beautiful, a specimen has been known to produce £20. at a sale. Pl. xi, fig. 192.

MULTILOCULAR. Many chambered.

MULTISPIRAL. (*Multus*, many; *spira*, spire.) A term applied to a shell when the spire consists of numerous whorls; or to an operculum of numerous volutions.

MULTIVALVE. (*Multus*, many; *valva*, valve.) Consisting of numerous valves. There are three kinds of multivalve shells: 1st. Those in which the valves are arranged in pairs, and produce a flattened figure, as Pedunculated Cirripedes, fig. 34 to 43; 2nd. Those in which they are arranged circularly, as Sessile Cirripedes, the valves of which are of two kinds; the *opercular*, consisting of several valves, which close the aperture, and the *parietal*, consisting of those which surround the body of the animal in a circular form, fig. 14 to 33. 3rd. Those in which they are arranged in a straight line, as Chiton, fig. 227.

MUREX. Linn. (*A sharp rock.*) *Fam.* Canalifera, Lam. siphonostoma, Bl.—*Descr.* Turrited, ventricose, thick, with three or more longitudinal, continuous, branched, spinose or fringed varices; spire prominent, acute; aperture oval, terminating in a posterior, partly closed canal, outer lip varicose, inner lip smooth, laminar; operculum horny, concentric, pointed.—*Obs.* This genus contains some of the most exquisitely beautiful shells in existence, the richness of their colouring, the ramifications of their varices, would render most species the finest possible subject for the exercise of the painter's art in still life. The most remarkable are the Rosebud Murex, with its pink-tipt fringes, the Venus Comb, with its long rows of parallel spines; the Ducal Murex, the Royal Murex, and many others, which follow each other in a tortuous direction on the spire. The Ranellæ have only two rows of varices, and have a posterior as well as an anterior canal. The genus Typhis consists of several small species resembling Murex in every respect, excepting that of having a tubular opening on the upper part of the whorl between each varix. See TYPHIS. The most beautiful Murices are brought from tropical climates. Pl. xvii. fig. 395, 396. The genus Trophon, consisting of Murex Magellanicus, &c. may very well be separated from the other types. M. Reeve's Monograph of Murex, including the latter, contains nearly 200 species.

MURICANTHUS. Sw. A sub-genus of Murex, thus described: "Varices numerous, foliated; spire short; margin of the outer lip with a prominent tooth near the base; Radix. *Sw.* Zool. Ill. 2nd series, pl. 113, Melanomathus. En. Méth. 418. f. 2." Sw. p. 296. The latter of the two species quoted, however, does not agree with the description, having no prominent tooth on the margin of the outer lip.

MURICATED. (*Muricatus.*) Having sharp points or prickles.

MURICIDEA. Sw. A genus of "Muricinæ," Sw. thus described: "Spire more produced, as long or longer than the body whorl; varices numerous; no internal channel at the top of the aperture." Sw. p. 297, and consisting of the following incongruous species, "Lamellosa. Chem. f. 1823, 4. Magellanica. En. M. 419. f. 4. Peruviana. Ib. f. 5. senticosa, Ib. f. 3. scaber. En. Méth. 419. f. 6. hexagona. Ib. 418. f. 3. erinacea. Mart. f. 1026." Sw. p. 297.

MUSCULAR IMPRESSIONS are the marks or areas formed on the

interior surface of shells by the muscular fibres which attach the animals to them. Lamarck has divided the Conchifera into two kinds: 1st. Monomyaria, those which have but one adductor muscle, and consequently have but one impression in each valve, as the Common Oyster, fig. 180; wnd. The Dimyaria, those which have two, and consequently have two impressions in each valve. There are other smaller impressions in some shells besides the principal. The palleal impression is a mark or scar passing near the margin of the shell. See Introduction.

MYA. Auct. *Fam.* Myaria, Lam. Pyloridea, Bl.—*Descr.* Transverse, oval, thick, gaping at both extremities, rounded anteriorly, acuminated posteriorly; hinge with one large dilate, compressed tooth in one valve, and a suture in the other, containing the cartilage; muscular impressions two, distant, large, irregular; palleal impression with a large sinus.—*Obs.* Mya may be known by the large, prominent, broad tooth in one valve. In Anatina there is one in each valve, and, in Lyonsia, accessory pieces. Lutraria has cardinal teeth and a ligamentary pit. Few species of Mya are known. They belong to the Northern Hemisphere. M. truncata. Pl. iii. fig. 71.

MYCETOPODA or MYCETOPUS. D'Orb. *Fam.* Nayades, Lam. *Descr.* Shell elongated, soleniform, inequivalve, inequilateral, gaping anteriorly; muscular impressions very complex.—*Obs.* These shells are said to terebrate like Pholas. M. solenoides. Pl. viii. fig. 151.

MYARIA. Lam. A family belonging to Lamarck's order Conchifera Dimyaria. Containing the following genera:

1. Anatina. Ligament in a spoon-shaped prominence on the hinge of each valve, shell thin. Fig. 69.
2. Mya. Spoon-shaped prominence in one valve; shell thick. Fig. 71.
3. Anatinella. A spoon-shaped process in both valves. Fig. 70.
4. Lyonsia. An internal bony appendage on the hinge. Fig. 491, 492.
5. Myochama. Flat valve attached, a bony appendage on the hinge. Fig. 73.
6. Cleidothærus. Deep valve attached, a bony appendage. Fig. 75, 76.
7. Cumingia. Ligamentary pit in both valves, spoon-shaped. Fig. 87.

MYOCHAMA. Stutch. (*Mya* and *Chama.*) *Fam.* Myaria, Lam.—*Descr.* Inequivalve, irregular, attached, subequilateral; attached valve flat, with two marginal, diverging teeth, and one end of a little testaceous appendage fixed between them by a horny cartilage; free valve convex, with umbo incurved and two very minute, diverging teeth, between which the other end of the testaceous appendage is placed; external surface of both valves conforming to the grooves or undulations of the shell to which the specimen is attached; muscular impressions two in each valve; palleal impressions with a short sinus.—*Obs.* This new genus, of which only one species is known, the M. anomoides from New South Wales, differs from Anomia and Anatina in being attached by the surface of one of the valves, from which circumstance the word Chama is added to its name; the little testaceous appendage bringing it near the Myariæ. M. anomoides. Pl. iii. fig. 73, 74.

MYOCONCHA. Sow. (*Mya* and *Concha.*) *Fam.* Cardiacea, Lam. *Descr.* Oval, equivalve, oblique; umbones terminal; ventral margin rounded; hinge with an external ligament, and one oblique, elongated tooth in the left valve; impression of the mantle not sinuated.—*Obs.* The fossil genus has the general form of Mytilus or Modiola, but the hinge of the Conchæ generally.

MYODORA. Gray. Reeve, Conch. Icon. Bivalve, for the most part triangular, inæquivalve; left valve concave, right valve flat; anterior side rounded; posterior side flexuous, truncated; hinge, with linear projections on each side of a triangular ligamentary pit, and a bony appendage. *Ex.* Myodora striata, Pl. xxvii. fig. 574.

MYOPARA. Lea. (*Myoparo*, a piratical oar-galley.) *Fam.* Arcacea, Lam. A genus founded on a minute fossil bivalve shell, somewhat resembling Isocardia in form, but having a series of teeth placed on each side of the umbones. M. costatus, Pl. vii. fig. 135.

MYRISTICA. Sw. A genus of "Pyrulinæ," Sw. thus described: "Subpyriform; spire strong, spiny, or tuberculated, nearly as long as the base; umbilicus either partially or entirely concealed; inner lip vitreous, thin; the outer with an internal and ascending canal; the basal channel wide. Hippocastanea. En. M. 432. f. 4. lineata, Ib. f. 5. melongena. En. Méth. 435. f. 3. nodosa. Chem. 1564. 5." Sw. p. 307. *Ex.* P. Melongena. Pl. xxvi. fig. 552.

MYRTEA. Turt. Venus spinifera, Auct. Lucina spinifera Nonnull. The shells of this genus are described as "Oval, triangular, equivalve, nearly equilateral, closed. Hinge of one valve with a single tooth, and lateral one on each side; of the other valve with two teeth, the lateral ones obscure. Ligament external." British Channel and Mediterranean.

MYSCA. Turt. A genus composed of species of Unio, Auct. which are distinguished by having "strong, transverse, notched, cardinal and long lateral teeth." Unio pictorum.

MYSIA. Leach. A genus composed of Tellina rotundata, montagu and other similar species.

MYTILACEA. Bl. The fourth family of Lamellibranchiata, Bl. The shells are described as regular, equivalve, frequently with a thick, horny epidermis. A toothless hinge and a linear ligament. This family contains the genera Mytilus and Pinna.

MYTILACEA. Lam. A family belonging to the first section of Conchifera Monomyaria, Lam. described as having the ligament partly interior, occupying the greater part of the hinge line, which is straight. The shell is rarely foliaceous. The Mytilaceæ cannot easily be confounded with the Malleaceæ, because the former are generally regular and the latter are irregular, and have a thick internal coating of pearl, beyond which the external coating extends. The genera may be thus distinguished:

1. Mytilus. Umbones terminating in a point. Fig. 158.
2. Dreissina. The same, with a septiform plate. Fig. 159.
3. Modiola. Anterior margin rouonded beyond the umbones. Fig. 160.
4. Pinna. Open at the posterior extremity. Fig. 162.
5. Lithodomus. Cylindrical, living in holes. Fig. 161.

MYTILUS. Auct. *Fam.* Mytilacea. Lam.—*Descr.* Equivalve, cuneiform, oblique, smooth, with umbones terminal, pointed, and posterior side broad, rounded; hinge linear, with a long, partly internal ligament; muscular impressions two in each valve, that on the posterior side large, irregular; that on the anterior small; palleal impression irregular.—*Obs.* The Linnæan genus Mytilus included the Modiolæ, which differ from the mytili in the rounded anterior side; and the Pinnæ, which are large shells, gaping at the posterior extremity. M. achatinus, Pl. ix. fig. 158.

MYXOSTOMA. Troschel, 1847. Cyclostoma Peteveriana, Thesaurus Conchyliorum, Pl. xxv. fig. 100, 101.

NÆARA. Gray. A genus composed of Anatina longirostrum, Lam. and other similar species. Pl. xxiv. fig. 493, 494, 495.

NAIA. Sw. A sub-genus of Castalia, Lam. thus described: "Oval cardinal teeth beneath the bosses, and deeply sulcated, C. corrugata. *Lam.* En. Méth. 248. f. 8, picta. *Sw.* En. Méth. 248. f. 6." Sw. p. 379. Pl. viii. fig. 148.

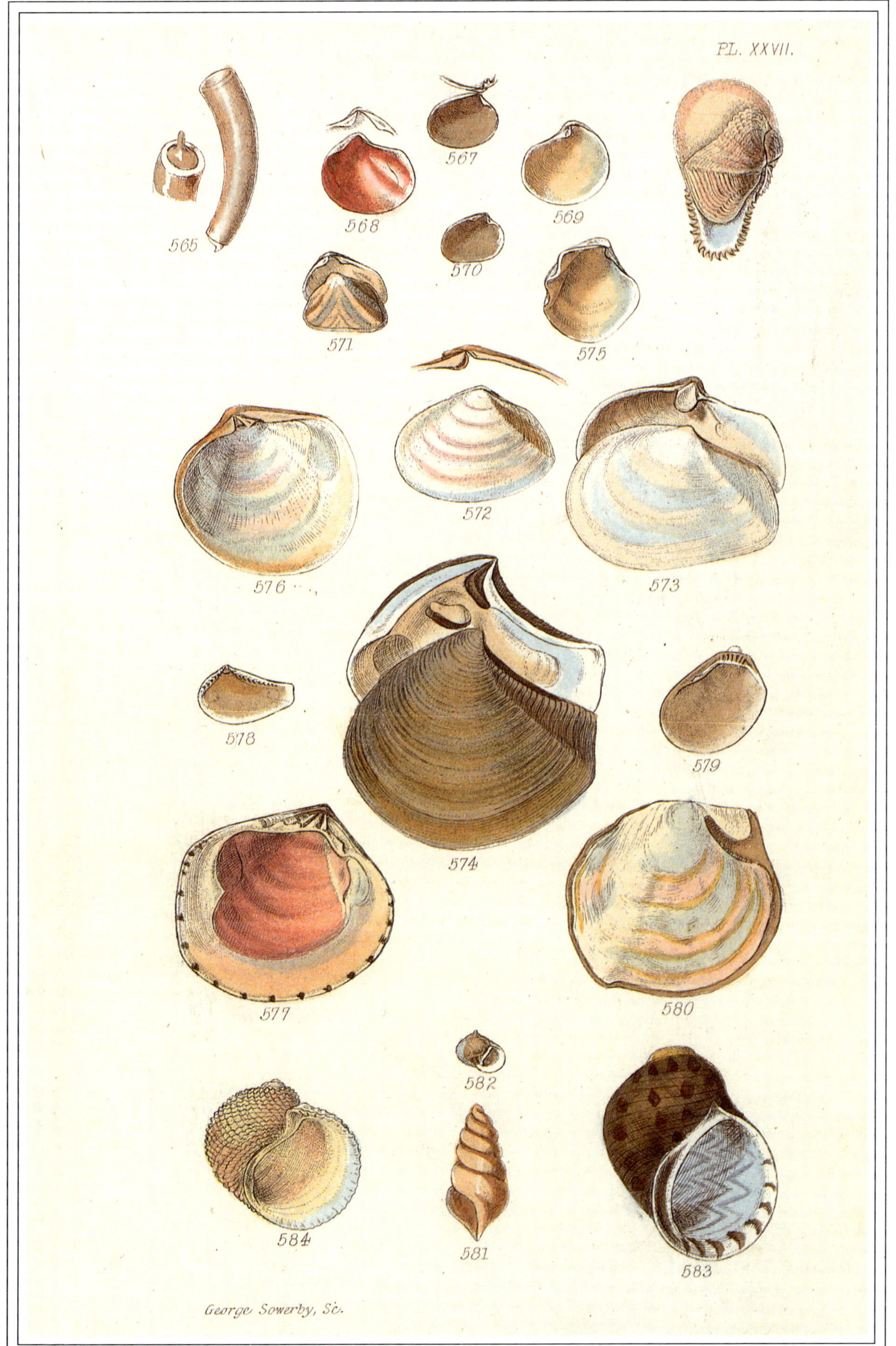

565. Cæcum trachea.
566. Triomphalia globosa.
567. Turtonia minuta.
568. Poronia rubra.
569. Kellia orbicularis.
570. Montacuta videntata.
571. Pythina Deshayesiana.

(567–571: See Kelladiæ)

572. Syndosmya alba.
573. Cochlodesma prætenuis.
574. Myodora striata.
575. Cryptodon sinuosum.
576. Diplodonta rotundata.
577. Circe scripta.
578. Leda caudatu.
579. Nucinella miliaris.
580. Hemipecten Forbesianus.
581. Spiralis.
582. Stoastoma pisum.
583. Paludomus neritoides.
584. Vanicoro cidaris.

NANINIA. Gray. A genus composed of the planorbicular species of Helix, with large umbilici, and outer lip thin, included in the sub-genus Helicella, Fer. *Ex.* H. citrina. Pl. xiv. fig. 280.

NASSA. Lam. A genus of small shells united to Buccinum by some authors, but separated by others on account of the little tooth-like projection terminating the columella. N. arcularia. Pl. xix. fig. 423.

NATICA. Brug. *Fam.* Neritacea, Lam. Hemicyclostomata, Bl.—*Descr.* Globose, thick, generally smooth; spire short, pointed, with few volutions; aperture semilunar, entire; outer lip thin; columellar lip oblique, nearly straight, callous; umbilicus with a spiral callosity, terminating behind the columella, and sometimes filling up the cavity; operculum shelly in some species, horny in others; epidermis thin, light, semitransparent.—*Obs.* The straight, callous, smooth edge of the columella and the callosity serve to distinguish this genus from Nerita, Neritina, Neritopsis and Helix. Pl. xv. fig. 327, 328.

NATICARIA. Sw. A sub-genus of Natica, thus described: "Oval; convex above; umbilicus small, open, placed very near the top of the aperture; inner lip reflected; small. N. melanostoma, Mart. 189. f. 1926, f1927. cancellata, *Sw.* Ib. 189. f. 1939. bifasciata, Griff. Cuv. 1. f. 2." Sw. p. 346.

NATICELLA. Guild. A sub-genus of Natica, thus described: "Operculum horny; shell globose, but generally depressed; umbilicus nearly filled up by a vitreous deposition of the inner lip; spire obtuse. N. aurantia. Mart. 189. f. 1934, 1935." Sw. p. 345.

NAVICELLA. Lamarck, 1822. Catillus, Humphrey (named in a catalogue) 1817. Cimber, Montf. 1810. (*A little ship.*) *Fam.* Neritacea, Lam. Hemicyclostomata, Bl.—*Descr.* Transversely oval, symmetrical, smooth; aperture entire, oval; dorsal surface convex; outer lip thin; inner lip flat, straight edged; spread over the front surface of the body whorl, and sometimes hiding the apex; apex incurved; operculum testaceous, flat, sub-quadrate, with a lateral articulation.—*Obs.* This well known genus, of which there are several species, is named Cimber by Montfort. The shells are brought from India, the Isle of Fance and the Moluccas. Fifteen species are enumerated in a Monograph of the genus by the Author, Thes. Conch. No. 11. Ex. n. Elliptica. See our Pl. xv. fig. 323.

NAUTELLIPSITES. Parkinson. A generic name proposed to include such species of Nautilus as have been compressed, so as to assume an oval instead of round form. The genus Ellipsolites of De Montfort consists of species of Ammonites similarly deformed.

NAUTILACEA. Bl. The fifth family of Polythalamacea, Bl. the shells of which are described as more or less discoidal, compressed, symmetrically convolute; the last whorl much larger than the others; which are entirely hidden beneath it and advancing beyond the last but one, so as constantly to form a large oval aperture, which is always, however, modified by the last whorl. The septa are united in the greater number of instances and pierced by a siphon. This family contains the genera Orbulites, Nautilus, Polystomella and Lenticulina.

NAUTILACEA. Lam. The sixth family of Polythalamous Cephalopoda, Lam. containing the genera Discorbites, Siderolites, Polystomella, Vorticialis, Nummulites, Nautilus. To these may be added Simplegas and Endosiphonites. Fig. 472 to 476.

NAUTILUS. Auct. (*A little boat.*) *Fam.* Nautilacea, Lam. and Bl.—*Descr.* Convolute, discoid, chambered, symmetrical; spire partly or entirely concealed by the last whorl; aperture modified by the last whorl, wide, sinuated on the dorsal margin; interior surface pearly; septa dividing the chambers simple: siphon discontinuous.—*Obs.* The shell named Nautilus by Pliny is the Argonauta of modern authors, a thin shell, not chambered. The Nautili are known from the Ammonites by the septa being simple, not sinuated as in the latter genus, and in general the volutions of the spire are not visible. Three or four species are known inhabitants of the Pacific Ocean and Australian Ocean. The fossil species are found in the tertiary, and also in the secondary strata, as low down as the Mountain limestone. Five species are described in Pl. ix. of the Author's Thesaurus Conchyliorum. N. pompilius, Frontispiece.

NAYADES. Lam. A family of the order Conchifera Dimyaria, Lam. described as containing fresh-water bivalve shells, with or without teeth on the hinge. They are all pearly within, and have a thick, rather smooth epidermis without. This family contains a great variety of shells, which have been separated into an immense number of genera, but which G. B. Sowerby, sen. gives very good reasons for uniting under one generic name. The most generally received distinctions are as follows:

1. Castalia. Two cardinal, one lateral, ribbed teeth. This genus is removed from the family of Trigonacea. Fig. 140.
2. Unio. Teeth various. Fig. 142, 145, 149, 148, 147, 151, 141.
3. Hyria. Trigonal, alated. Fig. 143, 150.
4. Anodon. No teeth. Fig. 152.
5. Iridina. Hinge crenated. Fig. 150.

NEARA. Gray, 1830. A genus composed of bivalve shells, formerly included in the genus Anatina, having a small spoon-shaped process and posterior lateral tooth in one valve, and an undefined ligamental pit, with no lateral tooth in the other. *Ex.* N. longirostratum, fig. 493, 4; and another species, fig. 495.

NECTOPODA. Bl. The first family Nucleobranchiata, Bl. containing the genera Carinaria and Firola; the latter is not a shell.

NEMATOPODA. Bl. The first class of the sub-type Malentozoa, Bl. containing all the mollusca with multivalve shells, except Chiton, and divided into the families Lapadicea and Balanidea, corresponding with Lamarck's sessile and pedunculated Cirripedes, and with the Linnean genus Lepas.

NEMATURA. Benson. *Fam.* Turbinacea, Lam.—*Descr.* Thin, nearly oval, somewhat compressed from back to front; spire acute, consisting of few rounded whorls; last whorl large, but contracted near the aperture; aperture small, oblique, rounded anteriorly; peritreme continuous, thin; operculum spiral, horny, with few volutions.—*Obs.* The distinguishing character of this genus is the contraciton of the last whorl near the aperture, in which respect it is nearly resembled by the shell called Cyclostoma lucidum. Two recent and one fossil species, all very minute, are described by Sowerby in Loudon's Magazine of Natural History, New Series. Pl. xiv. fig. 305.

NERINEA. Defr. *Fam.* Canalifera, Lam.—*Descr.* Turrited, oblong, sub-canaliculated, consisting of numerous whorls; aperture with a strong fold on the columella, one on the outer lip, and one on the inner lip at the edge of the body whorl.—*Obs.* This genus is only found in a fossil state, and usually in the Oolitic beds; no other shell resembles it; the strong, prominent folds on the three upper angles of the subquadrate aperture presents a singular appearance in a section. One species has been named N. Hieroglyphus. *Ex.* N. Goodhalii. Pl. xvi. fig. 374.

NERITA. Auct. *Fam.* Neritacea, Lam. Hemicyclostomata, Bl.—*Descr.* Smooth or ribbed, semiglobose; spire short, sometimes flat, consisting of few volutions; aperture large, semi-lunar; outer lip thick, entire; inner lip thickened, dentated at the edge, spread over the body whorl, forming a flattened disc; operculum shelly, spiral, with an appendage by which it is locked under the sharp edge of the columella.—*Obs.* These marine shells are known from Neritina by the thickness of the

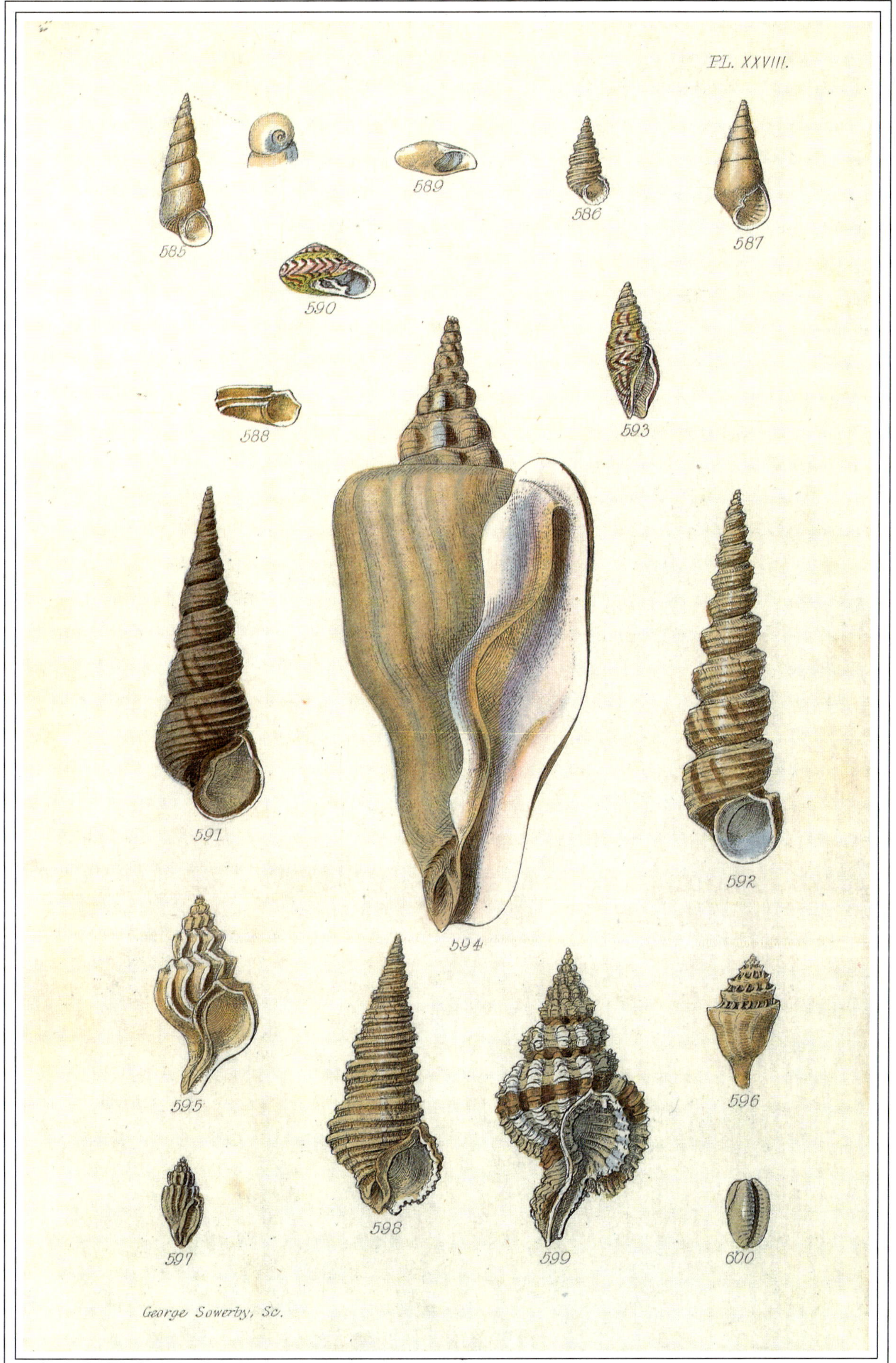

585. Chemnitzia varicula.
586. Alvania ascaris.
587. Odostomia plicata.
588. Adeorbis sub-carinata.
589. Teinostoma politum.
590. Camitia pulcherrima.
591. Mesalia brevialis.
592. Eglesia spirata.
593. Daphnella marmorata.
594. Cyrtulus serotinus.
595. Trophon scalariformis.
596. Conopleura striata.
597. Mangelia coronata.
598. Fastigiella carinata.
599. Hindsia acuminata.
600. Pachybathron marginelloides.

shell and the want of the thick, horny, dark coloured epidermis; from Natica, by the flat area produced by the spreading of the thickened columellar lip. N. Peloronta. Pl. xv. fig. 330.

NERITACEA. Lam. A family of the first order of Trachelipoda. Lam. containing the following genera:

1. NAVICELLA. Apex terminal, not spiral; inner lip septiform. Fig. 323.
2. NERITA. Columellar lip septiform, edge with distinct teeth; shell thick. Fig. 330.
3. NERITINA. Shell thin; columellar lip septiform, edge denticulated; generally a thick, dark coloured epidermis. Fig. 324 to 326.
4. NATICA. Having an umbilicus behind the columellar lip, with a spiral callosity. Fig. 327, 328.
5. NERITOPSIS. Edge of the columellar lip with a deep notch. Fig. 331.
6. PILEOLUS. Patelliform; apex central; columellar lip septiform, leaving the aperture small. Fig. 322.
7. JANTHINA. Columellar lip linear; aperture angulated. Fig. 333.

NERITELLA. Humph. 1797. NERITINA, Lamarck, 1822.

NERITINA. Lamarck, 1822. NERITELLA, Humph. *Fam.* Neritacea, Lam.—*Descr.* Thin, semiglobose, obliquely oval, smooth, flattish in front; spire short, sometimes depressed, consisting of few rapidly increasing whorls; aperture semicircular; outer lip thin, sharp; columellar lip broad, flat, its inner edge straight, denticulated; operculum testaceous, semicircular, sub-spiral, with an articulating process on the inner edge.—*Obs.* This genus of fresh-water shells differs from Nerita in the minuteness of the denticulation of the columellar, as well as in the characters mentioned in our observations upon the latter genus. N. Spinosa, (Clithon, Montf.) fig. 352. N. virginea, fig. 324. N. perversa, Lam. (Velates, Montf.) fig. 326. The Monograph, in Pl. 10 of the Thesaurus Conchyliorum, contains 116 species. Our Plate xv. fig. 324, 325.

NERITOPSIS.Gray. *Fam.* Neritacea, Lam.—*Descr.* Sub-globose, thick, cancellated; spire short, composed of few rapidly increasing whorls; aperture transverse, sub-orbicular; outer lip thickened within; columellar lip thick, rather flat, with a large rounded notch in the centre of its inner edge.—*Obs.* This genus most nearly resembles Nerita, from which it differs in the peculiar notch of the columella. N. granosa. Pl. xv. fig. 331.

NICANIA. Leach. ASTARTE, Sowerby. The same as CRASSINA of Lamarck.

NEVERITA. Risso, 1826. NATICA glaucina, and similar species.

NISSO. Risso, 1826. The perforate species of EULIMA; Genus BONELLIA, Deshayes, 1836.

NITIDELLA. Sw. A genus of "Columbellinæ," Sw. thus described: "Bucciniform, small, ovate, smooth, glassy; aperture effuse; outer lip slightly thickened, faintly inflexed, and generally striated internally; inner lip somewhat flattened above; base of the pillar with one or two slight internal folds, or a single angular projection. Columbella nitida, *Lam.* (fig. 17, *c.* 151.)" Sw. p. 313. Pl. xxvi. fig. 560.

NOBIA. Leach. *Order*, Sessile Cirripedes, Lam. This genus resembles Pyrgoma, Auct. consisting of a conicial paries, supported upon a funnel-shaped cavity in the madrepore, but differs in its operculum, which consists of two valves, whereas that of Pyrgoma has four. N. grandis. Pl. i. fig. 29.

NODOSARIA. Lam. and ORTHOCERA have been united by Sowerby under the name of the first. *Fam.* Orthocerata, Lam. and Bl.—*Descr.* Straight, chambered, elongated; chambers more or less ventricose; septa perforated by a central siphon.—*Obs.* This genus consists only of fossils found in sub-appenine tertiary beds. It is placed by De Blainville in one of his divisions of the genus Orthoceras, which is characterized as "species not striated, and with chambers very much inflated." N. æqualis. Pl. xxii. fig. 465.

NODOSE. Having tubercles or knobs.

NOGROBS. Montf. A fossil appearing from the figure and description to resemble Belemnites.

NONION. Montf. A genus of microscopic Foraminifera.

NONIONINA. D'Orb. A genus of microscopic Foraminifera.

NOTREMA. Rafinesque. A shell described as composed of three integral valves, concerning which De Blainville puts the query, "ne seroit-ce pas plutôt une Balanide mal observée?"

NOVACULINA. Benson. (*Novacula*, a razor.) *Fam.* Solenacaea, Lam.—*Descr.* Equivalve, inequilateral, transversely elongated; external ligament communicating with the interior of the shell by an oblique channel; beaks prominent; hinge line nearly straight, with one narrow curved cardinal tooth in one valve, entering between two similar teeth in the other; siphonal scar long; extremities of the shell gaping; epidermis thin, light brown, folding over the edges and connecting the dorsal margins. *Hab.* Jumna, Gooti, and Ganges. Pl. iii. fig. 63.

NUCINELLA. S. Wood. Biv. Crag. 1850. A genus formed for the reception of a very minute crag fossil belonging to the same family as the Nuculæ and Pectunculi; but differing in the arrangement of the teeth. N. miliaris. Pl. xxvii. fig. 579.

NUCLEOBRANCHIATA. Bl. The fifth order of the second section of Paracephalophora Monoica, Bl. the shells of which are described as symmetrical, more or less curved, or longitudinally rolled up and very thin. This order contains, *Fam.* 1. Nectopoda, containing Carinaria; *Fam.* 2. Pteropoda, containing Atlanta, Spiratella and Argonauta.

NUCLEUS. (*A kernel.*) Anything forming a centre around which matter is gathered. The nucleus of shells is the first formed part; the first deposit of shelly matter to which the successive layers are added; the apex of the spiral cone, of which most shells are composed. (See CONE.) The nucleus is formed within the egg in oviparous, and within the old shell in viviparous mollusca. It is frequently more transparent and light than the remainder of the shell, and sometimes falls off; when this occurs the shell is said to be decollated.

NUCULA. Lamarck, 1801. (*A small nut.*) *Fam.* Arcacea, Bl. and Lam.—*Descr.* Equivalve, inequilateral, transverse, covered with an epidermis; hinge linear, with a series of sharp, angulated teeth, arranged in a line on each side of the umbones, and central ligamentary pit; muscular impressions two, simple; palleal impressions not sinuated.—*Obs.* The row of teeth on each side of the umbones, and the ligamentary pit in the centre of the hinge prevent the pretty little shells of this genus from being confounded with any other. Thirty-four figures are enumerated in the catalogue by Sowerby, sen. which accompanies the Conchological Illustrations of the author. The new species, to the amount of 24, have been figured in parts 14 to 16, of the above mentioned work. Recent Nuculæ are found from the frozen to the torrid zones, and the fossil species occur in nearly all the beds from the Pliocene to the Carboniferous system. Pl. vii. fig. 137.

NUMMULACEA. Bl. The third family of Cellulacea, Bl. described as containing shells or calcareous bodies, which are characterized as discoidal, lenticular; without the slightest traces of whorls to be seen externally. The whorls are numerous, internal, and divided into a great number of cells, which are separated from each other by imperforate septa. This family contains the genera Nummulites, Siderolites, Vorticialis, Helicites, Orbiculina, Placentula.

NUMMULITES. Lam. (*Nummus*, money.) *Fam.* Nautilacea Lam.—*Descr.* Orbicular, convolute, shewing no trace of spire externally; interior divided into cells spirally arranged.—*Obs.* The singular fossils composing this genus receive their name from their external resemblance to a battered coin. N. lenticulina. Pl. xxii. fig. 472, 473.

NUX. Humph. CYCLAS, Lam.

NYMPHACEA. Lam. A family belonging to the order Conchifera Dimyaria, Lam. Ligament external, placed on a prominent fulcrum. This family contains the following genera:

1. SANGUINOLARIA. Rostrated, gaping; two cardinal teeth in each valve, including *Soletellina* and *Lobaria*. Fig. 98, 99.
2. PSAMMOBIA. Quadrate; valves closed, including Psammotæa. Fig. 100.
3. CORBIS. Thick, fimbriated; a cardinal tooth in the centre of a pit. Fig. 101.
4. GRATELOUPIA. A series of small teeth filling a triangular area. Fig. 102.
5. EGERIA. One single and one double cardinal tooth. Fig. 103.
6. LUCINA. Rounded; anterior muscular impression tongue-shaped. Fig. 104.
7. TELLINA. An anterior fold in the ventral margin; lateral teeth. Fig. 105, 106.
8. TELLINIDES. No anterior fold; no lateral teeth. Fig. 107.
9. DONAX. Margin denticulated; shell wedge-shaped. Fig. 108.
10. CAPSA. Margin not denticulated, no lateral teeth. Fig. 109.

OBELISCUS. Humph. PYRAMIDELLA (part.) Lamarck.

OBLIQUE. (*obliquus*, lat.) In a slanting direction. The whorls of spiral univalves generally take an oblique direction in reference to the imaginary axis of the shell. A bivalve is said to be oblique when it slants off from the umbones. An example of this is seen in Avicula, fig. 163.

OBSOLETE. (*obsoletus*, lat.) Worn out, out of use. This term is used to express an indistinctness of character, which sometimes is used to express an indistinctness of character, which sometimes results from the action of sea-water upon unprotected parts of the shell, and sometimes from the deposits of enamel formed in age, and covering the early striæ, ribs, teeth, &c. thereby rendering them less acute.

OBTUSE. (*obtusus*, blunt.) The application of this term is not peculiar to conchology. It is most frequently used to express the character of the spire. *Ex.* The apex of Megaspira, fig. 294.

OCEANUS. Montf. ("Corne d'ammon vivant," Fr.) NAUTILUS umbilicatus, Auct.

OCTHOSIA. Ranz. CLITIA, Leach.

OCTOCERA. Bl. The first family of the order Cryptodibranchiata, Bl. containing the genus Octopus. A species of which being found in the Argonauta, or Paper Sailor, has given rise to the long continued controversy as to whether it is really the constructor of the shell, or whether it is a mere pirate, and having destroyed the true animal of the Argonaut, has possessed itself of the habitation. This question is now set at rest. See ARGONAUTA.

OCTOGONAL. (*octogonum*.) Having eight angles. For an example, see Dentalium, fig. 2.

OCTOMERIS. Sow. (οκτω, *octo*, eight; μερος, *meros*, part.) *Fam.* Balanidea, Bl.—*Order*, Sessile Cirripedes, Lam.—*Descr.* Eight principal valves circularly arranged, forming a compressed cone, attached by a jagged base; aperture enclosed by an operculum, consisting of four valves in pairs.—*Obs.* The only genus of Sessile Cirripedes agreeing with this in the number of principal valves in Catophragmus, Sow. which is, however, sufficiently distinguished by the several rows of smaller valves by which the principals are surrounded at the base. O. angulosus. Pl. i. fig. 24.

ODONTIS. Sow. MONODONTA, Lam.

ODOSTOMIA. Fleming, 1842. *Descr.* "Shell conical; aperture ovate; peristome incomplete, retrally, and furnished with a tooth on the pillar." A genus originally composed of several small species of land shells. Turbo plicatus, Spiralis, Unidentatus, &c. Mont. Since applied to some minute marine shells, nearly resembling Chemnitzia. *Ex.* O. plicata. Pl. xxviii. fig. 587.

OLIVA. Auct. (*An olive.*) *Fam.* Convoluta, Lam. Angyostomata. Bl.—*Descr.* Oblong, cylindrical, thick, smooth, shining; spire very short, with sutures distinct, aperture elongated, notched at both extremities; outer lip generally thick; columella thick, obliquely striated, terminated by a tumid, oblique, striated varix; a raised band passing round the lower part of the body whorl.—*Obs.* The shells composing this well known genus present a great variety of rich markings and brilliant colours. They are marine and tropical. Fossil species are found sparingly in the London Clay and Calcaire-grossièr. The ancillariæ are distinguished from this genus by the sutures of the whorls being covered by enamel. Mr Reeve's Monograph contains 99 species. The genus is thus divided in the British Museum arrangement, STREPHONA and OLIVELLA, the O. porphyria and the common form; SCAPHULA, the wide-mouthed cymbiform species, O. auricularia; AGARONIA, Gray, the thin subulate species, with the mouth widening at the bottom. Pl. xxi. fig. 457.

OLIVELLA. Sw. A genus of "Olivinæ," Sw. thus described: "Oliviform; spire (typically) rather produced; the tip acute; inner lip not thickened; outer lip straight; base of the pillar curved inwards, and marked by two strong plaits; upper plaits obsolete or wanting; aperture effused at the base only; biplicata, Tank. Cat. 2332. purpurata. Zool. Ill. ii. 58, f. 1. mutabilis. *Say*. eburnea. Zool. Ill. ii. 58, f. 2. conoidalis. *Lam*. No. 57. oryza. *Lam*. No. 62."

OLYGYRA. Say. "Helicina," Lamarck, was first applied by Lamarck to Rotella, and afterwards to the genus of operculated land shells, to which "Olygyra" should perhaps in strictness be now given.

OMALAXIS. Desh. Subsequently BIFRONTIA. Desh. Fig. 354.

ONISCIA. Sow. (G. B.) *Fam.* Purpurifera, Lam. Entomostomata, Bl.—*Descr.* Oblong, sub-ovate, slightly turbinated, cancellated; spire short; aperture elongated; terminating anteriorly in a very short, recurved canal; outer lip thickened, denticulated within; inner lip spread over a portion of the body whorl, granulated.—*Obs.* The granulated inner lip is the principal character by which this genus is distinguished from Cassidaria. In Oniscia the canal is not so produced. Mr. Reeve's Monograph contains 7 species. C. oniscus, Pl. xviii. fig. 409.

ONUSTUS. Humph. A genus proposed by Humphrey and adopted by Swainson who describes it thus: "Shell trochiform, the surface irregular, and often covered with extraneous bodies, cemented and incorporated with the calcareous substance of the shell; the under part of the body whorl flattened or concave, umbilicate. O. Solaris. Mart. 173. f. 1700, 1701. Indicus. Ib. 172. f. 1697, 1698." A thin lamina extending beyond the angle of the body whorl from the outer lip gives a concavity to Phorus Indicus, and is considered by some authors sufficient to distinguish it from the genus Phorus.

ONYTHOCHITON. Gray. Chiton undulatus, and similar species.

OPERCULAR. Of, or belonging to, the operculum. A term applied to the valves which compose the operculum of multivalve shells, as distinguished from the parietal valves, or those which are arranged circularly and form the body of the shell.

OPERCULINA. D'Orb. A genus of microscopic Foraminifera.

OPERCULUM. (*A cover or lid.*) The plate or plates with which many molluscous animals enclose the aperture of their shells, when retired within them. The operculum is sometimes *horny*, as in Trochus; and sometimes *testaceous* or shelly, as in Turbo. It is *spiral* when from a central or sub-central nucleus, the successive layers take a revolving direction, as in Trochus. It is *concentric* or *annular* when the outside edge of each layer entirely surrounds the preceding one. It is *unguiculated*, when the laminæ are placed side by side, as in Purpura. The opercula of multivalve shells are composed of two or four pieces, which are called the opercular valves. The shelly or membranaceous plate with which some of the animals enclose the aperture of their shells, during the wintry part of the year, for the purpose of protecting them while in a torpid state, and which they get rid of by dissolving the edges, when preparing to emerge from their temporary retirement, must not be considered as the operculum, as it does not belong to or form part of either the animal or its shell, but is produced for the occasion by a secretion of the animal, being deposited in a soft state and subsequently hardening. It is called the *epiphragm*, and may easily be distinguished from the true operculum by the texture, and by the circumstance of their being soldered to the edge of the aperture. The operculum, on the contrary, is moveable, and is always composed of a series of successive layers, corresponding with the growth of the shell.

OPIS. Defr. A genus described by De Blainville as consisting of species of Trigonia which have the umbones sub-spiral, with a large, striated tooth on the hinge. Opis cardissoides, Trogonia, Lam. Opis similis, Sow. Min. Con. pl. 232. f. 2.

ORAL. (*Os, oris*, mouth.) Applied to that part of a shell which corresponds with the mouth of the animal, but very seldom used in this sense.

ORBICULA. Lam. (*Orbis*, an orb.) *Fam.* Brachipoda, Lam. Palliobranchiata, Bl.—*Descr.* Inequivalve, irregular, sub-orbicular, compressed, attached by a fibrous substance passing through a fissure near the centre of the lower valve; upper valve patelliform, with the umbo central; muscular impressions four in each valve, semilunar. South America and West Indies.—*Obs.* Discina, Lam. is an Orbicula. Crania is known from this genus by having no fissure in the lower valve, but being attached by its substance. Hipponyx has only two muscular impressions in each valve. Mr. Sowerby's Monograph of this genus in the author's Thesaurus Conchyliorum contains 6 species. O. lævis, Pl. xi. fig. 201.

ORBICULAR. (*Orbiculus*, a little orb.) Of a round or circular form.

ORBICULINA. Lam. A genus of microscopic Foraminifera.

ORBIS. Lea. A minute fossil, described as "orbicular, with flat quadrate whorls and aperture square," in other respects resembling Solarium. O. Rotella, Pl. xvi. fig. 355, 356.

ORBITINA. Risso. A genus said to be established upon the nuclei of two land shells.

ORBULITES. Lam. a genus separated from Ammonites on account of the last volution covering the spire. This is generally considered as characterizing the Nautili, and distinguishing them from the Ammonites; but there are so many gradations that it seems impossible to maintain the distinction in this respect. Fig. 479, O. crassus, fig. 480, O. discus. Pl. xxii.

OREAS. Montf. Part of Cristellaria, Lam. A genus of microscopic Foraminifera.

ORTHIS. Dalman. (ὀρθος, *orthos*, straight.) *Fam.* Brachiopoda, Lam. One of the generic divisions of Brachiopoda by Dalman, thus described: "Hinge rectilinear, with umbones distant; the larger valve with a transverse, basal, smooth area, with a triangular pit." O. basalis, Pl. xi. fig. 207.

ORTHOCERA. Lam. See Nodosaria.

ORTHOCERATA. Lam. A family of Polythalamous Cephalopoda, Lam. containing the following genera:–

1. Conularia. Conical, externally striated; no siphon. Fig. 469.
2. Amplexus. Cylindrical; margins of the septa reflected. Fig. 463.
3. Orthoceratites. Straight, gradually conical; septa simple; siphon central. Fig. 464.
4. Nodosaria. Divided externally into lobes. Fig. 465.
5. Belemnites. Straight, conical; septa simple; siphon lateral; apex solid; internal cast, or nucleus, pyramidal, separable. Fig. 466 to 468.
6. Conilites. Like Belemnites, but external shell thin at the apex. Fig. 470.

ORTHOCERATA. Bl. The first family of Polythalamacea, Bl. containing the genera Belemnites, Conularia, Conilites, Orthoceras and Baculites. De Blainville remarks that the genera included in this family are all fossils, and known very imperfectly, in consequence of the greater number of the specimens being only casts.

ORTHOCERATITES. Auct. *Fam.* Orthocerata, Lam. and Bl.—*Descr.* Straight, conical, divided into numerous chambers by simple septa perforated by a central siphon. O. annulata, Pl. xxii. fig. 464.

OSTEODESMA. Desh. Periploma, Schum.

OSTRACEA. (*Ostracées*, Lam.) A family belonging to the second section of the order Conchifera Monomyaria, the shells of which are described as irregular, foliaceous, sometimes papyraceous, with the ligament wholly or partly interior. The principal difference between the Ostracea and the Pectinides consists in the absence of the auricles and the foliated structure of the shells, for, although the Spondylus has ex-foliations or spines upon the external surface, the shell itself is compact and firm. This family contains the genera Gryphæa, Ostrea, Vulsella, Placuna, Anomia, which may be thus distinguished:–

1. Pedum. Flat, turned up at the sides, an hiatus for the passage of a byssus. A triangular disc on the hinge. Fig. 179.
2. Ostrea. Foliaceous, irregular, hinge on a small triangular disc. Including Dendostrea, Ostræa, Exogyra, Gryphæa. Fig. 180 to 183.
3. Placuna. Two diverging ribs near the umbones. Fig. 184.
4. Placunanomia. The same, but attached by fibres passing through a hole in one valve. Fig. 189 to 191.
5. Anomia. No hinge ribs, attached by a bony substance passing through a hole in one valve. Fig. 189 to 191.
6. Vulsella. Tongue-shaped, a ligamentary pit on the hinge. Fig. 185.
7. Mulleria. Doubtful. Fig. 192.

OSTRACEA. Bl. The first family of the order Lamellibranchiata, Bl. containing the genera Anomia, Placuna, Harpax, Ostrea (including Dendostrea, Sw.) and Gryphæa.

OSTREA. Auct. (οστρεον, *ostreon*, a bone.) *Fam.* Ostracea Lam. and Bl.—*Descr.* Irregular, inequivalve, generally inequilateral, foliaceous, attached by part of the lower valve; hinge sometimes slightly crenated; destitute of teeth; with a ligament spread upon the lower part of a central, triangular area, which is divided into three parts; upper valve much flatter than the lower; muscular impressions one in each valve,

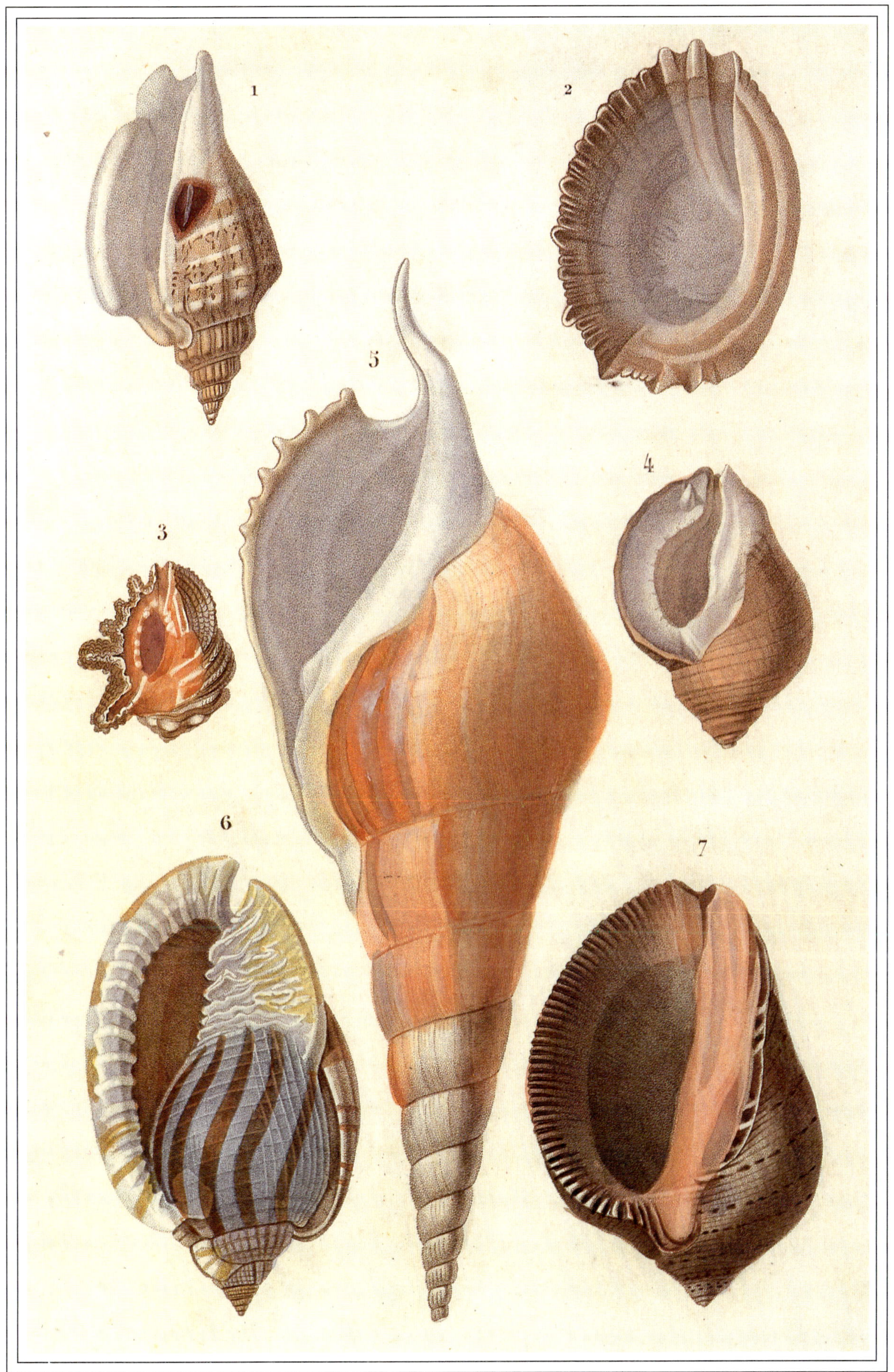

1. *Strombe variable*. (Strombus variabilis, *Swain.*)
2. *Concholépas du Pérou*. (Concholepas Peruvianus, *Lamk.*)
3. *Ricinule digitée*. (Ricinula digitata, *Lamk.*)
4. *Licorne lèvre épaisse*. (Monoceros crassilabrum, *Lamk.*)
5. *Rostellaire bec-arqué*. (Rostellaria curvirostris, *Lamk.*)
6. *Casque zèbre*. (Cassis undata, *Martini.*)
7. *Pourpre persique*. (Purpura persica, *Lamk.*)

large, sub-central, sub-orbicular; with one very minute.—*Obs*. The Linnean genus Ostrea includes the Pectens and many other genera so different from each other, that without any desire to increase the number of genera, it was found necessary by subsequent authors to separate them. The common Oyster is the type of this genus as at present constituted, and is well known to be abundant in various parts of the world. Those which depart farthest from this type are the Gryphæa, Lam. with a prominent, incurved umbo in the lower valve. The Dendostrea, Sw. with margins characterized by strongly angulated folds, throw out arms from the lower valve, by which they are attached to stems of sea-weed, &c. Fig. 180, O. edulis. Fig. 181. O. folium. (Dendostrea, Sw.) Fig. 182, Gryphæa incurva. Fig. 183, Exogyra conica. Pl. x.

OTIDES. Bl. The first order of Scutibranchiata, Bl. containing the genera Haliotis and Ancylus.

OTION. Leach. (ωτιον, a little ear.) Included by Darwin in his work on Cirripedes, with Cineras, under the name Conchoderma defers. *Order*. Pedunculated Cirripedes, Lam.—*Descr*. Body sub-quadrate, supported on a fleshy pedicle with a gaping aperture and two posterior auricular tubes; valves five, separate, two semilunar, placed at the sides of the aperture, two terminal, very small, one dorsal, minute.—*Obs*. Otion differs from Cineras in having two cylindrical posterior tubes, and in the extreme minuteness of three out of five of the valves. Found on spars floating in the sea, &c. (Lepas aurita, Linn.) O. Cuvieri. Pl. ii. fig. 43.

OTIS. Humph. Auricula, Lam.

OVATE. (*Ovatus*.) Egg-shaped or oval.

OVEOLITHES. Montf. A microscopic shell resembling Bulla.

OVIPAROUS MOLLUSCA. Those which produce their young in eggs. Used in distinction from the Viviparous Mollusca, whose young are perfectly formed before they leave the body of the parent.

OUTER LIP. See Labrum.

OVULUM. Brug. (*Ovum*, an egg, dim.) *Fam*. Convoluta, Lam. Angyostomata, Bl.—*Descr*. Ovate or fusiform, smooth, convolute, spire covered; aperture narrow, with a canal at each extremity; outer lip crenulated, inflected; inner lip smooth, callous towards the spiral extremity; dorsal area wide, sometimes indistinctly marked.—*Obs*. The Ovula were placed by Linnæus in his genus Bulla, from which they are very remote. They differ from Cypræa in having the inner lip smooth. We have given representations of their different forms as follows: O. Ovum, fig. 442. O. verrucosum, (Calpurnus Montf.) fig. 441. O. Volva, the weaver's shuttle (Radius, Montf.) fig. 422. O. gibbosum, (Ultimus, Montf.) fig. 443. The Monograph in the Thesaurus Conchyliorum , Pl. 9, enumerates forty-eight species of this beautiful genus of shells. See our plate xx. fig. 441 to 443.

OXYANASPIS. Darwin. Cirripedes. Lepadæ, P. 133. Pl. iii. fig. 1. A genus of Pedunculated Cirripedes, the shells of which are thus described, "Valves 5, approximate; scuta with their umbones in the middle of the occludent margin; carina rectangularly bent, extending up between the terga, with the basal end simply concave."

OXYSTOMATA. Bl. The fifth family of Asiphonbranchiata, Bl. This family appears to have been formed for the express purpose of providing a place in the system for the genus Janthina, which seems to bear so little analogy with other genera of Mollusca, that conchological writers have been puzzled to known where to place it.

PACHYBATHRON. Gaskoin. A genus established for the reception of a singular shell resembling Marginella, but having the columellar lip spread over the body whorl, and the teeth continued across it in folds, giving the front of the shell the appearance of a Cypræa. I think Marginella Kieneriana, Petit. Sowerby's Thesaurus Conchyliorum, Pl. lxxviii. fig. 198, 199, 200, will be found to approach this shell, and almost lead it into the Marginellæ. *Ex*. P. Marginelloides. *Gaskoin*. West Indies. Pl. xxviii. fig. 600.

PACHYLABRA. Sw. Pachystoma, Guild. A sub-genus of Ampullaria, the outer lip of which is thickened within. *Ex*. Ampullaria globosa.

PACHYMYA. Sow. (παχυς, *pachus*, thick, and *Mya*.) *Fam*. Cardiacea? Lam.—*Descr*. Obliquely elongated, equivalve, thick sub-bilobed, with beaks near the anterior extremity; ligament partly immersed attached to prominent fulcra.—*Obs*. This singular fossil is shaped like Modiola, but the shell being extremely thick, and the ligament attached to a prominent fulcrum, it is difficult to know where to place it. Pachyma Gigas. Pl. vii. fig. 130.

PACHYSTOMA. Guild. (παχυς, *pachus*, thick; στόμα, *stoma*, mouth.) A genus composed of such species of Ampullaria, Auct. as have the edge of the aperture thickened and grooved within so as to form a sort of ledge upon which the operculum rests. Ampullaria globosa and corrugata are examples of this variation. The name Pachylabra is given to such species by Swainson, who objects to the above name on account of its having been previously used to a genus of fishes. Pl. xxv. fig. 539.

PACHYTOMA. Sw. A sub-genus of Helicina, thus described, "Aperture entire; the inner lip very thick; the spiral whorls hardly convex; P. occidentalis. Zool. J. iii. 15. f. 6–10. viridis, Zool. Journ. i. pl. 6. f. 7." Sw. p. 337.

PACLITES. Montf. A genus composed of species of Belemnites, Auct. described towards the extremity, with a pore, at the apex, and a straight lengthened aperture. *Ex*. B. ungulatus, Bl.

PÆCILASMA. Darwin. Cirrip. P. 99, including Trilasmis, Hinds. A genus of Pedunculated Cirripedes, the shell of which is thus described, "Valves 3, 5, or 7 proximate; carina extending only to the basal points of the terga; with its lower end either truncated or produced into a deeply imbedded disc, scuta nearly oval, with their umbones at the vertical angle."

PADOLLUS. Montf. 1810. A genus composed of species of Haliotis, with a strongly marked spiral groove. *Ex*. H. tricostalis, Lam. Pl. xv. fig. 339.

PAGODELLA. Swainson. Should be Pagodus, Gray. A sub-genus of Trochus, thus described: "Trochiform; generally thin, and always not pearlaceous; aperture and pillar perfectly united and entire; operculum horny. P. major. Mart. 163. f. 1541, 1542. P. tectum. P. persicum. Ib. f. 1543, 1544." Sw. p. 351.

PAGODUS. Gray, 1839. See Pagodella.

PALLEAL IMPRESSION. (*Pallium*, a mantle.) The mark or groove formed in a bivalve shell by the muscular attachment of the mantle, which, being always found near the margin of the shell, is sometimes termed the marginal impression. In bivalves with two muscular impressions it passes from one to the other. If in passing, it takes a bend inwards posteriorly, it is said to be sinuated, and that part is called by Mr. Gray, the Siphonal scar.

PALLIOBRANCHIATA. Bl. The first order of the class Acephalophora. Bl. The animals of this order are described as more or less compressed, included between the two valves of a bivalve shell, one inferior, the other superior, joining at the back and opening in front. The Palliobranchiata in the system of De Blainville correspond with the Brachiopoda in the system of Lamarck, and the shells may be known by their being symmetrical. This order contains in the first section of symmetrical bivalves, Lingula, Terebratula, Thecidium, Strophomena, Plagiostoma, Dianchora and Podopsis; in the second section, Orbicula and Crania.

PALMATED. Flattened like a palm, as the fronds or fringes of some Murices.

PALMINA. Gray. Differing from Otion in having but one auricle.

PALUDINA. Lam. *Fam.* Peristomata, Lam. Cricostomata, Bl.—*Descr.* Varying in form from oval to globose, in some instances oblong, covered with a greenish horny epidermis; spire acute, composed of rounded whorls; aperture ovate; peritreme entire, slightly modified by the last whorl; operculum horny, concentric. Europe, North America, East Indies, China, &c.—*Obs.* The construction of the operculum distinguishes this genus of fresh-water shells from Valvata and Cyclostoma. The Paludinæ are viviparous. P. Achatina, Pl. xv. fig. 321.

PALUDOMUS. Swainson. A genus of the family of "Melanianæ," Sw. described as differing from Melania in having the spire shorter than the aperture. Sw. p. 340. Mr. Reeve's Monograph contains 15 species. See our Plate xxviii. fig. 583.

PANDORA. Brug. *Fam.* Corbulacea, Lam. Pyloridea, Bl.—*Descr.* Thin, inequivalve, pearly within, rounded anteriorly, rostrated posteriorly; right valve flat with a cardinal tooth, or short rib, and a slit containing the cartilage with a narrow plate on the dorsal edge turned towards the left valve; left valve concave, with a receptacle for the cardinal tooth of the right valve and the internal cartilage; no external ligament. Europe, America, Ceylon, &c.—*Obs.* This well known genus is in no danger of being confounded with any other shell. P. rostrata, Pl. iv. fig. 90.

PANOPÆA. Menard. *Fam.* Solenacea, Lam. Pyloridea, Bl.—*Descr.* Equivalve, inequilateral, oval, gaping at both extremities; hinge with an acute cardinal tooth in each valve, and a large callosity near the umbones supporting the ligament; muscular impressions two, distant, oval; palleal impression with a large sinus. Britain, North America, Mediterranean, Australia, &c.—*Obs.* This genus resembles Mya in general appearance, but differs in having an external ligament and a sharp tooth, instead of the broad spoon-shaped process in the hinge of the latter genus. P. Australis. Pl. iii. fig. 65, 66.

PAPER SAILOR. A common name given to the Argonauta.

PAPILLARY. (*Papilla*, a teat.) Shaped like a teat. This term is applied by conchologists when the apex of the spire of a univalve shell is rounded like a teat and not spiral up to the extreme point; as the apex of Cymba, fig. 434.

PAPYRACEOUS. (*Papyrus*, a kind of paper made of the flags of the river Nile in Egypt.) Of a thin, light texture, resembling that of paper. An example of this is to be seen in the Argonauta, commonly called the "Paper Sailor," fig. 485, and in the Pholas papyracea, fig. 56.

PAPYRIDEA. Sw. A sub-genus of Cardium, thus described: "Shell heart-shaped, or transversely oval; inequilateral; the anterior side almost always gaping; representing the Pholadæ. P. Soleniforme, Wood, Conch. pl. 56. f. 3.—apertum, Ib. 56. f. 2.—transversum, Sow. Conch. f. 4.—ringens, Wood, pl. 53. f. 1, 2." Pl. xxiv. fig. 503, 504.

PARACEPHALOPHORA. Bl. The second class of the type Malacozoa, Bl. divided into the sub-classes: P. dioica, P. monoica, P. hermaphrodita.

PARIES. (*A wall.*) The principal part of a multivalve shell, forming a circular wall round the body of the animal, and composed of one or more valves which are called the parietal valves.

PARIETAL VALVES. The principal valves of multivalve shells surrounding the body like a wall; as distinguished from the opercular valves, or those which compose the operculum.

PARMACELLA. Cuv. (*A little cell.*) *Fam.* Limacinea, Lam. and Bl.—*Descr.* Haliotoid, internal, thin; spire flat, consisting of one or two rapidly increasing whorls; aperture as large as the whole shell, with the dorsal margins inflected.—*Obs.* This description applies to Parmacella of Cuvier. The shell figured in Sowerby's Genera under that name is Cryptella of Webb. Pl. xiii. fig. 256, 257, 258.

PARMOPHORUS. Bl. A genus composed of Emarginula elongata, Auct. and other species of a similarly elongated form. Australian. p. elongatus. Pl. xii. fig. 242.

PARTULA. Ferussac. *Fam.* Colimacea, Lam. Auriculacea, Fer.—*Descr.* Conical, smooth; spire equal to the aperture in length, consisting of few whorls; aperture auriform; outer lip reflected, broad; inner lip reflected, with a slight prominence on the columella. 25 species are given in Reeves' monograph. P. australis, fig. 302.

PASITHÆA. Lea. A genus formed of some pyramidal shells, described as resembling Melania, but separated from that genus on account of being marine fossils. P. striata, Pl. xiv. fig. 317.

PATELLA. Linnæus. (*A dish* or *platter.*) *Fam.* Phyllidiana, Lam. Retifera, Bl.—*Descr.* Symmetrical, compresso-conical, nearly regular, oblong or oval; apex sub-central, inclining towards the anterior margin; aperture oval, forming the base of the shell; internal surface smooth; with a muscular impression shaped like a horse-shoe, with the ends bending forwards, encircling and dividing the space all round, except where the interruption occurs to receive the head of the animal; external surface ribbed, grooved, striated or banded radiately. Helcion is a name given to P. pellucida, fig. 230. On rocks and sea-weeds in all climates.—*Obs.* Patelloida differs from Patella in the construction of the animal; Siphonaria, in the lateral siphon; and Ancylus, in the oblique twist of the anix, as well as in the nature of the animal. The Patellæ are marine. P. Oculus. Pl. xii. fig. 229, 230.

PATELLIFORM. (*Patella*, a dish; *forma*, shape.) Shaped like a dish, or like shells of the genus Patella.

PATELLOIDA. Quoy and Gaimard. Lottia, Gray.—*Fam.* Phyllidiana, Lam.—*Descr.* Patelliform, rather flat; apex obtuse, leaning towards the posterior margin; muscular impression not symmetrical, but widest on the right side near the head of the animal; central disc of a variable brown colour. On rocks and sea-weeds in all climates.—*Obs.* The shells of this genus so closely resemble patella that it is almost impossible to make the distinction from the shells alone. They are, however, generally flatter, and have the apex placed somewhat nearer the posterior margin. The animals are very distinct. P. Antillarum. Pl. xii. fig. 231.

PATELLOIDEA, Bl. or patelliform shells. The third family of the order Monopleurobranchiata, Bl.; the animals of which are described as depressed, flattened, covered by a wide external shell, which is patelliform and non-symmetrical. This family contains the genera Umbrella and Siphonaria.

PATROCLES. Montf. A genus of microscopic Foraminifera.

PALULARIA. Sw. A sub-genus of "Anodontinæ," Sw. thus described: "Shell nearly equilateral, round or cordate; no teeth, P. ovata, Sw." *Ex. Conch.* pl. 36, rotundatus, Ib. pl. 137.

PAVONIA. D'Orb. A genus of microscopic Foraminifera.

PAXYODON. Schum. Hyria, Lam.

PECTEN. Brug. (*A comb.*) *Fam.* Pectenides, Lam. Subostracea, Bl.—*Descr.* Inequivalve, ribbed longitudinally, nearly equilateral, with a triangular auricle on each side of the umbones; hinge linear, destitute of

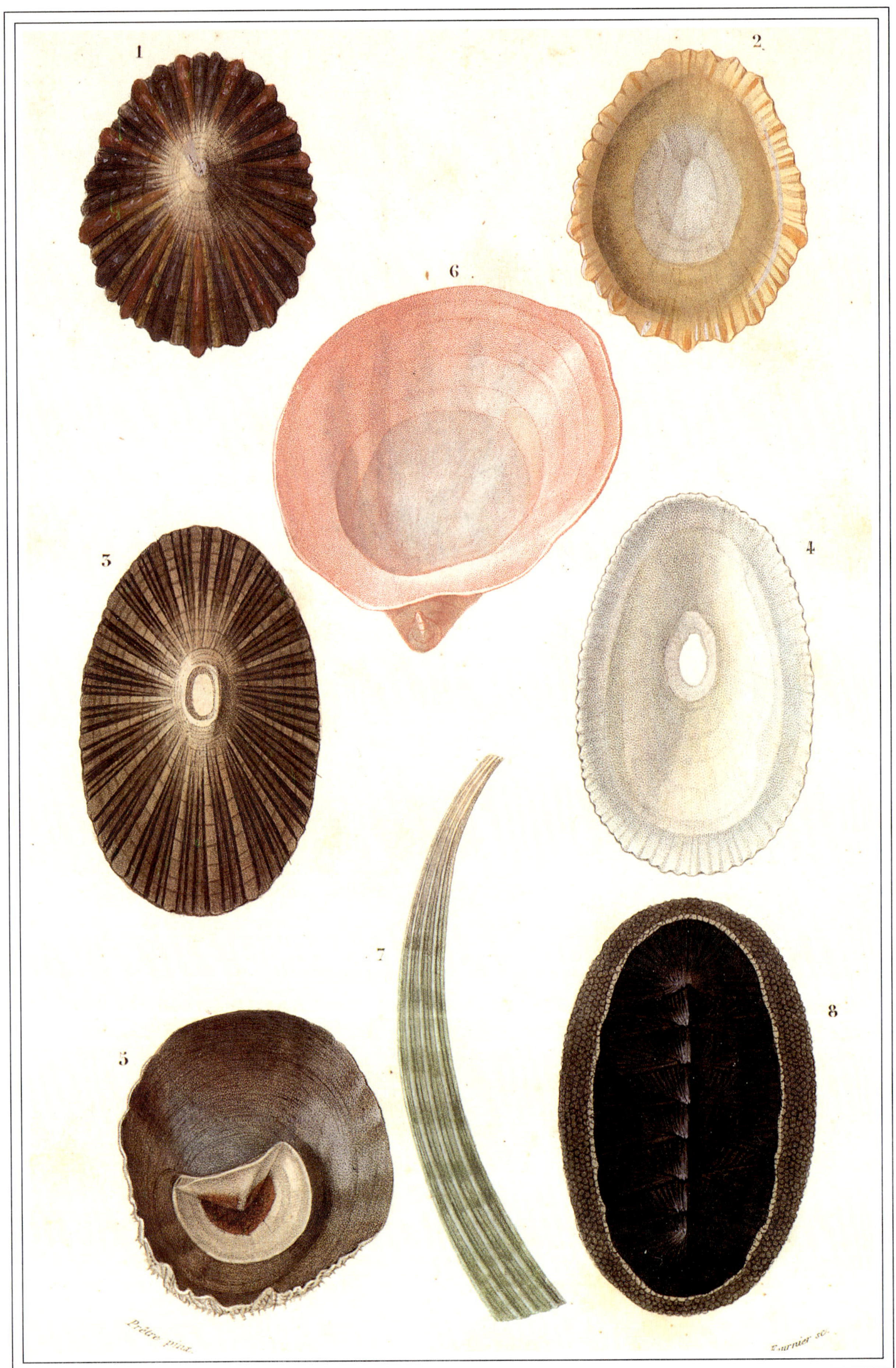

1, 2. *Patelle commune*. (Patella vulgata, *Lin.*)
3, 4. *Fissurelle en bateau*. (Fissurella nimbosa, *Lk.*)
5. *Calyptrée scabre*. (Calyptraea equestria, *Lk.*)
6. *Cabochon bonnet hongrois*. (Pileopsis hungarica, *Lk.*)
7. *Dentale éléphantine*. (Dentalium elephantinum,)
8. *Oscabrion écailleux*. (Chiton squamosus, *Lin.*)

teeth, having a central pit containing the cartilage; muscular impressions one on each valve, large, subcentral.—*Obs.* This genus of beautiful shells, to which the well known Scallop belongs, contains numerous species, some of which are found in the British Seas. The Hinnites Pusio (P. Pusio of some authors) has been separated on account of the irregularity of the external surface of one valve. The Monograph of this genus in Thesaurus Conchyliorum, by the author, contains 101 species. Plates 12 to 20. Fig. 171 to 173. Pl. x.

PECTENIDES. Lam. A family belonging to the second section of the order Conchifera Dimyaria, Lam. including the following genera:

1. Pecten. Unattached, including *Decatopecten* and *Hinnites*. Fig. 171, 172, 173.
2. Lima. Unattached, gaping. Fig. 174.
3. Plagiostoma. Unattached, with an area between the umbones. Fig. 176.
4. Dianchora. Attached by the point of the umbo. Fig. 175.
5. Spondylus. Attached, irregular, a triangular area in one valve, divided by a slit. Fig. 177.
6. Plicatula. Plicated, a very small area in one valve. Fig. 178.

PECTINATED. (*Pecten*, a comb.) Marked in a regular series of ridges.

PECTUNCULUS. (*Pecten*, dim.) *Fam.* Arcacea, Lam. and Bl.—*Descr.* Equivalve, sub-equilateral, orbicular, thick, covered with a velvety epidermis, striated longitudinally; ventral margin denticulated within; hinge semi-circular, with a series of small teeth on each side of the umbones, which are separated by a small triangular disc in each valve bearing the ligament; muscular impressions two in each valve, strongly marked, united by an entire palleal impression.—*Obs.* Linnæan conchologists have mixed this genus with Arca, from which it is, however, totally distinct, not only in the roundness of the general form, but also, and principally, in the curve of the hinge line; in fact the characters of this genus are so strongly marked that there is no danger of confounding it with any other. It does not contain many species; two or three are British. The fossil species occur in London Clay and Calcaire-grossiér. The Monograph by Mr. Reeve contains nineteen species. The generic name, Axinea of Poli, claims the priority. Pectunculus pilosus. Pl. vii. fig. 134.

PEDICLE or PEDUNCLE (*Pedunculus*, a little foot.) The stem or organ of attachment of the class of shells called in the system of Lamarck "Pedunculated Cirripedes," consisting of a fleshy tendinous tube, by the lower end of which they are attached to sub-marine substances.

PEDICULARIA. Sw. A genus of "Scutibranchia," thus described: "Shell irregular, sub-patelliform; a thick, large, obsolete apex on one of the longest sides, and an internal callous rim within, on one side only; circumference undulated, irregular. P. Sicula, Sw." Sw. p. 357. Sicily. A singular shell probably of the nature of the Cypraedae, which is found attached to corals, conforming its shape to the irregularity of their surface, and fitting closely. *Ex.* Pl. xxiv. Fig. 513.

PEDIPES. Adanson. *Fam.* Auriculacea, Bl. Colimacea, Lam.—*Descr.* Sub-globose, longitudinal, thick, striated; spire equal to the aperture in length; aperture sub-ovate; peritreme sharp, thickened within, modified by the last whorl; columella with three strong plaits on the inner edge; outer lip with one fold.—*Obs.* This genus contains but one or two small recent species, in some respects resembling Auricula, from which it is known by the thickness of its shell, and its globular form. Coast of Africa. Pl. xiv. Fig. 299, P. Adansoni.

PEDUM. Lam. (*A shepherd's crook.*) *Fam.* Pectinides, Lam. Sub-ostracea, Bl.—*Descr.* Irregular, inequivalve, sub-equilateral, attached by a byssus passing through a sinus in the lower valve; hinge toothless, with a triangular area in each valve, separating the umbones; ligament contained in a groove running across the area; muscular impressions one in each valve, large, sub-orbicular; both valves flat, narrow at the dorsal, broad at the ventral extremities; lower valve with raised edges over-wrapping the upper.—*Obs.* This singular genus, of which only one species is known, differs from all the other Pectinides, not only in shape and structure, but also in the mode of attachment, which is by means of a byssus passing through a sinus in the lower valve; and not, as in Ostræa, by a part of the outer surface. P. Spondyloideum is the only species at present known. Moluccas. Pl. x. fig. 179.

PEDUNCLE. See Pedicle.

PEDUNCULATED. (*Pedunculus*, a little foot.) Attached to external objects by a hollow fleshy tube, called the Peduncle.

PEDUNCULATED CIRRIPEDES. Lam. An order consisting of molluscs which have multivalve shells, supported on a peduncle. The genera which it contains are thus distinguished:

1. Pentelasmis. Five valves. Fig. 34.
2. Cineras. Five very minute valves distant from each other. Fig. 42.
3. Otion. The same, but the animal has two auricles. Fig. 43. The genus Palmina, Gray, has but one.
4. Octolasmis. Shaped like Pentelasmis, abut with 7 or 8 valves. Fig.41.
5. Lithotrya. Five valves, peduncle scaly, with a plate at the base. Fig. 39.
6. Scalpellum. Shape square, valves 13, peduncle scaly. Fig. 35.
7. Smilium. Same, but the peduncle hairy. Fig. 36.
8. Ibla. Four valves, one pair long, one pair short, peduncle hairy. Fig. 40.
9. Brismeus. Even at the base. Fig. 38.
10. Pollicipes. Principal valves in pairs, with many smaller valves at the base. This genus has been divided into *Pollicepes*, and *Capitellum*, the latter of which is founded upon Pollicepes Mitellus, Auct. Fig. 37 and 37*.

PELAGUS. Montf. A genus composed of species of Ammonites, which have the spire covered by the last whorl, as in Nautilus, and have an umbilicus. Orbulites. Bl.

PELLUCID. Transparent.

PELORUS. Montf. Polystomella, Bl. A genus of microscopic Foraminifera.

PELORONTA. Oken. Nerita *Peloronta*, Auct. 330.

PENEROPLIS. Montf. A genus of microscopic Foraminifera.

PENICILLUS. Brug. Aspergillum, Auct.

PENTAMERUS. Sow. (Πεντε, *pente*, five; μερος, *mgros*, part.) *Fam.* Brachiopoda, Lam.—*Descr.* Equilateral, inequivalve; one valve divided by a central septum into two parts; the other by two septa, into three parts; umbones incurved, imperforate.—*Obs.* Dalman remarks upon this genus Gypidia, that it is most probably identical with Pentamerus, Sow.; but rejects the name for two reasons; 1st. That it has already been applied to a class of insects; 2nd. He disputes the fact of the shell being quinquelocular, *i.e.* not counting the triangular foramen in the hinge of the larger valve as one of the divisions. Pl. xi. Fig. 212, 213.

PENTELASMIS. Leach. See Lepas. (Πεντε, *pente*, five; 'ελασμα, *elasma*, plate.) *Order.* Pedunculated Cirripedes, Lam.—*Descr.* Compressed, conical, composed of five valves; lower lateral pair sub-trigonal; upper lateral pair elongated, sub-quadrate; dorsal valve accurate, peduncle elongated, smooth. Found on floating wood in the sea.—*Obs.* This genus should have been described under the name

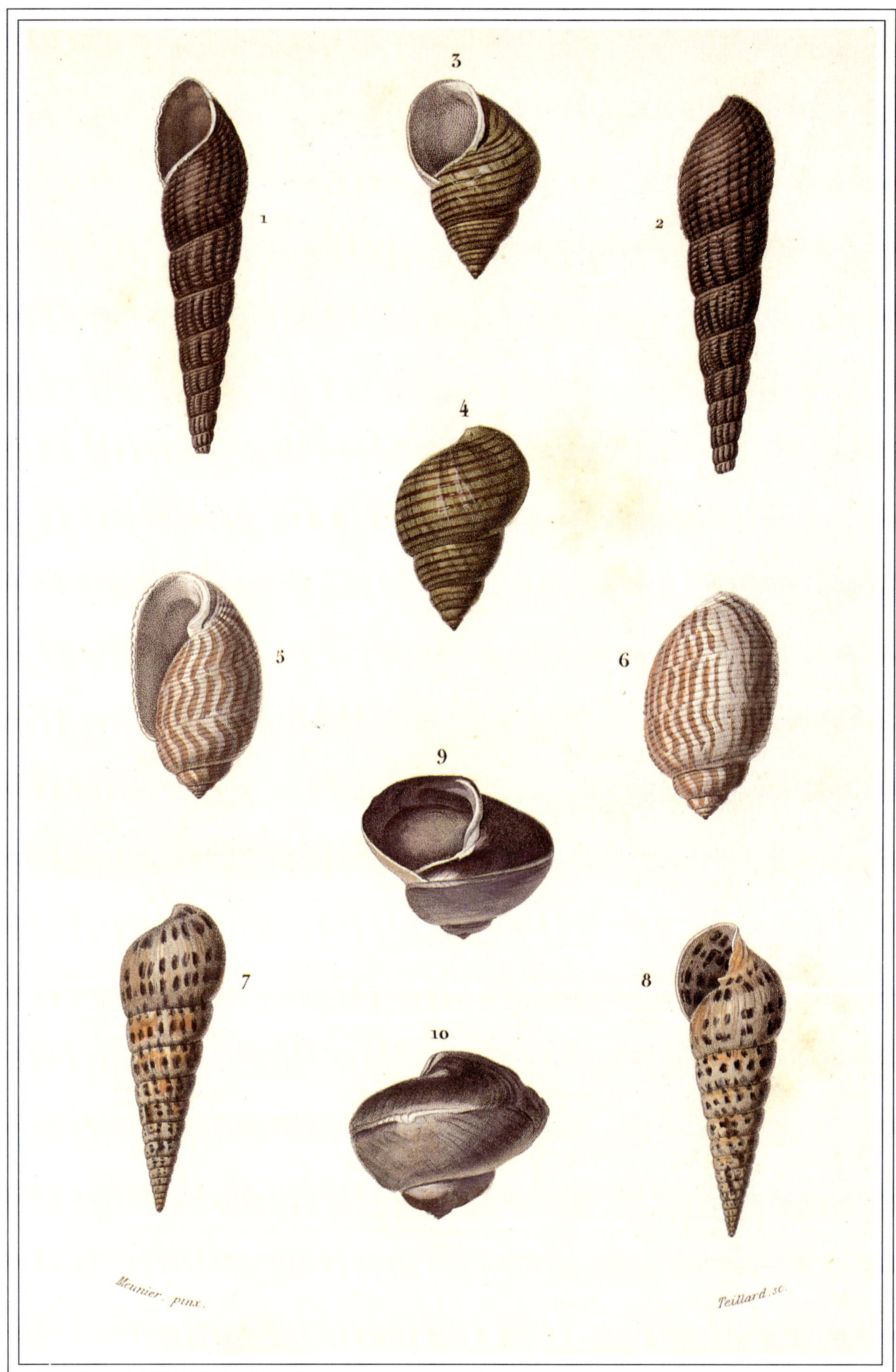

1, 2. *Mélanie tronquée*. (Melania abra, *Desh.*)

3, 4. *Paludine du Bengale*. (Paludina Bengalensis, *Lamk.*)

5, 6. *Tornatelle brocard*. (Tornatella flammea, *Lamk.*)

7, 8. *Pyramidelle tachetée*. (Pyramidella maculosa, *Lamk.*)

9, 10. *Janthine commune*. (Janthina communis, *Lamk.*)

LEPAS; it is known from all others of the order by the number of valves. Pentelasmis is the genus Anatifera of Lamarck. Lepas anatifa, Linn. Fossil species of this marine genus are found in the Calcaire-grossièr of Paris, and in other similar beds. P. lævis. Pl. ii. fig. 34.

PENULTIMATE WHORL. The last whorl but one.

PERA. Leach. A genus composed of CYCLAS amnica, and other similar species. pl. xxiv. fig. 500.

PERDIX. Montf. DOLIUM *Perdix*, Auct.

PERFORATED. (*Perforatus.*) Bored through, as the apex of Fissurella, fig. 245, and Dentalium, fig. 2.

PERFORATION. (*Perforo*, to bore or pierce.) A round opening, and having the appearance of being bored, as in Haliotis, fig. 338. Sometimes the term is applied to an umbilicus which penetrates a shell through the axis to the apex, as Eulima splendidula, fig. 348.

PERIBOLUS. Brug. A genus founded upon young specimens of CYPRÆA, with their outer lips not formed.

PERIOSTRACUM. A name used by Mr. Gray to signify the substance which covers the outer surface of many shells, called the *Epidermis* by most conchological writers. "Drap Marin" is the name given to this substance by French Naturalists.

PERIPLOMA. Schum. *Fam.* Myariæ. A genus thus described: "Shell very thin with the left valve more ventricose than the right; hinge toothless, ligament double, the external portion thin, the internal part thick, placed upon prominent, sometimes spoon-shaped hinge laminæ, and supported by a transverse bone; muscular impressions two, distant, palleal impression sinuated posteriorly." *Genus*, Osteodesma, Deshayes. *Ex.* P. inæquivalvis. Pl. iii. fig. 72.

PERISTOMATA. Lam. A family belonging to the first section of the order Trachelipoda, containing the following genera:–

1. AMPULLARIA. Globose or discoidal; operculum concentric; including *Pachystoma, Lanistes, Ceratodes.* Fig. 318 to 320.
2. PALUDINA. Oval; operculum concentric. Fig. 321.
3. VALVATA. Globose; operculum spiral. Fig. 322.

PERISTOME. The edge of the aperture, including the inner and outer lips.

PERITREME. A term used to express the whole circumference of the aperture of a spiral shell. In descriptions, it is said to be notched or entire, simple, reflected, round or oval, &c. as the case may be.

PERLAMATER. Schum. (*Mother of Pearl.*) MELEAGRINA Margaritifera, Lam. The pearl oyster.

PERNA. Auct. ("Pernæ concharum generis," Plin.) *Fam.* Malleacea, Lam.—*Descr.* Sub-equivalve, irregular, compressed, foliaceous; hinge straight, linear, composed of a series of transverse, parallel grooves, containing the cartilage and intermediate spaces bearing the ligament; anterior margin with a sinus for the passage of a byssus; posterior ventral margin oblique, attenuated.—*Obs.* This genus is known from Crenatula by the straightness, number and regularity of the grooves in the hinge and the sinus, for the passage of the byssus. P. Ephippium. Pl. ix. fig. 166. Thesaurus Conchyliorum, Pl. 97, fig. 189 to 191.

PERSICULA. Schum. A genus formed of MARGINELLA *Persicula*, Auct. and other species having the spire concealed. Pl. xx. fig. 438.

PERSONA. Montfort, 1800. (*Mask.* A genus composed of TRITON *Anus*, Auct. and similar species. Pl. xviii. fig. 401.

PETRICOLA. Lam. (*Petrus*, a stone; *cola*, an inhabitant.) *Fam.* Lithophagidæ, Lam.—*Descr.* Equivalve, inequilateral, transversely ovate or oblong, rather irregular, anterior side rounded; posterior side more or less attenuated, slightly gaping; hinge with two cardinal teeth in each valve; muscular impressions two in each valve; palleal impression entire; ligament external.—*Obs.* The Petricolæ are found in holes made by the animals in rocks, madrepores, & C. They may be known from Saxicava by the regularity of their form and the teeth on the hinge. Pl. iv. fig. 91, 92.

PETRIFIED FINGERS, CANDLES, SPECTRE CANDLES, &c. are vulgar terms by which fossils of the genus Belemnites were formerly known.

PHAKELLOPLEURA. Guild. A genus composed of those species of CHITON, Auct. which have bunches of hairs or hyaline bristles on each side of each valve on the margin. The Chiton fascicularis, found on our own coasts, is a well knwon example. Pl. xxiv. fig. 506.

PHANEROPTHALMUS. *Adams*, Sowerby's Thesaurus, f1850. A sub-genus of Bullidæ, the shells of which are thus described: "concealed, oval, entirely open, without more trace of a spire than a curved process at the left border; the right border prolonged into a point slightly turned on itself."

PHARAMUS. Montf. LENTICULINA, Bl. A genus of microscopic Foraminifera.

PHARETRIUM. König. (φαρετρεων, *pharetrion*, a quiver.)—*Descr.* A testaceous body composed of two conical sheaths, one within the other, perforated at the apex, and joined together near the oral margin. In describing this genus, which appears to be the same as ENTALIS of Defrance, Mr. König expresses the supposition that it may probably belong to the class Pteropoda. P. fragile, Pl. i. fig. 3.

PHARUS. Leach. MS. Gray. Syn. Brit. Mus. (undescribed.) CERATISOLEN, Forbes. British Mollusca, P. 255.

PHASIANELLA. Lamarck, EUTROPIA. Humphrey, Gray's Synopsis. (*Phasianus*, a pheasant.) *Fam.* Turbinacea, Lam. Ellipsostomata, Bl.—*Descr.* Smooth, oval, variegated; aperture entire, oval; outer-lip thin; inner-lip thin, spread over a portion of the body whorl; columella smooth, rather thickened towards the base; operculum horny, spiral within; testaceous, incrassated without. Britain, Mediterranean, &c.; the fine large species are Australian. Some fossil species are found in the tertiary beds.—*Obs.* The shells composing this genus are richly marked with lines and waves of various and delicate colours, and if the genus be restricted to those species which are smooth, and which have a thick shelly operculum, we may regard it as well defined; but there are some spirally-grooved species of TURBO, Linn. which, from their oval shape, have been considered as belonging to this genus. Such species should not, in our opinion, be retained in this genus; they belong to Littorina. P. variegata, Pl. xvi. fig. 367.

PHILINE. *Ascanias.* A sub-genus of Bullidæ, the shells of which are thus described by Adams in his Monograph in Sowerby's Thesaurus: "shell concealed in the mantle, thin, involute on one side, destitute of distinct spire or columella; aperture large and wide."

PHITIA. Gray. CARYCHIUM, Müller.

PHOLADARIA. Lam. A family of the order Conchifera Dimyaria, Lam. The animals contained in this family live in cavities bored by themselves in rocks, wood, &c. Theya re cylindrical in form. Lamarck here places PHOLAS and GASTROCILÆNA, the last of which belongs more properly to the family of Tubicolaria, where we have enumerated it. Pholas has been divided into *Pholas*, fig. 55, *Martesia*, which has the valves nearly closed; and Pholadidæa, fig. 56, which has the cup-shaped extension. The genus Pholadomya, fig. 67, has been added, although of doubtful character. The genus Galeomma, fig. 58, 59, has also been recently added.

PHOLADIDÆA. Leach. PHOLAS Papyracea, Auct. Remarkable for the cup-shaped process at the posterior extremity. Pl. ii. fig. 56.

PHOLADOMYA. Sow. (*Pholas* and *Mya.*) *Fam.* Pholadaria, Lam.—*Descr.* Thin, rather hyaline, equivalve, inequilateral, ventricose,

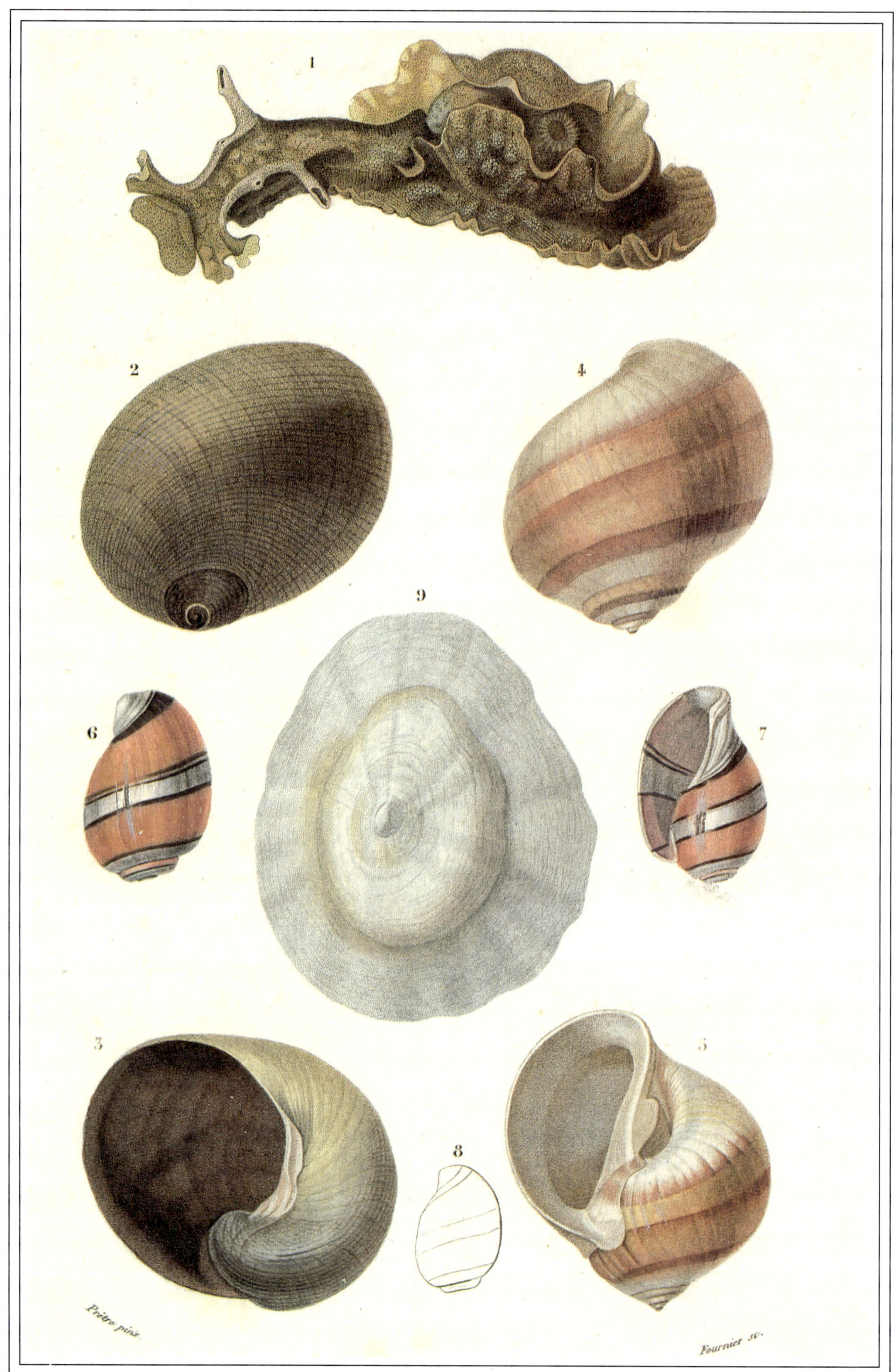

1. *Aplysie ponctuée.* (Aplysia punctata, *Cuv.*)
2, 3. *Sigaret déprimé.* (Sigaretus haliotoideus, *Lamk.*)
4, 5. *Natice flammulée.* (Natica canrena, *L.k.*)
6, 7, 8. *Bulle banderolle.* (Bulla aplustre, *Lin.*)
9. *Ombrelle de la méditerranée.* (Umbrella mediterranea, *Lamk.*)

posteriorly gaping, elongated, anteriorly short, rounding; ventral margin rather gaping; hinge with an elongated pit, and lateral plate in each valve; ligament external, short, muscular impressions two in each valve, rather indistinct; palleal impression with a large sinus.—*Obs.* The only recent species of this genus is from the island of Tortola. Several fossil occur in rocks of the Oolitic series. P. candida. Pl. ii. fig. 57.

PHOLAS. Auct. (Φωλεω, *pholeo*, to lie hid in a cavity.) *Fam.* Pholadaria, Lam. Adesmacea, Bl.—*Descr.* Transverse, oblong, equivalve, inequilateral, imbricated, gaping on both sides, the anterior hiatus being generally the largest, although sometimes nearly closed, with the dorsal margin surmounted with one or more laminar accessory valves; hinge callous, reflected, with a long curved tooth protruding from beneath the umbones in each valve.—*Obs.* This genus of marine shells, dwelling in holes formed in rocks, wood, &c. is easily distinguished from any other nearly allied genus by the curved, prominent, rib-like teeth. The monograph of the family in Pt. 10 of Sowerby's Thesaurus Conchylium contains, besides Triomphalia, 42 species. The principal forms of which are represented by Ph. Costata and Candida, Thes. fig. 21, 22, 23, and 8, 9, with *one* accessory valve. Ph. Dactylus, our fig. 56 (Dactylina) with several accessory valves; Ph. Crispata, Thes. fig. 37. (Zirfœa) with *no* accesssory valve. Ph. tridens, Thes. fig. 60, 61 (Calona) with tube. Ph. papyracea, our fig. 56 (Pholadidæa) with a cup-like termination; and Ph. striata, Thes. f. 40 (Martesia) enclosed by various shields. (P.. ii. fig. 55, 56.

PHOLEOBIUS. Leach. Part of the genus Saxicava, Auct.

PHONEMUS. Montf. A genus of microscopic Foraminifera.

PHORUS. Montf. Trochus agglutinanas, &c. Auct. Remarkable for the adhesion of little pebbles, dead shells, &c. to the outer edge of the whorls, which are taken up in the course of the growth of the dead shell. From this circumstance they are called "Collectors, Carriers, &c." Recent species are brought from the East and west Indies; fossil species are fouond in the Tertiary beds. The genus Onustus, *Humphreys*, has for its type, Phorus Indicus, a very thin species, with the margin of the body whorl extending in a broad keel at the angle. Pl. xvi. fig. 360.

PHOS. Montf. *Fam.* Purpurifera? Lam.—*Descr.* Turrited, thick, cancellated, varicose; spire pointed, generally longer than the aperture; aperture rounded or oval; outer lip having internal ridges, with a sinus near the anterior termination; columella with an oblique fold; canal short, forming externally a raised varix.—*Obs.* The raised external surface of the canal, brings this genus near to Buccinum, while, in general appearance, most of the species more resemble Murex. They have, however, no truce varices on the whorls, but merely raised bars. Pl. xvi. fig. 416, P. senticosus.

PHYLLIDIANA. Lam. A family belonging to the first section of the order Gasteropoda, Lam. The genera belonging to this family may be distinguished as follows:

1. Chiton. Composed of eight valves; valves contingent. Fig. 227.
2. Chitonellus. The same, with the valves distant. Fig. 228.
3. Patella. Conical, symmetrical. Fig. 229, 230.
4. Patelloida. Differing from Patella in the animal. Fig. 231.
5. Siphonaria. With a siphonal scar on one side. Fig. 231*.
6. Scutella. Siphonal scar nearer to the side of the head. Fig. 510, 511.

PHYLLONOTUS. Sw. A sub-genus of Murex, thus described: "Canal moderate; varices foliated, laciniated, compressed, or resembling leaves; inflatus. Mart. 102. fig. 980, eurystoma. Zool. Ill. ii. 100. imperialis Ib. pl. 109." Sw. p. 296.

PHYSA. Drap. A genus formed for reserved species of Limnæa, Auct. P. castanea. Pl. xiv. fig. 310.

PHYSETER. Humph. Solarium, Lam.

PILEOLUS. Cookson. (*A little cap.*) *Fam.* Neritacea, Lam.—*Descr.* Patelliform, with the apex sub-central, straight. In the lower disc, or under surface, the centre of which is rather raised or cushion-shaped, is placed the lateral, narrow, semilunar aperture, with the outer lip marginated and the inner lip crenulated.—*Obs.* This interesting genus is known only in a fossil state. Two species are found in the upper layer of Oolite, above the Bradford clay. The spire, although internal, connects this genus in some degree with Neritina. Still there is no danger of confounding them. P. plicatus. Pl. xv. fig. 332.

PILEOPSIS. Lamarck. 1822. Capulus, Montf. 1810.

PILIDIUM. Forbes and Hanley. A genus established on anatomical grounds for the reception of a little patelliform shell, the P. fulvum, British Mollusca, p. 441, pl. 62, fig. 6, 7.

PILLAR. The usual English name for the column which forms the axis of spiral shells, around which the whorls revolve. See Columella.

PINNA. Auct. (*The fin of a fish.*) *Fam.* Mytilacea, Lam.—*Descr.* Equivalve, inequilateral, oblique, wedge-shaped, thin, horny; umbones terminal; hinge rectilinear, without teeth; anterior margin sinuated, to admit the passage of a byssus; posterior margin truncated, gaping; muscular impressions two in each valve; posterior large, sub-central; anterior small, terminal, sometimes double.—*Obs.* The beautiful large shells of which this genus is composed, are possessed of a large, flowing, silky byssus, of which gloves and hose have been manufactured. They have received their name from their resemblance to the pectoral fins of some fishes. some species attain very large dimensions, and measure two feet in length. A fabulous story is told with regard to animals of this genus, namely, that a certain small species of crab is in the habit of taking refuge from its enemies in the shell of the Pinna, into which it is received with great hospitality and kindness by the "*blind slug*," which inhabits it. In return for which kindness, he occasionally goes abroad to procure food for both. On his return he knocks at the shell, which is opened to receive him, and they share the supplies together in convivial security! Some species are smooth, although the greater number are imbricated or crisped outside. P. saccata. Pl. ix. fig. 162.

PINNATED. (From *Pinna*, a fin.) When a protuberant part of a shell is spread out and flattish, as in Rostellaria columbaria, fig. 403, it is said to be *alated*, or winged, but when the protuberant part is radiated or ribbed, like the fin of a rish, it is *pinnated*, as in Murex pinnatus, and Murex tripterus. (Conch. Illustr.)

PIRENA. Lam. A genus of fresh-water shells, rejected by De Ferussac and other authors, who place Lamarck's two first species with melanopsis, and his two last with Melania. P. terebralis, Pl. xiv. fig. 316.

PISIDIUM. Leach. a genus of river shells separated from Cyclas principally on account of a difference in the animal. The species of Pisidium, however, are less equilateral than the Cyclades, and the posterior or ligamentary side of the latter is the longer, while that of the former is the shorter. Pl. v. fig. 112.

PISIFORM. (*Pisum*, a pea; *forma*, shape.) Shaped like a pea or small globular body.

PISUM. Megerle. (*A pea.*) Pisidium, Leach.

PITHOHELIX. Sw. A sub-genus of "Geotrochus," Sw. Sw. p. 332.

PITONELLUS. Montf. Rotella, Auct.

PLACENTA. Schum. Placuna, Auct.

PLACENTULA. Schum. A genus of microscopic Foraminifera.

PLACUNA. Brug. (πλακους, *placos*, a cake.) *Fam.* Ostracea, Lam. and

Bl.—*Descr.* Compressed, thin, equivalve, nearly equilateral planorbicular, fibrous, foliaceous; hinge flat, with two diverging ribs in one valve, and two corresponding grooves in the other, containing the cartilage; muscular impressions one, large, circular, central, and one or two smaller in each valve.—*Obs.* The two best known species of this well defined genus are the P. placenta, commonly called the Chinese Window Shell, and the P. Sella, called the Saddle Oyster, from the anterior margin being turned up so as to resemble a saddle. The genus may be known from all others by the divering costa on the hinge. Placunanomia is the only genus resembling it in this respect, but this is easily distinguished by a perforation through the shell. These shells are used in China to glaze windows. Pl. xi. 184, P. Placuna.

PLACUNANOMIA. (Sw. *Placuna* and *Anomia.*) *Fam.* Ostracea, Lam. and Bl.—*Descr.* Thin, foliaceous, compressed, sub-equivalve, sub-equilateral, irregular, flat near the umbones, plicated towards the margins, attached by a bony substance passing through a fissure in the lower valve; hinge flat, with two diverging ribs in one valve, corresponding with two diverging grooves, containing the cartilage, in the other; muscular impressions one in each valve, central, sub-orbicular.—*Obs.* The specimens from which Mr. Broderip described this singular genus, were brought by Mr.Cuming from the gulf of Dulce in Costa Rico. Another species is from one of the Philippine Islands. They partake of the characters of several genera, having the hinge like Placuna, and being attached by a process passing through the lower valve, like Anomia. P. Cumingii, Pl. xi. fig. 189, 190, 191.

PLAGIOSTOMA. Sow. Min. Con. (πλαγιος, *plagios*, oblique; στομα, *stoma*, mouth.) *Fam.* Pectenides, Lam. Palliobranciata, Bl.—*Descr.* Sub-equivalve, inequilateral, oblique, auriculated on each side of the umbones, radiately striated; hinge straight in one valve, with a triangular notch in the other.—*Obs.* This genus, one species of which is spinous, and another smooth, is only known in a fossil state. It is found in the Lias and chalk. P. spinosum. Pl. x. fig. 176.

PLAIT or FOLD. A term applied to the prominences on the columellar lip of some univalve shells, particularly in the sub-family of Volutidæ. *Ex.* Voluta, fig. 433; Cymba, 434; and Melo, fig. 435.

PLANARIA. Brown. A minute fossil resembling Planorbis in appearance, but differing in being a marine shell, and having a reflected outer lip. From Lea's Contributions to Geology. P. nitens. Pl. xiv. fig. 312.

PLANAXIS. Lam. (*Plana*, flat; and *axis.*) *Fam.* Turbinacea, Lam. Entomostomata, Bl.—*Descr.* Sub-ovate, pyramidal, solid; spire measuring ½ or ⅓ of the axis, consisting of a few whorls; columella contiguous to the axis, flat, truncated, and separated from the outer lip by a short canal; outer lip thickened and denticulated within; operculum horny, thin, with a terminal nucleus.—*Obs.* This is a genus of small marine shells found in the West Indies, &c. P. sulcata. Pl. xvi. fig. 365.

PLANE. (*Planus.*) Flat, planed, as the columellar lip of Purpura, fig. 414.

PLANORBICULAR. (*Planus*, flat; *orbis*, an orb.) Flat and circular, as Ammonites, fig. 478.

PLANORBIS. Müll. (*Planus*, flat; *orbis*, an orb.) *Fam.* Lymnacea, Lam. and Bl.—*Descr.* Thin, horny, convolute, planorbicular, nearly symmetrical; spire compressed, concave, consisting of numerous gradually increasing whorls, which are visible on both sides; aperture transversely oval, or nearly round; peritreme entire; outer lip thin; inner lip distinct, spread over a part of the body whorl.—*Obs.* This is a genus of shells abounding in all climates in ditches and stagnant pools, not liable to be confounded with any other, excepting the discoidal species of Ampullaria, which may be distinguished by the aperture being broadest in the opposite direction. It is further to be remarked that the discoidal Ampullariæ are dextral shells, and the Planorbes are sinistral or reversed; and although the latter are sometimes so flat and orbicular that it is difficult to know which is the spiral side, it may nevertheless always be ascertained by a careful examination. Fossil species are found in the fresh-water strata of the Isle of Wight, and the neighbourhood of Paris. P. corneus. Pl. xiv. fig. 311.

PLANORBULINA. D'Orb. A genus of microscopic Foraminifera.

PLANULACEA. Bl. The second family of Cellulacea, Bl. The microscopic Foraminifera contained in this family are described as very much depressed, not spiral, chambered, cellular, and having the septa indicated by grooves on the external surface of the shell, which increase in length from the apex to the base: some of the small cellular cavities are to be seen on the margins. This family contains the genera Renulina and Peneroplis.

PLANULARIA. Defr. PENEROPLIS, Montf. A genus of microscopic Foraminifera.

PLANULINA. D'Orb. A genus of microscopic Foraminifera.

PLANULITES. Lam. DISCORBITES of the same author. A genus of microscopic Foraminifera.

PLATIRIS. Lea. (πλατυς, *platus*, wide; ιρις, *iris.*) A genus including several species of Nayades, referred to IRIDINA, Lam. The genus Platiris is divided into two sub-genera. Iridina, species which have crenulated margins; I. Ovata, I. exotica, Spatha, Lea; those with smooth or very slightly crenulated hinges, S. rubeus, S. Solenoides, Mycetopus, D'Orb. Fig. 151.

PLATYLEPAS. (πλατυς, *platus*, wide; λεπας, *lepas*, rock.) *Order.* Sessile Cirripedes, Lam. *Fam.* Balanidea, Bl.—*Descr.* Conical, depressed, consisting of six valves, each divided internally by an angular plate jutting from the centre (like the buttress of a wall); operculum consisting of four valves in pairs.—*Obs.* This genus differs from Balanus, Coronula, &c. in the internal structure of the valves. De Blainville's description of Chthalamus partly agrees with this. Pl. i. fig. 19.

PLAXIPHORA. Gray. Chiton Carmichælis, &c.

PLECTOPHORUS. Fer. (πλῆκτρον, *plectron*, spur; φορέω, *phoreo*, to carry.) A genus consisting of small testaceous appendages fived on the posterior extremity of a species of slug. P. corninus. P.. xiii. fig. 260.

PLEIODON. Conrad. IRIDINA, Lam. *Fam.* Nayades, Lam.

PLEKOCHEILUS. Guild. AURICULA Caprella, Lam. CARYCHIUM undulatum, Leach. (CAPRELLA, Nonnull.) This proposed genus is described as scarcely umbilical, dextral, oval, spiral; with the spire elevated, obtuse; the two last whorls very large, ventricose; aperture entire, elongated; columella with a single plait; the plait concave, inflected. Fig. 522, 523.

PLEUROBRANCHUS. Cuv. (Πλερα, *pleura*, the side; *Branchiæ*, gills.) *Fam.* Semiphyllidiana, Lam. Subaplysiacea, Bl.—*Descr.* Internal, thin, haliotoid, slightly convex towards the spiral apex; aperture entire.—*Obs.* This is a very light shell, delicately coloured, resembling Aplysia, but differing in the integrity of the margin. P. membranaceus. Pl. xii. fig. 232.

PLEUROCERUS. Rafinesque. A genus very imperfectly described in the "Journal de Physique" as "oval, or pyramidal; aperture oblong; outer lip thin; inner lip truncated at the columella, which is smooth and tortuous, not umbilicated. Operculum horny or membranaceous." De Blainville, in giving this description, remarks that he has neither seen the animal nor the shell of this genus, which he imagines to have been formed from the "Paludine Coupée de M. Say."

PLEURORYNCHUS. Phillips. (Πλευρα, *pleura*, the side; ρυγχος,

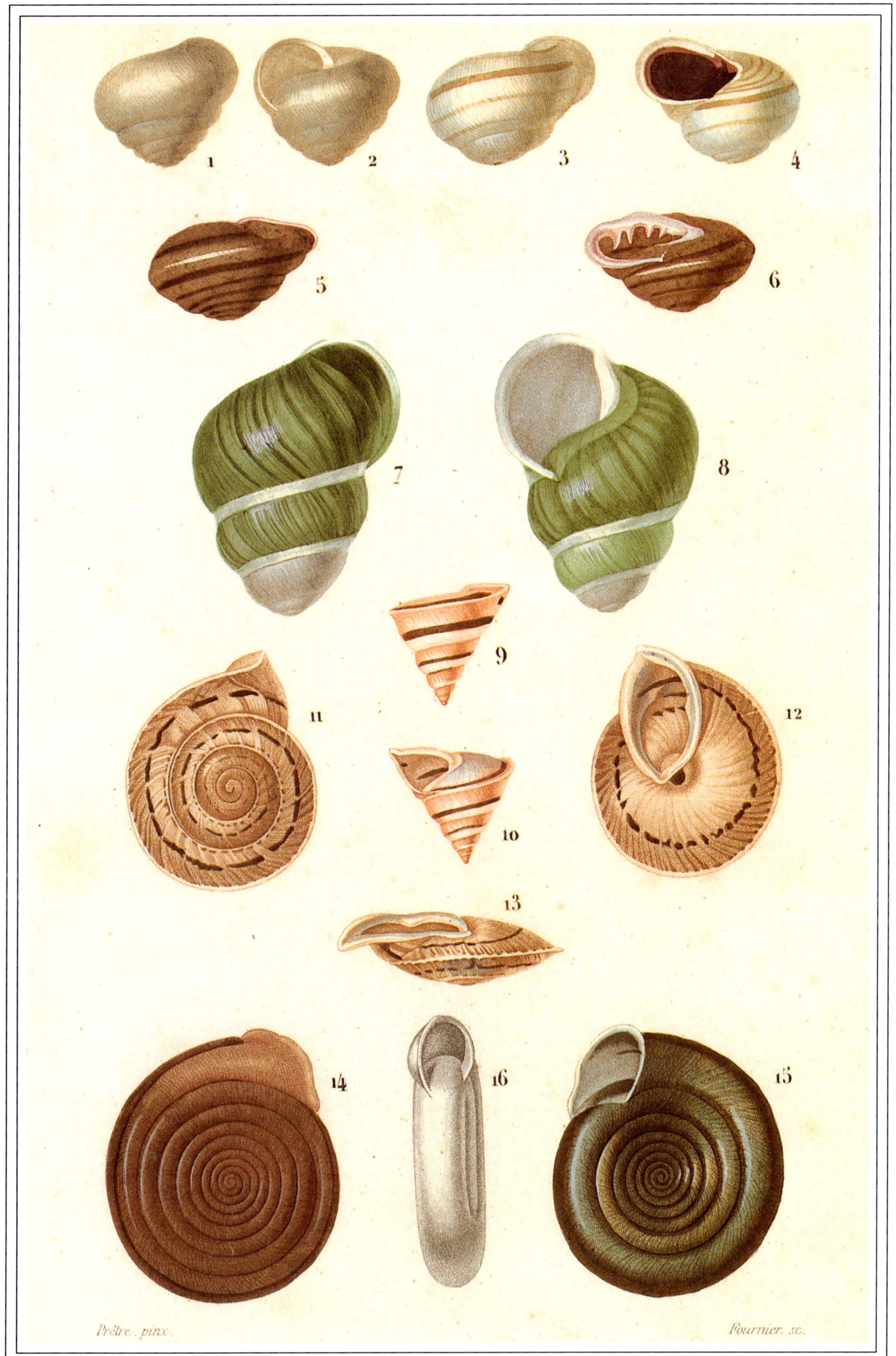

1, 2. *Hélice trochiforme*. (Helix epistylium, *Mull.*)
3, 4. *Hélice macrostome*. (Helix vittata, *Mull.*)
5, 6. *Hélice sinuée*. (Helix sinuata, *Mull.*)
7, 8. *Hélice multicolore*. (Helix, polychroa, *Swain.*)
9, 10. *Hélice Pyramidelle*. (Helix pyramidella, *Wagner.*)
11, 12, 13. *Hélice de Lister*. (Helix Listeriana, *Gray.*)
14, 15, 16. *Hélice polygire*. (Helix polygirata, *Born.*)

rynchus, a beak.) A genus founded upon a very singular species of CARDIUM, distinguished by the short anterior side, and the elongation of the hinge line into auricular processes, which are truncated at the extremities. C. Hibernicum from the Black Rock near Dublin, which is vulgarly called "Asses-hoof," and C. elongatum (Sow. Min. Con. vol. 1. 82.), form part of this genus. Pl. xxiv. fig. 505.

PLEUROTOMA. Lam. *Fam.* Canalifera, Lam. Siphonostomata, Bl.—*Descr.* Fusiform, thick, in general ribbed or striated transversely; aperture oval, terminating anteriorly in an elongated canal; outer lip thin, with a fissure near its spiral extremity; columella smooth, nearly straight. Found principally in tropical climates.—*Obs.* This genus, which nearly resembles Fusus in other respects, may be known by the notch in the outer lip. The species differ in the length of the canal. Swainson has designated this genus a family, and divided it into the following genera: Brachytoma, in the description of which he says that the spire and aperture are of equal length, including the species strombiformis: Pleurotoma, in which the channel is so much lengthened, as to be little shorter than the spire: Clavatula, having the long narrow slit of Pleurotoma, in which the channel is so much lengthened, as to be little shorter than the spire: Clavatula, having the long narrow slit of Pleurotoma, but with a very short canal: Clavicantha, having the canal equally short, but the sinus or notch, instead of being linear and long, is short and wide; the surface is rough, and the whorls either coronated with prickles, or with compressed nodules resembling spines: Tomella, which has the spire and canal fusiform, but the spire of very few whorls, and the inner lip considerably thickened within where it joins the outer lip. Fig. 379, 389, P. marmorata; 381, P. Strombiformis, (Clavatula, Sw.) The name "Turris," Humphrey, is prior to the above, and also to the application of "Turris" to the turrited mitres. Mr. Reeve's Monograph of the genus Pleurotoma, contains 369 species, including the Clavatulæ. Pl. xvi.

PLEUROTOMARIA. Defr. *Fam.* Turbinacea, Lam.—*Descr.* Turbinated, spiral; aperture sub-quadrate, with rounded angles; outer lip with a deep slit near its union with the spire.—*Obs.* This genus, which is only known in a fossil state, abounds in inferior Oolite, Oxford clay, and casts are found in a limestone bed in Norway. The Scissurellæ differ in being very minute shells, and are not so trochiform as the species of Pleurotomaria, P. reticulata, Pl. xv. fig. 341.

PLICACEA. Lam. A family of the order Trachelipoda, Lam. containing the following genera:

1. PYRAMIDELLA. Pyramidal, with numerous whorls. Fig. 342.
2. TORNATELLA. Cylindrical, with few whorls. Fig. 343, 344.
3. RINGICULA. Margin reflected. Fig. 540, 541.

PLICADOMUS. Sw. A sub-genus of Pupa, thus described: "spire moderate, regular and thick, but gradually conic; the tip obtuse; aperture perpendicular; inner lip wanting; outer lip semicircular; the margin dilated and reflected. P. sulcata, Chem. 135, f. 1231, 1232." Sw. p. 332.

PLICATED. (*Plicatus*, folded.) Applied to spiral plaits on the columella of some shells. *Ex.* Voluta, fig. 433. Also to the angular bendings in the margins of some bivalve shells. *Ex.* Dendrostæa, fig. 181.

PLICATULA. Lam. (*Plicatus*, folded.) *Fam.* Pectenides, Lam. Subostracea, Bl.—*Descr.* Irregular, sub-equivalve, sub-equilateral, attached by a small part of the surface of one valve, strongly plicated; umbones separated by a small, external ligamentary area; hinge with two cardinal teeth in each valve, two approximate in one valve, received between two distant in the other; cartilage placed between the cardinal teeth; muscular impressions one in each valve.—*Obs.* The cardinal teeth resembling those of Spondylus, distinguish this genus from others of the Lamarckian family Pectenides. Very few species are yet known, they are brought from the East and West Indies and the Philippine Islands. Fossil species are found in several of the supra-cretaceous beds. Seven species are enumerated in the Monograph by the Author, Part 8, Thesaurus Conchyliorum. *Ex.* Pl. gibbosa, Pl. x. fig. 178.

PNEUMOBRANCHIA. Lam. The second section of the order Gasteropoda, Lam. containing the family Limacinea, fig. 256 to 263.

PODOPSIS. Lam. This genus appears to have been described from specimens of a species of Spondylus, with the triangular disc broken out, so as to present a similarly shaped foramen, which was supposed to afford a passage for a large byssus.

POLINICES. Montfort. 1810. A genus composed of NATICA Mammilla, and other similar species with mammillated spires, and the umbilicus filled with enamel. Pl. xv. fig. 327.

POLLIA. Gray. TRITONIDEA, Sw. The name given by Gray was pre-occupied by a genus of Lepidopterous Insects.

POLLICIPES. Leach. (*Pollex*, a thumb's breadth; *pes*, a foot.) *Order.* Pedunculated Cirripedes, Lam.—*Descr.* Conical, compressed, consisting of numerous valves, mostly in pairs, three or four pairs forming the principal part of the shell, and surrounded at the base by two or three rows of smaller valves, supported on a scaly, short pedicle.—*Obs.* This description will be found to exclude Scalpellum, and Smilium, the valves of which are more equal. The P. Mitellus, Auct. (fig. 37*), has been separated as a genus under the name of Mitellus by some authors, and it is certainly very different from P. polymerus, fig. 37, and P. cornucopia. Pl. ii. fig. 37, 37*.

POLLONTES. Montf. MILIOLA, Bl. A genus of microscopic Foraminifera.

POLYBRANCHIATA. Bl. (Πολυς, *polus*, many; *branchiæ*, gills.) The fifth family of the order Lamellibranchiat6a, Bl. containing the genera Arca, Pectunculus and Nucula, which have a series of small teeth on the hinge.

POLYDONTES. Montf. (Πολυς, *polus*, many; οδος, *odos*, tooth.) A species of Helix, shaped like CAROCOLLA, AND HAVING A NUMBER OF TEETH IN THE APERTURE.

POLYGONAL. MANY-SIDED.

POLYGONUM. SCHUM. (Πολυς, *polus*, many; γωνια, *gonia*, an angle.) A genus composed of species of TURBINELLA, Auct. which have large continuous costæ, so as to present the appearance of many-sided shells. T. polygonus, fig. 383. This generic name may be used to include all those species of Turbinella, Auct. which have very small folds on the columella. Pl. xviii.

POLYGYRA. Say A genus of Heliuciform shells, characterized by the large number of close set whorls, constituting the spire. *Ex.* P. Septemvolvus. Pl. xiii. fig. 275, 276.

POLYLEPAS. Bl. (Πολυς, *polus*, many; λεπας, *lepas*, rock, Linn.) SCALPELLUM, Auct.

POLYMORPHINA. D'Orb. A genus of microscopic Foraminifera.

POLYPHEMUS. Montf. A genus composed of species of ACHATINA, Auct. which have elongated apertures, short spires, and an undulation in the outer lip. P. Glans. Pl. xiv. fig. 288.

POLYPLAXIPHORA. Bl. The second class of the sub-type Malentozoa, Bl. containing the genus Chiton.

POLYSTOMELLA. Lam. A genus of microscopic Foraminifera.

POLYTHALAMACEA. Bl. (Πολυς, *polus*, many; Θαλαμος, *thalamos*, chambers.) The third order of Cephalophora, Bl. the shells of which are described as straight, more or less symmetrically convolute, divided into several chambers. The septa are sometimes, but not always, pierced by one or more siphons. This order is divided into the families,

Orthocerata, Lituacea, Cristacea, Ammonacea, Nautilacea, Turbinacea, Turriculacea, all of which contain genera of chambered shells. De Blainville arranges these families according to the degree in which the spires revolve. The first being straight, as the Orthocerata, and the last being so closely coiled up, that the last whorl covers the rest, as in the Nautilacea.

POLYTHALAMIA. Lam. The first division of the order Cephalopoda, Lam. containing the following families of chambered shells, viz. Orthocerata, Lituacea, Cristacea, Sphærulacea, Radiolata, Nautilacea, Ammonacea. Fig. 463 to 484.

POLYTROPA. Sw. A genus of Scolyminæ, Sw. thus described: "Bucciniform; but the base narrow, and ending in a straight and contracted, but rather short, channel; spire longer, or as long as the aperture; exterior foliated, or tuberculated; inner lip flattened, as in *Purpura*; basal notch small, oblique; no internal channel; crispata. En. Méth. 419, f. 2. Chem. 187, f. 1802. Capilla, Pennant, pl. 72, f. 89, imbricata. Mart. 122. f. 1124. ? rugosa. Chem. f. 1473–4." Sw. p. 305. Pl. xxvi. fig. 546.

POLYXENES. Montf. A genus of microscopic Foraminifera.

POMATIA. Gesner. (Gray, Syn. B. M. p. 133.) A genus of the family of "Cyclostomidæ," described as having "an elongated shell with reflexed lips, and a horny spiral operculum." Also a sub-genus of Snails, containing Helix pomatia, Auct. (Gray's Turton, p. 135.)

POMATIAS. Hartman, 1821. Species of Cyclostoma, of a turrited tapering form, with reflex lips. Cy. patula, Thesaurus Conchyliorum. Pl. xxviii. fig. 171.

POMUS. Humph. Part of Ampullaria, Lamarck.

PORCELLANA. Adanson. Marginella, Auct. Monograph, Thes. Conch. Pl. viii.

PORODRAGUS. Montf. A genus composed of species of Belemnites, placed by De Blainville in the section characterized as swelled near the apex, and straightened towards the base.

PORONIA. Recluz. See Kelliadæ. P. rubra. Pl. xxvii. fig. 568.

POSIDONIA. Brong. A genus formed on the cast of a bivalve shell, common on schists from Dillemberg.

POSTERIOR. (*After*, *behind*.) The posterior or hinder part of a bivalve shell, is that in which the siphonal tube of the animal is placed. It is known in the shell, by the direction of the curve in the umbones, which is from the posterior towards the anterior; also by the ligament, which is always placed on the posterior part of the hinge, when it exists only on one side of the umbones; and by the sinus (when there is one) in the palleal impression, which is always near the posterior muscular impression. In some shells, however, it is very difficult for a learner to trace these marks; such bivalves, for instance, as have the ligament spread out on both sides of the umbones; such as are nearly symmetrical, and have the umbones consequently straight, and a single muscular impression near the centre of the valve. The Brachiopodous bivalves have a different position, with relation to the animal, from the other bivalves, so that the hinge line is the posterior extremity, and the part where the valves open, is the anterior. The posterior extremity of the aperture of a spiral univalve shell, is that nearest to the spire. In patelliform shells the anterior and posterior extremities are distinguished by the muscular impression, which is annular, enclosing a central disc in the inner surface of the shell, excepting where it is interrupted by the place where the head of the animal lies, which of course is anterior. The posterior is marked *p.* in fig. 119, and 387. See Anterior.

POSTERO-BASAL MARGIN of a bivalve shell is the posterior side of the margin opposite the hinge.

POSTERO-DORSAL MARGIN is the posterior side of the hinge.

POTAMIS or POTAMIDES. Brong. A genus of fresh-water shells resembling Cerithium in the characters of the aperture, but which may be known from that genus by the thick, horny epidermis with which they are coated. (Cerithium, Sow.) We think that these shells should be placed near Melania. P. muricata. Pl. xvii. fig. 377.

POTAMOMYA. A genus of shells resembling Corbula, in every respect, except that of being inhabitants of fresh-water. Fig. 498, 499, represents one of these fresh-water Corbulæ. Pl. xxiv.

POTAMOPHILA. Sow. (Ποταμις, *potamis*, river; Φιλιος, *philios*, choice.) "Conques fluviatiles," Lam.—*Descr.* Thick, equivalve, inequilateral, trigonal, covered with a greenish brown, smooth, horny epidermis; hinge thickened, broad, with one central, notched cardinal tooth in one valve, and two in the other, with indistinct lateral teeth; ligament large, supported on prominent fulcra; muscular impressions two in each valve, sub-orbicular.—*Obs.* The name given to this shell refers to its place of abode, being found in rivers. It is the Venus sub-viridis of some authors, although being a fresh-water shell, and having an incrassated hinge, and a smooth, thick epidermis, it is most distinct from that genus. It is described by Bowdich under the name Megadesma, on account of its large ligament, and by Lamarck under that of Galathæa, a name previously used by hin for a genus of Crustacea. P. radiata, fig. 115. Megadesma appears to be the preferable name, since it has the right of priority over Potamophilia. It is found in Africa. Pl. v. fig. 115.

PRIAMUS. Beck, 1837. Halia, Kisso, 1826. A genus composed of Achatina Priamus, Lam. Buccinum Stercus-Pulicum, Chemn. Conch. 9. t. 120. f. 1026–7. This shell is ascertained to belong to a marine mollusc, having a horny operculum, and therefore is justly considered to form a distinct genus, allied to the Bucicna and Struthiolariæ. Pl. xxv. fig. 545.

PRISODON. Schum. Hyria, &c. Auct. Fig. 144.

PRODUCEA. (*Productus*, prominent.) A term applied to the spire of univalve shells, or to any other prominent portion.

PRODUCTA. Sow. (*Productus*, produced.) *Fam.* Brachiopoda, Lam.—*Descr.* Equilateral, inequivalve, thick, striated; one valve generally convex, with the margin reflected; hinge rectilinear, transverse.—*Obs.* The peculiarity of this genus, from which it derives its name, is the manner in which the anterior margins of the valves are drawn out and overwrap each other. The genus is only known in a fossil state. Species occur in Mountain Limestone, and Transition Limestone of older date. P. depressa. Pl. xi. fig. 266*.

PROSERPINA. Gray? Fig. 274, represents a small shell belonging to the Helix tribe, to which it is believed, Mr. Gray has applied the name Proserpina nitida. We do not know how the genus is defined. Pl. xiii. fig. 274.

PROTO. Defr. A fossil shell resembling Turitella, but having a spiral band reaching to the centre of each valve. p. terebralis, Bl.

PSAMMOBIA. Lam. *Fam.* Nymphacea, Lam.—*Descr.* Transverse, oblong, slightly gaping at both ends; hinge with two cardinal teeth in one valve, one in the other; ligament supported upon a prominent fulcrum; muscular impressions two in each valve, sub-orbicular, distant; palleal impression with a large sinus; epidermis thin.—*Obs.* The genus thus described includes Psammotæa of Lamarck, which, according to him, only differs in the number of teeth, and which he says are but "Psammobies dégenerés." The difference appears to be accidental. This genus differs from Tellina in not having a posterior fold in the margin. Pl. iv. fig. 100.

PSAMMACOLA. Bl. (ψαμμος, *psammos*, sand; *cola*, an inhabitant.) A

ated, acute; columella flattened; operculum horny, with the nucleus lateral, thin towards the columella.—*Obs.* True purpuræ are to be found in the Lamarckian genera Buccinum, Ricinula, and others. They may be generally distinguished by the flatness of the columellar lip, and by the short canal or emargination, which is not reflected or raised, as in Buccinum. The species are very numerous and very variable in form, inhabiting the seas of temperate and tropical climates. The animals secrete a purple liquor, which has been used advantageously for dyeing; the origin of the famous Tyrian dye. Reeve's Monograph contains about 80 species. *Ex.* P. persicula. Pl. xix. fig. 44.

PURPURIFERA. Lam. (*Purpura*, purple; *fero*, to carry.) A family belonging to the second section of Lamarck's order Trachelipoda, the shells of which are described as having a very short recurved, or ascending canal, or else only a notch between the inner and outer lips. The name Purpurifera has been given to the family, because the animals which it includes and particularly the genus Purpura, contain the colouring matter from which the ancients obtained the well-known splendid purple. This family contains the following genera.

1. Cassis. Outer lip thick, reflected, denticulated, canal turned suddenly over the back; spire short; including *Cassidea* and *Cypræcassis*. Fig. 410 to 412.
2. Cassidaria. Canal turned gently upwards. Fig. 407, 408.
3. Oniscia. Inner lip granulated; canal short. Fig. 409.
4. Buccinum. Outer lip thickened not reflected; canal short; including *Cyllene* and *Phos*. Fig. 416, 421, 422, 425.
5. Nasa. The same, with a notch or tooth at the extremity of the columella; including *Cyclops*. Fig. 423, 424.
6. Dolium. Swelled, grooved spirally; outer lip not reflected. Fig. 420.
7. Purpura. Aperture large; columellar lip flat; including Tritonidea. Fig. 414, 415.
8. Monoceros. The same, with a tooth on the outer lip. Fig. 417.
9. Concholepas. Patelliform; aperture as large as the shell. Fig. 417.
10. Ricinula. Columellar and outer lips granulated, denticulated, outer lip digitated; including *Tribulus*. Fig. 413.
11. Trichotropis. Hairs on the epidermis, along the keels. Fig. 429.
12. Terebra. Elongated, with a spiral groove near the suture of the whorls. Fig. 428.
13. Bullia. Short; aperture wide; outer lip marginated. Fig. 427.
14. Eburna. Like Buccinum, but the outer lip not thickened. Fig. 426.
15. Harpa. With varices at regular intervals. Fig. 419.

PUSIA. Sw. A sub-genus of Tiara (Mitra.) (Sw. Malac. p. 320.)

PUSIODON. Sw. A genus of "Lucerninæ," Sw. (Helix) thus described: "Shell flattened, smooth; the body-whorl large, and much dilated at the aperture; spire small, flat, of three or four contracted whorls; aperture very oblique, sinuated, or obsoletely toothed at the base of the outer lip, which is spreading and sub-reflected; inner lip obsolete; umbilicus open. Zonaria Chemn. 132. f. 1188. auriculata, Zool. Ill. I. pl. 6." Sw. Malac. p. 330.

PUSIONELLA. Gray. Fusus Nifal, &c.

PUSIOSTOMA. Sw. A genus of the family "Columbellinæ," Sw. Thus described: "general form of Columbella, but the outer lip is only toothed in the middle, where it is greatly thickened; inner lip convex between the granular teeth; punctata, E. M. 374. f. 4. mendicaria, 375. f. 10. turturina, 314. f. 2. fulgurans. Lam." Sw. malac. p. 313.

PUSTULARIA. Sw. A genus of "Cypræinæ," sw. thus described: "Shell generally marked by elevated pustules; aperture narrow and linear; the extremities more or less produced; the teeth continued beyond, and frequently forming elevated striæ across the lips. P. Cicercula, P. Globulus." Sw. Malac. p. 324.

PYCNODUNTA. Fischer. A genus of brachiopoda. Pl. xii. fig. 117, 118.

PYLORIDEA. Bl. The ninth family of the order Lamellibranchiata, Bl. the shells of which are described as nearly always regular, rarely otherwise, nearly always equivalve, gaping at both extremities; hinge incomplete, the teeth becoming gradually obsolete; two distinct muscular impressions; palleal impression very flexuous posteriorly. This family is divided into: Section 1. Ligament internal; Pandora, Thracia, Anatina, Mya, Lutricola. Section 2. Ligament external; Psammocola, Soletellina, Solen, Sanguinolaria, Solenocurtus, Solinomya, Panopæa, Glycimeris, Saxicava, Byssomya, Rhomboides, Hiatella, Gastrochæna, Clavagella, Aspergillum.

PYRAMIDAL. (*Pyramidalis.*) Resembling a pyramid in form. *Ex.* Cerithium Telescopium, fig. 378.

PYRAMIDELLA. Lam. (*A little pyramid.*) *Fam.* Pliacea, Lam. Auriculacea, Bl.—*Descr.* Pyramidal, smooth, polished; spire long, pointed, composed of numerous whorls; aperture small, modified by the last whorl, rounded anteriorly; outer lip slightly expanded; columella tortuous, with several folds. This is a genus of small, polished, marine shells. Pyramidella Terebellum. Pl. xv. fig. 342.

PYRAMIS. Schum. 1817. Testus, Montfort, 1810. Trochus Obeliscus. Lamarck.

PYRAZUS. Montf. Part of the genus Potamis, Brongniart.

PYRELLA. Sw. A genus consisting of Turbinella Spirilla, Auct. and similar species, having a long channel, a pyriform outline, and one strong plait at the base of the columella, the apex of the spire is enlarged. P. Spirillus, fig. 344. (The proper term would be Spirilla.) Pl. xxxi. fig. 550.

PYRIFORM. (*Pyrum*, a pear; *forma*, shape.) Shaped like a pear, i.e. large and rounding at one end, and gradually tapering at the other. *Ex.* Pyrula, fig. 390.

PYRGO. Defr. A genus of microscopic Foraminifera.

PYRGOMA. Auct. (Πυργος, *pyrgus*, a tower.) *Order* Sessile Cirripedes, Lam.—*Descr.* Composed of a single conical, hollow paries, with a small aperture closed by an operculum of four valves, and supported upon a cup-shaped base.—*Obs.* The genera into which Leach has divided this genus are Pyrgoma, Adna, and Megatrema; his genera Nobia and Savignium differ in having but two valves for the operculum. Pyrgoma differs from Creusia in having the body of the shell, i.e. the parietal cone, simple, not divided into valves. Pl. i. fig. 31. Pl. xxiv. fig. 489, 490.

PYRULA. Lamarck. Family Canalifera, generally turbinate, with few angular whorls; aperture terminating in a canal; columella smooth. The Ficulæ being removed, there remain a considerable number of species under this name, typified by P. Melongena, &c.

PYRUM. Humph. Pyrula, Lam.

PYTHINA. Hinds. Voyage of the Sulphur. P. 70. Pl. xix. fig. 8, 9. A bivalve shell thus described, (translation) "transverse, subæquilateral, æquivalve. One valve with one small central and two lateral teeth; the other valve with two lateral teeth; ligament internal; two rounded muscular impressions; palleal impression rather straight, without a sinus. There is only one species described, the P. Deshayesiana. Pl. xxvii. fig. 571.

QUADRATE. (*Quadratus.*) Square, applied when the outline of shells is formed by nearly straight lines meeting at right angles.

QUINQUELOCULINA. D'Orbigny. A genus of microscopic Foraminifera.

QUOYIA. Desh. MS. Planaxis decollatus Quoy et Gaimard.

RADIATING. (*Radians.*) A term applied to the ribs, striæ, bands of colours, &c. when they meet in a point at the umbones of a bivalve shell, and spread out towards the ventral margin.—*Ex.* The bands of colour in Tellina radiata, fig. 105.

RADICATED. (*Radix*, a root.) Attached, and as it were rooted by means of a fibrous byssus.

RADIOLATA. Lam. A family belonging to the dorer Cephalopoda, Lam. The shells belonging to it are described as discoidal, with the spire central, and the chambers radiating from the centre to the circumference. This family contains the genera Rotalina, Lenticulina, and Placentula.

RADIOLITES. A genus belonging to the family of Rudistes, differing from Sphærulites, in having both the valves more conical.

RADIUS. Montf. A genus composed of Ovulum Volva, Auct. and other similar species, having a long attenuated canal at each extremity. Pl. xx. fig. 442.

RADIX. Montf. A genus composed of species of Limnæa, having a short spire and wide aperture.—*Ex.* L. aperta, fig. 309.

RADSIA. Gray. Chiton Barnesii, and similar species.

RAMIFIED. (*Ramus*, a branch.) Branched out.—*Ex.* The varices of some Murices, &c.

RAMPHIDOMA. Schum. Pollicipes, Leach.

RAMOSE. (*Ramosus*, branched. Spread out into branches.) *Ex.* Murex inflatus, fig. 395.

RANELLA. Auct. (*Rana*, a frog.) *Fam.* Canalifera, Lam. Siphonostomata, Bl.—*Descr.* Oval or oblong, depressed, thick, with two rows of continuous varices, skirting the outline, one on each side; spire rather short, pyramidal, acute, aperture oval, terminating in a canal at each extremity; outer lip thickened within, crenulated, or denticulated, forming an external varix; inner lip spread over a protion of the body whorl.—*Obs.* The shells composing this well-defined genus, are for the most part covered with tuberculations, and granulations, and from the colour and squat shape of some species, have been likened to frogs. The Ranellæ are mostly inhabitants of the East Indian seas. The few fossil species known, occur in the tertiary beds. The two continuous rows of varices skirting the spire, distinguish this genus from Triton, which it nearly approaches, and into which some species run by imperceptible gradations. Mr. Reeve's Monograph contains 50 species. Pl. xvii. fig. 393, 394.

RANGIA. Desmoulins. Gnathodon, Gray.

RAPANUS. Schum? A genus consisting of species of Pyrula, Auct. which are thin, much inflated, with short canals. P. papyracea. Pl. xvii. fig. 389.

RAPELLA. Sw. A genus of "Pyrulinæ," Sw. thus described: "Shell ventricose, generally thin, almost globose; the base suddenly contracted, and forming a short canal, the channel almost obsolete; umbilicus large, partly concealed by the inner lip. R. papyracea. En. Méth. 436, f. 1." Sw. p. 307. Rapanus, Schum. Fig. 389.

RAPHANISTER. Montf. A species of madrepore, described as a shell.

RAPUM. Humph. Turbinella, Lam.

RAZOR SHELL. A common name by which shells of the genus Solen are known in the market.

RECTILINEAR. (*Rectus*, right; *linea*, a line.) In a straight line. *Ex.* The hinge of Byssoarca Noœ, fig. 132.

RECURVED. (*Re*, back; *curvo*, to bend.) Turned backwards; the term, when applied to symmetrical conical univalves, is used to signify that the apex is turned towards the posterior margin, as in Emarginula, fig. 241.

REFLECTED. (*Reflected*, to fold back.) Turned, or folded backwards. *Ex.* The edge of the outer lip in Bulinus, fig. 282, is *reflected*, while that of Cypræa, fig. 445 to 450, is *inflected.*

REGISTOMA. Hassell, 1824. Pupina vitrœa, Thesaurus Conchyliorum, Pl. iv. fig. 6.

REMOTE. (*Remotus*, distant.) Remote lateral teeth in a bivalve shell, are those that are placed at a distance from the cardinal teeth. *Ex.* The lateral teeth of Aphrodita, (fig. 123) are remote; those of Donax, (fig. 108) are near.

RENIELLA. Sw. A sub-genus of Malleus. Lardn. Cyclop. Malac. p. 886. Gray states it to be only a distorted specimen of Vulsella, Syn. B. M. p. 145.

RENIFORM. (*Ren*, a kidney; *forma*, shape.) Shaped like a kidney. *Ex.* The aperture of Ampullaria, fig. 318.

RENULINA. Lam. A genus of microscopic Foraminifera.

REOPHAX. Montf. A genus of microscopic Orthocerata, Bl.

REPENT. (*Repens*, creeping.) A term applied to those shells, which, being attached by the whole length of their shell, give the idea of creeping or crawling. *Ex.* Vermilia, fig. 7.

RETICULATED. (*Reticulatus.*) Resembling net-work.

RETIFERA. Bl. The first family of the order Cervicobranchiata, Bl. containing the genus Patella.

REVERSED or Sinistral Shells, are those in which the aperture is on the left side of the shell, while it is held with the mouth downwards, and towards the observer. *Ex.* Balea, fig. 296. Attached bivalves are said to be reversed, when the left valve is free, instead of the right; a circumstance which sometimes occurs in Chama and Ostrea.

RHEDA. Humph. Hyalæa, Lam.

RHINOCLAVIS. Sw. A genus of "Cerithinæ," Sw. thus described: "channel curved backwards, in an erect position; inner lip very thick, with a tumid margin; pillar generally with a central plait; operculum ear-shaped; lineatum. En. M. 443, fig. 3, Vertagus. Ib. f. 2, subulatum. Lam. No. 23, fasciatum. Mart. 157, f. 1481. obeliscus, En. Méth. 443, f. 4; faluco, Ib. f. 5, (aberrant), semi-granosum. Ib. 443, f. 1, asperum. Mart. 157, f. 1483.

RHINOCURUS. Montf. A genus of microscopic Foraminifera.

RHINODOMUS. Sw. A genus of "Scolyminæ," Sw. thus described: No internal grove; shell clavate; the spire longer than, or equal with the aperture; the whorls with ridges or longitudinal varices, and rendered hispid by transverse grooves; inner lip wanting; pillar with a terminal fold; aperture striated; outer lip with a basal sinus. R. senticosus, Chem. tab. 193. f. 1864–1866.

RHIZORUS. Montf. A genus described from a microscopic shell, appearing to be a cylindrical Bulla.

RHODOSTOMA. Sw. A sub-genus of "Turbiniæ," Sw. p. 344.

RHOMBOIDAL. (ῥομβοειδος, *rhomboeidus.*) Having a rhombic form, i.e. four-sided; two sides meeting at acute, two at obtuse, angles. Conchologists are not very strict in the application of this term, for, indeed, a perfect rhomboidal figure could not be found among shells.

RHOMBOIDES. Bl. A genus described as resembling Byssomya as to the shell, but differing as to the animal. Mytilus rugosus, Gmelin. Hypogæa barbata, Poli.

RHOMBUS. Montf. (ῥομβος, *rhombos*, a rhomb.) A genus consisting of species of Conus, having a rhomboidal or quadrilateral form and a coronated spire. *Ex.* Conus nocturnus, fig. 459.

RICINULA. Lamarck, 1812. "Sistrum," Montfort, 1810, has the

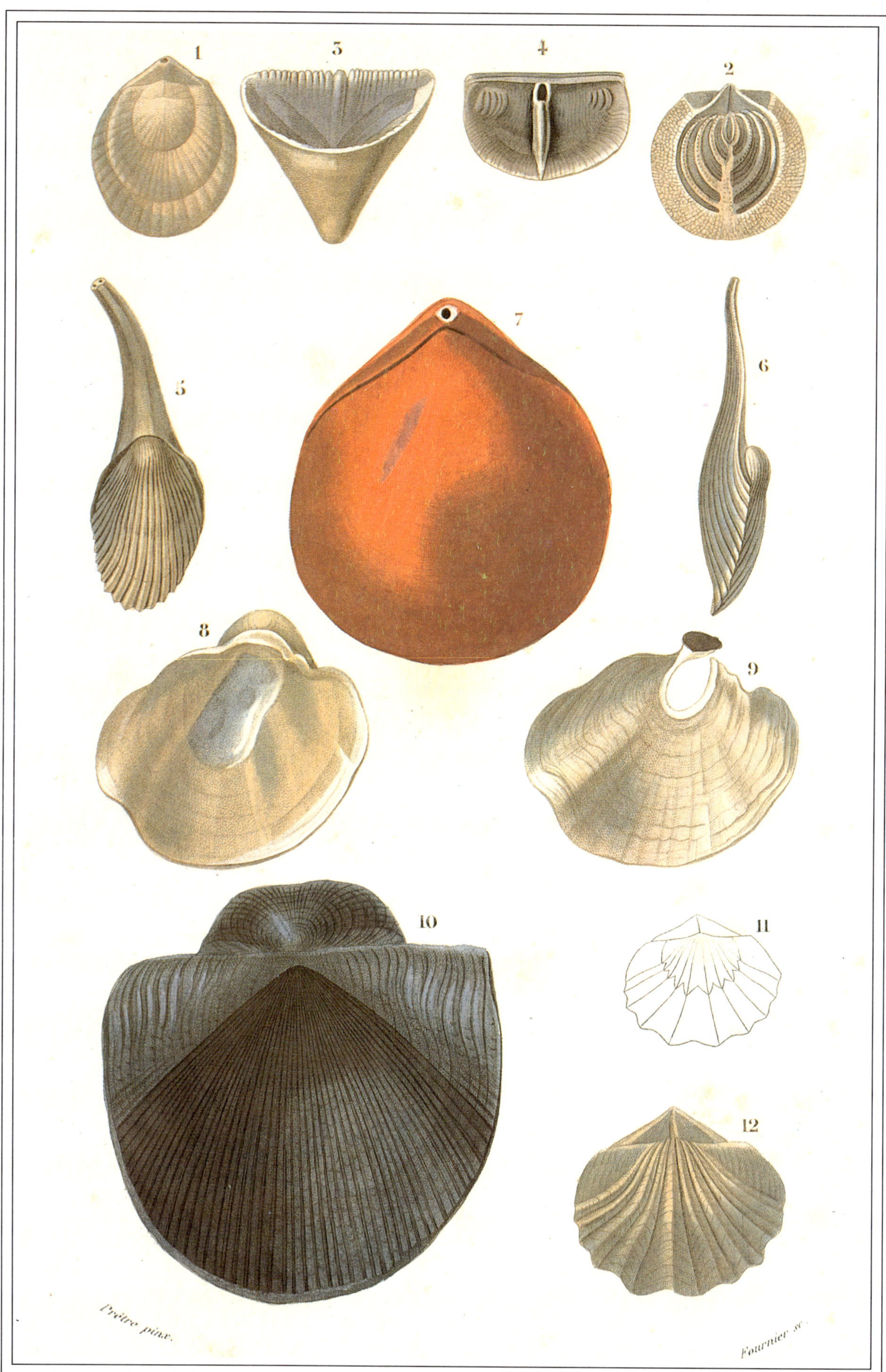

1, 2. *Thécidée rayonnante*. (Thecidea radians, *Def.*)

3, 4. *Calcéole sandaline*. (Calceola sandalina, *Lamk.*)

5, 6. *Térébratule lyre*. (Terebratula lyra, *Lamk.*)

7. *Térébratule lenticulaire*. (Terebratula lenticularis, *Desh.*)

8, 9. *Anomie pélure d'oignon*. (Anomia ephippium, *Lin.*)

10. *Producte treillissé*. (Productus antiquatus, *Sow.*)

11, 12. *Térébratule de Say*. (Terebratula Sayi, *Morton.*)

priority. (Resembling the seed-vessel of the *Ricinus.*) *Fam.* Purpurifera, Lam. Entomostomata, Bl.—*Descr.* Sub-ovate, thick, tuberculated; spire short; aperture narrow, terminating anteriorly in a short canal; outer lip thickened, denticulated within, digitated without; columellar lip spread over a portion of the body whorl, and granulated.—*Obs.* This interesting genus is composed of some neat little shells allied to Purpura, from which they are distinguished by the finger-like branching of the outer lip, and the granulations of the columella. More than 50 species are described in Reeve's Monograph. R. Horrida, Pl. xix. fig. 413.

RIGHT. See DEXTRAL.

RIMULA. Couthoy. CEMORIA, Leach.

RIMULARIA. Defrance. A genus consisting of a minute species of EMARGINULA, Auct. which has a fissure near the margin, but not reaching it. R. Blainvilii, fig. 243.

RIMULINA. D'Orbigny. A genus of microscopic Foraminifera.

RINGICULA. Deshayes. A genus founded on Auricula ringens of Lamarck and several small fossils, resembling in some respects Pedipes of Adanson; they would belong to Tornatella, were it not for the lips being thickened and marginated. Pl. xxv. fig. 540, 541. A. ringens.

RISELLA. Gray, 1840. Small, vertically depressed species of Trochidæ, with flat undersides. Tr. Melanostomus.

RISSOA. Freminville. *Fam.* Ellipsostomata, Bl. Melaniana, Lam.—*Descr.* Oblong, turrited, acuminated; spire long, consisting of numerous whorls; aperture round or oval, pointed posteriorly, dilated anteriorly; outer lip slightly thickened, emarginated, operculum horny.—*Obs.* The Rissoæ are small white, marine shells, considered by some authors as resembling Melaniæ, but placed by Sowerby near the Scalariæ. They are principally from the shores of the Mediterranean, and are also very abundant on the British shores, as well as the East and West Indian. K. reticulata. R. reticulata. Pl. xv. fig. 346.

ROBULUS. Montf. A genus of microscopic Foraminifera.

ROLLUS. Montf. A genus composed of CONUS Geographus, Auct. Pl. xxi. fig. 462, and other species, rather cylindrical in form, and having a coronated spire.

ROSALINA. D'Orb. A genus of microscopic Foraminifera.

ROSTELLARIA. Lamarck, 1801. (From *rostrum*, a beak.) *Fam.* Alatæ, Lam. Siphonostomata, Bl.—*Descr.* Turrited, fusiform, thick, smooth or ribbed; aperture oval, terminating anteriorly in a long canal, posteriorly in a channel running up the spire; outer lip dilated, thickened, sometimes digitated, running up all or part of the spire, with a sinus near the anterior canal; inner lip smooth, spread over part of the body whorl and of the spire. The Red Sea and the Indian Ocean produce the few known species of this genus.—*Obs.* HIPPOCHRENES is the name given by De Montfort, to those fossil species which have the outer lip simple and very much dilated. Four recent species are enumerated in the Thesaurus, Pt. i. by the Author. Ex. R. Curvirostrum. Pl. xviii. fig. 402.

ROSTRATED. (From *rostrum*, a beak.) Having one or more protruding points, as Tellina rostrata.

ROTALIA. Lam. A genus of microscopic Foraminifera. The same as Rotalites of De Montfort.

ROTELLA. Lam. 1822. Previously HELICINA, Lamarck. (*A little wheel.*) *Fam.* Turbinacea, Lam.—*Descr.* Orbicular, generally smooth, shining; spire conical, depressed, short; aperture subtrigonal; outer lip thin, angulated near the centre; inner lip spread over the surface of the whorls, forming a thickened disc. Operculum horny, orbicular, spiral, with numerous whorls.—*Obs.* The pretty little shells thus described are found in seas of tropical climates. They are distinguished from other genera of the family by their lenticular form and the orbicular callosity of the under surface. Fig. 357, R. vestiaria. Pl. xvi.

RUDISTES. Lam. A family of the order Conchifera Monomyaria, Lam. the shells of which are described as irregular, very inequivalve, without distinct umbones; the ligament, hinge and animal entirely unknown. The shells contained in this family may be thus distinguished.

1. CALCEOLA. Large valve conical; attached by a flat space between the umbones, which form the extremities of the shell. Fig. 194.
2. HIPPURITES. Large valve cylindrical, with two internal lobes or varices. Fig. 198.
3. SPHÆRULITES. Large valve attached, including *Radiolites*. Birostrites is proved to be the cast of a Sphærulites. Fig. 193, 196.
4. HIPPONYX. Flat valve attached, upper valve conical. Fig. 199, 200.

RUDISTES. Bl. The second order of the class Acephalophora, Bl. containing the genera Sphærulites, Crania, Hippurites, Radiolites, Birostrites and Calceola.

RUDOLPHUS. Lam. MONOCEROS, Auct.

RUFOUS. Reddish brown.

RUGOSE. Rough, rugged.

RUPELLARIA. Fl. de Belvue. An unfigured shell placed by De Blainville in a division of the genus Venerirupis.

RUPICOLA. Fl. de Belvue. A shell described by De Blainville as an equivalve, terebrating species of ANATINA. A. rupicola, Lam.

SABINEA. A genus of shells resembling small species of LITTORINA, as L. Ulvæ, &c. of our shores.

SADDLE OYSTER. PLACUNA Sella, so called on account of a resemblance in shape to a saddle; the part near the umbones being flat, and the ventral margins being turned up in a sort of fluting or peak.

SAGITTA. (*An arrow.*) An ancient name for Belemnites.

SALIENT. (*Saliens.*) Jutting out, prominent.

SALPACEA. Bl. The second family of the order Heterobranchiata, Bl. containing no genera of shells.

SANDALINA. Schum. CREPIDULINA, Lam. A genus of microscopic Foraminifera.

SANGUINOLARIA. Lamarck, 1801. (*Sanguis*, blood.) *Fam.* Nymphacea, Lam. Pyloridea, Bl.—*Descr.* Equivalve, inequilateral, transverse, sub-ovate, rounded anteriory, sub-rostrate posteriorly, compressed, thin, covered with a shining epidermis, gaping at the sides; hinge with two cardinal teeth in each valve, and an external ligament supported upon a prominent fulcrum; muscular impressions two in each valve, lateral, irregular, palleal impressions with a large sinus.—*Obs.* This description is made to exclude some of Lamarck's species of Sanguinolaria, such as S. occidens, S. rugosa, which are Psammobiæ; and to include others which he has left out. The Sanguinolariæ are sub-rostrated posteriorly, while the Psammobiæ are sub-quadrate, and have a posterior angle. S. rosea. Sandy shores of tropical climates. Pl. iv. fig. 98.

SARACENARIA. Defr. A genus of microscopic Foraminifera.

SAVIGNIUM. Leach. A genus of Sessile Cirripedes, described as composed of four valves soldered together, and a convex bivalve operculum; the ventral and posterior valve on each side being soldered together, in other respects resembling PYRGOMA. Pl. i. fig. 30.

SAXICAVA. Fl. de Belvue. Journ de. Ph. an. 10. (*Saxum*, a stone; *cava*, a hollow.) *Fam.* Lithophagidæ, Lam. Pyloridea, Bl.—*Descr.* Transverse, irregular, generally oblong, inequilateral, sub-equivalve, gaping anteriorly; ligament external; muscular impressions two, lateral; palleal impression interrupted, not sinuated; hinge, when young with sometimes two or three minute, obtuse, generally indistinct, cardinal teeth; which become obsolete when full grown—*Obs*. Several genera have been founded only upon the difference between the young and old shell of the same species of this genus. The Saxicavæ are found in the little hollows of rocks; in cavities on the backs of oysters, of roots of seaweeds, &c. in northern and temperate climates. S. rugosa. Pl. iv. fig. 94.

SCABRICULA. Sw. A sub-genus of Mitræ, consisting of species which have a roughened external surface, &c. Sw. Malac. p. 319.

SCABROUS. Rough.

SCALA. Klein. SCALARIA, Auct.

SCALARIA. Lamarck, 1801. *Fam*. Scalariana, Lam. Cricostomata, Bl.—*Descr*. Turrited, oval or oblong; spire long, composed of rounded, sometimes separate whorls, surrounded by regular concentric ribs; aperture oval, peristome reflected, continuous, entire—*Obs*. The typical species of this genus, commonly called the Wentletrap, (S. pretiosa) is celebrated for the beautiful appearance caused by the numerous ribs encircling the whorls, and formerly produced an immense price in the market. It is brought from China. There are many smaller species, some of which are equally elegant. Fig. 351, S. Pallasii, Kiener. The Monograph in Sowerby's Thesaurus contains 93 species.

SCALARINA. Lam. A family belonging to the first section of the order Trachelipoda, Lam. The shells belonging to it are described as having the inner and outer lips continuous, without a canal, emargination, or other division. In this respect the family is stated to differ from the Turbinacea, and is therefore separated. The genera may be distinguished as follows:–

1. VERMETUS. Irregularly twisted, like Serpula. Fig. 345.
2. EULIMA. Pyramidal; apex contorted; including *Bonellia*. Fig. 347, 348.
3. RISSOA. Pyramidal, straight, consisting of a few whorls. Fig. 346.
4. SCALARIA. With external varices. Fig. 351.
5. CIRRUS. Trochiform. Fig. 349.
6. ENOMPHALUS. Orbicular. Fig. 350.
7. DELPHINULA. Few whorls, rapidly increasing. Fig. 352.

SCALLOP. The common name for shells of the genus Pecten, the larger species of which were worn by pilgrims to the Holy Land in the time of the Crusades.

SCALPELLUM. Leach. 1817. (A little knife or lancet). *Order*, Pedunculated Cirripedes, Lam. *Descr*. Flat, quadrated, acuminated, composed of thirteen valves, one dorsal, arcuated; one pair apicial, acuminated: one pair ventral; two pair lateral, small, sub-quadrate; pedicle scaly. *Obs*. This genus and *Smilium*, are the only Pedunculated Cirripedes which have thirteen valves; in the latter genus, which we think should at any rate be united to this, the valves are somewhat differently placed, and the pedicle is said to be smooth. Scalpellum vulgare. British. Pl. ii. fig. 35. and S. peronii, Pl. ii. fig. 36.

SCAPHA. Klein. (*A boat*.) NAVICELLA, Auct.

SCAPHA. Voluta vespertilio, &c.

SCAPHANDER. Montf. A sub-genus of Bullidæ represented by BULLA lignaria, Auct. Fig. 251. Several species are described in Adams' Monograph, No. 11. Sowerby's Thesaurus.

SCAPHELLA. Sw. A genus of the family "Volutinæ," Sw. thus described: "Shell smooth, almost polished; outer lip thickened internally; suture enamelled; lower plaits the smallest; apex of the spire various: 1. fusiformis. Sw. Bligh. Cat. 2, undulatus. *Ex*. Conch. pl. 27. 3. Junonia, Thesaurus Conchyliorum, pl. 49. fig. 44. stromboides. 5. papillosa. Sw. Sow. gen." Sw. Malac. p. 318.

SCAPHITES. (*A boat*.) *Fam*. ammonacea, Lam. and Bl.—*Descr*. convolute, chambered, closely related to the Ammonites, from which it differs in the last whorl being eccentrically straightened, and lengthened, and again incurved towards the extremity. Only known in a fossil state. S æqualis. Pl. xxiii. fig. 481.

SCAPHULA. Sw. A genus of "OLIVINÆ," Sw. thus described: "Spire very short, thick, abtuse, and not defined; aperture very wide, with only two or three oblique plaits at the base. OLIVA patula, *Sow*. Tank. Cat. 2331. (*b*") (Sw. P. 332.) and O. auricularia, Lamarck.

SCARABUS. Montf. (*Scarabæus*, a kind of beetle.) *Fam*. Colimacea, Lam. Auriculacea, Fer.—*Descr*. Oval, somewhat compressed, smooth, with slightly raised varices; spire equal in length to the aperture, pointed, consisting of various whorls; aperture ovate, rounded anteriorly, pointed posteriorly, modified by the last whorl; outer lip sub-reflected, with several prominent folds on the inner edge; inner lip spread over a portion of the body whorls, with several prominent folds.—*Obs*. The shells of this genus are found like the Auriculæ, in marshy places. C. Imbrium is said to have been found on the tops of mountains, by Captain Freycinet. S. imbrium. Pl. xiv. fig. 299.

SCHIZOCHITON. Gray. Ch. incisus, having a notch in the margin.

SCHIZODESMA. Gray. A genus composed of species of MACTRA, Auct. with the ligament placed in an external slit. M. Spengleri. Pl. iv. fig. 81.

SCISSURELLA. D'Orbigny. (*Scissus*, cut.) *Fam*. Turbinacea, Lam.—*Descr*. Sub-globose, umbilicated, with a spiral groove terminating at the margin of the outer lip in a slit; spire short; aperture oval, modified by the last whorl; outer lip sharp, with a deep slit near the spire. Recent on the coast of Britain; fossil in the Calcaire-grossièr.—*Obs*. This genus, consisting of small shells, is known from Pleurotomaria by the shortness of the spire; the latter genus being trochiform. S. elatoir. Pl. xv. fig. 340.

SCOLYMUS. Sw. A genus of the family "Scolyminæ." Sw. (Turbinella) thus described: "Sub-fusiform, armed with foliated spines; spire shorter; pillar with distinct plaits in the middle." The species enumerated are, "cornigerus, pugilaris, Globulus, Rhinoceros, ceramicus, Capitellum, umbilicaris, mitis." Sw. Malac. p. 304.

SCROBICULARIA. Schumacher. A genus belonging to the Tellinidæ, having no lateral teeth, but small cardinal teeth and the internal cartilage placed in an oblique spathular fulcrum in each valve. S. piperita, Forbes and Hanley, Brit. Mollusca, pl. xv. fig. 5.

SCONSIA. Gray, 1847. Cassidaria striata, *Lamarck*, &c.

SCORTIMUS. Montf. A genus of microscopis Foraminifera.

SCROBICULATED. (*Scrobiculus*, a little ditch or furrow.) Having small ditches or furrows marked on the surface.

SCUTELLA. Brod. (*Scutellum*, a little shield.) *Fam*. Phyllidiana, Lam.—*Descr*. Shaped like Ancylus, pearly within; apex posteriorly inclined, central, involute; muscular impressions two, oblong, ovate, lateral; aperture large, ovate.—*Obs*. This genus is intermediate between Ancylus and Patella; while in the aspect of the beak, the observer is reminded of Navicella. BRODERIPIA, Gray, contains part of this genus typified by S. rosea. pl. xxiv. fig. 508, 509. Scutella crenulata.

SCUTIBRANCHIATA. Bl. (*Scutum*, a shield; *branchiæ*, gills.) The third order of Paracepalophora Hermaphrodita, Bl. containing animals with patelliform, but not symmetrical shells, and divided into the families Otidea and Calyptracea.

SCUTUM. Montf (*A shield*) PARMOPHORUS ELONGATUS, Lam.

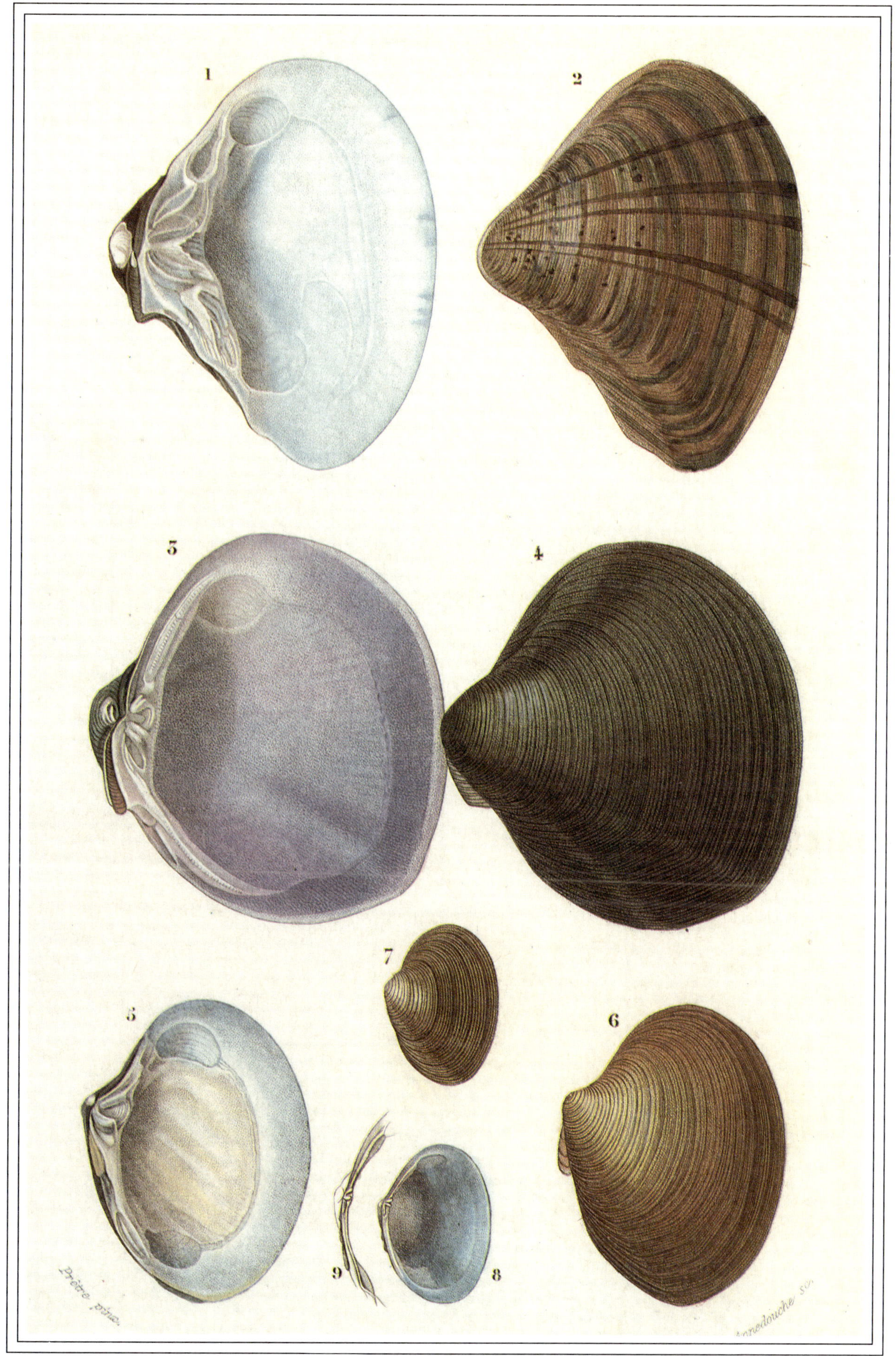

1, 2. *Galathée à rayons*. (Galathea radiata, *Lamk*.)
3, 4. *Cyrène cordiforme*. (Cyrena cordiformis, *Desh*.)
5, 6. *Astarté d'Islande*. (Astarte Islandica, *Desh*.)
7, 8, 9. *Cyclade des rivières*. (Cyclas rivicola, *Lamk*.)

SECURIFORM. (*Securis*, an axe; *forma*, shape.) Hatchet-shaped. *Ex.* Pedum. fig. 179.

SEDENTARY ANNELIDES. Lam. The third order of the class Annelides, Lam. distinguished from the other two orders by the circumstance of the animal being enveloped by a shelly tube which it never entirely leaves. The order is divided into the families Dorsalia, Maldania, Serpulacea, and Amphitrites. Fig. 1 to 13.

SEA DATE. The common name for Pholas Dactylus in the market, given to it on account of its cylindrical shape. Fig. 35.

SEGMENTINA. Fleming, 1824. Nautilus Lacustris, Montagu. Test. Brit. Planorbis nitidus, Drap. tab. 2. Fig. 17 to 19.

SEMICORDATE. Half heart-shaped.

SEMIDISCOIDAL. Forming the half of a circular disc.

SEMILUNAR. Half moon-shaped.

SENECTUS. Humph. A genus of "Senectinæ," thus described by Swainson: "Imperforate; the base produced into a broad flat lobe, spire rather elevated and pointed; the whorls convex; aperture perfectly round; not more oblique than *Helix*; inner lip entirely wanting, imperialis. Mart. 180. f. 1790. marmoratus. 1. M. 448. f. 1," Sw. p. 348.

SEMIPHYLLIDIANA. Lam. The second family of the order Gasteropoda, Lam. the genera of which are distinguished as follows:–

1. Umbrella, round, flat; apex central, muscular impression not interrupted. Fig. 332.
2. Pleurobranchus, apex lateral, sub-spiral. Fig. 232.

SENOCLITA. Schum. Cineras, Leach. See Conchoderma.

SEPTARIA. Lam. See Teredo.

SEPTUM. (Lat.) An enclosure, applied to the thin plate of Crepidula, Fig. 239; also to the plates dividing the chambers of multilocular shells.

SERAPHYS. Montf. 1810. Terebellum convolutum, Lam. Fig. 451.

SERPULA. Auct. (*A little serpent.*) *Fam.* Serpulacea, Lam.—*Descr.* Tubular, narrow, pointed at the apex, gradually widening towards the aperture, attached irregularly, sometimes spirally, twisted, imbricated; keeled or plain; aperture generally round, with the edge simple, or angulated by the termination of external ribs or keels.—*Obs.* This description is intended to include the genera Serpula, Spirorbis, Vermilia, Galeolaria, &c. The Serpulæ abound in all seas, on rocky shores, at any time covered by water, attached to any kind of marine substance, whether movable or stationary. The fossil species occur in almost all tertiary strata. Pl. i. fig. 4 to 7.

SERPULACEA. Lam. The fourth family of the order Sedentary Annelides, Lam. containing the following genera of tubular, irregular shells.

1. Serpula, attached by a small portion of the shell. Fig. 4.
2. Spirorbis, attached by the whole length, coiled. Fig. 5.
3. Galeolaria, with the open extremity raised, and the aperture tongue-shaped. Fig. 6.
4. vermilla, attached by the whole length, straight or waved. Fig.
5. Spiroglyphus, which hollows a bed in the body to which it is attached. Fig. 8.

Sowerby* gives satisfactory reasons for reuniting the whole of the preceding under the name Serpula.

6. Magilus, which burrows in coral; outer lip reflected. Fig. 9 to 10.
7. Leptoconchus, outer lip reflected. Fig. 11.
8. Stylifer, spiral, thin, globular, living in Starfish. Fig. 12, 13.

The three last genera should certainly find some outer place in the system.

SERPULORBIS. Sassi, 1827.

SESSILE CIRRIPEDES. Lam. (*Sessilis*, low, dwarfish.) An order of Cirripedes, consisting of those which are attached by the base of the shells, containing the genera Tubicinella, Balanus, Coronula, Acasta, Pyrgoma, Creusia. To which may be added some other genera enumerated in explanation of figures 14 to 33. The shells of the Sessile Cirripedes consist of two different sets of valves: 1st. The *parietal* valves, or pieces arranged in a circle, side by side, around the body of the animal, (an arrangement designated *coronular* by De Blainville.) 2nd. The *opercular* valves, or pieces placed so as to enclose the aperture. Between those opercular valves the ciliæ protrude which characterize the class. Besides these two sets of valves, there is generally a shelly plate, serving as a sort of foundation to the rest. The Sessile Cirripedes may be thus arranged.

1. Tubicinella. Six parietal valves, tube-shaped, opercular valves perpendicular. Fig. 14.
2. Coronula. Six parietal valves, opercular valves horizontal. Fig. 15, 16, 17, 18.

These two genera fix themselves in the skin of the Whale. The latter has been divided into the genera Chelonobia, Cetopirus, Diadema, and Chthalamus.

3. Platylepas. Valves divided, each having a prominent internal plate. Fig. 19.
4. Clitia. Parietal valves four, opercular valves two, valves dove-tailed into each other. Fig. 20.
5. Elmineus. Parietal valves four, opercular valves four. Fig. 22.
6. Conia. Parietal valves four, thick and porous at the base. Fig. 21.
7. Octomeris. Parietal valves eight. Fig. 24.
8. Catophragmus. Parietal valves numerous, irregular. Fig. 23.
9. Balanus. Parietal valves six; opercular valves four, placed against each other conically in pairs. This genus has been divided into acasta, Conoplea, Chirona, and Balanus. Fig. 25, 26, 27.
10. Creusia. Parietal valves, four supported on the edge of a funnel-shaped cavity. Fig 28.
11. Pyrgoma. Paries simple, supported on a cavity. This genus has been divided into the genera Nobia, Savignium, Pyrgoma, Adna, Megatrema, and Daracia. Fig. 29 to 33.

SETIFEROUS. Hairy.

SHANK SHELL. The vulgar name for the shell designated Murex Rapa. It is used in Ceylon for ornamental purposes.

SIDEROLITES. Monft. A genus of microscopic Foraminifera.

SIGARETUS. Lam. *Fam.* Macrostomata, Lam.—*Descr.* Suborbicular, oblique, haliotoid, thick; spire depressed, consisting of two or three rapidly increasing whorls; aperture wide, entire, modified by the last whorl, the width exceeding the length; columella tortuous; inner lip spread thinly over part of the body whorl; epidermis thin.—*Obs.* This genus is distinguished from Natica, by the width of the aperture, and the absence of the umbilical callosity. It may be known from Stomatia, and Stomatella, by the texture, which in Sigaretus, is never pearly as in Stomatia, the former being partly an internal shell. Mostly brought from tropical climates. S. concavus. Pl. xv. fig. 334.

SILIQUA. Megerle. (A husk, or pod.) Leguminaria, Schum. A genus composed of species of Solen, Auct. which have an internal rib. Fig. 51, Solen radiatus.

SILIQUARIA. (Lamarck, 1801.) *Fam.* Cricostomata, Bl. Dorsalia,

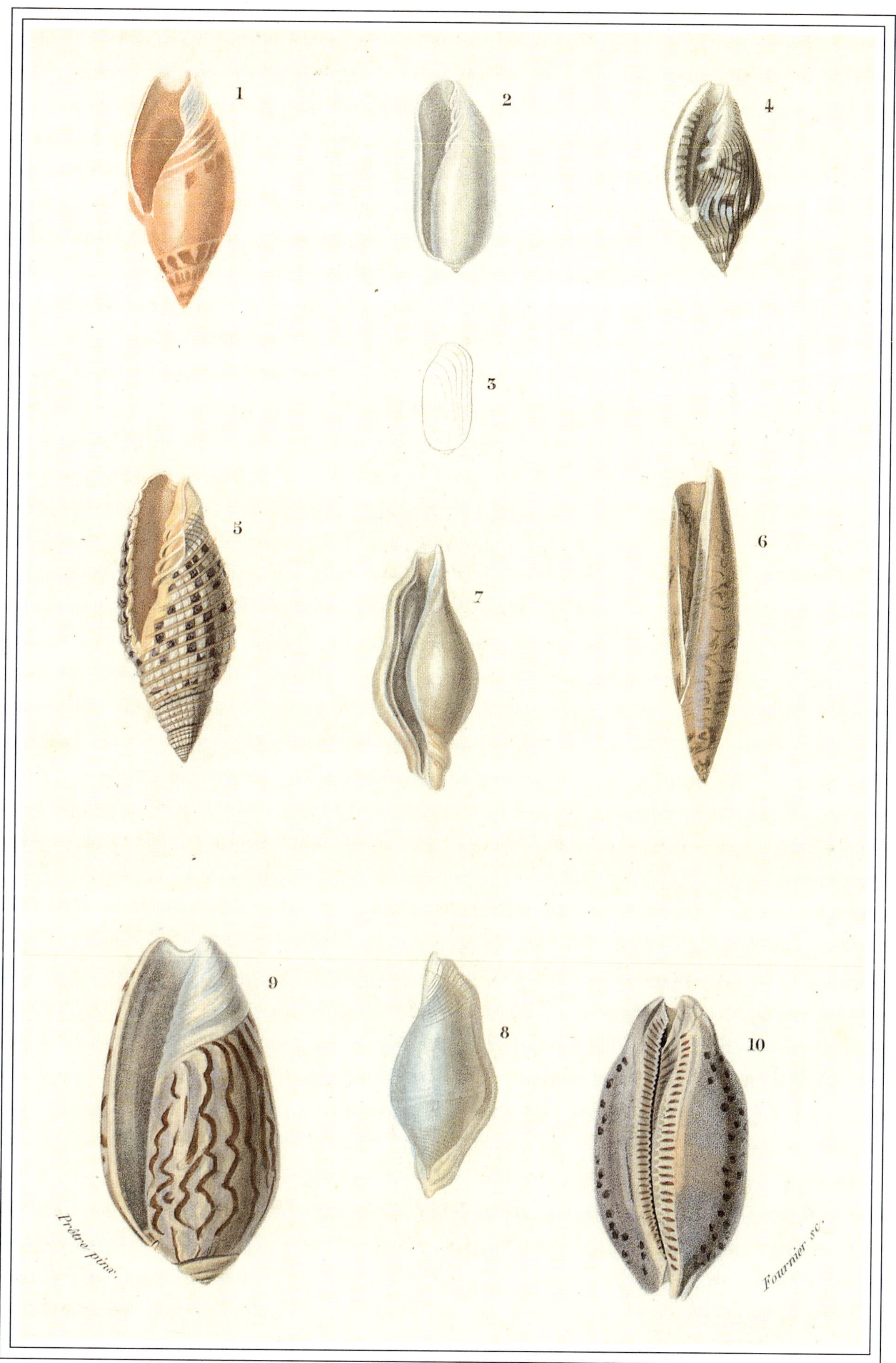

1. *Ancillaire bordée.* (Ancillaria marginata, *Lamk.*)
2, 3. *Volvaire hyaline.* (Volvaria pallida, *Lamk.*)
4. *Marginelle d'Adanson.* (Marginella Adansoni, *Kiener.*)
5. *Mitre scabriuscule.* (Mitra scabriuscula, *L.*)
6. *Tarière subulée.* (Terebellum subulatum, *Lamk.*)
7, 8. *Ovule intermédiaire.* (Ovula intermedia, *Sow.*)
9. *Olive du Pérou.* (Oliva Peruviana, *Lamk.*)
10. *Porcelaine bouffonne.* (Cypræa scurra, *Chemn.*)

Lam.—*Descr.* Tubular, regose, spiral near the apex, irregularly twisted near the aperture, with a longitudinal fissure radiating from the apex, and proceeding through all the whorls and sinuosities of the tube.—*Obs.* This genus was included in Serpula by Linnæus, from which, however, it is distinguished by the longitudinal slit. The recent species are found in the sponges with siliceous spiculæ, in the Mediterranean; the fossils in tertiary beds. Pl. i. fig. 1.

SIMPLE. (*Simplex*, lat.) Single, entire, uninterrupted, undivided.

SIMPLEGAS. Mont 1, 83. (*Simplex*, simple; γαστηρ, *gaster*, belly.) A genus described by De Blainville, as being discoidal, and having the spire uncovered like Ammonites, but having the chambers divided, by simple septa, like Nautilus.—*Obs.* The septa of the shell named Simplegas by De Montfort, are evidently sinuous, according to his figure. S. sulcata, Pl. xxii. fig. 475.

SINISTRAL. (*Sinister*, left.) On the left side. A sinistral shell is a *reversed* one. The sinistral valve of a bivalve shell may be known, by placing the shell, with its ligamentary or posterior part towards the observer; the sides of the shell will then correspond with his right and left side.

SINUOUS. Winding, serpentine. The septa of Ammonites are sinuous. The muscular impression of the mantle, or palleal impression of some bivalve shells, is sinuated near the posterior muscular impression.

SINUS. (*Sinus*, a winding, or bay.) A winding or tortuous excavation. The sinus in the outer lip of Strombus, fig. 406; and that in the muscular impression of Venus, will be indicated by the letter *s*.

SIPHON. (Σιφον, siphon.) A pipe, or tube. A shelly tube passing through the septa of chambered shells. It is said to be *dorsal*, *central*, or *ventral*, according to its situation near the outer, or inner parts of the whorl. See Introduction.

SIPHONAL SCAR. The name applied by Mr. Gray to the opening or winding sinus in the palleal impression of a bivalve shell, in the place where the siphonal tube of the animal passes.

SIPHONARIA. Sow. (Σιφον, siphon.) *Fam.* Phyllidiana. Lam. Patelloidea, Bl.—*Descr.* Patelliform, depressed, inclining to oval, ribbed; apex nearly central, obliquely inclining towards the posterior margin; muscular impression partly encircling the central disc, but interrupted in front, where the head of the animal reposes, and at the side by a siphon, or canal passing from the apex to the margin.—*Obs.* This siphon, which is in some species very distinct, serves to distinguish this genus from Patella. S. Sipho. Pl. xii. fig. 231*.

SIPHONOBRANCHIATA. Bl. (*Siphon*, and *Branchiæ*, gills.) The first order of Paracephalophora Dioica, Bl. divided into the families Siphonostomata, Entomostomata, and Angiostomata.

SIPHONOSTOMA. Guild. A sub-genus of Pupa, consisting of several elongated species, which have the aperture detached from the whorls; such as P. costata, and fasciata.

SIPHONOSTOMATA. Bl. (Σιφον, siphon; στομα, *stoma*, mouth.) The first family of Siphonobranchiata, Bl., the shells of which are extremely variable in form, but always have a canal or notch at the anterior extremity of the aperture. This family partly answers to the Canalifera of Lamarck and the genus Murex in the system of Linnæus. It contains the genera Pleurotoma, Rostellaria, Fusus, Pyrula, Fasciolaria, Turbinella, Columbella, Triton, Murex, Ranella, and Struthiolaria.

SIPHUNCLE. (Siphunculus.) A small siphon.

SISTRUM. Montf. (1810,) claimed a prior name for Ricinula, Lamarck. Fig. 413.

SKENEA. *Flem.* Typified by S. planorbis. A marine shell of depressed form. Pl. 74, fig. 25.

SMILIUM. Leach. *Fam.* Pedunculated Cirripedes.—*Descr.* Thirteen pieces, ten of which are in pairs, lateral, subtriangular; one posterior dorsal, linear; all smooth; peduncle hairy.—*Obs.* This genus is now included in Scalpellum. Pl. ii. fig. 36, S. Peronii.

SNAIL. The common garden Snail, so destructive to our vegetables, belongs to the genus Helix. The water snail, found in ponds, is Planorbis.

SOL. Humph. A genus consisting of several species of the genus Trochus, and corresponding with the sub-genus Tubicanthus, Sw. Malac. Fig. 349.

SOLARIUM. Lamarck. Architectoma, Bolter. (*A terrace or gallery.*) *Fam.* Turbinacea. Lam. Goniostomata, Bl.—*Descr.* Discoidal beneath, conical above, with a wide umbilicus, the spiral margin of which is angulated and crenulated; aperture trapezoidal; peritreme thin, sharp; columella straight; operculum horny, subspiral.—*Obs.* The Solarium Perspectivum, is commonly called the Staircase Trochus, from the angulated edges of the whorls being seen through the umbilicus, which reaches to the apex, and presents the appearance of a winding gallery. The species are not numerous, they belong to tropical climates. A few fossil species occur in the tertiary formations. S. Perspectivum. Pl. xvi. fig. 353.

SOLDIANA. D'Orb. A genus of microscopic Foraminifera.

SOLEN. Auct. (*A kind of shell-fish*, Plin.) *Fam.* Solenacea, Lam. Pyloridea, Bl.—*Desc.* Bivalve, transversely elongated, sub-cylindrical, equivalve, very inequilateral, gaping at both extremities, umbones terminal, close to the anterior extremity; hinge linear, with several small cardinal teeth, and a long external ligament; muscular impressions distant, anterior, tongue-shaped, placed behind the cardinal teeth, posterior irregular, sub-ovate; palleal impression long, bilobed posteriorly.—*Obs.* The above description of the genus Solen, is framed so as to admit only those species which are commonly called Razor Shells, with the umbones terminal, and the anterior muscular impression behind them. They are found buried deep in the sand, in a perpendicular position, their situation being pointed out by a dimple, on the surface. They are abundant in temperate climates. Some of the Lamarckian Solenes will be found in the genus Solenocurtus, Bl. Pl. ii. fig. 60, 61.

SOLENACEA. Lam. A family of the order Conchifera, Dimyaria, Lam. The shells belonging to it are described as transversely elongated, destitute of accessary pieces, gaping only at the lateral extremities; ligament external.—The genera may be thus distinguished.

1. Solen. Razor shells, truncated at the extremities. Fig. 60.
2. Panopæa. Broad, with prominent tooth. Fig. 65, 66.
3. Solenocurtus. Rounded at the extremities, with internal bar. Fig. 61.
4. Solenimya. No teeth, epidermis over-reaching the shell. Fig. 68.
5. Glycimeris. Thick, fulcrum of the ligament prominent. Fig. 67.
6. Lepton. Flat, scale-shaped. Fig. 62.
7. Novaculina. Umbones nearly central; covered by a thin epidermis. Fig. 63.
8. Glauconome. Oval, margins close. Fig. 64.

SOLENELLA. Sowerby, 1832. (*Solen.*) *Fam.* Arcacea, Lam.—*Descr.* Oval, equivalve, subequilateral, compressed, covered with a thin, shining, olive-green epidermis; hinge with three or four anterior, and numerous sharp posterior lateral teeth, arranged in a straight line; muscular impressions two, lateral; palleal impression with a large sinus; ligament external, prominent, elongated.—*Obs.* This genus partakes of

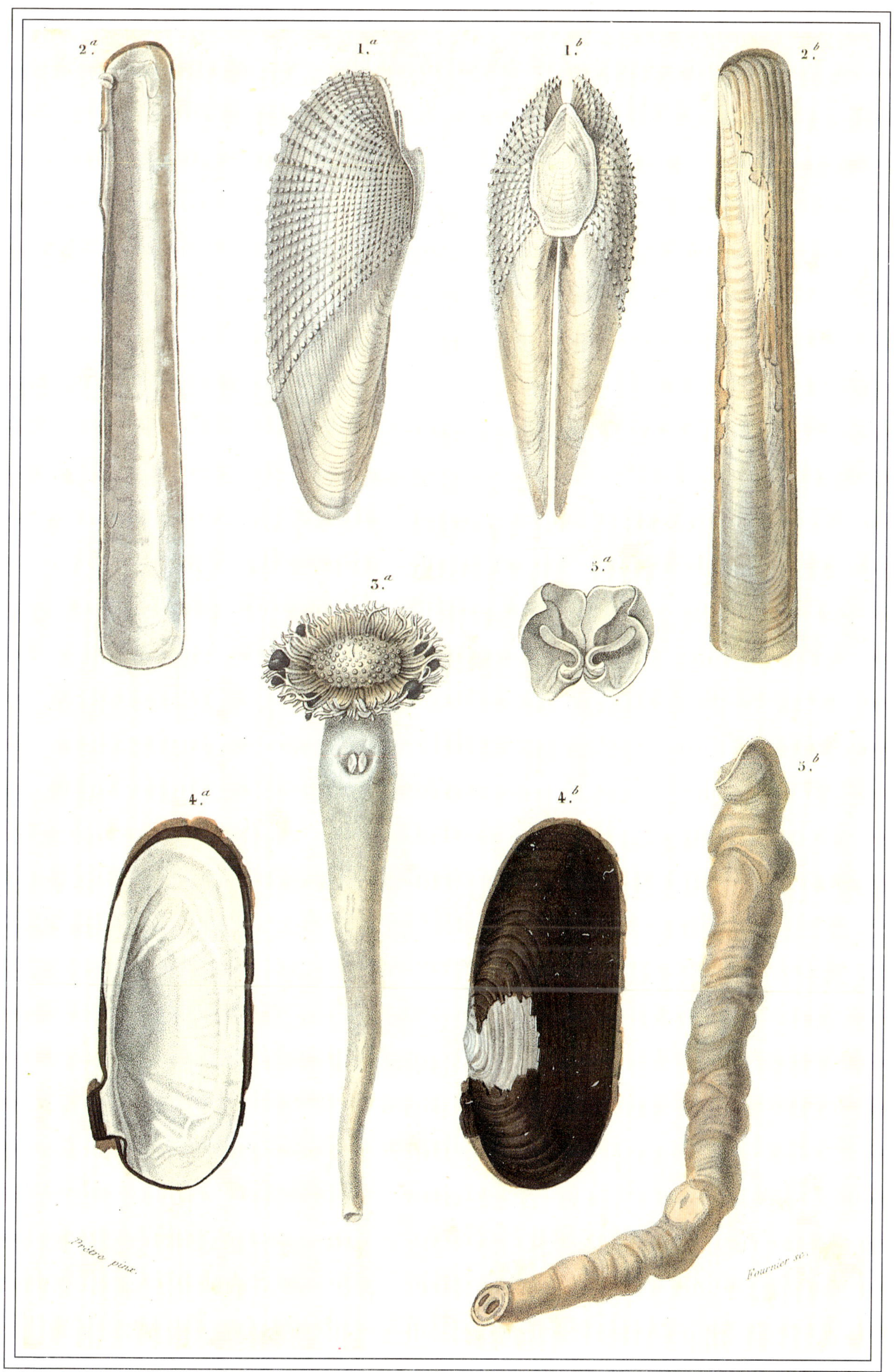

1.*a et* 1.*b* *Pholade dactyle*. (Pholas dactylus, *Lin.*)
2.*a et* 2.*b* *Solen silique*. (Solen siliqua, *Lin.*)
3. *Arrosoir de Java*. (Aspergillum Javanum, *Lamk.*)
4.*a et* 4.*b* *Glycimère silique*. (Glycimeris siliqua, *Lamk.*)
5.*a et* 5.*b* *Taret commun*. (Teredo navalis, *Lin.*)

sub-central, sub-orbicula. The Mediterranean, East and West Indies, and China, produce Spondyli most abundantly.—*Obs*. This genus is remarkable for the richness and beauty of the spines and foliations, which adorn the external surface of most of the species, the splendid colours by which many of them are varied, and the natural groupings formed by their attachment to each other. Forty species are enumerated in the Thesaurus Conchylium, Pl. 8 by the Author, Pl. 83 to 89; our Pl. x. fig. 177, and frontispiece.

SPORULUS. Montf. A genus of microscopic foraminifera.

SQUAMOSE. (*Squama*, a scale.) Scaly, covered with scales, as the pedicule of Pollicipes Mitellus, fig. 37*.

STENOPUS. Guild. (Στεὺς, narrow) πoὺς, foot.) A genus nearly "allied to the Linnæn Helices, from all of which it differs in the curious contraction of the pedal disc, and the caudal tentaculum furnished with a gland beneath." The shell is described as heliciform, umbilicated, transparent, with the aperture transverse. The two species described are Stenopus cruentatus and lividus; they are both from the Caribbæan Islands, Guild. Zool. Journ. xii. p. 528, tab. 15, f. 1 to 5. St. cruentata, f. 515, 516. Including Nanina, Gray, Helia, Citrina, f. 280.

STOASTOMA. C. B. Adams. A genus of minute operculated land shells, of a globose form, and semicircular aperture, with a nucleus or concentric operculum. The outer lip is not reflected, and it is produced beyond the columella, from which it is separated by a little groove. In the absence of more accurate knowledge of the animal, I should hesitate to regard this as more than an interesting group of Helicinæ, not more distinct from other groups of the same genus thus they are from each other. Mr. Cuming's collection contains 12 species. En. S. pisum (Jamaica.) Pl. xxviii. fig. 582.

STOMATELLA. See Stomax.

STOMAX. Montf. 1810. Stomatia, Lamarck, 18701. *Fam*. Mocrostomata, Lam.—*Descr*. Sub-orbicular, oblong, auriform, variegated without, irridescent within; spire depressed; aperture entire, very wide, oblique; peritreme uninterrupted.—*Obs*. This genus is known from Haliotis by being destitute of the series of holes; is distinguished from Sigaretus by the substance of the shell, the latter being internal, and never pearly. Our description includes Stomatella, Lam. The Stomatiæ are marine, and belong to the East Indies and New Holland. S. Phymotis. Pl. xv. fig. 335.

STREPHONA. Brown. 1756. Olivia, Lamarck.

STORILLUS. Montf. 1, 131. A genus of microscopic Foraminifera, included in the genus rotallites in M. De. Blainville's system.

STRAPAROLLUS. Montf. A genus containing some species of Helix. Auct. Generic characters not defined.

STREPTAXIS. Gray. *Fam*. Colimacea, La,.—*Descr*. Ovate, or oblong; when young, sub-hemispherical, deeply umbilicated, with rapidly enlarging whorls. At length the penultimate whorl is bent towards the right and dorsal side of the axis, and the umbilicus becomes depressed, and often nearly closed. The mouth is lunulate, the edge slightly thickened and reflected, and often with a single tooth on the outer side of the inner lip.—*Obs*. This genus of land shells is separated from Helix on account of the eccentricity of the penultimate whorl. S. contusa. Pl. xiii. fig. 269, 270.

STRIATED. (*Stria*, a groove.) Marked with fine grooves or lines.

STRIGOCEPHALUS. Defr. Pentamerus, Sow.? Gypidia. Dalman.

STROMBUS. Auct. *Fam*. Alatæ, Lam. Angiostomata, Bl.—*Descr*. Oblong, turrited, rather ventricose, solid; aperture generally lengthened, terminating posteriorly in a short canal, and anteriorly in an emargination or truncated canal; outer lip, when young, thin; when full grown, thickened and expanded, lobed at the spiral extremity, sinuated anteriorly, near the caudal canal. *Obs*. This well known genus includes some species of immense size, commonly called conch shells. Most of the recent species are brought from the Indian Ocean. Very few fossil species are known. The young shells have very much the appearance of cones, the outer lips being thin. There are also several species which do not, even when full grown, thicken their outer lips very considerably. The genus Strombus is distinguished from Rostellaria, by the notch in the outer lip, which in the latter genus is close to the canal. Fifty-seven species are enumerated in the Thesaurus Conchyliorum. S. pugilis, Pl. xviii. fig. 406.

STROPHOMENA. Rafinesque. Orthis, Dalman.

STROPHOSTOMA. Deshayes, 1827. A fossil shell, of the family of Colimacea, Lam. in some degree resembling Anostoma, having the aperture turned upwards the spire, it is, however, umbilicated, and it is said to have an operculum, resembling that of Cyclostoma. It is the Ferussina of Grateloup, 1826, one year earlier, and therefore the right name. Pl. xxv. fig. 534, 5, 6.

STRUTHIOLARIA. Auct. (*Struthio*, an Ostrich.) *Fam*. Canalifera, Lam.—Descr. Oblong, turrited, thick; spire turrited, composed of several angulated whorls; aperture oval, sub-quadrate, oblique; outer lip thickened, reflected, advancing in the centre, receding towards the extremities; inner lip thickened expanded over the columella and part of the body whorl.—*Obs*. This singular genus, consisting of three of four recent species, is named "Pied D'Autruche" by the French, on account of some resemblance in the outer lip to the foot of the Ostrich. From New Zealand. Fig. 391, S. straminea. Four species are described in the author's monograph, Thesaurus Conchyliorum, Pl. 1. *Ex*. Pl. xvii. fig. 391.

STYLIFER. Brod. (*Stylus*, a style; *fero*, to bear.)—*Descr*. Thin, pellucid, turbinated; apex a little out of the perpendicular, aperture wide anteriorly, gradually narrowing towards the spiral extremity, where it terminates acutely.—*Obs*. This is a genus of small, transparent shells, found burrowing in the rays of Starfish. There are but two or three species at present known, one of which is elongated like Terebra, the other nearly globular. S. astericola. West Indies, Gallapagos, and Britain. Pl. i. fig. 12, 13.

STYLINA. Flem. Stylifer, Brod.

SUB. (*under*.) Used as a prefix and signifying nearly. Thus a bivalve-shell, the valves of which are nearly alike, would be described as *sub*-equivalve.

SUB-APLYSIACEA. Bl. The first family of the order Monopleurobranchiata, Bl. containing several genera of Mollusca without shells, and the genus Pleurobranchus.

SUB-BIVALVES. A term of distinction applied by De Blainville, to those spiral univalves which have an operculum; these, as they consitute two distinct pieces, he considers as forming a medium between univalves and bivalves.

SUB-MYTILACEA. Bl. The sixth family of the order Lamellibranchiata, Bl. the shells belonging to which are described as free, rather pearly, regular, equivalve; hinge dorsal, laminated; ligament external; two muscular impressions; palleal impression not sinuated. This family, with the exception of the last genus, agrees with the family Nayades of Lamarck, and contains the genera Anodon, Unio, and Cardita.

SUB-OSTRACEA. Bl. The second family of Lamellibranchiata, Bl. the shells of which are described as of a compact texture, sub-symmetrical; with the hinge rather complex; one single, sub-central, muscular impression, without any traces of palleal impression. This family

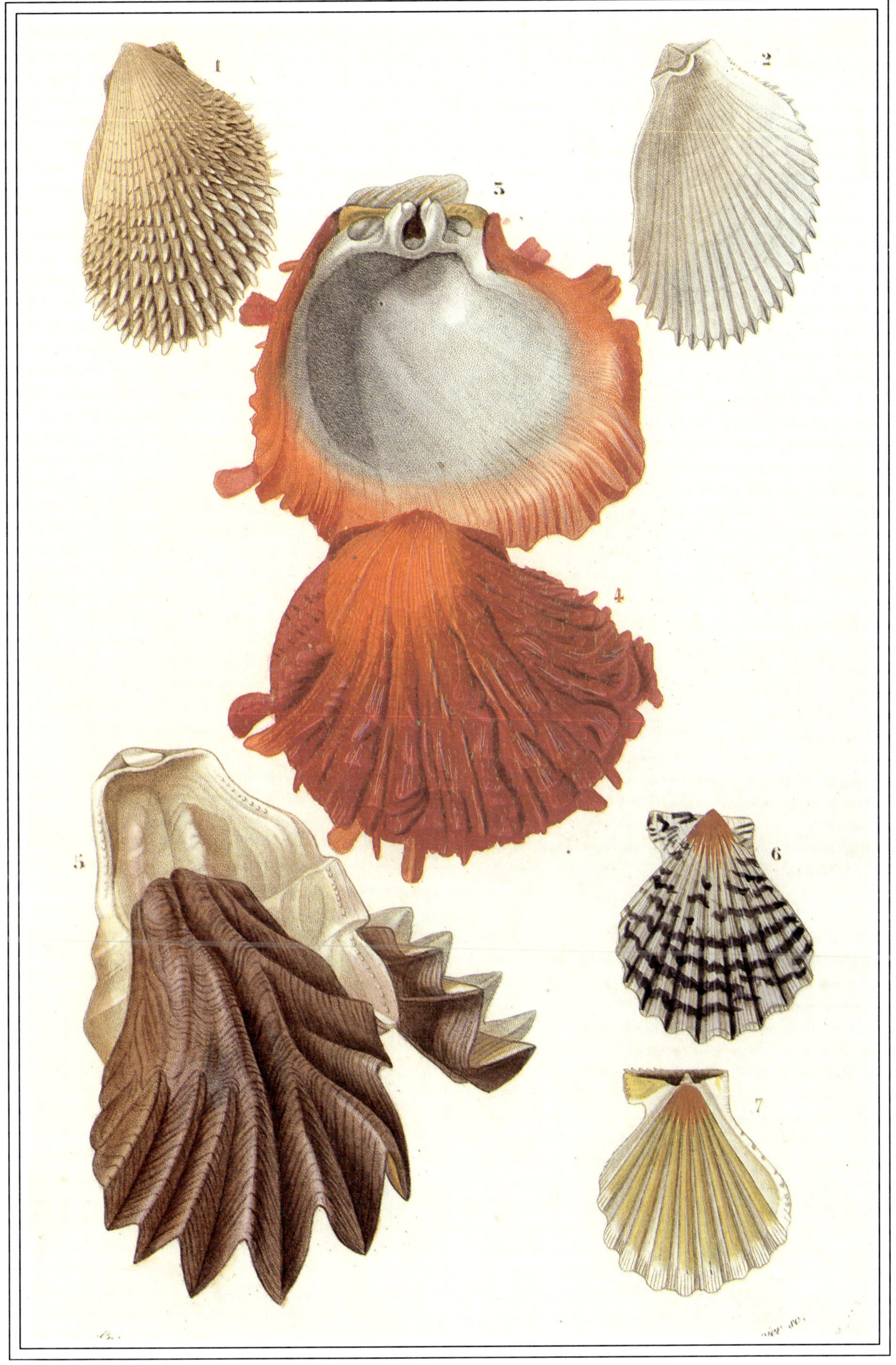

1, 2. *Lime écailleuse*. (Lima squamosa, *Lamk*.)
3, 4. *Spondyle safrané*. (Spondylus crocastus, *Desh*.)
5. *Huitre feuille*. (Ostrea folium, *Lamk*.)
6, 7. *Pecten tigré*. (Pecten tigris, *Lamk*.)

corresponds with the Pectenides of Lamarck, and part of the genus Ostrea in the system of Linnæus. It contains the genera Spondylus, Plicatula, Himnites, Pecten, Pedum, Lima.

SUB-SPIRAL. Not sufficiently spiral to form a complete volution.

SUBULA. Bl (*An awl.*) A generic name under which M. De Blainville includes TEREBRA maculata, Auct. f. 428, together with nearly all the species of Terebra, enumerated by Lamarck and other authors; only leaving in the latter genus those species, which being more bulbous, or ventricose, nearly resemble Buccinum in general form. These last mentioned species, such as Terebras buccinoidea, have been formed into a new genus by Mr. Gray, under the name Bullia. If both these genera were adopted, the genus Terebra would be extinct. Pl. xx. fig. 428.

SUBULATE. (*Subula*, an awl.) A term applied to shells which are long and pointed as in Terebra. Fig. 427, 428.

SUBULINA. Beck, 1837. A genus founded on the high-spired Helix octona, fig. 514. Macrospira, Guilding, 1840.

SUCCINEA. Drap. (*Succinum*, amber.) *Fam.* Colimacea, Lam. Limacinea, Bl. *Sub-genus*, Cochlohydra, Fer.—*Descr.* Ovate, rather elongated; aperture large, entire, longitudinal; spire short; outer lip thin, continuous with the thin, sharp-edged columella; inner lip spread over a part of the body-whorl.—*Obs.* The shells belonging to this genus of partly amphibious mollusca, are distinguished from Linnæa by not having a fold on the columella. The S. amphibia is of a bright amber colour. Pl. xiii. fig. 265, 266.

SULCATED. (SULCATUS, lat.) Having grooves or furrows.

SULCI. Grooves or furrows.

SUTURE. (*Sutura*, lat.) A seam, stitch, joining together. Applied particularly to the line which marks the joining of the whorls of the spire. The suture is distinguished as *simple*, as in most cases; or *double*, when accompanied by a parallel groove close to it; *marginated*, when produced into a ledge by the matter which fills up and covers it; *obsolete*, when it is filled up so as not to be visible, as in the case of Ancillaria.

SYCOTYPUS. Brown, 1756. A generic name applied to Pyrula ficus, &c.

SYLVICOLA. Humph. CYCLOSTOMA, Lam.

SYMMETRICAL. (συν, *syn*, similar; μετον, *metron*, proportion.) Both sides alike. Although the term is used thus as one of distinction, it is to be observed that no shells are strictly and perfectly symmetrical; even in the Nautilus, the apex verges in a slight degree towards one side of the shell. Two kinds of univalve are symmetrical, or nearly so; 1st. Those which are symmetrically convolute, as the Nautilacea and the Ammonacea, which are spiral; 2nd. Those which are not spiral, but simply conical, as the patelliform shells. Bivalves belonging to the Brachiopoda are also symmetrical. *Ex.* Patella, fig. 229. Ammonites, fig. 478.

SYMPHYNOTA. Lea. A genus of Nayades, in which Mr. Lea proposed to include species of the genus UNIO, the valves of which are connate, or united at the dorsal margin. We believe that this distinction, as a genus, has been abandoned by its author. The fact is, that all the Uniones are Symphynotæ when in a young state. In Unio Alatus, (fig. 147) and Dipsas plicatus, (fig. 142) it will be observed that the valves have not separated at the dorsal edge, but are broken lower down. Pl. vii. fig. 142, 147.

SYNDOSMYA. Recluz. A Tellinæform genus of shells, having a cartilaginiferous pit in each valve, and distinct lateral teeth. *Ex.* S. alba. Pl. xxvii. fig. 572.

TALONA. Gray, 1840. Pholas tridens. See monograph of the genus Pholas in Sowerby's Thesaurus Conchyliorum, Pl. 10. sp. 39, fig. 60, 61.

TAPADA. (Gray Turton. p. 127) A division of the genus HELIX, containing HELIX aperta, Auct. or the Tapada snail.

TAPES. Schum. PULLASTRA. Sow. T. litteratus. See monograph, Thesaurus Conchyliorum, Pl. 13, 14; and our figure, Pl. vi. fig. 120.

TECTURA. "Tecture," Aud. and Edw. Ann. Sci. Nat. 1830. LOTTIA, Gray.

TECTUS. Montf. A genus composed of species of the genus Trochus, having elevated, conical spires, and columella notched or truncated by a spiral fold. Trochus maculatus, presents an example. Pl. xvi. fig. 359.

TEINOSTOMA. H. and A. Adams. A genus formed of two interesting shells collected in W. Colombia, by Mr. Cuming. They are formed like the Rotellæ, and the Nassa neritoidea, but have the aperture quite simple and smooth, with the outer lip produced into a peak. *Ex.* T. politum. Pl. xxviii. fig. 589.

TELEBOIS. Montf. a genus of microscopic Foraminifera.

TELESCOPIUM. Chemn. CERITHIUM Telescopium, Auct. fig. 378.

TELLINA. Linn. *Fam.* Nymphacea, Lam. Conchacea, Bl.—*Descr.* Sub-equivalve, inequilateral, compressed, rounded anteriorly, slightly beaked or angulated posteriorly, the posterior ventral margin having a flexuosity; hinge with two cardinal and generally two lateral teeth in each valve; muscular impressions, two in each valve, remote; palleal impression with a large sinus.—*Obs.* The fold or bending in the posterior margin distinguishes this genus from others which it nearly resembles. It is composed of some bivalves of great beauty and variety, which are dound in nearly all climates. Fig. 105, t. radiata, 106, T. lingua-felis. Mr. Hanley's monograph of this genus in Sowerby's Thesaurus Conchyliorum, contains 207 species, very variable in form. Pl. v. fig. 105, 106.

TELLINIDES. Lam. *Fam.* Nymphacea, Lam.—*Descr.* Subn-equivalve, inequilateral, transverse, compressed, rounded anteriorly, slightly beaked or angulated posteriorly; hinge with two cardinal teeth in each valve, and one lateral tooth in one valve, very near the cardinal teeth. Muscular impressions two, distant, palleal impression with a large sinus. *Obs.* This genus is distinguished from Tellina in having but one lateral tooth near the cardinal teeth. T. rosea, Pl. v. fig. 107.

TENUIPEDES. (*Tenuis*, slender; *pedes*, feet.) The second section of the order Conchifera Dimyaria, divided into the families Mactracea, Corbulacea, Lithophagidæ, Nymphacea.

TERACLITA. Schum. CONIA, Acut.

TEREBELLUM. Browne, 1756. Turritella, Lamarck.

TEREBELLUM. Lamarck, 1801. (*Terebra*, an augur?) *Fam.* Convolutæ, Lam. Angyostomata, Bl.—*Descr.* Smooth, slender, oblong, subcylindrical; spire obtuse, short, sometimes hidden; (Seraphs, Montf.) aperture long, narrow posteriorly, wider anteriorly; outer lip slightly thickened, truncated, unconnected at the base with the columella; inner lip thin, smooth, nearly straight, spread over a portion of the body-whorl, continued in a ridge above the sutures of the spire.—*Obs.* Montfort has separated the fossil species with hidden spires, under the name Seraphs. (T. convolutum, Lam.) Only one recent species is known. Of this there are several varieties, one spotted, one marked in sub-spiral lines, another in patches. It is brought from the East Indies. T. convolutum; T. subulatum. Pl. xxi. fig. 451, 452.

TEREBRA. (*An augur, a piercer.*) *Fam.* Purpurifera, Lam. Entomostomata, Bl.—*Descr.* Subulate, elongated, pointed, turrited; spire long, consisting of numerous whorls; aperture small, terminating in a short, reflected canal; outer lip thin; columella tortuous; operculum horny. The recent species are mostly tropical.—*Obs.* Nearly all the species enumerated by Lamarck and other authors are included by De Blainville in his genus Subula; those few species which that conchologist left in the present genus, being shorter and more ventricose than the others, approximate in shape to some of the Buccina, and are distinguished by Mr. Gray under the generic name Bullia. It seems strange, that De Blainville, being convinced of the necessity of separating the two groups, and consequently applying a new generic term to one of them, should have given that term to the larger number and the more typical species of the Lamarckian genus. Fig. 427, Bullia vittata. (Terebra.) Fig. 428, Terebra maculata. (Subula.) The Monograph of this genus in the author's Thesaurus, Pl. v. contains 109 species. Plates 41 to 45. Our Plate xx. gig. 427, 428.

TEREBRALLA. Sw. A genus of "Cerithinæ," Sw. thus described: "Outer lip much dilated, generally uniting at its base to the inner lip; leaving a round perforation at the base of the pillar; channel truncate; operculum round: Palustre. Mart. f. 1472." Sw. p. 315.

TEREBRATING SHELLS. (*Terebro*, to pierce.) Shells which reside in holes pierced in rocks, wood, &c. by means of some corrosive secretion of the animal. *Ex.* Pholas, Teredo, &c.

TEREBRATULA. Brug. (*Terenratis*, bored.) *Fam.* Brachiopoda, Lam.—*Order.* Palliobranchiata, Bl.—*Descr.* Inequivalve, equilateral, oval or sub-trigonal, ventricose, or compressed, attached by a tendon passing through an opening in the dorsal, or upper and larger valve, the umbo of which advances beyond that of the other valve; hinge destitute of a ligament, with two teeth in the dorsal valve, locked into corresponding cavities in the ventral, or lower valve, and with two curious processes originating at the umbo of the lower valve, presenting, in some species, the appearance of fine winding tape, advancing towards the front of the valve, and again receding to the centre, where the ends unite; muscular impressions two, placed near the centre of each valve.—*Obs.* The Terebratulæ are included in the genus Anomia in the system of Linnæus. The recent species are not very numerous – they are found in all climates. The fossil species are more numerous than the recent ones, occurring in the secondary and tertiary formations. Mr. Sowerby, sen's Monograph in the 7th part of the author's Thesaurus Conchyliorum, contains 40 recent species. Plates 68 to 72. P. Psittacea, Pl, xi. fig. 202.

TEREDINA. (From Teredo. *Fam.* Tubicolæ, Lam. Adesmacea, Bl.—*Descr.* Valves equal, inequilateral, with prominent umbones, as it were soldered to the outside of the rounded end of a shelly tube, of which they form a part; aperture of the tube partly divided; a flat accessary valve placed on the unbomes.—*Obs.* This genus, which is only known in a fossil state, is distinguished from Teredo, by the valves being fixed on the tube, and the tube being closed at one extremity. T. personata, Pl. ii. fig. 46, 47.

TEREDO. Auct. (*A piercer.*) *Fam.* Tubicolæ, Lam. Adesmacea, Bl.—*Descr.* Valves equal, inequilateral; presenting when closed, an orbicular figure, with a large angular opening in front, and a rounded opening at the back; placed at the anterior extremity of an irregular, flexuous, elongated tube, open at both ends; the anterior termination divided in a double aperture opened and closed at the will of the animal by two operrcula. *Obs.* This genus of Molluscous animals, is remarkable for boring holes in wood, which are filled by their elongated tubes, and give it a honey-comb appearance. fig. 48. T. Navalis. Fig. 49, a piece of bored wood. Pl. ii.

TERMINAL. When the umbones of a bivalve shell are placed at or near the extremity, as in Mytilus, fig. 158, Pinna, fig. 162, they are said to be *terminal*. The same term is also applied to the nucleus of an operculum, when it forms an extreme point, or is close to one of the edges.

TESSELATED. (Wrought in chequer-work.) A term applied to the colouring of shells, when arranged in regular defined patches like a tesselated pavement.

TESTACELLA. Lamarck, 1801. (*Testa*, a shell.) *Fam.* Limacinea, Lam. and Bl.—*Descr.* Haliotoid, compressed; aperture wide, oblique; columella flat, oblique, spire short, flat, consisting of less than two whorls.—*Obs.* This shell which is extremely small compared with the animal, is placed upon its back, near the posterior extremity. The animal is found in some of our gardens, and very much resembles the common garden slug. t. Haliotoidea. Pl. xiii. fig. 261.

TESTACEOUS. (*Testa*, a shell). Shelly. Testaceous Mollusca, are soft animals having shells. A testaceous operculum is one composed of shelly matter.

TETRACERA. Bl. The first family of the order Polybranchiata, Bl. containing no genera of testaceous mollusca.

TEXTILLA. Sw. A sub-genus of Conus, consisting of Conus ballatus, &c. Sw. Malac. p. 312.

TEXTULARIA. Defr. A genus of microscopic Foraminifera.

THALAMUS. Montf. A genus described as resembling Conilites, but curved and granulated.

THALLEPUS. Sw. A genus of "Aplysianiæ," Sw. thus described: "Body more slender and fusiform;" (than Aplysia,) "the lobes of the mantle short, and incapable of being used for swimming; tentacula two, large, ear-shaped; eyes not visible. T. ornatus, *Sw.* Sp. Now." Sw. p. 349.

THALLICERA. Sw. A generic name under which Swainson distinguishes Ampullaria Avellana, Auct. Pl. xxv. fig. 338.

THECIDIUM. *Fam.* Brachiopoda. Lam. *Order*, Palliobranchiata. Bl.—*Descr.* Lower valve concave, sub-trigonal, with the umbo produced into a triangular, slightly incurved beak, and with two short, pointed processes advancing from beneath the umbones; upper valve flat, rounded square, with a short, blunt appendage, formed to fit between the tooth-like process of the other valve; its inner surface ornamented with symmetrically curved ridges. Thecidium Mediterranean, Sowerby's Thesaurus Conchyliorum, Pl. 73. fig. 30, 31, 32. Our Plate vii. fig. 216.

THECOSOMATA. Bl. The family of the order Aporobranchiata, Bl. containing the genera Hyalæa, Cleodora, Cymbulia, Pyrgo.

THELICONUS. Sw. A sub-genus of Conus. Lardn. Cyclop. Malac. p. 312.

THELIDOMUS. Sw. A generic name under which Swainson has described a division of the genus Helix, and which he has also used to designate a genus in the family of "Rotellinæ," founded upon an aggregate of loose particles collected and agglutinated in a spiral form by the larva of an insect. Sw. Malac. p. 330 and 353.

THEMEON. Montf. A genus of microscopic foraminifera.

THEODOXUS. Montf. a division of the genus Nerita. fig. 324, N. virginea.

THETIS. Sow. (*A sea nymph.*) A genus of fossil shells, described as resembling Mactra, but not having the internal ligament, and having several small, acuminated, cardinal teeth, but no lateral teeth. It resembles Tellina in some degree, but has not the posterior fold.

THIARA. Megerle. Part of the genus Melania, Lamarck.

THIARELLA. Sw. A sub-genus of Mitra, Lardn. Cyclop. Malac. p. 319.

THRACIA. Leach. *Fam.* Lithophagidæ, Lam. Pyloridea, Bl. A genus described as intermediate between Anatina, and Mya, and in some degree resembling Corbula. T. corbuloides, Pl. iv. fig. 93.

THUNDER-STONES. One of the vulgar appellations which have been applied to shells of the genus Belemnites.

THYATIRA. Leach. A genus composed of Amphidesma *flexuosa.*

Cryptodon. Turton. (First with characters.)

TIARA. Sw. A genus of "Mitranæ," Sw. thus described: "Aperture narrow, linear, or of equal breadth throughout; outer lip and base of the body-whorl contracted, the former generally striated; an internal canal at the upper part of the aperture; shell (typically) turrited, and equally fusiform; representing the *Muricidæ* and Cymbiola." Sw. Malac. p. 319. The principal difference between Tiara and Mitra appears to be that in the latter, the aperture is more linear and contracted in the centre. Mitra Episcopalis is an example.

TINOPORUS. Montf. A genus of microscopic Foraminifera.

TIRANITES. Montf. A division of the genus Baculites.

TOMELLA. Sw. A genus of "Pleurotominæ," Sw. thus described: "Fusiform, smooth; the spire of very few whorls, and not longer than the channel; inner lip with a thick callosity at the top; the slit short and side; lineata, En. Méth. 440, f. 2, clavicularis, IB. f. 4. filosa. En. Méth. 440, f. 6. lineolata. Ib. f. 11." Sw. p. 314. Pl. xxvi. fig. 551.

TOMOGERUS. Montf. 1810. ANASTOMA, Fischer. Described under the later name, ANASTOMA, see fig. 271.

TONICIA. Gray, Syn. B. M. p. 126. A genus composed of those species of Chiton which have the margin smooth. Ch. elegans, &c.

TORNATELLA. Lamarck. ACTEON, Montf. *Fam.* Plicacea, Lam.—*Descr.* Oval, spirally grooved; spire short, rather obtuse, consisting of few whorls; aperture long, narrow, rounded anteriorly; outer lip simple; inner lip thin, slightly spread, columella spiral, incrassated, confluent with the outer lip. The recent species are few. Several fossil species occur in London Clay, Inferior Oolite and Calcaire-grossièr. Monoptygma, Lea, resembles this genus, but has a fold in the inner lip. T. solidula, Pl. xv. fig. 343.

TORNATINA. Adams, 1850. A subgenus of Bullidæ, thus described: "Shell cylindrical or fusiform, spire conspicuous, apex papillated, suture chanelled, columella callous, with a single plate." Sixteen species are described in Mr. Adams' Monograph, Pt. x. Sowerby's Thesaurus.

TORTUOUS. (*Tortuosus*) Twisted. This adjective is sometimes applied as a specific name; as Area tortuosa.

TRACHELIPODA. Lam. (τραχηλος, *trachelos*, a neck; ποδα, *poda*, foot.) The third order of the class Mollusca, in the system, of Lamarck. The trachelipoduos mollusca are described as having the posterior part of the body spirally twisted and separated from the foot; always enveloped in a shell. The foot is free, flat, attached to the case of the neck. Shell spiral, and enclosing the animal when at rest. This order contains the families, Colimacea, Lymnacea, Melaniana, Peristomiana, Neritacea, Janthinea, macrostomata, Scalariana, Plicacea, Canalifera, Alata, Purpurifera, Columellaria, Convolutæ. The genera belonging to these families, are represented in the plates, fig. 264 to 462.

TRANSVERSE. (Crosswise.) A shell is said to be transverse, when its width is greater than its length, that is, when it is longer from one side to the other than from the umbones to the ventral margins. The term is applied by some authors to express the direction of the lines of growth in bivalve shells, and the spiral lines in spiral shells. See CONCENTRIC.

TRAPEZIUM. Meg. CYPRICARDIA, Lam.

TRAPEZIFORM, or

TRAPEZOID. (τοαπεζωον, *trapezion*, *trapezium*: ειδος, *eidosform.*) Having four unequal and unparallel sides. *Ex.* Cucullæa, fig. 133.

TRIBULUS. Klein. RICINULA, Lam.

TRICHOTROPIS. Brod. and Sow. (Τοιχος, *trichos*, hair; τοοπις, *tropis*, keel.) *Fam.* Purpurifera, Lam.—*Descr.* Turbinated, keeled, thin, umbilicated; aperture longer than the spire; entire; columella obliquely truncated; outer lip thin, sharp; epidermis horny, produced into long hairs at the angels of the shell; operculum horny, with the nucleus lateral.—*Obs.* Although the shells of this genus have something of the shape of Turbo, they are distinguished from that genus at once by the thinness of the shell. They are also known from Buccinium, by the absence of a canal. Only two or three species are known, which belong to the Northern and Arctic Oceans. T. bicarinata. Pl. xx. fig. 429.

TRIDACNA. Auct. *Fam.* Tridacnacea, Lam. Chamacea, Bl.—*Descr.* Equivalve, regular, inequilateral, radiately ribbed, adorned on the ribs with vaulted foliations, waved at the margins, with a large anterior hiatus close to the umbones, for the passage of a large byssus, by which the animal fixes itself to marine substances; hinge with a partly external ligament; two laminar teeth in one valve, one in the other.—*Obs.* The beautiful shells composing this genus are of a delicate white colour, tinged with buff. One species, the T. gigas, attains a remarkable size, measuring from two to three feet across, and weighing five hundred pounds. Tridacna is distinguished from Hippopus by the large opening in the hinge. t. elongata. Pl. ix. fig. 157.

TRIDACNACEA. Lam. A family belonging to the first section of the order Conchifera Dimyaria, Lam. described as regular, equivalve, solid, and which are remarkable for the deeply sinuated or undulated ventral margin. This family contains the genera:

1. HIPPOPUS. Valves closed at or near the hinge. Fig. 156.
2. TRIDACNA. An hiatus near the hinge. Fig. 157.

TRIDENTATE. (*Tridentatus.*) Having three teeth, or salient points. *Ex.* Hyalæa tridentata. Fig. 226.

TRIGONA. Schum.? Triangular species of CYTHEREA, such as C. lævigata, Triplas corbicula, ventricosa, bicolor, &c. The author found, however, in preparing the monograph of Cytheræa, No. 12, Thesaurus Conchyliorum, that the triangular pass by so many gradations into the rounded or oval forms, that it was impossible to find a resting place. Pl. vi. fig. 117*b*.

TRIGONOCÆLIUS. D'Nyst, 1835. A genus of bivalve shells, resembling Pectunculus, but distinguished by a triangular pit in the area of the hinge. *Ex.* T. aurita. Pl. vii. fig. 136.

TRIGONACEA. Lan. a family belonging to the order Conchifera Dimyaria, containing the genera Trigonia and Castalia, the latter of which ought to be removed to the Nayades. Fig. 139, 140.

TRIGONAL. Triangular, having three sides.

TRIGONELLA. Humph. MACTRA, Auct.

TRIGONIA. Brug. (τοιγωνον, *trigonon*, triangular.) *Fam.* Trigonata, Lam. Camacea, Bl.—*Descr.* Equivalve, inequilateral, transverse, sub-trigonal, costated and granulated without, pearly and irridescent within, denticulated on the inner margin, rounded anteriorly truncated posteriorly; hinge with four oblong, compressed, diverging teeth in one valve, receiving between their grooved sides, two similar teeth in the other; ligament external, thick; muscular impressions two in each valve.—*Obs* Only one recent species of this marine genus is known, the T. pectinata, which comes from New Holland; and was formerly so rare, that a much worn odd valve has been sold for a considerable sum. It is of a brilliant pearly texture within, tinged with purple or golden brown. Fossil species occur in Lias, upper and lower Oolite, and Green-sand. t. Pectinata. Pl. vii. fig. 139.

TRIGONOSEMUS. König. A genus composed of species of TEREBRATULA, Auct. which have one valve produced into a beak, perforated, or as it were truncated at the apex, differing from Terebratula lyra, Lam. T. lyra. Pl. xi. fig. 208.

TRIGONOSTOMA. A sub-genus of Helix, with a trigonal aperture. Gray's Turton, p. 139.

TRIGONOTRETA. König. A genus composed of species of Terebratula, Auct. which have the hinge of the larger valve produced into a triangular disc, divided by a triangular foramen in the centre. Spirifer, Sowerby, belongs to this genus. Fig. 214, 215.

TRILASMIS. Hind, Voy. Sulphur, p. 71, Pl. xxi. fig. 5. A small pedunculated Cirripeda, described as having two principal valves and a carina. From the characters of the animal and shell, however, Mr. Darwin has felt obliged to add several species to this group, and those species having the terga developed, and the scuture divided, could not properly be called trilasmis. In Mr. Darwin's work they are described under the name Pæcilasma.

TRILOBATE. (Τρεις, three; λοβος, division, lobe.) Divided into three lobes or principal parts. *Ex.* Malleus, Fig. 165.

TRILOCULINA. D'Orbigny. A genus of microscopic Foraminifera.

TRIPARTITE. (*Tripartitus*) composed of or divided into three separate parts.

TRIOMPHALIA. Sowerby, jun. (Τοια, three; ὀμφάλιον, umboes.) Pro. Zool. Soc. and Thesaurus Conchyliorum, p. 500. No. 10. A remarkable form of bivalve shell, differing from the Pholades in several particulars–1st. It has no curved processes in the hinge; 2nd The right valve is produced at the hinder end into a gongue or lappel; 3rd The left valve extends its ventral covering, so as completely to overlap the other anteriorly, Pl. xxvii. fig. 566.

TRIPHORIS. Deshayes. A genus composed of small reversed species of Cerithium, Auct. which have the anterior canal closed at the anterior of the aperture, but opened at the extremity, and a small tubular opening on the upper part of the whorls, making three openings on the body whorl. This genus stands in the same relation to Cerithium as the Typhis to Murex. Pl. xvi. fig. 375, 376.

TRIPLEX. Humph. Murex, Linn.

TRIPLODON. Spix. Hyria, Auct.

TRIPTERA. Quoy et Gaimard, Cuviera, Fer. Described in the Voyage de la coquille, and represented as a molluscous animal destitute of a shell.

TRIQUETRA. Bl. Triangular species of Venus Auct.

TRISIS. Oken. Arca tortuosa, Auct.

TRISTOMA. Described as Triphora.

TRITON. Montfort, 1810. *Fam.* Siphonostomata, Bl. Canalifera, Lam.—*Descr.* Oblong or oval, thick, ribbed or tuberculated, with discontinuous varices placed at irregular distances; spire prominent, mammillated; aperture round or oval, terminating anteriorly in a generally long, slightly raised canal; columellar lip granulated or denticulated; outer lip thickened, reflected, generally denticulated within; epidermis rough; operculum horny.—*Obs.* However nearly allied the Tritons may apper to the Murices and Ranellæ there are still to be traced in the shells of each of those genera, several constant and well marked distinctions, by which they may be at once recognized. In the Ranellæ, the varices run in two rows along the spire; in the Murices, they form three or more rows; but in the Tritons, they do not follow each other, *i.e.* they do not occur in the same part of each volution. The large species of Triton are sometimes used as trumpets. The Tritons are brought from the Mediterranean, Ceylon, the East and West Indies, and South Seas. Reeves' Monograph contains 102 species. Fig. 398 to 401.

TRITONIDEA. Sw. A genus of "Buccininæ," Sw. thus described: "Shell bucciniform, but the basal half is narrowed, and the middle more or less ventricose; spire and aperture equal. Pillar at the base with two or three obtuse and very transverse plaits, not well defined; outer lip internally crenated and with a superior siphon; inner lip wanting, or rudimentary." This genus is the same as the one first distinguished by Mr. Gray under the name of Polia. The latter name, as stated by Mr. Swainson, cannot stand, having been previously occupied for a genus of Lepidopterous Insects. Tritonidea articularis. (Pollia, Gray.) Pl. xix. fig. 415.

TRIVIA. Gray. A genus composed of those small species of Cyopræa, Auct. which are characterized by small ridges on the dorsal surface and have the anterior of the columella internally concave and ribbed. C. Pediculus. Auct. Pl. xxi. fig. 449, 450.

TROCHATELLA. Sw. A sub-genus of Helicinæ, consisting of those species which are acute and trochiform. Pl. xxv. fig. 532, 533.

TROCHIA. Sw. A genus of the family Buccininæ, thus described: "shape intermediate between Purpurea and Buccinum; whorls separated by a deep groove; inner lip when young, depressed, when adult, thickened, convex and striated; basal canal very small. T. sulcatus. E. M. 422. f. 4." Sw. Malac. p. 300.

TROCHISCUS. Sowerby. Tr. Norrissii.

TROCHITA. Schumacher. Trochatella, Lesson. Infundibulum, Montf. The spiral species of Calypræa.

TROCHIDON. Sw. A sub-genus of "Trochinæ," Sw. Lardn. Cyclop. Malac. p. 351.

TROCHILÆA. Sw.? Pileolus, Auct.

TROCHURUS. Humph. Monodonta. Lam.

TROCHUS. Linn. (*A top.*) *Fam.* Turbinacea, Lam. Goniostomata, Bl.—*Descr.* Turbinated, thick, striated, tunerculated or smooth; spire elevated, conical, consisting of numerous whorls; under surface discoid; aperture more or less depressed in an oblique direction, generally angular; columella arcuated, more or less prominent at its union with the outer lip, contiguous to the axis of the shel; operculum horny, orbicular, with numerous whorls.—*Obs.* Lamarck distinguished this genus from Turbo by the general form, which is more conical, and the aperture, which is angulated, while that of Turbo is rounded. Monodonta or Odontis is only separated on account of the notch at the termination of the columella. But these characters glide so imperceptibly from one genus to the other, that there is no line of demarcation to be found but in the operculum. Accordingly, Sowerby (in Gen. of Sh. 37.) has stated his reasons for considering as Trochi, all the species which have horny opercula; and as Turbines, all those which have testaceous opercula. The Trochi are found in all climates. Pl. xvi. fig. 358 to 360.

TROPÆUM. Sow. Crioceratites.

TROPHON. Montfort, 1801. Murex Magellanicus, Auct. Fusus Antiquus, and several other species which belong more properly to Fusus than to Murex. T. scalariformis, Wood. Pl. xxviii. fig. 595.

TRUMPET SHELL. A large species of Triton (variegatus), used by the natives of South Sea Islands as a trumpet, to call warriors and herds of cattle together. It answers the purpose tolerably well, producing a very sonorous blast.

TRUNCATED. (*truncus*, cut short.) Terminating abruptly, as it were cut short. *Ex.* solenensis, fig. 60.

TRUNCATULANA. D'Orb. A genus of microscopic Foraminifera.

TRUNCATELLA. Risso, 1813. A genus composed of several species of land shells which have been confounded by some authors with Cyclostoma. The genus is thus described: "Shell turriculated, cylindrical, decollated or truncated at the apex, no epidermis; aperture oval, short, with lips continuous, simple." *Ex.* Truncatella truncatulina, Lowe, Zool. Journ. t, 5. p. 80. Our Plate xxv. fig. 520, 521. It is found on the shores of Britain, the Mediterranean, and West Indies.

TUBA. Lea. A genus of small fossil shells, described as resembling Turbo, but with the aperture more like that of Melania. Lea. Contrib. Geol. Pl. xvi. fig. 369.

TUBERCLE. (*tuberculus*). A small swelling excrescence, or knob.

TUBERCULATED. Having a number of small lumps or pimples, as Turrilites, fig. 483.

TUBICINELLS. Lam. (*Tubicen*, a trumpeter.) *Order*, Sessile Cirripedes, Lam.—*Descr.* A cylindrical tube, composed of six elongated valves jointed together side by side, striated, longitudinally, surrounded by concentric rings; aperture circular, enclosed by an operculum of four valves, placed perpendicularly in an epiphragm.—*Obs.* The Tubicinellæ are found with nearly the whole shell buried in the thick skin of the whale. T. Balænarum. Pl. i. fig. 14.

TUBICOLARIA. Lam (*Tuba*, a tube; *cola*; an inhabitant.) A family of the order Conchifera Dimyaria, Lam. consisting of bivalves soldered as it were within, or connected with, a testaceous tube. The genera contained in this family may be thus distinguished.

1. Aspergillum. Valves fixed, tube perforated and fringed. Fig. 44.
2. Teredina. Valves fixed, prominent, tube closed at one end. Fossil. Fig. 46, 47.
3. Clavagella. One valve fixed, the other free. Fig. 45.
4. Teredo. Both valves free, tube open at both ends. Fig. 48, 49.
5. Fistulana. Valves free, tube closed at one end, straight, long. Fig. 53, 54.
6. Gastrochæna. Valves free, tube closed at one end, short, bulbous. Fig. 52.

TUBIVALVES. Bl. Shells composed of two valves connected in a tube, corresponding with the family Tubicolæ of Lamarck.

TULIPARIA. Sw. A sub-genus of "Coronaxis," Sw. Lardn. Cyclop. Malac. p. 311.

TURBINACEA. Bl. The sixth family of Polythalamacea, Bl. containing the genera Cibicides and rosallites, microscopic foraminifera.

TURBINACEA. Lam. A family of the first section of the order Trachelipoda, Lam. containing the following genera.

1. Solarium. With umbilicus reaching to the apex; including *Bifrontia* and *Orbis*. Fig. 353 to 356.
2. Rotella. A callosity on the under side. Fig. 357.
3. Phasianella. Oval; operculum shelly. Fig. 367.
4. Planaxis, Columellar lip flat; aperture notched. Fig. 365.
5. Turbo. Top-shaped; mouth generally round; operculum shelly. Fig. 368.
6. Trochus. Top-shaped; mouth generally angulated; operculum horny, consisting of many whorls; including *Elenchas*. Fig. 358, 359, 361.
7. Margarita. Operculum horny, consisting of few whorls; pearly. Fig. 362.
8. Littorina. Similar, not pearly; including *Assiminea*. Fig. 363, 363*.
9. Phorus. Attaching dead shells, stones, &c. Fig. 360.
10. Monodonta or Odontis. A notch and prominent point at the lower part of the aperture. Fig. 366.
11. Lacuna. With an umbilicus. Fig. 364.
12. Turritella. Elongated, screw-shaped. Fig. 369 to 371.

TURBINATED. (*Turbo*, a top.) Top-shaped, the term is applied generally to those shells which are large at one extremity, and narrow to a point at the other. *Ex.* Trochus, fig. 358; Turbinellus, fig. 382.

TURBINELLUS. Lamarck. Cynodonta. Schum.? Scolymus, Swainson. (*A little top.*) *Fam.* Canalifera, Lam. Siphonostomata, Bl.—*Descr.* turbinated, thick, wide near the apex, generally tuberculated; spire short, depressed, mammillated; aperture rather narrow, terminating anteriorly in an open canal; outer lip thickened within; columella having from three to five prominent, compressed, transverse folds. The species of this genus are mostly tropical.—*Obs.* The Turbinelli are a well marked genus of marine shells, the species of which are numerous. No fossil species are known. The genus Cancellaris makes the nearest approach to Turbinellus in some characters, but may be distinguished by the roundness of its form, the raised lines inside the outer lip, and the obliquity of the folds on the columellar. Pl. xvii. fig. 382 to 384. Seventy-two species are enumerated in Reeve's Monograph.

TURBO. Auct. (*A top.*) *Fam.* Cricostomata, Bl. Turbinacea, Lam.—*Descr.* Turbinated, solid, ventricose, generally rounded, sub-effuse anteriorly, entire; operculum shelly, solid, incrassated on the outer side, horny and sub-spiral on the inner side. The Turbines are mostly tropical.—*Obs.* The only certain means of distinguishing this extensive genus of marine shells from Trochus, is the operculum, which in the later genus is horny, spiral, and composed of a great number of whorls. The Trochi, however, are in general more conical, and flatter at the under side of whorls, and this constitutes Lamarck's distinction between the genera. Reeve's Monograph contains about thirty species. T. setosus. Pl. xvi. fig. 368.

TURGID. (*Turgidus.*) Puffed up, swollen, inflated. This term is applied synonymously with Ventricose.

TURRICULA. Humph. Melania, Auct.

TURRICULACEA. Bl. The seventh family of the Order Polythalamacea, Bl. containing the genus Turrilites, fig. 483.

TURRILITES. Lam. (*Turris*, a tower; λιθος, a stone.) *Fam.* Turriculacea, Lam. Ammonacea, Bl.—*Descr.* Chambered, turrited, spiral; septa sinuous and lobate, perforated by a siphon; aperture rounded, with the outer lip expanded. This genus, which is distinguished from the other Ammonacea by having the spire produced, *i.e.* not being convolute, consists of several species, occurring only in chalk-marl. Pl. xxiii. fig. 483.

TURRIS. Montf. 1810. A genus composed of those species of Mitra, Auct. which have the whorls angulated, with the aperture lengthened and undulated.

TURRITED. The spire of a univalve shell is said to be *turrited* when the whorls of which it is composed are regulated so as to have the appearance of little turrets rising above each other, as in Mitra, fig. 431. Vulpecula, Gray.

TURRITELLA. Lam. Terebellum, Browne. (*A little tower.*) *Fam.* Turbinacea, Lam. Cricostomata, Bl.—*Descr.* Turrited, elongated, generally grooved spirally; spire pointed, consisting of numerous whorls; aperture rounded or angulated; inner and outer lips thin, confluent anteriorly; operculum horny.—*Obs.* The shells composing this well-defined genus, are commonly called screws, a name to which the spiral grooves of most of the species seems to entitle them. Mr. Reeve's Monograph contains sixty-five species. T. imbricata. Pl. xvi. fig. 370.

TURTONIA. Hanley. See "Kelliadæ," T. minuta, Pl. xxvii. fig. 567.

TYMPANOSTOMA. Schum. (*Timbrel mouth.*) Potamis, Brongn. Potamus muricata, fig. 377.

TYPHIS. Montf. A genus composed of Murex tubifer, Auct. and other similar species, which have the canal closed and a perforated tube between each varix on the angulated part of the whorls. Besides the fossil species originally described, there are now five species known, which are figured in part 200, of the Conchological Illustrations by the Author. Typhis tubifer, Pl. xvii. fig. 397. Pl. xxvi. fig. 554, 555, 556.

ULTIMUS. Montf. (*The last.*) A genus composed of Ovulum gibbosum, Auct. and other species in which the canals are not distinctly defined, nor elongated. This fanciful name is given to the genus on account of its being described in the last page of the book. Pl. xx. fig. 443.

UMBILICATED. (*Umbilicatus.*) having an umbilicus, as Nautilus umbilicatus.

UMBILICUS. (*A navel.*) The hollow formed in spiral shells when the inner side of the volutions do not join each other, so that the axis is hollow. The umbilicus is marked with the letter *u* in Helix aglira, fig. 279. The term is also used to express any small, neat, rounded hollow.

UMBO. (*The boss of a buckler or shield.*) The point of a bivalve shell above the hinge, constituting the apex or nucleus of each valve, from which the longitudinal rays diverge, and the lines of growth, commencing at the minutest circle, descend in gradually enlarging concentric layers to the outer margin. The umbones will be marked with the letter *u*, in Cytherea, fig. 117.

UMBRELLA or UMBELLA. (*A little shade.*) *Fam.* Semi-phyllidiana, Lam. Patelloidea, Bl.—*Descr.* Patelliform, sub-orbicular, compressed, rather irregular; apex slightly raised, placed near the centre; margin acute; internal surface with a central, callous, coloured disc, surrounded by a continuous, irregular muscular impression.—*Obs.* This genus is known from Patella, by its continuous muscular impression. It is commonly called the Chinese Umbrella shell. There are but two species at present known; the U. Mediterranea, and the U. Indica. Pl. xii: fig. 233.

UNDATED. (*Unda*, a wave.) Waved.

UNDULATED. (*Undulatus.*) Minutely waved.

UNGUICULATED. (*Unguis*, a nail or hoof.) An unguiculated operculum is one in which the layers are disposed laterally, and the nucleus constitutes part of the outer edge.

UNGULINA. Daud. (*Ungula*, a nail or claw.) *Fam.* Mactracea, Lam. Conchacea, Bl.—*Descr.* Equivalve, sub-orbicular, sub-equilateral, with margins entire, simple, closed all round; hinge with one short, sub-divided cardinal tooth in each valve, and a very minute additional tooth in one valve, an oblong ligamentary pit divided into two portions, one of which receives the cartilage, the external ligament is immediately below the umbones; muscular impressions, two in each valve, oblong; impression of the mantle entire. Coast of Africa. U. transversa, Pl. iv. fig. 88.

UNI-AURICULATED. Having one Auricle. See Auriculated.

UNICORNUS. Montf. Monoceros, Auct.

UNIO. (*A pearl.*) *Fam.* Nayades, Lam. Submytilacea, Bl.—*Descr.* Inequilateral, equivalve, regular, free, pearly within, covered by a mooth epidermis without; umbones prominent, generally corroded; muscular impressions two in each valve, lateral, distant; the anterior composed of several small divisions; hinge varying in age, species, and individuals.—*Obs.* The above description is framed so as to include all the genera of the Lamarckian Nayades, together with Castalia, which are placed in the family Trigonacea, they are all fresh-water shells, commonly called fresh-water muscles. The distinctions of the various genera into which they have been divided, will be found in their respective places, and under the name of Nayades. They are all represented in figures 140 to 152. Of these fig. 145 to 148, are more generally considered as forming the genus Unio. Pl. viii.

UNIVALVE. (*Unus*, one; *valva*, valve.) A shell consisting of a single piece, as distinguished from Bivalves and Multivalves, which are composed of two or more principal pieces. Spiral shells having an operculum, are called sub-bivalves by some authors.

UPPER-VALVE. The free valve in attached bivalves.

UTRICULUS. Brown. A sub-genus of Bullidæ, the shells of which are thus described by Mr. A. Adams, in his Monograph of Bullidæ in Sowerby's Thesaurus—"Shell small, oblong-ovate; outer lips nearly the whole length of the last whorl, and entire; spire very short, volutions prominent."

UVIGERNA. D'Orb. A genus of microscopic Foraminifera.

VAGINA. Megerle. Solen *vagina*, Auct.

VAGINULA. (*A little sheath, the husk of corn.*) *Class*, Pteropoda, Lam.—*Descr.* Pyramidal, slightly inflated in the centre, thin, fragile; aperture oblong, with the edges turned slightly outwards.—*Obs.* The little shells of this genus, which are only known in a fossil state, differ from Cuvieria in being pointed at the extremity. Found in the tertiary beds of Bordeaux. V. Daudinii, Pl. xii. fig. 225.

VAGINULINA. D'Orb. A genus of microscopic Foraminifera.

VALVATA. Muller, 1774. *Fam.* Peristomata, Lam. Cricostomata, Bl.—*Descr.* Thin, turbinated; spire short, composed of from three to six rounded whorls; aperture circular; peritreme acute, entire; operculum horny, spiral.—*Obs.* This genus of small shells resembles Cyclostoma, from which the recent species may be known by the horny texture of the external surface, being fresh-water shells. Europe and North America. The fossils of course belong to the fresh-water formations. V. piscinalis, fig. 322.

VALVES. (*Valva*, a door, a folding piece.) The two pieces composing a bivalve shell, which close upon each other, turning upon a hinge consisting of a ligament, cartilage, and teeth. See Bivalve, Multivalve, and Univalve.

VALVULINA. D'Orb. A genus of microscopic Foraminifera.

VANICORO. Quay and Gaimard. A genus of beautiful shells, something like Sigaretus in form, admitted by Mr. Sowerby in the genus Neritopsis, but differing from that genus in the form of the columella. The type is Nerita cancellata, Chemnitz. Mr. Cuming's collection contains twenty-four species, all of which are cancellated. The operculum is thin, horny, and semicircular, only half enclosing the animal. Ex. V. cidaris. Pl. xxvii. fig. 584.

VARIX. (*A swelling vein.*) A varix is formed on the outer surface of a spiral shell, by the thickened, reflected edge of a former aperture, after fresh deposits of testaceous matter have increased the size by adding to the growth of the shell beyond it. In this manner there are frequently many varices, or edges of former apertures, in various parts of the spire and the body whorl. They are sometimes placed at regular distances from each other, as in Harpa, fig. 419; sometimes *continuous*, as in Ranella, fig. 394; sometimes *discontinuous*, as in Triton, fig. 398; sometimes *ramose*, as in Murex, fig. 395; sometimes *simple*, as in Scalaria, fig. 351; sometimes *spinose*, as in Murex spinosus. The term *varix* has also been applied to any swelling ridge, such as that on lower part of the columella of Ancillaria, fig. 456.

VELATES. Montf. Neritina perversa, Auct. Pl. xv. fig. 326.

VELLETIA. Gray? A genus described as differing from Ancyllus in being dextral. Velletia lacustris, Ancylus lacustris, Auct. Sowerby Gen. fig. 2.

VELUTINA. Fleming, 1822. *Fam.* Macrostomata, Lam.—*Descr.* Subglobose, covered with a velvety epidermis; spire short, composed of two rapidly enlarged ventricose whorls; aperture large, sub-ovate; peritreme thin, entire, separated from the last whorl; columella tortuous, thin.—*Obs.* This shell does not resemble any other genus in the family. Northern Seas. Pl. xv. fig. 337.

VENERICARDIA. Lam. A genus composed of the shorter species of Cardita. Pl. vi. fig. 121.

VENERIRUPIS. Lam. (From *Venus* and *rupis*, a rock.) The oblong species of Venus Auct. which live in cavities of rocks and stones. This genus is united by Sowerby with some other species of Venus under the name Pullastra. V. Vulgaris, Pl. iv. fig. 97.

VENTRAL. (*Venter*, the belly.) The margin of a bivalve shell opposite the hinge. The under valve in Brachiopodous bivalves is the ventral valve. The ventral surface of an univalve spiral shell is that which faces the observer when the aperture is placed towards him. The ventral part of the whorls of symmetrical convolute shells, is the inner part, that which is nearest to the spire.

VENTRAL SIPHON. In symmetrical convolute univalves, is one placed near the inner edge of the whorls.

VENTRICOSE. (*Ventricosus.*) Swelled, rounded out, (*bombé Fr.*) as Harpa ventricosa, fig. 419.

VENUS. Auct. (*Goddess of Beauty.*) (Dosina, Gray.) *Fam.* Marine Conchacea, Lam. Conchacea, Bl.—*Descr.* Equivalve, inequilateral, sub-globose, sub-ovate, transverse, externally rugose, striated, ribbed, cancellated or smooth; margins entire simple, close; hinge with three more or less distinct cardinal teeth, diverging from the umbones in each valve; muscular impressions two, lateral, distant; palleal impressions sinuated posteriorly; ligament external.—*Obs.* This extensive genus, including some bivalves of splendour and beauty, justifying the name given to it, may be known from Cytherea by the absence of a lateral tooth, which is found near the cardinal teeth in the latter. Artemis is distinguished not only by its beautiful form, but by the deep angular sinus in the palleal impression. Found mostly in temperate and tropical climates. A monograph will appear in No. 13 of Thesaurus Conchyliorum by the Author. Pl. vi. fig. 119. 119*a*.

VERMETUS. Adanson. *Fam.* Scalariana, lam. Cricostomata, Bl.—*Descr.* Spiral at the apex, irregularly twisted towards the aperture; aperture round, small.—*Obs.* This shell resembles the Serpulæ in general appearance, although it is regularly spiral near the apex. The animal is known to be a true mollusc, rather nearly allied to that of the genus Dentalium, which is also placed wrongly in the Lamarckian system. Vermetus Lumbricalis. Coast of Africa. Pl. xv. fig. 345.

VERMICULAR. (*Vermicularis.*) Worm-shaped, tubular serpentine. *Ex.* Vermilia triquetra, fig. 7.

VERMICULARIA. Lam. Vermetus, Adanson; afterwards Vermetus, Lam.

VERMILIA. Lam. A genus composed of species of Serpula, which are attached by the whole length of the shell, no part being free. Vermilia triquetra. Pl. i. fig. 7.

VERTEBRALINA. D'Orb. A genus of Microscopic Foraminifera.

VERTEX. Apex.

VERTIGO. Müll. *Fam.* Colimacea, Lam.—*Descr.* Cylindrically fusiform, sinistral, hyaline; aperture marginated, sinuated, denticulated on the inner edge; peristome sub-reflected.—*Obs.* This genus of minute land shells, resembles Pupa, but is a reversed, hyaline shell. Vertigo pusilla. Pl. xiv. fig. 293.

VERRUCA. Schum. Clitia, Leach.

VESICA. Sw. A sub-genus of Bulinus, Sw. p. 360.

VEXILLA. Sw. A genus of "Nassinæ," Sw. thus described: "General shape of *Purpura*, the inner lip flattened and depressed; the outer, when adult, thickened, inflected and toothed; aperture wide; picta *Sw.* Chem. pl. 157. fig. 1594–5." Sw. Malac. p. 300. Pl. xxv. fig. 544.

VIRGULINA. D'Orb. A genus of microscopic Foraminifera.

VITRELLA. Sw. A sub-genus of "Bullinæ," Sw. Lardn. Cyclop. Malac. p. 360.

VITRINA. Drap. (*Vitreus*, glassy.) *Fam.* Limacinea, Lam. and Bl.—*Descr.* Ovate thin, glassy, fragile; spire short; last whorl large; aperture wide, transverse; peritreme simple; columella spiral, linear.—*Obs.* This genus of land-shells is not known in a fossil state. The recent species are found among moss and grass, in shady situations. De Ferussac has divided this genus into Helicolimax, fig. 263, and Helixarion, fig. 262.

VITULARIA. Sw. A genus of "Muricinæ," Sw. thus described: "General habit of *Muricidea*, but the inner lip is depressed and flattened, as in the *Purpurinæ*; varices simple, nearly obsolete. Tuberculata, *Sw.* En. M. 419. fig. 1. (*Murex vitulinus*, Auct.)" Sw. p. 297. Pl. xxvi. fig. 553.

VIVIPARA. A generic name given by Montfort, and retained by some authors on the ground of priority for Paludina, Lam. on account of the animals being *viviparous*, i.e. the young being perfectly formed before they leave the ovaries.

VIVIPAROUS. See Vivipara.

VOLUTA. Auct. (*Volvo*, to revolve.) *Fam.* Columellaria, Lam. Angyostomata, Bl.—*Descr.* Sub-ovate, rather angulated, thick, generally tuberculated, smooth; spire short, conical, with a mammillated apex; aperture generally angulated, large, terminating anteriorly in a deep notch; columella smooth, with several plaits, of which the lowest is the largest; outer lip thickened within.—*Obs.* The genus Voluta, as left by Linnæus, is only characterized by the folds on the columella, and includes many shells which, although they agree in this respect with the genus, are yet quite opposite to each other in all other characters. Thus the Auriculæ, which are land shells, and have the aperture entire, are mixed up with others which are marine, and have a canal, as Turbinellæ, and the Fasciolariæ, and others which have merely a notch, as the true Volutes. This genus, as it is circumscribed at present, includes a great number of beautiful shells, most of which are rich in colouring. Cymba and Melo have been separated by Mr. Broderip from the genus Voluta of Lamarck, for reasons stated in their respective descriptions. Fifty-eight species are described in the Monograph by the author, in Thesaurus Conchylium, Pl. xlvi. to lv. vol. 5. Our Pl. xx. fig. 443.

VOLVARIA. Lam. (*Volva*, a shuttle.) *Fam.* Columellaria, Lam.—*Descr.* Cylindrical, convolute, spirally striated; spire very short, nearly hidden; aperture narrow, as long as the whole shell; columella with three oblique plaits; outer lip dentrated.—*Obs.* The Volvariæ are only known in a fossil state, and resemble some species of Bulla in general form, but are distinguished by the plaits on the columella. V. concinna. Pl. xx. fig. 439.

VOLUTELLA. Swainson. (*A little volute.*) A genus composed of those species of Marginella, Auct. which have the spire concealed, and the aperture smooth within. Fig. 438, Persicula of Schumacher.

VOLUTILITHES. Sw. (*Voluta*, and λιθος, *lithos*, a stone.) A genus composed of some fossil species of Voluta, which have the plaits on the pillar generally numrous, indistinct, and sometimes wanting altogether, with a pointed spire. V. spinosa, Pl. xx. fig. 436.

VOLUTION. See Whorl.

VOLVULA. Adams. Sowerby's Thesaurus, Pt. xi. 1850. A genus of Bullidæ, the shells of which are thus described: "Sub-cylindrical, beaked at both ends; spire concealed; aperture narrow; inner lip with a single obsolete fold."

VORTICIALIS. Lam. A genus of microscopic Foraminifera.

VULSELLA. Lam. (*A little tongue.*) *Fam.* Ostracea, Lau. Margaritacea, Bl.—*Descr.* Equivalve, irregular, longitudinal, compressed, oblong; umbones separated by a slight area in both valves; hinge with a large pit in the centre, containing the cartilage, the ligament being spread over the areas; muscular impressions, one on each valve, sub-central, oblong.—*Obs*. This genus differs from Ostræa in the equality of valves, and in having a hollow pait in the hinge for the cartilage. Vulsella lingulata, Pl. xi. fig. 185.

WATERING-POT. Aspergillum, fig. 44, commonly so called on account of the resemblance of its perforated termination to that of the spout of a watering-pot.

WENTLE TRAP. Scalaria pretiosa, commonly so called.

WHORL. A complete turn or revolution round the imaginary axis of a spiral shell. The last whorl is called the *body-whorl*. The whorls are described as *non-contiguous*, when they do not touch each other; *continuous*, in the opposite case. *Depressed* when they are flat. They are *angulated*, *keeled*, or coronated; *distinct*, or indistinct. they are sometimes, as in Cypræa, hidden by the last whorl.

YETUS. Adanson. CYMBA, Broderip.

XYLOPHAGA. Turton. (ξυλον, *zylon*, wood; φαγω, *phago*, to eat.) *Fam*. Tubiscolæ, Lam.—*Descr*. Equivalve, globose, closed at the back; with a large, angular hiatus in front; hinge with a small curved tooth advancing from beneath the umbones in each valve.—*Obs*. This shell, which is found in a cylindrical cavity, eaten in the wood by the animal, resembles Teredo, but has not the shelly tube, nor the posterior hiatus. X. dorsalis, Pt. x. fig. 50, 51.

XYLOTRYA. Leach. XYLOPHAGA, Sow.

ZARIA. Gray, 1840. A division of the genus Turritella represented by T. duplicata, &c.

ZIERLIANA. Gray. The short strombiform, thick-lipped species of Mitra. M. Ziervogelii.

ZIRFÆA. Leach. 1817. Pholas crispata, without accessory valves. See Monograph of Pholas, Sowerby's Thesaurus Conchylium. No. 10, fig. 37.

ZONITES. Montf. A genus formed of Helix Algira, and other similar species with depressed spires and large umbilici; included in the sub-genus Helicella. Pl. xiii. fig. 279.

ZUA. Leach. A genus described under the word "CIONELLA." The manuscript name by Leach having them published by Gray, claims the priority.

ZURAMA. Leach. A sub-genus of Helix. H. pulchella, Auct. Gray's Turton, p. 41.

ZYZIPHINUS. Leach. MS. Gray, 1840. Tochus zyziphinus and similar species.

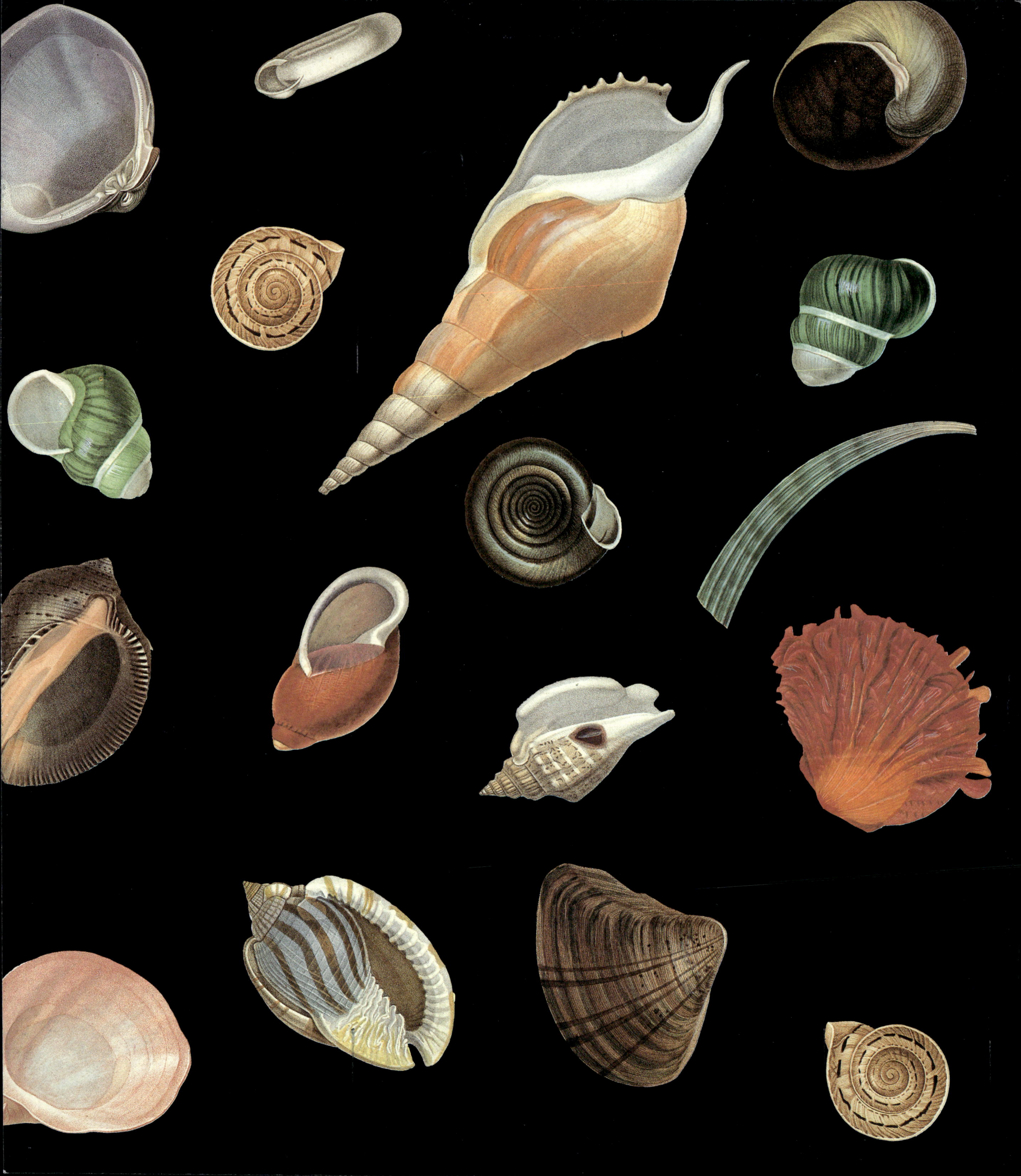